PRINCIPLES OF FINANCE

THE PRINCIPLE OF SELF-INTERESTED BEHAVIOR
People act in their own financial self-interest

THE PRINCIPLE OF RISK AVERSION
When all else is equal, people prefer higher return and lower risk

THE PRINCIPLE OF DIVERSIFICATION
Diversification is beneficial

THE PRINCIPLE OF TWO-SIDED TRANSACTIONS
Each financial transaction has at least two sides

THE PRINCIPLE OF INCREMENTAL BENEFITS
Financial decisions are based on incremental benefits

THE SIGNALING PRINCIPLE
Actions convey information

THE PRINCIPLE OF CAPITAL MARKET EFFICIENCY
The capital markets are efficient

THE PRINCIPLE OF RISK-RETURN TRADE-OFF
There is a trade-off between risk and return

THE PRINCIPLE OF VALUABLE IDEAS
Extraordinary returns are achievable with new ideas

THE OPTIONS PRINCIPLE
Options are valuable

THE BEHAVIORAL PRINCIPLE
When all else fails, look at what others are doing for guidance

THE TIME-VALUE-OF-MONEY PRINCIPLE
Money has a time value

PRINCIPLES OF FINANCE

With Corporate Applications

PRINCIPLES OF FINANCE

With Corporate Applications

DOUGLAS R. EMERY

*The Koffman Fellow and
Professor of Finance
Binghamton
State University of New York*

JOHN D. FINNERTY

*General Partner
McFarland Dewey & Co.
and
Professor of Finance
Fordham University*

WEST PUBLISHING COMPANY

St. Paul   New York   Los Angeles   San Francisco

COPYEDITING: *Bob Burdette*
INTERIOR DESIGN: *John Rokusek*
ILLUSTRATIONS: *Rolin Graphics*
COMPOSITION: *G&S Typesetters, Inc.*
COVER DESIGN: *Diane Beasley Design*
COVER PHOTOGRAPH: *Hans Wendler, The Image Bank*

98 97 96 95 94 93 92 91   8 7 6 5 4 3 2 1 0

Library of Congress Cataloging-in-Publication Data

Emery, Douglas R.
    Principles of finance with corporate applications / Douglas R. Emery, John D. Finnerty.
        p.   cm.
    Includes bibliographical references and index.
    ISBN 0-314-79213-9
    1. Corporations—Finance.   I. Finnerty, John D.   II. Title.
HG4026.E47   1991
658.15—dc20   90-43415
                                                                                              CIP

To Cindy and Louise

We wish there were innovative words to be said.
Alas, the best we can do is offer our heartfelt,
but wholly inadequate, thanks.

About the Authors

Douglas R. Emery

The Koffman Fellow and Professor of Finance in the School of Management at the State University of New York at Binghamton. Doug earned an MBA and Ph.D. from the University of Kansas. He has also been on the faculties of the University of Missouri—Columbia, Washington University in St. Louis, Purdue University, and the University of Calgary. His current research interests include the theory and application of financial decision models, fixed income securities, and the effects of reputation. In addition to his research in finance, his work has appeared in the *Journal of Accounting Research*, *Psychometrika*, *Organizational Behavior and Human Performance*, and the *Journal of Marketing Research*. Doug is an Associate Editor of *Decision Sciences*.

John D. Finnerty

General Partner of McFarland Dewey & Co., an investment banking firm in New York City, and Professor of Finance in the Graduate School of Business Administration at Fordham University. John earned an M.A. from Cambridge University, which he attended under a Marshall Scholarship, and a Ph.D. from the Naval Postgraduate School. His current research interests include liabilities management and securities valuation. He has worked for Morgan Stanley & Co., Lazard Frères & Co., and was chief financial officer of the College Savings Bank. He is the author of *Corporate Financial Analysis*, and co-holds four patents on financial products. John is an Associate Editor of *Financial Management* and Vice President of the Fixed Income Analysts Society.

Contents in Brief

CONTENTS

APPLICATIONS

PREFACE

The finance discipline has matured to the point where there exists a sound body of theory that represents our collective understanding of finance. In this book, we have summarized the theory of finance—the agreed upon common body of knowledge—by setting down, for the first time, the Principles of Finance. Our Principles of Finance are a set of fundamental tenets designed to help the student develop intuition about financial decision-making. It is our firmly held belief that if you understand the "first principles," every problem and issue can be addressed and solved with these principles; essentially, if you understand the general theory, you can use it to solve specific problems.

Our Principles of Finance provide an integrated view of the theory of finance, so that financial decision-making can be treated as an application of a coherent body of theory. By understanding the Principles of Finance, rather than simply memorizing a collection of seemingly disparate decision rules, students will be better able to cope with the unforeseen and inevitable changes and problems they will encounter in the future.

After covering the basics, we show how to apply these insights to the world of corporate finance, using financial modeling. Many of our applications come from the "real world," with which John Finnerty is so intimately familiar. Some of the applications involve well-known companies. In other applications, we have changed the name "to protect the innocent." All of the applications are designed to illustrate how theory is useful and immediately applicable to the real world.

Of course, like every discipline, there is always more to learn—no matter how large and well understood the common body of knowledge becomes. We are honest about the limits of our understanding. We indicate what is known, what is believed, and what is still being debated. The latter represents the very important process of research, in which many faculty are engaged. The efforts of a great many people over many years have gone into the development and testing of the theory of finance. We cite many important contributions to the finance literature by a broad range of scholars at the ends of the chapters.

Students often hear about the supposed conflict between research and teaching. In our opinion, this is very misleading. There is no inherent conflict between the creation and the dissemination of knowledge. There are those who expend more of their effort on one process than the other, but virtually all of us are involved in both processes to at least some extent.

INNOVATIONS OF SPECIAL NOTE

FINANCIAL CONTRACTING   In addition to providing the first formal enumeration of the Principles of Finance, this book further modernizes the teaching of finance by containing a separate chapter on financial contracting. This is in addition to (1) consistent recognition throughout the book of the existence of asymmetric information, and the attendant agency problems that are created by it, and (2) the explicit application of the important theoretical concepts of this material to specialized topics.

OPTIONS   Our treatment of options is contained in the first section of the book, and we use the term *option* in its broadest sense: any right without an obligation attached to it. These innovations enable us to apply the important insights of option theory to a wide variety of topics. Thus, for example, option concepts are applied to financial contracting, capital budgeting, and capital structure, among many others.

A PRACTITIONER'S PERSPECTIVE   John Finnerty's almost 15 years of experience in the everyday world of finance brings a unique perspective to this book. John can speak credibly to students about the tremendous value of understanding the theory of finance in a world of practice because of his first-hand experience.

INTERNATIONALIZATION   A great deal is heard today about the importance of internationalizing the curriculum. We believe that our country's continued economic well-being demands that we be international in our thinking. It is imperative that today's firms incorporate into their decision-making the specific constraints and additional market imperfections introduced by operating in an international economy. However, the theory of finance does not stop at the border. Thus, the concepts and principles developed in this book are readily applicable to international transactions. With this in mind, we treat the international aspects of finance as both a point of view and a particular market environment in which to operate.

LEARNING AIDS

PRINCIPLES FIRST   The book is divided into two sections. The Principles section builds the conceptual foundation for the balance of the book. This enables us to construct an integrated model of financial decision-making. After reading Chapter 2, Principles of Finance, students will know quite a bit about what is known and what is not known about finance.

APPLICATIONS NEXT   The Applications section applies the basic principles to a broad range of financial topics that we feel fit logically into four areas: (1) Long-Term Investment Decisions; (2) Long-Term Financing Decisions; (3) Investment and Financing Interactions; and (4) Short-Term Decisions: Managing the Firm. This provides significant latitude for professors to select particular application topics for coverage in whichever order they choose. For the most part, students will have gained the necessary conceptual background in the Principles section to be able to follow all of the applications material.

PRACTICE PROBLEMS   The problems at the end of each chapter are numerous, with 30 or more per chapter, and were written by the authors specifically for this book. The problems are differentiated according to the type of instructional purpose: Problems in problem set A are very straightforward. They review the chapter material and can be answered by direct reference to the text material. Problems in problem set B also relate fairly closely to the material in the chapter but are somewhat more complex. Problems in problem set C are extensions of material presented in the chapter. The C-type problems are designed to challenge the students with complex situations, puzzles, or the examination of more subtle implications of the material in the chapter. Occasionally, problems are drawn from material in earlier chapters to reinforce the retention of important concepts.

LEAD-IN PROBLEMS   Most of the applications chapters begin with a real-world problem or issue that a corporation has faced. A "solution" to the problem is given at the end of the chapter, which indicates what the company actually did, why it did so, and what alternative courses of action it might reasonably have taken instead.

DECISION SUMMARY BOXES   Along with the applications in the chapter, we provide summaries of the important dimensions of each decision situation—a sort of "what really matters" for each decision. These summaries are identified as *Decision Summary Boxes* and are located in the Summary Section of each of the applications chapters (10 through 26). They provide a set of policy guidelines that are consistent with financial theory, yet take into account those areas where "gaps" in the theory make it difficult, if not impossible, to make unambiguous financial policy choices (e.g., the choice of a dividend policy).

NEW TERMS AND JARGON   Terms are defined and redefined in early usage to minimize effort wasted on looking up definitions. Examples given early in the book are deliberately drawn from everyday experience, to minimize student feelings of being overwhelmed by new jargon. Important, as well as specialized, terms appear in boldfaced type in their first usage, and often again in their first usage in subsequent chapters. These words are included in the glossary.

GLOSSARY   The glossary is extensive and is designed to serve as a convenient reference source, both for usage in later chapters and after graduation. Also, the definitions of many of the terms in the glossary cite one or more sections of the book in which a more complete definition can be found, often in context.

HUMOR   We interrupt the dry dullness from time to time to bring you occasional messages of humor and levity. Our tone is purposefully somewhat informal, in the spirit of not taking ourselves too seriously.

TARGETED AUDIENCE

This book was written for use in the core finance class in MBA and other masters programs in accounting, business, or management, and for advanced courses in undergraduate programs. There is an abundance of applications material, so the book can also be used subsequently in advanced masters courses and as a text for case classes at both the graduate and undergraduate levels.

We assume throughout the book that students have familiarity with the standard prerequisites in business/management programs: college level algebra, financial accounting, microeconomics, and probability and statistics. Although we explicitly assume that students have this background, we provide reminders of basic definitions and concepts that will have been covered in prerequisite courses. Also, while an understanding of mathematics is necessary, we facilitate the learning process by providing simple examples and analogies. By providing both verbal/logical *and* rigorous mathematical descriptions, we hope to enlist each student's "learning strength," as well as have the descriptions reinforce one another.

Finally, this book has been written with the intent that it will become a useful future reference tool for students as they move through their business careers. For example, the abundance of applications material will provide a reference source for material not covered in class; the inclusion of reference section numbers in the glossary facilitates later reference use; and the decision summary boxes provide an easily accessed summary of the important dimensions and concepts connected with particular topics.

SUPPLEMENTARY MATERIALS

INSTRUCTOR'S MANUAL Written by Raj A. Padmaraj of Bowling Green State University, the instructor's manual provides instructor guidance on how best to use the book as a teaching tool. The first part provides chapter-by-chapter **teaching notes** that contain an outline and summary, including key concepts and definitions, demonstration problems with transparency masters for class usage, supplementary problems with solutions, and suggestions for problem assignments. A guide for cross referencing to other texts is also given. The second part contains a **test bank** with solutions that is also available on computer disk.

SOLUTIONS MANUAL The solutions manual contains solutions to all of the end-of-chapter problems and is available separately for students. It was written by the authors, in conjunction with D. Katherine Spiess of the University of Missouri—Columbia.

STUDY GUIDE Written by Daniel T. Winkler of the University of North Carolina at Greensboro, the study guide provides the student with a helpful perspective on how to get the most out of the book, including a guide to self-study, and serves as a useful companion to the book. For each chapter, it furnishes an overview, learning objectives, chapter highlights, key terms, worked problems, and a set of exercises with complete solutions.

SOFTWARE Written by Hugh S. McLaughlin of Bentley College, computer software in the form of LOTUS 1-2-3 spreadsheets designed to be used on a personal computer is available to adopters at no cost. This software covers specific decision/valuation models such as the Black-Scholes option pricing model, capital budgeting project analysis, and lease versus buy analysis, among others. Each topic includes a master model that can be used for calculation, problems that ask the student to complete the logic of partially created models, and problems that ask the student to use the model for computational purposes.

ACKNOWLEDGMENTS

As with any book, this book is not simply the work of its authors. Many people have contributed to its creation and development from initial concept to finished product. In particular, we deeply appreciate the invaluable comments and suggestions we have received from the following people who read all or part of various drafts of the manuscript:

Sankar Acharya New York University

James S. Ang Florida State University

Ronald C. Braswell Florida State University

Greggory A. Brauer	University of Washington
Ivan E. Brick	Rutgers University
Douglas Carman	Southwest Texas State University
Richard P. Castanias	University of California—Davis
Susan Chaplinsky	University of Michigan
Larry Y. Dann	University of Oregon
John R. Ezzell	Pennsylvania State University
Mona J. Gardner	Illinois State University
Chinmoy Gosh	University of Connecticut
Atul Gupta	Bentley College
Puneet Handa	New York University
Shalom J. Hochman	University of Houston
Keith M. Howe	DePaul University
Mai E. Iskandar	Northern Illinois University
O. Maurice Joy	University of Kansas
Ronald J. Kudla	University of Wisconsin—Eau Claire
Bruce R. Kuhlman	University of Toledo
Raman Kumar	Virginia Polytechnic Institute and State University
Edward C. Lawrence	University of Missouri—St. Louis
Scott Lummer	Texas A&M University
Richard D. MacMinn	University of Texas—Austin
Gershon N. Mandelker	University of Pittsburgh
Terry Maness	Baylor University
Surendra K. Mansinghka	San Francisco State University
Ronald W. Melicher	University of Colorado
Mark J. Moran	Case Western Reserve University
Dennis T. Officer	University of Kentucky
Debra K. Reed	Texas A&M University
Ralph W. Sanders, Jr.	Tulane University
Barry Schachter	Tulane University
Lemma W. Senbet	University of Maryland
Dennis P. Sheehan	Purdue University
David C. Shimko	University of Southern California
D. Katherine Spiess	University of Missouri—Columbia
Robert J. Sweeney	Marquette University
John Thatcher	Marquette University
Daniel T. Winkler	University of North Carolina—Greensboro

We also thank Robert J. Kueppers of Deloitte & Touche who reviewed portions of the manuscript dealing with accounting issues and Stephen B. Land, Esq., of Howard, Darby & Levin and Jeffrey D. Summa of Deloitte & Touche, both of whom reviewed portions of the manuscript dealing with tax issues. As we remind you repeatedly in the book, taxes play an important role in financial decision-making, and the tax law changes frequently. It is therefore important to check on the current tax provisions that may affect a financial decision when you undertake a financial analysis.

We are grateful to too many other people for their help and encouragement to mention them all individually. We appreciate the support of current colleagues and that of our former colleagues at Lazard Frères & Co., Morgan Stanley & Co., and the University of Missouri—Columbia. We are particularly grateful to several individuals who have helped shape our thinking. Helpful discussions with friends and colleagues over the years have contributed greatly to the book. These included, but were certainly not limited to, discussions with Victor Marek Borun, Fordham University; Uphinder S. Dhillon, SUNY—Binghamton; Louis H. Ederington, University of Oklahoma; Adam K. Gehr, Jr., DePaul University; Paul C. Grier, SUNY—Binghamton; Bradford D. Jordan, University of Missouri—Columbia; Dennis J. Lasser, SUNY—Binghamton; Dean Leistikow, Fordham University; Wilbur G. Lewellen, Purdue University; James A. Miles, Pennsylvania State University; Philip C. Parr, Eastern Washington University; Richard H. Pettway, University of Missouri—Columbia; George E. Pinches, University of Kansas; Gabriel Ramirez, SUNY—Binghamton; Jong-Chul Rhim, University of Southern Indiana, Anthony Saunders, New York University; David P. Stuhr, Fordham University; F. Katherine Warne, Southwestern Bell; and Frank M. Werner, Fordham University. Special thanks go to David J. Loschky and John D. Stowe, both of University of Missouri—Columbia, for their encouragement, friendship, and the innumerable insights they have engendered over the years.

We thank John Finnerty's current partners and associates at McFarland Dewey & Co. who have provided a stimulating environment within which to apply the principles of finance and a laboratory for testing new analytical techniques based on these principles.

John Finnerty is especially grateful to Arthur R. Taylor, Dean of the Fordham University Faculty of Business, for providing him with the opportunity to return to full-time teaching. Nothing crystallizes your thinking on a subject better than teaching it to others.

Many students, both graduate and undergraduate, suffered through class testing of the material in this book, putting up with inconveniences such as last minute changes and incomplete tables and figures at the back of the chapters. We appreciate and have benefited from their many ideas for improving the presentation. Of particular note are the contributions of Su-Jane Chen, Karen K. Dixon, Barbara Finnegan, David N. Ketcher, Chang-Hwan Lee, Ken Motamed, Mary Peters, Chris Prestigiacomo, and Christina VanCook. In addition to our own class usage of the material, we especially appreciate the help of Keith M. Howe, Scholes Professor of Finance at DePaul University, and his students for class testing some of the chapters.

We thank all of the people at West Educational Publishing who helped with the project, including Nancy Hill-Whilton, Susanna Smart, Ann Hillstrom, and especially our editor, Dick Fenton. The insights, thoughtfulness, and patience of our production editor, Mark Jacobsen, in the face of an entirely unreasonable production schedule deserve a note of special thanks. We are deeply indebted to Rich Wohl, our friend and original editor at West, who helped initiate and shape this project, offered valuable insights along the way, and strongly encouraged us throughout the process.

Lifelong appreciation goes to our fathers, E. Ward Emery and John P. Finnerty, to Doug Emery's undergraduate professor, mentor, and friend, William Graziano of Baker University, and to John Finnerty's great uncle, O. K. Taylor, who started his career at what is now Exxon Corporation as an office boy and retired many years later as deputy treasurer. After years of trying they finally got it across to us: "When in doubt, always go back to first principles."

In this book we say a great deal about the 12 Principles of Finance that are explained in Chapter 2. In writing this book we regularly encountered a 13th principle—the unlucky one that is the bane of all authors. We call it the Underestimation Principle. Its circularity highlights its inevitability: Writing a book always takes longer than you think—even when you take into account the Underestimation Principle! So we sincerely thank our spouses and families for their tremendous forbearance during the long and arduous process that culminated in this book. Yes, it did take considerably longer than we originally estimated, and it even took longer than every subsequent estimation. But we never lied; it's just that the basic principles always assert themselves.

Douglas R. Emery
Binghamton, NY

John D. Finnerty
Spring Lake, NJ

A Few Words
from a Practitioner
on the Importance of Theory

This book explains the theory of finance and illustrates its application to problems in corporate finance. Students, as well as practitioners, tend to view theory as a not-so-necessary evil. They often say that theory seems to get in the way of good financial practice. We think that view comes from a misunderstanding of the role that financial theory plays in promoting our understanding of financial behavior and in preparing us to deal with problems we have not previously encountered.

It is easy to learn how to cope with routine problems. Many financial managers develop a list of rules for dealing with such problems. But what happens when the financial manager encounters a problem that doesn't conveniently fit one of the rules? No list can ever be complete, so if you adopt the list-of-rules approach you will inevitably encounter a problem that doesn't fit. That's why understanding financial theory is so important.

A thorough understanding of financial theory enables you to transcend simple rules. You need to understand the basis for the rules—the theory—in order to be able to deal with situations to which the rules do not apply. Financial theory enables you to understand what is going on in the financial world. Believe it or not now, once you have a sound conceptual view of finance, you will understand financial transactions that now seem puzzling, ones you might have read about in the *Wall Street Journal*. Understanding the theory of finance enables you to identify a point of departure for evaluating a newly encountered problem, to ask the questions necessary to elicit the information you need, and to process this information and develop a solution to the problem.

Theory is as important to finance as it is to other disciplines. Consider other professions, such as law or medicine. Some law schools emphasize the theory of the law; others dwell on the current statutes in the state in which the law school is located. Some medical schools stress the importance of research and theory; others dwell on current practices. If you encounter a difficult legal or medical problem that cannot be solved with routine practices, and thus requires special interpretation, who would you want working on your behalf? Someone who possesses a working knowledge of the theory will be able to give you better advice than another who does not have such knowledge.

We must be honest and tell you that the theory of finance is not complete—we know of no theory that is. First, there are significant controversies that have yet to be resolved—and on which research efforts continue in earnest. We explain the arguments on both sides of each controversy and tell you where we think the weight of the evidence lies. Second, there are several areas in which financial managers appear, on the basis of current financial theory, to be acting incorrectly—perhaps even irrationally—and we offer potential reasons for such apparent conflicts between practice and theory.

We present 12 Principles of Finance in Chapter 2 as the underpinning for financial theory. One deserves special comment. The first principle, the Principle of Self-Interested Behavior, is the most basic. Without this principle, we cannot explain financial behavior. Regrettably, some individuals have misapplied this principle. I have had the unfortunate experience of encountering, at one time or another, individuals who "crossed over the line" by pursuing self-interested behavior without regard to the law. They paid a heavy price: in two cases, the price included time in jail and banishment from the securities industry for life. In a third case, the price was high even though it did not include time in jail. If you pursue a career in finance, you will likely encounter one or more situations in which you could make literally millions of dollars by, for example, trading on insider information (what is called exploiting asymmetric information for ill-gotten gain—illegally using information that others don't have). Our Principle of Self-Interested Behavior explicitly excludes such behavior; individuals should behave in accordance with the established rules and regulations to ensure sound ethical—and legal—behavior. There is nothing wrong with pursuing self-interested behavior—just as there is nothing wrong with trying to minimize your taxes—*provided you always play by the rules of the game*.

To return to the issue raised at the outset, students and practitioners often have little patience for theory. Yet, I have always marvelled at how well certain individuals I have met have succeeded in finance without the benefit of any formal training in finance. Indeed, some of the more successful traders and sales people I have known didn't even have college degrees. But what they all had in common was an acquired understanding of the principles of finance—those generalities that hold across so many specific situations—and a well-honed ability to apply them. They probably couldn't articulate them but they surely understood what the principles implied about financial behavior. And they exhibited an unusual adeptness at applying the Principle of Self-Interested Behavior to exploit that understanding. Whether it's a bond trader deciding which bonds to buy, a stock portfolio manager deciding which stocks to sell, an investment banker determining the structure of a new security, or a corporate treasurer deciding what type of security to issue, what seems to distinguish those who are successful from those who are not is their grasp of financial theory and their ability to apply it in *any* situation.

So my advice to you is to take some time to understand the basics—the theory—because it's in your own self-interest.

John D. Finnerty, General Partner
McFarland Dewey & Co.

PRINCIPLES

INTRODUCTION

The discipline of finance concerns, first, valuation. In its various forms, the question What is something worth? is one that is asked again and again. Finance is also concerned with decision-making. For example, how should a firm obtain the money it needs to operate? The two functions are interrelated because financial decisions depend on value, as in the case of a firm's decision whether to purchase a particular asset, such as a truck. The decision criterion for such a decision is buy the asset only if it is worth at least as much as it costs. Although this point may seem obvious, it can easily be overlooked in a complex situation, as in the heat of a takeover battle.

In your financial accounting classes you learned about accounting for the firm: The **balance sheet** describes (accounts for) the firm's current financial position. It depicts the financial condition of the firm at one instant in time, much like a photograph. The **income statement** describes (accounts for) the profitability of the firm's operations during the latest accounting period, say a quarter of a year. It provides a measure of the firm's performance. The **statement of cash flows** summarizes (accounts for) the sources and uses of cash by the firm during the latest accounting period, reflecting the flow of resources into and out of the firm in terms of their associated cash flows. It is similar to a map in that it depicts the firm's path from the previous balance sheet to the current balance sheet.

While both finance and accounting are concerned with a firm's assets and liabilities, they differ from each other in at least one major respect: They tend to focus on different periods of time. Accounting, with its emphasis on review, generally has a historical outlook. One of its major purposes is to account for what has happened in the past; for example, accountants update a firm's balance sheet to determine the firm's current financial position or audit a firm's financial statements to verify their accuracy. In contrast, the decision-making emphasis of finance gives it a focus on the future. Picking up from the accounting view of the firm's current position, finance concentrates on the questions What do we do now? and Where do we go from here?

To answer these questions, a firm gathers information, analyzes it, and decides on a particular course of action.

THE THREE AREAS OF FINANCE

The discipline of finance is divided into three subareas. Each of the subareas concerns the same set of transactions, but each deals with them from a different viewpoint. Figure 1-1 characterizes the relationships among the various subparts of finance in relation to the system of markets you studied in economics.

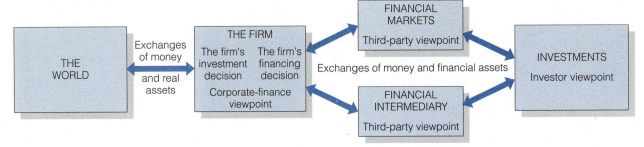

FIGURE 1-1

One characterization of the financial world.

Corporate finance is an area of finance that deals with the operation of a corporation from that firm's viewpoint. Broadly speaking, corporate finance can be further broken down in terms of the two sides of the balance sheet. The asset side involves what is called the **investment decision** because it is concerned with (decisions affecting) the assets in which the firm should invest. The liabilities and owners' equity side involves what is called the **financing decision** because it is concerned with obtaining the funds (financing) from investors so that the firm can obtain the assets in which it has decided to invest. Decisions in corporate finance all reflect certain basic Principles of Finance.

Investments is an area of finance that also concerns the firm's financing decision, but from the other side of each transaction. Investments studies it from the viewpoint of the investors rather than from the corporation's viewpoint. Confusion about terms can arise between **investments** and the firm's investment decision. You can think of the two as a sequential chain: Investors invest in (provide financing for) the firm by purchasing the financial securities the firm issues; the firm in turn invests in (purchases) assets.

Financial markets and intermediaries, the third area of finance, also deals with the firm's financing decision, but from yet another viewpoint, that of a third party. In the case of financial markets, the viewpoint is that of an independent observer of the transaction. In the case of financial intermediaries, the viewpoint is that of an intermediary, or go-between, who facilitates transactions between investors and firms.

Generally, the firm's investment decision concerns the exchange of money for **real assets**. Real assets can be **tangible assets**, such as equipment and raw materials, or **intangible assets**, such as patents, copyrights, trademarks, and technical expertise. The firm's investment decision ties into its production decision in the following manner: The firm purchases plant, equipment, and other real assets in exchange for money; it hires labor and purchases raw materials in exchange for money; it manufactures a product using the real assets together with the labor and raw materials; and it sells the product in exchange for money. All of these transactions (decisions) affect only the asset side of the firm's balance sheet.

The firm's financing decision concerns the exchange of money for **financial assets**. Financial assets are contracts that provide for the exchange of money at various points in time. For example, a **bond** provides for a specified set of cash payments to its owner, who has previously exchanged money to purchase the bond. Financial securities, such as stocks and bonds, are financial assets. Other contracts for the exchange of money, such as short-term bank loans, accounts payable, and accounts receivable are also financial assets.

The positions of the financial securities issuer and the investor in those securities are mirror images of each other, but they involve inherent conflicts that must be resolved contractually. The mirror-image relationship means that a financial security, such as a bond, is an asset for the investor, but it is a liability for the firm. While this is obvious if you think about it, it is important to keep in mind. (Also note that while a share of stock is not, strictly speaking, a liability of the firm, it too imposes certain obligations and responsibilities on the firm.)

THE ROLE OF SCIENCE IN THE STUDY OF FINANCE 1.2

When a person hears the word science, words such as chemistry, biology, and physics generally come to mind. But science is broader than this. Webster defines science as "the observation, identification, description, experimental investigation, and theoretical explanation of a class of phenomena." In this book, we describe the study, or science, of *finance*.

Even if you have never studied finance, you no doubt have some awareness of the stock market. Have you ever wondered what the "Dow" is or why it changes every day? (Actually, it may change from minute to minute with each trade of a stock that composes the Dow.) If you heard about the "takeover fight" involving RJR Nabisco, Inc., did you wonder what it was all about?[1] Such questions stem from human curiosity, which is the starting point for science. Science is essentially a quest for understanding.

But why do we want to understand something? Sometimes, it is simply curiosity, but in other cases, our drive for understanding is based on a desire to improve our world. When we understand something, we can use that understanding to predict an outcome. For example, we know that under "normal" circumstances, if we lower the price of a product, we will sell more units of that product. You might recall from an economics course that this phenomenon is referred to as a downward-sloping demand curve. Because we understand downward-sloping demand curves (at least to some extent), we can use that understanding to predict changes in product sales under a carefully specified set of circumstances.

And why do we want to be able to predict? Accurate prediction can be used to *prescribe* a method of obtaining a particular desired outcome. Continuing with our price-demand example, suppose our firm has decided to discontinue manufacturing a particular product. Suppose further that we want to eliminate our existing inventory of that product quickly to make room for inventory of other products. Because we can predict something about the price-demand relationship, we might decide to lower the price to sell off the inventory more quickly.[2]

Our understanding of the financial world is embodied in the theory of finance. While the theory of finance is not perfect or complete, we can use such predictions to prescribe better decision-making techniques, at least to the extent that this body of theory can predict outcomes. Therefore, understanding the theory of finance is a prerequisite to good financial decision-making. Rules of thumb are limited in their scope. They can take you only so far. *At some point, you must think!* A rule of thumb can be used to solve problems that are familiar. In other words, a rule of thumb is good for solving problems that are not really problems.

---

[1] We will tell you about the battle for control of RJR Nabisco in Chapter 22.
[2] Of course, lowering the price is not the only thing we could do to speed the sale of the inventory, but it is a method that generally works.

In contrast to rules of thumb, principles, derived from a useful body of theory, provide a foundation for solving problems you have never before encountered; problems that are *truly* problems. Remember, if decision-making can be programmed into a computer, as rules of thumb can be, *you* are not needed (except to write the program and input the data, and you can probably even pay someone else to do that).

Our study of finance, then, is essentially a quest for better theories that will provide better understanding so that we can prescribe better decision-making techniques. An important tool for adding to the theory of finance is a technique called **modeling**.

1.3   ## MODELING

A **model** is a method of depicting reality. There are many different types of models. Most of us have built physical models of things such as cars, ships, and airplanes. Most people use a road map to determine their route to an unfamiliar place. A photograph or picture is yet another type of model encountered in everyday life. In other courses of study, you have no doubt used charts and graphs, which we will also use in our study of finance.

Many of the models used in finance are **mathematical models**. The primary benefit of using a mathematical model is its precision in specifying relationships. This does not mean that every mathematical model represents reality perfectly. It simply means that there will be no question about the relationships specified in a mathematical model.

Returning once again to our price-demand example, when we say that lowering the price of a product will increase sales, we really mean that the statement is true under "normal" circumstances. In essence, we have a set of circumstances, *assumptions*, under which the statement will be true. The idea that a statement holds under "normal" circumstances is actually a model of a particular situation. A mathematical model extends this notion by expressing the assumptions—the circumstances—as mathematical relationships.

AN EXAMPLE OF A SIMPLE MATHEMATICAL MODEL

Suppose you want to drive from one place to another, 100 miles away. A highway with a speed limit of 55 miles per hour connects the places. You estimate you will average 50 mph. How long do you expect it will take to get from one place to the other?

The answer, of course, is 2 hours. But how do we know that? Because of a time-distance-speed model. Time equals distance divided by speed, or

$$T = \frac{D}{S} \tag{1.1}$$

where T, D, and S denote time, distance, and speed, respectively. Equation (1.1) is a simple model, used frequently, though we may not think much about its being a mathematical model.

THE PARTS OF A MATHEMATICAL MODEL

Broadly speaking, a mathematical model is made up of three parts: **parameters**, **variables**, and **relationships**.[3] D and S are the parameters in the time-distance-speed model given in Equation (1.1). The use of parameters creates a model that can be applied to a large number of situations. In short, parameters allow us to generalize. By expressing distance as D, rather than specifying a particular value, our model can be applied to *any* situation.[4]

Variables are the outcomes for which the model solves. That is, they are the values to be predicted. We use a model to predict outcomes on the basis of a set of parameter values. In the example given, the model tells us we need to leave one place at least 2 hours before we need to be at the other place. T is the only variable in our time-distance-speed model.

To the extent we have control over the parameter values, we can predict outcomes based on possible parameter value choices. By examining the predicted outcomes, we can prescribe the best choices of the parameter values to achieve a particular outcome. For example, if we are running a little short on time, we can use the model to tell us that we need to average 52 rather than 50 mph to keep an appointment. When used in this application, we are actually rearranging the model so that $S = D/T$. This rearrangement illustrates how the distinction between parameters and variables can become "blurred." S and T have exchanged roles (as well as positions in the model) from what they were in Equation (1.1), so that S is a variable and T is a parameter. The roles are determined by the model's point of view.

The relationships embodied in a model can be established by a variety of methods. In some cases, relationships—how one parameter affects another—are estimated empirically as they might be for the time it takes to perform a maintenance function. Other relationships are specified by contractual agreement as in the case of the amount of money you will earn working as an assistant to one of your professors. Finally, many relationships are specified on a logical, conceptual, or theoretical basis as in the case of expecting a downward-sloping demand curve.

JUDGING THE USEFULNESS OF A MODEL

What is it that makes a model useful? Is our time-distance-speed model a useful model? Most people think it is a useful model, but why? It is certainly not because the model is complete and all-inclusive. Look at all of the things left out of our time-distance-speed model: contingencies for gas stops, fixing a flat tire, reduced speed due to road construction, bad weather. If you think about it, you can see that the use of "average" speed covers up a great deal of complexity. In spite of all of its missing factors, it is a very useful model.

Because a model is an approximation of reality, its usefulness is judged by the *accuracy* of its predictions. In short, what we really want to know is whether the model's predictions agree with our experiences. In the case of our time-distance-

---

[3] We use the terms **parameter** and **variable** because novice students may be more familiar with these terms. Models in economics often use the terms **exogenous variable** in place of parameter and **endogenous variable** in place of variable.

[4] For example, suppose the two towns in our example had been 200 miles apart but everything else is as described previously. Then we need only put the value 200, rather than 100, into Equation (1.1) to find that we expect it to take 4 hours rather than 2 to get to our destination. Therefore, the use of parameters allows us to apply our model to an infinite number of different situations, rather than using it only for the situation at hand.

speed model, it does. Think about it. Odds are that you used a time-distance-speed model the last time you estimated the time to drive someplace.

A model's accuracy is sometimes constrained by the availability and/or cost of data. For example, suppose you want to borrow some money and would like to calculate the amount of interest you will have to pay. You would like to pay as low an interest rate as possible. If rates will be lower tomorrow, you may be better off waiting until tomorrow to borrow the money. If rates will be higher tomorrow, you may be better off borrowing the money today. We know how to calculate the amount of interest once we know the interest rate. What we do not know is whether the rate will be lower today or tomorrow. In such cases, where accurate information cannot be obtained, although the relationship expressed is theoretically correct, the model may not be very useful.

Even if information can be obtained, it may not be worth the **cost**. For example, suppose you want to buy a pen; nothing fancy, just an everyday pen. You like Cross pens. You have at least three alternatives:

a. Drive to all of the stores in town that sell Cross pens, determine the lowest price for the style you want, drive back to the store offering the lowest price, and buy the pen;

b. Let your fingers do the walking and call all of the stores in town that sell Cross pens, determine the lowest price, drive to the store offering the lowest price, and buy the pen; or

c. Stop at a store that sells Cross pens while you are on your way to this class and pay whatever price is demanded to buy the pen.

If you are like us, you will probably choose alternative c because the difference in prices among the various stores normally will not justify the search costs associated with alternatives a and b.

Similarly, when we choose to use one model rather than another, we often make a trade-off between prediction accuracy and cost. Sometimes it is not worth the time, effort, and resources necessary to estimate the parameter values required to use a more complex but more accurate model. That is, the added cost associated with using the more accurate model cannot be justified.

IMPERFECT MODELS

Returning once again to our price-demand example, you can see that a downward-sloping demand curve is a form of model. Of course, the predictions of such a model can be more or less accurate. There is a famous example in marketing about a product that had an upward-sloping demand curve. In other words, the firm sold more units when it increased the price. Think about it: Raise the price and sell more units. Sounds backwards, doesn't it? That is exactly why it is such a famous example. The product is the synthetic beach sandal, commonly called flip-flops.[5] When first offered for sale, very few consumers purchased flip-flops. Apparently, the price was so low that consumers did not believe that flip-flops could be worth purchasing. When retailers understood this problem, they raised the price. With a higher price, consumers started trying the product, and sales increased—hence the upward-sloping demand curve. Of course, after consumers found that the product was worth using, competition drove the price back down. Today, flip-flops have a down-

---

[5] A friend of ours calls them "go-aheads" because, as he says, "Did you ever try going backward in them?"

ward-sloping demand curve, just like most other products. (You might say the demand curve for flip-flops, flip-flopped. Of course, *we* wouldn't dare say that.)

In the case of the temporary upward-sloping demand curve for flip-flops, were the factors that normally create a downward-sloping demand curve missing? Would not a lower price make the product affordable to more people? Of course it would. However, in that case, there was a factor present in the situation that is unusual: the price was *so* low that virtually anyone could afford them, creating an initial impression that the incredibly low price identified a useless product. This is reflected in the fact that the demand curve changed from upward- to downward-sloping once consumers discovered that the product was indeed worthwhile, even if it was very inexpensive.

In new product situations, such as with flip-flops, even if the factors that normally create a downward-sloping demand curve are not the whole story, they are a good place to *start*. It is the same with other models in finance. Even when a model does not predict perfectly, it can nevertheless provide useful insights and represent a good starting point for solving new and challenging problems.

THREE MODELS OF THE FIRM   1.4

Our view of the firm has evolved over a number of decades, and it continues to evolve. To express this evolving view, three models of the firm are presented below. The first model is essentially a "pure" view of the firm. It is an idealized look that provides broad categories of parts and interactions among those parts. As with a downward-sloping demand curve, it is a good starting point for understanding and analyzing the firm's financial decisions.

THE INVESTMENT-VEHICLE MODEL

This model of the firm is essentially the one presented in Figure 1-1. Investors provide funds (financing) in exchange for financial securities. In this world, there are only two types of financial securities: equity and debt. **Equity** denotes ownership of the firm, and is typically represented by shares of **common stock**. A person who owns all the shares of common stock owns the firm. If more than one person owns shares in the firm, each person's ownership portion is simply the number of shares he owns divided by the total number of existing shares. **Debt** denotes a legal obligation to make contractually agreed upon future payments, identified as **interest** and repayment of the **principal** (original debt amount). Debtholders have simply loaned the firm money and have no claim of ownership as long as the firm meets its payment obligations. The firm's managers use the funds provided by investors to buy (and sell) real assets, such as plant and equipment, and other inputs, such as labor, raw materials, and semifinished (finished) goods. In the investment-vehicle model, the firm's managers are neutral intermediaries who act only in the best interest of the shareholders, the owners of the firm. Sometimes, especially in the case of small firms, the owner is the manager. When this happens, obviously, there is no chance for conflict between the owner and the manager because they are one and the same.

The investment-vehicle model of the firm is embodied in the typically stated goal that managers should *maximize shareholder wealth*. In a "perfect" world (one without owner-manager conflicts) maximizing shareholder wealth is a theoretically correct managerial goal. Because it is correct in a "perfect" world, the investment-vehicle model is the best starting point for analyzing financial decisions.

THE ACCOUNTING MODEL

While the investment-vehicle model of the firm is not wrong, it must be operationalized. The accounting model of the firm is, in some sense, a subset of the investment-vehicle model because it is a method of operationalizing the investment-vehicle model. The accounting model is embodied in the balance sheet view of the firm, an abbreviated version of which is illustrated in Figure 1-2. As previously noted, the firm's investment decision concerns the asset side of the balance sheet, and the firm's financing decision concerns the liabilities and owners' equity side of the balance sheet. The accounting model represents the outcome of the actual financing and investment decisions of the firm, regardless of whether those decisions were in the best interest of the firm's owners.

THE SET-OF-CONTRACTS MODEL

The set-of-contracts model of the firm builds on the accounting model.[6] The accounting model includes many of the explicit contracts to which a firm is a party, such as loans, accounts payable, and accounts receivable. The set-of-contracts perspective of the firm has been developed in recent years to include implicit as well as explicit contracts to which the firm is a party. Implicit contracts include legally mandated requirements, such as workplace safety standards, and a manufacturing company's product liability. A firm also may have implicit contracts with employees that require the employee to expend his best effort. Shareholders have an implicit contract with the managers that requires the managers to act in the best interests of the shareholders. Less visible explicit contracts include things such as outstanding guarantees on previously sold products, promised employee severance pay, and future pension obligations to employees when they retire.

Many contracts depend on the occurrence of particular future outcomes, as where a firm has agreed to provide two weeks' notice prior to dismissing an employee. The obligation of providing two weeks' notice is *contingent* upon the decision to dismiss the employee. In other words, the obligation is not relevant *unless* an employee is actually dismissed. This type of contract is called a **contingent claim**.

A loan is another example of a contingent claim; the lender's claim to the firm's assets is contingent on the firm's actions. If a firm fails to make contracted loan payments, the lender can make a claim on the firm's assets, as by putting a lien on the firm's inventory. Loosely speaking, such a lien restricts the firm from selling the asset without paying off the lender. Therefore, if a firm fails in its contractual obligation to a lender, the lender will have some control over the firm's actions. That ability to exert control is contingent on the firm's contractual failure. Without such a failure, the lender has no control over the firm's actions.[7]

1.5   ## OWNERSHIP, CONTROL, AND RISK

Business firms today are often very large and complex organizations. However, by tracing the development of a firm, starting as one person's idea and evolving into a large complex organization, we can highlight the modern view of a firm—the set-

---

[6] In other areas of business, the set-of-contracts model is sometimes referred to as the **stakeholder** model.
[7] In practice, this scenario is further complicated by whether, or exactly when, the borrowing firm files for protection under the bankruptcy laws.

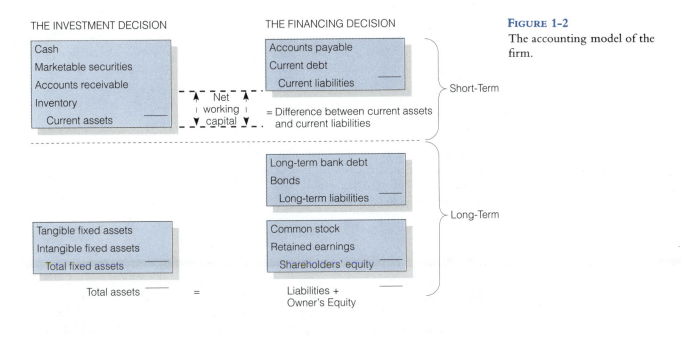

FIGURE 1-2
The accounting model of the firm.

of-contracts model. Consider the following fictionalized account of Henry Ford's automobile manufacturing firm.

START-UP

Henry started with the idea of producing a car that would be inexpensive enough to make buying a car affordable for a large number of people. Using his own money, he purchased raw materials, built one vehicle by himself, and sold the car to a satisfied customer, earning a profit. He reinvested the revenue from the sale, purchased additional raw materials, and manufactured more vehicles. Figure 1-3 illustrates Henry's balance sheet. Note that the basic accounting identity, total assets equals liabilities plus owners' equity, must always hold. Note also the financing decision represented by the right-hand side of the balance sheet. Henry provided the entire financing himself. (We use TA to denote the liabilities plus owners' equity to emphasize that the accounting identity, total assets = liabilities plus owners' equity, must always hold.) Henry is also the manager of the firm. In fact, at this point, besides suppliers and customers, Henry is the only person involved in the firm.

Henry's primary motivation in starting this firm was to earn money. But what happens if the firm is unsuccessful? That is, what happens if Henry cannot sell his cars for a profit? Eventually, Henry can run out of money. Under some circumstances, then, Henry can lose all the money he invested, but no one else stands to lose anything.

FIGURE 1-4

Balance sheet for Henry's firm after the bank loan.

Cash .... C′		
Raw materials .... R′		
Tools .... T′	Bank loan .... B′
Garage .... G′	Henry's equity .... HE′
Total Assets .... TA′	Liabilities + Owner's Equity ...... TA′

At this initial point, we want to note three things: First, Henry has exclusive **ownership** of the firm and its assets. Second, Henry has complete **control** of the firm and its assets (within legal limits). Third, Henry is bearing all the **risk** associated with this firm's investment.

DEBT

Building one car at a time was OK, but it occurred to Henry that if he could purchase a sufficiently large amount of raw materials with each of his orders, he could save money on shipping charges. Henry (and therefore the firm) did not have enough money to make such large orders. So Henry went to a bank and borrowed money, promising to repay the money out of revenues from future sales of his cars. Figure 1-4 illustrates the revised balance sheet for Henry's firm. Note that the firm's financing—its **capital structure**—is now made up of two parts. The two parts of the firm's new capital structure are debt and equity. (Recall that equity denotes ownership, whereas debt is a legal obligation that the company has to the debtholders according to a specified contract.) As the only equityholder, Henry still has exclusive ownership of the firm and its assets. Henry also retains direct control over the firm and its assets because he is the manager of the firm. However, Henry is now constrained by the obligations which the company has undertaken to obtain the loan from the bank. (Henry could be indirectly liable if he has provided his personal guarantee for the loan.)

As with Henry, the bank's primary motivation for making this loan was to earn money. Toward this end, Henry has to agree to repay the loan *plus* pay an interest charge. But what happens if the firm is unsuccessful? That is, what happens if Henry cannot sell his cars for a profit? Under some circumstances, the company might not have sufficient cash to pay the bank what the company has promised. Because it is possible the bank will not be fully repaid, the bank is bearing some of the risk of Henry's firm and its investment. But how much risk?

On the downside, if it is not fully paid, the bank may still receive something, whereas Henry will have lost all of the money he invested. On the upside, if the firm does well, the bank will receive only the loan repayment plus promised interest, whereas Henry will get all of the "excess net revenue"—everything above the amount promised to the bank. Therefore, Henry does worse than the bank on the downside and better than the bank on the upside, so Henry is bearing more risk than the bank. Of course, the bank must trust Henry to act responsibly and not run off to South America with all the firm's money, leaving the bank with nothing.

You can see that this situation is more complex than the one in which Henry provided all the financing for the firm. Let's review the situation: First, Henry retains exclusive ownership of the firm. Second, Henry still controls the firm's assets, but he is constrained by the firm's obligations to the bank. Third, the bank now bears some of the risk of the firm and its investment. Fourth, Henry bears all of the **re-**

sidual risk (all of the rest of the risk of the firm and its investment), which is the majority of the firm's risk.

EMPLOYEES

After a while, Henry has a large number of orders for cars, so large that it would take him longer than the rest of his life to build those cars, and more orders are coming in every day. To fill those orders, Henry hires some employees. The balance sheet of the firm does not change; however, Henry now has some implicit obligations to these employees, and the employees have some implicit obligations to the firm. Therefore, although neither the balance sheet nor the ownership of the firm has changed, Henry's control over the firm's assets is further constrained.

MULTIPLE EQUITYHOLDERS

Demand for Henry's cars continues to grow. Now, although Henry has enough employees to build the cars on backorder, he does not have sufficient money to purchase enough raw materials to build them. He goes to the bank, but the bank refuses to loan more money. In short, the bank manager says that loaning more money would place the bank at too much risk. The bank will agree to loan more money only if Henry puts up more money, but Henry doesn't have any more money; all of his money is already invested in the firm. So the bank suggests that Henry find other people to provide the required additional equity financing, and Henry does. He sells shares in his firm to new shareholders and creates a board of directors. Figure 1-5 illustrates the firm's new balance sheet.

Where do Henry and his firm stand now? First, the firm is no longer exclusively Henry's. The firm has other shareholders who are part owners. Second, although Henry is still the manager and still has control over the firm's assets, he is now even more constrained because in addition to the debt and employee obligations, Henry has an obligation to act in the best interests of the other shareholders. Third, the bank continues to bear some of the risk of the firm. Fourth, Henry no longer bears all of the firm's residual risk. He and the new shareholders now share the residual risk of the firm in direct proportion to the number of shares each person owns.

Let's also take a moment to point out the new shareholders' motivation for making this investment. As with Henry and the bank, their motivation is to make money. And the more money the firm makes, the more money each shareholder makes (in proportion to the number of shares each person owns). Since all of the shareholders, including Henry, have the same motivation, it might appear that all their interests are identical. However, Henry is the only shareholder who has direct control over the firm's assets. Therefore, the other shareholders have to trust Henry to act in their best interests.

Cash	C″	Bank loan	B″
Raw materials	R″	New shareholders' equity	O″
Tools	T″	Henry's equity	HE″
Garage	G″		
Total Assets	TA″	Liabilities + Owners' Equity	TA″

FIGURE 1-5

Balance sheet after going public.

SEPARATION OF OWNERSHIP FROM CONTROL

More time has now passed, and Henry's firm is operating more successfully than ever before, but Henry is now tired of working for the firm. He has decided that he can retire and live off the returns from his investment. So Henry hires special employees, **managers**, to run the firm—to make the operating decisions. As with some of the other changes already examined, hiring managers to run the firm will not change anything on the firm's balance sheet. Nevertheless, this change is a *very important* change: Henry no longer has direct control over the firm and its assets. The hired managers now have control over the firm's assets, and Henry has become like the other shareholders. In particular, he must now trust these hired managers to run the firm for his benefit, just as the other shareholders had to trust him previously.[8]

At this point, Henry's firm has become a very large and complex organization. At the start, the right-hand side of the balance sheet was very simple; its total was made up solely of Henry's equity. Now, it has become complex, involving explicit as well as implicit contracts among the many participants. You should be able to see that each of the changes in the firm that were noted above adds to the potential for conflicts of interest among the various parties. For example, consider a shareholder who does not have direct control over the firm's assets. This shareholder may be willing to place the firm at great risk to have a chance at earning a high return because she has other assets and can "afford" to take the risk. Contrast this shareholder with the manager of the firm who is not a shareholder. The manager has direct control over the firm's assets but may be unwilling to place the firm at great risk, regardless of the potential return, because the manager is not willing to suffer the possible loss of her job. There are also many other potential conflicts of interest that can arise in complex organizations. Chapter 9 further explores this fascinating and complex area of finance. More important, this theme—that there are conflicts among the various stakeholders of the firm (stockholders, bondholders, banks, employees, customers, etc.) that must be resolved and that shape the behavior of the firm—will recur repeatedly in future chapters.

1.6

THE ROLE OF THE CORPORATION

The corporate form is the predominant form of business organization in the United States in total output of goods and services. Corporations issue a variety of financial securities, which are traded in the capital markets. This section discusses the advantages the corporate form of organization has over the primary alternative forms.

THE CORPORATE FORM AND ITS BENEFITS

There are three basic forms of business organization: sole proprietorship, partnership, and corporation. In a **sole proprietorship**, a single individual owns all the assets of the business directly and is directly responsible for all its liabilities. The sole proprietor has **unlimited liability** with respect to the losses and liabilities of the business; that is, the sole proprietor's entire personal net worth is at risk. A sole proprietorship is not a taxable entity. Instead the income from the proprietorship is

---

[8]In actual situations, an owner like Henry can negotiate to become a member of the firm's board of directors, perhaps even the chairman. In fact, a majority owner can elect the whole board and install himself as chairman.

added to his other income to determine his income taxes. Most small businesses are set up as proprietorships because they are easy to organize.

A **partnership** is similar to a proprietorship except that there are two or more owners. In a **general partnership** all partners have unlimited liability, including unlimited liability for actions taken entirely by other general partners. The partners share in profits and losses, often in proportion to their respective capital contributions to the partnership. As with a proprietorship, the income from the business is taxed directly to the general partners; a partnership does not pay income taxes. Oil and gas ventures and real estate ventures are often organized as partnerships because that form of organization permits the co-venturers to apply partnership tax losses against other income to reduce their tax liability.

The partnership form has another disadvantage besides unlimited liability. If a general partner leaves the partnership or dies, the partnership must be dissolved. This would be very inconvenient if there were a very large number of partners. Many states permit **limited partnerships**, in which there are one or more limited partners in addition to the general partners. The general partners run the partnership with unlimited liability. The limited partners contribute capital and share in partnership profits or losses. But a limited partner's liability with respect to the partnership is limited to the capital she has invested. In addition, limited partners are typically permitted to leave the partnership by selling their partnership interests to other investors, thereby avoiding the need to dissolve the partnership.

A **corporation** is legally a "person" that is separate and distinct from its owners, who are its **stockholders**. A corporation is empowered to own assets, incur liabilities, sell securities to raise capital, and engage in other specified activities. The officers of a corporation are considered agents of the corporation and are authorized to act on its behalf.

The corporate form of organization has four major advantages over sole proprietorships and partnerships:

- *Limited liability.* Stockholder liability for the debts and other obligations of the corporation is limited to the loss of the shares which the individual owns. If a corporation goes bankrupt or loses a large product-liability suit, the most its shareholders can lose is their respective investments. In a proprietorship or a general partnership, the owners can lose considerably more, in the extreme case virtually their entire collective net worth.

- *Permanency.* A corporation's legal existence is not affected when some of its shareholders sell their shares. It is thus more permanent than a proprietorship or a partnership.

- *Better access to external sources of capital.* Because of its permanency and its ability to borrow money or to sell additional shares to raise funds, a corporation has greater financing flexibility than the other two forms.

- *Transferability of ownership.* Selling shares in a corporation is normally easier than trying to sell a proprietorship or a general partnership interest (which would require reconstituting the partnership).

The corporate form does have a significant drawback, however. A corporation must pay taxes on its income. Operating income that is to be paid out to stockholders in the form of dividends is thus exposed to income taxation twice, first to the corporation and then to the shareholder.

In an attempt to combine the advantages of the partnership and corporate forms without their respective disadvantages, some businesses have recently formed **master limited partnerships**, sold a portion (or in some cases all) of the limited partnership interests to the public, and qualified the limited partnership units for trading on the New York Stock Exchange. For example, California Federal Savings and Loan Association set up Cal Fed Income Partners L.P. in September 1986 to invest in income-producing real estate.[9] A wholly owned subsidiary of the bank served as the general partner, and the limited partnership units were sold in a **public offering**.

Master limited partnerships are designed to give investors the limited liability, permanency, better access to capital, and transferability of ownership that the corporate form provides but without exposing operating income to two layers of taxation. Master limited partnerships have been set up to operate real estate and oil and gas businesses. One publicly-traded master limited partnership owns more than 100 Burger King restaurants that it leases to Burger King franchisees. Another owns the Boston Celtics basketball team. You should not be surprised to learn that Congress has recently passed legislation that has resulted in certain master limited partnerships being taxed like corporations.

THE RIGHTS OF OWNERSHIP

As already noted, a corporation's common stockholders are the corporation's owners. As the owners, they have the following rights:

- *Dividend rights.* Common stockholders have the right to share equally on a per-share basis in any distribution of the company's earnings in the form of dividends.[10] This right is limited to the extent that the payment of dividends on common stock is at the discretion of the company's board of directors and is also subject to legal and other restrictions, which are discussed in Chapter 18.

- *Voting rights.* Common stockholders have the right to vote on certain matters, such as the annual election of directors. In most cases, each share of common stock entitles its holder to one vote.[11] A corporation's articles of incorporation typically specify either of two voting procedures: majority voting or cumulative voting. Under **majority voting**, with one vote per share, stockholders vote for each director separately, casting one vote per share for each director they support, and the candidates receiving the largest numbers of votes are elected to the board. Alternatively, under **cumulative voting**, the directors are voted on jointly, and a stockholder can, if he wants, cast all his votes in favor of a single candidate.[12] Cumulative voting makes it easier for a minority-stockholder group to elect a representative of its own to the board.

    Stockholder votes are usually routine. The corporation pays the cost of the

[9] Cal Fed Income Partners L.P. prospectus, November 20, 1986.

[10] Some companies have two or more classes of common stock. In such cases, each common stockholder shares equally with other common stockholders of the same class.

[11] Many companies have multiple classes of common stock with disproportionate voting rights. For example, Ford Motor Company has two classes of common stock. Class B stock, owned by members of the Ford family, controls 40% of the voting power, even though the class B stock represents less than 10% of the total outstanding common stock of the company. The Securities and Exchange Commission has initiated efforts to restrict companies in the future from having more than one class of common stock with disproportionate voting rights.

[12] For example, suppose there are 10 directors up for reelection and you own 100 shares. In that case, you have $100 \times 10 = 1,000$ votes. Under majority voting, you can vote 100 shares for each of 10 different candidates. Under cumulative voting, you can cast all 1,000 votes for a single candidate (or you can allocate them as you like among between 2 and 10 candidates).

solicitation of shareholder votes. The company's managers and directors recommend a slate of directors, propose outside auditors, and recommend how shareholders should vote on any issues that are put to a vote. Shareholders rarely vote against these recommendations, particularly in the case of large publicly traded companies. Occasionally, though, a dissident group emerges and wages a **proxy fight** in an effort to gain control of the corporation. Dissidents rarely win (when they do, it is usually following an extended period of extremely poor corporate performance) at least in part because the insiders—the managers and perhaps large shareholders—have a significant financial advantage.

■ *Liquidation rights.* Common stockholders have the right to a pro rata share in any distribution of the residual assets of the corporation in the event of liquidation. **Residual assets** are what remain after the corporation has settled all its obligations and made distributions to senior securities holders.

■ *Preemptive rights.* Common stockholders may have the right to subscribe pro rata to any new issue of the corporation's shares. Such offerings, **rights offerings**, are described in Chapter 14.[13] Very few large publicly traded companies now grant their shareholders preemptive rights. Preemptive rights are often found where a single shareholder group, such as a founder's family, controls a high percentage of a company's shares and wishes to maintain its proportionate ownership interest through subsequent new share issues.

When a company has two or more classes of common stock with differences in dividend, voting, liquidation, or preemptive rights, the different classes of stock will usually trade at different prices, with the price differential reflecting the value investors attribute to the differential rights.[14]

A FEW WORDS OF ADVICE   1.7

As you study finance, there are a few things we would like to encourage you to keep in mind. These are things we have found to be helpful to our students.

MULTIPLE TERMS FOR ESSENTIALLY THE SAME THING: A JARGON

Whenever you first encounter a new subject, there are new terms you must learn. Finance is no different from the other subjects you have studied in that regard; it has its own language, or jargon. When we learn a new language, it is good to *add vocabulary in sequence* rather than trying to learn all of it at once. A rich language has many terms for essentially the same thing, but each term has subtle differences that make it the "best" term to use in a particular situation. While this richness provides more precise communication and is welcome in technical situations, it can be overwhelming at first. For now, we will keep it simple, concentrating on the basic concepts rather than forcing you to memorize new terms. While the new terminology is essential, we will endeavor to familiarize you with the terminology of finance in a way that promotes your understanding of the basics. Ultimately, however, it is very important that you learn the language of finance. Unless you understand it, you will find it very difficult to comprehend fully the more subtle concepts of finance.

---

[13] For example, a shareholder who owns 10% of a corporation's shares and who has preemptive rights thereby has the right to subscribe for 10% of any new common stock issue by the corporation.
[14] Levy (1983) documents the value investors attach to voting rights.

FINANCIAL CALCULATORS

The other piece of advice we have for you is to *purchase a financial calculator*. You may have a calculator that will add, subtract, multiply, and divide. You may even have a scientific calculator that will automatically perform particular statistical or scientific calculations. While scientific calculators are useful for courses in statistics, engineering, and chemistry, in today's world you really need to have proper equipment to do the job right—and this is a course in finance. Costs for financial calculators are low in relative terms. Currently, you can purchase a basic financial calculator for $15 to $20, with more sophisticated financial calculators costing up to several hundred dollars. Because it is applicable to personal financial transactions such as car loans, student loans, and home mortgages, the basic financial calculator also can be useful to you well beyond this course in finance.

1.8   PHILOSOPHY AND OUTLINE OF THE TEXT

This book was written with an overriding belief that if a person understands the "first principles," every problem and issue can be addressed and ultimately solved in the best manner by applying these principles. Essentially, it is our view that if you understand the general, you can always apply that understanding to a specific situation. And once you understand the principles and the structure of the financial world, applications of those principles can be interesting and even fun. For this reason, we have divided the book into two sections.

The Principles section presents the theories and concepts of finance. Chapter 2 provides an overview of the Principles of Finance, presenting and discussing each one separately. Chapters 3 through 9 explore the financial world and develop the principles, relying upon observation as well as logical and mathematical analysis.

The Applications section applies the Principles of Finance to the world of corporate finance and is divided into four parts: (1) Long-Term Investment Decisions deals with the firm's decision to purchase and/or develop assets for use in its business, such as building a new plant; (2) Long-Term Financing Decisions concerns the firm's choice of financing mix and the decisions that affect this choice, such as how much money to borrow, how large a cash dividend to pay, and whether to reacquire outstanding common stock; (3) Investment and Financing Interactions deals with the complications that arise when the investment decisions and the financing decisions are interdependent, as in the cases of leases, mergers and acquisitions, and international transactions; and (4) Short-Term Decisions concerns the short-term and day-to-day financial management of the firm, the part of corporate finance with which most corporate treasurers occupy themselves on a daily basis.

REFERENCES

Ball, Ray, and Philip Brown. "An Empirical Evaluation of Accounting Income Numbers." *Journal of Accounting Research* 6 (Autumn 1968): 159–78.

Cornell, Bradford, and Alan C. Shapiro. "Corporate Stakeholders and Corporate Finance." *Financial Management* 16 (Spring 1987): 5–14.

Donaldson, Gordon. *Managing Corporate Wealth: The Operations of a Comprehensive Financial Goals System.* New York: Praeger, 1984.

Grossman, Sanford J., and Joseph E. Stiglitz. "On Value Maximization and Alternative Objectives of the Firm." *Journal of Finance* 32 (May 1977): 387–415.

Jensen, Michael C., and William H. Meckling. "Theory of the Firm: Managerial Behavior, Agency Costs and Ownership Structure." *Journal of Financial Economics* 3 (October 1976): 305–60.

Jensen, Michael C., and Richard S. Ruback. "The Market for Corporate Control: The Scientific Evidence." *Journal of Financial Economics* 11 (April 1983): 5–50.

Kaplan, Robert, and Richard Roll. "Investor Evaluation of Accounting Information: Some Empirical Evidence." *Journal of Business* (April 1972): 225–27.

Levy, Haim. "Economic Evaluation of Voting Power of Common Stock." *Journal of Finance* 38 (March 1983): 79–93.

Seitz, Neil. "Shareholder Goals, Firm Goals and Firm Financing Decisions." *Financial Management* 11 (Autumn 1982): 20–26.

Treynor, Jack L. "The Financial Objective in the Widely Held Corporation." *Financial Analysts Journal* 37 (March/April 1981): 68–71.

2

PRINCIPLES OF FINANCE

In this chapter, we describe the "first principles" of finance. These principles provide the basis for understanding financial transactions and making financial decisions. They consist of a set of fundamental tenets that form the basis for financial theory and for decision-making in finance. They are based on logical deduction and/or empirical observation. Some of them may seem innocuous to you; others may seem counterintuitive when you first encounter them. Please bear with us, in spite of any initial (very healthy) skepticism on your part. Even if every principle is not absolutely correct in every instance, it is generally accepted that each principle is a valid characterization of an important aspect of the financial world.

2.1 THE PRINCIPLE OF SELF-INTERESTED BEHAVIOR:
People Act in Their Own Financial Self-Interest

In order to build a useful model, one that prescribes how to make the best decisions, it is necessary to have a reasonably accurate assumption about human behavior. While there may be exceptions at the individual level, we assume that as a group, people act in an economically rational way. We also assume that nonfinancial considerations do not exist, at least to start the analysis. Ignoring nonfinancial considerations is like ignoring air friction if you were going to drop a food-relief package from an airplane and needed to know where the package would land. The answer won't be exactly correct if air friction is disregarded. However, there are at least three benefits to attacking the problem without air friction. First, you can begin to understand how packages fall from airplanes in a relatively simple environment. Second, you can make a rough estimate of where a package actually will land. Third, you can introduce air friction into the problem after you understand the basic idea of how packages fall from airplanes. In a similar way, nonfinancial considerations are added to the specific situation *after* considering the financial ones.

The Principle of Self-Interested Behavior may be a little difficult to accept initially, for a couple of reasons. First, you may think of several apparent exceptions to this principle. When you think of a philanthropist's (or your) contribution to a charity, you might think such gifts violate this principle. This is not the case. The Principle of Self-Interested Behavior does not imply that such generosity does not exist or that it is not desirable. However, we would not think of giving money to other investors as "rational" behavior.

A second reason that might make it difficult to embrace this principle is the counseling most of us receive that "money isn't everything." The Principle of Self-Interested Behavior is certainly not denying the truth of such a statement or the importance of "human" considerations. In fact, it can be reasonably argued that if it weren't for periodic selfless behavior by some exceptional individuals, the world would be much less hospitable. This principle does not imply that money is *the most important thing* in everyone's, or even anyone's, life. It states that when all else is equal, each party to a financial transaction will choose the course of action that is most financially advantageous to that party. This principle has been found to be a good explanation of actual behavior because the large majority of transactions involve nonpersonal considerations where getting the most good out of available resources is the primary consideration.

There is an important corollary to the Principle of Self-Interested Behavior. Often competing desirable actions can be taken. While people take the most advantageous action, taking that action eliminates the possibility of taking other desirable actions. The **opportunity cost** of an alternative is the difference between its value and the value of the best possible alternative. Opportunity cost provides an indication of the relative importance of a decision. When the difference in value between an alternative and the best possible alternative is small, it follows that the cost of incorrectly choosing the inferior alternative is small. Similarly, when the difference is large, the cost of not making the best choice is large. For example, suppose a person sells a car for $3,200, without much forethought. The person finds out the next day that the car could have been sold for $3,300. That person has incurred an opportunity cost of at least $100. This probably would not be considered significant by most people. In contrast, however, if that same person had discovered the next day that the car could have been sold for $4,500, the opportunity cost of at least $1,300 on an asset worth $4,500 probably would be considered significant by most people.

In some cases, opportunity costs are subtle and very difficult to define, but their importance cannot be overstated.

A relatively recent application of the Principle of Self-Interested Behavior is called **agency theory**. Agency theory analyzes individual behavior in situations that involve a principal-agent relationship where one person, an **agent**, is responsible for taking action on behalf of another person, a **principal**. Recall the set-of-contracts model discussed in Chapter 1. Many of the contracts making up a firm can be viewed as agency relationships. Examples of agents in principal-agent relationships include employees such as salespeople, pension fund managers, lawyers, executors, and agents of real estate, travel, and insurance. A critical consideration involving principal-agent relationships is the problem of **moral hazard**. Moral hazard refers to situations where the agent can take unseen actions for personal benefit when such actions are costly to the principal. By carefully analyzing individual behavior, agency theory helps lead to more effective provisions for contracts between a principal and an agent. A typical goal of such contract provisions is to reduce conflicts of interest, thereby mitigating moral hazard problems. Agency theory is discussed at length in Chapter 9.

THE PRINCIPLE OF RISK AVERSION:
When All Else Is Equal, People Prefer Higher Return and Lower Risk

2.2

In a way, the Principle of Risk Aversion is simply a method of operationalizing the Principle of Self-Interested Behavior. It is based on logic and is fairly straightforward. We are not going to give you formal definitions for **return** or **risk** yet because we want to avoid getting bogged down in intricacies. However, to appreciate the justification for this principle, simply ask yourself: If you are faced with two alternative choices that are identical, including their riskiness, except that alternative A provides a higher return than B, which alternative would you choose? We would say that if you are rational, you would choose A. Similarly, if you are offered two alternatives that are identical (including their return) except that A is riskier than B, which alternative would you choose? If you are like most people, you would choose B. In the interest of full disclosure, we should point out that the choice with respect to risk is less predictable than the choice with respect to return. People, generally, although not universally, behave as though they are averse to risk. For example, during periods when bond investors are concerned that business conditions are deteriorating, a "**flight to quality**" often occurs as certain bond investors sell corporate bonds and purchase less risky government bonds. As a practical matter, though, there will be the occasional incorrectly predicted result when we assume that all people are always averse to risk, in just the same way that our car might have a flat tire and cause the time-distance-speed model described in Chapter 1 to underestimate our travel time.

You are undoubtedly wondering how often (if ever) someone gets a choice between alternatives that are truly "identical except for." Some things are "hidden" in this assumption. It is like the use of "average" speed in the time-distance-speed model. The fact that you never face such a choice or that you don't travel at a single speed does not destroy the model's usefulness. This principle simply provides a starting point from which to build a useful model of the financial world.

There is a notable exception to the Principle of Risk Aversion we should mention (since you've probably already thought of it)—gambling. Some people think of investing in the stock market and buying a lottery ticket as similar activities because both have outcomes that are uncertain. However, we believe there is an important distinction between investing and gambling. Gambling generally has a negative expected value; on average, you lose money. If you buy all the lottery tickets and win all of the prizes in a lottery, you will have less money after playing the game. In contrast, while it is certainly possible to lose money investing in financial securities, such investments have a positive *expected* value; on average, you earn money.

The reason gambling is sometimes an exception to this principle is that the choices people make while gambling are often **risk-seeking** rather than **risk-averse**. This exception, however, is relatively unimportant. Many people gamble small sums, in most cases because they find it fun. Such recreational gambling does not violate the Principle of Risk Aversion. The number of people who exhibit risk-seeking behavior by regularly betting sums that are large in relation to their income or net worth represents only a very small percentage of the population.

2.3 THE PRINCIPLE OF DIVERSIFICATION:
Diversification Is Beneficial

The Principle of Diversification is really quite straightforward and requires little explanation. A prudent investor will not invest her entire wealth in a single company. Such a policy would expose the investor's entire wealth to the risk that the company might fail. By dividing one's investment among multiple companies, the entire investment will not be lost unless all of the companies fail, which is much less likely than the possibility that one of them will fail. The Principle of Diversification builds on the Principle of Risk Aversion. We will prove in Chapter 7 that an investor can achieve higher return, lower risk, or both, by investing in a group of securities, a **portfolio**, rather than by investing exclusively in one security.

THE PRINCIPLE OF TWO-SIDED TRANSACTIONS: *Each Financial Transaction Has At Least Two Sides*

The Principle of Two-Sided Transactions also seems very straightforward, yet it is sometimes forgotten when things become complex. Understanding financial transactions requires that we not become short-sighted and forget that while we are following self-interested behavior and making decisions in *our* financial self-interest, everyone else is also acting in *his* own financial self-interest as well, including those with whom we are transacting business. Consider the sale of an asset—or, should we say the purchase of an asset? That is just the point. For every sale there is a purchase; for each buyer there is a seller. When we analyze one side of a transaction, we must keep in mind that there is someone else analyzing the other side.

An example of the confusion regarding the Principle of Two-Sided Transactions that sometimes occurs in the news media involves the reporting of stock market transactions. Media commentators sometimes refer to "profit takers selling off their holdings" and causing a decline in the price of a particular common stock. The implication in talking about "selling off" seems to be that more selling than buying took place. You have undoubtedly read in the newspaper that changes in market prices are the result of an "imbalance" between the amount of buying and the amount of selling that is taking place. This is, of course, not true. When financial securities (e.g., a bond or share of stock) are bought and sold, there is a buyer and a seller for each security that changes hands. And if you will recall the Principle of Self-Interested Behavior, it does not make sense to say that those on the buying side deliberately bought a stock that was going to decline in value. They thought the stock would maintain or increase its value. It just happened that the buyers turned out to be wrong! Quite simply, it is these differences in expectations that give rise to most securities transactions in the first place.

We can describe this sort of situation as a disequilibrium where, loosely speaking, more people believe the stock is overvalued than believe the stock is undervalued. This difference in beliefs may lead to more **sell orders** than **buy orders**, but in spite of the disequilibrium in orders (those *willing* to buy or sell), there is *exactly* one share purchase for each share sale that occurs. In such situations, people buy or sell until the market price reaches what they think is the correct value of each share. (It is also possible that they may change their opinion about what the price ought to be, especially if they had thought that the price was too low, yet the price keeps falling!)

Most situations are **zero-sum games**, situations in which one player can gain *only* at the expense of another player. So you might say that in most situations, my gain is your loss and vice versa. This is exactly the kind of situation we have been describing with the buyer-seller illustration. In the buy-sell transaction, a higher price costs the buyer and benefits the seller; a lower price costs the seller and benefits the buyer. Nevertheless, some transactions are not zero-sum games. For example, some years ago, companies could sell **zero-coupon bonds** to tax-exempt investors and realize additional value relative to selling standard corporate bonds. The added value was due to a provision in the tax law that allowed a company to accelerate its deductions of interest expense.[1] A company could share a portion of this added value

---

[1] An explanation of exactly how the specification of interest deductions for tax purposes created additional value for issuers of zero-coupon bonds is given in Chapter 5. The explanation is postponed until then so that background information necessary to help you understand the explanation can be presented.

with investors by paying a higher rate of interest than would otherwise have been required, so that both could benefit.

Exceptions such as zero-coupon bonds are of particular interest because they are chances for everyone to be better off. But as you will often see, it is not so clear, in the bigger picture, that "everyone" really is better off. In the case of zero-coupon bonds, issuers and investors were both better off. But they benefited at the expense of other taxpayers because in the wider context of the issuers, investors, and other taxpayers, the issuance of zero-coupon bonds really was a zero-sum game (as the U.S. Treasury recognized in 1982 when it changed the tax law to eliminate the generous tax treatment that zero-coupon bonds had enjoyed). Reducing one group of taxpayers' tax payments may cause other taxpayers to bear a larger portion of the cost of government spending.

The vast majority of financial transactions that are not zero-sum games are the result of certain provisions in the tax code. As the foregoing example illustrates, it is possible under certain conditions for two entities (e.g., a securities issuer and a securities investor) to make an agreement in which both come out ahead by structuring the transaction so that the government collects less total tax from the two entities than if the transaction had not taken place. While it is clear that the two entities are indeed better off, the possibility that everyone is better off rests on the government's ability to create tax provisions that reduce taxes for entities that act in ways that help society as a whole. Since this is a finance textbook, we will not dwell on the debate over the government's ability to write such tax provisions. Suffice it to say that with but a few exceptions, entities seek out ways to pay less in taxes. But this is consistent with the Principle of Self-Interested Behavior, which implies that tax-created exceptions to the usual zero-sum-game condition will be sought out and exploited whenever possible.

2.5   THE PRINCIPLE OF INCREMENTAL BENEFITS:
Financial Decisions Are Based on Incremental Benefits

The Principle of Incremental Benefits states that the value from choosing a particular alternative is determined by whatever changes the alternative will make in the future outcome—changes from what the outcome would have been if the alternative had not been chosen. That is, the value of an alternative is the total sum of all the incremental changes in future outcomes that it will cause. The term **incremental** is very important: Only the difference in the outcomes with and without the decision is relevant to the decision's value. For example, if General Motors spends nothing this year on advertising its products, some people will nevertheless buy GM products. Thus, the value to GM of advertising its products is based on the difference between future sales they would make *with* the advertising expenditure and future sales they would make *without* the advertising expenditure. And GM's decision, whether or not or how much to advertise, is based on the expenditure compared with the profit from the incremental sales that result from the advertising. In other words, the advertising decision is based on the *net* change in profit.

In many situations, applying the Principle of Incremental Benefits involves carefully identifying items that are irrelevant to the value of a decision, as opposed to simply identifying those that are relevant. For example, suppose you are going to buy one of two identically priced TVs. You are considering various features of the TVs to determine which will be better for you. The Principle of Incremental Benefits implies that a sales tax that applies equally to both TVs is not relevant to the choice. In this example, the application is relatively transparent, but this principle is perhaps not as straightforward as some of the other principles.

Like many of the other principles described in this chapter, the Principle of Incremental Benefits can get lost when things become complex. But, in addition, this principle may be more tricky because it is easily overlooked, even in some relatively simple situations where attention to incremental changes is especially important. One situation where it may be difficult to accept and apply this principle involves the concept of a **sunk cost**, a cost that has already been incurred and will not be altered by subsequent decisions.

During the development of the Lockheed Corporation's L-1011 tri-star jet, critical discussions occurred over whether to continue the project. When the jet was first proposed, there was enthusiasm in the corporation about its potential. But after considerable work on the project, it became clear that the tri-star project would not be nearly as valuable as had first been thought. When some decision-makers at Lockheed proposed abandoning the tri-star, others argued against such a strategy because of the millions of dollars that Lockheed had already spent on the development of the tri-star. The decision to continue with the project proved to be a disaster for Lockheed. Bankruptcy was only narrowly avoided, and the tri-star project was eventually scrapped.

If Lockheed decision-makers had applied the Principle of Incremental Benefits, they might have concluded much earlier that the potential benefits from finishing the project were insufficient to justify the remaining development costs. Concentrating on previous expenditures obscured the fact that in such cases, the company should proceed with a project only if the necessary remaining costs are less than the projected final benefits from the project. Whatever expenditures have already been made are not relevant to the decision to continue the project because they cannot be changed. Previous expenditures are sunk costs.

In spite of the Principle of Incremental Benefits, some individuals seem to have an emotional reaction connected with sunk costs. These individuals continue to own an asset, even though they know they could sell the asset and reinvest their money more profitably. Clearly, these people are not applying the Principle of Incremental Benefits because they are continuing to incur an opportunity cost. Identifying such situations can be especially difficult because at sometime in the future, if the asset is sold for more than its historical cost, the decision-maker points to that fact and claims a "profit," even if greater profit could have been realized if the asset had been sold earlier and the money reinvested elsewhere. That is, the "profit" might hide the fact that an opportunity cost is being incurred.

THE SIGNALING PRINCIPLE: 2.6
Actions Convey Information

If you have ever asked someone how she would act in a particular situation and later observed that same person actually faced with the situation, you know that people very often act differently from the way they say they will. And yet, based on the Principle of Self-Interested Behavior, we can often predict how people will act.

Because of self-interested behavior, a decision to buy or sell an asset can often provide information about the condition of the asset or about a decision-maker's expectations or plans for the future, to name just a few possibilities. For example, when the chief executive officer of a company announces at a securities analysts' meeting that he is very encouraged about his company's prospects for future earnings growth but the company is, at the same time, reporting to the Securities and Exchange Commission that company executives, including the chief executive officer, are selling large numbers of their own shares of the company's stock, the chief executive's prognosis is highly suspect. In this case, actions probably speak louder than words.

A number of applications of the Signaling Principle have occurred in finance. For example, the announcement of dividend declarations, stock splits, new securities issues, and a variety of other financial decisions can convey useful information in the sense that they may "signal" a change in management's expectations regarding a company's future earnings.

Of course, in other cases, decisions may be misinterpreted and presumed to provide information they do not actually convey. For example, recall the temporarily upward-sloping demand curve for flip-flops, discussed in Chapter 1. In that case, many consumers incorrectly thought the incredibly low price for a pair of flip-flops signaled that the product was worthless. The flip-flop example is a variation of a problem that is known as **adverse selection**. Loosely speaking, the problem of adverse selection arises when participation in a market is such an apparently negative signal that it discourages the inclusion of good-quality products in the market. In such cases, poor-quality goods will dominate the market. The problem of adverse selection also occurs in used-equipment markets where the question comes up whether the equipment offered for sale is actually worthless as opposed to no longer needed. The concept of signaling is discussed in more detail in Chapter 5.

2.7   THE PRINCIPLE OF CAPITAL MARKET EFFICIENCY:
The Capital Markets Are Efficient

The term **capital market** refers to a market in which financial assets, or securities, such as stocks and bonds, are traded (i.e., bought and sold). Probably the most well known capital markets are the New York Stock Exchange and the American Stock Exchange, which together with the other stock exchanges and the over-the-counter market, are referred to collectively as the **stock market**. But there are many other capital markets where different kinds of financial securities are traded. Examples of other financial assets include various types of options, futures, commercial paper, preferred stock, straight bonds, and convertible bonds. We use the stock market for illustrative purposes at this point because it is probably somewhat more familiar to you. A more complete description of the capital markets is given in Chapter 4.

Formally, the Principle of Capital Market Efficiency states that

Market prices of financial assets that are traded regularly in the capital markets reflect all available information and adjust fully and quickly to "new" information.

How do share prices react to new information? Suppose an oil company were to announce the discovery in the United States of a massive new oil field comparable to the North Slope of Alaska. What stock market trading prices would change? Clearly, the share price of the discovering company would rise. But what about other oil company stocks? Because of the increase in the supply of oil, the price of oil would decline, bringing down the value of the oil reserves owned by other companies. Therefore, we would expect that share prices of the other oil companies would tend to fall (unless of course they were participating in the new discovery). Other share prices might change as well. For example, cheaper oil should lead to cheaper plastic and increased business for a plastics manufacturer and therefore higher share prices for plastics manufacturers. The share prices of banks to which Mexico is heavily in-debted might also decrease because the lower price of oil would adversely affect Mexico's ability to repay its debt. Alert traders who recognized these effects would act upon the information by buying the shares of the oil company that made the discovery and selling the shares of oil companies not involved in the discovery, buy-ing the shares of companies like plastics manufacturers that would benefit from the lower price of oil and selling the shares of lenders to Mexico that would be hurt by a lower price of oil. This buying and selling activity is the mechanism by which new information becomes reflected in share prices. As you might have gathered by now, an event like a major oil discovery would provide many opportunities to make a great deal of money quickly in many different capital markets. This opportunity to profit from new information provides the incentive to act (recall the Principle of Self-Interested Behavior) that causes share prices to respond to new information.

The efficiency of the capital markets depends importantly on how quickly new information becomes reflected in share prices. For a machine, perfect efficiency means there is no wasted energy—no loss to friction—and this is certainly one as-pect of capital market efficiency. The capital markets are well organized, and the cost of making a transaction (buying or selling) is very low, especially when compared to transaction costs in the real asset markets (such as machines, real estate, and raw ma-terials). It is generally much easier, cheaper, and faster to buy and sell financial assets than it is to buy and sell real assets. For example, a full-service brokerage house such as Merrill Lynch would charge a sales commission of about 1% of the sales value to execute an order to buy or sell 1,000 shares of stock selling for $60 per share, a $60,000 transaction. Somewhat lower (higher) percentage commission rates would be charged to handle larger (smaller) transactions. In contrast, a real estate brokerage firm such as Century 21 would charge about 7% of the sale value to sell a $60,000 house. We'll talk more about why this difference exists but for now, let's just note the difference.

In addition to convenience, low cost, and high speed, the capital markets are un-imaginably large, with an incredibly large number of participants and very intense competition. When anything happens that might alter the value of a financial asset, there are lots of people paying close attention because there is a tremendous amount of money at stake. And those people can buy or sell their financial assets in minutes or even seconds. This explains why transaction costs and operational efficiencies play an important role in determining the degree of **informational efficiency**, the speed with which prices fully reflect new information. The lower the transaction costs and the smaller the other impediments to trading activity, the more quickly and more easily market participants can act on new information, and the more quickly share prices will adjust to reflect the new information.

In an efficient market in which there are no impediments to trading, the price of each asset would be the same everywhere in the market, except for transitory differ-ences during periods of disequilibrium. In such a market environment, if price dif-ferentials exist, traders would immediately capitalize on those differences by engag-ing in **arbitrage**. Arbitrage is the act of buying and selling an asset simultaneously, where the sale price is larger than the purchase price, so that the difference provides a riskless profit.[2] As long as selling prices exceed buying prices, traders would earn a riskless arbitrage profit, and they would continue to do so until the price differential no longer existed. Economists refer to this phenomenon as the **law of one price**. The law of one price may not hold strictly when there are transaction costs or other

[2] Arbitrage is discussed further in Chapter 5, which explores the Principle of Capital Market Efficiency in greater depth.

impediments to trading, but it is a good approximation of reality. Arbitrage activity will ensure that whatever price differentials exist are smaller than the cost of arbitraging them away. In commodity markets, one observes small differences in price, as for example a difference between the New York and London prices of gold due to the cost of shipping gold from one place to the other. In the capital markets, with such low shipping costs, differences in the prices of any particular security tend to be zero.

The Principle of Capital Market Efficiency is probably the easiest to accept yet the hardest to internalize of all of the Principles of Finance. We all know there are people who win the lottery and occasionally people amass vast fortunes trading in the stock market. How can we become a winner? How can we start with a small sum and amass a great fortune trading in stocks? (The answer to both questions is the same: only with luck or illegal activity!) If there were such a way, of course, everyone would do it. But then, instead of one great fortune, there would be a multitude of smaller "fortunes." Yet hope springs eternal!

The logic of the Principle of Capital Market Efficiency is impeccable, and the amount of empirical research that generally supports it is voluminous.[3] Nevertheless, investors continue to search for "bargains" in the stock market, and just about every major brokerage house regularly publishes a list of "undervalued stocks." If a stock appears on such a list, investors will evaluate the security and bid up the stock's price if they agree with the brokerage analysts' conclusion. In an efficient market, a stock does not remain undervalued for very long. But in an efficient market can there be so many undervalued stocks that brokerage houses can regularly identify and publish extensive lists of them? What special powers do their analysts possess that enable them to identify such undervalued companies? If you are skeptical of the value of such lists, you are not alone. People who are unusually prescient are more likely to "trade for their own account" (i.e., take the profits for themselves) rather than publish a list from which others can profit, because of self-interested behavior.

Later, in Chapters 4 and 5, we will detail how competition, size, and the similarity of assets all combine to make the capital markets extremely efficient. And still later, we may surprise (and perhaps frustrate or annoy) you by assuming that the capital markets are **perfect** (100% efficient—no loss due to friction) in order to build a decision model. In fact, a perfect market is the best approximation we have of the capital markets. Like the assumption of risk aversion, assuming perfect capital markets, while not correct 100% of the time, allows us to create very useful decision models.

2.8

THE PRINCIPLE OF RISK-RETURN TRADE-OFF:
There Is a Trade-Off between Risk and Return

If people prefer higher return and lower risk (the Principle of Risk Aversion) and they act in their own financial self-interest (the Principle of Self-Interested Behavior), then, logically, competition will force people to have to make a trade-off between the return and the risk of their investment. Relatively speaking, high return and low risk will not be simultaneously achievable because that is what *everyone* wants.

---

[3]There are studies that show evidence of imperfections that are not large enough to profit from, after taking transaction costs into account. One apparent exception to capital market efficiency is the superior investment performance of stocks with low price/earnings ratios. We suspect that this apparent violation of market efficiency is the result of improperly adjusting for risk, but we await the results of future research that will address the question more fully.

The Principle of Risk-Return Trade-Off is another way of saying that if you want to have a chance at some really great outcomes, you have to take a chance on having a really bad outcome. Even without providing a formal definition of **risk**, we can agree on some of the effects of risk. One important dimension of risk is that higher risk brings with it an increase in the chance of a bad outcome. The Principle of Risk-Return Trade-Off builds on this notion, and while it seems to rest largely on common sense, there is a tremendous amount of analytical and empirical research that supports it, just like the work that supports the Principle of Diversification and the Principle of Capital Market Efficiency.

There is a corollary to the Principle of Risk-Return Trade-Off and the Principle of Risk Aversion that is important to point out: There is a reduced return that most people are willing to accept in exchange for a reduction of risk. When an asset is bought or sold, its return can be adjusted by altering its sale price. A lower (higher) purchase price increases (decreases) its return. Capital markets offer such opportunities, and each participant chooses his place on the risk-return spectrum.

THE PRINCIPLE OF VALUABLE IDEAS: *Extraordinary Returns Are Achievable with New Ideas*

2.9

The Principle of Valuable Ideas is the one you have been waiting for. It says that you might find a way to get rich after all. One way to earn an extraordinary return is to create a valuable new product or service.

The majority of valuable new ideas occur in the physical asset markets. Unlike a financial asset that is either identical or extremely similar to an almost infinite number of other financial assets, physical assets are more likely to be unique. For example, the founders of Apple Computer became very wealthy by inventing and successfully introducing the personal computer. The value of this device is immediately evident when you consider how much more difficult and tedious financial analysis would be without a personal computer to assist you.

Physical assets can be unique in a number of ways. Consider patents. Thomas Edison became a very wealthy man from having invented a large number of unique products such as the light bulb, the phonograph, the motion picture, and many others. If patent protection had not been available, it is unlikely that he would have become so wealthy (or worked so hard to create inventions). The ability to hold the exclusive rights to produce a unique product provides incentives and enhances the value of a physical asset. Even without patent protection, some companies have been successful at building brand loyalty by convincing consumers that they are the only companies that can produce particular types of products; this generates a high proportion of repeat purchases and purchases of related products.

In many cases, the uniqueness of a physical asset revolves around an idea. When someone comes up with a new idea, there is some chance that the idea can be transformed into **extraordinary positive value**, a value larger than appropriate for the risk involved in implementing the idea. There are many examples of new ideas that have made an individual or even many individuals very wealthy. We have already mentioned Apple Computer and Thomas Edison. Another example involves a man named Ray Kroc who bought a small chain of hamburger stands and by applying his ideas about how to operate the business, made himself and a large number of other people very wealthy. You may have heard of Ray's little chain; it's called McDonald's. The list of such products and services is almost endless, and the potential for new products and services *is* endless.

You may find it difficult to reconcile the Principle of Valuable Ideas with the Principle of Capital Market Efficiency. Together, they state that the capital markets are efficient, and yet even in the capital markets, even with all the competition, a *new* market, product, or service can be created that provides an extraordinary return. The critical difference between the two principles is that the Principle of Valuable Ideas speaks to the return that is associated with being the creator of the opportunity, whereas the Principle of Capital Market Efficiency speaks to the return associated with simply purchasing part of an opportunity that has become known to everyone. The founders of Apple Computer earned a tremendous rate of return on their investment as a result of their innovations. But as other people became aware of the unique advantages that Apple Computer offered, those advantages became fully reflected in the company's share price. So once the stock became actively traded, because of capital market efficiency, a purchaser of Apple Computer common stock could expect only to earn a rate of return commensurate with the risk of investment.

2.10 THE OPTIONS PRINCIPLE:
Options Are Valuable

An **option** is defined as a right, without an obligation, to do something. In other words, the owner (the buyer of the option) can require the **writer** (the seller of the option) to make the transaction specified in the option contract (e.g., sell a parcel of land), but the writer cannot require the owner to do anything. Often, in finance, an explicit option contract refers to the right to buy or sell an asset. The right to buy an asset is termed a **call** option, and the right to sell an asset is referred to as a **put** option. Call options are frequently used by real estate developers. A call option allows the developer to gain consent of all necessary parties prior to investing a large amount of money, money that could be lost if one of the parties later refused to sell his land. Perhaps you have never heard insurance referred to that way, but insurance can be modeled (thought of) as a put option. Suppose you have fire insurance on your house and it burns down. The insurance settlement can be viewed as selling the destroyed house to the insurance company for a price equal to the amount of the insurance coverage. You may decide to use the money to build a new house, but that is your choice.

There is an important corollary that might help you understand the logic underlying the Options Principle: An option cannot have a negative value to the owner because the owner can always decide to do nothing. So if there is absolutely no chance that the transaction named in the option will *ever* have positive value to the owner now or at *any* time in the future, the option will be worthless, but the option can never have a negative value. However, even the smallest probability that the transaction specified in the option contract will have a positive value to the owner at *some* time in the future gives the option some positive value, however tiny that value might be.

When people hear the word **options**, they usually think of explicit financial contracts such as a call option or a put option. However, we use the term **option** in its broadest sense: a right that has no obligation attached to it. With such a broad definition, you can see that options are widespread. In fact, they exist in many situations without being noticed. So the importance of options extends well beyond their easily identified existence because many assets contain "hidden" options.

An example of a hidden option involving bankruptcy occurs because of **limited liability**. Limited liability is a legal concept stating that the financial liability of an asset owner is limited in some manner. For example, the stockholders of a corporation enjoy limited liability because if the corporation declares bankruptcy, they risk losing only their respective equity investments in that corporation. In the extreme, an individual can declare personal bankruptcy and seek protection from her creditors under the law. So in the extreme, the law provides the option to default, not to repay fully the individual's debts. This, of course, is not an option you think of right away as being valuable, but it is nevertheless a valuable option.

Another example of an option that is not immediately obvious to many people involves taxes. Taxes on capital gains income are paid only in the year that the owner sells the asset. At the owner's option, then, capital gains tax can be avoided by retaining ownership; that is, as long as you do not sell an asset, you do not have to pay capital gains tax. Again, this is an option that is attached to all assets and is valuable to tax-paying investors, even though it is rarely the first option that comes to mind when options are being discussed.

Hidden options such as those in the two examples just given dramatically complicate the process of accurately measuring the value of an asset. In some cases, such options actually provide an alternative method of valuing the asset, as we shall see with valuing shares of common stock. Chapter 8 presents methods for valuing options, describes their pervasive existence, and discusses their importance in greater detail. For now, we hope you can see that an asset plus an option is more valuable than the asset alone.

THE BEHAVIORAL PRINCIPLE: *When All Else Fails, Look at What Others Are Doing for Guidance* 2.11

In a sense, the Behavioral Principle is simply an application of the Signaling Principle. The Signaling Principle says that actions convey information. The Behavioral Principle deals with an effort to use such information.

To help you understand the Behavioral Principle, we want you to imagine that you have earned your MBA and that you have been working for about a year and a half for a single medium-size corporation in three positions. Recently, the hard work and long hours you have been putting in have been noticed by your boss, Mr. Womack, the company's financial vice-president. In recognition of your accomplishments, Mr. Womack has invited you and your spouse to his home for dinner along with several other members of the department and their spouses. You and your spouse are just congratulating each other for having successfully navigated the very formal cocktail hour when you arrive at the dining room, which is larger than your whole apartment. As you seat yourselves in your assigned seats, you and your spouse simultaneously nudge each other, motioning toward the silverware. There is more silverware at your place setting alone than you have in your whole kitchen. And you have not a clue about which piece should be used for which food. What do you do?

There is only one reasonable way to proceed. Unobtrusively, look down the table as each course is served and use the same piece of silverware that Mr. Womack is using. But suppose this is not possible—you can't see Mr. Womack very well from where you sit. What should you do? You can simply "check out" the people immediately around you. Most of us will go with the majority if there isn't someone we especially trust.

Now change the scenario from dinner to finance. Suppose you are a financial manager and you are facing a major decision that seems to have no single, clearly correct course of action. For example, suppose that the board of directors has asked you to assess how the company is currently being financed and to recommend any changes that you deem appropriate. How a company is financed determines its **capital structure**, which is discussed in Chapters 15 and 16. For now, suffice it to say that financial theory has not yet been able to prescribe, unambiguously, an *optimal* capital structure for a firm. As a second example, suppose your company is trying to determine its optimal action concerning dividends. Again, financial theory has not yet been able to prescribe, unambiguously, an optimal dividend policy. What should you do? One reasonable approach is to look for guidance in what other companies similar to your company have done in the recent past and are currently doing. You can either imitate the companies that you feel are most likely to be the best guides, or you can imitate the majority. In particular, the policy choices revealed by other companies in the same industry can provide useful guidance. This form of behavior is sometimes referred to as the "industry effect." We refer to it as the **Behavioral Principle of Finance** and state it thus:

When all else fails, look at what others are doing for guidance.

In practice, the Behavioral Principle is typically applied in two types of situations. In some cases, such as capital structure choice, financial theory does not provide a clear solution to the problem. In other cases, financial theory provides a clear solution, but the information required to determine the correct solution would be very expensive and time-consuming to gather. Valuation of certain assets is an example of the latter case. It is often less costly to determine a value for an asset, such as a company or piece of real estate, by inferring that value from the prices at which similar assets have recently changed ownership. In cases such as these, companies use the Behavioral Principle to arrive at an inexpensive approximation of the correct answer.

We have just cited two appropriate applications of the Behavioral Principle: (1) the case where there is a limit to our understanding; (2) the case where its use is more cost-effective than obtaining sufficient information to answer the question using the most accurate method. Another application that sometimes occurs in practice is *not* appropriate: "blind imitation" to minimize personal cost and risk. We want to leave you with an important warning to avoid this misapplication.

The Behavioral Principle can be tricky to apply. You have to decide when there is no single, clearly correct, best course of action. Further, once having decided that there is no best course of action, you must decide if there is a "best" other company or group of companies to look to for guidance. Finally, you must extrapolate from their revealed policy choices to decide which course of action is most appropriate in your particular situation. The Behavioral Principle is, admittedly, a second-best principle. It leads to approximate solutions in the best of situations and "the blind leading the blind" in the worst. Still, it is useful in certain situations, despite its shortcomings.

As with several of the other principles, there is an important corollary to the Behavioral Principle. Application of the Behavioral Principle in many competitive situations gives rise to the **free-rider** problem. In such situations, when a "leader" expends resources to determine a best course of action and a "follower" receives the benefit of the expenditure by simply imitating, the leader is subsidizing the follower. For example, McDonald's does extensive research and analysis concerning the placement of its restaurants. Other fast-food chains have at times chosen their new restaurant locations by simply building near a McDonald's restaurant. Patent and copyright laws are designed to protect innovators, at least to some extent, from the free-rider problem to reward the introduction of valuable new ideas that improve society. The free-rider problem is discussed in more detail in Chapter 9.

THE TIME-VALUE-OF-MONEY PRINCIPLE: *Money Has a Time Value*

2.12

In chapter 1 we presented a simple example of a time-distance-speed model. Here, we present what we consider to be the time-distance-speed model of finance. This model is based on two concepts that you are likely to be familiar with. The first is that if you own something, you are entitled to do whatever you like with it, within legal bounds. The second concept is that if the item you own is money, you can "rent" it to someone else. That is, another person or institution, such as a bank, can use your money for some period of time, and that borrower will pay you interest for the use of your money. These concepts make up what is called the **time value of money**. Simply stated, the time value of money is how much it costs to "rent" money.

In its simplest form, the time value of money can be thought of as the opportunity to earn interest on a savings account at a bank, savings and loan association, or credit union. If a person were to keep a sizable amount of money idle, say in cash at home instead of in a savings account, that person would be incurring an opportunity cost. If one keeps money in cash at home, one is forgoing the opportunity to earn interest on it. Clearly, earning some interest is better than earning no interest. For this reason, we think of the interest rate as a measure of the opportunity cost. In fact, because of capital market efficiency, we can use our capital market alternatives as benchmarks against which to measure all other investment opportunities: Do not make the investment unless it is at least as good as comparable capital market investments.

Let's consider an example involving the time value of money. Suppose someone deposits $1,000 in a savings account today and the institution is paying 7% per year. One year from today, the account will have $1,070. To generalize, call the amount that is deposited in the account today PV (for *Present Value*), and the promised payment from the institution at some point in the future FV (for *Future Value*). Let r denote the interest rate. Then the amount of interest earned over a time period is the interest rate times the amount deposited at the beginning of the period, $r(PV)$. So the amount in the account at the end of the period, FV, can be expressed as

$$FV = PV + r(PV) = (1 + r)PV \qquad (2.1)$$

In words, Equation (2.1) states that the future value equals the present value plus the interest earned, or equivalently, the future value equals the present value times 1 plus the interest rate.

Equation (2.1) is based on earning $r(PV)$ for the time the money is in the savings account. That is, the quantity r is expressed per **time period**, like 7% per year. But suppose the money remains in the account for two time periods? At the end of the first year, the account contains $1,070. By reapplying Equation (2.1), at the end of 2 years, the account contains

$$FV = \$1,070(1.07) = \$1,144.90$$

Note that the account will earn $70 interest the first year and $74.90 interest the second year. This is because the interest paid at the end of the first year itself earned interest the second year, amounting to $4.90 (7% of $70). In this way, interest **com-**

pounds when funds are left in an account for more than one interest period. The process of compounding interest can be handled by extending Equation (2.1). Let n represent the number of time periods the money remains in the account. Then

$$FV = PV(1 + r)^n \qquad \text{(2.2)}$$

Analogous to the time-distance-speed model discussed in Chapter 1, you can think of r as the average speed and n as the time traveled. FV and PV can be thought of as places and the difference between them (FV—PV) is analogous to distance. In this way, we can talk about how long it takes to get from one amount of money, PV, to another, FV, when time depends on the average "speed," r. If we want to get there faster, we have to go at a higher rate of speed. Of course, just like driving, a higher rate of speed might be dangerous and/or illegal because of the Principle of Risk-Return Trade-Off.

Having demonstrated the logic of Equation (2.2), we want to make one more transformation. Like the time-distance-speed model, Equation (2.2) can be re-arranged. When written as

$$PV = \frac{FV}{(1 + r)^n} \qquad \text{(2.3)}$$

it is in the form in which it is most often used. In words, Equation (2.3) states: A dollar today is worth more than a dollar that will be received in the future because interest can be earned on today's dollar in the interim. Thus, to determine the present value of an amount of money that will be received in the future, divide the future value by the quantity $(1 + r)^n$, which reflects the cost to rent money at interest rate r from now until the time n periods from now when you expect to receive the payment. We will show you throughout this book that this model can be used to evaluate the present value of future payments, the "financial distance" between future value and present value, in *any* financial situation, just as the time-distance-speed model can be used to estimate physical distance when you know travel time and average speed.

To use the present-value model, you must estimate the amounts to be received in the future, referred to as **expected future cash flows**. Next, you must estimate the appropriate "rental" rate for each of the expected future cash flows from now until you expect to receive each of them. This rental rate has many different names, but the generic term for it is the **discount rate**. Estimating the discount rate corresponds to estimating the *average* speed. The analogy is especially appropriate between speed and discount rate because of the use of averages. Averages are used because it is simply impossible to take into account all contingencies that might occur from now until the time you expect to receive the future cash flow. Finally, you must estimate the time between now and when you expect to receive the future cash flows.

Equation (2.3) is often referred to as the basic **discounted cash flow framework** for valuation. It is simple in the form given, but like motion equations in the physical sciences, it becomes more complex as you take into account the many sources of friction and other complicating factors. The financial model becomes complex as we combine multiple expected cash flows and allow the discount rate to change over time. Equation (2.3) can be used to value any asset, provided that we can calculate the expected future cash flows and determine an appropriate discount rate for each element of the cash flow stream. This involves, among other things, selecting a discount rate for each cash flow that accurately reflects the riskiness of that cash flow. But applying the model to the valuation of a particular asset can prove difficult. Estimating expected future cash flows requires skill, and selecting the appropriate discount rate(s) often represents a more difficult challenge, even for an expert in finance. One of the principal objectives of this book is to give you the knowledge necessary to apply Equation (2.3) in any valuation situation you might encounter. In particular, the book provides the theoretical foundation you will need to apply the guiding principles and select the most suitable discount rate(s).

According to the Time-Value-of-Money Principle, the primary dimensions of any financial situation are the expected future cash flows, the discount rate, the timing of the cash flows, and the present value. These variables can be represented with a mathematical model. As simple as this statement sounds, there will be a great temptation to forget this important point later on when things become more complex. The importance of this principle (and for that matter all of the principles) rests on its ability to keep our thinking clear and logical. If we cannot represent a concept in a formal mathematical relationship, mistakes can occur much more easily.

SUMMARY

So there they are, the Principles of Finance. We will refer back to them again and again as we develop decision-making procedures for a variety of situations. What we have tried to do in this chapter is to give you an overview of the principles and some intuitive feel for them. By relating them as much as possible to the everyday world with which you are familiar, we hope you are able to see that these principles are simply careful statements about known relationships.

These principles, when combined and built upon, produce useful, and sometimes surprising, insights. Yet once these insights are understood, they become common sense—as with the principle that states What goes up must come down. Taking the analogy one step further, we now know that this principle is not literally correct: Voyager II will never return to earth; it went up, but it will never come down. In spite of this violation, the principle has provided immeasurable benefits to humankind and a foundation for modern technology. So too, the Principles of Finance provide a foundation for decision-making in the financial world because the financial models we build throughout the rest of the book are applications of these principles.

As our "first" application of these principles, consider the goal of a firm. What is the appropriate goal? In Chapter 1, we noted that the investment-vehicle model of the firm embodies the often-stated goal of *maximizing shareholder wealth*. You can now see that this goal is a direct application of the Principle of Self-Interested Behavior. The shareholders are the owners of the firm. Since the owners are entitled to a return (rent) from the use of their money, how do they want the firm to act? The answer of course is they want the firm to act in their best interest—to maximize their wealth. You should keep this goal in mind as we analyze the decisions of the firm throughout the rest of the book.

PROBLEMS

PROBLEM SET A

A1. Define the term **opportunity cost**.

A2. What is a **principal-agent relationship**?

A3. Cite an example in which the problem of **moral hazard** can arise in a principal-agent relationship.

A4. Define the term **portfolio**.

A5. What is a **zero-sum game**?

A6. Define the term **sunk cost**.

A7. Cite an example that involves information signaling.

A8. Describe a situation in which the problem of **adverse selection** can arise.

A9. Define the term **arbitrage**.

A10. Suppose **buy orders** are placed for twice as many shares of a stock as the number of shares offered for sale in a 1-hour period. What would be the relationship (higher, lower, or the same) between the reported trading price just prior and just after that 1-hour period, assuming no other events?

A11. Define the term **option**.

A12. An investor deposits $1,000 into a bank account that pays interest at the rate of 10% per annum (payable at the end of each year). If she leaves the money and all accrued interest in the account for 5 years,

    a. How much money does she have after 1 year?

    b. How much money does she have at the end of the fifth year?

A13. How would your answers to problem A12 change if interest was paid quarterly, that is, at the end of each quarter in an amount equal to 2.5% of the account balance?

A14. What is the present value of $10,000 to be received 7 years from today when the annual discount rate is 12%?

PROBLEM SET B

B1. Explain how the Signaling Principle is derived directly from the Principle of Self-Interested Behavior.

B2. Describe in your own words what is meant by the term **efficient capital market**.

B3. Define the term **limited liability**. How does limited liability create an option for a borrower?

B4. *USA Today* reported on September 3, 1987, that on August 5, 1987, executives of Teradyne had told Wall Street analysts that "business was jumping" and that on August 6 the company's chairman sold 24,800 shares (which his secretary said belonged to his daughter) for $32 each, or $793,600. Interpret these events in light of the Signaling Principle.

B5. Explain how the Behavioral Principle is derived directly from the Signaling Principle.

B6. Cite two appropriate and two inappropriate applications of the Behavioral Principle.

B7. Describe a situation where you might want to guard against the **free-rider** problem.

B8. Explain in your own words the idea of compounding interest.

B9. What is the present value of $5,000 to be received in two equal installments ($2,500 each), 4 years and 5 years from today, when the annual discount rate is 10%?

B10. A bond pays 8% interest (i.e., 8% of its principal amount) at the end of each year it remains outstanding. The $1,000 principal is to be repaid at the end of 6 years. The interest cost of other identical bonds (i.e., the discount rate at which they are trading in the marketplace) is 10%. Calculate the present value of the stream of payments from the bond. Explain why this present value represents the price an investor should be willing to pay for the bond.

B11. Explain why the Principle of Two-Sided Transactions is important to financial decision-making.

B12. Describe in your own words why financial decisions are based on incremental benefits. How does a sunk cost affect the incremental benefit from a decision?

PROBLEM SET C

C1. In April 1987, International Business Machines Corp. introduced a new family of personal computers. The April 3 issue of the *Wall Street Journal* reported that this event would trigger "a new phase of competition in the computer industry." Explain how you would expect the prices of other personal computer manufacturers' common stock to react to this announcement.

C2. How do the Principles of Self-Interested Behavior and Two-Sided Transactions relate to the Principle of Capital Market Efficiency?

C3. Cite an example in which it is not possible to measure *exactly* the opportunity cost of an alternative. Is it possible to measure exactly the opportunity cost of an alternative in most situations?

C4. In our discussion of the Principle of Capital Market Efficiency, we introduced the concept of **arbitrage.** We also said we would later on assume that the capital markets are **perfect.** How can the concept of arbitrage be used as the basis for a definition of a **perfect capital market?**

REFERENCES

Akerlof, George A. "The Market for 'Lemons': Quality Uncertainty and the Market Mechanism." *Quarterly Journal of Economics* 84 (August 1970): 488–500.

Black, Fischer, and Myron Scholes. "The Pricing of Options and Corporate Liabilities." *Journal of Political Economy* 81 (May/June 1973): 637–54.

Fama, Eugene. "Efficient Capital Markets: A Review of Theory and Empirical Work." *Journal of Finance* 25 (May 1970): 383–417.

Fisher, Irving. *The Theory of Interest.* New York: Augustus M. Kelley, 1965 (reprinted from the original edition published in 1930).

Hamada, Robert S. "Portfolio Analysis, Market Equilibrium and Corporation Finance." *Journal of Finance* 24 (March 1969): 13–31.

Jensen, Michael C., and William H. Meckling. "Theory of the Firm: Managerial Behavior, Agency Costs and Ownership Structure." *Journal of Financial Economics* 3 (October 1976): 305–60.

Leland, Hayne E., and David H. Pyle. "Informational Asymmetries, Financial Structure, and Financial Intermediation." *Journal of Finance* 32 (May 1977): 371–87.

Manne, H. G. "Mergers and the Market for Corporate Control." *Journal of Political Economy* (April 1965): 110–20.

Markowitz, Harry. "Portfolio Selection." *Journal of Finance* 7 (March 1952): 77–91.

Miles, James, and Dosoung Choi. "Comment: Evaluating Negative Benefits." *Journal of Financial and Quantitative Analysis* 14 (December 1979): 1095–99.

Miller, Merton H., and Franco Modigliani. "Dividend Policy, Growth, and the Valuation of Shares." *Journal of Business* 34 (October 1961): 411–33.

Modigliani, Franco, and Merton H. Miller. "The Cost of Capital, Corporation Finance, and the Theory of Investment." *American Economic Review* 48 (June 1958): 261–97.

Myers, Stewart C., and Nicholas S. Majluf. "Corporate Financing and Investment Decisions When Firms Have Information that Investors Do Not Have." *Journal of Financial Economics* 13 (1984): 187–221.

Sharpe, William F. "Capital Asset Prices: A Theory of Market Equilibrium Under Conditions of Risk." *Journal of Finance* 19 (September 1964): 425–42.

Smith, Clifford W., Jr. "Applications of Option Pricing Analysis." In James L. Bicksler, ed., *Handbook of Financial Economics*. North-Holland, 1979, 79–121.

Smith, Clifford W., Jr., and Jerold B. Warner. "On Financial Contracting: An Analysis of Bond Covenants." *Journal of Financial Economics* 7 (1979): 117–61.

Spence, Michael. "Competitive and Optimal Responses to Signals: Analysis of Efficiency and Distribution." *Journal of Economic Theory* 7 (1974): 296–332.

Tobin, J. "Liquidity Preference as Behavior Towards Risk." *Review of Economic Studies* 26 (February 1958): 65–86.

THE TIME VALUE OF MONEY

In this chapter we develop the mathematical tools for measuring the time value of money and show you how to determine the value, at *any* point in time, of cash flows that actually occur at other points in time. Equation (2.3) provides a starting point for the analysis by showing how to compute the present value of a single expected future cash flow. Equation (2.3) is extended in this chapter to determine the present value of multiple cash flows.

A very practical benefit to be gained from studying the time-value-of-money formulas is that you will learn how to apply them to your personal financial transactions (which will help you when you act in your own financial self-interest.) This chapter will enable you to understand how payments are determined for installment debt contracts, such as mortgages and car loans.

In Chapter 1 we discussed financial calculators and recommended that you should have one. The time-value-of-money formulas are programmed into financial calculators. While some people still use factor tables, they often then use calculators for multiplication involving the factors. At this point in time, the cost of a financial calculator is small enough and the convenience great enough that a financial calculator is part of the necessary equipment for participating in the business world. Often we will use the term **calculator** to mean a financial calculator.

NET PRESENT VALUE   3.1

The present value of an expected future cash flow—Equation (2.3)—is one method of determining what an expected future cash flow is *worth* today. A second method of determining the present value of an expected future cash flow is to find out what it would *cost* today in the marketplace to buy an asset that would provide the same expected future cash flow; in other words, determine the current market value of the expected future cash flow as reflected in the value of an asset that will generate it. By comparing the present value (what the expected cash flow is worth) with the price at which the asset can be purchased (what the expected cash flow would cost), we can determine whether buying the right to the expected cash flow (that is, the asset) is a good decision. The difference between the present value of the expected cash flow stream and the cost of the asset is a measure of the value of the decision to purchase the asset. This measure is the **net present value**, or NPV, of the asset:

NPV = net present value = present value − cost.

*A decision with a **positive NPV** will increase wealth because the asset costs less than it is worth.*

*A decision with a **negative NPV** will decrease wealth because the asset costs more than it is worth.*

The Principle of Capital Market Efficiency states that current market prices of financial securities reflect all available information. That is, financial securities are fairly priced. Another way to state this principle is to say that the NPV from investing in financial securities is zero. At this point, most people ask: If the NPV is zero, why would anyone purchase a financial security? The answer is to earn a profit. A zero NPV implies that the investor will earn an *appropriate return* for the investment risk; not a zero return. The Principle of Risk-Return Trade-Off implies that investors who take more risk will earn a larger profit, on average. Of course, with risky investments, the outcome may be extremely good, extremely bad, or anywhere in between. At the time of investment, however, the investor's expectation must be favorable, or he would not be willing to make the investment. So the decision to purchase a risky financial security (NPV = 0) is a decision to take risk in order to have a chance at a higher return than would be earned by a safe investment, such as depositing the money in a federally insured savings account.

It is almost impossible to *overstate* the importance of the net-present-value concept. NPV appears in connection with virtually every topic in this book, and virtually all financial decisions in some way or another involve the assessment of the net present value associated with each of several courses of action. This is because, in the context of a firm, firms pursuing the goal of maximizing shareholder wealth will pursue positive-NPV decisions. Therefore, it is very important to remember that

NPV measures the value resulting from a financial decision.

3.2 DEFINITIONS, ASSUMPTIONS, AND SOME ADVICE

Before we go any further with deriving and using time-value-of-money formulas, there are several definitions and assumptions that are important to state explicitly. By detailing them now, we hope to facilitate your understanding and provide a useful guide that you can easily refer to later on as you follow the derivations and work the problems at the end of the chapter. It might be helpful to read through the complete list of notation and assumptions now, even though some of the terms are not explained until later.

ASSUMPTIONS

ASSUMPTION 1   Whenever it is not stated otherwise, it is assumed that expected future cash flows will occur at the end of the time period in which they are expected to occur.

ASSUMPTION 2   Positive-value cash flows are inflows, and negative-value cash flows are outflows from the decision-maker's viewpoint (the company or individual). In other words, the algebraic sign indicates whether the amount is an inflow (+) or outflow (−).

ASSUMPTION 3   Unless otherwise stated, "now" is the instant before $t = 0$. That is, $t = 0$ cash flows (in or out) are just about to occur.

ASSUMPTION 4   There is a single appropriate discount rate for a given situation or problem. This assumption is relaxed later on, but in this chapter, things are kept simple to concentrate on learning the basic valuation formulas.

NOTATION	
CF_t	The net cash flow at time t. E.g., CF_3 denotes the net cash flow at time period 3.
CF	The net cash flow for each period for an annuity.
FV_n	The future value amount at time t. E.g., FV_5 denotes the future value at time period 5.
FVA_n	The future value of an n-period annuity at time n.
k	The nominal annual discount rate.
m	The number of compounding periods per year.
n	A number of time periods.
NPV	The net present value.
PV	A present value amount.
PVA_n	The present value of an n-period annuity.
PVA_∞	The present value of a perpetuity.
r	The effective discount rate per period. E.g., $r = .05$ denotes 5% per time period.
r_a	The effective annual discount rate.
t	A time period. E.g., $t = 3$ denotes time period 3.

Equations (2.2) and (2.3) were derived in our discussion of the Time-Value-of-Money Principle in Chapter 2. Equation (2.3) is the **present value formula** and is restated here for convenience:

The Present Value Formula

$$PV = \frac{FV_n}{(1 + r)^n} = FV_n \left\{ \frac{1}{(1 + r)^n} \right\} \qquad (2.3)$$

The bracketed amount on the right-hand side of the present value formula is often referred to as a **present value factor**.

Equation (2.2) is the **future value formula** and is also restated here for convenience:

The Future Value Formula

$$FV_n = PV(1 + r)^n \qquad (2.2)$$

The amount $(1 + r)^n$ is often referred to as a **future value factor**.

ADVICE

1. Valuation problems are often easier to understand with the aid of a time line, which serves as a visual aid. It has been our experience in connection with complex valuation problems that the error rate is lower when a time line is used to depict the problem.

2. As you read through the rest of the chapter, duplicating our calculations in the examples will significantly help to develop your ability to use your calculator accurately and quickly. Likewise, following through our algebraic derivations will help you understand the time-value-of-money concept.

3.3   MULTIPLE EXPECTED FUTURE CASH FLOWS

In the previous chapter, we noted that the present value formula is extremely important and very versatile as well. The example below demonstrates the versatility of the present value and future value formulas. In the example, there is a set of expected cash flows in which the flows are of different sizes and each of the flows is expected to occur at a different point in time. The value of the set of expected cash flows is determined at various points in time.

EXAMPLE ■   Suppose you expect to receive the cash flows given in Table 3-1 in the time periods indicated. Assume the discount rate is 10%.

Question 1   What is the present value of the set of expected cash flows given in Table 3-1?

Figure 3-1 provides a visual aid to understanding this problem. Now compute the present value of the set of cash flows by applying the present value formula (2.3) to each cash flow with $r = 10\%$ and n set equal to the time period when the cash flow is expected to occur:

$$\text{PV} = \frac{3,000}{(1.1)^0} + \frac{2,000}{(1.1)^1} + \frac{8,000}{(1.1)^2} + \frac{5,000}{(1.1)^3}$$

$$= 3,000 + 1,818.182 + 6,611.570 + 3,756.574$$

$$= \$15,186.326$$

Figure 3-2 illustrates the above calculation. Looking at Figure 3-2, you should be able to see how each application of the present value formula leads to the present value of the expected cash flow. Note that by entering the single expected cash flow, the time it will occur, and the interest rate per period, a calculator can compute each

TABLE 3-1   Simple Time-Value-of-Money Example

Time	0	1	2	3
Cash flow	$3,000	$2,000	$8,000	$5,000

FIGURE 3-1

Time line for the cash flows in Table 3-1.

FIGURE 3-2

Present value calculation for the cash flows in Table 3-1.

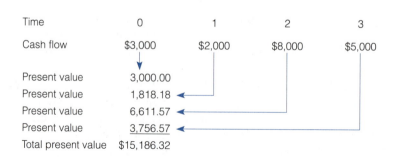

of the present values directly. For example, FV = 8,000, $n = 2$, $r = 10\%$; then PV = 6,611.57 for the third payment. (NOTE: Some calculators require that the future cash flows and present value have opposite algebraic signs.) The total present value is simply the sum of the individual present values.

Question 2 What is the future value at time period 4 ($t = 4$) of the set of expected cash flows given in Table 3-1?

Figure 3-1 again provides a visual aid to understanding the problem by indicating the time and amount of the cash flows. Given the answer to question 1, there are two methods of computing the answer to question 2. We will show you both methods.

Method A To compute the future value at $t = 4$, apply Equation (2.2), the future value formula, to each cash flow with $r = 10\%$ and n set equal to the difference between $t = 4$ and the time period when the cash flow is expected to occur.

$$FV_4 = 3,000(1.1)^4 + 2,000(1.1)^3 + 8,000(1.1)^2 + 5,000(1.1)^1$$
$$= 4,392.30 + 2,662.00 + 9,680.00 + 5,500.00$$
$$= \$22,234.30$$

Figure 3-3 illustrates the calculation for method A. Again, as with computing the present value, you should be able to see how the future-value formula is applied to each of the cash flows and the total future value is the sum of the individual future values. It is helpful to verify these calculations yourself.

Method B Having already computed the present value of this set of cash flows to answer question 1, there is a shortcut for computing the combined value of the set at any other point in time. The future value at $t = 4$ can also be computed by simply applying the future value formula directly to the total present value, with $r = 10\%$ and $t = 4$:

$$FV_4 = PV(1 + r)^4 = \$15,186.326(1.1)^4 = \$22,234.30$$

A comparison of method B with method A for answering question 2 illustrates how much easier it is to value a set of cash flows at *any* other point in time, once the total value has been determined at a single point in time. Note that as with all these calculations, a calculator can be used directly. Thus, with PV = 15,186.326, $n = 4$, and $r = 10\%$, FV is computed to be 22,234.30.

Question 3 What is the total value at $t = 2$ of the set of expected cash flows given in Table 3-1?

Having already computed both the present value and FV$_4$, there are three methods for calculating FV$_2$: (1) proper application of both the future and present value formulas to each of the individual cash flows; (2) application of the future value formula to PV, with $r = 10\%$ and $n = 2$; and (3) application of the present value for-

FIGURE 3-3

Future value calculation for the cash flows in Table 3-1.

mula to FV_4, with $r = 10\%$ and $n = 2$. Calculations for all three methods produce the single correct answer:

1. $FV_2 = 3{,}000(1.1)^2 + 2{,}000(1.1)^1 + 8{,}000 + \dfrac{5{,}000}{(1.1)^1}$

    $= 3{,}630.00 + 2{,}200.00 + 8{,}000 + 4{,}545.45$

    $= \$18{,}375.45$

2. $FV_2 = PV(1 + r)^2 = \$15{,}186.326(1.1)^2 = \$18{,}375.45$

3. $FV_2 = \dfrac{FV_4}{(1 + r)^2} = \dfrac{22{,}234.30}{(1.1)^2} = \$18{,}375.45$ ■

3.4 ANNUITIES

Any question concerning a time-value-of-money calculation can be answered using the present value and/or the future value formula. This is a very powerful statement. However, in complex situations, the calculations can be very tedious. Fortunately, just as with the shortcuts for answering questions 2 and 3 in the example given above, other formulas can solve more complex problems. These other formulas are extensions of the present value and future value formulas.

Any pattern of expected cash flows could be programmed into a calculator. Two additional formulas that are programmed into virtually every financial calculator are those used for valuing **annuities**. These two formulas are very useful for answering some more complex, yet fairly routine, time-value-of-money problems.

An **annuity** is a series of identical cash flows that are expected to occur each time period for a specified number of time periods. Annuities occur in many different financial transactions. One example of an annuity is an installment debt contract, such as a contract to borrow money for the purchase of a car or house: A bank or other financial institution gives the borrower a lump sum of money in exchange for an agreement to repay a fixed amount every month for a specified number of months. The series of payments represents an annuity.

Valuing an annuity is relatively easy because the payments occur in a regular manner (same amount every period for n periods), and therefore the combined amount can be calculated by applying a single formula.

THE FUTURE VALUE OF AN ANNUITY

We started our discussion of the time value of money in Chapter 2 with an example in which money was deposited in a savings account for one or more time periods. Building on the notion of saving money, consider now a savings plan that calls for depositing the same amount every period for n time periods. What will the investment from such a savings plan be worth at the end of the n periods? To analyze this question, let CF denote the amount deposited each time period (i.e., $CF_1 = CF_2 = \ldots = CF_n = CF$). Recall that by convention, the amount is assumed to be deposited at the end of each time period. Figure 3-4 illustrates an annuity consisting of n payments.

FIGURE 3-4
Time line for an annuity.

The future value of an annuity can be computed by applying the future value formula (2.2) to each payment and then summing the individual values to get the total. Starting with the last payment and summing backward to the first payment at time $t = 1$, the future value of the annuity at n, FVA_n, is

$$FVA_n = CF(1 + r)^0 + CF(1 + r)^1 + CF(1 + r)^2 + \\ \ldots + CF(1 + r)^{n-2} + CF(1 + r)^{n-1} \tag{3.1}$$

Figure 3-5 illustrates the calculation of Equation (3.1). Note that the first payment (at $t = 1$) earns interest for $(n - 1)$ time periods, *not* n time periods, and also note that the last payment is assumed to occur exactly at the end of the annuity, so it does not earn any interest—$(1 + r)^0 = 1$.

Equation (3.1) has a CF in every term on the right-hand side. If the CF is factored out, the equation can be rewritten as

$$FVA_n = CF[(1 + r)^0 + (1 + r)^1 + (1 + r)^2 + \\ \ldots + (1 + r)^{n-2} + (1 + r)^{n-1}] \tag{3.2}$$

The bracketed part on the right-hand side of Equation (3.2) can be expressed as a sum, with the greek capital sigma denoting summation:

$$FVA_n = CF \sum_{t=0}^{n-1} (1 + r)^t \tag{3.3}$$

Although we will not go through the mathematical proof here, many textbooks in mathematics contain a proof that the summation on the right-hand side of Equation (3.3) can be rewritten as a formula involving simply r and n;

$$\sum_{t=0}^{n-1} (1 + r)^t = \frac{(1 + r)^n - 1}{r} \tag{3.4}$$

By substituting Equation (3.4) into Equation (3.3), the future value of an annuity can be expressed as

$$FVA_n = CF \left[\frac{(1 + r)^n - 1}{r} \right] \tag{3.5}$$

The quantity in brackets on the right-hand side of Equation (3.5) is often referred to as a **future value annuity factor** just as $(1 + r)^n$ is often called a future value factor. The particular values for CF, n, and r along with Equation (3.5) are all that is

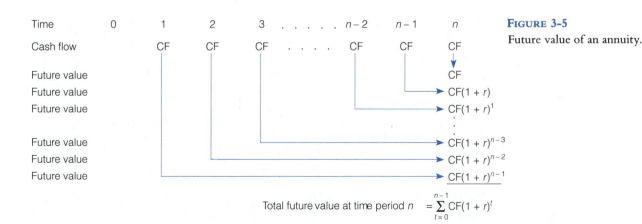

FIGURE 3-5

Future value of an annuity.

needed to determine the future value of the annuity, no matter how many payments the annuity has. As is the case with the future value and present value factors, virtually all financial calculators have the future value annuity factor programmed into memory. By entering values for CF (the payment, usually denoted "pmt" on the key), n (the number of payments in the annuity, usually "n" on the key), and r (the discount rate, usually "i," "k," or "r" on the key), the calculator can compute the future value of the annuity at $t = n$ (usually "FV" on the key). NOTE: The value of r must be expressed in the same time units as n; for example, if n is measured in years, then r is the effective interest rate per year.

EXAMPLE ■   If a person saves \$2,000 per year for 30 years and the money earns 5% interest per year, how much money (principal plus interest) will have accumulated at the end of the 30 years?

Figure 3-5 depicts the problem if $n = 30$. Since the stream of cash flows is an annuity, its future value can be computed by applying Equation (3.5):

$$FVA_n = CF\left[\frac{(1 + r)^n - 1}{r}\right] = \$2,000\left[\frac{(1 + .05)^{30} - 1}{.05}\right]$$

$$FVA_{30} = \$2,000\ (66.43885)$$
$$= \$132,877.70$$

■

THE PRESENT VALUE OF AN ANNUITY

As with all the present and future values considered thus far, the present value of an annuity can be computed via several methods. But as with the others, we can build on what we have already established. Since the future value of an annuity can be computed with Equation (3.5), the value of the annuity at any other point in time can be easily computed by properly applying the present value formula (2.3) to the future value annuity formula (3.5). The present value of an annuity is the present value of the future value of the annuity:

$$PVA_n = FVA_n\left[\frac{1}{(1 + r)^n}\right]$$

$$= CF\left[\frac{(1 + r)^n - 1}{r}\right]\left[\frac{1}{(1 + r)^n}\right]$$

$$= CF\left[\frac{(1 + r)^n - 1}{r(1 + r)^n}\right] \tag{3.6}$$

The quantity in brackets on the right-hand side of Equation (3.6) is often referred to as the **present value annuity factor**, just as part of the present value formula is called the present value factor. The particular values for CF, n, and r (with r and n given in identical time units) are all that is needed to determine the present value of the annuity. As with the future value, present value, and future value annuity formulas, calculators have the present value annuity formula programmed into their memory. By entering values for CF (the payment, usually denoted "pmt" on the key), n (the number of payments in the annuity, usually "n" on the key), and r (the discount rate, usually "i," "k," or "r" on the key), the calculator can compute the present value of the annuity at $t = n$ (usually denoted "PV" on the key).

EXAMPLE ■   A bank expects to receive future car loan payments of \$200 per month for the next 36 months from one of its customers, with the first payment due

1 month from today. If the interest rate on the loan is 1% per month, how much money is being borrowed? In other words, what is the present value of the loan?

The present value annuity formula, Equation (3.6), can be used to compute the answer to the question with CF = $200, n = 36, and r = 1%:

$$\text{PVA}_n = CF\left[\frac{(1 + r)^n - 1}{r(1 + r)^n}\right] = \$200\left[\frac{(1.01)^{36} - 1}{.01(1.01)^{36}}\right]$$

$$= \$200\ (30.1075)$$

$$= \$6,021.50 \qquad \blacksquare$$

THE PAYMENTS OF AN ANNUITY

We have shown you how to compute the present and future value of an annuity, given a set of payments and an interest rate. When a person borrows money, however, it is often helpful to be able to verify the required payments based on the borrowed amount and interest rate, which are stated in the contract. Just as we rearranged the future value formula to derive the present value formula, the annuity formulas can be rearranged to solve for the necessary payments:

$$CF = \text{PVA}_n\left[\frac{r(1 + r)^n}{(1 + r)^n - 1}\right] \qquad (3.7)$$

and

$$CF = \text{FVA}_n\left[\frac{r}{(1 + r)^n - 1}\right] \qquad (3.8)$$

The bracketed amounts on the right-hand side of Equations (3.7) and (3.8) are simply the inverse of the present and future value factors, respectively. By entering values for r, n, and either the present or future value, a calculator can be used to solve for CF (usually denoted "pmt" on the key). (You may need to enter a value of zero for whichever value, present or future, is not needed, depending upon your calculator.)

EXAMPLE 1 ■　Consider a $1,000 loan that is to be paid off in three equal periodic installments. If the interest rate is 10% per period, what must the amount of each payment be?

From Equation (3.7):

$$CF = \text{PVA}_n\left[\frac{r(1 + r)^n}{(1 + r)^n - 1}\right] = \$1,000\left[\frac{.1(1.1)^3}{(1.1)^3 - 1}\right]$$

$$CF = \$1,000[.40211] = \$402.11$$

By entering PV = $1,000, r = 10% per period, and n = 3, a calculator can also compute the payment directly as $402.11. ■

EXAMPLE 2 ■　A person is saving money for a down payment on a house. How much must be saved at the end of every month to accumulate a total of $12,000 at the end of 5 years if the money is invested at a rate of .5% per month?

From Equation (3.8):

$$CF = \text{FVA}_n\left[\frac{r}{(1 + r)^n - 1}\right] = \$12,000\left[\frac{.005}{(1.005)^{60} - 1}\right]$$

$$CF = \$12,000[.0143328] = \$171.99$$

As in the first example, a calculator will compute the payment value of $171.99 from inputs of FV = 12,000, r = .5%, and n = 60. ■

AMORTIZING A LOAN

When a bank or other financial institution makes a loan, a loan amortization schedule is often made up to show how the loan is **amortized**, or paid off over time; that is, how the **principal** (the original amount borrowed) will be repaid in addition to the interest. An amortization schedule represents in tabular form the relationships among the parts of the loan, such as the payments, the principal, and the interest rate. Since a loan typically has the structure of an annuity, an amortization schedule also provides a representation in tabular form of the relationships among these items for an annuity.

EXAMPLE ■   Consider again the $1,000 loan that is to be paid off with an annuity consisting of three equal payments and an interest rate of 10% per period. We determined that the payments must be $402.11 per period to pay off the loan. What does the amortization schedule look like for this loan?

The amortization schedule for this loan is given in Table 3-2. ■

VALUING ANNUITIES NOT STARTING TODAY

In some cases, an annuity is expected to start at a time other than $t = 0$ (with the first payment at $t = 1$). There are several methods that can be used to compute the present value of such an annuity. One method involves the tedious application of the present value formula to every expected future cash flow. A second, easier method, involves applying the present value formula to the present value annuity formula, in much the same way that we derived the present value annuity formula from the future value annuity formula. A third method involves computing the difference between the present value of two different annuities. The first annuity extends from now until the end of the one in question. The second annuity extends from now until the start of the one in question. The difference between the two values is the value of the annuity in question.

TABLE 3-2   A Loan Amortization Schedule

	1	2	3
Period:			
a. Principal at start of period	$1,000.00	$697.89	$365.57
b. Interest for the period (10% of starting principal)	100.00	69.79	36.56
c. Balance a + b	1,100.00	767.68	402.13
d. Payment	402.11	402.11	402.11
e. Principal at start of next period c − d	697.89	365.57	.02[a]

[a] Not zero, due to rounding error.

EXAMPLE ■ What is the present value of $5,000 to be received at the end of each of the years 4 through 7 when the effective interest rate is 12% per year? Figure 3-6 illustrates the timing of the cash flows.

Method A Applying Equation (2.3) gives

$$PV = \frac{\$5,000}{(1.12)^4} + \frac{\$5,000}{(1.12)^5} + \frac{\$5,000}{(1.12)^6} + \frac{\$5,000}{(1.12)^7}$$

$$= \$3,177.590 + \$2,837.134 + \$2,533.155 + \$2,261.746$$

$$= \$10,809.625$$

Method B The present value annuity formula computes the value of an annuity one period *before* the first cash flow occurs (first payment at $t = 1$, whereas the annuity is said to start at $t = 0$). So the present value annuity formula with $n = 4$ and $r = 12\%$ will give us the value of the annuity as of $t = 3$. The present value formula can then be used to compute the present value of the set of expected cash flows:

$$PV = \$5,000 \left[\frac{(1.12)^4 - 1}{.12(1.12)^4} \right] \left[\frac{1}{(1.12)^3} \right]$$

$$= \$15,186.746\ [.71178]$$

$$= \$10,809.625$$

This calculation is illustrated in Figure 3-7. It is important to note that the present value formula uses $n = 3$ (*not* 4) because the reference point for the annuity occurs *one period before the first payment occurs*.

Method C An annuity with the first cash flow occurring during a time period subsequent to $t = 1$ can be viewed as the difference between two other annuities. The annuity shown in Figure 3-6 can be represented as the difference between the annuity shown in Figure 3-8 and the annuity shown in Figure 3-9. That is, the net cash flow in each period in Figure 3-6 equals the cash flow for that period in Figure 3-8 minus

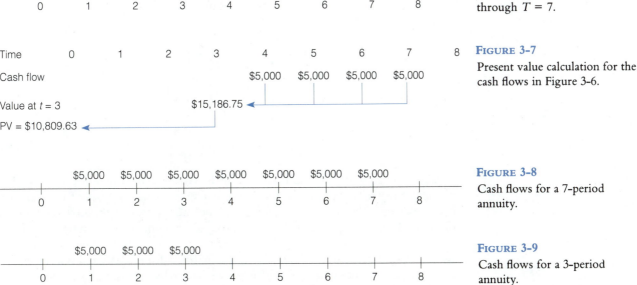

FIGURE 3-6
Cash flows occurring $T = 4$ through $T = 7$.

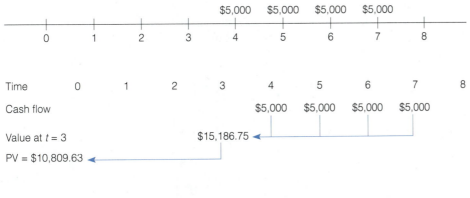

FIGURE 3-7
Present value calculation for the cash flows in Figure 3-6.

FIGURE 3-8
Cash flows for a 7-period annuity.

FIGURE 3-9
Cash flows for a 3-period annuity.

the cash flow for that period in Figure 3-9. (The cash flows cancel each other out in the first three periods.)

So the present value of the annuity in Figure 3-6 equals the present value of a 7-period annuity minus the present value of a 3-period annuity:

$$PV = \$5,000 \left[\frac{(1.12)^7 - 1}{.12(1.12)^7} \right] - \$5,000 \left[\frac{(1.12)^3 - 1}{.12(1.12)^3} \right]$$

$$= \$22,818.783 - \$12,009.156$$

$$= \$10,809.627$$

Methods B and C are similar in the effort necessary to solve the problem. (The difference in answers is due to rounding.) Each requires two time-value-of-money calculations and one arithmetic calculation. Method A will take longer to apply because it requires n time-value-of-money calculations and a summation. We suggest that you adopt the method that is easiest for you to understand and use. ■

PERPETUITIES

An annuity that goes on forever is a **perpetuity**. Perpetuities exist in some situations; however, an important reason for studying them is that they can be used as a simple and fairly accurate approximation of a long-term annuity. As you may have already noticed, the present value factor becomes smaller as n becomes larger. That is, 1 over $(1+r)^n$ becomes small as n becomes large. So the further in the future a cash flow is expected to occur, the smaller is its present value. Therefore, the later payments in a very long annuity add very little to the present value of the annuity. For example, at a discount rate of 10% per year, a payment of $100 has a present value of $5.73 if it is expected to be received 30 years from today, but it has a present value of only 85 cents if it is expected to be received 50 years from today. Because of the declining present value of each subsequent future cash flow in an annuity, the present value of an annuity has a maximum value, no matter how many payments are expected. The maximum value of an annuity is therefore the value of an infinite annuity, that is, the maximum equals the value of a perpetuity.

To derive the present value of a perpetuity, we can start with the present value of an annuity and then let n become very large. In mathematical terms, we are taking the limit of the function as n approaches infinity. Let us start by rewriting the present value annuity formula

$$PVA_n = CF \left[\frac{(1 + r)^n - 1}{r(1 + r)^n} \right]$$

$$PVA_n = CF \left[\frac{(1 + r)^n}{r(1 + r)^n} \right] - CF \left[\frac{1}{r(1 + r)^n} \right]$$

$$PVA_n = \left[\frac{CF}{r} \right] - \left[\frac{CF}{r(1 + r)^n} \right] \tag{3.9}$$

When the present value annuity formula is written in the form of Equation (3.9), it is easier to see what happens to the present value as the number of payments, n, becomes large. The number of payments does not appear in the first term on the right-hand side of Equation (3.9), so the first term is unaffected as n becomes large. But as n grows larger, the denominator of the second term on the right-hand side also grows larger. (The term $(1+r)$ is greater than 1 for a positive discount rate, so each time it is multiplied by itself, it grows larger by a factor of r.) Since the denominator grows with increases in n, and n does not appear in the numerator, the second term becomes smaller as n becomes larger. In the limit, as n tends toward infinity, the second term becomes zero.

To see this by example, try CF = $100 and r = 10%. Then with n = 25, the second term is $92.30; with n = 50, the second term is $8.52; with n = 75, it is $.79; with n = 100, it is $.073, and so forth. From this analysis, the present value of a perpetuity must equal the first term on the right-hand side of Equation (3.9) or

$$PV_{perpetuity} = PVA_\infty = \frac{CF}{r} \qquad (3.10)$$

where ∞ denotes that PVA_∞ is the limiting value as n becomes infinite.

EXAMPLE ■   What is the present value of $1,000 per year, forever, at a discount rate of 8% per year?

The answer can be computed using Equation (3.10):

$$PVA_\infty = \frac{CF}{r} = \frac{\$1000}{.08} = \$12,500.00 \qquad ■$$

NOMINAL AND EFFECTIVE INTEREST RATES   3.5

HOW FREQUENCY OF COMPOUNDING AFFECTS THE ACTUAL RATE

In the discussion and each of the examples thus far, we have been careful to specify the discount rate so that it is consistent with the frequency of the cash flows, for example, 1% per *month* with *monthly* payments. In practice, the discount rate is often specified as a **nominal annual rate** (rate per year), even when interest is paid more frequently than once per year. The term **nominal** means that the rate is an annual rate "in name only." That is, the true annual rate may be different, depending on the frequency with which interest is paid during the year. It is necessary to specify the **compounding period** in order to know exactly what the true discount rate is. The compounding period is the length of time between interest payments. For example, the compounding period might be monthly, quarterly, yearly, or any other time interval that may be specified in a contract.

The term **effective rate** refers to the true rate per time period and depends upon both the compounding period and the nominal rate. The effective rate equals the nominal annual rate divided by the number of compounding periods per year. For example, monthly compounding with a 12% nominal annual rate specifies an effective rate of 1% per month. If we denote k as the nominal annual rate and m as the number of compounding periods per year,

$$r = \frac{k}{m} \qquad (3.11)$$

> **NOTE**: *Calculations are always made using an effective rate unless it is otherwise specified in the formula.*

We will analyze the effect that the compounding period has on the time value of money by starting with an example.

EXAMPLE 1 ■   How does the compounding period affect the future value at the end of one year of $10,000 invested today at a 12% nominal annual rate?

To answer this question, compare the future value amounts based on various compounding periods. Let us consider yearly, semiannually, quarterly, monthly, and weekly compounding periods.

Yearly compounding From Equation (3.11), r equals 12% per year. The future value at the end of one year, FV_1, can then be computed from the future value formula:

$$FV_1 = PV[1 + r]^n = \$10,000[1.12]^1 = \$11,200.00$$

Semiannual compounding From Equation (3.11), r equals 6% per half year. So the future value at the end of one year (two half years), FV_2, can again be computed from the future value formula:

$$FV_2 = \$10,000(1.06)^2 = \$11,236.00$$

Quarterly compounding r equals 3% per quarter, so the future value at the end of 1 year (4 quarters), FV_4, is

$$FV_4 = \$10,000(1.03)^4 = \$11,255.09$$

Monthly compounding r equals 1% per month, so the future value at the end of 1 year (12 months), FV_{12}, is

$$FV_{12} = \$10,000(1.01)^{12} = \$11,268.25$$

Weekly compounding r equals 0.2308% per week, so the future value at the end of 1 year (52 weeks), FV_{52}, is

$$FV_{52} = \$10,000(1.002308)^{52} = \$11,273.59$$

The future values based on the various compounding periods are listed in Table 3-3. From this series of future values, you should be able to see that the actual interest amount (and therefore the *rate* also) increases with more frequent compounding. That is, the effective annual rate increases as the length of the compounding period is decreased.   ◼

The **effective annual rate** can be computed from the effective rate per compounding period by "compounding r for 1 year." That is, the effective annual rate is the rate that will be earned in 1 year when the principal is invested at a rate of r per compounding period. In this example, the amount of interest earned in 1 year ranges from \$1,200.00 with annual compounding to \$1,273.41 with weekly compounding. The effective annual rate, denoted r_a, is given in each case by the amount of interest that is earned in 1 year, $(FV_{year} - PV)$, divided by the present value, or

$$r_{annual} = r_a = \frac{FV_{year} - PV}{PV} \tag{3.12}$$

which can be rewritten as

$$r_a = \frac{FV_{year}}{PV} - 1 \tag{3.13}$$

Table 3-3 lists the effective annual rates for the different frequencies of compounding considered in the example.

A more direct method of computing r_a can be developed by combining the effective rate with the future value formula. Let m denote the number of compounding periods per year; for example, with quarterly compounding, $m = 4$. Then, sub-

TABLE 3-3 Future Values and the Effective Annual Rates for the Different Frequencies of Compounding

Compounding Frequency	PV	FV$_{year}$	Yearly Interest (FV$_{year}$ − PV)	Effective Annual Rate r_a = (FV$_{year}$ − PV)/PV
Yearly	$10,000	$11,200.00	$1,200.00	12.0000%
Semiannually	10,000	11,236.00	1,236.00	12.3600
Quarterly	10,000	11,255.09	1,255.09	12.5509
Monthly	10,000	11,268.25	1,268.25	12.6825
Weekly	10,000	11,273.59	1,273.59	12.7359

stituting Equation (3.11) into the future value formula, the future value at the end of 1 year, FV$_{year}$, can be written as

$$FV_{year} = PV\left[1 + \frac{k}{m}\right]^m \tag{3.14}$$

Substituting Equation (3.14) into Equation (3.13), we have

$$r_a = \frac{PV\left[1 + \frac{k}{m}\right]^m}{PV} - 1 \tag{3.15}$$

which, by canceling the PVs, reduces to

$$r_a = \left[1 + \frac{k}{m}\right]^m - 1 \tag{3.16}$$

EXAMPLE 2 ■ What is the effective annual rate for a nominal annual rate of 12% with quarterly compounding?

With $m = 4$ and with $k = 12\%$, Equation (3.16) gives

$$r_a = \left[1 + \frac{.12}{4}\right]^4 - 1 = [1.03]^4 - 1 = 1.125509 - 1 = .125509 = 12.5509\%$$

Note that Equation (3.16) produces the same value for r_a as the one we calculated in Table 3-3 for a 12% nominal annual rate with quarterly compounding.

Because of the similarity between Equation (3.16) and the future value factor, the future value function on a calculator can also be used to compute the answer to the above example: $1 invested for 4 time periods at 3% per period has a future value of $1.125509. The earned interest of $.125509 on an investment of $1 yields an effective rate of 12.5509%. ■

CONTINUOUS COMPOUNDING

Since the effective annual rate increases as the length of the compounding period is shortened, a logical next question is What is the most frequent compounding possible? We computed r_a for weekly compounding, but we can examine daily compounding, hourly compounding, compounding by the minute, by the second, or even compounding by fractions of a second. As the compounding period becomes immeasurably small, we say that the frequency of compounding becomes **continuous**. In contrast to continuous compounding, the compounding we have considered thus far is **discrete compounding**, where interest is computed at the end of each compounding period.

Building further on our example 1, Table 3–4 lists future values computed by application of the future value formula and effective annual rates computed with Equation (3.16) for a number of values for m. Notice that the change in the future value for each doubling of m is smaller than the previous change.

Table 3–4 shows r_a for various values of m. As already noted, when m becomes large enough, compounding can be considered to be continuous. Recall that we derived the perpetuity formula by taking the limit of the annuity formula as n approaches infinity. Similarly, we can examine smaller and smaller compounding periods by taking the limit of FV_{year} as m approaches infinity. We will not present the mathematical proof here, but it can be shown that

$$\lim_{m \to \infty}\left\{\left[1 + \frac{k}{m}\right]^{m}\right\} = e^{k} \tag{3.17}$$

where e is a number that is approximately equal to 2.718.[1] Equation (3.17) is generally found on your calculator with either an "e^{x}" or "exp" on the key. Substituting Equation (3.17) into Equation (3.16), for continuous compounding, we have

$$r_a = e^{k} - 1 \tag{3.18}$$

EXAMPLE ■ What is the effective annual rate for a nominal annual rate of 12% with continuous compounding?

Applying Equation (3.18), we have

$$r_a = e^{k} - 1 = e^{.12} - 1 = 1.1274969 - 1 = 12.74969\%$$

Notice that the effective annual rate with continuous compounding is only slightly larger than it is with $m = 6654$ (12.74956% versus 12.74969%), which compounds the interest approximately 18 times per day. For that matter, all of the effective annual rates in Table 3–4 are nearly identical. From this it should be evident that a large value for m in Equation (3.16) will produce a good approximation for the effective annual rate with continuous compounding. ■

TIME-VALUE-OF-MONEY FORMULAS WITH CONTINUOUS COMPOUNDING

Equation (3.17) can be modified to compute the future value factor with continuous compounding: k is the nominal rate for 1 year. k times n is the nominal rate for n years. That is, k times n is the total nominal interest rate for n years. Since k is used in Equation (3.17) to compute a future value factor 1 year into the future, k times n can be similarly used in the equation to compute a future value n years into the future. Thus the future value factor with continuous compounding is e^{nk}. As with any other compounding period, the present value factor is the inverse of the future value factor, often expressed as e^{-nk}. (Recall that a function with a negative exponent equals 1 over the same function with the same positive exponent. Thus, 2^{-2} equals 1 over 2^{2}, or ¼.)

The formulas for the present value and future value of an annuity with continuous compounding can be obtained by modifying the formulas for discrete compounding

---

[1] The exponential function occurs frequently in the mathematical and natural sciences. The number e is the base for what are called **natural logarithms**, usually denoted ln; ln is the inverse function of e. That is, $ln[e^{x}] = x$.

TABLE 3-4 The Effective Annual Rate as a Function of Compounding Frequency

m	FV_{year}	r_a
104	$11,274.19	12.7419%
208	11,274.58	12.7458
416	11,274.77	12.7477
832	11,274.87	12.7487
1664	11,274.92	12.7492
3328	11,274.944	12.74944
6654	11,274.956	12.74956
∞	11,274.969	12.74969

TABLE 3-5 Time-Value-of-Money Formulas with Continuous Compounding and Continuous Annuity Cash Flows

Present value formula	$PV = FV_n [e^{-nk}]$
Future value formula	$FV_n = PV[e^{nk}]$
Present value annuity formula	$PVA_n = CF \dfrac{[e^{nk} - 1]}{ke^{nk}}$
Future value annuity formula	$FVA_n = CF \dfrac{[e^{nk} - 1]}{k}$

periods by substituting k for r and e^{nk} for $(1 + k)^n$ in each formula. There is, however, one additional complication with the annuity formulas. The cash flows in the annuities are assumed to occur continuously. That is, CF is the total amount of cash flow that will occur in 1 year, but it is spread out so that it occurs evenly over the year. Table 3-5 provides the time-value-of-money formulas with continuous compounding and continuous cash flows.

EXAMPLE 1 ■ What is the present value of $1,000 expected to be received 3 years from today if the discount rate is 10% per year compounded continuously?
From the present value formula:

$$PV = \$1,000e^{-3(.1)} = \$1,000(.740818) = \$740.82 \qquad \blacksquare$$

EXAMPLE 2 ■ What is the present value of $2,000 per year received continuously for 5 years if the discount rate is 10% per year compounded continuously?
From the present value annuity formula:[2]

$$PVA_5 = \frac{\$2,000[e^{5(.1)} - 1]}{[.1e^{5(.1)}]} = \$2000 \left[\frac{(1.64872 - 1)}{(.1)(1.64872)} \right] = \$7869.37 \qquad \blacksquare$$

[2]The answer to this question can also be approximated with your calculator by using a very small compounding period and cash flow: Let the compounding be 4,000 times per year; then each compounding period has a cash flow of $.50 ($2,000/4,000) and an approximate effective rate of .0025% (10%/4,000). On our calculator, with pmt = .50, i = .0025%, and n = 20,000 (5 years @ 4,000 per year), PV = $7,869.31, an error of only 8 cents on an amount of almost $8,000.

EXAMPLE 3 ■ Here is a more complex example. What is the future value of $1,000 received at the end of each year for 5 years if the discount rate is 6% per year compounded continuously?

First, we must determine the effective annual rate to apply to the cash flows since the cash flows will occur annually rather than uniformly spread over the year. Applying Equation (3.18), the effective annual rate is

$$r_a = e^{.06} - 1 = .061837 = 6.1837\%$$

The future value can then be computed by applying the future value annuity formula for yearly compounding with $r = 6.1837\%$ and $n = 5$:

$$\text{FVA}_5 = \frac{\$1,000[(1.061837)^5 - 1]}{(.061837)} = \$5,657.80 \qquad ■$$

MORE ABOUT EFFECTIVE RATES

We have described how to determine an effective rate from a nominal annual rate by dividing k by the number of compounding periods (Equation (3.11)). We have illustrated how to compute the effective annual rate from the effective rate per compounding period by compounding the effective rate over one year (Equation (3.16)). Although we have illustrated how to compute these two effective rates (annual and per compounding period), there is an effective rate for *every* time period. That is, just as there is an effective annual rate in each case, there is also in each case an effective quarterly rate, an effective weekly rate, and so on. For example, suppose a rate is given as a 12% nominal annual rate with monthly compounding. What is the effective quarterly rate? Just as the effective annual rate in this case is the effective monthly rate compounded for 1 year, the effective quarterly rate is the effective monthly rate compounded for 1 quarter. So the effective quarterly rate, r_q, is

$$r_{\text{quarterly}} = r_q = (1 + r)^3 - 1 \qquad \textbf{(3.19)}$$

Since $r = 1\%$ per month,

$$r_q = (1.01)^3 - 1 = 3.0301\%$$

From this example, you should be able to see that the effective rate for *any* time period can be computed from the effective rate for any other time period simply by compounding the rate for the smaller time period over the longer time period. What is not obvious is that the relationship works both ways. That is, the effective rate for the shorter period can also be calculated from the effective rate for the longer time period by reversing the calculation.

The effective rate for one time-length can be computed from the effective rate for any other time-length simply by compounding the former rate by the ratio of the time-length of the second to the time-length of the first. In other words, the effective rate for the shorter period can be obtained from the effective rate for the longer period by compounding the rate for the longer period by *part* of a compounding period. Denote C1 as a time-length (e.g., monthly, daily, etc.) and r_1 as the effective rate per C1. Define C2 and r_2 similarly for a second time-length. Then, in equation form, we have

$$r_2 = [1 + r_1]^{C2/C1} - 1 \qquad \textbf{(3.20)}$$

You should be able to see that Equation (3.19) equals Equation (3.20) with C1 = 1 month and C2 = 3 months (1 quarter of a year).

EXAMPLE 1 ■ What is the effective monthly rate for a nominal annual rate of 12% with quarterly compounding?

r_1, the effective quarterly rate, can be obtained from the nominal annual rate by dividing k by 4, so $r_1 = 3\%$. A quarter of a year equals 3 months, so C1 is 3 times C2 and C2/C1 equals ⅓. Then, by Equation (3.20)

$$r_2 = [1 + r_1]^{C2/C1} - 1 = (1.03)^{.3333} - 1 = .9901\%$$

The effective monthly rate with quarterly compounding is therefore less than the effective monthly rate with monthly compounding (.9901% versus 1%). This is consistent with what we have already established about effective discount rates: The effective rate increases with more frequent compounding.

As in the case of effective annual rates, the future value function on a calculator can be used to determine any effective rate: $1 invested for .3333 time periods at 3% per time period has a future value of $1.009901. The earned interest of $.009901 on $1 of investment yields an effective rate of .9901% per month. ■

EXAMPLE 2 ■ We have shown you how to determine the effective quarterly rate with a nominal annual rate of 12% and monthly compounding by compounding the monthly rate for 3 months. A second method for determining this rate is to apply Equation (3.19) to r_a for this problem; r_a for this case is given in Table 3-3 as 12.6825%. Then, from Equation (3.20), r_q is

$$r_q = [1 + r_a]^{1/4} - 1 = (1.126825)^{.25} - 1 = 3.0301\%$$ ■

EFFECTIVE RATES WITH CONTINUOUS COMPOUNDING

The formula for computing effective rates with continuous compounding is based on k, the nominal annual rate. Just as we multiplied k by n to create the time-value-of-money formulas with continuous compounding, we can multiply k by any portion or multiple of a year in Equation (3.18) to compute an effective rate for a time period other than 1 year. Thus, for any portion of a year, say α, the effective rate, r_α, is

$$r_\alpha = e^{\alpha k} - 1 \qquad\qquad (3.21)$$

EXAMPLE ■ What is the effective quarterly rate for a 12% nominal annual rate with continuous compounding?

From Equation (3.21):

$$r_{.25} = e^{(.25)(.12)} - 1 = e^{.03} - 1 = 3.0454\%$$

Note that the effective quarterly rate for continuous compounding is higher than the effective quarterly rate for monthly compounding (3.0454% versus 3.0301%). More frequent compounding raises the effective rate. ■

HOW OFTEN SHOULD YOU COMPOUND?

After seeing how the effective annual rate increases with shorter compounding periods, students often ask the question If the nominal annual rate is constant, how often *should* you compound? If you are borrowing money, your answer will be as infrequently as possible, but if you are lending money, you would like to compound as often as possible. The Principle of Two-Sided Transactions reminds us that in each case there is a financial entity on the other side of the transaction. Therefore, the compounding period is often set in the same way the interest rate is set—competitively. As long as both sides understand what the effective rate is, that is all that really matters. So our answer to the question of compounding frequency is to apply the following rule of thumb:

Compound frequently enough so that more frequent compounding will not make any material difference to either party in the transaction.

The above statement says that at some subjective point, neither the borrower nor the lender will be willing to quibble over the difference in value. Recall how the future value amount increased with each increase in the number of compounding periods per year in our illustration on compounding-period effect. In our example, the difference between weekly compounding and continuous compounding is only $1.38 per year (11,273.59 versus 11,274.97). Most people would consider this difference small enough to disregard. However, the difference between annual compounding and quarterly compounding is $55.09 per year (11,200.00 versus 11,255.09), an amount which some people might consider significant.

Notice that we have stated this rule of thumb in terms of dollar amount, not in terms of effective annual rate. This is deliberate because the larger the amount of principal, the greater the difference caused by any difference in the effective annual rate due to the compounding period. That is, in our example, if we change the principal amount to $100 (instead of $10,000), the difference between annual and quarterly compounding is only 55 cents. Similarly, if the principal amount is $10 million, the difference between weekly and continuous compounding is $1,380. Thus, the significance of a difference in effective annual rates depends upon the size of the principal amount.

3.6 PARTIAL TIME PERIODS

In the previous section, you might have wondered about our use of fractional exponents to represent partial time periods. For example, .25 was used to determine the effective quarterly rate from the effective annual rate. Using the time-value-of-money formulas with partial time periods requires knowledge of the assumptions underlying the formulas so that you can correctly interpret, and modify if necessary, the values computed by applying those formulas.

We find a time line particularly helpful for solving problems involving partial time periods. If you have any trouble following the examples given below, try expressing each situation as cash flows on a time line.

SINGLE CASH FLOWS

Computing present and/or future values of single cash flows between partial time periods is fairly straightforward; it requires only the use of a fractional exponent, except in cases where a contract specifies that partial periods will be ignored.

EXAMPLE ■ What is the present value of $1,000 to be received 46 months from today if the effective annual discount rate is $r_a = 12\%$?

Method A   With a stated effective annual rate and no stipulations concerning partial time periods, the present value can be computed using the present value formula, Equation (2.3), with $n = 3.83333 (= {}^{46}\!/_{12})$:

$$PV = \frac{1,000}{(1.12)^{3.83333}} = \$647.64$$

Method B   A more complex method of computing this present value is to compute the effective monthly rate as .94888%, using Equation (3.20), and use monthly compounding with Equation (2.3), so that $n = 46$:

$$PV = \frac{1,000}{(1.0094888)^{46}} = \$647.64 \qquad \blacksquare$$

ANNUITIES WITH PARTIAL TIME PERIODS

In contrast with the single-cash-flow formulas, annuity formulas are not normally used with factional time periods, except in the case of a contract that requires partial payments for partial time periods.

EXAMPLE 1 ■   What is the value 3.75 years from now of a 3-year annuity, with the first \$1,000 payment being made 1 year from today, if the discount rate is $r_a = 10\%$?

The value of this annuity 3 years from today is given by Equation (3.5) as \$3,310. The future value can be computed by simply treating the future value of the annuity as a single payment of \$3,310 at $t = 3$ and compounding that amount for .75 time periods, producing an answer of \$3,555.27 ($= 3,310[1.1]^{.75}$). ■

EXAMPLE 2 ■   What is the present value of a 4-year annuity, with the first \$5,000 payment being made 9 months from today, if the discount rate is $r_a = 8\%$?

Three months ago, this annuity would be a "normal" 4-year annuity. So the value of this annuity 3 months ago (at $t = -.25$) is given by Equation (3.6) as \$16,560.63. The present value can be computed by simply compounding that amount for .25 time periods, producing an answer of \$16,882.35 ($= 16,560.63[1.08]^{.25}$). ■

SOLVING FOR A DISCOUNT RATE   **3.7**

Often, a person knows the timing and amounts of the expected future cash flows and, armed with an appropriate discount rate, can compute the present value. We have also shown you how to solve for the periodic payments of an annuity when the discount rate and either the present or future value is given. In other cases, however, the present value is already known from a market price, but the discount rate is not known. When the discount rate is not known, it is often helpful to compute the discount rate that is implied by the expected cash flows (both future and present) in order to provide a comparison with other investment alternatives. All of the equations given thus far can be inverted or solved by trial and error to determine what discount rate equates the investment with the present or future value of the expected future cash flows. Financial calculators are also programmed to solve for the discount rate for a variety of basic problem types.

EXAMPLE 1 ■ Suppose a bank promises to pay you $10,000 three years from today if you give the bank $7,938.32 today. What interest rate will you be earning if you make the investment?

If we rearrange either the future or present value formulas, we can solve for r:

$$r = \left[\frac{FV}{PV}\right]^{1/n} - 1 \qquad (3.22)$$

Applying Equation (3.22) to this example, we have

$$r = \left[\frac{10,000}{7938.32}\right]^{.3333} - 1 = 1.08 - 1 = 8.00\% \qquad ■$$

Although it is possible to solve for r algebraically in this case, in many cases this is not possible. In fact, most calculators use a trial-and-error computer program to solve for r, even for the type of example just given. To use a calculator to solve the problem, simply put in values for the known parameters, FV = 10,000, PV = 7,938.32, and n = 3. The discount rate for an annuity can be obtained with a calculator in a similar manner.

EXAMPLE 2 ■ If the present value of $1,000 per month for four years is $40,648.56, what effective annual rate is implied?

This problem must be solved in two steps. First, compute the monthly effective discount rate by entering n = 48 (4 years @ 12 months per year), pmt = 1,000, and PV = 40,648.56 into a calculator and have the calculator compute r, which equals .70%. Second, r_a can be obtained by compounding .7% per month for 12 months via Equation (3.20):

$$r_a = (1.007)^{12} - 1 = 8.7311\%$$

An alternative to the second step is to enter PV = $1, n = 12, r = .7% into a calculator and have the calculator compute FV, which equals $1.087311. Then r_a can be computed by subtracting 1 from the earned interest to obtain r_a = .087311, or 8.7311%. ■

THE ECONOMIC MEANING OF A DISCOUNT RATE

While it is a mathematical exercise to solve for a discount rate, what does its value mean? Recall from Chapter 2 that earning interest is an opportunity, and therefore the discount rate can in some situations be interpreted as a measure—an approximation—of the opportunity cost. There are two required conditions for interpreting a discount rate as a measure of opportunity cost: (1) the rate is comparably measured for each alternative (e.g., they are both effective annually compounded rates, not an effective annually compounded rate and an effective quarterly compounded rate), and (2) the alternatives are not encumbered by special conditions. Thus, comparing the effective annual rates on alternative loans is a valid comparison when the loans are otherwise equivalent. Note that comparing the nominal annual rates on alternative loans with different compounding periods is not a valid comparison, even if the loans are otherwise equivalent.[3]

---

[3] Similarly, when a loan requires that another transaction be made with the lender, such as the requirement that the borrower also buy a car or a piece of furniture, even the effective annual rate may be meaningless because the borrower does not have the opportunity to borrow the money per se. The lender may be taking a loss on the loan in order to sell the product. This problem is examined later on in this chapter.

ANNUAL PERCENTAGE RATE (APR) LEGISLATION   3.8

As part of the Consumer Protection Act, Congress passed a law in 1968 called the Truth-in-Lending Act, known as Regulation Z. Regulation Z has been amended several times since its passage, but has remained in force for more than 20 years.

The purpose of the Truth-in-Lending Act is "to promote the informed use of consumer credit by requiring disclosures about its terms and cost." In other words, the act requires financial institutions to disclose interest charges in a uniform way, so that consumers will be able to compare costs and benefits in financial transactions across alternatives. For example, by requiring that financial institutions disclose a common measure of the cost of a loan, consumers are better able to shop for the lowest-cost loan. While the Principle of Capital Market Efficiency holds for publicly-traded securities in the capital markets, there have been violations in the market for consumer loans that are fostered by misinformation and/or complex and confusing loan procedures for consumers. More simply put, uninformed people have paid higher rates for loans than they would otherwise have paid in a competitive market because they did not understand the true financial cost they were incurring.

ADD-ON INTEREST

One example of a confusing method of determining interest payments is "add-on interest." Unlike the compound-interest procedures we have described thus far where interest is paid on the remaining balance of a loan, add-on interest is paid on the original principal amount every period for the total life of the loan. This means that the rate that is stated in the contract sounds much lower than either the effective annual rate or the nominal annual rate.

EXAMPLE ■ Consider a $10,000 car loan with 36 equal payments and add-on interest at 6%. The payments for this loan would be computed in the following manner: 6% of $10,000 times 3 (for the 3 years) equals $1,800, plus $10,000 gives a total of $11,800. This total of $11,800 is then divided by 36 to determine the required payments of $327.78 per month for 36 months. What is the effective annual rate on this 6% add-on interest loan?

Payments of $327.78 per month for 36 months and a present value of $10,000 implies, via calculator, an effective monthly rate of .92358%. This effective monthly rate produces an effective annual rate of $r_a = 11.6636\%$ and a nominal annual rate of $k = 11.0830\%$. You can imagine the confusion uninformed consumers might have if this $10,000 loan requiring 36 equal monthly payments of $327.78 each is quoted by various institutions as (1) "a 6% loan," (2) "an 11% loan," (3) "an 11.0830% loan," or (4) "an 11.6636% loan." ■

This is only one example of the many different ways that loans could have been quoted prior to the passage of the Truth-in-Lending Act. Congress felt that uninformed people could be (and were being) taken advantage of by the use of so many different terms and definitions. In an effort to protect consumers from overly complex financial contracts, Congress defined the **annual percentage rate**, or APR.

WHAT IS AN APR?

Section 226.14(b) of Regulation Z states that the annual percentage rate shall be computed by multiplying the periodic rate by the number of periods in a year. So the Truth-in-Lending Act specifies k, the **nominal annual rate** as the **annual percentage rate**, or APR, which must be disclosed in all financial contracts with financial institutions. Therefore, institutions still have some ability to manipulate the effective annual rate by altering the compounding period. For example, where governmental regulations have limited the nominal interest rate on deposits, some competitive institutions have gone to continuous compounding in order to pay (and advertise) the highest effective interest rate possible. In the case of loans, some competition-sensitive institutions have used techniques such as rounding off decimals in order to produce a lower APR. Still, in spite of a few problems, Regulation Z has had a major impact on consumer loan contracts by forcing greater uniformity of such contracts.

One of the complicating factors associated with computing an APR in practice is the treatment of front-end charges, that is, fixed charges paid at the time the loan is made. In an effort to ensure that such costs are fully disclosed, the APR must include these charges. Therefore, in cases where there are fixed charges for initiating the loan, the stated APR will actually be larger than k, the nominal annual rate.

In spite of the potential for manipulating the compounding period, the compounding period for a mortgage loan on a house or an automobile loan is generally equal to the time between payments, which in most cases is monthly. Typically, then, the APR equals the nominal annual rate $k\%$ with monthly compounding, except for any adjustment for front-end fixed charges. Of course, this will not necessarily be true in all cases. So, after learning about the time value of money, if *you* cannot understand how the payments are determined for a loan contract and what the effective annual rate of interest is, our advice is not to sign the contract until the lender specifies your debt service obligation for you, period by period!

SPECIAL FINANCING VERSUS A DISCOUNT ON THE PRICE

Over the last decade, reduced financing costs have often been used as part of the sales promotion for consumer goods, such as cars and furniture, as well as for housing purchases, such as condominiums. In short, "creative" financing has become part of the package in many types of consumer purchases. Promotions involving "special financing" became more popular as interest rates rose and became more volatile in the early 1980s than they had been over the previous three decades. However, like many of the complexities that the Truth-in-Lending Act eliminated from consumer transactions, "special financing" can cause considerable confusion about which alternative is most advantageous. In this section, we provide an example and some guidelines for making choices among alternatives where "special financing" is part of the package.

Often the discount rate creates the most confusion in connection with alternatives that contain "special financing." The stated rate in the "special financing package" is not the discount rate that should be used for decision-making purposes because it is not a correct measure of the opportunity cost of borrowing the money. The special rate offered, such as 3.9% for purchasing a new car, is only a means for determining the payments; in a sense, it is bogus. You cannot borrow money at that rate *unless* you purchase a particular product. In most special-financing offers, the seller is deliberately choosing to loan the consumer money at a cost below the opportunity cost for the money. The question the consumer must answer is Does the savings on the interest lower the total cost of the product sufficiently to make the purchase a good economic choice?

Recall from our discussion of the Time-Value-of-Money Principle that the interest rate can be used as a measure of the opportunity cost for using the money. Therefore, the discount rate used to evaluate special-financing offers is the opportunity cost for money—the rate at which you can borrow money for *any* comparable use. That is to say, it is the rate that is appropriate for the lender to charge, based on the risk of making the loan.

Whereas we described the special rate as bogus, the cash flows are real. Note that the stated price may also be bogus, but again, the monthly payments must be made. The question that is relevant is What is the present value of the set of promised future payments? In other words, what is the real price you are paying for the product?

EXAMPLE ■ An automobile manufacturer is currently offering a choice of special financing or a cash discount on the purchase of a particular model of car that you have already decided you will buy. The current price for the car is $10,000. The manufacturer is offering either $600 cash back, for a net cash price of $9,400, or will loan you the $10,000 with a 2.9% nominal annual interest rate and monthly payments for the next 36 months. Suppose that currently you can borrow $9,400 from a bank with monthly payments for the next 36 months at an APR of 9% in order to pay cash for the car. Should you borrow from the bank or from the automobile manufacturer?

Method A There are two methods of solving this problem. Because the terms of both loans require equal monthly payments for the next 36 months, one method is simply to compare the monthly payments. Based on PV = $9,400, *n* = 36, and a discount rate of .75% per month (APR = 9%), the bank will require payments of $298.92. Based on PV = $10,000, *n* = 36, and a monthly discount rate of .2417% (APR = 2.9%), the car company will require payments of $290.37. Therefore the special financing provides the better deal.

Method B The second method of determining the best choice of financing is to compute the present value of the payments required by the car company and compare that present value with the cash price. The difference is a net present value. Based on a discount rate of .75% per month (the opportunity cost), the present value of an annuity of 36 monthly payments of $290.37 is $9,131.21. This is less than the $9,400 cash price, so the special financing is the better deal. The NPV of $268.79 ($9,400 − $9,131.21) is the present value of the difference in the monthly payments found with method A. ■

PROBLEM SOLVING: A REVIEW   3.9

Solving problems reinforces our understanding of important relationships among variables, such as the inverse relationship between a present value and the discount rate: All else being equal, a higher discount rate produces a lower present value. Although we can memorize particular relationships, solving the end-of-chapter problems can verify and improve your understanding of these relationships, so that they are more than just words. Problem solving comes easier to some students than others, but it is a skill that can be learned. In this section, we provide a reminder about algebraic manipulation and outline an approach to problem solving that we hope will be helpful.

Sufficient information is a necessary prerequisite to the solution of any problem, including mathematical problems such as those at the end of each chapter. In mathematical terms, information can be provided in two forms: (1) as a value for a parameter, such as the discount rate is 10%, or (2) as a relationship, such as the present value formula. Recall from algebra that you must have at least as many equations as you have unknowns to compute a unique solution to a problem. So, for example, the present value formula cannot be used to determine a present value without the additional information concerning future cash flows and a discount rate. While this may seem silly because it is so obvious, when a problem involves a large number of variables, parameters, and relationships, it is an important fact to remember. This notion provides a starting point for systematically solving problems. Consider our special-financing example in the previous section of this chapter. We can specify four generalized steps, in the form of questions, necessary to solve that problem:

- **What must be determined?** The question can be answered by comparing the present value of one alternative with the present value of the other alternative. Thus, you need to determine two present values.

- **What is already known?** The cash price is $9,400, so the present value of the cost under the price-discount alternative is known without further calculation. The basis for determining the payments under the special-rate alternative is $10,000. The special rate is $k = 2.9\%$, with 36 monthly payments. The opportunity cost for money—the "normal" borrowing rate—is 9% APR, or $r = .75\%$ per month.

- **What relationships exist?** The relevant relationships are used in conjunction with what you already know to compute the needed inputs. So far, we have one part of the answer: present value of the price-discount alternative. We also have one of the two inputs necessary to compute the other part of the answer, the discount rate. What we do not have yet is the payment schedule for the special financing. The annuity relationship can be used to compute the payment schedule for the special-financing alternative, so the annuity relationship is the only additional information needed to solve the problem.

- **What inputs are needed?** The payment schedule and the discount rate are necessary to compute a present value.

Listed below in Table 3-6 are the set of variables and parameters and a source of information about each for this example. The subscripts d and s denote price *discount* and *special* financing, respectively.

The last step in solving a problem involves using known relationships in conjunction with known values. In virtually every case, this last step involves algebraic manipulation of some sort. We assume students have some knowledge of algebra;

TABLE 3-6 Sources of Information for the Special-Financing Example

Variable	Source of Information
Price	given
Cash Discount	given
PV_d	Price less Cash Discount
PV_s	present value formula using CF_s, r, and n
CF_s	annuity formula using Price, k_s, and n
r	given
k_s	given
n	given

however, like many skills, our skill at algebraic manipulation deteriorates if it is not used regularly. Thus, many students find it helpful to review some of the basics of algebra.

Probably the most important concept with respect to algebraic manipulation is the rule that whatever you do to one side of the equation, you must also do to the other side of the equation. You can think of this rule like the balance scale often depicted in the picture of the blindfolded lady of Justice. So, for example, if you add something such as 12, or *n*, or PV to one side of an equation, you must add an equivalent amount to the other side of the equation. Likewise, if you multiply the equation by some value, you must multiply each side of the equation by the same value. Using steps like multiplying–dividing through an equation and adding/subtracting equal amounts to both sides of an equation to solve for a particular variable is a matter of practice for the types of situations you will encounter here.

As you work through the end-of-chapter problems, keep in mind that where the example in the chapter may tell you A and B and ask for C, often the practice problem is simply a "rearrangement" such as giving you B and C and asking you to determine A.

SUMMARY

This chapter introduced the mechanics of the time value of money. The present value and future value formulas were used to compute the value of money at times other than when it will be received. Annuity formulas allow somewhat more complex problems to be solved in a routine manner. We showed you how compounding frequency affects the time value of money, and we defined the difference between a nominal and an effective rate. We explained how the existence of multiple practices of computing interest costs led to the Truth-in-Lending Act, which has reduced confusion over the actual cost of consumer borrowing. Finally, we provided a brief review of problem solving.

We showed you in this chapter that present value depends on the discount rate. Because the discount rate measures the opportunity cost of forgoing a comparable alternative, there is only one discount rate that "correctly" measures the present value of a particular expected future cash flow at a particular point in time. However, as was noted, that rate can change from one point in time to the next because of market conditions. Therefore, it is very important to remember that present value is inversely related to the discount rate. That is,

an increase in r lowers the present value; a decrease in r raises the present value.

PROBLEMS

PROBLEM SET A

A1. You expect to receive the following future cash flows at the end of the years indicated: $500 in year 2, $1,200 in year 4, $800 in year 5, and $1,500 in year 6. If the discount rate is 7% per year;
   a. What is the present value of all four expected future cash flows?
   b. What is the value of the four flows at year 5?
   c. What is the value of the four flows at year 10?

A2. The following future cash flows will be received at the end of the years indicated: $1,000 in year 1, $1,400 in year 2, $900 in year 4, and $600 in year 5. If the discount rate is 8% per year;
   a. What is the present value of all four expected future cash flows?
   b. What is the value of the four flows at year 5?
   c. What is the value of the four flows at year 3?

A3. What is the present value of $500 per year for 8 years if the discount rate is 8.5% per year?

A4. What is the future value at the end of year 6 of a 6-year annuity of $1,000 per year if the discount rate is 10%?

A5. What is the future value, at the end of year 5, of $1,200 per year for each of the next 5 years if the discount rate is 7% per year?

A6. What is the future value 10 years from now of an annuity of $350 per year for each of the next 7 years if the discount rate is 10% per year?

A7. What is the present value of a 6-year annuity of $1,000 per year, if the discount rate is 10% per year?

A8. What are the monthly payments on a 3-year $5,000 loan if the interest rate is 1% per month?

A9. What are the annual payments for a 4-year $4,000 loan if the interest rate is 9% per year? Make up a loan amortization schedule for this loan.

A10. What is the present value of a stream of $1,500 payments received at the end of each of years 3 through 9 if the discount rate is 10% per year?

A11. What is the present value of a stream of payments consisting of $800 per year forever if the discount rate is 11% per year?

A12. If the discount rate is 8% per year, what is the present value of $1000 per year for: (a) 10 years? (b) 20 years? (c) 50 years? (d) 100 years? (e) forever?

A13. What is the effective annual rate for a nominal annual rate of 15% with monthly compounding?

A14. What is the effective annual rate for a nominal annual rate of 15% with continuous compounding?

A15. What is the present value of $3,400 to be received 3 years from today if the discount rate is 11% per year compounded continuously?

A16. What is the present value of $15,000 per year received continuously for 5 years if the discount rate is 12% per year compounded continuously?

A17. What is the present value of $4,500 to be received 31 months from today if the effective annual discount rate is $r_a = 10\%$?

PROBLEM SET B

B1. What is the future value of $20,000 received as a lump sum at the end of each year for 5 years if the discount rate is 10% per year compounded continuously?

B2. What is the effective quarterly rate for a nominal annual rate of 12% with semiannual compounding?

B3. What is the effective quarterly rate for a 15% nominal annual rate with continuous compounding?

B4. What is the value 4.35 years from now of a 4-year annuity, with the first $1,200 payment being made 1 year from today, if the discount rate is $r_a = 10\%$?

B5. What is the present value of a 6-year annuity, with the first $2,500 payment being made 7 months from today if the discount rate is $r_a = 12\%$?

B6. You expect to receive $2,000 3 years from today. If the present value of this amount is $1,423.56, what is the annual discount rate?

B7. You expect to receive $1,000 sometime in the future. If the present value of this amount is $592.03 and the discount rate is 10% per year, when is the cash flow expected to occur?

B8. How long does it take a present value amount to double if the discount rate is (a) 4%? (b) 9%? (c) 15%?

B9. If an annuity of $5,000 per year for 8 years has a present value of $27,469.57, what is the annual discount rate?

B10. What is the present value of a 15-year annuity with payments of $1,800 per year, where the first payment is expected to occur 4 years from today and the discount rate is 7.3% per year?

B11. Suppose you expect to receive $1,000 per year for each of the next 15 years, except that you will not receive any payments in years 3 and 5. What is the present value of this amount if the discount rate is 12% per year?

B12. Create a loan amortization schedule for borrowing $7,500 at an interest rate of 20% per year, to be paid off in four equal annual payments.

B13. Bob's Bank has offered you a $40,000 mortgage on a house. Payments are to be $374.90 per month for 30 years. (a) What effective monthly interest rate is Bob charging? (b) What is the APR on this loan? (c) What is the effective annual rate on this loan?

B14. Performance Auto is offering you a choice of either special financing or a price discount on their new sports car, the QT-123. The stated price for the car is $31,000, but you can pay $25,500 cash and "drive it home today." Alternatively, you can borrow the $31,000 from Performance Auto and make monthly payments for 3 years with an APR of exactly 1% per year. If the best financing currently available is to borrow money from Bob's Bank for 3 years at 12% APR with monthly installment payments and you have decided to buy a QT-123 from Performance Auto, should you take the special financing or borrow the money from Bob's Bank and pay the cash price?

B15. Harry's Home Finance is offering to loan you $10,000 for a home improvement. The loan is to be repaid in monthly installments over a 9-year period. If the rate on this loan is 15% nominal annual, compounded weekly, what would your monthly payments be if you accepted Harry's offer? (Note that there are more than 4 weeks in a month!)

B16. Suppose your parents have decided that after you graduate at the end of this year, they will start saving money to help pay for your younger sister to attend college. They plan to save money for 5 years before she starts college, and the instant after they make the last payment, they will withdraw the first payment for her. The payments to her will be $4,000 per year at the start of each of her 4 college years. If they save an equal amount at the end of every month for 5 years and the effective monthly interest rate earned on their savings is .45%, how much must they save each month in order to be able to make the four payments with no money left over?

B17. What are the monthly payments on a 3-year $10,000 loan (36 equal payments) if the discount rate is a 10% effective annual rate?

B18. Suppose you would like to be paid $20,000 per year during your retirement, which starts in 20 years. Assuming that the $20,000 is an annual perpetuity and the discount rate is an effective 4% per year, how much should you save per year for the next 20 years so that you can achieve your retirement goal?

PROBLEM SET C

C1. Annuities have payments that occur at the end of every period. An **annuity due** is an annuity whose payments occur at the start of every period. Make a time line for this problem, and you will be able to see that a simple way to value an annuity due is to view it as an annuity with "n-1" payments *plus* a payment at $t=0$. (a) What is the present value of an 8-year *annuity due* of $750 per year if the discount rate is 8.2% per year? (b) What is the future value at the end of 6 years of a 6-year *annuity due* of $400 per year if the discount rate is 10.4%?

C2. Harry's Home Finance is offering to loan you $10,000 for a home improvement. The loan is to be repaid in monthly installments over a 9-year period. If the interest rate on this loan is 15% nominal annual, compounded continuously, what would your monthly payments be if you accepted Harry's offer?

C3. Billy Bob won a lottery that will pay him $10,000 per year for 10 years. He got the first payment 9 months ago, so the second payment will occur 3 months from today. Billy Bob has decided to sell the rest of the payments and is offering them to you for $61,825.00. If the appropriate discount rate on this stream of expected future cash flows is a 10% *effective* annual rate; (a) What is the present value of this set of cash flows? (b) What is the net present value of buying this set of expected future cash flows from Billy Bob for $61,825.00?

C4. What is the future value, 1.75 years from now, if the present value is $900 and the discount rate is 12% nominal annual, compounded semiannually?

C5. (a) What is the present value of $5,000 per year received at the end of each year for 20 years if the discount rate is a nominal 8% annual rate, compounded continuously (b) Under the same conditions except that the money is received continuously over each year, what is the present value?

C6. (a) What is the present value of $10,000 per year received at the end of each year in perpetuity with a 7.4% nominal annual discount rate? (b) Under the same conditions except that the money is received continuously over each year, what is the present value?

C7. Suppose your parents have decided that after you graduate at the end of this year, they will start saving money to help pay for your younger brother to attend college. They plan to save money for 5 years before he starts college and to save during his college years. They plan to contribute $4,000 per year at the start of each of his 4 college years. Your parents will thus make monthly payments for 8 years, 5 prior to and 3 during your brother's college education. The effective monthly interest rate earned on their savings is .45%. How much must the monthly savings be under these conditions?

C8. What is the present value of $1,000 every 2 years forever, with the first payment 2 years from today, if the discount rate is a 12% effective annual rate?

C9. What is the present value of $500 every 4 years forever, with the first payment 2 years from today, if the discount rate is a 12% effective annual rate?

C10. A company advertising early-retirement programs promises to repay you forever whatever amount you pay them per year for 12 years. What discount rate are they promising?

C11. Suppose you would like to be paid $30,000 per year during your retirement, which starts in 25 years. Assuming that the $30,000 is an annual perpetuity and the discount rate is an effective 6% per year, what should you save *per month* for the next 25 years so that you can achieve your retirement goal?

C12. Suppose you are paying $31.73 per week for 10 years to repay a $10,000 loan. (a) What is the effective weekly rate on this loan? (b) What is the APR? (c) What is the effective annual rate?

C13. What are the monthly payments on a $50,000 25-year loan if the interest rate is 13% nominal annual with continuous compounding?

REFERENCES

Fisher, Irving. *The Theory of Interest*. New York: Augustus M. Kelley, 1965 (reprinted from the original edition published in 1930).

Hirshleifer, J. *Investment, Interest and Capital*. Englewood Cliffs, N.J.: Prentice-Hall, 1970.

4

THE CAPITAL MARKETS

In this chapter we describe the environment surrounding the firm's financing decision—the market environment within which the firm funds its capital expenditure program and manages the right-hand side of its balance sheet. The firm must choose its overall mix of liabilities and shareholders' equity, determine the types of liabilities (i.e., debt) it will incur, and issue debt and equity securities to raise the funds it needs to operate its business. Recall that a firm's financing decision can be viewed from at least three different perspectives: the firm's, an investor's, and that of an intermediary or independent third party. For the most part, our viewpoint will be that of a firm; more specifically, a corporation.

4.1 THE CAPITAL MARKETS

In order to carry on its business, a firm invests in various **real assets**. These include tangible assets, such as land, plant and equipment, and intangible assets, such as patents and trademarks. A firm's assets are recorded on the asset side of the balance sheet. To obtain the funds needed to purchase real assets, a firm issues financial assets, or **securities**.[1] These securities are recorded on the liabilities and shareholders' equity side of the balance sheet. In a similar way, households incur debt to purchase real assets such as automobiles and homes. Securities exist because the amounts of saving by individuals, institutions, corporations, and governments during any period differ from the amounts of their investments in real assets. Securities have value because they are backed by the real assets of the firm that issued them. The ability of certain classes of assets to support large amounts of debt is one factor that accounts for the leveraged buyout boom of the 1980s.

THE IMPORTANCE OF THE CAPITAL MARKETS

The purpose of the capital markets is to bring the users and suppliers of capital together. The capital markets allocate financial capital accumulated by savers to corporations, governments, and others who would like to invest in real assets but currently lack sufficient funds. If every individual, company, institution, and government could generate just enough funds, and no more, to meet its need for funds to purchase real assets every period, capital markets would not be needed. Each economic unit would be self-sufficient. But in our modern economy, the entities most responsible for real-capital formation, manufacturing corporations, are collectively

---

[1] This definition is broader than the legal definition of what constitutes a "security." In particular, our definition would include a bank loan agreement as a security, even though a bank loan agreement is not, from a strictly legal standpoint, a security. But a bank loan is a substitute for issuing bonds, which fall within the legal definition of a security, so that the broader definition adopted here is appropriate from a financial standpoint.

net users of funds, while households and financial institutions, such as banks, insurance companies, and pension funds, are net suppliers of funds. Capital markets act as a conduit for funds from net-funds suppliers to net-funds users. How efficiently this conduit operates will determine to a great extent how efficiently real resources are allocated in the economy.

In a competitive market system such as ours, resources are allocated primarily on the basis of price. The expected rate of return for any security is inversely related to its price, other things being equal. A higher price translates into a lower expected rate of return and vice versa. Recall the Principle of Risk Aversion: All else equal, people prefer higher return and lower risk. Net users of funds must outbid other net users of funds by offering higher expected returns (or the same return but with lower risk) in order to obtain the funds they need. Recall the Principle of Self-Interested Behavior. Net funds suppliers will seek the highest risk-adjusted expected returns. While there are government restrictions, institutional constraints, and other factors that can impede this process at times, the interplay of supply and demand in the capital markets will determine the prices of financial assets—the expected returns they will provide—and how the available financial capital will be allocated among end users. Moreover, as a consequence of self-interested behavior, we can also expect that those end users with the most profitable investment opportunities will be the ones who are willing to offer the highest expected returns for each level of risk. Accordingly, the pricing mechanism in the capital markets must work efficiently if real resources are to be allocated to their most efficient uses.

FINANCIAL ASSETS

Companies issue financial assets, or securities, to raise funds. Securities are of two basic types: **debt** and **equity**. The distinction between debt and equity is important but can at times prove tricky when investment bankers become unusually creative. The major distinction between the two involves ownership. Equity denotes ownership; debt is a legal obligation of the corporation to make specified payments (which are specified in the debt contract). If a person, or group of persons, owns all of the equity of a corporation, that person or group *owns* the corporation. As owners, equityholders are entitled to all the rights associated with private property. In contrast, debtholders must be repaid according to whatever contract terms are specified in the debt contract. If the corporation fails to meet the terms of the debt contract, ownership of the corporation can be transferred from the equityholders to the debtholders.

DEBT SECURITIES   Debt embodies a legal obligation to make certain contractually specified payments. Debt securities, such as bonds, are certificates evidencing an obligation to repay borrowed funds.[2] A corporate bond and a bank loan agreement are examples of debt securities. Debt obligations consist of **short-term debt**, which is repayable within 1 year of its issuance date, and **long-term debt**, which is repayable more than 1 year from its issuance date. Short-term debt consists chiefly of trade credit (i.e., payables for delivered goods), commercial paper, short-term bank loans, and in the case of bank issuers, certificates of deposit. Long-term debt securities consist chiefly of bonds. Debt securities come in an enormous number of

[2]Under the Internal Revenue Code, a financial instrument must have a stated maturity date in order to qualify as "debt" for tax purposes. However, perpetual debt (i.e., with no stated maturity) does exist in other countries. For example, the Canadian Pacific Railroad and the British government have issued perpetual bonds (the latter perpetuities are called **consols**).

varieties. But they all have at least one thing in common: a promise to pay stated amounts of principal and interest on stated dates.

Corporations often enter into financial arrangements that are not, strictly speaking, debt. A lease is a debt equivalent in that a company must make regular payments, similar to making principal and interest payments, in order to maintain the uninterrupted use of the equipment. Other debt-equivalent financial arrangements are more difficult to detect.

EQUITY SECURITIES   Equity securities are certificates evidencing partial ownership of the corporation. Debt securities rank senior to equity securities in that all current debt payments must be made before equityholders can receive any dividends. Also, debtholders must be repaid in full before equityholders can receive anything in the event the corporation is liquidated.

Most equity securities are of two basic types: **common stock** and **preferred stock**. Preferred stock is really a hybrid, combining certain features of debt and certain features of common stock. Legally, preferred stock is an equity security because it is not an obligation for borrowed money; typically payments on preferred stock can be made only out of current profits and retained earnings.[3] Preferred stock ranks senior to common stock in the payment of dividends and the distribution of any liquidation proceeds. In addition, some companies have issued **preference stock**, which is structured just like preferred stock but is junior to preferred stock (and senior to common stock).

CONVERTIBLE SECURITIES   A second type of debt-equity hybrid is the convertible security. It is of two basic types: **convertible bonds** and **convertible preferred stock**. These are securities that can, at the option of the owner, be exchanged for (converted into) common stock on certain specified terms. Therefore, a convertible security can be modeled as a "straight" security plus an option.

Certain hybrids are so unusual that they prompt the question Is it really debt, or is it really equity? For example, in February 1983, MAPCO Inc. sold an issue of adjustable-rate convertible debt. The interest payable on each bond was approximately equal to, and would move up with, the dividends on the common stock into which the bond could be converted. There was no conversion premium; the market value of the underlying common stock equaled the market value of the bond at the time the convertible bonds were issued. Each bond was redeemable as soon as 1 year after its issuance at $550 (versus $1,000 face amount). Is it debt or equity? Or is it both? Although we will show you in Chapter 8 that this type of security can be viewed conceptually as either debt plus an option or equity plus an option, the tax laws require a definitive designation. MAPCO booked $550 of each bond as debt and the remaining $450 as equity.[4] MAPCO also tried to deduct the "interest" expense for tax purposes, but the Internal Revenue Service (IRS) ruled that the security was equity and refused to allow the interest deduction. Final verdict: Conceptually, it can be viewed as either in combination with an option; it is part debt and part equity from an accounting standpoint; it is all equity for federal tax purposes. It may come as no surprise that no more of this type of security has been issued since the IRS ruling.

The distinction between debt and equity is important because of the tax-deductibility of interest. Section 385 was added to the Internal Revenue Code in 1969 to pro-

---

[3] The corporate law of some states also permits payments to be made to preferred stockholders out of additional paid-in capital.
[4] MAPCO, Inc., prospectus, February 3, 1983.

vide taxpayers guidance in structuring debt instruments to qualify as debt for tax purposes. But specifying exactly what constitutes debt (and exactly what constitutes equity) has proven very difficult. The principal difficulty arises in connection with privately held companies where one or more shareholders contribute capital and wish to characterize it as debt rather than equity so that any interest/dividend payment is tax-deductible. The IRS has never issued final regulations under Section 385, and it withdrew its most recent proposed regulations in 1983. As a result, there is no official guidance, although there is a body of case law on the subject. The inability of the IRS to issue final regulations under Section 385 not only illustrates the difficulty of distinguishing between debt and equity in some cases but also creates a practical problem you may experience in the future if you try to finance a business with a high degree of leverage that includes substantial "loans" from shareholders.

OTHER FINANCIAL ASSETS   There are a number of other financial assets traded in the capital markets. Futures and options are among the more important of these. Some options are issued by corporations, but most are written by investors against shares of common stock that are already outstanding. For example, a corporation can issue call options on its own stock—**warrants**.

The tremendous variety of securities that are traded in the marketplace has important implications regarding how effectively the capital markets perform their capital-allocation function. The revolution in securities innovation over the past decade has substantially increased the variety of securities available and benefited both issuers and investors; each participant is better able to issue or invest in securities whose risk-return characteristics suit their risk-return preferences.

THE MARKETS FOR STOCKS AND BONDS

Stocks and bonds are traded either on an organized exchange or in the over-the-counter (OTC) market. The New York Stock Exchange (NYSE) is the largest exchange, handling about 80% (in number of shares and aggregate market value of shares traded) of all shares traded on organized exchanges. The American Stock Exchange (AMEX) handles about 5-10% of the trading volume, and the regional exchanges (principally the Midwest, Pacific, Philadelphia, Boston, and Cincinnati Stock Exchanges) handle the remaining 10–15%. However, the bulk of the trading volume on the regional exchanges involves NYSE-listed stocks, and just about any stock listed on the NYSE can also be purchased in the OTC market. Accordingly, one of the important functions of the regional exchanges and the OTC market is to provide price competition for NYSE-listed stocks.

ROLE OF THE EXCHANGES   The principal function of the securities exchanges is to provide a continuous market with stable prices so that investors can resell securities easily. The securities exchanges bring together buy and sell orders from all over the United States and foreign countries. The exchanges provide anonymity to investors because brokers do the trading.

The exchanges are generally organized along the lines of the NYSE, so we will describe the operation of the NYSE. The main trading floor of the NYSE is roughly the size of a football field. There is an annex where bonds are bought and sold. On the floor of the exchange are several U-shaped counters. Each of these contains a number of **trading posts**. At each post is a **specialist** who is responsible for maintaining an orderly, continuous market (that is, with smooth changes in price) in each of the stocks assigned to that specialist by the NYSE Board of Governors. Each specialist can act as either a **broker**, executing orders for other brokers in return for a commission, or a **dealer**, buying and selling shares of the stocks for himself. They act as dealers in order to smooth stock price fluctuations. For example, during a day when imbalances between sell orders and buy orders occur, specialists customarily buy or sell shares themselves and change the price of the stock by a smaller amount than would otherwise be necessary to balance supply and demand. Specialists have considerable discretion in setting market prices. They earn the **bid-ask spread** on every share that passes through their hands, and their monopoly position can generate substantial income if the stocks for which they are responsible are actively traded. Of course, specialists also bear considerable risk; recall the Principle of Risk-Return Trade-Off.

The NYSE also includes commission brokers, floor brokers, floor traders, and odd-lot dealers. **Commission brokers** act as agents who buy and sell securities for brokerage houses such as Merrill Lynch. **Floor brokers** are freelance brokers who do not work for a particular brokerage house but execute orders for commission brokers; for example, when a commission broker has an order flow too large to handle alone. **Floor traders** trade for themselves; they do not buy for other brokers or for the public. Although floor traders trade free of commission because they are NYSE members, other costs, such as transfer taxes and clearing fees, have reduced the volume of floor trading in recent years. **Odd-lot dealers** combine transactions of fewer than 100 shares (**odd lots**) into trades of 100 shares or multiples of 100 shares (**round lots**) and then execute these round-lot transactions.[5]

At the end of 1989, there were 1,720 companies listed on the NYSE, and there were 2,246 stock issues (common and preferred) with an aggregate market value in excess of $3 trillion listed there.[6] Average daily volume has increased steadily and dramatically in recent years, averaging more than 165 million shares per day in 1989. In general, NYSE-listed common stocks are actively traded; price quotations are almost continuously available throughout the trading day; and the closing share prices, which one can find in most major financial publications, are reliable indicators of share value. At the end of 1989, there were 1,058 equity issues listed on the AMEX with an aggregate market value of approximately $131 billion, equivalent to less than 5% of the value of NYSE-listed stocks.[7] Trading volume declined in 1989 to an average of 12.4 million shares per day, representing about 7.5% of NYSE trading volume.

OVER-THE-COUNTER MARKETS   The term **over the counter** originated years ago when dealers sold securities to investors directly from dealer inventories or over the dealer's counter. Now, over the counter connotes the trading of securities other than on an organized exchange. The broker-dealers who trade in the OTC market are linked to one another by various electronic means. There is no monopolistic market maker, as in the case of the NYSE, but a variety of competing market makers. However, there is also no one charged with the responsibility to maintain an orderly market in each stock, so that OTC share prices are potentially more volatile than the prices of NYSE-listed stocks.

Currently, virtually all federal, state, and municipal debt obligations are traded over the counter, although some zero-coupon securities derived from U.S. government bonds are also exchange-traded. More than 90 percent of corporate bonds are

---

[5] There are certain high-priced stocks for which 10 shares constitute a round lot. Exchange transactions take place in round lots.

[6] *New York Stock Exchange Fact Book* (New York: New York Stock Exchange, 1990), 31.

[7] *American Stock Exchange Fact Book* (New York: American Stock Exchange, 1990), 8.

traded over the counter, although many are also listed on the NYSE. Because most corporate bond trading takes place away from the exchanges, even for NYSE-listed bond issues, the bond quotations for exchange-listed bonds that are published in the financial press should be used with caution. The prices may not reflect the most recent trades if those trades took place over the counter.

The OTC stock market is smaller than the OTC bond market. About 40% by share volume and 20% by dollar value of all stock trading in the United States takes place in the OTC market. There are roughly 30,000 equity securities traded in the OTC market. However, the vast majority of these are seldom traded, and reliable price quotations are often impossible to obtain. Of all the OTC issues, at the end of 1989, 4,963 were included in the National Association of Securities Dealers Automated Quotations (NASDAQ) system, a computerized communications system for the OTC market that started in 1971. It provides up-to-date bid-ask dealer quotes for OTC stocks. NASDAQ has greatly improved the quality of pricing information available to market participants. In addition, roughly 3,000 to 4,000 additional OTC issues not included in NASDAQ are also fairly actively traded. NASDAQ has established listing requirements similar to the listing requirements the exchanges have adopted, to limit inclusion to the better-capitalized and more actively traded OTC stocks.[8] The daily pricing information provided for stocks included in the NASDAQ National Market System (NMS) is similar to the price quotations for exchange-listed stocks: open, high, low, close, and change from the previous day's close. For other OTC stocks, typically only closing bid-ask quotations are provided, and then only for actively traded OTC stocks.

OTC MARKETS VERSUS THE EXCHANGES A stock will trade in the OTC market only if some broker-dealer is willing to make a market in the stock. Because investors deal with market makers in buying and selling OTC stocks, the OTC markets are **negotiated markets**. In contrast, the exchanges are **auction markets**, conferring monopoly power on the specialist to act as intermediary (i.e., auctioneer).

THIRD AND FOURTH MARKETS The term **third market** refers to over-the-counter trading in exchange-listed securities by nonmember firms. The third market grew rapidly between 1965 and 1972 as financial institutions sought to avoid paying the high exchange-mandated commission charges. But the introduction of negotiated commissions, beginning in 1971 (and complete abolition of fixed commissions on May 1, 1975), greatly reduced the commission differential. Third-market proportionate volume is still less than its 1972 peak, but the third market performs a useful function during periods when trading on the NYSE is suspended or the NYSE is closed (e.g., after-hours trading). Also, third-market participants do not own exchange seats, which are expensive to buy and maintain. Consequently, their overhead costs tend to be lower, and they tend to charge lower brokerage fees. Nevertheless, most trading in exchange-listed stocks tends to take place on the exchanges.

The term **fourth market** refers to over-the-counter trading in which large in-

[8] For example, the NYSE requires minimum pretax income of $2.5 million in the last year and $2 million in each of the preceding 2 years, minimum net tangible assets of $18 million, and a minimum of 1.1 million publicly-held shares among its listing requirements. *1990 NYSE Fact Book,* 28. The AMEX requires minimum pretax income of $750,000 for the last year or 2 of the last 3 years, minimum stockholders' equity of $4 million, and a minimum of 500,000 publicly-held shares among its listing requirements. *1990 AMEX Fact Book,* 11. NASDAQ National Market listing requires at least $4 million of net tangible assets, pretax income of $750,000 for the last year or for 2 of the last 3 years, $400,000 of net income for the last year or for 2 of the last 3 years, and a minimum of 500,000 publicly-held shares. *NASDAQ Fact Book* (Washington, D.C.: National Association of Securities Dealers, 1990), 43.

stitutions deal with each other directly, thus saving brokerage commissions. The potential commission savings are great enough for very large trades that institutions often find it advantageous to check with other institutions for interest in a transaction before contacting a broker. Thus, the fourth market, like the third market, owes its existence primarily to efforts by market participants to reduce the impact of frictions that exist in the exchanges' auction markets.

THE ROLE OF FINANCIAL INTERMEDIARIES

Financial intermediaries, like the capital markets, play an important role in facilitating the smooth flow of financial capital from net funds suppliers to net funds users. They stand between these two groups, issuing their own securities to net funds suppliers, such as small savers, and investing the proceeds in securities issued by net funds users, such as manufacturing companies. The intermediary transforms funds from one form, which it tailors to appeal to net funds suppliers, into another form, which it tailors to appeal to net funds users. For example, a bank will issue small-denomination certificates of deposit to individuals and invest the proceeds in a bank loan or a bond issue of a large manufacturing company. In general, it would be very expensive and time-consuming for the manufacturing company to sell its bonds in small denominations directly to individual investors.

Financial intermediaries exist because they provide

- **Lower transaction costs.** Financial intermediaries are continually dealing in the capital markets. Because they are in frequent contact with investors, they can locate buyers for a company's securities more readily than the issuing company could, which can reduce transaction costs.

- **Greater diversification.** Recall the Principle of Diversification; diversification is beneficial. A small investor can achieve greater diversification by investing in the securities of an intermediary, which can pool thousands of investors' funds and purchase a broadly diversified portfolio of securities. Because of brokerage commissions and institutional restrictions (e.g., most bonds have a minimum denomination of $1,000 and a round lot is 10 bonds, or $10,000), financial intermediaries make it easier and cheaper for individual investors to realize the benefits of diversification.

- **Convenience.** A financial intermediary can tailor securities to meet investors' preferences. For example, a company might want to issue bonds with a fixed interest rate and a 10-year maturity. A financial intermediary can tailor securities to suit investors' preferences—issue some floating rate, some fixed rate, and a variety of different maturities—and purchase the 10-year fixed-rate bonds.

- **Reduction in default risk.** A financial intermediary may provide its own financial guarantee to reduce the degree of default risk investors face. For example, the Government National Mortgage Association (GNMA) issues securities that are backed by the full faith and credit of the United States government and hence involve no default risk. The funds are ultimately invested in home-mortgage loans, which do involve significant default risk.

Financial intermediaries operate with the intention of making a profit. The forgoing benefits potentially have real value for issuers and investors. As a consequence of self-interested behavior, financial intermediaries must not only realize some of this potential value but also pass some of it along to issuers and investors in order to justify their using intermediaries rather than dealing directly with each other.

THE ROLE OF THE FINANCIAL PRESS

According to the Principle of Capital Market Efficiency, the market prices of securities that are traded regularly react quickly (at most within hours) to new information. But how is this information conveyed to the marketplace? Much of it is brought to market participants by the financial press. When a major corporate announcement takes place, the news is broadcast over the Dow Jones broad tape. TV-type monitors on traders' desks display these announcements. Self-interested behavior would suggest that when a major announcement occurs and a trader realizes its significance, the trader will act upon the information immediately if she can realize a profit by doing so. In many cases, much of the opportunity for profit will have passed by the time the story appears in the next day's *Wall Street Journal*! By increasing the speed with which information can be disseminated in the capital markets, developments in the electronic media have undoubtedly increased capital market efficiency. As long as there is self-interested behavior, the faster and more widely the financial press can spread information, the faster securities prices will adjust to new information.

EFFICIENT RESOURCE ALLOCATION 4.2

This section takes a closer look at how the capital markets allocate financial resources. The crucial variable is the discount rate, often referred to as the **opportunity cost of capital**. The opportunity cost of capital is the price per unit of financial capital that users of funds must pay suppliers of funds for the use of their capital. In the case of debt, the opportunity cost of capital is also referred to as the **rate of interest**. The opportunity cost of capital is important because it will determine who will lend, who will borrow, how much capital each lender will supply, and how much capital each borrower will use. Actually, there is no one rate of interest at any particular point in time but a variety of interest rates, depending on the length of the borrowing period (e.g., lenders normally demand a higher rate of interest in return for agreeing to lend for 30 years than for agreeing to lend for just 1 year), the creditworthiness of the borrower (Exxon Corporation can borrow more cheaply than we can), and a number of other factors that we will discuss later in the chapter. Also, because of market imperfections, such as transaction costs, the interest rate borrowers pay is generally higher than the interest rate individuals receive under comparable circumstances. But we will leave these complications for later.

A PERFECT CAPITAL MARKET

To illustrate the role that the opportunity cost of capital plays in allocating capital, let us begin with a somewhat idealistic situation that eliminates the complexities that characterize actual capital markets. Suppose that there is a single **perfect capital market**. That is, one in which

1. There are no barriers to entry that would keep some potential suppliers of funds or some potential users of funds out of the market;
2. There is **perfect competition**; that is, each capital market participant is sufficiently small that its actions cannot affect the rate of interest;
3. Financial assets are infinitely divisible;

4. There are no transaction costs connected with borrowing and lending (e.g., no loan application fees or brokerage commissions);

5. Information is fully available to every capital market participant without charge;

6. There are no taxes (or if there are taxes, every market participant is taxed in an identical manner, so that taxation will not produce any distortions);

7. There are no government or other restrictions on trading, including no restrictions on **short selling** (this term is defined later in the chapter); and

8. Bankruptcy is costless.

THE PRICE FOR WAITING

In such a market, every market participant faces identical borrowing and lending opportunities. There is a single riskless borrowing rate which we can speak of as "the rate of interest." This unique rate of interest is determined through competition among lenders of funds and borrowers of funds, and plays a very important role in the capital market.

If the prevailing rate of interest is 10% per year, a person who lends $10,000 today will receive $11,000 (the original $10,000 plus $1,000 interest) 1 year from today. A person who lends $10,000 today must forgo $10,000 of consumption today. But in return for waiting 1 year, the lender will be able to consume $11,000 when the loan is repaid with interest in 1 year's time, an addition of $1,000 worth of consumption. In this sense, the 10% rate of interest represents the price for waiting.

Figure 4–1 illustrates how the capital markets allow people to trade off consuming (spending) now against future consumption. Suppose an individual knew with certainty that he would receive C dollars in cash flow today and C dollars 1 year from today. If there were no capital market, the individual could consume no more than C today and more than C 1 year from today only if he could store some of today's unused cash flow. Being so limited could be very inconvenient, especially for someone who did not receive the same cash flow each year.

The capital market expands an individual's choice between spending dollars today and spending dollars in the future. The line in Figure 4–1 indicates all of the possible combinations of spending on consumption today (measured along the horizontal axis) and spending on consumption 1 year from today (measured along the vertical axis). The slope of the line represents the rate at which the individual can trade off

FIGURE 4-1

The line of all possible combinations of consumption now and next year.

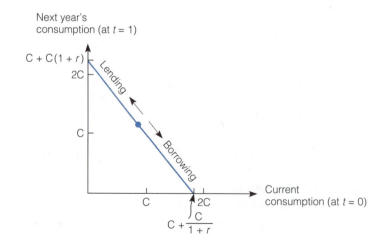

current consumption for future consumption and vice versa. Mathematically, the slope equals $-(1+r)$, where r denotes the rate of interest. Given her income, the individual can consume C today and C 1 year from today. Alternatively, she can lend the entire current income C at interest rate r, consume nothing today, and consume $C + C(1+r)$ at time $t=1$. At the opposite extreme, she can borrow the amount $C/(1+r)$ at interest rate r, consume $C + C/(1+r)$ today, and consume nothing at time $t=1$. Of course, combinations along the line between these two extremes are also possible.

A numerical example might help make this a little clearer. Suppose C = $10,000 and r = 10%. The individual can consume $10,000 today and $10,000 1 year from today if he neither borrows nor lends. Alternatively, he can lend $10,000 at 10% interest, receive $11,000 1 year from today, and consume $21,000 (cash flow of $10,000 plus loan proceeds of $11,000). At the other extreme, the $10,000 of future cash flow has a present value of PV = $9,090.91 (= $10,000/1.1). Thus, the individual could borrow $9,090.91 against cash flow 1 year from today and consume $19,090.91 today but nothing 1 year from today.[9] By borrowing or lending, the individual could achieve any position along the line in Figure 4-1.

SMOOTHING CONSUMPTION PATTERNS

Individuals are unlikely to have identical consumption preferences. The capital markets permit individuals to tailor their consumption patterns to suit their preferences, subject of course to remaining within the set of consumption patterns that are feasible. In terms of Figure 4.1, an individual can wind up anywhere along the line but cannot be above the line because combinations above the line are not attainable under the conditions given.[10]

Consider two individuals, each of whom will receive C dollars today and C dollars 1 year from today. Denote them Miser and Spendthrift. Miser would like to consume .5C today and $C + .5C(1+r)$ one year from today. How does she accomplish this? She lends .5C and receives back $.5C(1+r)$ 1 year from today. Spendthrift, on the other hand, would like to consume 1.5C today and $C - .5C(1+r)$ one year from today. So he borrows .5C to augment today's consumption but must agree to pay back $.5C(1+r)$ 1 year from today. Figure 4-2 illustrates Miser's and Spendthrift's consumption–combination choices.

The capital market permits each individual to shift wealth across time to achieve that individual's most preferred consumption pattern, within the constraint of the individual's total wealth.

AGGREGATE INVESTMENT OPPORTUNITIES

Another way of viewing an individual's alternative consumption choices is to express them as capital market investment opportunities. By default, this period's consumption decision is, in essence, an investment decision. The more the individual invests now (defers consumption), the more the wealth (potential consumption) that

---

[9] Note that the slope of the line is $-21,000/19,090.91 = -1.1$, or $-(1+r)$.

[10] Readers who are familiar with economic theory will recognize the line in Figure 4-1 as the individual's consumption-possibilities curve. We could superimpose an indifference map in order to determine which point on the consumption-possibilities curve would make the individual best off. The optimal point would occur where the consumption-possibilities curve is tangent to an indifference curve. At the point of tangency, the individual's marginal rate of time preference (the rate at which he is willing subjectively to trade off current consumption for future consumption) equals the market rate of interest.

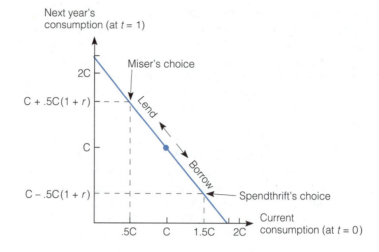

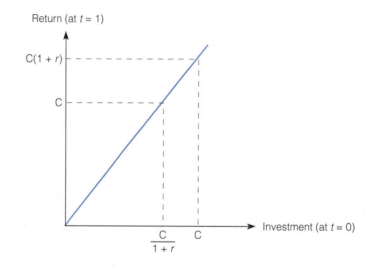

individual will have next year. Figure 4–3 expresses the current period's decision as an investment decision. The line proceeding up and to the right from the origin is a line of all possible investment amounts. If our individual invests all that is available, C, then 1 year from now, the investment will return $C(1+r)$; the future value is $(1+r)$ times the present value. Likewise, investing $C/(1+r)$ now will return C 1 year from now; the present value is the future value divided by $(1+r)$. An investment of $.5C$ will return $.5C(1+r)$, and so forth. Thus, the capital market investment-opportunities line has a slope of $(1+r)$.

In addition to capital market investment opportunities, market participants can invest in real assets. Figure 4-4 presents a real asset investment-opportunities curve. It shows the combinations of investment today and return 1 year from today that may be realized by investing in real assets.[11] Note that the real asset investment-

---

[11] The alert reader will realize that the smoothness of the investment-opportunity curve rests on the assumption that investment opportunities are divisible into "very small" pieces. That is, there is not the "lumpiness" that characterizes actual capital investment projects.

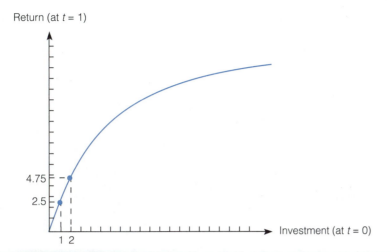

opportunities curve in Figure 4-4 is not a straight line. This reflects the diminishing returns that one can expect from investments in real assets. Recall the Principle of Valuable Ideas. Quite simply, some ideas are more valuable than others. In the extreme, some ideas are actually costly; they will not return enough to be worthwhile.

The opportunity to invest in real assets greatly expands the set of investment possibilities beyond those shown in Figure 4-3. More importantly, comparing capital market and real asset investment opportunities simultaneously will lead us to a very important result: a criterion for determining how much to invest in real assets.

Because of self-interested behavior, people will invest in the most profitable real asset investment opportunity first, the next most profitable opportunity second, and so on. In Figure 4-4, the scale is represented in millions of dollars, so that the first $1 million of investment produces a return of $2.5 million. Investing the second $1 million produces a return of $2.25 million. Investing additional $1 million amounts would produce successively smaller returns. But how much should the *total* amount of investment be?

To determine the optimal amount of total investment, individuals must review their alternatives and opportunity costs. If you can earn r per period by investing in the capital market, why would you ever invest in a real asset investment opportunity of identical risk that returned less than r? The answer is that you would not. And this is exactly where the net-present-value (NPV) rule originates. *Do not buy an asset that is not worth what you have to pay for it.* In other words, do not buy an asset with a negative NPV.

Figure 4-5 superimposes the real asset investment-opportunities curve on the capital market investment-opportunities line. We have noted that the slope of the capital market investment-opportunities line is $(1+r)$ and the return to investment is r. If individuals apply the decision rule stated above, they will invest in real assets only if the asset will return at least r. These opportunities are contained in the part of the curve where the slope is greater than or equal to $(1+r)$. Therefore, the optimal total investment amount can be determined by a line parallel to the capital market investment-opportunities line, tangent to the real asset investment-opportunities curve. Figure 4-6 illustrates this concept by including this parallel line.

In Figure 4-6, the optimal total investment amount is I*. With a total investment amount of I*, the total return at $t = 1$ is R*. A normal total return would be I*(1+r) = R* −NFV* (because the triangles AR* NFV* and BOI* are congruent). Conse-

Capital market investment-opportunities line superimposed on the real asset investment-opportunities curve.

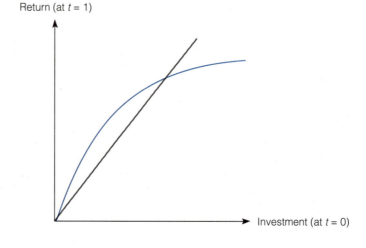

The optimal total investment, I^*, and corresponding increase in present value, NPV*.

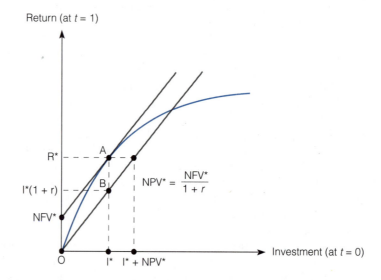

quently, the aggregate excess return at time $t=1$ will be NFV*. NFV* has a present value of NPV* ($= $ NFV*/[1+r]). For individuals with money to invest, our description is straightforward. But what about individuals who have no money to invest?

Suppose an individual does not have the cash necessary to invest in an attractive real asset investment opportunity. Must the individual pass up the opportunity? No! The capital market allows both positive and negative investment; that is, lending *and* borrowing. Therefore, when an individual has an attractive real asset investment opportunity but lacks the cash to undertake the opportunity, that individual can obtain the necessary cash by borrowing in the capital market.[12]

Returning to our notion of Miser and Spendthrift, we can see how investing in real assets makes *both* of them better off. The value added by investment I* is NPV* in terms of $t=0$ dollars and NFV* in terms of $t=1$ dollars. Let the individual's por-

---

[12] We are using the term **borrowing** loosely. Actually, an individual can obtain *any* type of financing because the risk-return trade-off makes the various types of financing equivalent. Any difference in the discount rate between different types of financing reflects a difference in risk. Risk differences are explored in Chapter 7.

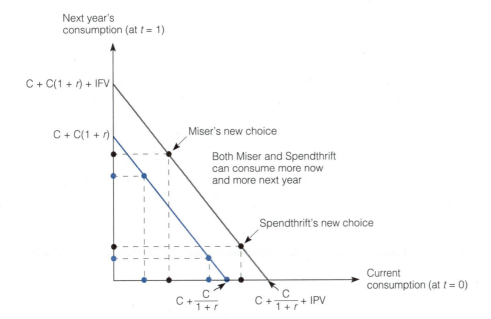

FIGURE 4-7

An illustration of how real asset investment opportunities improve the consumption combinations for *all* individuals.

tion of the added value be IPV at $t=0$ and IFV at $t=1$. The individual's position can then be determined by adding these amounts to the individual's income, as shown in Figure 4-7, which is adapted from Figure 4-2. In Figure 4-7 we can see that both Miser and Spendthrift will be able to consume more now and more next year with investment I* in real assets. Furthermore, all individuals will not be as well off with any investment other than I*. Thus, the opportunity to invest in real assets improves every individual's set of consumption possibilities, regardless of her personal consumption preferences.

The capital markets bring together the aggregate choices for investing in real and financial assets and borrowing for either consumption or investment purposes. So the capital markets play a crucial role because they determine the trade-offs individuals face among all of these choices. These trade-offs are embodied in, or represented by, the rate of interest. The rate of interest, then, is a measure of the opportunity cost of choosing one alternative over another. The rate of interest is the opportunity cost of capital.

FISHER SEPARATION

The development of net present value as a criterion for choosing investments illustrates a point initially recognized by the American economist Irving Fisher more than a half century ago.[13] Fisher discovered that the criterion for determining the optimal amount of capital investment need not have anything to do with individuals' relative preferences for current and future consumption. Provided individuals have free access to the capital markets (they can lend or borrow freely at the prevailing rate of interest), each individual can create his own consumption pattern by borrowing or lending appropriate amounts. As illustrated in Figure 4-7, the investment decision is *separable* from individuals' consumption preferences. All individuals, regardless of the relative preferences for current and future consumption, are best off if

---

[13] Fisher (1965).

the enterprise invests I* in real assets; that investment program maximizes *everyone's* consumption possibilities. A business enterprise should maximize NPV because that will give the owners of the enterprise the widest range of consumption possibilities. This result, that capital investment decisions are separable from consumption decisions, is often referred to as **Fisher's separation theorem**.

Fisher's separation theorem has an important implication for corporate enterprises. Today's large corporations, some with literally hundreds of thousands of shareholders, can operate viably only if shareholders delegate operating responsibility to professional managers. According to Fisher's separation theorem, the corporation's shareholders can all agree on a single overriding corporate objective: *maximize the NPV of the corporation's investments*.

Fisher's separation theorem rests on the assumption of a perfect capital market. To the extent that actual capital markets deviate from this ideal, Fisher's separation theorem may be only an approximation. In the next chapter, we discuss the existence of market imperfections.

4.3   MARKET COMPLETENESS

Over the past decade, a veritable revolution in securities innovation has taken place. This revolution has introduced into the capital markets a wide variety of new financial instruments. New forms of debt, new types of preferred stock, new classes of convertible debt instruments, and new types of options and financial futures have broadened the choices available to investors. To appreciate the significance of these developments, we must introduce the concept of a **complete capital market**.

A COMPLETE CAPITAL MARKET

A **complete capital market** is one in which there is a distinct marketable security for each and every contingency in the world. An incomplete capital market is one in which the available securities do not **span** all possible contingencies; there are fewer types of securities than contingencies. In a practical sense, in a complete and perfect capital market, there would be no benefit to securities innovation because the range of securities available would permit investors to invest in whatever return distributions they desire.

Actual capital markets are incomplete. There are infinite contingencies and only a finite number of securities. As a result, the Principle of Valuable Ideas applies—new ideas may provide extraordinary returns. This contributes to an explanation of the continuing innovations in the securities markets. New securities may increase the degree of market completeness. For example, new forms of options and futures may allow investors to invest in a return distribution that was previously not available.

SPANNING

A simple example will help convey the notion of completeness. Imagine a situation in which there are two possible future states of the world (i.e., two contingencies), prosperity (*P*) and depression (*D*). Suppose there is only one security available, which pays 100 per unit if state *P* occurs but only 20 per unit if state *D* occurs. Now we introduce an investor, who wishes to realize 50 in state *P* and 10 in state *D*. The investor can accomplish this by buying a half unit of the security. But suppose the investor wanted to realize 100 in state *P* and 50 in state *D*. One unit would provide enough in state P but not enough in state D. Two and one-half units would provide enough in state D but too much in state P.

Now suppose a financial innovator comes along and introduces a new security that pays 50 in state P and 40 in state D. If the investor buys x units of the old security and y units of the new security that satisfy the equations

$$100x + 50y = 100$$
$$20x + 40y = 50 \qquad\qquad \textbf{(4.1)}$$

the investor would be able to realize exactly 100 in state P and exactly 50 in state D. The two equations can be solved to yield $x = .5$ and $y = 1$. The investor should buy half a unit of the old security and one unit of the new security. As a result of the new security's introduction, the available securities now *span* the two contingencies. The securities market is complete; the investor can identify a pair of securities amounts x and y to achieve any combination of returns in states D and P the investor desires.[14] You should be able to show that this statement would not be true if, for example, the new security would pay 75 in state P and 15 in state D.[15]

SECURITIES INNOVATION

The preceding example illustrates the role that securities innovation plays in expanding investors' choice sets. The new security enabled the investor to accomplish something that was not previously possible; it made the market more complete. But securities innovation is driven by the innovator's profit motive: self-interested behavior. An innovation will be introduced only if the innovator can profit by doing so. For example, suppose that all transactions were costless and that a second innovator tried to introduce a second new security that would pay 75 in state P and 30 in state D. One unit of such a security would produce exactly the same distribution of returns as a combination consisting of a half unit of the old security and a half unit of the first new security. It would be redundant, and therefore its introduction could not be profitable.

If there were market imperfections, introducing the second new security *could* be profitable if, for example, it involved lower transaction costs than existing securities. As a general rule, securities innovation is profitable only if it reduces the impact of market imperfections or makes the capital markets more complete.

Chapter 14 describes a variety of securities innovations, but providing two examples here might help make the forgoing concepts more meaningful. It is mutually advantageous for a nontaxpaying corporation to issue preferred stock to a taxpaying

---

[14] In mathematical terms, the set of securities will span the set of contingencies, provided that the set of linear equations, one per contingency as in Equation (4.1), has a solution. If there are N contingencies and N linearly independent equations, then there is a unique solution. In that case, there would be N distinct securities. If there are more than N securities but only N contingencies, there may be more than one possible solution. In that case, certain securities would be redundant. But as long as N of the securities were distinct from one another, an investor could achieve whatever distribution of returns across the N contingencies the investor desires.

[15] In this case, Equation (4.1) would take the form

$$100x + 75y = 100$$
$$20x + 15y = 50$$

This system of equations is inconsistent. It has no solution because the first equation can be rewritten as $20x + 15y = 20$, which clearly cannot hold if the second equation does and vice versa. The two securities are redundant because $1\frac{1}{3}$ units of the new security produces exactly the same distribution of returns as the old security.

corporation. The taxpaying corporation can deduct 70% of the dividends it receives from its taxable income. Interest paid to corporate debtholders does not enjoy this advantage. Due to the tax advantage, preferred stock provides a lower (pretax) dividend yield than the yield of a comparable debt instrument. However, the market value of fixed-dividend-rate preferred stock can change dramatically as interest rates change. This makes fixed-dividend-rate preferred stock unattractive as a short-term investment vehicle for corporations with temporary excess cash balances. So in 1982, investment bankers introduced adjustable-rate preferred stock (ARPS), the dividend rate on which adjusts quarterly in accordance with a dividend formula. But the dividend formulas could not capture the movement in market dividend yields precisely, so that the market value of ARPS varied with interest rate changes, though not as much as the value of fixed-dividend-rate preferred stocks. Investment bankers in 1984 introduced Dutch-auction-rate preferred stock (DARPS) whose dividend rate is reset to market levels by a Dutch auction every 7 weeks.[16] The market value of DARPS is much more stable than the market value of ARPS, reducing investors' liquidity risk substantially. Both ARPS and DARPS were intended to make the capital markets more complete. The more than $10 billion of DARPS that were issued within 3 years of the security's introduction attests to its success.[17]

SELLING SHORT

An investor can take either a **long** investment position or a **short** investment position in a market asset. A long position involves buying the asset and holding it. An investor does this because the investor expects the asset to increase in value, or at least hold its approximate value and provide a flow of dividends or interest during the holding period. A short position involves borrowing an asset, such as bonds or shares of stock, from its owner and selling it to a third party. Does this sound illegal? Let us assure you that it is not. However, selling securities short is normally done by only a small percentage of investors. They generally do it because they expect the prices of the securities they borrow and sell short to decline. If a price decrease occurs, the short seller is able to buy back the securities at a profit and return them to their owners. Of course, short selling requires a long buyer who is bullish (i.e., who expects price appreciation), who will buy the securities from the short seller. Aside from brokerage commissions, the Principle of Two-Sided Transactions applies; it is a zero-sum game: The short seller's gain is the long buyer's loss if price decreases, and the long buyer's gain is the short seller's loss if price increases. Short selling can also be used in **hedging** a long position because gain on the short position, if the short position is designed correctly, will offset some or perhaps all of the loss on the long position (and vice versa).

Short selling is more complicated than buying a long position for the following reasons:

- A short sale of an NYSE-listed stock can only occur on an **up-tick**, that is, following a trade that raised the stock's price. This rule is intended to prevent short selling from exacerbating a decrease in share prices.
- The short seller must compensate the owner of the borrowed securities for any dividends or interest paid during the period the securities are borrowed.

[16] In a Dutch auction, bids come from the seller and are lowered until a buyer agrees to purchase. This contrasts with the English aution, in which bids come from potential buyers and are raised until the seller agrees to sell.

[17] See Alderson, Brown, and Lummer (1987), for an interesting analysis of the new security.

- A short seller may have to provide cash or securities as collateral to the owner of the borrowed securities.

- The owner of the securities can demand them back at any time, which could force the short seller to repurchase them (i.e., to **cover** the short) at a disadvantageous time. In such situations, the short seller's broker tries to borrow the same securities from a different owner in order to maintain the short position.

Short selling increases investors' choice sets because each security can be held in a long position or can be sold short. Returning to the example summarized in Equation (4.1), suppose the new security would still pay 50 in P but would pay -20 in D (e.g., as shares of common stock might). The investor should "buy" x units of the old security and y units of the new security that satisfy the following equations:

$$100x + 50y = 100$$
$$20x - 20y = 50 \qquad (4.2)$$

The solution to the system of equations is $x = 1.5$ and $y = -1$. The investor should buy 1.5 units of the old security and sell short 1 unit of the new security. If short selling were not permitted, then only long positions would be possible ($x > 0$ and $y > 0$). In that case, the two securities would not span the two contingencies. But short selling is permitted, subject to the aforementioned restrictions. Short selling is often used by sophisticated investors to achieve a more desired future-return distribution.

OPTIONS AND FUTURES

Recall that an **option** is a contract that gives its holder the right, without any obligation, to buy a specified amount of securities (typically 100 shares in the case of a standardized market-traded stock option) at a specified price (a **call** option) or to sell a specified amount of securities (again, typically 100 shares) at a specified price (a **put** option) within some stated time period. The specified price is the **strike price**. The Options Principle states that options are valuable, because they confer a right that carries no obligation. A **financial-futures contract** (or more simply, a **financial future**) is a standardized contract to deliver a specified quantity of a specific financial instrument during a stated future delivery month.

Therefore, a **future** is simply a buy/sell transaction that is agreed upon now, but exchange of the asset and selling price will take place at a specified time in the future. Neither side has an option or a choice about its behavior. However, either party to the transaction can buy/sell its obligation prior to when the transfer is scheduled to take place.

OPTIONS MARKETS The Chicago Board of Options Exchange (CBOE) began operations in 1973. Today it is the largest options exchange in the world in aggregate dollar value of contracts traded. Among U.S. securities exchanges, only the NYSE is bigger. Most stock options are traded on one of four exchanges—the CBOE, the AMEX, the Philadelphia Stock Exchange, and the Pacific Stock Exchange. There is a small over-the-counter market that deals primarily in the nonstandardized options that the four exchanges do not handle.

Option prices are determined on the options exchanges by "open outcry." For example, on the CBOE there are competing market makers for each option who can trade only for their own accounts, in contrast to the major stock exchanges where there is a single market maker for each stock. In addition, there are floor brokers who execute buy and sell orders for their customers. Option prices are determined through competition among market makers in response to buy and sell orders conveyed by the floor brokers.

The four options exchanges jointly own and clear all their option trades through the Options Clearing Corporation (OCC). The OCC interposes itself between every option buyer and every option seller. It substitutes its promise to deliver for the option seller's promise to deliver, which reduces transaction costs by obviating the need for the buyer to evaluate the option seller's creditworthiness. The OCC effectively makes all call option contracts for a particular security, strike price, and expiration date perfect substitutes for one another, and similarly for put option contracts.

In recent years, the number of traded options has proliferated. In addition to options on common stocks, there are traded options on foreign currencies, on debt instruments such as U.S. Treasury securities, on stock market indexes such as the Standard & Poor's 500 Index, and on futures contracts.

FUTURES MARKETS   Financial futures are traded on financial securities, such as Treasury bills, Treasury notes, and Treasury bonds, Eurodollar time deposits, and U.S. certificates of deposit; foreign currencies; stock indexes such as the Standard & Poor's 500 Index and the NYSE Composite Index; precious metals; and economic indexes such as the Consumer Price Index.

Financial futures are traded on organized exchanges. The first financial futures traded on an exchange in the United States were foreign exchange futures, which began trading at the International Monetary Market (IMM) of the Chicago Mercantile Exchange in 1972. Trading in each financial future takes place in a trading ring on the exchange floor. Exchange members who wish to trade the future enter the trading ring and indicate their intention to transact business by open outcry or appropriate hand signals. When a buyer and seller agree on contract terms, the latest price is posted on a board near the trading ring.

Unlike the stock exchanges and the options markets, there are no central market makers on the futures exchanges. As a result, futures prices can exhibit considerable volatility. To limit this volatility, the futures exchanges have established price limits; futures prices cannot change by more than the indicated limit on any particular day.

SIGNIFICANCE OF OPTIONS AND FUTURES   The development of organized options markets and futures markets was one of the most significant financial developments of the 1970s. These new financial instruments increased the ability of investors to alter their return distributions. As a result, financial risk could be reallocated within the capital markets to enable participants to invest in return distributions that better match their preferences.

4.4   THE TERM STRUCTURE OF INTEREST RATES

Up to this point, we have assumed that funds are borrowed or invested for exactly 1 year. In actuality, a tremendous variety of maturities are available. Banks can borrow literally overnight in the Federal funds market. At the other extreme, telephone companies have typically been able to issue bonds with maturities up to 40 years. Industrial companies, electric and gas utility companies, municipalities, and the U.S. Treasury regularly issue bonds with maturities up to 30 years, although General Electric Capital Corporation sold a 60-year debt issue in October 1989 (which will mature about the time the authors reach their 100th birthdays). There is virtu-

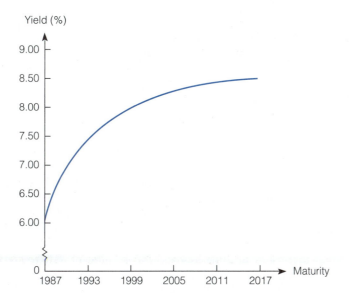

FIGURE 4-8
The term structure of interest rates on June 26, 1987.

ally a continuum of maturities possible between these extremes for each type of issuer.

MEANING OF THE TERM STRUCTURE

We observe in the bond markets that the interest rate required to sell a bond issue generally increases with the maturity of the bonds. There are a number of ways to characterize this interest rate/maturity relationship. One method is to plot the **term structure of interest rates**. The term structure of interest rates is the relationship between the yields on zero-coupon U.S. Treasury bonds and the maturities of those U.S. Treasury bonds as of a particular date for a collection of zero-coupon U.S. Treasury bonds that spans the available maturity spectrum, currently 0 to 30 years.

A **zero-coupon bond**, also referred to as a **pure-discount bond** or a **single-payment bond**, pays no periodic interest but makes a single lump-sum payment at maturity. For example, a zero-coupon bond with a face amount of $1,000 that matures in 5 years will have a present value of PV = $1,000/(1.10)^5 = $620.92 per bond when the effective annual rate is 10% per year. The investor pays $620.92 today for the promise of receiving $1,000 in 5 years.

Figure 4–8 depicts the term structure of interest rates as of Friday, June 26, 1987. It is based on the yields of CATS (Certificates of Accrual on Treasury Securities), which were created from U.S. Treasury bonds by Salomon Brothers Inc.[18] The yields at which bonds trade are affected by the taxability of their returns, whether they were created by a securities firm that issued receipts against Treasury bonds held in trust (like the CATS) or were created by stripping bearer U.S. Treasury bonds, as well as other factors.[19] Consequently, two different zero-coupon U.S.

---

[18] Salomon Brothers Inc created CATS by purchasing registered U.S. Treasury bonds, depositing them in a trust, and having the trust issue certificates (i.e., the CATS) representing separate entitlements to receive different interest payments and the principal repayment at maturity.

[19] The first zero-coupon U.S. Treasury bonds were created by physically detaching coupons from bearer U.S. Treasury bonds. Securities firms "stripped" U.S. Treasury bonds in this manner because they discovered they could earn a riskless arbitrage profit by buying Treasury bonds, stripping coupons, and selling the various pieces to investors who were willing to pay the highest prices for them.

Treasury bonds that mature on a particular date may trade at different yields. As a result, picking any particular type of zero-coupon U.S. Treasury bonds, such as CATS, will lead to a term structure that may only approximate the true term structure. However, investors pursuing arbitrage opportunities will ensure that any such approximation is a close one.

EXPLAINING THE TERM STRUCTURE

The term structure depicted in Figure 4–8 is upward-sloping, as it usually is. Long-term rates typically exceed short-term rates. However, there have been periods in our history when the reverse was true; the term structure was downward-sloping (also described as inverted). A downward-sloping term structure occurred between the fourth quarter of 1980 and the fourth quarter of 1981 when interest rates were at historically high levels. Note that the term structure tends to "flatten out" as maturity increases. Typically, when maturity exceeds 20 years, the yield differentials that exist with longer maturities become less and less significant. There are four basic theories that might explain the observed shape of the term structure.[20]

EXPECTATIONS HYPOTHESIS   The expectations hypothesis states that the interest rate expectations of market participants determine the shape of the term structure. Simply put, if market participants expect interest rates to increase in the future, the term structure will be upward-sloping. If they expect interest rates to decrease in the future, the term structure will be downward-sloping.

The following example illustrates the basis for the expectations hypothesis. Suppose an individual can invest $1,000 in either of two alternatives: a 2-year bond that will pay 10% interest per year or a 1-year bond that will pay 8% interest followed by reinvestment in a second 1-year bond at whatever the 1-year rate is next year. How will the individual decide between these alternatives? She must decide whether investing in the 1-year bond and reinvesting the proceeds in another 1-year bond will produce a greater expected return at the end of 2 years than investing in the 2-year bond. Investing $1,000 in the 2-year bond will produce a total return (principal plus compound interest) of $1,210 at the end of 2 years. Investing $1,000 in the 1-year bond will produce an expected return of $1,080(1 + f)$ at the end of 2 years, where f denotes the expected rate of interest on a 1-year bond that is issued 1 year from today. Thus: (1) investors invest in the 1-year bond if $1,080(1 + f) > \$1,210$; (2) investors are indifferent between the two bonds if $1,080(1 + f) = \$1,210$; and (3) investors invest in the 2-year bond if $1,080(1 + f) < \$1,210$. But $1,080(1 + f)$ is greater than (equal to) (less than) $1,210 only if f is greater than (equal to) (less than) 12.04%. If $f > 12.04\%$, all investors would want to own 1-year bonds. Similarly, if $f < 12.04\%$, they would all want to hold 2-year bonds. In order for investors to be willing to hold some of each, $f = 12.04\%$.

In this example, next year's expected 1-year rate of interest—the **forward rate**—of $f = 12.04\%$ is greater than the current 1-year interest rate—the **spot rate**—of 8%, and the term structure is upward-sloping; the 2-year yield (10%) exceeds the current 1-year yield (8%). Suppose instead that investors expected the 1-year interest rate to fall to, say, 6% next year. Under the expectations hypothesis, the yield on a 2-year bond y would have to satisfy the equation

$$(1 + y)^2 = (1.08)(1.06) = 1.1448, \text{ and therefore } y = 6.995\%$$

---

[20] For a more extensive discussion of the term structure and the associated theories, see Malkiel (1970).

In this second case, the yield curve would be downward-sloping since the 2-year rate would be less than the current 1-year rate.

The expectations hypothesis is capable of explaining any shape of the term structure. It says simply that investor expectations dictate the shape at any point in time. There is empirical evidence that the expectations hypothesis is capable of providing at least a partial explanation for the term structure.[21] It also has a certain intuitive appeal. However, it cannot by itself explain the term structure. The expectations hypothesis implies that investing in short-term Treasury securities should provide the same expected rate of return as investing in long-term Treasury securities. Ibbotson and Sinquefield have found that over the period 1926–1987, Treasury bills provided an average annual rate of return of 3.5% versus 4.3% and 4.8%, respectively, for long-term and intermediate-term U.S. government bonds.[22] For such differentials to persist over such an extended period, there must be some explanation for the premium rate of return that investors in longer-term bonds realize vis-à-vis Treasury bills.

LIQUIDITY PREFERENCE   The expectations hypothesis ignores risk. This is a significant omission because the Principle of Risk Aversion implies that investors who are offered two alternatives that provide the same expected return will always choose the one that involves lower risk. In the preceding example, if the individual's intended holding period was 2 years, the expected 1-year yield 1 year hence was 12.04%, and 1-year and 2-year yields were 8% and 10%, respectively, the individual would choose the 2-year bond. Why? Because it has the same expected return as the sequence of 1-year bond investments but without any reinvestment risk.

The liquidity-preference theory argues that investors generally prefer shorter maturities because shorter-term bonds exhibit less price volatility than longer-term bonds. Shorter-term bonds involve less risk because they can be converted into cash prior to maturity with less risk of loss of principal due to unexpected interest rate changes. As a consequence, investors require a yield premium to compensate for this risk, to induce them to hold longer-term bonds.

The liquidity-preference theory contends that the term structure should be generally upward-sloping, as has been the case. While there is some empirical support for the pure liquidity-preference theory of the term structure, the combined expectations-hypothesis/liquidity-preference theory has greater support than either theory on its own.[23]

INFLATION UNCERTAINTY   Not only future interest rates are uncertain; so are future inflation rates. Annual inflation rates have exhibited considerable volatility since 1970. Suppose for the moment that short-term interest rates fully reflect investors' inflation expectations and that inflation uncertainty is the only source of uncertainty regarding future interest rates. In that case, the individual in our previous example would prefer the 1-year bond over the 2-year bond even if his intended holding period was 2 years.[24] The 1-year-bond and 2-year-bond alternatives would provide the same expected return in nominal dollars (i.e., before adjusting for the effects of inflation). But investing in the 1-year bond would involve less inflation risk because interest rates would adjust at the end of the first year to reflect any changes in

---

[21] See Cargill (1975).

[22] Ibbotson and Sinquefield (1989), p. 72. The lower rate for long-term bonds versus intermediate-term bonds probably reflects changes in inflation and hence interest rates in the past several decades.

[23] See McCulloch (1975).

[24] See Brealey and Schaefer (1977) for a more formal development of the explanation of the term structure based on inflation uncertainty.

inflation expectations for the second year. The individual would invest in the 2-year bond only if that alternative provided a yield premium large enough to compensate for the greater inflation risk.

Inflation uncertainty, like liquidity preference, argues that the term structure will generally be upward-sloping. However, the two theories have different policy implications. Inflation uncertainty argues that all investors should have a relative preference for very short-term investments, regardless of their investment horizons. Liquidity preference, on the other hand, argues that the best strategy for investors is to match the maturity of their investments to their investment horizons. Which theory provides the more accurate explanation for the term structure will have to be decided empirically.

SEGMENTED MARKETS   The segmented-markets theory enjoys some degree of acceptance among market practitioners, although there is, as yet at least, no real empirical support for it. The segmented-markets theory holds that different classes of institutional investors have different maturity preferences because of differences in liability structure, tax position, and so on. For example, pension funds that have very long-term liabilities invest primarily in very long-term securities. Insurance companies that have written large volumes of so-called guaranteed investment contracts maturing in 5 to 10 years concentrate in that maturity range. Money-market funds face tight limitations on permissible maturities that confine them to very short-term securities.

Taken to its logical extreme, the segmented-markets theory contends that the securities markets are segmented by maturity. Each investor is confined to a particular maturity segment and never purchases a security that is outside that segment. As a result, so the argument goes, the term structure is determined by the interaction of supply and demand within separate maturity segments.

The segmented-markets theory per se is incapable of explaining why the term structure is generally upward-sloping (unless perhaps one can argue that there is a systematic shortfall in supply across maturity segments, which causes yield premiums to increase with maturity). It also ignores the inherent substitutability of investment alternatives. Investing in a 1-year bond and rolling that investment over 1 year later is a perfectly adequate substitute for investing in the 2-year bond. As a consequence of self-interested behavior, we would expect that once yield differentials became wide enough, investors could be induced to invest outside their preferred maturity segments. In any case, securities firms and certain other investors that do not face maturity restrictions could be expected to engage in arbitrage to eliminate unwarranted yield differentials. The expectations-hypothesis/liquidity-preference/inflation-uncertainty theories therefore provides a much better explanation of the term structure than the segmented-markets theory.

SIGNIFICANCE OF THE TERM STRUCTURE

In an efficient market, the term structure of interest rates at a particular point in time reflects investors' expectations regarding future interest rates. Indeed, strict adherents to the expectations hypothesis argue that one need *only* examine the term structure in order to gauge how interest rates are likely to behave in the future. Empirical evidence suggests that the term structure does contain useful, though not completely reliable, information regarding future interest rates.[25]

[25] Evidence presented by Fama (1976) indicates that forward rates are the best predictors of future spot interest rates, even though these predictions are not always accurate.

Consider again the example discussed earlier in this section. If the 1-year interest rate is 8% and the 2-year interest rate is 10%, what can we say about the 1-year interest rate (the 1-year "spot rate") 1 year from today? The forward rate, we found previously, is $f = 12.04\%$. Under the expectations hypothesis, the forward rate equals the expected 1-year spot rate one year hence. If the expectations hypothesis holds strictly, we would expect the 1-year interest rate to increase to 12.04% in 1 year from 8% today. Extrapolating to longer maturities, the current term structure can be used to formulate the expectations regarding future spot rates and regarding the future term structure.

Because the expectations hypothesis does not provide a complete explanation for the term structure, the forward rates embodied in the term structure are imperfect predictors of future spot rates. Also, as with any prediction, conditions may change and cause actual rates to deviate, perhaps substantially, from the predicted rates. Nevertheless bond analysts do use the term structure to obtain information about expected future interest rates, which they use in bond valuation.

TERM STRUCTURE AND THE YIELD CURVE

The term structure of interest rates consists of a plot, like the one illustrated in Figure 4-8, of yield versus maturity for a collection of zero-coupon U.S. Treasury bonds that spans the available maturity spectrum. Another way to characterize the interest rate/maturity relationship is to plot the **yield curve**. The yield curve for any issuer shows for each maturity the interest rate that investors would demand in order for a regular coupon-paying bond of that maturity to be worth **par** (i.e., price equals face amount). Because issuers normally sell regular coupon-paying bonds rather than zero-coupon bonds, issuers and investors typically find the yield curve for the issuer's debt more meaningful than the term structure of interest rates. In particular, the yield curve shows the yield the issuer would have to offer investors in order to sell regular coupon-paying bonds of any particular maturity.

The term structure and the yield curve are equivalent ways of characterizing the interest rate/maturity relationship for Treasury debt (or for the debt of any issuer for that matter). Returning to the preceding example, suppose bonds pay interest once each year. The term structure of interest rates tells us that investors discount payments to be received 1 year from today at the rate of 8% per annum and payments to be received 2 years from today at the rate of 12% per annum.

Consider a 1-year regular coupon-paying bond. Suppose its face amount is $1,000. The bond pays interest at a coupon rate r. At the end of 1 year, each bond pays $1,000(1+r)$. In order for the price of the bond to equal its face amount, the following equation must be satisfied:

$$1,000 = \frac{1,000(1 + r)}{1.08}, \text{ so } r = 8\%.$$

Next consider the 2-year bond. The bond pays $1,000r$ at the end of 1 year and $1,000(1+r)$ at the end of the second year. In order for the price of the bond to equal its face amount, the following equation must be satisfied:

$$1,000 = \frac{1,000r}{1.08} + \frac{1,000(1 + r)}{(1.12)^2} \tag{4.3}$$

so, $r = 11.77\%$. Note that

$$1,000 = \frac{1,000r}{1.1177} + \frac{1,000(1 + r)}{(1.1177)^2} \tag{4.4}$$

when $r = 11.77\%$. We call 11.77% the **yield to maturity** of the 2-year coupon-paying bond. Similarly, 8% is the yield to maturity of the 1-year coupon-paying bond. Chapter 6 describes how yield to maturity is used in bond valuation.

The yield curve shows the yield to maturity investors require for a bond of each maturity. The procedure just illustrated can be used to derive a yield curve from a particular term structure, or it can be used in reverse to obtain a term structure from a particular yield curve. Since the vast majority of bonds are coupon-paying, what we observe directly in the bond market are yields to maturity, which represent points on, or at least approximately on, various issuers' yield curves. There is also a public market for zero-coupon Treasury bonds that enables us to observe, at least approximately, the term structure. We use the qualifier "approximately" because a variety of factors (among the more important of which is taxes) can affect bond prices and yields. When bonds sell at significant discounts from or premiums to their face amounts, the observed yields may deviate significantly from the yield at which a new par-value bond can be sold.

In the simple example just considered, the term structure passed through the points 8% at 1 year and 12% at 2 years. The yield curve passed through the point 8% at 1 year and 11.77% at 2 years. What's the difference between these two curves? The term structure provides the discount rates that investors would use to discount each payment in a payment stream. The yield curve provides the discount rates that investors would use to discount every payment in a payment stream of the indicated maturity, under the assumption that each payment in the stream is discounted at the same rate. For example, the term structure indicates that a single payment to be received in 2 years should be discounted at a 12% rate. The yield curve indicates that every payment in a 2-year stream should be discounted at an 11.77% rate. Equations (4.3) and (4.4) illustrate the equivalence of the two approaches: Discount each payment according to the term structure, or discount every payment at the appropriate yield to maturity.

This example also illustrates another aspect of the relationship between the term structure and the yield curve. When the term structure is upward-sloping, as in Figure 4–8, the term structure will be above the yield curve (e.g., 12% > 11.77%). The opposite is true when the term structure is downward-sloping. When the term structure is flat, the yield curve coincides with it.

SUMMARY

The capital markets allocate financial capital accumulated by savers to corporations, government entities, and others who would like to invest in real assets but lack sufficient funds to meet their current needs for capital. In this way, they act as a conduit for funds from net funds suppliers to net funds users. How efficiently this conduit operates in allocating funds to their most profitable uses will determine to a great extent how efficiently real productive resources are allocated in the economy.

In this chapter we described the capital markets in the United States, how they operate, and the types of financial assets, or securities, that are bought and sold in these markets. Corporations issue securities in the capital markets to raise funds.

In a perfect and complete capital market, investors are able to create whatever return distributions they need to cover every contingency. Our study of the capital markets shows that in such a world, enterprises should invest in all projects that have a positive NPV and should not invest in any projects that have a negative NPV.

The capital markets in the United States are organized into either auction markets, like the NYSE and the other stock exchanges, or dealer markets, like the OTC markets for stocks and bonds. Most stocks are traded in the OTC market, but the greatest dollar volume of trading in stocks takes place on the NYSE. In contrast, the bulk of the trading in bonds occurs in the OTC market.

There are a great variety of debt securities and equity securities issued and traded in the capital markets. The variety has grown tremendously in recent years. These securities innovations have been designed to satisfy previously unfulfilled investor preferences. They have served to make the capital markets more complete. Chapter 14 describes the more frequently issued securities in greater detail. But it will be useful to keep in mind that capital market frictions and the incompleteness of the capital markets create profitable opportunities for financial innovation.

As part of its allocative function, the capital markets establish the prices of securities. The next chapter discusses the efficiency with which the capital markets perform this important operation.

PROBLEMS

PROBLEM SET A

A1. What is the purpose of the capital markets?

A2. What is the major distinction between debt and equity?

A3. What is a **convertible** security?

A4. Define the term **round lot**.

A5. What is the role of a **financial intermediary**?

A6. What is the role of the **financial press**?

A7. What are the eight conditions that create a perfect capital market?

A8. How do efficient capital markets help people who have valuable ideas but no capital?

A9. What is **Fisher's separation theorem**?

A10. What is the **term structure of interest rates**?

A11. Suppose 1-year bonds pay 9% this year and are expected to pay 10% next year. Under the expectations hypothesis of the term structure of interest rates, what should 2-year bonds currently pay?

A12. What is meant by the term **liquidity preference**?

A13. What is meant by the term **inflation uncertainty**?

A14. What is a **segmented market**?

A15. Suppose there are two possible outcomes, P and D, and two securities you can invest in, x and y. The payoffs for the securities under the alternative outcomes are

	x	y
P	200	80
D	80	120

How many units should you purchase of each security so that you will have a payoff of 110, no matter which outcome occurs?

A16. Suppose there are two possible outcomes, P and D, and two securities you can invest in, x and y. The payoffs for the securities under the alternative outcomes are

	x	y
P	100	50
D	20	40

How many units should you purchase of each security so that you will have a payoff of 100 if P occurs and 110 if D occurs?

A17. What is a **short position**?

A18. What is a **long position**?

PROBLEM SET B

B1. Discuss the importance of **limited liability** to the valuation of a corporation. (*Hint:* you might want to refer back to our discussion of the role of the corporation in Chapter 1.)

B2. How do the capital markets help people who are saving for retirement?

B3. Tim Kinney's income this year is $42,000. Next year it will be $110,000. If Tim has $20,000 in current debts, must have $70,000 for consumption next year, and wants to have no debts at the end of next year, what is the maximum Tim can spend this year if his market-opportunity-cost discount rate is 10%?

B4. Explain in your own words how the capital markets help people who want to consume sooner *and* those who want to postpone their consumption until later.

B5. Suppose you have the opportunity to buy an asset today for $50,000 and the asset will be worth $75,000 one year from today with certainty. Given current economic conditions, should you buy the asset? How would the fact that you do not have the $50,000 for the investment affect your decision?

B6. What are **specialists**, and what do they do?

B7. Why is **Fisher's separation theorem** significant to a corporation?

B8. Why might inflation uncertainty cause investors to invest in short-term securities?

B9. Suppose 2-year bonds pay 12% per year and 1-year bonds pay 11% per year. Ignoring any preference for liquidity, how much would next year's 1-year bond have to pay for you to be indifferent between investing in a 2-year bond versus investing in two sequential 1-year bonds?

B10. What is the difference between the term structure of interest rates and the yield curve?

B11. What are the similarities and differences among warrants, options, and futures?

PROBLEM SET C

C1. How do the capital markets help people, directly *and* indirectly, who want to buy a house?

C2. How do the capital markets help the following three types of people: (a) young professionals, (b) middle-aged managers, (c) retired executives.

C3. Explain how efficient capital markets lead to the conclusion that corporations should use the net-present-value rule for their decision-making. What role does Fisher's separation theorem play in this line of reasoning?

C4. How does the notion of segmented markets reduce, but not eliminate, the impact of the expectations hypothesis on the term structure of interest rates?

C5. Explain what a complete capital market is, in your own words.

C6. What are the similarities and differences between negotiated markets and auction markets?

REFERENCES

Alderson, Michael J., Keith C. Brown, and Scott L. Lummer. "Dutch Auction Rate Preferred Stock." *Financial Management* 16 (Summer 1987): 68–73.

Baron, David P. "A Model of the Demand for Investment Banking and Advising and Distribution Services for New Issues." *Journal of Finance* 37 (September 1982): 955–76.

Bower, Nancy L. "Firm Value and the Choice of Offering Method in Initial Public Offerings." *Journal of Finance* 44 (July 1989): 647–62.

Brealey, Richard A., and Stephen Schaefer. "Term Structure and Uncertain Inflation." *Journal of Finance* 32 (May 1977): 277–90.

Cargill, Thomas F. "The Term Structure of Interest Rates: A Test of the Expectations Hypothesis." *Journal of Finance* 30 (June 1975): 761–72.

Fama, Eugene F. "Forward Rates as Predictors of Future Spot Rates." *Journal of Financial Economics* 3 (October 1976): 361–77.

Feldman, David. "The Term Structure of Interest Rates in a Partially Observable Economy." *Journal of Finance* 44 (July 1989): 789–812.

Fisher, Irving. *The Theory of Interest*. New York: Augustus M. Kelley, 1965 (reprinted from the original edition published in 1930).

Froot, Kenneth A. "New Hope for the Expectations Hypothesis of the Term Structure of Interest Rates." *Journal of Finance* 44 (June 1989): 283–305.

Hirshleifer, J. *Investment, Interest and Capital*. Englewood Cliffs, N.J.: Prentice-Hall, 1970.

Ibbotson, Roger G., and Rex A. Sinquefield. *Stocks, Bonds, Bills, and Inflation: Historical Returns (1926–1987)*. Charlottesville, VA: Institute of Chartered Financial Analysts, 1989.

McCulloch, J. Huston. "An Estimate of the Liquidity Premium." *Journal of Political Economy* 83 (January-February 1975): 95–119.

Malkiel, Burton G. *Term Structure of Interest Rates: Theory, Empirical Evidence and Applications*. New York: McCaleb-Seiler, 1970.

Martin, John D., Samuel H. Cox, Jr., and Richard D. MacMinn. *The Theory of Finance: Evidence and Applications*. Chicago: Dryden Press, 1988.

Mikkelson, Wayne H., and M. Megan Partch. "Valuation Effects of Security Offerings: An Empirical Investigation." *Journal of Financial Economics* 15 (January-February 1986): 31–60.

Nachman, David C. "Spanning and Completeness with Options." *Review of Financial Studies* 1, no. 3 (Fall 1988): 311–28.

Smith, Clifford W., Jr. "Investment Banking and the Capital Acquisition Process." *Journal of Financial Economics* 15 (January-February 1986): 3–29.

5

CAPITAL MARKET EFFICIENCY: EXPLANATION AND IMPLICATIONS

This chapter is devoted to exploring the fundamental financial concept embodied in the Principle of Capital Market Efficiency. We explain how capital market efficiency results logically from the application of other principles to the capital market environment. We also develop the explanation through an analogy with the physical sciences. Through this analogy we hope to facilitate your understanding of the Principle of Capital Market Efficiency.

As we stated in Chapter 2, capital market efficiency means that prices of securities that are traded in the capital markets reflect all available information and adjust fully and quickly (at most, within hours) to new information.[1] We described the concept in Chapter 2 but deferred the explanation of the factors that tend to promote capital market efficiency and those that tend to impede it. We explain in this chapter why it makes sense that the capital markets *should be* efficient.

The capital markets have evolved to perform certain important functions. To explain capital market efficiency, we must first explain these functions and how the capital markets should operate. You will then be able to see (1) how new information comes to be reflected in securities prices; (2) how market frictions, such as transaction costs, can impede this process and thereby pose a threat to market efficiency; and (3) how information regarding disparities in value will create opportunities for profit in the absence of significant market imperfections. Exploiting these opportunities will produce riskless profits for the first person to recognize each opportunity and at the same time eliminate the disparities (and opportunities). The competition to find and exploit such opportunities lies at the heart of capital market efficiency.

When it was first put forth, the idea that the capital markets have so few frictions that they may be thought of as **perfect**, meaning entirely frictionless, was very startling to the world of finance and economics. This notion has a number of very interesting implications, most notably that investors cannot consistently earn abnormally high risk-adjusted rates of return (other than through extraordinarily good luck). This rather surprising implication has spawned considerable criticism of the notion and skepticism regarding the initial evidence in support of it. We hope that you will be able to see the logic in this principle more easily when viewed in terms of our analogy; we are confident that at least initially, you will find the implications of capi-

---

[1] Three forms of capital market efficiency have been defined. Our Principle of Capital Market Efficiency refers to the **semistrong-strong form of capital market efficiency**. The semistrong-form requires that prices fully reflect all publicly available information. The **weak-form** requires simply that prices reflect all of the information in past security prices. The **strong-form** requires that prices reflect all available (both public *and* private) information. It is interesting to note that the insider-trading scandals of the 1980s (and many earlier decades) appear to provide substantial evidence that the capital markets are not efficient in the strong-form.

tal market efficiency somewhat difficult to accept. These implications not only caused an uproar among financial economists and people in the securities industry when this concept was first put forth, but they are also a major reason for the inherent difficulty students have in understanding finance.

AN ANALOGY   **5.1**

We begin with a simple analogy to the physical sciences in which the notion of **efficiency** plays a critical role, as it does in finance. In both cases, true efficiency represents an ideal because there are various frictions that impede a system (i.e., a machine or market) from being perfectly efficient. But understanding the implication of efficiency and assessing the significance of the factors that impede efficiency is important to understanding how well (that is, how "efficiently") the machine works. So too for the capital markets.

ENERGY CONSERVATION

An important law in the physical sciences, the law of energy conservation, states that energy is neither created nor destroyed when energy is transformed from one form into another inside a closed system. This law implies that no machine can be more than 100% efficient. That is, the energy output from a machine can never exceed the energy input to the machine. Simply stated, you can't get something for nothing! In the financial world, schemes that seem to provide more output than input are known as "scams." Such things are illegal and yet persist. We will talk more about them later.

An example of the limits of a machine's capability can be seen in the technology of refrigeration. Suppose it is a hot summer day and you are a poor graduate student who cannot afford the utility cost of air conditioning, let alone the initial cost of the air conditioner itself. But on this particular day it is so hot that you hit the limit of endurance. You go into the kitchen and open the refrigerator door to feel a blast of cool refreshing air across your face. Thinking you have solved the problem, you decide to stay in the kitchen with the refrigerator door open. What will happen?

A refrigerator works just like an air conditioner, so why shouldn't it work to have the kitchen cooled by the refrigerator? A refrigeration unit uses its power to take heat from inside itself to outside itself. But outside itself is still *inside* the kitchen, so the kitchen is not cooled at all. In fact, since the refrigerator is substantially less than 100% efficient, energy escapes in the form of heat with each transfer, and the kitchen will actually heat up if the door to the refrigerator is left open.

The law of energy conservation prevents a machine's efficiency from exceeding 100%, but machines with an efficiency equal to 100% don't exist either; energy is lost to friction. If the refrigerator were 100% efficient, we could say that the transaction was costless in terms of increased temperature. But as we have said, transactions are not costless.

FRICTION IN THE CAPITAL MARKETS: TRANSACTION COSTS

Our analogy with the capital markets is that the transfer of assets from one party to another is like a transfer of heat from one area to another within the kitchen. The total wealth of the parties is analogous to the temperature in the kitchen, where lower temperature corresponds to higher wealth. It makes no more sense to say that the total wealth of a group of people can be increased by the simple transfer of assets among them than it does to say that opening the refrigerator door can cool the kitchen. The only thing involved is a transfer from one to another. It is certainly possible to make one individual better off at the expense of another individual, just as it is possible to decrease the temperature inside the refrigerator by increasing the temperature outside it. In other words, it is possible to make unbalanced transfers between people. (For example, if you like, you can pay us $1,000 for an asset that is worth only $800.) But the wealth of the two individuals, taken together, cannot be increased by a transfer between them any more than the kitchen can be cooled by a transfer of heat within its boundary.

Continuing with our analogy, just as the kitchen will heat up as a result of a number of heat transfers within its boundary, the total wealth of two parties will be dissipated by transfers of assets between them. The dissipation occurs because of several factors that we will lump together and call **transaction costs**. Examples of transaction costs include commission fees and the time and money involved with transferring assets, such as moving lumber from one place to another. Transaction costs are very much like friction; they slow down the process and use up resources (energy). In fact, they are often referred to as **friction costs** because of this similarity.

5.2   LIQUIDITY AND VALUE

THE REASON FOR CAPITAL MARKETS: LIQUIDITY

Throughout history, society has evolved by developing new ideas and procedures that facilitate life, retaining those that prove useful and discarding those that are not useful or become useless because of other innovations. In ancient history, individuals were responsible for all of their own needs. Over time, cooperative societies developed where individuals specialized in certain tasks. Still later, a barter society developed where individuals exchanged goods and services to meet their needs. Finally, money was used to represent goods and services because it was more easily transferred from one person to another. The use of money as a medium of exchange and storage of resources has proved so useful that today its logic is rarely questioned.[2]

Simply stated, money allows for the easy transfer of resources much as liquids (as opposed to solids) are able to flow through a tube. Analogous to the notion of how easily a liquid flows through a tube, depending upon how thick it is, assets are referred to as being more or less **liquid**. In the financial world, **liquidity** refers to how easily assets are transferred without loss of value. That is, there is high (low) liquidity if it is easy (hard) to convert assets to cash with no impairment in value. Cash is the most liquid asset since it is most easily transferred from one entity to another. Real property (for example, a building) is one of the less liquid types of assets because it generally takes longer than securities to find a buyer who is willing to pay the highest price and transaction costs are generally greater.

Probably the primary reason that money is used by society is its liquidity. Money allows us to exchange our efforts for another person's efforts without having to trade our services directly. Money also allows us to exchange one asset for another easily. Suppose you own 100 shares of Exxon common stock and would like to reinvest the

---

[2]It is interesting to note that a very sophisticated form of barter, **counter trade**, has developed in international trade. See "More Companies Turn to Barter Deals," *Financial Times*, February 11, 1986, 17. Barter is also a mainstay of the "underground" economy where one or both parties prefer a noncash transaction for illegal motives such as tax evasion and/or reducing the likelihood of being caught dealing in illegal substances.

funds in General Motors common stock (perhaps because you believe that oil and gas prices are about to drop). While you might be open to the possibility of trading the Exxon shares for General Motors shares, it is generally much easier to sell the Exxon shares for cash and then buy the General Motors shares for cash rather than trying to locate a person who wants the exact other side of the trade you are looking for.

The stock market facilitates the exchange of assets. Without that **market,** you would have to incur higher costs to make a transaction, costs in the form of time and effort, as well as various out-of-pocket costs. The stock market reduces the *total* transaction costs. In many markets, such as the New York Stock Exchange (NYSE), there is a **market maker** who facilitates liquidity by transacting in the asset. For example, when your order to sell 100 shares of Exxon common stock and your order to buy General Motors common stock are executed on the NYSE, the **specialist** (market maker) handling each stock, rather than another individual investor like yourself, may be on the other side of the transaction.

Most markets have been set up to increase the liquidity of the assets that are traded by reducing the transaction costs associated with the transfer of an asset. Think about what you would do if there were no stock market and you wanted to sell your 100 shares of Exxon common stock. One possibility that might be very attractive would be to set up a stock market yourself, provide a service to other people, and earn money. If you were the first to set up such a market, it is likely that you would earn a positive net present value (NPV) for your efforts. Setting up a new market that provides increased liquidity for a particular type of asset reflects the existence of a profitable opportunity summarized in the Principle of Valuable Ideas; one who creates a viable new market provides a service that can earn a positive NPV for the market maker. Creating a viable market can also make the Principle of Capital Market Efficiency come true. Of course, this is exactly why the capital markets exist. There are real benefits to the participants, which can be exploited for profit by those who are clever enough to do so.

AN UNEXPECTED BENEFIT: A MEASURE OF VALUE

Although markets are created in response to a need for liquidity, there is an additional benefit when market transactions are made public. The prices at which those transactions take place provide a measure of value that is visible to everyone. Consider the following example.

Suppose you are going to invest approximately $10,000 in a 3-month Treasury bill. Such securities are sold on a **discount basis**. You pay a price that is less than $10,000 now to purchase a Treasury bill that will pay $10,000 at the end of 3 months. The difference, the **discount**, depends on the current market rate of interest for 3-month Treasury debt. What price should you be willing to pay for the Treasury bill? There are a couple of ways to establish a "fair price" for the bill. One way is to call your broker and ask for the current prices at which 3-month Treasury bills are trading. Another is to look in the finance or business section of a major metropolitan area newspaper or in the third section of the *Wall Street Journal* to find the prices at which 3-month Treasury bills closed the previous day. But which price is likely to be more accurate? The current quote you obtain from your broker is the more accurate because that quote should reflect trading that has taken place since yesterday's close. Nevertheless, except during periods of great volatility, the previous day's closing price is a very close approximation of the security's current "fair market value."

A large proportion of financial market transactions are reported publicly, with the information conveniently available, virtually as transactions take place. Thus, "fair market prices" for many financial assets, like particular stocks, bonds, options, and futures, are freely observable at any time. So if you want to know what a share of IBM is worth, observe the most recent actual transaction price, and you have a very accurate estimate of its value. After all, two parties actually transferred a share at that price; they didn't just talk about it, or *offer* to buy or sell it, and it isn't an average of many transactions from the last few weeks or months—they actually bought/sold it within the last few minutes, and either one of them would have been willing for *you* to have been the other party in the transaction. (In fact, in most cases, they would not have known the difference if you had been!) So even though the primary reason for the creation of a market is to provide liquidity for an asset, a "spin-off" benefit from the existence of markets is that they provide an inexpensive, fast, and accurate method of estimating the price at which an asset can currently be bought or sold. Transaction prices from the market provide an estimate of an asset's current "fair market value."

5.3   ARBITRAGE: STRIVING FOR EFFICIENCY

Having described the capital markets in Chapter 4 and outlined above the reasons for their existence, we now turn to their operation. In this and the next section we will present two concepts that are very important to the operation of the capital markets: arbitrage and signaling. Following these two sections, we will detail the important implications that arbitrage and signaling, among other concepts, have for the capital markets.

ARBITRAGE: GET RICH QUICK

Suppose the current price of a security in a particular market differs from the current price of that same security in a different market and that this information is available to one or more market participants. Someone who possesses this information can exploit it for profit by engaging in what is called **arbitrage**: buying an asset in one market for the purpose of immediately reselling the asset at a higher price in another market.[3] Arbitrage is an important factor in the efficient operation of any market, but especially a capital market. When people first learn about arbitrage, their usual reaction is to say that it sounds wonderful, but they are skeptical about the existence of such opportunities. In spite of their (very healthy) skepticism, market prices do in fact differ between two markets for short periods.

Consider an asset that is traded in two markets, such as shares of stock of a particular company. Suppose shares of Exxon common stock are trading at a higher price on the Pacific Stock Exchange than on the NYSE. Then it would be possible to buy Exxon shares on the NYSE and resell them on the Pacific Stock Exchange for more than you paid for them. When there is a price differential, arbitrage is possible by simply buying at the lower price and selling at the higher price. The transactions taken together "lock in" a profit equal to the price differential multiplied by the

---

[3] We start by using the dictionary definition of **arbitrage**, or what may be termed "riskless arbitrage." The term **arbitrage** is also used in the sense of "risk arbitrage" to describe the purchase of shares of companies that are expected to increase in value in the future for reasons such as becoming a takeover target. Such purchases involve a large element of speculation. In the last subsection of this section, we discuss arbitrage versus speculation.

number of shares simultaneously purchased and sold. This profit is thus "riskless"; the purchased and sold shares offset one another exactly. There are people who earn a living exploiting arbitrage opportunities they observe while watching multiple capital markets that trade the same asset.

AN ALTERNATIVE DEFINITION OF A PERFECT MARKET In Chapter 4 we defined a perfect capital market formally with eight requirements. An alternative way of defining a perfect capital market is to say that it is a market in which *there are never any arbitrage opportunities*. While one definition might be preferred to another, depending upon the focus, viewing a perfect capital market as one that has no arbitrage opportunities can provide important insight into what we mean by a perfect capital market environment.

COMPETITION: IF IT'S THAT EASY . . .

Having told you what arbitrage is and that opportunities for earning a riskless arbitrage profit do exist, we assume that if you are like most of us, you are thinking of applying the Principle of Self-Interested Behavior and wondering how you might participate in such a delightful process. Surely, you would like to be able to buy things at one price and simultaneously sell them for a higher price. Well, you're not alone. Consequently, what would you predict would be the frequency, and size, of differences in trading prices on two markets for a particular asset like a share of Exxon stock? That's right—not very often and not very much. And the larger the difference you're looking for, the less likely it is to occur. If you had to think that one through, there was a short cut: the Principle of Capital Market Efficiency. You were probably already applying it with your skepticism when we first told you about arbitrage.

An important implication of investor arbitrage is that when one investor discovers an arbitrage opportunity and trades securities to exploit this opportunity *and* other investors become aware of this opportunity by monitoring that person's trading activity, the competing investors will (eventually) eliminate the arbitrage opportunity. In March 1990, the *Wall Street Journal* reported that Edward O. Thorp, a "one-time university professor and mathematical whiz" who had developed strategies for exploiting price discrepancies between a company's common stock and securities convertible into its common stock, had closed his money management business and returned $200 million of his clients' money.[4] Mr. Thorp had published some of his ideas in a 1967 book entitled *Beat the Market* and had set up an investment partnership in 1969 that traded securities utilizing his strategies, which earned returns averaging 19% per annum. Mr. Thorp said he withdrew from the money management business in 1990 because his ideas had become so widespread that only those investors with the lowest transaction costs could utilize his arbitrage strategies profitably.

Now, if you think about it, you will see that competition among people engaged in arbitrage is an important contributing factor to capital market efficiency. The very existence of people, **arbitrageurs**, who are constantly looking for arbitrage opportunities insures that prices for a particular asset will not differ very much among the various markets on which the asset is traded. If it is easy to access both markets, there won't be any need for arbitrageurs because people making a transaction will buy or sell their asset for the best price provided by the two markets. When the two

---

[4]"Money-Manager Math Whiz Calls It Quits," *Wall Street Journal*, March 15, 1990, C1.

markets are not easily accessed simultaneously, then it is worthwhile for arbitrageurs to incur the cost of accessing both markets simultaneously and making transactions that push the two markets toward identical prices for a given asset. Of course, in time, competition among arbitrageurs will drive the net present value of being an arbitrageur to an equilibrium value of zero. Careful now—that does not mean the arbitrageur has a zero profit.

> *When the NPV is zero, participants are getting exactly a fair return for the effort they are expending and an appropriate positive return for any risk they are taking on, and capital market efficiency is enforced.*

Another important factor that contributes to the competitive environment of the capital markets is the homogeneity of financial assets. The term **homogeneity** refers to the degree of similarity among items. Financial assets are *very* homogeneous. As an example, consider a very simple financial asset, a $10 bill. Would you exchange one $10 bill for another (assuming both are real)? Would you exchange a $10 bill for two $5 bills? For the most part, people are indifferent to such exchanges. Forms of money are very homogeneous. Virtually any positive incentive (such as additional money) will induce people to exchange one form of money for another.

Homogeneity is not limited to forms of money. Consider financial securities. Suppose there are two securities that are exactly alike except for their expected future return. The Principle of Risk Aversion says that investors will invest in the alternative with the higher expected return. As with forms of money, shares of stock are also homogeneous, as are bonds. Investors are relatively indifferent to owning shares in one company versus another, except for differences in return and risk. For example, most people do not have strong feelings, beyond the financial considerations of return and risk, about owning shares of stock in IBM versus Xerox. Further, corporate bonds are similar to government bonds, except that corporate bonds are riskier, and for that matter, bonds are relatively similar to stocks, except that stocks are riskier. When you think about it, you can see that financial assets are very homogeneous, especially in comparison with physical assets such as houses. Because of this difference in homogeneity, investors in financial assets can concentrate on the risk and return of an asset. When investors find two identical or even very similar investment opportunities, they will make transactions to increase the return on their investments, just as arbitrageurs do. Therefore, even though not all investors are primarily pursuing arbitrage opportunities, arbitrageurs must compete with the investing population as well as one another.

LIMITS TO ARBITRAGE: TRANSACTION COSTS

Having told you that arbitrage opportunities do exist from time to time, and yet the Principle of Capital Market Efficiency is alive and well because it is a natural result of people applying the Principle of Self-Interested Behavior, we need to reconcile the occasional arbitrage opportunity with capital market efficiency. How far apart do prices have to be for arbitrage opportunities to exist? Conceptually, any difference in price is an opportunity. However, in practice, transaction costs are not zero, and therefore if the difference between the prices is too small, arbitrageurs will not make a transaction because it will not be profitable. As you have probably already surmised, an arbitrage transaction is worth making only if the benefit exceeds the cost of the transaction.

As with any business, arbitrageurs have two types of transaction costs: **fixed** and

variable. Variable transaction costs are those relevant for evaluating a specific arbitrage opportunity. For example, suppose that a stock sells for 31⅛ in London and 31⅜ in New York, and that it will cost you ¹⁄₁₆ to buy in London, ¹⁄₁₆ to sell in New York, and ¹⁄₁₆ for transfer and communications costs. Consequently, it will cost you ³⁄₁₆ to make ¼ point. If you can buy and sell 1,000 shares, you make $62.50. Sounds good because you will have more than covered your variable costs. You will have earned a riskless arbitrage profit.

But what about the cost of setting up your office, setting up communication lines, educating yourself, paying your support staff? Those costs are the *fixed transaction costs*, and they must be considered too. Fixed transaction costs are an important consideration when you are making the decision whether to spend your time watching the market for certain assets, watching so closely that you will know when arbitrage opportunities occur. In other words, the fixed transaction costs are important to the question whether you should enter, or continue to be in, that line of business. If arbitrage opportunities cease to exist, those in the business will be driven out because they will not be able to earn a fair return to cover their fixed costs. If arbitrage opportunities occur sufficiently often, other people will be attracted to become arbitrageurs to earn a positive NPV. The additional transactions will push the market toward equilibrium by eliminating arbitrage opportunities and reducing the return to what is appropriate for the risk involved with being an arbitrageur.

When two or more markets for the same asset exist, the differential between trading prices in any two markets for that asset will exceed the variable cost of making a transaction only for brief periods. Only for as long as it takes arbitrageurs to buy and sell enough assets to reduce the price differential to less than the variable costs of making another transaction.

Because of arbitrage, on average, *the price differential between markets is smaller than the variable transaction costs* for an asset traded in two markets. But how do variable transaction costs compare among different assets? How do the transaction costs of buying a used car in Los Angeles, transporting it to Chicago, and selling it compare with the costs of buying, transporting, and selling a share (or 100 shares, or 1,000 shares) of stock? Unless you have someone who wants to drive across the United States from Los Angeles to Chicago, getting a car from Los Angeles to Chicago can be costly in time (yours or someone you pay) as well as gas and oil. In contrast, the ownership of shares of stock can be transferred quickly and easily, with transactions made virtually simultaneously via telecommunications, and all at a relatively low cost.

Transaction costs for buying and selling financial assets are low relative to transaction costs for physical assets, for several reasons. The most important of these reasons is simply their physical differences. That is, a few sheets of paper or some marks on a magnetic tape or disk are vastly easier to transport than 3,000 pounds of automobile. A second important reason is market size; the number of financial assets changing hands every day is incredibly large. When there are many transactions taking place each day, the fixed transaction costs of the person "making the market" are less, on a per-transaction basis, because there are more transactions over which to spread the fixed costs.

Since the transaction costs for financial assets are so low, in both relative and absolute terms, price differentials for financial assets in different markets are tiny compared with price differentials for physical assets in different markets. Even on a percentage basis, price differentials for financial assets are relatively small because of low transaction costs and high competition among arbitrageurs. The low price differentials among markets reflect capital market efficiency, and a large body of empirical evidence supports the Principle of Capital Market Efficiency.[5]

ARBITRAGE VERSUS SPECULATION

We compared the cost of transporting shares of stock with the cost of transporting a car. Consider the idea of arbitraging used cars between areas of the country that have different market values for the same type of car.[6] It might not be possible to buy and sell used cars in two markets simultaneously because the car may need to be at both the purchase point and sale point for careful inspection, which would eliminate the possibility of *simultaneous* purchase/sale. Literally speaking, a transaction that involves holding the asset for any positive time is not arbitrage.

We cannot be specific about the time that determines where riskless arbitrage leaves off and speculation begins. But we can say that when the asset is held for any positive time, risk is introduced into the transaction, and the longer the time between purchase and sale, the greater the risk. People who buy and sell a particular asset but are not strictly speaking arbitrageurs are **traders**. Traders are engaged in short-term speculation.

The importance of the continuum from arbitrage to speculation is that in many cases, traders anticipate price changes using less than perfect information. Traders are involved in "small gambles." Of course, if you accept our description of gambling as having a negative expected value (from Chapter 2), these "educated speculations" are not true gambles. They are investments because they average a positive return. After all, if the average return was not positive, the trader could not continue to do business indefinitely while sustaining losses.

"Slightly" speculative transactions, which anticipate price changes, smooth the transition from one price level to another. New information does not generally occur in a complete and correct form. The first inkling of new information may come in the form of a "rumor." An asset trader's talent for determining more quickly than other traders which rumors are true and which are false is extremely valuable because facts can translate directly into price changes that can be turned into profit.

While some talents can't be taught—and interpreting information may be one of them—we can point out that some actions carry with them subtle implications about a firm's current condition and/or its prospects for the future. In the next section we talk about how observations along one dimension can provide information about another dimension. These observations can generate new information and provide a basis for interpreting existing imperfect information.

5.4   ## SIGNALING AND INFORMATION GATHERING

Underlying the Principle of Capital Market Efficiency is an important corollary: Market participants react quickly to events that convey useful information. This quick reaction, which is the mechanism that makes a market informationally effi-

---

[5] Fama (1970) provided the first comprehensive summary of the empirical support for the efficient-markets hypothesis. A wealth of additional evidence has been furnished by studies published since Fama's. Some of the subsequent studies find limited evidence of market inefficiency (e.g., see *Journal of Financial Economics* 6, nos. 2/3). However, even with some inefficiency, it is not clear that investors can profit from such imperfect pricing when both variable and fixed transaction costs are taken into account.
[6] This is not a hypothetical example. Auto brokers are extensively involved in this process.

cient, is due in part to the Signaling Principle, which states that actions convey information.

An important concept connected with the Signaling Principle is the notion of **asymmetric information**: information that is known only to certain people. Recall that the term **signaling** refers to using actual behavior to infer things you can't observe directly or find out in other ways. Thus, signaling involves inferences concerning asymmetric information; actions convey the asymmetric information and in so doing eliminate the asymmetric information. In future chapters we will discuss the signaling aspects of corporate dividend changes and capital structure changes, among others, to explain how such changes affect the value of the firm. In an efficient market, participants will react to the information signals contained in the announcement of such changes by making securities purchase and sale decisions. Executing the purchase and sale transactions will cause securities prices to change, which is the mechanism by which the information content of the signals is reflected in securities prices.

WHAT IS SIGNALING?

In 1970, George Akerlof published a paper in the *Quarterly Journal of Economics* entitled "The Market for 'Lemons': Quality Uncertainty and the Market Mechanism." In that paper he provides an example of signaling and outlines the problem of **adverse selection**—a process of inferring "negative" information about a product or service. The problem of adverse selection can discourage the inclusion of "good-quality" products and/or services because offering the product or service is an apparently negative signal, as you will see in Akerlof's example.

Akerlof's application is to the used-car market. An individual decides to sell his car. The question is *why* does he want to sell the car? One possible answer is that the car is not functioning properly; in other words, the car is a "lemon." This possibility gives rise to a paradox. If the seller wants to sell the car because it is a "lemon," buyers would be foolish to buy the car. But if the car is a "good" car that buyers would like to buy, why should the seller want to sell the car? The logical conclusion to this paradox is that used-car prices depend upon how often sellers voluntarily sell "good" cars. If the only reason for selling a car was that it was not worth fixing, all used cars would be worthless. (We have friends who argue that used cars are in fact worthless!) Of course, we've all heard stories about used cars turning out to be exceptionally good as well as exceptionally bad. Because there are reasons for selling a car other than its "not being worth the trouble to repair" and people have different levels of tolerance for car trouble, all used cars are not worthless. There is some probability that buying a used car will turn out well and some probability that it will turn out poorly. Many of our friends who are not skilled at determining the quality of used cars always buy new cars to protect themselves from this problem. Others, who are skilled in evaluating the quality of a used car, put that skill to use and pay less for their dependable transportation. The savings represent the difficulty and cost, in time, effort, and money, of obtaining and using this valuable skill.

Since Akerlof's paper was published, there have been many applications of the concept of signaling to financial transactions. Most of the applications are too technical to be detailed here, but it should be obvious that the number of daily events that can be thought of as information signals is virtually infinite. Companies make visible decisions nearly every day that provide an almost continuous flow of information about their current operations and directions for the future. For example, decisions concerning new equipment and raw materials, like how much to buy and who to buy from, occur regularly. Other less frequent but telling information signals include decisions concerning financing, like decisions to issue new stock or bonds or to change the quarterly dividend the company pays its stockholders. Still other signals are not company decisions at all but decisions made by people outside the company, like decisions to buy products from the company.

CONDITIONAL SIGNALS: WATCHING MANAGEMENT

An important thing to note about information signals is that some are "sent" intentionally and others are sent inadvertently. Suppose you are listening to a chief executive officer (CEO) of a corporation speak about the company's prospects for the future. The CEO paints a rosy picture, outlining the company's plans for expanded production facilities to handle the projected increase in sales that will result in "big profits" for the next several years. The CEO is dynamic, enthusiastic, and persuasive. A week later, you find out that 10,000 of 15,000 shares the CEO owned were sold just 3 days after you heard the better-things-are-coming speech. How does it make you feel to learn that the CEO sold that stock? After hearing about the stock sale, what do you think the CEO *really* believes about the company's prospects for the next several years? Now it is possible that the CEO sold the 10,000 shares to pay for a new yacht, and there are other possible explanations for the behavior, some of which would not reflect negatively on the company's prospects. However, most of us would consider it a negative signal if a person sells an asset while telling everyone else to buy it because it is a great investment. (Share sales by insiders are often regarded as a leading indicator of an imminent change in a company's profitability.)

Selling a large part of their ownership in the company is generally considered a negative information signal from management. While that is a relatively straightforward conclusion, there are many other signals that can be positive or negative, depending upon other facts or decisions. When a company announces that it plans to borrow money, you would want to know why. Without any other information, that announcement cannot be construed as positive or negative. Borrowing can be a positive signal of new investment opportunities, a negative signal of low sales or poor management, or a neutral signal of replacing worn-out equipment.[7]

INTERPRETING SIGNALS: A VERY VALUABLE TALENT

Most information is easily and costlessly available if you just wait long enough. IBM's sales data for 1988 are easily obtained from library data. But knowing what IBM's sales were for 1988 is not going to help you determine whether, in the future, shares of IBM's stock will sell for more or less than they do now. Some information, like the number of shares owned by management and how much money a company has borrowed, is published on a regular basis (every quarter or year) as required by the Securities and Exchange Commission (SEC). However, just like the sales figure from the library, it is unlikely that the information can be profitably used *after* it is published. Traders (or **speculators** who own the stock for longer periods) are constantly searching for new information that will tell them if shares of a stock are going to increase or decrease in value in the future, so that they will know whether to buy or sell the shares now. Competition to obtain information before prices re-

---

[7] As will be explained in Chapter 14, studies have found that market participants generally react negatively to the announcement of additional corporate borrowing, although the magnitude of the reaction is not significant statistically. See Smith (1986).

flect that information is extremely intense. The competition is intense because the more often a trader or speculator obtains valuable new information first, the more money she makes. (Such competition has lead some people to breach ethical, and legal, standards, creating "insider-trading scandals.")

Of course, the more current the information is, the more difficult and costly it will be to obtain. For example, a trader dealing in shares of Sears's common stock might pay someone to check local stores for the number of customers at various times and make statistical estimates of current sales, so that when Sears announces the latest sales figures, the trader has anticipated any change in share price that is due to an increase or decrease in sales. Profits that a trader earns are the result of the cost, in time, effort, and money, of gathering information and using it to make informed trades.

When considering information like recent sales figures or levels of borrowing, we are dealing with "hard facts." However, just as there is a continuum from arbitrage to speculation, there is a continuum for the quality of our information. That continuum might be described, from one end to the other, as starting with hard information, moving to interpretive, to speculative, intuitive, and finally blind guess.

The process of interpreting information involves inductive reasoning. Most of us are familiar with **deductive reasoning** where a *general* fact provides accurate information about a *specific* situation. For example, if a friend tells you he has just bought a cat, you can predict that the animal has four legs and a tail with a high probability of being correct. In contrast, **inductive reasoning** attempts to use a *specific* situation to make *general* conclusions. Therefore, accuracy depends critically on having a great deal of information. For example, suppose a friend tells you he has just bought an animal that has four legs and a tail. Without more information, making an accurate prediction of what kind of animal your friend got is virtually impossible. The pieces of information that are uncovered for use with inductive reasoning may be obvious—such as knowing that your friend had planned to visit a person whose cat recently had kittens. However, such pieces of information are often quite subtle, such as spotting a few cat hairs on your friend's knee.

Because information can be drawn from truly obscure facts and interpreted in an infinite number of ways, a person's talent for dealing with new and/or uncertain information is like any other talent a person might have for activities like reading, music, mathematics, sports, and art. To some extent it is possible to teach people how to go about interpreting new and/or uncertain information. But like the other activities just mentioned, there can be great differences in abilities among people, even if the people have received identical training. Also, like those other activities, an exceptional talent for dealing with new and/or uncertain information and interpreting information signals correctly has extraordinary value. For those of us who do not possess that unusual talent, it is still important to understand the process.

THE COLLECTIVE WISDOM   5.5

Having described several important concepts related to the operation of the capital markets, we now move on to applying those concepts and examining their implications for the capital markets. In this section we examine how competition for information can make stock prices good "predictors" of the future. With an infinite number of ways to interpret new and/or uncertain information and so many people competing for information, the question arises: Is one person consistently right? The answer is no, but there is information in their "collective wisdom."

AVAILABLE INFORMATION AND STOCK PRICE MOVEMENT

In our overview of the Principle of Capital Market Efficiency in Chapter 2, we said that *market prices reflect all available information*. A logical implication of this statement is that any transaction you can make in an efficient market has an NPV equal to zero (i.e., the cost equals the value). Often, when people hear this statement, they ask: Then why bother to invest? These people have forgotten that a zero NPV includes a profit that is appropriate for the risk of the investment. So the answer to the question is To earn a profit. (And, perhaps, a large profit if you are willing to take on considerable risk.)

Another important implication of the above statement concerns the movement of prices. *Price movements are random in an efficient market*. If you think about it, this *must* be the case. If price movements could be predicted before new information arrived, the information would already be here! Instead, price movements take place only after someone can better assess an asset's value based on new information. Thus, because price movements depend upon information arrival and information arrives randomly, price movements must reflect that randomness.

It is important to distinguish between anticipated and unanticipated new information. Some information, such as earnings and dividend announcements, is available at regular intervals (e.g., quarterly in the case of earnings announcements by publicly-traded companies). It is therefore anticipated by market participants, who will use whatever other information is available to formulate expectations and may then enter into securities transactions in anticipation of the release of the new information. As a result, in an efficient market, if traders are sufficiently skilled that they can anticipate the new information perfectly, market prices would fully reflect the new information even *before* the official announcement. When the new information is not perfectly anticipated—as, for example, when market participants expect an earnings increase, but instead there is an earnings decrease—there will be price adjustments both before and after the announcement. At the other extreme, some information cannot be anticipated (for example, a fire that destroys a company's production facilities or the discovery of a revolutionary product or process). The occurrence of such events is essentially random in nature. In such cases, the market is able to react only after the event occurs and is disclosed to market participants. In between, there are varying degrees of anticipation. For example, a tender offer for a company may be anticipated if there have recently been tender offers for other companies in the same industry but may not be anticipated by market participants under some other circumstances. For example, after the leveraged buyout of Northwest Airlines in 1989, similar offers for United Airlines and American Airlines quickly followed. One frequently observes such "industry effects." How effectively market participants anticipate new information will determine how market prices react to the new information.

Over time, information can arrive that causes our total information about the likelihood of a particular outcome to move from unlikely to likely, to actual occurrence. Continuing the earnings-announcement example, securities analysts generate earnings forecasts and subsequently revise them up to the time of the earnings announcement as new information becomes available to them. While each securities analyst may have perfectly valid reasons for each earnings forecast revision, the series of earnings forecasts (and revisions of them) taken collectively behaves as though it were a random process. With each infinitesimal change in the likelihood of an outcome affecting the value of a stock, there will be a change in the fair market value of that stock, just as a change in earnings expectations (resulting from an earnings forecast revision) changes the value of a stock. Since a variety of new information is arriving almost continuously and the interpretation of all the available information is going on continuously, there will be many changes in prices, and these price changes will behave randomly. In fact, stock prices are almost constantly changing for exactly this reason.

At first glance, all the movements of stock prices appear to occur because we are not sure what a stock is worth. At this point, we hope you can see that the movement in stock prices is the result of constantly reassessing what a stock is worth. Price changes are the result of competition in an ongoing interpretation of all the available information, so random stock price movement is the result of *rational* behavior.

THE STOCK MARKET AS AN IMPORTANT LEADING ECONOMIC INDICATOR

Random stock price movement implies that no single person can consistently predict future stock prices correctly. Although traders are using information that lies somewhere along the continuum we mentioned, as a general rule, much of their information will not be "hard facts," and therefore their decisions will be "educated guesses." Now, if one trader has extraordinary talent to interpret information and predict future stock prices with great accuracy, he will very quickly amass a fortune. People observing this talent will value that trader's opinion more highly than the opinions of others. These people, then, by watching, would be interpreting the information available to them. They would have another signal to watch: the expert trader.

While some traders are more successful than others, no single trader, analyst, or firm has yet been consistently accurate enough to convince the rest of the world that he is *the* expert. As a group, however, their work and competition create prices that reflect the probabilities of future events more accurately than any single trader, analyst, or firm. In fact, stock prices are so accurate at assessing the probabilities of future events that stock market indexes such as the Standard & Poor's 500 Index of common stock prices are among the most accurate leading economic indicators known. Traders, or their representatives (who provide a valuable service for which traders are willing to pay), expend a lot of resources doing things like counting customers at Sears stores so they can translate those statistics into sales estimates, the sales into profit estimates, the profit into dividend estimates, the dividend estimates into predicted stock value, and finally, the predicted stock value into decisions to buy or sell.

The important point is that on average, the **collective wisdom**, embodied in a competitive price, provides a much more accurate assessment of value than any single assessment. Of course, it is always possible to find an individual's assessment that at a particular point in time, turns out to be more accurate than the market's assessment. However, that is after the fact. What has not yet been observed is an individual's assessment that is consistently, over a long time, more accurate than the market's competitive price. There have been many "temporary successes" that for a time appear to be better than the market, but even random guesses achieve some successes. For example, if you always pick heads when a coin is flipped, you'll choose correctly 50% of the time. Think about the following example.

Consider all of the market prognosticators who are trying to predict the stock market's general direction. Suppose that there are 4,096 market prognosticators whose predictions are evaluated quarterly and that each quarter each forecaster is just as likely to pick the stock market's direction correctly as to predict it incorrectly. With a .5 probability of being correct each time, we can use the binomial probability distribution to show that during an average year, 256 will be "correct" in every quarter (= $[.5]^4$ = 6.25%; 6.25% of 4,096 = 256). Over a typical 2-year period, 16 will have correctly "predicted" the stock market's movement each quarter. Even over a 3-year period, on average, one of the prognosticators will be exactly right *every* quarter. In spite of the equal likelihood of being right or wrong in any one quarter, 1 out of 4,096 prognosticators on average will make 12 correct predictions in a row (2^{12} = 4,096). Someone can therefore have a good "run," even if she does not possess any extraordinary predictive powers. Perhaps that's why one's duration as a market "guru" must be short-lived! In fact, a review of the financial press would reveal that different forecasters from time to time have appeared unusually prescient. But each one's period in the limelight has been limited. (Note that 4,096 is a *very* small number of prognosticators when compared with the number of market participants.) In any case, the competitive market price reflects the collective wisdom about the probabilities of all the possible outcomes, taking into account the cost of being wrong as well as the benefit of being right.

5.6   VALUE CONSERVATION

We said at the beginning of this chapter that perfect, meaning entirely frictionless, markets are efficient. Another important, and startling, implication of perfect markets is the concept of **value additivity**. In a capital market free of any imperfections such as asymmetric information, asymmetric taxation, and transaction costs, the value of the whole must equal the sum of the values of the parts; in such a market environment, the value of the firm equals the sum of the values of all of its assets. Were this not the case for any particular firm, there would be a profitable arbitrage opportunity. As discussed earlier in the chapter, in the absence of impediments to arbitrage, agents would exploit this opportunity until further profits were no longer possible, at which point value additivity would have been restored.

THE LAW OF VALUE CONSERVATION

The law of value conservation in finance is analogous to the law of energy conservation in the physical sciences. If value is conserved across transactions, as it is in a perfect market, value additivity will exist among assets. In the case of two assets, value additivity can be stated, ***The value of two assets combined equals the sum of their two individual values***. Algebraically, it can be represented as

$$V(A + B) = V(A) + V(B). \tag{5.1}$$

Notice that Equation (5.1) describes the process of separating assets as well as combining them. Also notice that Equation (5.1) is easily generalized to apply to more than two assets.

The two people most responsible for introducing the concept of value conservation into financial economics are Franco Modigliani and Merton Miller.[8] These two men are commonly referred to as MM (pronounced "M 'n' M"). Their work changed the thinking of financial economists. In fact, one indication of the signifi-

---

[8]Particularly important papers written by MM that relate to value conservation include Miller and Modigliani (1961), Modigliani and Miller (1958).

cance of their work is that Modigliani's contribution was cited when he was awarded the 1985 Nobel Prize in economics. Building on MM's work, Lawrence Schall coined the phrase **value-additivity principle** to describe the principle embodied in Equation (5.1).[9]

In the absence of any new information, an efficient market represents a zero-sum-game environment. Value additivity is the result of competition within such an environment; it is an implication of the combined effect of capital market efficiency and two-sided transactions. That is, value additivity results when it is always the case that one person's gain is another person's loss. A word of caution is in order. As we pointed out in Chapter 2 and will discuss further here, the one significant factor that can cause capital markets to deviate from being a zero-sum-game environment is taxes. (We also pointed out, however, that even in the presence of taxes, the capital markets still represent a zero-sum-game environment when we include the government in the game.)

It sounds so simple to say that value is neither created nor destroyed when assets are exchanged, and yet countless hours of work have gone into debate over this issue. The fundamental question is whether an asset can be worth different amounts, depending upon whether it is attached to another asset. The Principle of Valuable Ideas says, in effect, that it may be possible to combine assets in value-increasing ways. But the Principle of Capital Market Efficiency says it isn't possible if people are already aware of the value-increasing possibility. Once again, how do we resolve this apparent contradiction? A financial asset is really only a set of expected cash flows. If we combine cash flows from various sources, can they be worth more in total after they are combined than they are worth in total now? The answer, and resolution, is *It is possible only if we are the **first** ones to think of making this valuable combination.* If the owners of the separate cash flow streams know that the cash flows are worth more when combined, they will either make the combination themselves or charge us the equivalent combined value for the assets because they *could* combine the cash flows themselves.

Similarly, the reverse question can be asked. Can cash flows be worth more if they are split up? Again, the answer is Only if we are the first ones to think of a value-increasing dissection.

To appreciate the concept underlying the law of value additivity, consider once again our example of a very simple financial asset, a $10 bill. Would you exchange a $10 bill for nine $1 bills? Of course not, but how about exchanging it for 11 of them? More interested? Value additivity says that breaking a $10 bill into several smaller assets does not change the total value—you'll still have $10 worth of assets. Similarly, suppose you have two $5 bills. Can combining the two bills by exchanging them for one $10 bill make the total worth more than the sum of the two taken separately? No.

But now consider a $10 bill that has been torn into four equal pieces, each piece given to a different person. Individually, the pieces are all worthless, or are they? Suppose you know the four people that hold a piece. You point out to each of them that his piece is worthless but you will be happy to take the piece off his hands at no cost to him. If they all give you their pieces, you will have an asset worth $10. Assuming each person knows that the other three pieces are obtainable, the holders are not likely to *give* their pieces to you. The holders would be willing to *sell* their pieces to you for $2.50 each. But then why should you bother with the transaction? It would cost you $10 for an asset worth $10. If the four individuals don't want to bother spending the time, effort, and money to get together and make the deal

[9]Schall (1972).

themselves, you might get them to sell their pieces for less then $2.50 each. If they sold you the pieces for $2 each, you would make a "commission" of $2 on the transaction, and they would be paying a transaction cost of 50 cents each.[10]

The capital markets are just a more sophisticated application of our $10-bill analogy. Value additivity holds exactly when all the parts are included. That is, when the loss due to "friction costs" is included, there is perfect conservation of value. More importantly, however, value additivity is the best approximation of a situation in which the transaction costs are small enough to be insignificant with respect to the transaction, which is exactly the case with the capital markets.

A CHANCE FOR A BIGGER PIE TO SPLIT: LOWERING YOUR TAXES

We've already mentioned that taxes can create a situation in which the environment is no longer a zero-sum game involving market participants; that is, taxes can create an environment in which value can be created in a transaction. But we haven't said exactly how this can happen. Essentially, this situation can arise whenever two parties pay taxes at different rates. When one party records a dollar of revenue and the other party records a dollar of expense in a single transaction, an asymmetry in taxes occurs if the two parties pay taxes at different rates. This is so because the revenue increases taxes collected and the expense decreases taxes collected. But since the increase and decrease are at different rates, the amounts involved are not equal. The result is that the government may collect more or less taxes on the revenue than it gives up on the expense. This means that there can be a net advantage to the two parties if the transaction reduces their collective tax bill.

For the most part, because people understand this phenomenon, the government generally collects fewer tax dollars when such asymmetries occur. Of course, in many of these cases, people are doing exactly what the government was encouraging them to do. For example, the government uses the tax code to encourage saving for retirement by creating special advantages to Individual Retirement Accounts to reduce the future burden on social programs. It has sometimes encouraged investment in new capital equipment to spur the economy by providing an investment tax credit.

An example of an asymmetry in taxes that Congress may not have intended involves **zero-coupon bonds**. Recall from Chapter 4 that a zero-coupon bond (sometimes called a **pure-discount bond**) is a bond that makes no interest payments between the time it is issued and the time it matures. For example, a zero-coupon bond might be sold for $100 when it is issued and pay $1,000 twenty years later. The interest that would otherwise be paid in cash is effectively compounded over the life of the bond; that is, the discount, the difference between the face amount paid at maturity and the issue price ($900 in the example), represents "imputed interest." Prior to July 1982, the Internal Revenue Code permitted the issuer and the holders to allocate equal amounts of the discount to each year of the bond's existence, rather than allo-

---

[10] Note that an interesting sunk-cost problem could arise. If you bought three of the pieces for $2.50 each and the holder of the fourth piece discovers that information, he could bargain for a higher price. How much higher? The $7.50 you have already paid is a sunk cost. If your three pieces are not worth anything without the fourth piece, the fourth person can demand up to $9.99, and you would be better off making the transaction, in spite of the $7.50 you already spent! (Of course, you might take nothing rather than let the fourth person "fleece" you. Acting out of frustration would be due to emotional rather than financial considerations.) To avoid this problem, you could bargain with each person separately and purchase options from them before making any transactions. While the options would complicate the valuation problem by creating more "pieces," the whole would still be worth exactly $10.

cate the discount on the basis of how interest would truly compound. In our example, the discount would be allocated $900/20 = $45 in the form of implicit interest for each of the 20 years. This amount was both the amount claimed by the company and the amount recorded as income by each bondholder. As you should recall from Chapter 3, interest actually accrues slowly at first but accelerates over a zero-coupon bond's life because of compounding; that is, the interest earned on the accumulated interest grows from one year to the next. The actual interest accrued is $12.20 in the first year and $108.75 in the last year in our example.[11] Thus, the company is overstating its interest expense for tax purposes in the early years and understating its interest expense in the later years. This "incorrect" allocation of the interest expense causes a shift in the firm's tax payments: Less taxes are paid in the early years and more taxes are paid in the later years than would be paid under the "correct" allocation. While the magnitude of the underpayment in the early years exactly equals the magnitude of the overpayment in the later years, this shift is valuable to the firm because of the time value of money; the firm can invest the tax underpayments in the early years so that it will have more than enough money to cover the added cost of the tax overpayments in the later years.

The shift in tax payments is good for the firm, but the Principle of Two-Sided Transactions reminds us to look at the other side of the transaction—the bondholders' position in the scheme of things. Sure enough, the shift in tax payments is bad for the bondholders. However, in spite of the apparent bad position for the bondholders, several billion dollars worth of zero-coupon bonds were issued in the years 1979 through 1982. What was the common characteristic of the buyers of these zero-coupon bonds? They were primarily tax-exempt investors, such as pension funds. Such investors pay no taxes, so that the shift in interest payments for tax purposes is irrelevant to them. The decrease in taxes collected from the issuing corporations was not being offset by an increase in taxes collected from the bondholders. In the spring of 1982, the number of new zero-coupon bonds being issued each month was dramatically accelerating. When the IRS realized that this asymmetry in taxes was occurring on a large scale and significantly affecting the taxes being collected, it asked Congress to change the tax law. In July 1982, the rule for allocating interest expense/income for a zero-coupon bond was changed to the "scientific method" to recognize correctly the amount of interest accruing each year.[12]

Zero-coupon bonds are only one of many examples of asymmetries that have occurred, or still exist, in the tax code. Among others, significant attention has been given to the problem of asymmetries that occur in the area of leasing. Although the majority of asymmetries exist by design to provide incentives for decisions that the Congress has deemed "socially desirable," many people spend considerable effort looking for tax asymmetries that they can exploit for profit.

APPARENT EXCEPTIONS TO VALUE ADDITIVITY

Many people are reluctant to believe that value conservation is the best approximation of the valuation of assets traded in the capital markets. To some extent, this skepticism may rest on the hope for an easy way to riches or on what they perceive as exceptions to the conservation of value. There are some apparent exceptions worth mentioning. The first concerns a privately owned company that issues its stock to

---

[11] You should be able to verify this using what you learned in Chapter 3.
[12] Tax Equity and Fiscal Responsibility Act (1982).

the public for the first time. It is virtually always the case that the total price paid for the shares is larger when the shares are sold in a public offering than when the shares are sold privately. This situation may appear to be a clear and legal violation of the law of value conservation and therefore a violation of value additivity. We will try to provide some insight into why this is not necessarily a violation of value additivity. The insight is essentially that "going public" increases the liquidity of shares. (Recall from Chapter 4 that liquidity refers to how easily an asset can be converted into cash.)

Consider the owners of a privately held company who have decided that they want to sell shares of stock in their company. The first step in the process is to find potential buyers for the stock. It can take substantial time, anxiety, and money to locate buyers. In many markets there are specialists who are paid to search for potential buyers. After locating one or more potential buyers, each of the parties (the firm and each buyer) must assess the value of the firm. This is a second task that can require considerable time, effort, and money. After valuing the firm, negotiations are necessary to reach agreement for the sale to one or more parties.

When a potential buyer is considering the purchase of shares, she must consider the possibility of any resale due to unforeseen future events. Purchasers in a private transaction face significant restrictions on their ability to resell their shares unless they register them under the U.S. securities laws. Assume for the moment that the shares in question are unregistered. Buyers must be concerned about what would happen if it becomes necessary to resell all or part of the shares soon after their purchase. Who will buy them? Realistically, "sophisticated purchasers" (i.e., high net-worth individuals and financial institutions) will be the only potential buyers for the unregistered shares unless the holder can convince the company to go to the time, trouble, and expense of registering the shares before the resale. What will these *other* investors be willing to pay for the shares? The current buyers will have an awareness of the resources used to get this far in the negotiations for *this* sale. All of these contingent possibilities increase the risk involved for the buyer. Because of the higher risk, the Principle of Risk-Return Trade-Off tells us that the buyers will lower the price they are willing to pay for shares to raise their expected return to compensate for the higher risk involved in buying unregistered shares.

Now consider the same scenario but with the resources that the current owners put into finding potential buyers going instead into registration for public sale and possibly listing on a stock exchange. In this second case, when potential buyers consider the purchase of shares, one aspect of risk and transaction costs has been removed. With shares registered for public sale, there is a much higher likelihood that a resale could be transacted quickly and at low cost. Holders can sell in the public market; they are not restricted to "sophisticated investors" as they are in the case of a private transaction. (Of course, trading on an exchange does nothing to guarantee the resale price.)

The process of "going public" appears to add value to the company. However, from our discussions in this chapter, we hope you can see that value has not actually been created. Rather, transaction costs have been reduced: There is a broader market, so the time and cost of locating buyers have been reduced. Investment risk has been reduced because purchasers will have greater liquidity and the valuation is more likely to be correct because of the publication of prices and the number of people valuing the company. Finally, the costs of transferring ownership from one party to another have been reduced. In short, the increased liquidity of the shares due to their public registration and their being traded in the stock market is valuable.

There is one other apparent exception to value additivity we want to mention. It is an example of an apparent "money machine" that is illegal and yet persists—the

pyramid scheme: a "scam" where the con artist tells victims that they can earn an extraordinary return on their money, such as 10% per quarter, with no risk. The con artist takes the money, then returns the investment with interest one quarter later and inquires about reinvesting. The victim is pleased because he has gotten his money back with tremendous interest, as promised. Usually the victims reinvest their money and can be called upon to cajole some friends into investing. The con artist takes in invested money, using the new money coming in to pay off any investors who want to quit. Of course, most investors want to keep their money invested in such a great investment, so the outflow for "quitters" is small for quite a while. In the meantime, a lot of money comes in. From the start, the amount of promised money exceeds the amount of money actually held by the con artist, but over time, the difference between promised returns and funds available grows and eventually becomes enormous. At some point, the con artist "disappears," along with whatever money actually remains.

This may seem to be an unlikely scheme at first because of the difficulty of pulling it off. The scheme is illegal, and there are many checks to prevent its occurrence. However, in each of the last three decades there have been one or more pyramid schemes that have been at least partially successful for the con artist. The most recent (we hope) is the J. David Co. scandal in 1984 in which investors lost $80 million and because of which J. David Dominelli was sentenced to 20 years in prison for fraud.[13] In each case, people lost significant amounts of money.

This scheme is not an exception to value additivity because the cash to pay interest to those who wish to withdraw is obtained from others who have been sucked in. Value is not created; it is simply transferred from one group of participants to another, with a sizable "commission" being taken by the promoter.

PERFECT CAPITAL MARKETS   5.7

We have spoken about how market imperfections such as transaction costs can impede market efficiency, chiefly by interfering with the arbitrage process. In the extreme, an ideal market environment is the one we described in Chapter 4 as a **perfect capital market**. Throughout the rest of the book we will use the notion of a perfect capital market as a starting point for our analysis.

Do the conditions specified for a perfect market in Chapter 4 describe existing capital markets? Pun intended, the answer is yes, very well, but not *perfectly*. How far the conditions in any market deviate from these eight conditions will determine how "imperfect" the market is. For example, if there are few participants in the market for a common stock and the flow of information to investors is very poor because there are no securities analysts who monitor the stock and prepare research reports on it, the market for the stock may not always behave efficiently.

The Principle of Capital Market Efficiency states that the capital markets are efficient, but how far is "efficient" from perfect? We don't have a precise way of separating the two concepts, but the eight conditions listed in Chapter 4 provide us with guidance in looking for important exceptions to a perfect capital market. If you think back over this chapter, you might see that we've already told you how the capital markets are imperfect. Let's summarize.

One significant market imperfection is the existence of asymmetric taxes. Having

---

[13] There were a number of articles about the J. David Co. scandal in the *Wall Street Journal* in 1984. Summaries can be found in *The Wall Street Journal Index*, 1984.

told you this, we should point out that tax laws change with considerable regularity. Therefore, in general, we will refrain from getting into too much detail concerning the tax laws. Later on, we do point out some tax asymmetries that have existed for a considerable period of time and are relevant to major corporate decisions. However, please be warned that even those tax asymmetries might be changed by Congress. It is important for you to remember to check for tax asymmetries as a potential explanation for transactions that otherwise would appear to be a zero-sum game.

A second significant market imperfection concerns the availability of information. In our discussion on speculation we pointed out the importance and cost of obtaining information. New information relevant to pricing a security is not costless and available to everyone. However, since competition impounds new information into prices so quickly and information is published almost as quickly, it is a good approximation of the environment to say that information is freely available to everyone. Signaling is an important component of the flow and interpretation of information. As with tax asymmetries, information flow—sending signals—is a potential explanation for transactions that otherwise would appear to be a zero-sum game.

In January 1990, Smith Barney, Harris Upham & Co. sold to investors 4 million shares of The Inefficient-Market Fund, Inc., which is designed to capitalize on imperfect information. The prospectus for the offering states that the fund's investment objective was to achieve long-term capital appreciation by investing at least 50% of its assets in equity securities of companies with market capitalizations under $500 million that "Smith Barney believes are inefficiently valued."[14] The prospectus goes on to state:

> In the opinion of Smith Barney, inefficiently valued stocks are those stocks that are underowned by institutions [institutional investors own fewer than 50% of the outstanding securities] and underfollowed by Wall Street [five or fewer research analysts from recognized major Wall Street firms make research available] and therefore are considered undervalued. . . . Undervalued securities are those whose price reflects the reality that the marketplace as a whole imperfectly absorbs and responds to available information with respect to certain issuers.[15]

You might want to check on how the fund is performing. Also, the clearly articulated investment objective would form the basis for an interesting empirical study. In any case, we think that there is probably an important linkage between the number of research analysts that follow a particular company, the quality of information about the company that is available to investors, and the accuracy with which shares are valued. What we don't know is how strong this linkage is.

A third imperfection we have discussed is the existence of transaction costs. As unbelievable as this may sound, transaction costs are considerably less important than the other two imperfections already mentioned. Transaction costs are usually symmetrical. Although they may inhibit arbitrageurs, traders, and speculators from making transactions, friction costs do not bias prices upward or downward, nor do they provide an incentive for making a transaction. That is, they do not create profit in and of themselves, except for the financial intermediary collecting a commission or finding a way to structure a transaction that reduces transaction costs. The significant effect that transaction costs *can* have is to favor one *type* of transaction over an-

---

[14] The Inefficient-Market Fund, Inc., prospectus, January 17, 1990.
[15] Ibid, 3. The bracketed definitions are taken from elsewhere in the prospectus.

other. For example, the existence of fixed transaction costs favors less frequent larger transactions over more frequent smaller transactions.[16]

In spite of the existence of capital market imperfections generally and the three discussed here in particular, a perfect market is a very good approximation for most segments of the capital markets. The assumption that the law of value conservation holds—that value is neither created nor destroyed through splitting or combining cash flows—is the best starting point for financial analysis. In future chapters we will use this starting-with-a-clean-slate approach in our analysis.

SUMMARY

In this chapter, we have explained how the Principles of Self-Interested Behavior, Two-Sided Transactions, and Signaling combine with the homogeneity of financial assets, low transaction costs, and large size in a very competitive market environment and lead us to the Principle of Capital Market Efficiency. This fundamental principle, which is a critical part of the fabric that underlies the remaining chapters of the book, states that at any point in time, capital market prices reflect all available information and adjust fully and quickly to new information. While disparities in valuation can occur, these will prove temporary, provided transaction costs and other frictions are relatively insignificant, because arbitrage activity will tend to eliminate them quickly and restore efficient pricing.

Capital market efficiency has several important implications.

- ***Price movements in an efficient market are random*** because market participants will react to each new piece of information that becomes available, and the events that generate this new information occur randomly.

- ***Market prices at any point in time will reflect the up-to-date collective wisdom*** of the market participants about the "correct" value of each asset.

- ***Market participants will interpret each new event*** and make buy and sell decisions accordingly. This involves the interpretation of corporate events, such as dividend or capital structure changes, as signals regarding possible changes in the corporation's financial condition or prospects. We will point out situations in future chapters where signaling effects, as in the case of a stock split, may be the most important consequence of a particular corporate policy decision.

- ***Conservation of value across transactions,*** which leads to value additivity. In the special case of perfect capital markets where there are no frictions such as asymmetric taxation or transaction costs and information is fully and costlessly available to everyone, the value of combined assets exactly equals the sum of their individual values. As a result, the law of value conservation holds; value is neither created nor destroyed when assets are combined or separated. Transaction costs appear to cause only minor departures from value additivity because they are not biased. That is, in most cases, both parties to a transaction must pay approximately equivalent transaction costs.

[16] Transaction costs include price discounts to reflect illiquidity. The prospectus for The Inefficient-Market Fund noted that a substantial portion of the smaller-capitalization stocks in which the fund would invest had illiquid markets. But illiquidity also entails greater risk, and under the Principle of Risk-Return Trade-Off, the smaller-capitalization, less liquid stocks should, in an efficient capital market, provide a higher expected return to compensate for this risk.

Taxes can cause the capital markets to deviate from being a zero-sum-game environment. Accordingly, you should look for tax-related factors that might be responsible for transactions that would otherwise seem to be zero-sum games. In practice, tax-related factors are often the driving force behind a transaction such as the wave of zero-coupon bond issues that occurred in the early 1980s. Aside from special tax consequences, value additivity is a good approximation of the valuation of assets in the capital markets. In spite of capital market imperfections, the perfect market ideal is a good approximation of the capital markets and serves as the best starting point from which to analyze capital market transactions.

PROBLEMS

PROBLEM SET A

A1. For what reason were the capital markets originally created?

A2. What is meant by the term **liquidity**?

A3. Explain how public securities prices provide a measure of value.

A4. What does it mean to sell a financial security on a **discount basis**?

A5. Define the term **riskless arbitrage**.

A6. How can arbitrage be used to define a perfect market?

A7. Respond to the following: "Why should I invest in the capital markets when I don't earn any money; that is, I get a zero NPV?"

A8. What do we mean when we say that financial assets are very **homogeneous**?

A9. What do we mean by the term **collective wisdom**?

A10. Why is it important to distinguish between anticipated and unanticipated new information?

A11. What is the **value-additivity principle**?

A12. What is a **zero-coupon bond**?

A13. Describe what we mean by the term **asymmetric taxes**.

A14. Describe what we mean by the term **asymmetric information**.

A15. Cite and briefly discuss three types of capital market imperfections that may affect corporate decision making.

PROBLEM SET B

B1. Originally, the capital markets were created to bring users and suppliers of capital together. In addition to this important purpose, we now find that there are important "side" benefits. Cite and discuss three benefits that capital markets provide for society.

B2. Explain the importance of **arbitrage** to the efficiency of the capital markets.

B3. Is the following statement true or false? Since arbitrageurs sell assets for more than they paid for the assets, arbitrageurs must make a lot of money. Justify your answer.

B4. Explain how an increase in the liquidity of a financial security can appear to be a violation of value additivity.

B5. Explain how the homogeneity of assets contributes to the efficiency of the capital markets.

B6. Describe the problem of **adverse selection** in your own words.

B7. Applying the Signaling Principle involves inductive reasoning. Cite an important aspect of inductive reasoning that can make some applications of this principle extremely difficult.

B8. Evaluate the following statement: As I understand the evidence, price movements are random. If this is the case, clearly the capital markets are not functioning well.

B9. Describe the law of value conservation in your own words.

B10. Explain how a continuing violation of value additivity would create an arbitrage opportunity, using algebraic representation.

PROBLEM SET C

C1. Comment on the following statement: If *all* markets were perfect, it would be both a blessing and a curse.

C2. Using our Principles of Finance, explain why a market rate of return is often referred to as an opportunity cost of capital (or opportunity cost discount rate).

C3. If payments for a $20,000 five-year car loan are $300.99 twice a month, what is the APR for the loan? What is the effective annual rate for this loan?

C4. Both fixed and variable transaction costs for arbitrageurs inhibit capital market efficiency. How would the effect of relatively large fixed and small variable transaction costs differ from that of relatively small fixed and large variable transaction costs?

C5. Smiling John's retirement service offers the following deal: "You pay us $10,000 a year for 12 years, with the first payment today, and we'll pay you $1,000 a month forever after." What *effective annual* rate is John offering? (This can be approximated via an algebraic solution, but the exact solution will be obtained using trial and error. If you don't see how to get the exact answer, try to make a good approximation.)

C6. a. With regard to Smith Barney's The Inefficient-Market Fund, Inc., why would imperfect information be expected to result in systematic undervaluation of small-capitalization common stocks?

   b. If smaller-capitalization stocks tend to be less liquid than stocks generally, explain why this apparent undervaluation may be illusory.

   c. If smaller-capitalization stocks were truly undervalued prior to the fund's establishment, if the fund begins to earn above-normal returns (more than the risk of the investment would require), what would you expect to happen to the relative valuation of smaller-capitalization stocks? [So the stock market is efficient after all?]

C7. Suppose you will receive $10,000 once a year forever, and the first payment will be made 3 months from today. What is the present value of this stream if the *effective* annual rate is 20%, compounded annually?

C8. Transaction costs are often cited as definite proof that capital markets are not perfect.

   a. Explain why although this is literally true, transaction costs do not generally cause actual capital market prices to be a bad approximation of perfect capital market prices.

   b. Explain how the magnitude of the bid-ask spread and the proportionate transaction costs purchasers and sellers must pay affect your answer to part a.

C9. Define the term **opportunity cost** and explain why it is an important concept in the process of determining the value of an asset.

C10. In our discussion of the Principle of Self-Interested Behavior, we said that it is important to take opportunity costs into account. How is the opportunity cost of alternative investments accounted for in an NPV calculation?

C11. Explain how the Principle of Self-Interested Behavior, the Signaling Principle, and the Behavioral Principle relate to the Principle of Capital Market Efficiency.

REFERENCES

Ackerlof, George A. "The Market for 'Lemons': Quality Uncertainty and the Market Mechanism." *Quarterly Journal of Economics* 84 (August 1970): 488–500.

Chari, V. V., and Ravi Jagannathan. "Adverse Selection in a Model of Real Estate Lending." *Journal of Finance* 44 (June 1989): 499–508.

Cootner, Paul H., ed. *The Random Character of Stock Market Prices*. Cambridge, Mass.: M.I.T. Press, 1964.

DeBondt, Werner F. M., and Richard Thaler. "Further Evidence on Investor Overreaction and Stock Market Seasonality." *Journal of Finance* 42 (July 1987): 557–81.

Fama, Eugene F. "Efficient Capital Markets: A Review of Theory and Empirical Work." *Journal of Finance* 25 (May 1970): 383–417.

Jennings, Robert H., and Laura T. Starks. "Earnings Announcements, Stock Price Adjustment, and the Existence of Options Markets." *Journal of Finance* 41 (March 1986): 107–25.

Miller, Merton, and Franco Modigliani. "Dividend Policy, Growth, and the Valuation of Shares." *Journal of Business* 34 (October 1961): 411–33.

Modigliani, Franco, and Merton Miller. "The Cost of Capital, Corporation Finance, and the Theory of Investments." *American Economic Review* 48 (June 1958): 261–97.

Radcliffe, Robert C. *Investment: Concepts, Analysis, Strategy*, 3d. ed. Glenview, Ill.: Scott, Foresman/Little, Brown Higher Education, 1990.

Schall, Lawrence D. "Asset Valuation, Firm Investment, and Firm Diversification." *Journal of Business* 45 (January 1972): 11–28.

Smith, Clifford W., Jr. "Investment Banking and the Capital Acquisition Process." *Journal of Financial Economics* 15 (January-February 1986): 3–29.

Tax Equity and Fiscal Responsibility Act of 1982, Section 231. Washington, D.C.: Government Printing Office, 1982.

6

APPLICATION OF THE PRESENT VALUE MODEL TO STOCKS AND BONDS

In the previous chapter we spent a good deal of time explaining the extent to which the capital markets are efficient and the important implications of that fact. Capital market efficiency implies that prices accurately reflect all available information. But what does "reflect all available information" imply about the "correct" price of a particular security? In this chapter we apply the Time-Value-of-Money Principle to show what determines "correct" prices, or what we will call **fair prices,** for financial securities.

The value of any financial security can be represented as the present value of its expected future cash flows. By now, you know that there are a great number of different financial securities. This chapter explores the relationships among variables that affect the value of two particular types (corporate bonds and common stocks), but the relationships apply to any financial security. Bonds and stocks are illustrated because they represent a very large proportion of all existing financial securities and because they represent two distinct types. A bond has a set of explicitly promised future payments. In contrast, common stock has no explicitly promised future payments, only the expectation that at least at some point in the future, there will be cash dividends to stockholders.

REQUIRED AND EXPECTED RATES OF RETURN 6.1

Before proceeding, we want to define and distinguish between two different rates of return which are often confused with each other. One is called the **required rate of return** and the other is called the **expected rate of return**. Distinguishing between these two concepts is critical when dealing with time-value-of-money mechanics. We have glossed over this distinction thus far by implicitly assuming in each situation that the two rates were equal.

THE REQUIRED RATE OF RETURN   The required rate of return is the rate of return that perfectly reflects the riskiness of the expected future cash flows. We can describe it as the minimum rate of return a person must earn to be willing to invest. In other words, it is the opportunity cost of capital for that risk level since investors will require at least what they can earn on a comparable investment in the capital markets. In Chapter 7 we begin to explore some of the important dimensions that determine a required rate of return.

THE EXPECTED RATE OF RETURN   The expected rate of return is the rate of return investors *actually* expect to earn if they make the investment. It is the rate of return that would make the NPV of the investment equal zero. In Chapter 3 we solved for the discount rate and implicitly assumed that the NPV equals zero. Note that such a procedure does not imply that the NPV is *actually* zero (because that depends on how the expected rate of return compares with the required rate of return).

The confusion between these two rates of return arises because in a *perfect* capital market, the two rates are always equal; NPVs are zero; all investments are fair; and everyone can *expect* to earn the rate that is appropriate for the risk they bear. (Of course, the actual outcome is likely to be different from the expected outcome for risky investments, but that is the nature of risk.) However, it is important to note that both the required rate of return and the expected rate of return are unique for each investment, and for positive-NPV investments the expected rate of return is greater than the required rate of return.[1]

6.2   VALUING A BOND

There are many different types of bonds, but all of them can be described by their pattern of promised future payments. The typical bond promises that **coupon payments** (also called **interest payments**) will be made periodically over the life of the bond and that the **principal amount** of the bond (or simply **principal**, the original amount borrowed) will be repaid in one or more installments over the life of the bond.[2] Coupon payments are determined by the **coupon rate**. The end of the bond's life is the **maturity date**. The coupon rate, frequency of coupon payments, par value, and maturity date of the bond are specified in the contract that creates the bond, the **bond indenture**. Most **corporate bonds** issued in the United States have a par value of $1,000 and require coupon payments every 6 months.

THE FAIR PRICE OF A BOND

Consider the fair price of a bond that pays $40 every 6 months for the next 2 years plus a $1,000 payment at the time of the last interest payment. Suppose the required rate of return for this bond—the rate an investor would demand in order to be willing to invest—is 10% nominal annual. Then the fair price of the bond, computed as the present value of the future payments, is

$$\frac{40}{(1.05)} + \frac{40}{(1.05)^2} + \frac{40}{(1.05)^3} + \frac{40}{(1.05)^4} + \frac{1,000}{(1.05)^4} = \$964.54 \qquad (6.1)$$

If you can buy the bond for less than $964.54, it would be a positive-NPV investment for you, whereas if you must pay more than $964.54, it would be a negative-NPV investment.

The Principle of Capital Market Efficiency requires that the market price of a

[1] We are ignoring the mathematical problem of multiple roots and certain other complications for now. These problems are examined in Chapter 11.

[2] When a bond issue is repaid in multiple installments, the method of repayment is called a **sinking fund**. Typically, bond issues that have a sinking fund require annual payments that begin after some specified grace period. Although sinking fund payments are certain from the corporation's viewpoint, it is only probabilistic that an individual bondholder will have to accept early repayment of the principal. Equation (6.1) is formulated to value an individual bond without a sinking fund from the bondholder's point of view; it can also be used to value the total bond issue from the corporation's viewpoint, including issues with sinking funds, by including the schedule of sinking fund payments.

bond be equal to its fair price. So if this bond was actively traded, you could get a very accurate estimate of its fair price by simply getting a quote for its most recent sale.[3] Obtaining a quote from a broker would save the trouble of computation. So why bother with the formula? Don't bother with the formula unless you have more than just publicly available information. If you want to estimate a fair price for a bond that is actively traded, find the most recent price paid for it.

However, consider another question: How was it decided that the required rate of return for the bond is a 10% nominal annual discount rate? Although trading prices for many bonds are published daily and are available by phone through investment services, required rates of return are not as easily obtained. The answer to this second question also relies on the Principle of Capital Market Efficiency. Since the market price equals the fair price and the expected cash flows are the same from either viewpoint, the expected rate of return implied by the market price must equal the required rate of return implied by the fair price. Thus, to estimate the required rate of return, compute the expected rate of return for the bond. To compute the expected rate of return, set the bond's market price equal to the present value of its future cash flows (i.e., set NPV = 0) and solve for the discount rate.

The benefit of knowing a required rate of return for a market-traded security might not be obvious. After all, you can observe the current market price, and in an efficient capital market, that is a fair price. However, there are several potential uses for the required rate of return. The most important use is for valuing comparable nonmarket-traded assets. This is especially important in the case of bonds because, of all financial securities, bonds are perhaps the most homogeneous.

THE YIELD TO MATURITY

In practice, investors generally compute the **yield to maturity** as an estimate of a bond's expected rate of return. The yield to maturity (YTM) is simply the APR (annual percentage rate) that equates the bond's market value with the present value of its promised future cash flows. For the typical corporate bond, the yield to maturity equals two times the effective 6-month rate implied by the bond's market price.

EXAMPLE 1 ■   Suppose you look in today's (April 10, 1991) *Wall Street Journal* and see the following bond quote in the NYSE bond section.

Bonds	Cur Yld	Vol	High	Low	Close	Net Chg.
Texco 5¾ 99	7.3	330	78½	77½	78¼	+½

From this quote, you know that

1. Texaco (the spelling in the quote is an abbreviation) pays owners of these bonds $28.75 every 6 months (one-half of 5.75% of $1,000);

2. assuming that the bond does not have a sinking fund, Texaco will pay owners $1,000 per bond at the bond's maturity in 1999;

---

[3] Of course, for bonds that are not traded regularly, Equation (6.1) is very useful. In fact, as noted in Chapter 4, certain market quotes for bonds listed in the financial press may not reflect bond values accurately, so that Equation (6.1) should be used in place of actual trading prices in such situations.

3. the **current yield**[4] on this bond is 7.3%;

4. 330 of these bonds were traded yesterday;

5. yesterday's high price, low price, and **closing price** (the price for the last trade before the market closed) for this bond are $785.00 (10 times 78½), $775.00, and $782.50, respectively; and

6. yesterday's closing price is $5 higher than the previous day's closing price (10 times ½).

By looking in *Moody's Bond Guide*, you can find out that this bond paid interest yesterday, April 9, 1991, and confirm that the bond matures on April 9, 1999, and that it does not have a sinking fund. What is the expected rate of return from buying this bond for $782.50 today?

First, determine the expected effective semiannual rate, using a financial calculator (or trial and error) by equating the present value of the bond's expected future cash flows to the current market price. The expected effective semiannual rate is the rate, r, that solves the equation:

$$782.50 = \frac{28.75}{(1 + r)} + \frac{28.75}{(1 + r)^2} + \cdots + \frac{28.75}{(1 + r)^{16}} + \frac{1,000}{(1 + r)^{16}} \qquad (6.2)$$

A rate of 4.862% gives a present value of $782.52, so r is very close to 4.862%. The yield to maturity for this bond is the APR, two times r, or 9.724%. In practice, investors would say that the bond has about a 9.75% YTM. By contrast, the expected *effective* annual rate of return for this bond is $[(1 + .04862)^2 - 1]$, which is .0996, or 9.96%.   ■

EXAMPLE 2 ■   The preceding example is convenient in that the bond paid interest "yesterday." Suppose instead that the interest payment had been made 2 months ago? Then the price quoted would not have been the actual price you would have paid for the bond. Although the price would have looked the same in the quote listed in the financial press, the actual price paid would be the quote plus a prorated portion of the next interest payment, or $792.08 (= $782.50 + [⅔]28.75). In practice, although there are more complex and more precise formulas, the basic method of calculating the yield to maturity is the same as in the preceding example.[5] That is, it would be assumed that the interest payment was made yesterday and that there are

---

[4]The **current yield** equals the annual coupon payment divided by the closing price. The current yield measures the rate of income from the coupon payments but ignores the gain or loss that will result from the difference between the purchase price and the principal repayment. The yield to maturity is a better measure of return because it measures the total return from owning a bond. Given current technology, there is little need for the bond quote to include the current yield. It appears that the current yield is still in the bond quote simply because of tradition, and traditions are sometimes hard to break.

[5]Bond professionals employ a relatively complex formula. For a $1,000-par-value bond that repays principal in full at maturity the formula is:

$$P + 1,000 \left[\frac{r}{2}\right] \left[\frac{A}{E}\right] = \sum_{t=1}^{T} \frac{1,000r/2}{[1 + YTM/2]^{t-1+(D/E)}} + \frac{RV}{[1 + YTM/2]^{T-1+(D/E)}}$$

where

A = the number of days elapsed between the beginning of the current interest period and the settlement date (accrued days);
D = the number of days to elapse between the settlement date and the next interest payment date;
E = the number of days per semiannual interest period;
P = market price (excluding accrued interest);
r = the annual coupon rate;

16 more periods until the bond matures. (If there were more than 90 days—half-way—since the last interest payment, it would be assumed that there were 15 more periods until maturity. The effect of such assumptions is examined in some of the problems.) To determine the effective semiannual rate of return in this case, Equation (6.2) is modified to adjust for being 2 months into the interest period. The effective semiannual rate in this second example is the rate, r, that solves the equation:

$$792.08 = \left[\frac{28.75}{(1 + r)} + \frac{28.75}{(1 + r)^2} + \cdots + \frac{1028.75}{(1 + r)^{16}}\right][1 + r]^{1/3} \quad \textbf{(6.3)}$$

By trial and error, a rate of 4.894% gives a present value of $792.04, so r in this case is very close to 4.894%. The YTM is then 2 times 4.894% = 9.79%, and the expected *effective* annual rate is $[(1 + .04894)^2 - 1]$, which is .1003, or 10.03%.

   If the investment is large enough, using the exact 9.96% effective annual rate in the first example and the exact 10.03% effective annual rate in the second example, rather than the approximation of 9.75% in both cases, can be important. But for small investments, most investors would not consider this difference significant. It is not significant because on a relative basis, the difference in price is small. In fact, the transaction cost of buying the bond is much larger than the difference in present values implied by the difference in rates. The bond would be worth $795.00 at the lower effective annual rate of 9.96% rather than $792.08 at 10.03%. This difference of only $2.92 compares with a transaction cost of about $35 for an investor buying one bond.[6]   ■

BOND VALUES AND CHANGING ECONOMIC CONDITIONS

You may have noticed that the market prices for the bonds in the examples just given were not equal to their par value. Although usually a bond is sold initially for a price very close to its par value, whenever economic conditions change so that the required rate of return for a bond changes, the fair price for the bond will change. The fair price changes because every present value depends on the discount rate, and with identical cash flows, a change in the discount rate requires a change in the present value.

   Because a change in the required rate of return causes a change in a bond's fair price, owning a bond is risky; its value can change over time. Note that this is also true for government bonds. A government bond can be riskless (or as close as possible to being riskless) only in the sense that the future cash flows will occur as promised. However, if you sell the bond before its maturity, there is a large probability

---

RV   = the redemption value per $1,000 par value (typically 100% of par value if the bond is redeemed at maturity);

T = the number of semiannual coupons payable between the settlement date and the maturity (or redemption) date;

YTM = the nominal annual yield to maturity.

The left-hand side of the equation represents the sum of the market price plus accrued interest. The right-hand side represents the sum of the present value of the interest payment stream plus the present value of the redemption value.

   As with our comment on compounding frequency (often enough so that more frequent compounding is not material to either party), unless the amounts involved are very large, a small rounding in quoting a YTM is probably not material enough to bother with a more complex formula.

[6] Purchasing one bond involves a relatively high commission. Ordering five or more bonds typically involves an incremental brokerage commission of $5-$10 when a discount brokerage house is used and somewhat higher commission charges when a full-service broker is used.

FIGURE 6-1

Hypothetical price paths for a discount bond and a premium bond.

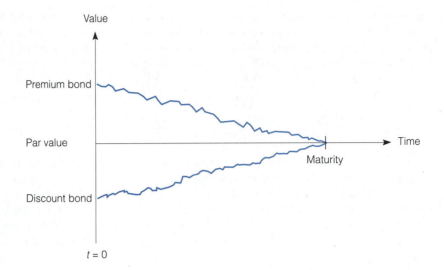

that you will sell it for more or less than the price you paid for it. Required rates of return change from time to time. The changes in bond prices that have taken place in the post-World War II era have resulted primarily from changes in the expected rate of inflation.

Recall from Chapter 3 that the present value of a future positive cash flow stream is inversely related to the required rate of return. Therefore, a bond's fair price is inversely related to its required rate of return. That is, if the bond's required rate of return increases, the fair price decreases, and vice versa. This phenomenon is further explored in the problems at the end of this chapter.

BOND VALUES AND MATURITY

While a bond's value may vary over time from its par value, it will converge to its maturity value as the time to maturity expires, except where the firm is expected to default on the maturity payment. This means that although the value of the bond may have a random component, the path of a bond's value is somewhat constrained, ending at its maturity value. This idea is illustrated in Figure 6-1 by hypothetical price paths for both a discount bond (selling below par) and a premium bond (selling above par).

6.3

VALUING COMMON STOCK

The method we will show you for valuing common stock differs from the method of valuing the typical corporate bond in two important respects. First, the horizon is *infinite* rather than finite. Although some bonds have infinite lives and even have a special name (an example of a bond with an infinite life is the **consol** mentioned in Chapter 4), they do not exist in the U.S. capital markets.[7] Second, as previously mentioned, the future cash flows are not specified contractually.[8] The future cash flows must be estimated on the basis of expectations about what the firm's earnings and dividend policy will be in the future.

[7] Consols exist in the European capital markets. Under the Internal Revenue Code, a bond must have a stated maturity to qualify as debt and permit the issuer to deduct interest payments for tax purposes.
[8] Recall from Chapter 4 that unlike common stock, preferred stock does provide for regular quarterly cash dividend payments at a specified rate.

From a financial point of view, the value of a share of common stock depends *entirely* on the cash flows that will be distributed to its owners (and the rate at which such cash flows are discounted). This seems like a strong statement, but if you imagine owning stock that would *never* provide any cash to its owner, it would be like owning stock in a nonprofit organization such as the United Way.

THE FAIR PRICE OF A SHARE OF COMMON STOCK

The future cash flows of a share of common stock are the future cash dividends and future sale price.[9] So the value of a share of stock today, denoted P_0, can be expressed as the present value of the expected future cash dividends, denoted D_0, D_1, D_2, . . . , D_n, for time periods 0, 1, 2, . . . , n, plus the present value of the expected future cash sale price of the share of stock at time n, denoted P_n, or

$$P_0 = \frac{D_1}{(1 + r)} + \frac{D_2}{(1 + r)^2} + \cdots + \frac{D_n}{(1 + r)^n} + \frac{P_n}{(1 + r)^n} \qquad (6.4)$$

where r is the required rate of return for this stock.[10] Applying Equation (6.4) is conceptually just like bond valuation. However, the specification of the parameter values for a share of stock can be a very difficult task because the expected cash flows are so uncertain. As we examine stock valuation further, you should note that each specific formula represents a special case or rearrangement of Equation (6.4). The cases differ because of the assumptions made to characterize the situation specifically, but they all fit the general case: The fair price equals the present value of the expected future cash flows.

Since a stock's fair price is the present value of two components, we normally think of the return from owning stock as made up of two parts. The first part, based on dividends, might be called the income part since the cash dividends paid periodically during the ownership of the stock are similar to income from any other source. The second part, based on the increase (or decrease) in value, might be called the capital-gain part since it represents the gain, or growth, in the value of the stock from the time of purchase until the time of sale.

Equation (6.4) provides for the sale of the stock at the end of time period n, but at what price will it be sold? Its value to a second owner who buys it at time period n and owns it for the next m periods after time period n can be determined in a similar manner: As with the first owner, the second owner has the expectation of selling the stock in the future (at time $n+m$). Therefore, we can apply the concept embodied in Equation (6.4) a second time to value the stock for the second owner. P_n, the stock's value at time n, can be expressed as

$$P_n = \frac{D_{n+1}}{(1 + r)} + \frac{D_{n+2}}{(1 + r)^2} + \cdots + \frac{D_{n+m}}{(1 + r)^m} + \frac{P_{n+m}}{(1 + r)^m} \qquad (6.5)$$

If Equations (6.4) and (6.5) are combined, P_0 can be rewritten as

$$P_0 = \frac{D_1}{(1 + r)} + \frac{D_2}{(1 + r)^2} + \cdots + \frac{D_{n+m}}{(1 + r)^{n+m}} + \frac{P_{n+m}}{(1 + r)^{n+m}} \qquad (6.6)$$

[9]Changes in value caused by other kinds of distributions, such as stock dividends or stock repurchases, will be accounted for by changes in the future cash dividends and the sale price.

[10]For now, we are ignoring tax considerations and treating cash dividends as though payments occur annually rather than quarterly as they typically do, and thus compounding yearly. These simplifications might significantly affect valuation in practice, but we believe that they are appropriate now so that we can concentrate on the important concepts.

Reapplying this same concept again and again for all future owners implies that the fair price for the stock can be expressed as the present value of an infinite stream of expected future cash dividend payments, or

$$P_0 = \frac{D_1}{(1 + r)} + \frac{D_2}{(1 + r)^2} + \cdots = \sum_{t=1}^{\infty} \frac{D_t}{(1 + r)^t} \qquad (6.7)$$

Equation (6.7) is a very general expression for the value of a share of stock. This is because it is given in terms of the stock's expected future cash dividends without any specific assumption about the pattern of those future cash dividends or when the share of stock will be sold. The payments can be expected to occur in an erratic way or in any pattern, such as increasing or decreasing at particular rates across particular time periods. Further, the shares can be expected to be sold in the future to subsequent owners any number of times.

BUT WHAT DETERMINES FUTURE DIVIDENDS?

If the value of a share of stock is based on expected future cash dividends, a logical next question is What determines future dividends? There are two factors that determine the cash dividends: (1) the firm's earnings and (2) its dividend policy. A firm's earnings are important since a firm cannot distribute cash (pay a dividend) to its owners if there is not enough cash in the cash account. There are only three ways a firm can obtain cash: (1) sell some of its products, assets, or services; (2) borrow additional money; or (3) sell additional shares of stock. While any of these methods can be used to obtain the necessary cash to pay a dividend, usually we think of the firm selling either current assets (like manufactured inventory) or services for more than the cost of producing them, so that the firm earns a profit from which to pay dividends. In the short term, the firm can also use financing proceeds and/or asset-sale proceeds to help manage its cash position. But in the long run, it makes little sense for a firm to sell off its fixed assets (after a while, the firm would deplete its plant and equipment) or to go to the capital markets for additional financing in order to pay cash dividends. So in the long run, the cash necessary for dividends is expected to come from the firm's earnings.

Since a firm can choose between the two alternatives of reinvesting its earnings or distributing the earnings to the shareholders in the form of dividends, a **dividend policy** is established to guide the firm in determining the amount of money that will be paid out in cash dividends. A simple but very convenient way to characterize a dividend policy is to compute what is called a payout ratio. A **payout ratio** expresses the firm's cash dividend as a proportion of the firm's earnings:

$$\text{Payout Ratio} = \frac{\text{Dividends}}{\text{Earnings}}$$

In any particular year, a firm may deviate, even substantially, from a "target" payout ratio. However, most firms follow a pattern of dividend payments that can be characterized over a number of years by an average payout ratio. While using an average payout ratio to describe a dividend policy oversimplifies the important issues connected with dividend policy, it is accurate enough to allow us to analyze stock valuation without requiring an in-depth study of dividend policy at this point. Chapters 17 and 18 are devoted to the importance of dividend policy and its management, and they contain an in-depth discussion of the issues involved in choosing and managing a dividend policy.

THE GORDON GROWTH MODEL 6.4

One particular assumption about the pattern of expected future cash dividend payments that has been applied to the infinite stream of dividends in Equation (6.7) is called the Gordon Growth Model, named after Myron J. Gordon. The assumption underlying the Gordon Growth Model is that cash dividend payments will change at some average rate, denoted g in the model, from one period to the next, forever into the future. This characterization of cash dividends is very useful because it is general enough to apply to many situations (for example, the rate of change can be positive or negative) and because it is a good *approximation* of actual patterns of dividends. While the infinite-horizon assumption may seem at first to be inaccurate (after all, corporations do not really live forever, at least not so far), it is a good approximation because as with any cash flow, the further in the future that a dividend will occur, the smaller is its present value. Therefore, distant future dividends contribute very little to the present value of the stock.

If cash dividend payments change at the rate of g from one period to the next forever into the future, the dividend payment for period t, D_t, can be expressed as the previous dividend, D_{t-1}, times 1 plus the growth rate. D_{t-1} is a function of D_{t-2}, and so forth, so that D_t can be expressed as a function of any dividend between now and time t, or

$$D_t = [1 + g]D_{t-1} = [1 + g]^2 D_{t-2} = \cdots = [1 + g]^{(t-1)}D_1 = [1 + g]^t D_0 \quad \textbf{(6.8)}$$

Since Equation (6.8) holds for all future dividend payments, every future dividend payment can be expressed as a function of D_1, the next dividend payment, or

$$D_t = D_1[1 + g]^{(t-1)} \quad \textbf{(6.9)}$$

If each of the future dividend payments in Equation (6.7) is represented by the expression in Equation (6.9), P_0 can be rewritten as

$$P_0 = \frac{D_1}{(1 + r)} + \frac{D_1(1 + g)}{(1 + r)^2} + \frac{D_1(1 + g)^2}{(1 + r)^3} + \cdots$$

$$= D_1 \sum_{t=1}^{\infty} \frac{[1 + g]^t}{[1 + r]^{(t+1)}} = D_1 \left[\frac{1}{r - g} \right]$$

or

$$P_0 = \frac{D_1}{(r - g)} \quad \textbf{(6.10)}$$

Recalling that the present value annuity factor equals $1/r$ for a perpetuity, it should seem reasonable that the factor for a growing infinite annuity equals $1/[r-g]$, as shown in Equation (6.10).

We used the notion of hypothetical subsequent owners to show that the fair price for a share of stock can be expressed in terms of an infinite stream of future cash dividends and a required rate of return as it is in Equation (6.7). We can use this same notion to create a valuation formula for a stock's fair price, P_t, at any point in time, t. P_t can be expressed in terms of the next dividend payment, D_{t+1}, a growth rate, and a required rate of return whenever dividends beginning at a level D_{t+1} are expected to change at the rate of g from one period to the next, forever into the future. So whenever g is expected to be the same each period forever into the future from time $t + 1$ onward, P_t, can be written as

$$P_t = \frac{D_{t+1}}{(r - g)}$$ (6.11)

Equation (6.11) is just a more general statement of Equation (6.10). That is, Equation (6.10) is Equation (6.11) when $t=0$.

By rewriting D_{t+1} as $(1 + g)D_t$ in Equation (6.11), we can see that the stock's price in the Gordon Growth Model grows at the same rate as the dividend payments from one period to the next. We can rewrite Equation (6.11) as

$$P_t = \frac{(1 + g)D_t}{(r - g)} = (1 + g)\left[\frac{D_t}{(r - g)}\right]$$

The fraction in brackets is similar in form to Equation (6.11); it expresses the fair price of the stock at time $t - 1$, so that P_{t-1} can be substituted for the bracketed amount:

$$P_t = (1 + g)P_{t-1}$$

EXAMPLE ■ Suppose Firestone is expected to pay a dividend of $3.00 next year on its common stock, has a required rate of return of 12%, and dividend payments are expected to grow at a rate of 4% per year forever. Applying Equation (6.11), the fair price for a share of Firestone common stock is $37.50 (= 3/[.12 − .04]). ■

AN IMPORTANT COMMENT ON THE RELATIONSHIP BETWEEN g AND r

One of the first questions students ask when they see Equation (6.11) is What happens if g equals r or if g is greater than r? The question arises because Equation (6.11) implies that the stock's value is infinite if g equals r and that it is negative if g is greater than r, neither of which makes economic sense. Very simply, g can never be greater than or equal to r. While we won't prove this statement at this point, briefly consider the following argument: g is the rate at which the cash dividend is expected to grow *every period, forever*. As noted above, in the long run, dividends are paid from a firm's earnings. For cash dividends to grow at the rate of g, the earnings of the firm must grow at a rate that equals or exceeds g (at least, on average over a long time) in order for the firm to have the income to pay the dividends. Although it is easy to imagine a very high growth rate of earnings in some cases, any situations you can imagine will involve a *finite* time period. No business can grow forever at a rate faster than the rate of growth of the nation's economic activity. If a business grew fast enough for long enough, the growth rate of the business and the growth rate of economic activity would converge because in the limit, the business would become 100% of the nation's economic activity!

One other comment concerning g might be helpful. Even though g acts like a discount rate, in that it compounds amounts, it is a *growth* rate. Be careful to distinguish between the two; it is easy to mix up the rates when you are computing stock values.

FORMING EXPECTATIONS AND MEASURING STOCK VALUE

In the simple example given above using the Gordon Growth Model to value Firestone stock, dividends were expected to grow at a constant rate forever into the future from *now* on. In most situations, it is possible to be more specific with our expectations about the near future than our expectations about the more distant future. In the same way, it is often possible to describe expected cash dividend payments for the near future more specifically than simply an "average rate of change" every period. As we approximate further into the future, the extra effort becomes less worthwhile because of the lower present value of the payments. From some point on, an average rate of change forever into the future is the most *efficient* estimate we can make, even if it is not the most accurate. In many cases a more accurate estimate is not worth the additional resources necessary to produce it.

EXAMPLE 1 ■ A firm is operating in a new industry that has recently caught on with the public, and sales for the firm are growing at the rate of 80% per year. This high rate of growth in sales is expected to translate into a 25% growth rate in cash dividends for each of the next 4 years, after which time the growth rate in dividends is expected to be 5% per year forever. If the latest annual dividend, paid yesterday, is $0.75 and the required rate of return for the stock is 22%, what is the stock worth today?

To solve this problem, first compute the set of expected future cash dividends, which is

Time	0	1	2	3	4	5	6 ...
Dividend	.75	.938	1.172	1.465	1.831	1.923	2.019 ...
Growth		25%	25%	25%	25%	5%	5%	5% ...

Second, compute a fair price for the stock at a future point in time, using Equation (6.11). To be able to use Equation (6.11), you must pick a point in time after the growth rate in dividends has become constant forever. Using time 5 as our future sale point, the hypothetical sale value for the stock, P_5, is $11.875. Finally, compute the present value of the expected future sale price and add that to the present value of all the expected cash dividends between now and then. Applying Equation (6.4), with n equal to 5,

$$P_0 = \frac{.938}{(1.22)} + \frac{1.172}{(1.22)^2} + \frac{1.465}{(1.22)^3} + \frac{1.831}{(1.22)^4} + \frac{1.923}{(1.22)^5} + \frac{11.875}{(1.22)^5} = \$8.295$$

You should note that the choice of time period 5 for the hypothetical sale is somewhat arbitrary. Any fair price from period 3 onward can be used. (Period 3 is not a misprint, dividends will grow at the 5% rate from period 4 on, and therefore dividend 4 can be used to compute P_3, which is $10.77. Again, the present value of the dividends and the sale price equals $8.295. Try it!) ■

EXAMPLE 2 ■ Suppose that a firm is currently in a building stage and is not expected to change its annual cash dividend while new projects are being developed over the next 3 years. The dividend has been $1 per year and is therefore expected to be $1 for each of the next 3 years. After the projects have been developed, earnings are expected to grow at a high rate for 2 years as the sales resulting from the new projects are realized. The higher earnings are expected to result in a 40% increase in dividends for 2 years. After these two extraordinary increases in dividends, the growth rate of dividends is expected to be 3% per year forever. If the required rate of return for this stock is 12%, what is the stock worth today?

As with example 1, the first step is to compute the set of expected future dividends.

Time	0	1	2	3	4	5	6	7 . . .
Dividend	1.00	1.00	1.00	1.00	1.40	1.96	2.019	2.079 . . .
Growth		0%	0%	0%	40%	40%	3%	3% 3% . . .

Second, compute the fair price of the stock for a point where the growth rate in the dividends is expected to be constant forever. This time, we will use dividend 5 to compute the stock price for time 4. This is the earliest point that satisfies the constant-growth criterion. Therefore,

$$P_4 = \frac{D_5}{(r - g)}$$

With $D_5 = \$1.96$, $g = 3\%$, and $r = 12\%$, P_4 equals $\$21.778$. Finally, applying Equation (6.4) to this set of expected future cash flows,

$$P_0 = \frac{1.00}{(1.12)} + \frac{1.00}{(1.12)^2} + \frac{1.00}{(1.12)^3} + \frac{1.40}{(1.12)^4} + \frac{21.778}{(1.12)^4} = \$17.132$$

6.5   GROWTH VERSUS INCOME

Recall that the value of a share of stock can be broken into two parts: income and capital gain. Suppose you have a choice between two investments: (1) buy stock in a firm that emphasizes income by paying out all or most of its earnings in cash dividends, or (2) buy stock in a firm that emphasizes capital gain by retaining and reinvesting all or most of its earnings. Which alternative is the better investment?

In this section we explore the impact that growth and income have on the value of a share of stock to establish conditions under which stockholders should have a preference for either growth or income. To help you follow our analysis, we will tell you the answer now: When all else is equal, a firm should invest its earnings in positive-NPV investments and pay out its residual earnings in dividends when the firm has only negative-NPV projects to invest in.

DIVIDEND GROWTH, RETAINED EARNINGS, AND THE PAYOUT RATIO

Retaining and reinvesting earnings corresponds to pursuing growth and providing a larger capital gain to shareholders. In contrast, paying out earnings as cash dividends corresponds to providing current income to shareholders. Thus, one way to think of the question of growth versus income is to pose it as a question of dividend policy: retaining earnings versus paying cash dividends. We said that for now we would characterize a firm's dividend policy by the average **payout ratio**, the ratio of its cash dividends to its earnings. A lower payout ratio increases retained earnings and provides lower dividends, whereas a higher payout ratio provides higher dividends but slows the growth of retained earnings (and the growth of the firm). Therefore, in addition to being a simple but convenient way to describe a firm's dividend policy, the payout ratio is also a relative measure of the firm's pursuit of growth (retained earnings) versus income. A high payout ratio emphasizes income, but at the expense of growth; a low payout ratio emphasizes growth, but at the expense of income.

Typically, firms vary their payout ratios over the life of the firm. Many firms in new and fast-growing industries pay no dividends for a number of years because such firms have many opportunities to invest the firm's retained earnings in. As a firm grows, becomes well-established, and new opportunities become more rare in its industry, the firm tends to increase its payout ratio. U.S. firms in well-established industries have average payout ratios of roughly 50% of their earnings.

A GROWTH VERSUS INCOME EXAMPLE

Indy-Sission, Ltd. is an Indianapolis manufacturer of various types of knives. Indy-Sission is having trouble deciding whether to pursue growth. Indy expects to earn $2 million next year, and it follows a dividend policy of paying out 60% of each year's earnings in the form of cash dividends on its 1 million outstanding shares of common stock. This policy is expected to result in a growth rate for cash dividends of 4% per year, forever. If the required rate of return for this stock is 10% per year, what is a share of Indy's common stock worth today?

First, determine next year's expected **earnings per share** (EPS_1) for Indy, the firm's total expected earnings divided by the number of shares. $EPS_1 = \$2 (= \$2$ million/1 million shares). Since Indy's payout ratio is 60%, next year's dividend is expected to be $.6(2.00) = \$1.20$. Therefore, applying Equation (6.11), the current value of a share of Indy's common stock is

$$P_0 = \frac{D_1}{(r - g)} = \frac{1.2}{(.1 - .04)} = \$20.00$$

Suppose that Indy faces two alternatives to the current policy of retaining and reinvesting 40% of its earnings every year. The first alternative is to become a "pure" income stock by changing to a 100% payout ratio, not retaining and reinvesting any of its earnings in the future. The second alternative is to undertake a 5-year growth plan where all the firm's earnings will be retained and reinvested, and no cash dividends will be paid out for the next 5 years. After the 5-year plan is completed, the firm will return to its current dividend policy of a 60% payout ratio. If you own stock in Indy, which alternative should you prefer? The alternative that produces the highest value for the stock, for sure, but which one does that?

THE INCOME ALTERNATIVE   If Indy pays out all of next year's earnings as dividends, the expected dividend per share will equal the expected EPS_1 of $2.00. Not retaining and reinvesting any of the firm's earnings leads to a zero growth rate in earnings since the firm will not be investing any additional principal from which to earn additional future income. With no growth in earnings and a 100% payout ratio, the growth rate in dividends will also be zero. As with previous examples, we can value the stock by applying Equation (6.11) with the parameter values for the situation at hand. If Indy announces today that it will adopt the income alternative, each share of stock will be worth

$$P_0 = \frac{D_1}{(r - g)} = \frac{2.0}{(.1 - 0)} = \$20.00$$

Because the income alternative with its 100% payout ratio produces the same fair price for the stock as the current policy of a 60% payout ratio, shareholders should not care whether the firm follows the current policy or adopts the income alternative.

THE GROWTH ALTERNATIVE   As in the previous examples of stock valuation where the next dividend is not expected to grow at a constant rate forever, the first task is to specify the set of expected future dividends. If Indy retains all of its earnings for the next 5 years, no dividends will be paid until year 6. In year 6, dividend payments will resume, and normal growth in dividends is expected after the year-6 dividend because of the return to a permanent payout ratio of 60%. Since the dividend in year 6 is estimated to be 60% of the expected earnings in year 6, it is necessary to determine the expected earnings in year 6 in order to estimate D_6. If the firm expects to earn its required rate of return of 10% on its retained and reinvested earnings, the expected future earnings per share in year 6, EPS_6, can be computed by starting with EPS_1 and "growing" it to EPS_6. Earnings for the second year, EPS_2, are expected to be the same as they are for the first year, except that there will be the additional return on the reinvested funds, or

$$EPS_2 = EPS_1 + .1(EPS_1) = EPS_1(1 + .1)$$

Likewise, EPS_3 is a function of EPS_2 and so forth, so that

$$EPS_6 = EPS_5(1.1) = EPS_4(1.1)^2 = \ldots$$

and

$$EPS_6 = EPS_1(1.1)^5 = 2(1.1)^5 = \$3.221$$

So $D_6 = .6(\$3.221) = \$1.933$. Dividend 7 and those beyond are an increasing function of D_6 with g equal to the normal 4% rate: $D_7 = D_6(1 + g) = \$1.933(1.04) = \$2.010$; $D_8 = D_6(1 + g)^2 = \$2.091$; $\ldots$ If the growth alternative is adopted, the expected future dividends for Indy are then

Time	0	1	2	3	4	5	6	7	8	...
Dividend	0	0	0	0	0	0	1.933	2.010	2.091	...
Growth	0%	0%	0%	0%	0%	NA	4%	4%	4%	...

In addition to the set of expected future dividends, we need a hypothetical future sale price in order to compute the present value of the stock. Since dividends are expected to grow at 4% forever into the future after year 6, D_6 can be used to compute P_5, the fair price at time 5:

$$P_5 = \frac{D_6}{(r - g)} = \frac{1.933}{(.1 - .04)} = \$32.217$$

As always, the current fair price is the present value of all the expected future cash flows. Since no dividends will be paid between now and the hypothetical sale date, the current fair price under the growth alternative is simply the present value of P_5, or

$$P_0 = \frac{P_5}{(1 + r)^5} = \frac{32.217}{(1 + .1)^5} = \$20.00$$

Because the growth alternative produces the same fair price for the stock as both the income alternative and the current policy, Indy's shareholders should be indifferent to which of the three alternatives the firm adopts.

INVESTMENT OPPORTUNITIES

In the growth-versus-income example, there are no differences among the three alternatives examined. The critical assumption that makes the three alternatives identical is the assumption that the firm earns exactly its required rate of return of 10% on all of its new investments. What happens if the firm earns more or less than the required amount? That is, suppose the firm's investments have positive or negative NPVs?

POSITIVE-NPV INVESTMENTS   Suppose that under the growth alternative the firm expects to be able to earn a rate of return on its new investments greater than the 10% required rate of return. In other words, suppose that the growth alternative represents a positive-NPV investment. Specifically, assume that the project has a total positive NPV of $1,886,000 and the firm expects to earn 12% on the 5-year expansion plan, but the usual 10% on regular growth after that. In this case, EPS_6 would be expected to grow from EPS_1 at a 12% rate, and therefore $EPS_6 = \$2(1.12)^5 = \$3.525$. D_6 would be $.6(3.525) = \$2.115$, and P_5 would be 35.247. Therefore, P_0 would be 21.886, which exceeds the current value of $20.00 and provides a positive NPV of $1.886 per share (= 21.886 − 20.00). Note that the price increase per share could also have been calculated simply by dividing the NPV of the project by the number of shares (= 1,886,000/1,000,000). So if Indy's expected rate of return is 12% on the proposed expansion rather than its required rate of return of 10%, shareholders should prefer the growth alternative to both the current policy and the income alternative. Of course, any expected rate of return on new investments that is above 10% will make the growth alternative preferable.

NEGATIVE-NPV INVESTMENTS   Now consider the effect that earning less than the required rate of return on the proposed expansion would have on the stock's value. This time assume that the expected rate of return is only 8% on Indy's 5-year expansion plan and the project has a negative NPV of −$1,753,000. Work through the numbers this time, and you will see that the value of the stock under the growth alternative would be only $18.247, which is less than the current value of $20.00 and would provide an NPV of −$1.753 per share (= 18.247 − 20.00). Note again that this number is the project NPV divided by the number of shares (= −1,753,000/1,000,000). So if the 5-year expansion plan is a negative-NPV investment, shareholders should prefer both the current policy and the income alternative to the growth alternative.

With any investment (positive or negative NPV), the value of an investment to the shareholders is simply the NPV of the project. Therefore, the aggregate value added to shareholder wealth by an investment is the NPV of the investment, and the per-share value added to shareholder wealth is the NPV of the investment divided by the number of shares outstanding. Once again, we can see why a firm should take on positive-NPV investments and avoid negative-NPV investments.

REQUIRED AND EXPECTED RATES OF RETURN FOR STOCKS   6.6

Thus far we have used a required rate of return, r, to determine the fair price for a share of stock, but we have said nothing about the specific determinants of r (beyond the general notion that r depends on the risk-return trade-off). At any point in time, a stock (or any asset) has a *single* required rate of return that is based on its characteristics that determine its risk. Since we develop models in the next two chapters for specifying a required rate of return for an asset, we will not discuss the particular characteristics that determine an asset's required rate of return at this point. What is important to understand now is the relationship among the various parameters that determine a stock's value. As we explore this relationship, please keep in mind that we are applying the Principle of Capital Market Efficiency and taking the stock's fair price as being equal to its market value.

ESTIMATING A STOCK'S REQUIRED RATE OF RETURN

In the bond valuation section, we asked the question Why should a person go to the trouble of valuing a bond that is trading regularly in a capital market? The same question is relevant to stock valuation, and our answer is the same: The Principle of Capital Market Efficiency applies. For a stock that is publicly-traded, the current market value as observed in the most recent price paid for a share of the stock is the best estimate of the fair price. As in the case of bonds, although market values are visible, required rates of return are not. And also like the bond valuation model, the stock valuation model provides a good way to estimate a required rate of return. For a stock, the required rate of return is sometimes referred to as the stock's **capitalization rate**.

Rearranging Equation (6.11) with $t = 0$ provides a model for estimating a stock's required rate of return, or capitalization rate:

$$r = \frac{D_1}{P_0} + g \tag{6.12}$$

EXAMPLE ■ Suppose you look in today's *Wall Street Journal* and see the following stock quote in the New York Stock Exchange section:

52 Weeks		Stock	Div.	Yld %	P-E Ratio	Sales 100s	High	Low	Close	Net Chg.
High	Low									
83½	64⅝	GMot	5.55	7.5	8	19820	75¼	74¼	74⅜	−⅝

From this quote, you know that

1. the highest and lowest price paid in the last 52 weeks for a share of General Motors's common stock on the NYSE is $83.50 and $64.625, respectively;
2. GM's estimated annual dividend rate (based on the latest quarter's dividend) is $5.55;
3. GM's dividend yield is 7.5% (= $5.55/$74.375);
4. GM's P/E ratio is 8; it is the closing price divided by the latest 12 months' earnings per share;
5. 1,982,000 shares (19,820 times 100) changed ownership yesterday;
6. yesterday's high, low, and closing prices for GM common stock are $75.25, $74.25, and $74.375, respectively; and
7. yesterday's closing price was $.625 (⅝ times $1) lower than the previous day's closing price.

If GM's dividend growth rate is expected to be 4.5% per year forever, next year's dividend rate is expected to be $5.80 ($D_1 = \$5.55(1.045)$) and

$$r = \frac{D_1}{P_0} + g = \frac{5.80}{74.375} + .045 = .123$$

So the implied capitalization rate equals 12.3%.   ■

ESTIMATING THE DIVIDEND GROWTH RATE

Arriving at the 12.3% capitalization rate in the previous example is straightforward as long as we don't ask how the growth rate was estimated. When we introduced the topic of stock valuation, we indicated that estimating the future cash flows was a difficult task. By using the Gordon Growth Model and g, the difficulty is simply shifted from estimating the dividends themselves to estimating g!

As we saw in the Indy-Sission growth-versus-income example, dividend growth, earnings growth, and the payout ratio are interdependent. If the payout ratio is constant, growth in a firm's dividends depends directly upon growth in the firm's earnings. In turn, growth in earnings depends upon (1) how much is retained and (2) what rate of return is earned on the investments. If all three factors are constant, the relationship among the factors can be expressed as

$$g = (1 - POR)i \tag{6.13}$$

where POR is the payout ratio and i is the expected rate of return on future investments. Recall that for Indy-Sission, POR is .6 and i is 10% which, by Equation (6.13), produces the same growth rate of 4% that was given in the example.

The relationship in Equation (6.13) provides a method of further decomposing the process of estimating future dividends. To estimate g, we can estimate the firm's expected future payout ratio and the firm's expected rate of return on its future investments. Decomposing g may make the task easier because firms tend to follow certain patterns in their payout ratios, and expected rates of return tend to fall into groups for particular types of investments. However, in some sense, decomposing g into an expected rate of return and a POR simply shifts, once more, the difficulty of what must be estimated. This time it is shifted from g to the expected rate of return on future investments.

It may provide you with some sense of relief to know that the buck stops here! The value of the stock depends upon the expected rate of return on the firm's current and future investments. Value is increased by positive-NPV investments and decreased by negative-NPV investments, so the task of the firm is to earn a rate of return on its investments that equals or exceeds the required rate of return on those investments.

A REQUIRED RATE OF RETURN EXAMPLE

U.S. Hair, Inc. (USH) is a "fly-by-night" distributor of barber-shop supplies. USH has had earnings totaling $20 million over the last 6 years and has paid a total of $8 million in dividends over the same time period, for a payout ratio of 40%. USH expects to have an EPS next year of $3.00 and expects to pay $1.20 dividend per share. USH stock is currently selling for $24.00 per share. If USH expects to earn 15% on its future investments, what is the required rate of return on USH's stock?

With POR = .4 and i = .15, from Equation (6.13), g = .09. Then, with D_1 = 1.2, P_0 = 24.00, and g = .09,

$$r = \frac{D_1}{P_0} + g = \frac{1.2}{24.00} + .09 = .14$$

So USH has a required rate of return of 14% but is expected to have future investments that have positive NPVs since its expected rate of return is 15%, which exceeds the 14% required rate of return.

Now go through the same computations again with the same values, except with the expected rate of return on future investments, i, set equal to 10%. You'll find that, with i = 10%, r is equal to 11%. In this case USH has a required rate of return of 11%, which exceeds its 10% expected rate of return. Therefore, in this case, USH is expected to have future investments that have negative NPVs.

Finally, go through the computations one more time, with i = 12.5%. This time you'll find that the required rate of return, r, equals the 12.5% expected rate of return. The implication for this last case is that USH is expected to have future investments that have NPVs equal to zero.

In each case, the value of the stock was assumed to be $24.00 per share, and we examined the impact of various assumptions about the expected rate of return on future investments on the estimated required rate of return on the stock. Even though the *estimate* of r depends upon the expected rate of return on future investments, we want to remind you that in fact the stock has only *one* required rate of return—in spite of the problems associated with estimating its actual value.

THE PRICE-EARNINGS RATIO

Like conversations about football and the weather, many investors will join into a discussion concerning the investment potential of a stock and feel good about their contribution to the conversation, regardless of any knowledge they might have about the stock. In this type of conversation, a statistic that is often mentioned as a measure of a stock's investment potential is the **price-earnings ratio**, commonly referred to as the **P/E ratio**, or simply **P/E**. A stock's P/E ratio is its market price per share divided by the firm's annual earnings per share. Recall that stock quotations in the financial press list a stock's P/E ratio, although the ratio given is "casual" because it is based on recent *past* earnings, rather than expected *future* earnings. Often investors will refer to a stock as selling at a "high" or "low" P/E to indicate that the stock has good or bad investment potential. But what does that mean? As with many things, it is unclear what a high or low P/E really indicates without obtaining additional information. Let's work through the relationships to find out why conventional wisdom holds that a high P/E is good and a low P/E is bad in a stable market environment. After that we will show you how the reasoning connected with this conventional wisdom is muddled, by illustrating some situations that can destroy or even reverse that conventional wisdom.

By substituting the dividend growth rate expression in Equation (6.13) into Equation (6.12), and writing D_1 in terms of EPS_1 and POR, we can express the firm's required rate of return, r, as

$$r = \frac{D_1}{P_0} + g = \frac{(POR)(EPS_1)}{P_0} + (1 - POR)i \qquad (6.14)$$

Rearranging the equation we have

$$r = (POR)\left[\frac{EPS_1}{P_0}\right] + (1 - POR)[i] \qquad (6.15)$$

When r is expressed in the form of Equation (6.15), you can see that r is composed of two components: (1) the first term on the right-hand side is the "income component," which is based on earnings from the firm's current operations; (2) the second term on the right-hand side is the "growth component," which is based on the firm's expected rate of return on future investments. The firm's payout ratio, POR, weights the proportional contribution of each component.

Look at Equation (6.15). You should be able to see that, for any given r and POR, the smaller $[EPS_1/P_0]$ is, the larger i must be. Since $[EPS_1/P_0]$ is the inverse of the P/E ratio, a small $[EPS_1/P_0]$ corresponds to a high P/E ratio. Therefore, since a low EPS_1/P_0 corresponds to a high value for i, the conventional wisdom is With all else equal, the higher the P/E ratio, the higher must be the expected rate of return on future investments; or, more simply stated, a "high" P/E ratio corresponds to good future investment opportunities.

An important warning   While we have just explained the logic embodied in the conventional wisdom that high P/E ratios are good and low P/E ratios bad, we must hasten to add that there are some important and frequent possibilities that can alter such a conclusion. The valuation formulas we have used here rely on expectations (averages). But actual values almost never equal the average. A firm's earnings vary randomly from year to year, even though its average earnings may be relatively stable over several years. In such cases, a firm can have a very "high" P/E ratio during a bad year and a very "low" P/E ratio during a good year, yet in both cases, the firm may not have changed fundamentally over a number of these good and bad years. So remember: A "high" P/E ratio can be the result of "low" recent earnings rather than a "high" expected rate of return on future investments.

A second possibility that can alter the conventional wisdom about P/E ratios is the possibility that earnings are not reflecting the actual timing of income. A firm may only now be recording a change in its accounts, even though the change actually occurred some time ago. For example, the firm might be recognizing (in the accounting sense) a bad debt that has existed for several years. Or a firm might now sell a piece of land that had become very valuable a long time ago. Since the land would be listed on the firm's balance sheet at its book, or historical, value rather than its current market value, selling the land would appear to create a large profit. Of course, the firm did not have to sell the land in order for the land to be worth more than the firm had paid for it. The increase in the value of the land had already taken place. (We hope you can see that it is not necessary to sell stock you own to know that it has gone up or down in value.) Similar possibilities exist that would lower, rather than raise, a firm's reported earnings.

A third possibility that can alter the conclusion about P/E ratios is changes in the firm's accounting procedures. For example, if a firm changes how it accounts for its inventory from the first-in-first-out basis (FIFO) to the last-in-first-out basis (LIFO), the firm's reported earnings will tend to be lower in times of inflation (accountants would say more "conservative"). Of course, the profitability of the process of buying raw materials, manufacturing a product, and selling the product is not altered in any way by the method used to account for the process.[11] Only the number that is reported as a *measure* of profit is affected by the method of accounting. A change in the measure of earnings can cause a change in the P/E ratio that really indicates nothing new about the value of the firm. In such cases, the conventional wisdom about P/E ratios can become meaningless.

Having told you that a firm's earnings may not accurately reflect the firm's current situation, we need to point out one more thing lest you conclude that our "accounting brethren" are dishonest and/or totally worthless. Over an extended period, like 10 years, it is difficult to continue to hide either good or poor performance with such things as changes in accounting procedures and extraordinary items. In the long run, a firm's cumulative reported earnings provide a reasonably accurate picture of the firm's past performance. However, within a limited period, like a few years, the accounting numbers may appear to tell a very different story from the one an objective observer would tell.

In short, maintain a healthy skepticism about P/E ratios. You need a lot more information than just a P/E ratio to estimate the value of a share of stock. After all, if all you needed were a P/E ratio, you probably wouldn't need this course! Still, like football and the weather, it's nice to have an "opinion".

---

[11] One exception to this statement concerns income taxes. If the firm also changes its method of inventory accounting for tax purposes to LIFO, the change will increase cost of sales and defer income taxes, which will benefit shareholders *and* result in a higher P/E ratio.

MEASURING THE EXPECTED NPV OF FUTURE INVESTMENTS

Another way of thinking about the difference between the required and expected rates of return, and measuring the impact of that difference on the value of the stock, is to compute the expected NPV of the firm's future investments. The NPV of future investments for a firm is just what the name implies, and as you should expect, it is positive if the expected rate of return exceeds the required rate of return and negative if the expected rate is less than the required rate.

If Equation (6.15) is rewritten with the expected rate, i, equal to the required rate, r, we have

$$r = (\text{POR}) \left[\frac{\text{EPS}_1}{P_0} \right] + (1 - \text{POR})[r] \qquad (6.16)$$

Rearranging Equation (6.16), the present value of the share of stock can be expressed simply as

$$P_0 = \frac{\text{EPS}_1}{r} \qquad (6.17)$$

The expression for P_0 in Equation (6.17) is the share's value if the expected rate of return on future investments equals the required rate of return. It can also be thought of as the present value of the equity-owned portion of the firm's current operations. But suppose i is not equal to r? In such cases, P_0 is higher or lower than the present value of the firm's current operations by however much the firm is expected to gain or lose on its future investments. P_0 can be expressed as the value of the firm's current operations plus the expected NPV of its future investments, or

$$P_0 = \frac{\text{EPS}_1}{r} + \text{NPVFI} \qquad (6.18)$$

where NPVFI denotes the expected NPV of the firm's future investments.

EXAMPLE ■ A financial analyst has just told you that she has analyzed the fast-hardware industry and estimates that the required rate of return for the industry is currently 15%. You are thinking of buying stock in McHandy, a company that is invested solely in this industry. If McHandy expects to earn $4.20 per share next year (which you feel represents a good estimate of the company's long-run prospects) and McHandy's stock is selling for 30½, what is the expected NPV of McHandy's future investments?

The value of McHandy's stock based on its current operations is computed to be $28.00 by applying Equation (6.17). Since the market value of the stock is $30.50, NPVFI is positive and equals $2.50. Therefore, McHandy is expected to increase its value in the future by making good future investments, ones that are expected to earn more than their required rates of return and thus have a positive NPV. ■

6.7

LIMITS TO USING THE STOCK VALUATION MODEL

At this point, a few words of caution about using the stock valuation model are appropriate. In some ways the model is true by definition—it must always hold. Mathematically, the value of a share of stock can be represented as the present value of its expected future cash flows. Unfortunately, there will always be an infinite number of combinations of parameter values that will produce a particular P_0 when they are inserted into one of the valuation equations. Thus, in this case, the problem of estimating parameters so that we can use the model is especially difficult since we can never be sure that any *one* of the parameter estimates is correct, and each one depends upon the others.

For example, suppose $D_1 = \$2.16$, $r = 15.75\%$, POR = .55, and $i = 20\%$. Then, by Equation (6.13), $g = 9\%$ and the Gordon Growth Model, by Equation (6.10), implies a fair price of $32.00 for the stock. But the same estimates for D_1 and POR, with $r = 16\%$ and $i = 20.556\%$ also imply a fair price of $32.00. If we observe a market value of $32.00, which set of parameter values is correct? Or is there yet a third set of values that are the "true" values?

AVAILABILITY OF INFORMATION   As we pointed out in Chapter 1, a major constraint on the use of any model is the ability to acquire the necessary inputs to the model—estimating the parameter values. If the necessary information cannot be obtained, the model will not be useful. In this case, the problem can be stated in mathematical terms by saying that we have too many unknowns and/or not enough equations. When we apply the model, additional information must be brought in, which is equivalent to providing additional equations. Computing historical growth rates and looking at other firms in an industry are two examples of methods of obtaining additional information. However, care must be taken because even though an application of the model may appear to be valid, an "answer" will be obtained whether or not it is valid. That is, you get an "answer" no matter what parameter values you use.

INFORMATION COST   A second major obstacle to using the stock valuation model is a corollary to the problem of information availability. The obstacle is the cost of obtaining the information needed to use the model. The value of any answer obtained from the model must be weighed against the cost of using the model. As with any model, if the cost of obtaining sufficiently accurate information is too high, the model is not worth using. In the case of publicly-traded stocks, for many investors, applying the Behavioral Principle by using the market price is the most cost-effective method of estimating a stock's true value. Also, it is a good starting point for estimating other parameter values in the valuation process.

SUMMARY

Probably the most important contribution of this chapter is the insight and understanding that is gained from exploring the relationships among the variables that affect the value of a security. The present value model can be used to determine a fair price for a security because any security can be represented as the present value of its expected future cash flows. When the future cash flows are relatively certain, as in the case of bonds, the fair price is easily determined if the security's required rate of return is known. Applying the Principle of Capital Market Efficiency, a bond's implied required rate of return, its **yield to maturity**, can be determined by equating the market price with the formula for a fair price.

In some cases, as in valuing stocks, estimating the expected future cash flows is a very difficult process. This causes difficulty in determining both the value of the security and its implied required rate of return. For a share of common stock, we established the following important points:

1. The expected future cash flows are the stock's future dividends.
2. The pattern of dividends will be determined by the firm's future earnings and the firm's dividend policy. For now, we characterized the firm's dividend policy in terms of an average payout ratio.

3. Future earnings depend upon the firm's actual rate of return, so expected future earnings depend upon the firm's expected future rate of return.

Therefore, in the final analysis, the value of a share of stock depends upon the expected future returns from the firm's investments. This is a very simple and powerful statement, but predicting the expected future returns from a firm's investments is a very difficult task. Of course, predicting the future is always a difficult task! There are analytical tools that can help you; we have described several in this chapter. Nevertheless, some events cannot be predicted. Perhaps the most important contribution the model presented in this chapter can make is to help us think about, and identify the important dimensions of, the problem of valuing a financial security. Try to keep the challenge of predicting the future in mind as you improve your understanding of the mechanics of valuing stocks and bonds by slugging through the end-of-chapter problems.

PROBLEMS

PROBLEM SET A

A1. What is a **required rate of return**?

A2. What is an **expected rate of return**?

A3. What are **coupon payments**, and what is a **coupon rate**?

A4. What is a **maturity date**?

A5. RCA made a coupon payment yesterday on its "6.25s00" bonds that mature on October 9, 2000. If the required rate of return on these bonds is 9.2% nominal annual and today is April 10, 1991, what should be the market price of these bonds?

A6. Dow made a coupon payment yesterday on its "7.75s01" bonds that mature on April 9, 2001. If the required rate of return on these bonds is 8.4% nominal annual and today is April 10, 1991, what should be the market price of these bonds?

A7. DuPont's "8.45s06" bonds closed yesterday at 103. If these bonds mature on October 9, 2006, and today is April 10, 1991, what is the yield to maturity of these bonds? What is their effective annual rate of return?

A8. GMAC's "8¾s02" bonds closed yesterday at 95¼. If these bonds mature on April 9, 2002, and today is April 10, 1991, what is the yield to maturity of these bonds? What is their effective annual rate of return?

A9. IBM's "9⅜s" bonds closed yesterday at 95⅛. If a coupon payment was made yesterday, April 9, 1991, and the yield to maturity on these bonds is 10%, when do these bonds mature?

A10. ATT's "7⅛s05" bonds closed yesterday at 92¾. If a coupon payment was made yesterday, April 9, 1991, and the yield to maturity on these bonds is 8%, when do these bonds mature?

A11. What do we mean by the term **payout ratio**?

A12. Assume that IBM is expected to pay a total cash dividend of $5.60 next year and that dividends are expected to grow at a rate of 6% per year forever. Assuming annual dividend payments, what is the current market value of a share of IBM stock if the required rate of return on IBM common stock is 10%?

A13. What required rate of return is implied by the Gordon Growth Model for a stock that is selling for $25.00 per share, and is expected to pay a single cash dividend next year of $1.80, and whose growth in dividend payments is expected to be 2% per year forever?

A14. Suppose that GM is expected to pay $4.00 in cash dividends next year at the rate of $1.00 per quarter and that the required rate of return on GM stock is 14%. If GM is currently selling for $37.50 per share, what is the expected growth rate in dividends for GM based on the Gordon Growth Model?

A15. Suppose GM has a payout ratio of 55% and an expected rate of return on its future investments of 15%. What would be GM's expected growth rate?

A16. Cite and explain three reasons why a P/E ratio may not be a reliable indicator of a stock's expected future performance.

A17. Aloada White's Laundry Co. has a 20% required rate of return and is selling for $19.50 per share. If Aloada expects to earn $3.15 per share next year, what is its NPVFI currently?

A18. Cite and discuss two important factors that limit the usefulness of the stock valuation model.

PROBLEM SET B

B1. A quick look in the NYSE bond-quote section will tell you that GMAC has many different issues of bonds outstanding. Suppose that four of them have identical coupon rates of 7¼% but mature on four different dates. One matures in 2 years, one in 5 years, one in 10 years, and the last in 20 years. Assume that they all made coupon payments yesterday.

    a. If the yield curve was flat and all four bonds had the same yield to maturity of 9%, what is the fair price of each bond today?

    b. Suppose that during the first hour of operation of the capital markets today, the term structure shifts and the yield to maturity of all these bonds changes to 10%. What is the fair price of each bond now?

    c. Suppose that in the second hour of trading, the yield to maturity of all these bonds changes once more to 8%. Now what is the fair price of each bond?

    d. Based on the price changes in response to the changes in yield to maturity, how is interest rate risk a function of the bond's maturity? That is, is interest rate risk the same for all four bonds, or does it depend on the bond's maturity?

B2. Philadelphia Electric has many bonds trading on the New York Stock Exchange. Suppose PhilEl's bonds have identical coupon rates of 9⅜% but that one issue matures in 1 year, one in 7 years, and the third in 15 years. Assume that a coupon payment was made yesterday.

    a. If the yield to maturity for all three bonds is 8%, what is the fair price of each bond?

    b. Suppose that the yield to maturity for all of these bonds changed instantaneously to 7%. What is the fair price of each bond now?

    c. Suppose that the yield to maturity for all of these bonds changed instantaneously again, this time to 9%. Now what is the fair price of each bond?

    d. Based on the fair prices at the various yields to maturity, is interest rate risk the same, higher, or lower, for longer- versus shorter- maturity bonds?

B3. Gehr's Gears, Inc. has bonds outstanding that mature in 14 years and 25 days from today. The bonds have an annual coupon rate of 15% and pay interest every 6 months. The bonds are currently selling for $1,100.

   a. Assuming a coupon payment was made yesterday and there are 29 more coupon payments remaining to be paid in the life of the bond, what is the YTM on this bond? What is the effective annual rate of return for this bond under these assumptions?

   b. Assuming a coupon payment was made yesterday and there are 28 more coupon payments remaining to be paid in the life of the bond, what is the YTM on this bond? What is the effective annual rate of return for this bond under these assumptions?

   c. Assuming a coupon payment was made, as it actually was, 155 days ago and there are 29 more coupon payments remaining to be paid in the life of the bond, what is the YTM on this bond? What is the effective annual rate of return for this bond under these assumptions?

B4. Exxon's "6s00" mature on June 13, 2000. What effective annual rate of return will you earn if these bonds are selling at 85 on April 13, 1991? What is the yield to maturity of this bond?

B5. Duke Power's "7⅜s03" bonds had a closing price of 92 yesterday, April 9, 1991. If these bonds mature on March 9, 2003, what is their yield to maturity? What is the effective annual rate of return on these bonds?

B6. Kay Patteris owns a bond that matures in 6 years and 110 days from today. The bond has an annual coupon rate of 6% and pays interest every 6 months. Currently, the bond is selling for $825.

   a. Assuming a coupon payment was made yesterday and there are 13 more coupon payments remaining to be paid in the life of the bond, what is the YTM on this bond? What is the effective annual rate of return for this bond under these assumptions?

   b. Assuming a coupon payment was made yesterday and there are 12 more coupon payments remaining to be paid in the life of the bond, what is the YTM on this bond? What is the effective annual rate of return for this bond under these assumptions?

   c. Assuming a coupon payment was made, as it actually was, 70 days ago and there are 13 more coupon payments remaining to be paid in the life of the bond, what is the YTM on this bond? What is the effective annual rate of return for this bond under these assumptions?

B7. Gebhardt Corp. has recently undertaken a major expansion project that is expected to provide growth in earnings per share of 400% within the coming year and 75% growth in each of the subsequent 3 years. After that time, normal growth of 3% per year forever is expected. The cash dividend was 10 cents per share this last year and is expected to be that amount for each of the next 5 years. In the sixth year, it is expected that the payout ratio will be 80% of the earnings per share, and the payout ratio is expected to remain at that level forever. If the required rate of return on Gebhardt common stock is 32% per year and the latest earnings per share was 25 cents, at what price should Gebhardt Corp. common stock be selling in the market?

B8. Explain in your own words why the growth rate in the Gordon Growth Model, g, cannot be larger than the required rate of return, r.

B9. Stowe-Away Travel, Inc. (Stowe) has a required rate of return of 18%, is expected to pay a dividend next year of $1.28, has a payout ratio of 50%, and is currently selling for $16.00 per share. What is Stowe's expected rate of return on future investments? What is Stowe's NPVFI?

B10. Losh Key Corporation common stock is selling for $25.00 per share with an expected cash dividend next year of $1. Short-term prospects are excellent for Losh Key: A 25% annual growth rate in dividend payments is expected for the 3 years following next year's dividend. After that, a normal growth rate of 4% per year forever is expected. What required rate of return is implied by the current $25.00 price?

B11. The copy service Quick Quality in Quantity (Q3) has a payout ratio of 80%, a required rate of return of 10%, and is expected to pay a dividend next year of $2.00. If Q3 is selling for $25 per share, what is its expected rate of return? What is Q3's NPVFI? What is the expected market value of a share of Q3 four years from now?

B12. Suppose a bond pays $90 per year forever. If the bond's required rate of return is 10.3%, what is the bond selling for in the capital markets?

PROBLEM SET C

C1. Managers of Biden-Time Co., makers of Mickey Moose watches, are currently considering suspending the company's cash dividends for the next 3 years to invest the money in a project they call Court Jesters. Biden-Time's current operations are expected to earn $.85 per share next year and with a constant payout ratio of 75% are expected to grow at 5% per year forever. Under the Court Jesters plan, earnings are expected to grow at 17% per year for the investment years. After the investment, the company expects to have a payout ratio of 70% and a growth rate in earnings of 6.5% forever. If the required rate of return on Biden-Time's stock is 20% per year, what is the NPV per share of the Court Jesters plan?

C2. The Ronald Raygun Co. currently has a payout ratio of 40% and a growth rate for its cash dividends of 5% per year. The stock has a required rate of return of 18%, and the company earned $2.20 per share this last year.

   a. What should be the current market value of a share of Raygun stock?

   b. What is the expected net present value of Raygun's future investments (NPVFI) in part a?

   c. Mr. Raygun is currently considering an expansion plan that would require all earnings to be retained for the next 4 years, so that the next cash dividend under this plan would be paid 5 years from now. Under the plan, growth in earnings is expected to be 10% per year for the next 4 years. Upon completion of the 4-year plan, the firm is expected to have the same 40% payout ratio and 5% growth rate that it has currently. Mr. Raygun is leaning toward undertaking the plan. What do you think the company should do?

   d. What is the NPVFI of Raygun's future investments under the expansion plan in part c?

   e. What is the expected rate of return on the Raygun expansion plan described in part c?

C3. A **consol** is a bond with an infinite maturity. Suppose an investment firm offered to provide you with a portfolio of consols that would pay you $10,000 per year forever, starting 10 years from today. To purchase the portfolio, you must pay the investment firm $500 per month for the next 10 years. What would be your effective annual rate of return if you undertook this opportunity?

C4. Here is a time-value-of-money puzzle for you: Suppose your professor can get you in on an investment that will pay you $280 per month for 20 months. To make this investment, you pay no money now, but you must borrow the principal amount of $2,600 from your professor's bank at 6% per month. The loan must be repaid in one lump sum at the end of the 20 months. *No prepayment of principal or interest is allowed.* Payment of both principal and interest for the loan will be $8,338.55 at the end of the 20 months. What conditions would make this loan favorable for you?

C5. Gin & Tech (G&T), a bar that caters to engineers, is about to issue new bonds. The bonds will make ten coupon payments of $200 every other year, starting 1 year from today. G&T will pay a maturity value of $1200 with the last coupon payment. If you buy one of these bonds for $1,100, what will be your effective annual rate of return?

C6. Philip Quick, owner of a chain of self-service gas stations, has several investments. One of them is 2,000 shares of Getty Oil. Getty is expected to pay a dividend next year of $2.38 and has expected growth of 6% per year forever. If Getty is selling for $19.45 per share, what is Phil's expected rate of return on Getty Oil? Another of Phil's investments is 1,200 shares of ConEdison, which has an expected growth rate in dividends of 4% per year forever, sells for $41⅞, and is expected to pay a dividend of $3.35 per share next year. What is Phil's expected rate of return on ConEdison? Now the real question: How can Phil's expected rates of return be different for these two investments? Why doesn't Phil sell the one with the lower expected rate of return and buy more of the one with the higher rate of return?

C7. Rowdy Ron's Dilapidated Diner (aka, R2D2) expects to pay a $2 dividend on its stock next year. Short-term prospects are excellent: A 20% annual growth rate in the dividend is expected for the next 3 years following the $2 dividend. After that, the annual growth rate is expected to drop to a normal 6% forever. The required rate of return for R2D2 is 14% per year, R2D2 maintains a constant payout ratio of 55%, and the stock is selling for $37 per share.

    a. Assuming the short-term growth is connected with a single project and R2D2 will invest only in projects that have a zero NPV after that project is finished, what is the NPV per share of the project?

    b. Under the same assumptions as in part a, what is the expected rate of return on the project?

C8. Explain how a positive-NPV investment enhances the value of a share of stock.

REFERENCES

Brigham, Eugene F., and James L. Pappas. "Duration of Growth, Changes in Growth Rates, and Corporate Share Prices." *Financial Analysts Journal* 22 (May-June 1966): 157–62.

Fama, Eugene F. "Components of Investment Performance." *Journal of Finance* 27 (June 1972): 551–67.

Francis, Jack Clark. *Investments: Analysis and Management.* New York: McGraw-Hill, 1986.

Fuller, Russell J., and Chi-Cheng Hsia. "A Simplified Common Stock Valuation Model." *Financial Analysts Journal* 40 (September-October 1984): 49–56.

Jacobs, Nancy L., and R. Richardson Pettit. *Investments.* Homewood, Ill.: Richard D. Irwin, 1984.

Johnson, Ramon. *Financial Valuation and Analysis.* Dubuque, Iowa: Kendall/Hunt, 1981.

Reilly, Frank K. *Investment Analysis and Portfolio Management.* Hinsdale, Ill.: Scott Foresman, 1985.

Sharpe, William F. *Investments*, 3rd ed. Englewood Cliffs, N.J.: Prentice-Hall, 1985.

Siegel, Jeremy J. "The Application of the DCF Methodology for Determining the Cost of Equity Capital." *Financial Management* 14 (Spring 1985): 46–53.

Van Horne, James C., and William F. Glassmire, Jr. "The Impact of Unanticipated Changes in Inflation on the Value of Common Stocks." *Journal of Finance* 27 (December 1972): 1081–92.

7

RISK, RETURN, AND ASSET PRICING MODELS

This chapter further explores the Principles of Finance. For example, we can build on the Principle of Self-Interested Behavior and the Principle of Risk Aversion by deriving the Principle of Diversification, which states that diversification of investments is beneficial. Building further, by introducing the Principle of Capital Market Efficiency, we can derive the Principle of Risk–Return Trade-Off, which states that in choosing among alternative investments, investors face a trade-off between risk and return. All of the analysis is done in the context of the present value model, with special attention to the discount rate.

We have told you that a required rate of return can be thought of as an opportunity cost. But suppose no comparable opportunity exists from which to estimate a required rate of return? What are the factors that determine a required rate of return? In other words, how does the market determine a required rate of return? In this chapter we derive a model for determining a required rate of return where return is expressed as a function of risk. The model expresses the required rate of return for any asset as a "base" return to a riskless asset *plus* an added return to compensate for the riskiness of the asset. By now, expressing return as a function of risk should come as no surprise, but there are some surprises when we determine what constitutes the risk of an asset. Most importantly, we will demonstrate that the risk of an asset—and therefore, as a consequence of the Principle of Risk-Return Trade-Off, its return—depends critically on how the asset's expected future cash flows covary with the composite cash flow stream for the portfolio (group) containing all investment opportunities.

7.1 PROBABILITY CONCEPTS

Since the required-rate-of-return model that we will derive draws on certain concepts and definitions from probability theory, we will begin by presenting the concepts of probability theory that we will need later. For those of you who are familiar with probability and statistics, this section and the next will serve as a brief review.

RANDOM VARIABLES

The best starting point for our discussion of risk is the notion of a **random variable**. We will present a formal definition momentarily, but first we will explain the concept. Intuitively, a random variable is a variable whose value is subject to uncertainty. For example, Exxon Corporation's earnings for next year can be modeled as a random variable. We might have some idea of what constitutes a reasonable range of possible values for this random variable, and a large number of securities analysts make their living by making educated guesses about the actual value, but we will not know for sure what outcome the earnings random variable will actually have until it occurs and it is reported.

More formally, a **random variable** is a function that assigns a real number to each and every possible outcome of a random experiment. To continue our example, the real number in question is the actual value of Exxon's earnings for next year. The earnings value reflects the result (the outcome) of Exxon's efforts in competitive markets (the random experiment).

The definition of a random variable states two important features. As its name suggests, a random variable is not perfectly predictable (i.e., it is random). In addition, a random variable *must* assign a real number to each and every possible outcome. This may seem to be a trivial point, but it is important because it enables us to quantify alternative outcomes. Consider a simple experiment like flipping a fair coin, which you have no doubt encountered before in a probability and statistics class. Suppose you flip a coin 10 times and record the outcomes as H for each heads and T for each tails. If five H's and five T's were recorded, how would you quantify the average outcome? We must define a random variable to assign values to H and T. Any two real numbers can be used. Given the two values, the average is easily computed. For example, if outcomes are denoted by the typical 0 for heads and 1 for tails, the average of the values obtained from the experiment is .5. As just noted, *any* two numbers could be used to represent heads and tails, such as 52 and 87, which, with an equal number of outcomes, gives an average of 69.5. The point to remember is that assigning a number to each possible outcome makes it possible to quantify, or in other words *model*, the financial world.

Random variables are said to be either **discrete** or **continuous**. A discrete random variable can take on only a specified discrete set of possible values; for example, 1, 2, 3, 4, 5, or 6 (the possible outcomes from the roll of a die). A continuous random variable can take on any value within a specified continuum; for example, Exxon's earnings for next year can be any value, including negative outcomes. (The fact that we round dollar amounts to the nearest penny for convenience means that the earnings random variable is only approximating a continuous random variable. But it is easier to treat it as truly continuous rather than to work with billions of discrete values!)

PROBABILITIES

If the outcome of an experiment is uncertain, we also need a means for assessing the relative likelihood of each possible outcome. We accomplish this goal by assigning a probability to each and every possible outcome. More formally, a **probability function** assigns a real number, called a **probability**, to each and every member of a specified set of outcomes of a random experiment. The probability function must satisfy two conditions: (1) each probability is nonnegative; (2) the probabilities sum to 1.0. The first condition divides the specified set of outcomes into those that are possible (positive probability) and those that are not (zero probability). The second condition ensures that the specified set of outcomes includes all possible outcomes. In practice, we will delete all zero-probability outcomes and consider only those that have a positive probability. In our coin toss example, unless we have a very unusual coin, we can ignore the possibility that the coin will land and remain on its edge.

The probability function for a discrete random variable X takes on only discrete

FIGURE 7-1
Mean value.

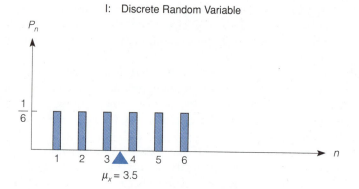

I: Discrete Random Variable

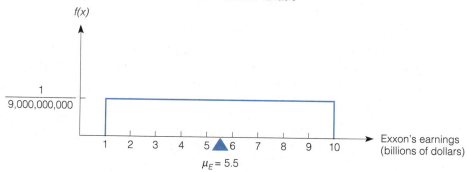

II: Continuous Random Variable

values, $p_1, p_2, \ldots, p_N$, when there are N possible outcomes. By definition, these values cannot be negative and must sum to 1.0:

$$p_n \geq 0 \text{ for all } n; \text{ and}$$

$$\sum_{n=1}^{N} p_n = 1 \qquad (7.1)$$

For example, heads and tails are equally likely if the coin is a fair coin. We would say that the probability of heads is ½ and the probability of tails is ½. Similarly for a fair die, the probability of each face occurring is ⅙. Note that both probability functions satisfy our definition. Panel I of Figure 7-1 illustrates the probability function for a discrete random variable defined as the outcome of the roll of a six-sided fair die.

The probability function for a continuous random variable X (called the **probability density function**, or *pdf*) is a function $f(x)$ defined over the continuum of possible outcomes so that $f(x) \geq 0$ for all x, and the area under the curve is 1.0:

$$\int_a^b f(x)\, dx = 1 \qquad (7.2)$$

where X can take on any value between a and b. Equations (7.1) and (7.2) are perfectly analogous to one another; integrating in the continuous case is analogous to summing in the discrete case. For example, if Exxon Corporation's earnings for next year might be anywhere within the range from $a =$ \$1 billion to $b =$ \$10 billion with equal likelihood across the range, $f(x) = 1/9,000,000,000$, and the area under $f(x)$

between a and b is easily seen to be 1. Panel II of Figure 7-1 illustrates the probability density function for this continuous random variable.

EXPECTED VALUE

Thus far, we have referred to future expected cash flows without saying precisely what we mean by **expected**. While there is certainly a general notion of what it means, a precise definition is necessary to avoid ambiguity and build an exact model.

The term **expected** refers to the **expected value**, or mathematical expectation, of a random variable (or any specified function of a random variable). Expected value may be thought of as the long-run average (mean) of any function of a random variable, the average value we would obtain if we repeated a random experiment a very large (i.e., large without bound) number of times. The expected value of a function of a discrete random variable is computed as the sum, over all possible outcomes, of each outcome for the function multiplied by the probability of its occurrence. In mathematical notation, for a function $g(X)$ of the random variable X, the expected value of $g(X)$, denoted $E[g(X)]$, is computed as

$$E[g(X)] = \sum_{n=1}^{N} p_n g(x_n) \qquad (7.3)$$

where $E[\ ]$ denotes the expected value, p_n denotes the probability of outcome n, x_n is the value of X associated with outcome n, and there are N possible outcomes. $E[g(X)]$ is the weighted average of the possible values for $g(X)$ with the probabilities p_n serving as the weights.

As an example, suppose profit for a firm equals 20% of its sales and the firm's sales can be \$1,000, \$2,000, \$3,000, or \$4,000 with equal probability (.25 each). Then, with $g(X) = .2x_n$, expected profit can be computed from Equation (7.3) as \$500 ($= .25[200] + .25[400] + .25[600] + .25[800]$).

For a continuous random variable X, the expected value of a function $g(X)$ is computed by integrating the function $g(X)$ multiplied by the probability density function $f(x)$ over the range of all possible values of X. In mathematical notation,

$$E[g(X)] = \int_a^b g(x) f(x) \, dx. \qquad (7.4)$$

Since $f(x)$ in the continuous case plays the same role as the probabilities p_n in the discrete case, we can also interpret $E[g(X)]$ in Equation (7.4) as the probability-weighted average outcome.

The expected value represents the average outcome if the process is repeated many times (literally, an infinite number of times). However, when we face only a single trial (e.g., one flip of the coin or actual realized earnings in one year), we may be concerned with the total probability distribution across all possible outcomes rather than being concerned exclusively with the expected value. This is so because in many cases, any single outcome might deviate tremendously from its expected value. For example, in the case of a single flip of a coin, an actual outcome *never* equals its expected value: With outcomes denoted 0 and 1, the expected value equals .5, which is different from both of the possible outcomes. In spite of this and other limitations, expected values are nevertheless very useful as summary measures in situations that have uncertain outcomes.

MEAN VALUE

The mean value of a random variable X (as opposed to some function of the random variable) is defined as the expected value of X itself. Mean value is usually denoted by the greek letter μ, and often subscripted by a number or letter to indicate the random variable to which the mean refers. The mean can be computed from Equation (7.3) or (7.4), depending upon whether the random variable is discrete or continuous, respectively, by setting $g(X) = X$; that is

$$\mu_x = E[X] \qquad (7.5)$$

For example, if X represents the outcome from the roll of a single die, the expected value of X is, from Equation (7.3)

$$\mu_x = E[X] = \sum_{n=1}^{6} \frac{1}{6}(n) = 3.5$$

Graphically, the mean value of a random variable locates the "weighted center" of the probability function. Figure 7-1 illustrates this concept. The expected value is like a fulcrum that balances the probability-weighted values that lie on either side of it. As a second example of the mean-value calculation, if we assume that Exxon Corporation's earnings next year might be anywhere within the range from $a = \$1$ billion to $b = \$10$ billion with equal likelihood, the expected value is $\mu = \$5.5$ billion, as illustrated in Panel II of Figure 7-1.[1]

Mean value is a very useful summary measure. When comparing two random variables, their respective mean values tell us how the random variables are expected to occur "on average."

VARIANCE AND STANDARD DEVIATION

Knowing the mean, or average value, of a random variable is only part of the story. It is also useful to know the dispersion of possible outcomes because the actual outcome is uncertain and may differ (perhaps substantially) from the mean. The **variance** of a random variable is a measure of its dispersion of possible outcomes; that is, the variance is a measure of how much the outcomes can vary above and below the mean. The variance is not the only possible measure of dispersion. For example, the **range**, the difference between the highest and lowest possible values, is another measure of dispersion.

One problem with the variance is that if we know a particular value for a variance but nothing else, the value is meaningless without additional information. For example, if we tell you that the variance of X is 100, that fact is meaningless unless you are given more information, such as 100 is the variance of prices for a television or a single compact disk. In the case of the compact disk, it would be considered large, whereas for the TV, it is a relatively small price variance.

The variance is usually denoted σ^2, and is sometimes subscripted by a number or letter to identify the random variable it refers to. The variance of X is defined as the expected value of the squared deviations from its mean, or $g(X) = (X - \mu_x)^2$, so

$$\sigma_x^2 = E[(X - \mu_x)^2] \qquad (7.6)$$

The **standard deviation** of a random variable is simply the square root of its variance. It is denoted by the greek letter σ, and is sometimes subscripted to indicate

---

[1] You can see graphically that $5.5 billion is the center of this probability density function. The mean value can be calculated by applying Equation (7.4) with $g(X) = X$, $a = \$1$ billion, and $b = \$10$ billion.

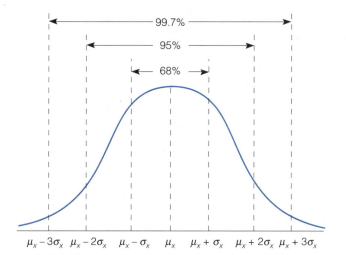

which random variable it refers to. The standard deviation is useful because it has a convenient interpretation and is measured in the same units as the mean. That is, variance is measured in units squared whereas standard deviation is measured simply in units. In the TV-CD example given above, the price variance of 100 is actually 100 dollars squared, whereas the standard deviation is $10.

Figure 7-2 illustrates the bell-shaped probability density function for what is known as the **normal random variable**. This form of probability function is frequently encountered in statistical analyses of problems in finance. When it applies, we know that there is a 68% chance (probability) that any single outcome will fall within one standard deviation (plus or minus) of the mean; there is a 95% probability that an outcome will fall within two standard deviations of the mean; and there is a 99.7% probability that an outcome will fall within three standard deviations of the mean.

COVARIANCE AND CORRELATION COEFFICIENT

Covariance is a measure of the manner and extent to which two random variables "covary." Covariance can be positive, negative, or zero. A positive covariance indicates that when one random variable has an outcome that exceeds its mean, the other random variable also tends to exceed its mean. A negative covariance indicates the reverse; a higher outcome for one random variable tends to be associated with a lower outcome for the other. A covariance equal to zero indicates that a simple pairing of outcomes does not reveal any regular pattern. At the risk of causing confusion, we feel we should point out that a covariance of zero does not rule out the possibility that there is a systematic relationship between the two random variables that may be very complex. A zero covariance indicates only that the process of pairing outcomes will not reveal a simple systematic relationship between the random variables.

The covariance of two random variables, say X and Y, is usually denoted as $\text{cov}(X, Y)$, or sometimes σ_{xy}. It is computed as the expected value of the product of their deviations from their means, or $g(X, Y) = (X - \mu_x)(Y - \mu_y)$, so

$$\text{covariance} = \text{cov}(X, Y) = \sigma_{xy} = E[(X - \mu_x)(Y - \mu_y)] \qquad (7.7)$$

The value calculated for the covariance between two random variables is sensitive to the particular units in which each random variable is measured. The **correlation**

coefficient removes this sensitivity to units of measurement. While covariance can take on any value, the correlation coefficient can take on only values between minus 1 and plus 1. The correlation coefficient is usually denoted by the greek letter ρ, and is sometimes subscripted to indicate the pair of random variables to which it refers. The correlation coefficient equals the covariance divided by the product of the individual standard deviations, or

$$\rho_{xy} = \frac{\text{cov}(X, Y)}{\sigma_x \sigma_y} \tag{7.8}$$

Dividing by the respective standard deviations causes the units of measurement in the numerator and denominator to cancel out, leaving ρ unit-free.[2]

STANDARD PROBABILITY DISTRIBUTIONS AND MODEL BUILDING

You probably recall from your past course work that there are quite a few "standard" probability distributions, such as the normal probability distribution, which is characterized by the bell-shaped probability function illustrated in Figure 7-2. Others include the binomial, student's-t, exponential, chi-square, and poisson. These standard probability distributions are useful in building mathematical models.

Suppose we want to model a particular stock's rate of return. We can compute actual return outcomes for the stock over time and use that empirically observed distribution as the basis for our model. In that case, every stock will have a slightly different return distribution that is based on the particular sample observed for that stock over the observation period. But if we can use a standard type of distribution to represent each stock's return, then we can model the returns simply, by estimating the parameter values that characterize that distribution rather than enumerating a large and cumbersome sample of outcomes. For example, mean and variance (or its square root, standard deviation) completely characterize the normal probability distribution. With just these two parameter values, we can draw precisely the bell-shaped curve in Figure 7-2. If a stock's rate of return follows a normal probability distribution—and prior studies have demonstrated that the normal probability distribution is a reasonable approximation of the true distribution in certain cases[3]—then complete information about the variability of a stock's return can be determined once the mean and variance have been specified. In other words, if stock returns are normally distributed and we know the mean and variance for the distribution, we know *all* there is to know about the stock's return. That is a very powerful and very useful statement.

Parameterizing standard probability distributions that have known mathematical relationships provides us with the power to generalize, which, if you recall from Chapter 1, is a primary goal of science. Statistics enters the process when the model is operationalized. We can use the tools of statistics to estimate parameter values. For

[2] The correlation coefficient also provides a measure of *linearity* between the two random variables. That is, ρ measures how well one random variable can be approximated by a linear function of the other random variable. In the extreme, when ρ is either $+1$ or -1, either random variable can be expressed as a perfect linear function of the other. Therefore, if $\rho = \pm 1$, when we know an outcome of X we can compute the corresponding outcome for Y from the function $Y = mX + b$, where m is the slope coefficient and b is the intercept, both of which are known constants. Keep in mind, however, that there may be complex nonlinear functions for the relationship between X and Y, despite ρ being small or even equal to zero.
[3] More accurately, stock rates of return tend to follow what is called a **lognormal probability distribution**; the logarithm of the continuously compounded rate of return (as well as the logarithm of the share price) follows a normal probability distribution.

example, the sum of all the outcomes divided by the number of outcomes is a well-known statistic called the **mean of the sample**, which we use to infer the mean of the underlying probability distribution. In the balance of this chapter we will take parameter values such as the mean and standard deviation as given and concentrate our discussion on developing the financial concepts that we will need later in the book. We will disregard the statistical work, often difficult and time-consuming, that goes into estimating such parameter values in practice.

THE EXPECTED RETURN OF AN INVESTMENT   7.2

The rate of return from an asset over any past time period can be computed from actual outcomes. But how can we specify a single value to represent the expected *future* rate of return from the asset when there is uncertainty about the future outcomes? One possibility is to use the expected value of the rate of return. Recall that there is a drawback to using the expected value: While it is the average outcome if the experiment is repeated an infinite number of times, often you can only get *one* of those outcomes. That is, if you own an asset for the next year, the asset will provide you with a single realized (actual) rate of return, which may turn out to be positive, zero, or negative, and may be very different from the mean of its possible outcomes for the next year. Once an outcome for that year has occurred, the experiment is not repeated. (Although the second year can be in some sense a repeat, conditions may have changed so that the possible outcomes for the second year are quite different from those of the first year.) Thus, if you have the good fortune or misfortune of having a good or bad outcome, after the fact it does not really matter what the expected value was.

In spite of the drawback noted above, investment decisions must be made before the outcome is known. The **law of large numbers** states that with a sufficient number of investments, the good and bad outcomes tend to cancel each other out, and the average of the outcomes will approximate the mean more and more closely as the number of investments increases.[4] It is in this sense that the expected value is a good measure of the expected future outcome when you make investments. We define the expected future outcome from an investment in an asset in the following manner:

DEFINITION

The **expected future rate of return** of an asset is the expected value (mathematical expectation) of its future possible rates of return.

THE RISK OF AN INVESTMENT   7.3

Risk can be defined in many ways. But for our purposes, risk must be quantified if we are going to allow for it properly in a mathematical model. We know of no definition that is universally accepted, but we will use a widely accepted definition.

When thinking about what constitutes risk, people usually come up with two no-

---

[4]Literally, the law of large numbers states that the mean of the outcomes approaches the expected value in the limit (i.e., as the number of trials increases without bound).

tions: (1) Uncertainty about the outcome, and (2) the possibility of what might be called a **negative outcome**. By the term **negative outcome** we mean an outcome that is truly distasteful. Failing to win a lottery is not a good outcome, but it is doubtful that people think of not winning a lottery as a serious setback. So most people do not think of buying a lottery ticket as a risky investment. Without intending to encourage you to participate, or dissuade you from participating in a lottery, we again point out that although it is not particularly risky, lottery tickets are negative-NPV investments because the expected value of the prize is less than the cost of the ticket. After all, the government or other organization running the lottery takes out some of the money paid for tickets.

A good definition of **risk**, then, should include a measure of variability and a measure of the possibility of negative outcomes. The standard deviation of the rate of return reflects variability both above and below the mean return. So, strictly speaking, the standard deviation is not as good a measure of risk as it might otherwise be since something with a relatively large standard deviation of the rate of return, like a lottery ticket, may be interpreted as having a large degree of risk when it is not really very risky. However, when an asset has a rate-of-return distribution that is approximately symmetrical around the mean, as the normal distribution is, it will always be the case that the larger the standard deviation, the riskier the investment.

In spite of its apparent shortcomings, the standard deviation of the rate of return (standard deviation for short) is a relatively good measure of risk, for several reasons. First, rate-of-return distributions tend to be approximately symmetrical. Second, existing empirical evidence indicates that using other measures of risk that appear to be conceptually superior to the standard deviation does not produce better descriptions or empirical approximations of rates of return, even though such methods are more complex and costlier to apply. Therefore, as a practical matter, standard deviation is a good indicator of risk. Finally, the theoretical models of required rates of return developed here, which incorporate standard deviation as the risk measure, are well known and provide a good starting point for understanding the important components of a required rate of return. We define the risk of an investment in the following manner:

DEFINITION

The standard deviation of the rate of return on total investment measures the **risk** of the total investment.

7.4   INVESTMENT PORTFOLIOS

With respect to investment returns, an important distinction needs to be made between the rate of return earned on an individual asset and the rate of return earned on a *set* of assets. While no one wants a low return on any asset, given a choice between a high return on a particular asset and a high return on the total set of assets, investors would prefer a high return on the *set* of assets. The distinction becomes important because the manner and extent to which the rates of return on the assets that compose the set covary with one another, as well as the risk of each asset, affect overall portfolio risk.

A set of assets is called a **portfolio**. The overriding concern for investors is the rate of return on, and risk of, the portfolio rather than the rates of return from the individual assets that make up the portfolio. Portfolio risk measures the investor's total exposure to risk. Of course the expected rate of return and risk of a portfolio are functions of the expected returns and risks of the individual assets, but what kind of functions? To explore the relationship between the portfolio's risk/return and the risks/returns of the individual assets, we will start by examining a simple portfolio made up of only two assets.

TWO-ASSET PORTFOLIOS

Denote the rate of return to asset 1 as X_1 with expected return μ_1 and standard deviation σ_1, and denote the return to asset 2 as X_2 with expected return μ_2 and standard deviation σ_2. Consider a portfolio containing the two assets that has a proportion w_1 of portfolio value invested in asset 1 and the remainder $(1 - w_1)$ invested in asset 2. The expected rate of return to the portfolio, μ_p, is

$$\mu_p = E[w_1 X_1 + (1 - w_1) X_2] = E[w_1 X_1] + E[(1 - w_1) X_2]$$
$$= w_1 \mu_1 + (1 - w_1)\mu_2 \tag{7.9}$$

Equation (7.9) states that the expected rate of return on the portfolio is simply the combination of the expected returns to the individual assets, weighted by the proportions of money invested in each asset. So the portfolio's expected return is a well-behaved function (more specifically, a linear function) of the expected returns from the individual assets. However, the portfolio's risk is related to the risk of the individual assets in a more complex fashion.

The standard deviation of the return to the portfolio, denoted σ_p, is the square root of the variance of the portfolio:

$$\sigma_p = \{E[(\{w_1 \mu_1 + (1 - w_1)\mu_2\} - \{w_1 X_1 + (1 - w_1) X_2\})^2]\}^{1/2}$$
$$= \{w_1^2 \sigma_1^2 + (1 - w_1)^2 \sigma_2^2 + 2w_1(1 - w_1)\rho\sigma_1\sigma_2\}^{1/2} \tag{7.10}$$

where ρ denotes the correlation coefficient between the rates of return on the two assets. So, in the case of risk, the standard deviation of the portfolio is not a simple weighted average of the standard deviations of the individual assets. (There is a single exception to this statement, which will be explored later.)

To explore how the expected returns and risks of individual assets combine to create the expected return and risk of a portfolio, consider our two-asset portfolio further. Figure 7-3 graphs the two assets in terms of expected return on the vertical

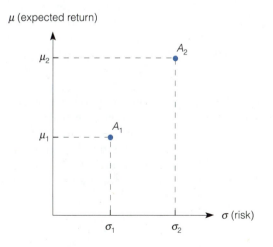

FIGURE 7-3
Asset 1 and asset 2.

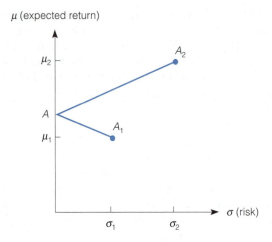

axis and risk (standard deviation) on the horizontal axis. If all the money is invested in either asset 1 or asset 2, the portfolio investment will be at A_1 or A_2, respectively. But of particular interest is the case where a positive fraction of the portfolio is invested in each asset. Equation (7.9) expresses the relationship between the expected returns to the assets and the expected return to the portfolio, and Equation (7.10) expresses the relationship between the risks of the assets and the risk of the portfolio. We can explore the combined effect of Equations (7.9) and (7.10) by putting in a value for the correlation coefficient, ρ, and looking at all possible values for w_1 between 0 and 1. We first consider three special cases: $\rho = -1.0$, $\rho = +1.0$, and $\rho = 0$.

PERFECT NEGATIVE CORRELATION   Consider first the case where $\rho = -1.0$. Figure 7-4 graphs the portfolio risk-return combinations given by Equations (7.9) and (7.10) for $0.0 \le w_1 \le 1.0$ when $\rho = -1.0$. Setting $\rho = -1.0$, Equation (7.10) can be reduced to

$$\sigma_\rho = w_1(\sigma_1 + \sigma_2) - \sigma_2 \qquad (7.11)$$

The most interesting thing about the case illustrated in Figure 7-4 is that it is possible to invest in the two risky assets so that the risk of the portfolio is actually zero. Since the two assets are perfectly negatively correlated, when the realized rate of return of asset 1 is high, the realized rate of return of asset 2 is low, and vice versa. When asset 1 has a medium return, asset 2 also has a medium return. Therefore, when the two assets are combined in the proportions represented by portfolio A in Figure 7-4, high and low returns always cancel each other out exactly. The portfolio earns the same rate of return every period. The idea that you might be able to invest in two assets, both of which are risky, and yet have your total investment be riskless is not at all intuitive. Harry Markowitz pointed out this phenomenon in 1952 and started a revolution in the way people think about investing.[5]

Figure 7-4 illustrates the special case in which the minimum value of portfolio risk is $\sigma_p = 0.0$. When $\rho = -1.0$, we can determine analytically the exact proportions to invest in the two risky assets, w_1 and $(1 - w_1)$ so that the portfolio is riskless. These proportions can be derived simply by setting Equation (7.11) to zero and solving for w_1. (This task is problem A19 at the end of this chapter.) In the more general case, where $-1.0 < \rho < +1.0$, the minimum value of σ_p is not already known.

[5] Markowitz (1952).

For the general case, the minimum point of the function, Equation (7.10), can be found with the aid of calculus.[6]

So what can we say in general about how to invest in two risky securities when $\rho = -1.0$? Individuals may have specific preferences about investments, but would you invest all your money in asset 1? Of course not. By investing at least some of your money in asset 2, you can earn a higher expected return with less risk. Look again at Figure 7-4. The line AA_2 *dominates* the line AA_1 because there is a point on AA_2 that has the same risk but higher return for every point on AA_1. Therefore, we have our first generalization about how to invest:

GENERALIZATION 1

When $\rho = -1.0$, *never* invest all of your money in the lower-return–less-risky asset.

Of course, people willing to take more risk may want to invest all their money in asset 2. Because of this, our generalization may seem somewhat limited. But Generalization 1 is a first step in building *general rules for investment* that apply to *everyone*.

Are there two securities to invest in that are perfectly negatively correlated? No, not that we know of. So let's consider some other cases that are more interesting because they are more realistic. But keep our starting point in mind because we are going to build on it.

PERFECT POSITIVE CORRELATION   Unlike the first case, it is both realistic and easy to find two assets that have perfect positive correlation between their rates of return. A simple example of such a situation is two identical securities, such as two shares of common stock in the same company. When $\rho = +1.0$, Equation (7.10) can be reduced to $\sigma_p = w_1\sigma_1 + (1 - w_1)\sigma_2$. In this case the risk of the portfolio *is* a simple weighted average of the risks of the individual securities. This, of course, is the single exception we mentioned earlier to our statement that the risk of the portfolio is not a simple linear function of the risk of the individual assets.

The possible expected returns to portfolio combinations for values of w_1 between 0.0 and 1.0 when $\rho = +1.0$ are shown in Figure 7-5. They form a straight line between A_1 and A_2. So while it is realistic to have two assets that have perfect positive correlation between their returns, this case really isn't very interesting either, because portfolio risk is simply a weighted average of the individual securities' respective risks. As a consequence, there is no portfolio interaction, and thus there is no useful investment generalization we can make from it.

ZERO CORRELATION   The case where $\rho = 0.0$ is depicted in Figure 7-6. It is somewhat like the perfect negative correlation case in that the same generalization can be made in this case even though it is not possible to create a riskless portfolio with just these two assets. That is, since the line of possible combinations moves from A_1 up and to the left (the "hook"), there is a set of combinations that is domi-

---

[6]Take the derivative of the equation with respect to the decision variable (in this case, w_1), set it equal to zero, and solve for w_1. To check that you have determined a minimum (as opposed to a maximum) show that the second derivative is positive at that point. (A negative second derivative at the point of interest would identify a maximum value of the function.)

FIGURE 7-5
Perfect positive correlation,
$\rho = +1.0$.

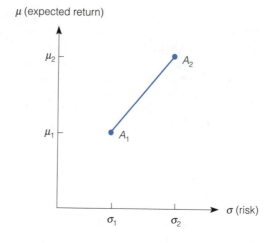

FIGURE 7-6
Zero correlation, $\rho = 0.0$.

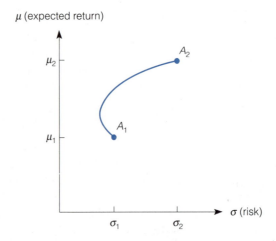

nated by other possible combinations. Again, Generalization 1 holds for *everyone*: Never invest all your money in the lower-return–less-risky asset.

PosITIVE CORRELATION   Having treated the three special cases, we now consider what happens to the portfolio risk-return combinations when the correlation coefficient is positive but not equal to 1.0. This case is typical and leads us to more interesting generalizations than the three special cases could about how you should invest your money. If we start with Figure 7-6 ($\rho = 0.0$) and make ρ increasingly positive, the "hook" from A_1 will gradually disappear as ρ becomes increasingly positive. Figure 7-7 shows the curve linking all possible combinations of portfolio risk and return for assets 1 and 2 when $\rho = .4$. Notice that the curve is not a straight line. Compared with $w_1 = 1.0$ (all the money invested in asset 1), a portfolio with $w_1 = .5$ has an expected return exactly halfway between the expected returns of assets 1 and 2 but has a standard deviation that is only about one-fifth the way toward asset 2 from asset 1. Think about that. The trade-off between how much expected return you get and how much risk you take on is more favorable to the investor in the area where $w_1 > .5$ than it is where $w_1 < .5$. In mathematical terms, the slope is greater when w_1 is close to 1.0 and smaller when w_1 is close to zero. We can also look

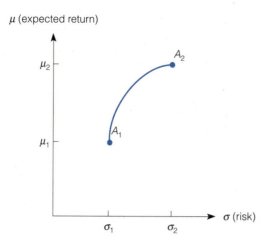

FIGURE 7-7
Positive correlation, $\rho = 0.4$.

at the investment possibilities by starting with $w_1 = 0.0$ (all the money invested in asset 2): By investing half of the money in asset 1, risk can be decreased 80% of the way toward σ_1, but expected return decreases only half the way toward μ_1.

While some people may be so risk averse that they would not invest anything in asset 2 and others may have such little risk aversion that they want to invest all their money in asset 2, many people will find it attractive to diversify.

GENERALIZATION 2

When asset returns are not perfectly positively correlated, diversification can increase the ratio of the expected rate of return on the portfolio to the risk of the portfolio.

In other words, Generalization 2 states that when asset returns are not perfectly positively correlated, diversification can change the risk-return trade-off among our set of possible investments as we move along the curve in Figure 7-7.

PORTFOLIOS WITH MORE THAN TWO ASSETS: AN EXPANDED FRAMEWORK

We have considered some of the interesting things that happen when two assets are combined in a portfolio. The number of assets was restricted to two to keep things simple. But portfolios can have any number of assets in them with an infinite number of proportions of money invested in each asset. To expand our thinking, imagine all of the various stocks that are publicly-traded frequently on the NYSE, the AMEX, or through the National Association of Securities Dealers Automated Quotation (NASDAQ) system as representing all the possible assets we can invest in. That gives us more than 8,000 assets. In addition to these individual assets, we can form an infinite number of portfolios containing different proportions of these 8,000 assets (stocks).

While it is impossible to list all of the possible asset combinations, we can show you what the set of risk-return combinations looks like based on numerical estima-

FIGURE 7-8
All possible combinations
of risky assets.

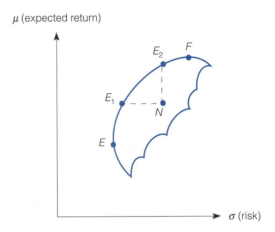

tions of actual rates of return from stocks. Figure 7-8 shows what the set of returns of all possible portfolios of stocks looks like. (It reminds us of an umbrella without a handle.)

As before, the important concern is What can we say about how investors, regardless of anything specific to them, should invest their money when they face this set of investment alternatives? Should they invest in portfolio N shown in Figure 7-8, which lies in the middle of the "umbrella"? No, because they can instead invest in portfolio E_1, which has the same expected return but lower risk. Or, they can invest in portfolio E_2, which has the same risk but a higher expected return. This same criticism can be made of any portfolio that does not have the highest possible expected return for a given risk level. Or, equivalently, any portfolio that does not have the lowest risk for a given expected return level. Clearly this set of portfolios— the ones on the curve between points E and F—is more "interesting" than the others, and so this set is referred to by a particular name, the **efficient frontier**.

DEFINITION

The **efficient frontier** is the set of portfolios that have the highest expected rate of return for a given level of risk (or equivalently, the lowest risk for a given expected rate of return).

The concept of an efficient frontier brings us to our next important generalization. If you are going to invest in the stock market, in *which* portfolios should you consider investing? Regardless of how much or how little risk you are willing to take, when this "umbrella" represents all of your alternative investments, you should invest somewhere on the efficient frontier.

GENERALIZATION 3

Never invest your money in a portfolio that lies below the efficient frontier.

A RISKLESS ASSET   7.5

What traits would a riskless asset possess? In the world we are modeling, a riskless asset is simply an asset with a zero standard deviation. That is to say, there is no uncertainty about the rate of return the asset will provide in the next time period; the realized rate of return will always equal the expected return. Is there such an asset? Literally, no. Among other possibilities, there is some chance that the obligor, regardless of who it is (even the U.S. government) might fail to make timely payment.[7] But for practical purposes, some investments have a small enough standard deviation to be considered "riskless." Most financial economists think of U.S. government 90-day Treasury bills as riskless investments because they regard the risk of default by the U.S. Treasury as negligible. Although such investments are not *literally* riskless, we will go along with the majority and assume them to be essentially riskless.[8]

INVESTING IN THE RISKLESS ASSET

Surprisingly, the existence of a riskless asset allows us to generalize further about how everyone should invest their money in *risky* assets. Combining our investment in a risky portfolio of assets with investment in a riskless asset resembles the two-asset portfolio problem we have already examined, so we can draw on what we have already learned about two-asset portfolios. However, please carefully identify the items we refer to: asset 1 is the riskless asset; asset 2 is a risky portfolio; and the total portfolio is a combination of asset 1 (the riskless asset) and asset 2 (the risky portfolio).

Equations (7.9) and (7.10) again provide us with expressions for the expected rate of return and standard deviation of the return from the total portfolio, but Equation (7.10) can be further simplified. With $\sigma_1 = 0.0$, as is the case for a riskless asset, Equation (7.10) reduces to

$$\sigma_p = \{(1 - w_1)^2 \sigma_2^2\}^{.5} = (1 - w_1)\sigma_2 \qquad \textbf{(7.12)}$$

Equation (7.12) shows that the risk of the total portfolio (the combination of the riskless asset and the risky portfolio), σ_p, is a simple linear function of the risk of asset 2 (the risky portfolio), σ_2. Therefore, whatever risky portfolio we choose for asset 2, the set of all possible total portfolio risk–return combinations of asset 1 and asset 2 forms a straight line between the riskless asset and the chosen risky portfolio. Figure 7-9 depicts this relationship for an arbitrarily chosen risky portfolio, N, from among our "umbrella set" of all possible portfolios. The most interesting point about this new set of possible investment combinations is that some of the possible combinations along the line from the rate of return to the riskless asset, r_f, to the rate of return to N dominate a part of the efficient frontier! The problem is further complicated because how much of the efficient frontier is dominated depends on our choice of N. This brings us to the next logical question: Is there a risky portfolio that is the best one to choose? Yes.

---

[7] You never know—the earth might be destroyed by a huge meteorite during the next period.
[8] Recall that we noted in Chapter 6 that United States government bonds are not perfectly riskless because of inflation risk; 90-day Treasury bills simply have a short enough life that the inflation risk is small enough to be ignored.

FIGURE 7-9
Combinations involving a risky
portfolio and the riskless asset.

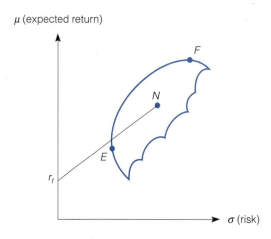

FIGURE 7-10
Combinations involving the best
risky portfolio and the riskless
asset.

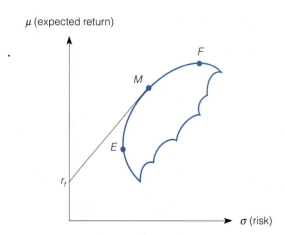

CHOOSING THE BEST RISKY PORTFOLIO

Figure 7-9 suggests the following decision rule, which builds on the notion of domi-
nating some portion of the efficient frontier: Choose the risky portfolio that dominates the largest portion of the efficient frontier.[9] If we follow this rule, the best risky
portfolio is the one that produces a line of combinations tangent to the efficient frontier. This best risky portfolio is called M. Figure 7-10 depicts combinations of M and
the riskless asset that take us to our next generalization:

GENERALIZATION 4

Always invest part of your money in the tangent portfolio M and the rest in the
riskless asset unless you are willing to take on more risk than the risk of the
tangent portfolio.

---

[9] This criterion is not arbitrary. We show later that it leads to a set of combinations that dominate the
efficient frontier everywhere except for equivalence at one point.

As with the other generalizations, the important thing about Generalization 4 is that it applies to everyone. Under the conditions we have modeled thus far, you should invest *your* money this way. The proportions you invest in the riskless asset and *M* are determined by your willingness to take on risk, but the choice of *M* is the same for everyone except those who are willing to take on more risk than they would take on by investing all their money in *M*. That means that a large number of people will want to invest some of their money in the risky portfolio, *M*. Further generalizations about how everyone should invest their money are possible if we introduce the opportunity to borrow money to invest.

BORROWING AND PORTFOLIO SEPARATION

The idea of borrowing can be introduced into the model by representing the borrowed amount as a *negative* proportion invested in the riskless asset (asset 1). That is, in our two-asset portfolio model, the investor is borrowing money to invest when w_1 is negative. This idea is tantamount to saying that what we owe you is negative to us but positive to you. The person loaning the money is investing in the borrower, so the borrowed amount is simply a negative investment. (The Principle of Two-Sided Transactions strikes again!)

One problem with using negative values for w_1 to represent a borrowed amount is that the implied borrowing rate of interest is the same as the lending rate of interest. At first, this is a very bothersome assumption to people because they know that when they go to a bank or similar institution, the bank posts a higher rate for borrowing and lower rate for lending (the rate paid on deposits). Different borrowing and lending rates are certainly a fact of life for most of us. However, consider large investors such as corporations. Many corporations invest and borrow in the commercial paper market. One day a corporation is a lender, but the next day that same corporation may be a borrower. The commercial paper rate is generally quoted as a single rate. In our model, we can quote a single rate for the borrowing and lending rate because one component of the differential between the borrowing and lending rates in practice is the financial intermediary's charge for transacting in small amounts. In other words, one part of the financial intermediary's profit is simply a charge for providing the service (a transaction cost) of separating large amounts into small amounts or putting small amounts together to make large amounts. Therefore, assuming the borrowing rate to be equal to the lending rate is for the most part equiva-

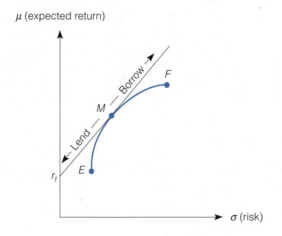

FIGURE 7-11
Combinations involving the riskless asset and lending and borrowing.

lent to assuming costless transactions, and markets in which transactions are costless are a good approximation of efficient capital markets.

Allowing w_1 to be negative requires no change in Equations (7.9) and (7.10). So when the possibility of borrowing (negative investment in asset 1) is added to the model, the line of investment possibilities is simply extended past M, continuing to climb with the same slope. Figure 7-11 depicts the line linking possible investment combinations when borrowing at the riskless rate is possible. It is called the **capital market line**, or CML. The CML intersects the efficient frontier at M and dominates the efficient frontier everywhere else. Figure 7-11 leads to another important generalization:

GENERALIZATION 5

Invest your money in the risky portfolio, M, and set the return and risk levels of your total investment by lending or borrowing to achieve your most desired position along the CML.

This is a very powerful statement. In fact, one implication of Generalization 5 is so important that like other important concepts, it has its own name. This implication is called the **portfolio separation theorem**, and it is usually stated as follows:

PORTFOLIO SEPARATION THEOREM

The choice of portfolio to invest in is not based on the investor's attitude toward risk.

Instead of choosing risky assets on the basis of your attitude toward risk, you should invest your money in M, the portfolio that creates an investment opportunities line that runs from the rate of return on the riskless asset and is tangent to the efficient frontier. The amount of risk you take on, and its commensurate return, is determined by your positive or negative investment in the riskless asset. This is a very different basis for investing from those people employed prior to the development of modern portfolio theory. When you really think about it, this is a startling approach to picking investments, and it is extremely unlikely that anyone would arrive at such an approach intuitively. A careful modeling of the world of stock investments by Harry Markowitz and William Sharpe produced surprising conclusions that began a revolution in the way the world thinks about investing.[10] And there is more. Generalization 5 states that everyone should invest in the risky portfolio M. But what is M?

THE MARKET PORTFOLIO

In the model derived thus far, everyone invests in the same set of risky assets. Thus, everyone owns a portion of every asset that is in this special portfolio M. Any asset

---

[10] Markowitz (1952); Sharpe (1964).

available in the market that is not in M cannot have an owner since everyone owns a part of the same set of assets. But every asset that is available in the market must have an owner, so every asset must be included in M. Therefore, M includes every asset that is available in the market and is called the **market portfolio**, which is why it is denoted M, for "market." In this model of the world, then, investors invest some money in every asset available. In other words, each investor completely diversifies his ownership of risky assets by owning some of everything. But what proportion of your money should be invested in each asset? This question is more easily analyzed with a simple example of a market rather than the stock market with its more than 8,000 stocks.

Consider a market with three risky assets, 1, 2, and 3, worth $100, $200, and $300, respectively. Suppose there are two investors, A and B, investing $450 and $150 each in the risky portfolio M with the rest of their money invested in the riskless asset. Investor A owns 75% of this market of risky assets, and B owns 25% of the market, so A owns 75% of each asset and B owns 25% of each asset. The investors own an identical mix of assets, but what proportion of each investor's portfolio is invested in asset 1? The answer is one-sixth because asset 1 is $100/$600, or one-sixth, of the total value of this market of risky assets. If an investor C decides to invest in this market, C should invest one-sixth of her money in asset 1, one-third ($200/$600) in asset 2, and one-half ($300/$600) in asset 3. In this way, C would be investing in the market portfolio for this market.

If we translate our three-asset example into a large market of risky assets like the stock market, the principle for determining the market portfolio is the same, but the tricky part is identifying the analogous value of each asset. An asset's value is not the market value *per share* but the market value of all the stock in a corporation. That is, the asset value to use in determining the proper investment proportions is the market value per share multiplied by the number of shares the corporation has outstanding. For example, if IBM is selling for $150 per share and there are 100 million shares of IBM, the stock market value of IBM is $15 billion. To determine the proportion of money to invest in each stock, first sum the stock market values of all the corporations in the market; then the corporation's stock market value divided by the sum of all stock market values is the proportion of the portfolio to invest in the stock. Continuing our hypothetical example of IBM, if the sum of the values for all stocks was $2 trillion, M would contain .75% ($15 billion divided by $2 trillion) invested in IBM stock.

If determining proportions to invest in each stock sounds tedious, that is because it would be! Fortunately, when such information is valuable to one set of people, other people apply the Principle of Valuable Ideas and recognize the potential to make a positive-NPV investment by producing the information for a profit or by creating investment funds that approximate the market portfolio. Currently, information about the composition of the market portfolio can be purchased from a variety of information services. In addition, a number of investment managers and mutual fund providers have created so-called stock index funds, which invest in a portfolio of common stocks that matches the composition of the Standard & Poor's 500 Index, a diversified collection of common stocks that is generally accepted as a good proxy for the (common stock) market. For example, the oldest and largest such fund, the Wells Fargo Equity Index Fund, had approximately $16 billion under management at year-end 1989.

The real value of deriving this portfolio model, in our opinion, is to identify the determinants of the value of an asset. With that in mind, it may be somewhat surprising to learn that a major determinant of the value of a stock, or any asset for that matter, is the correlation between its rate of return and the rate of return to the market portfolio. Other major determinants of value include market imperfections, such as tax or informational asymmetries, and innovative ideas that have positive or negative NPV (the Principle of Valuable Ideas).

7.6   THE CAPITAL ASSET PRICING MODEL

We have described how to construct portfolios and explained how to evaluate their returns. We will now take a closer look at how to evaluate the returns of the individual securities that compose the market portfolio. We will show you that, as you might already expect on the basis of our discussion thus far, the returns to a particular security are tied to the security's incremental contribution to the riskiness of the market portfolio.

Generalization 5 prescribes a rule for investing in risky assets when the return to the investor is defined as the expected value of the future rate of return and risk is defined to be the standard deviation of that expected return. The prescribed line of investment possibilities, called the CML (capital market line) and depicted in Figure 7-11, defines the risk-return combinations that an investor can achieve by combining an investment in the market portfolio with lending or borrowing at the riskless rate. In the middle 1960s, several financial economists working independently on generalizations about investing in portfolios asked the question How does an individual stock's return contribute to the makeup of the capital market line?[11] In other words, can the required rate of return of an individual security be determined from the CML? The answer is yes, the model can be inverted to identify the determinants of the required rate of return of each security in the market. The resulting model is a particularly simple one in which the risk premium depends only on the correlation between the security's return and the return on the market portfolio.

THE SECURITY MARKET LINE

There are two critical assumptions we need to make in order to accomplish the inversion of the model: (1) the capital markets are perfect, and (2) they are in equilibrium. In Chapter 4, we defined several conditions that had to be satisfied for a market to be perfect. We noted in Chapter 5 that these conditions are equivalent to assuming that the capital markets are arbitrage-free, that is, that there are no opportunities for a riskless arbitrage profit. We also noted that the capital markets are efficient as a consequence of their being arbitrage-free. Thus, once again, we apply the Principle of Capital Market Efficiency: The capital markets are efficient, so the expected rates of return must equal the required rates of return. If you recall our statements in the previous chapter on required and expected rates, we said there is no better estimate of the market value of, or the required return of, a particular stock than the one we observe in the market. However, if we can identify the determinants of a required rate of return, then we can create an estimate for the required rate of return of a stock or asset that is *not currently observable* in the market for risky assets.

To accomplish the inversion of the CML and determine the required rate of return of a security j, we need the market portfolio M and the individual security j, and we

---

[11] It is likely that others were working on this same question but, in particular, William Sharpe, John Lintner, and Jan Mossin published papers on this question in 1964, 1965, and 1966, respectively, and Jack Treynor wrote an article in the same period that never appeared in a journal. The published papers are included in the references at the end of the chapter.

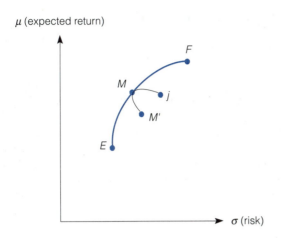

μ (expected return)

σ (risk)

FIGURE 7-12
Risk-return combinations involving portfolios M, M', and security j.

introduce into the model one other portfolio, M'. M' is defined to be identical to M *except that* M' does not include an investment in security j. We can again apply the two-asset portfolio approach. This time, we are examining the two-asset combinations that can be made by combining M' and j. The important thing we know in this case is that the curve linking possible risk-return combinations associated with M' and j includes, at one point, the market portfolio M. This must be the case because the market portfolio M must include security j. In particular, the market portfolio lies on the efficient frontier, so it must include the optimal (i.e., highest expected return for a given level of risk) combination of portfolio M' and security j.

Figure 7-12 depicts the risk-return combinations involving j, M', and M. At the point M, the slope of the line of possible combinations connecting j and M' must equal the slope of the CML. Note that because the market portfolio M includes security j and lies on the efficient frontier, the curve $M'Mj$ (joining M', M, and j) cannot lie outside the curve EMF (joining E, M, and F). Also, the curves $M'Mj$ and EMF can only intersect at the point M because at that point portfolio M contains the optimal mix of M' and j. Other combinations of M' and j are suboptimal and hence must lie under the efficient frontier.

The slope of the CML is the difference between μ_m and r_f, or $\mu_m - r_f$, divided by the difference between the σ_m and σ_f, which is σ_m since σ_f equals zero. In other words, the slope of the CML is its rise over its run, or

$$\text{CML slope} = \frac{(\mu_m - r_f)}{\sigma_m} \qquad (7.13)$$

The slope of the curve $M'Mj$ at the point M can be obtained with the aid of calculus (by taking the derivative of the function $\mu = f(\sigma)$ at that point), but we will spare you the mathematical details.

$$\text{slope of } M'Mj \text{ at the point } M = \frac{(\mu_j - \mu_m)\sigma_m}{\text{cov}(j,m) - \sigma_m^2} \qquad (7.14)$$

Both of the curves pass through the point M, and at M they have identical slopes. Therefore, we can set Equation (7.13) equal to Equation (7.14) and solve for μ_j. In other words, we can determine the required/expected rate of return to security j that is implied by the CML. Solving for μ_j, we get

$$\mu_j = r_f + \left\{ \frac{\text{cov}(j,m)}{\sigma_m^2} \right\} (\mu_m - r_f) \qquad (7.15)$$

Equation (7.15) is called the **security market line** (SML) because it specifies the required/expected rate of return of security j that is implied by the CML when the market is in equilibrium.

In more general terms, a stock is a capital asset. If the SML prices stocks by specifying an appropriate return, can we generalize and use it to specify a required return to *any* capital asset? Yes, if the model is appropriate to the situation. By using the more general concept that j is a capital asset, rather than specifically a stock, Equation (7.15) becomes one form of what is called the **capital asset pricing model**, or CAPM. Just as the name implies, it is a model for pricing capital assets.

In words, the CAPM states that the required rate of return of any asset can be expressed as the sum of the rate of return of the riskless asset and a risk premium to compensate for the risk of the particular asset. Or more simply stated, any asset's required rate of return equals the riskless rate of return adjusted for the risk of the asset. This statement is very appealing, and it might make you wonder why we have gone to such great lengths to derive this model. Why didn't we simply assert this statement in the first place? The importance of the derivation is that it shows that the appropriate risk adjustment is **not** an adjustment that is immediately obvious. The risk adjustment is based on how an asset's rate of return covaries with the rate of return on the market portfolio. (Had you guessed that covariance with the market is the critical determinant?) This adjustment is appropriate because it reflects how an individual asset contributes to an investor's risk in his total investment portfolio.

BETA

If we know the exact return distribution of all of the assets in the market, and the covariance of each asset's return with the return on the market portfolio, we can specify a required rate of return using Equation (7.15). But suppose we do not have all of the specific information necessary to apply Equation (7.15). In that case, we are taking the CAPM out of the perfect capital market environment in which it was derived and putting it into the real world. In the case of individual stock returns, how they vary with respect to the market portfolio's return can be estimated by applying a statistical method called **linear regression**. We can express the actual historical rate of return on a stock r_j as a linear function of the actual historical excess rate of return on the market portfolio $(r_m - r_f)$, so that

$$r_j = r_f + \beta_j(r_m - r_f) \tag{7.16}$$

We can then apply the technique of linear regression to estimate β_j from historical data by collecting a sample of simultaneous observations of r_j, r_m, and r_f, and fitting Equation (7.16) to the historical data to estimate the value of the regression coefficient β_j.

If we take the expected value of the expression on each side of Equation (7.16), we get

$$\mu_j = r_f + \beta_j(\mu_m - r_f) \tag{7.17}$$

Comparing Equations (7.15) and (7.17), we can see that

$$\beta_j = \frac{\text{cov}(j,m)}{\sigma_m^2} \tag{7.18}$$

Because of Equation (7.18), the covariance between a common stock's rate of return and the excess rate of return of the market portfolio divided by the variance of the market portfolio has come to be called the common stock's **beta**. Beta is particularly

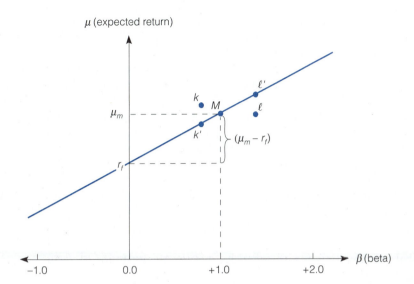

FIGURE 7-13
The security market line.

important because it is a *linear* measure of how much an individual asset contributes to the standard deviation of the market portfolio. So the beta of an asset is a simple, well-behaved measure of the risk of the individual asset.

Figure 7-13 is a graph of expected return expressed as a function of β, that is, the SML (security market line). Note that the beta of the market portfolio equals 1.0. The value-weighted average of all common stock betas equals 1.0. Also, note that the beta of the riskless asset equals 0.0. So it is possible to create an artificial riskless asset.[12] The SML is the graphical representation of Equations (7.15) and (7.17). The riskless rate of return is the vertical intercept of this line, and the slope of the line is the quantity $\mu_m - r_f$, the expected excess return on the market portfolio. That is, the rise divided by the run is $\mu_m - r_f$ divided by 1. Finally, note that beta can be negative. Accordingly, an asset can have a required rate of return that is *less* than the riskless rate of return. At first glance, this seems counterintuitive: How can any asset have an expected rate of return that is less than the riskless rate of return? But remember that these are assets held in a fully diversified portfolio, the market portfolio. Therefore, the measure of risk for the individual asset depends on how the standard deviation of the portfolio return changes when that asset is added to the portfolio. When an asset with a negative beta is added to the market portfolio, the standard deviation of the portfolio decreases. Hence, while the notion of negative risk is counterintuitive, in this context, at least, it is explainable.

ARBITRAGE AND THE SML

As the name **security market line** suggests, the [beta, expected return] combinations for all securities that compose the market portfolio must lie along the SML. Consider a security l whose [beta, expected return] combination lies below the SML, as represented by the point l in Figure 7-13. Would anyone want to invest in asset l? No, because there is an asset whose [beta, expected return] combination, located at l' on the SML, is superior. Asset l' has the same β as asset l. Thus, both contribute identically to portfolio risk but asset l' has a higher expected return. In a perfect capital market, an asset such as l would give rise to an arbitrage opportunity.

[12]Black (1972).

Investors could sell asset l short, buy asset l', and reap an arbitrage profit whose expected value is $\mu_{l'} - \mu_l$ without altering portfolio risk. How long would such an arbitrage opportunity continue to exist? Until the price of asset l had been driven down to such an extent that the [beta, expected return] combination for asset l shifted to the SML. That is, until the [beta, expected return] combinations for assets l and l' are equal.

Can a security whose [beta, expected return] combination lies above the SML, such as security k depicted in Figure 7-13, exist for long? Not in a perfect capital market because investors would purchase asset k and sell asset k' short, and thereby earn an arbitrage profit whose expected value is $\mu_k - \mu_{k'}$, without altering portfolio risk. Such activity would continue until the market value of asset k had been driven up to such an extent that the [beta, expected return] combination for asset k shifted to the SML.

In a perfect capital market environment, that is, one in which there are no impediments to arbitrage activity (e.g., no restrictions on short selling), the [beta, expected return] combinations for all securities *and* for all portfolios of securities must lie along the SML.

ASSUMPTIONS UNDERLYING THE CAPM

We feel it is important to be explicit about the formal assumptions underlying the derivation of the CAPM, so at this point we will list them. While the list may cause you to wonder if the model has any relevance because the assumptions do not seem very realistic, we split them into two groups according to how they are viewed by scholars. The first group consists of those assumptions that if they do not hold, may compromise the insights of the model. The second group consists of assumptions that appear to hold in the real world, or if they are not very realistic, it is generally believed that violation of them does not destroy the conclusions of the model.

CRITICAL ASSUMPTION 1   The derivation of the CAPM assumes that the mean and standard deviation of a sample of observations are what statisticians call **sufficient statistics** for describing the probability distribution of the rate of return from the asset. This implies that for purposes of the model, the mean and standard deviation of observed outcomes contain *all* of the relevant information that exists about the security. There are several more specific assumptions that will cause this very broad assumption to hold. For example, the mean and standard deviation of a sample are sufficient statistics for the parameters of the normal distribution as well as several other probability distributions that seem to approximate the return from an asset. So this broad assumption holds if the returns to the assets are assumed to follow any one of several specific probability distributions.[13] However, the mean and standard deviation of a sample are not sufficient statistics for *all* possible return distributions. There are several ways of saying this, but the "bottom line" is If there is important information about the return distribution that we do not get from its mean and standard deviation, CAPM may be missing one or more important determinants of the required rate of return from an asset.

CRITICAL ASSUMPTION 2   A second assumption made in the derivation of the CAPM is that the market is in equilibrium. That is, we applied the Principle of Capi-

[13] Alternatively, it may be assumed that investors are expected utility maximizers. In that case, investor "utility functions" that are quadratic functions of dollar returns will ensure that the mean and standard deviation are sufficient for purposes of characterizing the probability distribution of the rate of return. However, the best functional form to assume for such investor utility functions is still a matter of debate.

tal Market Efficiency. On the one hand, this assumption reflects a widely held belief. On the other hand, if this assumption is violated, the CAPM cannot be tested because the model is formulated on the assumption that the capital markets *are* efficient. Therefore, any test of the CAPM is really a joint test of the model *and* market efficiency. If a test of the CAPM fails, we cannot say for sure whether the model is somewhat incorrectly specified or the market is not exactly efficient. At this time, most people believe that the model identifies a major determinant of an asset's return and that the capital markets are very efficient. Therefore, although it is unlikely that the model is a perfect representation of reality, the model is useful in a practical way because it approximates reality and identifies an important determinant of an asset's return.

CRITICAL ASSUMPTION 3   The CAPM is a 1-period model. Asset returns are defined to be over the next period, and investors are assumed to be maximizing their returns over the single period. The period can be of any length. However, no relationship with a subsequent period is assumed. Therefore, it is possible that investors with differing investment horizons should be acting in different ways to maximize their benefit from their wealth. That is, if investors have differing "utilities" from wealth, depending upon when it is received, it is possible that a more complex model is necessary to describe required rates of return.

OTHER ASSUMPTIONS   The CAPM is derived in a perfect market environment. Recall that the characteristics of a perfect capital market were enumerated in Chapter 4. This list of characteristics sometimes makes people skeptical whether the CAPM can have any relevance. But while we encourage skepticism in your investing, scholars have extensively investigated the impact of relaxing each of these assumptions on the conclusions of the model. They have found that very similar conclusions are reached with considerably more complex models, and therefore the benefits from such increased complexity do not appear to be worth the increased effort it takes for people to understand and apply the more complex models.

APPLYING THE CAPM   7.7

The principal conclusion emanating from portfolio theory is Generalization 5. Investors should invest in some mix of the market portfolio and the riskless asset. This is a rather inconvenient prescription in the real world since transactions are not only costly but much more costly when buying or selling a small number of shares. This conclusion can be translated into a more practical prescription by asking, Can the return to the market portfolio be accurately approximated with a relatively small number of assets? The answer to this question is yes. The basic conclusion of portfolio theory can be restated as the underlying reason for the Principle of Diversification. The remaining question is the one we raised in our discussion of that principle: How much diversification is necessary to get "all" the benefits?

APPROXIMATING THE MARKET PORTFOLIO

In our discussion of the expected return of an asset, we mentioned the law of large numbers as a justification for using the mean of the distribution to represent the expected future return of the asset. The notion of large numbers, and more specifically random samples, can also be used here. The law of large numbers can help determine an accurate approximation of the market portfolio. Recall the procedure

FIGURE 7-14

Portfolio standard deviation as a function of portfolio size.

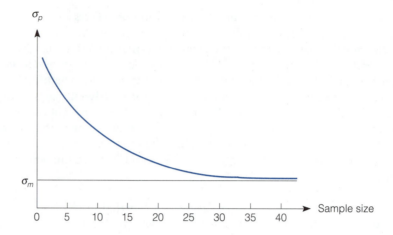

for estimating the unknown mean of some probability distribution. Compute the sample mean for a "reasonably large" random sample. Now the definition of "large" does not necessarily depend on the size of the underlying population. A large sample in statistics may contain only 25 to 30 observations. Based on this fact, we can predict that approximately equal investments in 25 to 30 randomly chosen stocks produces a portfolio with a realized rate of return that is consistently close to the realized return on the market portfolio. (This result has also been demonstrated empirically innumerable times.) So a portfolio of 25 to 30 stocks randomly chosen from all traded stocks must have an expected return that is very close to the expected return on the market portfolio. How accurate the approximation is will be a function of how large a random sample of assets is in the approximation portfolio. Figure 7-14 graphs the standard deviation of a portfolio of randomly selected securities as a function of the size of the random sample.

It is possible to achieve a similar approximation of the market portfolio with fewer securities, using a technique called **stratified random sampling**. This technique is widely used in opinion polls to reduce the cost of taking the poll; stratifying the random sample reduces the size of the random sample necessary for a given level of confidence that the opinions are truly representative of the target population. With a stratified random sample, the population to be sampled is broken down into "key" segments, and a random sample is taken from each segment. With stocks, the segments might be industry segments that taken together are representative of the entire stock market. Using stratified random sampling, it is possible to use a random sample of between 7 and 10 stocks to approximate the market portfolio.[14] With prices per share averaging $30 and a purchase of 100 shares for each stock in the portfolio, a carefully chosen portfolio with a market value of $25,000–$30,000 can be used to approximate the market portfolio.

Recall from our discussion of the capital markets in Chapter 4 that there are portfolio investment funds of various types generally grouped under the heading of **mutual funds**. For investing amounts smaller than $25,000 and for investors not wanting the responsibility of managing their own portfolio, investors can invest in mutual funds to approximate the market portfolio. Currently there are index funds, such as those based on the Standard & Poor's 500 Index. In fact, an important reason for the existence of mutual funds is to provide the opportunity to all investors to diversify inexpensively.

[14] Brennan (1975).

DIVERSIFIABLE AND NONDIVERSIFIABLE RISK

Beta measures the risk that an individual asset adds to the market portfolio (or a well-diversified approximation of it). The weighted average of the betas of the individual assets equals the beta of the portfolio, which, if you recall, equals 1.0 for the market portfolio. As Figure 7-13 shows, the expected return to an individual asset or portfolio is a linear function of beta. Look back at Equation (7.15). By expressing the covariance in terms of standard deviations and the correlation coefficient, Equation (7.15) can be rewritten as

$$\mu_j = r_f + \left\{ \frac{(\mu_m - r_f)}{\sigma_m} \right\} \sigma_j \rho \qquad (7.19)$$

In this form, the risk adjustment is expressed as the product of the slope of the CML and the standard deviation of the individual asset's future return multiplied by the correlation coefficient. But what if the risk-return trade-off did not depend on diversification? Then the risk adjustment would simply be the risk-return trade-off (the slope of the CML) multiplied by σ_j. Equivalently, viewed from another perspective, if investors are paid for the total risk inherent in an individual asset, the risk adjustment would also equal the risk-return trade-off multiplied by σ_j. Therefore, if the required return to an asset is based simply on its risk if it is held alone rather than its risk if it is held as part of a portfolio, the return to a nondiversified investor investing in asset j, denoted μ_{jn} would be given as

$$\mu_{jn} = r_f + \left\{ \frac{(\mu_m - r_f)}{\sigma_m} \right\} \sigma_j \qquad (7.20)$$

which can be rewritten as

$$\mu_{jn} = r_f + \left\{ \frac{(\mu_m - r_f)}{\sigma_m} \right\} \sigma_j \rho + \left\{ \frac{(\mu_m - r_f)}{\sigma_m} \right\} \sigma_j (1 - \rho) \qquad (7.21)$$

The three terms on the right-hand side of Equation (7.21) can be identified as (1) the return to the riskless asset; (2) the return for taking on what is called **nondiversifiable** (or **systematic**) risk; and (3) the return for taking on what is called **diversifiable** risk. **Nondiversifiable** (or **systematic**) **risk** is risk that cannot be eliminated by further diversification. **Diversifiable** (or **unsystematic**) **risk** is risk that can be eliminated by diversification. Viewed this way, the two different terms for risk in Equation (7.21) represent another way of showing how diversification reduces the risk of a portfolio. People who invest in a nondiversified portfolio, such as a single security, take on more risk than those who invest in that security as part of a well-diversified portfolio.

Every asset has both diversifiable and nondiversifiable risk. However, looking back at Equation (7.19), which is the CAPM expression for the required return of an asset, and comparing it with Equation (7.21), we note that the market will pay investors to take on nondiversifiable risk, but there is no return paid for taking on diversifiable risk. This makes sense because, in a market that contains a large number of risky assets, as the U.S. stock market does, it is both easy and relatively inexpensive to diversify. And investors are not able to require payment for something that is negative to them when it can be easily (and virtually costlessly) eliminated. In other words, because investors have a choice of whether to take on diversifiable risk, when they invest they cannot require payment for taking it on.

BUT WHAT HAPPENS IF YOU DO NOT DIVERSIFY?

The required returns of an asset when the owner is diversified and nondiversified are specified by Equations (7.19) and (7.21), respectively. The Gordon Growth Model (Chapter 6) is a method of converting a required rate of return from a stock into a market value for the stock. Let us use the Gordon Growth Model to value security j for two prospective buyers. One investor will add this to a diversified portfolio, and the other investor will sell all his existing investments and invest solely in security j. The value of security j to the diversified investor, denoted V_d, can be expressed in the Gordon Growth Model as

$$V_d = \frac{D_1}{\mu_j - g} \tag{7.22}$$

where D_1 is the cash dividend expected next period and g is the growth rate of dividends forever. Similarly, the value of security j to the nondiversified investor, denoted V_n, can be expressed in the Gordon Growth Model as

$$V_n = \frac{D_1}{\mu_{jn} - g} \tag{7.23}$$

The relationship between V_n and V_d can be determined from the relationship between μ_{jn} and μ_j. Comparing Equation (7.21) with Equation (7.19), we can see that unless $\sigma_j = 0.0$ or $\rho = 1.0$, μ_{jn} is always greater than μ_j. Therefore, with g and D_1 identical in Equations (7.22) and (7.23), $V_n < V_d$. For example, suppose $\mu_j = 10\%$, $\mu_{jn} = 12\%$, $D_1 = \$2$, and $g = 5\%$. Then $V_d = \$40$, and $V_n = \$28.57$.

In words, then, the value of the security to the diversified investor is always greater than it is to the nondiversified investor. But the Principle of Two-Sided Transactions reminds us that there are two sides to each transaction. We have established the relative value of the stock to the diversified purchaser and the nondiversified purchaser, but what about the value to the seller of the stock? Following the Principle of Self-Interested Behavior, current owners of the shares will sell to the highest bidder. In a bidding competition between diversified and nondiversified investors, diversified investors can "afford to" bid a higher price. Therefore, the prices that are observed in the stock market quotations reflect the higher value that diversified investors are willing to pay for the shares. If a nondiversified investor is going to purchase shares, she must pay the higher (diversified) price.

The nondiversified investor, then, faces three alternatives: (1) Do not invest in the stock market. (2) Receive a lower rate of return than is appropriate for the risk of investing in stocks by paying a higher price for the shares. (3) Diversify. We want to emphasize that under the second alternative, while nondiversified investors have the alternative of investing in stocks, the prices they pay for the shares are the higher prices appropriate for a diversified investor. As long as there are diversified investors actively seeking positive-NPV investments, attempts by nondiversified investors to purchase shares will have no impact on the market price of a share because they will be outbid or they will pay the same price as diversified investors and, from a risk-return perspective, actually overpay. This statement remains true even if there are a sizable number of nondiversified investors! This is a striking example of the robustness of the conclusions of the CAPM. It is assumed that all investors invest in the market portfolio, but even if that assumption is violated, competition ensures that prices will be set *as though* all investors did invest in the market portfolio.

MULTIFACTOR MODELS   7.8

Critical assumption 1 underlying the CAPM states that the mean and standard deviation contain all the information about the asset's future return that is needed to formulate the asset pricing model. But suppose there is more to an asset's future returns than the mean and variance are capable of capturing? Essentially, according to the CAPM, an asset's expected future return varies with a single factor: the expected return on the market portfolio. But what if there are other factors on which required rates of return depend?

For the sake of illustration, consider the rate of return on the common stock of a company, GIOC (for Great Investment Opportunity Corporation). The rate of return on GIOC stock can be expressed as the sum of two components, the riskless rate r_f, plus an uncertain, or risky component, which we will denote R (for risky). Letting r_G denote the rate of return on GIOC stock, we have

$$r_G = r_f + R \qquad (7.24)$$

The uncertain component R is affected by a variety of factors, some that affect all companies and others that are specific to GIOC (and perhaps a handful of similarly situated companies). To be perfectly general, suppose that there are K independent factors that contribute to systematic risk. In that case, the rate of return on GIOC stock would be expressed as

$$r_G = r_f + R(F_1, F_2, \ldots, F_K) + \epsilon \qquad (7.25)$$

where F_k denotes factor k ($k = 1, 2, \ldots, K$), $R(\cdot)$ is some function of the factors, and ϵ denotes the incremental return due to nondiversifiable risk.

THE ARBITRAGE PRICING THEORY   7.9

Equation (7.25) embodies a more general model of a required rate of return. But exactly what do the F_k's consist of? And what does the function $R(\cdot)$ look like? Currently there is considerable debate among financial economists concerning these questions. For example, in applications of the CAPM, are multiple factors being approximated by the return on the market portfolio, thus masking the true determinants of a required rate of return? At this point, no single opinion has emerged, but there is one model that has received considerable attention because it relaxes the assumption of a single determinant. This alternative model is called the **arbitrage pricing theory**, or APT. As the name implies, the APT relies on the concept of arbitrage. In particular, the APT relies on arguments similar to those we presented in Chapters 2 and 5, to develop an asset pricing model that characterizes a market equilibrium that is free of arbitrage opportunities. (Recall that an alternative definition of a perfect capital market is one that is free of arbitrage opportunities.)

THE APT: A MULTIFACTOR LINEAR MODEL

Like the CAPM, the APT is built on the Principle of Capital Market Efficiency. The APT simply represents an alternative approach to securities valuation within the same framework. The APT relates asset returns within a multivariate framework in which the return relationships are linear. While the APT takes as its starting point the Principle of Capital Market Efficiency, it does not attempt to specify any particular set of determinants on the basis of conceptual arguments. Instead, the APT asserts that an asset's expected rate of return depends on a linear combination of a set of factors whose identity must be determined empirically. Thus far, in empirical tests of the APT, a variety of different factors have emerged as possible determinants of actual common stock returns.[15] A statistical method called **factor analysis** has been used to attempt to identify relevant factors.[16]

The APT model looks strikingly like an extended CAPM, even though it is derived in a very different way. We will not derive the APT model here, but we will show you its operational form.

$$r_j = r_f + \beta_{j1}(\mu_{f1} - r_f) + \beta_{j2}(\mu_{f2} - r_f) + \ldots + \beta_{jK}(\mu_{fK} - r_f) \qquad (7.26)$$

where K is the number of factors that affect an asset's return; $\mu_{f1}, \mu_{f2}, \ldots, \mu_{fK}$, are the expected returns to factors $1, 2, \ldots, K$, respectively; and $\beta_{j1}, \beta_{j2}, \ldots, \beta_{jK}$, are the asset's sensitivities to factors $1, 2, \ldots, K$, respectively. APT formulations typically include the expected excess return on the market portfolio, the sole factor in the CAPM, as an explanatory variable.

The APT, then, is a multifactor model of the general form of Equation (7.25) in which the F_k's that determine an expected return are to be identified empirically, assuming $R(\cdot)$ is a simple linear function.

APPLYING THE APT

To illustrate the APT, let's assume there are three relevant factors: the excess rate of return on the market portfolio, $F_1 = r_m - r_f$, the rate of growth of real gross national product (GNP) relative to the riskless rate of return, $F_2 = r_{GNP} - r_f$, and the rate of consumer price inflation (CPI) relative to the riskless rate, $F_3 = r_{CPI} - r_f$. Note that the respective impacts of the second and third factors must be incremental to the impact of the excess return on the market portfolio. If the impact of F_2 can be explained completely in terms of the impact of F_1, then $\beta_2 = 0$, and F_2 is not a necessary part of the model, even though it does exist. A similar statement holds for F_3. Which factors are important as a practical matter is of course an empirical question.

Suppose that the riskless rate is 8% and that the beta coefficients are $\beta_1 = 1.2$, $\beta_2 = 0.2$, and $\beta_3 = 0.3$. If the rate of return on the market portfolio is 16%, the rate of growth of real GNP is 3%, and the rate of consumer price inflation is 6%, then if $\epsilon = 0$,

$$\begin{aligned} r_G &= 8\% + 1.2(r_m - 8\%) + 0.2(r_{GNP} - 8\%) + 0.3(r_{CPI} - 8\%) \\ &= 8\% + 1.2(16\% - 8\%) + 0.2(3\% - 8\%) + 0.3(6\% - 8\%) = 16.0\% \end{aligned}$$

THE APT MODEL VERSUS CAPM

As a practical matter, the APT model is simply an alternative formulation that describes actual stock returns about as well as the CAPM. The CAPM endures thus far not because it is conceptually superior but probably because it is relatively simple and it was the first one put forth. Subsequent improvements (added complexities) or

---

[15] A number of empirical investigations of the APT are cited in the references. The first test was by Gehr (1978).

[16] One of the difficulties that arises with this research is that in some cases, the quantified factors have not appeared to be associated with identifiable real world factors. That is, some quantified factors cannot be identified as something familiar, such as a measure of inflation or unemployment.

alternative formulations have not been shown to provide significantly better descriptions of actual stock returns than those produced by the CAPM. Neither have these alternative models provided such an increase in understanding (additional insights) that scholars have agreed that one of them is unequivocally superior in a conceptual sense. Perhaps that means that the expected excess return on the market portfolio adequately incorporates the effect of the plausible alternative factors. Perhaps instead it means that the additional factors that contribute significantly to expected asset returns have yet to be identified or that the return relationships are nonlinear. These are subjects for future research. At this point, without sufficient reason to replace the CAPM, financial economists seem to feel comfortable continuing to view an asset's required return as a function simply of the expected excess return on the market portfolio, which was the first coherent conceptual model of the required rate of return on an asset.

SUMMARY

This chapter demonstrates the Principle of Diversification by showing the benefits of diversification to investors. By applying the Principle of Two-Sided Transactions and the Principle of Self-Interested Behavior, it was shown that stock prices depend on the value of the stock to diversified investors. People who invest without diversifying are not receiving as much return as possible for the risk they are taking. Therefore, you should invest without diversifying *only* if you have valuable information about the stock that is not already incorporated into its price, an extremely rare occurrence in an efficient capital market. Otherwise, Generalization 5, which follows from portfolio theory, provides practical guidance for investing: Invest in that combination of a well-diversified portfolio of risky assets and the riskless asset that is most consistent with your willingness to take on risk.

This chapter also demonstrates the Principle of Risk-Return Trade-Off by deriving a function for the trade-off between risk and return. This function is called the capital asset pricing model, or CAPM. In the CAPM, portfolio risk is defined as the standard deviation of the future rate of return from the total portfolio. With this definition of portfolio risk, the risk of an individual asset depends upon the correlation between the returns on the asset and the return on the market portfolio, which is measured by the asset's beta coefficient. Beta measures how much the individual asset contributes to the standard deviation of the future rate of return of a well-diversified portfolio.

Current models of required rates of return, such as the CAPM, are not perfect representations of asset valuation. There are empirical tests that reveal imperfections involving even the most complex forms of the CAPM, as well as the APT. However, the CAPM identifies a very important and nonintuitive determinant of an asset's required return, namely, the expected excess return on the market portfolio. The APT broadens our view of asset pricing by allowing for the inclusion of additional factors that might affect required returns. However, the APT does not itself identify these specific factors. But suppose potential factors are identified that are in addition to, or represent an alternative to, the factor identified by the CAPM. For example, the reputation of a firm or the size of the trading market for its shares might have an effect on a stock's required return. If we hypothesize that one or more additional factors are important determinants of a stock's required return, the APT provides a method of empirically testing such hypotheses.

As a practical matter, the expected excess return on the market portfolio can be viewed as the principal determinant of an asset's required return. Like the time-distance-speed model, the CAPM provides a good starting point for understanding and action.

PROBLEMS

PROBLEM SET A

A1. Define the term **random variable**. Give two examples of discrete random variables and two examples of continuous random variables.

A2. Explain the meaning of the term **expected value** in your own words.

A3. Why is knowing only the variance (but not the mean) of a random variable of very limited value?

A4. What are the two necessary dimensions that make up risk?

A5. How is risk defined in the models contained in this chapter? What are the shortcomings of this definition? Why is this definition useful as it is applied to investment models, in spite of these shortcomings?

A6. Explain in your own words why an investor should not be concerned about the risk and returns of individual assets but should be concerned only about the risk and return of her entire portfolio.

A7. Explain in your own words how it is possible to invest in two risky assets that are perfectly negatively correlated (i.e., $\rho = -1.0$) and earn a riskless return.

A8. Define the term **efficient frontier**. Why is it intuitively appealing to want to be invested in a portfolio that is on the efficient frontier?

A9. State the **portfolio-separation theorem** and explain why it is such an important finding.

A10. What is the beta of a stock whose covariance with the market portfolio returns is .0045 if the variance of the rate of return on the market portfolio is .002?

A11. Define the term **excess return on the market portfolio**.

A12. Define the CML.

A13. Define the SML.

A14. What is the difference between the CML and the SML?

A15. Why are random variables an important tool of mathematical model building?

A16. Define the term **arbitrage**.

A17. Define the terms **diversifiable risk** and **nondiversifiable risk** and explain the difference between the two.

A18. Why is it that the market will pay an investor for taking on nondiversifiable risk but will not pay an investor for taking on diversifiable risk?

A19. Solve Equation (7.11) for the proportion of investment in each asset, w_1 and $(1 - w_1)$, that makes investment in the portfolio riskless when the correlation coefficient ρ equals -1.0.

A20. According to the CAPM, what would be the required rate of return on an asset that has a beta of 1.35 when the expected rate of return on the market portfolio is 12% and the riskless rate of return is 7%?

PROBLEM SET B

B1. Given the probability distribution for rates of return for stock X and stock Y, compute (a) the expected return for each stock, $E(X)$ and $E(Y)$; (b) the variance of the rate of return for each stock; (c) the covariance between the rates of return for stock X and stock Y; and (d) the correlation coefficient between the rates of return for stock X and stock Y.

| Probability | Rates of Return | |
	Stock X	Stock Y
.1	−10%	4%
.3	0	8
.3	6	0
.2	10	−5
.1	20	15

B2. Given the statistical sample of monthly returns for the market and stock XYZ, compute (a) the average return for the market and stock XYZ over these 12 months; (b) the variance of the rate of return for each over these 12 months; (c) the covariance between the rates of return for the market and stock XYZ over these 12 months; (d) the correlation coefficient between the rates of return for the market and stock XYZ for these 12 months; and (e) the beta for stock XYZ, using linear regression for these 12 months.

Month	Market	XYZ	Month	Market	XYZ
JAN	8.02	17.23	JLY	−2.63	−14.22
FEB	3.15	10.59	AUG	1.74	2.31
MAR	2.20	−3.01	SEP	−2.33	−9.83
APR	−1.51	1.27	OCT	7.41	21.53
MAY	7.31	14.32	NOV	−4.28	0.61
JUN	1.29	−6.78	DEC	2.76	−1.78

B3. It has been said that asset pricing models do not work very well because the actual monthly returns are often considerably larger or smaller than the return specified by the model. Explain why this is or is not a valid criticism of asset pricing models.

B4. Discuss the implications that the portfolio separation theorem has for the job of a corporate financial manager.

B5. What is the beta of an asset whose correlation coefficient with the market portfolio's returns is .62 and variance is .1 if the variance of the market portfolio's rate of return is .0025?

B6. Discuss the differences and similarities of the CAPM and the APT.

B7. Respond to the following statement: First you say σ measures the risk of investing. Then you say β measures the risk of investing. Which is right?

B8. According to the CAPM, an asset with a beta of zero has a required rate of return equal to the riskless rate, r_f. Does this mean that the asset is riskless? Can an asset with a positive standard deviation of return, σ, have a beta of zero?

B9. If the required rate of return on an asset with a beta of 1.4 is 17% and the riskless rate of return is 7%, what is the expected rate of return on the market portfolio?

B10. The Principle of Diversification states that diversification is beneficial. However, in an efficient capital market, the value of a share of stock does not reflect whether the share's owner is diversified. Why is this the case?

B11. Suppose the expected rate of return and variance of the market portfolio are .11 and .0016, respectively. If the riskless rate of return is .06, what will be the required rate of return on a stock whose rate of return variance is .12 and correlation with the market portfolio's returns is .46?

B12. What is the expected rate of return and standard deviation of the return for the next year on a stock that is selling for $30 now and has probabilities .2, .6, and .2 of selling for 1 year from now at $24, $33, and $39, respectively? Assume that no dividends will be paid on the stock during the next year and ignore taxes.

B13. What is the beta of a stock when its expected rate of return is 15%, its standard deviation of return is 25%, its correlation coefficient with the market is .2, and the return to the market portfolio is 14% with a standard deviation of 4%? Assuming the market for this stock is in equilibrium, what is the riskless rate that is implied by the information given?

B14. Stock A has a beta of 2.0 and a required rate of return of 15%. The market rate of return is 10%. What will be the required rate of return on stock B, which has a beta of 1.4?

PROBLEM SET C

C1. Explain why M *must be* the "market portfolio," that is, why M must include some of every possible asset.

C2. Discuss the following statement: Since capital markets are so efficient, developing new information about the value of a company must be a worthless undertaking.

C3. Figure 7-8 shows what the group of all possible portfolio combinations for stocks in the stock market looks like. Is it possible that any two of these portfolios have a correlation coefficient between them that is equal to *minus* 1.0? If it is possible, give an example. If it is not possible, explain why.

C4. Using calculus, find the value of w_1 (as a function of the correlation coefficient, ρ, and the standard deviations of the rates of return, σ_1 and σ_2) that provides the two-asset investment portfolio with the minimum risk that is possible, assuming $0.0 \leq w_1 \leq 1.0$.

C5. Suppose that r_f is 5% and r_m is 10%. According to the SML and the CAPM, an asset with a beta -2.0 has a required rate of return of **negative** 5% ($= 5 - 2[10 - 5]$). Can this be possible? Does this mean that the asset has negative risk? Why would anyone ever invest in an asset that has an expected and required rate of return that is negative? Explain.

C6. Consider the following statement: The way to make a lot of money is to use other people's money for investing. That is, if you borrow and invest the borrowed money, you will make a lot of money. Several of our Principles of Finance indicate that this statement is not correct. Briefly describe how four of the principles explicitly or implicitly imply that this statement is false.

C7. Explain in your own words how the SML can be derived from the CML.

C8. The Principle of Capital Market Efficiency states that the capital markets are so efficient that market prices for securities reflect all available information about the security. In other words, a security's market price is the best estimate of the value of the security that can be made. If we believe that this is true, why do we bother to try to create models that accurately value a security? Why don't we simply use the latest trading price since it is the best possible estimate?

C9. Respond to the following statement: Since all I can expect to earn from investing in a security that is on the SML is a zero NPV, I don't see why it's worth my trouble to invest in financial securities that are traded in an efficient capital market.

REFERENCES

Black, Fischer. "Capital Market Equilibrium with Restricted Borrowing." *Journal of Business* 45 (July 1972): 444–55.

Blume, Marshall E. "Betas and Their Regression Tendencies." *Journal of Finance* 30 (June 1975): 785–96.

Breeden, Douglas R., Michael R. Gibbons, and Robert H. Litzenberger. "Empirical Tests of the Consumption-Oriented CAPM." *Journal of Finance* 44 (June 1989): 231–62.

Brennan, Michael J. "The Optimal Number of Securities in a Risky Asset Portfolio When there are Fixed Costs of Transaction: Theory and Some Empirical Evidence." *Journal of Financial and Quantitative Analysis* 10 (September 1975): 483–96.

Brigham, Eugene F., Dilip K. Shome, and Steve R. Vinson. "The Risk Premium Approach to Measuring a Utility's Cost of Equity." *Financial Management* 14 (Spring 1985): 33–45.

Brown, Stephen J. "The Number of Factors in Security Returns." *Journal of Finance* 44 (December 1989): 1247–62.

Brown, Stephen J., and Mark I. Weinstein. "A New Approach to Testing Asset Pricing Theories: The Bilinear Paradigm." *Journal of Finance* 38 (June 1983): 711–43.

Chen, Nai-Fu. "Some Empirical Tests of the Theory of Arbitrage Pricing." *Journal of Finance* 38 (December 1983): 1393–1414.

Cho, D. Chinhyung, Cheol S. Eun, and Lemma W. Senbet. "International Arbitrage Pricing Theory: An Empirical Investigation." *Journal of Finance* 41 (June 1986): 313–29.

Fama, Eugene F. "Components of Investment Performance." *Journal of Finance* 27 (June 1972): 551–67.

Friend, Irwin, Yoram Landskroner, and Etienne Losq. "The Demand for Risky Assets Under Uncertain Inflation." *Journal of Finance* 31 (December 1976): 1287–98.

Gehr, Adam K., Jr. "Some Tests of the Arbitrage Pricing Theory." *Journal of the Midwest Finance Association* 7 (1978): 91–105.

Harrington, Diana R. *Modern Portfolio Theory, the Capital Asset Pricing Model and Arbitrage Pricing Theory: A User's Guide*, 2nd ed. Englewood Cliffs, N.J.: Prentice-Hall, 1987.

Haugen, Robert A. *Modern Investment Theory*. Englewood Cliffs, N.J.: Prentice-Hall, 1986.

Keim, Donald B., and Robert F. Stambaugh. "Predicting Returns in the Stock and Bond Markets." *Journal of Financial Economics* 17 (December 1986): 357–90.

Latham, Mark. "The Arbitrage Pricing Theory and Supershares." *Journal of Finance* 44 (June 1989): 263–81.

Lintner, John. "The Valuation of Risk Assets and the Selection of Risky Investments in Stock Portfolios and Capital Budgets." *Review of Economics and Statistics* (February 1965): 13–37.

Lintner, John. "Security Prices, Risk and Maximal Gains from Diversification." *Journal of Finance* 20 (December 1965): 587–616.

Litzenberger, Robert H., and Krishna Ramaswamy. "The Effect of Personal Taxes and Dividends on Capital Asset Prices." *Journal of Financial Economics* 7 (June 1979): 163–95.

Markowitz, Harry M. "Portfolio Selection." *Journal of Finance* 7 (March 1952): 77–91.

Markowitz, Harry M. *Portfolio Selection: Efficient Diversification of Investments*. New York: Wiley, 1959.

Modigliani, Franco, and Gerald A. Pogue. "An Introduction to Risk and Return." *Financial Analysts Journal* 30 (March-April 1974): 68–80, (May-June 1974): 68–86.

Mossin, Jan. "Equilibrium in a Capital Asset Market." *Econometrica* (October 1966): 768–83.

Mullins, David W., Jr. "Does the Capital Pricing Model Work?" *Harvard Business Review* 60 (January-February 1982): 105–14.

Reinganum, Marc R. "The Arbitrage Pricing Theory: Some Empirical Results." *Journal of Finance* 36 (May 1981): 313–22.

Roll, Richard. "A Critique of the Asset Pricing Theory Tests. Part I: On Past and Potential Testability of the Theory." *Journal of Financial Economics* 4 (March 1977): 129–76.

Roll, Richard. "Performance Evaluation and Benchmark Errors." *Journal of Portfolio Management* 6 (Summer 1980): 5–12.

Rosenberg, Barr. "The Capital Asset Pricing Model and the Market Model." *Journal of Portfolio Management* 7 (Winter 1981): 5–16.

Ross, Stephen A. "The Arbitrage Theory of Capital Asset Pricing." *Journal of Economic Theory* 13 (December 1976): 341–60.

Sharpe, William F. "A Simplified Model for Portfolio Analysis." *Management Science* 10 (January 1963): 277–93.

Sharpe, William F. "Capital Asset Prices: A Theory of Market Equilibrium Under Conditions of Risk." *Journal of Finance* 19 (September 1964): 425–42.

Sharpe, William F. *Investments*, 3rd ed. Englewood Cliffs, N.J.: Prentice-Hall, 1985.

Tobin, James. "Liquidity Preference as Behavior Towards Risk." *Review of Economic Studies* 25 (February 1958): 65–86.

Trzcinka, Charles. "On the Number of Factors in the Arbitrage Pricing Model." *Journal of Finance* 41 (June 1986): 347–68.

OPTIONS

The Options Principle states that options are valuable. Options exist in many situations. In some cases they are explicit and obvious. For example, the term **options** brings to mind the various options that are traded on the Chicago Board Options Exchange (CBOE), which is the largest options market in the world. In fact, the dollar value of options contracts traded on the CBOE ($4.7 billion) exceeded the dollar volume of equity traded on the AMEX in 1989.

While market-traded options are explicit, in other situations options may be difficult to spot, and an option might be inadvertently overlooked. Recall that the Options Principle uses the term option in its broadest sense: *any* right that has no obligation attached to it. In this chapter we discuss important areas in which options are found and illustrate methods for determining the value of an option. For the most part, we examine options on assets that have only a single terminal cash inflow in a perfect capital market environment. This provides a sufficiently simple environment in which to investigate some of the important generalizations that can be made about options.

As just noted, an **option** is the right, without the obligation, to do something. The optionholder (the buyer of the option) can require the optionwriter (the seller of the option) to make the transaction specified in the option contract, but the option does not allow the writer to require the holder to do anything. There are two basic forms of option contracts. The right to buy an asset is referred to as a **call option**, and the right to sell an asset is referred to as a **put option**.

In addition to valuing options, an option pricing model (OPM) can be used to value other assets. Thus, an OPM provides an alternative valuation method to asset pricing models such as the CAPM and APT. As in the case of asset pricing models, option pricing models are not yet perfect and complete. Progress is being made, however, and new insights into the valuation process continue to emerge from research in this area.

One consideration in the discussion of options is the tremendous amount of jargon connected with them. Unfortunately, it is necessary to take some time to learn the various terms. This is especially important because there are multiple terms for many of the concepts and parameters. Table 8-1 contains a miniglossary of terms connected with options to familiarize you with the terminology. To aid the learning process, we will try to use a single term consistently for a concept or parameter, so that it is easier for you to concentrate on understanding the concepts.

Definitions for three fundamental terms are needed to start our discussion. The first is the term **exercise**. The optionholder **exercises** the option when she chooses to make the transaction specified in the option. For example, a call is exercised when the call optionholder decides to purchase the asset according to the option's terms. The second term is the **strike price** (also referred to as the **exercise price**, or in the case of call and put options, **call price** or **put price**, respectively). This is the price at which the transaction specified in the option contract can be enforced. A call

TABLE 8-1   A Glossary of Option-Related Terms (equivalent terms are given in parentheses)

American option An option that can be exercised any time during its life.

Buy (purchase) (take a long position) To purchase an option.

Call an option (call) (exercise) To exercise a call option.

Call option The right without the obligation to purchase a specified asset at a specified price within a specified time period.

Call price (strike price) (exercise price) The price at which the asset will be purchased if a call option is exercised.

Clear a position Eliminate a position by selling a long position or buying a short position.

Contingent claim (option) A claim that is contingent on one or more outcomes. For example, an option will be exercised just prior to its expiration if it is in-the-money. The value of the option is contingent upon the value of the underlying asset.

Covered call optionwriter A person who sells (writes) a call option on an asset that he owns.

Create (sell) (take a short position) (write) The "seller" side of an option transaction.

European option An option that can only be exercised at the time of its expiration.

Exercise (call) (put) When the optionholder enforces the sale on the terms specified in an option contract.

Exercise price (strike price) (call price) The price for which the asset will be exchanged if the option is exercised.

Exercise value (intrinsic value) The value to the optionholder of exercising the option. In the case of a call, the exercise value is the greater of either 0 or the underlying asset's value minus the option's strike price. In the case of a put, the exercise value is the greater of either 0 or the option's strike price minus the underlying asset's value.

Expiration (maturity) When an option contract ceases to exist (be valid).

Expire (mature) Cease to exist.

Hedge A transaction that reduces the risk of an investment.

In-the-money For a call option, this is when the value of the underlying asset exceeds the strike price. For a put option, this is when the value of the underlying asset is less than the strike price.

Long (long position) (own) The holding of an option contract, the holder of which determines whether and when the contract will be exercised; possession of the right without the obligation (to buy or sell).

Mature (expire) Cease to exist.

Maturity (expiration) When an option contract ceases to exist (be valid).

Option The right without the obligation to purchase (call option) or sell (put option) an asset.

Optionholder (own an option) (take a long position in the option) (purchaser of the option) The person in the long position side of the option transaction.

Optionwriter (sell an option) (take a short position in the option) The person in the short position side of the option transaction.

Out-of-the-money For a call option, this is when the value of the underlying asset is less than the strike price. For a put option, this is when the value of the underlying asset exceeds the strike price.

Position Having a claim (owing) (long), or obligation with respect to (owing) (short), an option. That is, having bought or sold an option.

Purchase (buy) (take a long position) To purchase an option.

Put an option To exercise a put option.

Put-call parity The relationship between the value of a put and the value of a call.

Put option The right without the obligation to sell a specified asset at a specified price within a specified time period.

Put price (strike price) (exercise price) The price at which the asset will be sold if a put option is exercised.

Sell (take a short position) (write) To create and sell an option.

Short (short position) (owe) The obligation to deliver (call option) or take (put option) securities in the event an option is exercised; responsible for the obligation without the right (to buy or sell).

Strike price (exercise price) The price for which the asset will be exchanged if the option is exercised.

Take a position Buy or sell. That is, to have some amount that is owned or owed on an option or asset.

Time to expiration (time to maturity) The time remaining until the option expires.

Time to maturity (time to expiration) The time remaining until the option expires.

Time value of an option The difference between the market value and the exercise value of an option.

Underlying asset (asset) The asset on which the option is written. That is, the asset on which the optionwriter is obligated to transact if the optionholder chooses. The value of an option is contingent upon the value of the underlying asset.

Warrant A long-term call option issued by a corporation. The option is to purchase shares of the issuing corporation's stock. The shares are newly created at the time the option is exercised.

Write (sell) (take a short position) To create and sell an option.

optionholder exercises the option by requiring the optionwriter to sell the underlying asset to the optionholder in exchange for the strike price. Finally, we need to distinguish between American and European types of options. An **American option** can be exercised by the holder at any time during the life of the option. A **European option** can be exercised only at the time of its maturity.

AN OPTION AS A CLAIM TO PART OF AN ASSET'S RETURN DISTRIBUTION

8.1

In the previous chapter we described an asset as a set of possible rates of return, where the asset is completely characterized by its expected rate of return, μ, and its standard deviation, σ. The expected rate of return from owning the asset for the next time period is based on the *current* value of the asset. For example, we know from Chapter 6 that a corporate bond selling for $875.38, which matures in exactly 10 years and carries an 8% coupon rate, has an expected rate of return (yield to maturity) of 10%. But if the same bond were selling for $934.96, it would have an expected rate of return of 9%.[1] Of course, the actual outcome can turn out to be quite different from the expected outcome. A rate of return distribution for an asset is simply the probability distribution for the set of all possible rates of return, based on the current value of the asset.

A hypothetical rate of return distribution for an asset, such as a share of common stock, is given in Figure 8-1. Suppose we partition the distribution into two parts: one part above and the other part below the expected value. The owner of an asset, person AO, prefers the possible outcomes that are larger than the expected rate of return (those to the right of μ) to those possible outcomes that are smaller than the expected rate of return (those to the left of μ). Of course, this same statement can be made if we partition the distribution into two parts at *any* point. Outcomes to the right of the "split point" can be viewed as "good" outcomes, and those to the left can be viewed as "bad" outcomes. For any "split point," AO would have to be paid to agree to give up the "good" possible outcomes but would have to pay someone else to get her to agree to accept the "bad" possible outcomes.

The "split point" is the strike price for the option. When an asset owner is paid for giving up "good" outcomes, the owner has sold a call option on the asset. When an owner pays someone else to take the "bad" outcomes, the asset owner has purchased a put option on the asset.

Now let us examine options on a simplified asset that has only one expected future cash flow: its terminal liquidation value. Assume further that the asset owner cannot affect this future cash flow by his action. Therefore, control of the asset has no value.[2] In such cases, the asset's rate of return depends only on its terminal liquidation value.

Suppose the distribution of future terminal liquidation values is that given in Panel I of Figure 8-2, with the current market value of the asset being $25. This distribution "maps" one-to-one from the distribution shown in Figure 8-1. That is, each outcome in one distribution corresponds to one, and only one, outcome in the other distribution. For example, a $30 outcome provides a 20% rate of return be-

---

[1] Recall that bond prices vary over time. Changes are due primarily to interest rate changes and to a lesser extent to firm-specific changes.

[2] This might seem like a strong assumption. It is for a physical asset. It is not for a financial security such as a share of common stock. The value of asset control is discussed in the next chapter. For shares of common stock in a large corporation that is widely held and publicly-traded, the value of control (voting rights) is relatively small.

FIGURE 8-1
A hypothetical rate of return
distribution for an asset.

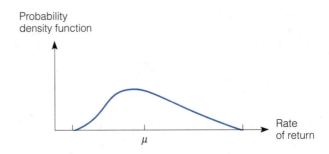

FIGURE 8-2
Probability density function of
terminal liquidation values for
the asset.

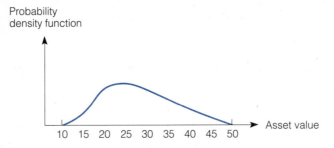

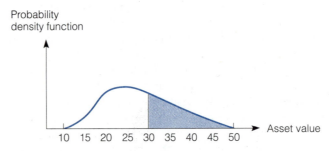

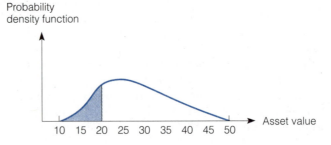

cause the current value of the asset is $25 (20% = [30 − 25]/25). The expected termi-
nal liquidation value is assumed to be $27.50, but the asset can turn out to be worth
anything from $10 to $50.

Suppose a person, CO, wants to own all of the "good" outcomes above $30 but
does not want to suffer any of the "bad" outcomes below $30. Then CO must pay

the asset owner, AO, to induce AO to agree to give up all outcomes above $30, should one of them occur. In other words, CO buys a call option from AO with a strike price of $30; AO sells a call option to CO. CO has a long position in the call option, and AO has a short position in the same option.[3] The call option gives CO the right to buy the asset for $30.

Panel II of Figure 8-2 illustrates the claim portion of the return distribution for a call option with a strike price of $30. A call option gives the optionholder the right to claim all of the "good" outcomes (those above the strike price) by exercising the option. The optionholder can avoid "bad" outcomes (those below the strike price) by simply not exercising the option. Therefore, if the terminal liquidation value of the asset is less than $30, CO will not want to exercise the option. But if its value is more than $30, say $35, CO can buy the asset from AO for $30 and sell the asset to someone else for $35, thereby gaining $5. The $5 gain is referred to as the option's **exercise value**. The exercise value of an **in-the-money** option is the positive difference between the asset's value and the option's strike price. The exercise value is zero for an **out-of-the-money** option (the option owner will "walk away from the option" rather than exercise an out-of-the-money option).

Now consider a put option. Suppose the asset owner, AO, does not want to have outcomes below $20. Since the outcomes below the $20 "split point" are "bad" outcomes, AO must pay a person, PO, to induce PO to agree to accept such an outcome if it occurs. In other words, AO buys a put option from PO with a strike price of $20; PO sells a put option to AO. AO has a long position in the put option, and PO has a short position in the same option.

Panel III of Figure 8-2 illustrates the claim portion of a return distribution for a put option with a strike price of $20. A put option gives the optionholder the right to avoid all of the "bad" outcomes by exercising the option. The optionholder can claim the "good" outcomes simply by failing to exercise the option (if she owns the asset). Therefore, if the terminal liquidation value is above $20, AO will accept the outcome and let the put option expire without exercising it. But if it turns out to be less than $20, AO will sell the asset to PO for $20. AO's gain is the exercise value of the put, which equals the difference between the $20 strike price and the value of the asset.

If you think about it, you should be able to see that insurance can be modeled as simply a put option on the insured asset. For example, if you have collision insurance on a car and there is an accident that completely destroys the car, the insurance company covers your loss (in an agreed-upon way, such as all but $100 if you have "$100 deductible" insurance). In effect, you had a "bad" outcome (an accident), so you sell the damaged car to the insurance company for the strike price (which is typically the market value of the car if it had not been damaged minus the $100 deductible).

INVESTING IN PART OF AN ASSET'S RETURN DISTRIBUTION

Suppose an asset owner, AO, sells a call option with a strike price of $30 and simultaneously buys a put option with a strike price of $20. Then AO's distribution of possible outcomes is given in Figure 8-3. AO has a long position in the asset, a long position in the put option, and a short position in the call option. In this case, AO will always have outcomes between $20 and $30 because those below $20 will be forced onto PO and those above $30 will be expropriated by CO. The "spikes" on

---

[3] Recall from Chapter 4 the notions of long and short positions. A long position is the ownership of an asset. A short position is the mirror image of a long position. That is, the short seller *owes* the asset or, in the case of an option, has the obligation without the right.

FIGURE 8-3

Distribution of terminal liquidation values for a long position in the asset, a long position in a put option ($S = \$20$), and a short position in a call option ($S = \$30$).

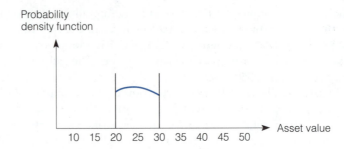

either side of the distribution represent the combined probabilities of outcomes above $30 and below $20.

If we extend the notion of combinations of positions (long or short) in assets, call options, and put options, you should be able to see that a person can create any kind of return distribution he desires. This is valuable because, for example, if you have information about the future, you do not have to purchase assets to reap the value of that information. Instead, you can purchase or sell one or more options, which is what buying and selling parts of the outcome distribution is all about.

As in the case illustrated in Figure 8-3, you can make transactions that provide the kind of return distribution that *exactly* suits your needs and/or any special information you have about the future. Just as a farmer can "lock in" a price for the commodities she produces by selling futures contracts, information specialists can profit from their efforts by making transactions in the option markets. As we noted in Chapter 4, option markets make the capital markets more complete. Individuals, or institutions such as savings and loans, who do not want to take risk can protect themselves, for a price, through option transactions. Such transactions are referred to as **hedging**. A hedge is like insurance.

One very interesting aspect of creating a particular outcome distribution through combinations of positions in assets, call options, and put options is that often an outcome distribution can be created in multiple ways. One of the more interesting facts that comes out of such multiple ways of creating the same outcome distribution is the relationship between the value of a call option and that of a put option with an identical strike price. This relationship is referred to as **put-call parity**.

PUT-CALL PARITY   Suppose a person wants to be able to claim the "good" outcomes above a "split point" of $30. In the examples given above, CO obtained this outcome distribution by purchasing a call option with a strike price of $30. In such a case, CO has claim to the outcome distribution shown in Figure 8-4. Now suppose that the asset owner, AO, who currently has only a long position in the asset, wants to have the same outcome distribution. AO can obtain this outcome distribution by purchasing a put option with a strike price of $30. If the outcome turns out to be above $30, AO will get that outcome because of the long position in the asset; if the outcome turns out to be below $30, AO will exercise the put option, thereby obtaining an outcome of $30. Thus, Figure 8-4 illustrates the claim to the outcome distribution for two investment positions: (1) owning (a long position in) a call option ($S = \$30$), and (2) owning both the asset and a put option ($S = \$30$).[4]

In terms of claims to the outcome distribution, then, owning a call option is equivalent to owning the asset *and* a put option with the same strike price as the call option. The only difference between these two positions is due to the time value of

---

[4] Note that Figure 8-4 is identical to Panel II in Figure 8-2.

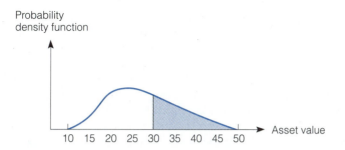

FIGURE 8-4
Claim portion of the outcome distribution for either (i) a long position in a call option ($S = \$30$) or (ii) a long position in the asset and a long position in a put option ($S = \$30$).

money. With a long call position, the claimant invests only the value of the call option. In the case of the long asset-long put combined position, the claimant must invest the value of the put option *plus* the value of the asset. Therefore, the call option position is more valuable by exactly the time-value-of-money difference between the two investments. The impact of the time value of money is explained below, and, using that analysis, we return to put-call parity later.

THE DETERMINANTS OF OPTION VALUE 8.2

Suppose the call option in our example had a strike price of $0? Then AO will have sold the entire return distribution to CO, since the lowest possible outcome for the value of the asset is $10.[5] We know that the option will *always* be exercised because it will *always* end "in-the-money" (with a positive exercise value—at least $10). The result will be that CO will always get the outcome minus the strike price of $0 ("needed" to exercise the option). In a perfect capital market environment, CO will require all of the return since CO will be taking all of the risk. Therefore, AO will have in effect sold the asset to CO because control of the asset is assumed to have no value in our simplified world. And, since the strike price of the call option is $0, there are no time-value-of-money considerations to account for.

Similarly, if the strike price of a put option purchased by AO was $60, AO will *always* exercise the option since the put will *always* end "in-the-money" (the maximum outcome for the value of the asset is $50). By purchasing such a put option, AO will be paying PO to take *all* the risk. Again, in a perfect capital market environment, PO will require all of the return for taking on all of the risk, and in this simplified world, AO will have in effect sold the asset to PO.

The only difference between these put and call scenarios involves time-value-of-money considerations. In the case of the call, payment for the asset takes place with the sale of the option since the strike price is $0. That is, no money will be involved in exercising the option. But in the case of the put option, AO pays PO the option's value at the time of the sale (now). That money can earn its time value for PO until the option's expiration (later), at which time PO will pay AO $60.[6] Please bear with us as we postpone the exact valuation considerations for the time value of money just a little longer.

From the above descriptions and examples, you should be able to see that a major

---

[5] Of course, having assumed a truncated return distribution simplifies the situation.

[6] It is interesting to note that the put option in this case would have the identical outcomes and therefore the same value as a *futures contract*, even though you recall from Chapter 4 that options and futures are different types of financial securities. This is another example where multiple, but equivalent, valuation methods can be used to model a transaction.

factor in determining the value of an option is the *portion of the asset's return distribution to which the optionholder has claim*. But what determines this portion? There are three underlying determinants of this claim portion. Two are straightforward; the third is more subtle. First, in the examples just given, it should be clear that the claim portion will be larger or smaller depending upon the strike price of the option. Second, the return distribution would be shifted up or down if the asset's current market value is more or less than $25, which would also affect the size of the claim portion. So the relationship between the strike price and the asset's current market value directly affects the value of the option, and therefore, the **strike price** and the **current market value** of the underlying asset are two of the determinants of the value of an option.

The effect of these two determinants on an option's value is the following: **(1)** The strike price affects put and call options in *opposite* directions. The value of a put option is *directly* related to its strike price, whereas the value of a call option is *inversely* related to its strike price. That is, a higher strike price increases (decreases) the value of a put (call) option. **(2)** The current market value of the underlying asset also affects put and call options in *opposite* directions, but the effects are reversed from that of the strike price effects. The value of a call (put) option is *directly (inversely)* related to the value of the underlying asset. That is, an increase in the market value of the underlying asset causes an increase (decrease) in the value of a call (put) option.

Less obvious is the importance of the third determinant of the value of an option, the **risk** (standard deviation of the rate of return) of the underlying asset. Figure 8-5 illustrates the claim portion of the outcome distributions for call options with identical strike prices on two different assets that have identical current market values but different risk levels. Panel I is based on an asset that has an outcome distribution with a low σ, whereas Panel II is based on an asset that has an outcome distribution with a high σ. As you can see, the call option on the asset shown in Panel II has a much larger probability (the area under the curve) of having a "good" outcome than does the call option on the asset shown in Panel I. Therefore, the call option in Panel II is worth more than the call option shown in Panel I.

This is a general result that applies to both calls and puts: **(3)** The value of an

FIGURE 8-5

Claim portion of the outcome distribution for a call option on a low-risk underlying asset and a high-risk underlying asset.

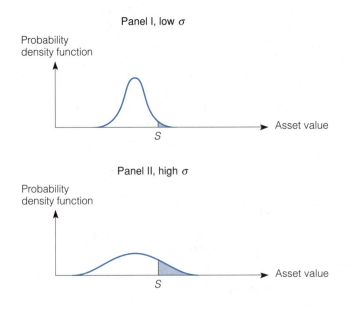

Panel I, low σ

Panel II, high σ

option is *directly* related to the risk of the underlying asset. That is, an increase in the risk (standard deviation of the rate of return) of the underlying asset increases the value of an option (a decrease in risk decreases the option's value). This is because there is a greater probability that the option will have positive exercise value, and therefore the option has a greater expected future cash flow.

Recall that an option conveys a right without an obligation. One way to see the impact that a change in the risk of the underlying asset has on the value of an option is to note that an increase in risk increases the number of "good" outcomes to be claimed and increases the number of "bad" outcomes to be avoided. "Good" outcomes are claimed with a call by exercising it. "Bad" outcomes are avoided with a put by exercising it. In both cases, the right is valuable.

Another way to understand the impact that the risk of the underlying asset has on the value of an option is to examine the option's expected future cash flow. An increase in the probability of a "good" outcome increases the expected future cash flow of a call option since "good" outcomes can always be claimed by exercising the option. By contrast, an increase in the probability of a "bad" outcome does not decrease the expected future cash flow of a call option since "bad" outcomes can always be avoided by not exercising the option. Likewise, an increase in the probability of a "bad" outcome increases a put option's expected future cash flow since the option can be exercised to avoid the "bad" outcomes.

The second major factor in determining the value of an option is the time value of money, which itself depends on time and the required rate of return. Therefore, the fourth determinant of the value of an option is its remaining **time until expiration.** Understanding why time is a determinant of option value is fairly straightforward. If you have a choice between two options, where the only difference between the options is the time until they expire, which option would you prefer to own? If you think about it, you can never be worse off with the option that has the longer time until expiration (although it may not make you any better off). Therefore, as with risk, there is a general result that applies to both calls and puts: **(4)** The value of an option is *directly* related to its remaining time until expiration. That is, an increase in the remaining time until expiration will never decrease the value of an option. (Another way to think about this is to say that more time allows more chance for the option to be in-the-money.) You should notice that this result was stated as "will never decrease" rather than "increases." Although there will be an increase in most situations, it is possible to have a situation where an increase in the time to maturity does not add value, but additional time can never take away value because the optionholder *always* has control—the right without the obligation.

The fifth (and final) determinant of the value of an option, already mentioned, is the **required rate of return**. **(5)** The value of a call (put) option is *directly* (*inversely*) related to the required rate of return. That is, an increase in the discount rate increases (decreases) the value of a call (put) option. One way to see the impact of the time value of money is to note that the option seller (writer) is paid for the option now and can earn the time value of money on that sale price until the option expires.

An important issue that remained unresolved for many years was the determination of the correct discount rate to apply to these funds to compute the time value of money. Fisher Black and Myron Scholes (1973) showed that the correct rate is the riskless rate of return. Needless to say, this answer is not immediately obvious from intuition. In fact, this answer eluded scholars for many years. While we do not present a proof that the discount rate must be the riskless rate, we can provide some intuition to help you understand this very important result.

Consider the case of a long position in the underlying asset and a short position in the call option: a writer of a call option who owns the asset. This combined position is referred to as a **covered call option**. As with our previous examples, assume that the asset has a single terminal cash flow. A covered call optionwriter, AO in the examples above, is paid for relinquishing all of the possible outcomes above the strike price. AO can therefore invest the proceeds received from the sale of the call option for the rest of the life of the option. The time value of money to be earned on the funds during this time would appear to depend upon the asset in which AO chooses to invest. This is not the case.

Recall that *value is a function of both risk and expected return*. Value can remain constant if a change in expected return (expected future cash flow) is exactly offset by a change in risk (and therefore required rate of return). This must be true for future value as well as present value. Therefore, if AO invests in a high-risk investment to get a high expected return, the future value is determined by the required rate of return to that investment, which is also high. Likewise, for low-risk investments: low expected return and low required return. In a perfect capital market environment, whatever investment is made will be along the security market line (SML) in accordance with the risk-return trade-off. Therefore, the time value of money can be determined on the basis of assuming that AO invests in the riskless asset.

For example, suppose AO receives $100 for a call option and invests the $100 at $r_f = 6\%$ per year for the half of a year left in the life of the option. The expected future cash flow of $103 (= $100[1.06]^{.5}$) has a present value of exactly $100 at its required rate of return of 6% per year. Alternatively, AO can invest the $100 in a risky asset that has an expected and required rate of return of 12% per year. The expected future cash flow for this second alternative is a higher amount, $106 (= $100[1.12]^{.5}$), but it also has a present value of exactly $100 at its required rate of return of 12% per year. The difference between the two expected future cash flows is simply the result of the risk-return trade-off and has no impact on *value*. While AO has a choice of a sure $103 or an expected $106, if AO takes the expected $106, the actual outcome may turn out to be $95, $110, or any other value. If there were a difference in *value* between these alternative investments the risk-return trade-off would not be at equilibrium. Therefore, since no extra value can be created using one expected/required rate of return combination versus *any* other combination, it is simplest to use the riskless rate of interest to account for the time value of money in the valuation of options.

The time value of money also plays a role in determining the value of an American option on an asset that has one or more cash flows in addition to its terminal liquidation value. A typical situation in this regard is a market-traded option on a dividend-paying stock. While the time value of money does play a role in such cases, this technical complexity is not examined here. We leave the determination of the value of such options to more in-depth investigations of option valuation.[7]

A CAUTIONARY WORD ABOUT UNDERSTANDING OPTION VALUATION

The above discussion includes specific statements about how the value of an option is affected by a change in one of the parameters. While such relationships are important, we want to discourage you strongly from memorizing these relationships. Instead, you should work on understanding the reasons for their existence. Once you

[7] See, for example, Cox and Rubinstein (1985) or Jarrow and Rudd (1983).

understand these reasons, you can always take a little time and think through how a change in the value of a particular parameter will affect the value of an option.

PLACES TO LOOK FOR OPTIONS 8.3

We have said that options exist in *many* forms but have mentioned only a few. In this section we cite a number of other places to look for options to help you develop insight into their pervasive existence.

PUBLICLY-TRADED OPTIONS As we noted in the introduction to this chapter, the CBOE has become one of the largest capital markets in the world. While the CBOE is the largest market for publicly-traded options, standardized puts and calls are also traded on the AMEX and Philadelphia Stock Exchange, among others. Warrants are also sometimes traded on the stock exchanges. A **warrant** is essentially a long-term call option on a stock. Warrants generally have very long lives when they are issued, such as 10 years or longer. They are issued by a corporation on its own stock. Consequently, unlike standardized stock options, such as those traded on the CBOE, when a warrant is exercised, it creates new equity in the firm. If you look in the Money & Investing section (section C) of the *Wall Street Journal*, you will see yet other publicly-traded options, such as stock index options and currency options.

INSURANCE As we have already noted, insurance can be viewed as a form of put option on the insured asset. For example, if a fire damages a fire-insured house (a "bad" outcome), the owner can, loosely speaking, "sell" the house to the insurance company for the insured amount. Of course, usually the insurance company pays the homeowner to repair the house to restore it to some prespecified condition. Still, in spite of additional complexity, a put option model of insurance provides the best starting point for valuing insurance.

REAL ESTATE OPTIONS Options have been used for many years in the area of real estate. For example, suppose a person is trying to develop a new shopping mall. The development depends on many things, such as securing several contiguous parcels of real estate, obtaining financing, and gaining commitments from retailers to lease shops. The development can only proceed if *all* the pieces fall in place. Rather than invest in each piece of land sequentially, the developer can purchase call options from the landowners with agreed upon strike prices. Then, *if* everything comes together, the developer has claim to the land for a particular price. Without the call option, the "later" landowners could hold out for extraordinary prices. Actually, the "last" landowner could require just short of the total positive NPV of the project.

To see this point, suppose the NPV of the project is $5 million at the start of the development, based on estimates for purchasing all the pieces. Suppose further that after all but one parcel of land have been purchased, the NPV of the project is $4 million and that the "last" piece of land was expected to cost $100,000. Assuming the investment project *must* have this parcel of land to be completed, the owner of the land can refuse to sell for the expected $100,000 price. How much will the developer be willing to pay for the land? The developer will be better off as long as the price for the land is less than the $4 million in positive NPV. That, of course, is considerably more than what the land was "worth" before the project was this far along. Now, however, if the landowner sets a price of $2 million for the land, the developer will be $2 million ahead, even after paying the "inflated" price. A call option can keep the developer from being "caught" in the position of having to give up a substantial portion of the positive NPV of the project to a "holdout."

CONVERTIBLES   A convertible bond or share of convertible preferred stock can be converted into shares of common stock at the option of the securityholder. A security such as a convertible bond can be viewed as a "straight" security (a "normal" corporate bond) *plus* a call option on shares of the firm's common stock. As in the case of warrants, the common shares are normally newly created. However, unlike a warrant, the option connected with a convertible security cannot be separated from the "straight" security.

CALL PROVISION ON A CORPORATE BOND   The vast majority of corporate bond indentures include a provision that allows the *firm* to redeem the bond for a preset amount prior to maturity. Therefore, the typical corporate bondholder is not simply a bondholder. She has a long position in (owns) the asset (a straight bond) and also has a simultaneous short position in (has written) a call option. The firm is on the "other side of the transaction." It has a short position in the asset (a straight bond) and a long position in the call option.

"HIDDEN" OPTIONS

As noted in our overview of the Options Principle, the importance of options extends well beyond their easily identified existence because many assets often contain "hidden" options. Whenever a situation is such that a claim on an asset is contingent upon the occurrence of particular outcomes, there is probably a "hidden" option involved. For example, recognizing a tax loss upon the sale of an asset requires (is contingent upon) an outcome where the market value of the asset has declined. "Hidden" options dramatically complicate the process of accurately measuring the value of an asset. This may seem to be an obvious statement because the option is "hidden." However, even in cases that are known to contain an option, the careful identification of the option for valuation purposes can pose a significant analytical puzzle. This is because an outcome distribution can be created using different investment positions. For example, in Figure 8-4 it was shown that a long call option position is equivalent to the combination of a long position in the asset plus a long position in the put option. Therefore, a "hidden" option can be valued as either a put option *or* a call option.

REFUNDING A HOME MORTGAGE   When a mortgage on a home permits prepayment of the loan (mortgage), the borrower can refinance the home loan at a lower interest rate if rates go down after the loan is made. In effect, then, the right to refinance the loan involves a hidden call option; the homeowner can take out a new (lower interest) loan and use the proceeds to prepay the high interest loan. The prepayment of the home mortgage loan is analogous to a corporation calling an outstanding high-coupon bond and refunding it. A penalty charge for prepayment of a loan can be viewed as part of the strike price for this "hidden" call option.

TAX-TIMING OPTIONS   We noted this option in our overview of the Options Principle. One such option occurs with respect to capital gains. There are others, such as the option firms have to refinance outstanding debt, which is analogous to the homeowner's option to refinance home mortgage debt, as just discussed.

OPTIONS CONNECTED WITH CAPITAL INVESTMENTS   In Chapter 13, we discuss options the firm has in connection with its capital investment projects. Such options include product price setting, as well as postponing, expanding, and abandoning an investment project, among others. A particularly important option that we implicitly noted in Chapter 6 is that of "growth opportunities." Recall the net present value of future investments, NPVFI. Much of this value may come from a firm's growth opportunities (options) in new areas that are created by its existing areas of investment.

VARIABLE COST REDUCTION   Also in later chapters we will talk about operating leverage and choices that involve fixed costs versus variable costs. When production is suspended, variable costs are no longer incurred, whereas fixed costs must still be paid. Thus, choosing a production process with relatively more variable cost and less fixed cost provides a "hidden" option on those costs.

COMMON STOCK AS A CALL OPTION

One "hidden" option is so important that we separate its description from the others. In our overview of the Options Principle, we pointed out that limited liability creates the option to default and not fully repay a debt. We now know from put-call parity that this option can be modeled in multiple ways, but for simplicity we will illustrate the relationship using a European call option and common stock in a simple firm that is partly financed by zero-coupon debt. (Recall that zero-coupon debt requires a single payment at maturity covering both interest and principal.) When the debt contract is created for this firm, it is as though the debtholders have written the stockholders a European call option on the firm's assets. The debt payment is the strike price. When the debt matures, if the firm is worth more than the strike price (debt payment) the stockholders will "buy back" the firm from the debtholders for the strike price (i.e., the stockholders will make the debt payment) and claim the residual value of the firm. If, however, the firm is worth less than the strike price, the stockholders will simply refuse to exercise their call option, and the debtholders "keep" the firm.

The above situation can be further generalized. Whenever *any* payment is due, interest or principal, the shareholders have in effect a decision whether they should "exercise" their call option. If the value of the firm's assets is greater than the payment due, the shareholders will exercise their option and "buy back" the assets from the debtholders by making the required payment. Each required payment is, in effect, the strike price of an option.

Therefore, when a firm has one or more debts, it is as though the shareholders have a call option on the firm's assets.

Although the strict equivalence between shares of common stock and a simple European call option holds *exactly* only under certain restrictive conditions, it is generally a good approximation. More importantly, as we will see in Chapter 9, viewing shares of stock in this way provides very important insights into the practical management of a corporation.

It is interesting to note that the "hidden" default option makes a standard corporate bond even more complex than already noted. We have pointed out that most firms have a long position in a call option for refinancing the bond, which they can and will exercise if the value of the bond increases by a sufficient amount. In addition, the firm has the "hidden" default option, which it can and will *fail* to exercise if the value of the firm decreases by a sufficient amount. While valuing a bond was shown to be a "straightforward" task in Chapter 6, you should be able to see now that determining the exact value of even this "simple" asset is more complex than it might appear at first.

8.4   SOME GENERALIZATIONS ABOUT OPTION VALUE

Thus far, we have established the fact that the value of an option on an asset depends upon five things:

1. the underlying asset's current value, denoted P_0;
2. the option's strike price, denoted S;
3. the risk (standard deviation of the rate of return) of the underlying asset's value, denoted σ;
4. the option's remaining time until expiration, denoted T;
5. the riskless rate of return, denoted r_f for an effective rate and k for an APR.

Now let us consider other facts that can be logically deduced about the value of an option.

1. Recall the corollary to the Options Principle: ***An option cannot have a negative value*** because the optionholder can always decide to do nothing. If there is absolutely no chance that the transaction named in the option will *ever* have positive value to the optionholder now or at *any time* in the future, the option will be worthless, but the option can never have a negative value. Of course, even the smallest probability that the transaction named in the option will have positive value to the owner at *some* time in the future gives the option some positive value, however tiny that value might be; hence, the principle that options are valuable.

2. ***An American option that is traded in an efficient capital market is never worth less than its exercise value***. (Recall that for an in-the-money option, the exercise value is the positive difference between the strike price and the asset's value, and for an out-of-the-money option, the exercise value is zero.) This is because an American option can be exercised at any time during its life. If such an option is ever worth less than its exercise value, a riskless arbitrage opportunity will exist: a person can purchase and exercise the option, thereby earning a riskless arbitrage profit. Riskless arbitrage opportunities do not exist in an efficient market. Another way to see the same concept is to say that if the option were ever worth less than its exercise value, an owner wanting to liquidate her option could exercise rather than sell it.

3. Based on points 1 and 2 above, ***the minimum value of an American option is its exercise value*** (either zero or positive).

4. ***The maximum value of an American call option is the value of the asset***. Recall our example of a strike price of $0. An American call option is never worth more than the underlying asset because if it were, buying the asset would strictly dominate buying the call option. That is, in the case of financial assets, there would be a riskless arbitrage opportunity for someone to purchase the asset and

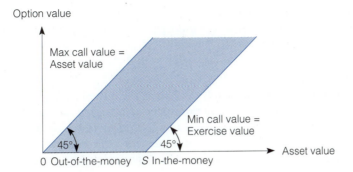

FIGURE 8-6
Minimum and maximum value
for an American call option.

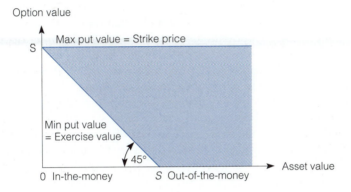

FIGURE 8-7
Minimum and maximum value
for an American put option.

sell the call option if the option could be sold for more than the amount for which the asset could be bought.[8]

5. Maximum and minimum values for an American call option are shown graphically in Figure 8-6. The line up from the origin is at a 45° angle because the maximum option value equals the asset value. Similarly, there is a one-to-one linear relationship between the exercise value and the value of the asset when the option is in-the-money. Therefore, the line extending up from the strike price is also at a 45° angle. For example, consider a call option with $S = \$35$ where the underlying asset has a current market value $P_0 = \$42$. Therefore, the call option's exercise value is currently $7 (= 42-35). If the market value of the underlying asset increased by $3 to $45, the exercise value would increase by an identical $3 amount to $10 (= 45-35).

6. ***The maximum value of an American put option is its strike price***. An American put option is never worth more than its strike price because if it were, there would be a riskless arbitrage opportunity. A person could sell the put option, earn the time value of money on the proceeds, and have more than enough to pay off the strike price at expiration, thereby earning a riskless arbitrage profit if the put was sold for more than the strike price. (The arbitrageur would end up owning the asset as an additional bonus.)

7. Maximum and minimum values for an American put option are shown graphically in Figure 8-7. The line from S on the asset-value axis to S on the option-value axis makes a 45° angle with the asset-value axis. In this area the put option

[8] This may not hold for physical assets, because of transaction costs. If the call is not exercised there may be costs associated with disposing of an otherwise worthless asset.

is in-the-money. For every dollar decrease in asset value there is an equal increase in the exercise value of the put option. For example, with $S = \$35$ and $P_0 = \$30$, the exercise value is $\$5$ ($= 35\text{-}30$). If the market value of the asset decreased by $\$4$ to $\$26$, the exercise value would increase by an identical $\$4$ amount, to $\$9$ ($= 35\text{-}26$).

8. The **time value of an option** is defined as the difference between its market value and its exercise value. *The time value of an option increases (decreases) as the value of the underlying asset moves toward (away from) the strike price*. The time value of an option is at its maximum when the value of the underlying asset exactly equals the strike price. Also, as noted earlier, the time value of an option is directly related to the option's remaining time until expiration. Figure 8-8 illustrates these points. Option A in Figure 8-8 has a longer time remaining until expiration than option B.

9. Point 2 above states that the exercise value is the minimum value for an American option because the optionholder can exercise it at any time. Because the total value of an option is its exercise value *plus* its time value (the difference between the option's market value and its exercise value), *it is generally better to sell rather than exercise an option prior to its expiration*.

An exception to this rule involves an American put option that is far enough in-the-money that the time value of money to be realized on exercising the option and reinvesting the strike price exceeds the time value of the option that is sacrificed when the option is exercised. To see this point another way, consider the extreme case of an asset that has become worthless and has no chance of becoming valuable. In such a case, the put holder should exercise the option to receive the proceeds (the strike price) and reinvest them to earn the time value of money on the proceeds.

Another exception to the sell-rather-than-exercise rule can occur with respect to cases where there are predictable changes that will occur in the value of the underlying asset. One such situation can occur when there are expected future cash flows associated with the asset that occur before the option expires. The value of the asset will decrease by the value of the cash flows because a future owner will not receive those cash flows. For example, the value of a share of common stock decreases by the value of a cash dividend. So for short-maturity options on stocks with expected dividend payments that are virtually certain to occur, there may be a point where it is more profitable to exercise rather than continue to hold a call option. This is due to the time value of the option being

FIGURE 8-8

Contrasting values of otherwise identical call options with different times until expiration and the maximum time value of an option.

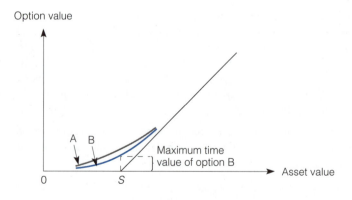

less than the present value of the dividend payments. Any potential purchaser of the option will reach the same conclusion the instant before a dividend payment will occur.

Generally, however, and especially for call options on assets that have only an uncertain terminal cash flow (such as the market value of the asset), prior to the expiration date it is better to sell rather than exercise an option as long as the capital market is efficient.

PUT-CALL PARITY   8.5

We introduced the concept of put-call parity in an earlier section. At this point, we will be more explicit about how the time value of money is accounted for in the difference between the value of a put option and the value of a call option. Recall that the outcome distribution shown in Figure 8-4 can be claimed by either ownership of (a long position in) a call option ($S = \$30$) or ownership of both the asset and a put option ($S = \$30$). The only difference in value between these two positions is the amount of money that will be invested. In the case of the call option, the owner invests the value of the call by purchasing the option and must pay $30 when the call is exercised. Thus, in one case, the investor commits the value of the call option now and the present value of the strike price in the future. In the other case, the investor commits the value of the put option now and the value of the asset now. Then, if the outcome is above the strike price, the owner ends up owning the asset in either case. If the outcome is below the strike price, the owner ends up with the strike price in cash but does not own the asset in either case. Therefore, we have the following relationship:

$$-P_0 - \text{PUT} = -\text{CALL} - S_0 \qquad (8.1)$$

where P_0 is the current value of the underlying asset, PUT is the current value of the put option, CALL is the current value of the call option, and S_0 is the present value of the strike price.

Recall that the present value of the strike price is invariant to the risk of the investment, so we can use the riskless rate to compute the present value of S. With a riskless APR of k and continuous compounding, $S_0 = Se^{-Tk}$, where T is the time until expiration. Substituting this expression into Equation (8.1) and rearranging, we can express the value of either option in terms of the other (and the present value of the strike price and the current value of the asset):

$$\text{CALL} = \text{PUT} + P_0 - Se^{-Tk} \qquad (8.2)$$

$$\text{PUT} = \text{CALL} + Se^{-Tk} - P_0 \qquad (8.3)$$

AN APPLICATION OF PUT-CALL PARITY

Just as common stock can be modeled as a form of call option, insights into the value and nature of other securities can be obtained by modeling them in different, but equivalent, terms. We noted previously that a convertible bond is a security that includes an embedded call option. We said a convertible bond can be modeled as being a straight bond plus a call option on shares of the firm's common stock. Put-call parity allows us to see that under certain conditions, a convertible bond can also be modeled as stock plus a put option. As in the case of approximating common stock as a European call option, it is generally a good approximation, even though a convertible bond is *exactly* equivalent to shares of stock plus a put option only under specific conditions.

One insight to be gained from the stock plus put option view of convertible debt involves how corporations view the issuance of convertible debt. Often, a financial manager will refer to convertible debt as **deferred equity**. The implication of this term is that the convertible bondholders are viewed as already being equityholders in the firm. Of course, because of the put option, these particular equityholders have the value of their equity somewhat protected because except in the case of bankruptcy, they can sell their equity back to the firm. This view may explain the general lack of concern by practicing financial managers over the issue of calling outstanding convertible debt to force its conversion into equity—it is already viewed as equity.

A second insight gained from the stock-plus-put-option view of a convertible bond is that when a firm does call outstanding convertible debt to force its conversion, the value to be obtained from calling is simply an out-of-the-money put option plus the difference between interest and dividend payments. We explore this topic further when the management of the firm's outstanding securities is discussed in more detail in Chapter 20.

8.6   VALUING OPTIONS

Thus far, we have not been very precise about the exact properties of the options we have been discussing. For example, in some cases, we have not said specifically whether an option was European or American. This lack of precision has been deliberate. It is intended to allow you to get a "feel" for some of the important generalizations about options. Of course, when we attempt to determine an exact value for an option, this lack of precision is not acceptable. Therefore, at this point, we will be more exact in our description of the particular option we are valuing.

The value of an option is, as with other financial securities, the present value of its expected future cash flows. But how is that present value computed? The present value of the expected future cash flows for a call option on an asset represented by a discrete random variable can be expressed as

$$E(\text{CALL}) = \left(\frac{1}{(1 + r_f)^T} \right) \left(\sum_{i=1}^{\infty} p_i \{ \max [(x_i - S), 0] \} \right) \tag{8.4}$$

where x_i is the asset's outcome, T is the number of time periods until expiration, and p_i is the **risk-adjusted probability** of outcome i.[9] Recall our discussion of how a change in the risk of the underlying asset affects the value of an option: The outcomes where the call is out-of-the-money, the "bad" ones, do not add anything to (or subtract from) the expected future cash flow. This is because they are eliminated by the max [ ] function in Equation (8.4).

THE REQUIRED RATE OF RETURN FOR AN OPTION

We have said that the value of any asset can be determined by discounting the expected future cash flows at the required rate of return. While this is conceptually a valid approach for determining the value of an option (an option is simply an asset

[9] Risk-adjusted probabilities are used to determine a "sure" expected value (sometimes called a **certainty equivalent**) that would be equivalent to the actual risky expected value. We use them here to reduce complexity (believe it or not!).

whose value is contingent upon the value of another asset), a major complication renders this approach impractical for valuing options: *The risk of the option depends upon the market value of the underlying asset.*

As we discussed in Chapter 5, the market value of an asset in an efficient market follows a random, unpredictable pattern. Thus, since every change in market value changes the risk of the option, the required rate of return changes every instant, which makes it virtually impossible to determine the value of the option. We can, however, make two general statements about option risk and required rate of return.

When a person owns an option, he has a claim to the "good" outcomes, *but* purchasing the option requires a smaller investment than does purchasing the underlying asset. Because of this, the standard deviation of the rate of return from owning an option is never less than the standard deviation of the rate of return from owning the underlying asset. Likewise, the beta is never less for owning the option than for owning the underlying asset. Therefore, *owning an option is never less risky than owning the underlying asset.*

Notice that we did not say the option is always riskier. This is because a call option with a strike price lower than the lowest possible outcome or a put option with a strike price higher than the highest possible outcome is equivalent to owning the asset in our simplified environment. Either is equivalent to owning the asset because either security would provide its owner with claim to the entire return distribution. (Recall that a call option with a strike price of $0 is the same as owning the asset in our simplified environment.) Because of this, *the risk of such an option in our simplified environment would be identical to the risk of owning the underlying asset.*

The above fact provides a lower bound on the risk of an option, and since in all other cases owning the option is riskier than owning the underlying asset, it leads us to our third general statement about the risk of an option: **The risk of an option increases as it becomes further out-of-the-money (or becomes less in-the-money).** Conversely, the risk of an option decreases as it becomes further in-the-money (or becomes less out-of-the-money). Another way to say the same thing is to say that the risk of a call (put) is *inversely* (*directly*) related to the value of the underlying asset.

Therefore, an option has a unique required rate of return for *every* possible value that the underlying asset can have. Consequently, even though it might be feasible to determine a required rate of return for an option at a single point in time, the determination of a required rate of return for an option is not useful because the risk of an option changes with each change in the value of the underlying asset.

A SIMPLE OPTION PRICING MODEL   8.7

Equation (8.4) can be used to begin building an option pricing model. Consider an asset with a very simplified set of only two possible outcomes, $60 and $160, with *risk-adjusted probabilities* .6 and .4, respectively. The risk-adjusted expected future cash flow is then $100 (= .6[60] + .4[160]). If r_f is 5%, the present value of the expected future cash flows is $95.24 (= 100/1.05).

What is a call option on this asset worth if it has a strike price of $150? In other words, what is the present value of this call option? If the asset's outcome turns out to be $60, the call option is worthless and will not be exercised. If the asset's outcome turns out to be $160, the option will be worth $10 at $t = 1$ (exercise value = asset value minus strike price = 160 − 150). Therefore, the risk-adjusted expected future cash flow is $4 (= .6[0] + .4[10]) and the present value of the option is $3.81 (= 4/1.05).

FIGURE 8-9

Possible outcomes and associated risk-adjusted probabilities for a two-state asset.

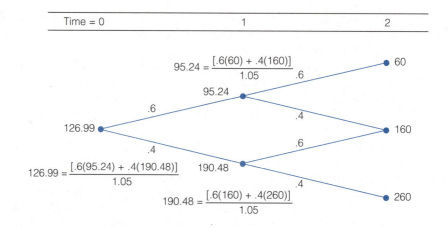

Now consider a similar option on a slightly more complex asset. This second asset has a 2-period life, where one of the possible outcomes after the first period is identical to those just given. Figure 8-9 presents the outcomes and associated risk-adjusted probabilities for the asset. At $t = 2$, the asset will be worth either $60, $160, or $260. At $t = 1$, there are two possible values. As in the example just given, one possibility is a value at time $t = 1$ of $95.24. The second possibility at $t = 1$ is based on the likelihood that the asset will be worth $160 or $260 at $t = 2$, which has a value at $t = 1$ of $190.48 (= {.6[160] + .4[260]}/1.05).

The value of a call option on this asset at time $t = 1$ was computed to be $3.81 if the asset is worth $95.24 at that time. Similarly, the value of the call option is $47.62 (= .6[160 − 150]/1.05 + .4[260 − 150]/1.05) if the value of the asset is $190.48 at $t = 1$. Therefore, the value of the call option at $t = 0$ must be $20.32 (= {.6[3.81] +.4[47.62]}/1.05).

The value of the call option can also be computed directly from Equation (8.4), thereby "skipping over" the option's possible values at $t=1$. To make such a computation, we need the risk-adjusted probabilities of the final outcomes. With independent outcomes, the risk-adjusted probability of a terminal outcome of $60 can be computed by multiplying the risk-adjusted probabilities along the "path" leading to that outcome: $(.6)(.6) = .36$. Likewise, the risk-adjusted probability of an outcome of $260 is $(.4)(.4) = .16$. The outcome of $160 can result from two paths, so its risk-adjusted probability is the sum of the risk-adjusted probabilities of each path: $(.6)(.4) + (.4)(.6) = .48$.[10] Then, from Equation (8.4), we have

$$E(\text{CALL}) = \left(\frac{1}{(1 + r_f)^T}\right) \left(\sum_{i=1}^{\infty} p_i \{\max [(x_i - S), 0]\}\right)$$

$$= \frac{.36[0] + .48[160 - 150] + .16[260 - 150]}{1.05^2} = 20.32$$

8.8   A MORE COMPLEX OPTION PRICING MODEL

The example just given with two periods can be extended. If the number of possible outcomes for the value of the asset increases, an option's value can be computed directly, if tediously, from the possible paths for the expected value of the asset as additional information arrives from one time period to the next. In fact, we can extend

[10] Since $160 is the only other possible outcome, this risk-adjusted probability can also be computed as $1 − .36 − .16 = .48$.

this notion and build what is called a **two-state option pricing model** (two-state OPM) for valuing an option.[11]

Think of describing the movement in the asset's expected present value during "small" time periods as either up (a little) or down (a little). When the risk-adjusted probability of an increase or decrease in value is constant over all periods, the risk-adjusted probabilities of the terminal outcomes can be computed using the binomial probability distribution. This is why the two-state OPM is often referred to as the **binomial option pricing model** (binomial OPM).

Theoretically, we can make the time periods and possible price movements in the two-state OPM so small that time is virtually continuous. Analyzing the effect of smaller and smaller time periods and price movements is analogous to examining the impact on the present value of more frequent compounding to learn something about continuous compounding, as we did in Chapter 3. In the two-state option pricing situation, we make the time periods and possible movements smaller and smaller to see what happens *in the limit* as the size of each time period approaches zero.

As in the case of using discrete compounding to estimate a present value for continuous compounding, an option value can be estimated by using the simple two-state approximation. Of course, the more complete and accurate the discrete description of asset value, the more accurate the estimate of option value. Such simplifications are especially useful for establishing crude estimates of the value of various "hidden" options.

THE BLACK-SCHOLES OPTION PRICING MODEL

Under a particular set of assumptions, as more time periods are used and the size of each time period approaches zero, the two-state OPM just described converges to the option pricing model derived by Fischer Black and Myron Scholes. Case Sprenkle (1961) developed an option pricing model that is accurate *except* in its treatment of the time value of money. But it was not until Black and Scholes (1973) proved that time-value-of-money adjustments *must* be made using the riskless rate that the model was complete. The Black-Scholes OPM is given as

$$\text{CALL} = P_0 N[d_1] - SN[d_2]e^{-Tk} \tag{8.5}$$

where

$$d_1 = \frac{ln[P_0/S] + Tk}{\sigma T^{1/2}} + \frac{\sigma T^{1/2}}{2} \tag{8.6}$$

$$d_2 = d_1 - \sigma T^{1/2} \tag{8.7}$$

$N[d]$ = the cumulative distribution function (cdf) for a standardized ($\mu = 0$, $\sigma = 1$) normal random variable: the probability that an outcome is less than or equal to d. $N[d]$ is given in Table 8-2 for values of d from $d = -3.09$ to $d = 3.09$, in increments of .01;

σ = the standard deviation of the (continuously compounded) rate of return on the underlying asset;

T = the time (in years) until the option expires;

k = the APR with continuous compounding for the riskless rate;

S = the strike price of the option;

P_0 = the current value of the underlying asset;

ln = the natural (base e) logarithm function.

[11] The two-state OPM was developed by Rendleman and Bartter (1979), among others.

TABLE 8.2 Cumulative Distribution Function for the Standard Normal Random Variable. For example, N[−1.15] = .1251 and N[1.57] = .9418.

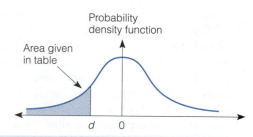

Probability density function

Area given in table

d	0.00	0.01	0.02	0.03	0.04	0.05	0.06	0.07	0.08	0.09
−3.0	.0013	.0013	.0013	.0012	.0012	.0011	.0011	.0011	.0010	.0010
−2.9	.0019	.0018	.0018	.0017	.0016	.0016	.0015	.0015	.0014	.0014
−2.8	.0026	.0025	.0024	.0023	.0023	.0022	.0021	.0021	.0020	.0019
−2.7	.0035	.0034	.0033	.0032	.0031	.0030	.0029	.0028	.0027	.0026
−2.6	.0047	.0045	.0044	.0043	.0041	.0040	.0039	.0038	.0037	.0036
−2.5	.0062	.0060	.0059	.0057	.0055	.0054	.0052	.0051	.0049	.0048
−2.4	.0082	.0080	.0078	.0075	.0073	.0071	.0069	.0068	.0066	.0064
−2.3	.0107	.0104	.0102	.0099	.0096	.0094	.0091	.0089	.0087	.0084
−2.2	.0139	.0136	.0132	.0129	.0125	.0122	.0119	.0116	.0113	.0110
−2.1	.0179	.0174	.0170	.0166	.0162	.0158	.0154	.0150	.0146	.0143
−2.0	.0227	.0222	.0217	.0212	.0207	.0202	.0197	.0192	.0188	.0183
−1.9	.0287	.0281	.0274	.0268	.0262	.0256	.0250	.0244	.0239	.0233
−1.8	.0359	.0351	.0344	.0336	.0329	.0322	.0314	.0307	.0301	.0294
−1.7	.0446	.0436	.0427	.0418	.0409	.0401	.0392	.0384	.0375	.0367
−1.6	.0548	.0537	.0526	.0516	.0505	.0495	.0485	.0475	.0465	.0455
−1.5	.0668	.0655	.0643	.0630	.0618	.0606	.0594	.0582	.0571	.0559
−1.4	.0808	.0793	.0778	.0764	.0749	.0735	.0721	.0708	.0694	.0681
−1.3	.0968	.0951	.0934	.0918	.0901	.0885	.0869	.0853	.0838	.0823
−1.2	.1151	.1131	.1112	.1093	.1075	.1056	.1038	.1020	.1003	.0985
−1.1	.1357	.1335	.1314	.1292	.1271	.1251	.1230	.1210	.1190	.1170
−1.0	.1587	.1563	.1539	.1515	.1492	.1469	.1446	.1423	.1401	.1379
−0.9	.1841	.1814	.1788	.1762	.1736	.1711	.1685	.1660	.1635	.1611
−0.8	.2119	.2090	.2061	.2033	.2005	.1977	.1949	.1922	.1894	.1867
−0.7	.2420	.2389	.2358	.2327	.2296	.2266	.2236	.2206	.2177	.2148
−0.6	.2743	.2709	.2676	.2643	.2611	.2578	.2546	.2514	.2483	.2451
−0.5	.3085	.3050	.3015	.2981	.2946	.2912	.2877	.2843	.2810	.2776
−0.4	.3446	.3409	.3372	.3336	.3300	.3264	.3228	.3192	.3156	.3121
−0.3	.3821	.3783	.3745	.3707	.3669	.3632	.3594	.3557	.3520	.3483
−0.2	.4207	.4168	.4129	.4090	.4052	.4013	.3974	.3936	.3897	.3859
−0.1	.4602	.4562	.4522	.4483	.4443	.4404	.4364	.4325	.4286	.4247
−0.0	.5000	.4960	.4920	.4880	.4840	.4801	.4761	.4721	.4681	.4641

Strictly speaking, this OPM applies only under the following assumptions:

1. The option and its underlying asset are traded in a continuously operating perfect market environment, including no restrictions on short positions.

2. The rate of return distribution from owning the underlying asset is the normal probability distribution, with known and constant σ over the life of the option contract.

3. The value of r_f is known and constant over the life of the option contract.

4. The option contract is European.

d	0.00	0.01	0.02	0.03	0.04	0.05	0.06	0.07	0.08	0.09
0.0	.5000	.5040	.5080	.5120	.5160	.5199	.5239	.5279	.5319	.5359
0.1	.5398	.5438	.5478	.5517	.5557	.5596	.5636	.5675	.5714	.5753
0.2	.5793	.5832	.5871	.5910	.5948	.5987	.6026	.6064	.6103	.6141
0.3	.6179	.6217	.6255	.6293	.6331	.6368	.6406	.6443	.6480	.6517
0.4	.6554	.6591	.6628	.6664	.6700	.6736	.6772	.6808	.6844	.6879
0.5	.6915	.6950	.6985	.7019	.7054	.7088	.7123	.7157	.7190	.7224
0.6	.7257	.7291	.7324	.7357	.7389	.7422	.7454	.7486	.7517	.7549
0.7	.7580	.7611	.7642	.7673	.7704	.7734	.7764	.7794	.7823	.7852
0.8	.7881	.7910	.7939	.7967	.7995	.8023	.8051	.8078	.8106	.8133
0.9	.8159	.8186	.8212	.8238	.8264	.8289	.8315	.8340	.8365	.8389
1.0	.8413	.8439	.8461	.8485	.8508	.8531	.8554	.8577	.8599	.8621
1.1	.8643	.8665	.8686	.8708	.8729	.8749	.8770	.8790	.8810	.8830
1.2	.8849	.8869	.8888	.8907	.8925	.8944	.8962	.8980	.8997	.9015
1.3	.9032	.9049	.9066	.9082	.9099	.9115	.9131	.9147	.9162	.9177
1.4	.9192	.9207	.9222	.9236	.9251	.9265	.9279	.9292	.9306	.9319
1.5	.9332	.9345	.9357	.9370	.9382	.9394	.9406	.9418	.9429	.9441
1.6	.9452	.9463	.9474	.9484	.9495	.9505	.9515	.9525	.9535	.9545
1.7	.9554	.9564	.9573	.9582	.9591	.9599	.9608	.9616	.9625	.9633
1.8	.9641	.9649	.9656	.9664	.9671	.9678	.9686	.9693	.9699	.9706
1.9	.9713	.9719	.9726	.9732	.9738	.9744	.9750	.9756	.9761	.9767
2.0	.9773	.9778	.9783	.9788	.9793	.9798	.9803	.9808	.9812	.9817
2.1	.9821	.9826	.9830	.9834	.9838	.9842	.9846	.9850	.9854	.9857
2.2	.9861	.9864	.9868	.9871	.9875	.9878	.9881	.9884	.9887	.9890
2.3	.9893	.9896	.9898	.9901	.9904	.9906	.9909	.9911	.9913	.9916
2.4	.9918	.9920	.9922	.9925	.9927	.9929	.9931	.9932	.9934	.9936
2.5	.9938	.9940	.9941	.9943	.9945	.9946	.9948	.9949	.9951	.9952
2.6	.9953	.9955	.9956	.9957	.9959	.9960	.9961	.9962	.9963	.9964
2.7	.9965	.9966	.9967	.9968	.9969	.9970	.9971	.9972	.9973	.9974
2.8	.9974	.9975	.9976	.9977	.9977	.9978	.9979	.9979	.9980	.9981
2.9	.9981	.9982	.9982	.9983	.9984	.9984	.9985	.9985	.9986	.9986
3.0	.9987	.9987	.9987	.9988	.9988	.9989	.9989	.9989	.9990	.9990

5. There are no cash flows associated with the asset over the life of the option contract, including no dividends when the asset in question is a stock.

The Black-Scholes OPM is *very* practical for two reasons. First, except for σ, the parameter inputs required to use the model are specified in the option contract or are readily observable in currently operating markets. Second, in most cases, this model provides a very good approximation of the true value of an option, even though the forgoing assumptions are not strictly satisfied, and in all cases, it is at least a good starting point for analysis. And this is true even though violations of the model's assumptions can dramatically complicate option valuation.

As you might expect by now, many violations of the perfect market environment assumption, such as transaction costs, do not significantly damage the model's usefulness. However, it may surprise you to find out that the distinction between an American and a European type of option is not important unless there are cash flows associated with the underlying asset during the life of the option. This is because, as we have already pointed out, it is generally better to sell, rather than exercise, an American option prior to its expiration. Thus, the Black-Scholes OPM can often be used to value American as well as European options.

EXAMPLE 1 ■ Suppose a non-dividend-paying stock is selling for $28 per share, the standard deviation of the rate of return from owning a share of this stock is .30, and the APR for the riskless rate of interest with continuous compounding is 6%. What is a call option on this stock worth if the option has a strike price of $30 and 9 months until expiration? To solve this, we first list the parameter values for the problem:

$$P_0 = 28;\ \sigma = .30;\ k = .06;\ S = 30;\ T = .75$$

In this case, then, $\sigma T^{1/2} = .259808$, and from Equation (8.6), d_1 is computed to be

$$d_1 = \frac{ln[P_0/S]}{\sigma T^{1/2}} + \frac{Tk}{\sigma T^{1/2}} + \frac{\sigma T^{1/2}}{2} = \frac{ln[28/30]}{.259808} + \frac{.75(.06)}{.259808} + \frac{.259808}{2}$$

$$d_1 = -.265553 + .173205 + .129904 = .037556 \approx .04$$

and from Equation (8.7):

$$d_2 = d_1 - \sigma T^{1/2} = .037556 - .259808 = -.222252 \approx -.22$$

From Table 8-2, we have

$$N[d_1] = N[.04] = .5160;$$
$$N[d_2] = N[-.22] = .4129;$$

and, finally, from Equation (8.5):

CALL $= P_0 N[d_1] - SN[d_2]e^{-Tk} = 28(.5160) - 30(.4129)e^{-.045} = \$2.61$ ■

Example 1 implies that according to the Black-Scholes OPM, an option like the one described in the problem should be selling in the market for a price of about $2½ to $2¾. As an exercise, look in the *Wall Street Journal* for market prices of call options that might be similar to the one described in this example and see if their value is approximately equal to $2.61.[12] Note that the time value of this call option equals the option's value because the option is out-of-the-money (the value of the option equals the sum of its time value and exercise value, the latter of which is zero).

EXAMPLE 2 ■ Suppose the same non-dividend-paying stock in the previous example was instead selling for $26 per share. With everything else the same, we would have

$$P_0 = 26;\ \sigma = .30;\ k = .06;\ S = 30;\ T = .75$$

As before, $\sigma T^{1/2} = .259808$. From Equation (8.6), d_1 is computed to be

$$d_1 = \frac{ln[P_0/S]}{\sigma T^{1/2}} + \frac{Tk}{\sigma T^{1/2}} + \frac{\sigma T^{1/2}}{2} = \frac{ln[26/30]}{.259808} + \frac{.75(.06)}{.259808} + \frac{.259808}{2}$$

$$d_1 = -.550795 + .173205 + .129904 = -.247686 \approx -.25$$

---

[12] Note that a standardized option contract that is traded on an organized exchange covers 100 shares of stock and that a call option on a dividend-paying stock will be worth less than a similar option on a stock that is not expected to pay any dividends during the life of the option.

and from Equation (8.7):

$$d_2 = d_1 - \sigma T^{1/2} = -.247686 - .259808 = -.507494 \approx -.51$$

From Table 8-2, we have

$$N[d_1] = N[-.25] = .4013$$
$$N[d_2] = N[-.51] = .3050$$

and, finally, from Equation (8.5):

$$\text{CALL} = P_0 N[d_1] - SN[d_2]e^{-Tk} = 26(.4013) - 30(.3050)e^{-.045} = \$1.69$$

Note that although the option is \$2 further out-of-the-money in this second example, the value of the call option (which is entirely time value) decreases by less than \$2 (from \$2.61 to \$1.69). ■

VALUING A PUT OPTION

A put option can be valued simply by substituting Equation (8.5) into Equation (8.3).

EXAMPLE ■   What is the value of a 9-month put option, with $S = \$30$, on a non-dividend-paying stock that is selling for \$28 per share if $\sigma = .30$ and $k = 6\%$? The value of a call option under the same conditions was just computed in Example 1, above, to be \$2.61. Therefore, from Equation (8.3):

$$\text{PUT} = \text{CALL} + Se^{-Tk} - P_0 = 2.61 + (30)e^{-.045} - 28 = \$3.29$$

Note that the time value of this put option equals \$1.29, which is the option's market value minus the exercise value of the option.

If we also extend Example 2, above, we find that the value of the same put option if the stock has a current value of \$26 is

$$\text{PUT} = \text{CALL} + Se^{-Tk} - P_0 = 1.69 + (30)e^{-.045} - 26 = \$4.37$$

Again, although the put option is \$2 further in-the-money, the value of the option does not increase by a "full" \$2. In this case, the major portion of option value is its exercise value, which is \$4, with the time value being only \$0.37. ■

COMBINING OPTION VALUES   8.9

A very important problem with respect to options, particularly in corporate finance, is how their values combine. While value additivity holds for traded options, value additivity does *not* necessarily hold for all options in all cases (because of complex interactions that can make their values interdependent). That is, the value of owning two options is not necessarily equal to the value of one of the options plus the value of the other, especially when exercising one option can affect the value of another option, as can be the case when the options are written on the same set of physical assets. This fact may seem obvious, but in a complex situation, it can easily be overlooked.

Suppose you own two "hidden" options, A and B, which cannot be separated from the ownership of the underlying asset. That is, if you own the asset, you have the options, such as in the case of corporate shareholders' limited liability—it exists as a matter of law. Panel I in Figure 8-10 is a Venn diagram of outcomes where those contained in the circle marked A are outcomes for which option A is in-the-money.

Panel I

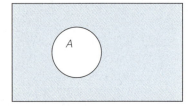

Panel II

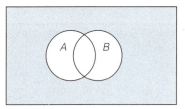

FIGURE 8-10

Outcomes covered by two options.

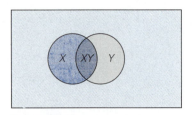

FIGURE 8-11

Valuation combinations of two options.

Denoting P_A as the value of asset A and S_A as the strike price for option A, the circle A contains all outcomes for which $P_A > S_A$. Option A is out-of-the-money for all other outcomes in the universe of all possible outcomes. The current value of option A is \$12,000.

Panel II in Figure 8-10 is a Venn diagram of outcomes for both options, with circle B defined for option B as circle A is for option A. The current value of option B is \$10,000, but of what additional value is the ownership of option B? Option A "covers you" for all of the outcomes in circle A and option B "covers you" for all of the outcomes in circle B. Since you own option A, however, option B adds "coverage" *only* for those outcomes that are not also in circle A. In other words, the intersection of circles A and B is redundant if you already own one of the options. Suppose the value of the overlap of the option coverage of outcomes is \$6,000. In this case, the value of combining options A and B, $V(A + B)$, is the sum of the values of the individual options, $V(A) + V(B) = \$22,000$ (= 12,000 + 10,000), *minus* the value of the intersection, $V(A \cap B) = \$6,000$, or

$$V(A + B) = V(A) + V(B) - V(A \cap B) = 22,000 - 6,000 = \$16,000 \quad \textbf{(8.8)}$$

Therefore, the value of owning two options is not always equal to the sum of the separate values of the individual options.

A similar situation can arise when the exercise of one option affects the value of another option, as in the case of some alternative uses for an asset. Suppose a firm has the option to build a new plant on a piece of land. Just prior to the implementation of the firm's plan, an alternative piece of land becomes available that would be a superior place for the firm to build its plant, all things considered, including total cost. In effect, the firm now has two options. But if the firm exercises the second option, the first option will become worthless. If you think about it, you will see that this scenario is simply an option view of an opportunity cost. However, even though they are different views, the NPV of an alternative action *must* be the same, whether it is valued using an OPM or a present value model.

A PORTFOLIO OF OPTIONS

We showed above that in certain circumstances, an additional option may not add its "full" value (or even any value in some cases) to the firm's wealth. Our corollary to the principle that options are valuable requires that having an additional option will never decrease the firm's wealth. Indirectly, this leads to another important generalization about combining options: ***The value of an option on a portfolio of assets is always less than or equal to the value of a portfolio of comparable options on the individual assets***.

To see this point, consider Figure 8-11, which presents a Venn diagram of outcomes for the values of two call options, one on asset X and one on asset Y. Denote the value of asset X as V_x and the strike price of the call option on asset X as S_x, with V_y and S_y similarly defined for asset Y and the call option on it. In the diagram, the area marked X contains all of the outcomes where

$$V_x - S_x \geq 0 \quad \textbf{(8.9)}$$

and the area marked Y contains all the outcomes where

$$V_y - S_y \geq 0 \quad \textbf{(8.10)}$$

The area marked XY contains all of the outcomes where both Equations (8.9) and (8.10) hold. A portfolio of the individual call options on assets X and Y has a positive value for the areas marked *X*, *Y*, and *XY*. This is because if one option is in-the-money and the other option is out-of-the-money, the optionholder will exercise the valuable one and incur no loss on the worthless one. An out-of-the-money option does not decrease the total exercise value of the portfolio of options, it only fails to increase the total exercise value.

In the area *XY*, the value of the portfolio of options is the same as the value of the option on the portfolio of assets because all of the individual options are in-the-money. In the areas *X* and *Y* (and outside *XY*), the value of the portfolio of options exceeds the value of the option on the portfolio of assets. This is because when the value of an asset is below the strike price on the associated option, the exercise value of the option on the portfolio of assets is reduced by however far that individual option would be out-of-the-money until the exercise value of the option on the portfolio is zero. When this exercise value reaches zero, there may still be individual options that are in-the-money and will provide value to the owner of the portfolio of options.

Let's summarize. In the area marked *XY*, the two alternatives are of identical value; in the areas marked *X* and *Y*, the value of the portfolio of options exceeds the value of the option on the portfolio of assets. Therefore, the value of a portfolio of options is always greater than or equal to the value of a single option on a portfolio containing all of the underlying assets.

Another way to see the intuition underlying this concept is to think about it in terms of diversification. An option is a claim on the "good" outcomes without the obligation to take the "bad" outcomes. In a portfolio of assets, the "good" and "bad" outcomes tend to cancel each other out. An option on each asset provides claim to only the "good" outcomes, whereas an option on the portfolio "sticks you" with both "good" and "bad" outcomes together.

COMPLICATING FACTORS   8.10

1. **Asymmetric information** can dramatically affect the value of an option. Also, the lack of information can make a person unwilling to trade in an option, especially if he thinks there are "informed" traders in the market: he can be "taken" by those "informed" traders! (This is an example of the adverse selection problem pointed out in our discussion of the Signaling Principle.)

2. **Tax considerations** can affect the value of an option, both in terms of market equilibrium prices and the ability of participants to make profitable arbitrage transactions. Recall our discussion of taxes in Chapter 5.

3. **Transaction costs** can also affect the value of an option. Again, recall our discussion of transaction costs in Chapter 5. We want to emphasize, however, that while transaction costs may inhibit arbitrage, as with taxes and imperfect information, it is the asymmetric ones that generally have a significant impact.

4. **Cash flows**, associated with the option or the underlying asset, which will occur during the life of the option, can both complicate and affect option value in a detectable way. Examples include dividends on common stock and interest payments on bonds.

5. **Margin requirements**, especially with respect to short sales for comparable positions, greatly complicate the valuation process. To the extent that they are asymmetric and restrict trading and/or represent added cash flows during the life of the option, margin requirements may have some practical impact on the value of an option.

6. *American versus European options*: As we have noted, the difference in value may not be very large. However, this distinction can add considerably to the complexity of determining an *exact* value for an option.

SUMMARY

As with any asset, (1) the value of an option depends upon its expected rate of return and risk, and (2) the value of an option does *not* depend upon individual investor attitudes or preferences. Therefore, option pricing models are in complete accordance with asset pricing models.[13] As an example of this consistency, we showed how shareholder equity can be modeled as a call option on the firm's assets. In spite of this consistency, using a discounted cash flow model to value an option is not practical because the risk (and therefore also the required rate of return) depends upon the value of the underlying asset, which may be changing constantly.

An option is a contingent claim, a claim on a portion of an asset's return distribution. In the simple environment examined in this chapter, an option's value depends on five factors. Any expected future cash flows (positive or negative) connected with an asset during the life of an option on that asset is a sixth factor that can also affect the value of the option.

Prior to the expiration date, it is generally better to sell, rather than exercise, a call option in an efficient capital market because the time value of the option is typically positive. The time value of an option is the difference between its market value and its exercise value. Exercising the option prior to the expiration date entails sacrificing the time value of the option; selling the option does not. The time value of an option is at a maximum when the value of the underlying asset equals the option's strike price, and declines as the difference between P_0 and S increases in either direction.

"Hidden" options can affect the value of an asset. Such options can be especially important because they are not always included in other valuation models. The accurate inclusion of the value of options such as these can be particularly tricky when there are multiple options, the values of which are interdependent. As we will show in Chapter 13, such dependence is important to the proper valuation of "hidden" options that are associated with a firm's capital investment projects.

Although great precision is required to determine the *exact* value of an option, we have tried to provide a "feel" for the important factors that affect option valuation and have presented several useful generalizations about options. In spite of the precision needed for determining an exact option value, complicating factors seldom significantly alter the generalizations presented here. More precise option pricing formulas are contained in many of the references, especially other books, cited at the end of this chapter.

PROBLEMS

PROBLEM SET A

A1. Broadly speaking, the value of an option depends on (a) the option's claim portion of the return distribution for the underlying asset and (b) the time

---

[13] A particularly interesting application of option pricing is the use of an OPM to estimate the σ of an asset. That estimate can then be used in another model such as the CAPM. For example, the standard deviation of the rate of return on the market portfolio, σ_m, can be obtained from an OPM for use in estimating beta. Such use of an OPM is similar to the use of the Gordon dividend growth model or the CAPM to estimate a required rate of return, such as a capitalization rate on a stock.

value of money. Name the parameters that determine each of these two factors and explain why each parameter is important.

A2. Explain why it is generally better to sell rather than exercise an American option. What general condition causes an exception to this rule?

A3. Cite a situation in which a person should exercise rather than sell an American call option.

A4. Cite a situation in which a person should exercise rather than sell an American put option on a stock that is expected to pay no dividends.

A5. What is the value of a call option with a strike price of $180 on the two-state asset shown in Figure 8-9?

A6. Suppose that the risk-adjusted probabilities for increasing and decreasing prices in Figure 8-9 were reversed; that is, an increase has a 40% chance and a decrease a 60% chance of occurring. What is the value of a call option with a strike price of $140 on such a two-state asset?

A7. Explain how insurance can be viewed as simply a put option.

A8. What is the relationship between the value of an American option and the value of a comparable European option? For example, is it always greater than, less than, or does the relationship depend on some parameter?

A9. Explain why an option on a portfolio of assets is never worth more than a portfolio of comparable options on the individual assets.

A10. Cite three situations involving "hidden" options.

A11. In your own words, explain how limited liability makes shares of common stock like a call option on the firm's assets.

A12. What is the maximum value for an American call option?

A13. Why would an American call option traded in an efficient capital market never be worth less than its exercise value?

A14. Cite and discuss four factors that can complicate the valuation of an option.

A15. Define the terms **option**, **call option**, and **put option**.

A16. What does it mean to take a position with respect to an option or security?

PROBLEM SET B

B1. What is the value of a put option with a strike price of $185 on the two-state asset shown in Figure 8-9?

B2. Suppose a stock is selling for $48.50 per share, the standard deviation of the rate of return from owning a share of this stock is 24% per year, and the APR for the riskless rate of interest with continuous compounding is 5%. According to the Black-Scholes OPM:
  a. What is a call option on this stock worth if the option has a strike price of $50 and 8 months until expiration?
  b. What is a put option on this stock worth if the option has a strike price of $50 and 8 months until expiration?
  c. What is a call option on this stock worth if the option has a strike price of $50 and 4 months until expiration?
  d. What is a put option on this stock worth if the option has a strike price of $50 and 4 months until expiration?

B3. According to the Black-Scholes OPM, what is the value of a 6-month put option with a strike price of $40 on stock selling for $37.75 if the standard deviation of the rate of return to the stock is 28% per year and the APR for the riskless rate of interest with continuous compounding is 7%?

B4. Suppose the standard deviation of a stock's rate of return is 25% per year and the APR for the riskless rate of interest with continuous compounding is 6%. According to the Black-Scholes OPM;

    a. What is a 6-month call option on this stock worth if the strike price is $30 and the stock is currently selling for $28? What are the time and exercise values of this option?

    b. What is a 6-month call option on this stock worth if the strike price is $30 and the stock is currently selling for $32? What are the time and exercise values of this option?

    c. What is a 6-month call option on this stock worth if the strike price is $30 and the stock is currently selling for $34? What are the time and exercise values of this option?

B5. Consider a 9-month call option with a strike price of $25 on a stock that currently sells for $25. According to the Black-Scholes OPM, if the APR for the riskless rate of interest with continuous compounding is 6%;

    a. What is the value of this option if the standard deviation of the rate of return to the stock is 35%?

    b. What is the value of this option if the standard deviation of the rate of return to the stock is 30%?

    c. What is the value of this option if the standard deviation of the rate of return to the stock is 25%?

B6. According to the Black-Scholes OPM, what is the value of a call option with a strike price of $110 and 3 months until expiration on an asset that has a current market value of $90 and a standard deviation of the rate of return equal to 30% per year if k is 10%?

B7. Consider a 6-month call option with a strike price of $20 on a stock that currently sells for $21. According to the Black-Scholes OPM, if the standard deviation of the rate of return to the stock is 30%;

    a. What is the value of this option if the APR for the riskless rate of interest with continuous compounding is 4%?

    b. What is the value of this option if the APR for the riskless rate of interest with continuous compounding is 7%?

    c. What is the value of this option if the APR for the riskless rate of interest with continuous compounding is 10%?

B8. Consider the following statement: A call option is a great way to make money. If the asset goes up in value, you get the increase, but if the asset goes down in value, you do not exercise the option and do not lose any money. Therefore, everyone should invest in call options. Is this statement true, false, or part true and part false? Explain why.

B9. What is the current value of a European call option with an exercise price of $20 and an expiration date 9 months from now if the stock is non-dividend-paying and is now selling for $24.38, the variance of the rate of return on the stock is .48, and the risk-free rate is 6%? What is the current exercise value of this call option? What is the current time value of this call option?

B10. We pointed out that common stock in a firm that has some debt can be viewed as being a call option. Can common stock in a firm that has no debt also be viewed as a call option? If so, explain how. If not, explain why.

B11. Suppose an asset with a two-period life similar to the one shown in Figure 8-9 has three possible terminal values: $150, $200, and $250. Probabilities for the valuation paths are .55 for an increase and .45 for a decrease.

    a. What is the value of a call option on this asset if the option has a strike price of 210 and the riskless rate is 10% per period?

    b. What is the value of a put option on this asset if the option has a strike price of 210 and the riskless rate is 10% per period?

c. Show that direct computation and put-call parity give identical answers to part b. That is, if you used one method to get the answer to part b, now use the other to show its equivalence. (*Hint:* Be sure to note that the riskless rate of return used in the Black–Scholes OPM is the nominal annual riskless rate of return, but the riskless rate of return given is the effective annual riskless rate of return.)

PROBLEM SET C

C1. What standard deviation of the rate of return to a stock is implied by the Black–Scholes OPM by the following situation? A 5-month call option with a strike price of $35 sells for $2.03, k is 6%, and the stock is currently selling for $32.75.

C2. Use put-call parity to show that the combination of buying an asset, buying a put with a strike price of S, and selling a call with a strike price of S, is equivalent to simply buying a riskless bond that has a maturity value of S.

C3. Suppose you live in a state that has a usury law prohibiting interest charges above 9% APR, but current market rates are 18% effective annual for a project for which you have the opportunity to provide 6-year debt financing. Show how you can use option contracts on an asset that is connected with the project to provide the project with a 6-year "loan" of $250,000, from which you will earn the market rate 18% per year with interest payments of $45,000 per year and a principal repayment of $250,000 at the end of 6 years.

C4. Show that the values of a European put and an American put are different when there is no chance that the option will be out-of-the-money during the remaining time until maturity.

C5. Why does the time value of an option increase (decrease) as the value of the underlying asset moves toward (away from) the strike price?

C6. A particular type of bond that has actually been issued from time to time allows for the bond to be redeemed, at the option of the bondholder, at either of two future points in time. Suppose such a bond can be redeemed for its face value after either 10 or 20 years. That is, at the 10-year point, the bond-holder makes a one-time decision to redeem or not. Clearly there is an option in this contract. Describe this complex bond in terms of one or more (a) option contracts and (b) bonds that are otherwise identical but do not have the two-points-of-redemption option.

C7. An investor is considering investing $5 million to acquire a thrift institution that currently has $1 billion of assets and zero net worth on its balance sheet. The thrift's liabilities consist principally of federally-insured deposits. Its assets include principally real estate loans, which were recently written down to their supposed "fair market value" by the thrift's regulators to enhance the thrift's saleability. What does option theory tell you about how the investor should view the prospective $5 million investment?

REFERENCES

Black, Fischer. "Fact and Fantasy in the Use of Options and Corporate Liabilities." *Financial Analysts Journal* 31 (July–August 1975): 36–41, 61–72.

Black, Fischer, and Myron Scholes. "The Pricing of Options and Corporate Liabilities." *Journal of Political Economy* 81 (May–June 1973): 637–54.

Brennan, Michael J., and Eduardo S. Schwartz. "Finite Difference Methods and Jump Processes Arising in the Pricing of Contingent Claims: A Synthesis." *Journal of Financial and Quantitative Analysis* 13 (September 1978): 461–74.

Cox, John C., and Stephen A. Ross. "The Valuation of Options for Alternative Stochastic Processes." *Journal of Financial Economics* 3 (January-March 1976): 145–79.

Cox, John C., Stephen A. Ross, and Mark Rubinstein. "Option Pricing: A Simplified Approach." *Journal of Financial Economics* 7 (September 1979): 229–63.

Cox, John C., and Mark Rubinstein. *Options Markets*. Englewood Cliffs, N.J.: Prentice-Hall, 1985.

Galai, Dan. "Empirical Tests of Boundary Conditions for CBOE Options." *Journal of Financial Economics* 6 (June-September 1978): 187–212.

Galai, Dan, and Ronald W. Masulis. "The Option Pricing Model and the Risk Factor of Stock." *Journal of Financial Economics* 3 (January/March 1976): 53–81.

Galai, Dan, and Meir I. Schneller. "Pricing of Warrants and the Value of the Firm." *Journal of Finance* 33 (December 1978): 1333–42.

Geske, Robert. "A Note on an Analytical Valuation Formula for Unprotected American Call Options on Stocks With Known Dividends." *Journal of Financial Economics* 7 (1979): 375–80.

Geske, Robert. "The Valuation of Compound Options." *Journal of Financial Economics* 7 (March 1979): 63–81.

Geske, Robert, and Richard Roll. "On Valuing American Call Options with the Black-Scholes European Formula." *Journal of Finance* 39 (June 1984): 443–55.

Gultekin, N. Bulent, Richard J. Rogalski, and Seha Tinic. "Option Pricing Model Estimates: Some Empirical Results." *Financial Management* 11 (Spring 1982): 58–69.

Hull, John. *Options, Futures, and Other Derivative Securities*. Englewood Cliffs, N.J.: Prentice-Hall, 1989.

Jarrow, Robert A., and Andrew Rudd. *Option Pricing*. Homewood, Ill.: Richard D. Irwin, 1983.

Macbeth, James D., and Larry J. Merville. "An Empirical Examination of the Black-Scholes Call Option Pricing Model." *Journal of Finance* 34 (December 1979): 1173–86.

Mason, Scott P., and Robert C. Merton. "The Role of Contingent Claims Analysis in Corporate Finance." *Recent Advances in Corporate Finance*, Edward I. Altman and Marti G. Subrahmanyam, eds. Homewood, Ill.: Richard D. Irwin, 1985.

Merton, Robert C. "Theory of Rational Option Pricing." *Bell Journal of Economics and Management Science* 4 (Spring 1973): 141–83.

Rendleman, Richard J., Jr., and Brit J. Bartter. "Two-State Option Pricing." *Journal of Finance* 34 (December 1979): 1093–1110.

Roll, Richard. "An Analytic Valuation Formula for Unprotected American Call Options on Stocks With Known Dividends." *Journal of Financial Economics* 5 (1977): 251–58.

Smith, Clifford W. "Option Pricing: A Review." *Journal of Financial Economics* 13 (March 1976): 3–51.

Sprenkle, Case. "Warrant Prices as Indications of Expectations." *Yale Economic Essays* 1 (1961): 179–232.

Sterk, William E. "Comparative Performance of the Black-Scholes and Roll-Geske-Whaley Option Pricing Models." *Journal of Financial and Quantitative Analysis* 18 (September 1983): 345–54.

Sterk, William E. "Option Pricing: Dividends and the In- and Out-of-the-Money Bias." *Financial Management* 12 (Winter 1983): 47–53.

Whaley, Robert E. "On the Valuation of American Call Options on Stocks With Known Dividends." *Journal of Financial Economics* 9 (1981): 207–11.

Whaley, Robert E. "Valuation of American Call Options on Dividend-Paying Stocks: Empirical Tests." *Journal of Financial Economics* 10 (March 1982): 29–58.

FINANCIAL CONTRACTING

Thus far, we have defined equity as ownership in the firm and debt as a legal obligation of the firm to make future fixed payments to the firm's debtholders. While this is a good starting point, the modern corporate environment is much more complex than this simple dichotomy implies. Recall from Chapter 1 our description of the **set-of-contracts model** of the firm, in which we touched briefly on this complexity. Similarly, in Chapter 4 we identified financial securities that are part equity and part debt. In this chapter we identify significant practical differences between two firms that would be otherwise conceptually identical in a perfect capital market environment. These practical differences are revealed by the set-of-contracts, or stakeholder, model of the firm, when the relationships among the claimants are viewed in the context of what is called **agency theory**, involving the analysis of situations where one person, an **agent**, acts on behalf of another person, a **principal**. As noted in Chapter 2, agency theory is an important application of the Principle of Self-Interested Behavior.

Most common stockholders of large publicly held corporations do not participate in the management of the company. Strictly speaking, they do not even own the company; they are shareholders who own shares of common stock which entitle them to voting rights and certain other rights that are specified in the company's articles of incorporation. Such corporations are operated by professional managers, some of whom may not own stock in the corporation. Managers' key decisions are subject to the review and approval of the corporation's board of directors. The board of directors serve as the stockholders' elected representatives, hiring the professional managers who operate the corporation. The directors have a legal responsibility to the stockholders to ensure that the corporation is being operated in a manner that is not prejudicial to the stockholders' interests. But the directors are typically nominated by top management. So two important questions arise: Are the professional managers' interests different from the nonmanagement stockholders' interests? And if they are, whose interests are the professional managers really promoting?

The divergence of the managers' interests from the stockholders' interests creates an **agency problem**: The agents (in this case the corporate managers) will tend to act in their own self-interest rather than in the interests of the stockholders. Therefore, steps must be taken, in the form of constraints, incentives, and punishments, to ensure that corporate managers act in the best interests of the corporation's common stockholders. Such constraints, incentives, and punishments impose costs that are part of **agency costs**.

Agency problems occur because of asymmetric information. If the principal knows everything that every agent does, an agent would never be able to take actions that were not in the best interest of the principal. Thus, if it were possible and not unreasonably costly for the principal to **monitor** the agent's actions perfectly, there would be no agency problems. Obviously, perfect monitoring, even if it were truly possible, is exorbitantly expensive. Most people would quickly conclude that "it's easier to do it myself."

Agency problems arise in connection with many of the other relationships in the set, or **nexus**, of corporate contracts that compose the modern corporation. For example, although debtholders lend the corporation money, it is the managers rather than the debtholders who decide how the money will be invested. As discussed in this chapter, managers may favor investments different from those the debtholders would choose if the debtholders could choose (even if managers are pursuing shareholder interests ahead of their own). In response to this possibility, debtholders require restrictions to protect their interests, and these restrictions can give rise to agency costs. A leveraged buyout (where a large proportion of debt financing is used to purchase—buy out—a firm) is a situation in which a large number of agency problems can arise. A leveraged buyout typically involves multiple classes of equity investors and multiple classes of lenders, each ardently following the Principle of Self-Interested Behavior. Resolving the inherent conflicts among these different classes of investors creates a host of agency costs.

Agency theory has also been used to explain a number of key issues in corporate finance, even though the situations do not on the surface appear to be principal–agent situations.[1] This chapter provides an overview of the financial contracting process in an agency theory framework. Agency cost considerations are relevant throughout the corporate decision-making process. Therefore, agency costs play an important role in many of the applications of the Principles of Finance that are contained in the remaining chapters.

9.1   PRINCIPAL–AGENT RELATIONSHIPS

Many situations involve a principal–agent relationship where an agent is responsible for taking action on behalf of a principal. Some of the more visible examples of agents in explicit principal–agent relationships include salespeople, pension fund managers, managers of cooperative organizations such as an agricultural co-op or a credit union, lawyers, executors, and agents of real estate, travel, and insurance. Principal-agent relationships are in fact ubiquitous since a majority of employees act as agents at some point for their employers, even if they are not legally defined as agents. In addition to explicit principal-agent relationships, many other situations can be described in the framework of the principal-agent relationship *as though* the two parties were principal and agent, even though the one party is not literally an agent for the other party.

Virtually any situation where one person or group of persons has delegated decision-making authority to another person or group can be described in terms of a principal-agent relationship. For example, the managers of a firm are employed by the owners (the stockholders) to make certain operating decisions. Often this relationship is even more complex; the executive managers report to a board of directors who are in turn elected by the stockholders. However, at each level there is a delegation of decision-making authority that can be modeled as a principal-agent relationship. Table 9-1 characterizes six of the more important relationships in corporate finance that can be modeled in a principal-agent framework.

Agency problems can occur whenever there is a potential conflict between the interests of the agent and those of the principal. Of course, if it were possible (and not prohibitively expensive) for the principal to know everything done by an agent, the

[1] Two particularly important applications are the choice of capital structure (Barnea, Haugen, and Senbet, 1985; Jensen and Meckling, 1976) and the design of new debt issues (Barnea, Haugen, and Senbet, 1980; Bodie and Taggart, 1978; Robbins and Schatzberg, 1986; Thatcher, 1985).

TABLE 9-1   Examples of Important Principal-Agent Relationships

Entity	Principals	Agent(s)
Publicly-held corporation	Stockholders	Managers
Publicly-held corporation	Debtholders and other lenders	Stockholders
Publicly-held corporation	Consumers	Firm
Closely-held company	Lenders to the company	Owner-manager(s)
Limited partnership	Limited partners	General partner(s)
Leveraged buyout fund	Investors	Fund manager

agent could always be forced through penalties to act in the principal's best interest, as the agent has agreed to do contractually. Alternatively, if the agent is paid according to a contract that perfectly matches the best interests of the principal, no conflict of interest arises and the principal does not need to know the actual decisions made by the agent. This is because in a "financial world," we know from the Principle of Self-Interested Behavior that the agent will act in her own best financial interest, and if that interest is in perfect accord with the principal's best interest, the agent will act in the principal's best interest. But our world is not characterized by perfect accord or perfect information. Thus, we must seek better financial contracts that minimize agency problems.

Even situations not previously thought of in terms of a principal-agent relationship can often be modeled as a principal-agent relationship. The basis for the model is the potential for conflicts of interest to arise between parties, where one party has decision-making authority but the other party has a financial interest in the outcomes from those decisions. For example, the stockholders and debtholders have a financial claim on the firm's assets. Yet the stockholders, because of ownership, have explicit control (through the managers) over the use of those assets. (We often speak in terms of stockholder decisions, even though the stockholders may have delegated the decision-making authority to managers.) This means that decisions concerning the use of the assets are made by the stockholders, but the debtholders' wealth depends upon the outcome from those decisions. For example, both stockholder and debtholder wealth may depend upon a decision to commit cash to undertake a new investment. A new investment may cause the firm to go bankrupt, whereby stockholders lose their investment and debtholders are not fully repaid the money they have been promised. In spite of the shared dependence on the outcome, it is the stockholders alone who make the decision to undertake the investment. Note that this is true even if the debt contract contains constraints. Within those constraints, the stockholders have complete control.

Many of the situations involving conflicts of interest analyzed in a principal-agent framework are modeled using what is called a **contingent claims** view of the firm. Recall from the previous chapter that stock can be modeled as an option on the firm's assets. Thus, many of the insights concerning options can be applied directly to conflicts of interest in a principal-agent framework. The expanded view of a firm as a complex set of contingent claims and principal-agent relationships involving the decision-making authority (control) over all, or a subset, of the firm's assets represents a major shift in the view of the firm. As we noted in Chapter 1, this view of the firm has evolved from the model of the firm as a single entity in a perfect capital market environment. However, the "clean-slate" view of a perfect capital market environment provides a very important basis for determining the effects of whatever capital market imperfections exist.

In Chapter 5 we said that an important continuing capital market imperfection is that of information asymmetries. When the interests of the agent and the principal for whom the agent is acting diverge, an information asymmetry can arise with respect to the decisions made by the agent. For example, is the agent putting forth "full effort" or "shirking"? Is the agent agreeing to contracts that involve side payoffs such as special travel to conduct personal business or enjoy a vacation? These examples may sound extreme, but such situations can become very complex. On the one hand, if the decision to travel was necessary for the employee to do the job, what is wrong with the employee getting personal benefit from the trip? That is, if the benefit to the employee is positive and the cost to the firm is zero, then why not allow the employee to take the side trip? The problem that arises is establishing that the firm is no worse off. The employer must make sure the employee's decision that resulted in the travel was not influenced by the side benefit the employee will receive as a result of choosing that alternative.

MONITORING

A principal can encourage an agent to act in the principal's best interest by incorporating in the contract appropriate constraints, incentives, and punishments for the agent. For example, managerial stock options and performance share plans are designed for this purpose. Nevertheless, because some of the agent's actions are not observed, a problem can arise that is referred to as **moral hazard**—whenever agents can take unobserved actions in their own interest, to the detriment of the principal. A natural and widely used method of controlling the problem of moral hazard is for the principal to **monitor** the agent's actions. Of course, monitoring is costly, and in most cases either impossible or prohibitively costly. The majority of contracts, therefore, involve either no monitoring or imperfect monitoring. Payments to agents under such contracts may be based primarily on one or more outcomes for the principal. A common example is a sales commission where an agent receives a percentage of a sales price. Partial and/or imperfect monitoring might consist of an audit of expenses to produce the sale, with a reduction in commission if those expenses exceed a certain level.

When a principal uses an agent on his behalf, the amount of monitoring is an important consideration in determining an efficient allocation of the principal's resources because of the costs involved. The probability that an agent will engage in improper behavior is related to the amount of monitoring. With no monitoring, agents are more likely to engage in improper behavior. Of course, not all agents will take self-interested actions to the detriment of the principal; therefore, devoting excessive resources to monitoring agent behavior may be wasteful. For any specific situation, there will be an optimal amount of monitoring that balances the possibility of lost resources due to improper agent action against resources spent monitoring the agent's behavior.

AGENCY COSTS

The agency costs involved in resolving principal-agent conflicts of financial self-interest consist of three parts:

1. Financial contracting costs, which include
   a. the transaction costs of setting up the contractual agreement (e.g., the costs of issuing bonds);

   b. the opportunity costs imposed by constraints that preclude otherwise optimal decisions (e.g., an inability to undertake a positive-NPV investment because of a restrictive bond covenant); and

   c. the incentive fees paid to the agent to encourage behavior consistent with the principal's goals (e.g., employee bonuses);

2. the costs to the principal of monitoring the agent (e.g., auditing costs); and

3. the loss of wealth the principal suffers as a result of the agent's pursuing divergent goals within an imperfect contract (e.g., excessive employee expense accounts).

Consequently, the existence of agency problems does not necessarily mean that the agents (e.g., corporate managers) will *not* act in the principals' best interest (e.g., maximize stockholder wealth); an agency problem simply makes it costly for the principal to ensure proper agent behavior. The agency cost is defined in terms of the Principle of Incremental Benefits: The agency cost is the incremental cost, above whatever cost would be incurred in a perfect market environment (capital or labor).

The principal's problem is to find the contract that will minimize the total agency cost connected with the relationship. In some cases, the optimal action may be simply to suffer the lost value associated with agents who sometimes "misbehave." In most cases, it will entail minimizing the total of the three contributing types of costs.

It is very important to note that agency costs are borne by the principal, not by the agent. The agent will refuse to participate in the contract if the conditions are not acceptable. Therefore, the agent must be induced to participate. Of course, one way an agent can make participation acceptable is to benefit from "misbehaving." Thus, the principal must assume that the agent will misbehave if given the chance. This point demonstrates the critical importance of the financial contracting process and once again illustrates the relevance of the Principle of Two-Sided Transactions: Participants must anticipate the actions of other participants. The failure to do so can be very costly.

SEPARATION OF OWNERSHIP AND CONTROL   9.2

The stockholder-manager principal-agent relationship arises because of the separation of ownership and control. Recall our fictionalized account of Henry Ford's auto firm in Chapter 1. When an individual owns all of the existing equity (shares) in a corporation that has absolutely no debt, she has total control over the firm's assets. When such a firm incurs a liability (debt), such as borrowing money from a bank or purchasing raw materials on credit, control over the firm's assets becomes subject to whatever constraints have been agreed to in the debt contract.[2] When the single equityholder sells additional equity, the new equityholders are granted a proportional interest in the firm's owners' equity (the value of all the firm's assets minus the value of all the firm's liabilities). However, control over the assets and the firm's decision-making process is maintained on a majority basis. Thus, as long as any single equityholder is more than a 50% shareholder, that shareholder can effectively control the assets, subject to any liability constraints. Of course, when every shareholder owns fewer than 50% of the shares, considerable control over a corporation may be exerted by minority shareholders, as in the case of the Ford family's signifi-

---

[2] Examples of such constraints include dividend restrictions, restrictions on additional borrowing, and the ability of a creditor to place a lien on some of the firm's assets.

cant influence over Ford Motor Company long after the family had ceased to own more than 50% of the stock. However, direct control can be *ensured* only through majority voting. This necessity encourages the creation of coalitions of shareholders, what might be called **block-voting.**

Few of today's major U.S. corporations have one owner or even a small group of owners that make up a majority coalition. And among the many owners there is room for only a few to be members of the board of directors and/or directly involved with the day-to-day management and decision-making of the corporation. Thus, in virtually all cases, employees are running and managing the firm. So who controls the assets?

In theory, the managers work for the stockholders. If management does not do a good job, the stockholders can fire them and hire new managers. Of course, as you might guess, such a process is cumbersome and difficult to accomplish in practice. Therefore, managers have considerable control over the firm and its assets, and have even been accused in some cases of using the firm's assets against the owners. In effect, then, the ownership and the control of a modern corporation and its assets are almost completely separated. Thus, the managers of a corporation with many stockholders can be viewed as agents for the stockholders. Whenever the goals of professional managers do not coincide with the goal of stockholders, the corporation's use of professional managers imposes agency costs on the corporation's stockholders.

STOCKHOLDERS' GOAL

Based on the Principle of Self-Interested Behavior, the theory of finance holds that the owners of the firm (the stockholders) want to maximize the present value of their investment. Thus, the stockholders' goal is for the firm to make the set of decisions that will *maximize stockholder wealth*. By now, you know that this implies that a firm's choices should provide the largest possible positive NPV. In a perfect capital market environment, managers would always act in the best interest of the stockholders by making the decisions that provide the largest positive NPV; with identical costless information available to everyone, no asymmetric information would exist. Therefore, managers could be rewarded for good decisions and punished for bad decisions, and they would never be able to take unseen actions that would hurt the stockholders. In the imperfect world in which we operate, however, managers may pursue other goals in spite of the stockholders' goal.

MANAGERS' GOALS

It has been argued that managers' goals are different from the stockholders' goal of maximizing stockholder wealth.[3] Managers are alleged to favor growth and large size, even at the expense of stockholder wealth, for a variety of reasons. Managers appear to value salary, power, and status, all of which are positively correlated with the size of the firm.[4] Larger size, it is argued, provides management with (1) greater job security due to a smaller chance of takeover and (2) a heightened ability to generate funds internally. Both of these aspects distance the firm from the watchful eye of the marketplace and increase existing management's security.[5] Faster growth creates more opportunities for the internal promotion of lower- and middle-level managers. Some models of the firm go so far as to include measures of growth or size among

[3] Wildsmith (1974).
[4] Gordon (1961).
[5] Galbraith (1967).

the elements of the firm's objective function.[6] In such models, a growth-maximizing (or size-maximizing) management pushes growth (or size) beyond the point at which stockholder wealth is maximized. Professional managers may be motivated to adopt policies that promote growth not only because growth creates new openings in the corporate hierarchy but also because the head of a growing division distinguishes herself as a productive member of the organization, one who is worthy of promotion.[7]

Corporate managers appear to have other objectives as well. These might include expense accounts for entertainment and travel, increased staff size, funds for discretionary investment, and minimizing the personal risk associated with decisions for which they are responsible.[8] Managers may even have goals for things such as a pleasant or impressive office decor. In short, it appears to be reasonable to approximate their goal as that of maximizing the present value of their own lifetime incomes—in other words, the pursuit of self-interested behavior, perhaps even at the expense of stockholder wealth.

DIVERGENCE OF STOCKHOLDERS' AND MANAGERS' GOALS

Managers may have different goals, but many of these goals are not in direct competition with the stockholders' goal of maximizing stockholder wealth. Therefore, it is most important that we examine (1) the particular decisions for which it is most likely, and most costly to stockholders, for managers to make self-interested suboptimal corporate decisions and (2) forces that naturally tend to limit goal divergence. Based on the findings, better contracts can be created.

A FEW WORDS ABOUT ETHICS

We have said that the goal of a corporation's managers should be to maximize stockholder wealth. By this we mean that corporate managers should evaluate the likely impact of each alternative course of action on stockholder wealth and should select only those that are consistent with the goal of stockholder wealth maximization. This book provides the tools for evaluating the impact of financial decisions on stockholder wealth.

We feel it important to emphasize that the goal of stockholder wealth maximization should be pursued subject to a fundamental restriction: Corporate managers should take only steps that are legal and ethically sound. You will no doubt encounter situations in your career in which there is a strong temptation to "play it close to the edge" or even "cross over the line" that separates ethical from unethical behavior in order to enhance a corporation's—and no doubt your own—position. But modest transgressions tend to lead to more serious transgressions and eventually to serious legal difficulties. In corporate history there are many examples of price fixing, insider trading, market manipulation, and similar activities that people undertook after convincing themselves that it was somehow in their firms' best interests to do so. We explicitly exclude such behavior when we talk about managers acting in the interest of maximizing stockholder wealth.

We have also said that managers may act in their own self-interest to the detriment of the stockholders. While we explicitly do not condone such behavior, we must also acknowledge that as a practical matter, it does appear to exist, at least to some ex-

---

[6] See, for example, Baumol (1958, 1962) and Marris (1963).
[7] Marris (1964).
[8] See, for example, Williamson (1964).

tent. For example, empirical evidence shows a difference in administrative costs (including management perquisites) based on a difference in monitoring.[9]

The important and overriding question with respect to financial contracting is how to prevent, or at least minimize, such behavior. As you might guess, the answer lies in reasonable monitoring procedures and in the use of contracts that minimize the *possibility* of conflicts of interest at the outset.

9.3   NATURAL DIVERGENCE OF GOALS

There are a number of relationships within a corporation where conflicts of interest arise naturally. In this section we examine several important relationships in which, and conditions under which, such a natural divergence can occur. In each case, the parties enter into contracts in order to try to resolve these conflicts. But such conflicts are unlikely to be completely resolved because no single contract can cover all possible contingencies.

STOCKHOLDER-DEBTHOLDER CONFLICT

Recall from the previous chapter that stock in a firm that has outstanding debt can be viewed as a call option: The stockholders have **limited liability**. That is, they have an option to default on outstanding corporate debt, and the corporate form limits their liability to their equity interests in the corporation. They are the residual claimants on the cash flow and the assets of the corporation that remain after debtholders and preferred stockholders (if any) are repaid in full. Debtholders have the senior-most claim on the corporation's cash flow and assets. The corporation's obligations to its debtholders are set out in bond indentures and loan agreements. The stockholder-debtholder relationship has at least five points at which there is a natural divergence of self-interests. In this relationship, the debtholders are modeled as the principals who must protect themselves against actions taken by the stockholders (modeled as the agents).

THE ASSET SUBSTITUTION PROBLEM   If the firm has debt outstanding, it may have an incentive to undertake relatively high-risk capital investment projects, even though such projects may reduce the overall market value of the firm. Figures 9-1 and 9-2 illustrate this possibility.

Dynamo Oil & Gas can invest in either of two projects, each of which would cost $3 million, which can be paid for out of cash-on-hand. Each pays off fully after 1 year. Project A's required rate of return is 17%, whereas because of higher risk, Project B's required rate of return is 25%. Clearly, Project A is a good investment, and Project B is a bad investment; Project A has a positive NPV, whereas Project B has a negative NPV. In fact, Project A has a higher expected payoff at the end of year 1 ($5 million versus $2.5 million for Project B) *and* a smaller standard deviation of the possible payoffs ($15 million versus $27.5 million for Project B).

But even though Project B has a negative NPV, Dynamo's stockholders would prefer it to Project A with its positive NPV. Why? Note that the unfavorable outcome associated with each project (Outcome 2) would leave the common stockholders with nothing at the end of the year. But the high-risk Project B would provide a substantially greater payoff to the common stockholders at the end of the year than Project A if the more favorable outcome (Outcome 1) occurs. Thus, Project B

---

[9]Akella and Greenbaum (1988).

FIGURE 9-1
Illustration of asset substitution.

Current Balance Sheet for Dynamo
(market values in millions of dollars)

Assets		Liabilities & Stockholders' Equity	
Cash	$ 3	Debt	$20
Fixed Assets	27	Common Stock	10
Total	$30	Total	$30

Low-Risk Project A

Investment: $3 million; Required rate of return: 17%
Payoffs (millions of dollars):

				Value of		
	Project Payoff	Probability	Firm		Common Stock	Debt
Outcome 1	$20	0.5	$50 =		$30	+ $20
Outcome 2	− 10	0.5	20 =		0	+ 20

Expected Value = $5.0   Standard Deviation = $15.0   NPV = $1.27 million
(= .5[20] + .5[−10])   (= [5/1.17] − 3)

High-Risk Project B

Investment: $3 million; Required rate of return: 25%
Payoffs (millions of dollars):

				Value of		
	Project Payoff	Probability	Firm		Common Stock	Debt
Outcome 1	$30	0.5	$60 =		$40	+ $20
Outcome 2	− 25	0.5	5 =		0	+ 5

Expected Value = $2.5   Standard Deviation = $27.5   NPV = −$1 million
(= .5[30] + .5[−25])   (= [5/1.25] − 3)

FIGURE 9-2
Transfer of wealth due to
asset substitution
(dollar amounts in millions).

Low-Risk Project A

Market Value of Dynamo
Immediately Before Investment:

Assets		Liabilities & Equity	
Cash	$ 3	Debt	$20
Fixed Assets	27	Common Stock	10
Total	$30	Total	$30

Market Value of Dynamo
Immediately After Investment:

Assets		Liabilities & Equity	
Cash	—	Debt	$20
Fixed Assets	31.27	Common Stock	11.27
Total	$31.27	Total	$31.27

High-Risk Project A

Market Value of Dynamo
Immediately Before Investment:

Assets		Liabilities & Equity	
Cash	$ 3	Debt	$20
Fixed Assets	27	Common Stock	10
Total	$30	Total	$30

Market Value of Dynamo
Immediately After Investment:

Assets		Liabilities & Equity	
Cash	—	Debt	$16
Fixed Assets	29	Common Stock	13
Total	$29	Total	$29

is clearly superior from the common stockholders' standpoint. But just the reverse is true for the company's debtholders. They get identical payoffs in the favorable outcome for each project but a greater payoff in the unfavorable state from Project A. Dynamo's common stockholders prefer the high-risk project, but its debtholders prefer the low-risk project.

Figure 9-2 shows the immediate impact on Dynamo's common stockholders and debtholders. We show you how to calculate the net present value of a capital investment project in Chapter 11, so we will skip the details of this calculation for now, but recall from Chapter 6 that the NPV of a project measures the change in the market value of the firm that results from undertaking the project. Project B is clearly undesirable because it decreases the total market value of the company. But Figure 9-2 indicates that the value of common stockholders' equity would increase if the company undertook Project B. Undertaking Project B would result in a transfer of wealth (1) from Dynamo's debtholders, who would lose three-quarters of the value of their investment if the project fails (which has probability 0.5) but would gain no additional value if it succeeds, (2) to Dynamo's common stockholders, who would gain if the project succeeds a large multiple of what they would lose if it fails.

Figures 9-1 and 9-2 illustrate the problem of **asset substitution** that confronts debtholders. The stockholders of a corporation will prefer projects that enhance their own wealth, and they may select projects that are adverse to the interests of the firm's debtholders. As a general rule, stockholders of leveraged companies gain at the expense of debtholders when the company's business risk increases or when riskier projects are selected over less risky ones. As in our example, stockholders may even prefer negative-NPV projects over positive-NPV projects. Note also that the temptation to behave in this manner is greater, the closer the company is to financial distress. The temptation is greater, of course, because the stockholders have less to lose in such a situation—their option never has a negative value.

THE GREEN CANYON PROJECT. The Hunt brothers' Green Canyon oil and gas drilling project illustrates the asset substitution problem.[10] Placid Oil Co., owned by trusts of the three Hunt brothers of Dallas, sons of the legendary H. L. Hunt, defaulted on its bank loan agreement in March 1986 after oil prices had plummeted. Placid filed for bankruptcy protection from its creditors in September 1986. Placid had sought to stretch out its loan payments in order to fund its Green Canyon project; the banks had insisted on Placid first using its available cash flow to service its debt before undertaking risky investments.

The Hunt brothers had embarked on the highly risky Green Canyon project, which would cost $340 million, in the hope that a massive oil and gas discovery (at one time the Hunts contended that they might find a 70-million-barrel oil reserve worth upwards of $1 billion) would enable them to pay down Placid's debt, help repay the debt of Placid's sister company Penrod Drilling Co., and repay personal debt that grew out of their unsuccessful, very expensive attempt to corner the world silver market in 1979–80.

---

[10]"Hunts' Empire May Unravel in U.S. Court," *Wall Street Journal*, 2 September 1986, A3, A18; "Hunts' Plan to Drill in the Gulf Runs into Stiffer Opposition from Lenders," *Wall Street Journal*, 23 December 1986, A4; "Hunts' Legal Victory on Drilling Project Exposes Their Lenders to Greater Risks," *Wall Street Journal*, 16 April 1987, A18; "Hunt Brothers Pin Hopes for Comeback on 'Crapshoot' in Oil," *Wall Street Journal*, 12 July 1988, A1, A14; "Placid Oil's Bank Settlement Outlines Hunts' Severe Moves to Save Company," *Wall Street Journal*, 25 July 1988, A20; and "Hunt for Black Gold at Green Canyon Ends in Red Ink," *Wall Street Journal*, 25 April 1990, A6. As one of these articles noted, perhaps the Hunt brothers were hoping to sink what was left of their legendary father's fortune into an effort to make a comeback just as celebrated as their father's gushers of the 1930s.

The Green Canyon project entailed drilling for oil and gas in very deep water in the Gulf of Mexico (one well, drilled through 2,243 feet of water, set a world water depth record) in a very hostile operating environment (hurricane gusts can reach 150 miles per hour) utilizing an untested technology (a one-of-a-kind floating drilling and production system). The Hunts were "betting the ranch" on one of the world's riskiest ventures. Many industry experts questioned the project's economic viability. The banks went to extraordinary lengths in their efforts to stop the project, arguing that if the project failed there would be little left of Placid for them to collect toward their loans.

Eventually, all three Hunt brothers' trusts and two of the Hunt brothers and their wives wound up in bankruptcy as their financial woes mounted. As for Green Canyon: Placid abandoned the project in April 1990.

The problem of asset substitution, illustrated by the Green Canyon Project, can be seen easily when the stock is viewed as a call option on the firm's assets: Recall that an increase in the variance of outcomes for the underlying assets increases the value of the option. If this increase in value more than offsets the negative NPV of the project, stockholders will want to undertake the project. This insight also illustrates the potential benefit and extraordinarily powerful insights that can often be achieved by viewing a situation in alternative ways (e.g., viewing common stock as an option).

How will debtholders react to the risk of asset substitution? They may try to restrict the firm's ability to engage in asset substitution through the use of indenture covenants that limit investments to projects in specified industries. They may also attempt legal action with respect to an existing contract, as is the case of the Green Canyon Project. Ideally, such limitations restrict *only* the targeted activities. However, to the extent such limitations are not able to eliminate completely the possibility of asset substitution, debtholders will require a higher rate of interest to compensate them for the residual risk of asset substitution. Such a higher rate is part of the agency costs borne by the stockholders. Another part of the agency cost involves the extent to which such limitations miss their target and unintentionally prevent a company from undertaking positive-NPV projects.

As an alternative to an extensive array of restrictive covenants, lenders can insist on the use of convertible bonds, which are convertible into shares of the company's common stock at the bondholder's option. The option on a convertible bond allows the securityholder to share in the upside if the projects the firm invests in are successful. Smaller, younger firms often issue convertible bonds, rather than straight bonds, precisely for this reason.

THE UNDERINVESTMENT PROBLEM A firm with risky debt outstanding may have an incentive to forgo a capital investment project that would increase the total market value of the firm. If business risk is held constant, any increase in total market value must be shared among the firm's common stockholders and debtholders. This problem is in some sense the reverse of the asset substitution problem. Where the asset substitution problem involves a predisposition on the part of stockholders in favor of high-risk projects, the underinvestment problem involves a predisposition against low-risk projects. Here again the characterization of stock as a call option on the firm's assets provides insight. We know that an increase in the variance of the outcomes for an underlying asset increases the value of the option. Conversely, a decrease in variance will decrease the value of the option. If such a decrease in value outweighs the positive NPV of a project, stockholders will refuse to undertake the project. Figure 9-3 illustrates such a situation.

FIGURE 9-3
Illustration of the
underinvestment problem
(dollar amounts in millions).

Before Investment

Crystal Manufacturing Company

Book Values

Assets		Liabilities & Equity	
Cash	$—	Debt	$40
Fixed Assets	50	Common Stock	10
Total	$50	Total	$50

Crystal Manufacturing Company

Market Values

Assets		Liabilities & Equity	
Cash	$—	Debt	$10
Fixed Assets	15	Common Stock	5
Total	$15	Total	$15

After Investment

Crystal Manufacturing Company

Book Values

Assets		Liabilities & Equity	
Cash	$—	Debt	$40
Fixed Assets	57	Common Stock	17
Total	$57	Total	$57

Crystal Manufacturing Company

Market Values

Assets		Liabilities & Equity	
Cash	$—	Debt	$18
Fixed Assets	27	Common Stock	9
Total	$27	Total	$27

Due to Crystal Manufacturing's precarious financial condition, its outstanding bonds are selling for 25 cents on the dollar. Imagine that Crystal discovers a superb investment opportunity that has an NPV of $5 million with virtual certainty (no it's not drug trafficking—remember what we said earlier about taking only legal and ethical steps to enhance stockholder wealth). The project would require a $7 million investment, which Crystal would have to raise externally. Will current or prospective stockholders be willing to make a $7 million equity contribution to fund the project? While the project would increase the total market value of the firm by $5 million, the value of the outstanding bonds would increase by $8 million because of the valuable new asset the company would have and because debtholders have first claim on the firm's assets in the event of bankruptcy. But the debtholders' gain comes at the stockholders' expense; stockholders would be asked to put up $7 million but would realize only $4 million (= $7 + 5 − 8)—a net decrease of $3 billion in stockholder wealth. Undertaking the project would be in the debtholders' interest but at the expense of the stockholders' interest.

Even after a debt contract has been made, stockholders control (through management) the decisions of the firm within the constraints imposed by the contract. Stockholders may at some point refuse to contribute further equity, which could work to the debtholders' detriment. As with the asset substitution problem, the underinvestment problem is most serious in the case of financially troubled firms.

CLAIM DILUTION: CAPITAL STRUCTURE CONSIDERATIONS   A substantial increase in the amount of debt outstanding will reduce a company's credit standing and cause the value of a company's outstanding debt to decrease. This is because the existing debtholders' claim on the firm's assets is *diluted* by the claim of the new debtholders. That is, all of the debtholders share in the first claim to the firm's assets in case of bankruptcy. The leveraged buyout of RJR Nabisco, Inc. illustrates this point. The buyout increased the company's outstanding debt from approximately

$5.7 billion to approximately $23.2 billion.[11] Following the announcement of the bid, outstanding RJR Nabisco bonds plunged roughly 20% in market value.[12] The outstanding debt did not have covenant restrictions that would prevent such extreme leveraging. Apparently, purchasers of the bonds expected the company's management to stick to its previous capital structure policy, which had involved only relatively modest amounts of debt. But the bondholders were rudely confronted with the problem of moral hazard: Once the debt is issued, the company's behavior may change to their detriment. As a result of the RJR Nabisco experience, there was near turmoil in the high-grade corporate bond market, particularly the market for bonds issued by consumer products companies, and calls for additional protective covenants to prevent other issuers from leveraging up and expropriating bondholder wealth.[13]

An interesting point to note about capital structure and claim dilution is that while a firm may deliberately change its capital structure to engage in claim dilution, a change in capital structure may be a natural consequence of poor economic conditions rather than a choice on the firm's part. In simple terms, the firm's capital structure is its proportion of debt financing. Because of the higher risk of equity, the value of equity varies more than the value of debt with a change in economic conditions. Thus, a downturn in economic conditions will decrease the value of equity more than the value of debt. When such a downturn occurs, then, the proportion of debt financing in the firm's capital structure (debt/[debt + equity]) increases.

CLAIM DILUTION: DIVIDEND POLICY In the absence of suitable protective covenants, common stockholders might be able to expropriate wealth from the debtholders by declaring a large cash dividend. Such a wealth expropriation would occur if the company's stock market value decreased less than the aggregate amount of the large cash dividend because the debtholders would share in the decline in firm value but the stockholders alone would get the dividend. Because of this risk, one of the protective covenants found in indentures of many bond issues (and in virtually all of those that are so-called junk, or high-yield, issues) is a dividend restriction. Such a restriction typically limits cash dividends to a fraction of earnings or cash flow, and in the case of very highly leveraged companies, may prohibit the payment of cash dividends altogether until long-term debt is repaid to some specified level.

ASSET UNIQUENESS When a firm's assets are unique, there is more risk associated with the disposal of those assets, should that become necessary. Thus, the collateral provided by the assets to the debtholders is of lower value. Although the assets might be highly sought after because of their uniqueness, it also might be the case that the assets become worthless (or perhaps even costly to dispose of). Therefore, a firm with unique assets will be required to pay a higher interest cost to compensate the debtholders for the increased risk.

MANAGER-STOCKHOLDER CONFLICT

We discussed certain aspects of the manager-stockholder conflict earlier in the chapter, pointing out that managers and stockholders may have different goals. We noted

[11] RJR Holdings Capital Corp., prospectus, May 12, 1989, p. 11.

[12] Margaret A. Elliott, "Rating the Debt Raters," *Institutional Investor*, December 1988, 109.

[13] "Takeover Fears Rack Corporate Bonds," *Wall Street Journal*, 25 October 1988, C1, C23; and "A Bruising Battle Over Bonds," *New York Times*, 27 November 1988, F1, F21.

that stockholders can try to achieve goal congruence by establishing appropriate financial incentives for corporate managers (through the board of directors) and by monitoring manager performance. Nevertheless, stockholder monitoring takes place at a distance, relying on a variety of information sources, such as the company's public disclosures, published financial statements, and exhibited financial policies. Here we point out several specific instances of goal divergence.

EMPLOYEE EFFORT   Some employees would like to get paid without having to put forth any effort. It has been said that 20% of the people do 80% of the work. The shareholders would of course like to have only 20%-type employees, in which case (conceptually) the shareholders would need only one-quarter as many employees ($X/100\% = 20\%/80\%$ implies that $X = 25\%$). The problem of an agent putting forth less than "full effort" is referred to as **shirking**.

EMPLOYEE PERQUISITES   The problem of moral hazard arises whenever the agent has the ability to take unobserved self-interested actions that are costly to the principal. One of the most obvious examples of such actions involves employee decisions that provide personal benefits, or **perquisites.** These include direct benefits, such as the personal use of a company car or personal sidetrips on company travel, and also indirect benefits such as an up-to-date office decor. The stockholders suffer a loss in their residual claim if employees are able to spend excessively on employee perquisites. While the distribution of perquisites is an obvious point of conflict, there are many other conflicts.

THE NONDIVERSIFIABILITY OF HUMAN CAPITAL   In Chapter 7 we defined diversifiable risk and nondiversifiable risk, and demonstrated that stockholders should be concerned only with nondiversifiable risk because they can diversify their investment portfolio in the capital market. This prescription was shown to hold with respect to **real capital**. However, in addition to real capital investments (the ones we typically think of, such as savings accounts, stocks, bonds, real estate, etc.), an individual has **human capital**, the unique capabilities and expertise that belong to an individual. Typically, a person's human capital is to a large extent invested solely in the firm for which she works. That is, employees devote the large majority of their day-to-day personal efforts to a single firm in exchange for salary and bonuses. This means that human capital is rarely well-diversified. Instead, it tends to be concentrated in an area or profession, and often in a specific firm. In fact, even if a person wants to, it is extremely difficult to diversify human capital. Professionals, such as corporate managers, engineers, physicians, accountants, and lawyers, simply do not have the time to become proficient in multiple areas; certainly not the number that might be necessary to provide reasonable diversification.

The nondiversifiability of human capital leads to yet other goal divergences between managers and stockholders. Managers may have distinctly different preferences concerning which investment projects the firm should undertake because they have differing attitudes toward diversifiable risk. The stockholders do not care about the random fluctuations in outcomes that are caused by diversifiable risk because their investments are well-diversified and such fluctuations tend to cancel each other out in the long run. In marked contrast, managers can be "wiped out" by a random fluctuation.

Consider for a moment the impact that bankruptcy would have on a well-diversified stockholder versus its impact on an employee. Suppose the firm goes bankrupt, and the stockholder's investment in the firm becomes worthless. This loss has no effect on the value of the other investments in the stockholder's investment portfolio, nor does it affect the stockholder's job. The employee, on the other hand, must seek new employment, even though the value of the employee's entire real capital investment portfolio is unaffected. The question of differential impact, then, comes down to job loss versus the loss of one part of an individual's investment portfolio. In the overwhelming majority of cases, an individual's most significant source of income is his job. Therefore, the impact of bankruptcy is much greater on the employee than it is on the stockholder. As a result of this differential impact, employees have a predisposition against investments that have a significant amount of diversifiable risk. And consequently they will try to avoid undertaking such a project, even if the project has a positive NPV.

ASSET UNIQUENESS   Another way that the nondiversifiability of human capital can cause the stockholders to incur an agency cost is with respect to the type of products and services that are produced by the firm. If the firm's products and/or services are unique (as opposed to generic), the employee's human capital will be even less well-diversified (i.e., this firm may be the only firm the employee can work for using her valuable personal skills). In such cases, the stockholders will have to pay the employees more than employees who appear to be otherwise comparable but are doing more generic work for other firms.

The distinction between the two effects of the nondiversifiability of human capital just noted is the point at which the agency costs are incurred. In the first case, the agency cost involves the possibility of passing up positive-NPV projects. That is, the effect is on the choice of *new* projects. In the second case, the agency cost involves higher wages paid to employees to induce them to work for the firm. That is, this second effect concerns an *existing* investment project.

FIRM-SPECIFIC INFORMATION AND SIGNALING   Because managers control the firm on a day-to-day basis, they often possess information that investors do not have. Based on the Signaling Principle, common stockholders and prospective common stockholders of a company interpret the firm's public announcements, such as dividend changes, new product announcements, or the issuance of new financial securities, to derive the informational content of such actions. For example, if it is believed that a company strives to pay out a fixed percentage of its "sustainable" earnings, an announced dividend increase would signal an expected increase in the firm's sustainable earnings. Of course, such signals are not simple because of the possibility that management might announce a dividend increase when it does not expect an increase in sustainable earnings, thereby emitting a false signal. In the next section we discuss some of the considerations connected with information interpretation.

CONSUMER-FIRM CONFLICTS

In the course of its business operations, a firm interacts with the consumers of its products and/or services. Such interactions can often be modeled as principal-agent relationships. Of course, it is important to keep in mind who the players are. In the situations in this section, the firm is modeled as the agent, and the consumer is the principal in the service/guarantees case, whereas their roles are reversed in the free-rider case.

SERVICE/GUARANTEES   The fundamental question that arises in the case of guarantees of product reliability and future service is whether the consumer can "trust" the firm to fulfill its obligations in a manner that will be agreeable to the consumer. In its agent role, the firm promises future service, should it become necessary. If the consumer (principal) believes the firm will live up to its promise, the firm can get full value for its products and services. The consideration of trust introduces the role of a firm's reputation into the consumer's purchase decision. In essence, a good reputation is the assurance that the consumer will actually get what the consumer feels he has paid for. Needless to say, a firm in financial distress may face an extremely difficult or even impossible task trying to convince consumers to trust it to provide future service. After all, when it comes time for service, the firm may be long gone.

THE FREE-RIDER PROBLEM   In our discussion of the Behavioral Principle, we introduced the free-rider problem. Recall that a free rider is someone who receives the benefit of someone else's expenditure (money, effort, or creativity) simply by imitation. The free-rider problem arises in a firm's business operations in connection with consumers duplicating and selling the firm's products and/or services without prior agreement. In this case, the consumer is modeled as the agent, the firm as the principal.

Consider the copying of books (photocopying or plagiarism), computer software, videotapes, audiotapes, and so on. Copyright laws are designed to protect the creator from such misuse. Likewise, patent laws are designed to protect the inventor from duplication of a valuable idea. The purpose of such laws is to provide incentives for people to be creative. In other words, our society has recognized the Principle of Valuable Ideas and encourages people to create value in this manner. In many cases these laws work very well. However, new products and technologies sometimes require the modification of existing laws. Such a modification was deemed necessary with respect to video-movie rentals. During the 1980s, royalties for movie rentals became mandated by law.

Another free-rider problem area involves international law. As markets become truly international, countries that do not recognize and enforce the copyright, patent, and royalty laws become places where pirated material can be easily created. Such pirated material represents lost sales to some extent, either in the country where the pirating has taken place or in other countries as the material makes its way into other markets, perhaps including the country of original creation.

How can the firm protect itself from unscrupulous consumers who free-ride? It is rumored that the Coca-Cola Company employed people to order Coke in establishments that did not sell their product. If the establishment failed to clarify that the cola product they actually served in response to the request was not Coke, Coca-Cola is said to have sued the establishment for violation of its trademark. While this may sound like a harsh measure on Coca-Cola's part, it may be one of the few methods available to a company to protect the value inherent in its trademark. (Perhaps Coca-Cola has reason to worry because many years ago Bayer lost its trademark for salicylic acid, aspirin, after the term had become so commonly used to refer to the drug, regardless of the manufacturer.)

FINANCIAL DISTRESS

As we noted in several cases, the problem of goal divergence can be exacerbated by the onset of financial distress. This is because financial distress can distort the agent's incentives, as in the case of (1) stockholder behavior with regard to debtholder wealth (e.g., asset substitution, underinvestment, and claim dilution), (2) managerial investment choice (e.g., an avoidance of good projects because they have diversifiable risk), and (3) the firm's credibility with consumers (e.g., a decrease in the value of guarantees of product quality and future service).

CLAIMANT COALITIONS   Financial distress can also create incentives for the firm's various claimants (or stakeholders) to form special coalitions among themselves—to "gang up" on one another. For example, suppose a firm is in financial distress, but the managers can contract with a bank for a loan to enable the firm to continue its operations, even though termination of the firm and the sale of its assets is a positive-NPV decision (i.e., liquidation would produce the largest present value). Each claimant will favor or oppose liquidation on the basis of its own outcome, not on the basis of maximizing total firm value.[14] The managers might want the firm to borrow the money from the bank and continue operations in an attempt to save their jobs, even though continuing the firm is not in the best interest of the stockholders. The stockholders might support the loan alternative over liquidation if they stand to get little or nothing from liquidation but would get a good return if the firm recovers, even if the loan is not in the best interest of the debtholders. The stockholders' position in this case is similar to their position in the underinvestment problem, and it too can be easily understood by applying the Options Principle to the characterization of stock as an option: Options are valuable, *but* the option is worthless if it expires out-of-the-money.

INFORMATION   **9.4**

Recall from Chapter 5 that asymmetric information is a significant capital market imperfection that can inhibit the accurate valuation of assets. Although information is not completely and costlessly available to all participants, market participants can apply the Signaling Principle to extract whatever information they can from observed corporate decisions. From an information-flow perspective, it would be nice if all decisions contained unequivocal information. In other words, the implications of an observed decision would be absolutely clear. However, as we noted in Chapter 5, there is a continuum of information contained in an observed action.

Because actions do not often provide unequivocal information, interpretation of information is a complex and difficult task. However, even when an action does provide unequivocal information, other problems can arise. For example, unequivocal information may make it possible for one party to take advantage of another. Thus, in some cases, the signaling entity may "camouflage" some decisions. One approach to this problem is to use a **randomized strategy**: The decision-maker randomly chooses (according to probabilities) among alternatives so that the choice will not always be identical and emit a consistent signal. In that way, observers cannot infer the exact parameter values of the decision-maker's "situation." For example, suppose it was observed that a corporation always reduced its price on a model that was about to be discontinued. If consumers knew the model was about to be discontinued, they might not think the reduced price made the model such a "good deal" after all, because the discontinuation would accelerate the obsolescence of the model. To avoid the implication that a reduced price signifies discontinuation, the corporation could have an occasionally (randomly determined) temporary price reduction.

Another important consideration concerning the potential information content of

---

[14]Bulow and Shoven (1978).

an observed action is the decision-maker's incentives for sending signals. Ideally, an agent—for example, a firm's managers—would have incentives to send accurate signals. The moral hazard problem that arises is that if the agents' earnings depend on their performance, they have an incentive to send signals that indicate "great" performance, even though their performance has been less than that. Thus, managers may have incentives to send false signals to the stockholders to imply better performance than has actually occurred. Or, in the case of stockholders modeled as agents, stockholders may have incentives to send false signals to debtholders and/or consumers to imply that better performance has occurred than is the case. Ideally, it is not cost effective for agents to send false signals. In other words, ideally, it would be a negative-NPV decision for one agent to **mimic** the activities of a "better" agent. If the incentives render an accurate signal as a positive-NPV decision, the signal is said to be **credible**.

Also in the context of the consumer-firm relationship, consider retail pricing. When is a "sale" really a sale? Some retailers have essentially continuous "sales." When is this or any other advertising claim credible? This represents a significant and ongoing asymmetric information problem.

There are many factors that determine an agent's incentives, such as rewards, punishments, ethical attitudes, the likelihood of being caught "misbehaving," and the agent's reputation. A few words of explanation about the relevance of an agent's reputation is in order since that relevance might not be immediately obvious.

REPUTATION   Reputation is relevant because a good reputation is valuable. When an agent has a good reputation, the agent can demand a higher price for whatever product or service the agent provides; that good reputation carries with it an implicit guarantee of satisfactory performance as in the case of the firm in the firm-consumer relationship. Therefore, the maintenance of that reputation is valuable to the agent, and conversely, its loss would be costly. The implicit cost of a lost good reputation increases the punishment that is associated with the agent's being caught misbehaving. Therefore, an agent with a good reputation has a greater incentive to behave properly compared with an agent who has no reputation or a bad reputation. Similarly, it may be valuable for an agent to earn a good reputation.

9.5   OPTIMAL CONTRACTS

An optimal contract balances the three types of agency costs (contracting, monitoring, and misbehavior) against one another so that the total cost is minimized. In some cases, the optimal contract involves a fixed wage and some degree of monitoring, as is typically the case for employees. In other cases, the cost of monitoring the agent outweighs the expected cost associated with agent misbehavior, and the optimal contract consists solely of a simple bonus arrangement based on the principal's outcome, as is the case for salespeople who earn only a commission based on a percentage of their sales.

Some of the decisions connected with the choice of a financial contract are similar to trade-offs an agent might make in an effort to earn a good reputation: An agent may forgo profiting from misbehaving in the short run, in order to earn a larger profit in the long run by increasing the value of her services through particularly exemplary short-run behavior. Similarly, with respect to the choice of a financial contract, an agent may agree to "severe" monitoring in order to earn a higher price for services than could be demanded without such severe monitoring. The principal agrees to the higher price for services because it is cost-effective relative to the cost of employing other agents at apparently lower explicit costs but with the possibility of agent misbehavior. In each case the participant is balancing the cost components against one another to achieve the lowest total cost.

Of course, it is virtually impossible for a financial contract to cover every possible contingency; one cannot conceive of everything that might go wrong. In any case, it is unlikely that attempting to deal with every possible situation would be optimal since it would involve tremendous time and expense. Each party must take reasonable precautions but must ultimately rely on the other parties to behave ethically and responsibly in those situations not explicitly covered by the agreement. If either party behaves unethically, the contractual provisions may not prove very effective anyway.

MANAGING FINANCIAL CONTRACTS 9.6

A financial contract is complex because it involves imperfect information in what can be modeled as a principal-agent relationship. In spite of this complexity, there are a number of important monitoring devices that may be cost-effective methods for reducing the problems of asymmetric information.

As already noted, share ownership tends to be widely dispersed in large corporations. For example, at year-end 1988, American Telephone and Telegraph Company had more than 2.6 million common stockholders, and General Motors Corporation had more than 1.7 million common stockholders. This diffusion of ownership exacerbates the problems associated with the separation of ownership and control discussed above, along with the possibility that corporate managers will pursue their own goals. However, a large number of empirical studies have reached conflicting conclusions about whether firms that are apparently manager-controlled differ in their profitability, growth rate, or correlation between profitability and executive compensation from firms that are apparently stockholder-controlled.[15]

Even with widely diffused share ownership—and managerial control—the stockholders do possess several devices for limiting managers' flexibility to pursue their own objectives at the expense of stockholder wealth and for providing managers with a financial incentive to align their goals with those of the company's stockholders. These devices include

- Stockholders have the right to elect the directors. Dissident stockholders can mount a proxy fight to elect new directors if they are dissatisfied with corporate performance. However, this may be of limited practical value because proxy fights are seldom successful (except perhaps when a group of stockholders that collectively controls a large block of shares bands together), and the recent practice of staggering directorships (for example, so that only one-third of the directors are elected each year) dilutes the effectiveness of this device.

- Incentive compensation plans, such as managerial stock options, performance shares, and bonuses tied directly to corporate profitability, can be designed to encourage stockholder wealth-maximizing behavior. A major drawback to bonuses based on accounting measures of profit (rather than stockholder wealth

[15] Elliott (1972), Kamerschen (1968), and Sorenson (1974) found no significant difference in either profitability or rate of growth between manager-controlled and owner-controlled firms. In contrast, Holl (1977), Palmer (1973), and Stano (1976) found a significant difference in profitability according to control type among firms possessing a high degree of monopoly power.

directly) is that such bonuses can sometimes be manipulated by managerial decisions about accounting procedures. Consequently, it is preferable to base a large component of managerial incentive compensation on appreciation in the firm's share price, through stock option or performance share programs, to "bond" more effectively managers' and stockholders' interests.

■ Stockholders have the right to sell their shares (except in special cases of restricted stock held by certain **insiders**). In particular, if poor corporate performance reduces the stock price and induces a takeover raid, stockholders can tender their shares to the prospective acquirer. The ability to sell their shares is potentially the most effective (though last-resort) measure open to the stockholders. However, so-called poison pills and similar antitakeover measures have blunted the threat of takeover as a device to enhance corporate performance.[16]

■ Competition in the managerial labor market may help promote strong corporate performance, both from fear of dismissal by the board of directors if performance falters badly and a desire to develop a reputation as a good manager to enhance the manager's future prospects.

Based on the available empirical evidence, it would seem that while these devices have not achieved unanimity of managers' and stockholders' interests, in most cases there is not a sharp divergence. However, ensuring that a sharp divergence does not occur requires continual monitoring by stockholders.

BOND INDENTURES AND LOAN AGREEMENTS

Bond covenants are the principal means by which bondholders prevent stockholders (or managers) from benefiting themselves at the bondholders' expense. Protective covenants are of two types. A **negative covenant** limits or prohibits altogether certain actions unless the lenders consent. A covenant might prohibit the incurrence of additional debt except under carefully specified conditions. A covenant might prohibit a company from pledging any of its assets for the benefit of other lenders unless the bondholders protected by the covenant receive an equitable pledge of assets at the same time. A **positive covenant** specifies certain actions that the firm must take. For example, a typical positive covenant requires a company to furnish financial statements at least quarterly. The requirement of sinking fund payments is another example of a positive covenant.

Covenants may also limit the payment of dividends, limit the firm's ability to merge or sell assets, or restrict its ability to enter into leases.[17] These and other restrictions impose a cost on stockholders to the extent they restrict the firm's operating flexibility, particularly if they cause the company to forgo positive-NPV investment opportunities. While it is possible to solicit lender consents to relax a restrictive covenant, such a process is cumbersome, time-consuming, and often expensive. In particular, the lenders will normally demand some form of payment, either an immediate cash payment or an increase in the coupon rate—in exchange for their

---

[16] Poison pills typically take the form of an option to purchase shares in the target company at a bargain price. The option becomes exercisable in the hands of the target company's stockholders once an "unfriendly" suitor (i.e., one not approved by the company's board of directors) acquires some specified percentage of the outstanding shares, often just 20%. Poison pill gets its name from the pill of cyanide foreign agents are supposed to swallow when capture becomes imminent; it prevents capture. Malatesta and Walkling (1988) conclude that poison pill securities reduce stockholder wealth.

[17] Smith and Warner (1979) find that 91% of the indentures for bonds issued to the public during 1975 included covenants limiting additional debt, 23% had covenants restricting dividend payments, 39% limited mergers, and 36% restricted sales of assets.

consent. For example, in April 1988, the owners of The Seven-Up Company and Dr. Pepper Company offered one group of bondholders[18] (1) a payment of $25 per $1,000 bond, (2) an increase in the coupon rate from $12\frac{1}{8}\%$ to $12\frac{3}{8}\%$ for the period from November 15, 1989, through May 14, 1992, and (3) a further increase in the coupon rate to $12\frac{5}{8}\%$ for the period from May 15, 1992, through May 15, 1997. At the same time, the firm offered other bondholders a similar financial incentive.[19] Both offers were in exchange for a consent to a leveraged buyout of the company.[20] The cost of the cash payment if all bondholders consented (a majority was required in each case) was $9.3 million. The increase in coupon rate, which would benefit every bondholder as long as holders of at least a majority of each issue consented, amounted to $934,000 per annum for the first increase and a further $934,000 per annum for the second.

The essential role of most bond covenants is to provide a form of monitoring. Some covenants are designed specifically to serve as an early warning system for bondholders. It is costly and time-consuming for bondholders to monitor a firm continuously. If the covenants are crafted correctly, a covenant violation will alert bondholders to the fact that the firm is not performing as they had expected and will issue the warning in time for the bondholders to insist that corrective action be taken, well before the onset of financial distress.

A study of long-term, senior nonconvertible industrial debentures sold between 1960 and 1980 considered the role of three types of bond covenants: the sinking fund provision, which obligates the issuer to make principal payments prior to maturity; the limitation on debt; and the limitation on dividend payments.[21] The study found that firms with higher financial leverage, which therefore have a greater incentive to expropriate wealth from bondholders, benefit to a greater extent than less highly leveraged firms from including in their debt issues covenants limiting debt and dividends. The study also found that smaller firms, for which asymmetric information between stockholders and bondholders is more likely, are more inclined to include covenants limiting debt and dividends than larger firms. Such covenants appear to be less important for larger firms because they generally have a longer-standing relationship with the capital market or perhaps finance in the public markets more frequently, which permits closer monitoring by bondholders (and securities regulators and underwriters). Also, all of the debentures in the study's sample provided for a sinking fund. A sinking fund reduces agency costs by mitigating the asset substitution problem; the cash that must be paid out to bondholders to satisfy the sinking fund requirement is not available for investment by the firm. Of course, the cost of this reduction is reduced flexibility with respect to future investments.

A call provision and the maturity structure of the debt also provide means of resolving agency problems associated with informational asymmetry, stockholder risk incentives, and forgone growth opportunities.[22] For example, having the option to call bonds for early redemption would eliminate the disincentive to pursue highly profitable projects whose benefits stockholders would have to share with bondholders if the bonds were not callable. Empirical research supports this rationale,

---

[18] The Seven-Up Company, Solicitation Statement for $12\frac{1}{8}\%$ Senior Subordinated Notes Due 1997, April 25, 1988, with $155.8 million outstanding principal amount.

[19] Dr. Pepper Company, Solicitation Statement for $12\frac{3}{4}\%$ Senior Subordinated Debentures Due 2001, April 25, 1988, with $218 million outstanding principal amount.

[20] The Seven-Up Company, Solicitation Statement, and Dr. Pepper Company, Solicitation Statement. Interestingly, both solicitation statements noted that legal counsel had determined that bondholder consents were *not* required for the leveraged buyout to proceed as planned.

[21] Malitz (1986).

[22] Barnea, Haugen, and Senbet (1980).

finding significant differences between firms that do and do not retain the right to call their bonds at any time (including just after issuance) for purposes other than refinancing at a lower interest cost.[23] The firms that retain this option tend to be faster growing, more highly leveraged, and less profitable (indicating greater default risk), and have outstanding debt of a longer maturity than the firms that do not have this option. These findings are consistent with the hypothesis that the call option is used to reduce the agency costs of debt.

OTHER MONITORING DEVICES

ACCOUNTING STATEMENTS   Audited financial statements are a routine monitoring device for agents in several of the relationships modeled in this chapter: manager-stockholder, stockholder-debtholder, firm-consumer. Such accounting statements provide an early warning system for principals (stockholders, debtholders, and consumers).

BOND RATINGS   Bond rating agencies such as Moody's or Standard & Poor's provide a monitoring service at the time of issuance and over the life of the bonds.

GOVERNMENT REGULATION   The U.S. government in the twentieth century has had an evolving role as a monitor. For example, the Food and Drug Administration (FDA) metes out punishments for violations of legally mandated minimum standards for product quality.

THE ENTIRE LEGAL SYSTEM   Theft, fraud, and many other forms of agent misbehavior are illegal. Therefore, the legal system provides a warning system and some protection for all types of principals.

NEW EXTERNAL FINANCING   Whenever a firm seeks additional financing of any kind (equity or debt, public or private, short- or long-term), the firm must provide information to prospective investors. Dissemination of that information facilitates a monitoring function by the firm's existing investors. Existing investors may be reassured that the firm has a healthy financial condition if the firm is able to convince new investors to invest a significant amount of money.

This concept of reassurance can be extended to the verification of valuable private information. Suppose a firm has a valuable new idea that would be damaged if it was released to the public, because of the free-rider problem. That is, others would steal the idea. In such cases, the firm may be able to issue new securities through investment bankers who underwrite the issue.[24] In other words, the firm tells the investment bankers about the valuable new idea underlying the project in which the funds raised will be invested but does not release the idea to the public until the idea is marketed. Investors are more confident about the value of the idea because the new security issue is underwritten. With an underwritten issue, not only do the investment bankers agree to market the new securities, but they actually purchase the securities before reselling them to the public. Taking ownership, even if for only a relatively short time period, is a much riskier proposition for the investment bankers than simply marketing the securities on a best-efforts basis in exchange for a commission. Presumably, investment bankers would not be willing to take on the additional risk if they perceived it to be significant.

[23] Thatcher (1985).
[24] Heinkel and Schwartz (1986).

CASH DIVIDENDS   The regular payment of cash dividends to common stockholders may help reduce the agency costs stockholders face by forcing the firm to raise capital externally more frequently than it otherwise would.[25] As noted above, new financing exposes management to the careful scrutiny of prospective investors, securities regulators, and underwriters.

REPUTATION   As noted in an earlier section, the agent's reputation can affect his incentives for providing accurate information. Returns from maintaining a good reputation, therefore, provide an incentive for the agent to furnish accurate information because injury to his reputation would be costly to the agent. The increase in the accuracy of information facilitates the monitoring process.

MULTILEVEL ORGANIZATIONS   The use of many levels of authority and the review of decision-making can also provide a form of monitoring. For example, theft by employees is more difficult when there are a larger number of employees who must participate to accomplish the theft.

MANAGERIAL BEHAVIOR IN PRACTICE   9.7

Leveraged buyouts illustrate a variety of agency problems. In a typical leveraged buyout, a group of outside investors, usually acting in concert with corporate management, offers to pay cash to acquire all the outstanding publicly held shares of a corporation that the buyout group does not already own. The purchase price is largely financed with debt (the reason for the term **leveraged buyout**). Three important questions arise in a leveraged buyout: Is the price offered existing stockholders "fair"? Will the transaction result in a transfer of wealth from current debtholders to the new common stockholders? How are the contractual arrangements among management, the new stockholders, and the new debtholders structured to avoid serious agency problems?

TENDER OFFERS

The first question arises as a result of asymmetric information. A price is said to represent "fair market value" when buyers and sellers who have full access to all available information voluntarily enter into transactions at that price. Outside stockholders do not have access to all the information management has at its disposal when it announces its purchase offer. As a consequence of self-interested behavior, one would expect management to offer a price sufficient to gain the shares it desires, but not one cent more. Another acquirer, if it had full access to management's information, might be willing to offer a considerably higher price. For example, in connection with the leveraged buyout of RJR Nabisco, Inc., the management-led group originally expressed its intention to bid $75 per share for the company's common stock and later raised its bid at least four times to approximately $109 per share.[26] The company's outside directors accepted a cash offer for 76% of the shares at a cash price of $109 per share from Kohlberg, Kravis & Roberts.[27] The subsequent bids, particularly management's final bid, which was more than 45% higher than its initial $75 bid, raised a serious question whether the initial bid was "fair."

[25] Rozeff (1986).
[26] RJR Nabisco, Inc., Offer to Purchase, December 6, 1988, 21–24.
[27] Kohlberg, Kravis & Roberts eventually acquired each remaining share in exchange for a package of preferred stock and convertible debentures. RJR Holdings Capital Corp., Offer, 18–27.

TRANSFER OF WEALTH FROM BONDHOLDERS TO STOCKHOLDERS

A leveraged buyout creates a firm with an equity financing component that is very small relative to the firm's liabilities. Therefore, a leveraged buyout can cause a capital-structure-induced claim dilution for existing bondholders that can in turn cause the market value of that company's bonds to plummet. As already noted, the prices of RJR Nabisco bonds fell roughly 20%.[28] The bonds that fell in price did not contain covenants that would protect bondholders against such claim dilution. Such protection has in practice taken either of two forms: (1) a provision that prohibits the transaction unless the bonds are redeemed, sometimes referred to as a "super poison put,"[29] or (2) a provision that requires an increase in the coupon rate sufficient to make the bonds worth par, referred to as a "rate-reset" mechanism.[30] The super poison put was invented largely in response to the RJR Nabisco leveraged buyout.[31]

The RJR Nabisco leveraged buyout resulted in at least two bondholder lawsuits. Metropolitan Life Insurance Co. charged that under contract law, RJR Nabisco owed its bondholders a "continuing duty of good faith and fair dealing."[32] ITT Corp. charged that the company violated securities laws by failing to disclose, to purchasers of a bond offering the preceding April, that management was considering a leveraged buyout.[33] The first lawsuit involves the issue of moral hazard; the second involves the issue of asymmetric information (and of the securities laws that are intended to remedy this problem).[34]

DESIGN OF CONTRACTUAL ARRANGEMENTS

A leveraged buyout poses difficult problems of contract design. The large proportion of liabilities increases the importance of efficient operation of the business in order to service the debt. It is not unusual to find management being given an equity interest of as much as 20% (through a combination of share purchases and stock options) to align the managers' objectives with those of the outside stockholders. Often, management's percentage equity stake will depend directly on how well the

---

[28] There are many other examples. Just prior to the RJR Nabisco announcement, Campeau Corporation acquired Federated Department Stores in a leveraged buyout. The transaction caused the prices of Federated's outstanding bonds to fall more than 17%. "A Bruising Battle," F21.

[29] The name derives from the bondholders' implicit put option: The bondholders have the right to sell the bonds back to the firm for par value (i.e., to exercise a put option).

[30] Note that neither provision fully protects bondholders if the bonds were worth more than par prior to the announcement of the leveraged buyout. In principle, this problem could be solved by requiring redemption at preannouncement fair market value.

[31] Harris Corporation sold the first debt issue with such a provision, which gives debentureholders, among other rights, the right to put the bonds back to the issuer for redemption at par within 90 days of a "Designated Event," which causes the bonds' credit rating to fall below Baa3/BBB− (i.e., to become junk bonds). Designated Events include (1) Harris consolidates with or merges into another company, (2) a single stockholder group acquires 20% or more of Harris's common stock, (3) Harris reacquires 30% or more of its common stock within a 365-day period, or (4) Harris distributes as a dividend assets representing 30% or more of the fair market value of its common stock within a 365-day period. Harris Corporation, prospectus, November 29, 1988, 8–9.

[32] "A Bruising Battle," F21.

[33] Ibid.

[34] Marais, Schipper, and Smith (1989) provide empirical evidence that, on average, (straight) debtholders lose but convertible debtholders do not lose in a leveraged buyout. The evidence of a loss to (straight) debtholders is consistent with the concept of claim dilution with respect to capital structure. The evidence of no loss to convertible debtholders is also consistent with this concept because (recall from Chapter 8) convertible bonds can be viewed as stock plus a put option. Viewing the convertible debtholders as stockholders explains why they do not incur the same loss as the straight debtholders.

company performs. In addition, the leveraged buyout firms involved in the transaction usually hold a majority of the director seats to be able to monitor the business's performance closely and control the voting if changes in management or in the company's business need to be made quickly.

Leveraged buyouts typically also involve very complex capital structures. Thus, agency problems may arise between different classes of debtholders and between different classes of equityholders. As a result, the debt and preferred stock agreements can be quite complex to deal with potential agency problems.

SUMMARY

In the large modern corporation, professional managers operate the business but may own only a tiny fraction of the outstanding common stock. There is reason to believe that in such an environment the various claimants to the firm's assets (including managers, stockholders, debtholders, other employees, and customers) do not have identical interests. The divergence of the interests of the various claimants creates agency problems: each claimant will tend to act in its self-interest rather than in the interests of the other claimants. Therefore, participants in a financial contract should take steps—in the form of incentives, constraints, punishments, and monitoring—to ensure that agents act in the principal's best interest. Such steps impose agency costs on the principals. Agency problems and agency costs arise in connection with many of the relationships that compose the nexus of contracts that make up a corporation. Financial distress is an important complicating factor that intensifies most agency problems and costs.

Stockholders are primarily interested in maximizing their wealth. Managers may pursue other goals, such as favoring corporate growth and size over profitability, seeking emoluments and perquisites, and trying to ensure their own security. Two very important dimensions that can cause goal divergence are (1) the moral hazard problem created by direct conflicts of interest, such as salary level and the employee's personal use of the firm's resources, and (2) the nondiversifiability of human capital. There are several devices that stockholders (and their board representatives) can use to limit managers' flexibility or desire to pursue their own goals at the expense of stockholder goals, including the right to elect the directors who hire and fire the managers, incentive compensation plans, and requiring audited financial statements. Ultimately, the stockholders have the right to eliminate their participation in the firm by selling their shares. If the market value of a poorly run firm falls sufficiently, another firm or investor can purchase sufficient shares to gain control and fire inept managers.

The corporate form of organization gives stockholders the option to default on outstanding corporate debt and limits their liability to their equity interests in the corporation. This means that stock can be modeled as a call option that the debtholders have sold to the stockholders. The stockholders' truncated option return distribution creates the problems of asset substitution, underinvestment, and claim dilution. In certain situations, stockholders may have incentives to pursue projects that are riskier than the firm's debtholders would approve (if they possessed such approval right), to eschew profitable projects that could benefit debtholders, to increase corporate debt substantially, or to pay themselves high dividends in the form of cash or corporate assets.

Once a transaction has been entered into (e.g., stock is purchased, money is lent, or a product has been purchased), the agent's behavior may change in some unforeseen manner. The principals can deal with this moral hazard in two ways: by creating incentives, constraints, and punishments that bond the agent's interests to those of the principal and discourage misbehavior and by closely monitoring the agent's performance. In the case of the manager-stockholder conflict, management contracts impose the incentives, constraints, and punishments, and the board of directors performs the monitoring function, meting out rewards and punishments. In the case of the stockholder-debtholder conflict, debtholders typically insist on certain contractual arrangements such as restrictive indenture covenants to protect their interests. Certain provisions of debt instruments—such as maturity structure, call provisions, sinking fund provisions, dividend restrictions, lease restrictions, and the convertibility feature, among others—are designed to mitigate the agency costs of debt. But it is impossible to foresee every contingency. Events, such as the leveraged buyout of a large firm that has historically maintained a very low proportion of debt in its capital structure, may sensitize bond investors to the need for additional protective covenants.

An optimal financial contract minimizes its total cost, which is made up of financial contracting costs (transaction costs, opportunity costs, and incentive fees), monitoring costs, and misbehavior costs. The existence of agency problems adds to the cost of financial contracting. **Agency cost** is defined as the incremental cost above whatever cost would be incurred in a perfect capital and labor market environment.

In future chapters we shall repeatedly encounter agency issues. Agency theory has been used to an increasing extent to explain financial contracting phenomena that were not previously well-understood. Agency cost considerations help explain the design of new securities issues (Chapter 14), the choice of capital structure (Chapter 15), dividend policy (Chapter 17), the design of asset-based financing arrangements (Chapter 21), and the design of merger or acquisition financing arrangements (Chapter 22).

PROBLEMS

PROBLEM SET A

A1. Describe and discuss the **asset substitution problem**.

A2. Describe and discuss the **underinvestment problem**.

A3. Define the term **moral hazard**.

A4. Define the term **free rider** and explain why it causes problems. Cite an example of the free-rider problem and a contract form that is typically used to reduce or eliminate the problem.

A5. Describe the concept and cite three examples of **agency problems**.

A6. Cite three goals managers might have that are not necessarily consistent with the goal of maximizing shareholder wealth.

A7. What is an **agency cost**? What are its three components? Cite an example of each one. Who bears the agency costs: the principal entirely, the agent entirely, or the two parties jointly?

A8. Describe the problem of **claim dilution**, using the notion of stock as a call option on the firm's assets.

A9. Cite and describe two ways that the uniqueness of assets creates agency costs for shareholders.

A10. How can employee perquisites create a conflict between the shareholders and the employees?

A11. How can product and service guarantees create an agency problem between the firm and its consumers?

A12. Define the term **credible signal**.

A13. Cite and briefly discuss four devices that naturally monitor agent behavior for the principal.

A14. Explain the concept of the **nondiversifiability of human capital**.

PROBLEM SET B

B1. Perfect monitoring in a perfect market environment always provides an optimal contract. Explain why monitoring is not always the best choice, even in a well-functioning market environment with low transaction costs.

B2. How does having a manager-stockholder reduce potential conflicts of interest?

B3. How does the nondiversifiability of human capital cause a conflict of interest between the managers and the stockholders regarding the firm's choice of investment projects?

B4. Explain how a manager's desire to maintain the ongoing value of a good reputation can facilitate shareholder monitoring of the manager.

B5. Explain why the stock price of a firm that is undergoing bankruptcy proceedings is virtually always positive and never negative.

B6. Explain how covenants in a bond indenture help to reduce a firm's agency costs, thereby reducing the firm's cost of financing.

B7. Using the stock-as-a-call-option view, explain why stockholders might choose not to undertake a low-risk project, even if the expected NPV of the project is positive. What group is on the other side of this transaction?

B8. Explain why debtholders typically require covenants in the bond indenture that restrict the firm's ability to take on additional debt. Cite two such covenants that are common and relate them to your explanation.

B9. Define and explain in your own words the concept of an optimal contract.

B10. Describe in your own words how financial distress can intensify conflicts of interest among the firm's claimants. Cite three specific examples of situations in which this can occur.

B11. What methods do shareholders have at their disposal for aligning managers' goals with their goals?

B12. Using the stock-as-a-call-option view, explain why stockholders might choose to undertake a high-risk project, even if the NPV of the project is negative. What group is on the other side of this transaction?

PROBLEM SET C

C1. Is it possible to have an agency problem if there is no asymmetric information? If so, cite an example; if not, explain why not.

C2. If you were a debtholder for a company, why would you be concerned about the firm's dividend policy?

C3. How can employee perquisites create an agency problem between managers and the *debtholders*?

C4. Explain in your own words how a complex multilevel organization provides a natural form of agent monitoring.

C5. How does convertible debt help to reduce the agency problem between the shareholders and the debtholders?

C6. We said that in cases of financial distress, various claimant coalitions can form.

Is it possible to predict what those coalitions will be when the firm is healthy? If so, explain how. If not, explain why.

REFERENCES

Akella, Srinivas, and Stuart I. Greenbaum. "Savings and Loan Ownership Structure and Expense-Preference." *Journal of Banking and Finance* 12 (September 1988): 419–37.

Barnea, Amir, Robert A. Haugen, and Lemma W. Senbet. "A Rationale for Debt Maturity Structure and Call Provisions in the Agency Theoretic Framework." *Journal of Finance* 35 (December 1980): 1223–34.

Barnea, Amir, Robert A. Haugen, and Lemma W. Senbet. *Agency Problems and Financial Contracting.* Englewood Cliffs, N.J.: Prentice-Hall, 1985, chap. 6.

Barry, Christopher T., and Laura T. Starks. "Investment Management and Risk Sharing with Multiple Managers." *Journal of Finance* 39 (June 1984): 477–91.

Baumol, William J. "On the Theory of Oligopoly." *Economica* 25 (new series) (August 1958): 187–98.

Baumol, William J. "On the Theory of Expansion of the Firm." *American Economic Review* 52 (December 1962): 1078–87

Baumol, William J. *Business Behavior, Value and Growth*, rev. ed. New York: Harcourt, Brace and World, 1967.

Bodie, Z., and Robert A. Taggart, Jr. "Future Investment Opportunities and the Value of the Call Provision on a Bond." *Journal of Finance* 33 (September 1978): 1187–1200.

Brickley, James A., and Fredrick H. Dark. "The Choice of Organizational Form: The Case of Franchising." *Journal of Financial Economics* 18 (June 1987): 401–20.

Bulow, Jeremy I., and John B. Shoven. "The Bankruptcy Decision." *The Bell Journal of Economics* 9 (Autumn 1978): 437–56.

Crutchley, Claire E., and Robert S. Hansen. "A Test of the Agency Theory of Managerial Ownership, Corporate Leverage, and Corporate Dividends." *Financial Management* 18 (Winter 1989): 36–46.

Diamond, Douglas W. "Reputation Acquisition in Debt Markets." *Journal of Political Economy* 97 (August 1989): 828–62.

Donaldson, Gordon. *Managing Corporate Wealth: The Operations of a Comprehensive Financial Goals System.* New York: Praeger, 1984.

Elliott, J. Walter. "Control, Size, Growth, and Financial Performance in the Firm." *Journal of Financial and Quantitative Analysis* 7 (January 1972): 1309–20.

Flannery, Mark J. "Asymmetric Information and Risky Debt Maturity Choice." *Journal of Finance* 41 (March 1986): 19–37.

Galbraith, John Kenneth. *The New Industrial State.* Boston: Houghton Mifflin, 1967.

Gordon, Robert A. *Business Leadership in the Large Corporation*, 2nd. ed. Berkeley, Calif.: University of California Press, 1961, 305–6.

Haugen, Robert, and Lemma Senbet. "New Perspectives on Informational Asymmetry and Agency Relationships." *Journal of Financial and Quantitative Analysis* 14 (November 1979): 671–94.

Heinkel, Robert, and Eduardo S. Schwartz. "Rights Versus Underwritten Offerings: An Asymmetric Information Approach." *Journal of Finance* 41 (March 1986): 1–18.

Hite, Gailen L., and Michael R. Vetsuypens. "Management Buyouts of Divisions and Shareholder Wealth." *Journal of Finance* 44 (September 1989): 953–70.

Holl, Peter. "Control Type and the Market for Corporate Control in Large U.S. Corporations." *Journal of Industrial Economics* 25 (June 1977): 259–73.

Jensen, Michael C. "Agency Costs of Free Cash Flow, Corporate Finance and Takeovers." *American Economic Review* 76 (1986): 323–39.

Jensen, Michael C. "Takeovers: Folklore and Science." *Harvard Business Review* (November/December 1984): 109–21.

Jensen, Michael C. "The Takeover Controversy: Analysis and Evidence." *Midland Corporate Finance Journal* 4 (Summer 1986): 6–32.

Jensen, Michael C. "Eclipse of the Public Corporation." *Harvard Business Review* (September/October 1989): 61–74.

Jensen, Michael C., and William H. Meckling. "The Theory of the Firm: Managerial Behavior, Agency Costs and Ownership Structure." *Journal of Financial Economics* 4 (October 1976): 305–60.

Jensen, Michael C., and Richard S. Ruback. "The Market for Corporate Control: The Scientific Evidence." *Journal of Financial Economics* 11 (April 1983): 5–50.

Kamerschen, David R. "The Influence of Ownership and Control on Profit Rates." *American Economic Review* 58 (June 1968): 432–47.

Lehn, Kenneth, and Annette Poulsen. "Free Cash Flow and Stockholder Gains in Going Private Transactions." *Journal of Finance* 44 (July 1989): 771–87.

Loderer, Claudio F., and Dennis P. Sheehan. "Corporate Bankruptcy and Managers' Self-Serving Behavior." *Journal of Finance* 44 (September 1989): 1059–75.

Malatesta, Paul H., and Ralph A. Walkling. "Poison Pill Securities: Stockholder Wealth, Profitability, and Ownership Structure." *Journal of Financial Economics* 20 (January/March 1988): 347–76.

Malitz, Ileen. "On Financial Contracting: The Determinants of Bond Covenants." *Financial Management* 15 (Summer 1986): 18–25.

Malitz, Ileen. "A Re-Examination of the Wealth Expropriation Hypothesis: The Case of Captive Finance Subsidiaries." *Journal of Finance* 44 (September 1989): 1039–47.

Marais, Laurentius, Katherine Schipper, and Abbie Smith. "Wealth Effects of Going Private for Senior Securities." *Journal of Financial Economics* 23 (June 1989): 155–91.

Marris, Robin L. "A Model of the 'Managerial' Enterprise." *Quarterly Journal of Economics* 77 (May 1963): 185–209.

Marris, Robin L. *The Economic Theory of "Managerial" Capitalism.* London: Macmillan, 1964.

Palmer, John P. "The Profit-Performance Effects of the Separation of Ownership from Control in Large U.S. Industrial Corporations." *Bell Journal of Economics and Management Science* 4 (Spring 1973): 293–303.

Robbins, Edward Henry, and John D. Schatzberg. "Callable Bonds: A Risk-Reducing Signalling Mechanism." *Journal of Finance* 41 (September 1986): 935–49.

Rozeff, Michael. "How Companies Set Their Dividend-Payout Ratios." In Joel M. Stern and Donald H. Chew, Jr., eds., *The Revolution in Corporate Finance.* Oxford: Basil Blackwell, 1986, 320–26.

Smith, Clifford W. Jr., and Jerold B. Warner. "On Financial Contracting: An Analysis of Bond Covenants." *Journal of Financial Economics* 7 (June 1979): 117–61.

Sorenson, Robert. "The Separation of Ownership and Control and Firm Performance: An Empirical Analysis." *Southern Economic Journal* 41 (July 1974): 145–50.

Stano, M. "Monopoly Power, Ownership Control, and Corporate Performance." *Bell Journal of Economics* 7 (Autumn 1976): 672–79.

Thatcher, Janet S. "The Choice of Call Provision Terms: Evidence of the Existence of Agency Costs of Debt." *Journal of Finance* 40 (June 1985): 549–61.

Wildsmith, J. R. *Managerial Theories of the Firm.* New York: Dunellen, 1974.

Williamson, Oliver E. *The Economics of Discretionary Behavior: Managerial Objectives in a Theory of the Firm.* Englewood Cliffs, N.J.: Prentice-Hall, 1964.

APPLICATIONS

Long-Term Investment Decisions

REQUIRED RATES OF RETURN

We begin our analysis of the firm's long-term investment decision by examining required rates of return. In Chapter 4 we introduced the concept of the opportunity cost of capital for a capital investment project. This is the rate of return you could earn in the capital market on an essentially comparable investment.[1] The opportunity cost of capital can be viewed as being a required rate of return since it is based on a currently available alternative opportunity, which must be forgone if you choose to invest in the project. For a capital investment project to be acceptable, the project's rate of return must be superior to the capital market opportunity cost: The investment must have a positive NPV.

Recall that financial management can be broken down into two parts: (1) the financing decision and (2) the investment decision. The financing, or capital structure, decision concerns the firm's choice between liabilities and owners' equity. In essence, it involves the components of the right-hand side of the balance sheet. The investment decision entails the firm's choice of assets, or the components of the left-hand side of the balance sheet.

In Chapter 6, we defined the required rate of return as the minimum rate of return that an investor must expect to earn to be willing to undertake the investment. The expected rate of return is the rate that the investor actually expects to earn if the investment is undertaken. In a sense, the required rate of return relates to the financing decision since the investor must earn that rate to be willing to provide financing. The expected rate of return can be viewed as relating to the investment decision since it is what the investor expects to earn if she invests. In perfect and complete markets, these rates are always equal. For example, an investment in a security that is traded in a perfect capital market is a zero-NPV investment: The investor expects to earn exactly the required rate of return.

Based on the Principle of Capital Market Efficiency, a perfect capital market environment is a good starting point for determining a required rate of return, just as it was in our discussions in Chapters 6 and 7. However, the investment decision often requires the firm to buy and sell real (physical) assets in markets that are not always efficient and/or well-behaved. As was discussed in Chapter 5, important differences between capital asset and real asset markets are due especially to differences in homogeneity (the similarity of assets), transaction costs, and the degree of competition.

Because real asset markets are not generally as efficient as the Western world's capital markets, we do not presume that real assets are fairly priced in most cases. Instead, we compute the expected NPV of an investment to decide whether to undertake the investment. The required rate of return, which we will estimate from the capital markets, is a necessary—and critical—input to measuring the NPV of an investment. It is critical because the present value of a future cash flow is inversely

---

[1] Such comparability can be difficult to define in some cases, but recall from Chapter 7 that nondiversifiable risk is the primary dimension. As a practical matter, then, investments are considered to be comparable when they have identical nondiversifiable risk.

related to the discount rate, r. The higher the discount rate, the lower the present value of the future cash flow. Clearly, then, using the wrong value for r can cause the NPV of an investment to be incorrectly measured, which may in turn cause poor investment decisions.

In Chapters 6, 7, and 8, we determined required rates of return for investing in financial securities such as bonds, stocks, and options. In this chapter we will apply these concepts to determine required rates of return for corporate investments in real assets. Because of the complexity of this topic, in this chapter, we will assume a perfect capital market environment (except for symmetric net corporate/personal taxes) for our investigation of required rates of return for investments in real assets. Later, in Chapter 15, the effect of certain capital market imperfections on required rates of return is examined when we discuss the firm's financing, or capital structure, decision.

10.1   THE OPPORTUNITY COST OF CAPITAL

The required rate of return for a prospective capital investment project is often referred to as simply the **cost of capital**. Unfortunately, the term **cost of capital** can be very misleading. It is *not* simply the firm's historical cost of funds, such as coupon payments on existing bonds, that determines the required rate of return. We must remember that the relevant cost of funds is an *opportunity cost*. It is the rate at which investors would provide financing for the project under consideration *today*.

Therefore, the cost of capital is ***not*** defined as the historical (or embedded) cost of funds for financing the firm's existing operations. This is very important to remember for two reasons. First, if the firm's historical cost of capital for its existing operations is used to evaluate potential new investment projects, the analysis will be wrong if market rates have changed. Observing capital markets for just a short time will convince you that market rates are not constant.

Second, even if the firm's current cost of funds is used to evaluate potential new investment projects, the rate will be wrong if the project does not have the same risk as that of the firm's existing operations. This is because the firm's current cost of funds reflects the average risk of *all* the firm's assets, but the project's risk may be very different from this average.

The required rate of return for any investment is the minimum rate of return that investors must expect to earn in order to be willing to finance the investment today. When management acts in the shareholders' best interest, the required rate of return will reflect the rate of return the firm could earn if it invested the funds in a capital market opportunity that is essentially comparable to the investment project under consideration. In a perfect capital market environment, of course, these two rates are the same. We point out this equivalence to reemphasize that at any particular moment, there is one rate of return for a given risk level in an efficient capital market. Any differential in the rate of return for comparable investments will be eliminated quickly by arbitrage activity.

10.2   CORPORATE VALUATION

We discussed the concept of value conservation in Chapter 5. Franco Modigliani and Merton Miller (MM) were most responsible for introducing this important concept in 1958 in an article about capital structure. MM demonstrate in the article that in a perfect and complete capital market, a firm cannot affect its market value by altering the way it is financed. The value of a firm depends only on the size of its expected future operating cash flow stream and the required rate of return on those expected future cash flows. Firm value does not depend on how that cash flow stream is divided between the debtholders and the shareholders. Therefore, a firm's capital structure—how the firm is financed—is irrelevant to the firm's value in a perfect capital market environment.

THE FINANCING DECISION

If the financing decision does not affect the value of the firm, you might be wondering why we would have any interest in it. There are at least three reasons. First, even if the financing decision does not affect the firm's value, it can provide us with important insight into the opportunity cost of capital. In other words, the financing decision can help us estimate the required rate of return for a potential new investment project, even if it does not affect the value of the project or the firm. Second, as a practical matter, even in an efficient capital market, mistakes can be made. It is important to understand the financing decision, if only to avoid making stupid mistakes in routine transactions during day-to-day operations. Finally, examining the financing decision in a perfect capital market environment provides a good foundation for understanding why and how certain market imperfections cause the financing decision to have some effect on firm value.

The value of a firm can be expressed as the value of the claims on its assets. With only simple equity and debt claims on the firm's assets,

$$V(\text{firm}) = V(\text{equity}) + V(\text{debt}) \tag{10.1}$$

where $V(\ )$ is a value function. Note that there is a practical difference between Equation (10.1) and the liabilities and owners' equity (right-hand) side of the balance sheet. The balance sheet is based on historical-cost-accounting methods, whereas Equation (10.1) is a market value equation. For example, $V(\text{equity})$ is the total market value of the equity of the firm; the current cost of purchasing all of the firm's outstanding shares of common stock. This value is often estimated by multiplying the current market value per share times the number of outstanding shares. For example, suppose a firm whose shares are currently selling for $48.25 has 2 million shares outstanding. $V(\text{equity})$ would be estimated to be $96.5 million (= [2]48.25).

THE INVESTMENT DECISION

Although the real asset markets may not be as efficient as the capital markets, once a financial claim on one or more real assets, such as a stock or bond, has been introduced into the capital market, the claim will trade for its single fair market value. This means that, again, value conservation will hold. Therefore, we can express the value of the firm as the sum of the values of the firm's individual assets, or

$$V(\text{firm}) = V(\text{asset a}) + V(\text{asset b}) + V(\text{asset c}) + \ldots \tag{10.2}$$

Similar to Equation (10.1), Equation (10.2) is a market value expression, but in this case it is for the asset (left-hand) side of the balance sheet. In this model, the firm is represented as a portfolio of its real assets.[2] The firm's investment decision consists

---

[2]Note that by equating Equations (10.1) and (10.2), a firm can be viewed as an intermediary between its investors and the real asset markets. This is essentially the view of the firm that is outlined in Figure 1-1.

of choosing which assets to add and/or remove from its portfolio. That choice is based on earning at least the required rate of return on each of the assets.

The model of the firm as a portfolio of assets is important because it lets us see that each asset must "rest on its own bottom." That is, each asset (or set of inter-related assets) has a unique value and earns a unique rate of return. An asset must earn at least its required rate of return in order to justify being included in the firm's asset portfolio. This notion is like the notion of contribution to portfolio risk we applied to derive the CAPM; where we established a required rate of return for each stock, based on what the stock contributes to the riskiness of the investor's portfolio. In this case, we are measuring the real asset's required rate of return by determining what that real asset would contribute to the riskiness of the firm's asset portfolio.

THE MARKET LINE FOR INVESTMENT PROJECTS

The derivation of the CAPM is based on shares of common stock. However, the fundamental notion of the CAPM can be extended to include all assets (financial and real). If we make this extension, we can build on the security market line (SML) and create what might be called the investment-project-market-line (IPML). The required rate of return for investment project j can then be expressed as function of the nondiversifiable risk of the project, its beta:

$$r_j = r_f + \beta_j(r_m - r_f) \qquad (10.3)$$

where r_j denotes the required rate of return on project j, r_f is the riskless rate, β_j denotes the beta for project j, and r_m is the required rate of return on the market portfolio. Choosing capital investment projects on the basis of the IPML would then consist of measuring the NPV of each project, using its required rate of return, r_j, obtained from the IPML.

EXAMPLE ■   Try-angle Designers, Ltd. is considering five potential new investment projects. Undertaking any single project does not preclude, or require, undertaking any of the others. Each project has a different beta, and therefore each has a different required rate of return. However, all of the projects cost $1,000 and promise a unique perpetual annual cash flow stream. The required rate of return on the market portfolio is 15%, and the riskless rate of return is 7%. Table 10-1 lists the beta, required rate of return, annual cash flow, expected rate of return, and NPV of each investment project. For example, the beta for project A is 1.30, so the required rate of return is 17.4% (= 7 + 1.30[15 − 7]). The annual cash flow for project A is $200, so its expected rate of return is 20% (= 200/1,000). Finally, the NPV for project A is $149.43, which is the present value of the expected future cash flows,

TABLE 10-1   Try-angle Designers, Ltd.'s Potential New Investment Projects

Project	Beta	Required Rate of Return	Annual Cash Flow	Expected Rate of Return	NPV
A	1.30	17.4%	$200	20%	$149.43
B	1.75	21.0	220	22	47.62
C	.95	14.6	140	14	−41.10
D	1.50	19.0	170	17	−105.26
E	.60	11.8	140	14	186.44

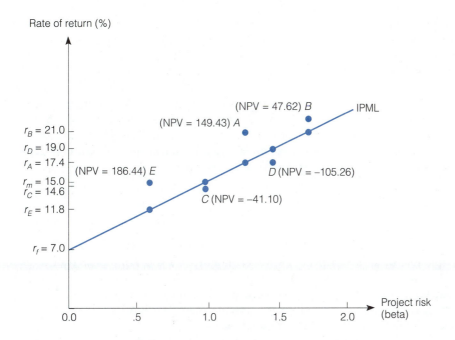

FIGURE 10-1
Try-angle Designers, Ltd.'s potential new investment projects and the IPML.

$1,149.43 (= 200/.174), minus its initial cost of $1,000. Try-angle should undertake projects A, B, and E, but Try-angle should reject projects C and D.

Figure 10-1 is a graph of the required and expected rates of return for the projects Try-angle is considering, along with the IPML. The required rates of return, of course, fall on the IPML since they were determined by the IPML equation. The expected rates of return for positive-NPV projects A, B, and E fall above the IPML, whereas they fall below the IPML for negative-NPV projects C and D. ■

VALUE AND THE RISK-RETURN TRADE-OFF   10.3

Although this chapter is focused on the concept of a required rate of return, it is imperative that we keep in mind how the rate of return (i.e., the discount rate), the expected cash flows, and the present value are related: Present value depends on both the required rate of return *and* the expected cash flows. When one of the parameter values changes, at least one other must also change. For example, if the required rate of return increases, the present value of the investment will decrease when the expected cash flows have remained constant. We have seen this in the case of a bond. With constant coupon payments, the market value of a bond changes whenever market interest rates change. Likewise, an increase in the expected future cash flows will increase present value *if* the risk, and therefore the required rate of return, has not changed. The relationship most easily forgotten with respect to this concept is that *present value can remain constant even if there are changes in both the expected future cash flows and the required rate of return*. The changes can exactly offset each other. This is precisely what the Principle of a Risk-Return Trade-Off means. Present value is constant, even though the required rate of return and expected cash flows change.

Consider the following simple example.

EXAMPLE ■ Suppose you have an asset that has an expected cash payment of $100 per year forever. The risk of this asset is such that the required rate of return is 10%. So the value of this asset is $1,000 (= 100/.1). Now suppose you have the opportunity to exchange this asset for an alternative asset that has an expected cash payment of $200 per year forever, but because of higher risk, the required rate of return on this alternative asset is 20%. Should you make the exchange?

The value of the alternative asset is also $1,000 (= 200/.2). Therefore, the decision of whether to make the exchange depends solely on your attitude toward risk. In other words, the choice represents a perfect risk-return trade-off. Even though the expected future cash flows are larger for owning the alternative asset, *there is no difference in value*. Such is the case when an investor moves *along* the SML or a firm moves *along* the IPML. ***Value is enhanced only when the increase (decrease) in expected return exceeds (is less than) the increase (decrease) in risk.*** ■

10.4   LEVERAGE

According to the CAPM, the required rate of return depends only on the nondiversifiable risk of an investment. However, nondiversifiable risk borne by the shareholders can be decomposed into two parts. Its primary determinant is often called **business** or **operating risk**. Its secondary determinant is referred to as **financial risk**. It is important to discriminate between these two types of risk because they affect required rates of return in different ways.

In many cases, business risk cannot be controlled by the firm. It is simply the inherent (nondiversifiable) risk of the investment. Less frequently, the firm's choice of production method affects the risk of the investment. By contrast, in virtually all cases, a firm's financial risk is determined by its capital structure, the components of the right-hand side of its balance sheet. To the extent that a firm chooses a particular level of total shareholder risk, it is said to be using **leverage**. More leverage increases risk. There are two types of leverage: **operating** and **financial**. The term **leverage** is derived from the mechanical lever that allows you to lift more weight than is possible by yourself. Financial leverage allows shareholders to control (lift, so to speak) more assets than is possible using only their own money.

OPERATING LEVERAGE

Operating leverage is determined by a firm's choice of fixed and variable cost functions. Multiple methods of producing a product and/or service may exist whereby a firm spends more on fixed costs and less on variable costs, or vice versa. A decrease in the variable cost per unit creates an increase in the contribution margin (the selling price minus the variable cost). With a larger contribution margin, the firm's profit is more sensitive to changes in the sales level of the product. That is, a small change in sales makes a large change in profit because the fixed costs are spent in either case. By contrast, an increase in the variable cost per unit causes a decrease in the contribution margin. With a lower contribution margin, the change in profit caused by a change in the sales level will not be as large. Therefore, lowering the variable cost per unit (by increasing fixed costs) increases the sensitivity of the firm's profit to changes in the level of sales. Such an increase in fixed cost is referred to as an increase in operating leverage.

EXAMPLE ■ Ms. Zoo's Tropical Ski Apparel, Inc. will purchase one of two alternative production methods for manufacturing ski caps. Method A costs $30,000 to install and $6 to make one cap. Method B costs $54,000 to install and $4 to make one cap. Ms. Zoo sells caps for $11 apiece. Which production method should Ms. Zoo purchase? The answer, of course, depends upon how many ski caps will be sold. For

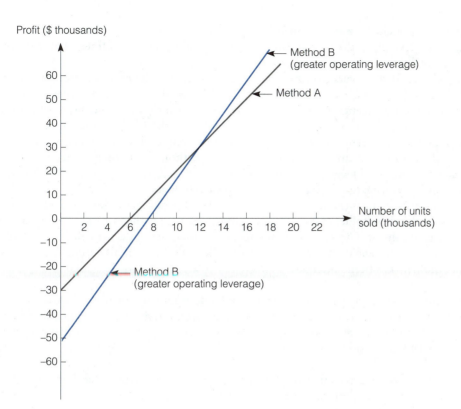

FIGURE 10-2
Illustration of differences in operating leverage.

simplicity we will ignore taxes and the time value of money. Profit will be the contribution margin times the number of caps sold (N) minus the fixed cost, so that profit for method A will be $5N - \$30,000$. Figure 10-2 illustrates Ms. Zoo's profit as a function of the number of ski caps sold for both methods. As could be predicted by our discussion above, Method B with its higher operating leverage (larger fixed and smaller variable costs) will make Ms. Zoo's profit more sensitive to the number of units sold. If the number sold turns out to be more than 12,000 (the point where $5N - 30,000 = 7N - 54,000$), then Method B will have been the better choice. If on the other hand sales turn out to be less than 12,000 units, then Method A will have been the better choice.

While operating leverage is important because of its impact on the risk of the investment, a firm's choice of operating leverage is limited by the number of possible different methods of producing a product and/or service. In some cases, the firm has no choice because there is a single (or significantly most efficient) method of production.

There are two particularly important things to remember about operating leverage. First, a firm's choice of operating leverage is generally unique for each investment rather than identical for all the firm's investments. Second, operating leverage affects the total risk of the investment project, and therefore it affects both the beta and required rate of return for the project.

FINANCIAL LEVERAGE

Operating risk depends principally on the nature of the investment project and to a lesser extent on the firm's choice of operating leverage. In contrast, financial risk depends principally upon the firm's choice of financial leverage. The firm's choice of financial leverage is the mix of debt, equity, and other sources of funds that make up its capital structure.

When a firm is leveraged (that is, partially financed with debt), the debt portion of its financing costs are fixed rather than variable. While the expected (mathematical expectation) payments to shareholders are larger than they are to debtholders, payments to shareholders can vary from one period to the next without affecting the operation of the firm. However, failure to make required debt payments can force the shareholders to turn the firm over to the debtholders. Loosely speaking, then, the use of financial leverage involves substituting fixed payments to debtholders for variable payments (e.g., cash dividends) to shareholders.

Graphically, financial leverage looks similar to operating leverage. The rate of return to the shareholders in an all-equity-financed firm is the same as the rate of return to the firm. The rate of return to the shareholders in a firm that is partially financed with debt is the rate of return to the firm after the fixed payment to the debtholders has been taken out.

EXAMPLE ■   Figure 10-3 illustrates shareholders' rate of return as a function of the rate of return to a firm with and without financial leverage. The leverage alternative assumes 50% debt financing. Figure 10-3 ignores taxes and assumes that the firm pays a 10% interest rate on its debt.   ■

We have come across the concept of financial leverage before. Recall from Chapter 7 (Generalization 5) that all investors in a perfect capital market should invest in

FIGURE 10-3

Illustration of the effect of financial leverage, assuming a 10% debt interest rate.

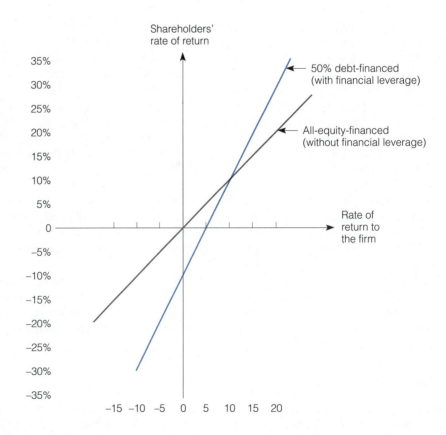

the same risky portfolio—the market portfolio. Investors set the expected return and risk levels of their total investment by lending or borrowing. This kind of lending and borrowing is simply personal financial leverage. There is a very important fact we learned in Chapter 7 about personal financial leverage: The choice of personal financial leverage (lending or borrowing) does not alter the total value of an investment; any change in return is exactly offset by a change in risk—the expected cash flows and required rate of return both increase but exactly offset each other, so that the value remains constant. In other words, the choice of personal financial leverage is simply the investor's choice of capital structure that places the investment at a particular point on the capital market line (CML). We will see that this same conclusion holds for a firm's choice of capital structure in a perfect capital market environment. Financial leverage is not a matter of value but a question of risk-return preference subject to a market-determined risk-return trade-off.

As with operating leverage, financial leverage also has two important corresponding (and almost reverse) things to remember about it. First, a firm's choice of financial leverage is for the most part made for the entire firm rather than being made separately for each of the firm's investments. Second, financial leverage affects the risk borne by each class of investor (debt, equity, etc.) but does not affect the required rate of return for the investment in a perfect capital market environment.

FINANCIAL LEVERAGE AND RISK BEARING   10.5

Even though financial leverage does not affect a firm's value in a perfect capital market environment and therefore does not affect the required rate of return to an investment, capital structure (the amount of financial leverage) can affect the required rates of return for each investor group (e.g., equity and debt). This is because a change in financial leverage causes a change in how the risk of the firm is borne by each investor group. To see this point, consider the following simple scenario.

AN EXAMPLE OF FINANCIAL LEVERAGE

Per-Pet, Inc. has an expected cash inflow each period forever with the following probability distribution:

Cash flow =	$250	$200	$150	$100	$50
Probability =	.2	.2	.2	.2	.2

The required rate of return for Per-Pet's expected future cash inflows is 15% per period. From this probability distribution you should be able to see that the expected cash inflow each period for Per-Pet is $150, and therefore, Per-Pet is worth $1,000 (= $150/.15) in a perfect capital market. Currently, Per-Pet is financed exclusively by equity, but the shareholders have heard the old adage that "the way to riches is by using someone else's money." The manager has pointed out that the firm could borrow $500 at 10% per period, so that the shareholders' expected rate of return on their remaining investment would increase to 20%. If $500 of financing is converted into debt, the firm would be taking on financial leverage and have a capital structure that would be half debt and half equity.

First of all, why would the debtholders accept a rate of return of only 10% when the firm's required rate of return is 15%? The answer, of course, is the risk-return trade-off: The debtholders will get their 10% return *every* period without fail—their return is riskless. But while the debtholders' return is riskless, the risk per dollar of investment for the shareholders will double from what it is now to what it will be under the proposed change in financial leverage. When the firm is all-equity-financed, the shareholders bear all the firm's risk, spread out over an investment of $1,000. With the proposed 50% debt capital structure, the shareholders also bear all the firm's risk, but the risk is spread out over an investment of only $500. Thus, the risk *per dollar invested* for the shareholders will be twice as large as it is currently, if the capital structure changes to 50% debt.

Another way to see the effect of financial leverage is to consider the return distributions to investors under each alternative. Based on the probability distribution for the cash flows, you should be able to show that the firm's expected return is 15% with a standard deviation of 7.07%. With the all-equity capital structure, the returns to the shareholders are the same as the returns to the firm: $\mu = 15\%$, $\sigma = 7.07\%$. With the half-equity–half-debt capital structure, the firm has the same expected return and standard deviation, but the cash flows are split between the shareholders and debtholders: The "first" $50 each period goes to the debtholders; any remaining cash inflow goes to the shareholders. Thus, the debtholders have an expected return of 10% ($50/$500) with a standard deviation of 0%. The shareholders have expected future cash flows per period, with the following probability distribution:

Cash flow	= $200	$150	$100	$50	$0
Probability	= .2	.2	.2	.2	.2
Rate of return =	40%	30%	20%	10%	0%

The symmetry of this distribution allows you to verify easily the manager's claim of an increase in the expected return for the shareholders to 20%. However, calculation of the standard deviation of this return shows that while the expected return has gone up, the standard deviation has also increased, from 7.07% to 14.14%. Thus, the shareholders "pay" for the increase in expected return with an increase in risk.[3]

What conclusions can we draw from this example? First, the return distribution for an investment project is not altered by a change in financial leverage in a perfect capital market environment. Second, the expected rate of return for the shareholders increases with an increase in financial leverage, but so does their required rate of return. The increased risk of the investment due to financial leverage exactly offsets the increase in expected return, so that there is no change in the shareholders' collective wealth. Currently, shareholders have $1,000 invested in Per-Pet. Under the proposed increase in financial leverage, shareholders will have $500 in cash to invest as they wish and $500 of invested value (= $100/.2) in the common stock of Per-Pet, for an unchanged total value of $1,000. Finally, under the proposed increase in financial leverage, debtholders give up $500 in cash for promised future payments worth *exactly* $500 (= 50/.1).

This example also demonstrates that because of financial risk, all investors do not bear the same level of risk. The shareholders bear more risk per dollar invested than do the debtholders. However, although a change in financial leverage causes changes in the required rates of return on both equity and debt, a change in financial leverage does not cause a change in the required rate of return for the investment project. The required rate of return for the project when it is all-equity-financed is 15% *and* the weighted average of debt and equity required rates of return under the levered alternative is also 15% (= .5[.2] + .5[.1]). This is not an accident. This must hold in all cases in a perfect capital market environment.

[3] The astute reader may notice that we have ignored the distinction between diversifiable and nondiversifiable risk. This was done for simplicity's sake. An equivalent example can be constructed in a more complex form, where only nondiversifiable risk matters.

THE WEIGHTED AVERAGE REQUIRED RATE OF RETURN   10.6

We always come back to opportunity cost: The required rate of return for an investment project can be described in terms of financing rates. Therefore, it can *always* be represented as the weighted average cost of the components of *any* financing package that will allow the project to be undertaken. For example, such a financing package could be 20% debt plus 80% equity, 55% debt plus 45% equity, and so on; or it could be 30% 30-year debt, 10% 180-day debt, 10% preferred stock, 15% 20-year convertible debt, and 35% common stock. The point is that the opportunity cost of capital is the rate required by investors based on the risk of the project—the investors can share that risk in any proportions they agree on. In a perfect capital market, each investor will require the fair rate of return for the amount of risk she is bearing, but the *average* will always be the same, regardless of the components. Certain capital market imperfections, such as asymmetric taxes, asymmetric information, and transaction costs, might cause the package to have an impact on the average cost, but we leave that part of the story for Chapter 15. For now, it is most important to understand how the required rate of return for each participant depends on the proportion of risk being borne by that participant.

SYMMETRIC NET CORPORATE/PERSONAL TAXES

Before revenue can be paid out to shareholders (e.g., a cash dividend payment), it is subjected to corporate taxes. That is, revenue comes into the firm; then, after deducting allowable expenses, the net income (i.e., revenue less expenses) is taxed before any of it can be paid out to shareholders. In contrast, interest is tax-deductible; when revenue is paid to debtholders in the form of interest payments, it is not subjected to corporate taxes before it is paid. Therefore, we must distinguish between the net (after-corporate-tax) cost of equity and the net (after-corporate-tax) cost of debt. Debt financing "saves" the corporate taxes on the revenue that goes to paying its cost. But that is only part of the story.

In addition to the difference in corporate tax treatment between debt and equity, there is also a difference in personal tax treatment: In effect, the personal tax rate is higher on income from debt than it is on income from equity. One reason for this difference is that taxes on interest income are paid each year as the income is earned, whereas taxes on capital gains income are deferred until the stock is sold, which might be indefinitely. Due to the complexity of the tax laws, we will not attempt to detail the relevant tax provisions here. At this point, we simply want you to be aware that there is a difference, so that it can be incorporated into the analysis.

In this chapter, we assume that the *net* tax difference is zero between debt and equity when both corporate *and* personal taxes are taken into consideration. This means that for debt and equity securities of identical risk, the required rate of return for debt will be higher than it is for equity, so that an investor will be able to pay the higher personal taxes assessed on income from debt securities. That is, investors have a higher before-personal-tax rate of return on debt than on equity of identical risk, but the after-personal-tax rates of return for the securities are identical. Therefore, even though the corporation saves the corporate tax on debt financing, the savings are lost because the firm pays an offsetting higher rate of return to the debtholders to compensate them for their higher taxes.

Essentially, in this chapter, we are investigating required rates of return in a perfect and complete capital market, except that there are symmetric net corporate/personal taxes. This is a simplified view of the world, but it builds a useful foundation for further study. In Chapter 15, the effect of *asymmetric* net corporate/personal taxes on required rates of return is investigated.

A REQUIRED RATE OF RETURN FORMULA

Before proceeding, we need to specify exactly what is meant by the components of a financing package. For simplicity, we will restrict the analysis to the proportions of financing provided by debt and equity. Let θ denote the ratio of debt financing to total investment value. For example, suppose an investment project has a total present value of $10,000 and $4,000 of debt will be used to finance the project. Then $\theta = .4$. It is important to note that θ does not depend on the initial cost of the investment project; θ depends only on the total value of the project and the amount of debt used to finance it. If our example project has an NPV of $2,000, then its initial cost must equal $8,000 since the NPV is the difference between the present value and the cost of undertaking the investment project. Note also that the shareholders of this project will be putting up $4,000 and getting $6,000 because they receive the NPV. They get 60% of the value in this case, even though they will be putting up only 50% of the initial cost. The investment project is referred to as 40% debt-financed and 60% equity-financed because those proportions reflect the distribution of the value of the project among the claimants. Proportions of the initial cost are not relevant because that would disregard the project's NPV.

The Per-Pet example demonstrates that the required rate of return to shareholders depends upon the financial leverage of the firm. The same phenomenon occurs with respect to the debtholders' required rate of return. The effect of financial leverage on the required rate of return to debtholders might be less obvious because, as long as there is no chance of default, the required rate of return to the debtholders will be the riskless rate. However, when default is possible, the required rate of return to the debtholders must increase to reflect the risk that debtholders will not receive full payment.[4]

Because it is very important to remember that the required rates of return to debt and equity depend upon the proportion of debt financing that is provided, we will denote these rates of return as functions of θ; $r_e(\theta)$ for equity and $r_d(\theta)$ for debt. The required rate of return to an investment project, denoted r^*, can then be written as

$$r^* = (1 - \theta)r_e(\theta) + \theta(1 - \tau)r_d(\theta) \tag{10.4}$$

where τ represents the corporate tax rate on income from the project. Equation (10.4) is often referred to as the **weighted average cost of capital,** denoted WACC. This is an especially typical term when it is applied to the firm's entire set of assets.

Note that the WACC is expressed as the after-corporate-tax rate of return. Since the returns to equity investors are paid after corporate taxes, $r_e(\theta)$, is also an after-corporate-tax rate of return (to equity). The return to debt, $r_d(\theta)$, is a pretax rate of return; it must be multiplied by $(1 - \tau)$ to convert it to an after-tax basis.

EXAMPLE ■   General Patent, Inc. makes innovative military equipment and has only long-term debt and common equity financing. Both securities are traded regu-

---

[4]Note that full payment includes the time value of money. That is, late payment reduces the value debtholders receive.

larly on a public securities exchange. Suppose we want to estimate the WACC for General Patent. To begin, we gather the following information:

current market value of GP's common shares (5 million shares outstanding)	$ 33.25/share
next year's expected cash dividend	$ 2.83/share
expected constant annual dividend growth	10%
total market value of equity (= 33.25[5])	$166.25 million
current market value of GP's bonds (70,000 bonds outstanding, 7.5% coupon, maturing in 17 years)	$800.00/bond
total market value of debt (= 800[70,000])	$ 56.00 million
General Patent's corporate tax rate	34%

Based on this information, we can use the dividend growth model to estimate $r_e(\theta)$. From Equation (6.12),

$$r_e(\theta) = \frac{D_1}{P_0} + g = \frac{2.83}{33.25} + .10 = .185$$

The yield to maturity on GP's long-term bonds, 10%, provides an approximation of $r_d(\theta)$.[5] GP's proportion of debt financing, θ, is .252 (= 56/[56 + 166.25]). From Equation (10.4), then, our estimate of GP's WACC is 15.5%:

$$r^* = (1 - \theta)r_e(\theta) + \theta(1 - \tau)r_d(\theta) = (.748)(.185) + (.252)(.66)(.10) = .155$$

■

The 15.5% WACC estimated for General Patent in the example just given can be used as a required rate of return for potential new investment projects that essentially duplicate (with respect to operating risk level and financing mix) GP's current operations. But how can we estimate a required rate of return for projects that are significantly different from the firm's current operations?

Conceptually, a firm could take a financing package to the capital market to establish the required rate of return for an investment project that has a risk level different from the firm's. This, of course, is cumbersome, and transaction costs could outweigh the benefits from such a strategy. In practice, a firm looks at existing market-traded securities of comparable risk to estimate the required rate of return rather than incurring the transaction costs of actually offering a potential financing package in the capital market. The required rate of return for an investment project is then derived from such market rates by adjusting the rates for any financial leverage difference between the firm and the market-traded securities. This procedure is outlined and an example presented later in the chapter.

MEASURING THE AFTER-TAX COST OF DEBT

The preceding example presented a simple method of approximating the after-tax cost of debt, by multiplying $(1-\tau)$ times the given pretax cost of debt, $r_d(\theta)$. We can measure this cost more precisely. In Chapter 6, we showed in Equations (6.2) and (6.3) how to calculate a bond's yield to maturity. The cost of debt and yield to maturity represent two methods of calculating what is essentially the same quantity; the

---

[5] The yield to maturity is only an approximation because of tax considerations.

cost of debt is measured from the issuer's viewpoint, and the yield to maturity is measured from the bondholders' perspective. The after-tax cost of debt, $(1-\tau)r_d\,(\theta)$, is the discount rate that renders the present value of the after-tax debt payment stream equal to the issuer's net proceeds:

$$NP = \sum_{t=1}^{T} \frac{DSAT_t}{[1 + (1 - \tau)\,r_d(\theta)]^t} \tag{10.5}$$

where NP is the net proceeds, $DSAT_t$ is the after-tax debt payment at time t (Debt Service After Tax), and T denotes the number of interest periods until the bond's maturity.

When applying Equation (10.5), it is important to bear three points in mind. Interest is tax-deductible in the period in which it is paid, but the tax benefit will be realized only if the issuer has ample other income to claim the interest deduction. Issuance expenses are not tax-deductible at the time of issuance but must be amortized over the life of the issue, which generates a series of tax deductions. If the offering price of the bond differs from the redemption amount, the difference must be amortized over the life of the issue, which gives rise to taxable income (if the bond is sold at a premium to its principal amount) or tax deductions (if the bond is sold at a discount).

EXAMPLE ■ Usurious Finance Company has just issued 5-year bonds that bear a 10% coupon rate and repay all principal at maturity. Each $1,000 bond was sold to investors for $990, and Usurious had to pay underwriting and other expenses amounting to $20 per bond. The company's marginal income tax rate is 40%.

Each bond pays after-tax interest of $30.00 (= 1000.00[1 − .4][.1]/2) per semiannual period. Expense amortization amounts to $2.00 per semiannual period (= 20/10), which generates a tax credit of $0.80 (= 2.00[.4]). Similarly, amortization of the discount is $1 (= [1,000 − 990]/10) per semiannual period and generates a tax credit of 40% of the claimed expense, or $0.40.[6] Therefore, the before-tax (DSBT) and after-tax (DSAT) debt payment stream for each bond is

Time	Item	DSBT	DSAT
0	net proceeds	970.00	970.00
1–10	interest	−50.00	−30.00
1–10	expense amortization	2.00	0.80
1–10	discount amortization	1.00	0.40
10	principal repayment	−1,000.00	−1,000.00

From Equation (10.5), the after-tax cost of debt must solve the equation

$$NP = \sum_{t=1}^{T} \frac{DSAT_t}{[1 + (1-\tau)r_d(\theta)]^t} = \sum_{t=1}^{10} \frac{28.80}{[1 + (1-\tau)r_d(\theta)]^t} + \frac{1,000.00}{[1 + (1-\tau)r_d(\theta)]^{10}}$$

[6] The Internal Revenue Code prescribes that if the difference between the redemption amount ($1,000 in the example) and the offering price ($990 in the example) is greater than or equal to (1) .25% of the redemption price multiplied by (2) the number of full years to maturity, then the issuer must amortize the discount under the scientific-interest method (as opposed to a straight-line basis). That is, if the discount or premium is too large, the amortization must be computed according to how interest would implicitly compound over the life of the bond. Problem C6 at the end of the chapter asks you to work out this type of amortization schedule.

A discount rate of 3.236% per semiannual period gives a present value of $970.00, so the APR of the after-tax cost of debt is 6.472% (= [2]3.236) and the effective annual rate is $(1 - \tau)r_a = 6.577\%$ (= $[1 + .03236]^2 - 1$). ■

A POTENTIAL MISUSE OF THE WEIGHTED AVERAGE COST OF CAPITAL   10.7

We have said that the required rate of return for an investment project must reflect the risk of the project and not the risk of the firm's other operations. But what happens if a firm incorrectly uses its weighted average cost of capital (WACC) for existing operations to evaluate all potential new projects, regardless of the risk? Figure 10-4 graphs the risk (beta) versus the expected return for a set of potential new investment projects available to a firm.

Assume that the firm's existing operations have a risk that is equal to the average risk of the entire set of potential new projects and that the rate *w* correctly reflects the WACC of the firm's current operations. The horizontal line *wc* in Figure 10-4 represents the use of the firm's WACC to evaluate the projects, where all projects with an expected rate of return above *w* are accepted and all those below *w* are rejected. If this decision rule is followed, the set of new investment projects undertaken by the firm will be riskier than are the firm's existing operations. This is because, taken as a group, the projects that would be accepted using this decision rule are riskier than the remaining set that would not be undertaken. (You can see this by visually estimating the center point of the groups, above and below *wc*, and comparing the two points.) Therefore, following such a decision rule will cause the risk of the firm to increase over time as new investment projects are undertaken. Of course, as a result, the firm's WACC will also increase to reflect the greater investor risk.

Taken to the extreme, misusing a firm's WACC to evaluate new investment projects could lead a firm with low operating risk, such as a utility, to take on high-risk investment projects, such as drilling exploratory oil wells, because of incorrectly computing the NPVs of the projects. The incorrect low rate could make the project appear to be very desirable, even though another company that regularly undertakes such projects finds the project to have a (correctly computed) negative NPV! Notice also that in addition to undertaking bad projects, the company will be incurring opportunity costs by passing up good projects.

Alternatively, consider what happens if the firm applies the IPML concept and

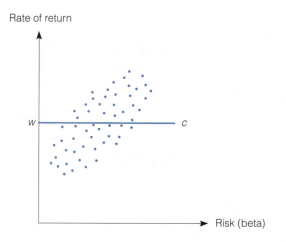

Rate of return

w ——————————————— *c*

Risk (beta)

FIGURE 10-4

Misapplication of the WACC concept to investment project selection.

FIGURE 10-5
Proper investment project
selection.

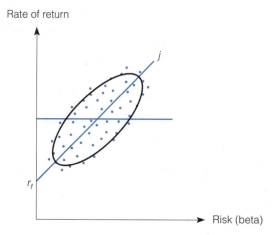

uses risk-adjusted required rates of return, such as those depicted by the line *rj* in Figure 10-5. As with the single rate of return decision rule, investment projects above the line will be accepted, whereas projects falling below the line are rejected. In this case, the average risk of the set above the line is approximately the same as that of the set that is rejected. So the application of project-specific risk-adjusted required rates of return does not as a matter of course cause the risk of a firm to increase over time. Of course, in other cases, the total risk could change. However, a change in total risk will not matter as long as the firm earns the rates of return sufficient to compensate for the risk.

You might recall that we have previously run across implications associated with increased firm risk in connection with the **asset substitution problem**. Asset substitution is a technique that shareholders can use to expropriate wealth from the debtholders. The firm deliberately undertakes riskier investments to reduce the value of the firm's outstanding debt. The value of the debt is reduced because of the increased risk of default. The present situation differs from the asset substitution problem in one major respect. In cases of asset substitution, shareholders are exhibiting knowledgeable self-interested behavior. The present case is simply the result of a misapplication of the concept of the opportunity cost of capital.

In practice, required rates of return reflecting **risk classes,** such as having a **hurdle rate** for each division of a firm, capture risk differences among potential new investment projects. Firms considering projects with varying degrees of riskiness often use a *set* of required rates of return, where each rate in the set corresponds to a particular risk class. Five risk classes will eliminate virtually all of the problem of shifting risk created by the misuse of a single discount rate.[7] Therefore, using more than five risk classes is probably unnecessary and a waste of resources. However, using at least three different risk classes appears to be valuable.[8]

10.8   **FINANCIAL RISK**

The operating risk of a firm is determined by the characteristics of the individual assets in which the firm has invested. Viewed in the context of portfolio theory

---

[7] Sundem (1975).
[8] Sundem (1975).

(Chapter 7), when a firm purchases an asset it is simply adding the asset to its existing portfolio of assets.[9] Therefore, it is the betas of the individual assets that combine to determine the operating risk of the entire firm.

In contrast to operating risk, financial risk depends on firm rather than individual project characteristics. In some sense, an individual asset or new investment project that is undertaken by an ongoing firm has no financial risk; only the firm has financial risk. This is because financial risk is created by financial obligation.

If a firm is *all*-equity-financed (no money owed at any time, no matter what), then the firm has no financial risk. Note that such a firm would not have even one creditor. All of the risk of this hypothetical firm would be its operating risk because the shareholders never owe anyone anything. Note also that in such a case, there is no possibility of, or option to, default. In effect, the shareholders do not enjoy the full benefits of limited liability. The firm could go bust, and the shareholders could lose everything they have invested in the firm, but if the firm is financed totally with equity, no loss can ever be inflicted on anyone other than the shareholders. Of course, the shareholders in an all-equity-financed firm cannot lose more than they have invested in the firm. However, they cannot benefit from limited liability and its accompanying option to default. Another way to look at this is to say that their limited liability is a put option with a strike price of zero. (Recall that a put option with a strike price of zero is worthless—of what value is selling your asset for $0?)

Because financial risk depends upon financial leverage, adjusting for the impact of financial risk must be done on the basis of whatever unit has responsibility for that financial obligation (e.g., debt payments). Except in very special cases, some of which are discussed in Chapters 20-22, the shareholders' obligation is not limited by the results of one investment project. Rather, financial obligation extends to the whole firm. When one project does poorly, the firm is still obligated to pay debts from the proceeds of all the firm's other projects. (Only when the firm's total performance from *all* its operations is inadequate to meet its promised obligations can the shareholders be relieved of their obligation—i.e., exercise their option to default.) Thus, in marked contrast to considerations of operating risk, financing considerations are generally not accounted for on a project-by-project basis. Instead, because financial obligations are at the level of the firm, the impact of financial leverage on required rates of return is determined by the capital structure of the whole firm.

Another difference between financial risk and operating risk is the extent to which a firm can control each type of risk. A firm can control its financial risk to a reasonable extent (and typically at reasonable cost) by its choice of capital structure and the maturities of its financial obligations. As previously noted, theoretically, a firm can have zero financial risk if it is financed *entirely* with equity. By contrast, the firm's operating risk is not as easily controlled. While the firm's choice of assets affects its operating risk via operating leverage (commitments to fixed as opposed to variable costs), the choice of assets is often constrained in some way. Technological considerations may force a firm to use certain processes that have a large component of either fixed or variable expense. For example, some products can be produced by one method only. Thus, whereas operating risk is not easily manipulated, financial risk is set by the financial policy of the firm and can be changed (although not costlessly) through recapitalizations that substitute debt for equity or vice versa.

---

[9] The diversification interaction of projects affects the problems of asset substitution and underinvestment discussed in Chapter 9. This problem is also addressed in Chapter 22, which deals with mergers and acquisitions.

SUBSIDIARIES

Whenever a firm splits itself into separate units, each of which enjoys limited liability with respect to its financing, the capital structure of each unit is the relevant consideration for assessing the impact of financing on the required rates of return. Therefore, if a firm is considering a new investment project where the financing will be obtained by creating a subsidiary for which the firm has limited liability, the required rates of return for financing that project must reflect the capital structure of the subsidiary.

10.9 THE IMPACT OF FINANCIAL LEVERAGE ON REQUIRED RATES OF RETURN

In a perfect capital market environment, value is always conserved, and value additivity holds, strictly. That is, the value of a package of securities always equals the sum of the values those securities would have if they were trading individually. From this fact, we know that the choice of financing package does not affect the value of a firm in a perfect (except for symmetric net corporate/personal taxes) and complete capital market. In short, capital structure is irrelevant in such an environment.

Capital structure irrelevance allows us to draw some important conclusions about the various required rates of return in Equation (10.4). Most importantly, if capital structure is irrelevant, the value of an investment project is unaffected by how the project is financed. This means that r^* *does not* vary with θ; r^* is constant for *all* values of θ because changes in θ do not affect the total value of the project or its expected cash flows. If the present value and the expected cash flows are constant, the third parameter in the present value equation (r^*) *must* be constant also. Of course, as was shown in the Per-Pet example, changes in financial leverage alter how the risk of the project is borne by the debt- and shareholders. Therefore, financial leverage *does* affect $r_e(\theta)$ and $r_d(\theta)$, even in a perfect capital market environment.

Based on the fact that r^* is constant across all possible values of θ, we can determine the values of $r_e(\theta)$ and $r_d(\theta)$ when θ takes on either of its extreme possible values. When the firm is all-equity-financed, $\theta = 0.0$, and the second term in Equation (10.4) drops out, so that $r^* = r_e(0)$. At the other extreme, when the firm is all-debt-financed, the first term drops out because $(1 - \theta) = 0.0$, and $r^* = (1 - \tau)r_d(1)$.[10] Since r^* does not depend upon θ in this environment, $r_e(0) = (1 - \tau)r_d(1)$.

The result that $r_e(0) = (1 - \tau)r_d(1)$ makes intuitive sense. The debtholders of a firm that is financed totally with debt would bear all of the firm's business risk. As such, the debtholders' risk would be the same as the risk borne by the shareholders if the firm were all-equity-financed. Therefore, these two returns must be equal because the risks are equal. The only difference between the all-debt and all-equity alternatives would be in how the taxes are paid—assuming an otherwise perfect capital market. For the all-debt alternative, the tax payments would be levied on the revenue (net of operating expenses) as personal interest income; there would be no corporate tax payments. For the all-equity alternative, there would be corporate tax payments, but lower personal tax payments.

A second implication that can be drawn from a perfect capital market analysis involves the rate that debtholders will require for financing only an infinitesimal fraction of the investment—$r_d(\theta)$ when θ is minutely greater than zero. We estab-

---

[10] We know of no corporation that is literally all-debt-financed ($\theta = 1.0$). Strictly speaking, θ is always less than 1.0. For convenience, rather than continuing to indicate that θ is as close to 1.0 as possible, we will simply refer to $\theta = 1.0$.

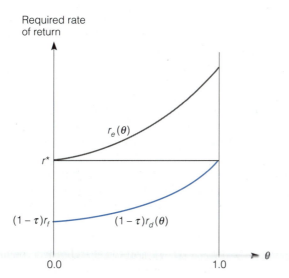

lished above that a firm that is truly 100% equity-financed has no chance of default. Such a hypothetical firm can borrow a *very small* amount of money in our assumed environment at the riskless rate of interest. Of course, the amount of funds that such a firm could borrow at the riskless rate may be only 1 cent for 1 minute. Still, conceptually, the rate on the first fraction of debt in a perfect capital market environment *must be* the required rate of return for the riskless asset, r_f.

Based on these two implications from a perfect market analysis (and hypothetical functions for $r_e(\theta)$ and $r_d(\theta)$), Figure 10-6 illustrates the relationships that can be established in a perfect capital market environment.

THE IMPACT OF FINANCIAL LEVERAGE ON BETA   10.10

Beta is the covariance between the stock's return and the return on the market portfolio, divided by the variance of the return on the market portfolio. In Chapter 7, we showed how beta can be estimated using linear regression. You may be wondering about the mechanics of how financial leverage affects beta. We know that financial leverage entails a perfect risk-return trade-off. In the case of the capital market line (CML), a change in personal financial leverage (lending or borrowing) moves the risk-return of the investment along the CML. It is similar for corporate financial leverage: A change in financial leverage simply moves the shareholders' risk-return along the security market line (SML).

The SML defines the required rate of return for a share of common stock as

$$r_e(\theta) = r_f + \beta_e(\theta)(r_m - r_f) \tag{10.6}$$

Similarly, the IPML defines the required rate of return for each of the firm's J investment projects as that given in Equation (10.3). As already noted, the firm's entire set of investment projects is simply a portfolio of investments. Therefore, the beta for the firm, β_F, is simply the weighted average of its project betas, or

$$\beta_F = \sum_{j=1}^{J} w_j \beta_j \tag{10.7}$$

where J is the firm's total number of investment projects and w_j is the proportion of firm value invested in project j ($j = 1, 2, \ldots J$). The required rate of return for the firm, r^*, then, can be expressed in terms of β_F as

$$r^* = r_f + \beta_F(r_m - r_f) \tag{10.8}$$

Comparing Equations (10.6) and (10.8) once again points out that the required rate of return for equity is not necessarily the required rate of return to use for measuring the NPV of a potential new investment project, even if the risk of the project is identical to the risk of the firm as a whole. The required rate of return to equity is *only* used to measure the value of the cash flows that are expected to go to the equityholders (as opposed to the value of the total cash flow coming into the firm). As shown in Figure 10-6, r^* and $r_e(\theta)$ are equal *only* if the firm has *no* financial leverage ($\theta = 0.0$).

What then must be the relationship between the beta for the firm, β_F (which is a weighted average of β_j, $j = 1, 2, \ldots J$), and the shareholders' beta, $\beta_e(\theta)$? β_F can be thought of as the beta for an all-equity investment in a portfolio of assets identical to that of the firm, $\beta_e(0)$. You might guess that to make the connection, we need to determine the role of debt. Just as there are equity betas and investment project betas, there are betas for debt securities. As with other investment portfolios, in a perfect capital market environment, the relationship among these betas is a weighted average and is given as

$$\beta_F = \theta\beta_d(\theta) + (1 - \theta)\beta_e(\theta) \tag{10.9}$$

where $\beta_d(\theta)$ is the beta for a debt proportion of θ.

10.11   A PRACTICAL PRESCRIPTION FOR ESTIMATING A REQUIRED RATE OF RETURN

When a firm takes on financial leverage, the risk borne by the debtholders is generally fairly low. If the debtholders bear no risk, $\beta_d(\theta)$ is zero. In such a case the debtholders will earn the riskless rate of interest, r_f. Even when the debtholders bear some of the firm's risk, the amount is typically small compared with other investment opportunities. As a practical matter, if we approximate $\beta_d(\theta)$ as zero, we can rewrite the relationship among the betas as

$$\beta_F = (1 - \theta)\beta_e(\theta) \tag{10.10}$$

We can then use Equation (10.10) to approximate a firm's beta.

EXAMPLE ■   Zelda Corporation is contemplating an expansion of its current operations. To evaluate the proposed expansion, the financial vice president has asked you to estimate the required rate of return to be used to compute the NPV of the project. How do you proceed?

First, you look in an investor's guide and find that the beta for shares of common stock in Zelda Corporation is estimated to be 1.6. Second, you note that the current market value of a share of Zelda is $8.125 and that there are 2 million shares outstanding, so the market value of Zelda's equity is $16.25 million. From Zelda's balance sheet you determine that the total book value of all of Zelda's liabilities is $9.75 million. Based on these figures, θ is estimated to be .375 ($= 9.75/[9.75 + 16.25]$).

Finally, from Equation (10.10), the β_F can be estimated to be

$$\beta_F = (1 - \theta)\beta_e(\theta) = (1 - .375)1.6 = 1.00$$

or about equal to the beta of the market portfolio. Therefore, Zelda should use the current estimate of r_m, the required rate of return on the market portfolio, to measure the NPV of the proposed expansion project.   ∎

ESTIMATING A REQUIRED RATE OF RETURN FOR A NEW INVESTMENT PROJECT

In the example just given, the investment project was of the same risk class as the firm's overall current operations. Now let us consider how a firm can estimate a required rate of return for a potential new investment project that is either in an area in which the firm has no experience or an area of the firm's current operations that has risk significantly different from the average risk of the firm.

EXAMPLE ∎   Poly-brands, Inc. is a multinational conglomerate with worldwide operations involving products and services that range from a ski resort in Vale, Colorado, to a high-tech ball-bearings manufacturing plant located in Bonn, West Germany. The audio division of Poly is considering an expansion of its compact-disk player manufacturing facilities located just outside of Tokyo. In order to measure the NPV of the proposed investment project, Poly needs to estimate the required rate of return for the project.

Poly's stock and bonds are traded regularly on major exchanges and we can estimate Poly's WACC. However, in this case, Poly's WACC is not a good estimate of the required rate of return for the project under consideration because the manufacture of compact-disk players has greater operating risk than the average risk of all of Poly's assets. Your job, Jim, should you decide to accept it, is to estimate the beta for this project.[11]

The steps for estimating the beta for this project are

1. Obtain estimates of stock betas for a sample of firms whose primary business is the manufacture of audio products, especially compact-disk players.

2. Estimate θ for each of the firms, using balance sheet data and the method given in the Zelda Corporation example.

3. Estimate each firm's beta by applying Equation (10.10). That is, the estimate of the firm's beta is its equity beta multiplied by $(1 - \theta)$.

4. The average of all the firm betas is the estimate of the investment project's beta.

Table 10-2 summarizes the above procedure, which indicates an estimated beta of 1.14.

The riskless rate is 8%, and the required rate of return on the market portfolio is 17%. The required rate of return for Poly's project is then calculated by applying the CAPM as:

$$r^* = .08 + 1.14 \,(.17 - .08) = .1826, \text{ or } 18.26\%$$ ∎

---

[11] Sorry to disappoint you, but this book will *not* self-destruct in 10 seconds! Of course, you could . . .

TABLE 10-2   Estimating the Beta of Poly-brands, Inc.'s Investment Project

Sample Firm	$\beta_e(\theta)$	θ	$(1 - \theta)\beta_e(\theta)$
A	1.70	.29	1.21
B	1.85	.45	1.02
C	1.95	.37	1.23
D	1.90	.43	1.08
E	2.00	.42	1.16
F	1.60	.35	1.04
G	1.65	.26	1.22
H	1.80	.34	1.19

Average beta = 1.14

10.12   THE IMPACT OF OPERATING LEVERAGE ON BETAS AND REQUIRED RATES OF RETURN

We said earlier that operating risk determines the required rate of return for an investment project. We also noted that often a firm has little control over an investment project's level of operating leverage because of technological, efficiency, or other production considerations. However, for those projects where a firm has a choice of operating leverage, how does operating leverage affect the beta and the required rate of return for the project?

The choice of operating leverage is similar to the choices of personal and corporate financial leverage. Higher operating leverage moves the required rate of return for a project along the IPML to a different risk-return level,[12] so the choice of operating leverage affects the project's beta and its required rate of return. The required rates of return for equity and debt simply reflect the allocation of risk between debtholders and equityholders. The rates can change if the risk allocation (i.e., the degree of financial leverage) changes, even if project risk does not change. But a change in the project's required rate of return will cause a change in the required rates of return for both debt and equity. Therefore, operating leverage affects all of the required rates of return; those for equity, debt, *and* the project. Note that this is distinctly different from the case of financial leverage. Financial leverage affects the required rates of return on equity and debt but not the required rate of return on the project in a perfect capital market environment.

REQUIRED RATES OF RETURN WITH A CHOICE OF OPERATING LEVERAGE

Because operating risk affects the beta of an investment project, the estimation method outlined above must have one more condition added to it when there is a choice of operating leverage. If there are significant differences in operating risk

---

[12] Any difference in the NPV of the project, based on operating leverage, would be expected to be the result of inefficiency in the real asset markets rather than in the capital markets. That is, the financing decision involves a perfect risk-return trade-off, whereas there may be a "best" choice of operating leverage for any investment project.

among potential production methods, the sample of representative firms must be restricted to those firms that are using a set of assets and production methods that are approximately equivalent to those in the proposed investment project.

EXAMPLE ■ Let us reexamine Poly-brands's investment project. Suppose there has been a recent technological advance in the production processes for manufacturing compact-disk players and that Poly's proposed project will use this new process. Suppose further that firms B, D, and F in Table 10-2 are relatively recent entrants into this product market and are using the new process. The other firms are more established, and their production process is no longer state-of-the-art. In this case, the sample should be split into two separate groups. Firms B, D, and F have an average implied firm beta of about 1.05. Firms A, C, E, G, and H have an average implied firm beta of about 1.20. In this modified case, then, the estimated beta for the required rate of return would be 1.05 rather than the average for all eight firms given previously (1.14). ■

SUMMARY

The required rate of return for an investment project does not depend on the firm that undertakes the project. The value of the project is based on its ability to generate future cash flows, just as the value of a share of stock is based on its expected future cash dividends. If one firm can generate higher expected future cash flows using the project's assets than other firms, the project will add more value to that firm than to the other firms. However, the risk of the asset is the same, regardless of which firm owns it. Therefore, the required rate of return for a project must be the same for all firms; differences in the value of a project among firms are reflected in the expected cash flows, not in the required rate of return. The process of evaluating proposed capital investment projects is examined in detail in the next three chapters.

In practice, you might be tempted to "add a few points" to a required rate of return "just for insurance." Ad hoc adjustments for "judgmental" factors should be avoided. This is not to belittle the valuable role that specialized judgment can play in a firm's choice of investment projects. But there are better methods of incorporating those important "other" factors into the decision-making process.

This chapter outlined a method for estimating the required rate of return for a capital investment project, based on the required rate of return on equity. It provides a good "back-of-the-envelope" estimate of the required rate of return for a project because the risk of the investment is by far the most important determinant of the required rate of return. The adjustment for risk must reflect the risk of the investment project rather than the risk of the firm's current operations. Adjustments for the particular financing package will matter only to the extent that there are capital market imperfections. The effect of capital market imperfections such as asymmetric taxes, asymmetric information, and transaction costs on the firm's financing decision is examined in Chapter 15. Adjusting for these imperfections leads to rate of return calculations that are more complex than the method developed in this chapter. These more complex methods are examined in Chapter 19.

Accurately estimating a required rate of return is a process sufficiently detailed that it is not usually done separately for each potential new investment project under consideration. Instead, firms use what are called risk classes. Required rates of return for various risk classes are established and reviewed periodically. Each prospective capital investment project is assigned to the appropriate risk class as part of its

DECISION SUMMARY BOX

- The required rate of return is a concept tied to the expected rate of return of comparable capital market investment alternatives. Therefore, it is important to disregard the historical cost of funds. Market rates change regularly because of changes in expected inflation and in the supply and demand for money. Investment decisions must be based on the alternatives that are *currently* available. The relevant question is What else can be done with the money *now*?

- The required rate of return is an opportunity cost of capital. It can be estimated from the prices of capital assets currently traded in efficient capital markets.

- The required rate of return depends on the operating risk of the particular project. Theoretically, each project should have its own required rate of return. In practice, however, investment projects are typically categorized by risk classes. Each risk class has associated with it a specific required rate of return.

- The required rate of return for a potential new investment project is the same as the required rate of return for the firm's current operations *only* if the nondiversifiable risk of the project is identical to the nondiversifiable risk of the existing firm taken as a whole.

- Present value is a function of both expected cash flows and the required rate of return. With a perfect risk-return trade-off, present value is constant, even when the other two parameters change.

- Except for capital market imperfections, changes in financial leverage involve a perfect risk-return trade-off. Therefore, the required rate of return for the project does not vary as the degree of financial leverage changes—in a perfect capital market environment.

- The required rate of return for an investment project does not equal either of the required rates of return on debt or leveraged equity. The required rate of return for a project is the *weighted average* of the current required rates of return on debt and leveraged equity, where the weights are the market-value proportions of debt and equity in the firm's capital structure. In a perfect capital market environment, this weighted average is constant across alternative financing packages and is equal to the required rate of return to *un*leveraged equity.

- The leverage ratio, θ, depends on market value, not on the initial cost of the investment. The cost and the market value differ by the NPV of the investment.

- Potential differences in the value of a project between one firm and another undertaking the project are reflected in the expected cash flows rather than the required rate of return.

- Large positive NPVs that do occur in potential new investment projects generally arise because of opportunities in the real asset market rather than in the capital asset market.

evaluation. The required rate of return for the risk class is used to calculate the project's NPV.

PROBLEMS

PROBLEM SET A

A1. Define what we mean by the firm's **financing decision** and the firm's **investment decision**. What entities are on the "other side" of these decisions?

A2. What is the NPV of a project that has an expected rate of return exactly equal to its required rate of return?

A3. Why is the required rate of return sometimes called the **opportunity cost of capital?**

A4. Suppose the expected rate of return on the market portfolio is 15% and the riskless rate of return is 9%. Suppose further that all of the projects listed below are perpetuities with annual cash flows (in $) and betas as indicated. If none of the projects requires or precludes any of the other projects and each project costs $2,000, (a) what is the NPV of each project, and (b) which projects should the firm undertake?

Project	A	B	C	D	E	F
annual cash flow	310	500	435	270	385	450
beta	1.00	2.25	2.22	0.65	1.37	2.36

A5. Stowe-Away Travel, Inc. is a diversified conglomerate with six different investment projects. The projects, their betas, and the proportion of the firm's value invested in each project are given below. (a) What is β_F for this firm? (b) If Stowe is 20% debt-financed, what is the beta for Stowe's equity, $\beta_e(.2)$?

Project	A	B	C	D	E	F
proportion of firm value	20%	10%	12%	10%	34%	14%
beta	1.00	2.25	2.22	0.65	1.37	2.36

A6. What are the two factors on which present value depends?

A7. If Goodyear has a debt-to-total-value ratio, θ, of 43% and its common stock has a beta of 1.32, what is the approximate value of Goodyear's firm beta, β_F?

A8. Define the term **leverage**. Distinguish between **operating leverage** and **financial leverage**.

A9. Give an example of a case where the expected future cash flows are increased but the present value of the flows remains unchanged.

A10. Tri-Knot, Ltd. has just issued some $1,000 par-value bonds with a 20-year life. The bonds have a 12% annual coupon rate, require semiannual coupon payments, and were sold for $970 each, less a cost of $12 per bond. If Tri-Knot's marginal tax rate is 35%, what is Tri-Knot's after-tax cost of debt, $(1-\tau)\,r_d(\theta)$ for this bond issue?

A11. Suppose a firm used a single discount rate to compute the NPV of all its potential investment projects, even though the projects had a wide range of nondiversifiable risk. Suppose further that the firm actually undertook all those projects that had a positive NPV. Briefly explain why such a firm would become riskier over time as it undertook investment projects.

PROBLEM SET B

B1. You are considering three stocks for investment purposes. The required rate of return on the market portfolio is 14%, and the riskless rate is 9%. Based on the information given below, which if any of these stocks should you invest in?

Stock	Beta	Current Price	Last Dividend	Growth Rate
A	1.3	$15	$1.2	5%
B	0.9	28	1.3	10
C	1.1	31	2.4	8

B2. What are the important differences in the way operating risk (versus financial risk) enters into the consideration of an investment project?

B3. The information given below has been gathered about O'ryan Swim-Where, Ltd. Based on this information, estimate O'ryan's WACC.

current market value of common shares (10 million shares outstanding) $ 23.63/share

next year's expected cash dividend	$ 1.92/share
expected constant annual dividend growth	8%
current market value of bonds (100,000 bonds outstanding, 8.5% coupon, maturing in 21 years)	$835.00/bond
corporate tax rate	34%

B4. Suppose that the value of a firm is not identical when it is computed using Equations (10.1) and (10.2). In particular, suppose that Equation (10.2) computes a value of $10 million, whereas Equation (10.1) gives a value of $8.5 million, both on the basis of market values in their respective asset markets. Assuming both values are correct, what transactions could you make to profit from this situation? Can you think of a second set of transactions you could use as an alternative way to profit from the situation?

B5. The treasurer of a large company is considering investing $50 million in 10-year Treasury notes that yield 8.5%. The company's WACC is 15%. Is this a negative-NPV project? Explain.

B6. Suppose a loan pays $200 now and requires only a single repayment of principal and all accrued interest after 4 years in the amount of $295.49. Ignoring taxes:
   a. What is the yield to maturity on this bond, assuming semiannual compounding?
   b. Create an amortization schedule showing the semiannual period-by-period accrued interest charges for this loan.

B7. Yukon, Etiquette, Inc. has a beta of 1.85 and is deciding whether to issue stock to raise money for an investment project that has the same risk as the market and an expected return of 20%. If the riskless rate is 10% and the expected return on the market is 15%, under what conditions should the company go ahead with the investment?

B8. The D. B. Spiess Finance Corporation is financed with 80% debt and 20% common equity. Its required rate of return on equity is $r_e = 25\%$ and its pretax cost of debt is 10%. Its marginal ordinary income tax rate is 40%. The riskless rate is 8% (pretax). Graph $r^*(\theta)$, $r_e(\theta)$, and $(1-\tau) r_d(\theta)$ for values of θ between 0 and 1. What have you assumed in drawing these curves?

B9. You plan to invest $10,000 in a security, borrowing $6,000 of the cost from a friend, thus putting up $4,000 of your own money. The cost of debt is 12%, and there are no taxes. With this arrangement, you expect a rate of return of 20% on your equity investment. What would your rate of return be without the leverage? That is, what would your rate of return be if the entire $10,000 was your own money?

B10. Describe how you would go about estimating a required rate of return for computing the NPV of a project.

B11. If payments for a $20,000 five-year car loan are $300.99 twice a month, what is the APR for this loan? What is the effective annual rate for this loan?

B12. Parr's Poultry Place, Inc. is considering two mutually exclusive 1-year investment proposals, A and B. A costs $100,000, and its expected payoff 1 year later is $114,000. The variance of its rate of return is 25%. B costs $50,000, and its expected payoff 1 year later is $56,000. The variance of its rate of return is also 25%. The expected rate of return and variance of rate of return on the market portfolio are 14% and 16%, respectively. The going rate on government bonds is 9%, and Parr has bonds outstanding with a current yield of 10.5%. The correlation coefficient, ρ, between the returns for A and the market is .8, whereas the correlation coefficient between the returns for B and the market is .32. Ignoring taxes and depreciation, what investment decision should Parr make concerning these investment proposals?

PROBLEM SET C

C1. Eastern Chemical Company has an oil and gas subsidiary that is considering the purchase of $100 million worth of proven oil and gas properties. Eastern's financial staff has compiled the following list of companies:

Company	Common stock beta	Debt ratio, θ
N.J. Chemical	1.35	0.35
Great Lakes Chemical	1.25	0.25
Johnson Chemical	1.50	0.45
Clark Chemical	1.40	0.40
Franklin Oil	1.40	0.50
Oscar Oil	1.45	0.50
VMB Oil & Gas	1.30	0.45
Peters Oil & Gas	1.55	0.60

All eight companies as well as Eastern pay income tax at a 34% marginal rate. Eastern's target debt ratio is 0.40, and its oil and gas subsidiary's target debt ratio is 0.50.

a. Calculate an estimate of the unlevered beta, β_F for the proven oil and gas project. Eastern's subsidiary has bonds outstanding with a yield to maturity of 15.15%.

b. Assuming a 10% risk-free rate and a 6% expected excess return on the market portfolio, calculate the required rate of return on unlevered equity, $r_e(0)$, for the project.

c. Calculate the weighted average cost of capital and show that $r^* = $ WACC.

C2. A company considering a capital investment project identifies five comparable companies and collects the following information:

Company	Beta	Debt ratio θ
A	1.10	0.25
B	1.20	0.30
C	1.15	0.20
D	1.30	0.50
E	1.25	0.25

The project should be one-third debt-financed, and the company's marginal tax rate is 34%.

a. Calculate the leveraged beta for the project.

b. The riskless interest rate is 9%, and the excess return on the market portfolio is 6%. Calculate the required rate of return on project equity.

c. The cost of debt for the project (before taxes) is 11%. Calculate the cost of capital for the project.

C3. Calimari Fisherys, Ltd. is financed with $\theta = .72$ proportion of debt, which is large enough that the beta of the firm's debt, $\beta_d(.72)$, is 0.32—too large to ignore. If the beta of Calimari's common stock is 3.1, what is the beta for the firm's assets, β_F?

C4. A company calculates its cost of debt and finds it to be 9.75%. It then calculates its cost of equity capital and finds it to be 16.25%. The company's chairman tells the chief financial officer that the company should issue debt because it is cheaper than equity. How should the chief financial officer respond to the chairman? (You may assume that the chief financial officer's job is secure!)

C5. **a.** Explain how to apply Equation (10.5) to calculate the cost of preferred stock. (*Hint*: Preferred stock dividends, expenses, and discount are not tax-deductible, and preferred stock dividends are typically paid quarterly.)

b. Suppose Usurious Finance Company issued preferred stock rather than debt, on the terms indicated in the example following Equation (10.5) in the text. Calculate the cost of preferred stock, both as an APR and as an effective annual rate.

C6. Suppose Usurious Finance Company, in the example following Equation (10.5), sold the 10% bonds to investors for $750 per bond. Assume issuance expenses of $20 per bond and a 40% marginal income tax rate. Usurious Finance would have to amortize the $250 discount per bond under what the IRS calls the "scientific-interest method." This is similar to the loan amortization we illustrated in Chapter 3, except that the interest charges are implicit rather than actual cash flows.

a. Calculate the investor's yield to maturity for these bonds.

b. Use the yield to maturity to allocate the discount period-by-period in such a way that the sum of (1) the cash interest paid during the period plus (2) the portion of the aggregate discount allocated to the period, all divided by (3) the accreted value of the bond as of the beginning of the period (offering price plus previously allocated discount), is the same every period (and equal to the APR yield to maturity divided by 2).

c. Calculate the after-tax debt payment stream.

d. Calculate the after-tax cost of debt.

C7. Suppose you have been offered the following deal: Pay us $7,072.12 at the end of each of the next 5 years, and we will pay you $200 per month at the end of each month forever after that. What effective annual interest rate would you be earning if you took this deal?

REFERENCES

Arditti, Fred D., and Haim Levy. "The Weighted Average Cost of Capital as a Cutoff Rate: A Critical Analysis of the Classical Textbook Weighted Average." *Financial Management* 6 (Fall 1977): 24–34.

Butler, J. S., and Barry Schachter. "The Investment Decision: Estimation Risk and Risk Adjusted Discount Rates." *Financial Management* 18 (Winter 1989): 13–22.

Chambers, Donald R., Robert S. Harris, and John J. Pringle. "Treatment of Financing Mix in Analyzing Investment Opportunities." *Financial Management* 11 (Summer 1982): 24–41.

Conine, Thomas E., Jr., and Maury Tamarkin. "Division Cost of Capital Estimation: Adjusting for Leverage." *Financial Management* 14 (Spring 1985): 54–58.

Fama, Eugene F. "Risk-Adjusted Discount Rates and Capital Budgeting Under Uncertainty." *Journal of Financial Economics* 5 (1977): 3–24.

Fuller, Russell J., and Halbert S. Kerr. "Estimating the Divisional Cost of Capital: An Analysis of the Pure-Play Technique." *Journal of Finance* 36 (December 1981): 997–1009.

Gahlon, James M., and Roger D. Stover. "Diversification, Financial Leverage, and Conglomerate Systematic Risk." *Journal of Financial and Quantitative Analysis* 14 (December 1979): 999–1014.

Gordon, M.J., and L.I. Gould. "The Cost of Equity Capital: A Reconsideration." *Journal of Finance* 33 (June 1978): 849–61.

Greenfield, Robert L., Maury R. Randall, and John C. Woods. "Financial Leverage and Use of the Net Present Value Investment Criterion." *Financial Management* 12 (Autumn 1983): 40–44.

Gup, Benton E., and Samuel W. Norwood III. "Divisional Cost of Capital: A Practical Approach." *Financial Management* 11 (Spring 1982): 20–24.

Haley, Charles W., and Lawrence D. Schall. "Problems with the Concept of the Cost of Capital." *Journal of Financial and Quantitative Analysis* 13 (December 1978): 847–70.

Hamada, Robert S. "Portfolio Analysis, Market Equilibrium and Corporation Finance." *Journal of Finance* 24 (March 1969): 13–31.

Harrington, Diana R. "Stock Prices, Beta and Strategic Planning." *Harvard Business Review* 61 (May-June 1983): 157–64.

Harris, Robert S., and John J. Pringle. "Risk-Adjusted Discount Rates-Extensions from the Average-Risk Case." *Journal of Financial Research* 8 (Fall 1985): 237–44.

Mandelker, Gershon, and S. Ghon Rhee. "The Impact of the Degrees of Operating and Financial Leverage on Systematic Risk of Common Stock." *Journal of Financial and Quantitative Analysis* 19 (March 1984): 45–58.

Miles, James A., and John R. Ezzell. "The Weighted Average Cost of Capital, Perfect Capital Markets, and Project Life: A Clarification." *Journal of Financial and Quantitative Analysis* 15 (September 1980): 719–30.

Modigliani, Franco, and Merton H. Miller. "The Cost of Capital, Corporation Finance, and the Theory of Investment." *The American Economic Review* 48 (June 1958): 261–97.

Myers, Stewart C. "Determinants of Corporate Borrowing." *Journal of Financial Economics* 5 (November 1977): 147–75.

Rosenberg, Barr, and Andrew Rudd. "The Corporate Use of Beta." *Issues in Corporate Finance*. New York: Stern, Stewart, Putnam & Macklis, 1983, 42–52.

Sundem, Gary L. "Evaluating Capital Budgeting Models in Simulated Environments." *Journal of Finance* 30 (September 1975): 977–91.

Turnbull, Stuart M. "Market Value and Systematic Risk." *Journal of Finance* 32 (September 1977): 1125–42.

Yagill, Joe. "On Valuation Beta, and the Cost of Equity Capital: A Note." *Journal of Financial and Quantitative Analysis* 17 (September 1982): 441–49.

11

CAPITAL BUDGETING: THE BASICS

The long-term portion of the firm's investment decision is commonly called **capital budgeting**, the process of determining a budget for investing capital. Or, more simply stated, capital budgeting is the process of deciding whether the firm should invest in specific long-term capital assets. Recall that capital assets include such things as land, plant, and equipment.

The firm's evaluation of a long-term investment project parallels that of an individual investor's investment decision, although the setting is somewhat different. In both cases the Principles of Finance play an important role:

1. The Principle of Valuable Ideas suggests places to look for potential investment project opportunities;

2. The Principle of Incremental Benefits requires the identification and estimation of the incremental expected future cash flows for the project;

3. The Principle of Risk-Return Trade-Off reminds us to consider the risk of the project when we are determining a required rate of return; and

4. Finally, the Time-Value-of-Money Principle requires an adjustment for that value in order to calculate the NPV of the investment.

Capital assets differ from current inputs such as labor and raw materials because of the time pattern of the cash flows associated with their purchase and use. The firm spends cash now to acquire assets in anticipation of realizing future cash inflows over several future years. To create its **capital budget**, a firm evaluates the future cash flows in relation to the initial cash flow to determine whether or not the proposed capital investment is in the firm's shareholders' best interest. The objective is to find assets that are worth more to the firm than they cost—to find assets that have a positive NPV. Capital budgeting plays a pivotal role in finance because the initial cash outflow is often substantial in relation to the expected periodic future cash inflows and because there is often tremendous uncertainty associated with the timing and amounts of the expected future cash flows.

The range of problems with which capital budgeting is concerned extends from purchasing a new piece of replacement equipment to the development of a totally new business or product line; for example, Boeing Company's decision to develop a new generation of more fuel-efficient commercial aircraft. The types of assets involved include tangible assets, such as land, plant, and machinery, and intangible assets, such as patents and research and development. In each case, a firm must decide whether the expected future cash flows are sufficient to justify the initial cash outflow. One special case, **mergers**, is saved for later discussion. Mergers represent mega-capital budgeting decisions. They are discussed in Chapter 22 along with the strategic, legal, tax, accounting, and other factors that make them so special.

In the previous chapter, we examined the determinants of a required rate of return for an investment project. In capital budgeting, the required rate of return is often referred to as the **hurdle rate**. In this chapter, we develop a framework within which to use that hurdle rate to make capital budgeting decisions.

ESTIMATING THE EXPECTED INCREMENTAL CASH FLOWS   11.1

The initial step in measuring the NPV of a project involves estimating the expected incremental after-tax cash flows associated with the proposed investment project. There are three important concepts involved with estimating expected future cash flows. First, as with any investment, the costs and benefits associated with a capital budgeting project are measured in terms of cash flow rather than earnings. This distinction is critical. Cash flows, rather than earnings, are important because only cash inflow can be used to pay cash dividends or invest in other new projects. Ultimately, only cash flow can be paid to the shareholders, either immediately or through reinvestment and later disbursement. And the *timing* of a cash flow affects its value because of the time value of money. Further, it is cash, not earnings, that is required to meet the firm's obligations. Failure to make liability payments when they are required for such things as interest, debt repayment, and taxes can cause the firm to pay penalty fees or may even cause bankruptcy for an otherwise healthy firm. Earnings calculations also reflect certain non-cash items, as discussed below. Finally, including non-cash items leads to ambiguity and subjective (non-financial) choices that might hide any principal-agent problems between management and the shareholders.[1]

The second important concept relative to estimating expected future cash flows is the Principle of Incremental Benefits: To evaluate a decision properly, the cash flows must be measured on an **incremental**, or **marginal**, basis. The relevant cash flows are the difference between the firm's cash flows with and without the proposed project. That is, if a cash flow will occur regardless of whether the project is undertaken, that particular cash flow neither enhances nor diminishes the value of the project. For example, consider a sequential set of capital budgeting decisions concerning the research and development of a new product: Initial funds are appropriated for research; subsequent funds may or may not be approved for product development, test marketing, and production. At each stage, previous expenditures are sunk costs. Therefore, at each stage of the decision-making process, only expenditures yet to be made and revenues *yet to be realized* are relevant to the decision of whether to proceed with the next step of the product-development process.

Third, the Principle of Incremental Benefits further requires that the measurement of the expected future cash flows be on an *after-tax basis*. The firm is concerned with after-tax cash flows in the same way that an individual is interested in "take-home" pay: ultimately, that is what can be used for consumption. Shareholders are interested in the *net* gain in wealth, and taxes diminish the wealth gain.

Finally, recall that cash flows are always assumed to occur at the end of the period unless it is explicitly stated otherwise. This assumption is made simply for computational convenience.

---

[1] Non-quantified items can be a very important component of a capital budgeting project. However, such items are introduced into the evaluation *after* the direct cash flows have been identified so that the items can be given careful and explicit consideration so as to minimize potential principle-agent conflicts.

ECONOMIC DEPENDENCE

A concept that is very important to the evaluation of a potential new investment project is the concept of **economic dependence**. When projects are **economically dependent** on each other, the costs and revenues from one project depend on the costs and revenues of the other project. That is, the sum of the costs and revenues the projects will have if they are undertaken alone do not add up to the costs and revenues that will occur if the projects are undertaken together. In some cases, proposed new projects cannot be formulated as economically independent of existing operations. For example, suppose that a consumer products company is considering investing in a plant to produce a new detergent that the company will add to its existing detergent lines. The new detergent is likely to detract from sales of the company's current detergents, and to the extent it does, the reduction in future cash flow from sales of existing detergents should be subtracted from the flow of cash to be received from sales of the new detergent.

Whenever possible, proposals are formulated so that they are economically independent of existing firm operations and other proposed projects. Such a formulation simplifies the evaluation of proposed projects. When a project is economically independent of the firm's current operations and other potential projects, the estimation of the incremental cash flows is considerably less complex. Also, the NPV of an economically independent project has the property of value additivity. That is, its NPV is an exact measure of the amount of wealth that the project will add to the firm.

Finally, formulating projects so that they are economically independent also reduces the amount of necessary evaluation. Consider three potential investment projects, A, B, and C. If the projects are not economically independent, the combination of each pair (AB, AC, BC) and all three projects together must be evaluated in addition to evaluating each project by itself. Thus, in the case of three projects, three evaluations are required if the projects are economically independent of one another, whereas seven evaluations are required if there is economic dependence among the projects. But what if there are two projects, D and E, in addition to A, B, and C, to be evaluated? By considering the case of five projects, it is easy to see that the number of evaluations required quickly gets out of hand when projects are not formulated to be economically independent of one another. In the case of five projects, the difference is between five evaluations on the one hand and 31 evaluations on the other.

MUTUALLY EXCLUSIVE AND DEPENDENT PROJECTS

Just as economic dependence affects the proposal preparation process, mutually exclusive and dependent proposals require special consideration. A collection of investment proposals is said to be **mutually exclusive** if acceptance of one of them automatically precludes acceptance of any of the others. For example, suppose a firm is considering a plant expansion at three alternative sites. If only one new plant will be built, the site alternatives are mutually exclusive of one another.

An investment proposal is said to be **dependent** on another if its acceptance is contingent on the other project's acceptance. For example, investment in a new pharmaceutical plant may be dependent on investment in research and development to develop a new drug to be produced there. As with economic dependence, when proposed projects are dependent on one another, the range of alternatives must be redefined. To continue the example, the research-and-development activity and the plant would be considered as one proposal. Also, the research-and-development project would be considered alone as a separate proposal.

TAX CONSIDERATIONS

Although some sections of the tax code are complex and are changed periodically, we can make some generalized statements about the effect of a capital budgeting project on the firm's tax liability. Three things affect the firm's taxes: revenues, expenses, and how and when those revenues and expenses are declared for tax purposes. Just as the timing of any cash flow affects its value, *when* a cash flow is recognized for tax purposes affects the present value of the taxes paid.

Recall our discussion in Chapter 5, which notes that tax asymmetries are one form of market imperfection. The example of a tax asymmetry given in Chapter 5 concerned the tax treatment of zero-coupon bonds. An implicit tax asymmetry can also occur whenever there is a discrepancy between the timing of a cash flow and the recognition of that cash flow for tax purposes. The present value of taxes paid is less on a revenue item, the further into the future that tax payment actually occurs. For example, suppose a firm takes in a cash advance of $1,000 on goods yet to be manufactured but to be delivered 6 months from today. If the tax on that revenue will be $100, the firm will earn $900. But if the tax need not be paid until the goods are delivered 6 months from now, the present value of the taxes paid is only $96.15 at an APR of 8% (= 100/1.04). Therefore, with the deferred tax treatment and an 8% APR required rate of return, it is as though the firm actually earned $903.85 (= 1,000 − 96.15) rather than $900.

Likewise, the present value of taxes saved is greater on an expense item, the sooner the reduction in taxes paid actually occurs. The most frequent discrepancy between cash flow timing and tax recognition occurs with respect to depreciation, depletion, and amortization expense.

Depreciation, depletion, and amortization expense, which we will refer to simply as **depreciation**, play an important role in the determination of cash flow. Over time, machines wear out. The accounting treatment of depreciation expense, whereby it is deducted each period, reflects this wear. Similarly, as a natural resource producer depletes its store of resources, it records **depletion** expense. Also, certain intangible assets, such as patents, copyrights, and licenses, have limited useful lives, and the cost of each is **amortized** over an appropriate period to reflect the gradual diminution in the value of the asset as the end of its useful life approaches.

For capital budgeting decisions, the important impact of depreciation is its effect on the timing of the firm's tax payments. Depreciation is a non-cash expense. The cash was expended to acquire or develop the asset. Depreciation is simply the recognition of the expense of that asset over time, as the asset is used over time. Because depreciation is deducted from revenue when calculating net income, it affects the timing of the firm's tax payments.

DEPRECIATION   The tax code requires that certain cash expenditures by a corporation to acquire assets be capitalized. **Capitalizing** the cash expenditure for an asset means that the cost of the asset cannot be deducted at the time it is purchased. Rather, the cost is deducted (or amortized) in two or more installments over time. The asset is depreciated; there is no immediately recognized expense, and therefore there is no immediate tax consequence. Instead, the expenditure is recognized as a prespecified series of expenses at various times in the future. By contrast, cash expenditures for items that are not required to be capitalized can be expensed immediately. Cash expenditures that are **expensed** are recognized for tax purposes at the time of expenditure and therefore have immediate tax consequences. However, they do not have any *subsequent* tax consequences since they do not involve the process of depreciation. To contrast these two different tax treatments, consider the following example.

EXAMPLE ■   An asset to be purchased by a corporation costs $1,000. The marginal tax rate for the corporation is 40%. How does the pattern of expenses recognized for tax purposes differ between (1) capitalizing the cash expenditure and depreciating the asset on on a straight-line basis over 4 years and (2) expensing the $1,000 now?

The pattern of expenses recognized over time for expensing versus capitalizing the expenditure for the asset is

Time	0	1	2	3	4	Total
Expensed	1,000	0	0	0	0	1,000
Capitalized	0	250	250	250	250	1,000

Note that the *total* amount of expenses claimed in both cases is $1,000; the only difference is the time at which the expense is claimed.

Taxes are paid on the basis of revenue minus expenses. If we denote the tax rate as τ, revenue as R, and expenses as E, then we can express the tax liability as

$$\text{tax liability} = \tau(R - E) = \tau R - \tau E \tag{11.1}$$

In this form it is easy to see that expenses reduce the tax liability and that revenue increases the tax liability. Of course, it is important to remember that since revenue also adds to cash inflow, more revenue is always preferred to less revenue unless τ is greater than or equal to 1.0. Likewise, since expense adds to cash *out*flow (in addition to reducing taxes), less expense is always preferred to more expense unless τ is greater than or equal to 1.0.

Continuing our example, we can now see that the reduction in taxes due to an expense is expressed in the second term on the right-hand side of Equation (11.1), τE, and the pattern of altered tax liability for expensing versus capitalizing will be

Time	0	1	2	3	4	Total
Expensed	400	0	0	0	0	400
Capitalized	0	100	100	100	100	400

Since the amounts given above are cash flows (as opposed to expenses claimed) and the total is the same in either case, we are clearly better off if we expense rather than capitalize because of the time value of money.   ■

In general, then, firms do not choose to capitalize their expenditures. Rather, the tax code *requires* that certain expenditures be capitalized.[2]

---

[2] We are assuming that the firm has sufficient income to use the tax credit or that loss carryforwards work properly. Exceptions to this assumption (and therefore this generalization) do occur, and when they do, they are often unique situations that require careful analysis.

INCREMENTAL CASH FLOWS

The cash flows associated with a capital investment project fall into four basic categories:

1. net initial investment outlay;
2. future net operating cash flow benefits to be realized from operating the asset;
3. non-operating cash flows required to support the initial investment outlay, such as those necessary for a major overhaul; and
4. net salvage value, which is the total of cash received and/or spent upon termination of the project.

Note that financing charges are *not* included in the incremental cash flow computations. Recall that this is because the required rate of return is an opportunity cost of capital that implicitly includes the financing cost. Therefore, only extraordinary financing costs, such as special transaction costs explicitly tied to the project, are included in the incremental cash flow computations. Such costs will most often be included in the net initial investment outlay.

1. NET INITIAL OUTLAY   The net initial investment outlay can be further decomposed into a. cash expenditures; b. changes in net working capital; c. net cash flow from the sale of old equipment; and d. investment tax credits.

As already noted above, cash expenditures that will be capitalized have no tax adjustment at the start of the project, whereas those that are expensed immediately for tax purposes must be adjusted for the immediate tax savings. Denote the net expenditure to be capitalized as I_0 and the net expenditure to be expensed immediately as E_0. Then the first component of the initial outlay can be expressed as

$$\text{cash expenditure} = -I_0 - E_0 + \tau E_0 = -I_0 - (1 - \tau)E_0 \qquad \textbf{(11.2)}$$

The negative signs indicate cash outflows.

Changes in net working capital at the start of a project are also part of the initial outlay for the project. Additional cash may be needed to open up an expansion outlet, or additional inventory and accounts receivable may be required to process a greater level of production and sales. The change in net working capital that is required to complete the project must be included in the initial outlay because if additional net working capital is required, cash must be invested for this purpose. Similarly, if the project reduces the firm's net working capital, those funds are freed up to be invested elsewhere.

The third component of the initial outlay is the net cash flow from the sale of old equipment. When an asset is sold, there is revenue and maybe an expense, but there may also be a tax effect. A tax effect will occur if the asset is sold for a net sale price that differs from the tax basis of the asset at the time of its sale (i.e., its net, or depreciated, book value). For example, suppose an asset was purchased for $2,000 5 years ago and there has been $300 of depreciation expense claimed for tax purposes for each of the past 5 years. The net book value of that asset is currently $500 (= 2,000 − 5[300]). If the asset is sold today for more than $500, then in effect, too much depreciation was claimed over the time the firm owned the asset. In such a case, the firm incurs a tax liability based on the difference between the sale price and the net book value. Likewise, if the asset is sold today for less than $500, too little depreciation was claimed over the time the firm owned the asset, and a tax credit is obtained on the difference between the asset's sale price and its net book value. If we denote the net sale price as S_0 and the net book value as B_0, then the after-tax cash flow associated with selling the old equipment is[3]

$$\text{net cash flow from the sale of old equipment} = S_0 - \tau(S_0 - B_0) = S_0(1 - \tau) + \tau B_0 \qquad (11.3)$$

Finally, the purchase of certain capitalized assets creates an investment tax credit for the firm. This aspect of the tax law has changed fairly often, so we include it only as a reminder to check the tax code at the time the project is to be undertaken. If the investment tax credit is denoted I_c and the change in net working capital is denoted ΔW, the net initial outlay, denoted C_0, can be expressed as

$$C_0 = -I_0 - \Delta W - (1 - \tau)E_0 + (1 - \tau)S_0 + \tau B_0 + I_c \qquad (11.4)$$

2. NET OPERATING CASH FLOW   The net operating cash flow during each period is calculated by starting with the **incremental change in cash revenue**. Let ΔR and ΔE denote, respectively, the changes in revenue and expense in each period that are associated with undertaking the project. Then the net operating cash flow is $\Delta R - \Delta E$ minus the tax liability on this amount. Therefore, the net operating cash flow, denoted CFAT (cash flow after tax), can be expressed as

$$\text{net operating cash flow} = \text{CFAT} = \Delta R - \Delta E - \text{tax liability} \qquad (11.5)$$

The tax liability depends in part upon whatever change in the depreciation expense will be caused by undertaking the project. For simplicity, we assume that all depreciation is on a straight-line basis, and therefore the change in depreciation expense is identical each period and denoted ΔD. Then the tax liability will be $\tau(\Delta R - \Delta E - \Delta D)$ and Equation (11.5) can be rewritten as

$$\text{CFAT} = \Delta R - \Delta E - \tau(\Delta R - \Delta E - \Delta D)$$

and, rearranging, we have

$$\text{CFAT} = (1 - \tau)(\Delta R - \Delta E) + \tau \Delta D \qquad (11.6)$$

In Equation (11.6), the cash flow is represented as the after-tax revenue minus expenses plus the "tax shield" from the depreciation expense. Equivalently, we can write

$$\text{CFAT} = (1 - \tau)(\Delta R - \Delta E - \Delta D) + \Delta D \qquad (11.7)$$

In Equation (11.7), cash flow can be thought of as net income plus depreciation.

3. NON-OPERATING CASH FLOWS   The treatment of non-operating cash flows parallels that of cash expenditures for the initial investment outlay. As with initial cash expenditures, some non-operating cash flows must be capitalized. Therefore, non-operating cash flows may be either capitalized or expensed immediately, and their effect on net cash flow will be either over multiple periods or wholly within the period of the cash flow. Non-operating cash flows that will be expensed immediately are simply multiplied by the factor $(1 - \tau)$ to adjust for the tax effect. Those that will be capitalized involve a cash outflow in the period of occurrence followed by a series of adjustments for the tax effect.

---

[3] The gain is taxed at ordinary income tax rates until all prior depreciation deductions have been fully 'recaptured.' If, as for example a result of inflation, the asset is sold for more than was initially paid for it, all prior depreciation deductions are recaptured, and the excess above the original purchase price is taxed as a capital gain, which in years past has often been taxed at a lower rate than ordinary income.

4. NET SALVAGE VALUE   The net salvage value of a project can be broken down into three parts: (a) sale of assets; (b) clean up and removal expenses; and (c) release of net working capital.

The adjustment of cash flows for the tax effects from the sale of assets was described above in our discussion of the net initial outlay. Equation (11.3) provides that adjustment. Cleanup and removal expenses are generally claimed for tax purposes in the same period they are incurred. Therefore, they are simply multiplied by the factor $(1 - \tau)$ to adjust for the tax effect. The release of net working capital is unaffected by tax considerations because it is simply an internal transfer of funds, such as exchanging inventory and accounts receivable for cash. Therefore, the released amount is simply added to the cash flow at the end of the project. With clean up and removal expenses denoted REX, expected sale price as S, and final book value as B, net salvage value can be expressed as

$$\text{net salvage value} = (1 - \tau)S + \tau B - (1 - \tau)\text{REX} + \Delta W \qquad \textbf{(11.8)}$$

The term **salvage value** typically refers to the expected before-tax difference between the sale price (S) and the clean up and removal expense (REX), that is salvage value = S − REX.

A SIMPLE EXAMPLE OF WORKING CAPITAL

The importance of including working capital considerations in the capital budgeting decision is often overlooked, at least partly because there may be some confusion about exactly what working capital is. In your accounting class, you were told that net working capital equals current assets minus current liabilities. But exactly what is working capital? To get a better understanding, consider the following simple (even silly) example about an entrepreneurial child named Terry.

It is a hot summer afternoon, and after watching people walk uncomfortably through the neighborhood because of the heat, Terry decides that there is money to made selling lemonade. Terry makes some lemonade and a sign, LEMONADE: 25¢. After several trips to the curb in front of the house, taking the sign, a table, a chair, some cups, and the lemonade, a customer walks by and asks Terry for a glass of lemonade. Terry pours the glass and says, "That will be 25 cents, please." The customer hands over a $1 bill, to which Terry responds, "Would you like to buy four glasses?" The customer is not that thirsty and asks for change. Terry puts the customer on hold, runs into the house, and borrows $3 worth of change from Mom. After returning and making change for the customer, Terry settles into selling lemonade all afternoon.

That evening at the dinner table, Dad asks about everyone's day. Terry proudly reports making $11 that day by selling lemonade. This prompts Mom to ask about the $3 in change. Terry hands over $3 to Mom and revises the profit figure down to $8. Mom, however, points out that money has a time value and that Terry had the use of the money all afternoon. Terry agrees and pays Mom the loan-shark rate of 5 cents interest on the $3 loan.

Terry's working capital was the $3 in change. It was put in at the start of the project, and when operations were shut down, it was there in the bottom of the cash register at the end of the project. The only cost of having the working capital was the time value of money. However, Terry could not operate the lemonade stand without the working capital. And, although the time value of money is trivial for $3 for an afternoon, it can be a substantial cost for a firm, as in the case of a 10-year project that requires $50,000 in working capital.

When we analyze a capital budgeting project, the cost of the time value of money associated with working capital is accounted for by the marginal cash flows. As was pointed out above, increases in working capital (which occur in the early stages of a project) are outflows; decreases in, and releases of, working capital (which occur mainly in the later stages of the project) are inflows. The topic of working capital management is dealt with in Chapters 25 and 26.

AN EXAMPLE OF INCREMENTAL CASH FLOW ANALYSIS

Rocky Mountain Chemical Corporation is considering a proposal to replace the packaging machines in its Texas plant. Each packaging machine currently in use has a net book value of $1,000,000 and will continue to be depreciated on a straight-line basis to a net book value of zero over the next 5 years. The plant engineer estimates that the old machines could be used for up to an additional 10 years. The purchase price for the new machines is $5 million apiece, which will be depreciated over a 10-year period on a straight-line basis to a net book value of $500,000 each. Each new machine is expected to produce a pretax operating savings of $1,500,000 per year over the machine it will replace. Rocky Mountain estimates that it could sell the old packaging machines for $250,000 each. Installation of each new machine is expected to cost $600,000 in addition to the purchase price; $500,000 of this amount will be capitalized in the same way as the purchase price, and the remaining $100,000 will be expensed immediately. Because the new machines are so much faster than the ones being replaced, Rocky Mountain's average raw materials inventory account will need to be increased by $30,000 for each new machine. Simultaneously, because of trade credit, accounts payable will increase by $10,000. Finally, it is expected that even though the new machines will have a net book value of $500,000 at the end of 10 years, it will be possible to sell the machines for only $300,000 with a removal and cleanup cost of $40,000. If Rocky Mountain Chemical Corporation has a marginal tax rate of 40%, what are the after-tax incremental expected future cash flows associated with each new machine?

The cash expenditures for the initial outlay in this case are the $5 million purchase price, the $500,000 capitalized installation cost, and the $100,000 expensed installation cost, so I_0 = $5.5 million, and E_0 = $100,000. The increases in the inventory and accounts payable accounts cause a required increase in net working capital of ΔW = $20,000.[4] The sale of the machine currently in use has two effects on future cash flows. The effect in the current period is given by Equation (11.3), with S_0 = $250,000, B_0 = $1 million, and τ = .4, for a total of $550,000. The second effect occurs in the depreciation expenses that will *not* be claimed for the old machine in each of the next 5 years. This second effect will be accounted for in the expected future annual cash flows. No investment tax credit has been specified. The net initial outlay can now be computed, using Equation (11.4):

$$C_0 = -I_0 - \Delta W - (1 - \tau)E_0 + (1 - \tau)S_0 + \tau B_0 + I_c$$
$$= -5,500,000 - 20,000 - .6(100,000) + .6(250,000) + (.4)(1,000,000) + 0$$
$$= -\$5,030,000$$

Note that the original purchase price of the old machine does not enter into this calculation. The original cost is a *sunk cost*; it was incurred in the past and hence can-

---

[4]Note that we have assumed the project will not cause a change in any other current asset or liability account. If changes in other accounts such as accounts receivable were expected, such changes would also be taken into account.

not be affected by the decision to replace or not to replace the old machine. Similarly, care must be taken to treat correctly sunk costs that have been incurred more recently. Dollars that have already been spent—for example on feasibility studies, prior research and development, and site preparation—are irrelevant for purposes of capital budgeting analysis. They are also sunk costs; whether or not the firm decides to proceed with the project, the timing and levels of prior capital expenditures cannot change because these expenditures have already been incurred.

The net operating cash flows resulting from purchasing the new machine can be calculated using either Equation (11.6) or (11.7). The change in revenue, ΔR, is zero, and the change in expenses, ΔE, is $-\$1,500,000$. Depreciation will increase $500,000 per year ($= [5,500,000 - 500,000]/10$) for the next 10 years because of the new machine, and it will decrease $200,000 per year ($1,000,000/5$) for the next 5 years because of the sale of the old machine. Since the change in depreciation, ΔD, for years 1 through 5 is $300,000 ($500,000 - 200,000$), Equation (11.6) specifies the net operating cash flow for years 1 through 5 to be

$$\text{CFAT} = (1 - \tau)(\Delta R - \Delta E) + \tau \Delta D$$
$$\text{CFAT(1 through 5)} = (1 - .4)(0 - (-1,500,000)) + (.4)(300,000) = \$1,020,000$$

For years 6 through 10, $\Delta D = \$500,000$, and the net operating cash flow per year is

$$\text{CFAT(6 through 10)} = (1 - .4)(0 - (-1,500,000)) + (.4)(500,000) = \$1,100,000$$

There are no non-operating cash flows that are anticipated over the life of this project, so no additional adjustments are necessary.

Even though these machines will be depreciated to a book value of $500,000 over 10 years, they are *expected* to have a market value of $300,000 at the end of the project's life. A removal and clean up expenditure of $40,000 is expected. From Equation (11.8), the net salvage value is

$$\text{net salvage value} = (1 - \tau)S + \tau B - (1 - \tau)\text{REX} + \Delta W$$
$$= (.6)(300,000) + (.4)(500,000) - (.6)(40,000) + 20,000$$
$$= \$376,000$$

NET-PRESENT-VALUE APPROACH   11.2

Discounted cash flow analysis lies at the heart of effective capital budgeting analysis. This section and the next describe the application of the two discounted cash flow approaches to evaluating capital investment projects that are the most widely accepted as being "correct": the net-present-value method and the internal-rate-of-return method. Following our discussion of these two important and very useful techniques, we will consider some other techniques that are often used. We will show you how these others might get you into trouble. But in order to understand why these other techniques don't work, you must first understand how the net-present-value method and the internal-rate-of-return method work.

HOW TO APPLY IT: DISCOUNT THE EXPECTED INCREMENTAL CASH FLOWS

The net present value (NPV) of a capital investment project is simply the present value of all the incremental after-tax cash flows connected with the project. As usual, cash outflows carry a negative sign, and cash inflows are positive quantities.

APPLICATION OF THE NPV CRITERION   Independent capital budgeting projects should be accepted if the NPV is positive and should be rejected if the NPV is negative. When the NPV = 0, the firm is indifferent between undertaking and not undertaking the project. In the case of mutually exclusive projects, the alternative with the largest positive NPV is accepted, unless the NPVs for all of the alternatives are negative, in which case, all of the projects should be rejected.

It is easy to interpret this criterion. When NPV is positive, the present value of the cash inflows exceeds the present value of the cash outflows; the project is worth more to the firm than it costs the firm to pursue it. Consequently, investing in the project would enhance the wealth of the firm's shareholders. As was illustrated in Chapter 6, investing in a positive-NPV project should increase the market value of stock in a publicly held firm.

EXAMPLE ■   Continuing our example of Rocky Mountain Chemical Corporation's packaging-machine replacement, if the after-tax required rate of return for this project is 12%, then the NPV for replacing a machine equals (000,000s omitted)

$$NPV = -5.03 + \sum_{t=1}^{5} \frac{1.02}{(1.12)^t} + \sum_{t=6}^{10} \frac{1.10}{(1.12)^t} + \frac{.376}{(1.12)^{10}}$$

$$= \$1,017,925$$

The project should be accepted because the NPV is positive.   ■

A MORE CONVENIENT COMPUTATION PROCEDURE

The analysis of the packaging machine given above is partitioned by years. That is, $CFAT_t$ for each year is computed, and then the NPV is given by the sum of the

TABLE 11-1   Alternative Groupings of Cash Flows for Rocky Mountain's Packaging-Machine Replacement (Millions of Dollars)

Item	Time											Total by Item	
	0	1	2	3	4	5	6	7	8	9	10		
Capitalized installation and equipment cost	−5.50											−5.50	$t = 0$
Expensed installation cost	−0.06											−0.06	$t = 0$
Change in net working capital	−0.02											−0.02	$t = 0$
Sale of old equipment	0.55											0.55	$t = 0$
Investment tax credit	0.00											0.00	$t = 0$
Lost depreciation from sale of old equipment		−0.08	−0.08	−0.08	−0.08	−0.08						−0.08/yr	$t = 1-5$
Depreciation		0.20	0.20	0.20	0.20	0.20	0.20	0.20	0.20	0.20	0.20	0.20/yr	$t = 1-10$
Change in revenues minus expenses		0.90	0.90	0.90	0.90	0.90	0.90	0.90	0.90	0.90	0.90	0.90/yr	$t = 1-10$
Sale of equipment											0.38	0.38	$t = 10$
Removal expense											−0.024	−0.024	$t = 10$
Return of net working capital											0.02	0.02	$r = 10$
Total by year	−5.03	1.02	1.02	1.02	1.02	1.02	1.10	1.10	1.10	1.10	1.476		

TABLE 11-2 Alternative NPV Computation for Rocky Mountain's Packaging Machine Replacement

Time	Item	CFBT[a]	CFAT	PV @ 12%
0	Capitalized installation and equipment cost	$-5,500,000$ $-I_0$	$-5,500,000$ $-I_0$	$-5,500,000$
0	Expensed installation cost	$-100,000$ $-E_0$	$-60,000$ $-(1-\tau)E_0$	$-60,000$
0	Change in net working capital	$-20,000$ $-\Delta W$	$-20,000$ $-\Delta W$	$-20,000$
0	Sale of old equipment	$250,000$ S_0	$550,000$ $S_0(1-\tau) + \tau B_0$	$550,000$
0	Investment tax credit	0	0 I_c	0
1–5	Lost depreciation from sale of old equipment	0	$-80,000/\text{yr}$ $-\tau D_{\text{old}}$	$-288,382$
1–10	Depreciation	0	$200,000/\text{yr}$ τD_{new}	$6,215,245$
1–10	Change in revenues minus expenses	$1,500,000/\text{yr}$ $\Delta R - \Delta E$	$900,000/\text{yr}$ $(1-\tau)(\Delta R - \Delta E)$	
10	Sale of equipment	$300,000$ S	$380,000$ $S(1-\tau) + \tau B$	$121,062$
10	Removal expense	$-40,000$ $-\text{REX}$	$-24,000$ $-(1-\tau)\text{REX}$	
10	Return of net working capital	$20,000$ ΔW	$20,000$ ΔW	
			NPV =	$1,017,925

[a] Note that non-cash items have zero before-tax cash flow.

present values of the CFAT$_t$'s. An alternative to this procedure is to compute the CFAT for each item (e.g., initial cost, change in working capital, etc.), in which case the NPV is given by the sum of the present values of the CFATs for the items. We find that we make fewer mistakes grouping by item because we think in terms of items rather than annual cash flows. To see the equivalence of the two procedures, imagine we are computing the sum of all of the entries in a table of numbers. It is as though in one case, we add the values in each row together and then sum row totals. In the other case, we add the values in each column together and then sum the column totals. Table 11-1 illustrates the two alternative cash flow groupings for the packaging-machine example. Table 11-2 illustrates the NPV calculation for the example, using item cash flow groupings. In Table 11-2, CFBT refers to the item's before-tax cash flow, and the formulas for each item's CFBT and CFAT are shown below the amount.

SENSITIVITY OF NET PRESENT VALUE TO THE DISCOUNT RATE

What is the relationship between the NPV of a capital investment project and the discount rate? When all cash flows after the initial cash flow are positive, as in the preceding example, NPV will decrease as *r* increases. For example, the NPV of the proposed investment in a new packaging machine at various discount rates is

r	0%	5%	10%	15%	20%	25%
NPV ($000)	5,946	3,348	1,571	315	−597	−1,277

When two or more projects are compared, a larger value for *r* makes projects with cash inflows concentrated in the early years more desirable. For example, consider two projects with associated cash flows:

	Investment	After-Tax Cash Flow			
		Year 1	Year 2	Year 3	Year 4
Project A	−100	50	50	25	25
Project B	−100	30	30	50	50

The NPV of each project at various discount rates is

	Net Present Value at Discount Rate of						
	0%	4%	8%	12%	16%	20%	24%
Project A	50.00	37.90	27.38	18.19	10.09	2.91	−3.47
Project B	60.00	43.77	29.94	18.07	7.80	−1.12	−8.92

Not only does the NPV of a project vary with the discount rate, but the relative NPVs of the projects can vary, depending on the discount rate used. For example, Project A is preferred if the discount rate is 16%, but Project B is preferred if it is only 8%. Consequently, determining the appropriate discount rate to use (i.e., determining the *actual* required rate of return) is critically important to the usefulness of the NPV criterion.

11.3   INTERNAL-RATE-OF-RETURN APPROACH

The **internal rate of return** (IRR) of an investment project is the discount rate that causes the NPV of the project to be zero. In other words, the IRR is the expected rate of return from a capital investment project.

HOW TO APPLY IT: SOLVE FOR THE DISCOUNT RATE

For the most part, as with other expected rates of return such as a bond's yield to maturity, the IRR must be calculated by trial and error, although there are handheld calculators that can perform this calculation in certain situations. Let *r* denote the hurdle rate. When all cash flows after the first are positive: if $r < \text{IRR}$, then $\text{NPV} > 0$; and if $r > \text{IRR}$, then $\text{NPV} < 0$.

Economically independent investment projects for which all after-tax cash flows but the first are positive are accepted if the IRR is greater than the hurdle rate and are rejected if the IRR is less than the hurdle rate. In the case of mutually exclusive proposals, the one with the highest IRR is often, but not always, chosen (provided at least one of the IRRs exceeds the hurdle rate), and the others are rejected. The IRR method can become more complex when one or more of the later after-tax cash flows is negative and also when two or more mutually exclusive projects are being compared.

EXAMPLE ■   Consider the proposed investment in a new packaging machine discussed earlier in the chapter. Using a calculator, you can easily verify that the IRR is 16.56%, which exceeds Rocky Mountain Chemical's 12% hurdle rate.   ■

COMPLICATIONS

In the preceding example, there is only one IRR. This is usually, but not always, the case.[5] To illustrate an exception to the usual unique IRR, consider an investment involving the following cash flows:

Year	0	1	2
Cash Flow	−$10,000	$25,000	−$15,600

There are two values for IRR—two discount rates that make NPV = 0: 20% and 30%. Whenever more than one reversal in sign occurs, more than one solution, or "root," is possible. In this example the signs of the net cash flows are −, +, −. In the packaging machine example, the initial flow is negative, but the rest (1–10) are all positive. (The number of roots cannot exceed, but may be less than, the number of reversals of sign.)

The relationship between the NPV and IRR methods is explored below. To summarize the discussion to this point, it can be said that in practice the two methods typically lead to the same acceptance or rejection decision. IRR requires more calculation unless the structure of the cash flows corresponds to what a handheld calculator or computer program requires.

NPV VERSUS IRR WITH MUTUALLY EXCLUSIVE PROJECTS   11.4

Firms often have to choose one project, and only one project, from a set of alternative projects. For example, a firm that plans to build a new assembly plant might have three possible locations and four possible plant configurations but needs only one plant and so must choose one location and one configuration. As already noted, such a set of projects is said to be mutually exclusive because the firm will choose one project from the set and reject all the others. The task is to choose the most profitable project, and you know by now, that means the one that provides the largest NPV.

[5] See Lorie and Savage (1955).

NATURE OF THE PROBLEM

Consider two proposals, A and B, that have the following expected cash flows:

	Expected Cash Flows (000s)						
Year	0	1	2	3	4	5	6
Project A	−200	75	75	75	75	75	75
Project B	−200	50	50	75	100	100	125

Proposal A has an IRR of 29.58%, and Proposal B has an IRR of 28.02%. If the hurdle rate is 15%, however, the NPVs of the two proposals are $83,836 and $91,533, respectively. Thus, the IRR method favors Proposal A over Proposal B, and the NPV method favors B over A. As illustrated in Figure 11-1, the hurdle rate would have to be greater than 20.56% for Proposal A to have a higher NPV than Proposal B.

The difference between the project choice implied by NPV and IRR becomes even more crucial when the sizes of the investment projects differ. For example, suppose the IRR from a $25,000 project is 30% and the IRR from a $100,000 project is 25%. One must determine that the implicit returns on the incremental $75,000 investment are inadequate before rejecting the $100,000 project.

DIFFERING ASSUMED REINVESTMENT RATES

A major conflict between NPV and IRR is caused by differing assumptions about the rate at which cash flows will be reinvested. The IRR method implicitly assumes that incremental after-tax cash flows are reinvested at the IRR, whereas the NPV method implicitly assumes that they are reinvested at the hurdle rate (or, equivalently in

FIGURE 11-1

Comparison of mutually exclusive proposals using the net-present-value and internal-rate-of-return methods.

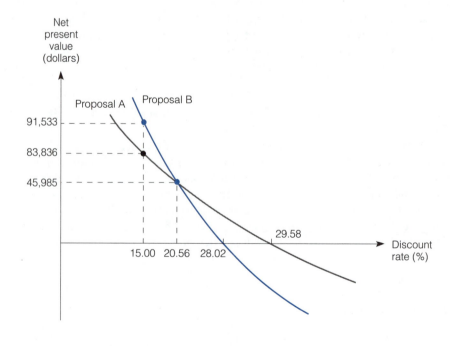

a perfect capital market, paid out to the shareholders). To illustrate, suppose that $100,000 is invested in a project that produces no income the first year, $200,000 the second year, and no income thereafter. The project's IRR is 41.4214%. If the firm's hurdle rate is 15%, the project's NPV is $51,229. Note that if $151,229 (= $100,000 investment + $51,229 NPV) is invested at 15% interest (compounded annually), the compound amount at the end of two years is $200,000, which is the payout at the end of the project's useful life. Alternatively, if $100,000 (= $100,000 investment + $0 NPV) is invested at 41.4214% interest, the compound amount at the end of two years is, once again, $200,000.

If the hurdle rate is computed correctly, it is the expected reinvestment rate in the long run. This is because over time, competitive forces drive the NPV from future projects of this type toward zero. In equilibrium, the future NPVs equal zero, at which point the reinvested cash flows earn exactly the hurdle rate. Therefore, as- suming that the hurdle rate has been correctly determined (it is the required rate of return on the investment), NPV is the decision rule to follow if IRR and NPV yield conflicting decisions. Because of this and other problems, NPV is the universally correct criterion to apply in capital budgeting studies.

PROFITABILITY INDEX   **11.5**

A third time-value-of-money-adjusted method involves calculating the **profit- ability index** (PI), or **cost-benefit ratio** as it is sometimes called. The PI for a project equals the NPV divided by the initial investment outlay:

$$PI = \frac{NPV}{C_0} \qquad (11.9)$$

where the variables are defined as in the previous two sections.

EXAMPLE ■   The PI for the new packaging machine is

$$PI = \frac{NPV}{C_0} = \frac{1.018}{5.03} = .202$$

Thus, the PI criterion indicates that the firm should accept the project.   ■

When a company evaluates mutually exclusive projects, however, the PI criterion can lead to the wrong decision.

EXAMPLE ■   Consider two projects that have the following characteristics:

	Project A	Project B
NPV	$40,000	$75,000
Initial investment outlay, C_0	10,000	25,000
PI	4.0	3.0

Project A has the higher PI, but Project B is more profitable. By investing an addi- tional $15,000, the firm can realize an additional $35,000 in NPV. Simply stated, the NPV of Project B exceeds the NPV of Project A, and NPV is the correct measure of value added by a project to the firm. So the NPV method is better than the PI method for evaluating mutually exclusive projects. ■

At this point it may not be very clear why we bother to compute the PI of a project. PI is a measure of the value of a project that ignores the size of the project, just as the IRR method does. However, in the next chapter, when we discuss a concept called **capital rationing**, we will show you that in certain situations the PI method is a useful tool for selecting the best *set* of projects to undertake among a large number of potential projects.

11.6   NON-PRESENT-VALUE METHODS

There are three non-present-value methods that are also widely used in capital budgeting. Their relative simplicity, which makes them so easy to use and understand, is deceiving. They are generally unreliable techniques, and exclusive reliance on them can lead to incorrect capital budgeting decisions. Because of their widespread use and their lack of reliability, it is important to study them and learn why they are deficient.

PAYBACK

The **payback** of a project is the time it takes the firm to recover its initial cash investment in the project without regard to the time value of money. The payback is calculated by simply summing the annual incremental after-tax cash flows for years 1, 2, etc. (without discounting them) until the sum equals the initial outlay.

EXAMPLE ■   The payback for Rocky Mountain's new packaging machine is

$$0 = -5.03 + \sum_{t=1}^{\text{PAYBACK}} \text{CFAT}_t$$

$$0 = -5.03 + 1.02 + 1.02 + 1.02 + 1.02 + .9314(1.02)$$

Therefore, payback in this case is 4.9314. Note that the incremental after-tax cash flow is assumed to be distributed uniformly throughout the year in which the end of the payback period occurs. ■

APPLICATION OF PAYBACK TO CAPITAL BUDGETING   Many companies use payback in the following manner to evaluate investment projects. They establish a maximum acceptable payback period, and only projects with a payback less than or equal to the maximum are eligible to be accepted. For example, if Rocky Mountain Chemical's management requires a payback of 5 years or less, the new packaging machine is acceptable.

PITFALL   You might be tempted to use payback to select from a set of mutually exclusive investment projects, thinking that a company should pursue the project that has the shortest payback period. But using payback ignores important dimensions of the problem. Payback ignores both the time value of money and all cash flows that occur after the corporation has recovered its initial investment. The following example illustrates the problem. Suppose the company's hurdle rate is 15% and that it is considering two investment projects that have the following cash flows:

	Expected Cash Flows (000s)						
	Investment	*Year 1*	*Year 2*	*Year 3*	*Year 4*	*Year 5*	*NPV*
Project A	100	50	50	25	25	—	12
Project B	100	60	40	30	30	30	34

Each has a 2-year payback, but Project B is clearly more desirable. As you should realize by now, an investment project's payback cannot be regarded as a reliable measure of its profitability.

PRACTICAL VALUE In practice, payback is often used in conjunction with other measures of profitability like NPV and IRR. Cash-poor companies often find payback a useful device for screening investment proposals because it provides management with some insight into the liquidity and riskiness of a project. Still, payback is not an adequate indicator of risk because it does not take into account the dispersion of possible returns or the portfolio effect within the context of the firm's other investments. Because of its weaknesses, payback should be viewed as at best a supplement to the discounted cash flow techniques. As long as a firm can obtain financing for good projects (those with a positive NPV) in the future, profitability rather than liquidity should be the primary determinant of project selection.

RETURN ON INVESTMENT

The term **return on investment** (ROI) is used by many companies to refer to their own measure of a project's profitability; ROI does not have a consistent definition for all companies. The **average rate of return on investment** (ARR) is one definition for ROI that measures the profitability of a proposed investment project as the ratio of the average annual incremental after-tax operating cash flow to the average investment:

$$ARR = \frac{ACF}{AI} \qquad (11.10)$$

where ACF denotes the average annual incremental after-tax operating cash flow over the life of the project and AI denotes the firm's average investment in the project. For example, assuming straight-line depreciation, the average rate of return on investment for an investment project requiring an initial cash investment of $2 million and providing an incremental after-tax cash flow of $250,000 per year is

$$ARR = \frac{\$250,000}{2,000,000/2} = 25.0\%$$

The ARR method contains a fatal flaw that makes it undesirable as a decision criterion. It averages cash flows across time periods, *totally* ignoring time-value-of-money differences. In addition, in applying the ROI method, companies often make the mistake of using accounting income rather than cash flow to measure investment returns.

To demonstrate the problem associated with using average rate of return, suppose a company whose hurdle rate is 10% is evaluating two projects that have the following cash flow streams:

| | After-Tax Operating Cash Flow | | | | | | | | | |
Year	0	1	2	3	4	5	6	7	8	NPV
Project C	−100	20	20	20	20	20	20	20	20	6.7
Project D	−100	0	15	20	20	20	20	30	35	−3.5

Both projects have an ARR of 40% (= 20/50), but Project C is profitable, whereas Project D is not. In addition, like payback, the ARR calculation does not properly take into account the length of a project's life. For example, suppose there is a Project E that also requires an investment of 100 but yields 20 per year for 9 years. Project E also has a 40% ARR but its NPV is 15.2, which exceeds Project C's NPV.

As indicated in Table 11-3 in the next section, ROI in various forms is fairly widely used. Some companies define ROI to be much like an IRR (rather than average) but use accounting earnings instead of after-tax cash flows. The widespread use of accounting earnings rather than after-tax cash flows is probably due to the practice of basing executive bonus plans on accounting earnings and in all likelihood creates an agency cost.

URGENCY

One variation on Ben Franklin's advice is "Why do today what you can put off until tomorrow?" The corollary to this statement as applied to capital budgeting is "Let's not replace it until we absolutely have to." No need for replacement studies. Wait until the machine breaks down, then air-freight in a new one. The specter of a costly period of downtime will be sufficient to convince management to eschew the studies and simply order the replacement equipment.

Such a policy has obvious disadvantages, yet the stories concerning plants that have critical equipment held together by "chewing gum and baling wire" have become a large component of industrial folklore. Capital projects and key pieces of equipment should be reviewed at regular intervals. A firm should develop a program of preventive maintenance and should estimate a likely replacement date each time it acquires an important piece of equipment. This will help to ensure that the assets are used with maximum efficiency and that equipment is replaced when it is most advantageous to do so—rather than when the baling wire finally snaps and the equipment becomes inoperable.

11.7   COMPARISON OF CAPITAL BUDGETING TECHNIQUES

The three time-adjusted approaches take into account the time value of money and are therefore superior to the methods that do not adjust for the time value of money. All three also lead to the same accept-reject decision for independent investment proposals as long as the IRR is unique. However, the IRR and PI methods may lead to an incorrect choice when there are mutually exclusive projects. Also, as we showed in Chapter 6, NPV is a *direct measure* of what the project will add to shareholder wealth. For these and other reasons discussed below, the NPV method is the best of the three rules.

INDEPENDENT PROPOSALS

The accept-reject criteria for the three time-adjusted approaches are summarized below:

Method	Accept Proposal	Reject Proposal	Indifferent
Net Present Value (NPV)	NPV > 0	NPV < 0	NPV = 0
Internal Rate of Return (IRR)	IRR > r	IRR < r	IRR = r
Profitability Index (PI)	PI > 0	PI < 0	PI = 0

where r denotes the firm's hurdle rate. The relationships are illustrated in Figure 11-2. When all future expected incremental cash flows are positive: if NPV > 0, then IRR > r and PI > 0, and vice versa; if NPV < 0, then IRR < r and PI < 0, and vice versa. In the in-between case, NPV = 0, IRR = r, and PI = 0. Because the project's IRR just equals the firm's hurdle rate (and, equivalently, the proposal's net present value is zero), the firm is indifferent to the project. Neither undertaking it nor failing to undertake it would affect the firm's value.

MUTUALLY EXCLUSIVE PROPOSALS

As we have noted, the three time-adjusted approaches may give contradictory results for mutually exclusive proposals. The problems associated with the IRR and PI methods when the sizes of the investment projects differ and the other problems associated with the IRR method have already been discussed.

If one must choose between the IRR method and the NPV method, NPV is supe-

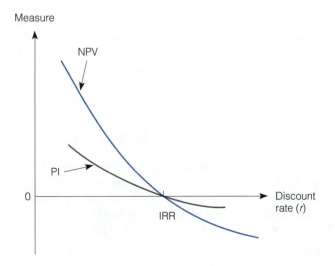

FIGURE 11-2

Relationships among net present value, internal rate of return, and profitability index.

TABLE 11-3   Results of a Survey of the Capital Budgeting Methods
Corporations Employ

Methods[a]				Number of Companies	Percentage of Companies
NPV	IRR	PBK	ROI		
✓	✓	✓	✓	32	17%
✓	✓	✓		17	9
✓	✓		✓	4	2
✓	✓			13	7
✓		✓	✓	17	9
✓		✓		13	7
✓			✓	7	4
✓				4	2
	✓	✓	✓	26	14
	✓	✓		15	8
	✓		✓	4	2
	✓			11	6
		✓	✓	15	8
		✓		4	2
			✓	7	4
				189	101%[b]

[a] *Method*   *Total*
NPV = net-present-value method   57%
IRR = internal-rate-of-return method   65
PBK = payback method   74
ROI = return-on-investment method   59
[b] Rounding error.

Source: Lawrence D. Schall, Gary L. Sundem, and William R. Geijsbeek, Jr., "Survey and Analysis of Capital Budgeting Methods," *Journal of Finance* 33 (March 1978), 282.

rior.[6] This is so for two reasons. First, under the IRR method, the assumed reinvestment rate varies with each set of cash flows. A higher (lower) IRR implies a higher (lower) reinvestment rate. Under the NPV method, the reinvestment rate is the required rate of return appropriate for the risk of each proposal. If the reinvestment rate measures the firm's opportunity cost of investing in one of the mutually exclusive projects, the NPV method takes this cost directly into account in the calculation for each project, whereas the IRR method does not. Second, as previously noted, the IRR calculation may produce multiple rates of return.

WHICH METHODS DO CORPORATIONS ACTUALLY USE?

Corporations use a variety of capital budgeting techniques, often in combination. Table 11-3 reports the results of a survey of corporations.[7] Roughly 1 in 6 corporations in the sample used all 4 techniques, and nearly as many used all but the NPV method. Each technique was used by more than half the companies. Somewhat surprisingly, the NPV method was the least-used technique, and the payback method

[6] See Hirshleifer (1970).
[7] See Schall, Sundem, and Geijsbeek (1978).

was the most frequently used technique. However, more recent studies indicate that the more theoretically correct techniques of NPV and IRR are becoming more widely adopted.[8] We hope that means that when you finish school and apply the things you've learned here, you'll be able to convince your employer to use the more sophisticated and more reliable discounted cash flow techniques that are available for capital budgeting.

The continued popularity of payback and return on investment is probably attributable to three factors. Payback is the easiest of the four techniques to understand; it boils down to "How soon do we get our money back?" Because it is the easiest to understand, it is also the most effective vehicle for communicating the economics of a proposed project to the widest audience, including financially unsophisticated, but voting shareholders. Note that payback alone is used by only 2% of the firms in the survey results reported in Table 11-3. Combining payback with other techniques has the advantage of presenting a theoretically correct analysis to those who understand NPV and/or IRR while at the same time providing a perspective on project economics for those who might not appreciate these more sophisticated techniques.

Second, as previously noted, many companies use payback as a risk-screening device. Projects with a payback that exceeds some predetermined cutoff are excluded from further consideration. This approach suffers from the deficiencies noted earlier in the chapter, but corporations may nevertheless use this simple approach to deal with risk.

Third, management compensation is often based on reported earnings. In such cases, agency problems can occur since managers may attempt to pursue those projects that will have the greatest bearing on their compensation. Hence, return on investment (calculated with earnings in place of after-tax cash flow) becomes a very important, if not the most important, technique for evaluating proposed investment projects. We'll say more about managerial incentives in the context of capital budgeting in Chapter 13.

THE CAPITAL BUDGETING PROCESS   11.8

We end our discussion of the basics of capital budgeting by providing an overview of how the capital budgeting process works in practice. The overall process can be broken down into five steps as a project moves from idea to reality:

1. Generation of ideas for capital investment projects;
2. Preparation of proposals;
3. The review of existing projects and facilities;
4. The evaluation of proposed projects and preparation of the capital budget;
5. Preparation of appropriation requests.[9]

IDEA GENERATION

The critical importance of generating new ideas should be obvious from the Principle of New Ideas. Unfortunately, we cannot teach people how to create new ideas

---

[8] See, for example, Oblak and Helm (1980).

[9] An excellent source for a more detailed description of the capital budgeting process in practice is Mike Kaufman, ed., *The Capital Budgeting Handbook*, Homewood, Ill.: Dow Jones-Irwin, 1986.

systematically. If we could, we would already be wealthy from having applied that process ourselves! However, while we do not have a process that ensures the creation of valuable new ideas, it is important to stress the value of new ideas, so that those ideas that do occur can be given serious consideration.

Where do new ideas come from? Ideas for investment projects may come from all levels within an organization. Often plant managers are responsible for identifying potential projects that will enable their plants to operate on a different scale or on a more efficient basis. Examples of such proposals are to add 10,000 square feet of production space to a plant or to replace a piece of equipment with a newer, more efficient machine. Plant managers screen out the less advantageous or less attractive proposals and send the ones that appear to be attractive to the divisional level, with supporting documentation.

Division management not only reviews the proposals sent in by the plant managers but adds projects of its own. For example, divisional management may wish to introduce a new product line or to combine two plants and eliminate the less efficient one, ideas that plant managers would be much less likely to initiate.

This bottom-up process results in proposals percolating upward through the organization. At each level, projects proposed by lower-level managers are screened, and some are forwarded to the next level. In addition, the managers at successively higher levels, who are in a position to take a broader view of the firm's business, add projects that were not visible to lower-level managers. At the same time, there is also a top-down process at work in most firms. Strategic planners will generate ideas regarding new businesses the firm should enter, firms it might acquire, and ways to modify its existing businesses to achieve greater profitability. Strategic planning is a critical element in the capital budgeting process. The top-down process complements the bottom-up process; the former generates ideas of a broader, more strategic nature, whereas the latter process generates ideas of a more project-specific nature.

In addition to the more standard bottom-up and top-down processes, some firms have a research-and-development group, either within a production division or as a separate department. A research-and-development group often provides new ideas for products that can be sent on to a marketing research department. The capital budgeting process in these types of situations usually proceeds sequentially:

1. Approve funds for research that may result in a product idea;
2. Approve funds for product development that may result in a usable product;
3. Approve funds for market research that may result in a production proposal;
4. Approve funds for plant and/or equipment for the production and sale of a new product.

Each stage involves a capital budgeting decision at one or more levels of the firm. Therefore, at each stage, a re-estimation of the NPV of going ahead is appropriate. With this kind of sequential appropriation of funds, an automatic **progress review** is enforced, which enables earlier cancellation of unsuccessful projects than would otherwise be possible.

Capital budgeting examples often concentrate on the final stage of the process outlined above in order to provide a less complex learning environment. Our examples are given with this concept in mind. However, while these "final-stage" examples are useful for illustrating the evaluation process, it is important to remember that approving funds for the investment frequently occurs as only one stage in a much larger and more complex process.

PROPOSAL PREPARATION

The originator of each proposal generally submits the proposal in writing, except for small expenditures. Sometimes proposals are not formally written in smaller privately owned companies, which tend to have relatively informal organizational structures. Most firms use standard forms, and these are typically supplemented by written memoranda for larger, more complex projects. Also, there may be consulting or other studies prepared by outside experts; for example, a set of standard economic forecasts prepared by economic consultants. The type and amount of information that the originator must provide depends on the nature of the project. A rough classification scheme for projects, in order of increasing complexity and difficulty follows:

1. **Government regulations and/or company policies** concerning such things as pollution control and health or safety factors. The critical issue in such proposals is whether the standards will be met in the most efficient manner—at the minimum present-value cost, rather than positive NPV per se. Engineering analyses of alternative technologies often provide critical information in such cases.

2. **Maintenance or replacement expenditures**. The central issue is cost reduction; the cost savings that result must be sufficient to justify the investment. Cost reduction involves not only the requirement that the purchase and installation of the equipment must be profitable to the firm's shareholders, but current action must also be more profitable than postponing action until some future time.

3. **Capacity expansion in current businesses**. Evaluating the economics of expanding existing facilities or adding new facilities to meet a growth in the demand for existing products is inherently more difficult than the first two classes of projects. It is necessary to prepare demand forecasts and make assessments of competitors' likely strategies. Marketing consultants may help, but the cash flow projections for this type of project are inherently subject to greater uncertainty than for maintenance or replacement projects.

4. **New products and new businesses**. Projects in this category, which include research-and-development activities, are the most difficult to evaluate. Their newness and long lead times make it very difficult to forecast product demand accurately. In many cases, the project is of interest primarily because it would give the firm an option to break into a new market. For example, a firm that possesses a proprietary technology might spend additional research-and-development funds trying to develop new products based on this technology. If successful, these new products could pave the way for future profitable investment opportunities. The Options Principle reminds us that in such cases, care must be taken to ensure that the value of the option is included as part of the projected cash flow stream.

EVALUATION OF PROPOSALS

The proposals generated at each level in the organization are submitted to higher authority for evaluation. Proposals surviving the review process at all stages compose the firm's **capital budget**. This document provides a list of the investment projects that are believed to have a positive NPV and contains a breakdown of proposed capital expenditures for the coming year by business unit for both new projects and projects from prior years that have not been completed. Frequently, the capital budget goes beyond this and provides projected annual capital expenditures over the firm's planning horizon (typically 5 years). Senior management must review and approve the budget before it is sent to the firm's board of directors for its approval.

APPROPRIATIONS

Inclusion in the capital budget seldom means automatic approval of the required expenditures. Most firms require that plant managers or division heads submit detailed appropriation requests before funds can be released for a project. Companies often prepare manuals that specify how the appropriations request should be prepared. This helps maintain upper management control over project costs; each appropriation request is screened at various levels. The degree of review required depends on the nature and cost of the project.

Managers at each level typically have upper limits on their authority regarding both expenditures on individual assets and the total expenditure for a budgeting period, so that larger projects require the approval of higher authority. For example, at the lowest level, a department head may have the authority to approve $15,000 in total equipment purchases for the year but must obtain specific approval from higher authority for any piece of equipment costing more than $3,000. A plant manger might have authorization limits of $100,000 per year and $20,000 per piece of equipment, and so forth. By maintaining such authorization limits, the larger the expenditure, the more extensive the review and greater number of inputs to improve the proposal. Multiple reviews make sense because a firm wishes to avoid making a negative-NPV investment. The hierarchical review structure reflects the obvious fact that misjudging a larger project is potentially more costly than misjudging a smaller one, hence the need for a greater number of reviews before deciding to proceed.

REVIEW AND PERFORMANCE MEASUREMENT

The capital-budgeting–strategic-planning process should include a system for reviewing the status of uncompleted projects to determine which, if any, should be discontinued and for measuring the performance of existing assets to see whether any should be sold or liquidated. The basic techniques of capital budgeting discussed in this chapter can be applied to the review and performance-measurement process. Chapter 13 contains special applications of these techniques for determining when it is most advantageous to dispose of an underperforming asset. This possibility is called the **abandonment option**.

SUMMARY

Financial analysis plays an important role in the capital budgeting process. Firms often spend large sums to invest in capital investment projects. The cost of the project may be spread over no more than a few years. But the returns from the investment are often distant and uncertain. Moreover, investing in one project may preclude investing in other (mutually exclusive) projects. Capital budgeting involves evaluating the profitability of such investments beforehand to determine which are likely to increase the value of the firm.

This chapter discussed six techniques you can use to assess the economics of proposed capital investments: payback, average rate of return on investment, urgency, net present value, internal rate of return, and profitability index. In performing capi-

DECISION SUMMARY BOX

The discussion in this chapter leads to the following guidelines:

- The Principle of Incremental Benefits is especially important to the capital budgeting process: discount the *incremental* expected future cash flows associated with the proposed project. When in doubt, incremental cash flows can be identified by comparing the firm with and without the proposed project.

- It is important to base the capital budgeting analysis on cash flow rather than earnings. Earnings are *not* incremental cash flows.

- Be sure to exclude all sunk costs.

- A set of proposed investment projects should be defined if possible so that it includes only economically independent and mutually exclusive proposals. Often, dependent proposals can be eliminated by combining them with the proposals on which they are dependent. Whenever this is not possible, the effects of economic dependence, including project-specific opportunity costs that are in addition to those accounted for in the discount

rate, must be carefully incorporated into the analysis.

- Cash flow should be calculated after taxes but without regard to the cash flows associated with financing, such as interest, dividends, and the proceeds from issuing new securities. The discount rate takes into account the financing cost and related considerations for the project.

- Because investment projects tend to have long lives, it is especially important to incorporate the time value of money into the analysis. The NPV, IRR, and PI methods all meet this fundamental criterion.

- As was shown in Chapter 6, positive-NPV projects increase the value of the firm's common stock, thereby increasing shareholder wealth. Therefore, a firm should

Accept all projects that have a positive NPV

and

Reject all projects that have a negative NPV.

tal budgeting studies, it is important to use cash flows rather than earnings or some other accounting measure to assess profitability because cash flow, rather than earnings, is what is available to meet a firm's cash obligations and to distribute to the firm's owners. Moreover, you should calculate these cash flows net of all project-related tax effects (i.e., on an after-tax basis).

Of the six capital budgeting techniques discussed, the NPV method is the superior method. Payback, average rate of return on investment, and urgency all suffer from serious shortcomings and can therefore produce incorrect accept-reject signals. Payback, average rate of return on investment, and urgency ignore the time value of money.

The NPV, IRR, and PI methods do not share these deficiencies. Used properly, they are reliable tools for assessing a capital investment project's worth to a firm's shareholders. However, because of different assumptions concerning the reinvestment rate, which can cause the NPV method and the IRR method to provide inconsistent rankings of mutually exclusive proposals, and the fact that the IRR and PI methods ignore size differences, NPV is the superior method.[10] The only exception to this general rule is in capital rationing situations, which we discuss in the next chapter. As we explain there, when a limit is placed on capital expenditures, the PI is

---

[10] It is interesting to note that in spite of this being generally acknowledged, the IRR method appears to be the more widely used method. This is probably due to its intuitive appeal as a measure of return. See Howe (1990) for a rate-of-return method that is consistent with NPV and PI, but provides the intuitive appeal of IRR.

a useful tool for picking the best subset of projects from among a group of "good" (positive-NPV) projects.

PROBLEMS

PROBLEM SET A

A1. Why is it desirable to formulate capital investment project proposals so that they are **economically independent** of other projects?

A2. Define the term **mutually exclusive**.

A3. Why are current tax laws very important to the proper evaluation of a capital investment project?

A4. The B.A. Friend Company has the alternative to **expense** or **capitalize** an asset it has just purchased for $9,000. If it capitalizes the asset, it will be depreciated to a book value of zero on a straight-line basis over 3 years. B.A. has a marginal tax rate of 38%, and the required rate of return on this asset is 12%. What is the present-value difference to B.A. between the alternatives of expensing or capitalizing the asset? B.A. expects to have sufficient income over the next 3 years to use all possible tax credits.

A5. Name the four typically cited components of the **incremental cash flows** associated with a capital budgeting project.

A6. Compare and contrast in words the two different models of net operating cash flow given in Equations (11.6) and (11.7).

A7. Name the four typically cited components of the **initial cash outlay** for a capital budgeting project.

A8. Describe the four terms on the right-hand side of Equation (11.8) in your own words.

A9. GAFF Corporation is contemplating a capital budgeting project with capital assets that will be depreciated to a book value of $10,000 but that GAFF expects to have a salvage value of $18,000. GAFF has a marginal tax rate of 34%. If cleanup and removal expenses are expected to be $1,000 and there will be no return of working capital, what will the net salvage value be on this project?

A10. What is a **profitability index**?

A11. Define the term **payback**.

A12. Why is the Principle of Valuable Ideas of critical importance to the capital budgeting process?

A13. Why are **sunk costs** excluded from the evaluation of a capital investment project?

PROBLEM SET B

B1. You currently have a machine that is making widgets for your company. The machine has 5 years of useful life left. Its current net book value is $50,000, and it is being depreciated to its expected zero salvage value in 5 years. It generates $60,000 per year in sales revenue, requiring $30,000 in operating expenses, excluding depreciation. If you sell the machine now, you could get $30,000 for it. You are considering buying a new machine to replace your current one. It will have a life of 5 years and a $5,000 salvage value, and it costs $65,000. It is expected to generate $70,000 in sales revenue, requiring

$25,000 in operating expenses, excluding depreciation. The required rate of return for this project is 10%; you use straight–line depreciation; and you are in the 40% tax bracket. Compute the NPV from replacing the old machine.

B2. You are considering two mutually exclusive projects. Both require an initial investment of $80,000. Project A will last for 6 years and have revenues of $100,000 and expenses, excluding depreciation, of $37,777.78 per year. Project B will last for 5 years and have revenues of $100,000 and expenses of $31,333.33 per year. Both projects will be depreciated on a straight–line basis over their lives to a zero book value. Assume you have a marginal tax rate of 45% and the required rate of return for this project is 12%.

   a. Calculate the NPV for each project.

   b. Calculate the IRR for each project.

   c. Graph the NPV of the projects as a function of the discount rate, including solving for the crossover point by trial and error.

   d. Assuming these projects cannot be repeated in the future, which one should you undertake?

B3. The NSF Grant Co. is considering a project that has a 5–year life and costs $2,500. It would save $500 per year in operating cost and increase revenue by $300 per year. It would be financed with a 5–year loan with an APR of 8%. The salvage value for the newly purchased equipment is expected to be zero. If the project requires an after–tax rate of return of 12% and Grant has a 40% tax rate, what is the NPV of the project? Use straight–line depreciation.

B4. The treasurer of a large company is considering investing $50 million in 4–year Treasury notes that yield 8.75% The company's weighted average cost of capital is 15%. Is this a negative–NPV investment? Explain.

B5. A capital investment project has the following expected cash flow pattern:

Period	0	1	2	3	4	5
Cash Flow	−100	25	50	50	25	10

The company considering the project has a 10% hurdle rate.

   a. Calculate NPV. Should the company accept the project?

   b. Calculate IRR. Should the company accept the project?

   c. Calculate payback period.

   d. Calculate ROI.

   e. What do payback period and ROI tell you about the project's acceptability?

   f. How would your answers to parts a or b change if you were told that the project is one of two mutually exclusive projects the company has under consideration?

B6. When is a firm's weighted average cost of capital an appropriate indicator of the required rate of return for a proposed capital budgeting project?

B7. A capital investment project has the following expected cash flow pattern:

Period	0	1	2	3
Cash Flow	50	100	−20	−50

The required rate of return for the project is 12%.

   a. Calculate NPV. Should the company accept the project?

   b. Calculate IRR. Should the company accept the project?

   c. Explain the meaning of the answer you obtained to part b.

   d. How would you resolve the inconsistency between the answers to parts a and b?

B8. Your supervisor, a Harvard Business School graduate, insists that ROI is the best criterion for selecting capital investment projects. He insists that NPV is just an "academic" approach.

a. Explain to your supervisor why the ROI criterion has certain limitations.

b. Illustrate those limitations with a numerical example.

B9. A company is considering two mutually exclusive projects that have the following expected cash flow patterns:

Period	0	1	2	3	4	5
A cash flow	−100	30	40	50	40	30
B cash flow	−150	45	60	75	60	60

The required rate of return for the project is 14%. Which project should the company accept? Justify your answer.

B10. Nassau Manufacturing Company is considering the following two capital investment projects:

		Cash Flow in Period				
Project	Initial Investment	1	2	3	4	5
A	−100	25	30	40	30	25
B	−50	10	15	25	15	15

Nassau's required rate of return for each project is 15%.

a. Calculate the NPV and IRR for each project.

Which project(s) should Nassau accept, assuming they are

b. Independent?

c. Dependent?

d. Mutually exclusive?

B11. American Tool & Die is considering purchasing a new metal stamping machine for $50 million. The machine will have a 4–year useful life with zero salvage value. The incremental after-tax cash flows are shown below (millions of dollars):

Year	1	2	3	4
Incremental free cash flow	30	25	20	20

American's target capital structure is 75% long-term debt. American's pretax cost of debt is 12%. The riskless rate is 10%, the premium on the market portfolio is 6%, American's beta is 1.25, and American's marginal income tax rate is 34%. Calculate the NPV for the project.

B12. The Lignite Mining Company is developing a new lignite mine in Texas that will cost $120 million. Lignite Mining plans to issue $40 million of common stock and incur $80 million of bank debt to raise the needed funds. Over the long term, Lignite Mining will maintain a capital structure consisting of ⅓ debt and ⅔ common equity. Lignite's cost of common equity is 20%, and its pretax cost of debt is 10%.

a. If Lignite Mining pays tax at a marginal rate of 34%, what is the company's weighted average cost of capital?

b. Under what circumstances is this weighted average cost of capital the appropriate discount rate to use for calculating the mining project's NPV?

B13. The Howe Fix-It Corp. is considering buying a new machine called a TX2 that costs $60,000. The TX2 requires $10,000 in setup costs that are expensed immediately and $10,000 in additional working capital. The TX2's useful life is 10 years, after which it can be sold for a salvage value of $20,000. The TX2 requires a maintenance overhaul costing $30,000 at the end of year 7. The overhaul is fully expensed when it is done. Howe uses straight-line depreciation, and the machine will be depreciated to a book value of zero on a 6-year basis. Howe has a tax rate of 40% and requires a 15% rate of return on projects like this one. The TX2 is expected to increase revenues minus expenses by $17,500 per year. What is the NPV of buying the TX2?

B14. Why is a change in net working capital an important and necessary part of the incremental cost of a capital budgeting project?

PROBLEM SET C

C1. A new product called QQ is being considered by JJ Corporation. An outlay of $6 million is required for equipment to produce the new product, and additional net working capital of $500,000 is required to support production and marketing. The equipment will be depreciated on a straight-line basis to a zero book value over 8 years. Although the depreciable life is 8 years, the project is expected to have a production life of only 6 years and will have a salvage value of zero at that time (removal cost = scap value). Revenues minus expenses for the first 2 years of the project are forecast to be $5 million per year but because of competition, revenues minus expenses in years 3 through 6 are projected to be only $3 million. The required rate of return for this project is 16%, and the relevant tax rate is 35%. Compute the NPV of the QQ project.

C2. The Doug E. Nuff Construction Company is considering a 33-year project the government wants it to undertake. Development and construction will take 3 years, and the project will operate for 30 years. The riskless rate is 5%; the rate of return on the market portfolio is 12%; the project's beta is 1.3. Doug's company is unleveraged. Doug expects to spend $250,000 for land, 1 year from the date the contract is awarded ($t = 1$). Construction of the building will cost $2 million, and the equipment will cost $3 million, both of which will be incurred at $t = 2$. There is a 5% investment tax credit on the building and a 7% investment tax credit on the equipment that can be claimed when operations commence ($t = 3$). The life of the building is 30 years, with a salvage value of $50,000, while the equipment has a 5-year useful life with no salvage value. The equipment will be replaced at 5-year intervals at a cost of $3 million upon each replacement. Straight-line depreciation will be used (over years $t = 4$ through $t = 8$, initially). To support operations, Doug expects to need $20,000 additional cash, to invest $60,000 in accounts receivable and $80,000 in inventory, and to maintain $60,000 in accounts payable. The investment in net working capital occurs at the start of operations ($t = 3$). The revenues from the project will amount to $800,000, fixed cost will be $100,000, and variable costs will be $150,000—all on an annual basis. At the end of the project, the company is expected to restore the surrounding area at a cost of $420,000. The tax rate is 40%. The value of the land is expected to be constant over the life of the project, and the building can be sold for its net book value at the end of the project. What is the minimum amount that the government would have to pay Doug at the time the contract is awarded ($t = 0$) to induce him to undertake the project?

C3. Brenda's Place (BP) is a national chain of short-order restaurants that has been very successful over the past 15 years. However, the growth potential in this market has declined and therefore BP's management is contemplating investing in a new business line—publishing. BP can enter this new field by purchasing and renovating a small building in downtown Chicago at a cost of $80,000, which will be depreciated on a straight-line basis to a zero book value over 10 years. Although the depreciable life is 10 years, the entire project is expected to be sold off for a salvage value of $50,000 at the end of 8 years. It is estimated that the project would increase sales by $100,000 per year during the next 2 years and by another $50,000 ($150,000 above current) in years 3 thru 8. Variable costs (including all labor and material) will be 60% of sales, and an increase of $10,000 per year in other annual operating expenses is expected. At the expected sales levels, about $80,000 of added receivables and inventories will be needed. Accounts payable are expected to increase by $20,000. BP is completely equity-financed and has a current cost of equity capital of 15%, which corresponds to a beta of 2.0. The publishing business is less risky and has an unleveraged beta of 1.4. The rate of return on the market portfolio is 10%. BP's tax rate is 40%. What is the NPV of this project?

REFERENCES

Beranek, William. "The Cost of Capital, Capital Budgeting, and the Maximization of Shareholder Wealth." *Journal of Financial and Quantitative Analysis* 10 (March 1975): 1–21.

Bierman, Harold, Jr., and Seymour Smidt. *The Capital Budgeting Decision*, 7th ed. New York: Macmillan, 1988.

Gitman, Lawrence J., and Vincent A. Mercurio. "Cost of Capital Techniques Used by Major U.S. Firms: Survey and Analysis of Fortune's 1000." *Financial Management* 11 (Winter 1982): 21–29.

Haley, Charles W. "Taxes, the Cost of Capital, and the Firm's Investment Decisions." *Journal of Finance* 26 (September 1971): 901–17.

Hirshleifer, J. *Investment, Interest and Capital.* Englewood Cliffs, N.J.: Prentice-Hall, 1970, 46–98.

Howe, Keith M. "A Note on Flotation Costs and Capital Budgeting." *Financial Management* 11 (Winter 1982): 30–33.

Howe, Keith M. "Perpetuity Rate of Return Analysis." *Engineering Economist* (1990).

Kaufman, Mike, ed. *The Capital Budgeting Handbook.* Homewood, Ill.: Dow Jones–Irwin, 1986.

Lorie, James H., and Leonard J. Savage. "Three Problems in Rationing Capital." *Journal of Business* 28 (October 1955): 227–39.

Oblak, David J., and Roy J. Helm, Jr. "Survey and Analysis of Capital Budgeting Methods Used by Multinationals." *Financial Management* 9 (Winter 1980): 37–41.

Petty, J. William, David F. Scott, Jr., and Monroe M. Bird. "The Capital Expenditure Decision-Making Process of Large Corporations." *Engineering Economist* 20 (Spring 1975): 159–72.

Pohlman, Randolph A., Emmanuel S. Santiago, and F. Lynn Market. "Cash Flow Estimation Practices of Large Firms." *Financial Management* 17 (Summer 1988): 71–79.

Quirin, G. David. *The Capital Expenditure Decision.* Homewood, Ill.: Richard D. Irwin, 1967.

Sarnat, Marshall, and Haim Levy. "The Relationship of Rules of Thumb to the Internal Rate of Return: A Restatement and Generalization." *Journal of Finance* 24 (June 1969): 479–89.

Schall, Lawrence D., Gary L. Sundem, and William R. Geijsbeek, Jr. "Survey and Analysis of Capital Budgeting Methods." *Journal of Finance* 33 (March 1978): 281–87.

Sick, Gordon A. "A Certainty-Equivalent Approach to Capital Budgeting." *Financial Management* 15 (Winter 1986): 23–32.

Weingartner, H. Martin. *Mathematical Programming and the Analysis of Capital Budgeting Problems*. Chicago: Markham, 1967.

Weingartner, H. Martin. "Capital Rationing: n Authors in Search of a Plot." *Journal of Finance* 32 (December 1977): 1403–31.

12

CAPITAL BUDGETING: SOME COMPLICATIONS

In this chapter, we apply the concepts presented in the previous chapter and introduce some dimensions that complicate the analysis of a firm's investment decision. One of these dimensions is economic independence. Whenever possible, investment projects should be formulated to be economically independent of each other. However, in some cases, it is not possible to formulate the proposal so that the proposed project is economically independent of other projects. In such cases, all or part of the proposed project will interact with existing operations and/or other projects. In the next section, we analyze an example in which a proposed new product would interact with the firm's current products.

Other topics covered in this chapter include optimal replacement cycles, taxes, and inflation. We show how these factors complicate the analysis of a proposed capital investment project. We also show, however, that proper treatment of all these relevant factors in a capital budgeting analysis is simply an application of time-value-of-money mechanics.

The chapter ends with a look at alternative methods of analyzing an investment project that might provide additional insights into the value of the project. These methods can be especially useful when it is not possible to determine a market-based estimate of the required rate of return for the project.

12.1 A NEW PRODUCT PROPOSAL

Headcleaner, Inc. manufactures a product called Clean-e-z that is used to clean magnetic tape heads on a videocassette recorder (VCR). Recently, the research laboratory at Headcleaner has developed a new method for cleaning VCR heads. The new process is being referred to by its laboratory name, Q-10. Q-10 is superior to Clean-e-z in every way, and therefore it is expected that the introduction of Q-10 would encroach upon, and ultimately eliminate, sales of Clean-e-z. In the meantime, the continuation of Clean-e-z would allow differential pricing of the two products as well as the opportunity to extract additional economic benefit from existing facilities that would otherwise have to be scrapped since they cannot be used to produce Q-10. In this case, there are economic dependencies connected with Q-10 that cannot be ignored. In addition, there are sunk costs connected with previous investments in production facilities for Clean-e-z that must be ignored.

A major question facing Headcleaner is how long it can enjoy monopolistic pricing power connected with Q-10. Although the product can be patented, competitors will be able to imitate the product sufficiently well that Headcleaner will not be able to obtain much of a price premium for Q-10 after competitors begin production of a similar product. It is estimated that development of an equivalent product will take 2 years from the time of discovery of the idea underlying Q-10. Therefore, once Headcleaner begins to market Q-10, the firm will enjoy monopolistic pricing power for at most 2 years. If a competitor were to discover the idea before Headcleaner begins marketing Q-10, the development time would be less than 2 years.

Consider first the Q-10 project by itself. An outlay of $6 million is required for equipment to produce the new product, and additional net working capital of $500,000 is required to support production and marketing. The equipment will be depreciated on a straight-line basis to a zero book value over 8 years, so depreciation will be $750,000 per year (= [6 million]/8). Although the depreciable life is 8 years, the project is expected to have a production life of only 6 years and a salvage value of zero at termination because of technological innovations such as the one under consideration.[1] Revenues minus expenses for the first 2 years of the project are projected to be $5 million per year, but because of competition, revenues minus expenses in years 3 through 6 are projected to be only $3 million per year. The required rate of return for this project is 16%, and the relevant marginal tax rate for this project is 35%. The value of the project, then, without regard to its effects on current operations, is

Time	Item	CFBT	CFAT	PV @ 16%
0	Equipment	−6.0	−6.0	−6.000
0	Δ Working capital	−0.5	−0.5	−0.500
1–6	Depreciation	0	0.263/yr	0.967
1–2	$\Delta R - \Delta E$	5.0/yr	3.25/yr	5.217
3–6	$\Delta R - \Delta E$	3.0/yr	1.95/yr	4.055
6	Salvage	0 ($B = 1.5$)	0.525 $(1 - \tau)S + \tau B$	.421
6	Δ Working capital	0.5	0.5	
			PV =	$4.160 million

The above calculation ignores the value of Clean-e-z sales, which although substantially reduced, are expected to continue for the next 2 years. Specifically, revenues minus expenses for Clean-e-z are expected to be $1.3 and $0.8 million per year before taxes, respectively, for the next 2 years. Production equipment for Clean-e-z currently has a book value of $3.0 million, 6 more years of straight-line depreciation at $500,000 per year to a zero book value, and an expected scrap value in 2 years of $250,000. Finally, $500,000 in net working capital will be released when the production of Clean-e-z is discontinued. If Q-10 is introduced now, the present value of Clean-e-z production and sales over the next 2 years is

---

[1]It is important to note that the useful life of an asset is not necessarily equal to its depreciable life. The Internal Revenue Code specifies one depreciable life for an asset for tax purposes. The useful life depends upon the specific use of the asset, among other things.

Time	Item	CFBT	CFAT	PV @ 16%
1–2	Depreciation	0	.175/yr	.281
1	$\Delta R - \Delta E$	1.3	.845	.728
2	$\Delta R - \Delta E$	.8	.520	.386
2	Salvage	.25 $(B = 2.0)$	.863 $(1 - \tau)S + \tau B$	1.013
2	Δ Working capital	.5	.5	

$$PV = \$2.408 \text{ million}$$

The total present value of the Q-10 project, then, appears to be the sum of the two present values, or $6.568 million. While this looks good, we must also determine the value of continuing Clean-e-z production without introducing Q-10. Headcleaner's production facilities for Clean-e-z could be used productively for another 6 years. Revenues minus expenses for Clean-e-z are currently $2.6 million per year. If this sales level were to continue for the next 6 years and the scrap value of Clean-e-z production equipment were to be zero at the end of 6 years, the present value of continuing Clean-e-z production without introducing Q-10 would be

Time	Item	CFBT	CFAT	PV @ 16%
1–6	Depreciation	0	.175/yr	.645
1–6	$\Delta R - \Delta E$	2.6/yr	1.690/yr	6.227
6	Salvage	0 $(B = 0)$	0 $(1 - \tau)S + \tau B$	0
6	Δ Working capital	.5	.5	.205

$$PV = \$7.007 \text{ million}$$

The continued production of Clean-e-z appears to be more valuable than the introduction of Q-10 at this time. However, the above calculation ignores the interaction of Clean-e-z sales with those of other competing products. The continued sales of Clean-e-z depend upon competitors not developing and introducing a product like Q-10. Once a competitor comes up with the idea, not only will Clean-e-z sales be hurt, but Headcleaner's projected 2 years of monopolistic pricing power will also be eroded or even eliminated. Therefore, we must consider postponing the introduction of Q-10 *temporarily* rather than putting it off until the Clean-e-z production facilities have been completely worn out. It is estimated that there is only a 20% chance of a competitor discovering the idea within the next year, a 25% chance in the year after, a 50% chance in the third year, and finally, if a competitor has not already discovered the idea before, it is a virtual certainty that one will discover the idea in the fourth year.

While a complete analysis could be developed that contains all the points at which the introduction of Q-10 would be possible, the decision facing Headcleaner is whether *any* postponement yields a greater NPV. Therefore, we need only compare the alternative of introducing Q-10 now (PV = $6.568 million) with that of introducing it later, say 1 year from now.[2]

---

[2] The choice of 1 year from now is of course somewhat arbitrary. "Later" is simply the next possible point at which introducing the product would be "reasonable."

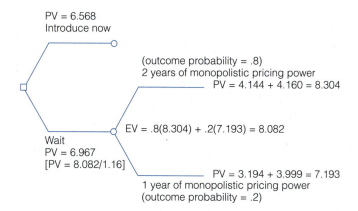

FIGURE 12-1

Diagram of Headcleaner's decision whether to wait to introduce Q-10 (in $ millions).

The present value of waiting a year is the discounted expected value of having either 1 or 2 years of monopolistic pricing power. If Headcleaner waits a year, there is a .20 probability it will have only 1 year of monopolistic pricing power, and therefore a .80 probability it will have 2 years of monopolistic pricing power. The expected value is then $8.082 million (= .8[8.304] + .2[7.193]), and the present value is $6.967 million (= 8.082/1.16). Therefore, the present value of waiting a year is $399,000 larger than the present value of introducing it now. Figure 12-1 presents a comparison of the two alternatives, and problems B2 and B4 at the back of the chapter provide additional information and ask you to verify the present values used in this example.

Although the largest present value, of those examined, appears to be achieved by continuing Clean-e-z production until the equipment is worn out, it is important to reiterate that this NPV is illusory: Competition eliminates this alternative. While Headcleaner can continue to produce only Clean-e-z, if a product like Q-10 is produced by a competitor, sales of Clean-e-z will not continue as they have been projected.

Also, note that it is not necessary to consider other waiting strategies at this time. We have shown that waiting 1 year is better than introducing now (6.967 vs. 6.568). Headcleaner still can decide later to postpone longer than 1 year. Since that decision need not be made at this time, Headcleaner can use whatever additional information becomes available within the next year to help make the subsequent decision.

EROSION AND ENHANCEMENT

The example just given illustrates a very important financial interaction between a product innovation, such as a new product or production process, and current products. When a product innovation is introduced there may occur what is called **erosion** of one or more existing products, as in the example above where the introduction of Q-10 eroded the sales of Clean-e-z. A reduction in sales may be an obvious consequence of an innovation. Perhaps less obvious is the decline in the market value of the production facilities for existing products caused by the innovation. Because of reduced or eliminated sales opportunities, the value of plant and equipment used by *other firms*, as well as that of the firm introducing the innovation, declines. Therefore, as perverse as it might seem, a firm may be best served by delaying the introduction of a product innovation until the innovation can be incorporated into the firm's natural replacement of equipment. Of course, a firm may introduce a product innovation sooner than it might have otherwise as a defensive move against its competitors.

Just as one interaction among products may cause a decrease in value, another interaction may cause an increase in value. Such an increase is called **enhancement**. Enhancement occurs when the production and/or sales of one product increases the value of another product. For example, an innovation that causes a reduction in the cost of making and/or installing a home swimming pool may cause an increase in the sales of swimming pool maintenance equipment.

It is extremely important to include economic dependencies that cause significant erosion or enhancement in order to measure correctly a project's NPV. Without their inclusion, you will not have measured the NPV, even though you may think you have!

12.2   EVALUATING REPLACEMENT CYCLES

An example of a machine replacement decision was presented in the previous chapter. The Rocky Mountain Chemical Corporation example involved a decision connected with specialized equipment that is subject to periodic technological design improvements. In such cases, the replacement decision is basically a one-time decision. Subsequently, when the chosen machine becomes worn out or technologically outmoded, its replacement will be essentially an entirely new project. In many cases, such a replacement decision is, in effect, a decision of whether to continue producing a product or even to remain in that line of business.

Often, replacement decisions are not like the Rocky Mountain example. Instead, many replacement decisions are fairly *routine*, involving machinery and equipment that does not change very much over time. The replacement of vehicles and standardized machinery, such as a stationary crane, are examples of such routine decisions. In those cases, the asset is replaced or overhauled because of worn-out parts rather than technological improvement. Essentially, the new asset is identical to the one it replaces. Routine replacement decisions follow a pattern, or **cycle**. The asset is purchased, maintained, and replaced on a regular basis, as, for example, a delivery vehicle for a shipping company like Emery World-Wide.

When choosing among alternative assets that fall into a replacement cycle, the firm often considers assets that have different life-cycle lengths. That is, the alternative assets have differing useful lives. When alternative assets in a routine replacement decision do not have identical life cycles, choosing the asset on the basis of the largest NPV is inappropriate because the alternative assets are not being valued on a comparable basis. For example, if a firm is choosing between two assets, one with a 5-year life and the other with a 10-year life, two sequential 5-year assets would be needed to do the job of one 10-year asset.

One way to choose among alternative assets in a replacement cycle decision, then, is to find a common horizon where some number of sequential replacements of one type of asset covers a production period equal to that for another type of asset. This approach can, however, be cumbersome. For example, comparing a 6-year type A asset with a 7-year type B asset would involve a horizon of 42 years—seven sequential purchases of A types versus six of B types. Further, you can see that if there was a C-type alternative with an 8-year life, the process becomes even more tedious. Equivalent annual cost is a more convenient method of choosing among alternative assets with differing replacement cycle lives.

EQUIVALENT ANNUAL COST

Just as the name implies, **equivalent annual cost** determines the equivalent cost per year of owning the asset over its entire life. The method is a very simple two-step application of time-value-of-money mathematics. The first step is to compute the present value of all the costs associated with owning the asset over its entire life. These costs include the purchase price, maintenance costs, and operating costs over the period of expected ownership. With the net initial outlay denoted C_0 and yearly CFAT costs denoted $C_1, C_2, \ldots, C_n$, where n is the length of the asset's life, the total present value of costs over the life of the asset, TC, is

$$TC = C_0 + \sum_{t=1}^{n} \frac{C_t}{(1 + r)^t} \tag{12.1}$$

where r is the required rate of return for the project.

The second step in the process is to determine the amount that, if it was paid out each year over the expected ownership life, has the same present value as the total present value of costs computed in step one. The amount computed for step two is an annuity that represents the *equivalent* annual cost. The equivalent annual cost, denoted EAC, is then given by the formula for determining the payments of an annuity, Equation (3.7):

$$EAC = TC \left[\frac{r(1 + r)^n}{(1 + r)^n - 1} \right] \tag{12.2}$$

A REPLACEMENT CYCLE EXAMPLE

Ozborn Agricultural Affiliates, Inc. (OA) is considering the purchase of a cornhusker machine. OA can buy two alternative machines, A or B. OA should choose the machine with the lower equivalent annual cost. Machine A costs $49,000 to purchase and install, has a 5-year life, and will be depreciated over 5 years on a straight-line basis to a book value of $4,000, so depreciation will be $9,000 per year for 5 years (= [49,000 − 4,000]/5). At the end of the 5 years, OA expects to be able to sell machine A for $10,000. For the expected production level, it will cost $25,000 per year to operate machine A. OA pays taxes at the rate of 40% on its cornhusker operation, and the required rate of return on this project is 12%. What is the equivalent annual cost for machine A?

The present value of all the costs is

Time	Item	CFBT	CFAT	PV @ 12%
0	I_0	−49,000	−49,000	−49,000
1–5	−ΔE	−25,000/yr	−15,000/yr	−54,072
1–5	Depreciation	0/yr	3,600/yr	12,977
5	Salvage	10,000	7,600	4,312
		(B = 4,000)	$(1 - \tau)S + \tau B$	
				TC = −$85,783

and the equivalent annual cost is given by Equation (12.2):

$$EAC = TC \left[\frac{r(1 + r)^n}{(1 + r)^n - 1} \right] = -85,783 \left[\frac{.12(1.12)^5}{(1.12)^5 - 1} \right] = -\$23,797$$

Machine B has a 10-year life but costs $72,000 to purchase and install. It will be depreciated over 8 years on a straight-line basis to a book value of zero, so depreciation will be $9,000 per year for the first 8 years (= 72,000/8) and zero for the last

2 years over which the machine will be used. Machine B is expected to require an overhaul at the end of year 6 that will cost $18,000 and will be expensed, rather than capitalized. At the end of the 10 years, OA expects to be able to sell machine B for a scrap value that will equal the cost of removal and cleanup. Machine B is slightly less expensive to run than machine A, costing $24,000 per year to operate at the expected production level. What is the equivalent annual cost for machine B?

The present value of all the costs is

Time	Item	CFBT	CFAT	PV @ 12%
0	I_0	−72,000	−72,000	−72,000
1–10	−ΔE	−24,000/yr	−14,400/yr	−81,363
1–8	Depreciation	0/yr	3,600/yr	17,883
6	Overhaul	−18,000	−10,800	−5,472
			TC =	−$140,952

and the equivalent annual cost is given by Equation (12.2):

$$\text{EAC} = \text{TC}\left[\frac{r(1 + r)^n}{(1 + r)^n - 1}\right] = -140,952\left[\frac{.12(1.12)^{10}}{(1.12)^{10} - 1}\right] = -\$24,946$$

OA should buy machine A because its equivalent annual cost is lower. Note that the revenues have been disregarded since both alternatives have the same revenues and risk.

Figure 12-2 compares the next 10 years of cornhusker machine production using the two machines. The comparison is made both on the basis of EAC and on the basis of the present value of total cost outlays over the common 10-year horizon. Figure 12-2 illustrates that the decisions implied by the equivalent annual cost method and an equivalent horizon comparison are identical in this example. In fact, the methods imply identical decisions in all cases. However, as noted earlier, the equivalent annual cost method is more convenient, especially when the lowest equivalent horizon is long or when several machines are compared.

REPLACEMENT FREQUENCY

The preferred shorter replacement cycle in the above example has an additional option associated with it. Because of the shorter life cycle, there is less chance that the firm will be economically forced to discard a machine that is mechanically sound but has been rendered useless by periodic technological advances. In essence, the firm has the option to change production technologies more often when it purchases the machine with the shorter life cycle. Therefore, if the two machines had identical

FIGURE 12-2

Comparison of equivalent annual cost and equivalent horizon methods.

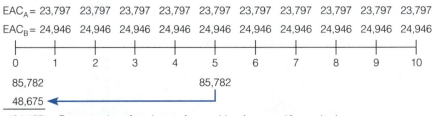

EACs (including removal costs), the machine with the shorter life cycle would be preferred. Although we do not have an option pricing model for conveniently determining an estimate for the value of more frequent replacement, it is nevertheless a valuable option.[3] There are other options with respect to capital budgeting as well. Several of these options are discussed in the next chapter.

The previous example involved a comparison between two alternative machines. It is also appropriate to make comparisons of differing replacement cycles with one machine. Salvage values and maintenance costs vary with the type and usage of a machine. (Salvage value is also a function of the potential future uses of the equipment.) One life cycle is not necessarily optimal for *all* situations. Let's investigate the replacement cycle decision, extending our cornhusker machine example to consider various life cycles for machine A. In each case, we assume that the depreciation schedule is as originally specified (straight-line over 5 years to a salvage value of $4,000), even though the actual usage will be different from this.

EXAMPLE 1 ■ Suppose that machine A could be replaced at the end of 4 years, rather than after 5 years. Having been used less, it is expected that it could be sold for $16,000 at the end of 4 years. In that case, the total cost over one life cycle will be

Time	Item	CFBT	CFAT	PV @ 12%
0	I_0	−49,000	−49,000	−49,000
1–4	ΔE	−25,000/yr	−15,000/yr	−45,560
1–4	Depreciation	0/yr	3,600/yr	10,934
4	Salvage	16,000	14,800	9,406
		$(B = 13,000)$	$(1 - \tau)S + \tau B$	
				TC = −$74,220

and the EAC = −$24,436. Therefore, the 5-year replacement cycle is preferred to the 4-year replacement cycle. We can, of course, also consider a longer replacement cycle. ■

EXAMPLE 2 ■ Suppose machine A could be used in the sixth year if, at the end of year five, an additional $1,000 were spent on maintenance. The machine is expected to have a zero salvage value at the end of the sixth year. Over a 6-year life, then, the total cost will be

Time	Item	CFBT	CFAT	PV @ 12%
0	I_0	−49,000	−49,000	−49,000
1–6	ΔE	−25,000/yr	−15,000/yr	−61,671
1–5	Depreciation	0/yr	3,600/yr	12,977
5	Maintenance	−1,000	−600	−340
6	Salvage	0	1,600	811
		$(B = 4,000)$	$(1 - \tau)S + \tau B$	
				TC = −$97,223

[3] A useful method of incorporating this option value into the analysis of the replacement problem without using an option pricing model is presented by Emery (1982).

and the EAC = −$23,647. Therefore, the 6-year replacement cycle is preferred to both the 5- and 4-year cycles. Problem B1 extends this example further by providing conditions for a 7-year replacement cycle for machine A and asking you to compute the EAC for that cycle.   ■

As was pointed out earlier, the choice of machine A (over B), with its shorter replacement cycle, provides more flexibility with respect to technological innovations. Similarly, flexibility in a machine's replacement cycle is also valuable because even if one cycle is projected at one point in time, the firm has the option to change when replacement will occur, depending upon conditions that develop. In this example, the EAC values for the various replacement cycles are close enough that the firm can choose to purchase machine A, run it for 4 years, and reevaluate the replacement decision at that time based on technological considerations, the condition of the machine, replacement cost, salvage values, maintenance experience over the 4 years, more accurate maintenance cost projections for its continued use, and so on.

EQUIVALENT ANNUAL ANNUITIES

The equivalent annual cost calculation annualizes the total cost of a project over its life. If you think about it, you can see that this same approach can be used to annualize any amount, such as a project's NPV, its total revenue, and so on. In those cases, the amount might be called an **equivalent annual benefit**, EAB. The general term for any annualized amount is **equivalent annual annuity**, or EAA. The EAA is a useful measure whenever the project horizon is indefinitely long, so that the assumption of an infinite, or permanent, stream is a good characterization of the situation.

EXAMPLE ■ Suppose one 5-year cycle of a machine has an NPV of $2,800. Assuming a required rate of return of 11%, the EAA for this project's NPV would be $757.60. With an infinite horizon of sequential replacement, the NPV from the sequence would be the present value of a perpetuity of EAA inflows, or $6,887.27 (= 757.60/.11).   ■

OTHER REPLACEMENT SCENARIOS

The one-time replacement decision was analyzed and illustrated in Chapter 11. Such decisions should be made using the one-time NPV decision criterion: Choose the asset with the largest NPV. In this section, we examined the replacement cycle decision, assuming that the project would be replaced periodically with an infinitely long horizon. *Routine* replacement cycle decisions can be made on the basis of equivalent annual cost: *Choose the asset with the lowest EAC.*

When the possibility of future technological advances in the asset exists, the replacement cycle decision is more complex. Among other things, the decision must include the option connected with a shorter replacement cycle, to make technological change sooner. In practice, technological advances are typically difficult to predict, but nevertheless the possibility of their occurrence can materially affect a firm's choice of asset.

12.3   INFLATION

In Chapter 4, we introduced the problem of inflation uncertainty. Later, in Chapter 6, we noted that U.S. government bonds are not truly riskless because of inflation uncertainty. We showed that with fixed payments, changes in the required rate of return cause changes in the value of the bonds. This phenomenon follows directly from the present value equation; asset value is a function of *both* the expected future cash flows and the required rate of return. The dependence of a bond's value upon changes in expected inflation results primarily from the fact that the payments are fixed. A change in bond values occurs because a change in expected inflation causes a change in the required rate of return.[4] If both the future cash flows *and* the required rate of return change in proportion to changes in the general levels of prices (i.e., in lockstep with the inflation rate), the value of the asset will not change. The key to properly measuring the effect of inflation on asset value, then, is to incorporate any differential impacts that inflation has on the parameters, but to ignore impacts that affect all the parameters equivalently.

For the analysis of a capital budgeting decision, the important point about inflation is that it should either be included in all of the estimates of the expected future cash flows and the required rate of return or excluded from every one of those estimates. When an estimate includes inflation, it is said to be stated in **nominal** terms, whereas when the estimate excludes inflation, it is said to be stated in **real** terms.[5] For proper measurement, then, all of the parameters in an NPV calculation must be expressed either entirely in real terms or entirely in nominal terms.

To investigate the effects of inflation, let us first consider its effect on the required rate of return. Denote the required rate of return in real terms as r_r, the required rate of return in nominal terms as r_n, and the inflation rate as π. The nominal required rate can be obtained by simply compounding the real rate and the inflation rate. So the relationship among these three parameters is

$$(1 + r_n) = (1 + r_r)(1 + \pi) \tag{12.3}$$

Multiplying through the right-hand side of Equation (12.3) and rearranging, the nominal rate can be expressed as a function of the real and inflation rates:

$$r_n = r_r + \pi + \pi r_r \tag{12.4}$$

Equation (12.4) may surprise you somewhat because you might have seen or heard the nominal rate expressed simply as the sum of the real and inflation rates, without including the cross-term, πr_r. Since the cross-term is relatively small compared to the other terms, the sum is a good approximation and is often used in practice. However, Equation (12.4) is a more accurate expression for this relationship.

A subtle problem that occurs when inflation is present is that while revenues and expenses inflate, the tax credits associated with depreciation do not inflate. This is because depreciation expense is based on the historical cost of the equipment. Thus, either the depreciation tax credits must be converted into real terms, or the expected revenue and expense cash flows must be converted into nominal terms. The problem is illustrated in the following example where the NPV of the project is computed in both real and nominal terms.

EXAMPLE ■ A machine with a 4-year useful life requires a total outlay of $10,000, all of which will be depreciated to a zero book value over 4 years on a straight-line basis, so depreciation will be $2,500 per year. The machine generates an incremental

---

[4] It is very important to note that the important measure is that of *expected* future inflation rate. This can be quite different from the inflation rate actually realized, although recent realized inflation rates are often highly correlated with expected future inflation rates.

[5] Recall from Chapter 3 that the term **nominal** means that the value is a value "in name only." Cash flows that are expressed in nominal dollar terms are not comparable in purchasing power to today's dollars, which is the reason the phrase "constant purchasing power dollars" is often used in place of the term **real**.

increase in operating income of $5,000 per year before taxes, and the firm pays taxes at the rate of 40% on this amount. Inflation is expected to be 8% per year, and the required rate of return in real terms is $r_r = 10\%$. What is the NPV of purchasing this machine?

First, we will compute the NPV of this project in real terms. To do this, the depreciation tax credits must be converted into real terms. The tax credit for the first year will be $\tau D = .4[2,500] = 1,000$. With 8% inflation, this will be worth $926 ($= 1,000/1.08$) in real terms, or dollars of constant purchasing power. The tax credit for the second year will be worth $857 ($= 1000/[1.08]^2$), with the other tax credits determined in a similar manner, by discounting them for the requisite number of years at the inflation rate. In real terms, then, the NPV is computed as

Time	Item	CFBT	CFAT (real)	PV @ 10%
0	I_0	−10,000	−10,000	−10,000
1–4	$\Delta R - \Delta E$	5,000/yr	3,000/yr	9,509
1	Depreciation	0	926	842
2	Depreciation	0	857	709
3	Depreciation	0	794	596
4	Depreciation	0	735	502
			NPV =	$2,158

To compute the NPV in nominal terms, we need the nominal required rate of return, which is given by Equation (12.4) as

$$r_n = r_r + \pi + \pi r_r = .10 + .08 + (.08)(.10) = 18.8\%$$

In nominal dollars, the first year's $\Delta R - \Delta E$ will be $5,400 ($= 5,000[1.08]$). The second year's $\Delta R - \Delta E$ will be $5,832 ($= 5,000[1.08]^2$), with the subsequent flows computed in a similar manner, by compounding them forward at the inflation rate. After converting the real net incremental cash flows associated with the revenues and expenses into equivalent nominal flows, the NPV of this project is computed as

Time	Item	CFBT	CFAT (nominal)	PV @ 18.8%
0	I_0	−10,000	−10,000	−10,000
1	$\Delta R - \Delta E$	5,400	3,240	2,727
2	$\Delta R - \Delta E$	5,832	3,499	2,479
3	$\Delta R - \Delta E$	6,299	3,779	2,254
4	$\Delta R - \Delta E$	6,802	4,081	2,049
1–4	Depreciation	0	1,000/yr	2,649
			NPV =	$2,158

If inflation affects various component cash flows differentially—for example, revenues are expected to increase 6% per year, whereas expenses are expected to increase 9% per year—those differentials should be incorporated into the analysis. This type of situation is posed in some of the problems at the end of the chapter. Differences in inflation rates among cash flows can cause complexity, as can differences in the effect of inflation on the required rate of return and the cash flows. Still, it merely complicates the problem; such complexity does not change the way we incorporate the effects of inflation. Whatever the case, the analysis should be cast in a consistent manner, *entirely in real terms or entirely in nominal terms.*

A FEW WORDS ABOUT THE TAX ENVIRONMENT   12.4

Since the nation was formed, there have been many different methods used by the United States federal government to collect taxes. In fact, even before the nation was formed, taxes were very important to our citizens (recall that the Boston Tea Party concerned tax provisions). Early in this century, the U.S. Congress instituted a procedure for collecting taxes, now familiar to most people, called an income tax. Since that time, the income tax has come to provide the primary source of tax revenue for the federal government. In spite of the fact that the income tax has existed for a long time, its provisions and tax rates have been changed frequently since it was first instituted. To show how often income tax rates have changed since the introduction of the federal income tax law, Table 12-1 presents the statutory federal tax rates on corporate income from 1909 through 1987. As you can see, the tax rate has changed fairly often.

Another example of how the tax laws have changed over the years is found in the provisions for capitalizing equipment expense—depreciation—and in provisions for claiming investment tax credit. In the past 30 years, there have been no less than five major changes in the depreciation rules in addition to numerous minor changes. The Tax Reform Act of 1986 brought out the *modified* ACRS (accelerated cost recovery system, pronounced "acres") provision. ACRS was introduced by Congress in 1981, superseding the asset depreciation range (ADR) method, which had been introduced approximately 4 years earlier. ADR was an attempt to specify carefully (once and for all!) the rules for using the three allowable depreciation methods which were, at that time, **double-declining-balance**, **sum-of-the-years'-digits**, and **straight-line**. The specification of these particular three depreciation methods as the allowable methods for federal income tax purposes had occurred many years earlier, but the rules governing their use had been modified fairly often during the intervening years. History does not make us optimistic that the modified ACRS procedure introduced in the 1986 law will endure for many years.

Because changes in the tax laws, including the federal corporate income tax, occur with considerable regularity, it is very important to *use the **current** tax laws to determine after-tax cash flows* for a capital budgeting decision, or for that matter, any financial decision. However, also because of these frequent changes, there is little point in memorizing all of the tax provisions. When you undertake a financial decision that is affected by taxes, you can and should determine exactly what the tax treatment for each item will be under current tax law. This can be done by consulting sources such as current tax guides (federal, state, or private) or tax experts within or outside your organization.

Please do not misinterpret our pointing out the futility of memorizing tax laws to mean that taxes are not important. Quite the contrary. *Taxes are a very important dimension* of corporate decision-making, but our approach here is to present the analysis in as general a framework as possible. As we have said, income taxes have been with us since 1909, but income tax rates and particular depreciation provisions seem to last only a few years. For this reason, we present taxes as an expense provision. In addition, even though the federal corporate income taxes are the largest part of a

TABLE 12-1   Statutory Corporate Income Tax Rates from 1909 through 1987

Year	Rate Brackets or Exemptions	Rate[a] (percent)
1909–1913	$5,000 exemption	1
1913–1915	No exemption after March 1, 1913	1
1916	None	2
1917	None	6
1918	$2,000 exemption	12
1919–1921	$2,000 exemption	10
1922–1924	$2,000 exemption	12.5
1925	$2,000 exemption	13
1926–1927	$2,000 exemption	13.5
1928	$3,000 exemption	12
1929	$3,000 exemption	11
1930–1931	$3,000 exemption	12
1932–1935	None	13.75
1936–1937	Graduated normal tax ranging from—	
	First $2,000	8
	Over $40,000	15
	Graduated surtax on undistributed profits ranging from—	7–27
1938–1939	First $25,000	12.5–16
	Over $25,000	19[b]
1940	First $25,000	14.85–18.7
	$25,000 to $31,964.30	38.3
	$31,964.30 to $38,565.89	36.9
	Over $38,565.89	24
1941	First $25,000	21–25
	$25,000 to $38,461.54	44
	Over $38,461.54	31
1942–1945	First $25,000	25–29
	$25,000 to $50,000	53
	Over $50,000	40
1946–1949	First $25,000	21–25
	$25,000 to $50,000	53
	Over $50,000	38
1950	First $25,000	23
	Over $25,000	42
1951	First $25,000	28.75
	Over $25,000	50.75
1952–1963	First $25,000	30
	Over $25,000	52
1964	First $25,000	22
	Over $25,000	50
1965–1967	First $25,000	22
	Over $25,000	48
1968–1969	First $25,000	24.2[c]
	Over $25,000	52.8[c]

TABLE 12-1 (*continued*)

Year	Rate Brackets or Exemptions	Rate[a] (percent)
1970	First $25,000	22.55[c]
	Over $25,000	49.2[c]
1971–1974	First $25,000	22
	Over $25,000	48
1975–1978	First $25,000	20
	Next $25,000	22
	Over $50,000	48
1979–1981	First $25,000	17
	$25,000 to $50,000	20
	$50,000 to $75,000	30
	$75,000 to $100,000	40
	Over $100,000	46
1982	First $25,000	16
	$25,000 to $50,000	19
	$50,000 to $75,000	30
	$75,000 to $100,000	40
	Over $100,000	46
1983–1986	First $25,000	15
	$25,000 to $50,000	18
	$50,000 to $75,000	30
	$75,000 to $100,000	40
	Over $100,000	46
1987[d]	First $50,000	15
	$50,000 to $75,000	25
	Over $75,000[e]	34

[a] In addition to the rates shown, certain types of "excess profits" levies were in effect in 1917–1921, 1933–1945, and 1950–1953.
[b] Less adjustments: 14.025% of dividends received and 2.5% of dividends paid.
[c] Includes surcharge of 10% in 1968 and 1969 and 2.5% in 1970.
[d] Rates shown effective for tax years beginning on or after July 1, 1987. Income in taxable years that include July 1, 1987 (other than as the first date of such year) is subject to a blended rate.
[e] An additional 5% tax is imposed on a corporation's taxable income in excess of $100,000. Maximum additional tax is $11,750; this provision phases out the benefit of graduated rates for corporations with taxable income between $100,000 and $335,000; corporations with income above $335,000, in effect, pay a flat tax at a 34% rate.

Source: Treasury Department, Office of Tax Analysis.

corporation's total tax bill, there are other tax provisions. For example, some, but not all, states have income tax provisions. A corporation may also face other taxes that are not directly related to its income.[6] Therefore, although they are closely related to a corporation's income, a corporation's total taxes are not necessarily exactly proportionate to its income. Furthermore, because of the variety of taxes a corporation faces, a corporation's marginal tax rate is rarely simply the federal income tax rate.

[6] For example, federal and state excise taxes, and state and local sales taxes. These taxes do not alter our analysis because in the case of excise and sales taxes, the tax amount is typically added directly onto the price of a product at the time the product is sold to a customer and consequently does not directly affect the corporation's incremental revenues and costs. In effect, such taxes are "taken off the top."

Because of the complexity of the tax laws, we do not attempt here to model taxes perfectly. In our presentations, we follow the convention of using a single marginal tax rate that people often think of as the federal income tax rate. However, taxes are more complex than this, and to the extent that a single rate can capture the tax effect, normally that rate is larger than the federal rate. To remind us of this, we generally use a tax rate in our examples that is different from the current maximum corporate tax rate (before surtax) of 34%.

DEPRECIATION

Throughout our examples and problems, we have assumed the use of straight-line depreciation. Very few, if any, corporations actually use straight-line depreciation for tax purposes or capital budgeting analysis (although most use it for financial reporting purposes). Straight-line depreciation is not used because of the time value of money. As long as the corporation has sufficient income that it can fully use all of its tax credits and deductions, the sooner it claims those credits and deductions, the sooner it can put the money to work earning more money. Of course, over the life of the investment, the total amount of depreciation tax deductions will be the same, regardless of the depreciation schedule that is used. However, the time value of money makes it more valuable to claim the tax deductions as soon as possible. This phenomenon was illustrated in Chapter 11 in our example showing that a corporation will prefer to expense rather than capitalize the cost of its equipment.

What depreciation method, then, is optimal for a corporation to use? This question can be answered by determining which allowable method provides the most advantageous time-value-of-money treatment for the tax credits (the product of depreciation deduction times the marginal tax rate). Of course, as we pointed out above, that answer is not necessarily the same from year to year because the allowable methods and procedures change with disturbing regularity. Therefore, there is little point in memorizing the fact that a particular method is optimal now; in all likelihood, that will not be the case by the time you use it.

There is tremendous value, however, in describing a general method for identifying the optimal depreciation schedule from whatever schedules are allowable at the time you must choose one. Even though there have been many allowable depreciation methods, as well as many different procedures for using them, the way to determine which method is optimal has not changed since the income tax laws first began requiring firms to capitalize equipment costs: ***A firm should use the depreciation method that provides the largest present value of depreciation tax credits.***

EXAMPLE ■ Suppose you are given a choice between using the straight-line method or the sum-of-the-years'-digits method to depreciate an asset that costs $110,000 and will have a salvage value of $20,000 at the end of 5 years. If the required rate of return for tax credits is 10% and the corporation pays a marginal tax rate of 40% on the income from this project, which method provides the more advantageous time-value-of-money treatment?

The sum-of-the-years'-digits method specifies the depreciation expense each year as a proportion of the difference between the purchase price and the salvage value. The procedure is as follows. First, sum the numbers 1, 2, 3, up to and including the number of years over which the asset will be depreciated. For depreciating an asset over 5 years, the sum of the years' digits is 15 (= 1 + 2 + 3 + 4 + 5), which can also be obtained from the formula $.5[n + n^2]$, where n is the number of years over which the asset will be depreciated. To determine the proportions to use each year, reverse the order of the digits and divide each digit by the sum of all the digits. Continuing with a 5-year asset, the first year's depreciation expense would be $5/15$ of the difference between the purchase price and the salvage value. Similarly, the proportions to apply in years 2 through five are $4/15$, $3/15$, $2/15$, and $1/15$, respectively.

The difference between the cost and salvage value in this case is $90,000. The straight-line method would specify a depreciation expense of $18,000 per year in each of the 5 years (= 90/5). This creates a CFAT of $7,200 (= τD = .4[18,000]) per year for each of the 5 years, which, at a discount rate of 10%, has a present value of $27,294. The sum-of-the-years'-digits method would specify depreciation expenses of $30,000 (= [5/15]90,000), $24,000 (= [4/15]90,000), $18,000, $12,000, and $6,000, which yield CFATs of $12,000 (= .4[30,000]), $9,600 (= .4[24,000]), $7,200, $4,800, and $2,400 in years 1 through 5, respectively. These CFATs have a present value of $29,021 at a discount rate of 10% (= $12,000/1.1 + 9,000/1.1^2 + \ldots$). Therefore, the sum-of-the-years'-digits method provides the larger present value of depreciation tax credits, and it should be chosen over the straight-line method. ∎

In this example, since the comparison is between straight-line depreciation and an "accelerated" method (one that allows the expense to be claimed more quickly than under the straight-line method) it is really not necessary to perform a present value calculation to determine which method provides the more advantageous treatment. As long as the firm can use the tax credits, accelerated depreciation provides the more advantageous treatment. Of course, for alternative accelerated depreciation rules, the optimal choice may not be so obvious.

OTHER METHODS OF PROJECT ANALYSIS   12.5

In our discussion of required rates of return in Chapter 10, we specified one method of incorporating the risk of the project into the analysis of the project. In that method, risk, as measured by the nondiversifiable business risk of the project, is fully reflected in the choice of discount rate. When the cash flows are discounted at the risk-adjusted required rate of return, the effect of risk is thereby included in the calculation of the project's NPV. To operationalize the impact of differential risk among projects, firms use risk classes, with a different required rate of return for each risk class. In some cases, the risk classes are represented by various divisions or groups of divisions of the firm. While this is the most widely used method of incorporating risk into the capital budgeting decision, other methods are also used, some of which are described in this section.

There are several problems with using the methods described below to incorporate risk into the analysis of a project. A major drawback most of them suffer from is that the distinction between diversifiable and nondiversifiable risk can easily be lost in the analysis. In other words, special care is necessary to ensure that the risk measure excludes diversifiable risk. Recall from Chapters 7 and 9 that diversifiable risk is not relevant to shareholders but can be very relevant to managers personally because of the difficulty of diversifying the manager's human capital.

The use of some of the methods discussed in this section, then, presents a particular problem because managers have an incentive to use them improperly. By deliberately including diversifiable risk, managers may be able to use risk as a basis for rejecting projects that have a large amount of diversifiable risk. Thus, these methods may inadvertently provide managers with a justification for rejecting projects that are undesirable from their viewpoint—even though the projects may be desirable from the shareholders' viewpoint. This aspect of capital investment analysis represents another example in which divergent interests can cause a conflict between the shareholders and the managers.

Despite the problem of including diversifiable risk, as well as other problems, the methods are presented and discussed because in some cases, they are tools that might provide additional insights into the value of an investment. They can be especially useful when it is not possible to determine a market-based estimate of the required rate of return for an investment. Generally, the use of the techniques described below requires more expertise than is provided here. However, it is important to know of their existence and the benefits and problems associated with using them. Additional expertise can be obtained from additional study or from support staff who are well versed in such quantitative methods. In fact, you have or will undoubtedly come across some or all of these methods in other course work.

BREAK-EVEN

The **break-even point** is where the total contribution margin exactly equals the total fixed cost of producing a product or service. The contribution margin is the difference between revenue and variable cost. For example, if revenue is $15 per unit for a product and the variable cost of producing a unit of the product is $10, the contribution margin is $5 per unit. With a total fixed cost of $500,000, break-even is 100,000 units ($= 500,000/5$). Break-even is the point at which the accounting income is zero. But accounting income ignores the opportunity cost associated with the time value of money (among other problems), so break-even is *not* the point at which the NPV equals zero. In spite of this, break-even is commonly used as a point of analysis, so it is important to understand the pitfalls of using break-even as part of the decision criteria.

It is easy for people to believe that as long as unit sales stay above the break-even point, the firm is "making money." However, this is true only in the sense that accounting income will be positive. If sales were to continue essentially at the break-even point forever, it is most likely that the firm would be better off if it exercised its abandonment option on the project.

Consider the break-even example just given. Suppose that the firm could sell off the entire project and everything connected with it for an after-tax net salvage value of $1.2 million. Then selling the project is a positive-NPV decision if unit sales will be exactly at the break-even point forever into the future. With sales forever at the break-even point, the firm's net cash flow from the project each year will equal the tax credit from the depreciation. It is likely that the firm can sell the project now and invest the money elsewhere to generate positive expected future cash flows that have a larger present value than the present value of the tax credits from depreciation.

The actual point of indifference is the level of unit sales at which the NPV from selling or abandoning the project is zero. Additional information is necessary to determine that point. Suppose that our project has 6 more years of useful life, after which it will have a net salvage value of zero. Suppose further that depreciation will be $150,000 per year for the next 4 years and zero for the last 2 years, the firm pays taxes on the income from this project at a marginal rate of 40%, and the required rate of return on the project is 12%. The level of sales for which the NPV of selling the project equals zero can be determined by setting the NPV from selling equal to zero and solving in a backward fashion for the CFAT for $\Delta R - \Delta E$, the CFBT for $\Delta R - \Delta E$, and finally for the sales level. The NPV calculation with these unknowns is

Time	Item	CFBT	CFAT	PV @ 12%
0	salvage	1,200,000	1,200,000	1,200,000
1–6	$\Delta R - \Delta E$	?	?	?
1–4	Depreciation (lost)	0	−60,000/yr	−182,241
			NPV =	0

and therefore the project must produce a present value of $1,017,759 (= 1,200,000 − 182,241). Solving for the corresponding annuity payment implies that the CFAT is $247,545 per year and thus the CFBT equals $412,575 per year (= 247,545/[1−.4]). The CFBT per year for $\Delta R - \Delta E$ is the total contribution margin minus the fixed cost. Denoting the number of units sold as Q, the contribution margin per unit as c, and the fixed cost per year as F, CFBT is given as

$$\text{CFBT} = cQ - F \tag{12.5}$$

and, solving for Q, we have

$$Q = \frac{\text{CFBT} + F}{c} = \frac{412,575 + 500,000}{5} = 182,515$$

Therefore, the indifference point—what might be called the "true" break-even—is a sales level of 182,515 units per year for the next 6 years. This sales level is almost twice the 100,000 level at which accounting income is zero. While the relationship between the indifference point and break-even is specific to the parameters of the situation, the indifference point is, in virtually all cases, considerably larger than what is commonly referred to as break-even.

Determining the indifference point of the project, the unit sales level per period at which the NPV of the project is zero, provides one with a "feel" for the project by putting the NPV in terms of the number of units that must be sold per year to have a worthwhile investment—and this applies to prospective new, as well as ongoing, projects. An additional "sense" of a project can be obtained by determining how sensitive the project's NPV is to variations in the annual sales level. This latter notion is called sensitivity analysis.

SENSITIVITY ANALYSIS

Sensitivity analysis is a technique that can provide some insight into a project's operating leverage. Operating leverage, as we have noted, affects the risk of a project. Therefore, the risk of the project's revenues depends upon the process that will be used to generate them. Recall that the term *leverage* comes from the mechanical lever, which allows a person to lift a heavy object with less effort than would otherwise be necessary. If you imagine a lever, where the pivotal point is called the fulcrum, break-even is the fulcrum for operating leverage.

Essentially, operating leverage refers to the effect that a change in sales will have on profit. A high (low) level of operating leverage means that a relatively small (large) change in sales will cause a relatively large (small) change in profit. Therefore, one way to get a feel for how much operating leverage a project has is to examine the sensitivity of its NPV to variations in the sales level.

In essence, it is the steepness of the slope (relationship) of profit as a function of

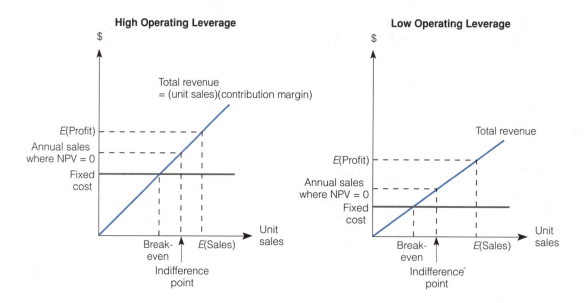

FIGURE 12-3

Comparison of high and low operating leverage. Note that E(sales) is the same in each case. Also note the difference in the slopes of the total revenue lines.

unit sales. The slope of the profit-to-sales relationship is determined by the contribution margin. A large contribution margin makes a steep slope; profits are very sensitive to changes in sales. A small contribution margin makes a relatively flat slope; profits are fairly insensitive to changes in sales. An increase in operating leverage, then, magnifies the effect that a change in sales has on profit.

Figure 12-3 illustrates the effect of two operating leverage functions on a firm's profit. Hypothetical values that illustrate the typical relationships among the break-even, the indifference, and the expected, sales levels for a positive-NPV project are shown. Notice that while the expected level of sales is identical for the two cases, break-even, the indifference point, and expected profit are all higher for the high-leverage case. These differences, of course, are due to the difference in risk between high and low leverage.

A common way to get a "feel" for the operating leverage of a project—its profit sensitivity—is to estimate optimistic, expected, and pessimistic levels for future annual sales. Extending the break-even example, suppose that optimistic, expected, and pessimistic estimates for future sales levels are, respectively, 250,000, 200,000, and 150,000. At the expected sales level, yearly CFBT for $\Delta R - \Delta E$ is given by Equation (12.5):

$$\text{CFBT} = cQ - F = 5(200,000) - 500,000 = \$500,000$$

The NPV for keeping the project, at the expected sales level, is

Time	Item	CFBT	CFAT	PV @ 12%
0	Salvage (forgone)	−1,200,000	−1,200,000	−1,200,000
1–6	$\Delta R - \Delta E$	500,000/yr	300,000/yr	1,233,422
1–4	Depreciation	0	60,000/yr	182,241
			NPV =	$ 215,663

Problem A4 asks you to verify that the NPV at the optimistic and pessimistic sales levels are $832,374 and −$401,048, respectively.

The range of NPV outcomes given by sensitivity analysis provides an estimate of the operating leverage of the project. If the optimistic and pessimistic sales estimates had been 75,000 and 400,000 instead of 150,000 and 250,000, respectively, the variation in the NPVs would have been much larger, ranging from −$1,326,115 to +$3,195,930. Comparisons such as these provide further insight into the nature of the project; however, as already noted, extreme care is necessary to exclude diversifiable risk from the analysis. When the variation in the sales level is due to economy-wide or industry-wide factors, such as total market size, it represents nondiversifiable risk for the most part. In contrast, when the variation is due to factors that are specific to the firm, such as market share, the risk is diversifiable for the most part.

Obviously, sensitivity analysis can be performed with respect to any parameter in the NPV computation. However, special care is also necessary when combining optimistic and pessimistic estimates for multiple parameters because the parameter values may be positively, negatively, or not at all correlated with one another. It is important to avoid the tendency to view the combinations of parameter outcomes as equally likely. For example, a high variable cost per unit, which causes the industry to set a high selling price, affects the total market size. Thus, a pessimistic market size is more likely to occur with a pessimistic variable cost.

DECISION TREES

As with some of the other techniques discussed in this chapter, you may have encountered decision trees in other course work.[7] If you have, you may recall that a decision tree is particularly valuable as a visual aid to identifying all of the relevant cash flows and their probabilities, thereby enhancing your understanding of a situation. In fact, we used a decision tree format for Headcleaner's postponement decision for Q-10 at the start of the chapter. You might also recall that we used a decision tree approach to derive the two-state option pricing model in Chapter 8. In that model, the set of possible outcomes is represented by what might be called "branches," where a subsequent outcome depends upon previous outcomes. All final outcomes result from following a "path" along what looks like the branch of a tree. A decision tree is similar to the two-state OPM, except that in addition to including "forks" for probabilistic outcomes, "forks" for managerial decisions are included in the picture. The application of a decision tree is illustrated in the following example.

Woody's Hazing, Inc. manufactures a line of window film for blocking out the sun, called Buckeye Vision. Recently, the research and development laboratory at Woody's has come up with a promising new idea. The question facing the company is whether to develop the idea further in the hopes that it will lead to a new product. The first decision, then, is whether to spend $600,000 further developing the idea, which creates a decision fork. If the development is undertaken, there is a probabilistic outcome fork where the outcome can be a major advance, a minor advance, or a bad idea. If it turns out to be a major or minor advance, Woody's is faced with a decision fork concerning whether to conduct a marketing research study of the new

---

[7]Particular analytical techniques you might encounter in other course work that also use the "decision tree" approach include the critical path method (CPM), and the program evaluation and review technique (PERT).

A decision tree. Note that the terminal NPV's (in $ millions) are given without supporting computations, to simplify the analysis.

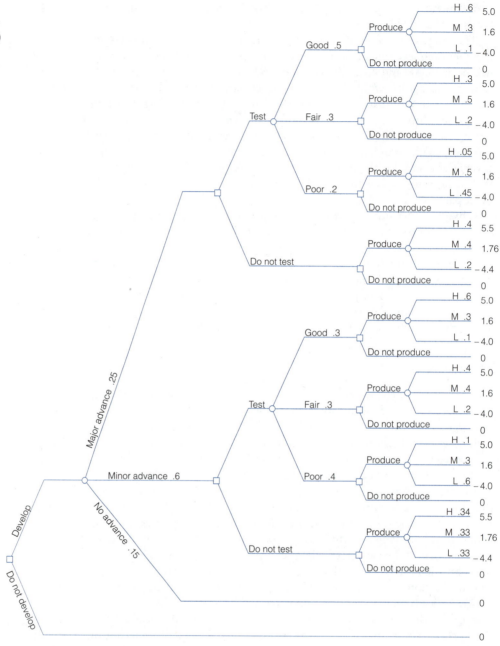

product at a cost of $250,000. The outcome from the test marketing will be an estimate of the demand for the new product as good, fair, or poor, and depending upon the demand forecast, Woody's can decide to start production of the new product or abandon the project.[8] Finally, if production is undertaken, actual sales for the product can turn out to be high, medium, or low.

[8] Of course, the interaction of the new product with the sales and production of existing products must be considered. Also, the postponement option, which was illustrated in the Headcleaner expansion example and which will be further explored in Chapter 13, is available at various points. These considerations are left out of this example to reduce the complexity of the example.

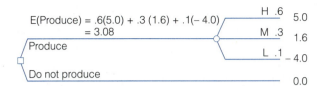

FIGURE 12-5
The production decision
(in $ millions).

In most cases, the probabilities for the outcome forks in a decision tree are what are called **subjective probabilities**, in effect, educated guesses that have been quantified into probabilities.[9] In this case, it has been estimated that further development of the new idea has a 25% chance of producing a major advance, a 60% chance of producing a minor advance, and a 15% chance of producing no advance. If a major advance occurs, the probabilities for good, fair, and poor outcomes from the marketing research are 50%, 30%, and 20%, respectively. Similarly, with a minor advance, good, fair, and poor outcomes from marketing research have probabilities of 30%, 30%, and 40%, respectively.

The entire decision tree for this problem is presented in Figure 12-4, including conditional probabilities for high, medium, and low demand, based on the marketing research outcome. The NPV of each outcome is given at the end of its branch. We will take the terminal NPV's as being given and not go into how they were estimated, for simplicity's sake. However, note that arriving at a terminal NPV depends upon the decision fork leading to that outcome. For example, the decision not to undertake production has a zero NPV. This is because, at the point *that* decision must be made, any development and marketing research costs are sunk costs. The NPVs also reflect timing differences when production is postponed to undertake test marketing.

As with any model building exercise, it is often helpful to approach the process in stages to avoid being overwhelmed by the problem. Although we actually constructed the decision tree shown in Figure 12-4 in stages, fitting it together by trial and error, it is presented in its entirety.[10]

Decision trees are solved in a backward fashion, from end to beginning, starting with each final outcome in a manner similar to solving for the indifference level of annual sales discussed in the section on break-even. The optimal choice at each decision fork is the path with the highest expected NPV. For example, with a major advance and a good outcome predicted by the marketing research, the expected NPV of production is $3.08 million (= .6[5.0] + .3[1.6] + .1[−4.0]). Therefore, with those outcomes, Woody's would choose to produce the product since the expected NPV of $3.08 from producing exceeds the zero NPV from not producing at that point. Figure 12-5 illustrates this computation. By contrast, with a minor advance and a poor outcome predicted by the marketing research, the expected value of production is −$1.42 million (= .1[5.0] + .3[1.6] + .6[−4.0]). Therefore, with

[9] While estimating such subjective probabilities can be a very difficult process, as with model building, the process often adds greatly to one's understanding of a situation.

[10] Sometimes it causes frustration (and perhaps confusion) when an instructor presents a solution to a problem that makes it appear very straightforward. The frustration occurs because it is not obvious that solving the problem from scratch takes a great deal of time. The student sees the instructor solve problems effortlessly and yet takes hours to slug through similar problems alone. We're sure your instructor is bright and capable, but remember that you do not see all the time the instructor spent making it look easy! You might find it comforting to know all the trouble it has taken to write this book, but frankly, we would find it embarrassing to tell you. We hope we are providing enough guidance so that you can follow the thought process for solving problems rather than being impressed by a "magic" solution that appears to have come out of a "black box."

this second example of outcomes, Woody's would choose not to produce the new product. By indicating the decision paths to be followed, based on probabilistic outcomes, the decision tree can be "pruned" so that the decision forks are eliminated and the presentation is simplified. For this example, the first "round" of decisions to be solved for is the set of final produce–do not produce decisions.

Following the production decisions, the next round is the set of decisions whether to test market the new product if the idea has lead to an advance. As with the decision to produce, expected values are computed to determine the optimal choice. If the decision will be to produce, regardless of the outcome from the marketing research, then the test marketing should not be undertaken. In such a case, the information from the marketing research study is not relevant to the decision since it will not alter the decision. In effect, the money would be wasted because the cost of $250,000 spent on the study exceeds the benefit from having the information that would be provided by the marketing research.

To determine whether to undertake the test marketing, we can examine the subparts of the problem that deal with that decision. Figure 12-6 illustrates the marketing research decision for the minor-advance outcome of the decision tree, including the expected values from the "pruned" production decisions. The total expected value from test marketing the new product is the expected value from the production decisions, based on the test outcome, minus the cost of test marketing the product. The computation of the total expected value from test marketing is illustrated in Figure 12-6. The expected value is $1.226 million.

To compute the expected value from producing the new product without first test marketing it, we need the probabilities of having high, medium, or low demand. These can be obtained by multiplying the probabilities of sequential outcomes and summing common final outcomes. For example, because high demand could occur whether the outcome from the market test would have been good, fair, or poor, the probability of high demand is the sum of the probabilities under each possible outcome. For example, a 30% chance of a good market test result followed by a 60% chance of high demand produces an 18% (30% times 60%) chance of that final outcome. The total probability of all of the possible high-demand outcomes is then $(.3)(.6) + (.3)(.4) + (.4)(.1) = .34$, or 34%. The calculations for the probabilities of medium and low demand are also given in Figure 12-6. Based on the probabilities for high, medium, and low demand, the expected value for producing the new product, without first test marketing it, equals $.9988 million.

Since the expected value from test marketing exceeds the expected value from producing the new product without the test, Woody's should test market the new product if product development has lead to a minor advance. The test marketing

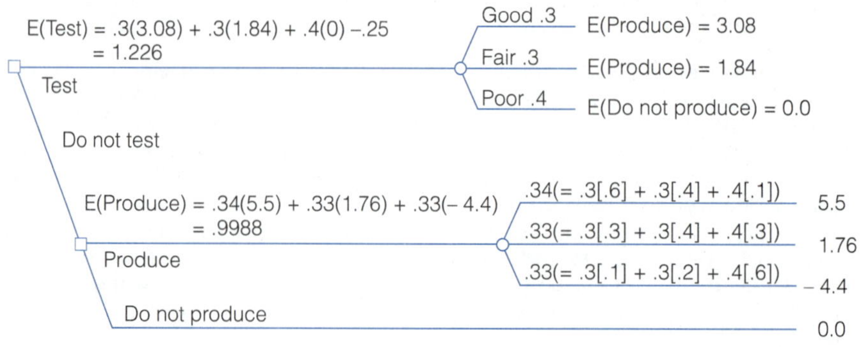

FIGURE 12-6

The test marketing decision if the development leads to a minor advance (in $ millions).

decision is also relevant if product development has lead to a major advance. Problem B13 asks you to determine the optimal choice for this outcome by calculating the relevant expected values.

THE EXPECTED VALUE OF ADDITIONAL INFORMATION An interesting extension to the decision as to whether or not to test market the product is to ask the question "Of what value is the additional information to be obtained from the test?" This value can be determined from the expected values calculated in Figure 12-6. The expected value without the test is $.9988 million. If the test marketing was costless, the expected value with the test would be $1.476 million. As long as the cost of running the test is less than the difference between the two, the test is valuable. Therefore, the value of the additional information from the test must be exactly this difference, which is given by

$$\text{Information value} = \text{EV(test)} - \text{EV(no test)} + \text{Cost of test} \qquad \textbf{(12.6)}$$

where EV denotes expected value. For this example, then,

$$\text{Information value} = 1.226 - .9988 + .25 = \$.4772 \text{ million}$$

THE EXPECTED VALUE OF PERFECT INFORMATION The idea of information value can be further extended to consider the **expected value of perfect information.** Suppose there is a test that would provide a perfect prediction of high, medium, or low demand. The probabilities of high, medium, and low demand are calculated in Figure 12-6 as .34, .33, and .33, respectively. If low demand is forecast, Woody's will choose not to produce the new product and will realize an NPV of zero. Otherwise, Woody's will produce the product and earn an NPV of either 5.0 or 1.6. Therefore, the expected value of this "perfect test," if it was costless, is $2.228 million (= .34[5.0] + .33[1.6] + .33[0]), and the expected value of perfect information, denoted EVPI, is

$$\text{EVPI} = \text{EV(perfect test)} - \text{EV(no test)} \qquad \textbf{(12.7)}$$

which in this case is

$$\text{EVPI} = 2.228 - .9988 = \$1.2292 \text{ million}$$

Therefore, in this example, Woody's would increase the expected value of the project by spending up to $1.2292 million for perfect test information if it were available. Knowing the EVPI is especially useful when a variety of alternative tests, each with a different cost, are being considered because any test with a cost that exceeds the EVPI can be immediately eliminated without further consideration. After all, since a test cannot provide better than perfect information, it cannot be worth more than perfect information!

We can now decide whether Woody's should spend $600,000 to develop the new idea by analyzing the "pruned" decision tree for this example, given in Figure 12-7. The expected value of developing the idea equals the outcomes weighted by their probabilities minus the $.6 million cost of developing the idea. This is shown to be $.6416 million in Figure 12-7. Thus, the development project has a positive NPV and should be undertaken.

From the complexity in this relatively simple (even simpleminded) example, you should be able to see that it is possible for the analysis of a real-world decision to overwhelm the decision-maker. Although computer software packages are available to help construct and solve decision-tree problems, such packages rarely deal suc-

FIGURE 12-7

The development decision and the "pruned" decision tree (in $ millions).

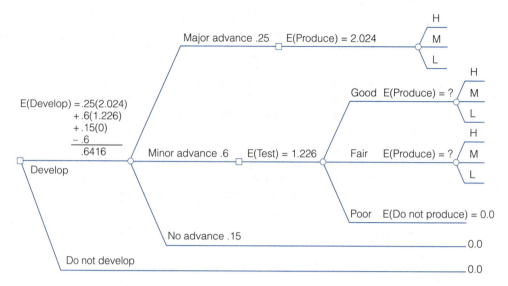

FIGURE 12-7

The development decision and the "pruned" decision tree (in $ millions).

cessfully with the question of risk. In the above example, we have "finessed" the question of differential risk and required rates of return by simply providing the NPVs. In cases such as this example, it can be argued that a variety of discount rates should be used to reflect risk differences among the various decisions. We have no general solution to this problem, other than to reiterate our warning about diversifiable risk, suggest that the analysis be kept as simple as possible by discarding pieces that are no longer relevant, and provide the following advice: As you build the model, apply the basic concepts developed in this chapter carefully to ensure that nothing that could have a significant bearing on the decision has been overlooked.

MONTE CARLO SIMULATION

Airline pilots receive some of their training on flight simulators. A flight simulator is a physical model that simulates (i.e., attempts to reproduce exactly) what it is like to pilot a particular type of aircraft under a variety of circumstances. Physically, the pilot sits in the model, which is an exact replica of the cockpit of the airplane being simulated. Video equipment provides a visual scene that appears for the pilot through the cockpit windows, while outside, the model is mounted on a complex set of hydraulic equipment that creates motion like that of flying. Flight simulators are very complex and very expensive to create and/or purchase, but a flight simulator can help pilots discover better methods of responding to emergency situations. Generally, the use of flight simulators is thought to produce better-trained pilots than would otherwise be possible. **Monte Carlo simulation** or more simply, **simulation**, is a technique that uses a mathematical model to simulate a capital investment or other phenomenon.

A simulation model is similar to sensitivity analysis in that it can be used to attempt to answer "what-if" questions. The model relies on random sampling from probability distributions of outcomes. Using a computer, a simulation model can assess the likelihood of particular outcomes by sampling (simulating) a large number of outcomes. Often, in statistics courses, a coin is flipped a number of times to illustrate that the number of resulting "heads" actually does turn out to be very close to the 50% that is theoretically estimated using probability theory. This is a simple simulation experiment. Flipping two coins and observing that both are "heads" about 25% of the time is a slightly more complex simulation experiment. With two coins, of course, the probability of two "heads" can be theoretically computed by multiplying the probabilities of the individual outcomes together; .5 for the occurrence of "heads" on the first coin times .5 for the occurrence of "heads" on the second coin equals .25 for the combined event. While the probabilities of combined outcomes in simple cases such as these coin examples can be determined using probability theory, it is not hard to imagine situations too complex to derive mathematically the probabilities of all the possible outcomes. By making assumptions about the joint probability distributions of the random variables, outcome probabilities can be determined for complex situations using a Monte Carlo simulation model.

We are not going to illustrate an application of simulation because of the complexity of such examples. However, as with the other methods discussed in this section, we will point out the major benefits and pitfalls of using simulation.

There are two major benefits from using simulation, both of which result from the model-building process. First, the process of building the simulation model can provide valuable insights into the problem at hand. The very framework that must be built requires extensive understanding. The model-building process fosters such an understanding, and insights are a by-product that comes with it. The second benefit is that a simulation model can describe a situation that may be indescribable in simple terms. That is, although we may not be able to immediately determine the answer, by dissecting the problem and evaluating the components, we can develop several methods of making a reasonable estimate. For example, the distance between two points can be estimated by summing the distance along various routes. So too with simulation models: A solution can be obtained by combining many simple components.

The major problem associated with using the simulation method is the difficulty of specifying the interrelationships among the parameters and variables. In the case of two coins, we can reasonably assume that the two flips are independent. As we pointed out with sensitivity analysis, there can be substantial complexity amongst the parameters. In modeling real-world phenomena, rarely do we know the exact relationships among the parameters and variables. A second problem, related to the first problem, is that often the model becomes so complex so quickly that the decision-maker gives up and employs someone else, such as support staff or a consultant, to build the model. If the major value to be obtained from using simulation is an increased understanding of the problem that results from building the model, having someone else build the model reduces, or even eliminates, that value. The only advice we can offer to minimize this problem is to work closely enough with the model builder to extract whatever understanding is to be obtained.

Finally, of all the methods discussed in this section, the problem of eliminating diversifiable risk from the analysis is probably most severe for simulation. It may be virtually impossible to identify and remove diversifiable risk from the analysis.

SUMMARY

In this chapter, we have pointed out a number of factors that complicate the capital budgeting decision. Admittedly, some, such as erosion and enhancement, can pose a serious challenge. However, other factors may increase the complexity of the analysis, and yet their inclusion is fairly straightforward from a conceptual viewpoint. For example, using the equivalent annual cost method to determine an optimal replacement cycle or to choose among equipment alternatives is simply an application of the time-value-of-money mechanics.

DECISION SUMMARY BOX

- Be sure to include the effects of all economic dependencies that cause **erosion** or **enhancement** in the value of existing or other potential projects.
- The minimum equivalent annual cost, EAC, can be used to identify the optimal replacement cycle for an asset. The minimum EAC can also be used to identify the optimal asset choice from among a set of alternative assets. Do not use EAC for choosing one-time projects or choosing among assets that are subject to substantial technological change.
- Be sure to use the *current* tax laws to determine after-tax cash flows.
- For tax and capital budgeting purposes, a firm should use the depreciation method that provides the largest present value of depreciation tax credits.
- Include the effect of inflation by representing all parameters, cash flows, and discount rates for a

decision on a consistent basis—in either real *or* nominal terms. Do not mix real and nominal amounts.
- A decision tree provides an excellent visual aid for understanding critical relationships. Among other things, the decision tree framework can be used for estimating the value of additional information.
- Be sure to distinguish between accounting break-even and the level of sales for which the NPV would be zero.
- Sensitivity analysis can provide insight into a project's operating leverage by examining "what-if" questions.
- EVPI, the expected value of perfect information, specifies a maximum value that can be gained from additional information.
- Be careful to exclude diversifiable risk when using simulation.

Four alternative methods of incorporating risk considerations into a capital budgeting analysis were presented, all of which are more complex mathematically than simply selecting an appropriate risk-adjusted discount rate, as discussed in Chapter 10. All four have certain deficiencies, in particular, difficulty in eliminating diversifiable risk, which make them inappropriate as the sole method of incorporating risk into a capital budgeting analysis. Despite this drawback, you should be aware of them because they may provide additional insights into a project, especially when it is not possible to obtain a good capital-market-based estimate of the risk-adjusted required rate of return.

PROBLEMS

PROBLEM SET A

A1. Define the terms **erosion** and **enhancement** as they relate to the firm's capital investment decisions.

A2. Explain the concept of an **equivalent annual cost** in your own words.

A3. The total present value of all costs associated with an asset over a 7-year life is $73,285. If the asset has a required rate of return of 11%, what is the EAC of using this asset?

A4. Verify that the NPV for the optimistic and pessimistic sales levels in the sensitivity example are $832,374 and -$401,048, respectively.

A5. A company is considering a capital investment project that has the following expected cash flows:

Time	0	1	2	3	4	5	6
Cash flow	−70	20	30	30	20	20	10
Abandonment	—	40	35	30	20	10	10

   a. If the required rate of return for this project is 13%, should the project be undertaken?

   b. If the company accepts the project, at what point in time should it expect to abandon the project?

A6. Suppose the expected value of a decision is $734,500. Suppose further that additional information about the likelihood of various outcomes from the decision could be gathered at a cost of $87,000, and if such information was gathered, the expected value of the decision would increase to $853,225. If perfect information was gathered, the expected value of the decision would be $1,010,000.

   a. What is the expected value of perfect information (EVPI) in this case?

   b. What is the information value of gathering the additional information?

A7. Define the term **simulation**.

A8. Define the term **sensitivity analysis**.

A9. The Canton Sundae Corporation is considering the replacement of an existing machine. The new machine, called an X-tender, would provide better sundaes, but it costs $120,000. The X-tender requires $20,000 in setup costs that are expensed immediately and $20,000 in additional working capital. The X-tender's useful life is 10 years, after which it can be sold for a salvage value of $40,000. Canton uses straight-line depreciation, and the machine will be depreciated to a book value of zero on a 6-year basis. Canton has a tax rate of 45% and requires a 16% rate of return on projects like this one. The X-tender is expected to increase revenues minus expenses by $35,000 per year. What is the NPV of buying the X-tender?

A10. A machine that costs $10,000 new can be replaced after being used from 4 to 7 years. Annual maintenance costs are identical for all possible replacement cycles. If the machine has a required rate of return of 12% and the net salvage values at the end of 4 to 7 years of use are those given below, what is the optimal replacement cycle? Ignore taxes and inflation.

Number of years of use	=	4	5	6	7
Net salvage value	=	$3,800	$2,800	$1,000	−$1,000

PROBLEM SET B

B1. In the section on replacement frequency in this chapter, the example considered a cornhusker machine. Suppose that machine A could be used for a seventh year if $18,000 is spent for maintenance at the end of year 6. This is in addition to $1,000 necessary at the end of year five to use the machine a sixth year. The net salvage value will be zero. What is the EAC for a 7-year replacement cycle?

B2. Verify that the NPV of $7.193 million shown in Figure 12-1 is correct. This is the value associated with 3 years of production of Clean-e-z and only 1 year of monopolistic pricing power for Q-10.

B3. Y.B. Blue Corporation is considering two alternative machines. Machine A will cost $50,000, have expenses (excluding depreciation) of $34,000 per year, and have a useful life of 6 years. Machine B will cost $70,000, have a useful life of 5 years, and will have expenses (excluding depreciation) of

$26,000 per year. Y.B. uses straight-line depreciation and pays taxes at the rate of 35%. The required rate of return for this project is 13%. Net salvage value is zero for each machine at the end of its useful life. Assuming the project for which the machine will be used is profitable, which machine should be purchased?

B4. Verify that the NPV of $8.304 million shown in Figure 12-1 is correct. This is the value associated with 3 years of production of Clean-e-z and 2 years of monopolistic pricing power for Q-10.

B5. A project's initial investment is $40,000, and it has a 5-year life. At the end of the fifth year, the equipment is expected to be sold for $12,000 when its book value is $5,000. The actual (including inflation net salvage value) after-tax cash flows for the next 5 years are expected to be (000's omitted)

Year	1	2	3	4	5
CFAT	20	25	10	10	10

The following rates are in real terms: the required rate of return for this project is 10%, the riskless rate is 7%, and the rate of return on the market portfolio is 9%. The tax rate is 46%, and the inflation rate is 3%.
   a. What is the implied beta of the project?
   b. What is the NPV of the project?
   c. What is the equivalent annual annuity of the project?

B6. Compare and contrast the concepts of break-even and net present value. Why is NPV the correct measure of project value? What insights concerning the choice of a capital budgeting project might the break-even point provide?

B7. In what way does a decision tree differ from the two-state option pricing model developed in Chapter 8?

B8. What are the potential benefits and pitfalls associated with using sensitivity analysis?

B9. A new product called AW-SUM is being considered by Egg Streams, Un-limited. An outlay of $16 million is required for equipment to produce the new product, and additional net working capital in the amount of $3.2 million is also required. The project is expected to have an 8-year life and the equipment will be depreciated on a straight-line basis to a zero book value over 8 years. Although the equipment will be depreciated to a zero book value, it is expected to have a salvage value of $2 million. Revenues minus expenses for the project are expected to be $5 million per year. The required rate of return for this project is 16%, and the relevant tax rate is 35%. Compute the NPV of the AW-SUM project.

B10. How does nondiversifiable risk create a pitfall in the use of simulation?

B11. Depreciation provides a sort of shield against taxes. If there were no taxes, there would be no depreciation tax shields.
   a. Does this mean that the NPV of the AW-SUM project in problem B9 would be less if there were no taxes?
   b. Compute the NPV of the AW-SUM project in problem B9, assuming a tax rate of 0% and that the required rate of return is 16%.

B12. Discuss the importance of the concept of economic dependence to a corporation such as IBM when it considers introducing a new product.

B13. Calculate the relevant expected values and determine the optimal choice for the test marketing decision in the Woody's Hazing example, assuming that product development has lead to a major advance.

PROBLEM SET C

C1. A machine has an NPV of $1500 for one 4–year replacement cycle. The required rate of return for this machine is 12%.
  a. What is the EAA (equivalent annual annuity) for the NPV of this machine?
  b. What would be the NPV from an infinite series of EAAs in part a?
  c. Show that the total NPV from earning an NPV of $1500 on this project at the start of every 4–year cycle, with an infinite series of future replacements is equal to the NPV computed in part b. (*Hint*: first compute the effective 4–year rate, then apply it to compute the present value of an infinite **annuity due** (payments at the *start* of the period) of $1500.)

C2. An increase in net working capital is an important and necessary part of the incremental cost of a capital budgeting project. The method we used to account for the impact of an increase in net working capital on the value of a project is to treat the increase as an outflow at the start of the project and as an inflow at the end of the project.
  a. Compute the cost in present value terms of a change in net working capital of $100,000 for a 10–year project if the hurdle rate for the project is 12%.
  b. Illustrate that this cost can also be accounted for by computing the yearly opportunity cost associated with the increase in net working capital. That is, 12% of $100,000 is $12,000 per year. Compute the present value of $12,000 per year for 10 years at 12%.
  c. Explain why these two methods of accounting for the cost of an increase in net working capital are equivalent.

C3. Letter–Fly, Unlimited, a conglomerate corporation with investments in overnight mail service and skeet–shooting franchises, is contemplating a 5–year investment project that requires an initial investment of $200,000 for equipment (depreciated over 5 years on a straight–line basis to a zero salvage value). The project also requires $25,000 in additional net working capital and is expected to have a salvage value of zero. The revenues from the project are expected to be $100,000 in the first year and to grow with inflation at 3.5% per year over the life of the project. Expenses are expected to be $25,000 in the first year and to grow at a different inflation rate of 6% per year. The general level of inflation for the economy is expected to be 5% per year. If the required rate of return on this project in real terms is 8% and taxes are paid at the rate of 32%, should Letter–Fly undertake the investment project?

C4. From one point of view, inflation does not create a problem in the evaluation of a capital budgeting project. From another point of view, inflation creates tremendous problems in the evaluation of a capital budgeting project. What are these two points of view?

C5. J. Hopkins, Inc. has decided to produce a new product. The product is most likely (probability = .75) to generate $700,000 per year in new revenues. If revenues are at or above this figure and this product is accepted by the public, its product life is permanent into the foreseeable future. However, while expected sales are high, there is a 25% chance that the product will not be well received by the public, in which case the project will be shut down after 1 year. Even if it is shut down after 1 year, it is expected that the project will produce revenues of $180,000. This product can be produced using either of two methods. Method A requires an initial investment in equipment of

$200,000 and annual expenses of $305,000. The equipment will be depreciated over 5 years to a zero book value on a straight-line basis, but it has an expected useful life of 10 years with a salvage value of zero. If the project fails, it will cost $50,000 to shut down. Method B requires an initial investment in equipment of $815,000 but annual expenses of only $75,000. The equipment for method B will also be depreciated over 5 years to a zero book value on a straight-line basis, but it has an expected useful life of 7 years with a salvage value of minus $50,000, due to removal costs. If the project fails, the salvage value for the project will be $75,000 if method B has been used. J. Hopkins has a tax rate of 37%, and this project has a required rate of return of 18%. How should J. Hopkins proceed with this project?

C6. What level of revenues per year in the previous problem would make J. Hopkins, Inc. indifferent to the project using method A?

C7. Ronald-Ray's Orchards, Inc. has always sent its payroll out to a local CPA firm for processing. Recently, Ron has been considering the purchase of a computer and necessary associated hardware to process the payroll himself. The CPA firm Ron currently uses charges $3,050 per year to process the payroll. Ron has investigated computer hardware and software, and found out that he can purchase the necessary hardware for $2,500 and a software package for $750 plus a $75-per-year charge to update the package, starting next year. To set the process up will take about 2 weeks of Ron's time (at $1,000 per week) and cost $4,000 for a consultant. After the procedure is set up, supplies and Ron's time will amount to $480 per year. The hardware, software, and consultant cost will be depreciated on a 4-year straight-line basis, but the useful life is expected to be 8 years with a salvage value of zero. If Ron's tax rate is 30% and the required rate of return for this project is 15%, should Ron undertake doing the payroll himself?

REFERENCES

Bey, Roger P. "Capital Budgeting Decisions When Cash Flows and Project Lives Are Stochastic and Dependent." *Journal of Financial Research* 6 (Fall 1983): 175–85.

Bey, Roger P., and J. Clayton Singleton. "Autocorrelated Cash Flows and the Selection of a Portfolio of Capital Assets." *Decision Sciences* 8 (October 1978): 640–57.

Brenner, Menachem, and Itzhak Venezia. "The Effects of Inflation and Taxes on Growth Investments and Replacement Policies." *Journal of Finance* 38 (December 1983): 1519–28.

Chen, Son-Nan, and William T. Moore. "Investment Decisions Under Uncertainty: Application of Estimation Risk in the Hillier Approach." *Journal of Financial and Quantitative Analysis* 17 (September 1982): 425–40.

Dyl, E. A., and H. W. Long. "Abandonment Value and Capital Budgeting: Comment." *Journal of Finance* 24 (March 1969): 88–95.

Emery, Gary W. "Some Guidelines for Evaluating Capital Investment Alternatives with Unequal Lives." *Financial Management* 11 (Spring 1982): 14–19.

Gaumnitz, Jack E., and Douglas R. Emery. "Asset Growth, Abandonment Value and the Replacement of Like-For-Like Capital Assets." *Journal of Financial and Quantitative Analysis* 15 (June 1980): 407–19.

Howe, Keith M., and Harvey Lapan. "Inflation and Asset Life: The Darby Versus the Fisher Effect." *Journal of Financial and Quantitative Analysis* 22 (June 1987): 249–58.

Howe, Keith M., and George M. McCabe. "On Optimal Asset Abandonment and Replacement." *Journal of Financial and Quantitative Analysis* 18 (September 1983): 295–305.

Rappaport, A., and R. A. Taggart, Jr. "Evaluation of Capital Expenditure Proposals Under Inflation." *Financial Management* 11 (Spring 1982): 5–13.

Robichek, A. A., and James C. Van Horne. "Abandonment Value and Capital Budgeting."
  Journal of Finance 22 (December 1967): 577–89.
Robichek, A. A., and James C. Van Horne. "Abandonment Value and Capital Budgeting:
  Reply." *Journal of Finance* 24 (March 1969): 96–97.
Van Horne, James C. "A Note on Biases in Capital Budgeting Introduced by Inflation."
  Journal of Financial and Quantitative Analysis 6 (March 1971): 653–58.

13

CAPITAL BUDGETING IN PRACTICE

In this chapter, we continue our investigation of factors that complicate the capital budgeting process, focusing especially on the important aspects of capital budgeting decisions in practice. The principle that options are valuable is straightforward, but its application in valuing a capital budgeting project can be very challenging. Similarly, opportunity costs play an extremely important role in determining the value of an investment project and should be included. Of course, they must first be identified. This chapter provides ideas for places to look for options and opportunity costs caused by interaction among existing and potential investment projects.

Another kind of interaction that can occur among projects arises from a practice called **capital rationing**, whereby management places certain limits on the firm's new investment projects, such as a limitation on the total amount of funds that can be expended on projects during the upcoming year. On the one hand, such artificial limits may cause a firm to pass up positive-NPV projects. On the other hand, what is called "soft" capital rationing provides management with a practical tool for planning and coordinating current and future capital investments. The distribution of managerial responsibility and the use of managerial incentives are two other useful tools for managing the firm's investment decisions.

The chapter ends with a discussion of additional practical considerations in the capital budgeting process. Some other factors that can be subtle and difficult to quantify in practice are pointed out. Finally, an overview, with practical reminders concerning the importance of the Principles of Finance, is given.

13.1 A PROPOSAL FOR CAPACITY EXPANSION

In addition to the new packaging machine proposal analyzed in Chapter 11, Rocky Mountain Chemical Corporation (RMC) has several other capital investment projects under consideration. If undertaken, these projects will be financed with funds from a new bond issue that RMC made earlier this month. One of the projects is a proposal to expand RMC's production capacity for one of its consumer products that is produced at its Colorado plant. The product is a relatively unique specialty facial soap, called Smooooth. This year's sales are running substantially ahead of last year's and are currently just about at the plant capacity of 10 million bars per year. It is projected that next year's sales could be over 11 million bars if RMC has the production capacity to produce that much soap. Further, it is projected that if RMC spends an additional $500,000 per year on advertising in each of the next 3 years, sales will be 12 million next year, 13 million the year after, and 14.5 million per year following that for the foreseeable future.

The proposal under consideration is to increase Rocky Mountain's production capacity for Smooooth soap by 65%. Before-tax initial outlays for the project are expected to total $1.85 million. Of this amount, $50,000 is an increase in working capital. Capitalized space and equipment costs will be $1.45 million, installation costs that must be capitalized will be $250,000, and costs associated with the installation that can be expensed immediately will be $100,000. This last amount can be expensed immediately because it stems from the temporary reassignment of current employees.[1] All of the capitalized expenses will be depreciated to a zero book value on a straight-line basis over 8 years. However, the additional facility is expected to be able to produce for 10 years if a substantial overhaul of the equipment is done at the end of the sixth year. The overhaul is expected to cost $200,000 and will be expensed (rather than capitalized) at the time of the overhaul. Depreciation, therefore, will be $212,500 per year $(= [1.45+.25]/8)$ for the first 8 years and zero for the last 2 years of the project. The salvage value of the new equipment (scrap value minus the cost of removal and cleanup) is expected to be zero at the end of the 10 years.

The wholesale price for Smooooth soap is $.612 per bar, and the variable costs of production amount to $.387 per bar, so RMC earns a contribution margin of $.225 per bar on Smooooth. The additional 4.5 million bars sold in years 3 through 10 will therefore generate an increase of $1,012,500 $(= \$.225$ times 4.5 million) in revenue minus expenses each year. The increase for years 1 and 2 will be $450,000 and $675,000, respectively. RMC's marginal tax rate is 40%, and the required rate of return for this project is 16%. What is the NPV of this project?

A computation of the net present value of the proposed expansion is given in Table 13-1. Notice once again that financing charges do not appear explicitly anywhere in the analysis, even though the funds for the project will come from RMC's recent bond issue. The financing opportunity costs are part of the project's required rate of return. The NPV of the project is computed to be $342,266; by trial and error, the IRR is found to be about 19.7%, which exceeds the hurdle rate of 16%. Finally, since the NPV is positive, the profitability index is also positive and equals .189 $(= 342,266/[1,700,000 + 60,000 + 50,000])$. At this point, it would be easy to think that the project should be undertaken. However, while the project looks good in this light, there is an important option that has been left out of the analysis thus far.

THE PRICE SETTING OPTION

The NPV computed for RMC's capacity expansion proposal is incomplete. Because the expansion project was assumed to be economically independent of existing operations, a valuable option has been left out of the analysis that creates an opportunity cost. Therefore, the NPV computation for the expansion is wrong. We failed to consider the alternative of raising the wholesale price for Smooooth soap.

Consider the possibility of raising the price from $.612 to $.629, and suppose such an increase in price will cause a decrease in demand for next year from what would have been about 11 million bars to 10.2 million bars. Since the plant's current production capacity is only 10 million, all of next year's production capacity could be sold at this higher price—and this is possible without any additional cash outflows for equipment, advertising, or net working capital. Based on the sales projections given in the proposal for the next 10 years, the demand for Smooooth soap at a wholesale price of $.629 is expected to exceed 10 million bars per year. With an increase of $.017 over the current price, RMC would have additional before-tax reve-

---

[1] Although these employees will be paid anyway, their wages become an opportunity cost if the project is undertaken. This is because the company will lose the work normally done by these employees while they help with the installation process. This phenomenon can also occur with respect to managerial time.

TABLE 13-1   NPV Analysis for Smooooth Production Capacity Expansion

Time	Item	CFBT	CFAT	PV
0	Capitalized installation and equipment cost	$-1,700,000$ $-I_0$	$-1,700,000$ $-I_0$	$-1,700,000$
0	Expensed installation cost	$-100,000$ $-E_0$	$-60,000$ $-(1-\tau)E_0$	$-60,000$
0	Change in net working capital	$-50,000$ $-\Delta W$	$-50,000$ $-\Delta W$	$-50,000$
1–3	Additional advertising expense	$-500,000/\text{yr}$ $-\Delta E$	$-300,000/\text{yr}$ $-(1-\tau)\Delta E$	$-673,767$
1–8	Depreciation	0 0	$85,000/\text{yr}$ τD	$369,205$
1	Change in revenues minus expenses	$450,000/\text{yr}$ $\Delta R - \Delta E$	$270,000/\text{yr}$ $(1-\tau)(\Delta R - \Delta E)$	$232,759$
2	Change in revenues minus expenses	$675,000/\text{yr}$ $\Delta R - \Delta E$	$405,000/\text{yr}$ $(1-\tau)(\Delta R - \Delta E)$	$300,981$
3–10	Change in revenues minus expenses	$1,012,000/\text{yr}$ $\Delta R - \Delta E$	$607,500/\text{yr}$ $(1-\tau)(\Delta R - \Delta E)$	$1,961,007$
6	Overhaul expense	$-200,000$ $-\Delta E$	$-120,000$ $-(1-\tau)\Delta E$	$-49,253$
10	Return of net working capital	$50,000$ ΔW	$50,000$ ΔW	$11,334$
			NPV =	$342,266

nues of $170,000 (= $.017[10 million]) per year, which provides an increase in after-tax revenues of $102,000 (= 170,000[1 − .4]) per year.

As an alternative to the expansion plan, then, RMC can increase its wholesale price and obtain an increase of $102,000 in its annual net CFAT—*with no other changes whatsoever in its after-tax cash flows.* A quick calculation on your calculator will show you that the present value of $102,000 per year for 10 years at a discount rate of 16% is $492,989, which is actually larger than the $342,266 generated by the expansion plan. Therefore, while the expansion plan is good (better than the status quo), the alternative of increasing the price is better. The analysis in Table 13-1 ignores the opportunity for RMC to increase the wholesale price for Smooooth soap, thereby overlooking a very significant opportunity cost.

Suppose that, based on extensive marketing research, RMC has determined the demand curve for Smooooth soap to be given as

$$\text{Demand} = \frac{2.538 \text{ million}}{(\text{price})^3}$$

We ask you in problem C7 to show that marginal revenue exceeds the $.387 marginal cost per bar for production levels up to 12,974,330. Accordingly, to optimize its price setting based on its *current* production capacity, RMC should set the demand equal to its desired production level of 10 million and solve for the price that will produce that demand, which is $.633. Of course, estimating a demand curve is not a trivial task. There are many dimensions that must be taken into account, such as consumers substituting other products and the likelihood that a competing product will become available. In spite of the cost and difficulty of obtaining it, an estimate of the demand curve for a product may be very valuable. In any case, the analysis for a proposed expansion should always include consideration of the price setting option and the opportunity costs associated with that option.

Another aspect of our analysis of RMC's price setting option involves the required rate of return. The required rate of return for the proposed wholesale price change should probably be less than the required rate of return for the capacity expansion proposal. This is because it is a less risky alternative. The firm will have more operating leverage, and hence more business risk, if it undertakes the expansion. If demand were to decline in the future, the price could be reduced under either alternative to stimulate demand. However, the firm's fixed costs will be higher under the expansion alternative. Using a discount rate that is less than 16% would of course raise the NPV of the price increase alternative.

Flexibility in product pricing is another illustration of the importance of "hidden options," and demonstrates once again the principle that options are valuable. Price flexibility is a very valuable tool that is available to the firm. Automobile manufactures have exercised this option and popularized cash rebates as a form of price reduction to stimulate demand. Similarly, firms should consider price *increases* among their alternative actions. We do not mean to imply that price stability may not also be beneficial; however, to be complete, any analysis must include consideration of the option to change the price of a product.

CAPITAL BUDGETING OPTIONS 13.2

There are many options connected with any investment a firm might undertake. In the capacity expansion example just given, the value of the price setting option was investigated. In the previous chapter, we analyzed the replacement decision and noted that a replacement option is always open to the firm. If an option is ignored, the firm may be incurring an opportunity cost. Therefore, the value of all of the options that are connected with a capital investment project must be considered if we are to measure the NPV of the investment correctly.

How does the firm value an option with respect to one of its proposed capital investment projects? Recall that an option is the right to do something without the obligation. The Options Principle is based on this tenet. When an option associated with a capital investment project is costless, it can only add to the value of that project. Of course, not all options are costless, and therefore the value of a capital investment project can be expressed as its "basic" NPV plus the value of all of the options associated with the project minus any cost associated with obtaining and/or maintaining those options, or

$$\text{Project value} = \text{NPV} + \text{Value of options} - \text{Cost of options} \qquad (13.1)$$

While Equation (13.1) is simple from one viewpoint, there is more to the story. We noted previously that we do not have an option pricing model for conveniently determining the value of more frequent replacement. Unfortunately, the same problem exists for many of the other options that are discussed in this section. It is important to understand that the lack of a convenient option pricing model does not diminish the importance of such managerial options, which have been shown to have substantial value. For example, a gold mine has been used to illustrate the value such options can have.[2] In that example, the option to shut down the mine during times when the price of gold is too low to make extraction profitable and reopen it

[2] Brennan and Schwartz (1985).

whenever extraction becomes profitable again, is shown to increase substantially the value of the mine.

Options are valuable, but recall from Chapter 8 that there are certain problems associated with combining option values. When an option associated with a capital investment project is exercised, other options are often precluded. In effect, at the time one option is exercised, other options are eliminated, and simultaneously many costs become sunk costs. Thus, the decision to exercise an option must include in the analysis the value of all alternative actions. Otherwise, the firm may incur an opportunity cost by choosing a suboptimal alternative.

Below, we discuss three other options that occur with respect to capital investment projects and provide a very important warning about including the value of such options in the decision to undertake a project.

FUTURE INVESTMENT OPPORTUNITIES

In Chapter 6, we presented a method of valuing stock called the Gordon Growth Model. We showed that probably the most important, as well as the most difficult, factor in determining the value of a stock is estimating the net present value of the firm's future investments, NPVFI. Likewise, future investment options can provide a significant source of value for a capital investment project, and they can be very difficult to value. In fact, in many cases, managers will argue that the largest part of the value to be obtained from undertaking the project is the option to identify additional more valuable investment opportunities in the future. For example, manufacturing and distributing a product now may mean that the distribution and marketing network is in place if a second product, based on a valuable new idea, is created. Expenditures on research and development are based on a similar notion, the possibility of discovering a new idea first in order to have the option of developing it into a product, production technique, and/or service.

THE ABANDONMENT OPTION

When a firm is making a capital budgeting decision, one of the options to be considered is the possibility of terminating the project earlier than originally planned. This is called the **abandonment option**. The abandonment value of a project is simply the NPV from terminating the project by selling or scrapping its assets.

The abandonment value of a project and/or asset depends upon many things, but it is enhanced by the existence of used-equipment markets. Generic and widely used brands of tangible assets are more likely to have active used-equipment markets. Intangible assets such as special production processes, patents, and copyrights are less likely to have organized secondary markets. Therefore, intangible assets tend to involve higher transaction costs to find buyers and are more difficult to sell than generic tangible assets. Of course, there are rarely any cleanup and/or removal costs associated with disposing of an intangible asset. Consequently, highly specialized tangible assets that are subject to technological obsolescence tend to have even higher transaction costs than intangible assets.[3]

---

[3] Mainframe computers in the 1970s are an example of such highly specialized equipment subject to technological obsolescence. Many universities were offered mainframe computers as "gifts" if the university would pay the cost of removal and reinstallation. Several universities made the mistake of accepting such "gifts," only to discover that they could have gotten greater computing capability for less money by purchasing a new machine! Corporations were sorry when universities began refusing such "gifts" because not only did the corporation then have to pay the removal cost, but in some cases it also lost a large tax benefit that would accrue from having made a "gift" to a nonprofit organization.

The importance of considering whether to *continue to develop* an investment was considered in the section on the capital budgeting process at the end of Chapter 11. This, of course, is simply the abandonment option during the development stage of a project. In addition to its importance during development, abandonment value should be considered periodically after a project is actually under way. A firm should review its current investments periodically because it is possible that abandoning an investment could have a positive NPV (bearing in mind that sunk costs should be ignored).

The abandonment option was also considered previously in our discussion of replacement decisions. It was pointed out that replacement decisions often provide natural opportunities for considering the abandonment of an investment. However, the abandonment option probably should be considered with respect to a firm's ongoing operations more frequently and systematically than simply whenever a replacement decision is being considered. This is particularly true when the firm is engaging in a process called capital rationing, in which the firm places an upper limit on the total amount of new investment. Capital rationing is discussed later in the chapter.

When a firm imposes capital rationing limits on its investment decisions, the firm will be incurring an opportunity cost whenever it passes up projects that have a positive NPV. Some of these forgone projects may be more valuable than the firm's current investments. One way of reducing this opportunity cost is for the firm to abandon less profitable current operations and use the sale or salvage proceeds to increase its capital budget so that it can undertake more attractive new investments. Therefore, when a firm engages in capital rationing, it is even more important that the firm review its current investments periodically to see if it could profit from abandonment.

EXAMPLE ■ Joe's Diner has been operating for about as long as anyone can remember. Pete has run it for the last 18 years since he took it over from his dad, Jack. Last month, Pete was approached by a developer about selling the place. The developer wouldn't say exactly what she had in mind, except that Pete could move the diner if he wanted to, because she was interested only in the land. At the end of their conversation, she offered Pete $350,000 for the land. Pete was confident that this was a fair price, indeed, the most he could hope to get for the place at this time. Pete thought about moving the diner, but after looking around, he realized that it was not feasible to move the physical structure, nor was there any place close enough to allow the retention of his clientele and the good name of Joe's Diner. The only alternative was to abandon the business.

To analyze his decision whether to sell the diner, Pete gathered the following information. The sale price of $350,000 would provide an after-tax amount of $280,000. The equipment could be sold at auction for about $30,000, on which he would have to pay $5,000 in taxes. The building needed renovation about every 10 years; the before-tax equivalent annual cost (EAC) of this periodic maintenance is $24,000, and the after-tax EAC, including the effect of depreciation, is $18,000. The annual revenues minus expenses from running the diner are $100,000 per year, and Pete pays taxes at the rate of 25% on this amount. Pete has determined that the required rate of return on this investment is 12%. The one thing that Pete almost forgot to include in the analysis was the opportunity cost for his time.

Recently, a friend offered Pete $35,000 per year, including retirement and other benefits, to come and work for him. Pete figured that it would not be exactly a 40-hour workweek, but it would average less than his 55-hour workweek in the diner. With the change in income sources, Pete's tax specialist estimated that the $35,000 per year would be taxed at a rate of 20%. Finally, Pete had been planning for quite a while to sell the diner and retire 12 years from now. It was estimated that the land would sell for the same price then as now, after adjusting for the effect of inflation. From this information, Pete computed the NPV from abandoning his investment in the diner as

Time	Item	CFBT	CFAT	PV @ 12%
0	Land sale	350,000	280,000	280,000
0	Equipment sale	30,000	25,000	25,000
1–12	EAC-building (saved)	24,000/yr	18,000/yr	
1–12	$\Delta R - \Delta E$ (forgone)	−100,000/yr	−75,000/yr	−179,637
1–12	Wages	35,000/yr	28,000/yr	
12	Land sale (forgone)	−350,000	−280,000	−71,869
			NPV =	$53,494

Notice that the positive and negative signs are reversed from what they would normally be because Pete is selling, rather than undertaking, the investment.

Postscript: Pete decided that he enjoyed what he was doing more than he would enjoy increasing his wealth by $53,494. This was not necessarily an irrational choice on Pete's part. For Pete, the nonmonetary values he was receiving from owning the diner exceeded $53,494. At the time, he said he was just relieved that his opportunity cost of staying in the diner wasn't larger; at some amount, he would have sold the diner because the nonmonetary values would not be large enough to overcome the opportunity cost. In fact, 2 years later, the developer came back and offered Pete $600,000 for the diner, and he took it.

An important point to understand in this example is that Pete needed to have an accurate estimate of the monetary opportunity cost of continuing to own the diner in order to make a rational decision concerning whether the nonmonetary values exceeded that cost. The nonmonetary values are not irrelevant; it is simply more accurate to include them *after* all other costs that are more easily quantified have been included. ∎

THE POSTPONEMENT OPTION

In the example involving an expansion of Rocky Mountain's Smooooth production capacity given earlier in this chapter, we pointed out the price setting option. We stopped the example at that point, but a logical next step in the analysis is to consider the idea of postponing, rather than canceling, the expansion alternative. A price increase now, followed by an expansion in production capacity, additional advertising, and perhaps even a decrease in price, may be superior to a simple price increase now. Of course, the analysis can become very complex when such additional alternatives are included because of interactions among the various alternatives. Decision trees (discussed and illustrated in the previous chapter) are a particularly useful device for dealing with this kind of complexity.

AN IMPORTANT WARNING ABOUT CAPITAL BUDGETING OPTIONS

We have said that although net present value is the most appropriate decision criterion, there are many different rules and analyses that are applied in practice to arrive at a decision whether to undertake a project. Often, people in practice talk about "gut feel," or special expertise, that allows a person to advocate undertaking a project that does not appear to have a positive NPV. Frequently, options are at the heart of the matter. It is difficult to quantify their value, so the "gut feel" approach is often simply to "guesstimate" that the project is a profitable investment and then proceed to undertake it. While this approach is not without any redeeming merit, it must be applied *very* sparingly. Otherwise, the value of one or more nebulous options can be used to justify undertaking *any* project, no matter how unprofitable the investment might appear or actually be.

It is probably best to quantify what the additional value for the options would need to be in order to justify the project and ask if that additional value is at all reasonable. For example, suppose a project appears to have an NPV of −$1 million, but an option that is connected with the project has been left out of the NPV calculation. Therefore, if that option is worth more than $1 million, the project actually has a positive NPV and should be undertaken. For the moment, let us assume that such an option exists and that the option can be characterized as a 25% chance of having an entry into a new market 5 years from now. Finally, assume the required rate of return for the project is 20%. For the present value of the option to exceed $1 million, the expected future value (5 years from now) must be greater than about $2.5 million ($= [1.2]^5 1,000,000 = 2,488,320$). With a 25% chance of achieving market entry, the future project within the option must then be expected to produce almost $10 million ($= .25[10] + .75[0] = 2.5$ million) in additional NPV (5 years from now) for the current project to have a positive total NPV. That is a lot of NPV!

A PROBLEM DEFINING INCREMENTAL CASH FLOWS: *The Case of Risk Differences*

13.3

In our discussion of required rates of return in Chapter 10, we introduced the concepts of operating risk and operating leverage. We noted that in some cases the firm can choose among different levels of operating leverage. For example, a choice between robotic and human manufacturing typically represents a choice between two levels of operating leverage. Robotic manufacturing has higher fixed costs to install but has lower variable costs to operate than human manufacturing. Therefore, the robotic manufacturing has a higher level of operating leverage. This difference in operating leverage creates a difference in the business risk of the alternative processes, and consequently there will be a difference in the required rates of return for the processes.

Consider two alternative manufacturing processes with different levels of operating leverage. Assume that the total production capacity is the same for the two processes and that the production process does not affect the sales for the product.[4] Because the sales revenue will be the same in either case, it would appear that the sales revenues are not incremental and can therefore be excluded from the analysis. However, this is not the case. Even though the expected revenues are the same in either

---

[4]This, of course, is not always the case. An example of a case where the production process apparently might affect the sales level is furnished by the Coors beer marketing campaign, which claims that the process of continuous refrigeration of the beer improves its quality.

case, because of the difference in risk between the two processes, the revenues *must* be included in the analysis.

The reason this problem occurs involves the proper definition of *incremental*. The increment for each alternative is measured from the status quo, *not* with respect to each other. Consequently, the contribution margin—the difference between the selling price and variable cost per unit—is the incremental amount, not the difference in costs. Therefore, the process should not be chosen on the basis of the lowest present value of costs because that approach will not always produce the correct decision. The process chosen must be the one that produces the largest NPV. This problem is illustrated in the following example.

EXAMPLE ■ Ronald–Ray's Orchards, Inc. manufactures apple cider. Currently, the level of production is limited by its production facilities, so Ron is considering an expansion of the firm's production capacity. There are two types of processes that can be installed for the expansion. One process is considerably more automated than the other, and therefore the operating leverage of the cider project would be higher if the more automated process were chosen. The total production capacity is the same for the two processes, and the expected value of the additional sales of cider is $100,000 per year. Ronald-Ray's marginal tax rate is 30%.

Process A costs $120,000 to install and has variable costs of $57,000 per year, whereas Process B costs $30,000 to install and has variable costs of $72,000 per year. Both investments would be depreciated on a straight-line basis to a zero book value over 8 years, but both have a 10-year useful life and expected salvage values of zero at the end of 10 years. Therefore, the depreciation tax credits will be $4,500 for A (= .3[120,000/8]) and $1,125 for B (= .3[30,000/8]) per year for the first 8 years and zero for the last 2 years of the project. Process A has a required rate of return of 15%, whereas the required rate of return for Process B is 12%. Which, if either, project should Ronald-Ray undertake?

First, consider the present values of the total cost of each process over the 10-year life. As shown below, these present values are $300,056 for A and $309,182 for B.

Process A

Time	Item	CFBT	CFAT	PV @ 15%
0	$-I_0$	120,000	120,000	120,000
1–8	Depreciation	0/yr	− 4,500/yr	−20,193
1–10	ΔE	57,000/yr	39,900/yr	200,249
			Total cost =	$300,056

Process B

Time	Item	CFBT	CFAT	PV @ 12%
0	$-I_0$	30,000	30,000	30,000
1–8	Depreciation	0/yr	− 1,125/yr	−5,589
1–10	ΔE	72,000/yr	50,400/yr	284,771
			Total cost =	$309,182

While A appears to have the lower total cost, *it is the wrong choice* because the NPV of the net cash flows (revenues minus expenses) depends upon which process is used to generate them. Therefore, the present value of the revenues depends on which process is used. With A, Ron would be spending much more now but less later to earn those revenues. With B, Ron spends less now but more later to earn the same revenues. Even though the revenues are expected to be the same in either case, if there is a downturn in demand and the revenues turn out badly, many of the expenses of Process A have already been incurred. With B, if the revenues turn out badly, the expenses will be less since a larger portion of the expenses for B are variable and thus are incurred only if needed to produce the product. Therefore, the revenues, which are the same in either case, are riskier if Process A is chosen.

Now consider the NPV of each process, including the revenues, over the 10-year horizon. As shown below, the NPV for Process A is only $51,258, whereas the NPV for Process B is $86,333. Therefore, Process B should be installed because it has a positive NPV that is substantially larger than that resulting from installing Process A.

Process A

Time	Item	CFBT	CFAT	PV @ 15%
0	I_0	$-120,000$	$-120,000$	$-120,000$
1–8	Depreciation	0/yr	4,500/yr	20,193
1–10	$\Delta R - \Delta E$	43,000/yr	30,100/yr	151,065
				NPV = $51,258

Process B

Time	Item	CFBT	CFAT	PV @ 12%
0	$-I_0$	$-30,000$	$-30,000$	$-30,000$
1–8	Depreciation	0/yr	1,125/yr	5,589
1–10	$\Delta R - \Delta E$	28,000/yr	19,600/yr	110,744
				NPV = $86,333

CAPITAL RATIONING 13.4

In spite of the efficiency of the capital markets, many firms engage in a practice known as **capital rationing**. Just as the name implies, capital rationing can limit (ration) the amount of new investment undertaken by a firm. A firm can impose such a limit in a number of different ways, but there are two widely used methods of capital rationing. One method is to use a discount (hurdle) rate that exceeds the required rate of return for the project by, for example, 3%. While this is a form of rationing, the use of a "higher" rate can be subtle because in many cases it is not explicitly acknowledged. Often, management argues on the basis of "conservatism," and a "few points" are added, or the number is "rounded up" when a required rate of return is established.

Another method of capital rationing is to set a maximum on parts of, and/or the total, capital budget. For example, a firm decides that it will invest a maximum of $1.2 million on new capital investment projects during the upcoming year. This second method of capital rationing is the more visible method because rationing is explicitly acknowledged. And because of this explicit acknowledgement, it appears to be the more widely used of the two methods. However, both methods are widely used.

One obvious consequence of using a higher discount rate is that for conventional investments with an initial outflow followed by a series of inflows, the NPV of the project will be understated. Some financial managers are not bothered by this fact because they like the idea that value is being "conservatively" measured. Likewise, limiting the total amount of money spent on new investment projects can also be viewed as being "conservative." This "conservatism," of course, creates an opportunity cost.

Management's eagerness to incur this opportunity cost is an agency cost that is associated with capital rationing. Recall that it is very difficult to diversify human capital. This fact led us to the proposition that while it is not relevant to shareholders, diversifiable risk is very relevant to managers personally. This fact has other implications as well. Because the managers' human capital is relatively undiversified, the risk of the managers' human capital investment in a project mirrors the total risk (diversifiable plus nondiversifiable) of the firm. Therefore, managers may be very much in favor of measuring investment values "conservatively" so that projects with a greater margin of safety will be chosen. In this way, the managers reduce the likelihood of bankruptcy, the risk of the firm, and the likelihood that they will lose their jobs. When management decides that the firm should incur the opportunity cost associated with choosing projects "conservatively" to reduce their personal risk, the loss in value is yet another agency cost the shareholders bear in connection with the separation of ownership and control.

Capital rationing has been, and continues to be, widely criticized by academic scholars. The criticism is based on the efficiency of the capital markets. The argument is that in a perfect capital market, a firm can *always* obtain the funds to undertake a capital investment project that has a positive NPV. This is because the project would dominate other capital market opportunities. That is, the project would have a positive NPV because the opportunity cost of capital would be more than met. Therefore, given that existing capital markets are very efficient, firms should simply obtain whatever additional funds are needed to undertake all capital investment projects that have a positive NPV. Of course, since we have identified several persistent imperfections in the capital markets, we must consider how those imperfections affect the firm's investment decisions.

The three major capital market imperfections identified in Chapter 5 are tax asymmetries, information asymmetries, and transaction costs. While the impact of these imperfections on the firm's value is considered in Chapter 15, where the firm's capital structure decision—the mix of debt and equity financing—is analyzed, we want to say a few words about their impact here because information asymmetry and transaction costs do appear to be potential explanations for the widespread use of capital rationing.

To obtain funds from the capital market, a firm must convince investors that it has a project available that has a positive NPV. The problem of adverse selection leads investors to raise the question "If this investment is so good, why is the firm willing to let me in on it? Why doesn't the firm want to keep all of the positive NPV for itself?" Of course, only the firm's managers know the answer to these, and other similar, questions. Consequently, there is an information asymmetry between investors and the firm. Investors will protect themselves by refusing to pay full value for participating in the investment. Given this "discount" in the value of the funds that a firm can obtain from outside investors, the firm must have special circumstances to be able to use the outside funds profitably. Such special circumstances include a "really good" new investment opportunity and a "really bad" set of current investments. The benefits from "really" good new investment opportunities are obvious, but let us examine the second case.

Additional funds can help the firm with a "really bad" set of current investments in the following way. After everyone learns that the firm's current investments are worth less than was previously believed, the market value of the firm will decline, and investors will incur a loss in value. By bringing in new investors prior to the decline in market value, the new investors will help the existing investors by sharing in the loss in value. By selling additional shares, the firm ensures that the loss that would have been borne only by the existing investors is smaller on a per-share basis. While we have not explained this idea fully, our brief discussion should increase further your appreciation of the importance of problems of asymmetric information.

Direct transaction costs associated with obtaining additional financing, such as the issuance costs of new bonds, are a second consideration with respect to capital rationing. As with asymmetric information considerations in the capital markets, we examine the impact of transaction costs in depth in later chapters, but we want to provide some insight into the problem here since it relates to the firm's use of capital rationing. Very simply stated, the cost of obtaining additional financing of any form is, at least to some extent, a declining function of the amount of new financing. That is, the cost, as a percentage of the amount of new financing, is lower when more funds are obtained. For example, as will be shown in Table 14–3, total flotation costs for $200 million worth of bonds might be 1%, whereas $10 million worth of bonds might have total flotation costs that are 6% of the value of the bonds. Therefore, when a firm has a capital investment project available that has a positive NPV but the firm does not have sufficient funds on hand to undertake the project, the transaction costs of obtaining the additional needed funds may cause the NPV to be negative and thereby make the project undesirable. We should note that in such cases, the firm may not be literally engaging in capital rationing. In effect, it may be measuring the project's NPV more accurately by including the cost of special financing transactions.

Another market imperfection that is given as an explanation for the widespread use of capital rationing takes place in the labor, as opposed to the capital, markets. When a firm undertakes a new capital investment project, it must have a manager for the project. Existing managers can often handle the management of additional small capital budgeting projects without too much difficulty. However, a large new project may require managerial expertise in addition to that which the firm's existing employees can provide.[5] While the firm may be confident of the high quality of its current employees, it cannot be so confident of being able to hire similar employees "off the street," so to speak. Many of the firm's current employees have been trained and have been able to grow into their current positions over time. From among many, they have been observed to be qualified for their jobs. Many others were not promoted because they were less qualified. Again, as between investors and the firm's managers, there is an information asymmetry between the firm and potential

---

[5] Of course, new employees may be assigned to current operations to allow existing employees to manage the new operations. Whatever the distribution of assignments, however, the firm must hire additional qualified managers.

new employees that could be hired to enable the firm to undertake a new project with a positive NPV. That information asymmetry causes an increase in the transaction costs associated with undertaking the proposed project and decreases the NPV of the project. As with capital market transaction costs, the firm may be simply including real costs to measure the project's NPV better rather than literally rationing capital. We discuss these adjustments in this section on capital rationing because in practice, such adjustments are referred to as capital rationing.

Agency costs provide a rationale for the fact that capital rationing is widely observed in practice. Certain other market imperfections can cause adjustments referred to as capital rationing to be in the best interest of the shareholders. We cannot say for certain whether agency costs and/or other market imperfections are causing firms to engage in capital rationing, but we suspect that both factors contribute to its use. In any case, virtually all firms do at least some amount of capital rationing; therefore, it is important to be able to function in an environment where capital is rationed.

13.5 PROJECT CHOICE UNDER CAPITAL RATIONING

How can a firm choose the best projects under capital rationing? Using a discount rate that is higher than the project's required rate of return for conventional investment projects that have a negative initial outflow followed by expected future inflows means that some projects with lower NPVs will be rejected, but the NPV criterion is still the best one for choosing projects. However, the decision criterion must be modified when the capital budget is limited by the total amount of funds available for new investment. The problem is that the firm needs to choose the best *set* of new projects. That is, it should choose the set of projects that provides the largest *total* NPV.

The problem is somewhat like a jigsaw puzzle since only infrequently can some fraction of a project be undertaken. Normally, a firm either undertakes or rejects a whole project. Consequently, a firm must fit together a total capital expenditure program that is less than or equal to the maximum amount of funds available. The rationing problem arises because each project adds a nondivisible expenditure that could cause the firm to over- or underspend its budgeted amount. We show that a method that ignores project size can be a useful tool for identifying the best projects to choose first. The profitability index measures NPV per dollar of investment. This is, in some sense, a measure of how good a project is without regard to the size of the project. Therefore, the profitability index can be a useful tool for choosing projects under capital rationing.

A CAPITAL RATIONING EXAMPLE

Suppose a firm has set a maximum of $1.3 million on its total capital budget this year. The firm has evaluated a large number of potential investments and discarded all of them except the set of projects listed in Table 13-2. While all of the projects listed have a positive NPV, the total funds required to undertake all of them is approximately $2.5 million, well in excess of the $1.3 million maximum. Which set of projects should the firm undertake?

As already noted, the firm should undertake the set of projects that produces the highest total NPV, but how can that set be determined? Table 13-3 ranks the projects given in Table 13-2 from largest to smallest by profitability index. Without regard to

TABLE 13-2 Choosing Projects under Capital Rationing

Project Number	Initial Outlay	NPV	Profitability Index
1	437,000	301,500	.69
2	382,000	214,000	.56
3	310,000	43,000	.14
4	260,000	55,000	.21
5	229,000	316,000	1.38
6	188,000	85,000	.45
7	135,000	124,000	.92
8	107,000	78,000	.73
9	93,000	122,000	1.31
10	86,000	95,500	1.11
11	82,000	59,000	.72
12	70,000	61,000	.87
13	55,000	21,500	.39
14	49,000	41,000	.84
15	38,000	60,000	1.58
Total	2,521,000	1,676,500	

TABLE 13-3 Projects Ranked by Profitability Index

Project Number	Initial Outlay	NPV	Profitability Index	Cumulative Outlay
15	38,000	60,000	1.58	38,000
5	229,000	316,000	1.38	267,000
9	93,000	122,000	1.31	360,000
10	86,000	95,500	1.11	446,000
7	135,000	124,000	.92	581,000
12	70,000	61,000	.87	651,000
14	49,000	41,000	.84	700,000
8	107,000	78,000	.73	807,000
11	82,000	59,000	.72	889,000
1	437,000	301,500	.69	1,326,000
2	382,000	214,000	.56	1,708,000
6	188,000	85,000	.45	1,896,000
13	55,000	21,500	.39	1,951,000
4	260,000	55,000	.21	2,211,000
3	310,000	43,000	.14	2,521,000

TABLE 13-4 Cumulative Outlay and Cumulative NPV Values

Project Number	PI	Cumulative Outlay	Cumulative NPV	Cumulative Outlay	Cumulative NPV	Cumulative Outlay	Cumulative NPV
15	1.58	38,000	60,000	38,000	60,000	38,000	60,000
5	1.38	267,000	376,000	267,000	376,000	267,000	376,000
9	1.31	360,000	498,000	360,000	498,000	360,000	498,000
10	1.11	446,000	593,500	446,000	593,500	446,000	593,500
7	.92	581,000	717,500	581,000	717,500	581,000	717,500
12	.87	651,000	778,500	651,000	778,500	651,000	778,500
14	.84	700,000	819,500	700,000	819,500		
8	.73	807,000	897,500	807,000	897,500	758,000	856,500
11	.72	889,000	956,500				
1	.69			1,244,000	1,199,000	1,195,000	1,158,000
2	.56	1,271,000	1,170,500				
6	.45						
13	.39			1,299,000	1,220,500	1,250,000	1,179,500
4	.21						
3	.14						

↑
optimal project set:
1, 5, 7, 8, 9, 10,
12, 13, 14, 15

size, a project with a higher PI is more desirable than one with a lower PI because it returns more NPV per dollar of initial investment. However, as we go down the list, there may come a point where skipping a project and undertaking two or more of the projects with lower PI values will provide a higher total NPV.

If the firm simply chooses the projects with the highest PI values until funds run out, it will choose the first 9 projects in Table 13-3 through Project 11, and undertake Project 2, and have a total NPV of $1.1705 million. However, a different set of projects provides the highest total NPV achievable. By deleting Projects 11 and 2 from the proposed set, the firm can undertake the rest of the set plus Projects 1 and 13, producing a total NPV of $1.2205 million. Making such substitutions requires trial and error, although judgment may limit the amount of time and effort involved. We can systematize the process and enhance our judgment by computing the cumulative outlay and cumulative NPV figures for the set. Table 13-4 provides cumulative figures for the projects starting from the top of the set ranked by PI and skipping selected projects. Three sets are illustrated, including the two already mentioned. As already noted, the second set identified in Table 13-4, where the total outlay is $1.299 million, produces the maximum total NPV of $1.2205 million. We can solve this problem via linear programming, as illustrated in the next section.

ZERO-ONE INTEGER PROGRAMMING

An analytical method, **zero-one integer programming**, can be used with the aid of a computer to determine the solution to a capital rationing problem. This method is particularly useful for problems that are more complex, such as those involving capital rationing constraints over multiple years.

Zero-one integer programming is a special case of linear programming. You may have encountered linear programming, and perhaps integer programming, in other course work. Because this topic is generally covered in other course work, we will not derive the technique or discuss it in great detail here. However, we will demonstrate how to formulate a capital rationing problem so that the optimal project set can be determined using zero-one integer programming. Our illustration should provide you with guidance should you ever be faced with a large and complex capital rationing problem. Zero-one integer programming algorithms are available in various software packages, including packages used on personal computers. The only drawback to its use on a PC is that the number of projects that can be considered is limited relative to the number that can be considered on a mainframe computer. Currently, problems involving up to 20 projects, or even more, can be solved easily on a PC.

As already noted, zero-one integer programming is a special case of linear programming. It is a special case because the variables can take on only the values 0 or 1. (Solution values with linear programming can be fractional, large or small, as well as positive or negative.) The objective function for the capital rationing problem is to maximize the total NPV subject to whatever capital rationing constraints exist. The problem is formulated by defining one variable for each project. In the final solution, a value of 1 for the variable representing a project indicates that the project should be undertaken, whereas a value of 0 for the variable indicates rejection of the project.

Suppose a firm will impose capital rationing constraints for the next several years and many of the projects under consideration require net outflows next year as well as this year. Such a situation is described in Table 13-5, which extends the set of projects considered in Table 13-2 by indicating the outflows that are required next year for each project.

TABLE 13-5 Projects: Two Years of Capital Rationing Constraints

Project Number	Initial Outlay	NPV	Year 2 Outlay
1	437,000	301,500	55,000
2	382,000	214,000	0
3	310,000	43,000	86,000
4	260,000	55,000	0
5	229,000	316,000	30,000
6	188,000	85,000	0
7	135,000	124,000	0
8	107,000	78,000	28,000
9	93,000	122,000	73,000
10	86,000	95,500	41,000
11	82,000	59,000	9,000
12	70,000	61,000	151,000
13	55,000	21,500	19,000
14	49,000	41,000	110,000
15	38,000	60,000	142,000
Total	2,521,000	1,676,500	744,000

Assume that in addition to this year's constraint of $1.3 million, a maximum capital budget of $400,000 is available for expenditure next year on these projects.[6] To formulate the problem, define the variables X_1 through X_{15} and denote NPV_1 through NPV_{15}, with subscripts corresponding to the project numbers. The X variables indicate whether or not the corresponding project will be undertaken. The objective is to maximize the total NPV resulting from taking on a set of projects. The total NPV is given by the function

$$\text{Total NPV} = \sum_{i=1}^{15} X_i NPV_i \qquad (13.2)$$

The capital rationing constraints can be expressed by defining the variables Y_1 through Y_{15} and Z_1 through Z_{15} to represent, respectively, the expenditures now and next year that are required for each project, so that in this example,

$$\sum_{i=1}^{15} X_i Y_i \leq \$1.3 \text{ million} \qquad (13.3)$$

and

$$\sum_{i=1}^{15} X_i Z_i \leq \$.4 \text{ million} \qquad (13.4)$$

By using a zero-one integer programming algorithm, the optimal solution to this problem can be determined to produce a total NPV of $1.1775 million with

$X_1 = 1$; $X_2 = 0$; $X_3 = 0$; $X_4 = 0$; $X_5 = 1$; $X_6 = 0$; $X_7 = 1$; $X_8 = 1$;
$X_9 = 1$; $X_{10} = 1$; $X_{11} = 1$; $X_{12} = 0$; $X_{13} = 1$; $X_{14} = 0$; $X_{15} = 1$;

so the firm should undertake Projects 1, 5, 7, 8, 9, 10, 11, 13, 15.[7] This set requires a total current expenditure of $1.262 million and a total expenditure next year of $397,000.

13.6 MANAGING THE FIRM'S INVESTMENT DECISIONS

Earlier in the chapter we pointed out the interaction between the capital budgeting decision and the abandonment decision. In fact, there are many interactions between capital rationing and the various options of price flexibility and replacing, postponing, accelerating, or abandoning investment projects. These interactions lead to the notion of a planning horizon whereby capital rationing can be used as a tool for managing interactions between the firm's investment and financing decisions.[8] For example, what appears to be capital rationing this year can be actually a method of ensuring the availability of funds for a project that is planned to be undertaken next

[6] The smaller amount allocated in next year's budget for investments made this year might be designed to enhance the firm's options on future investments. Limiting future commitments increases the firm's financial flexibility to undertake new investments in the future that might not be available, or even known about, today.

[7] We were delighted to find that software packages for this type of technique have come a long way. They are very "user friendly." At this point, we would attempt to solve only the most trivial capital rationing problems by hand.

[8] Interactions between the firm's investment and financing decisions provide the focus for Part 3 (Chapters 19 through 23).

year. Of course, plans can change for a number of reasons, as when a competitor makes the proposed project unattractive by price changes and/or the introduction of a new product. While planning does not guarantee a great outcome, it can substantially improve the expected value of the outcome. Therefore, the planning process is critical to good financial management.

CAPITAL RATIONING AS A PLANNING TOOL

The example of capital rationing presented in the previous section was given in what might be called an environment of **"hard" capital rationing**. "Hard" refers to how the maximum total expenditure is viewed, implying that under no circumstances can that maximum be exceeded. Of course, when a set of projects is particularly attractive, management may decide to exceed its self-imposed capital expenditure limit after all. In fact, firms often establish a condition that might be called **"soft" capital rationing**: The firm has set a target for its total amount of new investment, but depending upon the desirability of the particular set of proposals under review and the firm's condition at the time decisions are actually being made, the firm may over- or underspend relative to that target.

The techniques described above for capital rationing decisions are also useful in a "soft" capital rationing environment. By varying the maximum somewhat, the firm can use the techniques to get a good picture of the trade-offs among the alternative investment sets open to the firm. For example, a firm may find that a small increase in the total expenditure may allow the firm to undertake the next most desirable project, which management may consider a worthwhile trade-off. Computer software, using the zero-one integer programming algorithm, is particularly useful for "soft" capital rationing because once the problem has been formulated, the computer can be conveniently used to obtain solutions under alternative conditions simply by changing the constraint values. Whatever technique is employed, a complete analysis when the firm uses capital rationing will include consideration of at least some variation in the maximum expenditure limit.

MANAGERIAL AUTHORITY AND RESPONSIBILITY

Cooperation among members of an organization is a prerequisite to good decision-making generally, and it is particularly important with respect to capital budgeting decisions. Interpersonal relationships can play a very important role in a capital budgeting decision. Feuds between people and/or divisions hurt the firm. Members of any one functional area, such as marketing research, obviously must be able to work together successfully. In addition, cooperation among the various decision-making *levels* of the organization plays a critical role in the decision-making process. Perhaps somewhat more subtle is the need for members of *different functional areas* to be able to work together successfully as when marketing research and finance exchange information necessary to estimate expected future cash flows for a project. Procedures that provide authority by area and amount, with a hierarchy of amounts, are designed to minimize problems among individuals, levels, and areas. Unfortunately, while such procedures generally provide a net gain by reducing or eliminating the effects of certain kinds of problems, they may create others.

For example, in Chapter 11 we described a typical budgetary authority system where a manager could approve capital expenditures to some maximum amount. Such a rule apparently means that the manager is required to seek approval for projects with expenditures exceeding the stated maximum. However, a manager might break up the necessary expenditures for a project into smaller amounts that do not require additional approval and/or spread them out over time. In this way, the manager can undertake the project without having to obtain prior approval from a higher decision-making level in the organization. This may sound extreme, yet cases have been cited where a division of a corporation actually built and equipped a whole new plant using plant expense orders. In one such case, corporate headquarters discovered the new plant only after its managers submitted an expenditure request for a chimney because they could not figure out a method of breaking up the expense into smaller amounts that would not need approval.[9]

The problem illustrated by this example is that the division thought the firm needed the new plant but felt that corporate headquarters would turn down the project. In essence, the division thought they knew better than corporate headquarters. The division managers probably felt that corporate headquarters lacked the hands-on viewpoint. Of course, they might have been right. But they might just as easily have been wrong. The responsibility for that decision was not theirs. The viewpoint from the division level does not encompass the breadth of the higher level of decision-making authority.

Our point is that this example illustrates a tremendous breakdown of the system of authority and responsibility. The division's responsibility was to communicate its viewpoint to the higher levels in the best way. Headquarters had the responsibility of trying to understand that viewpoint, weighing it along with other information, and deciding on the best course of action.

At the other extreme, having top management review all decisions could lead to the absurd case where the CEO has to approve a salesman's purchase of a new pencil. In essence, budgetary authority is designed to reduce transaction costs. Lowering the level of decision-making authority within a firm may reduce the net cost of making the decision, including the opportunity cost of delay when time is critical.

The problems just cited point out the need to balance decision-making authority against transaction costs. In spite of these and other problems that can arise, recall from Chapter 9 that multiple layers of decision-making authority provide a monitoring function that substantially reduces the agency costs associated with operating an organization. Essentially, the multiple layers and divisions of authority make collusion among employees much more difficult, and it is less likely that employees will take self-interested actions at the expense of the shareholders. Therefore, the multiple layers may provide a form of agency cost reduction that also enters into the choice of decision-making authority for each level of the firm.

In practice, the kinds of procedures outlined in Chapter 11 in conjunction with intelligent and honest employees best using their abilities, provide methods of coping with the complexities encountered in practice and generally produce sensible capital budgeting decisions.

MANAGERIAL INCENTIVES AND PERFORMANCE EVALUATION

We noted earlier in this chapter that a capital rationing environment can provide additional opportunities for managers to enforce self-interested behavior with respect to the firm's investment decisions, thus increasing the firm's agency costs. This points out, once again, the desirability of contractual managerial incentives that reduce the firm's agency costs.

[9]See Bower (1970).

A typical example of poor incentives is the case where managers are evaluated on the basis of the firm's or the division's rate of return on the book value of assets, or what is often called ROI (return on investment). ROI does not have a consistent relationship with the NPV of a project. Therefore, ROI does not measure how successful the manager has been in choosing capital budgeting projects that add to the value of the firm.

Unfortunately, when managers are evaluated and rewarded on the basis of a particular measure of performance, it is not surprising that the managers act to maximize the value of that measure. Consequently, it is important to choose performance measures that are consistent with the firm's goals. Otherwise, you might get exactly what you asked for—even though it was not at all what you wanted!

POSTAUDITS

It is often extremely difficult to evaluate a decision after the fact. In many cases, the opportunity costs of forgone alternatives and options are simply impossible to measure. Also, as the cliche "hindsight is better than foresight" points out, the use of hindsight to measure what might be considered foresight can be entirely unreasonable. In some cases, outcomes occur that were not even thought possible, let alone predicted as likely to occur. Further, identifying and measuring the incremental cash flows that actually resulted from a decision can be impossible.

For example, suppose you own a grocery store and 2 years ago you installed optical scanners in the checkout counters. The scanners were installed for a variety of reasons. It was argued that they would dramatically improve the store's inventory management by reducing the chance of over- and understocking, reducing the time to take inventory, and reducing the cost of ordering. In addition, it was expected that the scanners would improve customer service by reducing the time for customers to check out. Now you are interested in determining whether installing the scanners was a good decision. What can be determined from a postaudit?

You can measure the current costs of ordering and taking inventory and compare them with prior costs, and it might be possible to establish a cost savings for any reduction in overstocking. However, estimating any incremental revenues associated with a reduction in the number of stockouts would be very difficult at best—how many sales would have been lost? An observed increase in sales can have been the result of many things, such as improved economy-wide conditions. Similarly, connecting the sales level to an improvement in the customer service level is not possible. Although you can survey your customers to measure any improvement in customer service, suppose total sales have not increased. You cannot establish what the sales level would have been if the scanners had not been installed. After all, competitors may also have put in scanners, so that your store might have experienced a substantial drop in sales had you not installed the scanners. In this case, it is not possible to measure precisely the incremental cash inflows that were generated by installing the optical scanners. At this point, only the financial condition of the entire store can be meaningfully established.

In spite of the problems of evaluating a decision after the fact, sensible evaluation procedures, sometimes called **postaudits**, can be useful and are often undertaken in practice. One valuable and typical procedure is to evaluate some or all of the expected future cash flow estimates. This process is often aimed more at improving the analysts' ability to forecast expected future cash flows on current and future projects than simply evaluating the analyst's performance. Some analysts have relatively consistent biases in their estimates (either optimistically above or pessimistically below). It might be possible to correct such a bias over time through the review and evaluation of the analyst's work.

A second form of postaudit is to determine the abandonment, versus continued operation, value of an entire project. Often, in situations like the optical-scanner example just discussed, determining the value of the entire operation is the only reasonable method of evaluating the project. Of course, while this may determine the project's current value, it does not indicate whether a particular decision was good or bad. The current value provides a measure of the outcome from the entire set of past decisions, but that outcome could be more the result of good or bad luck than good or bad decision-making.

DECISION-MAKING IN PRACTICE

In practice, there can be a great deal of "squish" in the decision-making process. Consequently, it is very important for a decision-maker to provide a rationally based system for making decisions. As with our warning about adding the value of options to a project's value, unfortunately a decision-maker can justify undertaking any project with enough "subjective add-ons."

It is often said that making estimates and planning are very complex and difficult processes because of uncertainty. Therefore, in the final analysis, decisions are subjective, and some would say that you can forget all the complex analysis—"Just take your best shot." While the first statement is true, the conclusion does not follow. Although a decision is certainly easier to make if it is simply the result of a coin flip or a "gut-feel-best-guess," the parameter estimates are no more accurate, and neither is the decision any better. In fact, the decision may lead to a disaster.

If a decision is worthy of consideration and can benefit from additional information, we should gather the most cost-efficient information set and make the decision based on that information. Sometimes, the most cost-efficient set is the information we have already gathered. In such cases, we choose the optimal alternative based on that information set. But, often, gathering additional information is a cost-effective method of making a better decision. And of course it makes no sense to expend resources gathering additional information and then disregard that information because it is not perfectly accurate.

Our purpose here is to provide a useful framework for making capital budgeting decisions. After all, if such decisions were trivial, there would not be much reason to study the process. By framing the analysis and decision criteria properly, the decision-makers' subjective judgments are enhanced and can be better understood. Of course, using the NPV framework will not save you from the effects of inaccurate forecasts of incremental cash flows or from the effects of using the wrong discount rate.

13.7   OTHER FACTORS THAT ARE DIFFICULT TO QUANTIFY

We have already mentioned a number of factors that are relatively difficult to quantify in a capital budgeting analysis, such as options, incorporating the effects of economic dependence, predicting the likelihood of technological advances, and hiring qualified managers. On the one hand, overlooking such factors that create opportunity costs can lead to bad decision-making. On the other hand, we have emphasized the importance of care in performing incremental analysis to reflect such factors (when they are important) while avoiding double-counting and/or over-estimating the impact of these factors, particularly with respect to options. Along with recommending care, we list other factors below that can also increase or decrease the value of a project. For the most part, these factors have a much smaller impact on the value of the project than some of the factors already mentioned, such as options connected with future investment opportunities.

1. Existing *working relationships with suppliers*—either good or bad.
   We noted the importance of interpersonal relationships within the company earlier in the chapter. This importance extends to relationships with individuals and departments in other firms. An individual working for a supplier can cause a costly delay because of a personal vendetta.

2. *Particular expertise* concerning an investment project, or the lack of it, among current employees.
   In our discussion of capital rationing, we pointed out the problems of information asymmetry in the labor markets and noted the difficulty of identifying high-quality employees that can manage a capital investment project. When transaction costs must be incurred to identify and hire additional qualified employees for an investment project, those costs decrease the NPV of the project. Similarly, when existing employees have expertise that can be used for an investment project, transaction costs associated with undertaking the project, such as training, will be lower, which in turn increases the project's NPV.

3. *Experience with quality* of machines and/or service from particular manufacturers.
   As with relationships with suppliers, good or bad service and/or parts availability from the manufacturer of a machine used for producing a product can decrease or increase the firm's expenses. Likewise, when a machine is known to have a better or worse "cost/quality" relationship, it will increase or decrease the NPV of the project. Also, improved knowledge of the expenses connected with using a machine may increase the accuracy of the forecast cash flows. Such improved knowledge is more likely when dealing with machines that use existing technology than machines using innovative technology.

The same warning we gave about options applies to the above and similar factors: As long as a person does not provide specific values that can be carefully examined, a proponent of a project can always find a long enough list of nebulous add-ons with which to "shout down" an opponent of the project. Don't be fooled. *A long list is not a substitute for a large net present value*!

SOME PRACTICAL ADVICE 13.8

Making decisions in a complex world is particularly difficult because no single approach *always* works best. As with earning extraordinary returns in the stock market, if it were that easy, everyone would already be doing it. At one extreme, the analyst-manager should gather all the relevant information to make the optimal choice. But of course there is more information to be gathered in virtually every situation, so with that strategy, the decision-maker would never make a decision; there would always be more information to be gathered. At the other extreme, gathering information costs money and takes time. Therefore, in order to minimize cost, one could conclude that the analyst-manager should never gather more information. Either approach may be optimal in a particular situation; however, both approaches are too extreme to be applied to every situation. Extreme solutions involving "always" or "never," such as always wait-never wait, always purchase more information-never purchase more information, are too simplistic to be consistently successful in complex situations. Our advice is to be wary of simplistic decision-making procedures that are like "cure-all" medicines, claimed to be appropriate for all situations.

Having told you to be wary, we must now tell you that the framework for decision-making described in Chapter 11 is *always* correct. The problem is that following the framework is sometimes extremely difficult because of a variety of complicating factors, such as opportunity costs and economic dependence. The tools we have described provide methods of coping in an environment where it is not only impossible to predict future outcomes but often impossible even to describe the possible outcomes. In other words, in some cases, we cannot even imagine some of the outcomes. For example, we are not aware of anyone who, on January 1, 1987, could have predicted the stock market crash on October 19, 1987, and the resulting impact on the cost of raising capital. When your investments depend on unknown future events, you simply do the best you can. We can talk about the possibility of a technological advance, but often we cannot say anything more about it than to make some nebulous statements about rendering an existing product obsolete. Also, some possible outcomes are so unlikely that they have no significant effect on the analysis, yet if one occurs, it will be catastrophic. As we have said before, we know of no way to teach a person how to generate new ideas. Our ability to teach a person to assimilate information is also limited.

In spite of the difficulties just noted, there are several Principles of Finance that are important to remember with respect to capital budgeting decisions.

VALUABLE NEW IDEAS Bad financing decisions can destroy a firm. On the other hand, while good financing decisions can contribute to a firm's profitability, the possibility of extraordinary success rests primarily on investment decisions. Because of the efficiency of the capital markets, rarely does great financial management make a firm extraordinarily profitable. The Principle of Valuable Ideas is alive and well: *Pursuing valuable ideas is the best way to achieve extraordinary returns*.

Valuable new ideas are not necessarily limited to new products. A valuable new idea can be related to many dimensions of the business. An improved management technique can be valuable. Ray Kroc employed valuable new management procedures in helping to make McDonald's a profitable corporation. He had many new ideas in addition to his idea of serving hamburgers quickly. For example, McDonald's introduced fast food in a family restaurant, a substantive change from the take-out hamburger joint.

Introducing new ideas in the form of products, services, management, and/or technology can reduce the value of current ideas or even render current ideas worthless. This was pointed out in the Headcleaner example in Chapter 12, but it can be seen in many places. For example, what are manual typewriters and many handheld calculators worth today in their ability to process work efficiently, compared with what they were worth when new?

MARKET EFFICIENCY Recall that in Chapter 6, when we derived models for valuing bonds and stocks, we asked the question "Why bother with a model for valuing a bond when the bond's value can be easily determined by looking at the latest trading price?" We said that the major value to be obtained from the model was to establish a required rate of return for measuring the opportunity cost. We also said that the physical asset markets are not as efficient as the capital markets and provided a list of reasons for this fact. But while transaction costs are higher and there is greater variance in trading prices for physical assets, there is valuable information contained in a market-traded price for a physical asset.

If you are not going to trust a market price, you should have a very good reason. This is true in the physical asset markets as well as the capital markets. Beware of an analysis that places a value on an asset that is very different from prices observed in a competitive market. Even if the market is less efficient than the capital markets, you need to have one or more good reasons why it should be different. When there is a market for an asset, you should *think long and hard before you conclude that a market price is "wrong."* Ask yourself what value you are bringing to the asset. That is, how will the way you are going to use the asset be sufficiently different that it is worth more to you than it is to other people? And if an asset will be used more profitably by others because, for example, they hold a patent, it is probably not good to compete with them for the use of that asset. It is probably considerably more profitable to put your efforts into searching for valuable new ideas for using assets more profitably than others, or at least as profitably as others.

TWO-SIDED TRANSACTIONS   Why is the other party to the transaction willing to sell the asset to you or purchase it from you? For example, why is the other party willing to sell you the asset for less than you think it is worth? Remember that the party on the other side of the transaction is acting in her best self-interest. Establishing reasons for the difference will help you understand the project you are analyzing.

SIGNALING   Watch the competition and try to understand their actions. Often, but not always, their actions contain information. The question is What information do the actions contain? The actions could simply be their application of the Behavioral Principle, which can lead to a "herd" mentality. If you are the first to recognize such behavior, you can profit from it.

Finally, *plan ahead*. Undertaking a major project is not as simple as discounting cash flows. It requires management. The NPV calculation provides the framework for making decisions. It is always correct. The difficulty is in correctly estimating the parameter values. But just because it is difficult or the process becomes complex, don't just blow it off and flip a coin. Use the information you have in the best way you can to decide whether to go ahead, quit, or seek additional information.

SUMMARY

In this chapter, we have pointed out additional factors that complicate the capital budgeting decision. A major focus has been on interactions among capital budgeting projects—with respect to both investment decision considerations and financing decision considerations. The inclusion of some factors, such as options and opportunity costs, can dramatically alter the value of an investment project. Capital rationing can be viewed as somewhat mechanical, but in its broader application, it can play a useful role as part of a planning process.

Use all the relevant information that is available. From one point of view, the

DECISION SUMMARY BOX

- Options and the opportunity costs they create play a very important role in the capital budgeting decision. The following options were identified:

  The expansion option.
  The price setting option.
  The abandonment option.
  The postponement option.
  The replacement option.
  Future investment opportunities.

- Often, a decision tree framework can be used for estimating the value of a capital budgeting option, in a manner similar to the two-state option pricing model.
- "Soft" capital rationing is useful as a framework for the planning process. Zero-one integer programming may be useful in this process and, with the right software, is convenient and easy to use.

- The profitability index can be used to enhance judgement when capital rationing is called for.
- Pursuing valuable new ideas is the best way to achieve extraordinary returns.
- Other factors, such as the level of expertise among employees, working relationships with other companies, and past experience with machines and/or service, can play a (minor) role in capital budgeting decisions.
- Watch how people act—the competition and those on the other side of your transactions.
- Have good reasons why you should be able to get a positive NPV from a project, especially if there is no innovative idea involved.
- The framework presented in this chapter for making capital budgeting decisions helps structure the decision and can enhance one's understanding of complex situations, even though its application is not as simple as "NPV."

capital budgeting process is not as easy as "NPV." However, the decision-making process based on maximizing NPV provides a *framework* for making the best possible capital budgeting decisions.

PROBLEMS

PROBLEM SET A

A1. Cite and briefly discuss six areas to look for options that might be connected with a firm's capital investment opportunities.

A2. Define the term **capital rationing**.

A3. Contrast the concept of "soft" capital rationing with that of "hard" capital rationing.

A4. Briefly describe the technique of zero-one integer programming.

A5. How can capital rationing be used as a tool for managerial planning?

A6. Why might it be important to review and assess (postaudit) the firm's decisions. What are some of the pitfalls associated with such a task?

A7. Explain briefly how the pricing of a product can interact with a firm's decision as to whether to expand production capacity.

A8. Why might the consideration of abandonment value be more important for a firm engaging in capital rationing than it is for firms that simply take on all positive-NPV projects?

A9. With respect to the Smooooth soap expansion example, at what price would RMC be indifferent between the expansion and an increase in the price? Assume that sales will be 10 million bars per year for 10 years at this price.

The current level of production for Adam's Gears, Inc. (the original gear) is limited by its production facilities, so Adam is considering an expansion of the firm's production capacity. Since the product has become essentially generic, raising the price is not an option for Adam. There are two types of processes that can be installed for the expansion. One process is considerably more automated than the other, and therefore the operating leverage of the expansion project would be higher if the more automated process were chosen. The total production capacity is the same for the two processes, as is the expected value of the additional gear sales, which is $1.3 million per year. Process A costs $1.56 million to install and has variable costs of $740,000 per year, whereas Process B costs $390,000 to install and has variable costs of $935,000 per year. Both investments would be depreciated on a straight-line basis to a zero book value over 8 years, but both have a 10-year useful life and expected salvage values of zero at the end of 10 years. Process A has a required rate of return of 15%, whereas the required rate of return for Process B is 12%. If Adam's Gears has a marginal tax rate of 30%, which, if either, project should Adam undertake?

A11. Cite and briefly discuss six factors that can be especially difficult to quantify for inclusion in a capital budgeting NPV calculation.

A12. Consider the following projects:

Project:	A	B	C	D	E	F	G
Initial cost:	10,000	20,000	20,000	15,000	30,000	40,000	20,000
NPV:	1,100	3,600	800	1,600	4,000	3,000	1,400

  a. Compute the profitability index for each project.
  b. If you were rationed to $115,000 for the initial investment, which projects should you choose?
  c. If you were rationed to $95,000 for the initial investment, which projects should you choose?

PROBLEM SET B

B1. What is the internal rate of return of a project that has an initial net outflow of 100, a $t = 1$ cash flow of +250, and a $t=2$ cash flow of -156?

B2. Based on the Principle of Two-Sided Transactions, what would you tell a firm that has "discovered" a large positive-NPV project that requires the firm to purchase the assets (which are necessary to undertake the project) from another corporation?

B3. Billy Bob's Big Eat'n Place has decided to purchase a new cornhusker. Billy Bob will buy one of two machines. Both machines cost $1,500. Machine A has a 4-year life, a salvage value of $1,000, and expenses of $475 per year. Machine B has a 5-year life, a salvage value of $500, and expenses of $460 per year. Whichever machine is used, revenues for this project are $1,200 per year, and machines will be replaced at the end of their lives. Using straight-line depreciation to the salvage value, a tax rate of 35%, and a discount rate of 20%, which machine should Billy Bob buy, and why?

B4. Cite an example of a situation in which "hard" capital rationing would be appropriate for at least a limited time.

B5. Rework the capital-rationing example in the chapter with a constraint of $.8 million.

B6. Respond to the following comment: First you tell us the value of a project is its NPV. Now you say that the project's value is its NPV plus the value of its options minus the cost of those options. Which is right?

B7. Rework the capital rationing example in the chapter with a constraint of $1.8 million.

B8. Suppose you are a section head considering a capital budgeting project. You have examined the proposed project, and according to every relevant piece of information you can find, you feel the project should be undertaken. After submitting your analysis, the division head informs you that the project has not been approved for funding. Briefly discuss the possible causes of the difference between your opinion of the project and that of upper management.

B9. The owners of Egg Sauce, Ltd. are tired of their business. In fact, they are so *exhausted* that they are considering abandoning the business. The building and land could be sold for $700,000 and would provide an after-tax amount of $640,000. The equipment could be sold at auction for about $55,000, and at that price, they could claim a tax credit of $5,000 in addition. The building needed renovation about every 10 years, the before-tax EAC of this periodic maintenance is $40,000, and the after-tax EAC, including the effect of depreciation, is $30,000. The annual revenues minus expenses (including all employee costs) from running Egg Sauce are $200,000 per year, and the firm pays taxes at the rate of 35% on this amount. The owners have determined that the required rate of return on this investment is 15%. At what after-tax sale price would the owners be better off selling than abandoning Egg Sauce?

B10. Cite and briefly discuss potential pitfalls encountered in estimating the value of future investment opportunities, in the context of our warning about capital budgeting options.

B11. Ivan's Onion-Brick Restaurant has been very successful for 10 years. However, the growth potential in Ivan's area has declined, and therefore Ivan is contemplating investment in a new business line—consulting. Ivan can enter this new field by purchasing and renovating a small building in downtown Newark at a cost of $100,000, all of which will be depreciated on a straight-line basis to a zero book value over 10 years. Although it will be depreciated to a zero book value, the entire project is expected to be sold off for a salvage value of $65,000 at the end of 8 years. It is estimated that the revenues from the project will be $100,000 per year during the next 2 years and $150,000 in years 3 thru 8. Variable costs (including all labor and material) will be 65% of revenues. At the expected revenue levels, Ivan expects to average about $30,000 in receivables, and accounts payable are expected to average $5,000. Ivan has determined that his required rate of return for this project is 17.31% and the tax rate is 35%. What is the NPV of this project?

PROBLEM SET C

C1. We have said that abandonment should always be considered with respect to the firm's current operations. Suppose a firm has the opportunity to sell one of its subsidiaries that is doing very poorly. As a general rule, why would it *not* be likely that a firm can "limit its losses" by selling off such subsidiaries?

C2. How might the agency costs associated with the separation of ownership and control contribute to a tendency for firms to expand rather than raise the prices of their products?

C3. Cite and discuss four broad factors that can cause the NPV of a capital budgeting project to be incorrectly measured.

C4. Use Figure 8-11 (in Chapter 8) to explain why a large number of options connected with a capital budgeting project might not necessarily be any more valuable than one option on the project.

C5. Rework the capital-rationing example with a constraint of $1.2 million.

C6. Capital rationing would not be a shareholder wealth-maximizing strategy in a perfect capital market. How might the capital market imperfections we noted in Chapter 5 (tax asymmetries, information asymmetries, and transaction costs) render capital rationing a rational tool?

C7. RMC's Smooooth soap has a marginal cost of $.387 per bar. Given the demand function

$$\text{Demand} = \frac{2.538 \text{ million}}{(\text{price})^3}$$

express total revenue as a function of quantity demanded; show that marginal revenue equals marginal cost when the quantity demanded is 12,974,330; and demonstrate that the optimal price is $.5805 per bar.

REFERENCES

Bower, J. L. *Managing the Resource Allocation Process: A Study of Corporate Planning and Investment.* Boston: Division of Research, Graduate School of Business Administration, Harvard University, 1970.

Brennan, Michael J., and Eduardo S. Schwartz. "A New Approach to Evaluating Natural Resource Investments." *Midland Corporate Finance Journal* 3 (Spring 1985).

Howe, Keith M. "A Note on Flotation Costs and Capital Budgeting." *Financial Management* 11 (Winter 1982): 30–33.

Howe, Keith M., and James H. Patterson. "Capital Investment Decisions Under Economies of Scale in Flotation Costs." *Financial Management* 14 (Autumn 1985): 61–69.

Joy, O. Maurice. "Abandonment Values and Abandonment Decisions: A Clarification." *Journal of Finance* 31 (December 1976): 1225–28.

Pinches, George E. "Myopia, Capital Budgeting and Decision Making." *Financial Management* 11 (Autumn 1982): 6–19.

Trigeorgis, Lenos, and Scott P. Mason. "Valuing Managerial Flexibility." *Midland Corporate Finance Journal* 5 (Spring 1987): 14–21.

Weingartner, H. Martin. "Capital Rationing: n Authors in Search of a Plot." *Journal of Finance* 32 (December 1977): 1403–31.

Woods, John C., and Maury R. Randall. "The Net Present Value of Future Investment Opportunities: Its Impact on Shareholder Wealth and Implications for Capital Budgeting Theory." *Financial Management* 18 (Summer 1989): 85–92.

LONG-TERM FINANCING DECISIONS

LONG-TERM FINANCING

This chapter examines a firm's long-term financing alternatives, methods of issuance, and markets in which securities can be issued. In this chapter, we focus the discussion on the major alternatives that are open to a firm. The firm's *choice* of financing mix from among these alternatives—its capital structure decision—is analyzed in the next chapter.

THE J. K. LINK FINANCING DECISION

J. K. Link, Inc. has decided to raise $100 million of long-term funds. Because of capital structure considerations (discussed in Chapters 15 and 16), the company has decided that the financing will take the form of a long-term debt issue. Its investment bankers have told the company's treasurer that the following three alternatives are available:

1. A domestic public issue of bonds maturing in 10 years that would bear a 9% coupon and require issuance expenses of $1 million;

2. A domestic private issue of bonds maturing in 10 years that would bear a $9\frac{1}{8}\%$ coupon and would require issuance expenses of $750,000; and

3. A 10-year issue of bonds that the investment bankers could sell to European investors (a "Eurobond issue") that would require a $9\frac{1}{8}\%$ coupon and would require issuance expenses of $1,250,000.

The third alternative looks unattractive because the coupon rate and issuance expenses are greater than a domestic public issue would require. The domestic private issue would require a higher coupon but involve lower issuance expenses than the domestic public issue, but the investment bankers have warned that the private issue might require the company to agree to certain restrictions that might limit its operating and financing flexibility in the future.

After discussing these three alternative sources of long-term funds in greater detail—and telling you about certain special features of the Eurobond market and bond covenants—we will return to this problem and provide a solution.

THE LONG-TERM FINANCING MENU

14.1

Each time a corporation chooses to raise funds externally, it must decide which type of securities to issue. Transaction costs play a role in this choice because transaction costs are proportionately smaller for larger issues. The fixed component of cost is spread out over a larger issue, and the variable costs are greater for issues that are small enough to impinge on the liquidity of the securities when they are later traded in the capital market.

TABLE 14-1 Breakdown of Principal Sources of Domestic External Long-Term Financing by U.S. Corporations, 1970–1989 (Dollar Amounts in Millions)

Year	Aggregate Domestic External Financing[a]	Percentage Represented by			Percent Change in S&P 500 Index During Year	Moody's Average of Yields on Aa-Rated Corporate Bonds
		Common Stock	*Preferred Stock[b]*	*Debt[c]*		
1970	$ 38,945	18.6%	3.6%	77.8%	0.10%	8.32%
1971	45,084	20.6	8.1	71.3	10.79	7.78
1972	41,957	23.1	8.0	68.9	15.63	7.48
1973	33,390	23.2	10.1	66.7	−17.37	7.66
1974	38,313	10.4	5.9	83.7	−29.72	8.84
1975	53,619	13.8	6.4	79.8	31.55	9.17
1976	53,356	15.6	5.2	79.2	19.15	8.75
1977	53,792	14.6	7.3	78.1	−11.50	8.24
1978	47,230	15.9	6.0	78.1	1.06	8.92
1979	51,102	15.2	7.1	77.7	12.31	9.94
1980	73,694	22.9	4.9	72.2	25.77	12.50
1981	70,441	33.4	2.6	64.0	− 9.73	14.75
1982	84,198	30.2	6.1	63.7	14.76	14.41
1983	119,949	37.0	6.0	57.0	17.27	12.42
1984	132,531	14.0	3.1	82.9	1.40	13.31
1985	201,269	14.4	3.2	82.4	23.93	11.82
1986	381,936	13.2	4.7	82.1	16.84	9.47
1987	367,863	11.8	6.3	81.9	2.03	9.68
1988	385,625	9.3	5.7	85.0	12.40	9.94
1989	325,034	8.0	4.1	87.9	27.25	9.46
Total	$2,599,328	18.3%	5.7%	76.0%		

[a] Aggregate amount raised through the issuance of common stock, nonconvertible preferred stock, nonconvertible debt, and convertible securities.
[b] Includes convertible preferred and preference stock.
[c] Includes convertible debt.

Sources: Federal Reserve Bulletin, Board of Governors of the Federal Reserve System, Washington, D.C., various issues; *Daily Stock Price Record: New York Stock Exchange,* Standard & Poor's Corporation, New York, various issues; *Moody's Industrial Manual,* Moody's Investors Service, Inc., New York, 1987, a31; and *Moody's Bond Record,* Moody's Investors Service, Inc., New York, April 1990.

Table 14-1 shows that debt, common stock, and preferred stock are the principal sources of external long-term financing that corporations used during the period 1970–1989. Over that 20-year period, debt, common, and preferred accounted for 76.0%, 18.3%, and 5.7%, respectively, of the aggregate domestic external financing of U.S. corporations.

DEBT VERSUS EQUITY FINANCING

Table 14-1 reveals that the aggregate sale of common stock is sensitive to stock market conditions. Corporate issuers try to take advantage of rising markets when the demand for common stock is relatively strong. New issue activity tends to increase during periods of rising share prices, such as 1971–1972, 1980–1983, and 1985–1986. Correspondingly, corporations are generally reluctant to sell new issues of common stock when the share price is "low" by historical standards. Thus, common stock new issue activity tends to diminish during periods of depressed or falling share prices, such as 1973–1974.

Similarly, the volume of fixed income security issues (i.e., preferred stock and debt) tends to vary with the level of long-term interest rates. During periods of rising long-term interest rates, such as 1979–1981, corporations tend to favor short-term borrowing in the hope that long-term interest rates will fall. When long-term interest rates do fall, as in 1984–1989, corporations begin to replace this short-term debt.

PUBLIC VERSUS PRIVATE FINANCING

Companies can sell securities to the public through a registered **public offering** or directly to institutional investors through a **private placement**. Securities sold in a public offering must be registered with the Securities and Exchange Commission (SEC) by filing a **registration statement**, which contains a prospectus describing the issuer and the securities. The issuer must distribute the prospectus to potential investors. After registration, the securities can be traded freely by investors.

FEATURES OF PRIVATELY PLACED SECURITIES
Privately placed securities are not registered and hence are not freely tradable. Consequently, securities regulations require companies to offer securities privately only to investors sophisticated enough to make an independent determination of their investment merits, such as life insurance companies, property and casualty insurance companies, credit companies, pension funds, and wealthy individuals. During the period 1980–1988, approximately 50% of preferred stock issues and 30% of long-term debt issues, by dollar value, were sold through private placements. With the exception of common stock issued to venture capital investors or investors in leveraged buyouts, virtually all common stock is sold in public offerings.

ADVANTAGES AND DISADVANTAGES OF A PRIVATE PLACEMENT
A private placement offers the following advantages in comparison with a public offering:

- *Lower issuance costs* for smaller issues. A private placement avoids the costs of registering the securities, printing prospectuses, and obtaining credit ratings and various other expenses. Also, the private placement agent's fee is generally significantly less than the selling and management portion of the underwriting spread for a comparable public offering, and the fee can be avoided if the issuer negotiates the private placement directly with investors.

- *Issues can be placed more quickly* for firms that do not qualify for what is called **shelf registration**. Shelf registration allows the firm to issue the new securities at any time during the subsequent 2 years after the registration statement becomes effective. Registering securities requires time to prepare the registration statement and have the SEC review it, although the short-form registration statement (a recently approved shortened form available to be used in some cases) and the shelf registration process have greatly expedited the public offering process.

- *Greater flexibility of issue size.* The private market is more receptive to smaller issues; issues of only a few million dollars each are not uncommon. Public debt and preferred stock issues of less than a $50 million principal amount are typically more costly because their small size decreases their liquidity and thus lessens their attractiveness to investors.

- *Greater flexibility of security arrangements* and other terms. Private investors are capable of analyzing complex security arrangements, and it is easier to tailor the terms of an issue to suit both sides of the transaction. It is also easier to obtain lenders' consents to a change in terms should the firm's circumstances change.

A private placement has the following disadvantages relative to a public offering:

- *Higher yield.* To compensate for illiquidity, purchasers of privately placed securities require a yield premium relative to publicly-traded securities. For example, during the period 1961–1977, the average yield on privately placed corporate bonds exceeded the average yield on comparable public issues by approximately 50 basis points (half of 1 percent).[1]

- *More stringent covenants and more restrictive terms.* Because of illiquidity, private purchasers insist on tighter covenant restrictions to compensate for the greater agency costs. Private lenders have insisted on tighter protection against "event risk," the risk that stockholders might initiate certain events, such as a leveraged buyout, that could expropriate bondholder wealth.

In early 1990, the SEC adopted Rule 144A under the Securities Act of 1933, which allows qualified institutional investors (generally those who own and manage $100 million or more of securities) to trade freely with each other in securities that have not been registered with the SEC. Rule 144A is likely to enhance the liquidity of the secondary private placement market and reduce the interest rate penalty that has typically resulted from the higher transaction costs associated with the private securities market.

UNDERWRITTEN VERSUS NONUNDERWRITTEN SALE OF SECURITIES

A company may choose to market its securities itself (as the U.S. government does), but the vast majority employ investment bankers in some capacity because of their expertise and experience. Table 14–2 shows the ranking of the 15 leading securities underwriters in the United States during 1989. Note that the 5 largest firms accounted for more than 60% of *all* underwritten securities offerings in 1989.

INVESTMENT BANKING   The **investment banker** serves as an intermediary between the issuer and the purchasers, and typically provides the following services:

- Advice regarding the type and terms of the security to be issued.

- Advice regarding markets: public or private, domestic or international.

- Assistance with preparing the required documentation. Private placements require an **offering memorandum** that describes the proposed terms of the issue and provides information concerning the issuer. Public offerings require the filing of a **registration statement** with the SEC and the distribution of a **preliminary prospectus** (which is filed with the SEC as part of the registration

[1] Zwick (1980).

TABLE 14-2 Leading Managing Underwriters for U.S. Securities Offerings in 1989[a]

Rank	Manager	Number of Issues	Amount (Millions of Dollars)	Percent of Total
1.	Merrill Lynch	428	$45,985	14.9%
2.	Goldman, Sachs	492	42,937	13.9
3.	First Boston	418	37,765	12.2
4.	Salomon Brothers	404	31,805	10.3
5.	Morgan Stanley	293	29,782	9.6
6.	Shearson Lehman Hutton	342	24,745	8.0
7.	Bear, Stearns	424	18,186	5.9
8.	Drexel Burnham Lambert	224	16,805	5.5
9.	Prudential-Bache	349	16,426	5.3
10.	Kidder, Peabody	196	8,799	2.9
11.	Paine Webber	114	4,745	1.5
12.	Donaldson, Lufkin & Jenrette	100	4,448	1.4
13.	UBS Securities	89	2,831	0.9
14.	Smith Barney, Harris Upham	79	2,809	0.9
15.	Dean Witter	24	2,573	0.8
All Others Combined		757	18,711	6.0
	Total	4,733	309,352	100.0%

[a] Full credit is given to the lead managing underwriter.

Source: Investment Dealers' Digest, January 8, 1990, 30.

statement) to prospective buyers during the marketing period and a final **prospectus** to investors to confirm their purchases. Figures 14–1 (a) and (b) show the cover page and the "prospectus summary" page from a typical prospectus. The registration statement and prospectuses contain detailed financial information regarding the issue and the issuer.

■ Pricing the new issue.

■ In connection with a **purchase-and-sale** offering, the investment bankers purchase the entire issue from the issuer at a fixed price and agree to reoffer the securities to the public at an initial price that represents a fixed **gross underwriting spread** over the price the issuer receives. In an underwritten offering, the securities firms bear the risk that the entire issue may not be saleable at the initial offering price; if it is not, they will sell the securities at the market clearing price and bear the loss.

SYNDICATED OFFERING PROCESS   The syndicated offering process involves the formation of an underwriting group, or syndicate, consisting of securities firms who purchase the securities from the issuer and agree to reoffer them to investors. The lead managing underwriter of a syndicated offering assembles a syndicate con-

2,795,000 Shares

MICROSOFT ®

Microsoft Corporation

Common Stock

Of the 2,795,000 shares of Common Stock offered hereby, 2,000,000 shares are being sold by the Company and 795,000 shares are being sold by the Selling Stockholders. See "Principal and Selling Stockholders." The Company will not receive any of the proceeds from the sale of shares by the Selling Stockholders.

Prior to this offering, there has been no public market for the Common Stock of the Company. For the factors which were considered in determining the initial public offering price, see "Underwriting."

See "Certain Factors" for a discussion of certain factors which should be considered by prospective purchasers of the Common Stock offered hereby.

THESE SECURITIES HAVE NOT BEEN APPROVED OR DISAPPROVED BY THE SECURITIES AND EXCHANGE COMMISSION NOR HAS THE COMMISSION PASSED UPON THE ACCURACY OR ADEQUACY OF THIS PROSPECTUS. ANY REPRESENTATION TO THE CONTRARY IS A CRIMINAL OFFENSE.

	Initial Public Offering Price	Underwriting Discount(1)	Proceeds to Company(2)	Proceeds to Selling Stockholders(2)
Per Share	$21.00	$1.31	$19.69	$19.69
Total(3)	$58,695,000	$3,661,450	$39,380,000	$15,653,550

(1) The Company and the Selling Stockholders have agreed to indemnify the Underwriters against certain liabilities, including liabilities under the Securities Act of 1933.

(2) Before deducting expenses of the offering estimated at $541,000, of which $452,000 will be paid by the Company and $89,000 by the Selling Stockholders.

(3) The Company has granted to the Underwriters an option to purchase up to an additional 300,000 shares at the initial public offering price, less the underwriting discount, solely to cover overallotments. If such option is exercised in full, the total Initial Public Offering Price, Underwriting Discount and Proceeds to Company will be $64,995,000, $4,054,450 and $45,287,000, respectively.

The shares are offered severally by the Underwriters, as specified herein, subject to receipt and acceptance by them and subject to their right to reject any order in whole or in part. It is expected that the certificates for the shares will be ready for delivery at the offices of Goldman, Sachs & Co., New York, New York on or about March 20, 1986.

Goldman, Sachs & Co.   **Alex. Brown & Sons**
                                                                                                Incorporated

The date of this Prospectus is March 13, 1986.

FIGURE 14-1(A)

Prospectus cover page.

PROSPECTUS SUMMARY

The following summary is qualified in its entirety by the more detailed information and Consolidated Financial Statements appearing elsewhere in this Prospectus. All information relating to the Company's Common Stock contained in this Prospectus, except as presented in the Consolidated Financial Statements, reflects the conversion of all outstanding shares of Preferred Stock into Common Stock on the date of this Prospectus.

The Company

Microsoft designs, develops, markets, and supports a product line of systems and applications microcomputer software for business and professional use. The Microsoft Software Product Line chart inside the front cover of this Prospectus illustrates the evolution and diversity of the Company's product line. Microsoft's systems software products include Microsoft® MS-DOS®, a 16-bit microcomputer operating system used on the IBM PC and IBM compatible computers, and computer language products in six computer languages. The Company offers business applications software products in the following categories: word processing, spreadsheet, file management, graphics, communications, and project management. The Company's products are available for 8-bit, 16-bit, and 32-bit microcomputers, including IBM, Tandy, Apple, COMPAQ, Olivetti, AT&T, Zenith, Wang, Hewlett-Packard, DEC, Siemens, Philips, Mitsubishi, and NEC. Microsoft develops most of its software products internally using proprietary development tools and methodology. The Company markets and distributes its products domestically and internationally through the original equipment manufacturer ("OEM") channel and through the retail channel primarily by means of independent distributors and dealers and by direct marketing to corporate, governmental, and educational customers.

The Offering

Common Stock offered by the Company	2,000,000 shares(1)
Common Stock offered by the Selling Stockholders	795,000 shares
Common Stock to be outstanding after the offering	24,715,113 shares(1)
Proposed NASDAQ symbol	MSFT
Use of Proceeds	For general corporate purposes, principally working capital, product development, and capital expenditures.

Selected Consolidated Financial Information
(In thousands, except per share data)

	Year Ended June 30,				Six Months Ended December 31,	
	1982	1983	1984	1985	1984	1985
					(Unaudited)	
Income Statement Data:						
Net revenues	$24,486	$50,065	$97,479	$140,417	$62,837	$85,050
Income before income taxes	5,595	11,064	28,030	42,843	18,219	29,048
Net income	3,507	6,487	15,880	24,101	9,996	17,118
Net income per share	$ .17	$ .29	$ .69	$ 1.04	$ .43	$ .72
Shares used in computing net income per share	21,240	22,681	22,947	23,260	23,253	23,936

	December 31, 1985	
	Actual	As Adjusted(1)(2)
	(Unaudited)	
Balance Sheet Data:		
Working capital	$57,574	$ 96,502
Total assets	94,438	133,366
Total long-term debt	—	—
Stockholders' equity	71,845	110,773

(1) Assumes the Underwriters' over-allotment option is not exercised. See "Underwriting."
(2) Gives effect to the sale of shares offered by the Company hereby. The net proceeds have been added to working capital pending their use. See "Use of Proceeds."

FIGURE 14-1(B)
Prospectus summary page.

sisting of those securities firms that it believes would be most able to market the issue successfully.

NONUNDERWRITTEN OFFERINGS Securities issues sold through investment bankers are not always underwritten. In connection with private placements, securities firms customarily serve as agent for the issuer. Such offerings are sold on a **best-efforts** basis; the securities firms do *not* purchase the securities and resell them, but rather, only use their best efforts to sell the securities on behalf of the issuer. Public offerings of the securities of smaller, less well known companies are also often handled on a best-efforts basis—usually because the issuer is unable to find a securities firm willing to accept the underwriting risk for a reasonable price.

SECURITIES FIRMS' COMPENSATION In connection with an underwritten public offering, the underwriters charge a gross underwriting spread calculated as a percentage of the aggregate public offering price of the issue. This spread has three components: a management fee, typically 15 to 20% of the total spread, which compensates the managing underwriters for their assistance in designing the issue, preparing the documentation, forming the syndicate, and directing the offering process; an **underwriting fee**, typically 15% to 20% of the total spread, which compensates for the underwriting risk; and a **selling concession**, typically 60% to 70% of the total spread, which serves as compensation for the selling effort.

Securities firms' compensation represents a significant portion of the issuer's out-of-pocket cost of floating a new issue. Table 14-3 provides average spread information for public offerings of various types and sizes during the period 1973–1989. It is generally most expensive, strictly in terms of the total cost of issuance, to issue common stock and least expensive to issue (nonconvertible) bonds. This reflects the greater risks involved in underwriting common stock issues and also the higher selling commissions required to distribute common stock issues, large portions of

TABLE 14-3 Underwriting Spread and Issuance Expenses as Percentage of Offering Price for Registered Public Offerings, 1973–1989

Issue Size (Millions of Dollars)	Common Stock			Preferred Stock			Convertible Preferred and Convertible Debt			Bonds		
	Underwriting Spread (%)	Issuance Expense[a] (%)	Total (%)	Underwriting Spread (%)	Issuance Expense[a] (%)	Total (%)	Underwriting Spread (%)	Issuance Expense[a] (%)	Total (%)	Underwriting Spread (%)	Issuance Expense[a] (%)	Total (%)
Under 10.0	8.68	6.16	14.84	8.83	2.65	11.48	7.17	4.74	11.91	4.72	1.46	6.18
10.0 to 24.9	6.41	2.19	8.60	5.62	1.15	6.77	4.28	1.65	5.93	1.89	0.56	2.45
25.0 to 49.9	5.62	1.26	6.88	2.69	0.76	3.45	2.93	0.86	3.79	2.17	0.59	2.76
50.0 to 99.9	5.12	0.89	6.01	1.95	0.31	2.26	2.54	0.52	3.06	1.43	0.31	1.74
100.0 to 199.9	4.74	0.57	5.31	2.65	0.31	2.96	2.17	0.30	2.47	1.07	0.19	1.26
200 to 500	4.66	0.38	5.04	3.27	0.18	3.45	2.15	0.14	2.29	1.07	0.12	1.19
Over 500	5.87	0.23	6.10	3.50	0.30	3.80	2.92	0.06	2.98	1.78	0.16	1.94
Average	5.87	1.67	7.54	4.07	0.81	4.88	3.45	1.18	4.63	2.02	0.48	2.50

[a] Includes legal fees, accounting fees, SEC filing fee, blue sky expenses, printing, mailing, and miscellaneous out-of-pocket expenses.
Source: Securities Data Company, Inc.

which are typically marketed to individual investors. Note also the significant economies of scale in issuing securities.

DIRECT SALES OF SECURITIES   Several finance companies and certain other issuers have bypassed the investment banking industry and issued securities directly to investors in order to reduce issuance expenses. This strategy is most effective when the issuer has a natural market it can exploit, such as current securityholders. For example, Sears Roebuck Acceptance Corp. offered $250 million of medium-term notes (maturing in 2 to 10 years) in December 1981 in a registered public offering. Nonfinancial companies seldom offer securities directly to the public. One exception is an innovative offering of "Energy Thrift Certificates" by Green Mountain Power Corporation beginning in 1979.[2] Another exception is a new issue dividend reinvestment plan used to reduce issuance expenses.

In most cases, the investment banker's superior access to market information and to the channels of distribution, which results from the investment banker's day-to-day interaction with prospective investors, makes it more economical for an issuer to sell securities through an investment banker.

COMMON EQUITY FINANCING   **14.2**

Large companies typically raise the bulk of new common equity internally, that is, by retaining a portion of earnings. But smaller or rapidly growing companies typically also issue new common stock to raise funds, and even large companies sometimes issue new common equity through sizable public offerings. In addition, many companies have instituted dividend reinvestment or employee stock purchase plans that generate additional common equity on a continuing basis.

PRINCIPAL FEATURES OF COMMON STOCK

A company's **corporate charter** limits the number of **authorized shares** of common stock. A company cannot issue shares unless it has authorized shares available. Increasing the number of authorized shares is normally noncontroversial, but it does require a shareholder vote. In practice, management often tries to ensure that it has enough shares authorized but not yet issued to meet any unforeseeable corporate needs.

Shares become **issued shares** when a corporation sells them to investors. Issued shares consist of **outstanding shares**, which are held by investors, and **treasury shares**, which the corporation has repurchased from investors. Earnings per share and book value per share calculations are based on the number of outstanding shares.

Table 14-4 shows the shareholders' equity section of the 1989 balance sheet and the 1989 earnings per share calculation for E. I. du Pont de Nemours and Company. This firm had 900 million shares of common stock authorized at year-end 1989, of which 685,333,800 were issued and outstanding with no shares in its treasury. Du Pont had an average of 700,505,538 common shares outstanding during 1989, and earned $3.53 per average outstanding share.

Shares of common stock are issued with or without **par value**. Because some

---

[2]Gatti, Mills, and McTague (1981). The certificates had a 360-day maturity with interest paid at maturity, like bank certificates of deposit. The certificates were sold exclusively within Vermont, thus avoiding the need to register them with the SEC. Green Mountain Power discontinued the ETC program in 1984.

TABLE 14-4   Shareholders' Equity and Earnings Per Share
of E. I. du Pont de Nemours and Company for 1989
(Dollar Amounts in Millions Except Per-Share Amounts)

	At 12/31/89
Preferred Stock, without par value:	
$4.50 Series—1,672,594 shares	$ 167
$3.50 Series— 700,000 shares	70
	237
Common Stock, $.60 par value;	
900,000,000 shares authorized;	
685,333,800 shares issued	411
Additional paid-in capital	4,399
Reinvested earnings	10,751
Common stockholders' equity	15,561
Total stockholders' equity	$ 15,798
Net income	$ 2,480
Preferred dividends	10
Available for common	$ 2,470
Average common shares outstanding	700,505,538
Earnings per common share	$ 3.53

states do not permit companies to sell shares at a price below par value, par values are generally very small. Par value therefore has little real significance.

Book value per common share is the ratio of (1) common stockholders' equity, adjusted for any liquidation premium on any preferred or preference stock the company may have outstanding, to (2) the number of common shares outstanding on that date:

$$\text{book value per common share} = \frac{\text{common stockholders' equity}}{\text{number of common shares outstanding}}$$

(14.1)

For example, Du Pont's book value per common share at year-end 1989 was[3]

$$\text{book value per common share} = \frac{\$15,561}{685.3} = \$22.71$$

Book value per common share is the value per share if the corporation's assets are sold and liabilities are paid off at the amounts shown on the balance sheet, including preferred stock paid off at its involuntary liquidation value. Of course, book

[3] Du Pont's preferred stock does not carry any liquidation premium. But to illustrate how a liquidation premium affects the book value per common share calculation, suppose that the liquidation premium is 5%. Thus, the liquidation value of the preferred stock would be $249 million, or $12 million greater than its face amount. Reducing common stockholders' equity by this amount leads to

Book value per common share adjusted for preferred stock liquidation premium $= \dfrac{\$15,549}{685.3} = \$22.69$

values generally bear no direct relation to the true liquidation values of a company's assets because book value is based on historical cost and accounting measures of depreciation.

SOURCES OF ADDITIONAL COMMON EQUITY

The principal sources of additional common equity capital are

- Retained earnings;
- Public offerings of shares of the company or a subsidiary;
- Rights offerings to the company's current shareholders;
- Conversion of outstanding convertible debt or preferred stock by the security-holders;
- Exchanges of common shares for outstanding debt or preferred stock;
- Direct placement of shares with institutional investors or, as newer companies have done, placement with larger companies that wish to make venture capital investments in return for licensing rights or other benefits;
- Sale of newly issued common shares through a new issue dividend reinvestment plan, employee stock plan, or a customer stock purchase plan; and
- Contribution of newly issued common shares to a pension plan in lieu of a cash contribution.
- Partnerships, limited partnerships, and master limited partnerships.

PUBLIC OFFERING

There are two principal methods for offering common stock publicly: negotiated offerings and competitive offerings. In a **negotiated offering**, the issuer selects its investment bankers, who help prepare the necessary documentation, and price and offer the issue to the public. In a **competitive offering**, the issuer puts the shares up for bid, and the bidding process determines which investment bankers will market the issue and at what price. With the exception of registered public utility holding companies, which are required to sell securities through competitive bidding, common stock is almost always offered on a negotiated basis. Common stock offered on a negotiated basis can be registered with the SEC on a **fixed-price basis**, a **formula basis**, or a **shelf basis**. Registration on a fixed-price basis requires that the offering price and underwriting spread be determined before the SEC declares the registration statement effective and the securities are offered to the public. A formula basis provides greater flexibility: The SEC declares the registration statement effective within certain pricing boundaries. (Typically, the offering price must fall within 50 cents above or below the prevailing market price, and the gross spread must not exceed some specified maximum.) Thereafter, the underwriters can determine the precise offering price and spread (within the boundaries) and confirm sales immediately. Underwriters bear less market risk under a formula basis than under the fixed-price procedure because the shorter time lag between pricing and selling the securities reduces the chance of significant market movement.

The shelf process offers the greatest flexibility of the three procedures. The issuer can register up to a 2-year inventory of shares. After the SEC declares the registration statement effective, the issuer can sell portions of this inventory whenever it chooses. One often-stated potential drawback to this procedure is that registering shares representing several offerings may adversely affect the company's share price because the registered but unissued shares "overhang" the market. However, a recent study found no support for this argument.[4]

COSTS OF THE OFFERING   The costs of a public offering consist of three components: (1) the gross spread paid the underwriters, (2) the market impact of the announcement of the offering and subsequent marketing activity, and (3) out-of-pocket expenses, such as lawyers' and accountants' fees, engraving and printing, and mailing. Out-of-pocket expenses tend to be fixed expenses and are therefore a significant cost factor only in connection with very small offerings. The gross spread was discussed above as compensation for the security firm. Of course, viewed from the other side of the issuing transaction, the gross spread is a cost to the issuing firm.

MARKET IMPACT   A variety of studies have found that a company's share price typically declines upon the announcement of a public offering.[5] This may seem puzzling. If the corporation intends to invest the issue proceeds in positive-NPV projects, the share price should increase. Does the tendency for the share price to fall indicate a tendency for corporations to invest in unprofitable projects?

Empirical evidence indicates that the share price falls because the offering sends a negative signal to investors. This reaction has been explained in terms of asymmetric information.[6] If management acts in its shareholders' best interest, it will refrain from issuing shares when it believes the company's stock is relatively undervalued in the market and will choose to sell new shares when it believes the company's shares are relatively overvalued. Accordingly, the announcement of the new issue may signal overvaluation and lead to a negative market reaction. Taking this line of reasoning a step further, the decrease in share price should be larger, the larger the size of the offering.[7]

The market impact of a new issue, denoted ΔP_a, can be measured as the percentage change in the share price between the day prior to the announcement date and the offering date, adjusted for market movement:

$$\Delta P_a = \frac{P_{-1} - P_0}{P_{-1}} - \frac{\text{SP}_{-1} - \text{SP}_0}{\text{SP}_{-1}} \qquad (14.2)$$

where P is share price, SP is the S&P 500 index, and the subscripts 0 and -1 denote the offering date and one day prior to the announcement date, respectively.

EFFECTIVE SPREAD   The effective spread is the gross spread plus the market impact:

$$\text{Effective Spread} = \text{Gross Spread} + \Delta P_a \qquad (14.3)$$

The effective spread is important because it is the *net* cost. For example, a 5% gross spread with a 2% price increase would be preferred to a 4% gross spread and a 2% price decline. Eliminating informational asymmetries with respect to future investment opportunities will increase the likelihood of receiving fair market value for new securities. Firms may be using underwriters to do just that. For example, a firm may be able to signal, through underwriters, that the firm has valuable private informa-

---

[4]Bhagat, Marr, and Thompson (1985).
[5]Asquith and Mullins (1986); Hess and Bhagat (1986); and Masulis and Korwar (1986). Also, Bowyer and Yawitz (1980) found that utility share prices fell relative to the Dow Jones Utility Index upon the announcement of an offering during both periods of generally rising share prices and periods of generally falling share prices.
[6]Myers and Majluf (1984).
[7]Masulis and Korwar (1986).

tion, without having to make the information public and available to competitors, which would reduce the value of the private information.[8]

Opportunities for issuers to reduce issuance costs may also occur because of market mechanisms. One such opportunity is increased institutional demand for an issue.[9] Institutional commission charges are substantially lower than retail commission charges. Thus, an issue targeted to institutional investors requires a smaller selling concession and hence gross spread than one targeted to retail purchasers.

TIMING   Issuers and their investment bankers typically expend a great deal of effort trying to time an offering appropriately. The objective, of course, is to realize the best possible price for the shares. Based on the Principle of Capital Market Efficiency, we know that selling shares prior to a decrease in the market requires luck rather than expertise. However, while expertise cannot insure peak pricing, it is still important because it can help us avoid "shooting ourselves in the foot." To minimize the timing risk, an issuer should adhere to the following guidelines:

- It is best not to offer shares too near an expiration date for options on the company's shares. Option-related buying and selling of the company's shares may affect the company's share price.[10]

- It is generally preferable to issue during periods when the calendar of competing issues is relatively light. During periods of a relatively smaller supply of new issues, the underwriters' sales forces can focus a greater proportion of their selling effort on your firm's issue.

- It is generally better to offer higher dividend yielding common stocks just before rather than just after the ex-dividend date. A company's share price may be above its equilibrium level just prior to the ex-dividend date but may be below its equilibrium level just after that date because of tax-oriented share trading around the ex-dividend date.[11]

- It is generally better to offer common stock during periods when investors are realigning their portfolios to increase the percentage of funds invested in common stocks, as occurred in 1982–1983.

- Companies with heavy common stock financing needs, such as utilities, often find it advantageous to make two smaller offerings in lieu of one larger one. This reduces the price risk as well as the potential market impact of the offering. The shelf registration process has reduced the cost of splitting an offering into multiple smaller offerings.

RIGHTS ISSUES

Instead of offering common stock directly to the general public, a company may offer new stock to its current shareholders on a privileged-subscription basis. Such offerings are called **rights offerings** because the company distributes to its shareholders **rights** to **subscribe** for additional shares at a specified price. The corporate charters of many companies give current shareholders the **preemptive right** to purchase newly issued stock or securities that can be converted into common stock. Preemptive rights give the shareholders the right to maintain their respective owner-

[8] Heinkel and Schwartz (1986).
[9] Finnerty (1983) discusses how such an opportunity developed during 1982 for certain electric utility common stock issuers.
[10] Klemkosky (1978).
[11] Finnerty (1981).

ship percentages of the company's common stock. In recent years, most large companies with widely dispersed shareholdings have eliminated preemptive rights. Companies outside the United States tend to rely on rights offerings to raise additional equity capital to a greater extent than U.S. companies.

HOW A RIGHTS OFFERING WORKS In a rights offering, the company distributes to each shareholder one right for each share the holder owns as of the specified **record date** for the offering. Rights are call options on newly issued shares. As with other market-traded options, a right has a time to expiration and a strike price. The time to expiration is called the **subscription period** and is defined by the **expiration date**, and it typically varies between 14 and 24 days. The strike price for a specified number of rights is called the **subscription price**. For example, on October 18, 1978, Long Island Lighting Company offered 6,402,515 additional shares of its common stock to its current shareholders on the basis of one new share for seven rights (i.e., each seven shares already owned) plus a subscription price of $17.15 per new share during the 18-day subscription period. At the time, the Long Island Lighting Company shares were trading at $18.375.

Shareholders can either (1) exercise the rights and subscribe for shares or (2) sell the rights if they are transferable (they usually are); otherwise, the rights will expire, worthless, at the close of business on the expiration date. If shareholders wish to purchase extra shares, they can purchase additional rights from other shareholders who choose to sell their rights, or if the company gives shareholders an **oversubscription privilege** to purchase the shares for which other shareholders fail to subscribe, they can buy them from the issuer to the extent they are available. In the 1978 Long Island Lighting Company rights offering, investors subscribed for 6,178,777 shares, representing 96.5% of the shares offered. Of these shares, 4,855,559 were subscribed for upon the exercise of rights, and 1,323,218 were subscribed for pursuant to the oversubscription privilege.

VALUE OF RIGHTS The Options Principle states that options are valuable. Because a right is a call option, then, it will always have a positive value prior to its expiration. Recall from Chapter 8 that the value of an option, and therefore a right, is a function of (1) the strike price, (2) the value of the underlying stock (3) the time to expiration, (4) the variance of the rate of return on the underlying stock, and (5) the riskless rate of interest. In addition, the value of a right depends on its **dilutive effect**, which is caused by its creation of new equity. Loosely speaking, the dilutive effect is the difference between the strike price (the new equity) and the market value (existing equity). Recall that when the value of the underlying stock is more than the strike price, a call option is in-the-money. The smaller the strike price relative to the share price, the more valuable the call option.

To encourage subscription, rights are issued in-the-money. That is, the issuer sets the subscription price at less than the market price of its stock on the record date. Because of the short time to expiration, the exercise value—which is based on the difference between the strike price and share price—is the major determinant of the value of a right. That is, with a very short life, the time value of the in-the-money option is negligible. Investment bankers generally recommend setting the subscription price so that the rights will have an initial value of no less than $0.15 to $0.20 each. Establishing this minimum rights value is intended to induce nonsubscribing shareholders to sell their rights rather than let them expire because they are worth less than the transaction costs of exercising them.

The initial value of each right just after the offering is announced, and when the stock is trading **rights-on** (i.e., the rights are still attached to the stock), is approximated by

$$R = \frac{P_R - S}{N + 1} \qquad (14.4)$$

where R is the value of the right, P_R is the market value of a share trading rights-on, S is the strike price, and N is the number of rights to purchase one new share. For example, the initial value of each right issued in connection with the 1978 Long Island Lighting Company rights offering was

$$R = \frac{\$18.375 - \$17.15}{7 + 1} = \$0.1531$$

Equation (14.4) is only an approximation of the value of a right because it ignores the time value of the right. It is a very good approximation because the time until expiration is very short, the right is significantly in-the-money so that the time value is small, and the dilutive effect of a single right is negligible.

After the ex-date, the stock is said to trade ex-rights because the purchaser of the shares is not entitled to receive the rights. On the ex-date, then, the share price decreases by the value of the right, which is no longer attached to it. Therefore, the share price ex-rights, denoted P_E, is

$$P_E = P_R - R \qquad (14.5)$$

In the case of the 1978 Long Island Lighting rights offering,

$$P_E = \$18.375 - \$0.1531 = \$18.2219$$

In a perfect capital market environment, the offering of rights does not affect shareholder wealth; the value of a right plus the value of a share ex-rights just equals the value of a share rights-on. Prior to the rights offering, seven shares were worth $7 \times \$18.375 = \$128.625$. For every seven shares outstanding, the firm issues one new share and receives \$17.15. On the ex-date, each share is thus worth ($\$128.625 + 17.15$) / ($7 + 1$) = \$18.2219. Immediately thereafter, the market value of each right will vary with the price of the firm's common stock:

$$R = \frac{P_E - S}{N} \qquad (14.6)$$

To continue the Long Island Lighting example, if the company's share price decreases to \$18, the market value of a right, denoted R', will be [12]

$$R' = \frac{\$18.00 - 17.15}{7} = \$0.1214$$

UNDERWRITTEN RIGHTS OFFERING Companies generally prefer to engage securities firms to "stand by" to purchase unsubscribed shares on an underwritten basis rather than reduce the subscription price to ensure a successful offering. Roughly two-thirds of all rights offerings are underwritten. The underwriters are paid a **standby fee** for each share offered for subscription plus a **take-up fee** payable

---

[12] Like Equation (14.4), Equations (14.5) and (14.6) are approximations that ignore the time value of the option. Also, actual values may deviate from theoretical values because of transaction costs. However, empirical evidence supports capital market efficiency by showing that arbitrage activity is generally successful at keeping the market value of a right close to its theoretical value. See Soldofsky and Johnson (1967).

on shares acquired by the underwriters through the exercise of rights during the subscription period and on shares remaining unsubscribed at the end of the period. In both cases, the underwriters would immediately sell the shares into the market. The standby fee, which is generally set between $0.20 and $0.50 per share, compensates for the underwriting risk. The take-up fee, which is generally set between $0.25 and $1.00 per share, compensates for the selling and other expenses the underwriters incur on the shares they actually handle. Flotation costs averaged 6.17% of the gross proceeds in underwritten rights offerings, and 2.45% of the gross proceeds in nonunderwritten rights offerings during the period 1971–1975.[13]

ADVANTAGES AND DISADVANTAGES OF A RIGHTS OFFERING   A rights offering provides shareholders with the option of retaining their proportionate ownership and voting interests in a company when it sells additional common shares. As a practical matter, this is probably beneficial only to shareholders with large holdings because of the separation of ownership and control; smaller shareholders can purchase additional shares in the market.

A rights offering may also be more beneficial than a public offering to a company that does not have broad market appeal or has concentrated stock ownership because it enables the selling effort to be focused on investors who already own shares and who are therefore familiar with the company. In addition, common stock issued in a rights offering can be purchased on margin, whereas common stock issued in a public offering cannot.

It is also often argued that a rights offering is beneficial to shareholders because they can buy shares at a "bargain price" or because they perceive the rights as a "dividend." But as already noted, a stockholder receives no benefits from the rights other than the option of retaining proportionate ownership; the company's share price falls following the ex-date, and the decrease in price offsets the value of a right, as in the case of a stock dividend.[14] The shareholder is just as well off following the rights offering as before it, provided she either sells the rights or exercises them but of course is worse off if she fails to sell or exercise them. Further, public offerings are consistently underpriced at issue, which involves a net wealth transfer away from the existing shareholders.

On the other hand, there are two principal disadvantages to a rights offering. First, a rights offering generally takes longer to complete. Second, a rights offering eliminates the possible transaction cost savings of selling large blocks of shares to institutions not currently holding the stock.

RIGHTS OFFERING VERSUS PUBLIC OFFERING   A company should issue new shares in the least costly manner. It is generally argued that a rights offering is less costly than a public offering. In spite of this argument, companies raise substantially more funds through public offerings than rights offerings. Also, the flotation costs associated with the sale of shares through nonunderwritten rights offerings to shareholders other than the parent company or some other holder of a large block of stock have been shown to be proportionately higher than the flotation costs in an underwritten public offering of the same size.[15] A rights offering can lead to lower flotation costs if there is a small group that holds a large percentage of the stock *and* that

---

[13] Smith (1977).
[14] Levy and Sarnat (1971).
[15] Hansen and Pinkerton (1982).

group commits to exercise its rights. Similar to public offerings, the announcement of a rights offering has a significant negative impact on the share price.[16]

The simultaneous existence of multiple methods of raising new external equity capital seems to imply that no single method is best in all cases.[17]

DIVIDEND REINVESTMENT PLANS

Many companies have instituted **dividend reinvestment plans** that give shareholders the opportunity to reinvest dividends, supplementary cash, and in some cases interest payments on the company's bonds and/or dividend payments on the company's preferred stock in newly issued shares of the company's common stock. The amount of new capital raised depends, of course, on the amount of dividends paid and shareholder decisions to reinvest. Companies also often provide **employee stock plans** that give their employees the right to subscribe for shares of the company's stock. Often such plans enable employees to purchase stock at a discount below the prevailing market price. The discount is intended to approximate the issuance costs.

MASTER LIMITED PARTNERSHIPS

Master limited partnerships are publicly-traded limited partnerships that operate businesses and are much like corporations except for their legal structure. Many are listed on the NYSE. A partnership is not taxable under the Internal Revenue Code; income is taxed directly to the partners, whether or not it is distributed to the partners in cash. A corporation, on the other hand, is taxable. Corporate operating income that is to be distributed to shareholders is taxed twice: as corporate net income *and* as shareholders' dividend income. The partnership structure eliminates a layer of taxation. However, if an entity is earning income, and has very heavy capital expenditure requirements, and needs to retain the bulk of its earnings, the limited partnership structure has a disadvantage in that the limited partners will owe tax on their respective pro rata shares of the partnership's income but will not receive cash from distributions to pay the tax. On the other hand, if the limited partnership reports tax losses, limited partners will get the benefit of these tax losses, whereas corporate shareholders cannot share in such losses. Several oil and gas producers have formed oil and gas master limited partnerships that pass through tax losses.

In recent years, a variety of companies have either restructured into limited partnership form or formed a subsidiary into a master limited partnership and floated a minority interest to the public. The list includes oil and gas producers, timber products producers, a collection of Burger King franchises, and the Boston Celtics professional basketball team. In each case, the organizers sought to utilize the tax advantages of the limited partnership structure.[18] The Revenue Act of 1987 changed the tax treatment of MLPs. Henceforth, newly formed limited partnerships that are publicly-traded, such as MLPs, would be taxed as corporations except for natural resource MLPs (e.g., oil and gas), oil and gas pipelines, and certain other kinds of partnerships with essentially passive income.

---

[16]White and Lusztig (1980).

[17]Heinkel and Schwartz (1986) provide a model that explains the simultaneous existence of three offering methods: underwritten public offering, underwritten rights offering, and nonunderwritten rights offering.

[18]Collins and Bey (1986).

DEBT AND PREFERRED EQUITY FINANCING

There are five principal classes of long-term corporate debt instruments: unsecured debt, secured debt, income bonds, tax-exempt debt, and convertible debt. Convertible bonds are discussed later in the chapter.

UNSECURED DEBT   Unsecured long-term debt consists of notes and debentures. By securities industry convention, the term **notes** is normally used to describe unsecured bonds with an original maturity of 10 years or less; the term **debentures** is normally used when the original maturity exceeds 10 years. Notes and debentures are issued on the strength of the issuer's general credit according to a financial contract (the bond indenture); they are not secured by specific property. If the issuer goes bankrupt, noteholders and debentureholders are classified as general creditors.

Debentures may be issued in different levels of seniority. **Subordinated debentures** rank behind (unsubordinated) debentures in payment of interest and principal and claims on the company's assets in the event of bankruptcy. Because of this subordinated position and its commensurate higher risk, subordinated debentures have a higher required rate of return than senior debt of the same company.

SECURED DEBT   There are several types of secured debt: mortgage bonds, collateral trust bonds, equipment trust certificates, and conditional sales contracts are the most common. An issue of **mortgage bonds** is secured by a lien on specific assets of the issuer, which are described in detail in the legal document, called a **mortgage**, that grants the lien. If the issuer defaults in the payment of principal or interest or in the performance of some other provision of the loan contract, lenders (or the trustee acting on their behalf) can seize the assets securing the mortgage bonds and sell them to pay off the debt obligation. If the proceeds are insufficient to satisfy the claim of the mortgage bondholders in full, they become general creditors for the balance of their claim. The extra protection the mortgage provides lowers the risk and hence lowers the required rate of return from that of comparable debentures. But the issuer sacrifices flexibility in selling assets because mortgaged assets can be removed from the asset pool only with mortgage bond holders' permission or if suitable replacement collateral is provided.

COLLATERAL TRUST BONDS   These securities are similar to mortgage bonds except that the lien is against securities; as for example, the common shares of one or more of the issuer's subsidiaries, rather than real property like plant and equipment.

EQUIPMENT TRUST CERTIFICATES AND CONDITIONAL SALES CONTRACTS   Such securities are frequently issued to finance the purchase of aircraft or railroad rolling stock.[19] These are similar financing mechanisms in which the borrower obtains title to the assets being financed only after the debt has been fully repaid.

INCOME BONDS   The issuer of an **income bond** is obligated to pay interest only if it has sufficient income available (hence the security's name). An earnings test is specified in the bond indenture, and interest must be paid if the company has sufficient income according to this test. By contrast, preferred stock dividends are paid at the discretion of the company's board of directors. Thus, investors should prefer

---

[19]Rice (1981) provides an excellent overview of equipment trust certificates and related methods of financing.

income bonds over preferred stocks, all else equal. But because the contingent nature of interest payments makes the risk of bankruptcy low for income bonds, issuers might find both securities to be of comparable riskiness. Moreover, in the past the fixed formula enabled issuers to deduct interest payments on income bonds for tax purposes, creating a significant cost advantage over preferred stock.[20]

TAX-EXEMPT CORPORATE DEBT   Corporations are permitted under the Internal Revenue Code to issue tax-exempt bonds for specified purposes. Congress grants tax-exempt bonding authority from time to time as an incentive to encourage investment in specified types of projects deemed to be in the public interest. The Tax Reform Act of 1986 sharply reduced the list of activities that qualify for tax-exempt corporate debt financing. Activities that still qualified following the Tax Reform Act of 1986 include solid waste disposal facilities and hazardous waste disposal facilities. When a project qualifies for tax-exempt debt financing, holders of the tax-exempt bonds do not have to pay federal income tax on the interest payments they receive, so they are willing to accept a lower interest rate than on taxable debt. This, of course, creates a tax asymmetry. Therefore, as a general rule, if a company plans to construct facilities that qualify for tax-exempt financing, it should use such financing to the maximum extent.

PRINCIPAL FEATURES OF LONG-TERM DEBT

The preceding discussion highlighted the principal differences among the various classes of long-term debt. More important from an analytical standpoint, long-term debt instruments share certain common features:

- A stated **maturity**.
- A stated **principal amount**.
- A stated **coupon rate of interest**.
- A **mandatory redemption** (or sinking fund) **schedule**. Long-term debt issues typically contain a **sinking fund**, which calls for a sequence of mandatory redemption payments (i.e., principal repayments) prior to the maturity date. Bonds are redeemed through the sinking fund at their face amount or through capital market purchases.[21] Long-term debt issues by utility companies represent an important exception; such issues typically have what is called a **bullet maturity**, which calls for a single lump sum repayment at maturity.
- An **optional redemption provision**. Issuers of long-term debt typically retain a call option on the debt. They retain the right to **call** the issue (or some portion of it) for early redemption according to a schedule of optional redemption (strike or call) prices that is specified at the time of issue. This right to redeem bonds is typically limited. Some bonds provide for a period immediately following issuance (e.g., 5 years) during which the bonds are **noncallable**; the issuer cannot

---

[20] One of the great puzzles in finance was why so many companies issued preferred stock rather than income bonds when income bonds seemed to offer greater advantages for both the issuer and lenders or investors. The issue is now moot. The Internal Revenue Service issued proposed rules for distinguishing debt from equity for tax purposes. Under the proposed rules, income bonds would generally be treated as equity, and "interest" on the income bonds would not be tax-deductible for the corporation. See McConnell and Schlarbaum (1981).

[21] If the bonds are selling at or above par value, the firm will call individual bonds that have been chosen randomly and pay the owner the par value. If the bonds are selling below par value, the firm can repurchase the bonds in the capital market if the sinking fund covenant does not require otherwise. Public debt issues generally give the issuer this option; private debt issues often do not.

call them at any price during this period. Most long-term issues contain a weaker provision; the bonds are only **nonrefundable**. Accordingly, the bonds can be called at the appropriate call premium and redeemed out of excess cash or the proceeds from an equity issue (or, in some cases, out of the proceeds of a junior debt issue), but during the period of nonrefundability the issuer is prohibited from issuing new debt that ranks senior to or on a par with the debt to be redeemed and using the proceeds to refund the outstanding issue. As noted in Chapter 9, the optional redemption provision may be useful in reducing a firm's agency costs, and there is empirical evidence suggesting that this is the case.[22]

PROTECTIVE COVENANTS   Debt issues provide for a financial contract that imposes restrictions on the long-term bond issuer that are designed to protect the bondholders. For public debt issues, this contract is called a **bond indenture**. A trustee acts as agent for the bondholders and monitors the issuer's compliance with the provisions of the indenture. For a private issue, it is called a **bond** (or **note**) **agreement**. These contracts specify the maturity, interest rate, and other terms mentioned earlier, and in many cases, include a number of restrictive covenants. These covenants typically specify certain financial tests that if not met limit the borrower's ability to (1) incur additional indebtedness (**debt limitation**), (2) use cash to pay dividends or make share repurchases (**dividend limitation**), (3) mortgage assets (**limitation on liens** and/or a **negative pledge clause**), (4) borrow through one of its subsidiaries (**limitation on subsidiary borrowing**), (5) sell major assets (**limitation on asset dispositions**), (6) merge with or into another company or sell substantially all its assets to another company (**limitation on merger, consolidation, or sale**), and (7) sell assets and lease them back (**limitation on sale-and-leaseback**). For example, a debt limitation covenant might prohibit the borrower from issuing additional long-term debt if (1) the issuer's interest coverage would, as a result of the issue, fall below some specified minimum (a **coverage test**) or (2) the resulting ratio of net tangible assets to long-term debt would fall below a specified minimum (an **asset-coverage test**). As a second example, a dividend limitation typically limits the amount of funds available for cash dividends or share repurchases to a specified sum plus some specified fraction of cumulative earnings (less the cumulative amount already used for this purpose) since the date of issuance of the bonds.[23]

Bond indentures and bond agreements also specify certain **events of default**. If the borrower fails to pay interest or repay principal promptly (subject possibly to a short grace period), defaults on another debt issue, or fails to adhere to one of the covenants (and fails to correct the deficiency when notified to do so by the trustee under the indenture or directly by lenders in the case of privately placed debt), the lenders (or the trustee acting on their behalf) can demand repayment of the debt. Often, however, bondholders will try to negotiate before pursuing default proceedings because generally the bondholders do not really want to take ownership of the firm.

CHOICE OF DEBT MATURITY

A debt repayment schedule that bunches the company's debt repayment obligations within a few brief periods involves greater insolvency risk (i.e., insufficient cash to meet required payments on time) than a debt repayment schedule that spreads these

---

[22] Thatcher (1985).

[23] See Chapter 9 for a discussion of the use of bond covenants in the financial contracting process.

repayment obligations over a reasonably long period. Also, if the company is rapidly growing and/or changing in significant ways (as in its investment risk), issuing shorter-maturity debt is an alternative to issuing convertible debt because it also provides the firm with the option to renegotiate its debt contract in the future.[24]

SIGNIFICANCE OF INCLUDING A SINKING FUND   A sinking fund has two important consequences. First, as noted in Chapter 9, the need to make principal repayments furnishes a monitoring device. Second, a sinking fund reduces the effective life of the debt, thereby reducing the bond's risk in the same way as a shorter maturity. When a debt issue provides for a sinking fund, the issue's maturity overstates the length of the period the original debt remains outstanding. For example, a debt issue that matures in 10 years but involves equal sinking fund payments at the end of years 6 through 10 has what might be thought of as an effective maturity of 8 years. On a time-weighted basis, the debt will be repaid in an average of 8 years. This effective maturity is called **average life**.

SETTING THE COUPON RATE

Most issuers of debt select a coupon rate that will make the bonds worth par. However, at times asymmetric taxes or asymmetric information can make it advantageous either to set the coupon rate below the prevailing market rate or to let the interest rate float according to some specified formula.

DEEP-DISCOUNT BONDS   In 1981 and 1982, many corporations issued so-called **deep-discount bonds**, which carried very low interest rates and were sold at prices well below their principal amounts. For example, Du Pont sold $600 million principal amount of 6% Debentures due 2001 at a price of 46.852% ($468.52 per $1,000 bond) on November 19, 1981. Recall that in Chapter 5 we discussed **zero-coupon bonds**, which would be the deepest-discount bonds possible since they make only a single payment at maturity. Among many others, Beatrice Foods sold $250 million principal amount of Zero Coupon Notes due February 9, 1992, at a price of 25.50% on February 2, 1982.

Certain investors, particularly pension funds, found the deep-discount bonds and zero-coupon bonds attractive. The bonds generally have a call price equal to their par value. Unless the bonds have a call price schedule that is well below their par value, it is unlikely that a firm would ever exercise its call option. While a reduced risk of a call benefits the bondholders it is of course at the expense of the issuer's refunding flexibility.

The discount also reduces the lender's reinvestment risk. In the case of a zero-coupon bond, the investor's "income" each period is effectively reinvested at the issue's yield to maturity, regardless of what interest rates are at the time. This immunizes the investor's total return against interest rate movements between the dates of issuance and maturity. The absence of reinvestment risk also enabled certain investors, such as pension funds, to match their investment income against future liabilities more closely than they could with alternative investments.

Issuers also found the deep-discount bonds and zero-coupon bonds attractive because of a tax asymmetry. Until May 1982, issuers were permitted to deduct an equal portion of the discount each period. Thus, interest could be deducted at a faster rate than it accrued, which substantially reduced the effective after-tax cost of the debt. Because most purchasers of zero-coupon bonds were tax-exempt, the manner of amortizing the discount did not affect them.

---

[24] See Chapter 9 for a discussion of how convertible debt can reduce agency costs.

FIXING THE COUPON RATE OR LETTING IT FLOAT   Industrial companies also issue floating-rate long-term debt, but they do so infrequently. However, companies such as banks and finance companies whose return on assets fluctuates with interest rate movements often find it prudent to issue such debt. For example, General Motors Acceptance Corporation issued $250 million principal amount of Adjustable Rate Notes Due November 15, 1990 on November 13, 1980. The interest rate on these notes was adjusted annually, beginning 2 years after the date of issue. On each adjustment date, it was set equal to 107.2% of the arithmetic average of the two most recent weekly average yields to maturity of U.S. Treasury securities adjusted to a constant maturity of 10 years.

Most companies have chosen to fix the interest rate on long-term debt issues and have adjusted the mix of fixed-rate and floating-rate debt by altering the mix of short-term bank debt and commercial paper on the one hand and fixed-rate longer-term debt on the other. Before deciding whether to issue floating-rate intermediate-term or long-term debt, a company should at least compare the prospective terms for such an issue against the following alternatives:

■ Issuing a sequence of shorter-term issues whose successive maturities match the successive interest rate adjustment dates.

■ Issuing fixed-rate debt that matures the day the floating-rate issue does.

In the first case, the sequence of shorter-term issues will involve roughly the same degree of interest rate risk as the longer-term floating-rate issue. The sequence of shorter-term issues will involve greater issuance expenses than the longer-term floating-rate issue, but companies can mitigate the issuance expenses by issuing **extendible notes**. These securities permit the issuer to reset the interest rate at regular intervals, typically every 2 or 3 years, but give holders the right to "put" the bonds back to the issuer immediately thereafter. As long as the issuer resets the interest rate at a market level, the put option will not be exercised, and the debt will thus effectively be rolled over.

In the second case, the floating-rate issue exposes the issuer to the risk that interest rates will change. Because of this, it is not surprising that industrial companies generally borrow long term on a fixed-rate basis to fund investments in fixed assets. By contrast, when the issuer's revenues are sensitive to movements in interest rates, borrowing on a floating-rate basis may actually reduce the company's financial risk by aligning the fluctuations in revenues and interest expense.

SETTING THE OPTIONAL REDEMPTION PROVISIONS

The optional redemption, or call, provision is a call option that gives the issuer the right to buy back the issue. Setting the optional redemption provisions involves two questions: Should the issue include a call option? If so, what form should it take? The answer to the first question would appear to be yes because most corporate debt issues include call provisions. By contrast, U.S. Treasury securities are generally noncallable for life. In a perfect capital market environment, an issuer does not derive any net benefit from including a call provision because lenders will require a yield premium sufficient to compensate them fully for the risk of a call.[25] However, market imperfections, such as tax asymmetries, agency costs, and transaction costs, may cause the call provision to matter.[26]

[25] Weingartner (1967) and Kraus (1973).
[26] See Boyce and Kalotay (1979) and Marshall and Yawitz (1980) concerning tax asymmetry arguments. See Bodie and Taggart (1978) and Barnea, Haugen, and Senbet (1980) concerning agency cost arguments. See Emery, Lewellen, and Mauer (1988) concerning the transaction cost argument.

Interestingly, within the past few years, some corporate issuers have begun to incorporate put options in their debt issues. The put option represents a mechanism for reducing agency costs by limiting the possibility of *claim dilution*, such as the loss in value that would result if a corporation effected a leveraged buyout and the bonds had to remain outstanding for their original term. The put option, by permitting holders to force early redemption, limits this impairment in value.

DESIGN OF CALL PROVISIONS   The call provision included in corporate debt issues has become highly standardized: The first year's call price is normally equal to the public offering price plus the coupon rate, and thereafter the annual call prices decrease by equal decrements to par, at which price the bonds are callable over the remaining years to maturity. The call provision also typically imposes certain limitations on the issuer's ability to exercise the option: in the public market, long-term manufacturing company debt issues are nonrefundable for 10 years but can be called and paid for out of excess cash or out of the proceeds of an equity issue; long-term electric utility debt issues are nonrefundable for 5 years; and long-term telephone utility debt issues are noncallable (for any reason) for 5 years.

It is unclear whether the conventional redemption schedule is optimal. There may be one or more alternatives that are equivalent or superior to currently used provisions, such as setting the call price equal to the market value of the bond.[27]

FREQUENCY AND TIMING OF DEBT ISSUES

The economies of scale noted in Table 14–3 make larger issues relatively more attractive. In addition, large issues ensure a relatively liquid secondary market for the bonds. Consequently, companies issue long-term debt in large discrete amounts, and most corporations plan these issues carefully. Due to capital market efficiency, arbitrage opportunities with respect to interest rate movement will not exist. However, if a firm will be making a transaction in any case, it may be possible to obtain a modest reduction in the total cost of the transaction with short-term management. For example, during periods of tight money or particularly volatile interest rates, the supply of funds for non-investment-grade bonds tends to shrink. Also, a large Treasury financing, for example, can temporarily depress the debt market. Therefore, issuers should remain flexible with respect to timing in order to prevent temporary factors from adversely affecting their cost of borrowing.

ISSUING PREFERRED STOCK AND PREFERENCE STOCK

Preferred stock and preference stock represent something of a hybrid, combining certain features of common stock and certain features of debt. Preferred stock and preference stock rank senior to common stock and junior to debt in claims on the corporation's operating income and claims on the company's assets in the event of liquidation. The only significant difference between preferred stock and preference stock is that preferred stock is senior; dividends must be paid in full on the preferred stock before the company can pay dividends on its preference stock. Companies normally issue preference stock only when charter limitations prevent them from issuing additional preferred stock. Because of the basic similarity between the two, the balance of this section will refer simply to preferred stock.

Preferred stock has the following principal features:

---

[27] One alternative form that has been proposed by Emery, Hoffmeister, and Spahr (1987) involves indexation of the call prices to changes in interest rates. The indexation is used so that the call price will be approximately equal to the market value of the bond.

■ A **par** (or **stated**) **value**. This par value is typically one of three quantities: $25, $50, or $100 per share. Issues that are to be sold predominantly to institutional investors are typically given a $100 par value. Issues targeted to individual investors are typically given a $25 par value so that a round lot (100 shares) would cost only $2,500.

■ A stated **dividend rate**. Preferred stock pays dividends quarterly, like common stock, but at a stated rate, like debt. Because of the contingent nature of preferred stock dividends, they are not deductible for tax purposes. Also, preferred stock issues typically have a **cumulative dividend feature**. That is, missed dividends are accumulated. This cumulative amount must be paid in full before any cash dividends can be paid on common stock.

■ An **optional redemption provision**. Preferred stock typically has optional redemption provisions similar to those found in debt issues.

■ **Redeemability**. Preferred stock may be **redeemable** or **nonredeemable**. Redeemable preferred stock contains sinking fund provisions similar to those found in sinking fund debentures. Nonredeemable preferred stock is perpetual, like common stock.[28] In general, the shorter the average life of the preferred stock issue, the more debtlike it is.[29]

FINANCING WITH PREFERRED STOCK   Utility companies have been the heaviest issuers of fixed-dividend-rate preferred stock. Preferred stock typically represents between 10% and 15% of an electric utility company's capitalization. Thrift and commercial banks have been the heaviest issuers of floating-rate preferred stock.

In recent years, the bulk of the fixed-dividend-rate preferred stock issues have contained sinking fund provisions. Previously, most such preferred stock issues were perpetual. The change is at least partly the result of a ruling by the National Association of Insurance Commissioners, which permits property and casualty insurance companies to value preferred stock issues for regulatory purposes at their face amount only if the issue's maturity does not exceed 40 years and it has a sinking fund that begins no later than 10 years from the date of issue and retires at least 2.5% of the issue per year. This ruling has reduced the breadth of the market for perpetual preferred stock issues and increased the liquidity premium on preferred stock issues with no sinking fund provision.

14.4   NEGOTIATED VERSUS COMPETITIVE OFFERINGS

A company can offer securities publicly using either competitive bidding or a negotiated offering. Under **competitive bidding**, the issuer specifies the type of securities it wishes to sell and invites securities firms to bid for the issue. In a **negotiated offering**, the issuer selects one or more securities firms to manage the offering and works closely with them to design the terms of the issue and determine the appropriate time to issue the securities. Currently, registered public utility holding companies are required to offer securities competitively but other companies are free to choose the offering technique.[30] Other electric utilities tend to offer debt and pre-

[28] The SEC requires companies to report redeemable and nonredeemable preferred stock separately. Only nonredeemable preferred stock can be included in stockholders' equity.
[29] The major rating agencies treat a sinking fund preferred stock issue as debt for purposes of their financial ratio analysis when the issue's average life is 10 years or less.
[30] Rule U-50 under the Public Utility Holding Company Act of 1935 requires competitive bidding. However, the SEC has granted individual exemptions during volatile market periods.

ferred stock by competitive bid (except during periods of heightened market volatility), but generally sell common stock on a negotiated basis. Railroads frequently sell equipment trust certificates through competitive bidding, but other industrial companies until recently seldom sold securities via competitive bidding.[31]

SHELF REGISTRATION PROCESS

The Securities and Exchange Commission instituted Rule 415, the so-called "shelf registration rule," on an experimental basis in March 1982 and then adopted the new rule on a permanent basis for large firms in November 1983. Rule 415 allows a company to register an inventory of securities of a particular type sufficient to cover its financing requirements for up to 2 years and sell the securities whenever it chooses. The securities remain "on the shelf" until the issuer finds market conditions sufficiently attractive to sell them.

The shelf registration process has improved companies' financing flexibility. In contrast to the prior procedure, the company does not have to file a new registration statement each time it offers securities, which reduces flotation costs. In addition, selling securities off the shelf avoids the 48-hour delay between the filing of a registration statement and the declaration of its effectiveness so that the offering can begin. Today, under Rule 415, securities can be sold within minutes. Also, a single shelf registration statement can cover many types of debt securities. This permits issuers to design the security at the time they sell it to exploit any special investor preferences and minimize the **reoffering yield.**

Rule 415 has effectively extended competitive bidding to issues of securities by the roughly 2,000 large corporations that qualify for use of the shelf registration statement. Securities firms and institutional investors can bid for securities that a company has on the shelf. Rule 415 appears to have had an impact on transaction costs, but the evidence is mixed.[32]

ARE COMPETITIVE OFFERINGS CHEAPER?

Which offering method is more likely to facilitate the lower cost of funds? The question has been hotly debated and empirical evidence is not conclusive.[33] However, a

---

[31] One notable exception is Exxon Corporation's use of the so-called Dutch auction competitive bidding process. See "Exxon Plan to Offer Its Notes at Auction Is Gaining Attention," *Wall Street Journal*, September 21, 1982, p. 43. In addition, most money market preferred stock issues are sold and then reoffered via the Dutch auction process.

[32] Kidwell, Marr, and Thompson (1984) found that debt issues sold off the shelf saved between 30 and 40 basis points (100 basis points equal 1%) relative to an otherwise identical negotiated debt issue. Bhagat, Marr, and Thompson (1985) found that syndicated equity offerings sold off the shelf had flotation costs (including underwriting spread, underpricing, and expenses) that were 13% lower than the flotation costs for syndicated equity offerings not sold under Rule 415 and that the flotation costs of nonsyndicated offerings were 51% lower under Rule 415. However, Fung and Rudd (1986) found no significant difference between the offering yields of bonds sold off the shelf and bonds sold in the traditional manner. But Fung and Rudd (1986) also found that offerings off the shelf had yields that averaged 10 basis points lower in periods of high interest rates and averaged 15 basis points higher in periods of low interest rates as compared to traditional underwritten bond offerings. Moore, Peterson, and Peterson (1986) found that the negative announcement effect for common stock offerings was not significantly different between shelf and traditional registrations.

[33] Sorensen (1979) finds that interest costs are generally greater in negotiated sales than in competitive sales. Parker and Cooperman (1978) found no significant difference in the cost of borrowing between the two techniques. Logue and Jarrow (1978) found no significant difference in the cost of equity capital between the two methods, with the increased market impact associated with the competitive offering process fully offsetting the lower underwriting spread. Fabozzi and West (1981) found no significant differ-

number of recent studies suggest that in general, the competitive process does not lead to significant cost savings, except perhaps during stable market periods when strong competition among bidding groups results in lower costs.[34] Competitive bidding generally results in lower underwriting spreads,[35] but competitive underwritings may involve wider spreads than negotiated underwritings during periods of great market uncertainty.[36] Moreover, the negotiated offering process offers greater flexibility in the design of the securities and the timing of the issue because the issuer has not committed in advance to a specific set of terms (e.g., maturity and redemption terms) or to a particular offering date (in competitive bidding, the date bids are to be received). It also gives securities firms the opportunity to form the most effective selling group for the issue (rather than splitting into competing bidding groups) and provides a stronger incentive for them to assess the demand for, and stimulate interest in, the issue prior to pricing because in contrast to a competitive bid, they know that they will have the securities to sell. An additional reason for using the negotiated process exists for industrial firms. In contrast to utilities, which have been frequent issuers of debt and equity securities, most industrial firms have few publicly-traded debt issues outstanding. Consequently, fewer pricing benchmarks would be available to bidders.

14.5   INTEREST RATE SWAPS

Interest rate swaps provide a mechanism by which lower-rated issuers might be able to borrow more cheaply than if they sold debt directly to investors in the public or private fixed-rate debt markets.[37] In the simplest form of swap, called a fixed-rate-floating-rate swap, two issuers of different credit standing borrow equal amounts simultaneously: the stronger credit sells fixed-interest-rate bonds, and the weaker credit borrows at a floating interest rate under a loan agreement of matching maturity. The two companies then swap interest payment obligations: the weaker-credit firm promises to pay interest on a fixed-rate basis to the stronger-credit firm, which promises to pay interest on a floating-rate basis. Thus, no principal changes hands, which limits the amount of bankruptcy risk involved in the swap arrangement. The interest rates are adjusted to compensate the stronger-credit firm for agreeing to enter into the swap arrangement. Because the interest rate credit differential on short-term loans is lower than the interest rate credit differential on longer-term loans, it is mutually advantageous to arbitrage between the fixed-rate and floating-rate markets by having the weaker-credit firm borrow on a shorter-term basis and the stronger-credit firm borrow on a longer-term basis. Typically, the stronger-credit firm, often a commercial bank, wishes to borrow on a short-term basis anyway. It simply uses its longer-term credit capacity to reduce its cost of short-term debt.

---

ence in borrowing costs between the two methods during periods of heightened bond market uncertainty (though the difference was not significant in a purely statistical sense, the negotiated process tended to produce lower borrowing costs during such periods) but that the competitive process tended to produce lower borrowing costs during relatively stable market periods as long as meaningful competition (i.e., three or more bids) existed for the issue. Bhagat (1986) found that the market reacted negatively to the announcement that the rule requiring public utility holding companies to use the competitive method to issue common stock had been suspended and reacted positively to reinstitution of the rule, which is consistent with the hypothesis that negotiated offerings are more expensive than competitive offerings.
[34] Fabozzi and West (1981).
[35] Logue and Jarrow (1978); Ederington (1975).
[36] Ederington (1976); Tallman, Rush, and Melicher (1974).
[37] Smith, Smithson, and Wakeman (1986); Bicksler and Chen (1986).

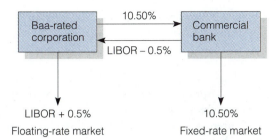

FIGURE 14-2
Fixed-rate/floating-rate swap.

EXAMPLE ■ Figure 14-2 illustrates a typical interest rate swap transaction. Suppose a Baa-rated company can borrow on a short-term basis at the London Interbank Offer Rate (LIBOR) plus 0.5% and on a long-term basis at 12% but that the commercial bank can borrow on a short-term basis at LIBOR and on a long-term basis at 10.5%. The bank borrows on a long-term basis, the Baa-rated company borrows on a short-term basis, and the two swap obligations, the company agreeing to pay the bank 10.5% and the bank agreeing to pay the company LIBOR minus 0.50%. The company saves 150 basis points (12% minus 10.5%) on its fixed-rate obligation but loses 100 basis points on its floating-rate obligation, for a net saving of 50 basis points. The bank also saves 50 basis points because it borrows effectively at LIBOR minus 0.50%. ■

The "flotation" costs associated with a swap are typically greater than in a public debt offering of the same maturity. Also, as of this writing, swap obligations have been either noncallable or callable under restrictive conditions. Thus, the cost of debt implicit in the swap should be calculated net of flotation costs and compared with other alternatives that provide for an equivalent call provision.[38]

Interest rate swaps have been enormously successful. Prior to their existence, some firms engaged in what are called **back-to-back loans**, a form of barter arrangement in the sense that a firm wishing to enter into such a transaction had to find another company that was willing to exchange loans. Interest rate swaps involve the exchange of interest payment obligations, rather than whole loans, and can be entered into with any number of large financial institutions. The success of the interest rate swap should therefore come as no surprise. Recall that the creation of a security market increases the liquidity of a security, thus increasing the value of the security by lowering transaction costs connected with buying and selling the security. In the same way, interest rate swaps reduced transaction costs by removing the need to find a bartering partner.

FINANCING WITH OPTIONS   14.6

Companies, particularly smaller ones, often find it more attractive to issue convertible bonds or bonds with warrants than to issue straight debt. In addition, smaller companies frequently include warrants as a "sweetener" to a new issue of common stock or a privately placed debt issue. A warrant is simply a long-term call option. It entitles the holder to buy common stock at a stated price for cash. A convertible bond (or convertible preferred share) entitles the holder to exchange the bond (or

---

[38] More exotic swap arrangements than the one discussed here are possible. For example, the two parties could borrow in different currencies and swap liabilities, then each could arrange a series of forward foreign exchange transactions to hedge its exchange rate risk. Such transactions can be of mutual benefit to multinational companies each of which has been a heavy borrower in a particular (but differing) currency but still has significant borrowing requirements. See Chapter 23.

preferred share) for a stated number of shares of the issuing company's common stock. Both types of securities thus incorporate an option.

WARRANTS

Recall that standardized call options traded in the options market are written by investors against outstanding shares of a company's stock. By contrast, warrants are issued by the company, often as part of a package that includes the issuer's common stock, preferred stock, or bonds. Warrants are like rights since the underlying security is newly issued equity. But warrants typically do not expire for several years, and some companies, such as Allegheny Corporation, have even issued perpetual warrants.

PRINCIPAL FEATURES OF WARRANTS   The provisions of a warrant are essentially the same as the provisions of a conventional call option. Figure 14–3 illustrates the relationship between the value of a warrant and the price of the underlying shares, which, of course, is just like the relationship we observed for other call options in Chapter 8.

A large and actively traded issue of warrants was sold by American Express Company in two **tranches**. American Express distributed 932,000 Common Share Purchase Warrants to its common stockholders on February 26, 1982, and sold an additional 900,000 such warrants to the public on March 31, 1982, at a price of $12.625 per warrant. Each American Express warrant entitled the holder to purchase at any time on or before February 28, 1987 one share of American Express common stock at a strike price of $55 per share.[39] The strike price represented a premium of 17.0% over the previous closing price of American Express common stock. The terms of the warrant permitted American Express to accelerate the expiration date if the price of American Express's common stock traded at or above a price of $95 per share for a period of 10 consecutive trading days. The American Express warrants were also redeemable on or after March 1, 1984, at a price of $40 per warrant. This redemption feature, like the redemption feature on a convertible bond, permits the issuer to force exercise of the call option. Some warrants provide for a "step-up"— an increase—in the strike price. Warrants, like those issued by American Express, provide for adjustment of the strike price if the issuer pays a common stock dividend, splits its common stock, distributes some of its assets (other than cash dividends), issues stockholders rights to purchase shares at a discount from the prevailing market price, and in certain other circumstances.[40] However, as is typically the case, American Express warrant holders are not entitled to vote or to receive dividends, and the strike price is not adjusted for cash dividend payments to common stockholders.

Warrants are often issued as part of a package of debt and warrants. For example, on April 14, 1983, MGM/UA Entertainment Co. issued $400 million of 10% Senior Subordinated Notes due April 15, 1993, along with 5,600,000 Common Stock Purchase Warrants.[41] The warrants were **detachable** after July 15, 1983; purchasers could sell the warrants for cash after that date and continue to hold the 10% Notes.

[39] American Express Company, prospectus, March 31, 1982.

[40] As is customary, the strike price is actually adjusted only if the dilutive factors would require an adjustment of at least 5%. In addition, the $40 redemption price and the $95 acceleration price of the American Express warrants would be adjusted along with the strike price.

[41] MGM/UA Entertainment Co., prospectus, April 14, 1983. The MGM/UA warrants contain two particularly noteworthy features. The strike price was unusually large relative to the current share price (55% above), and the warrant could be exercised either by paying cash or by surrendering 10% Notes, which would be valued at their face amount for purposes of the exercise transaction.

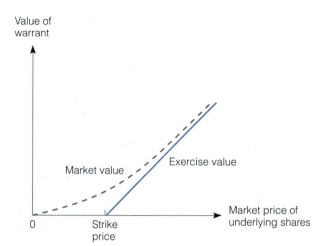

VALUING WARRANTS A warrant is a long-term call option. Because of this, a warrant can be valued in the same manner as any other call option; for example, by applying the Black-Scholes option pricing model. But there is one important caveat. As with rights, the issuance of warrants is dilutive because new shares are created. To take this dilutive effect into account, the call option value obtained from the Black-Scholes OPM must be divided by a dilution factor: [42]

$$W = \frac{C}{1 + P} \qquad (14.7)$$

where W denotes the value of the warrant, C denotes the value of a call option to purchase one common share on the same terms embodied in the warrant, and P denotes the proportionate increase in the number of common shares that would result from issuance and exercise of the warrants. Equation (14.7) is used to value warrants for a prospective warrants issue. Once the warrants have been issued, their dilutive impact is fully reflected in the issuer's common stock price, as a consequence of capital market efficiency, so that $W = C$.

FINANCING WITH WARRANTS Companies can sell warrants separately, as American Express did, or in combination with other securities, as MGM/UA Entertainment did. When a company issues warrants at their fair market price, the cash they receive is fair compensation for the potential equity interest given up because of the efficiency of the capital markets. Nevertheless, it may be possible to use warrants to create more efficient financial contracts by reducing the agency costs associated with financing the corporation. [43]

CONVERTIBLE SECURITIES

The principal features of convertible bonds and convertible preferred stock are sufficiently similar, at least with respect to the conversion feature, that we can concentrate on convertible bonds, but our comments will also apply to most convertible preferred (and preference) stock.

Convertible debt issues have the following principal conversion features in addi-

---

[42] Galai and Schneller (1978).
[43] See Chapter 9 for a discussion of optimal financial contracts.

tion to the coupon rate, maturity, and optional redemption features that typify a straight bond:

- Each bond is convertible at any time prior to maturity into common stock at a stated **conversion price**, which typically exceeds the issuer's share price at the time of issue. In other words, the conversion option is normally issued out-of-the-money. The conversion premium is typically 10% to 20%. Dividing the face amount of the convertible bond by the conversion price gives the **conversion ratio**, the number of shares of common stock into which each bond can be converted. The conversion terms are normally fixed for the life of the issue, although some convertible securities provide for one or more step-ups—increases—in the conversion price over time.

- The conversion price is typically adjusted for stock splits, stock dividends, rights offerings that involve a discounted offering price, or the distribution of assets (other than cash dividends) or indebtedness to shareholders if the adjustment is above some threshold amount (typically 1%).

- Bondholders who convert do not receive accrued interest; therefore bondholders rarely convert voluntarily just prior to an interest payment date.

- If the bonds are called, the conversion option will expire just before (typically between 3 and 10 days) the redemption date.

Many of the more recent convertible debt issues have contained provisions prohibiting the issuer from calling the issue for redemption within 3 years, or in some cases, 2 years, of their issuance. Some of these issues contain an exception, however, permitting optional redemption during the 2-year or 3-year period if the underlying share price equals or exceeds 150% of the stated conversion price over a specified period, typically 20 or 30 consecutive trading days.

VALUING CONVERTIBLE BONDS   A convertible bond can be modeled as a straight bond plus a nondetachable warrant. From the Options Principle, we know that the value of a warrant can never be negative. Therefore, in a perfect capital market environment, the value of a convertible bond can never fall below its value as a straight bond. Similarly, the value of a convertible bond can also never fall below its conversion value, the value of the common shares into which the bond can be converted. Figure 14-4 illustrates the relationship between the bond value, conversion value, and actual market value of a convertible bond.

FIGURE 14-4

Bond value, conversion value, and actual market value of a convertible bond.

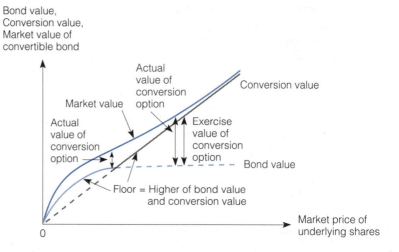

Modeled as a straight bond plus a warrant, a convertible bond can be valued by valuing the bond and warrant components separately. The value of a convertible bond exactly equals the sum of the bond and warrant component values in a perfect capital market environment.

CONVERTIBLE DEBT VERSUS CONVERTIBLE PREFERRED STOCK   The principal buyers of convertible securities are either entirely tax-exempt investors or those who cannot benefit directly from the corporate 70% dividends received deduction.[44] Consequently, under most market conditions, issuers of convertible securities have been able to obtain essentially the same terms (chiefly annual interest or dividend rate and conversion premium), whether they issued convertible debt or convertible preferred stock. Issuers who are in a taxpaying position and expect to remain in a taxpaying position for a number of years therefore find it cheaper to issue convertible debt rather than convertible preferred stock. In contrast, issuers who do not expect to be in a taxpaying position for a number of years typically issue convertible preferred stock. In addition, convertible preferred stock is typically perpetual, whereas convertible debt has a stated maturity and typically has a sinking fund.

To provide maximum flexibility, a company can issue what is know as **convertible exchangeable preferred stock**. Such securities are convertible preferred stock that is exchangeable at the option of the company into convertible *debt* of the company. The annual interest rate on the convertible debt issue equals the annual dividend yield on the convertible preferred stock issue, and the issues have equivalent conversion terms. The exchange feature permits a nontaxpaying company to reap the advantages of issuing the convertible security in preferred stock form while preserving the flexibility to reissue it, in effect, in the form of debt should it become a taxpayer before the issue is converted.

EXCHANGEABLE DEBENTURES

Companies have also issued bonds exchangeable for the common stock of other companies. The debentures are in effect "convertible" into the common stock of another company rather than that of the issuer. But in all other respects, the issue of exchangeable debentures is structured like a conventional convertible bond. Exchangeable debentures may be attractive to a company that owns a block of another company's common stock when it would like to raise cash and intends eventually to sell the block but wishes to defer the sale—either because it believes the shares will increase in value or because it wishes to defer the capital gains tax liability it will incur upon sale of the shares.

DOMESTIC VERSUS INTERNATIONAL FINANCING   14.7

A company can sell U.S.-dollar-denominated bonds to U.S. investors in the domestic bond market or to foreign investors in the Eurobond market. Alternatively, a company can sell bonds denominated in a foreign currency. However, issuing bonds denominated in a foreign currency involves a foreign exchange risk because the issuer must either realize foreign currency from its operations or purchase foreign currency to meet its future debt service obligations on this debt.

[44] The 70% figure is as of January 1, 1988. The rate for the dividends received deduction was reduced twice in the 1980s, and it is rumored that it will be reduced yet again. As we pointed out in Chapter 12, tax laws are changed with sufficient regularity that you should check the current provisions when they affect a decision.

DOLLAR-DENOMINATED BORROWING IN THE EUROBOND MARKET   A **Eurobond** is a bond issued outside the country in whose currency the bond is denominated. The Eurobond market developed during the 1960s when the U.S. government levied an interest equalization tax on the purchase of foreign securities by U.S. investors and imposed restrictions on capital exports by American companies. Large U.S. balance of payments deficits continued the outflow of dollar funds, and the U.S.-imposed withholding tax on interest payments by domestic corporations to foreign investors discouraged foreign investment of these funds in domestic bond issues for many years. Instead, foreign investors avoided this withholding tax by purchasing Eurobonds issued by special-purpose subsidiaries of U.S. companies established in the Netherlands Antilles, which enjoyed a special status as a result of its tax treaty with the United States. The 30% withholding tax was eliminated in 1984, permitting U.S. companies to sell debt directly to foreign investors free of this tax.

Companies headquartered in the United States issue dollar-denominated Eurobonds to investors in Europe (hence the prefix *Euro*) and other areas outside the United States. Eurobonds denominated in other currencies are also issued, but U.S. dollar-denominated bonds at times represent more than half the total Eurobond market.

Dollar-denominated Eurobond issues are as varied as domestic bond issues. Most are straight debt issues, but convertible Eurobonds and Eurobonds with warrants are not uncommon. Nevertheless, there are important differences between the domestic bond market and the Eurobond market:

- Eurobond investors typically possess assets denominated in several currencies. The relative attractiveness of dollar-denominated Eurobonds, and hence the relationship between bond yields in the domestic bond market and the dollar-denominated Eurobond market, depends on U.S. dollar exchange rates. When the U.S. dollar is appreciating relative to the other major currencies, Eurobond investors tend to increase their purchasing of dollar-denominated Eurobonds (as well as other dollar-denominated assets), which can drive Eurobond yields below domestic bond yields and create an attractive borrowing opportunity for U.S. corporations, giving rise to a so-called Eurobond window.[45]

- Because of investors' exchange rate sensitivity, Eurobond maturities are typically shorter and issue sizes generally smaller than in the domestic market.

- Eurobond investors tend to be more sensitive to the identity of the issuer and less sensitive to the issuer's credit standing than domestic investors. As a result, certain American companies that are very well known in Europe have at times been able to borrow more cheaply in the Eurobond market than some more highly rated (by the bond rating agencies) purely domestic U.S. companies.

- Eurobonds are generally **bearer bonds** that pay interest annually. Issuing bonds in bearer form makes it more difficult to refund them prior to maturity because most buyers can be contacted only when they come to the paying agent to claim their interest payments.

- The Eurobond market is essentially unregulated; it is a truly international market. Hence, Eurobond yields are somewhat less susceptible to government influence than domestic bond yields. Nevertheless, arbitrage activity ensures that Eurobond yields normally track domestic bond yields fairly closely.

[45] Finnerty, Schneeweis, and Hedge (1980) provide an interesting study of the behavior of Eurobond interest rates.

Annual interest payments on Eurobonds make it necessary to compare effective annual yields when comparing domestic and Eurobond borrowing alternatives. For example, suppose a company can issue a 10-year public debt issue at par bearing a 12% coupon in the domestic market or a 12⅛% Eurobond issue; the total issuance expenses are identical for the bonds. From Equation (3.16), the effective annual rate for the domestic bond is $(1.06)^2 - 1 = 12.36\%$, compared with a 12.125% (12⅛) effective annual rate for the Eurobond. Therefore, the Eurobond issue is slightly cheaper in spite of its higher coupon rate.

The Eurobond market offers companies an alternative to borrowing domestically. Table 14-5 presents the mix of domestic and international bond financing by U.S. corporations during 1970–1989. The volume of Eurobond financing dropped markedly in 1973 and 1974, following the elimination of capital export controls. Volume picked up again sharply in the 1979–1986 period when the strength of the U.S. dol-

TABLE 14-5 Volume of Domestic and International Bond Financing by U.S. Corporations, 1970–1989   (Dollar Amounts in Millions)

Year	Domestic[a]	International[a]	Total[a]	Percent Domestic	Trade-Weighted Dollar Exchange Rate[b]
1970	$30,315	$ 741	$31,056	97.6%	121.07
1971	32,123	1,098	33,221	96.7	117.81
1972	28,896	1,992	30,888	93.6	109.07
1973	22,268	874	23,142	96.2	99.14
1974	32,066	110	32,176	99.7	101.42
1975	42,756	268	43,024	99.4	98.50
1976	42,262	430	42,692	99.0	105.57
1977	42,015	1,130	43,145	97.4	103.31
1978	36,872	1,122	37,994	97.0	92.39
1979	39,690	2,872	42,562	93.3	88.09
1980	53,206	4,107	57,313	92.8	87.39
1981	45,092	6,178	51,270	88.0	102.94
1982	53,636	12,567	66,203	81.0	116.57
1983	68,370	11,969	80,339	85.1	125.34
1984	109,903	18,200	128,103	85.8	138.19
1985	165,754	33,660	199,414	83.1	143.01
1986	313,503	64,442	377,945	82.9	112.22
1987	301,349	49,977	351,326	85.8	96.94
1988	327,864	51,021	378,885	86.5	92.72
1989	262,875	47,639	310,514	84.7	98.60
Total	$2,050,815	$310,397	$2,361,212	86.9%	

[a] Includes convertible debt.
[b] Index for which March 1973 = 100.

Sources: "SEC Monthly Statistical Review," U.S. Securities and Exchange Commission, vol. 42, June 1983, pp. 5, 6, 10; "World Financial Markets," Morgan Guaranty Trust Company, New York, various issues; and *Federal Reserve Bulletin,* Board of Governors of the Federal Reserve System, Washington D.C., various issues.

lar and other factors brought about a sharp increase in the foreign demand for dollar-denominated bonds.

Because of the segmentation of the Eurobond market and the domestic bond market prior to the repeal of the 30% withholding tax, capital market efficiency did not always hold between the two markets. Eurobond borrowing enabled a U.S. corporation to expand the market for its debt. During the period January 1979–December 1983, issuers of Eurodollar bonds saved an average of 52 basis points, even after adjusting for the higher underwriting spreads Eurodollar bonds involve, relative to a comparable domestic debt issue.[46]

14.8

EVALUATING THE MERITS OF INNOVATIVE FINANCING ARRANGEMENTS

The rapid pace of securities innovation has produced an almost overwhelming menu of financing instruments, some involving complex and difficult-to-evaluate options structures. Confronted with the choice among existing financing alternatives and yet another innovative security, the corporate financial executive must try to strip away the veneer and determine whether the bankers' claim that the new security is truly innovative is valid. In other words, has the banker come up with a valuable new idea?

In addition to the pursuit of valuable new ideas, two important developments account for the revolution in securities innovation in recent years. First, the investment banking business has become more competitive, hence more transactional. Developing an innovative security provides an opportunity for the developer to solicit business from companies that have traditionally used other investment bankers and typically also to obtain the mandate to market the new security on a negotiated basis, rather than having to bid for securities "off the shelf" as with standard debt instruments. Second, inflation rates and interest rates have become more volatile, tax changes have become more frequent, and regulatory changes have become more profound as a result of the move toward deregulation in several areas. Financial innovation is, at least in part, a response to the changing economic and financial environment. For example, increased interest rate volatility led to the development of adjustable rate preferred stock—and a series of refinements—designed to eliminate the exposure of the securityholder's principal to interest rate changes.

A new security is truly "innovative" only if it enables an investor to realize a higher after-tax risk-adjusted rate of return and/or an issuer to realize a lower after-tax cost of funds than they could realize with previously existing securities. It is not enough just to be different; there must be real value to the issuing company's shareholders. A new security could accomplish this either by creating a pattern of risk-return combinations that investors could not have achieved previously and thereby making the financial markets more complete or by reducing taxes, transaction costs, or resolving informational asymmetries, thereby lessening the valuation impact of market imperfections.

SOURCES OF VALUE ADDED

Table 14-6 lists several innovative securities and identifies the sources of value associated with each of them. A new security can enhance shareholder value in any of the following ways:

---

[46]Kidwell, Marr, and Thompson (1986).

1. The smaller the yield at which the new security is sold relative to the yield at which the same debt service payment stream would be sold in one of the conventional security structures, the greater the market value of the company. The lower the yield at which the company can "sell" the available cash payment stream, the greater the cash proceeds the company realizes by entering into this commitment.

If a company can repackage a security's payment stream so that it either involves less risk or reallocates risk from one class of investors to another that is less risk sensitive and charges a smaller risk premium, shareholder value will be enhanced. Collateralized mortgage obligations (CMOs), stripped mortgage-backed securities, and interest rate swaps are examples. Second, if a company can form a diversified portfolio of assets more cheaply than investors can, the company can issue a security against that portfolio of assets and thereby reduce the investor's risk and hence the required yield. Mortgage pass-through certificates and receivable pay-through securities are examples. Third, if a company can securitize a loan so that it becomes publicly tradable, the lender's liquidity improves, resulting in a lower required yield. Negotiable certificates of deposit and commercial real estate-backed bonds are examples. Both can be traded in the public securities markets, unlike conventional certificates of deposit and most commercial mortgages.

2. The smaller the percentage underwriting commissions and other expenses, the greater the market value of the company. Lower transaction costs reduce the amount of proceeds that must be paid to third parties rather than invested in the issuer's business. If a company can structure a new issue so that underwriting commissions are reduced, shareholder value will be enhanced. Extendible notes are an example. Their maturity can be extended by mutual agreement of issuer and investors, effectively rolling over the notes without additional underwriting commissions.

3. The lower the agency costs associated with a particular security, the greater the market value of the firm, all else equal. If a firm can structure a new security to reduce agency costs, shareholder wealth can be enhanced. For example, interest rate reset notes protect bondholders against a deterioration in the issuer's credit standing prior to the reset date. Under the Principle of Capital Market Efficiency, without such protection we would expect bondholders to require a higher offering yield to compensate for this risk. Due to asymmetric information, they might charge a significant interest rate premium even if management has no plan to take steps, such as a leveraged buyout, that might trigger such a deterioration. Interest rate reset notes would be mutually advantageous in that case.

4. The smaller the tax liability associated with payments to holders of the new security, the greater the market value of the company. If a company can structure a new security to reduce investor taxes without increasing corporate income taxes, shareholder value will be enhanced as a result of this tax arbitrage. For example, a company that is currently not a taxpayer can create such an arbitrage by issuing adjustable rate preferred stock, auction rate preferred stock, or single point adjustable rate stock in lieu of commercial paper. Industrial companies and thrifts that have large tax loss carryforwards have accounted for a high percentage of auction rate preferred stock issues. Both auction rate preferred stock and commercial paper are purchased by corporate money managers, but preferred stock dividends are more valuable to a corporation than interest payments because the corporation is tax exempt on 70% of the dividends it receives. Consequently, auction rate preferred stock carries a lower pretax yield than similarly rated commercial paper.

Interestingly, adjustable rate preferred stock, auction rate preferred stock, and single point adjustable rate stock evolved sequentially. Auction rate preferred stock has proved the most enduring of the three.

TABLE 14-6   Several Innovative Securities and the Sources of Value Associated with Each.

Security	Distinguishing Characteristics	Risk Reallocation/ Yield Reduction	Enhanced Liquidity
Adjustable Rate Convertible Debt	Debt the interest rate on which varies directly with the dividend rate on the underlying common stock. No conversion premium.		
Adjustable Rate Notes and Floating Rate Notes	Coupon rate floats with some index, such as the 91-day Treasury bill rate.	Issuer exposed to floating interest rate risk but initial rate is lower than for fixed-rate issue.	Price remains closer to par than the price of a fixed-rate note of the same maturity.
Adjustable Rate Preferred Stock	Quarterly dividend rate reset each quarter based on maximum of 3-month T-bill, 10-year Treasury, and 20-year Treasury rates plus or minus a specified spread.	Issuer bears more interest rate risk than a fixed-rate preferred would involve. Lower yield than commercial paper.	Security is designed to trade near its par value.
Auction Rate Preferred Stock (MMP/DARTS/ AMPS/STAR)	Dividend rate reset by Dutch auction every 49 days (subject to a maximum rate of 110%, or under certain circumstances 125%, of the 60-day "AA" Composite Commercial Paper Rate). Dividend is paid at the end of each dividend period.	Issuer bears more interest rate risk than a fixed-rate preferred would involve. Lower yield than commercial paper.	Security is designed to provide greater liquidity than convertible adjustable preferred stock.
Collateralized Mortgage Obligations (CMOs) and Real Estate Mortgage Investment Conduits (REMICs)	Mortgage payment stream is divided into several classes which are prioritized in terms of their right to receive principal payments.	Reduction in prepayment risk to classes with prepayment priority. Designed to appeal to different classes of investors; sum of the parts can exceed the whole.	More liquid than individual mortgages.
Commercial Real Estate-Backed Bonds	Nonrecourse bonds serviced and backed by a specified piece (or portfolio) of real estate.	Reduced yield due to greater liquidity.	More liquid than individual mortgages.
Convertible Adjustable Preferred Stock	Adjustable rate preferred stock convertible on dividend payment dates into variable number of the issuer's common shares, subject to a cap, equal in market value to the par value of the preferred.	Issuer bears more interest rate risk than a fixed-rate preferred would involve. Lower yield than commercial paper.	Security is designed to provide greater liquidity than adjustable rate preferred stock (due to the conversion feature).

Reduction in Agency Costs	Reduction in Transaction Costs	Tax Arbitrage	Other Benefits
		Effectively, tax deductible common equity. Security has since been ruled equity by the IRS.	Portion of the issue carried as equity on the issuer's balance sheet.
		Designed to enable short-term corporate investors to take advantage of 70% dividends received deduction.	
Dividend rate each period is determined in the market-place, which provides protection against deteri-oration in issuer's credit standing (protection is limited by the dividend rate cap).		Designed to enable short-term corporate investors to take advantage of 70% dividends received deduction.	
	Most investors could not achieve the same degree of prepayment risk reduc-tion as cheaply on their own.		
			Appeals to investors who like to lend against real estate properties.
		Designed to enable short-term corporate investors to take advantage of 70% dividends received deduction.	

TABLE 14-6 (*continued*)

Security	Distinguishing Characteristics	Risk Reallocation/ Yield Reduction	Enhanced Liquidity
Convertible Exchangeable Preferred Stock	Convertible preferred stock that is exchangeable, at the issuer's option, for convertible debt with identical rate and identical conversion terms.		
Extendible Notes	Interest rate adjusts every 2–3 years to a new interest rate the issuer establishes, at which time note holder has the option to put the notes back to the issuer if the new rate is unacceptable.	Coupon based on 2–3 year put date, not on final maturity.	
Interest Rate Reset Notes	Interest rate is reset 3 years after issuance to the greater of (*i*) the initial rate and (*ii*) a rate sufficient to give the notes a market value equal to 101% of their face amount.	Reduced (initial) yield due to the reduction in agency costs.	
Interest Rate Swaps	Two entities agree to swap interest rate payment obligations, typically fixed rate for floating rate.	Effective vehicle for transferring interest rate risk from one party to another. Also, parties to a swap can realize a net benefit if they enjoy comparative advantages in different international credit markets.	
Master Limited Partnership	A business is given the legal form of a partnership but is otherwise structured, and is traded publicly, like a corporation.		
Mortgage Pass-Through Certificates	Investor buys an undivided interest in a pool of mortgages.	Reduced yield due to the benefit to the investor of diversification and greater liquidity.	More liquid than individual mortgages.
Negotiable Certificates of Deposit	Certificates of deposit are registered and sold to the public on an agency basis.	Issuer bears market price risk during the marketing process.	More liquid than non-negotiable CDs.

Reduction in Agency Costs	Reduction in Transaction Costs	Tax Arbitrage	Other Benefits
	No need to reissue convertible security as debt—just exchange it—when the issuer becomes a taxpayer.	Issuer can exchange debt for the preferred when it becomes taxable with interest rate the same as the dividend rate and without any change in conversion features.	Appears as equity on the issuer's balance sheet until it is exchanged for convertible debt.
Investor has a put option, which provides protection against deterioration in credit quality or below-market coupon rate.	Lower transaction costs than issuing 2 or 3-year notes and rolling them over.		
Investor is compensated for a deterioration in the issuer's credit standing within 3 years of issuance.			
			Interest rate swaps are often designed to take advantage of special opportunities in particular markets outside the issuer's traditional market or to circumvent regulatory restrictions.
		Eliminates a layer of taxation because partnerships are not taxable entities.	
	Most investors could not achieve the same degree of diversification as cheaply on their own.		
	Agents' commissions are lower than underwriting spreads.		

TABLE 14-6 (*continued*)

Security	Distinguishing Characteristics	Risk Reallocation/ Yield Reduction	Enhanced Liquidity
Receivable Pay-Through Securities	Investor buys an undivided interest in a pool of receivables.	Reduced yield due to the benefit to the investor of diversification and greater liquidity. Significantly cheaper for issuer than pledging receivables to a bank.	More liquid than individual receivables.
Single Point Adjustable Rate Stock	Dividend rate reset every 49 days as a specified percentage of the high-grade commercial paper rate.	Issuer bears more interest rate risk than a fixed-rate preferred would involve. Lower yield than commercial paper.	Security is designed to trade near its par value.
Stripped Mortgage-Backed Securities	Mortgage payment stream subdivided into two classes, (*i*) one with below-market coupon and the other with above-market coupon or (*ii*) one receiving interest only and the other receiving principal only from mortgage pools.	Securities have unique option characteristics that make them useful for hedging purposes. Designed to appeal to different classes of investors; sum of the parts can exceed the whole.	
Zero-Coupon Bonds (sometimes issued in series)	Non-interest-bearing. Payment in one lump sum at maturity.	Issuer assumes reinvestment risk. Issues sold in Japan carried below-taxable-market yields reflecting their tax advantage over conventional debt issues.	
Zero-Coupon Convertible Debt	Non-interest-bearing convertible debt issue.		

5. The greater the corporate tax shield, other things such as the corporate income tax rate remaining the same, the greater the market value of the company. If a company can structure a new security to increase the present value of tax shields available to the issuer or to reduce the issuer's income tax liability in some other manner without increasing the investors' tax liabilities commensurately, shareholder value will again be enhanced through tax arbitrage. For example, selling zero-coupon bonds to tax-exempt investors before the Tax Equity and Fiscal Responsibility Act of 1982 (TEFRA) resulted in such an arbitrage because the issuer could deduct the original issue discount on a straight-line basis, that is, faster than interest on the notes implicitly compounded. TEFRA changed the method of amortization to the scientific interest method, as interest implicitly compounds, and eliminated this arbitrage opportunity. Similarly, convertible exchangeable preferred stock and master limited partnerships can offer tax advantages to the issuer net of any increases in investor taxes.

Reduction in Agency Costs	Reduction in Transaction Costs	Tax Arbitrage	Other Benefits
	Security purchasers could not achieve the same degree of diversification as cheaply on their own.		
	Security is designed to save on recurring transaction costs associated with auction rate preferred stock.	Designed to enable short-term corporate investors to take advantage of 70% dividends received deduction.	
		Straight-line amortization of original issue discount pre-TEFRA. Japanese investors realize significant tax savings.	
		If issue converts, the issuer will have sold, in effect, tax-deductible equity.	If holders convert, entire debt service stream is converted to common equity.

Other reasons are often given to explain securities innovations; for example, a desire to achieve a particular accounting treatment or a particular regulatory treatment. The value added by innovations introduced only for their accounting advantages is highly suspect. An efficient capital market can see through accounting transformations to determine the true financial benefits, if any, arising out of a new financial instrument.

THE SEARCH CONTINUES

Securities firms will continue to search for innovative ideas. Yet the process of developing securities innovations is, or at least must eventually become, subject to diminishing returns. The most obvious and potentially most profitable innovations are exploited first, less obvious opportunities generally take longer to find, and less profitable opportunities tend to be put off for later development. In addition, changes in tax law close loopholes and foreclose tax arbitrage opportunities. But the existence of market imperfections coupled with changes in tax law, regulatory codes, and the economic and financial landscape will no doubt continue to generate profitable opportunities for securities innovations.

SOLUTION TO J. K. LINK'S FINANCING DECISION

Our discussion of the different debt financing alternatives should indicate to you that Link's treasurer has several questions that must be answered before she can accurately compare the financing alternatives: What are the mandatory redemption provisions and the optional redemption provisions? How often is interest compounded? What are the covenant restrictions, particularly on the private debt issue?

Suppose the investment bankers tell the treasurer that the three quoted interest rates all assume that the bonds are noncallable and mature in a lump sum at the end of 10 years. Also, the covenants for the domestic public issue and the Eurobond issue would be identical, but the domestic private issue covenants would be somewhat more restrictive. You know from the chapter that the domestic issues pay interest semiannually and that the Eurobond issue pays interest annually. Consequently, care must be taken to express all three costs on a comparable basis. This can be done by comparing the effective costs of the issues for a common time period. The role of covenants is more complex, so first let's compare the cost of funds for the three alternatives.

Assuming Link's marginal income tax rate is 34%, the domestic public debt issue has an effective semiannual cost of 3.02% on an after-tax basis:

Time	Item	CFBT	CFAT	PV @ 3.02%
0	net proceeds	99,000,000	99,000,000	99,000,000
1–20	interest payments	−4,500,000	−2,970,000	−44,103,112
1–20	flotation expense[47]	0	17,000	252,442
20	principal repayment	−100,000,000	−100,000,000	−55,149,330
				PV = 0

Proceeding in the same manner, the effective semiannual cost for the domestic private issue is 3.05%. Finally, the effective semiannual cost for the Eurobond issue is calculated in two stages. First, the effective annual cost is calculated in a manner similar to those above and is found to be 6.15%. The semiannual cost is then calculated from Equation (3.20)

$$r_{s-a} = [1 + .0615]^{.5} - 1 = 3.03\%$$

Therefore, the domestic public issue is the cheapest alternative. Had the private issue been the cheapest alternative, the treasurer would have had to weigh the immediate cost of money savings against the cost implicit in the reduced flexibility of more restrictive covenants.

---

[47] The flotation expense is amortized over the life of the issue on a straight-line basis for tax purposes. This treatment is like using straight-line depreciation for capital equipment—even though the cash outflow for the flotation cost is incurred now, it is expensed for tax purposes over the life of the issue.

SUMMARY

A company that needs to raise long-term funds externally has a number of alternatives available: common stock, preferred stock, straight debt, convertible debt, warrants, and any number of variations on these basic securities types. If the company decides to sell securities, it can do so in the public market or in the private market, and it can sell them directly to investors or engage a securities firm to assist it. The bulk of the securities issued by U.S. companies are sold in the domestic market in negotiated underwritten offerings.

The initial decision involves what type of security to sell. Most important, the firm must decide in light of its capital structure objectives and its current financial condition whether to sell debt or equity securities. Economies of scale involved in issuing securities make it impractical for a company to sell debt and equity securities each time it needs funds in the exact debt and equity proportions embodied in the company's target capital structure.

After deciding what type of security to sell, the company must determine which market offers the most attractive terms. The private market offers some advantages but also suffers some disadvantages relative to the public market. The private market is generally more attractive than the public market for small debt issues or for debt issues backed by complex security arrangements. The Eurobond market is another alternative capital market.

There are a number of sources of additional common equity capital: retained earnings, public offerings of new shares, rights offerings of new shares to current

DECISION SUMMARY BOX

- Many different types of financial securities make up the long-term financing menu. For example, among other things, securities may be equity, debt, or some combination; public or private; domestic or international.

- Issuing debt is the most widely used external financing method.

- New securities can be marketed in a variety of ways. For example, they may be underwritten by one or more investment banking firms, sold on a "best-efforts" basis by one or more investment banking firms, sold directly to the public by the firm, or, in the case of common stock, sold through either a rights offering or a dividend reinvestment plan to current shareholders.

- Issuance costs are proportionately lower for larger issues.

- Bonds have lower explicit issuance costs than common stock for comparable dollar amounts.

- Financial contracts are carefully constructed, and provisions such as the covenants contained in an indenture should be carefully examined. Contractual agreements may be able to reduce agency costs, but such provisions are not costless. For example, restrictive covenants may reduce a firm's interest cost, but only at the expense of the firm's flexibility.

- The exact payment schedule can affect a firm's cost of financing. Compounding affects the cost because of the time value of money. A sinking fund reduces the maturity of the issue. Therefore, a sinking fund may affect the cost of an issue because of differences in the term structure of interest rates.

- Flotation expenses are normally amortized for tax purposes on a straight-line basis over the life of the issue. This treatment is similar to depreciation on capital equipment.

shareholders, private placement of new shares, sale of new shares through a dividend reinvestment or employee stock plan, or a contribution of shares in lieu of cash to the company's pension plan. Public offerings account for most of the new common equity capital companies raise from external sources.

There are five principal classes of long-term corporate debt: unsecured debt, secured debt, income bonds, tax-exempt debt, and convertible debt. Debt instruments belonging to these five classes have certain principal features in common: a stated maturity, a stated principal amount, a stated coupon rate of interest (or interest rate formula, in the case of floating-rate debt), a mandatory redemption schedule, an optional redemption provision, and covenant restrictions designed to protect bondholders.

Preferred stock is a hybrid, combining certain features of debt and certain features of common stock. Sinking fund preferred stock is like debt except that dividend payments are made quarterly and are not tax-deductible, and missing a scheduled dividend payment will not force the issuer into default. Because of a tax asymmetry, preferred stock may be cheaper than debt for a nontaxpaying corporation. Issuing preferred stock in that case will not involve any sacrifice of tax shield benefits but will result in a lower offering yield. Preferred stock yields are generally lower than the yields on comparable debt instruments because of the 70% dividends received deduction available to corporate investors.

Financing with convertible debt (or convertible preferred stock) represents a form of what practitioners call deferred equity financing. The issue is debt (or preferred stock) until it is converted. A convertible bond (or convertible preferred share) derives its value from two sources: its value as a straight bond (or straight preferred share) and the value of the underlying common stock into which it can be converted. As was shown in Chapter 8, put-call parity allows the security to be modeled as a bond plus a call option or as stock plus a put option.

Warrants tend to be used less frequently than convertible securities in financing. They differ from conventional call options in that they are issued by the company that will issue the underlying common stock—and are therefore dilutive—and they are much longer-lived. Nevertheless, their similarity in structure to conventional call options enables us to use the Black-Scholes option pricing model to value them, provided adjustments are made for dividend-paying stocks and for the dilutive effect of issuing warrants.

In addition to the types of securities described in this chapter, the long-term financing menu includes less widely used alternatives, and the securities innovation process adds new ones periodically.

PROBLEMS

PROBLEM SET A

A1. What are the two features of debt and equity (one of each) that differentiate them from each other?

A2. What is the difference between public and private financing?

A3. Cite three advantages and the major disadvantage of private financing.

A4. Why does the par value of common stock have little real significance?

A5. What is by far the largest source of new external financing?

A6. What is by far the largest source of new equity financing?

A7. Name the three explicit transaction cost components of the **gross under-writing spread** in an underwritten public offering.

A8. Explain why the real transaction cost of an issue is the **effective spread** rather than the **gross spread**.

A9. What is a **rights offering**?

A10. What is a **dividend reinvestment plan**?

A11. What is the difference between secured and unsecured debt?

A12. What is a **convertible** security?

A13. What is the difference between a negotiated and a competitive offering?

A14. What is an **interest rate swap**?

A15. What is a **warrant**?

A16. What is a **Eurobond**?

A17. Show that the effective semiannual rate for the domestic private issue in J. K. Link's financing decision is 3.05%. Show that the effective annual rate for the Eurobond issue is 6.15%.

A18. Explain why **preferred stock** is viewed as a "hybrid" security.

PROBLEM SET B

B1. A debt issue bears a 10% coupon and has a sinking fund that makes equal payments at the end of years 4 and 5. Interest is paid semiannually at the end of each period. If the issuing firm nets a price equal to 95% of the face amount of the debt, what is the effective annual pretax cost of the debt?

B2. A new debt issue bearing a 12% coupon and maturing in one lump sum at the end of 10 years involves issuance expenses equal to 2% of the gross proceeds.

    a. Assume the issuing firm pays tax at a 50% marginal rate. What is the after-tax cost of debt?

    b. Suppose instead the firm is not a taxpayer and expects never to be. What is the after-tax cost of debt?

    c. Explain how your answer to part b would change if the firm expected to pay taxes at a 50% rate after 5 years.

B3. A company is considering issuing preferred stock that bears an 8% dividend rate (payable quarterly). The issue is perpetual. Issuance expenses are 1%.

    a. What is the cost of this preferred stock?

    b. How does your answer to part a change if the preferred stock matures in one lump sum after 10 years?

    c. How does your answer to part b change if the issue has a sinking fund calling for equal payments in years 9 and 10?

B4. Explain why a firm making a new securities issue, especially one that includes some component of equity, must be concerned with more than simply the explicit transaction costs such as underwriter fees.

B5. A new floating-rate debt issue pays interest annually based on the 1-year Treasury bill rate. Assume zero issuance cost. The issue matures in 5 years. The current 1-year Treasury bill rate is 9%, and the forecast 1-year rates over the next 4 years are 9.25%, 9.5%, 9.75%, and 10%. The coupon equals the beginning-of-period Treasury rate plus 100 basis points. There is no sinking fund.

    a. Project the debt service payment stream.

    b. Calculate the pretax cost of debt.

    c. Calculate the after-tax cost of debt, assuming a 34% tax rate.

B6. Consider a firm about to make a new equity issue. The firm feels it can make either a public offering or a rights issue to all existing shareholders. The firm wants to raise $14.4 million, net new equity capital. The current share price is $30, with 3 million shares outstanding. Under Plan I, a public offering would be made as follows: 600,000 new shares would be underwritten at a market price of $26 per share and a net price to the firm of $25 per share. Theoretically, after the issue is completed the market price per share will be $29.17. Under Plan II, a rights offering (one right per share issued to each current shareholder) would be made with the following features: 1 million new shares would be sold at $15 each; 3 rights would be necessary to buy each share. Total flotation costs would be $600,000 for Plan II. Theoretically, after the issue is completed, the market price per share should be $26.25. Assuming that the firm's actual goal is to maximize shareholder wealth, which of these plans would be better, and why?

B7. The A. B. Sea Company wishes to raise $100 million through a rights offering. It has 70 million shares outstanding, trading at $25 per share. It wishes each right to be worth at least $0.20 initially.
  a. Find the subscription price and subscription ratio.
  b. After the offering commences, the shares trade at a price of $23 per share. What is the value of one right?
  c. In what situations is a rights offering more appropriate than a general public offering?
  d. What is the principal drawback to a rights offering?

B8. Warrants are often referred to as "sweeteners" to a bond issue, as though the firm can "throw them into the deal" at no cost. Explain why it is, or is not, costless for the firm to include warrants with a bond issue.

B9. A company can sell a 1-year debt issue bearing a 10% coupon or a 2-year debt issue bearing a 12% coupon. The issuer's tax rate is 34%.
  a. Calculate the break-even refunding rate.
  b. How would you interpret your answer to part a?
  c. If the issuer sells the 1-year issue and at the end of 1 year the 1-year new issue rate is 13%, what is the issuer's actual realized cost of 2-year funds?
  d. If the issuer knew with certainty that the 1-year new issue rate 1 year hence would be 13%, which alternative should be accepted?

B10. Explain the role of debt covenants.

B11. A long-term debt issue in the amount of $100 million calls for mandatory redemption payments of $20 million each at the end of years 7, 8, and 9, and repayment of the remaining balance at the end of year 10. Calculate the issue's average life.

B12. What are the principal impulses to financial innovation?

B13. A Japanese bank can borrow at a fixed rate of 9% or at LIBOR. A manufacturing company can borrow at a fixed rate of 12% or at LIBOR + 1%.
  a. Is there a mutually advantageous opportunity to engage in an interest rate swap? Explain.
  b. Suppose the bank offers to pay the manufacturing company LIBOR in return for payments at $11\frac{1}{2}\%$. How should the manufacturing company respond?
  c. The manufacturing company proposes to pay $10\frac{1}{2}\%$ in return for LIBOR. Is such a swap advantageous for the bank?
  d. What fraction of the net cost benefit does each party realize under the swap terms in part c?

B14. In what sense is preferred stock
  a. "Expensive" debt?
  b. "Cheap" equity?

PROBLEM SET C

C1. A firm issues a 10-year debt obligation that bears a 12% coupon rate and gives the investor the right to put the bond back to the issuer at the end of the fifth year at 103% of its face amount. The issue has no sinking fund. Interest is paid semiannually. Issuance expenses are 1%. The issuer's tax rate is 34%.
  a. Calculate the after-tax cost of debt, assuming the debt remains outstanding until maturity.
  b. Calculate the after-tax cost of debt, assuming investors put the bond back to the firm at the end of the fifth year. (*Note*: Any unamortized issuance expenses and any redemption premium can be deducted for tax purposes in the year of redemption.)

C2. A CD broker calls the chief financial officer (CFO) of the Spring Lake Savings Bank and offers a "special deal." The broker has a client who is willing to purchase two CDs in the amount of $99,000 each. One bears a 7½% coupon rate, payable monthly in arrears, and the other bears a 7% coupon rate also payable monthly in arrears. Each matures in 5 years. In return for this special deal, the CD broker asks the CFO to pay a fee of 1¼% per annum (6.25% of face amount) on the 7½% CD and a fee of 2½% per annum (12.50% of face amount) on the 7% CD. The 5-year Treasury yield, semiannually compounded, was 9.50% at the time. The CD broker offers to let Spring Lake Savings pay the fees in 15 equal monthly installments beginning 1 month from the settlement date.
  a. Considering the two CDs collectively, specify Spring Lake Savings Bank's pretax debt service stream.
  b. The CD broker tells the CFO that the CDs are a great deal because the cost of funds for one is 8¾% (7½% + 1¼% per annum) and for the other is 9½% (7% + 2½% per annum), for a blended cost of 9.125%. Do you agree? Explain.
  c. Calculate Spring Lake Savings Bank's actual aggregate cost of funds for the two CDs.
  d. The chairman of Spring Lake Savings asks the CFO whether CD financing involves a lower cost of funds than the Treasury's cost of 5-year funds. How should the CFO respond?
  e. If Spring Lake Savings Bank's next best alternative is to sell a 5-year CD bearing a 9¾% coupon, payable monthly in arrears, which requires a CD brokerage fee of 0.25% per annum (1.25% of face amount) payable at settlement, should the CFO accept the special deal? Justify your answer.

C3. Explain why the shelf registration process might lead to a more efficient capital market.

C4. A convertible bond can be modeled as a call option plus a straight bond. A warrant is a call option. In a perfect capital market environment the combined market value of a warrant and a straight bond will be identical to the market value of a comparable convertible bond. Explain why you might expect the market value of the warrant-bond combination to be somewhat higher than the comparable convertible bond. *Hint*: This can be done using the Options Principle.

REFERENCES

Agmon, T., Aharon R. Ofer, and A. Tamir. "Variable Rate Debt Instruments and Corporate Debt Policy." *Journal of Finance* 36 (March 1981): 113–26.

Alderson, Michael J., Keith C. Brown, and Scott L. Lummer. "Dutch Auction Rate Preferred Stock." *Financial Management* 16 (Summer 1987): 68–73.

Alexander, Gordon J., and David B. Kuhnau. "Market Timing Strategies in Convertible Debt Financing." *Journal of Finance* 34 (March 1979): 143–56.

Asquith, P., and D. W. Mullins. "Equity Issues and Offering Dilution." *Journal of Financial Economics* 15 (1986): 61–89.

Barnea, Amir R., Robert A. Haugen, and Lemma W. Senbet. "A Rationale for Debt Maturity Structure and Call Provisions in the Agency Theory Framework." *Journal of Finance* 35 (December 1980): 1223–34.

Bhagat, Sanjai. "The Effect of Management's Choice between Negotiated and Competitive Equity Offerings on Shareholder Wealth." *Journal of Financial and Quantitative Analysis* 21 (June 1986): 181–96.

Bhagat, Sanjai, M. Wayne Marr, and G. Rodney Thompson. "The Rule 415 Experiment: Equity Markets." *Journal of Finance* 40 (December 1985): 1385–1401.

Bicksler, James, and Andrew H. Chen. "An Economic Analysis of Interest Rate Swaps." *Journal of Finance* 41 (July 1986): 645–55.

Bierman, Harold, Jr. "The Cost of Warrants." *Journal of Financial and Quantitative Analysis* 8 (June 1973): 499–504.

Block, Ernest. "Pricing a Corporate Bond Issue: A Look Behind the Scenes." In *Essays in Money and Credit*. Federal Reserve Bank of New York, 1964, 72–76.

Bodie, Zvi, and Robert A. Taggart. "Future Investment Opportunities and the Value of the Call Provision on a Bond." *Journal of Finance* 33 (September 1978): 1187–1200.

Bowyer, John W., Jr., and Jess B. Yawitz. "The Effect of New Equity Issues on Utility Stock Prices." *Public Utilities Fortnightly* 105 (May 22, 1980): 25–28.

Boyce, William M., and Andrew J. Kalotay. "Tax Differentials and Callable Bonds." *Journal of Finance* 34 (September 1979): 825–38.

Brennan, Michael J., and Eduardo S. Schwartz. "Convertible Bonds: Valuation and Optimal Strategies for Call and Conversion." *Journal of Finance* 32 (December 1977): 1699–1715.

Brennan, Michael J., and Eduardo S. Schwartz. "Analyzing Convertible Bonds." *Journal of Financial and Quantitative Analysis* 15 (November 1980): 907–29.

Collins, J. Markham, and Roger P. Bey. "The Master Limited Partnership: An Alternative to the Corporation." *Financial Management* 15 (Winter 1986): 5–14.

Davey, Patrick J. *Dividend Reinvestment Programs*. New York: Conference Board, 1976.

Dyl, Edward A., and Michael D. Joehnk. "Sinking Funds and the Cost of Corporate Debt." *Journal of Finance* 34 (September 1979): 887–93.

Dyl, Edward A., and William J. Sawaya. "The Bond Issue Size Decision Revisited." *Financial Management* 8 (Winter 1979): 60–67.

Ederington, Louis H. "Uncertainty, Competition, and Costs in the Underwriting of Corporate Bonds." *Journal of Financial Economics* 2 (March 1975): 71–94.

Ederington, Louis H. "Negotiated Versus Competitive Underwritings of Corporate Bonds." *Journal of Finance* 31 (March 1976): 17–28.

Emery, Douglas R., J. Ronald Hoffmeister, and Ronald W. Spahr. "The Case for Indexing a Bond's Call Price." *Financial Management* 16 (Autumn 1987): 57–64.

Emery, Douglas R., Wilbur G. Lewellen, and David C. Mauer. "Tax Timing Options, Leverage, and the Choice of Corporate Form." *Journal of Financial Research* 11 (Summer 1988): 99–110.

Esslen, Rainer. *The Complete Book of International Investing*. New York: McGraw-Hill, 1977.

Fabozzi, Frank J., and Richard R. West. "Negotiated Versus Competitive Underwritings of

Public Utility Bonds: Just One More Time." *Journal of Financial and Quantitative Analysis* 16 (September 1981): 323–39.

Finnerty, John D. "The Behavior of Electric Utility Common Stock Prices Near the Ex-Dividend Date." *Financial Management* 10 (Winter 1981): 59–69.

Finnerty, John D. "Financial Engineering in Corporate Finance: An Overview." *Financial Management* 17 (Winter 1988): 14–33.

Finnerty, John D. "How to Lower the Cost of Floating a New Stock Issue." *Public Utilities Fortnightly* 111 (March 17, 1983): 25–29.

Finnerty, Joseph E., Thomas Schneeweis, and Shantaram P. Hedge. "Interest Rates in the Eurobond Market." *Journal of Financial and Quantitative Analysis* 15 (September 1980): 743–55.

Fredman, Albert J., and John R. Nichols. "New Capital Dividend Reinvestment Plans of Electric Utilities." *Public Utilities Fortnightly* 108 (February 28, 1980): 19–28.

Fung, W. K. H., and Andrew Rudd. "Pricing New Corporate Bond Issues: An Analysis of Issue Cost and Seasoning Effects." *Journal of Finance* 41 (July 1986): 633–43.

Galai, Dan, and Meir I. Schneller. "Pricing of Warrants and the Value of the Firm." *Journal of Finance* 33 (December 1978): 1333–42.

Gatti, James F., John R. Mills, and Peter J. McTague. "The Feasibility of Small Denomination Consumer Note Issues As a Source of Funds for Non-Financial Borrowers." *Financial Management* 10 (Autumn 1981): 41–53.

Hansen, Robert S., and John M. Pinkerton. "Direct Equity Financing: A Resolution of a Paradox." *Journal of Finance* 37 (June 1982): 651–65.

Heinkel, Robert, and Eduardo S. Schwartz. "Rights Versus Underwritten Offerings: An Asymmetric Information Approach." *Journal of Finance* 41 (March 1986): 1–18.

Hess, A. C., and S. Bhagat. "A Test of the Price Pressure Hypothesis Using Announcement Data." *Journal of Financial Economics* 15 (1986).

Kalotay, Andrew J. "Sinking Funds and the Realized Cost of Debt." *Financial Management* 11 (Spring 1982): 43–54.

Kidwell, David S., M. Wayne Marr, and G. Rodney Thompson. "Eurodollar Bonds, Alternative Financing for U.S. Companies: A Correction." *Financial Management* 15 (Spring 1986): 78–79.

Kidwell, David S., M. Wayne Marr, and G. Rodney Thompson. "SEC Rule 415: The Ultimate Competitive Bid." *Journal of Financial and Quantitative Analysis* 19 (June 1984): 183–95.

Klemkosky, Robert C. "The Impact of Option Expirations on Stock Prices." *Journal of Financial and Quantitative Analysis* 13 (September 1978): 507–18.

Kraus, Alan. "The Bond Refunding Decision in an Efficient Market." *Journal of Financial and Quantitative Analysis* 8 (December 1973): 793–806.

Levy, Haim, and Marshall Sarnat. "Risk, Dividend Policy, and the Optimal Pricing of a Rights Offering." *Journal of Money, Credit, and Banking* 3 (November 1971): 840–49.

Litzenberger, Robert H., and David P. Rutenberg. "Size and Timing of Corporate Bond Flotations." *Journal of Financial and Quantitative Analysis* 7 (January 1972): 1343–59.

Logue, Dennis E., and Robert A. Jarrow. "Negotiation vs. Competitive Bidding in the Sale of Securities by Public Utilities." *Financial Management* 7 (Autumn 1978): 31–39.

McConnell, John J., and Gary G. Schlarbaum. "Returns, Risks, and Pricing of Income Bonds, 1956–76." *Journal of Business* 54 (January 1981): 33–57.

Marshall, William J., and Jess B. Yawitz. "Optimal Terms of the Call Provision on a Corporate Bond." *Journal of Financial Research* 3 (Summer 1980): 203–11.

Masulis, Ronald W., and A. N. Korwar. "Seasoned Equity Offerings: An Empirical Investigation." *Journal of Financial Economics* 15 (1986): 91–118.

Merton, Robert C. "On the Pricing of Corporate Debt." *Journal of Finance* 29 (May 1974): 449–70.

Miller, Merton H. "Financial Innovation: The Last Twenty Years and the Next." *Journal of Financial and Quantitative Analysis* 21 (December 1986): 459–71.

Moore, Norman H., David R. Peterson, and Pamela P. Peterson. "Shelf Registrations and

Shareholder Wealth: A Comparison of Shelf and Traditional Equity Offerings." *Journal of Finance* 41 (June 1986): 451–63.

Myers, Stewart C., and Nicholas J. Majluf. "Corporate Financing and Investment Decisions When Firms Have Information That Investors Do Not Have." *Journal of Financial Economics* 13 (June 1984): 187–222.

Parker, George G. C., and Daniel Cooperman. "Competitive Bidding in the Underwriting of Public Utility Securities." *Journal of Financial and Quantitative Analysis* 13 (December 1978): 885–902.

Rice, Michael D. *Equipment Financing.* New York: Salomon Brothers, 1981.

Scholes, Myron S. "The Market for Securities: Substitution versus Price Pressure and the Effects of Information on Share Prices." *Journal of Business* 45 (April 1972): 179–211.

Schwartz, Eduardo S. "The Valuation of Warrants: Implementing A New Approach." *Journal of Financial Economics* 4 (January 1977): 79–93.

Smith, Clifford W., Jr. "Alternative Methods for Raising Capital: Rights versus Underwritten Offerings." *Journal of Financial Economics* 5 (December 1977): 273–307.

Smith, Clifford W., Jr. "Raising Capital: Theory and Evidence." *Midland Corporate Finance Journal* 4 (Spring 1986): 6–22.

Smith, Clifford W., Jr., Charles W. Smithson, and L. Macdonald Wakeman. "The Evolving Market for Swaps." *Midland Corporate Finance Journal* 3 (Winter 1986): 20–32.

Smith, Clifford W., Jr., and Jerold B. Warner. "On Financial Contracting: An Analysis of Bond Covenants." *Journal of Financial Economics* 7 (June 1979): 117–61.

Soldofsky, Robert M., and Craig R. Johnson. "Rights Timing." *Financial Analysts Journal* 23 (July-August 1967): 101–14.

Sorensen, Eric H. "The Impact of Underwriting Method and Bidder Competition Upon Corporate Bond Interest Cost." *Journal of Finance* 34 (September 1979): 863–70.

Tallman, Gary D., David F. Rush, and Ronald W. Melicher. "Competitive versus Negotiated Underwriting Costs for Regulated Industries." *Financial Management* 3 (Summer 1974): 49–55.

Thatcher, Janet S. "The Choice of Call Provision Terms: Evidence of the Existence of Agency Costs of Debt." *Journal of Finance* 40 (June 1985): 549–61.

Turnbull, Stuart M. "Swaps: A Zero Sum Game?" *Financial Management* 16 (Spring 1987): 15–21.

Van Horne, James C. "Of Financial Innovations and Excesses." *Journal of Finance* 40 (July 1985): 621–31.

Weingartner, H. Martin. "Optimal Timing of Bond Refunding." *Management Science* 13 (March 1967): 511–24.

White, R. W., and P. A. Lusztig. "The Price Effects of Rights Offerings." *Journal of Financial and Quantitative Analysis* 15 (March 1980): 25–40.

Yawitz, Jess B., and Kevin J. Maloney. "Evaluating the Decision to Issue Original Issue Discount Bonds: Term Structure and Tax Effects." *Financial Management* 12 (Winter 1983): 36–46.

Zwick, Burton. "Yields on Privately Placed Corporate Bonds." *Journal of Finance* 35 (March 1980): 23–29.

CAPITAL STRUCTURE: WHY IT MATTERS

In the preceding chapter, we described some of the many alternative ways a firm can obtain long-term financing. In this chapter, we take up the question of whether some of these ways can be used to enhance the value of the firm. This question has been called "the capital structure puzzle."[1] *Puzzle* is a particularly appropriate term because our answer to this question has evolved in much the same way that a puzzle is pieced together. Currently, pieces are still being added to improve our understanding, but as yet we do not have the complete picture. In this chapter, we review and discuss the existing pieces of the puzzle and present our view of the picture. In the next chapter, we apply this view to derive guidelines for managing a firm's capital structure.

Recall that the mix of financing methods used by a firm is called the firm's **capital structure**. Loosely speaking, capital structure refers to the proportions of debt and equity that make up the liabilities and owners' equity side (right-hand side) of the firm's balance sheet. Often, people refer to the use of debt in a firm's capital structure as leverage. The term *leverage* is derived from the mechanical lever that allows you to lift more weight than is possible by yourself. Financial leverage allows the equityholders to control more assets than is possible with their own money. However, financial leverage also alters the degree of risk that is borne by the equityholders, and, as we will see, a primary consideration with respect to capital structure is how the risk of the firm is borne by those providing the financing.

In practice, the term *capital structure* often refers simply to the proportion of the corporation's financing that is provided by debt. The ratio of debt to total firm value is called the company's **leverage ratio**. U.S. corporations involved in manufacturing have had an average leverage ratio of between 45% and 55% from 1965 to 1985.[2] The primary industry in which the corporation does business appears to be an important determinant of a firm's choice of leverage ratio. Some people might argue that this pattern is the result of managers applying the Behavioral Principle of Finance when it is not appropriate: The patterns are due to managers imitating each other, and in fact the actions may carry no information. However, in this chapter, we investigate explanations based on valuation considerations resulting from capital market imperfections and systematic differences across industries in the availability of different forms of expenses to shelter operating income and in the availability of assets to support leverage. We argue that these considerations are responsible, at least in part, for the patterns of capital structure observed in practice.

---

[1] Myers (1984).
[2] Department of Commerce Quarterly Balance Sheet for non-farm, non-financial corporations.

AT&T's Capital Structure Decision

American Telephone and Telegraph Company (AT&T), at the time the world's largest business enterprise, announced on January 8, 1982, that it had reached agreement with the United States Department of Justice to divest itself of its 22 telephone subsidiaries by year-end 1983. The agreement modified a 1956 consent decree that had limited AT&T to the regulated telecommunications business. Following the divestiture, which would involve approximately three-quarters of its assets, AT&T would be free to pursue whatever business opportunities it wished to pursue. The divestiture would move AT&T abruptly out of a stable, regulated telephone company environment. The expectation was that AT&T would move into the competitive world of advanced information technology.

The following table shows AT&T's capital structure, that is, the mix of long-term funds that was financing its business at year-end 1982:

	Amount (billions)	Percent of Capitalization
Long-term debt	$ 44.105	40.9%
Preferred equity	1.851	1.7
Common equity	61.913	57.4
Total Capitalization	$107.869	100.0%

The 40.9% long-term debt ratio was in line with the degree of leverage in the capital structures of other highly regulated companies. (Most of AT&T's subsidiaries' debt was triple-A-rated.) But as AT&T's management contemplated its dramatic change in business environment, management questioned whether a change in capital structure should accompany the other changes. The fact that AT&T would be sharply reducing its size and entering into nonregulated businesses with possibly greater operating risk concerned AT&T's management.

After discussing the considerations relevant to a company's choice of capital structure, we will explain how AT&T reached (and then applied) its capital structure decision.

15.1   NATURE OF THE CONTROVERSY

The major controversy regarding capital structure concerns whether a firm's total value is affected by its choice of capital structure. The Principle of Capital Market Efficiency holds that financing transactions in a perfect and complete capital market are "fair" transactions, so financing that is obtained in such a capital market should be a zero-NPV transaction.[3] Therefore, in a perfect capital market environment—one with costless information, no taxes, and no transaction costs—capital structure doesn't matter. Unfortunately, although a perfect market analysis provides the best starting place for thinking about the problem, the realities of capital market imperfections must be included to arrive at more practical conclusions. As we noted in Chapter 5, taxes, asymmetric information, and transaction costs are important dimensions in the operation of the capital markets, and those dimensions affect our conclusions about capital structure.

[3]Just like investment decisions, financing decisions can be evaluated by measuring their NPV. Examples of such analyses are given in subsequent chapters, such as the analysis of a bond refunding given in Chapter 20 and the analysis of a lease financing given in Chapter 21.

There have been, and continue to be, conflicting arguments and conclusions about the significance of a corporation's choice of capital structure. We will start by enumerating six of them in the approximate chronological order in which they were put forth. The **traditional view** advocates the inclusion of a "significant" amount of debt in a corporation's capital structure. According to this view, debt is a relatively "cheap" form of capital, and firm value increases as the proportion of debt in the capital structure is increased. However, beyond some point, the higher debt level would increase the riskiness of the firm to such an extent that firm value would decrease if the proportion of debt in the capital structure was increased further.

The **perfect market view** concludes that capital structure is irrelevant to the value of the firm because investors can achieve any desired debt-equity mix on their own as cheaply as any company can. In a perfect capital market environment, the value of the firm consequently depends only on its expected future operating cash flows and the required rate of return that is appropriate for the risk of those cash flows. How the firm is financed does not affect its value.

The **corporate tax view**, a third school of thought, reaches the conclusion that the firm should be financed with the largest proportion of debt that is possible—essentially all financing should be provided by debt to maximize the value of the firm. This view is based on the tax advantage that debt enjoys relative to equity: interest (i.e., payments to debtholders) is tax-deductible by the firm, whereas dividends (i.e., payments to equityholders) are not. Debt financing creates a tax shield that shelters part of the firm's operating income. Each additional $100 of debt increases value by $100 times the tax rate, the value of the tax shelter created by the additional debt.

The **bankruptcy view** tempers the corporate tax view by noting that as the proportion of debt in the capital structure increases, so does the likelihood of bankruptcy. The bankruptcy view brought the capital structure debate full circle by providing a justification for the traditional view that debt is beneficial as long as leverage does not become excessive. Because the firm must trade off the tax benefits associated with a larger proportion of debt financing against the increased likelihood of incurring bankruptcy costs, an all-debt capital structure is too extreme. Accordingly, the bankruptcy view concludes that the proportion of debt financing should be large but less than 100% to reflect the potential cost of bankruptcy.

The **personal tax view** further tempers the corporate tax view. This view represents, in a sense, a rebuttal to the corporate tax view and the bankruptcy view by the proponents of the perfect market view. An additional tax aspect of debt financing is relevant. Even though income to shareholders is taxed twice (versus only once for income to debtholders), the personal tax rate charged on income to debtholders is substantially larger than the personal tax rate charged on income to shareholders because a significant portion of shareholders' returns is in the form of capital gains, whose tax can be deferred. The personal tax view concludes that the combined corporate and personal tax effects are not significantly different for debt and equity financing and that if bankruptcy costs are not significant either, then capital structure is not a significant determinant of a firm's value. Proponents of the personal tax view acknowledge that market imperfections exist but argue that their impact on capital structure choice is not significant.

Finally, there is the **signaling view**. According to the signaling view, the firm's financing transactions provide important signals to investors regarding management's expectations about the company's future earnings. For example, management may be willing to have the firm incur additional debt *only* if it believes the firm's prospects have improved sufficiently to enable the firm to service the additional debt.

It is widely believed that a firm's choice of capital structure, at least to some degree, affects the firm's value. In practice, capital structure matters, if for no other reason than that companies actually behave as though it mattered. The empirical evidence shows consistent patterns of leverage ratios, as though there were definite reasons for following certain policies. These patterns point out the possibility that some policies are superior to others that are not adopted. It might be argued that firms are all following the Behavioral Principle of Finance—in the extreme case, just copying each other—and that these patterns are simply "neutral mutations." It is our opinion that this explanation is too simplistic. In this chapter, we detail a set of conceptual reasons why capital structure affects the value of the firm. In the next chapter, we outline a practical method of managing capital structure that is consistent with this conceptual framework.

15.2   THE TRADITIONAL VIEW

The traditional view holds that there is an optimal capital structure that contains a positive amount of debt. Accordingly, a firm without any leverage could increase its total market value by exchanging some of its equity financing for debt financing. According to this view, as a firm increases its leverage, the required rates of return on equity and debt both increase because of the increase in financial risk. But for small amounts of debt, the required rate of return on debt increases very little with increases in the firm's leverage. As a result, substituting debt for equity initially leads to a lower weighted average required rate of return. The savings resulting from substituting a cheaper source of funds for equity more than offset the increase in the required rate of return on equity. But beyond some point, which determines the location of the optimal capital structure, the increase in the required rate of return on equity more than offsets the savings resulting from substituting debt for equity. By adopting the optimal capital structure, a firm minimizes its weighted average required rate of return and maximizes its total market value. A graphic representation of the traditional view is presented in Figure 15-1. In this figure, the measure of lev-

FIGURE 15-1

Traditional view of capital structure.

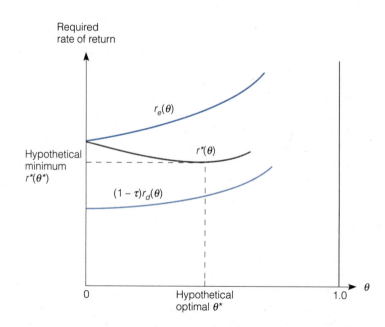

erage, the ratio of debt value to total value, is denoted as θ. The required rates of return on debt, equity, and the firm are denoted $r_d(\theta)$, $r_e(\theta)$, and $r^*(\theta)$, respectively.

Given the Principle of Capital Market Efficiency and our statement that capital structure does not matter in a perfect market environment, we hope you are skeptical of the traditional view's explanation of the relevance of capital structure. The view that debtholders can be "fooled" into providing capital at a lower rate of return than that required by the risk of the investment is wrong. Thus, the *reasoning* underlying the traditional view is incorrect. However, as we will detail in the remainder of this chapter, for a variety of other reasons, the conclusion that capital structure affects the value of a firm, and that therefore firms have an optimal capital structure that contains a positive amount of debt, is probably correct after all.

THE PERFECT MARKET VIEW   15.3

In Chapter 5, we discussed the concept of value conservation. We said two financial economists named Modigliani and Miller (MM) were most responsible for introducing this important concept. The first article introducing this concept was published in 1958, and the topic of the article is capital structure. In this article, MM demonstrate that in a perfect and complete capital market, a firm cannot affect its market value by altering the way it is financed. The value of a firm depends only on the size of its expected future operating cash flow stream and the required rate of return, not on how that cash flow stream is divided between the debtholders and the shareholders. Therefore, a firm's capital structure is irrelevant to the firm's value in a perfect market environment.

The crux of the MM argument is that investors can create the same capital structure through their own capital market transactions. Investors can use what MM call "homemade leverage." Recall from Chapter 7 (Generalization 5) that all investors should invest in the same risky portfolio, but investors set the expected return and risk levels of their total investment by lending or borrowing. The choice of personal capital structure (lending or borrowing) does not alter the total value of the investor's portfolio because any change in expected return is exactly offset by a change in risk.

Of course, as we have already mentioned, this perfect market view leaves out taxes, transaction costs (including bankruptcy penalties), and information considerations. With varying tax rates on corporate and personal income, individual investors may prefer that the income be classified as debt, equity, or some combination of the two. In the case of a preference for a combination of income types, the firm may be able to reduce aggregate transaction costs associated with issuing securities because of economies of scale. Also, transaction costs associated with bankruptcy, which are otherwise avoidable, make excessive leverage undesirable. Finally, it may be that capital structure (or capital structure changes) can be used less expensively than other methods to convey information to the public. All of these concerns are valid and will be addressed in this chapter.

CORPORATE RETURNS AND RISK BEARING

In Chapter 10, we examined the impact of capital structure on required rates of return. We used a simple example of a company called Per-Pet, Inc. to illustrate the fact that the required rate of return of a project does not depend on capital structure in a perfect market environment, even though the required rates of return to debt and equity may change in response to a change in the firm's financial leverage. The Per-Pet example illustrates the perfect capital market view. Rereading the Per-Pet example is strongly recommended because we build on the example later in the chapter.

Another way of illustrating the perfect market view of capital structure is with an arbitrage argument, presented below. Some people find one rather than the other presentation more enlightening, but both illustrate this view of capital structure.

AN ARBITRAGE ARGUMENT THAT CAPITAL STRUCTURE IS IRRELEVANT

In their path-breaking 1958 article, MM point out that in a perfect capital market environment, no profitable arbitrage opportunities can exist. Using this argument, they show that if two companies have identical operating profitability but different capital structures, arbitrage among investors will ensure that the two companies have equal market values.

Consider two companies operating in a perfect capital market environment. Each will generate $10,000,000 of operating income, and they are identical in every other aspect, except that Company A has debt in its capital structure and Company B has an all-equity capital structure. Suppose that investors currently value the two companies as indicated in Table 15-1. Company A has a higher market value, supposedly because of its leverage.

According to the perfect market view, this situation cannot persist because of the following profitable arbitrage opportunity: Shareholders of Company A can realize a greater return on their investment with no increase in either their investment risk or the amount of funds they have invested, by making the following transactions. First, sell their shares of Company A; second, borrow enough funds to create their own personal 50% leverage to duplicate Company A's capital structure; and third, use the proceeds from the sale of shares and the personal loan to purchase shares of Company B. To illustrate this opportunity, consider the following example.

Suppose an investor owns 1% of the shares of Company A. The first step in the arbitrage process is to sell these shares at their market value of $291,667 (1% of $29,166,667). The second step is for our investor to borrow an identical amount, $291,667, at an interest rate of 12% per period. This creates a personal capital structure that is 50% debt and 50% equity, exactly the capital structure of Company A.

TABLE 15-1 An Illustration of Capital Structure Arbitrage

Company	A	B
Leverage ratio (= debt/[debt + equity])	50%	0
Operating income	$10,000,000	$10,000,000
− Interest expense[a]	3,500,000	0
Net income	$ 6,500,000	$10,000,000
Market value of equity	29,166,667	50,000,000
Market value of debt	29,166,667	0
Total market value	$58,333,334	$50,000,000

[a] At a 12% interest rate.

The final step is to use the total funds to purchase $583,334 (= 291,667 + 291,667) of Company B shares, which happens to be 1.16667% (= 583,334/50,000,000) of the value of Company B. Now let's compare the return to our investor before and after the arbitrage transaction. Before the three-step transaction, the investor's return per period is 1% of Company A's expected net income, which equals $65,000. After the transaction, the investor's return per period is $116,667 (1.16667% of B's expected net income) minus an interest charge of $35,000 (12% of $291,667), which is a net amount of $81,667. Thus, without adding any funds, our investor has an investment with an identical amount of leverage (and therefore identical risk) that earns $16,667 per period more after completing the arbitrage transaction.

With self-interested behavior, arbitrage activity by investors will continue until the market prices of shares in the two companies are equal. Only when the share values are equal will there be no further profitable arbitrage opportunity. Problem B2 at the end of the chapter illustrates this process in reverse. It asks you to recreate the example with Company B worth more and show that the capital structure can be profitably "undone" by lending money at 12%.

TAX ASYMMETRIES   15.4

As we pointed out in Chapter 5, an important place to look for value-altering market imperfections is in the tax code. Whenever tax rates differ for the two sides of a transaction, there is a tax asymmetry that might be exploitable. How do taxes affect the relevance of capital structure in an otherwise perfect market environment? We have already mentioned some of the arguments concerning taxes. Here, we will start by introducing corporate income taxes and then sequentially add other tax considerations to the Per-Pet example introduced in Chapter 10 and assess the impact of each imperfection on the value of the firm.

CORPORATE INCOME TAXES

In 1963, MM published another article about capital structure in which they pointed out a significant tax asymmetry in corporate income tax law: Interest payments are tax-deductible to the firm, whereas dividend payments are not. MM argued that while the capital market is efficient enough to render capital structure essentially irrelevant otherwise, this corporate tax asymmetry causes debt to be more attractive for corporate financing purposes than equity. This is the corporate tax view.

Consider again our example of Per-Pet in Chapter 10. Per-Pet has an expected cash inflow each period forever with the following probability distribution:

cash flow =	$250	$200	$150	$100	$50
probability =	.2	.2	.2	.2	.2

The required rate of return for Per-Pet's expected future cash inflows is 15% per period. From this probability distribution you should be able to see that the expected cash inflow each period for Per-Pet is $150, and therefore, Per-Pet is worth $1,000 (= $150/.15) in a perfect capital market.

As before, let us start with an all-equity firm and examine the effect on the value of the firm of adding debt to the firm's capital structure. If the tax rate incurred on the firm's net income is 37.5%, the after-tax cash flows are simply the pretax flows ($250, $200, . . .) multiplied by 1 minus the tax rate (1 − .375). So the all-equity firm will have expected future after-corporate-tax cash flows that can be paid out to the shareholders every period according to the following probability distribution:

cash flow = $156.25 $125.00 $93.75 $62.50 $31.25
probability = .2   .2   .2   .2   .2

With a required rate of return to the shareholders of 15%, Per-Pet has a market value of $625.00 (= $93.75/.15). Now suppose $500 worth of debt is sold to investors, requiring $50 per period in interest payments, which will be $31.25 after-tax (= [1 − .375]50). Then the distribution of expected future after-corporate-tax cash flows available for shareholders will be

cash flow = $125.00 $93.75 $62.50 $31.25 $0
probability = .2   .2   .2   .2   .2

Due to the higher leverage, the required rate of return increases to 20%. The expected future cash flow to be paid out to shareholders after the capital structure change is then $62.50, and the market value of the equity portion of the firm equals $312.50 (= $62.50/.20), so that the total value of the firm is $812.50 = $500.00 + $312.50. By leveraging the firm, the shareholders end up with an investment value of $312.50 plus $500 in cash, so they have increased their wealth from $625 to $812.50 and are better off by $187.50.

The extra value for the shareholders can be traced to the tax asymmetry. The government collects fewer tax dollars from the leveraged firm. Specifically, with the all-equity capital structure, the firm pays an average of $56.25 (= $150[.375]) per period, whereas an average of only $37.50 (= $100[.375]) is paid per period with the leveraged capital structure.

PERSONAL TAXES

In 1977, Miller (without Modigliani) detailed the personal tax view. According to that view, the differential between tax rates on personal income from equity and debt securities cancels out the corporate tax asymmetry.

From an income tax perspective, the corporate tax example just given is incomplete. Before its net income is fully distributed to its investors, the corporation pays taxes on the income. But those same investors then pay personal income taxes on the income they receive. To model this process, we will assume that the debtholders' tax rate is 50%, whereas the shareholders have a lower tax rate of 20%. The lower rate for the shareholders is designed to incorporate the effect of shareholders actually receiving some of their income as capital gains, thereby paying a lower effective rate.[4]

With personal taxes, the shareholders must pay 20% of their income in taxes, in which case they receive an after-tax amount of 80% (100% minus 20%) of the corporate income (e.g., .8[156.25] = $125). With an all-equity capital structure, then, the shareholders will have the following distribution of cash flows:

cash flow = $125.00 $100.00 $75.00 $50.00 $25.00
probability = .2   .2   .2   .2   .2

With a required rate of return of 15%, Per-Pet has a market value of $500.00 (= $75.00/.15). Now suppose $250 worth of debt is sold to investors, requiring $50

[4]Recall that, even when there is no difference between the capital gains tax rate and the regular income tax rate, the effective capital gains rate is often much lower because the tax payment is deferred until the asset is sold.

per period in interest payments. The debtholders pay personal income taxes at the rate of 50%, so the debtholders receive an after-tax cash flow of $25 (= $50[1 − .5]) per period. With a required rate of return of 10%, the market value of this debt will be $250 (= $25/.10). With the "first" $50 paid to debtholders each period, corporate taxes paid, and then personal taxes paid by shareholders, the distribution of expected future after-tax cash flows to shareholders will be

cash flow =	$100.00	$75.00	$50.00	$25.00	$0
probability =	.2	.2	.2	.2	.2

The expected future cash flow to be paid out to shareholders after the capital structure change is then $50.00, and the market value of the equity portion of the firm equals $250 (= $50/.20), so that the total value of the firm is $500 = $250 + $250. By leveraging the firm, the shareholders end up with an investment value of $250 plus $250 in cash for a total value of $500. Consequently they are no better off as a result of leveraging the firm since they started with a total investment value of $500.

The irrelevance of capital structure demonstrated by this example depends upon the tax rates used. Denote τ_d, τ_e, and τ as the tax rates for debtholders, equity-holders, and the corporation, respectively. Miller shows that whenever

$$(1 - \tau_d) = (1 - \tau_e)(1 - \tau) \tag{15.1}$$

the net income tax effect is zero because the bias created by corporate and personal taxes exactly cancel each other out. However, it is very important to note that *the tax biases cancel each other out completely **only** when Equation (15.1) holds.*

In spite of the requirement that Equation (15.1) hold for there to be no net tax effect, we can draw some generalizations from the example: Even if personal taxes do not fully mitigate the conclusion of the corporate tax view of capital structure—more leverage is preferred to less—personal taxation may significantly reduce the amount of the benefit to leverage created by the corporate income tax. Further, it should be clear from the sequential modification of the Per-Pet example that taxes may affect firm valuation in a complex way. The Tax Reform Act of 1986 provides a basis for testing the relative importance of personal and corporate tax effects on capital structure choice. The Tax Reform Act of 1986 reduced the maximum personal income tax rate to 28% (excluding any surtax) from 50% but reduced the maximum corporate income tax rate only to 34% (excluding any surtax) from 46%. The 1986 law makes leverage relatively more attractive at the corporate level than at the personal level. The act also eliminated the investment tax credit, reduced the degree of acceleration in depreciation tables, and eliminated or reduced many other nondebt-related deductions. It also reduced the rate of personal taxation on interest income but eliminated the personal dividend exclusion and increased the rate of personal taxation on the capital gain component of equity returns. These tax changes should shift the optimal corporate financing mix toward increased debt. The magnitude of any such shift that actually occurs will provide evidence regarding the relative importance of the various tax-related factors that affect capital structure choice. Of course, as we pointed out in Chapter 12, tax laws change with almost alarming regularity. Therefore, companies do not act immediately following a change in the tax code, rather, waiting for a "shakedown" period.

FINANCIAL DISTRESS

The possibility that a firm may lose some, or perhaps all, of the value of interest deductions during periods of financial distress plays a role in determining how capital structure affects the valuation of the firm.[5] The implication is that financial distress also creates a tax asymmetry. Loss carryforwards and loss carrybacks are sometimes limited, so the corporate tax shields due to leverage may be lost during a period of financial distress. But even if all current losses can be fully carried forward and deducted from future income, the firm still loses the time value of money on the tax shields.

Tax credits due to expenses other than interest may also play a role in capital structure choice.[6] A firm need not be paying out all its revenue as interest to avoid paying any corporate income taxes. Other expenses, such as depreciation, also provide tax shields. The implication is that a firm with a large amount of "nondebt" tax shields can have the same total market value as another firm that has significantly more leverage in its capital structure. This in turn implies the possibility of a higher total value for the firm with a larger amount of "nondebt" tax shields but less debt because of the lower likelihood of bankruptcy and hence lower expected bankruptcy costs.

The tax asymmetry due to financial distress affects the argument between the corporate and personal tax views of capital structure. If the corporate view is correct and there is a net valuation benefit from leverage, then lost tax credits during times of financial distress reduce that benefit. In such a case, the lost tax credits mitigate the corporate tax view's extreme conclusion that the firm's financing should be essentially all debt. If the personal tax view is correct and leverage is otherwise irrelevant to the value of the firm, the possibility of lost tax credits would make any leverage undesirable. Few, if any, would want to defend a view this extreme. Nevertheless, it does follow logically from the personal tax view and the existence of bankruptcy risk.

Tax-Timing Options

In our discussion of the Options Principle, we referred to the importance of "hidden" options. One of the examples cited in that discussion is a "hidden" option involving capital gains taxes. Taxes on capital gains income are paid only in the year that the owner sells the asset. At the *owner's* option, then, tax can be postponed by retaining ownership. This option is called a tax-timing option and it creates a valuable tax asymmetry.[7]

In the case of a capital loss, individuals can choose to recognize the loss and reduce their current tax liability. In the case of a capital gain, individuals can defer their tax liability and earn the time value of money on the tax liability until the tax is actually paid. The present value of taxes *paid* on a gain are therefore less than the present value of taxes *reduced* by a loss because of the time value of money.[8]

You know that the value of any financial instrument can be represented as the present value of its expected future after-tax cash flows. Stocks and bonds, in particular, were valued this way in Chapter 6. Because the tax-timing option attached to each security—stock or bond—affects the expected future cash flows for the security, the tax-timing option is part of the value of the security. When the firm has an all-equity capital structure, there is one tax-timing option on the portfolio of outcomes resulting from corporate activities and market conditions. When a corpora-

---

[5] This concept was put forth by Brennan and Schwartz (1978), Kim (1978), and Wrightsman (1978).
[6] DeAngelo and Masulis (1980).
[7] Constantinides (1983).
[8] In addition to the time-value-of-money difference, prior to the Tax Reform Act of 1986 there was also a difference in the tax rates for long-term gains and short-term losses, which made the tax-timing option even more valuable than it is under the 1986 version of the tax code.

tion has both debt and equity in its capital structure, there is one tax-timing option on the stock and a second option on the bonds. Recall from Chapter 8 that the value of a portfolio of options on individual securities is always greater than a single option on a portfolio of those same securities. Based on this fact, the total value of a corporation may be larger when it is financed with both equity and debt.

In a capital market environment that is perfect except for income taxes, it would be possible for individual investors to create their own multiple tax-timing options through the use of homemade leverage. To replicate the tax-timing options on a leveraged firm, the shareholders must be able to turn stock issued by an unleveraged firm into marketable securities with the tax-timing option properties of either stocks or bonds. For this to be the case, three conditions must hold: The securities must replicate the expected future cash flows of stock and bonds in a leveraged firm; tax law must give the homemade security the same tax treatment; and the homemade security must be marketable. Current capital market conditions and tax law make it unlikely that individual investors could profitably create multiple tax-timing options on an unleveraged firm.

However, even if individuals could create homemade leverage that duplicated the tax-timing options of the leveraged firm, there would still be an optimal capital structure, at least in some sense. Whether firms or individuals capture the added value due to tax-timing options, the additional value is there to be had, and in equilibrium, an optimal package of financing will exist for each firm.

Net Effect of Taxes

Our first insight into why capital structure matters comes when we relax the assumption that there are no taxes: *Tax asymmetries may cause the firm's capital structure to affect its value*. The empirical evidence presented below appears to support the view that, on balance, taxes appear to favor a capital structure that includes at least some debt. Thus, the firm's choice of capital structure is an important policy tool that can be used to benefit a company's shareholders. To the extent there are systematic interindustry differences in the availability of tax shelter from depreciation and other sources besides interest deductions, we would expect to find systematic interindustry differences in leverage.

TRANSACTION COSTS 15.5

Transaction costs are market imperfections that may also cause capital structure to have an effect on the value of the firm in an otherwise perfect capital market environment. Three types of transaction costs have been identified as important to the firm's choice and management of capital structure: Agency costs, bankruptcy costs, and issuance costs.

Agency Costs

Recall from Chapter 9 that there are certain conflicts among the debtholders, shareholders, and managers. A major conflict that arises from the use of debt financing is the possibility that shareholders will expropriate wealth from the debtholders. Recall that there are several methods of expropriating wealth from the debtholders. One method involves asset substitution. Recall also that equity can be viewed as a call option on the firm. Therefore, since the value of an option is an increasing function of the variance of the value of the underlying asset, the shareholders may have an incentive to increase the variance of the investment outcomes. Suppose debtholders loan money to the firm on the premise that the firm will invest in a low-risk project, and therefore they agree to a low interest rate on the loan. Then if the firm invests in a high-risk project, the risk of the loan will increase, thereby increasing the required return on the loan and lowering the present value of the loan. For example, suppose the firm borrows money to invest in its business, and immediately thereafter the firm's managers do a leveraged buyout. What happens to the value of the debt?[9] The change in the present value of the loan is lost to the debtholders but gained by the shareholders.

Conflicts among the various claimants to the firm's assets, such as the asset substitution problem between the debtholders and shareholders, as well as many others, must be resolved in some way. When it is possible, contracts that eliminate these conflicts are created. For example, restrictive covenants, such as a restriction on dividend payments, are included in a bond indenture to eliminate certain potential conflicts. When it is not possible to create a contract that eliminates a particular conflict, investors will reduce the price they are willing to pay for the debt to reflect the fact that the conflict may be resolved in a way disadvantageous to them. When a firm issues new securities, the agency cost of the securities is the sum of all the costs of a special contract (e.g., restrictive covenants for a bond; these are costly because they eliminate some of the firm's options) plus any reduction in price that is due to potential conflicts that remain.

A firm's capital structure may also affect the firm's agency costs with respect to its labor contracts.[10] Employees are more likely to incur search costs for getting a new job when they work for a firm that is more likely to go bankrupt, and those costs are not consistent across all firms. The expected costs of the employees' job searches depend upon the uniqueness of the product or service of the firm. Employees performing more generic tasks have lower expected job search costs than do employees involved with tasks that are more specialized. Labor costs will reflect this difference. Therefore, all else equal, agency costs connected with labor are higher for firms providing more specialized products or services than they are for firms with less specialized products or services. Higher agency costs resulting from increasing leverage are likely to mean that the degree of specialization of a firm's product or service affects its choice of capital structure.

There is also an aspect of debt financing that reduces the firm's agency costs: those costs associated with the shareholders monitoring the managers. Whenever the firm issues new debt, prospective debtholders will analyze the firm very carefully to determine a fair price to offer for the new debt. Each time new debt is issued then, the shareholders are provided with a free outside "audit" of the firm. This outside audit reduces the cost to the shareholders of monitoring the managers to ensure that the managers continue to act in a responsible manner.

Another way the use of debt can involve a monitoring function is the use of a sinking fund provision. With a sinking fund, the firm must be able to meet the periodic required payments in addition to the interest payments. Difficulty in doing so can provide a relatively early warning that the firm is in trouble; an inability to meet them can trigger default. Obviously, this monitoring function is beneficial for debtholders, but it is also provides further monitoring of the managers for the benefit of the shareholders.

[9] As we pointed out in Chapter 9, debt covenants provide a mechanism for dealing with agency costs. In this example, a suitably designed debt limitation covenant would prevent the leveraged buyout (unless debtholders were compensated for agreeing to relax the covenant restriction).
[10] Titman (1984).

Securing debt by specifying specific tangible assets as collateral can play a role in reducing the agency costs of debt.[11] Secured debt limits the losses of the debtholders in case of bankruptcy, thereby limiting the amount of wealth that the shareholders can expropriate from the debtholders and hence reducing the monitoring costs of the debtholders. The limit on wealth expropriation imposed by secured debt also limits the ability of shareholders to pursue wealth expropriation strategies. In particular, the assets securing a debt instrument cannot be sold without the permission of the debtholders. This in turn makes it more likely that positive-NPV projects will be undertaken because shareholders will have to increase their wealth through new projects rather than wealth expropriation from debtholders.[12]

Remember that agency costs are borne by the firm (i.e., existing shareholders). Therefore, when the firm issues additional debt, the net agency cost of debt must be considered as an additional cost of leverage. However, the impact of debt agency costs on the valuation implications of capital structure is not straightforward. On the one hand, the agency cost of debt decreases any valuation benefit due to leverage. On the other hand, there are agency costs associated with obtaining *any* additional financing, debt or equity. When a firm seeks additional financing to undertake a desirable investment project, total transaction costs (including the agency costs) of the alternative methods must be compared.

The trade-off among the agency costs associated with the various claimants to the firm's assets (e.g., debtholders, shareholders, managers, creditors, customers, etc.) leads to a theory of optimal capital structure that involves the use of multiple types of securities to balance off the various classes of agency costs against one another.[13] One of the particularly appealing implications of this theory is that the optimal capital structure it implies involves multiple types of securities but does not depend upon the existence of income taxes. This is appealing since firms were being financed with combinations of debt and equity securities long before income tax laws existed.

BANKRUPTCY COSTS

With debt in its capital structure, a firm has an expected cost of bankruptcy. These costs include notification costs, court costs, and lawyer fees. They also include indirect costs, such as suppliers refusing to ship goods other than on a COD basis (or refusing to ship altogether) as financial distress sets in. Allied Stores and Federated Department Stores experienced financial difficulties beginning late in 1989 that led many suppliers to halt shipments to their department stores, which include such well-known chains as Bloomingdale's. Of course, the direct transaction costs of bankruptcy are paid only if it actually occurs. Therefore, it is important to note that with an ongoing firm that is not in imminent danger of financial distress, the cost is a mathematical expectation.[14] This expected value is considerably less than the actual cost when there is only a small chance of bankruptcy.

The expected bankruptcy costs depend in part on the degree of specialization of the firm's assets. The higher the degree of specialization, the lower the degree of liquidity and the greater the sales transaction costs. In the extreme case, a specially designed piece of equipment that is specific to just one company's production process might be worth just its scrap value should the company go bankrupt.

An argument based on a firm's type of assets, similar to the argument concerning

[11] Scott (1976); Stulz and Johnson (1985).
[12] Myers (1977).
[13] Jensen and Meckling (1976).
[14] Warner (1977a).

specialized assets, is that a firm with primarily tangible assets can borrow more than an otherwise comparable firm that has primarily intangible assets, such as patents and trademarks.[15] Intangible assets are less liquid and have higher sales transaction costs than do tangible assets, and their value may be more firm-specific (e.g., the value of a patent depends on how it is applied, which its inventor is uniquely positioned to accomplish), so the firm with more intangible assets has larger expected bankruptcy costs.

The effect of the possibility of incurring bankruptcy costs is like that of corporate income tax credits that are lost during times of financial distress: If all other factors combined create a net valuation benefit to leverage, bankruptcy costs make it undesirable for the firm to be financed *entirely* with debt. If there is no net benefit to leverage due to all other factors combined, the possibility of incurring bankruptcy costs would make leverage undesirable.

ISSUANCE COSTS

The cost of obtaining new financing affects the firm's management of its capital structure. As we pointed out in Chapter 14, the cost per dollar of additional financing declines with increases in the size of the issue. This means that a firm should not sell a series of small issues when it needs to raise funds externally. Rather, the firm should sell larger issues, less often, to reduce the net cost of issuance. This conclusion is not limited to the use of debt and does not imply a preference for any particular method of financing. However, it does imply that the dynamic management of the firm's capital structure is important to the value of the firm. A firm can waste resources on issuance expenses if it does not carefully manage its capital structure.

Concerning particular methods, recall from Table 14–3 that the combination of underwriting spread and issuance expenses for bonds appears to be lower than it is for other methods of obtaining additional outside financing. Therefore, whether or not other factors create a net valuation benefit to leverage, debt is attractive *relative* to equity when a firm has already decided that it is going to obtain additional outside financing.

NET EFFECT OF FRICTIONS

Our second insight into why capital structure matters comes when we relax the assumption that there are no transaction costs: *Transaction costs may cause the firm's capital structure to affect its value*. It appears that debt has the lowest total transaction cost among external financing alternatives (all transaction costs considered). Therefore, even if there were no net continuing valuation benefit due to tax asymmetries or other factors, debt may be the optimal external financing choice because of lower transaction costs whenever it is beneficial for a firm to obtain additional external financing to undertake a positive-NPV investment.

15.6 ASYMMETRIC INFORMATION AND SIGNALING

As with other financial decisions, the Signaling Principle plays an important role in analyzing the firm's capital structure decision. Also, as in other cases, the information content of any action related to capital structure can have a significant impact on the valuation of the firm.

---

[15] Malitz (1986).

SIGNALING FIRM QUALITY

Capital structure choice can have an impact on the value of a firm if the choice of structure conveys useful information to investors concerning a company's future earnings prospects.[16] For example, consider two identical firms, G and B. Investors can see no difference between the two firms, but managers in both firms know that G's expected earnings are 25% greater per period than B's. B's managers are delighted to have their company's stock valued identically with G's stock, but G's managers want everyone to know that their company has better future earnings prospects and should be more highly valued since both firm's have executive bonus compensation plans that include stock options. How can the managers of G demonstrate the information about higher expected earnings? One way is for G to take on more debt than B. G can promise a larger fixed payment than B because of its higher expected future earnings. With equivalent leverage, B will be taking on more risk. B will have more variability in shareholder returns and more chance of incurring bankruptcy costs than G because of the difference in their expected future earnings. In the extreme, G can set a debt level that would bankrupt B *for sure* if B imitated G. In that way, G can signal its superior expected future earnings.

Other examples of the potential information content of a firm's capital structure decision involve the interaction of investment and financing decisions. One argument is that corporations use underwriters, rather than rights offerings or direct public issues, because of the necessity of maintaining proprietary information.[17] The underwriter may be able to certify the value of the firm and its new projects by standing ready to purchase all the shares without revealing (and therefore destroying the value of) certain types of private information.

Another consideration is the involvement of the owners of the firm in financing new projects.[18] Suppose B and G are identical except for a new project that is about to be undertaken. G has a project with a large positive NPV, whereas B's new project has a zero NPV. The owners of G are eager to provide the financing for the new project themselves, using personal funds so that they alone will earn the large expected NPV. In contrast, the owners of B are indifferent to allowing outside investors to invest in the new project since it has a zero NPV. Generalizing the argument, then, the percentage of owner financing may be able to provide a credible signal of the owners' opinion of investment opportunities.

A similar type of asymmetric information problem arises with respect to the current market value of the firm. If shareholders know that the firm is currently overvalued, they would like to have partners to share in the decline in market value that will take place in the future when others realize the firm is overvalued. But if shareholders know that the firm is currently undervalued, they do not want to have new partners who will get a share of the increase in market value that will take place in the future when others realize the firm is undervalued. Shareholders of properly valued firms will be indifferent to having new partners. This leads to the idea that if additional financing is to be obtained, the firm will choose debt or equity depending upon whether they want or do not want new partners. That is, undervalued firms will issue new debt, whereas overvalued firms will issue new equity. Of course, in this simple world we have just described, shareholders of overvalued firms will not want to be identified as such, so they will mimic the undervalued firms by issuing debt instead of equity.

These concepts can be further generalized by considering both new project value

---

[16] Ross (1977).
[17] Heinkel and Schwartz (1986).
[18] Leland and Pyle (1977).

and the current market value of the firm simultaneously.[19] A simple description of combinations can be constructed by classifying each as good, OK, or bad. For example, the firm is OK (i.e., correctly valued) and the new project is good (i.e., has a large positive NPV). Let us further add that the firm has some ability to finance new projects with currently available funds. The interactions among currently available investment funds, the NPV of the new project, and any current under- or overvaluing of the firm makes various types and amounts of new financing more, or less, attractive to the firm's shareholders. With this kind of a classification scheme, we can analyze the conditions under which firms will or will not obtain additional financing, and further, if new financing is obtained, we can predict the conditions that will lead the firm to issue debt or equity.

The pattern that emerges from the simple world just described has been referred to as a "pecking order theory" of capital structure.[20] In this world, firms use retained earnings as their primary source of financing for new projects. Newly issued debt is less preferred than internal funds, but more preferable than other sources. Debt-equity combinations, such as convertible debt, are third in the pecking order, with smaller proportions of equity being preferred to larger proportions of equity. Last in the pecking order comes new financing that is all-equity. Although firms may have such a pecking order and want to avoid the dilemma of either selling new equity too cheaply or having to pass up a good project, there can be cases where a new project is sufficiently good that the firm will issue new equity and suffer current undervaluing, even if such cases occur infrequently.

FINANCIAL DISTRESS/BANKRUPTCY

Another informational asymmetry that can arise during times of financial distress is the problem of accurately determining the likelihood that the firm will continue as an ongoing concern.[21] This likelihood is important because it affects the value of certain goods, as was noted in Chapter 9 as a firm-consumer conflict. In the case of a manufacturer, the lack of available parts and service in the future may substantially reduce the market value of current goods, as it would, for example, with an auto manufacturer that is in financial distress. When the public puts a lower probability on the firm continuing in business than is actually the case, the firm will be forced to accept a lower price for its product than what the product is actually worth. The lower purchase price reduces the profit margin and hence the rate of return the manufacturer earns on the product. This forgone profit can be very substantial. In fact, while this cost is difficult to measure, it is probably the largest cost of financial distress/bankruptcy by a wide margin.

NET EFFECT OF ASYMMETRIC INFORMATION

Our third insight into why capital structure matters comes when we relax the assumption that information is freely available and costless: *It may be possible to use a firm's capital structure to reduce costs associated with the problem of asymmetric information*. It appears that during times of financial distress, firms are unable to get full market value for their products. The expected value of this cost reduces the net benefit of leverage to the firm. In contrast, the firm may be able to signal higher expected

---

[19] Myers and Majluf (1984).
[20] Myers (1984).
[21] Titman (1984).

future earnings and/or current market value through the judicious use of leverage, which adds to the net benefit of leverage. The asymmetric information argument tends to suggest systematic industry differences; for example, low leverage when product reliability and follow-up service are important concerns, as in the home appliance industry.

FINANCIAL LEVERAGE CLIENTELES   15.7

The personal tax view of capital structure choice suggests that both personal tax considerations and corporate tax considerations affect capital structure choice. It also suggests that investors will take their own tax situations into account in deciding whether to invest in highly leveraged firms. The idea that investors "sort" themselves into groups, where each group prefers the companies it invests in to follow a certain type of policy, is called the **clientele effect**. When applied to financial leverage, the clientele effect refers to those investors that prefer one type of security or capital structure over another for a particular reason. A similar concept in marketing is called **market segmentation**. A market segment is an identifiable group of consumers who purchase a product with particular attributes that are distinct from the attributes of alternative products, such as a market segment that buys luxury cars versus one that buys economy cars.

The existence of various leverage clienteles mitigates some, but not all, of the arguments given thus far in favor of capital structure relevance. With respect to taxes, some securities may be a more or less attractive investment for certain investors. For example, investors with a high marginal income tax rate may find debt securities less attractive, whereas tax-exempt investors may find debt securities relatively more attractive. Similarly, investors with a low marginal income tax rate may prefer firm leverage to personal leverage because of the higher corporate tax rate. Investors preferring a firm with a particular capital structure strictly because of their own risk preferences are able to avoid the transaction costs of a homemade increase or decrease in leverage by simply investing in a firm with their preferred amount of leverage.

Arguments concerning personal marginal tax rates lead to the hypothesis that an investor's marginal tax rate is a major determinant of the investor's preference for investing in firms with more or less leverage. Based on these arguments, investor preferences for corporate financial leverage should be inversely related to the investor's marginal tax rate.[22] That is, low marginal tax rate investors should prefer to invest in firms with high leverage and vice versa. Note that confirmation of this hypothesis would verify the important role of taxes, and yet there may be no firm valuation implications. In other words, the existence of leverage clienteles would not lead firms to choose a particular capital structure consistently. And yet investor preference may make it advantageous for a firm to issue one type of security relative to others at particular times.

Taxes and transaction costs reduce the return to shareholders. Therefore, investors should, and do, invest in securities that minimize their aggregate taxes and transaction costs for any particular combination of risk and return. The result of considering taxes and transaction costs is that a particular clientele group may be able to afford to pay a premium for a certain type of security. (The premium is measured relative to the prices of securities that are otherwise identical.) As long as a premium

---

[22]Farrar and Selwyn (1967) among others.

is offered, firms will have an incentive to adopt policies that make their securities appeal to the clientele willing to pay the highest premium. Such a policy is of course another application of the Principle of Valuable Ideas: new ideas have the potential for adding extraordinary value.

EXPLOITING OPPORTUNITIES TO ADJUST CORPORATE LEVERAGE

Over time, however, competition among firms will drive the premium to zero, and market equilibrium will return. In the aggregate, companies will supply just enough of each type of security so that all the positive-NPV opportunities resulting from capital structure choices have been exploited, the positive premiums have been fully extracted, and therefore all the premiums have been driven to zero. What remains after the premiums are gone are clientele groups and firms that are comfortable with one another. In equilibrium, the patterns can remain indefinitely since neither the clientele groups nor the companies have incentive to change. Whenever there are changes in laws (tax laws or any law affecting investments), it may be possible to "play the game" all over again as the market attains a new equilibrium. Each change creates the potential for new opportunities.

Thus, we have a fourth insight into why capital structure matters: *It may be possible to earn a premium for supplying a security or capital structure policy that is in short supply*. (Note that this gain must be weighed against the transaction costs of investors' rearranging their security holdings.) Whenever a law is changed that affects the taxes and transaction costs for a particular financial leverage clientele, opportunities may be created for firms to earn a positive NPV by altering their capital structure to exploit these opportunities. For example, the Tax Reform Act of 1986 reduced the personal tax rate relative to the corporate tax rate and imposed a constraint on home-made leverage. Investors may deduct interest expense on debt incurred to support investments only to the extent such interest expense does not exceed investment income by more than $5,000 per year. This constraint on homemade leverage will have its greatest impact on those financial leverage clienteles that previously maintained the highest degrees of personal leverage. Firms whose shareholders predominantly belonged to such clienteles thus had an opportunity to increase corporate leverage. Others have noted that the Tax Reform Act of 1986 created an incentive for corporations to increase leverage because of the change in tax rates. The aforementioned constraint suggests that this impact should be most pronounced among the least leveraged firms in each industry.[23]

15.8   A REVIEW OF THE EMPIRICAL EVIDENCE

Early attempts at addressing the capital structure question established that a firm's choice of leverage depends upon the industry in which the firm is doing business. Unfortunately, firms within the same industry are similar in a number of ways, including many of those dimensions which have been theorized to affect a firm's value through its capital structure. Subsequent studies that are more focused in their approach have indeed verified that a firm's choice of leverage is related not just to its industry but more specifically to many of the dimensions that have been shown theoretically to affect a firm's value. For example, a recent study shows significant differences in capital structure across industries, but also finds that more profitable

[23] Ben-Horim, Hochman, and Polmon (1987).

firms tend to use less debt in their capital structures.[24] (Note that the finding is that high profitability leads a firm to choose low leverage, *not* the other way around.)

As with earning extraordinary returns, if it were easy, a definitive answer to the capital structure puzzle would have been found long ago. Unfortunately, it is very difficult to examine this question because of the dynamic nature of the world, the economy, and the firm. A number of studies have analyzed the impact on value of financial security exchanges. These studies examined how the value of a firm changes when various financial securities are exchanged. When one type of security is exchanged for another, complicating changes in the firm's assets do not necessarily accompany the exchange. So a financial security exchange can often be viewed as being a relatively "pure" capital structure change. Other studies, **cross-sectional** in nature, examine many firms simultaneously in an attempt to identify capital structures that appear to be related to higher firm value. Rarely does a single study (of any type) provide an answer to more than one part of the capital structure puzzle. Taken in total, however, a picture is starting to emerge from the existing empirical evidence. There is at least some empirical support for each of the theoretical positions discussed above, which suggests that the complete answer to the question, Does capital structure matter?, will be multifaceted.

THE NET SIGNIFICANCE OF TAXES

Existing empirical evidence regarding the effect of leverage changes on the value of the firm indicates that leverage changes are accompanied by simultaneous changes in the firm's value in the same direction: Leverage-increasing (-decreasing) exchanges increase (decrease) firm value,[25] and exchanges that cause no change in firm leverage do not have a significant effect on firm value.[26] This evidence is consistent with the corporate tax view of capital structure. However, although the direction of the valuation change is consistent with the corporate tax view, the magnitude of the change is substantially smaller than what would be predicted on the basis of the corporate tax view alone. This smaller-than-predicted effect is consistent with the personal tax view that personal taxes play an important role in mitigating the corporate tax effect. In addition, somewhat conflicting results are contained in a cross-sectional study that does not find evidence that supports the significance of the corporate tax view.[27]

There is some supporting, *although mixed*, evidence that nondebt tax shields favorably affect the value of the firm.[28]

TRANSACTION COSTS

AGENCY COSTS   Empirical evidence supports the existence of the agency costs of debt generally and in particular the notion that corporations deliberately structure the optional redemption provisions of new debt issues to reduce agency costs.[29] There is also evidence that is consistent with the idea that agency costs are higher for firms that provide highly specialized products and/or services.[30]

[24] Kester (1986).
[25] Cordes and Sheffrin (1983); DeAngelo and Masulis (1980); Masulis (1980); Masulis (1983).
[26] Dietrich (1984).
[27] Bradley, Jarrell, and Kim (1984).
[28] Bradley, Jarrell, and Kim (1984); Cordes and Sheffrin (1983); DeAngelo and Masulis (1980); Long and Malitz (1985); Titman and Wessels (1988).
[29] Thatcher (1985).
[30] Titman and Wessels (1988).

BANKRUPTCY COSTS Direct bankruptcy costs have been shown to be relatively small.[31]

ISSUANCE COSTS Issuance costs may be an important determinant of capital structure. Evidence shows that debt ratios in the short term are negatively related to firm size, and it can be argued that this may reflect the relatively high costs faced by small firms when they issue long-term securities.[32]

ASYMMETRIC INFORMATION

SIGNALING There is substantial support for the idea that information is conveyed to the public when a firm makes a leverage-changing transaction.[33] Among these, on average, leverage-increasing announcements are good news, whereas leverage-decreasing announcements are bad news. This is consistent with the signaling view that good-quality firms can take on more debt than bad-quality firms. The one transaction that is an exception to this view is the issuance of new debt securities. New debt issues have not been found to have a significant impact on firm value.[34] But this exception is consistent with the view that the financing and investment decisions interact. The good news of a leverage increase is canceled out by the bad news that the firm is obtaining outside financing for its new project rather than financing it entirely with internally generated funds.

While the issuance of new debt securities may be neutral to slightly negative because of the "mixed signal," the issuance of new equity is not a "mixed" signal. It is a leverage-decreasing transaction, and the firm is obtaining outside financing for its new project. The evidence strongly supports the notion that the market interprets new equity offerings to be significantly bad news.[35] The issuance of convertible debt, which can be viewed as being part equity and part debt, has been found to be a more negative signal than the issuance of straight debt but a less negative signal than the issuance of straight equity.[36] Taken together, these results are very consistent with the pecking order theory of capital structure.

The direction of valuation changes predicted by the signaling view match those predicted by the corporate tax view. Therefore, it is very difficult to separate information effects from tax effects. However, there is evidence from preferred stock for common stock exchange offers, which do not involve corporate tax effects, that directly supports the signaling view (as opposed to direct support of the corporate tax view).[37]

BANKRUPTCY COSTS In contrast to the direct costs of bankruptcy, the indirect costs of bankruptcy, such as forgone profit, are very significant and frequently exceed 20% of the value of the firm.[38]

---

[31] Altman (1984); Warner (1977b); White (1983), among others.
[32] Titman and Wessels (1988).
[33] Finnerty (1985); Masulis (1980); Pinegar and Lease (1986); Vermaelen (1981).
[34] Dann and Mikkelson (1984); Eckbo (1986); Mikkelson and Partch (1986). The valuation impact of the announcement is negative but not significant statistically.
[35] Asquith and Mullins (1986); Kolodny and Suhler (1985); Masulis and Korwar (1986); Mikkelson and Partch (1986).
[36] Dann and Mikkelson (1984).
[37] Pinegar and Lease (1986).
[38] Altman (1984).

LEVERAGE CLIENTELES

The evidence regarding a leverage clientele effect is consistent with the prediction that a firm's leverage is inversely related to the average marginal tax rate of its shareholders: The shareholders of firms with less leverage have higher marginal tax rates.[39]

PRACTICE

Even though a company's shareholder mix can be expected to shift in response to a change in its capital structure, a sudden shift may be disruptive to its share price in the near term, and frequent major shifts may be disruptive over the longer term because transaction costs make it expensive for investors to buy and sell shares. In practice, the large majority of companies maintain a stable capital structure and appear to have a target capital structure that they adjust toward.[40] It appears, then, that firms depart from a stable capital structure only when significant changes in investment opportunities, earnings, tax position, or other factors identified as relevant to capital structure choice dictate.

SOLUTION TO AT&T's CAPITAL STRUCTURE DECISION

The new, partly regulated AT&T (its long distance telephone services continued to be regulated following the divestiture) came into being January 1, 1984. The following table compares AT&T's assets and capital structure pre- and postdivestiture:

	At 1/1/84 (billions)	At 12/31/83 (billions)
Total assets	$35.592	$149.530
Long-term debt	9.137	44.810
Preferred equity	1.523	1.523
Common equity	12.367	60.762
Total capitalization	$23.027	$107.095
Percent debt	39.7%	41.8%

AT&T's financial staff conducted an analysis of alternative capital structures and concluded that a reduction in its debt ratio to a range of 25% to 30% would be appropriate.[41] Important considerations in arriving at this decision were (1) AT&T's desire to attain a capital structure comparable to those of its most creditworthy competitors (those with senior debt rated double-A or better) in the regulated telecommunications services, nonregulated telephone equipment, and computer manufacturing industries, and (2) its intention to rely less heavily than it had previously on external financing.

AT&T's financial staff decided that the nonregulated portions of its business

[39] Harris, Roenfeldt, and Cooley (1983); Kim, Lewellen, and McConnell (1979).
[40] Marsh (1982); Taggart (1977).
[41] American Telephone and Telegraph Company, 1983 *Annual Report to Shareholders*, p. 8. The authors are indebted (no pun intended) to members of AT&T's financial staff for helpful discussions concerning AT&T's reformulation of its capital structure policy.

would support a debt ratio of 20% to 25% and that the regulated long distance telephone services business, being somewhat less risky, would support a debt ratio of 30% to 40%. The latter range is lower than AT&T's historical debt ratio target (40% to 45%) because AT&T's financial staff felt that the long distance telephone business is riskier than the local telephone business, which it had been forced to divest. Based on this analysis, AT&T's financial staff concluded that AT&T should set a (blended) debt ratio target of 25% to 30%.

How has AT&T done since the divestiture? AT&T made more or less steady progress in reducing its long-term debt ratio between 1984 and 1987:

Year	1/1/84	12/31/84	12/31/85	12/31/86	12/31/87
Long-term debt ratio	39.7%	36.4%	32.3%	33.6%	33.3%

In the fourth quarter of 1988, AT&T announced that it would recognize a $6.7 billion pretax charge to cover the cost of eliminating old network facilities and 16,000 related jobs. (Remember what we said at the beginning of the chapter regarding AT&T management's concern about an increase in operating risk.) The resulting reduction in common equity raised AT&T's long-term debt ratio to 41.5% (on a book value basis) at year-end 1988 (about what it was just prior to the divestiture). Standard & Poor's Corporation (S&P) maintained its double-A rating of AT&T's senior debt. Had AT&T not reduced its leverage between 1984 and 1987, it seems problematical whether its double-A rating would have withstood the downturn in AT&T's fortunes.

This example also gives us the opportunity to point out that, in practice, debt ratios are typically expressed on the basis of book values. Of course, it is the market value ratio that determines the riskiness of the debt. Therefore, even though it was not until the fourth quarter of 1988 that AT&T's book value debt ratio changed, AT&T's market value debt ratio had *already increased prior to the announcement*, reflecting the lower value of AT&T's equity. You, of course, already knew that because you understand the Principle of Capital Market Efficiency!

SUMMARY

The critical issue concerning capital structure is whether it affects the value of the firm. In their classic article on capital structure, MM show that a firm's capital structure has no effect on its value in a perfect capital market. Reflecting the Principle of Risk-Return Trade-Off, differences in required rates of return reflect differences in the risk of the investment—*not* differences in value—in a perfect market. In such a world, share valuation is based entirely on the profitability of a company's assets and its capital investment program, that is, the expected NPVs of future projects. Even if leverage enhanced investment value, shareholders could take out personal loans to create homemade leverage. Therefore, in a perfect market, firms cannot capture any value due to leverage since shareholders can do it themselves just as cheaply as the firm.

But our financial system contains some important persistent imperfections. Information is not costless and freely available to everyone, so the Signaling Principle (actions contain information) is a very important consideration. Capital structure and

DECISION SUMMARY BOX

A firm should establish its capital structure with a view to maximizing the wealth of its shareholders. Important considerations are

- *tax consequences*, both the firm's current and projected corporate tax rate and the personal tax positions of its investors;
- *total transaction costs* associated with financing the firm, including agency costs, issuance costs, potential bankruptcy costs, and day-to-day management costs;
- *market reaction* to the firm's choice of capital structure and any changes that might be made to it;
- *demand-supply imbalances* for securities that might be profitable, especially those resulting from changes in laws that might create profitable issuance opportunities;
- *transaction costs associated with the firm's investors rearranging their security holdings* because of a change in the firm's capital structure policy;
- any *legal or policy restrictions* on the firm and its shareholders that might affect the firm's choice of capital structure.

capital structure changes may provide important information about the firm to the public. Thus, a firm should be careful to choose the best method of financing, taking all costs into account—including how the firm's choices of financing transactions will be interpreted (i.e., the information content of its actions). An important understanding of observed empirical patterns of financing based on asymmetric information leads to the **pecking order theory** of capital structure, wherein the use and amount of newly issued outside equity provides negative information about the value of the firm and its prospects, on average.

There are other market imperfections. The system of corporate income taxation imposes a bias in favor of debt over equity, as do issuance costs. However, the system of individual income taxation, as well as direct and indirect financial distress/bankruptcy costs, have an opposite bias. Aggregate agency costs and tax-timing options both favor a mix of debt and equity rather than using one or the other exclusively. Taken together, these market imperfections lead to the belief that there is some optimal mix of debt and equity that maximizes the value of a firm.

The clientele effect, where personal investments are made in firms that have adopted capital structures that are best for the individual investors, may mitigate some of these considerations. To the extent that the supply of a particular type of security equals the demand for that type of security at the prevailing price, there will be no valuation consequences to capital structure choices, and capital structure will be irrelevant with respect to the investor's decisions to invest in that type of security. Changes in laws, particularly the tax code, sometimes create a demand for new types of securities or alter the demand for existing ones. Such changes in demand may in turn create profitable opportunities for a firm to supply a particular type of security to satisfy this new demand, thereby making one type of financing relatively more attractive to both issuer and investor. These opportunities are eliminated as the supply of new securities fulfills the demand for them.

There is not yet complete agreement about how capital structure affects the value of the firm. We expect future research to provide increased insight on this issue. In the meantime, we will try to provide some guidance in the next chapter about how firms can, and currently do, manage their capital structures in light of the many considerations relevant to it.

PROBLEMS

PROBLEM SET A

A1. Briefly explain the **corporate tax view** of capital structure.

A2. Briefly explain how the **personal tax view** of capital structure mitigates the **corporate tax view**.

A3. Give an example of a tax-timing option and explain why it is valuable.

A4. How can restrictive debt covenants reduce the likelihood of **asset substitution**?

A5. How can a new debt issue provide a monitoring function for a firm's shareholders?

A6. Cite two examples of how transaction costs might affect a firm's choice of financing.

A7. Why might potential new equity investors in a firm be leery of buying newly issued stock in a firm?

A8. Define the term **financial leverage clientele**.

A9. True or false: Issuing new stock in a firm whose stock is already publicly-traded significantly lowers the market value of the stock, on average.

A10. True or false: Issuing new debt in a firm whose stock is already publicly-traded significantly lowers the market value of the stock, on average.

A11. True or false: The explicit transaction costs connected with financial distress and bankruptcy are large as a proportion of the value of the firm.

A12. True or false: The explicit transaction costs connected with financial distress and bankruptcy are much larger than the implicit opportunity costs such as lost sales, depressed product price, and lost tax credits.

A13. Briefly explain in your own words why taxes would not be asymmetric if Equation (15.1) holds.

A14. Why might a firm that manufactures a unique product using specialized employee expertise tend to finance with less debt than an otherwise identical firm that manufactures a generic product?

PROBLEM SET B

B1. You invest $12,000 in Joe's Garage, Inc., borrowing $5,000 of the money at 10%. If you expect to earn 24% on your investment under this arrangement, what would you expect to earn if you put up the entire $12,000 from your own money? Ignore taxes.

B2. Consider two firms operating in a perfect capital market environment. Each will generate $10 million of operating income, and they are identical in every other respect, except that Company A has debt in its capital structure and Company B has an all-equity capital structure. Suppose that investors currently value firm A as indicated in Table 15-1, but the market value of the equity in B is $65 million. According to the perfect market view, this situation cannot persist. Suppose an investor owns 1% of the shares of B. Show how this owner can profit from arbitrage.

B3. Show how financial distress can affect the value of the firm through its tax credits, even when a firm is able to use completely all tax credits via loss carryforwards.

B4. Respond to the following statement: Since a firm can lower its interest cost by including more restrictive covenants in its bonds, a firm should use the most restrictive set of covenants it can in order to achieve the lowest interest cost.

B5. Miles's Manor, an unassuming resort in midstate Pennsylvania, currently has an all-equity capital structure. Miles's Manor has an expected income of $10,000 per year forever and a required rate of return to equity of 16%. There are no personal taxes, but Miles's pays corporate taxes at the rate of 35%, and all transactions take place in an otherwise perfect capital market.

    a. What is Miles's Manor worth?

    b. How much will the value of the firm increase if Miles's Manor leverages the firm by borrowing half the value of the unleveraged firm at a rate of 10% and the leverage causes the required rate of return on equity to increase to 18.89%?

B6. What is the basis for the view that a firm's total market value is invariant to its choice of capital structure? Cite three broad types of capital market imperfections that can cause the capital structure of a firm to have an effect on the value of that firm. Give three examples (one for each type) where such an imperfection would cause a firm's capital structure to have an effect on the value of that firm. Explain *how* each of the three examples you gave would cause a firm's capital structure to have an effect on the value of that firm.

B7. Dick's Pet-Way Corporation (DPC) is a chain of pet stores that has an expected cash inflow each year forever with the following probability distribution:

cash flow =	$1500	$1250	$750	$500
probability =	.25	.25	.25	.25

DPC's required rate of return is 20% per year. Assume all of DPC's income is paid out to the firm's investors.

    a. If DPC is all-equity-financed and there are no taxes, what would DPC be worth in a perfect capital market?

Now suppose DPC's corporate tax rate is 30%.

    b. If DPC is all-equity-financed and there are no personal taxes, what would DPC be worth in an otherwise perfect capital market?

In addition to corporate taxes, suppose DPC borrows $1,400 at a required rate of return on the debt of 10%. (*Hint*: Note that the required rate of return on equity increases to 23.89%.)

    c. If there are no personal taxes, what would DPC be worth in an otherwise perfect capital market? What would be DPC's leverage ratio, θ?

    d. If there are personal taxes on debt income at a rate of 37%, and personal taxes on equity income at a rate of 10%, what would DPC be worth in an otherwise perfect capital market?

    e. If there are personal taxes on debt income at a rate of 25%, and personal taxes on equity income at a rate of 10%, what would DPC be worth in an otherwise perfect capital market?

    f. Finally, compute the value of DPC as a 35.7% leveraged firm, with a 10% rate of return on the debt when there are no taxes at all in a perfect capital market.

B8. Suppose that a firm is operating with corporate and personal taxes in an otherwise perfect capital market and Equation (15.1) currently holds. In such a world, a firm would never take on any risky debt. Why not? (*Hint*: Consider what would happen in financial distress.)

B9. Miller (1977) showed that with corporate and personal income taxes in an otherwise perfect market, the gain from corporate leverage, G_L, for the stockholders can be expressed as

$$G_L = \left[1 - \frac{(1 - \tau)(1 - \tau_e)}{(1 - \tau_d)} \right] D$$

where τ, τ_e, and τ_d are as defined in Equation (15.1) and D denotes the market value of the corporation's debt.

  a. Explain how G_L changes in response to a change in τ, a change in τ_e, and a change in τ_d.

  b. Find a simple expression for G_L when the tax rates for debtholders and equityholders are equal. Relate this expression to the corporate tax view of leverage.

  c. Suppose high-grade taxable bonds (i.e., interest income is taxable to bondholders) trade at a 10% yield to maturity whereas high-grade tax-exempt bonds trade at a 7% yield to maturity. If equityholders are taxed at a 28% rate and corporations are taxed at a 34% rate, what is the gain from corporate leverage per dollar of debt?

B10. Describe the **pecking order theory** of capital structure. Briefly explain the logic underlying this theory.

PROBLEM SET C

C1. The operating head of your division approaches you, as division controller, and poses the following question: "If our company issues bonds that bear a 10% coupon, and sells them at par, then the company pays $100 per year in cash on the bonds, the cash yield is 10%, and the company's cost of debt is 10%. Our company's share price is $50, and each share pays $2.50 per year in dividends. If the company were to sell stock at the current market price, the company would have to pay $2.50 per year in cash on the stock, the cash yield is 5%, and therefore the company's cost of common equity is 5%, isn't it?"

  a. Is the operating head correct in his reasoning?

  b. Help the operating head resolve his confusion.

C2. Respond to the following comment: Thirty years ago, the traditional view held that capital structure mattered. The current view also holds that capital structure matters. I guess they had it right in the first place.

C3. Leverage increases the risk (and therefore the required rate of return) of the equityholders. Above some point, an increase in leverage also increases the risk (and required rate of return) of the debtholders. How is it possible, then, that in a perfect capital market environment the weighted average of the two are constant since both required rates of return are increasing?

C4. A comment was made by a journalist that the trouble with U.S. corporations was obvious from reading their balance sheets: They owed more money than they had! His conclusion was based on the firm's debt being larger than its equity. How would you respond to such a comment? Think about it before responding.

C5. The good fairy has decided to smile on you and has offered you a choice between two "great" outcomes. The alternatives concern an investment that has the same risk as the market portfolio and requires an initial investment of $10 million. The alternatives are (1) the cost of financing for the investment will be three standard deviations less than the current average market required rate of return for financing such investments, but the investment will have an otherwise zero NPV or (2) the expected future cash inflows from the investment will be three standard deviations larger than those that would make the investment have a zero NPV, but the cost of financing for the investment will be at the current average market required rate of return for financing such investments. Therefore, either alternative will provide you with a positive-NPV investment; alternative 1 does so by virtue of "great" financing, whereas alternative 2 does so by virtue of "great" investing. Which alternative should you choose, and why?

C6. Suppose a firm's earnings before interest and taxes forms an expected perpetuity of Y per year and that the firm has just issued an amount D of perpetual debt that pays interest at the rate $r_d(\theta)$ per annum. Let τ denote the firm's income tax rate and $r_e(0)$ its unleveraged, and $r_e(\theta)$ denote its leveraged, cost of equity capital. Assume there are no personal income taxes and all transactions take place in a perfect capital market except for corporate taxes.

  a. Show that the market value of the firm if it is unleveraged, V_U, would be

  $$V_U = \frac{(1-\tau)Y}{r_e(0)}$$

  b. Show that the total market value of the firm if it is leveraged (debt plus equity), V_L, is

  $$V_L = \frac{(1-\tau)[Y - r_d(\theta)D]}{r_e(\theta)} + D$$

  c. Explain why in the absence of other market imperfections the following must hold:

  $$\frac{(1-\tau)[Y - r_d(\theta)D]}{r_e(\theta)} + D = \frac{(1-\tau)Y}{r_e(0)} - \frac{(1-\tau)r_d(\theta)D}{r_d(\theta)} + D$$

  d. Show that in the absence of other market imperfections

  $$V_L = V_U + \tau D$$

  e. Explain why the model developed in parts a–d implies that in such a world the firm should be 100% debt-financed.

  f. What factors does the model omit that would imply that 100% debt financing is not optimal in practice.

REFERENCES

Altman, Edward I. "A Further Empirical Investigation of the Bankruptcy Cost Question." *Journal of Finance* 39 (September 1984): 1067–89.

American Bar Association. *Commentaries on Model Debenture Indenture Provisions.* Chicago: ABA, 1971.

Asquith, Paul, and David W. Mullins, Jr. "Equity Issues and Offering Dilution." *Journal of Financial Economics* 15 (January-February 1986): 61–90.

Barges, A. *The Effect of Capital Structure on the Cost of Capital.* Englewood Cliffs, N.J.: Prentice-Hall, 1963.

Barnea, Amir, Robert A. Haugen, and Lemma W. Senbet. *Agency Problems and Financial Contracting.* Englewood Cliffs, N.J.: Prentice-Hall, 1963.

Baron, David P., and Bengt Holmstrom. "The Investment Banking Contract for New Issues under Asymmetric Information: Delegation and the Incentive Problem." *Journal of Finance* 35 (December 1980): 1115–38.

Baxter, Nevins D. "Leverage, Risk of Ruin and the Cost of Capital." *Journal of Finance* 22 (September 1967): 395–403.

Ben-Horim, Moshe, Shalom Hochman, and Oded Polmon. "The Impact of the 1986 Tax Reform Act on Corporate Financial Policy." *Financial Management* 16 (Autumn 1987): 29–35.

Beranek, William. *The Effect of Leverage on the Market Value of Common Stock*. Madison, Wis.: Bureau of Business Research and Service, 1984.

Boness, A. James, and George M. Frankfurter. "Evidence of Non-Homogeneity of Capital Costs within 'Risk-Classes.'" *Journal of Finance* 32 (June 1977): 775–87.

Booth, James R., and Richard L. Smith. "Capital Raising, Underwriting and the Certification Hypothesis." *Journal of Financial Economics* 15 (January-February 1986).

Bowman, Robert G. "The Importance of a Market-Value Measurement of Debt in Assessing Leverage." *Journal of Accounting Research* 18 (Spring 1980): 242–54.

Bradley, Michael, Greg A. Jarrell, and E. Han Kim. "On the Existence of an Optimal Capital Structure: Theory and Evidence." *Journal of Finance* 39 (July 1984): 857–78.

Brennan, Michael J., and Eduardo S. Schwartz. "Savings Bonds, Retractable Bonds and Callable Bonds." *Journal of Financial Economics* 5 (August 1977): 67–88.

Brennan, Michael J., and Eduardo S. Schwartz. "Corporate Income Taxes, Valuation, and the Problem of Optimal Capital Structure." *Journal of Business* 51 (1978): 103–14.

Brennan, Michael J., and Eduardo S. Schwartz. "Optimal Financial Policy and Firm Valuation." *Journal of Finance* 39 (July 1984): 395–607.

Castanias, Richard P. "Bankruptcy Risk and Optimal Capital Structure." *Journal of Finance* 38 (December 1983): 1617–35.

Constantinides, George M. "Capital Market Equilibrium with Personal Tax." *Econometrica* (May 1983): 611–36.

Cordes, Joseph J., and Steven M. Sheffrin. "Estimating the Tax Advantage of Corporate Debt." *Journal of Finance* 38 (March 1983): 95–105.

Dann, Larry Y., and Wayne H. Mikkelson. "Convertible Debt Issuance, Capital Structure Change and Financing-Related Information: Some New Evidence." *Journal of Financial Economics* 13 (June 1984): 157–86.

Darrough, Masako N., and Neal M. Stoughton. "Moral Hazard and Adverse Selection: The Question of Financial Structure." *Journal of Finance* 41 (June 1986): 501–13.

DeAngelo, Harry, and Ronald W. Masulis. "Optimal Capital Structure under Corporate and Personal Taxation." *Journal of Financial Economics* 8 (March 1980): 3–30.

Dietrich, J. Richard. "Effects of Early Bond Refundings: An Empirical Investigation of Security Returns." *Journal of Accounting and Economics* 6 (No. 1, 1984): 67–96.

Eckbo, B. Espen. "Valuation Effects of Corporate Debt Offerings." *Journal of Financial Economics* 15 (January-February 1986): 119–52.

Emery, Douglas R., and Adam K. Gehr, Jr. "Tax Options, Capital Structure, and Miller Equilibrium: A Numerical Illustration." *Financial Management* 17 (Summer 1988): 30–40.

Emery, Douglas R., Wilbur G. Lewellen, and David Mauer. "Tax Timing Options, Leverage, and the Choice of Corporate Form." *Journal of Financial Research* 11 (Summer 1988): 99–110.

Ezzell, John R., and R. Burr Porter. "Flotation Costs and the Weighted Average Cost of Capital." *Journal of Financial and Quantitative Analysis* 11 (September 1976): 403–13.

Farrar, Donald E., and L. L. Selwyn. "Taxes, Corporate Financial Policy, and Returns to Investors." *National Tax Journal* 20 (1967): 444–54.

Finnerty, John D. "Stock-for-Debt Swaps and Shareholder Returns." *Financial Management* 14 (Autumn 1985): 5–17.

Flath, David, and Charles R. Knoeber. "Taxes, Failure Costs, and Optimal Industry Capital Structure: An Empirical Test." *Journal of Finance* 35 (March 1980): 3–29.

Fons, Jerome S. "The Default Premium and Corporate Bond Experience." *Journal of Finance* 42 (March 1987): 81–97.

Galai, Dan, and Ronald W. Masulis. "The Option Pricing Model and the Risk Factor of Stock." *Journal of Financial Economics* 3 (January-March 1976): 53–82.

Glenn, David W. "Super Premium Security Prices and Optimal Corporate Financing Decisions." *Journal of Finance* 31 (May 1976): 507–24.

Gordon, Myron J. *The Investment, Financing, and Valuation of the Corporation*. Homewood, Ill.: Richard D. Irwin, 1962.

Haley, Charles W., and Lawrence D. Schall. *The Theory of Financial Decisions*. 2nd ed. New York: McGraw-Hill, 1979.

Hamada, Robert S. "The Effect of the Firm's Capital Structure on the Systematic Risk of Common Stocks." *Journal of Finance* 27 (May 1972): 435–52.

Harris, John M., Jr., Rodney L. Roenfeldt, and Philip L. Cooley. "Evidence of Financial Leverage Clienteles." *Journal of Finance* 38 (September 1983): 1125–32.

Haugen, Robert A., and Lemma W. Senbet. "The Insignificance of Bankruptcy Costs to the Theory of Optimal Capital Structure." *Journal of Finance* 33 (May 1978): 383–93.

Haugen, Robert A., and Lemma W. Senbet. "New Perspectives on Informational Asymmetry and Agency Relationships." *Journal of Financial and Quantitative Analysis* 14 (November 1979): 671–94.

Haugen, Robert A., and Lemma W. Senbet. "Bankruptcy and Agency Costs: Their Significance to the Theory of Optimal Capital Structure." *Journal of Financial and Quantitative Analysis* 23 (March 1988): 27–38.

Heinkel, Robert, and Eduardo S. Schwartz. "Rights Versus Underwritten Offerings: An Asymmetric Information Approach." *Journal of Finance* 41 (March 1986): 1–18.

Ho, Thomas S., and Ronald F. Singer. "Bond Indenture Provisions and the Risk of Corporate Debt." *Journal of Financial Economics* 10 (December 1982): 375–406.

Jensen, Michael C., and William H. Meckling. "Theory of the Firm: Managerial Behavior, Agency Costs, and Ownership Structure." *Journal of Financial Economics* 3 (October 1976): 305–60.

Jones, E. Phillip, Scott P. Mason, and Eric Rosenfeld. "Contingent Claims Analysis of Corporate Financial Structures: An Empirical Investigation." *Journal of Finance* 39 (July 1984): 611–25.

Kalaba, Robert E., Terence C. Langetieg, Nima Rasakhoo, and Mark I. Weinstein. "Estimation of Implicit Bankruptcy Costs." *Journal of Finance* 39 (July 1984): 629–42.

Kalotay, Andrew J. "On the Advanced Refunding of Discounted Debt." *Financial Management* 7 (Summer 1978): 7–13.

Kane, Alex, Alan J. Marcus, and Robert L. McDonald. "How Big is the Tax Advantage to Debt?" *Journal of Finance* 39 (July 1984): 841–53.

Kester, W. Carl. "Capital and Ownership Structure: A Comparison of United States and Japanese Manufacturing Corporations." *Financial Management* 15 (Spring 1986): 5–16.

Kim, E. Han. "A Mean Variance Theory of Optimal Capital Structure and Corporate Debt Capacity." *Journal of Finance* 33 (March 1978): 45–64.

Kim, E. Han, Wilbur G. Lewellen, and John J. McConnell. "Financial Leverage and Clienteles: Theory and Evidence." *Journal of Financial Economics* 7 (March 1979): 83–110.

Kolodny, Richard, and Diane Rizzuto Suhler. "Changes in Capital Structure, New Equity Issues, and Scale Effects." *Journal of Financial Research* 8 (Summer 1985): 127–36.

Kraus, Alan, and Robert H. Litzenberger. "A State-Preference Model of Optimal Financial Leverage." *Journal of Finance* 28 (September 1973): 911–22.

Lee, Wayne L., Anjan V. Thakor, and Gautam Vora. "Screening, Market Signalling, and Capital Structure Theory." *Journal of Finance* 38 (December 1983): 1507–18.

Leland, Hayne E., and David H. Pyle. "Informational Asymmetries, Financial Structure, and Financial Intermediation." *Journal of Finance* 32 (May 1977): 371–88.

Linn, Scott C., and J. Michael Pinegar. "The Effect of Issuing Preferred Stock on Common and Preferred Stockholder Wealth." Working paper, University of Iowa, 1985.

Long, Michael S., and Ileen Malitz. "Investment Patterns and Financial Leverage." In Friedman, ed., *Corporate Capital Structure in the United States*. Chicago, Ill.: University of Chicago Press, 1985.

McConnell, John J., and Gary G. Schlarbaum. "Evidence on the Impact of Exchange Offers on Security Prices: The Case of Income Bonds." *Journal of Business* 54 (January 1981): 65–85.

Malitz, Ileen. "On Financial Contracting: The Determinants of Bond Covenants." *Financial Management* 15 (Summer 1986): 18–25.

Malkiel, Burton G. *The Debt-Equity Combination of the Firm and the Cost of Capital: An Introductory Analysis*. New York: General Learning Press, 1971.

Marsh, Paul. "The Choice Between Equity and Debt: An Empirical Study." *Journal of Finance* 37 (March 1982): 121–44.

Masulis, Ronald W. "The Effects of Capital Structure Change on Security Prices: A Study of Exchange Offers." *Journal of Financial Economics* 8 (June 1980): 139–78.

Masulis, Ronald W. "The Impact of Capital Structure Change on Firm Value, Some Estimates." *Journal of Finance* 38 (March 1983): 107–26.

Masulis, Ronald W., and Ashok N. Korwar. "Seasoned Equity Offerings: An Empirical Investigation." *Journal of Financial Economics* 15 (January-February 1986): 91–118.

Mauer, David C., and Wilbur G. Lewellen. "Debt Management Under Corporate and Personal Taxation." *Journal of Finance* 42 (December 1987): 1275–91.

Mikkelson, Wayne H., and M. Megan Partch. "Valuation Effects of Security Offerings and the Issuance Process." *Journal of Financial Economics* 15 (January-February 1986): 31–60.

Miller, Merton H. "Debt and Taxes." *Journal of Finance* 32 (May 1977): 261–75.

Miller, Merton H., and Franco Modigliani. "Some Estimates of the Cost of Capital to the Electric Utility Industry, 1954–57." *American Economic Review* 56 (June 1966): 333–91.

Miller, Merton H., and Franco Modigliani. "Some Estimates of the Cost of Capital to the Electric Utility Industry, 1954–57: Reply." *American Economic Review* 57 (December 1967): 1288–1300.

Modigliani, Franco, and Merton H. Miller. "The Cost of Capital, Corporation Finance and the Theory of Investment." *American Economic Review* 48 (June 1958): 261–97.

Modigliani, Franco, and Merton H. Miller. "Corporate Income Taxes and the Cost of Capital: A Correction." *American Economic Review* 53 (June 1963): 433–43.

Myers, Stewart C. "Determinants of Corporate Borrowing." *Journal of Financial Economics* 5 (November 1977): 147–75.

Myers, Stewart C. "The Capital Structure Puzzle." *Journal of Finance* (July 1984): 575–92.

Myers, Stewart C., and Nicholas S. Majluf. "Corporate Financing and Investment Decisions When Firms Have Information That Investors Do Not Have." *Journal of Financial Economics* (June 1984): 187–221.

Pinegar, J. Michael, and Ronald C. Lease. "The Impact of Preferred-for-Common Exchange Offers on Firm Value." *Journal of Finance* 41 (September 1986): 795–814.

Piper, Thomas R., and Wolf A. Weinhold. "How Much Debt Is Right for Your Company?" *Harvard Business Review* (July-August 1982): 106–14.

Rogers, Ronald C., and James E. Owers. "Equity for Debt Exchanges and Shareholder Wealth." *Financial Management* 14 (Autumn 1985): 18–26.

Ross, Stephen A. "The Determination of Financial Structure: The Incentive Signalling Approach." *Bell Journal of Economics* 8 (Spring 1977): 23–40.

Rubinstein, Mark E. "A Mean-Variance Synthesis of Corporate Financial Theory." *Journal of Finance* 28 (March 1973): 167–81.

Schipper, Katherine, and Abbie Smith. "A Comparison of Equity Carve-outs and Seasoned Equity Offerings: Share Price Effects and Corporate Restructuring." *Journal of Financial Economics* 15 (January-February 1986): 153–86.

Schwartz, Eli, and J. Richard Aronson. "Some Surrogate Evidence in Support of the Concept of Optimal Financial Structure." *Journal of Finance* 22 (March 1967): 10–18.

Scott, David F., Jr., and John D. Martin. "Industry Influence on Financial Structure." *Financial Management* 4 (Spring 1975): 67–73.

Scott, James H., Jr. "A Theory of Optimal Capital Structure." *Bell Journal of Economics* 7 (Spring 1976): 33–54.

Scott, James H., George H. Hempel, and John W. Peavy III. "The Effect of Stock-for-Debt Swaps on Bank Holding Companies." *Journal of Banking and Finance* 9 (June 1985): 233–51.

Smith, Clifford W., Jr., and Jerold B. Warner. "On Financial Contracting: An Analysis of Bond Covenants." *Journal of Financial Economics* 7 (June 1979): 117–61.

Solomon, Ezra. *The Theory of Financial Management*. New York: Columbia University Press, 1963.

Spence, A. Michael. "Job Market Signaling." *Quarterly Journal of Economics* (August 1973): 355–79.

Stiglitz, Joseph E. "A Re-Examination of the Modigliani-Miller Theorem." *American Economic Review* 59 (December 1969): 784–93.

Stiglitz, Joseph E. "Some Aspects of the Pure Theory of Corporate Finance: Bankruptcies and Takeovers." *Bell Journal of Economics and Management Science* 4 (Autumn 1972): 458–82.

Stiglitz, Joseph E. "On the Irrelevance of Corporate Financial Policy." *American Economic Review* 64 (December 1974): 851–66.

Stulz, Rene M., and Herb Johnson. "An Analysis of Secured Debt." *Journal of Financial Economics* 14 (December 1985): 501–21.

Taggart, Robert A., Jr. "A Model of Corporate Financing Decisions." *Journal of Finance* 32 (December 1977): 1467–84.

Thatcher, Janet S. "The Choice of Call Provision Terms: Evidence of the Existence of Agency Costs of Debt." *Journal of Finance* 40 (May 1985): 549–61.

Titman, Sheridan. "The Effect of Capital Structure on a Firm's Liquidation Decision." *Journal of Financial Economics* 13 (March 1984): 137–51.

Titman, Sheridan, and Roberto Wessels. "The Determinants of Capital Structure Choice." *Journal of Finance* 43 (March 1988): 1–19.

Vermaelen, Theo. "Common Stock Repurchases and Market Signalling: An Empirical Study." *Journal of Financial Economics* 9 (June 1981): 138–83.

Vermaelen, Theo. "Repurchase Tender Offers, Signalling, and Managerial Incentives." *Journal of Financial and Quantitative Analysis* 19 (June 1984): 163–81.

Warner, Jerold B. "Bankruptcy, Absolute Priority and the Pricing of Risky Debt Claims." *Journal of Financial Economics* (May 1977a): 239–76.

Warner, Jerold B. "Bankruptcy Costs: Some Evidence." *Journal of Finance* 32 (May 1977b): 337–47.

Weinstein, Mark I. "The Effect of a Rating Change Announcement on Bond Price." *Journal of Financial Economics* 5 (December 1977): 329–50.

Weinstein, Mark I. "The Seasoning Process of New Corporate Bond Issues." *Journal of Finance* 35 (December 1978): 1343–54.

Weston, J. Fred. "A Test of Capital Propositions." *Southern Economic Journal* (October 1963): 105–12.

White, Michelle J. "Bankruptcy Costs and the New Bankruptcy Code." *Journal of Finance* 38 (May 1983): 477–88.

Williams, Joseph. "Prerequisites, Risk, and Capital Structure." *Journal of Finance* 42 (March 1987): 29–48.

Wrightsman, Dwayne. "Tax Shield Valuation and the Capital Structure Decision." *Journal of Finance* 33 (May 1978): 650–56.

Yawitz, Jess B., Kevin J. Maloney, and Louis H. Ederington. "Taxes, Default Risk, and Yield Spreads." *Journal of Finance* 40 (September 1985): 1127–40.

16

MANAGING CAPITAL STRUCTURE

Corporations exercise great care in managing capital structure. Choosing an appropriate capital structure is difficult because, as the preceding chapter indicates, the factors involved are complex and the impact of each factor on the value of the firm is not clear cut. In principle, a corporation should balance the net advantage of additional leverage against the additional costs that would result. Unfortunately, the change in the present value of the expected costs of financial distress, agency costs, and the cost of reduced financing flexibility do not lend themselves to precise measurement.

A number of methods exist for analyzing the impact of alternative capital structures, but in the end, the choice of capital structure requires expert judgment. The analytical models suggest a range of reasonable capital structures rather than pinpointing the optimal one. This chapter describes how a firm can take into account the various factors relevant to the capital structure decision discussed in Chapter 15 to select an appropriate (as distinguished from *the* best) capital structure.

HEWLETT-PACKARD'S LEVERAGE CHOICE

To illustrate a practical situation, Figure 16-1 contains three annual statements of income, a year-end balance sheet, and three annual statements of changes in financial position which were prepared from the more detailed financial statements presented in Hewlett-Packard Company's 1987 annual report.[1] You are probably familiar with Hewlett-Packard. You may have even purchased one of the company's calculators to help you with this or other classes.

Hewlett-Packard is a large, well-established, highly profitable firm that designs, manufactures, and services electronic products and systems for measurement and computation. Proportionately, it has virtually no long-term debt. The company earned $644 million in 1987, a 14% after-tax rate of return on average shareholders' equity. At year-end 1987, the company had total assets of $8.1 billion, but only $88 million of long-term debt. Current liabilities include $979 million of short-term debt, up from $229 million a year earlier, but the firm's annual report noted that the increase was a temporary condition that resulted from the firm's worldwide cash management activities. In any case, there was $57 of shareholders' equity on a book basis (and considerably more on a market value basis) for each dollar of long-term debt, and the firm's cash and marketable securities were nearly 2½ times the firm's total debt. Also, Hewlett-Packard's annual report indicated an effective tax rate for 1987 of 33.0% (= 318/962).

Based on the knowledge you gained by reading Chapter 15, can you make a case that Hewlett-Packard is underleveraged? A firm as large and sophisticated as Hewlett-

---

[1] Hewlett-Packard Company, *1987 Annual Report to Shareholders.*

FIGURE 16-1

Summary financial statements for Hewlett-Packard Company (dollar amounts in millions).

Source: Hewlett-Packard Company, *1987 Annual Report to Shareholders.*

Statements of Income

	1987	1986	1985
Net revenue	$8,090	$7,102	$6,505
Costs and expenses	7,128	6,322	5,747
Pretax earnings	962	780	758
Provision for taxes	318	264	269
Net income	$ 644	$ 516	$ 489

Balance Sheet (10/31/87)

Assets		Liabilities and Shareholders' Equity	
Cash & marketable securities	$2,645	Current liabilities	$2,735
Other current assets	2,845	Long-term debt	88
Fixed assets	2,328	Other liabilities	134
Other assets	315	Deferred income taxes	154
		Shareholders' equity	5,022
Total assets	$8,133	Total liabilities and shareholders' equity	$8,133

Statements of Changes in Financial Position

	1987	1986	1985
Net income	$ 644	$ 516	$ 489
Noncash expenses	483	445	450
Funds from operations	1,127	961	939
Investment in fixed assets	507	499	632
Increase (decrease) in working capital, excluding cash	(7)	(97)	148
Dividends	60	56	57
Shares repurchased	220	287	240
Other used (provided)—net	(176)	(167)	(177)
Increase (decrease) in cash and marketable securities	$ 523	$ 383	$ 39

Packard would certainly not underleverage itself intentionally. What factors might account for the apparently low degree of leverage? What further information would you need to be able to determine whether Hewlett-Packard's shareholders could benefit from an increase in leverage? At the end of this chapter, we will answer these questions.

INDUSTRY EFFECTS   16.1

According to the Behavioral Principle, the capital structure choices of comparable companies offer some useful guidance to a firm that is reconsidering its capital structure or formulating a capitalization policy for the first time. Lending support to this application of the Behavioral Principle, several studies have identified systematic differences in capital structure across industries.[2]

Table 16-1 presents the results of a cross-sectional analysis of firms in the United

[2] Kester (1986); Bowen, Daley, and Huber (1982); Schwartz and Aronson (1967); Scott (1972); Scott and Martin (1975).

TABLE 16-1 Industry Differences in Leverage

Industry (SIC Code)	Net Debt/Equity Ratio Based on[a]	
	Book Value of Equity	Market Value of Equity
Comparatively High Leverage		
Nonferrous metals (3330,3341,3350)	3.79	1.11
General chemicals (2800)	2.95	1.26
Steel (3310)	1.97	1.67
Paper (2600)	1.73	1.36
Petroleum refining (2911)	1.55	1.12
Textiles (2200)	1.41	1.30
Cement (3241)	1.30	1.37
Comparatively Moderate Leverage		
Apparel (2300)	1.02	0.95
Tire and rubber (3000)	1.02	0.84
Motor vehicles (3711)	0.92	0.59
Plastics (2820, 3079)	0.84	0.79
Construction machinery (3530, 3531)	0.69	0.81
Comparatively Low Leverage		
Motor vehicle parts (3714)	0.49	0.50
Photo equipment (3861)	0.47	0.22
Alcoholic beverages (2082, 2085)	0.43	0.28
Pharmaceuticals (2380)	0.19	0.08
Household appliances (3630)	0.10	0.24

[a] Net debt is calculated by subtracting cash and marketable securities from the sum of short-term debt and long-term debt (including convertible debt and capitalized leases).

Source: W. Carl Kester, "Capital and Ownership Structure: A Comparison of United States and Japanese Manufacturing Corporations," *Financial Management* 15 (Spring 1986), 9.

States and Japan (companies from the two countries were grouped together into industry samples).[3] There are significant differences in leverage across industries. Metals, chemicals, and steel companies that have substantial tangible fixed assets are highly leveraged. Pharmaceutical and photo equipment manufacturers, much of whose assets are in the form of patents and other intangible assets, have comparatively low leverage. A regression analysis on factors that might account for these industry differences suggests that accounting profitability is a very important determinant.[4] But it is an inverse relationship: The more profitable firms tended to have less leverage than less profitable ones. Does that seem surprising? Perhaps it simply reflects the pecking order theory: The most profitable firms borrow least because of

[3] Kester (1986).

[4] Kester (1986) measured profitability as earnings before interest, taxes, noncash expenses, discontinued operations, and extraordinary items, divided by average total assets. The numerator represents cash flow from continuing operations that is available to service debt, which is also the principal factor the rating agencies use in assessing credit quality.

TABLE 16-2 Industry Differences in Leverage, 1951–1969

Industry (SIC Code)	1951		1960		1969		1951–1969[c]	
	Leverage[a]	Rank[b]	Leverage[a]	Rank[b]	Leverage[a]	Rank[b]	Leverage[a]	Rank[b]
Auto parts & acces. (3714)	.38	5[d]	.26	1	.34	1	.29	1
Steel (3310)	.37	3[d]	.32	3	.35	2	.33	2
Oil-integrated domestic (2912)	.32	2	.31	2	.37	3	.34	3
Textile products (2200)	.29	1	.38	4[d]	.47	6	.38	4
Chemicals (2800)	.38	5[d]	.38	4[d]	.42	4 ·	.40	5
Retail dept. stores (5311)	.37	3[d]	.41	6	.48	7	.42	6
Retail food chains (5411)	.45	8	.42	7	.46	5	.44	7
Aerospace (3721)	.52	9	.48	8	.54	8	.50	8
Air transportation (4511)	.44	7	.63	9	.60	9	.55	9

[a] Leverage measured as long-term debt plus short-term debt divided by total assets.
[b] Annual ranking from lowest leverage (1) to highest leverage (9).
[c] Average of the annual industry averages for 1951, 1954, 1957, 1960, 1963, 1966, and 1969.
[d] Denotes tie.

Source: Robert M. Bowen, Lane A. Daley, and Charles C. Huber, Jr., "Evidence on the Existence and Determinants of Inter-Industry Differences in Leverage," *Financial Management* 11 (Winter 1982), 10–20.

their ample internal cash generation. In addition, several of the industry dummy variables were positive and statistically significant.

Table 16-2 is based on the results of a second study, one that shows the stability of industry differences in leverage over time. This study measured the ratio of total debt to total assets at 3-year intervals between 1951 and 1969 for companies in nine industries (defined by four-digit SIC codes).[5] Table 16-2 presents the results for 1951, 1960, and 1969. The rankings did not remain fixed over the 19-year period, but they do appear fairly stable, particularly between 1960 and 1969. Domestic integrated oil companies, steel companies, and auto parts manufacturers were the least highly leveraged throughout the 19-year period. Aerospace and air transportation companies were the most highly leveraged.

The systematic differences in industry capital structure can be attributed to three principal factors: differences in the degree of operating risk; differences in the extent of tax shelter provided by accelerated depreciation (for tax purposes, that is), investment tax credit, and operating tax loss carryforwards; and differences in the degree to which assets will support corporate borrowing. All three factors are easy to explain.

DIFFERENCES IN OPERATING RISK

Recall from Chapter 10 the definitions of operating and financial leverage, and the difference between the two. In Chapter 10, we said that the operating leverage is the major determinant of the required rate of return for a project and showed how finan-

[5] Bowen, Daley, and Huber (1982).

cial leverage determines how the risk of the firm is distributed between the share-holders and the debtholders. We also showed that increasing the degree of leverage in a firm's capital structure increases the variability of the returns to its shareholders, thus increasing their financial risk. But beyond some point, an increase in financial leverage also increases the debtholders' financial risk as well as that of the share-holders.[6] Table 16-3 illustrates this point.

Table 16-3 shows how the firm's interest coverage varies with its return on assets and the degree of financial leverage in its capital structure. Interest coverage is measured as

$$\text{Interest Coverage Ratio} = \frac{\text{EBIT}}{\text{Interest Expense}} \qquad \text{(16.1)}$$

where EBIT denotes earnings before interest and income taxes. In the high-operating-risk case, for example a manufacturing company in a very competitive industry, the company's expected return on assets is assumed to be 12% but the actual return it realizes might be as low as 5% or as high as 19%. In the low-operating-risk case, for example an electric utility company, the firm's expected return on assets is assumed to be 10%, but the realized return varies within the narrower band from 7% to 13%.

If the firm belongs to an industry characterized by high operating risk, its interest coverage ratio might fall to 2.00 if its leverage ratio is .25 or only 1.00 if its leverage ratio is 0.50. With higher leverage, it would fail in the worst case to cover its interest charges. At the other extreme, if the firm belongs to an industry characterized by low operating risk, even in the worst case it would cover its interest charges by at least a factor of 1.55 as long as its leverage ratio does not exceed 0.50. Thus, the low-operating-risk firm could support greater financial leverage; the firm is capable of taking on a higher degree of financial risk than the high-operating-risk firm because of the lower degree of operating risk. Because operating risks vary from one industry to another, it is not surprising that capital structures also vary by industry.

DIFFERENCES IN ABILITY TO USE TAX CREDITS

With regard to the second factor that leads to interindustry differences in capital structure, the relative (to firm size) amount of tax shelter provided by accelerated depreciation, investment tax credit, and operating tax loss carryforwards is negatively related to the average degree of financial leverage in the capital structures of companies in the nine industries listed in Table 16-2.[7] One would expect that because of differences in capital intensity across industries, there would be differences in the availability of other sources of tax shelter.[8] These operating sources of tax shelter reduce a firm's ability to utilize the tax shelter benefits that would result from increased financial leverage. Greater availability of operations-related tax shelter should therefore reduce the degree of financial leverage that is optimal. Interindustry differences in the availability of operations-related tax shelter should therefore produce systematic differences in capital structure.[9]

---

[6] Recall that in a perfect capital market environment, the weighted average of the two is constant. See Chapter 10.

[7] Bowen, Daley, and Huber (1982) divided the total amount of operations-related tax shelter by total revenue in order to neutralize the effect of differences in company size. Larger companies will tend to have greater amounts of operations-related tax shelter benefits available just because of their size.

[8] The existence of such interindustry differences was first proposed by DeAngelo and Masulis (1980).

[9] Bowen, Daley, and Huber (1982) found a tendency for the capital structures of individual firms in an industry to gravitate toward the industry mean over a 5-year to 10-year period. This is an example of a concept you might recall from your statistics class called **regression toward the mean**.

TABLE 16-3 Degree of Operating Risk Affects the Capacity to Support Additional Leverage (Dollar Amounts in Millions)

| | High Operating Risk | | | | | | | | |
| | 5% Return on Assets | | | 12% Return on Assets | | | 19% Return on Assets | | |
	Low Leverage	*Modest Leverage*	*High Leverage*	*Low Leverage*	*Modest Leverage*	*High Leverage*	*Low Leverage*	*Modest Leverage*	*High Leverage*
Total assets	$100	$100	$100	$100	$100	$100	$100	$100	$100
Total debt/Total assets	.25	.50	.75	.25	.50	.75	.25	.50	.75
Total debt	$ 25	$ 50	$ 75	$ 25	$ 50	$ 75	$ 25	$ 50	$ 75
Earnings before interest and taxes	$5.0	$5.0	$5.0	$12.0	$12.0	$12.0	$19.0	$19.0	$19.0
Interest (at 10%)	2.5	5.0	7.5	2.5	5.0	7.5	2.5	5.0	7.5
Interest coverage	2.00x	1.00x	0.67x	4.80x	2.40x	1.60x	7.60x	3.80x	2.53x

| | Low Operating Risk | | | | | | | | |
| | 7% Return on Assets | | | 10% Return on Assets | | | 13% Return on Assets | | |
	Low Leverage	*Modest Leverage*	*High Leverage*	*Low Leverage*	*Modest Leverage*	*High Leverage*	*Low Leverage*	*Modest Leverage*	*High Leverage*
Total assets	$100	$100	$100	$100	$100	$100	$100	$100	$100
Total debt/Total assets	.25	.50	.75	.25	.50	.75	.25	.50	.75
Total debt	$ 25	$ 50	$ 75	$ 25	$ 50	$ 75	$ 25	$ 50	$ 75
Earnings before interest and taxes	$7.0	$7.0	$7.0	$10.0	$10.0	$10.0	$13.0	$13.0	$13.0
Interest (at 10%)	2.25	4.5	6.75	2.25	4.5	6.75	2.25	4.5	6.75
Interest coverage	3.11x	1.55x	1.04x	4.44x	2.22x	1.48x	5.78x	2.89x	1.93x

DIFFERENCES IN ABILITY OF ASSETS TO SUPPORT DEBT

Companies that have a relatively high proportion of intangible assets or very attractive growth opportunities tend to use less leverage than other companies. For example, a significant proportion of the market value of pharmaceutical companies and computer manufacturers is embodied in patents and trademarks. A high proportion of the market value of alcoholic beverage companies is embodied in trade secrets and patents covering their manufacturing processes and in consumer brand loyalty, which does not show up on the balance sheet. Table 16-1 indicates the comparatively low degrees of leverage of pharmaceutical companies and alcoholic beverage companies. In contrast, as also illustrated in Table 16-1, companies with relatively high proportions of tangible assets, such as steel companies and cement companies, tend to have relatively high degrees of leverage.

When differences in profitability, operating risk, and nondebt tax shields are controlled for, companies that spend comparatively large sums on advertising (such as alcoholic beverage manufacturers) and research and development (such as pharmaceutical companies) tend to use less debt.[10] The relatively low degree of leverage in

[10] Long and Malitz (1986) also found evidence that the availability of nondebt tax shields affects the degree of corporate leverage.

such cases may be due to the value that different types of assets have in financial distress. Recall from Chapter 9 that the use of intangible (versus tangible) assets affects a firm's agency costs. A patent may lose its value quickly when a high technology company goes into financial distress causing its brightest technicians and engineers to depart, and its customers to seek alternative sources of supply from financially healthy manufacturers. But investments in plant and equipment generally hold their value better in situations of financial distress. For example, there is a very active secondary market in aircraft. When assets are more readily marketable, the expected costs of financial distress will be consequently smaller, and the firm can bear a higher degree of leverage than it would otherwise.

16.2

SIGNIFICANCE OF DEBT RATINGS

Interindustry differences in capital structure are only part of the story. For example, should a firm simply adopt the industry average debt ratio? There are differences among firms in any particular industry with respect to tax position, size, competitive position, operating risk, business prospects, and other factors. There also appear to be important differences among firms with respect to their desired level of financial risk and degree of access to the capital markets, as reflected in the debt ratings they strive to achieve for their debt obligations. In practice, a firm's bond ratings are a very important factor affecting a firm's choice of capital structure.

INTERPRETATION OF BOND RATINGS

Figure 16-2 shows the rating definitions adopted by two of the major rating agencies, Moody's Investors Service, Inc., and Standard & Poor's Corporation. The highest four rating categories (Moody's Aaa, Aa, A, and Baa; Standard & Poor's AAA, AA, A, and BBB) constitute the range of what are called **investment grade ratings**. The lower ratings represent what are called **speculative grade ratings**. Each agency distinguishes different levels of credit quality within each rating category below triple-A. Moody's attaches numbers 1 (high), 2 (medium), and 3 (low); Standard & Poor's attaches + for the highest and − for the lowest. Thus, for example, a medium-grade single-A credit would be rated (Moody's/Standard & Poor's) A2/A and would be of somewhat lower quality than one rated A1/A+.

The distinction between investment grade ratings and speculative grade ratings is important because of restrictions placed on certain classes of institutional investors. Under regulations issued by the Comptroller of the Currency, bonds must generally be of investment grade quality in order to qualify as **legal investments** for commercial banks. In addition, various state laws impose minimum-rating and other standards that debt obligations (or their issuers) must satisfy for the bonds to qualify as legal investments for savings banks, trust companies, public pension funds, and insurance companies. In general, bonds rated speculative do not qualify as legal investments, but in many cases, more restrictive state regulators require ratings no lower than single-A for legal investment purposes.

If a firm's bonds fail to qualify as a legal investment, the market for them narrows. The institutions just mentioned are severely restricted in their ability to purchase bonds that fail to qualify as legal investments, and many face an absolute prohibition. Its bond rating is very important, then, to a firm that wants to ensure its uninterrupted access to the capital markets on acceptable terms.

The bond rating definitions in Figure 16-2 show that the ratings serve as indicators of the relative likelihood of financial distress, as judged by the rating agencies.

Bonds rated among the top three investment grade categories have investment attributes that range from "favorable" to "gilt edge" and a capacity to pay interest that ranges from "strong" to "extremely strong." Bonds rated in the lowest investment grade category (Baa/BBB) offer investors less protection than higher-rated bonds. They offer adequate protection but are more likely to be subject to adverse future developments. That is, the risk of financial distress prior to maturity is greater in the case of lower-rated bonds than with higher-rated bonds. Bonds rated speculative are significantly riskier, at best offering bondholders only "very moderate" protection and at worst already in default.

The choice of a bond rating objective by a firm thus involves a decision as to (1) the relative degree of risk of future financial distress it is willing to bear and (2) the relative degree of future access to the capital markets it would like to achieve. To the extent that a firm chooses a rating objective that still leaves the marginal benefit of additional leverage (measured as the incremental tax shield benefits obtainable) exceeding the marginal cost of additional leverage (measured as the incremental expected cost of financial distress), one could interpret the difference between the degree of leverage actually achieved and the degree of leverage that would equate marginal benefit and marginal cost as a "margin of safety." The desired margin of safety is determined by management's decision as to how much risk of future financial distress or restricted market access the firm is willing to bear.[11] A single-A rating would seem to be a reasonable rating target, but certain companies are more or less risk averse than this standard implies.

BOND RATING AND THE CHOICE OF FINANCIAL RATIO TARGETS

Once a firm has chosen its rating target, how can it decide what financial objectives are most consistent with achieving this target? The rating agencies apply a large number of criteria in reaching a judgment concerning the most appropriate rating. For example, in the case of industrial companies, Standard & Poor's evaluates the following nine factors:

1. degree of operating risk in the company's principal businesses;
2. the firm's market position in these businesses;
3. the firm's margins and other measures of its profitability;
4. quality of the firm's management;
5. conservatism of the firm's accounting policies;
6. fixed charge coverage;
7. leverage (including off-balance-sheet debt) in relation to the liquidation value of the firm's assets;
8. adequacy of cash flow to meet future debt service obligations, and
9. the firm's future financial flexibility in the light of its future debt service obligations and planned capital expenditure requirements.[12]

Each of these items bears on the risk of future financial distress. The rating agencies weigh their assessments of the factors they consider relevant and reach a decision. There is no all-purpose formula. More important, the foregoing list includes a

---

[11] Note that this decision contains an agency problem and can be a source of agency costs for the shareholders. The conflict is due to the nondiversifiability of human capital, which causes managers to avoid diversifiable risk, even though shareholders do not care about it. See Chapter 9 for a discussion of this concept.

[12] See *Debt Ratings Criteria: Industrial Overview* (New York: Standard & Poor's Corporation, 1986), 21–30.

Moody's Investors Service, Inc.[a]   *Standard & Poor's Corporation*[b]

INVESTMENT GRADE RATINGS

Aaa

Bonds which are rated Aaa are judged to be of the best quality. They carry the smallest degree of investment risk and are generally referred to as "gilt edge." Interest payments are protected by a large or by an exceptionally stable margin and principal is secure. While the various protective elements are likely to change, such changes as can be visualized are most unlikely to impair the fundamentally strong position of such issues.

AAA

Debt rated AAA has the highest rating assigned by Standard & Poor's. Capacity to pay interest and repay principal is extremely strong.

Aa

Bonds which are rated Aa are judged to be of high quality by all standards. Together with the Aaa group they comprise what are generally known as high grade bonds. They are rated lower than the best bonds because margins of protection may not be as large as in Aaa securities or fluctuation of protective elements may be of greater amplitude or there may be other elements present which make the long term risks appear somewhat larger than in Aaa securities.

AA

Debt rated AA has a very strong capacity to pay interest and repay principal and differs from the highest rated issues only in small degree.

A

Bonds which are rated A possess many favorable investment attributes and are to be considered as upper medium grade obligations. Factors giving security to principal and interest are considered adequate but elements may be present which suggest a susceptibility to impairment sometime in the future.

A

Debt rated A has a strong capacity to pay interest and repay principal although it is somewhat more susceptible to the adverse effects of changes in circumstances and economic conditions than debt in higher rated categories.

Baa

Bonds which are rated Baa are considered as medium grade obligations, i.e., they are neither highly protected nor poorly secured. Interest payments and principal security appear adequate for the present but certain protective elements may be lacking or may be characteristically unreliable over any great length of time. Such bonds lack outstanding investment characteristics and in fact have speculative characteristics as well.

BBB

Debt rated BBB is regarded as having an adequate capacity to pay interest and repay principal. Whereas it normally exhibits adequate protection parameters, adverse economic conditions or changing circumstances are more likely to lead to a weakened capacity to pay interest and repay principal for debt in this category than in higher rated categories.

SPECULATIVE GRADE RATINGS

Ba

Bonds which are rated Ba are judged to have speculative elements; their future cannot be considered as well assured. Often the protection of interest and principal payments may be very moderate and thereby not well safeguarded during both good and bad times over the future. Uncertainty of position characterizes bonds in this class.

BB

Debt rated BB has less near-term vulnerability to default than other speculative issues. However, it faces major ongoing uncertainties or exposure to adverse business, financial, or economic conditions which could lead to inadequate capacity to meet timely interest and principal payments. The BB rating category is also used for debt subordinated to senior debt that is assigned an actual or implied BBB− rating.

[a] Moody's applies numerical modifiers, 1, 2, and 3 in each generic rating classification from Aa through B in its corporate bond rating system. The modifier 1 indicates that the security ranks in the higher end of its generic rating category; the modifier 2 indicates a mid-range ranking; and the modifier 3 indicates that the issue ranks in the lower end of its generic rating category.

FIGURE 16-2

Bond rating definitions.

Sources: Moody's Investors Service, *Moody's Bond Record*, January 1990, and Standard & Poor's, *CreditWeek*, July 9, 1990. Reprinted by permission.

number of factors, the most important of which is the quality of management, that do not lend themselves to quantification.[13] Nevertheless, the values of certain key credit statistics for comparable companies whose debt carries the target rating offers useful guidance.

[13] Largely because of these qualitative factors and the somewhat imperfect link between current financial condition and future financial condition, studies that have attempted to discriminate among actual bond ratings on the basis of historical financial information have found that these models have a significant degree of predictive error. For example, see Pinches and Mingo (1973). There is evidence that agency costs play a role in the qualitative factors. See Iskandar (1986).

Moody's Investors Service, Inc.[a]	*Standard & Poor's Corporation*[b]

SPECULATIVE GRADE RATINGS (*continued*)

B	**B**
Bonds which are rated B generally lack characteristics of the desirable investment. Assurance of interest and principal payments or of maintenance of other terms of the contract over any long period of time may be small.	Debt rated B has a greater vulnerability to default but currently has the capacity to meet interest payments and principal repayments. Adverse business, financial, or economic conditions will likely impair capacity or willingness to pay interest and repay principal. The B rating category is also used for debt subordinated to senior debt that is assigned an actual or implied BB or BB− rating.

Caa	**CCC**
Bonds which are rated Caa are of poor standing. Such issues may be in default or there may be present elements of danger with respect to principal or interest.	Debt rated CCC has a currently identifiable vulnerability to default, and is dependent upon favorable business, financial, and economic conditions to meet timely payment of interest and repayment of principal. In the event of adverse business, financial, or economic conditions, it is not likely to have the capacity to pay interest and repay principal. The CCC rating category is also used for debt subordinated to senior debt that is assigned an actual or implied B or B− rating.

Ca	**CC**
Bonds which are rated Ca represent obligations which are speculative in a high degree. Such issues are often in default or have other marked shortcomings.	The rating CC typically is applied to debt subordinated to senior debt that is assigned an actual or implied CCC rating.

C	**C**
Bonds which are rated C are the lowest rated class of bonds and issues so rated can be regarded as having extremely poor prospects of ever attaining any real investment standing.	The rating C typically is applied to debt subordinated to senior debt which is assigned an actual or implied CCC− debt rating. The C rating may be used to cover a situation where a bankruptcy petition has been filed, but debt service payments are continued.

CI

The rating CI is reserved for income bonds on which no interest is being paid.

D

Debt rated D is in payment default. The D rating category is used when interest payments or principal payments are not made on the date due even if the applicable grace period has not expired, unless S&P believes that such payments will be made during such grace period. The D rating also will be used upon the filing of a bankruptcy petition if debt service payments are jeopardized.

[b] Plus (+) or Minus (−): The ratings from "AA" to "CCC" may be modified by the addition of a plus or minus sign to show relative standing within the major rating categories.

Table 16-4 shows how the values of ten key credit statistics vary across the six highest rating categories assigned by Standard & Poor's. Note how the interest coverage ratio, fixed charge coverage ratio, cash flow to long-term debt, and cash flow to total debt are all progressively better, the higher the company's senior debt rating. These four measures of a firm's ability to continue to service its debt on a current basis are probably more important than the other six indicators of credit quality. These other indicators also are generally better, the higher the debt rating. Taken together, the ten measures would go a long way toward distinguishing a stronger credit rating from a weaker one.

TABLE 16-4   Senior Debt Ratings as Indicators of Credit Quality[a]

Senior Debt Rating[b]	AAA	AA	A	BBB	BB	B
Interest coverage ratio	10.46x	8.21x	5.53x	3.05x	2.47x	1.87x
Fixed charge coverage ratio[c]	7.48	4.43	2.93	2.30	2.04	1.51
Cash flow/Long-term debt	309.03%	118.44%	75.40%	45.74%	27.02%	18.95%
Cash flow/Total debt	151.40	84.31	60.73	39.44	23.28	16.88
Pretax return on average long-term capital employed	25.60	22.05	18.03	12.10	13.80	12.01
Operating income/Sales	18.67	15.20	11.73	10.18	10.90	8.83
Long-term debt/Capitalization	8.85	18.88	24.46	31.54	42.52	52.04
Total debt/Capitalization, including short-term debt	17.85	24.87	29.11	34.02	45.85	55.69
Total debt/Capitalization, including short-term debt (including 8x rents)	27.44	38.69	43.00	47.02	58.30	63.45
Total liabilities/Tangible shareholders' equity and minority interest	74.44	103.28	109.16	130.54	186.50	238.51

[a] Median of the 3-year simple arithmetic averages for the period 1983–1985 for companies whose senior debt had the indicated rating.
[b] As assigned by Standard & Poor's.
[c] Based on full rental charges, rather than the one-third of rental charges used in the SEC fixed charge coverage calculation.

Source: Debt Ratings Criteria: Industrial Overview (New York: Standard & Poor's, 1986), 51.

Table 16-5 shows that the credit indicators vary over time. In particular, there was a noticeable deterioration in the credit statistics for single-A-rated companies between 1978 and 1982. This deterioration undoubtedly reflects the deterioration in the economy, which fell into a recession in 1982, but also reflects an apparent changing of the standards required to achieve a single-A rating. The credit statistics for a particular rating category at any moment in time are a somewhat imperfect indicator of credit quality. Therefore, many analysts use an average of 3 to 5 years' values for various credit measures in order to set benchmarks that are less susceptible to transitory effects.

Having selected a rating target, a firm can use the values of the key credit statistics of comparable companies whose debt has been assigned the target rating as a rough guide to the ratio targets it should set for itself. A method for accomplishing

TABLE 16-5 Deterioration in Credit Quality between 1978 and 1982 of Companies Whose Senior Debt Was Rated Single-A[a]

	1982	1981	1980	1979	1978
Interest coverage ratio	4.31x	5.55x	6.05x	7.47x	7.94x
Fixed charge coverage ratio[b]	2.70	3.48	3.97	4.85	4.76
Cash flow/Long-term debt	60.07%	72.53%	69.06%	69.31%	70.01%
Cash flow/Total debt	49.17	61.84	55.50	59.40	60.42
Pretax return on average long-term capital employed	16.00	20.83	22.15	23.71	22.28
Operating income/Sales	11.55	12.52	12.75	14.13	14.39
Long-term debt/Capitalization	26.23	25.36	25.74	25.98	26.56
Total debt/Capitalization, including short-term debt	29.66	29.36	30.25	30.53	29.63
Total debt/Capitalization, including short-term debt (including 8x rents)	40.34	40.59	40.38	38.53	39.33
Total liabilities/Tangible shareholders' equity and minority interest	102.26	103.81	105.11	102.85	97.61

[a] Credit statistics represent the annual simple arithmetic average for companies whose senior debt was rated single-A by Standard & Poor's.
[b] Based on full rental charges, rather than the one-third of rental charges used in the SEC fixed charge coverage calculation.
Source: Credit Overview: Industrial Ratings (New York: Standard & Poor's, November 1983), 26.

this is described later in the chapter. For now, three points of caution should be emphasized:

1. Quantitative factors are not the entire story. A deteriorating market position or perceived weaknesses in management will require above-average credit statistics.

2. Achieving an improved credit rating requires a proven track record. Simply achieving improved credit statistics will not necessarily guarantee a higher credit rating; the firm must demonstrate that it can maintain them.

3. The averages may change over time, as illustrated in Table 16-5.

There is empirical justification for our assertion that companies select financial ratio targets. Studies suggest that companies establish debt-to-equity ratio targets and that companies tend to adjust their actual debt-to-equity ratios to their respective targets over time, albeit somewhat slowly, as in the AT&T example in Chapter 15.[14]

IMPORTANT FACTORS AFFECTING A FIRM'S CHOICE OF CAPITAL STRUCTURE   16.3

There are at least four basic considerations involved in a firm's choice of capital structure. This section describes how to analyze each, and the next section illustrates the application of these techniques to Washington Chemical's choice of capital structure.

[14] Marsh (1982); Taggart (1977).

ABILITY TO SERVICE DEBT

A prudent financial manager will not recommend that her firm incur additional debt unless she is confident that the firm will be able to generate sufficient cash, even under adverse conditions, to service it; that is, to pay interest and repay principal on schedule. Many companies appear to maintain a margin of safety in the form of unused debt capacity to keep both the risk of financial distress and the risk that access to the capital markets might be interrupted at a tolerable level.

Various measures of debt servicing capacity are available. One is the interest coverage ratio defined by Equation (16.1). Rental (including lease) payments include an interest component. Fixed charges, which include interest expense and one-third of rental expense, represents a better indicator of true interest expense. To take these factors into account, we can calculate a fixed charge coverage ratio:[15]

$$\frac{\text{Fixed Charge}}{\text{Coverage Ratio}} = \frac{\text{EBIT} + \frac{1}{3} \text{ Rentals}}{\text{Interest Expense} + \frac{1}{3} \text{ Rentals}} \tag{16.2}$$

where EBIT again denotes earnings before interest and income taxes. In Equation (16.2), $\frac{1}{3}$ rentals approximates the interest component of rental expense.

To avoid default, a firm must meet its principal repayment obligations as well as its interest obligations on schedule. A more comprehensive measure of a firm's ability to service its debt obligations is

$$\frac{\text{Debt Service}}{\text{Coverage}} = \frac{\text{EBIT} + \frac{1}{3} \text{ Rentals}}{\text{Interest Expense} + \frac{1}{3} \text{ Rentals} + \frac{\text{Principal Repayments}}{1 - \text{Tax Rate}}} \tag{16.3}$$

In Equation (16.3), the amount of principal repayments must be divided by 1 minus the tax rate because principal repayments are not tax-deductible. They are paid with after-tax dollars, whereas interest expense and rental expense are tax-deductible.

A firm can evaluate the impact of alternative capital structures using **sensitivity analysis**. The firm calculates the interest coverage ratio, fixed charge coverage ratio, and debt service coverage ratio for each capital structure under different projected business scenarios and then compares the calculated values with benchmarks that reflect the firm's desired credit quality. Table 16-4 suggests the following rough benchmarks. If a company in an industry characterized by average operating risk wishes to meet minimum investment-grade standards, it should strive for an annual interest coverage ratio of no less than 3.05 and an annual fixed charge coverage ratio of no less than 2.30 under reasonably conservative "expected case" assumptions and a debt service coverage ratio of no less than 1.00 under "pessimistic" assumptions.[16]

A firm in a highly cyclical industry should set higher interest coverage and fixed charge coverage ratio standards to compensate for the higher level of operating risk, while one in a noncyclical industry can prudently set lower standards. For example, an electric utility firm can set lower coverage ratio standards than a manufacturing firm in a highly competitive industry.

A firm that wishes to maintain single-A-"type" ratios would aim toward an interest coverage ratio of at least 5.53 and a fixed charge coverage ratio of at least 2.93 if it is in an industry of "average" operating risk. Higher or lower standards would be

---

[15] The fixed charge coverage ratio in Equation (16.2) is the one specified by the Securities and Exchange Commission. However, some analysts prefer to use total rentals rather than one-third this amount. For example, see *Debt Ratings Criteria*, 50.

[16] The precise standard set for the debt service coverage ratio will depend, to a certain extent, on the company's confidence in its ability to refinance the debt.

appropriate for companies in industries that are more, or less, cyclical, respectively. More precise benchmarks can be obtained by calculating these three ratios for companies in the same industry that are of the desired credit quality.

ABILITY TO UTILIZE INTEREST TAX SHIELDS FULLY

We showed in Chapter 15 that one of the principal benefits of debt is the tax-deductibility of interest payments. But firms using debt financing must generate sufficient income from operations to claim the deductions.

A firm that does not pay taxes and does not expect to become a taxpayer has less incentive to incur additional debt. The tax shields would go unused, yet the additional debt would increase the risk of incurring the costs of financial distress. Absent any tax shield benefits, the added debt might be harmful to shareholders. Note that a firm that is not currently in a taxpaying position but expects to be in the future must also think twice before incurring additional debt. It can carry tax losses forward, but the added debt will be beneficial only if the expected present value of these tax shields plus the expected value of the reduction in agency costs exceeds the expected present value of the costs of financial distress.

Most companies as part of their regular planning process project their future tax positions. It is important for a firm to test alternative capital structures in light of the firm's projected taxpaying position under different business scenarios. As a practical matter, a firm's capital structure should probably contain no more debt than its future tax position will enable it to exploit. As noted earlier in this chapter, this means that companies in industries that have substantial other tax shelter opportunities, such as the oil and gas (depletion allowances) and steel (depreciation and loss carryforwards) industries, should have lower leverage ratios than companies in other industries.

As we noted in Chapter 11, there are frequent changes to the tax code. Such changes complicate this analysis. For example, it was pointed out in Chapter 15 that the Tax Reform Act of 1986 made sweeping changes in both corporate and personal taxation that have increased the value of corporate debt financing. Such changes, as well as changes in the other factors that affect the capital structure decision, can cause the firm's target capital structure to change over time.

The true tax advantage to additional leverage is difficult to estimate for an individual firm, but studies seem to indicate that the tax benefits to be derived from an additional dollar of borrowing are substantially less than the statutory tax rate and that the tax value of incremental interest deductions varies significantly across industries.[17] The lower the tax advantage to increasing leverage, the smaller the cost of maintaining any particular margin of safety.

PROTECTION AGAINST ILLIQUIDITY AFFORDED BY ITS ASSETS

A firm should not incur additional debt if doing so would involve a significant probability of insolvency. The risk of insolvency will depend not only on the projected coverage of debt service obligations out of earnings before interest and taxes but also on the firm's ability to generate cash through additional borrowing, sale of equity securities, or sale of assets. With regard to the latter, the more liquid a firm's assets, the higher the degree of leverage they are generally capable of supporting. Thus, a

---

[17]Cordes and Sheffrin (1983); Kane, Marcus, and McDonald (1984). One possible explanation for this difference is the variability of future borrowing. See Lewellen and Emery (1986).

real estate company or a credit company can generally support relatively high degrees of leverage.

DESIRED DEGREE OF ACCESS TO THE CAPITAL MARKETS

A firm that plans to undertake a substantial capital expenditure program will want to ensure its uninterrupted access to the capital markets on acceptable terms. To do so, it will have to maintain adequate credit strength. Prior to the development of the new issue junk bond market (the market for new issues of non-investment-grade debt), a firm that is large enough to sell debt publicly could have ensured reasonably uninterrupted access to this market on acceptable terms by maintaining a strong single-A credit standing. The rapid expansion of the junk bond market beginning in 1983 appeared to lessen the need to maintain such a high credit standing strictly for reasons of market access.[18] But the virtual collapse of the junk bond market in early 1990 emphasized the risk inherent in increasing leverage to such an extent that a firm's debt rating falls below investment grade.

We think the junk bond market collapse was due at least in part to bond investors and thrift insurance regulators finally appreciating that the Principle of Risk-Return Trade-Off also applies to junk bonds: The high rates of interest paid on junk bonds do not provide a free lunch but compensate for the higher default rate on junk bonds compared to investment grade bonds.[19] We also think the new issue junk bond market will eventually revive, though probably not on as grand a scale as before its 1990 collapse. Firms that are tempted by that market's reopening to achieve a degree of leverage consistent with a noninvestment grade rating should also bear in mind the Principle of Risk-Return Trade-Off: The benefits of higher leverage must be weighed against the higher risks, including the increased risk that market access may be impeded should the junk bond market once again contract sharply, suddenly, and unexpectedly.

CORPORATE DEBT MANAGEMENT OVER TIME

The four factors just discussed all affect a firm's capital structure target. Additional factors, in particular market imperfections, affect how a firm implements its long-term financing program in light of this target. While companies strive to achieve a target debt-to-equity ratio, their actual debt-to-equity ratios tend to move toward the respective targets rather slowly.

One of the more important factors affecting the specific issuance decision is the cost of issuance. Table 14-3 in Chapter 14 indicates the existence of significant economies of scale in securities issuance expenses. One large issue is cheaper than two or more smaller issues from the standpoint of transaction costs. A firm that needs only a relatively small amount of external funds would tend to draw down on bank lines of credit rather than issue securities. Similarly, the cost of servicing an outstanding debt issue, the cost of monitoring compliance with debt covenants (because they may differ between debt issues), the cost of refunding bond issues, and the cost of securing covenant waivers (when required or desired) are all subject to economies of scale.

Perhaps even more important is the difference in issuance expenses by security

---

[18] Perry and Taggart (1988) describe the development of the market and assess its significance.

[19] Two studies that document the higher default rates on junk bonds are Altman (1989) and Asquith, Mullins, and Wolff (1989).

TABLE 16-6   Summary of Corporate Sources and Uses of Funds 1978–1987[a] (in Billions)

	1978	1979	1980	1981	1982	1983	1984	1985	1986	1987[b]
Uses of Funds										
Capital investment[c]	$213.2	$249.4	$233.3	$288.1	$247.5	$300.7	$390.3	$352.4	$349.7	$372.1
Liquid assets and other	39.9	29.1	43.8	53.1	68.6	79.8	80.9	102.1	88.7	47.8
Total uses	$253.1	$278.5	$277.1	$341.2	$316.1	$380.5	$471.2	$454.5	$438.4	$419.9
Sources of Funds										
Internal cash generation	$217.2	$228.7	$237.1	$285.6	$287.3	$352.5	$402.6	$417.0	$426.2	$424.5
Cash dividends[d]	(48.0)	(54.7)	(61.7)	(67.6)	(72.0)	(78.0)	(81.0)	(82.9)	(89.1)	(95.3)
Net internal	169.2	174.0	175.4	218.0	215.3	274.5	321.6	334.1	337.1	329.2
Debt (net)	81.6	100.0	79.1	119.5	97.3	70.1	209.5	172.7	161.3	127.8
Equity issued for cash[d]	13.0	15.6	25.6	24.4	27.6	48.2	20.8	31.2	40.3	38.2
Equity retired[d,e]	(10.7)	(11.1)	(3.0)	(20.7)	(24.1)	(12.3)	(80.7)	(83.5)	(100.3)	(75.3)
Net equity issued (Retired)	2.3	4.5	22.6	3.7	3.5	35.9	(59.9)	(52.3)	(60.0)	(37.1)
Total sources	$253.1	$278.5	$277.1	$341.2	$316.1	$380.5	$471.2	$454.5	$438.4	$419.9

[a] Nonfarm, nonfinancial corporations.
[b] Estimated by Salomon Brothers Inc.
[c] Includes net receivables.
[d] Includes common and preferred stock.
[e] Net of equity issued upon conversion of debt or in a stock-for-debt swap.

Source: Prospects for Financial Markets (New York: Salomon Brothers, various issues).

type (or source of funds). Retained earnings involve no issuance expenses. Issuing securities does involve issuance costs. Debt is cheapest; preferred stock is next cheapest; and a new issue of common stock is most expensive, as Table 14–3 indicates. Relative issuance expenses are capable of explaining the pecking order theory of financing:[20] Firms first look to retained earnings to finance capital investment projects. To the extent they require additional funds, they prefer to issue debt securities rather than equity securities. If they can find profitable opportunities to issue an innovative security, such a security will jump, at least temporarily, to the top of the external financing pecking order.[21] Table 16–6 provides support for the pecking order theory. Internally generated funds provide the bulk of the funds for capital investment projects, and companies appear to be loath to issue common stock. Indeed, in each of the years between 1984 and 1987, nonfinancial corporations retired more equity than they issued.

A firm might deviate from the pecking order when it decides to pursue a capital investment project whose cost exceeds the amount of retained earnings available but the firm does not wish to reduce the cash dividend to common stockholders. It might also deviate to take advantage of an attractive but temporary financing opportunity; for example, the opportunity to issue tax-exempt securities prior to the date the authority to issue such securities expires. Just prior to passage of the Tax Reform Act of 1986, many companies rushed to issue tax-exempt industrial revenue bonds

[20] Myers (1986a) discusses the theoretical underpinnings of the pecking order theory.
[21] Myers (1986b) points out that the rewards to innovation are quickly eliminated as imitators enter the market.

and pollution control revenue bonds in anticipation of the severe restrictions that the act would impose on such forms of tax-exempt financing by corporations.

16.4   CHOOSING AN APPROPRIATE CAPITAL STRUCTURE

This section integrates the five considerations just discussed into a single framework for determining an appropriate capital structure. The basic framework for this analysis consists of a **comparative credit analysis**, which suggests a range of target capital structures that might be appropriate, and a **pro forma financial structure analysis**, which shows the impact of the alternatives within the target range on the firm's credit statistics and reported financial results, and indicates whether the firm will be able to utilize tax shield benefits fully. This enables the firm to select a specific target capital structure. We illustrate this method of analysis by demonstrating how a firm, Washington Chemical Corporation, decided that its capital structure should contain ⅓ debt and ⅔ common equity.

CHOICE OF DEBT RATING TARGET

In practice, the most widely used technique for selecting an appropriate capital structure utilizes a comparative credit analysis. This approach is an application of the Behavioral Principle that bases the choice of capital structure on the capital structures of comparable companies whose senior debt carries the desired bond rating. The approach involves the following steps:

- Select the desired rating objective.
- Identify a set of comparable companies and select from among these the companies whose senior debt has the desired senior debt rating.
- Perform a comparative credit analysis of these companies in order to define the capital structure (or range of capital structures) most consistent with this rating objective.

Earlier in this chapter we discussed five principal considerations that enter into the capital structure decision. The choice of rating actually encompasses three of the five. A debt rating provides the rating agency's assessment of the issuer's ability to service its debt. As such, the rating takes into account the degree of protection afforded by the liquidity of the firm's assets. In addition, as we noted in Chapter 15, the rating also affects the breadth of the market for the bonds and thus determines to a great extent the issuer's ease of access to the capital markets. The only two of the five considerations not encompassed in the choice of rating are the issuer's ability to utilize tax benefits and the debt management considerations, such as issuance expenses, that determine the pecking order of the various sources of funds. We must evaluate these factors separately.

The choice of rating objective is senior management's. As noted earlier, a rating of single-A seems to be a reasonable target that provides a compromise between ensuring relatively uninterrupted capital market access and realizing the full tax-saving potential of added leverage. However, more conservative companies and companies that have very heavy future financing programs might strive for a higher rating, and other companies that are willing to bear greater financial risk might set a lower rating target.

COMPARATIVE ANALYSIS

Table 16-7 illustrates a comparative credit analysis of specialty chemicals companies that are comparable to Washington Chemical Corporation. There are six specialty chemicals companies with rated debt outstanding. The senior-debt ratings (Moody's/Standard & Poor's) range from a low of Ba1/BB to a high of A2/A.

CHOICE OF FINANCIAL RATIO TARGETS   Washington Chemical's top management, upon the recommendation of the firm's chief financial officer, decided that a senior debt rating "comfortably within" the single-A range would be appropriate. Three of the companies in Table 16-7 have at least one senior debt rating in the single-A category, and Johnson Chemical and Wilson Chemical are rated in the middle of the single-A category by both agencies.

Washington Chemical's financial staff prepared the comparative credit analysis. The analysis shows that Washington Chemical is significantly more profitable than one of the A2/A issuers and only slightly less profitable than the other. Washington Chemical's debt-to-capitalization, cash-flow-to-debt, and fixed charge coverage ratios fall between the higher and lower of the two values for each ratio exhibited by the two A2/A specialty chemicals companies. Washington Chemical's ratios are substantially better than those of Myers Chemicals, which is a borderline triple-B–single-A. Washington Chemical concluded from this analysis that its financial condition is of medium-grade single-A quality.

One point regarding the ratios in Table 16-7 requires clarification. We have emphasized the importance of basing financial decisions on market values, but the financial ratios in Table 16-7, as well as those in Tables 16-4 and 16-5, are based on book values. Market values and the factors that create market values are not being ignored, but it is simply impractical to attempt to calculate all the ratios in Table 16-7 on the basis of market values. The rating agencies consider the market value of a firm's assets in assessing its leverage. But they view these assets on a liquidity basis rather than on a going-concern basis.[22] Thus, the true debt-to-capitalization ratio should value the common equity component on the basis of the liquidation value of the assets rather than on the basis of either the current book value of equity or the prevailing share price of the firm's common stock (which reflects the value of the firm on a going-concern basis). Assets such as proven oil and gas reserves that are relatively liquid will support a higher degree of leverage than less liquid assets. New plant and equipment will tend to support greater leverage than an equal book value amount of antiquated plant. But determining these liquidating values is necessarily subjective because liquid markets for fixed assets generally do not exist and appraisals generally are not available. Still, the quality of assets will tend to vary systematically from one industry to another. Thus, for a particular rating category, the debt-to-capitalization ratios for companies in one industry whose debt bears that rating, when compared to the debt-to-capitalization ratios for companies in another industry whose debt bears the same rating, will reflect interindustry differences in liquidating asset value, among other factors.

Similarly, the rating agencies evaluate the issuer's accounting methods to adjust the reported profit measures to a reasonably comparable basis for the issuers in each industry. They also use information reported in the footnotes to the financial statements to adjust long-term debt to include "off-balance-sheet liabilities" such as unfunded pension fund liabilities, noncapitalized lease obligations, and take-or-pay

[22]*Debt Ratings Criteria*, 26.

TABLE 16-7 Comparative Credit Analysis of Specialty Chemicals Companies with Rated Debt Outstanding (Dollar Amounts in Millions)

	Washington Chemical Corporation	Myers Chemicals Corp.	Northwest Chemicals Inc.	Delaware Chemicals Corp.	Western Industries	Johnson Chemical Inc.	Wilson Chemical Corp.
Senior debt rating (Moody's/Standard & Poor's)	—	A3/BBB+	Ba1/BBB−	Baa2/BBB−	Ba1/BB	A2/A	A2/A
Profitability:							
Operating profit margin	7.4%	5.9%	1.9%	4.5%	8.9%	4.1%	9.2%
Net profit margin	3.9	2.6	1.0	2.3	2.2	2.3	4.1
Return on assets	4.8	3.2	2.2	4.9	2.8	4.3	4.9
Return on common equity	10.3	9.2	5.0	13.9	8.8	10.8	10.0
Capitalization:							
Short-term debt	$16	$60	$10	$10	$16	$8	$36
Senior long-term debt	$158	$144	$ 49	$163	$110	$140	$245
Capitalized lease obligations	—	22	10	20	—	—	1
Subordinated long-term debt	—	—	—	13	80	8	—
Total long-term debt	158	166	59	196	190	148	246
Minority interest	—	—	3	2	—	—	—
Preferred equity	—	2	35	5	—	—	—
Common equity	321	253	165	334	162	278	659
Total capitalization	$479	$421	$262	$537	$352	$426	$905
Long-term debt ratio	33%	39%	23%	36%	54%	35%	27%
Total-debt-to-adjusted-capitalization ratio	35	47	25	38	56	36	30
Cash-flow-to-long-term debt ratio	60	42	45	35	27	51	63
Cash-flow-to-total-debt ratio	55	31	39	33	25	49	55
Liquidity:							
Current ratio	2.4x	1.9x	2.7x	2.1x	1.9x	2.2x	2.6x
Fixed Charge Coverage Ratio:							
Last 12 months	3.5x	2.3x	2.4x	3.3x	2.0x	3.3x	3.7x
Latest fiscal year	4.3	4.0	3.8	2.9	2.3	4.4	4.2
One year prior	5.6	3.0	3.2	2.7	2.8	5.4	5.7
Two years prior	6.3	4.0	2.8	2.2	3.8	7.9	4.9

contract obligations and other project-financing-related liabilities. The latter two tend to be greater in certain industries than in others.

Thus, an analysis like the one in Table 16-7 that is based on book values rather than true economic values is capable of providing meaningful conclusions. Such an analysis is necessarily imperfect. But if comparable companies are chosen carefully and differences between the comparable companies and the firm that is the object of the analysis are carefully weighed, the comparative credit analysis can lead to useful financial policy guidelines.

As noted, the choice of capital structure objective ultimately requires judgment. Before reaching a decision, Washington Chemical also consulted its investment bankers and evaluated its expected profitability. Washington Chemical believes that its profitability will exceed that of its single-A competitors. Thus, it might be a little more aggressive than its single-A competitors in its use of leverage. On the other hand, it might decide to issue debt publicly (rather than continue to borrow exclusively from banks), which would argue for conservatism. Based on its careful consideration of all these factors and the average ratios indicated in Table 16-4, Washington Chemical decided that the following financial ratio ranges would be consistent with its objectives:

Annual fixed charge coverage ratio: 3.50x to 4.00x

Annual cash-flow-to-total-debt ratio: 50% to 60%

Long-term debt ratio: 30% to 35%

In applying the third of these tests, Washington Chemical included the permanent component of short-term debt as part of long-term debt.

Pro Forma Analysis

Before deciding where to aim within each of these ranges (or whether to be more conservative in its use of leverage), Washington Chemical thought it important to

- Confirm its ability to utilize fully the implied volume of tax shield benefits, particularly under somewhat adverse conditions;

- Gauge the impact of these obligations on its future external financing requirements; and

- Determine what impact, if any, this capital structure policy might have on its dividend policy.

Table 16-8 contains a pro forma financial structure analysis. If Washington Chemical is to achieve and maintain a long-term debt ratio within its target range, 30%–35% of its financing will be long-term debt. Also, in evaluating its future financial condition, Washington Chemical realizes the importance of considering a reasonably pessimistic case as well as its expected case for the projected operating results. Consequently, there are four cases considered in Table 16-8 that correspond to two degrees of leverage (long-term debt ratio of 30% and 35%) and two operating scenarios (10% growth and 5% growth).

It is evident from Case 1 and Case 2 that Washington Chemical could justify a 35% long-term debt ratio in the expected case scenario. Both the fixed charge coverage and cash-flow-to-total-debt ratios increase steadily and remain comfortably within their respective target ranges. Moreover, Washington Chemical can utilize fully the tax benefits of ownership and can claim fully all interest deductions. Washington Chemical has established a policy of paying out one-third of its earnings as

TABLE 16-8 Pro Forma Financial Structure Analysis for Washington Chemical Corporation (Dollar Amounts in Millions)

		Projected Ahead				
	Initial	*1 Year*	*2 Years*	*3 Years*	*4 Years*	*5 Years*
Case 1: Leverage at upper end of range/expected case operating results:						
Pre-interest taxable income[a]	$61	$67	$74	$81	$89	$98
Interest	18	20	22	24	26	28
Surplus (Deficit)[b]	$43	$47	$52	$57	$63	$70
Earnings before fixed charges and income taxes[c]	$70	$77	$85	$93	$102	$113
Fixed charges[d]	20	22	24	26	28	30
Fixed charge coverage	3.5x	3.5x	3.5x	3.6x	3.6x	3.8x
Net income[c]	$30	$33	$36	$42	$45	$51
Noncash expenses	65	72	79	84	94	102
Cash flow[c]	95	105	115	126	139	153
Dividends	(10)	(11)	(12)	(14)	(15)	(17)
Internal cash generation	85	94	103	112	124	136
Capital expenditures	(125)	(125)	(125)	(135)	(150)	(160)
Cash required	$40	$31	$22	$23	$26	$24
External debt requirement[e]	$20	$17	$14	$15	$17	$17
External equity requirement[e]	$20	$14	$ 8	$ 8	$ 9	$ 7
Cash flow to total debt[f]	55%	55%	56%	57%	59%	60%
Case 2: Leverage at lower end of range/expected case operating results:						
Pre-interest taxable income[a]	$61	$67	$74	$81	$89	$98
Interest	18	19	21	23	25	26
Surplus (Deficit)[b]	$43	$48	$53	$58	$64	$72
Earnings before fixed charges and income taxes[c]	$70	$77	$85	$93	$102	$113
Fixed charges[d]	20	21	23	25	27	28
Fixed charge coverage	3.5x	3.7x	3.7x	3.7x	3.8x	4.0x
Net income[c]	$30	$33	$36	$42	$45	$51
Noncash expenses	65	72	79	84	94	102
Cash flow[c]	95	105	115	126	139	153
Dividends	(10)	(11)	(12)	(14)	(15)	(17)
Internal cash generation	85	94	103	112	124	136
Capital expenditures	(125)	(125)	(125)	(135)	(150)	(160)
Cash required	$40	$31	$22	$23	$26	$24

TABLE 16-8   (*continued*)

	Initial	Projected Ahead				
		1 Year	**2 Years**	**3 Years**	**4 Years**	**5 Years**
Case 2: Leverage at lower end of range/expected case operating results (continued):						
External debt requirement[g]	$17	$15	$12	$13	$15	$15
External equity requirement[g]	$23	$16	$10	$10	$11	$9
Cash flow to total debt[f]	55%	56%	57%	59%	61%	63%
Case 3: Leverage at upper end of range/pessimistic case operating results:						
Pre-interest taxable income[a]	$61	$64	$67	$71	$74	$78
Interest	18	20	22	24	27	30
Surplus (Deficit)[b]	$43	$44	$45	$47	$47	$48
Earnings before fixed charges and income taxes[c]	$70	$74	$78	$82	$86	$90
Fixed charges[d]	20	22	24	26	29	32
Fixed charge coverage	3.5x	3.4x	3.3x	3.2x	3.0x	2.8x
Net income[c]	$30	$30	$33	$33	$33	$33
Noncash expenses	65	70	72	77	82	88
Cash flow[c]	95	100	105	110	115	121
Dividends	(10)	(10)	(11)	(11)	(11)	(11)
Internal cash generation	85	90	94	99	104	110
Capital expenditures	(125)	(125)	(125)	(135)	(150)	(160)
Cash required	$40	$35	$31	$36	$46	$50
External debt requirement[e]	$20	$18	$17	$19	$23	$25
External equity requirement[e]	$20	$17	$14	$17	$23	$25
Cash flow to total debt[f]	55%	52%	50%	48%	46%	44%
Case 4: Leverage at lower end of range/pessimistic case operating results:						
Pre-interest taxable income[a]	$61	$64	$67	$71	$74	$78
Interest	18	19	21	23	26	28
Surplus (Deficit)[b]	$43	$45	$46	$48	$48	$50
Earnings before fixed charges and income taxes[c]	$70	$74	$78	$82	$86	$90
Fixed charges[d]	20	21	23	25	28	30
Fixed charge coverage	3.5x	3.5x	3.4x	3.3x	3.1x	3.0x
Net income[c]	$30	$30	$33	$33	$33	$33
Noncash expenses	65	70	72	77	82	88

TABLE 16-8   (*continued*)

	Initial	Projected Ahead				
		1 Year	2 Years	3 Years	4 Years	5 Years
Case 4: Leverage at lower end of range/pessimistic case operating results:						
Noncash expenses	65	70	72	77	82	88
Cash flow[c]	95	100	105	110	115	121
Dividends	(10)	(10)	(11)	(11)	(11)	(11)
Internal cash generation	85	90	94	99	104	110
Capital expenditures	(125)	(125)	(125)	(135)	(150)	(160)
Cash required	$40	$35	$31	$36	$46	$50
External debt requirement[g]	$17	$16	$15	$17	$20	$22
External equity requirement[g]	$23	$19	$16	$19	$26	$28
Cash flow to total debt[f]	55%	53%	51%	50%	48%	46%

[a] As computed for federal corporate income tax purposes. Estimated to grow at 10% per annum in the "expected case" and 5% per annum in the "pessimistic case."
[b] Calculated as pre-interest taxable income minus interest.
[c] Estimated to grow at 10% per annum in the "expected case" and 5% per annum in the "pessimistic case."
[d] Assumes rental expense of $6 million per annum.
[e] Calculated to preserve a ratio of 35% long-term debt financing to 65% additional common equity. In Case 1 for the initial year, net income is $26 and dividends are $10, leaving retained earnings of $16 for the year. Capital expenditures exceed internal cash generation by $40 (= $125 − 85). External financing plus the addition to retained earnings equals $56 (= 40 + 16), of which 35% must be long-term debt, indicating $20 (= .35 × 56) of external debt and $20 (= $40 − 20) of external equity.
[f] The amount of total debt at the end of the initial year is $174. The debt level for any single year projected ahead is the initial amount plus the sum of the annual external debt requirements up to the year in question. In Case 1 for the initial year, the debt level is $174 (= 16 + 158 from Table 16-7). The debt level projected ahead 2 years is $205 (= $174 + 17 + 14), so that cash flow to total debt equals 56% (= 115/205).
[g] Calculated to preserve a ratio of 30% long-term debt financing to 70% additional common equity. See footnote e for an explanation of the method of calculation.

cash dividends. Adhering to that policy and adhering to its target capital structure would require a modest amount of external equity financing ($46 million over 5 years if the long-term debt ratio is 35% and $56 million if it is only 30%). So Washington Chemical might have to compromise on its policy objectives.[23]

Under a more pessimistic operating scenario, Case 3 and Case 4 illustrate that Washington Chemical's fixed charge coverage and cash-flow-to-total-debt ratios would eventually fall below their respective target ranges. The deterioration is less severe in Case 4 because the long-term debt ratio is only 30%. However, the external equity financing requirement is greater. Because there is some likelihood that the pessimistic case will occur, Washington Chemical decided not to use the maximum leverage and financed itself with a leverage ratio of ⅓. Because the analysis in Table 16-8 shows that Washington Chemical can fully utilize all available tax deductions even in the pessimistic case, the firm has no plans to use leveraged lease or preferred stock financing. Thus, its financing ratios will be ⅓ conventional long-term debt and ⅔ common equity.

[23] We discuss dividend policy in Chapters 17 and 18. We explain there why there would be no advantage in a perfect capital market environment to a firm to pay cash dividends and sell new shares at the same time. In problem C8 at the end of Chapter 18, we ask you to reconsider the problem facing Washington Chemical in light of its apparently conflicting capital structure and dividend objectives.

OTHER ASPECTS OF THE CAPITAL STRUCTURE DECISION

Washington Chemical's target capital structure contains only long-term debt and common equity. Companies often adopt more complex capital structures that include one or more layers of subordinated debt, convertible debt, capitalized lease obligations, preferred equity, or other forms of capital.

SUBORDINATED DEBT   Holders of subordinated debt rank behind senior debtholders in the event of default. If strict priority was preserved in bankruptcy, a layer of subordinated debt would be just as beneficial to senior debtholders as additional equity. In addition, the interest payments to subordinated debtholders are tax-deductible, whereas payments to shareholders are not, which benefits the issuer. However, interest payments and principal repayments must be made in a timely fashion on subordinated debt as well as on senior debt for the issuer to avoid default.

In view of the greater exposure to default risk, the rating agencies generally rate subordinated debt one step below senior debt if the senior debt is rated investment grade and two steps below senior debt if the senior debt is rated speculative grade.[24] The rating differential typically adds about 25 basis points (a 0.25% higher coupon rate for debt that is issued at par value, or more in the case of speculative-grade issuers), to the cost of a new debt issue. Moreover, because strict priority is not always preserved in bankruptcy, the rating agencies will generally add nonconvertible subordinated debt to senior debt for purposes of their ratio calculations. In view of the higher interest cost, $1 of subordinated debt has a more severe impact than $1 of senior debt on a firm's coverage and cash-flow-to-debt ratios. Consequently, investment-grade manufacturing companies seldom find it advantageous to issue nonconvertible subordinated debt.

Finance companies, on the other hand, typically do issue subordinated debt. Because of the comparatively close matching of the maturity structures of their assets and their liabilities, credit companies can support a high degree of leverage. Because the bulk of their business consists of lending funds at a favorable spread over their funding costs, a well-run finance company will have the capacity to use fully the interest tax shields, even when it is very highly leveraged. The subordinated debt, like equity, will provide comfort to senior lenders and tax deductions to the issuer, which equity would not provide.

Subordinated debt is also typically a large component of a firm's capital structure in a leveraged buyout. Because of the extreme degrees of leverage in leveraged buyouts, agency problems are potentially acute. As pointed out in Chapter 15, agency costs are capable of explaining the significance of capital structure to firm valuation, even in the absence of tax factors. In the typical leveraged buyout, the outside equity investors (i.e., other than management) own the subordinated debt (or the junior subordinated debt if there is more than one class of subordinated debt). The subordinated debt enables the outside equity investors to resolve potential agency problems that could arise between themselves and the managers who are also shareholders. But the debt is subordinated to senior debt so as not to create additional agency problems vis-à-vis senior lenders.

Companies customarily issue convertible debt on a subordinated basis. Since both

---

[24] For example, a senior debt rating of A2/A would imply a subordinated debt rating of A3/A-. Conversely, a senior debt rating can be inferred from a subordinated debt rating when a company has only rated subordinated debt outstanding. For example, Western Industries has convertible subordinated debt outstanding, which is rated Ba3/B+. This implies the senior debt rating of Ba1/BB (i.e., up two notches because it is speculative grade) indicated in Table 16-7.

issuers and investors expect the issue to be converted into common equity within a matter of perhaps a few years anyway, it is appropriate that convertible debt be junior to nonconvertible debt with respect to bankruptcy priority. Hence, issuing convertible debt on a senior basis would not normally lead to significant cost savings.

CAPITALIZED LEASE OBLIGATIONS   Companies that cannot fully utilize the tax benefits of ownership often find it advantageous to lease assets from entities that can claim these tax deductions and are willing to pay something for them in the form of reduced lease payments. But failure to make a timely lease payment places a firm in default under the lease agreement. Consequently, lease obligations are really a form of secured debt obligation. The rating agencies customarily include capitalized lease obligations, which are reported on the face of the balance sheet, in long-term debt. The decision whether to take on capitalized lease obligations or to borrow on a conventional basis thus hinges principally on tax considerations, as discussed in Chapter 21.

PREFERRED EQUITY   As discussed in Chapter 14, preferred stock is a hybrid security, incorporating certain debt features and certain equity features. Failure to make a timely preferred dividend or preferred sinking fund payment will not put the issuer into default. Consequently, substituting preferred stock for a portion of a firm's debt will enhance the position of debtholders in the event of default. However, companies normally treat their preferred stock payment obligations as though they were fixed. Consequently, if a firm issues a significant amount of preferred stock, particularly if it contains a sinking fund, these payment obligations can impair the credit standing of the firm's debt securities.[25]

For a nonregulated firm, preferred equity financing can be a profitable alternative to debt financing when the firm does not expect to have to pay income taxes for several years and sells the preferred equity to corporate investors, who can avail themselves of the tax exemption on 70% of dividends received.[26] The growth in the market for adjustable rate preferred stock and money market preferred stock can be attributed in large part to the tax asymmetry that results when a nontaxable corporation issues such securities, rather than commercial paper, to corporate investors.[27]

16.5   EFFECTING CHANGES IN CAPITAL STRUCTURE

This chapter concludes with a discussion of a practical problem that frequently arises in capital structure analysis. Following a change in management or a change in management philosophy, a firm might reassess its capital structure in the manner described in this chapter. Suppose that it finds that its desired capital structure differs significantly from its current capital structure. What should the firm do?

The firm has two basic choices. It could alter its capital structure slowly by adjusting its future financing mix appropriately. For example, suppose a firm's target capital structure consists of 35% long-term debt and 65% common equity, and its current capital structure contains 25% long-term debt and 75% common equity.

[25] As long as preferred equity represents no more than 5% of a company's capitalization, if it is nonregulated, 10% if it is a natural gas or telephone utility, or 15% if it is an electric utility, the use of preferred equity financing will not normally impair the company's senior debt rating. *Corporate and International Ratings* (New York: Standard & Poor's Corporation, 1983), 83–84.
[26] Fooladi and Roberts (1986) demonstrate the existence of this tax arbitrage opportunity.
[27] Alderson, Brown, and Lummer (1987); Winger, Chen, Martin, Petty, and Hayden (1986).

The firm could cure this underleveraged condition by financing with, say, 50% long-term debt and 50% common equity until its long-term debt ratio reaches 35%. As noted earlier, evidence suggests that, on average, companies tend to move toward their target capital structures slowly. However, this means that the firm's capital structure continues to be suboptimal for as long as it takes the firm to correct the condition. Moreover, the firm's future financing mix would also periodically deviate from the desired 35%-65% mix.

Alternatively, the firm could alter its capital structure more quickly through an exchange offer, recapitalization offer, debt or share repurchase, or stock-for-debt swap. This would enable the firm to begin employing immediately a mix of financing that conforms to its desired capital structure. This approach is not without cost either. The firm will incur transaction costs, and there will be signaling effects associated with the capital structure change.

If a firm's capital structure deviates from its target capital structure and the deviation in capital structure corresponds to one full rating category or more, an exchange offer or some other type of transaction designed to effect an immediate change in capital structure is probably warranted. If the firm believes it is underleveraged, the announcement of such a transaction designed to increase the firm's leverage can be expected to increase the firm's share price.[28] If the firm is less than one full category away from its rating objective (e.g., it is a weak single-A and it wants to become a strong single-A), altering its retention ratio and its external financing mix is probably more appropriate.

SOLUTION TO HEWLETT-PACKARD'S LEVERAGE CHOICE

With the benefits of the guidelines for managing capital structure developed in this chapter, let us return to Hewlett-Packard's leverage choice. First, how significant an impact on Hewlett-Packard's credit statistics would result from a small increase in financial leverage?

Figure 16-3 provides a pro forma analysis of the effect of borrowing $100 million to finance a share repurchase. Such a transaction would not affect the asset side of the balance sheet. The $100 million size was selected arbitrarily. If we find that a $100 million borrowing with share repurchase would have a favorable impact, we can then consider larger transactions.

Borrowing $100 million to repurchase common stock would have an inconsequential impact on Hewlett-Packard's credit statistics. Because of the high level of short-term debt relative to long-term debt, the credit statistics based on total debt are more relevant than those based exclusively on long-term debt. Glancing back at Table 16-4, Hewlett-Packard's pro forma credit statistics in Figure 16-3 are consistent with a AAA rating, particularly when we take into account the amount of cash and marketable securities, which represent more than twice the amount of total debt.

Second, can Hewlett-Packard fully use the tax benefits of asset ownership and the added interest tax shields? A footnote to the financial statements in Hewlett-Packard's 1987 annual report reveals that Hewlett-Packard did not pay current federal income taxes in 1985 or 1987 and that the $21 million paid in 1986 was more than offset by the combined $26 million of refunds for 1985 and 1987. The footnote

---

[28] Masulis (1980, 1983) finds that the stock market has generally reacted favorably to exchange offers and recapitalizations that increase leverage but negatively when the transaction has the opposite effect.

FIGURE 16-3

Pro forma analysis of impact
of increase in leverage on
Hewlett-Packard Company
(dollar amounts in millions).

	Actual 1987	Pro Forma $100 Million Borrowing to Repurchase Shares
Interest and Fixed Charge Coverage:		
Earnings before interest and taxes	$ 1,047[a]	$ 1,047
Interest expense	85	95[b]
Interest coverage	12.32x	11.02x
Fixed charge coverage[c]	8.40	7.80
Cash Flow to Debt:		
Cash flow	$ 1,127	$ 1,120[d]
Long-term debt	88	188
Total debt	1,067	1,167
Cash flow to long-term debt	12.81x	5.96x
Cash flow to total debt	1.06	0.96
Debt to Capitalization:		
Long-term debt	$ 88	$ 188
Total debt	1,067	1,167
Capitalization	5,110	5,110
Long-term debt to capitalization[e]	1.72%	3.68%
Total debt to adjusted capitalization[f]	17.52	19.17
Cash and marketable securities	$ 2,645	$2,645
Cash and marketable securities to:		
Long-term debt	30.06x	14.07x
Total debt	2.48	2.27

[a] Year-end balance sheet lists $979 million of notes payable in addition to $88 million of long-term debt. Interest cost of total debt is assumed to be 8%.
[b] Interest cost of new debt is assumed to be 10% per annum.
[c] Reflects fixed charge component ($45 million) of rental expense.
[d] Assumes marginal income tax rate of 34%, indicating incremental after-tax interest expense amounting to $7 million per annum.
[e] Capitalization equals long-term debt plus shareholders' equity.
[f] Adjusted capitalization equals capitalization plus short-term debt.

also reveals an aggregate of $76 million of research and development tax credits plus $30 million of investment tax credits for the 3 years. The critical factor in determining whether Hewlett-Packard might benefit from an increase in leverage is the firm's ability to use the interest tax shields. Although they were not U.S. federal taxpayers during this time, Hewlett-Packard should examine the extent to which foreign borrowing might be used to reduce its foreign tax liabilities.

The Tax Reform Act of 1986 phased out the investment tax credit and reduced the tax benefits from accelerated depreciation. Therefore, Hewlett-Packard will not be able to generate additional investment tax credits in the future. However, the provision for research and development tax credits continues. Consequently, depending upon the size of Hewlett-Packard's future research and development budgets, the firm may not be able to use additional federal interest tax shields.

Figure 16-1 also indicates that at least over the past 3 years, Hewlett-Packard has internally generated more than $3.0 billion but needed only $1.6 billion for capital investment purposes. Indeed, the firm has spent $747 million repurchasing shares. The pecking order theory would explain the absence of long-term borrowing during this period.

We conclude that while Hewlett-Packard's financial statements might give the appearance of underleveraging, it is not clear that increasing the firm's leverage will increase its market value.

SUMMARY

Choosing an appropriate capital structure involves balancing the net tax advantage and agency cost benefits of additional leverage against the additional risk of insolvency and the cost of reduced financial flexibility that would result from increased leverage. Simultaneously, transaction costs and information effects must also be considered. Unfortunately, these costs do not lend themselves to precise measurement. As a result, the "best" capital structure cannot be pinpointed. From a practical standpoint, the best the firm can do under present circumstances is determine an appropriate capital structure based on its desired rating objective and the senior debt ratings and capital structure choices of comparable companies. This basic approach is reasonable in view of the evidence regarding systematic differences in observed capital structure across industries.

This chapter described and illustrated a procedure a firm can use to select an appropriate capital structure. The procedure involves two important steps. First, the firm conducts a comparative credit analysis. This involves identifying a set of comparable companies from an operating standpoint. These companies will have com-

DECISION SUMMARY BOX

The following procedures are useful in managing capital structure:

- Determine the *rating objective*. This objective reflects management's desired margin of safety with respect to the risk of financial distress and the risk of impeded access to the capital markets.

- Conduct a *comparative credit analysis* of companies with rated debt outstanding in order to determine the degree of leverage that is consistent with the chosen rating. It is particularly important to select companies with similar asset portfolios because asset type affects the costs of financial distress and the degree of leverage that can be supported at any rating level. It is also important to select companies that are comparable in size because other things being equal, the larger a firm, the proportionately more debt the rating agencies will tolerate at any rating level.

- Determine the values of the *key financial ratios that characterize leverage*. Three such ratios that are particularly meaningful are annual fixed charge coverage ratio, annual cash-flow-to-total-debt ratio, and long-term debt ratio. However, no three ratios can tell the whole story, so many analysts use

additional financial ratios to define the target capital structure.

- Conduct a *pro forma financial analysis* to test the firm's ability to use fully both the tax benefits of ownership under its planned capital expenditure program and the interest tax shields if it finances in accordance with its target capital structure. Also test the impact on financial ratios of different future operating scenarios to determine what adjustment to the target capital structure is appropriate in light of the firm's expected future operating environment.

- Determine the need for and desirability of a *share repurchase or other form of transaction* to adjust capital structure sharply.

- Specify the *long-term financing program* in light of the current capital structure, the capital structure target, transaction costs, and other market imperfections. This step involves determining the extent to which the firm should deviate from tapping long-term funds sources in the usual pecking order. For example, an opportunity to issue an innovative security or to take advantage of a temporary tax-advantaged opportunity would justify such a deviation.

parable operating risk profiles, and because corporate tax positions also tend to vary systematically across industries, are likely to have reasonably comparable tax situations. The values of the key financial ratios for each firm in the set are then calculated to determine the relationship between senior debt rating and financial structure within the set of comparable companies.

A bond rating serves as a surrogate for both the relative risk of financial distress and the relative degree of free access to the capital markets. A senior debt rating in the single-A range connotes very modest risk of financial distress and is usually sufficient to ensure uninterrupted access to the capital markets on acceptable terms. The choice of rating together with the results of the comparative credit analysis permit a firm to specify reasonable ranges of variation of the key financial ratios that define its financial structure.

The second step in the procedure involves conducting a pro forma financial structure analysis. This tests, among other things, the firm's ability to utilize fully both the tax benefits of ownership under its planned capital expenditure program and the interest tax shields if it finances itself in accordance with its target capital structure. If it cannot, then it should reduce its target debt ratio and substitute preferred equity and/or substitute lease financing for conventional debt financing. The result of this two-step process is a target capital structure that balances the advantages against the costs of a change in financial leverage.

PROBLEMS

PROBLEM SET A

A1. What are **coverage ratios**? Why should a firm and its investors be concerned with coverage ratios?

A2. What are the three principal factors that cause systematic differences among the capital structures that typify different industries?

A3. Cite five factors Standard & Poor's evaluates to determine a bond rating for an industrial company.

A4. Why is a pro forma analysis an important prerequisite to choosing a capital structure?

A5. What is the major reason that subordinated debt is typically rated lower than senior debt?

A6. A company's latest 12 months' EBIT is $30 million, and its interest expense for the same period is $10 million. Calculate the interest coverage ratio.

A7. The firm in the preceding problem also had $15 million of rental expense during the latest 12 months. Calculate the firm's fixed charge coverage ratio.

A8. The firm in the two preceding problems also had $6 million of principal repayments during the latest 12 months. Its marginal tax rate is 40%. Calculate the debt service coverage ratio.

A9. Explain why selecting a target senior debt rating is a reasonable approach to choosing a capital structure. Explain why a target senior debt rating of single-A is a prudent objective when there is only a very limited new issue market for non-investment-grade debt and investor willingness to purchase triple-B-rated debt is likely to be highly sensitive to the state of the economy.

A10. If a firm's capital structure is different from its target capital structure, explain how the firm could bring its capital structure into line with its target capital structure. How might the firm bring it into line quickly?

A11. A firm's capital structure consists solely of debt and common equity. What form would an exchange offer take if the firm believes it is

    a. Overleveraged?

    b. Underleveraged?

A12. How has the stock market generally reacted to the announcement of exchange offers and other transactions that will alter a firm's leverage significantly?

A13. Explain what is meant by the term **subordinated debt**. Why is convertible debt typically issued in the form of subordinated debt rather than senior debt? In what sense is subordinated debt advantageous, and in what sense is it disadvantageous, to senior debtholders?

PROBLEM SET B

B1. A firm has the following capital structure:

	Amount ($ millions)
Long-term debt	200
Common equity	400
Total	600

    a. Calculate the firm's current long-term debt ratio.

    b. Calculate the pro forma effect of issuing $50 million of long-term debt to raise cash for a capital investment project.

    c. Calculate the pro forma effect of exchanging $50 million of long-term debt for a like amount of common equity.

B2. Why should a firm's ability to use tax credits affect its capital structure?

B3. Bixton Company's new chief financial officer is evaluating Bixton's capital structure. She is concerned that the company might be underleveraged, even though the company has larger-than-average research and development and foreign tax credits when compared to other companies in its industry. Her staff prepared the following industry comparison:

Rating Category	Fixed Charge Coverage	Cash Flow/ Total Debt	Long-Term Debt/ Capitalization
Aa	4.00–5.25x	60–80%	17–23%
A	3.00–4.30	45–65	22–32
Baa	1.95–3.40	35–55	30–41

    a. If Bixton's objective is to achieve a credit standing that falls, in the words of the chief financial officer, "comfortably within the 'A' range," what target range would you recommend for each of the three credit measures?

    b. Before settling on these target ranges, what other factors should Bixton's chief financial officer consider?

    c. Before deciding whether the target ranges are really appropriate for Bixton in its current financial situation, what key issues specific to Bixton must the chief financial officer resolve?

B4. How does a firm's size (as measured by total assets or total sales, for example) affect its choice of capital structure under the comparable-firms approach?

B5. Sanderson Manufacturing Company would like to achieve a capital structure consistent with a Baa2/BBB senior debt rating. Sanderson has identified six comparable companies and calculated the following credit statistics:

Company	A	B	C	D	E	F
Senior debt rating	Baa2/BBB	Baa3/BBB−	Baa2/BBB	Baa1/A−	Baa1/BBB−	Baa2/BBB+
Return on assets	5.2%	5.0%	5.4%	5.7%	5.2%	5.3%
Long-term debt/cap	38%	41%	45%	40%	25%	43%
Total cap ($MM)	425	575	525	650	210	375
Cash flow/LT debt	39%	43%	28%	46%	57%	43%
Fixed charge cov	2.57	2.83	2.75	2.38	3.59	2.15

   a. Sanderson's return on assets is 5.3%, and it has a total capitalization of $600 million. What are reasonable targets for long-term debt/cap, cash flow/LT debt, and fixed charge coverage?

   b. Are there any companies among the six who are particularly good or bad comparables? Explain.

   c. Suppose Sanderson's current ratio of long-term debt to total cap is 60% but its fixed charge coverage is 3.00. What would you recommend?

B6. Why would lenders be willing to lend a larger proportion of the market value of tangible assets such as plant and equipment than of the market value of intangible assets such as "special" formulas and goodwill?

B7. Show that of the interest coverage ratio, fixed charge coverage ratio, and debt service coverage ratio, (1) the interest coverage ratio will always have the greatest value and (2) the debt service coverage ratio will always have the smallest value, as long as interest coverage exceeds 1. Under what circumstances will all three ratios have the same value?

B8. Suppose that a firm wishes to maintain a capital structure that is consistent with an A senior debt rating. Under what circumstances would the firm maintain a lower degree of leverage than a cross section of single-A-rated firms?

B9. A firm has $100 million of earnings before interest and taxes and $40 million of interest expense.

   a. Calculate this firm's interest coverage ratio.

   b. Calculate the pro forma interest coverage ratio assuming the issuance of $100 million of 10% debt with the issue proceeds to be invested fully in a plant under construction.

   c. Calculate the pro forma interest coverage ratio assuming the issuance of $100 million of 10% debt with the proceeds to be invested temporarily in commercial paper that yields 8%.

B10. International Oil and Refining Company has operations in the United States, where it is not currently a taxpayer but expects to be within 5 years (i.e., nontaxable for 4 years and fully taxable in years 5 and beyond). International can issue either 10% debt or 8% preferred stock to raise the $25 million of funds it needs to upgrade its U.S. refinery. Assume a tax rate of 40% and that each issue matures in a lump sum 10 years from the date of issue.

   a. Ignoring issuance expenses, which issue has the lower after-tax cost?

   b. Describe how issuing debt or preferred stock would affect holders of International's outstanding debt and preferred stock?

   c. Which security should International issue?

   d. If International is uncertain about its future tax position in the United States, what other alternatives might it consider?

B11. The Rapid-Weight-Gain Company (RWGC) wants to slim down its long-term debt ratio to 0.50 "as quickly as possible." Its current capital structure is

	Amount ($ millions)
Long-term debt	400
Common equity	100
Total	500

   a. How much common stock would RWGC have to issue to reduce its long-term debt ratio to 0.50?

   b. How much common stock would RWGC have to exchange for outstanding debt in order to reduce its long-term debt ratio to 0.50?

   c. Discuss the relative merits of alternatives a and b in light of RWGC's objective.

PROBLEM SET C

C1. Explain why a lease obligation is a form of secured debt. Construct a numerical example to demonstrate how lease financing displaces conventional debt financing dollar-for-dollar when the firm's capital structure is held fixed.

C2. Explain in your own words why you might expect to observe a negative correlation between financial leverage and operating leverage.

C3. Companies A and B are identical except for their capital structures. A has a debt ratio of 25%. B has a debt ratio of 33.33%. Suppose that the interest rate on both companies' debt is 10% and that investors can also borrow at a 10% interest rate.

   a. An investor owns 5% of the common stock of company A, half of which is financed through borrowings. What investment-loan package involving B will produce identical returns?

   b. An investor owns 10% of the common stock of B, none of which is financed through borrowings. What investment-loan combination involving A will produce identical returns?

C4. Using agency theory concepts, explain how restrictive covenants that disallow things such as leases and liens on the firm's assets might cause a firm to achieve a higher rating on its bonds than would be possible without such restrictive covenants.

C5. The development of the new issue junk bond market had important implications for capital structure choice. The existence of a viable junk bond market means that firms can comfortably maintain higher degrees of leverage than they could prior to the development of this market. Do you agree or disagree? Justify your answer.

C6. A firm's balance sheet includes something called **minority interest**, which appears below long-term debt and above preferred stock. Discuss whether minority interest should be treated as debt or equity, assuming

   a. It consists of outstanding common stock of a subsidiary, and the parent company has no intention of repurchasing or otherwise retiring that common stock.

   b. It consists of redeemable preferred stock of a subsidiary, which the firm is obligated to redeem in equal annual amounts over the next 5 years.

   What is your conclusion regarding whether minority interest is really debt or equity?

REFERENCES

Alderson, Michael J., Keith C. Brown, and Scott L. Lummer. "Dutch Auction Rate Preferred Stock." *Financial Management* 16 (Summer 1987): 68–73.

Altman, Edward I. "Measuring Corporate Bond Mortality and Performance." *Journal of Finance* 44 (September 1989): 909–22.

Asquith, Paul, David W. Mullins, Jr., and Eric D. Wolff. "Original Issue High Yield Bonds: Aging Analyses of Defaults, Exchanges, and Calls." *Journal of Finance* 44 (September 1989): 923–52.

Ben-Horim, Moshe, Shalom Hochman, and Oded Palmon. "The Impact of the 1986 Tax Reform Act on Corporate Financial Policy." *Financial Management* 16 (Autumn 1987): 29–35.

Bowen, Robert M., Lane A. Daley, and Charles C. Huber, Jr. "Evidence on the Existence and Determinants of Inter-Industry Differences in Leverage." *Financial Management* 11 (Winter 1982): 10–20.

Cordes, Joseph J., and Steven M. Sheffrin. "Estimating the Tax Advantage of Corporate Debt." *Journal of Finance* 38 (March 1983): 95–105.

DeAngelo, Harry, and Ronald Masulis. "Optimal Capital Structure Under Corporate and Personal Taxation." *Journal of Financial Economics* 8 (March 1980): 3–29.

Debt Ratings Criteria: Industrial Overview. New York: Standard & Poor's, 1986.

Fooladi, Iraj, and Gordon S. Roberts. "On Preferred Stock." *Journal of Financial Research* 9 (Winter 1986): 319–24.

Iskandar, Mai E. "The Role of Debt Characteristics in Bond Ratings." Ph.D. dissertation, The University of Missouri–Columbia, 1986.

Kane, Alex, Alan J. Marcus, and Robert L. McDonald. "How Big is the Tax Advantage to Debt?" *Journal of Finance* 39 (July 1984): 841–53.

Kester, W. Carl. "Capital and Ownership Structure: A Comparison of United States and Japanese Manufacturing Corporations." *Financial Management* 15 (Spring 1986): 5–16.

"The Leveraging of Corporate America: A Discussion of Corporate Capital Structure." In Donald H. Chew, Jr., ed., *Six Roundtable Discussions of Corporate Finance with Joel Stern.* New York: Quorum Books, 1986: 217–64.

Lewellen, Wilbur G., and Douglas R. Emery. "Corporate Debt Management and the Value of the Firm." *Journal of Financial and Quantitative Analysis* 21 (December 1986): 415–26.

Long, Michael, and Ileen Malitz. "The Investment-Financing Nexus: Some Empirical Evidence." In Joel M. Stern and Donald H. Chew, Jr., eds., *The Revolution in Corporate Finance.* New York: Basil Blackwell, 1986: 112–18.

Marsh, Paul R. "The Choice Between Equity and Debt: An Empirical Study." *Journal of Finance* 37 (March 1982): 121–44.

Masulis, Ronald W. "The Effects of Capital Structure Change on Security Prices: A Study of Exchange Offers." *Journal of Financial Economics* 8 (June 1980): 139–78.

Masulis, Ronald W. "The Impact of Capital Structure Change on Firm Value: Some Estimates." *Journal of Finance* 38 (March 1983): 107–26.

Myers, Stewart. "The Capital Structure Puzzle." In Joel M. Stern and Donald H. Chew, Jr., eds., *The Revolution in Corporate Finance.* New York: Basil Blackwell, 1986a: 100–11.

Myers, Stewart. "The Search for Optimal Capital Structure." In Joel M. Stern and Donald H. Chew, Jr., eds., *The Revolution in Corporate Finance.* New York: Basil Blackwell, 1986b: 91–99.

Perry, Kevin J., and Robert A. Taggart, Jr. "The Growing Role of Junk Bonds in Corporate Finance." *Journal of Applied Corporate Finance* 1 (Spring 1988): 37–45.

Pinches, George E., and Kent A. Mingo. "A Multivariate Analysis of Industrial Bond Ratings." *Journal of Finance* 28 (March 1973): 1–18.

Pinches, George E., and Kent A. Mingo. "The Role of Subordination and Industrial Bond Ratings." *Journal of Finance* 30 (March 1975): 201–6.

Schwartz, Eli, and J. Richard Aronson. "Some Surrogate Evidence in Support of the Concept of Optimal Capital Structure." *Journal of Finance* 22 (March 1967): 10–18.

Scott, David F., Jr. "Evidence on the Importance of Financial Structure." *Financial Management* 1 (Summer 1972): 45–50.

Scott, David F., Jr., and John D. Martin. "Industry Influence on Financial Structure." *Financial Management* 4 (Spring 1975): 67–73.

Taggart, Robert A., Jr. "A Model of Corporate Financing Decisions." *Journal of Finance* 32 (December 1977): 1467–84.

Winger, Bernard J., Carl R. Chen, John D. Martin, J. William Petty, and Steven C. Hayden. "Adjustable Rate Preferred Stock." *Financial Management* 15 (Spring 1986): 48–57.

17

DIVIDEND POLICY:
WHY IT MATTERS

This chapter discusses dividend policy. There are various interpretations of this term and therefore it is important to specify what we mean when we use it. In practice, the term *dividend policy* refers to the corporation's decision to pay out a portion of its earnings to its shareholders as dividends.

Recall from Chapter 6 that the ratio of dividends paid to earnings is called the company's **payout ratio**. The firm retains the balance of its earnings for reinvestment in its business. For simplicity, we have thus far characterized a dividend policy simply as a constant payout ratio. It is, of course, more complex than this. A firm's payout ratio typically varies over the life of the firm. For example, a small and rapidly growing company may retain *all* its earnings for many years to help finance its growth. More mature companies customarily pay out some portion of their earnings; on average, approximately 50% of the earnings of all U.S. corporations over the past half century have been paid out as dividends.

Further, dividend policy involves more than simply the payout ratio. Dividend payments are made in cash. (We reserve the special case of dividends paid in the form of additional shares for the next chapter.) Because a company has a variety of alternative uses for its cash, confusion often occurs among the dividend policy decision, the capital budgeting decision, and the capital structure decision.[1] For example, if paying cash dividends reduced capital expenditures by the amount of the dividend, the dividend decision would be a by-product of the investment decision. We would be unable to distinguish the stock market's reaction to an announced dividend change from its reaction to the change in the company's capital budget; the two policies would simply be mirror images of each other. Similarly, if the capital budget is held fixed but the cash to pay the dividend is financed by added borrowing, the dividend decision becomes a by-product of the capital structure decision.

When we discuss the impact of a company's dividend policy on how the stock market values its shares, we must isolate the impact of a change in cash dividends from the company's choices of capital investments and capital structure; otherwise, we would not be analyzing dividend policy exclusively. But if we hold both the capital budget and the capital structure fixed, the cash required for dividend payments must come from external sources. In a strict sense, then, a pure dividend policy decision involves only a *trade-off* between retaining earnings on the one hand and selling new shares to obtain the cash to pay dividends on the other. Although some companies (most notably electric utility companies) have paid regular quarterly cash dividends (in many cases averaging 70% or more of earnings) and *simultaneously* sold new issues of common stock, firms in other industries rarely maintain high payout

---

[1] Even the "high and mighty" have made this mistake. Martin Feldstein, at the time Chairman of the Council of Economic Advisers, and a colleague tried to explain dividend policies in Feldstein and Green (1983). But their model made dividend policy a mirror image of capital investment policy. See Bortz and Rust (1984).

ratios and sell new issues of common stock regularly. One aspect, then, of the dividend policy issue is Would the shareholders of such companies have been better off if, instead, the companies had retained the cash and sold fewer new shares?

Another complicating question concerning dividend policy is the method of payment. There are alternative means of distributing cash to shareholders. A company can make regular payments, say at quarterly intervals, or it can make larger irregular payments in the form of "extra" or "special" dividends. Alternatively, it can eschew dividends and use the cash to repurchase shares, which may have certain tax advantages for individual shareholders relative to cash dividends. The method-of-payment issue is discussed in the next chapter. This chapter focuses on the trade-off between retained earnings and dividend payments coupled with a new share issue.

ITT Corporation's Dividend Dilemma

In mid-1984, the management of ITT Corporation was in the midst of planning a strategic reorientation of the company. ITT had sold off several businesses and desired to increase the proportion of its resources devoted to industrial and defense technology. In line with this change, ITT was considering a reduction in its common stock dividend rate in order to have available additional internal funds for reinvestment in its business. Over the prior 5 years ITT's payout ratio had varied between 40% and 85%:

	1983	1982	1981	1980	1979
Dividends per share	$2.76	$2.70	$2.62	$2.45	$2.25
Earnings per share	4.50	4.74	4.70	6.12	2.65
Payout ratio	61%	57%	56%	40%	85%

ITT's payout ratio was very high relative to the payout ratios of technology companies, and it was high relative to large companies generally.

Press reports at the time suggested that ITT's common stock had attracted an investor clientele that preferred higher-yielding stocks. If ITT cut the common dividend, it would risk disappointing these investors, who might sell their shares and seek out higher-yielding common stocks. Therefore, a dividend cut could be disruptive to ITT's share price. But if ITT really felt that its payout ratio was too high—and that a higher proportion of its earnings should be reinvested in its business—a dividend cut would seem to be the appropriate decision.

As you read this chapter, think about what you might have recommended to ITT's chairman if you had been ITT's treasurer in mid-1984. We will tell you what action ITT took with respect to the dividend—and how the capital market reacted—at the end of the chapter.

Nature of the Controversy   17.1

The major controversy in the area of dividend policy concerns whether a firm's total value is affected by its choice of dividend policy. Based on value conservation, value additivity (Chapter 5) holds that splitting or combining cash flows cannot alter their total value. So in a perfect market environment—one with costless information, no taxes, and no transaction costs—dividend policy doesn't matter. Unfortunately, although a perfect market analysis provides the best starting place for thinking about the problem, the realities of capital market imperfections must be included to arrive at more practical conclusions. As we noted in Chapter 5, taxes, information asymmetries, and transaction costs are important persistent imperfections in the operation of the capital markets, and those imperfections affect our conclusions about dividend policy.

As in the case of capital structure choice, there have been, and continue to be, conflicting arguments and conclusions about dividend policy. We'll start by enumerating four of them in their approximate chronological order. The **traditional view** advocates high payout ratios. According to this view, shareholders prefer immediate dividends over less certain and more distant capital gains, which would presumably result if the cash were reinvested in the business instead of being paid out as dividends; a bird in the hand is worth two in the bush, some would say. The **tax differential view**, a second school of thought, reaches the opposite conclusion. It argues that shareholders prefer capital gains over dividends, and hence low payout ratios, because capital gains have generally been taxed at a lower rate than dividends (at least for individual shareholders). The Tax Reform Act of 1986 changed this; capital gains and dividends are now taxed at the same (nominal) marginal rate. Nevertheless, the tax differential view is worth examining because of the tax advantage capital gains have traditionally enjoyed and because immediate capital gains continue to have a time-value-of-money advantage over regular dividend income because the tax on a gain is deferred.[2] The **perfect market view** of dividends concludes that dividend policy doesn't matter. Because the capital markets are so efficient, a company's value is relatively insensitive to its choice of dividend policy when the firm's capital structure is held constant. Finally, there is the **signaling view**. According to the signaling view, dividend changes represent an important signal to investors regarding *changes* in management's expectations about the company's future earnings. It is widely acknowledged that dividend policy is relevant to share valuation, at least to the extent that dividend policy conveys information about the company's current and future operations and profits.

In practice, dividend policy is relevant if for no other reason than companies actually behave as though it matters. As with the choice of capital structure, the empirical evidence shows consistent patterns of dividend policy, as though there were definite reasons for following certain policies. These patterns point out the possibility that some policies are superior to other policies that are not adopted. It might be argued that firms are all following the Behavioral Principle—in the extreme case, just copying each other—and that these patterns are simply "neutral mutations." It is our opinion that while this is a possible explanation, it is too simplistic. In this chapter, we detail a conceptual basis for dividend relevance. In the next chapter we outline a practical method of managing dividend policy that is consistent with this conceptual framework.

17.2   THE PERFECT MARKET VIEW

Once again we call on the concept of value conservation and Miller and Modigliani (MM). After their article on capital structure, MM applied the concept to dividend

---

[2] Recall that capital gains are taxed at the time of the sale of the asset, not as they accrue. Consequently, the tax liability for capital gains is reinvested and earns the time value of money until the tax payment is actually made. This tax advantage of capital gains over dividend income is conceptually similar to the tax advantage of accelerated over straight-line depreciation.

policy. They showed that, in a perfect capital market, a company that fixes both its capital investment program and its capital structure cannot affect the wealth of its existing shareholders by paying out either more or less than its residual cash flow.[3] The crux of the MM argument is that the payment of a cash dividend that is financed by a new share issue leaves unchanged the wealth of the firm's existing shareholders (i.e., those individuals and entities who were shareholders just prior to the dividend and new share issue). The aggregate value of the shares outstanding prior to a dividend distribution will decrease by exactly the amount of the aggregate dividends paid. The value of the new shares must equal the amount of the dividend distribution in order to leave the firm's capital investment program and capital structure unaffected. Thus, the wealth of the existing shareholders is unaffected. Also, because of value conservation, the aggregate value of the firm is the same before and after the dividend-distribution-cum-new-issue. All that has happened is that value has been transferred from new shareholders to the existing shareholders; value has been neither created nor destroyed.

ILLUSTRATION OF DIVIDEND IRRELEVANCE

Consider a company that has decided to make, but has not yet announced, a major new capital investment in a project that will cost $10 million. The project has a positive NPV of $20 million. The company has $10 million in cash available to finance the capital investment project if it so chooses. The company has 10 million shares of stock currently outstanding, selling for $24 each, and no debt. Thus, the company's aggregate value is $240 million (= $24 x 10,000,000) prior to the project announcement, and it will be $260 million (= $240,000,000 + 20,000,000) following the announcement.

To determine whether paying dividends affects shareholder wealth, consider the following two alternatives facing the company: (1) pay no cash dividend and finance the project with cash, or (2) pay a cash dividend of $1 per share, and find some other source for the $10 million cash needed to finance the project. In order for the dividend–no-dividend alternatives to be equivalent for comparison purposes (that is, so we can determine which alternative is superior without having other factors influence our conclusion) the firm must sell $10 million worth of new shares in conjunction with the dividend alternative. The sale of new stock is to finance the project by replacing the $10 million in equity that was given up when the dividend was paid.

Under alternative 1, the company uses the cash to finance the project, rather than paying the cash out as a dividend. In that case, each share would be worth $26 (= $260,000,000/10,000,000). If the shareholders want the $10 million in cash they would have received had the money been paid out as a dividend, they can sell 384,615 (= 10,000,000/26) of their own shares to obtain it.

Under alternative 2, the company declares a $10 million cash dividend and sells $10 million worth of new equity immediately after paying the dividend. After paying the dividend (to be more precise, immediately after the shares begin trading ex-dividend), each share will be worth the predividend share price ($26) less the amount of the dividend ($1), or $25. Note that paying the dividend does not affect shareholder wealth. Prior to the dividend, a holder of one share owned a security worth $26; following the dividend payment, the holder of one share has a security worth $25 plus $1 of cash, or the same $26 in all.

To raise the $10 million it needs to finance the new project, the company must sell

---

[3] Miller and Modigliani (1961).

400,000 (= 10,000,000/25) new shares (assuming these shares are fairly priced). Immediately following the new share issue, the company will have 10,400,000 shares outstanding that are trading for $25 each, giving the company an aggregate value of $260 million. And $260 million is exactly the value it had prior to the dividend-distribution-cum-new-share-issue. Thus, the mere payment of the dividend has not altered the company's aggregate value or the wealth of its shareholders. It has simply enabled the holders of the original 10 million shares, in effect, to "cash in" a portion of their equity investment in the company.

CAPITAL MARKET IMPERFECTIONS   As we have already mentioned, this perfect market view leaves out taxes, transaction costs, and information asymmetries. For many individual investors there is a trade-off between cash dividends and capital gains: A cash dividend will reduce each shareholder's capital gain, or increase her capital loss.[4] If capital gains are taxed at a lower rate than dividends, shareholders will prefer the income to occur as capital gains rather than dividends if they have a choice. However, a cash dividend may be beneficial to a second group of shareholders who desire liquidity and would have to pay large commission charges if they were to try to "manufacture" their own dividends by selling portions of their shareholdings—especially if the second type of shareholder is tax-exempt and hence doesn't care about the tax differential between the two types of income. Finally, it may be that dividend policy can be used, less expensively than other methods, to convey information to the public. All of these concerns are valid and will be addressed. However, as we have done in other cases, we have started with the "clean slate" of a perfect market view.

IRRELEVANCE AND SEPARATION

In closing this section, we want to point out the interdependence of MM's two classic propositions, one dealing with capital structure (Chapter 15) and the other dealing with dividend irrelevance. In the forgoing example, it was assumed that the company sold new shares to preserve its capital structure. But if the choice of capital structure also does not affect a company's value, it might just as well have issued debt securities. If both capital structure and dividends are irrelevant, the required rate of return for evaluating a project is independent of both the firm's choice of capital structure and its choice of dividend policy. In that event, the firm's investment decisions would be truly separable from its financing decisions, and we could treat the two sides of its balance sheet as perfectly separable from one another. (In which case we would not have had to have gone to the trouble to write Part 3 of the Applications Section since it deals with the problems of investment-financing interaction.)

17.3   THE TRADITIONAL VIEW

The traditional view of dividend policy holds that within "reason," investors prefer larger cash dividends to smaller cash dividends. This conclusion is based on what is often referred to as the bird-in-the-hand fallacy. The term *fallacy*, of course, reveals the widely held opinion of the traditional view. However, as with the traditional

---

[4]A company's share price declines by the amount of the declared but as yet unpaid dividend when the shares begin trading on the ex-dividend date because after that time, purchasers will not be entitled to receive the dividend.

view of capital structure, while the argument is flawed, there may be some merit in the conclusion.

RISK

Dividends represent cash in hand, whereas reinvesting that cash in the hope of realizing greater dividends and/or additional capital gain sometime in the future represents a risky prospect. Consequently, aren't shareholders better off getting a dividend? At this point, we hope you recognize an opportunity to apply the Principle of Risk-Return Trade-Off and answer no, not necessarily.[5] The difference between the dividend now and later is, of course, risk and the time value of money. Therefore, because of the risk-return trade-off, if we want the dividend now, we must accept a lower rate of return on the investment in those shares. (The investor is still free to achieve a different risk-return profile, depending on how he reinvests the dividends.) Looking again at the perfect market analysis, the issue is whether the existing shareholders or some "new" shareholders are going to be investing the $10 million in the new project.

Any shareholder who decides that future dividends and capital gains are *excessively* risky (as opposed to being in accordance with the risk-return trade-off) can sell all or a portion of her shares. This involves transaction costs, but it does enable the individual shareholder to satisfy her own risk-return objectives. Moreover, if the firm can reinvest funds profitably and the firm's capital investment program and capital structure are held fixed, the mere payment of a dividend does not alter the firm's risk profile or the risk that its shareholders, as a group, must bear. Thus, the uncertainty of future dividends and capital gains does not by itself alter the MM dividend irrelevance argument.

The above argument notwithstanding, psychological theories have been advanced that provide a rationale for some individuals preferring cash dividends over capital gains.[6] These theories argue that because of psychological reasons, dividends and capital gains are not perfect substitutes for one another. For example, a lack of self-control provides a reason for an investor to prefer regular cash dividends: If the investor must sell stock to get income, he might have a tendency to sell too much stock too soon, thus depleting his capital before death. Such psychological reasons might be the basis for an explanation of dividend policy preferences as rational behavior in terms of agency costs. That is, an investor may choose to invest in a firm that follows a particular type of dividend policy to minimize the total agency costs of shareholding, including the investor's human frailties.

SHAREHOLDER PREFERENCE FOR CURRENT INCOME

A concept discussed in Chapter 15 that is also important in the study of dividend relevance is the **clientele effect**—the concept of investors "sorting" themselves into groups, each of which prefers the companies it invests in to follow a certain type of policy. When applied to dividend policy, the clientele effect refers to those investors that prefer one dividend policy over another for a particular reason. A similar concept in marketing is called **market segmentation**. A market segment is an identifiable group of consumers who purchase a product with particular attributes distinct

---

[5] Two noteworthy studies that have taken issue with the "bird-in-the-hand" argument are Brennan (1971) and Higgins (1972).
[6] Shefrin and Statman (1984).

from the attributes of other products; for example, luxury cars versus compact cars.

With dividend policy, there are natural clienteles for high-cash-dividend stocks and for low-cash-dividend stocks. For example, a pension fund might have a foreseeable future need for cash income to meet its obligations. There is considerable empirical evidence supporting the existence of investor clienteles.[7] For example, we have studied electric utility common stocks and have seen evidence of a clientele effect.[8] Electric utility common stocks are among the highest yielding common stocks; compared to other common stocks, a relatively high proportion of the total return utility common stocks provide investors is in the form of dividends (and a relatively small proportion is in the form of capital gains). These stocks have undoubtedly attracted a natural clientele of investors who look to the dividend stream as a source of regular income. However, shareholders who have a preference for current income could sell shares on a periodic basis to generate income. Therefore, in a perfect market, a preference for current income does not alter the conclusion that dividend policy is irrelevant.

Returning to our perfect market example, the irrelevance of dividend policy does not change when we introduce risk, nor does dividend policy matter when we introduce a shareholder preference for current income. But we will see later that this conclusion does depend on the perfect capital market environment.

17.4 THE TAX DIFFERENTIAL VIEW

In Chapter 11, we noted that the tax laws change with some regularity. As in the case of capital budgeting projects, it is imperative that you know the relevant tax laws with respect to dividends. Within the boundaries of current laws, there may be one or more tax asymmetries, as has been the case at various times in the past.

As we have already pointed out, at the time of this writing, dividends are effectively taxed more heavily than capital gains for individual investors because of the tax-timing option—the ability to postpone the tax liability on capital gains income. In addition, under the previous versions of the Internal Revenue Code, other differentials have also existed. For example, at one time, the first $100 ($200 for a joint return) of individual income from cash dividends was tax-exempt. Also, prior to the Tax Reform Act of 1986, only 40% of the capital gain realized upon the sale of a share of common stock held more than 6 months was subject to tax. The balance was tax-free. Thus, historically, the Internal Revenue Code has imposed a higher marginal tax rate on dividends individuals receive than on the capital gains they realize. This difference in the marginal rate was in addition to the reduction in the *effective* rate caused by the tax-timing option. We note this historical difference for two reasons. First, it illustrates once again the necessity of knowing the current tax laws. Second, there is a good chance that, by the time you read this, some or all of the above capital gains tax differential will have been restored.

Tax-exempt institutions, such as pension funds, do not have a tax bias in favor of capital gains. And the bias is reversed in the case of corporate shareholders. Under the Internal Revenue Code, as modified by the Tax Reform Act of 1986, corporate shareholders pay income tax at a 34% peak marginal rate but are permitted to claim

---

[7] Elton and Gruber (1970) and Lewellen, Stanley, Lease, and Schlarbaum (1978) found evidence suggesting that higher-payout firms tend to attract less heavily taxed investors and that lower-payout firms tend to attract more heavily taxed investors.
[8] Finnerty (1981).

a 70% dividends received deduction. A fully taxable corporate shareholder would therefore pay tax on dividend income at a rate no greater than 10.2% (= .30 × 34%) because only 30% of the dividends it receives are taxable. In contrast, corporate shareholders pay tax on long-term capital gains at rates up to 34%. Thus corporate investors may prefer dividends over capital gains from a purely tax standpoint.

As with the traditional view, the clientele effect mitigates the tax differential argument in a market that is perfect except for this tax asymmetry. Based on their tax positions, investors will have preference for investing in high- or low-cash-dividend stocks. These preferences create natural tax clienteles for various dividend policies. Firms offer dividend policies that appeal to different tax clienteles. Each tax clientele can invest in the shares of companies whose dividend policies best suit that clientele's tax posture. Of course, as long as there is a sufficient supply of investment opportunities for each group, no premium need be paid by investors to obtain a preferred investment instrument. With no premium, dividend policy would again be irrelevant—in spite of the tax asymmetry.

INFORMATION CONTENT AND SIGNALING   17.5

Dividend changes could have an impact on the price of a company's stock if such changes convey useful information to investors concerning a company's future earnings prospects. For example, suppose that a certain company has changed its dividend rate infrequently, and each time the rate was changed, the company's earnings have changed subsequently in the same direction as the dividend rate. Then investors will interpret future changes in the dividend rate as a signal that management's assessment of the company's earnings prospects has changed. A dividend increase would signal an improvement in the company's minimum sustainable level of earnings, and a dividend decrease would signal a worsening of the company's earnings prospects. As discussed later in the chapter, the empirical evidence supports the importance of dividend changes as a signaling device.

A study by John Lintner, based on interviews with corporate executives, found that financial managers thought their corporations should aim toward some long-term target payout ratio in order to give shareholders a "fair share" of the company's earnings. Lintner developed the following model to explain corporate dividend changes:[9]

$$DPS_1 - DPS_0 = ADJ [POR(EPS_1) - DPS_0] \qquad (17.1)$$

According to this model, a company that is currently paying dividends at the rate of DPS_0 per share and has a target payout ratio of POR will adjust (ADJ) its dividend rate, but less than fully, as its earnings per share (EPS) change. If a company always paid out its target ratio of earnings, then its dividends per share in the coming period would be $DPS = POR(EPS_1)$. But Lintner found that corporations "managed" their dividend payments so as to produce a smooth progression in dividends. Accordingly, $ADJ < 1$, so that dividends progress toward the target level over several periods rather than all at once. This, of course, reduces the likelihood that a dividend increase will have to be "rolled back" in the future. Because of this "stickiness," dividend changes serve as a signaling device. A company will not increase its dividend

[9]Lintner (1956).

rate unless it believes the increase is sustainable because of a higher sustainable level of earnings.

If dividend announcements do indeed convey useful information, it is reasonable to expect that the quality of the information these announcements convey would depend on the degree to which dividend changes conform to, or deviate from, an established dividend pattern. Such a pattern would have two important attributes: (1) the amount of each dividend change and (2) the timing of each change. For example, if a company has established a pattern of regular annual increases in its dividend rate and has demonstrated that this pattern of increases is sustainable by keeping its payout ratio relatively stable, any deviation from that pattern (i.e., an increase that differs from the preceding year's increase) would signal to investors a change in the firm's earnings prospects. Moreover, it would signal that a higher sustainable dividend *growth rate*, rather than just a higher sustainable *dividend level*, had been achieved. This argument presumes that insiders (who set the dividend rate) have information that is not available to investors outside the firm, that such information is used to determine future dividend payout streams, and that dividends are "sticky" in the sense that companies exhibit great reluctance to cut the dividend rate.[10]

The above argument also presumes that the structure of incentives is such that, taken in total, it favors accurate signals. As discussed in Chapter 9, the reputation of a firm can play an important role in discouraging false signals. Research demonstrates that such incentive structures are plausible[11] and that dividend changes have a discernible information content.[12]

A pattern consisting of regular annual dividend increases might take on added significance during periods of inflation. During such periods, it is not enough for a company simply to sustain any particular absolute dividend level because inflation would erode the value of the dividend in real terms. Investors might then use the dividend growth rate evident in the historical pattern—provided they believe the pattern is sustainable—to gauge the likelihood that the future rate of dividend growth will at least keep pace with inflation.

Unlike the traditional and tax differential views, the clientele effect does not mitigate the signaling view of dividend policy. Even in a market that is perfect except for information availability (and cost), dividend policy may be a dimension relevant to firm value. Because of the informational content of dividend changes, simply paying out residual cash flow on a year-by-year basis may not be in the shareholders' best interest. Such a policy would lead to a dividend level and a payout ratio that could fluctuate wildly, depending on year-to-year changes in the availability of attractive investment projects. Generally, companies manage their dividend policies so that dividend changes are orderly and consistent with changes in the company's earnings prospects. The next chapter describes an operational approach to dividend policy that is based on this guiding principle.

Our first insight into why dividend policy matters comes when we relax the assumption that information is freely available and costless. If it is costly to gather information, it is possible that **dividend policy may be the least expensive, and/or most accurate, method of conveying information** to shareholders. If this is the case, and the empirical evidence presented below supports this view, then dividend policy is an important tool that can be used to benefit a company's shareholders.

---

[10] Black (1976); Fama, Fisher, Jensen, and Roll (1969); and Friend and Puckett (1964) provide evidence that companies are reluctant to cut the dividend rate. Black's article also provides a useful and interesting summary of the issues surrounding the "informational content of dividend changes."

[11] See, for example, Bhattacharya (1979); Hakansson (1982).

[12] Aharony and Swary (1980); Ang (1987); Charest (1978); Eades (1982); Kalay (1980); Kwan (1981).

We have pointed out that various investor clienteles will exist when the perfect market assumption is relaxed: some because of taxes and others because of investor cash flow preferences, such as pension fund preference for dividend-paying stocks. While the existence of investor clienteles does not, by itself, cause dividend policy to matter, the story changes somewhat when other market imperfections are considered. Now we introduce transaction costs.

FLOTATION COSTS AND COMMISSION CHARGES

Shareholders who desire a stream of share-related income could sell portions of their holdings and create "homemade" dividends in lieu of the corporation paying a cash dividend. However, they will incur brokerage commissions. Alternatively, if the corporation pays a cash dividend and issues shares to preserve both its capital structure and planned capital investment program, it will incur the costs of floating the new issue. Either way, there will be transaction costs. The existence of brokerage commissions tends to favor dividend payments over share sales for shareholders who prefer current income. However, those same brokerage commissions cause a reverse preference for shareholders who prefer reinvestments, favoring retained earnings over dividends. For the firm, the existence of flotation costs, which are associated with new issues, tends to favor retained earnings over new issues as a means of raising equity capital for capital investment purposes. The questions with respect to transaction costs is Who pays the transaction costs, and how much are they in total?

A shareholder who desires an increased income stream would prefer real cash dividend payments over homemade dividends if the firm can sell new shares more cheaply than the shareholder can sell a few of her own shares. Of course, the reverse preference holds if it is cheaper for shareholders to sell their own shares. In general, brokerage commissions and flotation costs both vary inversely with the size of the transaction. These economies of scale make it cheaper for the company to sell a large block of shares than for individual shareholders to make small odd-lot sales. Consequently, it is generally cheaper for the company to pay dividends than for shareholders to manufacture homemade dividends. Market imperfections, then, rather than a shareholder preference for current income, may explain the existence of certain investor clienteles that prefer high-payout stocks. Regular dividend checks relieve investors of the inconvenience and significant brokerage charges involved in making frequent odd-lot sales.

Two trends have affected the difference between flotation costs and brokerage commissions in recent years. The growth of the discount brokerage industry has reduced brokerage commissions; however, the greatest commission reductions have occurred in connection with larger share transactions (i.e., those involving several hundred shares or more). In addition, the proliferation of new issue dividend reinvestment plans has permitted companies to reduce issuance costs substantially, perhaps to as little as 2% (versus 4% to 5% for normal-size public offerings). Dividend reinvestment plans offer shareholders the option to reinvest their dividends with little or no brokerage commission.[13] This reduces the penalty a high-dividend-payout policy would otherwise impose on shareholders who wish their dividends to be reinvested. However, it does not eliminate the tax bias in favor of capital gains

---

[13]Dividend reinvestment plans are discussed in Chapter 14.

because shareholders must recognize the reinvested dividends as income. Nevertheless, by reducing flotation costs, dividend reinvestment plans may have led to increased payout ratios for those firms, such as electric utility companies, whose investor clienteles desire a relatively high level of dividend income.

LEGAL AND POLICY RESTRICTIONS

Certain institutions are prohibited, either by law or by policy, from investing in the common stocks of companies that have not established a history of regular dividend payments over a sufficiently long period. Other investors, such as many trust and endowment funds, can spend only dividend income as a matter of policy. These investors exhibit a preference for at least some minimum level of regular dividend income to maintain institutional decision-making flexibility.

NET EFFECT OF TRANSACTION COSTS

We believe—and we think we have the support of the majority of our colleagues in the finance profession—that the tax bias in favor of capital gains (the time value of the postponed tax liability) exerts a stronger influence on what a company's dividend policy ought to be than transaction cost considerations or the legal and policy restrictions that are responsible for certain investors having a dividend preference. Consequently, we believe that the combined effect of the factors mentioned in this section favors retentions over dividends to some degree. The extent of this bias depends largely on the shareholder mix and on the tax positions and liquidity preferences of shareholders, all of which may change. For example, Figure 17-1 shows that between 1950 and 1988 the percentage of New York Stock Exchange-listed common

FIGURE 17-1

Growth in institutional ownership of New York Stock Exchange-listed common stocks.

Source: New York Stock Exchange Institutional Investor Fact Book 1990, 18–29.

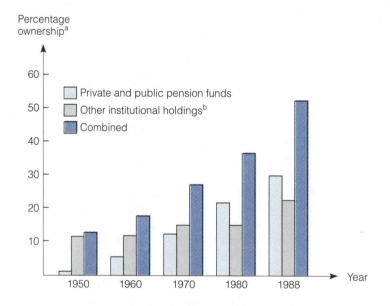

a Equity assets as a percentage of the aggregate market value of New York Stock Exchange-listed common stocks

b Insurance companies, open-end investment companies, and foreign institutions

stocks owned by institutional investors increased from 12% to 52% of the aggregate market value of the shares listed there.[14]

If individual shareholders are the largest group and consist chiefly of higher-marginal-tax-rate individuals, there is likely to be a *net* preference for capital gains over dividends. This is due to the time value of money connected with postponing the tax liability. (Also, for reasons discussed in the next chapter, this same group would prefer that the firm make cash distributions through share repurchases rather than cash dividends.) Conversely, for the same reason, if shareholders consist primarily of older retired individuals, other corporations, and tax-exempt institutions, there is likely to be a *net* preference for dividends. These considerations point up the importance of market imperfections to the relevance of dividend policy and consequently the importance of a company's understanding its shareholder mix, and their likely preferences when setting its dividend policy.

EQUILIBRIUM AND THE CLIENTELE EFFECT   17.7

The Principle of Valuable Ideas states that new ideas may be valuable when they are first applied. But the Principle of Capital Market Efficiency states that after others recognize the same opportunity and competition enters the picture, extraordinary returns are driven out of the investment. These principles can be applied to dividend policy clienteles.

Taxes and transaction costs reduce the return to shareholders. Therefore, investors should invest in a company that follows the dividend policy that is optimal for themselves. That is, they should (and do) invest in companies whose dividend policies minimize their taxes and transaction costs, holding all else (risk and return) constant. The result of including taxes and transaction costs is that a clientele group will be better off if they pay up to some maximum premium for shares of firms that follow their optimal policy. (The maximum premium is the additional cost if they invest in the next best company that is otherwise identical but does not follow their optimal policy.) As long as a premium is offered, companies have the incentive to change their policy and sell shares to the clientele group offering the premium. Such a policy would reflect the application of the Principle of Valuable Ideas.

Over time, however, competition among companies drives the premium to zero, and capital market equilibrium and efficiency return. In the aggregate, companies will supply enough of each type of stock so that all the positive-NPVs resulting from dividend policy choices have been extracted and the premiums have been driven to zero.[15] What remains after the premiums are gone are clientele groups and companies that are very comfortable with each other. In equilibrium, the patterns can remain indefinitely since neither the clientele groups nor the companies have any incentive to change. However, whenever there are changes in laws (tax laws or any law affecting investments), it may be possible to play the game all over again

---

[14] *New York Stock Exchange Institutional Investor Fact Book 1990*, (New York: New York Stock Exchange, January 1990), 18–29. Private and public pension funds collectively owned 30% of the New York Stock Exchange-listed common stocks at year-end 1988 (versus 1.2% in 1950). Moreover, nontaxable institutions' collective percentage ownership has increased more or less steadily over the past two decades. Ibid., 18–21.

[15] Just like investment decisions, financing decisions can be evaluated by measuring the NPV. Examples of such an analysis are given in Chapters 20 and 21. The first example involves a bond refunding decision, and the second involves a leasing decision.

as the market attains a new equilibrium. Each change represents a potential new opportunity.

Thus, we have a second insight into why dividend policy matters: *It may be possible to earn a premium for supplying a dividend policy that is in short supply*. So whenever a law is changed that affects the optimal dividend policy for a particular clientele, there may be opportunities for companies to earn a positive NPV by altering their dividend policy decisions to exploit these opportunities. For example, following the passage of the Tax Reform Act of 1986, which raised the effective tax rate on capital gains relative to the effective tax rate on dividends, Teledyne, which had used excess cash to repurchase shares and had not declared a cash dividend in 26 years, declared its first cash dividend on its common stock.[16]

17.8   A REVIEW OF THE EMPIRICAL EVIDENCE

A large number of empirical studies have attempted to resolve the controversy whether a company's choice of dividend policy can affect its shareholders' wealth. These studies generally fall into two categories: those designed to test investors' relative preference for dividends and capital gains and those designed to test the significance of dividend changes as a signaling device. The available evidence indicates that corporations typically adopt a target payout ratio and that they are reluctant to cut, from one period to the next, the nominal dividend per share amount. That is, companies tend to maintain or increase the actual cash payment per share, allowing the payout ratio to fluctuate around the target. This finding is consistent with the signaling view of the significance of dividend policy. The empirical record is less conclusive, although generally supportive of the view that investors exhibit a relative preference for capital gains over dividends. However, for the most part, this evidence was gathered prior to the Tax Reform Act of 1986. More will be learned as evidence is gathered about the post-1986 period. In the future, Congress may restore the favorable tax treatment previously accorded capital gains. This demonstrates very well our recommendation to know the *current* tax code and look for tax asymmetries in that code.

THE EVIDENCE: SIGNALING

Table 17-1 summarizes the dividend changes U.S. corporations announced during the period 1970–1989. Fewer than 3% of the dividend actions taken during the period involved dividend decreases or omissions; dividend increases and resumptions outnumbered decreases and omissions by more than 7 to 1, and lack of changes in the dividend rate outnumbered decreases and omissions by almost 30 to 1.

A variety of studies of the impact of dividend announcements on share prices have found that the stock market reacts favorably to announcements of dividend increases and adversely to announcements of dividend decreases, as the signaling view suggests.[17] Dividend increases signal that the company has achieved a higher level of

---

[16] Between 1972 and 1986, Teledyne purchased 71 million shares of its common stock, reducing its common shares by 86% to 12 million. See "Farewell Buybacks, Hello Dividends," *Fortune*, March 2, 1987, 129ff.

[17] Aharony and Swary (1980); Charest (1978); Eades (1982); Kwan (1981); and Pettit (1972). Bhattacharya (1979) and Hakansson (1982) have developed formal models in which dividend changes serve as a signal of how well the firm is doing. However, there is not unanimous agreement as to the significance of dividend announcements. See, for example, Watts (1973).

TABLE 17-1 Dividend Changes Announced by Publicly-Owned U.S. Companies, 1970–1989

Year	Number of Companies Taking Dividend Action	Dividend Increased	Dividend Resumed	Dividend Decreased	Dividend Omitted	Extra or Special Dividend Declared
1970	Approx. 9,800	828	75	201	284	910
1971	Approx. 9,800	885	111	154	213	841
1972	Approx. 9,800	1,563	107	73	103	980
1973	Approx. 9,800	2,197	116	37	114	1,105
1974	Approx. 9,800	2,120	139	86	228	1,097
1975	Approx. 9,800	1,648	129	186	266	1,013
1976	Approx. 9,800	2,624	137	74	117	1,047
1977	Over 10,000	2,984	120	68	138	968
1978	Over 10,000	3,211	105	46	105	997
1979	Over 10,000	2,968	71	46	131	829
1980	Over 10,000	2,445	51	88	160	719
1981	Over 10,000	2,160	45	103	198	640
1982	Over 10,000	1,590	46	258	315	515
1983	Over 10,000	1,833	66	106.	126	480
1984	Over 10,000	1,774	58	65	116	435
1985	Over 10,000	1,560	35	68	139	428
1986	Over 10,000	1,513	46	96	189	359
1987	Over 10,000	1,590	54	74	104	403
1988	Over 10,000	1,705	38	62	117	501
1989	Over 10,000	1,648	41	85	160	524
Total		38,846	1,590	1,976	3,323	14,791

Source: Standard & Poor's, *Annual Dividend Record,* 1974–1990.

sustainable earnings, and dividend decreases signal the reverse. In addition, a study by Fama and Babiak provides support for the Lintner model, discussed earlier in the chapter.[18] They studied the dividend records of 392 U.S. companies between 1946 and 1964 and found that on average, firms tended to pay out half their earnings (POR = ½) and tended to move one-third of the way toward this target each year (ADJ = ⅓).

EXAMPLE ■ For example, a company that earned $2.00 per share and paid dividends per share of $1.00 one year and expected to earn $2.90 in each of the next 3 years would pay dividends per share of $1.15 (= 1.00 + [.5(2.90) − 1.00]/3) the next year, $1.25 (= 1.15 + [.5(2.90) − 1.15]/3) the following year, and $1.32 (= 1.25 + [.5(2.90) − 1.25]/3) the third year, according to Equation (17.1). ■

[18] Fama and Babiak (1968).

THE EVIDENCE: SIGNIFICANCE OF TAXES

Taxes would affect share prices if investors could not find some means of offsetting the tax disadvantage (to individual investors) that high-yielding stocks suffer from. Various strategies that investors might employ either to postpone the tax on dividends or effectively to convert dividends to capital gains have been offered.[19]

For example, an individual can eliminate the taxes payable on dividend income by purchasing a single-premium life insurance policy from an insurance company that will invest the sum in common stocks. Income accrues tax-free. Individuals may liquidate the investment tax-free by borrowing the cash value of the policy. Many single-premium life insurance policies charge a very low net interest rate (what the borrower pays the insurance company, net of the yield the insurance company realizes on its profit), in some cases zero, on accumulated interest and dividend income that is borrowed but charge a net rate of 2% to 3% on borrowed principal. Such loans do not have to be repaid but are simply subtracted from the death benefit upon the death of the insured person. These and other dividend-income-tax-reducing schemes are a creation of the tax laws, in this case, the favorable tax treatment accorded life insurance. In addition to being able to create tax shelters like the one just described to offset the tax disadvantage of dividends to individual shareholders, as already noted, corporate shareholders should exhibit a relative preference for dividends over capital gains, and tax-exempt institutions should be indifferent between dividends and capital gains except to the extent of policy or legal restrictions on the expenditure of capital gain income. Consequently, whether the differential taxation of dividends and capital gains is important in practice is an empirical question.

If taxation is important, one should find that shares offering an above-average dividend yield provide an above-average pretax rate of return to compensate for the higher tax rates on dividends than on capital gains. One should also find that higher-yielding stocks are owned by investors with relatively low marginal tax rates and that lower-yielding stocks are owned by investors with relatively high marginal tax rates. On the first point, there is strong though not universal support.[20] On the second point, there are studies that furnish evidence of a clientele effect.[21] In addition, one study found that during the period 1920–1960, corporate payout ratios tended to decrease following an increase in the differential tax rates on dividends and capital gains, and that the reverse occurred when this differential narrowed.[22] The weight of the evidence, then, currently falls on the side of dividend relevance.

However, bear in mind that its relevance may be very small! There are distinguished scholars whose research and analysis have brought them to the conclusion that dividend policy is only a very minor piece in the valuation puzzle.[23] As we noted in Chapter 14, bad financing decisions can destroy a firm. But, although good finan-

---

[19] Miller and Scholes (1978).

[20] See, for example, Litzenberger and Ramaswamy (1979, 1982) and Blume (1980), all of which find that the marginal income tax rate implied in share prices is significantly greater than zero. On the other hand, Black and Scholes (1974) and Miller and Scholes (1982) find no significant difference between the pretax returns high-payout stocks and low-payout stocks provide investors.

[21] See note 7 for citations regarding the clientele effect.

[22] Brittain (1966).

[23] Measurement difficulties may account, at least in part, for the lack of agreement among the studies cited in note 20. The statistical tests should really test the relationship between expected dividend yield and expected pretax returns, but one cannot measure either expected dividends or expected returns directly. For example, unexpectedly high earnings could result in a larger-than-expected dividend (given a set payout ratio) and a higher share price that together produce a higher-than-expected total return. In such a situation, it is not a higher expected dividend but higher-than-expected earnings that account for the unusually high total return.

cing decisions, such as an optimal dividend policy, can contribute to the profitability of a firm, the possibility of extraordinary success rests primarily on the firm's investment decisions: *The principle of pursuing valuable new ideas is the best way to achieve extraordinary returns*.

THE SHARE REPURCHASE ALTERNATIVE   17.9

Corporations that wish to distribute cash to their shareholders typically do so by declaring cash dividends. As an alternative to a cash dividend, the corporation could repurchase shares of common stock. For example, International Business Machines announced a tender offer for up to 4 million shares of its common stock in February 1977. At the time, IBM had more than $6 billion in cash and marketable securities on its balance sheet. The tender offer resulted in IBM reacquiring 2,546,000 shares at a cost of $280 per share, an aggregate cost of approximately $713 million.

SHARE REPURCHASE VERSUS DIVIDENDS

We have demonstrated that when the firm is expanding, shareholders are indifferent between (1) dividend payout with the issuance of new shares and (2) retention of earnings—in a perfect capital market environment (including the absence of all taxes), the two alternatives leave shareholder wealth unchanged. Similarly, when the firm is contracting (the mirror image of expanding) shareholders are indifferent between dividend payout and using earnings to repurchase outstanding shares—in a perfect capital market environment, the two alternatives leave shareholder wealth unchanged. The following examples illustrate this point.

EXAMPLE 1 ■ Suppose that Letts, Knot, Kidder, Selves, a "Big-Three" CPA firm, has determined that it has $50 million cash available for distribution. Letts has 10 million shares outstanding. It expects to earn $2.50 per share, and the current market value per share is $25. The firm could pay a cash dividend of $5 per share, implying an ex-dividend value of $20 per share, or a P/E (price-earnings) ratio of 8. Alternatively, the firm could use the $50 million to repurchase 2,000,000 (= 50,000,000/25) shares. Following the share repurchase, each share would be worth

$$\frac{10,000,000(\$25) - \$50,000,000}{10,000,000 - 2,000,000} = \$25$$

Thus, as long as the firm repurchases shares at the current market price of $25, a shareholder who does not sell will have the same wealth per share as a shareholder who does sell, namely $25 per share. The only difference is that one person has the wealth in the form of cash and the other has the wealth in the form of stock. Moreover, each shareholder would have the same $25 per share wealth if Letts, Knot, Kidder, Selves paid the $5 dividend; in that case, every shareholder would have their wealth in the same form: $5 in cash plus a share of stock worth $20.   ■

Note that to the extent the firm pays a repurchase price in excess of the market price, there is a transfer of wealth to the shareholders who sell from those who do not.

EXAMPLE 2 ■   To continue the Letts example, suppose the firm decides to spend $50 million to buy shares for $30 each from the firm's retired chairman (who sits on the compensation committee of Letts's board of directors). The firm can purchase $1,666,666\frac{2}{3}$ (= $50,000,000/30$) shares. Following the share repurchase, each share will be worth

$$\frac{10,000,000(\$25) - 50,000,000}{10,000,000 - 1,666,666\frac{2}{3}} = \$24$$

There is a transfer of wealth *to* the retired chairman amounting to $8,333,333.33 (= $[30 - 25]1,666,666\frac{2}{3}$), and there is a transfer of wealth *from* the remaining shareholders amounting to the same $8,333,333.33 (= $[25 - 24]8,333,333\frac{1}{3}$). In the past, many firms have paid a premium to buy back shares from a takeover raider. When they do, they expropriate a portion of the other shareholders' collective wealth. ∎

The effect of a share repurchase on shareholder wealth is often misunderstood by less sophisticated market participants who judge the impact in terms of EPS (earnings per share). In example 1, the firm's shares should trade at a P/E ratio of 8 following the distribution of the $50 million in cash, regardless of whether the cash is distributed as a dividend or through share repurchase, because of the risk-return trade-off—the same amount of equity is invested in either case. Neither the firm's capital structure nor its capital investment policies are affected by the method of cash distribution. The share repurchase alternative would result in projected EPS of

$$\frac{\$2.50(10,000,000)}{8,000,000} = \$3.125$$

However, although the EPS is higher with the share repurchase, each share would still be worth

$$\$3.125(8) = \$25$$

The increase in projected EPS is just offset by the decline in the P/E ratio (from 10 to 8). The confusion over the impact of share repurchases results from the mistaken belief that share repurchase will not alter the P/E ratio. But if the P/E ratio remained unchanged, the risk-return relationship would differ between the alternatives, which would be inconsistent with the Principles of Capital Market Efficiency and Risk-Return Trade-Off.

ADVANTAGES OF REPURCHASING SHARES In example 1, the share repurchase program does not affect shareholder wealth, which remains $25 per original share following the repurchase. But this conclusion depends on our assumption of a perfect capital market. Asymmetric taxes can alter this conclusion. Because of the tax factors noted earlier in this chapter, taxable individual shareholders would generally suffer a lesser tax liability, and hence realize greater wealth, if the firm repurchases shares in lieu of making a dividend distribution. Historically, capital gains have been taxed at a lower rate than dividends for individual investors. If dividends are taxed at a 50% rate and capital gains are taxed at a 20% rate, shareholders in the above example would have to pay $25,000,000 (= $[.5]50,000,000$) in aggregate taxes on the dividend distribution but no more than $10,000,000 (= $[.2]50,000,000$) in aggregate taxes on the share repurchase (depending upon the tax basis of each shareholder). On the other hand, dividends paid to other corporations are taxed at a lower rate than capital gains because of the 70% dividends received deduction. Consequently, corporate shareholders will generally prefer dividends to capital gains. The overall net tax advantage (or disadvantage) of share repurchase versus dividends will

TABLE 17-2 Stated Objectives of Corporate Share Repurchase Programs

Objective	Number of Times Mentioned in Walsh Study [a]			Number of Times Mentioned in Lees Study [b]		
	Primary Objective	Secondary or Lesser Objective	Total	Primary Objective	Secondary or Lesser Objective	Total
Obtain shares for executive stock options and other compensation programs	57	35	92	38	26	64
Obtain shares for acquisitions	15	53	68	2	23	25
Improve earnings per share	8	34	42	2	24	26
Obtain shares for conversions	10	26	36	0	16	16
Temporary investment of surplus cash	4	17	21	0	8	8
Support share price	1	19	20	2	9	11
Increase debt-to-equity ratio	1	13	14	1	7	8
Exploit attractive investment opportunity	7	2	9	17	23	40
Reduce cost of servicing small holders	0	8	8	1	4	5

[a] Objectives reported by a sample of 113 corporations that repurchased shares of their own common stock in 1973.
[b] Objectives reported by a sample of 72 corporations that repurchased shares of their own common stock during the period 1978–1982.

Sources: Francis J. Walsh, Jr., *Repurchasing Common Stock* (New York: The Conference Board, Report No. 659, 1975): 7, and Francis A. Lees, *Repurchasing Common Stock* (New York: The Conference Board, Research Bulletin No. 147, 1983), 6.

thus depend on the shareholder mix. In Section 17.10, we consider a strategy that combines the two alternatives by offering shareholders an option.

WHY DO FIRMS REPURCHASE THEIR SHARES?

The IBM example illustrates one of several reasons corporations have given for repurchasing their shares. Table 17-2 summarizes the results of two studies concerning corporate motives for repurchasing shares.[24] In interpreting these results, it should be kept in mind that firms may be loath to announce that they have excess cash available or that they wish (for tax reasons) to substitute a share repurchase for a cash dividend. Consequently, the stated objective may mask the true objective.

DISTRIBUTE CASH TO SHAREHOLDERS The most widely recognized motive, and the one that has received the most attention in the financial literature, is the distribution of surplus funds in lieu of a dividend distribution. The substitutability of one for the other is most vividly demonstrated by the sharp increase in the magnitude of share repurchases in 1973 and 1974. In connection with the wage and price controls program in 1973–1974, the federal government imposed dividend limitations. However, it did not impose any restrictions on share repurchases. The volume of share repurchases increased from 44 million shares in 1972 to 144 million in 1973 and 90 million in 1974.

Corporations that find themselves with a substantial amount of excess cash to dis-

[24] Walsh (1975) and Lees (1983) provide a more detailed study of motives corporations have for repurchasing their own stock. While the two studies are dated, we believe that the survey results they report cover the range and reflect the relative importance of the corporate motives for repurchasing common stock.

tribute generally prefer to repurchase shares rather than declare a "special" or "extra" dividend. This is due to a potential tax asymmetry. The share repurchase can effectively convert dividend income into a long-term capital gain.[25]

Tandy Corporation has been one of the stronger proponents of the view that a firm should repurchase shares rather than pay cash dividends. Prior to passage of the Tax Reform Act of 1986, Tandy had never paid a cash common stock dividend; between 1973 and 1984, Tandy repurchased more than $700 million of its common stock, including $100 million and $355 million cash tender offers and two exchange offers worth approximately $125 million, all with the avowed intention of reducing its shareholders' tax liability on Tandy's cash distributions.[26] Soon after the act became law, Tandy introduced a regular quarterly cash dividend in January 1987.

The aforementioned tax advantage exists for one-time share repurchase programs. However, if a firm substituted a program of regular share repurchases for periodic dividend payments, there is a danger that the Internal Revenue Service would claim that such repurchases do not satisfy Section 302 of the Internal Revenue Code, thus creating a tax liability for shareholders.[27] We have noted that the tax position of corporate shareholders differs from that of individuals. Corporations are entitled to a 70% dividends received deduction, and corporate shareholders therefore generally prefer dividends over capital gains.

Since 1960, the percentages of New York Stock Exchange-listed stocks owned by corporations and nontaxable institutions have increased substantially while the corresponding percentages for stock owned by individuals has decreased. As a result, institutions hold roughly half the aggregate market value of New York Stock Exchange-listed common stocks.[28] Because of the different preferences of the different investor groups, it is important for a corporation contemplating a share repurchase program as a means of distributing excess cash to take into consideration its shareholder mix. Generally, some stockholders of the firm will prefer a cash dividend, while others will prefer share repurchase as a means of cash disbursement.

ELIMINATE SMALL SHAREHOLDINGS   The cost of servicing a small shareholder account (e.g., printing and mailing annual and quarterly reports, proxy materials, dividend checks, etc.) is roughly the same as the cost of servicing a large shareholder account. Therefore, the cost of servicing small shareholder accounts is proportionately greater. Corporations frequently try to reduce the overall cost of servicing shareholders by offering to repurchase small shareholdings. For example, on August 2, 1982, LTV Corporation announced an offer to repurchase common shares from its shareholders who owned 20 or fewer shares. LTV offered a premium of $1 over the closing price the day the shareholder's order was received plus a bonus of $5 for each shareholder tendering her entire account.[29] Such a transaction may benefit both the larger shareholders who remain, by reducing future servicing costs,

---

[25] Under Section 302 of the Internal Revenue Code, the share repurchase must also satisfy one of the following three conditions in order for any gain to qualify for long-term capital gain treatment: (1) the payment is deemed "not essentially equivalent to a dividend," (2) the repurchase results in a "substantially disproportionate" reduction in the shareholder's interest in the firm, or (3) the repurchase completely terminates the stockholder's interest in the firm.

[26] Tandy Corporation, *1977 Annual Report to Shareholders*, June 30, 1977.

[27] See note 25. Although the IRS could (in keeping with Section 302) take this position even with respect to a one-time share repurchase program instituted by a widely held firm, it has not, to our knowledge, done so.

[28] *New York Stock Exchange Institutional Investor Fact Book 1990*, 18–29.

[29] "LTV Offering To Buy Shares," *New York Times*, August 3, 1982, D4.

and the small ones that are bought out, by giving them more than they could otherwise net for their shares. The benefits depend on the total reduction in future servicing costs.

Offers to repurchase small shareholdings generally involve a price that represents a premium of between $0.50 and $1.00 per share over the prevailing market price plus a bonus of between $5.00 and $10.00 if the entire shareholding is tendered. The bonus typically approximates the annual cost of servicing a shareholder account. The premium price, together with the opportunity to avoid the disproportionately high brokerage commissions on odd-lot transactions, provide a strong inducement to sell.

INCREASE LEVERAGE   A corporation that wishes to increase its leverage can either borrow funds and use the proceeds to repurchase shares or offer its shareholders the opportunity to exchange their shares for a new issue of debt.

EXPLOIT PERCEIVED UNDERVALUATION   The firm's common stock is "undervalued" and therefore provides an attractive investment opportunity (i.e., one with a positive NPV) is perhaps the reason most frequently articulated by corporations when announcing a share repurchase program.[30] For example, more than 200 companies announced share repurchase plans within one week of the October 1987 stock market crash, citing the sharply lower share prices that resulted from the crash and their belief that their shares were now undervalued.[31] Shareholders would benefit if the share repurchase announcement caused the stock market to revalue the firm's shares upward. Remaining shareholders might benefit further if management was unusually prescient. But these benefits depend on management's ability to identify when a firm's stock is undervalued and, in turn, on the stock market's recognition of this. In an efficient capital market, a stock is "undervalued" from the standpoint of a firm's management only if management possesses information that is not currently available to the market and that information would lead investors to revalue the firm's shares upward if it were available to them. Based on the Principle of Self-Interested Behavior, if investors believe that management possesses significant nonpublic information (for example, regarding the firm's earnings prospects), they would react to the announcement of the share repurchase program by bidding up the price of the firm's shares. The announcement of the share repurchase program serves as a proxy for the release of the nonpublic information. But it is more difficult for the market to gauge the significance, if any, of the share repurchase announcement than it would be for it to gauge the significance of the nonpublic information, were it disclosed publicly. Because of the ambiguity of the share repurchase announcement for valuation purposes—in the extreme, the firm may really be using excess cash to retire shares in lieu of dividend distribution—the announcement of a share repurchase program may not cure the information asymmetry and the resulting perceived "undervaluation."

Whether the announcement of a share repurchase program can lead to an increase in a firm's share price is an empirical question, that is considered later in the chapter.

---

[30] There is probably some reluctance on the part of corporations to announce that they lack sufficient attractive external investment opportunities. Whether or not they really regard the firm's stock as undervalued, management is in many cases actually distributing cash that is excess in the sense that they cannot find positive-NPV projects.

[31] "More Than 200 Firms Set Buy-Back Plans Since Market's Crash," *Wall Street Journal*, October 26, 1987, 17.

For now, suffice it to say that at least two major studies have provided evidence regarding managements' ability to identify when their stocks are undervalued.[32] If management does have this ability, repurchasing shares would prove beneficial to the remaining shareholders (i.e., those who do not sell their shares back to the firm), at least over the longer term. Note that in an efficient capital market, even if a firm could exploit nonpublic information to benefit one group of shareholders (those who hold) at the expense of another (those who sell), such a situation could not continue for very long. Rational investors would refuse to sell shares to the firm until they were satisfied that the transaction price fully reflected any significant nonpublic information the firm was trying to exploit.[33]

INCREASE REPORTED EARNINGS PER SHARE Corporations undertaking share repurchase programs frequently state as one of their objectives a desire to increase reported earnings per share. This presumes that the firm's shares continue to trade at the same price-earnings ratio, in which case the share price would be higher following the repurchase and the firm's shareholders would therefore benefit. However, what should be compared is (1) the combined value of the dividend plus the value of a share immediately thereafter if the corporation uses the cash to make a dividend distribution and (2) the value of a share immediately following the repurchase if the corporation uses an identical sum to make share repurchases. As we have demonstrated, if shares are repurchased at a "fair" price, the two alternatives leave (the remaining) shareholders in an identical position. The effect of the increase in reported earnings per share exactly offsets the amount of the dividend.

If a premium price is paid, however, the increase in earnings per share, and hence the subsequent share price, will not fully compensate for the dividend forgone. In that case, selling shareholders would benefit at the expense of the remaining shareholders, the increase in reported earnings per share notwithstanding. In such cases, the remaining shareholders would be better off if the firm instead made a dividend distribution.

CONSOLIDATE INSIDERS' CONTROL POSITION Although it is seldom stated explicitly as an objective, it is apparent that some corporations have repurchased shares to consolidate the position of existing management or certain large shareholders (collectively called **insiders**). This most often takes the form of block purchases from contentious minority shareholders, sometimes at a substantial premium over the prevailing market price. The financial press uses the pejorative term **greenmail** to describe such repurchases. In other cases, it takes the form of repurchases intended principally to reduce the "public float" in the stock—that is, the percentage held by persons not affiliated with the insider group. In the extreme case, an insider group might purchase sufficient shares to "take the firm private" so that the firm is no longer subject to the Security and Exchange Commission reporting requirements. In yet other cases, the repurchases are designed simply to reduce a firm's liquidity and hence its attractiveness as an acquisition candidate, thereby enhancing management's security.[34] In each of these cases, however, the repurchase program is not necessarily consistent with the objective of maximizing the wealth of the firm's

---

[32] Finnerty (1976); Jaffe (1974). These studies suggest that managers in many cases have information regarding their respective firms that is not generally available to market participants and that they are able to profit from this insider information.

[33] Vermaelen (1981).

[34] Note that this strategy can backfire. The repurchases reduce the number of shares outstanding, thereby reducing the number a takeover raider would need to buy to gain control.

shareholders generally. Because of this, there is a potential agency problem connected with the insider control position.

ELIMINATE PERCEIVED MARKET OVERHANG   One of the secondary reasons sometimes given—and one of the reasons stated in connection with the IBM tender offer mentioned at the beginning of this section—is to eliminate **market overhang**, the problem posed by certain large holders who might want to liquidate some or all of their holdings but who are reluctant to sell because they might have to sell at a significant discount to dispose of their shares. The repurchase program provides liquidity and even a premium if the firm's tender is at a premium. Such cooperation by the firm (and its managers) can build and/or maintain a favorable reputation for cooperative and ethical behavior. Such a reputation may reduce the firm's agency costs.

EVIDENCE REGARDING THE STOCK MARKET'S REACTION

The stock market's reaction is probably influenced by the general profile of repurchasing firms that has emerged from studies of the financial and operating characteristics of these firms. These studies have shown that firms that repurchase their shares are generally less leveraged, less profitable, and slower growing than other firms.[35] These results are broadly consistent with the vew that such firms lack positive-NPV investment opportunities.

The stock market's reaction to a share repurchase announcement also depends importantly on *how* the firm decides to implement the share repurchases. Methods for implementing a share repurchase program are discussed at greater length in Chapter 18. Briefly, the two principal methods are an **open market purchase** program and a **tender offer**. An open market purchase program involves purchasing shares of common stock on the open market at prevailing prices, in competition with other prospective investors. A tender offer, as already noted, involves a one-time offer to purchase a stated number of shares, typically at a single fixed price that exceeds the prevailing share price at the time of the tender offer announcement. Recent evidence suggests that the announcement of a tender offer is more likely to elicit a favorable stock market reaction than the announcement of an open market program. At least four studies have demonstrated that tender offers generally have a favorable share price impact around the time the firm announces the tender offer and that any price rollback that occurs when the tender offer terminates is generally not significant, except perhaps when the tender offer is oversubscribed and the firm elects to prorate its purchases among tendering shareholders.[36]

Apparently a tender offer is a more positive signal than an open market purchase. However, this doesn't mean a firm should always choose the tender offer method because the tender offer is typically more expensive and can have other disadvantages, particularly if the tender offer is oversubscribed. Of course, these are probably just the reasons why the tender offer is interpreted as the more positive signal!

TRANSFERABLE PUT RIGHTS   17.10

A firm cannot compel its shareholders to sell their shares; it can only offer to repurchase them. As discussed in Chapter 18, firms often use the **fixed-price tender**

---

[35] See Finnerty (1975); Marks (1976); Norgaard and Norgaard (1974).
[36] Dann (1981); Dielman, Nantell, and Wright (1980); Masulis (1980); Vermaelen (1981).

offer method to repurchase shares, offering shareholders the opportunity to sell their shares back to the firm at a premium above the prevailing market price. Typically, the firm also states a maximum number of shares it is willing to repurchase at the stated tender price. Each shareholder is free to accept the offer (and sell his shares to the firm), or reject the offer (and retain her shares). But if the aggregate number of shares tendered exceeds the maximum, the firm is permitted to prorate the number of shares it repurchases from each holder so that shareholders may sell fewer shares than they had intended.

Announcing a fixed-price tender offer is tantamount to giving shareholders a put option. The stated tender price serves as the strike price. When the tender price exceeds the prevailing share price, the put option is in-the-money. In any case, we know from the Options Principle (options are valuable) that the option has value (a time value) even if it is currently out-of-the-money—the tender price is below the market price. Shareholders can realize the value of the tender put option only if they exercise the option; they cannot sell it separately from their shares, so if they do not exercise, the option expires worthless.

Those shareholders with a relatively low tax basis in their shares will have less of an incentive to sell their shares than a higher-tax-basis shareholder because of the higher capital gains tax liability. When a tender offer is undersubscribed, the premium over market price paid to the selling shareholders results in a transfer of wealth from the shareholders who "remain behind." Moreover, if the tender offer is prorated there is a tax inefficiency: Some investors with low tax bases, and hence greater tax liabilities as a result of tendering, will sell shares while investors with higher tax bases, and hence smaller potential tax liabilities, will not sell all their shares.

Transferable put rights are designed to mitigate these deficiencies.[37] A transferable put right represents the right to sell back to the firm one share of the firm's common stock at a fixed price (the strike price) within a stated period (the time to maturity). In Chapter 14, we discussed rights offerings, which involve the distribution of call options to a firm's shareholders. Those options involve the right to *buy* from the firm one share of the firm's common stock at a fixed price within a stated period. Transferable put rights and the conventional rights offering are symmetrical; the former involves put options, and provides the right to sell shares, the latter involves call options, and provides the right to buy shares.

HOW A TRANSFERABLE PUT RIGHTS OFFERING WORKS   On August 15, 1988, The Gillette Company issued one put right for each 7 shares held as of August 12.[38] Each put right entitled the holder to sell one share of stock to the company on or before September 19 at a price of $45 (net to the seller in cash), a significant premium above the $34⅞ closing price on August 12 (a Friday). Gillette had 112,100,227 shares outstanding, and the company would repurchase 16,014,318 shares (one-seventh of the shares outstanding) at a cost of approximately $721 million if all the put rights were exercised.

VALUE OF TRANSFERABLE PUT RIGHTS   Recall from Chapter 8 that the value of an option, and therefore a put right, is a function of (1) the strike price; (2) the value of the underlying asset (3) the time to expiration; (4) the variance of the rate of return on the underlying asset; and (5) the riskless rate of interest. In addition, the

---

[37] Kale, Noe, and Gay (1989).
[38] The Gillette Company, Summary of Rights Offer, Transferable Share Repurchase Rights, August 15, 1988.

value of a put right depends on its **antidilutive effect**, resulting from the decrease in the number of shares outstanding. (Recall that rights have a dilutive effect, resulting from an increase in the number of shares.)

Similar to a rights offering, put rights are issued in-the-money to encourage exercise, as in the Gillette example. That is, the issuer sets a positive exercise value by setting the repurchase (strike) price *above* the market price of the stock on the **date of record**. (Recall that for a *call* rights offering the strike price is set *below* the market price.) Because of the short time to expiration, the time value of the option is small and therefore a relatively less significant determinant of the value of the put right.

Given our characterization of a put right and our description of how a transferable put rights offering works, we hope you can now see the symmetry between a put rights offering (in-the-money put options issued to current shareholders) and the conventional rights offering described in Chapter 14 (in-the-money call options issued to current shareholders). In light of this symmetry in structure, you should not be surprised to learn that the basic expression for valuing a put right is symmetrical to Equation (14.4) for valuing a (call) right.

The initial value of a put right just after the offering is announced and when the stock is trading rights-on (i.e., the rights are still attached to the stock) is approximated by

$$R = \frac{S - P_R}{N - 1} \tag{17.2}$$

where R is the value of one put right, P_R is the market value of a share trading rights-on, S is the strike (repurchase) price, and N is the number of rights to sell one share assuming the issuer distributes one put right per share. For example, the initial value of each right issued in connection with the Gillette put rights offering was

$$R = \frac{\$45.00 - 34.875}{7 - 1} = \$1.6875 \text{ per Gillette share}$$

Note the symmetry between Equations (14.4) and (17.2). A conventional (call) rights issue results in 1 new share for every N outstanding; a put rights issue results in 1 fewer share for every N previously outstanding, when all rights are exercised.

Similar to the case of a conventional (call) rights offering, after the ex-date the stock trades ex-rights because a purchaser is not entitled to the put rights. On the ex-date, then, the share price decreases by the value of the right which is no longer attached to it. Therefore, the share price ex-rights, denoted P_E, is

$$P_E = P_R - R \tag{17.3}$$

and thereafter the market value of each put right will vary with the price of the firm's (ex-right) shares:

$$R = \frac{S - P_E}{N} \tag{17.4}$$

To continue the Gillette example, the put rights began trading August 16, closing at $10⅝ while the stock closed at $33¾ per share. Substituting into Equation (17.4), the value of each put right, as we have characterized them, would be

$$R = \frac{\$45.00 - 33.75}{7} = \$1.6071 \text{ per Gillette share}$$

Since Gillette issued one put right per 7 common shares, the approximate market value of the put rights Gillette issued is

$$(7)1.6071 = \$11.2497$$

which *exceeds* the observed market price. Surprised?

There is one additional factor that can affect the value of a put right that we have left out of Equations (17.2) and (17.4): *Taxes*. Put rights enable low-tax-basis share-holders to realize the value of the option by selling the put right, thereby avoiding the capital gains tax liability they would incur if they sold their shares. Avoiding (or at least deferring) this tax liability is valuable, and depending upon the supply of put rights offered by low-tax-basis shareholders and the demand for put rights by high-tax-basis shareholders, the put price can be bid up above the sum of its exercise value plus its time value. To the extent it is bid up above the sum of these values, low-tax-basis shareholders effectively realize a greater proportion of the value of the tax savings relative to a fixed-price tender offer—at the expense of high-tax-basis shareholders.[39]

The following generalized version of Equation (17.4) has been developed to re-flect these tax considerations:[40]

$$R = \frac{(1 - \tau_g)S + \tau_g B - P_E}{(1 - \tau_g)N} \tag{17.5}$$

where τ_g denotes the capital gains tax rate and B the tax basis of the marginal pur-chaser of put rights. To continue the Gillette example, suppose the marginal pur-chaser had a tax rate of 18% and a tax basis of $30 per share. Then the value of the Gillette put rights is $1.4895 (= [(1 − .18)45 + .18(30) − 33.75]/[(1 − .18)7]) per Gillette share and $10.4265 (= [1.4895]7) per put right, implying a time value of the option of $0.1985 (= 10.625 − 10.4265) for these hypothetical parameter values. This is the best example we have found that illustrates so clearly how tax factors *can* affect option valuation.

ADVANTAGES OF TRANSFERABLE PUT RIGHTS   Put rights offer four potential advantages over fixed-price tender offers: (1) low-tax-basis shareholders are able to realize value for their rights without having to incur the tax liability that the sale of their shares would trigger; (2) only shareholders with low tax bases remain, which will make a takeover more costly to a potential raider; (3) there is a tax efficiency gain (at the expense of the U.S. Treasury) because low-tax-basis shareholders sell their rights rather than their shares; and (4) there is no risk of oversubscription.

Transferable put rights represent an innovative share repurchase strategy. The only potential drawback we can see is that because of tax law complexity, share-holders may be forced to incur significant transaction costs in the form of effort (or cost of tax advice) necessary to determine the correct tax treatment of the receipt and exercise of the put rights. We think this problem will prove relatively minor in the long-run, as investors become more familiar with put rights, and we expect that transferable put rights will become more widely used in the future because of their inherent advantages.

17.11	POLICY IMPLICATIONS

While some investors prefer high-payout stocks, others prefer capital gains, princi-pally for tax reasons. As one would expect, dividend-oriented common stock inves-

[39] Kale, Noe, and Gay (1989).
[40] Ibid., 147.

tors generally gravitate toward high-payout common stocks, such as electric utility stocks, and capital-gain-oriented common stock investors generally gravitate toward more rapidly growing companies that distribute little or no dividends, such as the common stocks of younger high technology companies. Thus, a significant change in dividend policy would tend to induce a shift in shareholder mix. Following a period of transition, there might be little if any change in the company's stock market value because former shareholders who objected to the new dividend policy would simply have sold out to new shareholders who liked the new policy. In this way, changes in shareholder mix would tend to lessen, or even eliminate, any longer-term impact of a change in a company's dividend policy on its share price.

Even though a company's shareholder mix can be expected to shift in response to a change in its dividend policy, a sudden shift may be disruptive to its share price in the near term, and frequent major shifts may be disruptive over the longer term because transaction costs make it expensive for investors to buy and sell shares. A company should strive to maintain a stable dividend policy, departing from an established dividend policy only when significant changes in its investment opportunities or earnings prospects dictate.

SOLUTION TO ITT'S DIVIDEND DILEMMA

On July 10, 1984, ITT Corporation announced a cut in its common dividend rate, to 25 cents per quarter from 69 cents per quarter. It announced the dividend action at the end of the trading day. The next day, ITT's share price fell by nearly a third relative to the market: ITT's share price fell to $21⅛, from $31 (a decrease of 32%), while the Standard & Poor's 500 Index fell 1.5%. ITT apparently had a sound business purpose in cutting its dividend rate, so why would there be such a severe stock market reaction?

At the time, a number of securities analysts complained that prior to the cut, ITT management had led them to believe that the dividend rate would not be cut in the near future. The severe drop in price and the securities analysts' complaints suggest that the sharp dividend reduction had caught investors by surprise. It would appear that ITT's management might have felt that a dividend reduction should not be a possibility—until it had already become a reality. From the material presented in this chapter, you should be able to see that if information is an important component of dividend policy, ITT's actions could be interpreted as contradictory signals. On the one hand, they appeared to say that their dividend rate would not be cut. On the other, a short time later the dividend rate was cut. Investors had to interpret this information.

At least three broad possibilities exist: (1) ITT ran into major difficulties between the time ITT management seemed to indicate that there would be no dividend cut and the time of the cut; (2) ITT management had planned the dividend cut as a business strategy, was less than forthcoming about its plans, but in conjunction with the cut was fully revealing its plans and beliefs about ITT's prospects; or (3) ITT management had planned the cut because ITT was doing poorly, was less than forthcoming about its plans, and was still not entirely forthcoming concerning its beliefs about ITT's future prospects when it cut the dividend rate. In this case, it may be that only additional information would allow investors to determine which of these possibilities is closest to the true situation. Investors who believed that (3) was a real possibility might have been convinced (2) was most likely the case if ITT had been able to signal in advance that a dividend cut was imminent.

Another possible contributing factor is that the cut in the dividend rate caused ITT's dividend clientele to be no longer interested in owning ITT's common stock. If this was the case, the clientele's sudden desire to rebalance their portfolios could have created a rush of sell orders, forcing down the market-clearing price. If investors had anticipated the dividend cut by one or two quarters, they might have been able to sell their ITT shares in a more orderly fashion, causing less of a market price disruption.

Although we cannot identify exactly the contributions of these factors, ITT's share price rose throughout the rest of July. By the end of July, it had risen to $24⅛ (an increase of 14%) while the Standard & Poor's 500 Index remained virtually unchanged. Over the balance of the summer, ITT's share price moved in parallel with the index. It would thus appear that roughly half of the decrease on July 11 could be explained as a permanent reaction to the negative signal, with the other half resulting from the disruptive effect of the sudden unexpected dividend cut.

We believe there is a valuable lesson to be learned from ITT's experience. If a company is seriously considering a dividend cut, it should make a reasonable effort to inform investors of this possibility or at least not deny the possibility if asked. At a minimum, a firm should avoid giving confusing or misleading signals. When a large dividend cut occurs, a shifting of dividend clienteles is also likely to occur. Ensuring the quality of information that is available to investors affords the most effective means of minimizing the disruptive impact on the share price when such shifts occur.

SUMMARY

A company should establish its dividend policy with a view to maximizing shareholder wealth. Its payout policy should be determined chiefly in keeping with its investment opportunities and internal funds needs. But also important are

1. anticipating how the market will interpret the firm's changes, *or* lack of changes, in its dividend policy;

2. taking advantage of changes in laws that create a demand for innovative dividend policies that might be profitable;

3. balancing shareholder preferences for capital gains and dividends;

4. taking shareholder preferences for liquidity into account;

5. balancing the relative transaction costs of selling shares for the firm versus the shareholders; and

6. taking into account any legal or policy restrictions on the firm and its shareholders concerning dividend policy.

The critical issue in dividend policy is whether the dividend decision should be made actively or passively. If passively, a company would simply pay out any funds that it could not invest profitably, in which case its dividend policy would simply be the mirror image of its capital investment program. If actively, the company would have to set its payout ratio and manage its dividend rate to maximize shareholder wealth.

In their classic article on dividend policy, MM show that in a perfect market with both the capital investment program and capital structure fixed, a firm's choice of dividend policy does not affect its value or the wealth of its shareholders. In such a world, share valuation is based entirely on the company's capital investment pro-

DECISION SUMMARY BOX

The analysis and empirical evidence reviewed in this chapter suggest the following dividend policy guidelines:

- A firm should make orderly changes in its dividend rate to avoid destabilizing its share price and to maximize the usefulness of its dividend policy as a signaling device. In particular, a company should determine at each decision point whether it should continue its current quarterly dividend rate or can sustain a higher rate into the foreseeable future. Of course, if earnings prospects have materially worsened since the last decision point, the company must consider cutting the dividend rate to a lower but sustainable level.

- The appropriate dividend action depends on the company's future earnings prospects and anticipated funds requirements.

- A firm should determine what percentage of its earnings it expects to have available for distribution over its planning horizon (typically 5 years). This percentage depends on its earnings prospects, the availability of attractive investment opportunities, and the firm's chosen capital structure policy.

- A firm should determine whether a higher or a lower payout ratio is warranted in view of the firm's particular shareholder mix but should avoid setting the target payout ratio at a level that would trigger the need for an additional equity issue. The payout ratios of comparable firms provide a useful guide in this regard. Generally, a shareholder mix dominated by upper-income individual shareholders would argue for a payout ratio somewhat below that justified solely on the basis of residual earnings considerations, whereas a shareholder mix dominated by corporate shareholders, retired individuals, and tax-exempt institutions would argue for the opposite.

- A firm that has a large amount of cash to distribute should consider repurchasing shares in lieu of increasing its dividend rate. The firm's shareholder mix will determine which strategy, or whether a combination of the two, is best. A shareholder mix dominated by individuals will generally prefer a share repurchase; a shareholder mix dominated by corporate investors will generally prefer one or more dividend distributions.

- A firm planning to repurchase its shares should consider doing so through a transferable put rights offering.

---

gram—the expected NPVs of future projects. Dividend policy does not matter; shareholders can manufacture homemade dividends just as easily as the firm can declare and pay real dividends. Consequently, dividend policy can be passive. In a perfect market, companies can simply distribute excess funds.

But our financial system contains some important persistent imperfections. Information is not costless and freely available to everyone. Dividend policy plays an important role as a signaling device. Thus, simply paying out residual earnings year by year is inadvisable because such a policy would in most cases cause the dividend rate to fluctuate wildly and thus reduce its information value. In order for dividend changes to serve as an effective signaling mechanism, a company must prevent its dividend rate from fluctuating wildly from one period to the next. A company can smooth out fluctuations by building cash surpluses during periods of lower capital expenditure requirements and then drawing down these cash balances during periods of higher capital expenditure requirements.

There are other market imperfections also. The system of individual taxation imposes a bias in favor of capital gains and against dividends. The system of corporate taxation does just the opposite for corporate investors. Depending upon the circumstances, tax-exempt pension funds may have preferences in either direction. At least partly as a result, high-income individual investors appear to gravitate toward low-payout firms, and corporate investors should prefer high-payout firms. Also, transaction costs for the firm impose a bias in favor of retained earnings over new share issues. However, transaction costs for investors impose at least some bias in favor of dividends over retained earnings for investors who want some minimum level of dividend income. The clientele effect, which involves investors investing in firms that have adopted dividend policies that are best for them, may mitigate some or all of these considerations, with the exception of the signaling implications.

When a firm has cash available for distribution to its shareholders, it can re-purchase shares in lieu of distributing the cash as dividends. Share repurchases are generally more beneficial from a tax standpoint to individual shareholders, but non-taxable institutional shareholders may prefer, and corporate shareholders generally will prefer, a dividend distribution. A firm's shareholder mix helps determine whether a share repurchase program is preferable to a dividend distribution—or whether the corporation should use some combination of the two.

A share repurchase program should have a valid business purpose that is consis-tent with the enhancement of shareholder wealth. Firms have a variety of reasons for repurchasing shares of their own stock in addition to wishing to distribute excess cash. Potential reasons include a desire to eliminate small shareholdings, increase lev-erage, buy back "undervalued" shares, neutralize the dilutive impact of employee stock option programs, increase reported earnings per share, consolidate insiders' control, or eliminate market overhang. These reasons are not all necessarily consis-tent with shareholder wealth maximization, so there are agency problems associated with share repurchases. If a share repurchase program is planned, a transferable put rights offering may be the most advantageous method of implementation because of its fewer agency problems and greater tax-efficiency.

We don't know yet exactly how dividend policy affects the value of the firm. We expect future research to provide increased insight into this issue. In the meantime, we will try to provide some guidance in the next chapter about how firms can, and currently do, manage dividends in light of the many considerations connected with dividend policy.

PROBLEMS

PROBLEM SET A

A1. Briefly explain the **traditional view** of dividend policy.

A2. Briefly explain the **tax differential view** of dividend policy.

A3. Briefly explain the **signaling view** of dividend policy.

A4. Define the term **dividend clientele** and briefly explain how the existence of dividend clienteles mitigates the tax differential view of dividend policy.

A5. True or False: The empirical evidence shows that on average, a dividend decrease affects the firm's stock price negatively but a dividend increase has no effect on the firm's stock price.

A6. True or False: A large majority of firms follow a dividend policy that spec-ifies a fixed payout ratio, so that the dollar amount each quarter fluctuates according to the firm's earnings.

A7. Cite two examples of how transaction costs might affect a firm's choice of dividend policy.

A8. Briefly explain how a change in a law might create a positive-NPV opportunity for a firm with respect to its dividend policy.

A9. What is meant by the phrase "bird-in-the-hand fallacy" when referring to the traditional view of dividend policy. Briefly explain how the counterargument invalidates the traditional view that shareholders benefit from a large dividend payout.

A10. In what sense are share repurchases and dividend payments substitutes for one another? Under what circumstances, if any, are they perfect substitutes?

A11. Common stock of the I. M. Wright Company has a current market value of $47. If Wright issues transferable put rights to its shareholders, and 5 put rights are required to sell one share back to the company for $55, what would you expect a put right to be worth, ignoring taxes?

PROBLEM SET B

B1. What is the basis for the view that a firm's total market value is invariant to its choice of dividend policy? Cite three broad types of capital market imperfections that might cause the dividend policy of a firm to have an effect on the value of that firm. Give three examples (one for each type) where such an imperfection would cause a firm's dividend policy to have an effect on the value of that firm. Explain *how* each of the three examples you gave would cause a firm's dividend policy to have an effect on the value of that firm.

B2. How might the cost of issuing new stock affect a firm's choice of dividend policy?

B3. Common stock of Wee-Bee Nuts, Inc. has a current market value of $23. Wee-Bee is planning to issue transferable put rights to its shareholders, with 4 put rights required to sell one share back to the company for $30. Ida B. Confused has a tax basis of $17.50 per share for her shares in Wee-Bee. If Ida's capital gain tax rate is 14%, what would you expect a put right to be worth to her?

B4. Cite three broad reasons why an unexpected cut in a firm's dividend rate might cause a severe drop in the market price of the firm's stock.

B5. Explain why a firm's share price falls on the dividend ex-date. By how much would you expect it to fall? Does it matter whether the dividend is paid in cash or additional stock?

B6. If the price of a share of common stock can be expressed as the present value of the future dividend stream, how could it be that dividend policy is irrelevant?

B7. Under what circumstances might the introduction of a dividend reinvestment plan increase shareholder wealth?

B8. Consider a firm that has decided to make, but has not yet announced, a large "bonus" cash dividend amounting in the aggregate to $5 million. The firm has 1 million shares outstanding that sell for $20 each. The firm has no debt; there are no taxes; and all transactions take place in a perfect capital market. Using calculations like those in the illustration of dividend irrelevance in a perfect capital market, show that shareholders will be indifferent between whether the firm pays out the "bonus" as a dividend or uses the money to buy back $5 million of its shares.

B9. Suppose a firm has a choice of paying out a cash dividend or reinvesting the money in projects that are expected to earn their required rate of 16.5% over the next 7 years. If the riskless rate is 8%, will the shareholders be better off with one or the other alternatives, or are the alternatives equally beneficial?

B10. How can a consistent policy of never decreasing the per share dollar amount of the cash dividend that a firm pays each period facilitate monitoring (a) of the firm's managers as agents by the firm's shareholders (as principals)?, and (b) of the firm's shareholders as agents by the firm's debtholders (as principals)?

B11. A corporation's common stock is trading at a P/E ratio of 12. Its projected earnings per share are $2.00, and its share price is $24. All its shareholders are tax-exempt.

   a. An open market purchase would result in projected earnings per share of $2.30. How would you expect the announcement of the share repurchase program to affect the firm's share price?

   b. How might your answer to part a change if the firm instead announced a tender offer?

B12. A firm recently paid out $10 million in cash dividends. Within the same month, the firm announced the issue of $20 million in new 20-year debentures to raise capital for an expansion. Discuss why a firm might decide to pay a dividend in spite of the need for expansion capital and the flotation costs associated with the new issue.

B13. Cardinal Computer Corporation has developed a phenomenally successful software package that makes it very easy to combine spreadsheet modeling and basic financial calculations. As a result, Cardinal has $20 million of excess cash that is available for distribution to its shareholders. All of Cardinal's shareholders invested at the firm's inception and consequently have a negligible tax (cost) basis in their Cardinal shares. Cardinal has 10 million shares outstanding.

   a. Assuming dividend income is taxed at a 40% rate and capital gains income is taxed at a 20% rate, calculate the impact on shareholder wealth of a $20 million cash dividend distribution and a $20 million share repurchase.

   b. Under what circumstances, if any, would Cardinal's shareholders be better off having Cardinal retain and reinvest the cash in short-term financial instruments rather than pay it out to shareholders?

B14. Suppose the tax code was changed so that capital gains were taxed at a fixed and constant rate of 10% on the gain at the time the asset is sold. What impact do you think such a change in the tax law would have on the average payout ratio of firms traded on the NYSE?

PROBLEM SET C

C1. A recent article in the *Wall Street Journal* ("Payouts Become Crucial Weapon in Appeasement," January 31, 1989) argues that cash dividends have become a "crucial weapon in corporate America's war of appeasement with raiders and other demanding investors."

   a. When might an increase in the dividend rate lead to an increase in a company's share price?

   b. Under what circumstances would a company prefer to pay out the cash in the form of a "special" or "extra" dividend?

   c. Does this renewed interest in cash dividends imply that the bird-in-the-hand argument for increased cash payouts is valid after all?

C2. Respond to the following comment: Thirty years ago, the traditional view held that dividend policy mattered. The current view also holds that dividend policy matters. I guess they had it right in the first place.

C3. **a.** How does the stock market normally react to the announcement of a dividend reduction?

   b. How would you explain the reaction in part a?

   c. Suppose you were told that a company announced a cut in its dividend rate to 25¢ per quarter from 50¢ per quarter but that the price of the company's shares closed $1 higher on the announcement date than it did the previous day (up from $61 to $62 per share). Is this inconsistent with your answer to part b?

   d. Under what circumstances might the events in part c occur simultaneously?

C4. Explain why companies exhibit a reluctance to cut their dividend rate.

C5. Our discussion in this chapter leads to a conclusion that is somewhat less than completely satisfying. Specifically, we do not provide a prescription that specifies *exactly* how to maximize shareholder wealth through dividend policy. If you will recall, our prescription concerning capital structure was somewhat similar. Now the question: Suppose the good fairy can tell you exactly how to optimize both your firm's capital structure policy and your firm's dividend policy. While the good fairy wants to be good to you, he does not want to be too good to you and has offered to provide you with the optimal prescription for your firm's capital structure policy *or* your firm's dividend policy, but not both. Based on what you now know of the potential gains to be had from each policy, which one would you choose to optimize? Explain your reasoning.

C6. It has been argued by a journalist that utilities should not be allowed to pay cash dividends because such a prohibition would (a) reduce their need to raise external capital, thus (b) reducing their transaction costs, so that (c) they will have a lower cost of capital, consequently (d) lowering utility rates and (e) making consumers better off. Do you think a legal restriction preventing utilities from *ever* paying a cash dividend would result in this chain of events? If not, where does the logic break down?

C7. Dividend policy interacts with the firm's investment and capital structure policies. In Chapter 15 we said that issuing new equity is considered to be a negative signal. The logic of this empirical observation is that if the project is "really good" the shareholders would rather borrow than take on additional partners. In light of this, how might a firm's dividend policy give rise to an opportunity cost with respect to its investment opportunities if its capital structure is held constant?

C8. A company plans to issue one put right for each outstanding share of common stock. N put rights will entitle the holder to tender one share of common stock to the company at a price of S. The current share price (i.e., rights-on) is P_R. Ignore shareholder income taxes.

   a. Assuming that all the put rights are exercised, develop an expression for the share price ex-rights in terms of N, S, and P_R.

   b. Use the expression developed in part a together with Equation (17.3) to obtain Equation (17.2).

   c. Develop Equation (17.4) using the reasoning applied in part a.

C9. Repeat problem C8 without ignoring shareholder income taxes. Let τ_g denote the marginal investor's capital gains tax rate and B her tax basis in the shares to be tendered. Note that the rights are taxed when they are issued.

   a. Assuming that all the put rights are exercised, develop an expression for the share price ex-rights.

b. Show that if the marginal investor buys a put right and tenders it to the company, the following condition must be satisfied for the transaction to have zero arbitrage profit:

$$(1 - \tau_g)S + \tau_g B - (1 - \tau_g)NR = P_E$$

c. Use the expression developed in part b to obtain Equation (17.5).

d. Obtain an expression analogous to Equation (17.2) for the case in which $\tau_g > 0$.

REFERENCES

Aharony, Joseph, and Itzhak Swary. "Quarterly Dividend and Earnings Announcements and Stockholders' Returns: An Empirical Analysis." *Journal of Finance* 35 (March 1980): 1–12.

Ang, James S. *Do Dividends Matter? A Review of Corporate Dividend Theories and Evidence.* Monograph 1987-2, Graduate School of Business Administration, New York University, New York, 1987.

Bhattacharya, Sudipto. "Imperfect Information, Dividend Policy, and the 'Bird-in-the-Hand' Fallacy." *Bell Journal of Economics* 10 (Spring 1979): 259–70.

Bierman, Harold, Jr. *Financial Policy Decisions.* New York: Macmillan, 1970: 143–57, 176–87.

Black, Fischer. "The Dividend Puzzle." *Journal of Portfolio Management* 2 (Winter 1976): 5–8.

Black, Fischer, and Myron Scholes. "The Effects of Dividend Yield and Dividend Policy on Common Stock Prices and Returns." *Journal of Financial Economics* 1 (May 1974): 1–22.

Blume, Marshall E. "Stock Returns and Dividend Yields: Some More Evidence." *Review of Economics and Statistics* (November 1980): 567–77.

Bortz, Gary A., and John P. Rust. "Why Do Companies Pay Dividends?: Comment." *American Economic Review* 74 (December 1984): 1135–36.

Brennan, Michael. "A Note on Dividend Irrelevance and the Gordon Valuation Model." *Journal of Finance* 26 (December 1971): 1115–21.

Brittain, John A. *Corporate Dividend Policy.* Washington, D.C.: Brookings Institution, 1966.

Charest, Guy. "Dividend Information, Stock Returns and Market Efficiency—II." *Journal of Financial Economics* 6 (June/September 1978): 297–330.

Dann, Larry Y. "Common Stock Repurchases: An Analysis of Returns to Bondholders and Stockholders." *Journal of Financial Economics* 9 (June 1981): 113–38.

Dielman, Terry, Timothy J. Nantell, and Roger L. Wright. "Price Effects of Stock Repurchasing: A Random Coefficient Regression Approach." *Journal of Financial and Quantitative Analysis* 15 (March 1980): 175–89.

Eades, Kenneth M. "Empirical Evidence on Dividends as a Signal of Firm Value." *Journal of Financial and Quantitative Analysis* 17 (November 1982): 471–500.

Elton, Edwin J., and Martin J. Gruber. "Marginal Stockholder Tax Rates and the Clientele Effect." *Review of Economics and Statistics* 52 (February 1970): 68–74.

Fama, Eugene F., and Harvey Babiak. "Dividend Policy: An Empirical Analysis." *Journal of the American Statistical Association* 63 (December 1968): 1132–61.

Fama, Eugene F., Lawrence Fisher, Michael Jensen, and Richard Roll. "The Adjustments of Stock Prices to New Information." *International Economic Review* 10 (February 1969): 1–21.

Feldstein, Martin, and Jerry Green. "Why Do Companies Pay Dividends?" *American Economic Review* 73 (March 1983): 17–30.

Finnerty, John D. "The Behavior of Electric Utility Common Stock Prices Near the Ex-Dividend Date." *Financial Management* 10 (Winter 1981): 59–69.

Finnerty, Joseph E. "Corporate Stock Issue and Repurchase." *Financial Management* 4 (Autumn 1975): 62–66.

Finnerty, Joseph E. "Insiders and Market Efficiency." *Journal of Finance* 31 (September 1976): 1141–48.

Friend, Irwin, and Marshall Puckett. "Dividends and Stock Prices." *American Economic Review* 54 (September 1964): 656–82.

Gordon, Myron J. "Dividends, Earnings, and Stock Prices." *Review of Economics and Statistics* 41 (May 1959): 99–105.

Gordon, Myron J. *The Investment, Financing and Valuation of the Corporation.* Homewood, Ill.: Richard D. Irwin, 1962.

Gordon, Myron J. "Optimal Investment and Financing Policy." *Journal of Finance* 18 (May 1963): 264–72.

Graham, Benjamin, David L. Dodd, and Sidney Cottle. *Security Analysis,* 4th ed. New York: McGraw-Hill, 1962.

Griffin, Paul A. "Published Earnings, Dividend Announcements and Analysts Forecasts." *Journal of Finance* 31 (May 1976): 631–50.

Hakansson, Nils H. "To Pay or Not to Pay Dividends." *Journal of Finance* 37 (May 1982): 415–28.

Higgins, Robert C. "Dividend Policy and Increasing Discount Rates: A Clarification." *Journal of Financial and Quantitative Analysis* 7 (June 1972): 1757–62.

Jaffe, Jeffrey F. "Special Information and Insider Trading." *Journal of Business* 52 (July 1974): 410–28.

Kalay, Avner. "Signaling, Information Content, and the Reluctance to Cut Dividends." *Journal of Financial and Quantitative Analysis* 15 (November 1980): 855–69.

Kale, Jayant R., Thomas H. Noe, and Gerald D. Gay. "Share Repurchase through Transferable Put Rights." *Journal of Financial Economics* 25 (November 1989): 141–60.

Kwan, Clarence C. Y. "Efficient Market Tests of the Informational Content of Dividend Announcements: Critique and Extension." *Journal of Financial and Quantitative Analysis* 16 (June 1981): 193–206.

Laub, P. Michael. "On the Informational Content of Dividends." *Journal of Business* 49 (January 1976): 73–80.

Lees, Francis A. *Repurchasing Common Stock.* New York: The Conference Board (Research Bulletin No. 147), 1983.

Lewellen, Wilbur G., Kenneth L. Stanley, Ronald C. Lease, and Gary G. Schlarbaum. "Some Direct Evidence on the Dividend Clientele Phenomenon." *Journal of Finance* 33 (December 1978): 1385–99.

Lintner, John. "Distribution of Incomes of Corporations Among Dividends, Retained Earnings, and Taxes." *American Economic Review* 46 (May 1956): 97–113.

Lintner, John. "Dividends, Earnings, Leverage, Stock Prices and the Supply of Capital to Corporations." *Review of Economics and Statistics* 44 (August 1962): 243–69.

Litzenberger, Robert H., and K. Ramaswamy. "The Effect of Personal Taxes and Dividends on Capital Asset Prices: Theory and Empirical Evidence." *Journal of Financial Economics* 7 (June 1979): 163–95.

Litzenberger, Robert H., and K. Ramaswamy. "The Effects of Dividends on Common Stock Prices: Tax Effects or Information Effects." *Journal of Finance* 37 (May 1982): 429–43.

Marks, Kenneth R. "The Stock Price Performance of Firms Repurchasing Their Own Shares." *The Bulletin,* New York University Graduate School of Business Administration (1976-1): 6–7.

Masulis, Ronald W. "Stock Repurchase by Tender Offer: An Analysis of the Causes of Common Stock Price Changes." *Journal of Finance* 35 (May 1980): 305–21.

Miller, Merton H., and Franco Modigliani. "Dividend Policy, Growth, and the Valuation of Shares." *Journal of Business* 34 (October 1961): 411–33.

Miller, Merton H., and Myron S. Scholes. "Dividends and Taxes." *Journal of Financial Economics* 6 (December 1978): 333–64.

Miller, Merton H., and Myron S. Scholes. "Dividends and Taxes: Some Empirical Evidence." *Journal of Political Economy* 90 (1982).

Norgaard, Richard, and Corine Norgaard. "A Critical Examination of Share Repurchase." *Financial Management* 3 (Spring 1974): 44–49.

Pettit, R. Richardson. "Dividend Announcements, Security Performance, and Capital Market Efficiency." *Journal of Finance* 27 (December 1972): 993–1007.

Pye, Gordon. "Preferential Tax Treatment of Capital Gains, Optimal Dividend Policy and Capital Budgeting." *Quarterly Journal of Economics* 86 (May 1972): 226–42.

Shefrin, Hersh M., and Meir Statman. "Explaining Investor Preference for Cash Dividends." *Journal of Financial Economics* 13 (June 1984): 253–82.

Tandy Corporation. *1977 Annual Report to Shareholders*, June 30, 1977.

Van Horne, James C., and John G. McDonald. "Dividend Policy and New Equity Financing." *Journal of Finance* 26 (May 1971): 507–19.

Vermaelen, Theo. "Common Stock Repurchases and Market Signalling: An Empirical Study." *Journal of Financial Economics* 9 (June 1981): 139–83.

Walsh, Francis J., Jr. *Repurchasing Common Stock*. New York: The Conference Board, Report No. 659, 1975.

Walter, James E. "Dividend Policies and Common Stock Prices." *Journal of Finance* 11 (March 1956): 29–41.

Walter, James E. "Dividend Policy: Its Influence on the Value of Enterprise." *Journal of Finance* 18 (May 1963): 280–91.

Watts, Ross. "The Information Content of Dividends." *Journal of Business* 46 (April 1973): 191–211.

MANAGING DIVIDEND POLICY

The previous chapter discussed reasons why a firm's choice and implementation of its dividend policy might affect its stock market value. This chapter explains how firms can select an appropriate dividend policy and determine how best to implement it. The discussion focuses on the dividend policy decision for a firm whose shares are publicly-traded. In addition, the chapter also addresses the dividend policy considerations peculiar to a closely-held firm.

MAJOR PHARMACEUTICAL COMPANY'S DIVIDEND PROBLEM

The board of directors of Major Pharmaceutical Company will discuss at its next meeting whether to increase Major's quarterly dividend. In preparation for that meeting, Major's board chairman has asked the company's treasurer to study the company's dividend policy and to recommend appropriate dividend action to the board.

Table 18-1 presents Major's 10-year dividend history. Major's payout ratio has decreased slightly over the period 1981–1990 (note the difference between the 5-year averages), whereas the average payout ratio of comparable pharmaceutical companies has increased more or less steadily from roughly 40% to roughly 50% during the same period. In addition, Major paid out a slightly lower percentage of available cash flow during the latter half of this period than it had during the first half. Major's financial forecast predicts earnings per share of $5.00, $6.00, and $7.20 in 1991, 1992, and 1993, respectively.

Major's **cash flow per common share** is the cash flow from operations minus preferred stock dividends, divided by the number of common shares outstanding. (Recall that **cash flow from operations** equals the sum of net income plus noncash expenses that were deducted when calculating net income.) The firm's financial forecast predicts cash flow per common share available for reinvestment or common dividends of $6.20, $7.40, and $8.80 in 1991, 1992, and 1993, respectively. However, Major will have to increase its capital expenditure budget substantially above historical levels in 1992 and 1993 in order to complete the development of its new arthritic painkiller and to purchase additional plant and equipment to accommodate production of the new drug.

Major's treasurer must now analyze this historical and projected financial information, and take into account any other considerations that may have a bearing on the dividend decision in order to formulate a recommendation. The treasurer's list of questions to be studied includes

■ Is an increase in the dividend rate likely to enhance the wealth of Major's shareholders?

TABLE 18-1 Ten-Year Dividend History for Major Pharmaceutical Company[a]

Year	Dividends Per Share	Earnings Per Share	Payout Ratio		Cash Flow Per Share Available for Common Dividends	Cash Flow Coverage of Common Dividends[b]	Quarterly Common Dividend Increased		
			Major	Index for Drug Companies			In Qtr.	From	To
1981	$0.40	$1.20	33.3%	39.4%	$1.53	3.83x	I	$0.09	$0.10
1982	0.46	1.32	34.8	41.0	1.58	3.43	II	0.10	0.12
1983	0.54	1.50	36.0	40.9	1.87	3.46	II	0.12	0.14
1984	0.64	1.85	34.6	41.7	2.50	3.91	I	0.14	0.16
1985	0.72	2.07	34.8	43.2	2.69	3.74	I	0.16	0.18
5-Year growth rate	15.1%	14.3%			15.9%				
5-Year average			34.7	41.2		3.67			
1986	0.84	2.45	34.3	42.4	3.06	3.64	I	0.18	0.21
1987	0.96	3.10	31.0	44.6	4.19	4.36	I	0.21	0.24
1988	1.12	3.73	30.0	45.6	4.66	4.16	I	0.24	0.28
1989	1.28	4.01	31.9	51.6	4.83	3.77	I	0.28	0.32
1990	1.44	4.25	33.9	48.0	5.51	3.83	I	0.32	0.36
5-Year growth rate	13.7%	13.6%			13.2%				
5-Year average			32.2	46.4		3.95			
10-Year growth rate	14.4%	15.4%			15.5%				
10-Year average			33.5	43.8		3.81			

[a] Adjusted for stock splits.
[b] Calculated as the ratio of cash flow per share available for common dividends to dividends per share.

- Is Major's current payout ratio appropriate?

- What should Major's payout ratio be, relative to the payout ratios of other drug companies?

- Would a share repurchase program be more beneficial to Major's shareholders than a cash dividend?

- In view of Major's heavy capital expenditure requirements, should Major temporarily cut the dividend rate or should it pay a **stock dividend** instead of a cash dividend in order to conserve cash?

The responses to these and related questions will determine a firm's dividend policy: How much of its earnings and cash flow should a firm distribute to its shareholders? In what forms should it distribute the cash? How should it time these

TABLE 18-2   Industry Differences in Payout Ratio

| | Five-Year Industry Average | | Ten-Year Average |
Industry	*1967–1971*	*1972–1976*	*1967–1976*
Life insurance	20.1%	25.5%	22.8%
Aerospace and aircraft	32.8	25.4	29.1
Building materials	41.5	31.1	36.3
Business equipment	34.9	38.5	36.7
Paper and paper products	45.7	32.2	38.9
Oil	47.9	34.6	41.2
Drugs and health care	49.7	38.9	44.3
Metals and mining	49.9	38.9	44.4
Steel	53.8	37.3	45.6
Textiles	48.5	44.9	46.7
Chemicals	55.3	42.3	48.8
Foods	57.0	47.3	52.1
Electric utilities	68.5	69.5	69.0
Average	46.6	39.0	42.8

Source: Allen Michel, ''Industry Influence on Dividend Policy,'' *Financial Management* 8 (Autumn 1979), 26.

distributions? Later in the chapter, we will help Major's treasurer prepare her recommendation.

INDUSTRY DIFFERENCES   18.1

Payout ratios have been shown to vary systematically across industries.[1] We suspect that these differences are due, at least in part, to the comparable investment opportunities that firms within a particular industry face and the systematic differences in investment opportunities that exist across industries.

Table 18-2 summarizes differences in industry payout ratios. The electric power industry had the highest payout ratios by a wide margin during the period 1967–1976. The life insurance and aerospace and aircraft industries generally had the lowest payout ratios during the period. Because of these systematic differences in payout ratio, Major's treasurer can apply the Behavioral Principle and use the payout ratios of firms in the same industry as a guide in selecting an appropriate payout ratio. Of course, because Major's situation differs to some degree from those facing other firms in the same industry, the payout ratios of these other firms are only a guide; Major can do better than the blind application of the Behavioral Principle.

DIVIDEND POLICY IN PRACTICE   18.2

The actual dividend policies of corporations provide a useful backdrop for our discussion of how a corporation can select an appropriate dividend policy.

[1] Michel (1979). An earlier study came to the same conclusion. See also Harkins and Walsh (1971).

CHARACTERISTICS OF CORPORATE DIVIDEND POLICIES

Dividend policies of publicly-traded firms commonly exhibit the following characteristics:

- *Predilection for paying common dividends.* Smaller and younger firms generally do not pay cash dividends to their common stockholders. At some point in its life cycle, a firm decides that it is sufficiently "mature" to begin paying dividends. This may be due to a desire to demonstrate the firm's stability, a decline in profitable investment opportunities, investor desires for at least some minimal level of cash distributions, a desire to broaden the market for the firm's stock to include investors who are prohibited from buying non-dividend-paying stocks, or other factors. Among New York Stock Exchange-listed firms, for example, each year during the postwar period, between 75% and 90% of the listed common stocks paid cash dividends during the year.

- *Dividends more stable than earnings.* Figure 18-1 illustrates the pattern of corporate earnings and dividends during the postwar period and the corresponding movement in the average annual payout ratio. Dividends are more stable than earnings; this is true for individual firms as well as in the aggregate.

- *Regularity of dividend payments.* Dividend-paying firms typically make quarterly payments. Some firms make semiannual or annual payments, and no more than a handful of operating firms make monthly distributions. Once they begin paying common dividends, firms strive to continue making regular payments. Table 18-3 illustrates the longevity of the dividend payment records of firms listed

FIGURE 18-1

Corporate dividends and earnings during the postwar period.

Source: Economic Indicators (Washington, D.C.: Government Printing Office, various issues).

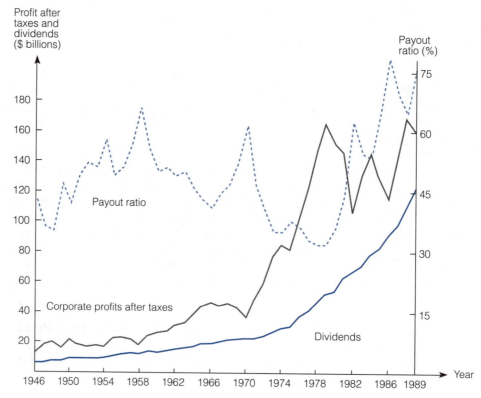

TABLE 18-3   Longevity of Dividend Payment Records of New York Stock Exchange-Listed Common Stocks

	Number of Firms That Have Paid Dividends over a Period of Consecutive Years								Number of Firms Listed Year-End
	100 or More	75–99	50–74	25–49	20–24	20 or More	10–19	Less than 10[a]	1983
Quarterly payments	6	41	134	448	86	715	201	602	1518
Annual payments	37	85	232	403	84	841	201	476[b]	1518

[a] Includes stocks that have not paid dividends.
[b] Includes stocks that do not make quarterly dividend payments.
Source: New York Stock Exchange Fact Book, 1984, 35.

on the New York Stock Exchange as of year-end 1983. Roughly half had made quarterly payments on an uninterrupted basis for 20 years or longer. In fact, corporations frequently highlight the length of their uninterrupted dividend records when announcing dividend declarations.

■ *Reluctance to cut the dividend rate.* Beyond the regularity of dividends, as noted in Chapter 17, firms exhibit a strong aversion to cutting an established dividend *rate* (i.e., a total dollar amount per period). This is probably because of the negative signal. Looking back at Table 17-1, you can see that the numbers of dividend decreases and omissions increased sharply—and the numbers of dividend increases and resumptions decreased sharply—during the recession periods 1974–1975 and 1980–1982. Investors generally interpret dividend reductions as a signal that the firm's earnings prospects have worsened. As in the ITT example in Chapter 17, this can adversely affect a firm's share price and, in some cases, the share prices of other firms in the same industry. For example, Consolidated Edison Company of New York announced on April 23, 1974, that it would omit its second quarter 1974 dividend. Its share price fell by 43% between April 22, 1974, and May 15, 1974. During the same period, many other electric utility stocks decreased in value as investors feared that other electric firms would reduce their dividend rates.[2]

■ *Extra or special dividends to supplement regular dividends.* Table 17-1 also indicates that a minority of firms declared "extra" or "special" dividends during the period 1970–1989. In addition to a "regular" quarterly dividend, a firm may pay an extra dividend at regular intervals, say at each year-end. Such dividends tend to be considerably more variable in amount than "regular" dividend payments. They are generally paid during periods of temporarily higher earnings to bring the firm's payout ratio up to its target level. Special dividends are often declared when a firm finds itself with substantial excess cash it wishes to distribute to its

[2] Interestingly, the impact of General Public Utilities' dividend reduction in 1979 and eventual elimination in 1980 did not affect all firms in the industry because the cause of the reduction, the Three Mile Island nuclear accident, was so specific.

shareholders.[3] Consequently, extra and special dividends are less effective devices for signaling a change in a firm's earnings prospects.

- *Regular timing of dividend increases.* Most firms review their dividend policies at least once annually, often during the same quarter each year.

In contrast to the timing of regular dividends, extra and special dividend announcements occur predominantly near the end of the firm's fiscal year; which is the October-December quarter for the majority of firms. This suggests that firms pay extra (or special) dividends when the year-end review reveals unexpectedly high or unsustainably high earnings for the year and the firm wishes to pay out its target percentage of earnings but does not wish to signal falsely a higher sustainable level of earnings. Many firms in cyclical businesses, for example General Motors Corporation, declare extra or special dividends during periods when earnings are at a cyclical peak and increase the regular dividend rate only when they believe they have reached a higher level of sustainable earnings.

DIVIDEND MECHANICS

A dividend must be declared by the firm's board of directors, and a firm can only declare and pay cash dividends only out of legally available funds.[4] Similarly, **stock dividends** and **stock splits** must be declared by the board.

DECLARATION OF DIVIDENDS

When a firm's board of directors declares a dividend, it specifies a **record date** and a **payment date**. The time line presented in Figure 18-2 shows the relative timing of the key dividend-related dates. Each shareholder of record (i.e., owner of shares according to the firm's stock ownership record) as of the close of business on the record date will receive a check dated on the payment date for the dividends declared on the shares owned. Because stock transactions must be settled by the fifth business day following the transaction, the major stock exchanges and securities dealers (in the over-the-counter market) establish an **ex-dividend date** 4 business days prior to the record date. On that date the shares begin trading **ex-dividend**, that is, without dividend rights. Consequently, a stock normally opens for trading on the ex-dividend date at approximately the preceding day's closing price less the amount of the dividend per share.

LEGAL LIMITATIONS ON DIVIDEND PAYMENTS

Two forms of legal restrictions on dividend payments are important. With the possible exception of the financially strongest firms, bond indentures, loan agreements, and preferred stock agreements typically contain restrictions on the amount of common dividends a firm can pay. You may recall from Chapter 9 that such limitations are designed to minimize the firm's agency costs.

State laws also impose dividend restrictions to prevent excessive cash distri-

---

[3] For example, in 1979 Western Pacific Industries Inc. declared a $23 special dividend following the sale of its Western Pacific Railroad unit. "Western Pacific Industries Declares $23-a-Share Payout," *Wall Street Journal*, November 8, 1979, 20. An interesting question is whether shareholders would have been better off if the firm had repurchased some of its common stock instead of paying a special dividend.

[4] Legal restrictions on dividend payments are discussed below.

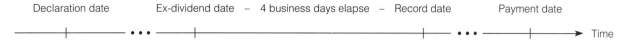

FIGURE 18-2
A time line for dividend-related events.

butions to common stockholders. Most states have laws prohibiting a firm incorporated in their state from paying dividends if doing so would render the firm insolvent. Many states also have laws prohibiting firms incorporated in their state from making dividend payments out of any account that falls outside a legally defined "surplus." In some cases, this surplus includes only retained earnings; in other cases, it includes paid-in capital as well; and in still other cases, a firm is permitted to distribute current earnings, even though prior losses had eliminated its surplus.

The forgoing limitations are seldom troublesome to a financially healthy firm. But a firm that has experienced large operating losses will have to ensure that its dividend policy will not cause it to violate existing dividend restrictions, even if this is otherwise contrary to the shareholders' best interest.

DIVIDEND POLICY GUIDELINES   18.3

Establishing a firm's dividend policy requires that a variety of conflicting and sometimes confusing considerations be taken into account beforehand. Chapter 17 discussed reasons why almost any dividend decision of a firm with a diversified shareholder mix may disappoint at least some of its shareholders. Nevertheless, a firm should strive to balance the desires of all of its shareholders against one another.

But is there a unique optimal dividend policy? As noted in Chapter 17, many financial experts believe that a firm's shareholders do not realize any net benefit from the firm's paying out cash in excess of residual earnings over the longer term. Most of those who hold this view acknowledge at least the possibility that dividend changes have informational value. If these experts are correct, there is generally no unique optimal dividend policy for a firm, and dividend policy should be largely passive. But as also noted in Chapter 17, there are good reasons for believing that dividend policy is not inconsequential to the stock market value of the firm. Unfortunately, the complexity of the considerations involved makes managing dividend policy an art more than a science.

In concept, a firm could commission a detailed study of its shareholder mix and the relationship between past dividend changes by firms in its industry on the one hand and resulting share price changes on the other. However, shareholder mixes change, particularly as institutions have come to play an ever larger role in the equity markets, and past statistical studies of the relationship between dividend changes and share price changes have been largely inconclusive. Moreover, these studies are expensive in terms of both dollars and scarce management time.

The problem of determining the optimal payout ratio is illustrated in Figure 18-3. The optimal payout ratio is P^*. That payout ratio leads to the maximum shareholder wealth, W^*, which consists of dividends plus the market value of outstanding shares. A higher or lower payout ratio leads to lower shareholder wealth. But payout ratios "near" P^* lead to values of shareholder wealth "near" W^*. The shape of the curve determines the size of the penalty that results from paying out more or less than P^*. In practice, if we had the ability to draw the curve in Figure 18-3 we would probably find that for most firms there is a range of payout ratios within which the

FIGURE 18-3
Target payout range.

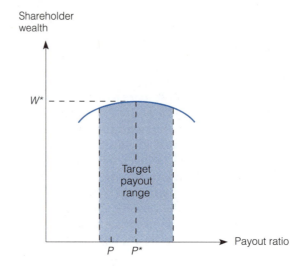

curve is relatively flat. Once inside that range, the cost of obtaining the information required to change the payout ratio from, say, P to P^* would likely exceed the benefit shareholders could realize as a result of that change.

Applying the Behavioral Principle provides a good starting point for establishing a target payout range like that illustrated in Figure 18-3. Factoring in the firm-related and investor-related considerations discussed in Chapter 17 then enables a firm to decide where its long-term target payout ratio should lie. The goal, then, is to determine an appropriate long-term target payout ratio.

A THREE-STEP APPROACH TO THE DIVIDEND DECISION

Determining an appropriate dividend policy for a firm involves a three-step approach.

1. *Estimating future residual funds.* The starting point for any analysis leading up to the dividend decision is the firm's cash flow projection over a reasonable time horizon, typically 5 years. The projected levels of capital expenditures and operating cash flow are most important in this regard. At a minimum, a firm should pay out, over time, that portion of its cash flow that would otherwise be invested in negative-NPV projects. Based on the investor-related considerations discussed below, a firm may decide to pay out more than this minimum level. However, because of the costs associated with floating new equity issues, it is generally inadvisable for a firm to pay out so much more than the minimum that the dividend decision alone triggers the need for a new equity issue.

There are many factors that complicate this analysis. Capital budgeting projects often come in large units and are subject to substantial variation from their projected timing and cost. As economic and business conditions change, so will the desired portfolio of capital expenditure projects. Similarly, future operating cash flow is not entirely predictable. Thus, analyzing even the most carefully prepared cash flow projections will suggest a range of distributable amounts, a range of funds needs, and hence a range of **feasible target payout ratios**.

2. *Determining an appropriate target payout ratio.* An analysis of the payout ratios of comparable firms, essentially those in the same industry and of nearly the same size and with similar product mix and other operating characteristics, will suggest a

range of **customary payout ratios** for (that segment of) the industry. As illustrated later in this chapter, a firm should consider the range of feasible target payout ratios together with the range of customary payout ratios and any special shareholder mix considerations in setting its long-term target payout ratio.

3. *Setting the quarterly dividend rate.* Because of the informational content of dividend changes, a fluctuating regular dividend rate is generally undesirable. Investors could find the dividend signals confusing. Such confusion would exacerbate the asymmetric information problem, leading to higher perceived risk and therefore a decline in the firm's share price.[5] Such a policy might also lead to shifts in the shareholder clientele.

A firm should increase its dividend rate, then, only if it believes it can sustain the higher rate. Similarly, if earnings prospects worsen materially, at some point the firm will have to cut its dividend rate or compromise its capital spending plans, and capital structure decisions, and perhaps even trigger the need for a new equity issue. If an increase in the dividend rate is deemed appropriate, investment bankers generally counsel firms to make a significant increase in lieu of several tiny increases and accordingly advise that any change be no smaller than 5% of the previous rate. Such a recommendation springs from their belief that a dividend increase should be at least this large to be considered meaningful by investors; that is, in order to serve as an effective signal.

Given its target payout ratio and its earnings projections, a firm should establish its quarterly dividend rate at the highest *comfortably sustainable* level. That is, the dividend rate should be sustainable at least over the planning horizon, and prudence dictates setting the actual rate somewhat below the expected maximum to compensate for the uncertainty of the earnings and funds forecasts.

It is important to recognize, however, that the informational value of dividend changes is necessarily transitory and that such information is either confirmed or denied by subsequent events. The primary goal with respect to the informational content of dividends should be to reinforce management's public statements about the firm's prospects. In this regard, there appear to be advantages to selecting a particular quarter in which to review the dividend policy annually, thus creating a predictable pattern.

SELECTING AN APPROPRIATE DIVIDEND POLICY   18.4

This section applies the dividend policy guidelines just developed to the dividend decision confronting Major Pharmaceutical Company. Major's Financial Planning Group has prepared a 5-year plan, which Major's board of directors has tentatively approved. Table 18-4 provides the projected values of certain financial variables drawn from the 5-year plan.

---

[5]There is at least one situation in which a fluctuating regular dividend rate would not be confusing to investors. If a firm paid out a fixed percentage of its earnings each quarter and if investors understood this policy, the dividend changes would not be confusing. But in that case, dividend policy would be passive; dividend changes would mirror earnings changes, and dividend changes would have no informational content beyond the information conveyed by the latest earnings announcement. You should be able to see why such a myopic dividend policy would be ill-advised: Not only would it rob dividend policy of its potential signaling value, but it would also tie the dividend rate to short-run earnings rather than to the long-run availability of residual cash flow. We should stress that the use of a target payout ratio that we are recommending involves projecting a feasible average payout ratio over the firm's planning horizon. The projected annual payout ratios will deviate around this average, and the actual payout ratios are likely to deviate even more, depending principally on the profitability of the firm's operations.

TABLE 18-4 Setting Dividend Policy for a Firm in a Relatively Noncyclical Business
(Dollar Amounts in Millions Except Per Share Amounts)

	Initial	Projected Ahead				
		1991	1992	1993	1994	1995
Earnings per common share		$ 5.00	$ 6.00	$ 7.20	$ 8.50	$10.00
Number of common shares (Millions)		× 10	× 10	× 10	× 10	× 10
Earnings available for common		$50.0	$60.0	$72.0	$85.0	$100.0
Depreciation		10.0	12.0	14.0	17.0	20.0
Other noncash charges		2.0	2.0	2.0	2.0	2.0
Cash flow available for reinvestment		$62.0	$74.0	$88.0	$104.0	$122.0
Capital investment requirement—Net[a]		$40.0	$60.0	$80.0	$72.0	$60.0
Target debt ratio		25%	25%	25%	25%	25%
To maintain target debt ratio:						
Additional borrowing to fund capital expenditures—Net[b]		$ 10.0	$ 15.0	$ 20.0	$ 18.0	$ 15.0
Required retained earnings[c]		30.0	45.0	60.0	54.0	45.0
Residual earnings		20.0	15.0	12.0	31.0	55.0
Discretionary cash flow[d]		22.0	17.0	14.0	33.0	57.0
Alternative policy 1:						
Dividend per share	$ 1.44	$ 1.60	$ 1.76	$ 1.92	$ 3.16	$ 4.40
Payout ratio		32%	29%	27%	37%	44%
Year-end debt[e]	$100.0	$104.0	$119.6	$144.8	$161.4	$163.4
Year-end equity[f]	300.0	334.0	376.4	429.2	482.6	538.6
Debt ratio	25%	24%	24%	25%	25%	23%
Cash flow coverage[g]		3.88x	4.20x	4.58x	3.29x	2.77x
Alternative policy 2:						
Dividend per share	$ 1.44	$ 1.68	$ 1.92	$ 2.16	$ 3.08	$ 4.00
Payout ratio		33%	32%	30%	36%	40%
Year-end debt[e]	$100.0	$104.8	$122.0	$149.6	$165.4	$163.4
Year-end equity[f]	300.0	333.2	374.0	424.4	478.6	538.6
Debt ratio	25%	24%	25%	26%	26%	23%
Cash flow coverage[g]		3.69x	3.85x	4.07x	3.38x	3.05x
Alternative policy 3:						
Dividend per share	$ 1.44	$ 1.80	$ 2.16	$ 2.56	$ 2.96	$ 3.36
Payout ratio		36%	36%	36%	35%	34%
Year-end debt[e]	$100.0	$106.0	$125.6	$157.2	$171.8	$163.4
Year-end equity[f]	300.0	332.0	370.4	416.8	472.2	538.6
Debt ratio	25%	24%	25%	27%	27%	23%
Cash flow coverage[g]		3.44x	3.43x	3.44x	3.51x	3.63x

[a] Gross capital expenditures minus depreciation expense.
[b] Calculated as one-fourth of capital investment requirement—net; this preserves debt ratio of 25%.
[c] Calculated as three-fourths of capital investment reqirement—net; this preserves debt ratio of 25%.
[d] Calculated as cash flow available for reinvestment plus additional borrowing to fund capital expenditures—net minus the sum of capital investment requirement—net and depreciation.
[e] Calculated as beginning-of-year debt plus additional borrowing to fund capital expenditures—net plus (aggregate dividends paid minus discretionary cash flow). As a result, it is assumed that excess cash is used to reduce debt (e.g., pay down bank lines).
[f] Calculated as beginning-of-year equity plus earnings available for common less aggregate dividends paid.
[g] Calculated as cash flow available for reinvestment divided by aggregate dividends paid.

SATISFYING THE FUNDS NEEDS OF THE BUSINESS

Major's board of directors has tentatively approved a 5-year capital expenditure budget of $385 million on positive-NPV projects. After allowing for depreciation, this budget provides for net capital investment amounting to $40.0 million in 1991, $60.0 million in 1992, $80.0 million in 1993, $72.0 million in 1994, and $60.0 million in 1995.

Major's chief financial officer has previously determined that 25% debt financing ($\theta = .25$) is appropriate in view of Major's desire to maintain its Aa3/AA− senior debt rating. Major's board has approved that policy decision. Maintaining this debt ratio would require the additional borrowing levels and the required retained earnings figures shown in Table 18-4. Residual earnings, simply the difference between forecast earnings and required retained earnings, are projected to decrease slightly in 1992 and 1993 and to increase sharply thereafter. Over the 5-year period, Major projects aggregate residual earnings of $133.0 million and aggregate discretionary cash flow of $143.0 million.

TARGET PAYOUT RATIO

The projected residual earnings of $133.0 million represent 36.2% of projected earnings available for common amounting to $367.0 million for the 5-year period. Having read Chapter 17, Major's treasurer is reluctant to recommend this target without first taking Major's shareholder clientele and other relevant factors into consideration.

A detailed analysis of Major's shareholder group would be expensive and time-consuming. However, Major's treasurer realizes that as long as their dividend policies are clearly articulated and stable, particular industries and particular firms tend to attract certain shareholder clienteles.

As illustrated in Table 18-1, Major's payout ratio has averaged 33.5% over the past 10 years and 32.2% over the past 5. Major's financial staff has also analyzed the payout policies of Major's closest 10 competitors in the *ethical* drug segment of the pharmaceutical industry from which Major derives more than 90% of its sales revenue and operating income. The average payout ratio for these firms was 37.8% in 1989, within a range from 21.1% to 50.2%, and 40.6% in 1990, within a range from 18.6% to 53.7%. Based on this analysis, Major's treasurer believes that a payout ratio in the range from 30% to 40% would be appropriate for Major. Because of Major's heavy capital expenditure programs in 1992 and 1993, she believes it appropriate that Major's payout ratio continue to be below the industry average, at least through 1993.

ANALYZING THE IMPACT OF ALTERNATIVE DIVIDEND POLICIES

Table 18-4 also examines the impact of three alternative dividend policies. A firm would normally wish to examine a larger number of alternatives before deciding on the appropriate dividend action, but these three alternatives will illustrate how a firm can weigh the various dividend policy trade-offs.

The current indicated annual dividend rate is $1.44 per share. Policy 1 continues the pattern of 16 cents per share per annum increases through 1993 to conserve cash for Major's capital expenditure program and then provides for increases in 1994 and 1995 ($1.24 each year) large enough to have paid out in total approximately 35% of aggregate earnings projected for the 1991–1995 period. That percentage, of course, represents the midpoint of what Major's treasurer believes is the appropriate target payout range. Policy 3 provides for roughly equal annual dividend increases amounting to 36 cents per share per annum for 1991 and 1992 and 40 cents per share per annum thereafter to signal Major's prospects for greater sustained earnings growth. Policy 2 represents a middle ground, with each year's dividend level between the respective year's dividend levels under Policy 1 and Policy 3. For comparability, each policy results in the same aggregate dividend payout over the 5-year period. Consequently, each policy would result in the same year-end-1995 balance sheet. Of course, the firm's accounting statements between now and then will differ under the alternative policies, but that will not affect the real economic activity of the firm. The only potential for significant differences among the alternatives is whatever difference they might make in the public's perception of their information content.

Policy 1 conserves cash in 1991, 1992, and 1993 but results in the most variable payout ratio and cash flow coverage. The abnormally large dividend increases in 1994 and 1995 are probably not sustainable. Thus, Policy 1 would probably send confusing signals to the marketplace.

Policy 3 would probably send the right dividend signal because it provides for a very stable payout ratio and it connotes sustained earnings growth. However, the debt ratio is volatile. It exceeds Major's target debt ratio by a significant margin in 1993 and 1994.

Of the three policies, Policy 2 would appear the most reasonable, even though the aggregate payout during 1991–1993 would exceed residual earnings for that period. The payout ratio is relatively stable in 1991–1993. While it is toward the lower end of the target range, it is in line with Major's historical payout ratios. Policy 2 also provides for larger dividend increases in 1991, 1992, and 1993 than in the past with only a slightly above-target debt ratio in 1993 and 1994. The analysis in Table 18-4 implies that an annual dividend increase of 24 cents per share probably could be sustained at least through 1995.

As this example illustrates, determining the appropriate dividend action requires judgment. Seldom will a particular dividend action satisfy the target payout ratio and target debt ratio year-by-year. A firm must weigh the trade-offs and settle on a dividend action that is consistent with (1) a reasonably stable payout ratio that lies within the target range, (2) a reasonably stable debt ratio, and (3) a reasonably stable progression of dividend changes that appropriately reflects changes in the firm's earnings and cash flow prospects.

SPECIAL CONSIDERATIONS FOR THE PRIVATELY-HELD FIRM

The preceding example applies only to publicly-traded firms. In most cases, privately-held firms do not have informational effects to worry about. However, tax considerations and the owners' liquidity needs are of great importance.

The owners of a closely-held firm can normally benefit by having the corporation retain earnings and reinvest funds rather than paying them out as dividends. Double taxation is avoided, and if the firm is sold, the reinvested earnings will have benefitted from deferred taxes and be taxed at capital gains rates that might be lower than ordinary income tax rates. For this reason, Internal Revenue Service regulations prohibit *excessive* earnings retention. But the definition of "excessive" is not entirely clear. Privately-held firms are generally smaller than publicly-traded firms. They consequently have less financial flexibility and somewhat more variable liquidity requirements. Somewhat greater retentions are therefore warranted to compensate for the higher liquidity risks privately-held firms face. Minimizing dividend payouts, especially until a surplus has been built up, may therefore be financially prudent as well as beneficial from a tax standpoint.

SPECIAL AND EXTRA DIVIDENDS   18.5

As discussed earlier in this chapter, firms in cyclical businesses often pay extra or special dividends during periods when earnings are at a cyclical peak. Such a policy is prudent because it preserves the integrity of changes in the regular dividend rate as a signaling device while at the same time, enabling the firm to pay out a stable percentage of its earnings, which corresponds to the longer-term ratio of residual earnings to total earnings.

Alternatively, a firm could set a higher regular dividend rate to achieve the same aggregate dividend payout over time. This would require either (1) additional borrowing during cyclical troughs with the borrowings being repaid during cyclical peaks or (2) the buildup of excess cash balances during cyclical peaks with the cash balances being drawn down to pay dividends during cyclical troughs. The former policy would worsen a firm's liquidity position during cyclical troughs when it might already be strained for other reasons. The latter policy would involve excess cash balances. For firms in highly cyclical businesses, a policy of regular dividend payments supplemented by occasional extra or special dividend payments is less risky from a financial standpoint and more efficient from a cash management standpoint than a policy consisting exclusively of regular dividend payments.[6]

STOCK DIVIDENDS AND STOCK SPLITS   18.6

Firms do not always pay dividends in cash. Frequently firms pay **stock dividends**. For example, if a firm declares a 5% stock dividend, a common stockholder of the firm will receive 5 new shares for each 100 shares of the firm's common stock she already owns.

A firm can achieve much the same financial effect as a stock dividend through a **stock split**. While there is a technical difference between the two, stock dividends and stock splits represent alternative means of recapitalizing a firm's capital accounts. However, neither one affects the net worth of the firm or the proportionate ownership interest of any of its shareholders.

STOCK DIVIDENDS

A stock dividend increases proportionally the number of shares each shareholder owns. The fair market value of the shares distributed in the stock dividend is transferred from the retained earnings account to the "paid-in capital" and "capital contributed in excess of par value" accounts on the firm's balance sheet.

Table 18-5 illustrates the balance sheet impact of a 100% stock dividend for a firm whose shares are selling at $30. The $30 million fair market value of the 1 million shares that constitute the dividend is transferred out of retained earnings. The declaration of the stock dividend does not affect each share's par value. So $10 million

---

[6] Finnerty (1986) illustrates how a firm involved in a highly cyclical business might set its dividend policy.

TABLE 18-5   Comparison of the Balance Sheet Impact of a 100% Stock Dividend and a Two-for-One Stock Split

Common Stockholders' Equity Initially	
Paid-in capital ($10 par value; 1,000,000 shares)	$ 10,000,000
Capital contributed in excess of par value	20,000,000
Retained earnings	70,000,000
Common stockholders' equity	$100,000,000
Common Stockholders' Equity Following 100% Stock Dividend	
Paid-in capital ($10 par value; 2,000,000 shares)	$ 20,000,000
Capital contributed in excess of par value	40,000,000
Retained earnings	40,000,000
Common stockholders' equity	$100,000,000
Common Stockholders' Equity Following Two-for-One Stock Split	
Paid-in capital ($5 par value; 2,000,000 shares)	$ 10,000,000
Capital contributed in excess of par value	20,000,000
Retained earnings	70,000,000
Common stockholders' equity	$100,000,000

(= [10]1,000,000) is added to paid-in-capital, and the $20 million balance is added to capital contributed in excess of par value. The firm's net worth remains $100 million.

STOCK SPLITS

Table 18-5 also illustrates the balance sheet impact of a comparable stock split (a 2-for-1 split). A stock split alters the par value of the shares but does not involve any transfer of balances between the components of common stockholders' equity. In the case of a 2-for-1 split, the par value of each share is halved. Thus, paid-in capital is unchanged.

STOCK DIVIDENDS VERSUS STOCK SPLITS

Table 18-5 illustrates the difference in accounting impact between stock dividends and stock splits. There is also an important difference in practice. Firms usually use stock dividends when they are making relatively small stock distributions, whereas relatively large stock distributions are typically made through stock splits. For example, the rules of the New York Stock Exchange prescribe that firms should make share distributions of less than 25% through stock dividends rather than stock splits.

FINANCIAL IMPACT OF STOCK DIVIDENDS AND STOCK SPLITS

The 100% stock dividend and 2-for-1 stock split illustrated in Table 18-5 each doubled the number of shares outstanding but did not affect the firm's liquidity position, capital expenditure program, leverage, or any operating variable. Consequently, barring any informational effects, a stock dividend or a stock split should leave the stock market value of a firm unchanged. Hence, a proportional reduction in the firm's share price should occur.

Suppose the firm in Table 18-5 earned $5.00 per share prior to the stock dividend or stock split, earning $5 million in the aggregate. A 100% stock dividend or 2-for-1 stock split would double the number of shares outstanding but not alter the $5 million aggregate earnings. Thus, earnings per share would be $2.50 per share following the dividend or split, and barring informational effects, the market value of a share would be halved to $15.00. The same earnings pie has simply been sliced into a greater number of pieces. So what is the value to shareholders of a stock dividend or of a stock split?

According to the Signaling Principle, actions convey information. The principal benefit of a stock dividend or stock split is probably the information it conveys. Approximately half the shares listed on the New York Stock Exchange, for example, tend to trade in the range between $10 and $30 per share in any particular year, as illustrated in Table 18-6. Stock dividends and stock splits are therefore usually associated with firms that have (or at least believe they have) excellent growth prospects. A stock split, in particular, may signal management's expectation that the firm's share price would, in the absence of the split, move out of, or further above the top end of, this customary trading range. If so, investors ought to react favorably to the news of an impending stock split. In connection with a stock split, firms frequently announce their desire to reduce the price of a share to a more popular trading range. More importantly, there is evidence that investors react positively to this signal.[7] A stock split, normally involving a greater reduction in share price than a stock dividend, is likely to have the greater informational content of the two.[8]

Second, firms often maintain the cash dividend per share following a stock dividend and maintain or reduce less than proportionately the cash dividend following a stock split. Such action causes an increase in the cash dividend payout. That increase in cash dividends is generally interpreted as signaling that management has raised its expectations of future earnings.

By reducing the share price to a more popular trading range, a stock split, and to a lesser degree, a stock dividend, may increase trading activity in a stock and thus improve its liquidity. By increasing the number of shares outstanding (and increasing the volume of trading activity), a stock split, and to a lesser degree, a stock dividend, may broaden the ownership of a firm's shares. However, the evidence on both points is not conclusive.

STOCK DIVIDEND VERSUS CASH DIVIDEND

Firms sometimes declare a stock dividend in lieu of a cash dividend to conserve cash and yet convey information. However, a stock dividend is more expensive administratively than a cash dividend. Moreover, when a firm substitutes a stock dividend for a cash dividend because of financial difficulty, it is likely that investors will view this as negative rather than positive information.[9]

---

[7] Charest (1978).

[8] Correspondingly, a **reverse stock split**, which reduces the number of shares outstanding and raises the share price proportionately, generally elicits a negative reaction. See Woolridge and Chambers (1983).

[9] A series of small stock dividends may also distort downward a firm's perceived earnings per share growth. Securities analysts generally adjust earnings per share comparisons for stock splits and large stock dividends but fail to adjust for small stock dividends. Similarly, the Dow Jones Industrial Average is not adjusted for small stock dividends.

TABLE 18-6 Distribution of Prices of New York Stock Exchange–Listed Common Stocks, 1967–1988

Price Group	As of January 6, 1967		As of January 7, 1972	
	Number of Firms	Percentage of Total	Number of Firms	Percentage of Total
Under $10	77	6.1%	105	7.4%
$10–$19⅞	282	22.3	350	24.8
$20–$29⅞	327	25.8	355	25.2
$30–$39⅞	251	19.9	241	17.0
$40–$49⅞	139	10.9	173	12.3
$50–$59⅞	73	5.8	71	5.1
$60–$99⅞	102	8.0	91	6.5
$100 and over	14	1.2	25	1.7
Total	1,265	100.0%	1,411	100.0%
Closing Value of Dow Jones Industrial Average	808.74		910.37	

Source: New York Stock Exchange.

REPURCHASING COMMON STOCK

Whether a corporation can increase shareholder wealth by reacquiring shares remains a somewhat controversial subject. In Chapter 17, we showed that in a perfect capital market environment, shareholders are indifferent not only between dividend payout and retention but also between a dividend distribution and a share repurchase program. We also noted that shareholder wealth may be affected by the manner in which a firm implements a share repurchase program.

FACTORS AFFECTING THE SHARE REPURCHASE DECISION

A corporation should weigh several important factors before deciding whether and how to implement a share repurchase program.

TAX ADVANTAGE TO REPURCHASING SHARES FROM INDIVIDUALS As discussed in Chapter 17, there is a tax asymmetry between dividend and capital gains income that causes individual investors to favor capital gains over dividends but causes corporate shareholders to have the opposite preference. This difference parallels the tax differential view of dividend policy. Because of the tax asymmetries, taxable individual shareholders generally suffer a lesser tax liability and hence realize greater wealth if the corporation repurchases shares in lieu of distributing a cash dividend. So if the shareholder body consists entirely, or at least predominantly, of individuals, there will be a net tax advantage to repurchasing shares.

As of February 3, 1978		As of December 31, 1984		As of December 31, 1988	
Number of Firms	Percentage of Total	Number of Firms	Percentage of Total	Number of Firms	Percentage of Total
283	18.0%	219	14.5%	366	22.3%
561	35.7	448	29.6	464	28.2
457	29.0	384	25.3	343	20.9
163	10.4	238	15.7	227	13.8
64	4.1	112	7.4	94	5.7
22	1.4	56	3.7	72	4.4
18	1.1	50	3.3	54	3.2
4	0.3	8	0.5	25	1.5
1,572	100.0%	1,515	100.0%	1,645	100.0%
770.96		1211.57		2168.60	

REACTION OF INVESTORS The effect of a share repurchase program on a firm's share price depends chiefly on two factors: (1) how investors react to the information that the firm intends to repurchase shares and (2) how the execution of the share repurchase program affects the market value of the repurchaser's stock. On the latter point, it is important to note that Securities and Exchange Commission rules governing share repurchase programs are intended to minimize the market impact of such programs.

The reaction of investors to the announcement of a share repurchase program will be influenced by the firm's public statements regarding the program and on the method adopted to effect the share repurchase. When a firm has a valid business purpose for undertaking a repurchase program, announcing this purpose increases the likelihood that the stock market will react favorably to the repurchase program. In addition, as discussed in Chapter 17, there is empirical evidence that tender offers generally have a more significant and more lasting impact on shareholder wealth than open market repurchase programs.

Among the possible negative implications of a repurchase announcement is the implication that the firm lacks attractive investment opportunities. If this reduction in attractive investment opportunities has not yet been reflected in the share price, the share price will probably fall. Such would tend to be the case if a so-called growth stock firm announced a large repurchase program and said simply that it thought that purchasing its stock represented a "good investment." However, the firm might avoid this negative reaction by demonstrating a purpose for the program that the investment community would find acceptable—perhaps repurchasing shares to have them available upon the conversion of securities.

Among the positive implications, a share repurchase might signal management's confidence in the future of the firm's business. If significant improvements in profitability had followed previous repurchases by the firm, one might expect an increase in the share price unless there were other negating factors. Second, if it was believed that institutional holders of the firm's stock wished to sell but were unwilling to accept the discount necessary to liquidate a major position, the announcement of a tender offer would signify additional liquidity to help facilitate the sale of large blocks and thereby help eliminate a portion of the "overhang" from the market. This factor was mentioned in connection with IBM's 1977 tender offer.[10]

A careful review of recent securities analysts' reports on a firm will provide some clue as to how the investment community might react to the announcement of a repurchase program. For example, if it is generally believed that a firm has substantial excess liquid assets, as was the case with IBM in 1977, the announcement is less likely to elicit a negative reaction than would otherwise be the case, even if the firm is regarded as a "growth stock" firm. In any case, it is important for a firm to explain its rationale to minimize the risk of an adverse reaction.

POSSIBLE IMPACT ON DEBT RATINGS   Most stock repurchase programs do not have a material impact on the firm's credit statistics. However, a large repurchase program might have an adverse ratings impact if the firm's debt rating is already in jeopardy; for example, if Standard and Poor's Corporation has placed the firm's name on its Credit Watch List for a possible downgrading. The higher leverage that would result from the repurchase might, in the rating agencies' view, decrease the firm's financial flexibility, and this factor could contribute to a downgrading. However, this factor is likely to be important only if (1) the share repurchase program is large relative to the firm's capitalization and (2) the rating is already in jeopardy.

EFFECT ON ACCOUNTING FOR THE ACQUISITION OF ANOTHER COMPANY   A repurchase program might prevent a firm from accounting for an **acquisition** on a **pooling-of-interests** basis. The pooling-of-interests and **purchase** methods of accounting for acquisitions are discussed in Chapter 22. Not being able to use pooling-of-interests accounting reduces the flexibility of firms that wish to account for acquisitions in this manner. However, although the financial statement impact of purchase accounting differs from that of pooling-of-interests accounting, the operating characteristics and tax position of the combined firms are not affected. Accordingly, the choice of accounting method should not affect the stock price of the combined entity.[11] This suggests that accounting considerations are less important than firms generally believe.

IMPLEMENTING A SHARE REPURCHASE PROGRAM

Having decided that a share repurchase program would be in its shareholders' best interests, a firm must then decide how best to implement the program. There are five basic methods of share repurchase, each with certain advantages and disadvantages.

OPEN MARKET PURCHASES   A corporation can repurchase shares of its common stock on the open market at prevailing prices, using one or more dealers to

---

[10]"Hot Stock," *Fortune*, April 1977, 67–68.
[11]Hong, Kaplan, and Mandelker (1978) find that the pooling-of-interests method does not lead to abnormal stock price behavior for acquiring firms.

purchase the shares on its behalf. An open market share repurchase program averages the firm's repurchase price during the repurchase period. Approximately two-thirds of the shares repurchased in the United States are bought in open market purchases. Firms typically institute such programs in order to satisfy share requirements—for example, for stock option and other employee benefit programs. Repurchases are made daily subject to SEC regulations governing the timing, price, volume, and coordination of share purchases, which are designed to minimize the impact of the share repurchase program on the firm's share price.

PRIVATELY NEGOTIATED BLOCK PURCHASES   Privately negotiated **block** purchases from large institutional shareholders are most often made in conjunction with, rather than as a substitute for, an open market purchase program.[12] Large blocks can often be purchased at a discount from the prevailing market price, particularly when the transaction is initiated by the seller. Firms also frequently purchase large blocks, often at large premiums, from contentious or potentially threatening minority shareholders. As noted in Chapter 17, there are agency problems associated with such repurchases, so it is not clear that the repurchases are always in the *collective* shareholders' best interest.[13]

CASH TENDER OFFER   The offer can be either an offer to purchase a stated number of shares at a fixed price or a **Dutch auction**. A firm that wishes to repurchase a relatively large number of its shares quickly can announce a fixed-price cash tender offer, specifying the number of shares it seeks and the price it is willing to pay. Such an offer has the advantage of providing an equal opportunity to all shareholders to sell their shares back to the firm. However, transaction costs for tender offers are generally higher than for other types of share repurchase programs (in particular, premiums paid to induce tendering). At the same time, there is evidence that perhaps because of their higher cost, tender offers are generally a more positive signal than open market purchase programs.

The Dutch auction tender offer procedure is a variation that gives a firm greater flexibility in determining the price at which the shares are to be purchased. A Dutch auction "reverses" the tender by having the individual shareholders offer their shares for prices in a range specified by the firm. Holiday Inns, Inc. used this procedure in January and February 1985 in its tender offer for up to 8 million of its common shares. Table 18-7 furnishes the details regarding this tender offer. Holiday Inns specified minimum and maximum amounts of shares (2.5 million if at least this number of shares was validly tendered, and 8 million, respectively) and minimum and maximum prices ($46 and $49, respectively). Each shareholder was asked to specify the minimum price (within the firm's range) he was willing to accept for the shares tendered. If fewer than the specified minimum number of shares were validly tendered, the firm would have to pay the maximum price it specified. Otherwise, the firm would select a price within the specified range and pay that price for all shares tendered at that price or at a lower price (subject to the requirement that it purchase at least the specified minimum number of shares). Holiday Inns purchased

---

[12] A **block** is generally defined in terms of some minimum number of shares or some minimum market value. The NYSE defines a block as consisting of the lesser of (a) 10,000 (or more) shares or (b) shares (regardless of the number) with a market value of $200,000 or more, which are sold in a single transaction.

[13] See Chapter 9 for a discussion of agency problems.

TABLE 18-7   Holiday Inns, Inc.'s Tender Offer for up to 8 Million Shares of its Common Stock

Tender date:	January 14, 1985
Length of tender period:	17 days
Tender method:	Dutch Auction
Purpose for the offer:	Firm's board believes the firm's stock represents an "attractive investment."
Number of shares sought:	
Maximum:	8,000,000 (firm reserved the right to increase the maximum to 10,000,000 shares).
Minimum:	2,500,000
Number of shares outstanding:	34,786,931
Percentage of shares sought:	
Maximum:	23.0% (up to 28.7% if maximum increased)
Minimum:	7.2
Pre-tender closing share price:	$44.00
Tender offer price:	
Maximum:	$49.00
Minimum:	46.00
Tender offer premium:	
Maximum:	11.4%
Minimum:	4.5
Dollar value of tender:	
At maximum price:	$392 million ($490 million if maximum increased)
At minimum price:	368 million (460 million if maximum increased)
Number of shares tendered:	6,300,000
% of outstanding tendered:	18.1%
Success ratio:	78.8%
Source of funds:	$500 million bank credit agreement.
Expenses:	
Dealer/Manager fee:	$0.15 per share purchased
Soliciting dealer fee:	None

Source: Holiday Inns, Inc., Offer to Purchase, January 14, 1985.

all 6.3 million shares tendered (78.8% of the amount it sought) at the maximum price it specified, $49 per share. Note that if the specified maximum price is the price that the firm would have specified in a fixed-price tender offer, the Dutch auction would lead to a lower cost when the minimum number of shares is tendered at prices lower than the maximum price.

Two of the more important considerations in connection with a tender offer are (1) how to set the tender offer premium and (2) whether to use a soliciting dealer (or group of dealers). In general, the premium should be just large enough to attract the desired number of shares, and in most cases, the tender offer premium ranges from 10% to 25%. When a large number of (institutional) shares are held by shareholders who have indicated a desire to sell, a smaller premium (perhaps 5% or less) could probably be offered. On the other hand, an above-average premium (perhaps 20% or greater) would normally have to be offered if trading volume is very low and the shares are very widely held. Care should be taken not to set the tender offer premium so high as to make it likely that the offer will be heavily oversubscribed because that might signal the firm's vulnerability to a hostile takeover bid. On the second question, firms tendering for their own shares generally find it advantageous to use dealers in lieu of increasing the tender premium in order to acquire the desired number of shares.

TRANSFERABLE PUT RIGHTS   As explained in Chapter 17, a fixed-price tender offer conveys to shareholders nondetachable put options, which are normally in-the-money at least initially. Shareholders can realize value for their options only by tendering shares to the firm, which might give rise to a large tax liability. Instead, a firm can distribute put rights to its shareholders. Those who do not wish to sell shares can sell the put rights to investors who wish to tender. Put rights are thus more tax efficient than a fixed-price tender offer, and there is no risk of oversubscription because the number of puts issued limits the number of shares that shareholders can tender.

EXCHANGE OFFER   Instead of offering cash for shares of its common stock, a firm might offer debt securities or preferred stock. The success of such an offer depends on the common stockholders' willingness to exchange a security that enjoys a relatively liquid market for a security for which a liquid market might never develop. Compensating shareholders for this risk might necessitate a large premium. Probably for this reason, the vast majority of common stock repurchase programs have involved cash purchases.

Table 18-8 provides a summary of the advantages and disadvantages of the five repurchase methods. Regardless of the method of repurchase chosen, a publicly-traded firm must comply with SEC regulations. These involve certain disclosure requirements and restrictions on a firm's simultaneously engaging in both a share repurchase program and a sale or other distribution of its common stock or securities that are convertible into its common stock. It is also important for a firm to determine whether any of its loan agreements or other contracts include restrictive provisions that might bear on stock repurchases. A firm should also review its listing agreements with stock exchanges, its corporate charter, and the laws of the state in which it is incorporated before it instatutes a share repurchase program.

WHEN IN DOUBT . . .   18.8

It seems appropriate to close this chapter by recapping what we know and don't know about dividend policy and how this affects a firm's choice of dividend policy. We do know that in a perfect capital market environment, dividend policy does not matter. In such an environment, each shareholder can costlessly tailor the firm's dividend policy to suit her own preferences so that dividend policy per se does not affect value.

But the world is not perfect; information is costly to gather, and there are taxes, transaction costs, and legal and policy restrictions, all of which may cause dividend policy to affect a firm's value. Just how much dividend policy really matters we don't know. A variety of empirical studies have provided evidence that dividend policy matters to at least a modest degree—although some people remain unconvinced—

TABLE 18-8 Summary Comparison of Share Repurchase Methods

Advantages	Disadvantages
Open Market Purchases	
■ No premium over market price	■ If blocks do not materialize, daily volume limitations make it difficult to complete program quickly
■ Can extend over long period, thereby providing long-term support to the market	■ Risk that market price can appreciate independent of the repurchase program before the program is completed
■ Holders who desire liquidity receive cash	■ Danger that buying can drive up market price leading to a de facto premium
■ Less market impact than tender offer or exchange offer if program is not completed successfully	
Private Block Purchases	
■ Blocks can often be purchased at a discount from market price	■ Success of program dependent on locating blocks (private block purchases therefore normally used to supplement open market purchase program)
■ Attracts less attention than other methods	■ May provide less long-term support to the market
	■ Preferential treatment toward the selling shareholders may become an issue with other shareholders if blocks are purchased at a significant premium
Tender Offer	
■ Allows repurchase of significant number of shares quickly at a (maximum) price fixed at the outset of the program	■ Normally requires premium of 10%–25% over market price (Dutch auction may reduce this)
■ Provides an equal opportunity to all shareholders to sell their shares	■ Higher transaction costs than open market purchase program
■ Evidence indicates that tender offers have more positive market impact after repurchase program completed than open market purchase program	■ Oversubscription or undersubscription can embarrass firm
■ More effective than open market purchase at drawing out "loose" shares	■ Oversubscription may indicate vulnerability to hostile takeover
■ Provides means of eliminating small holdings	
■ Holders who desire liquidity receive cash	
Transferable Put Rights	
■ Allows repurchase of significant number of shares quickly at a (maximum) price fixed at the outset of the program	■ Higher transaction costs than open market purchase program and than tender offer (e.g., if fees are paid to list the put rights for trading on a stock exchange)
■ Reduces agency costs by providing an equal opportunity to all stockholders to sell their shares	■ Put rights taxed as a dividend upon distribution but give rise to a short-term capital loss if they expire worthless; variety of additional tax consequences that are complex
■ More effective than open market purchase at drawing out "loose" shares	
■ Holders who desire liquidity receive cash	
■ Transferability enables nontendering shareholders to receive value for their rights	
■ More tax efficient than a tender offer	
■ No risk of oversubscription	
■ Relatively low-tax-basis shareholders retain their shares, which will make the firm more costly to a takeover raider	

(continued)

TABLE 18-8 (*continued*)

Advantages	Disadvantages
Exchange Offer	
■ If preferred stock is offered in the exchange, there is a tax advantage to shareholders who exchange and hold the preferred	■ Higher transaction costs than open market purchase program
■ Transaction cost savings to shareholders who exchange and hold	■ Shareholders are offered a less liquid security they may not wish to hold; therefore, exchange offer may require larger premium than a tender offer
	■ Oversubscription or undersubscription can embarrass firm

but provide no clear guidelines to how a firm can select the truly "optimal" dividend policy. Thus, while our understanding of dividend policy has come a long way, we're not ready to uncork the champagne just yet.

So where does this leave us? In practice, the best a corporation can do is to try to find a reasonable dividend policy, communicate that policy clearly, and then make orderly changes in its dividend rate as its earnings and cash flow prospects change. But what constitutes a "reasonable" dividend policy? The method illustrated in this chapter represents an important application of the Behavioral Principle: When in doubt, look at the dividend policies of comparable firms for guidance. To return to our dinner analogy, the firms in the industry are sitting around the table, and the first course arrives. Some of the guests reach for the small fork, some for one of the larger forks, and some for a spoon (and there always seems to be at least one that reaches for a knife and cuts its dividend rate); that is, the firms exhibit a range of payout ratios and a variety of dividend policies. You check to see what the majority of guests are doing (what is the average payout ratio?) but most particularly at those you think will provide the most reliable guide (either because of their expertise or comparability), ignoring those you decide are not competent and comparable (the poor fellow who is served soup and immediately grabs a fork). Then you select the utensil you think most appropriate.

It's important to keep in mind that we are not blindly imitating. The systematic differences across industries (in terms of investment opportunities, tax positions, and business and other risks) provide a rationale for looking to the dividend policy choices of comparable firms for guidance.

SOLUTION TO MAJOR PHARMACEUTICAL COMPANY'S DIVIDEND PROBLEM

As noted in the chapter, Major Pharmaceutical Company's treasurer concluded on the basis of a very careful study of the firm's projected earnings and cash flow, and comparable firms' dividend policies, that a payout ratio in the range from 30% to 40% would be appropriate for Major. Based on this analysis, Major's treasurer recommended an increase of 24 cents per share per annum when Major's board reconsidered the dividend rate at the February board meeting. Such an increase exceeded the increases in prior years but Major's treasurer felt that the larger increase was appropriate in view of Major's improved earnings prospects. After reading a number of securities reports prepared by analysts who follow Major, the treasurer also concluded that the recommended dividend increase was larger than analysts were expecting. And, since Major was also projecting higher-than-expected future earnings, she expected that the announcement of the dividend increase would probably have a favorable impact on Major's share price. In fact, it did.

SUMMARY

Corporate dividend policies exhibit a predilection toward paying at least some minimum level of dividends on a regular basis, a desire to maintain both a stable payout ratio and a stable dividend rate and to make orderly changes in the dividend rate, and a strong aversion to cutting an established dividend rate. There also appear to be systematic industry differences in payout policies.

DECISION SUMMARY BOX

The following considerations are important to the management of dividend policy:

- A firm must first determine how much cash it has available for distribution. If the firm believes it is in an excess cash position, it is necessary to determine, in the light of future requirements for cash and future prospects for cash generation, the amount of the excess.
- Having determined how much cash is available for distribution, the second step involves deciding how best to distribute the cash. The most important factor is how the method of distribution is likely to affect shareholder wealth. Particularly important in this regard are tax effects and the composition of the shareholder body. Individual shareholders who have owned their shares long enough to qualify for long-term capital gains treatment will generally prefer a share repurchase program over a dividend distribution. Corporate shareholders who can claim the 70% dividends received deduction will generally prefer a dividend distribuion over a repurchase program.
- The costs of each type of distribution must be evaluated. Share repurchase programs are generally more expensive than dividend distributions, particularly if the firm repurchases shares by tendering at a significant premium over the prevailing share price.

- If management believes the firm's shares are undervalued and wishes to signal this belief, a tender offer is likely to be superior to a cash dividend. Recent evidence suggests that a tender offer can have a lasting positive price impact. However, this is likely to be the case only if the firm's subsequent operating performance confirms management's judgment concerning the undervaluation of the firm's shares.
- Announcing a share repurchase program (or a large extra or special dividend) might have a negative impact on a firm's share price if it was previously believed the firm had superior growth prospects. Firms may therefore be tempted to retain most of the excess cash and pay it out over time through increases in the regular dividend. However, this policy will prove harmful to shareholders if (1) they could have invested the funds more profitably themselves and (2) it is perceived that the buildup of excess cash indicates the diminishing growth prospects anyway.
- A share repurchase program reduces the number of outstanding common shares. Consequently, earnings per share, cash flow per share, and book value per share will be higher following a repurchase program than following an equivalent cash dividend. However, the Principle of Capital Market Efficiency tells us that simply altering per share figures does not affect firm value. Nevertheless, many firms like to maintain a smooth pro-

gression in earnings per share, and the impact of share repurchases on reported financial results can be an important consideration for such firms.

- A dividend change sends a signal. A large dividend increase that the firm could not sustain would send a false signal to the market. A large dividend increase followed by a dividend reduction might harm the firm's credibility. Consequently, if the firm does not expect the condition that gave rise to the excess cash to persist, it should repurchase shares or declare an extra or special dividend rather than increase the regular dividend by the full amount of the excess cash. If its cash generation prospects have improved, it might signal this by increasing the regular dividend by an amount that can be sustained and pay the balance through share repurchases or as an extra or special dividend.
- Most common stock investors, particularly individuals, would prefer regular dividend payments over irregular cash distributions. There are at least three principal reasons for this. First, regular dividend payments facilitate individual financial planning by each shareowner; each is paid on a regular basis, and payments are reduced or suspended only under adverse conditions. Second, certain institutions are limited by legal or policy constraints to stocks that pay regular dividends. For example, many university endowments are subject to rules that do not permit the use of capital gains to cover operating expenses. Third, the receipt of dividend income is a passive means of providing liquidity to a shareholder without the costs and inconvenience associated with selling shares to create a "homemade dividend."

- A firm can use a share repurchase program to eliminate small shareholdings. This will enhance shareholder wealth if the present value of the dividend and servicing cost savings exceeds the cost of the repurchase program.

The chapter outlined and illustrated the application of a set of dividend policy guidelines. A firm should determine its expected residual earnings and set its dividend rate at a level consistent with its financial policies earnings and cash flow prospects. It can look to the payout ratios of comparable firms as well as to the fraction of projected earnings it expects to represent residual earnings to determine an appropriate long-term target payout ratio. Firms often supplement regular dividend payments with extra dividend payments during peak earning periods to stabilize both the payout ratio and the regular dividend rate.

Five basic methods are available for repurchasing shares: open market purchases, privately negotiated block purchases, cash tender offer, transferable put rights, or exchange offer. Any of the first four could be used by a firm wishing to distribute excess cash. A firm wishing to eliminate small shareholdings would use the tender offer method. A firm wishing to buy a relatively large percentage of its outstanding shares would generally use either the tender offer or the put rights method. While a tender offer is more expensive than an open market repurchase program, empirical evidence indicates that probably because of its more positive statement (higher cost) and higher risk, the tender offer method has a more positive impact on a firm's value.

In the final analysis, striving for *the* optimal dividend policy and *the* optimal dividend rate at any particular time is probably not cost-effective, even if it were possible. A firm should seek to pay out a reasonable and stable percentage of its earnings, to make orderly changes in its dividend rate, and to supplement its dividend payments with occasional share repurchases because of the associated tax advantages. As with many other aspects of financial policy, "satisficing" rather than "optimizing" in the near term may indeed constitute the optimal policy over the longer term when all things—like time and effort—are considered.

PROBLEMS

PROBLEM SET A

A1. Define the term **ex-dividend date**.

A2. Among the following alternatives, what is the most common pattern of dividend policy: (a) a stable payout ratio where dividend payments vary with earnings; (b) a stable payment rate per share where dividend payments are more stable than earnings; (c) dividend payments that vary each year according to the firm's capital investment opportunities; (d) a stable payment rate per share with a once-a-year "extra payment" based on the firm's earnings so that dividend payments are more stable than earnings.

A3. What is a **record date** for a dividend payment?

A4. Briefly describe our three-step approach to the dividend decision.

A5. True or False: Typically, a firm has a target payout ratio that it aims for over time, but the payout ratio for any particular quarter can be substantially different from this target.

A6. What is the difference between a stock dividend and a stock split, and what conditions make one more likely to be used than the other?

A7. Why might transaction costs cause a firm to find it advantageous to repurchase small shareholdings that are outstanding?

A8. What are the major advantages of a share repurchase over a cash dividend?

A9. Why might a large share repurchase have a potential impact on a firm's debt rating?

A10. True or False: To pay a cash dividend, it is only necessary for the firm to have sufficient retained earnings to afford the dividend payment. If false, cite two factors that could preclude a firm from paying a dividend.

A11. True or False: Dividends are normally paid quarterly, whereas bond interest payments are normally made semiannually.

A12. Can it *ever* happen that either a person owns shares of stock but does not receive the same cash dividend per share paid to other shareholders, or a person no longer owns shares of stock but does receive a cash dividend?

A13. Shore Electronics Corporation's common stock is selling for $44 per share and its common stockholders' equity is shown below:

Paid-in capital ($4 par value; 5,000,000 shares)	$ 20,000,000
Capital contributed in excess of par value	30,000,000
Retained earnings	50,000,000
Common stockholders' equity	$100,000,000

    a. Show the impact of a 50% stock dividend.

    b. Show the impact of a 3-for-2 stock split.

    c. Describe how the stock market would react to each event. How would you explain the difference in reaction?

A14. With respect to a share repurchase program, describe the principal differences between an open market purchase program and a tender offer.

A15. Describe how a Dutch auction tender offer works and how a Dutch auction tender offer differs from a single-fixed-price tender offer.

A16. What are the principal advantages of the transferable put rights method of share repurchase relative to the fixed-price tender offer method?

PROBLEM SET B

B1. A–Mart Inc.'s current share price is $25. A–Mart expects to earn $5.00 per share and pay a dividend of $2.00 per share next year. Investors expect a 10% dividend growth rate forever into the future. All transactions take place in a perfect capital market.
  a. What rate of return on the stock are investors expecting?
  b. Suppose that A–Mart announces that it is going to switch to a 100% payout policy and will issue common stock whenever necessary to finance capital expenditures. What will happen to A–Mart's share price? Explain.

B2. Describe conditions under which a firm might find it advantageous to substitute a stock dividend for an increase in its cash dividend.

B3. Illustrate how a firm's repurchasing its own shares can be viewed as being equivalent to the firm's paying a cash dividend. Ignore taxes and assume a perfect capital market environment.

B4. Illustrate how a firm's repurchasing its own shares will increase the firm's leverage. Ignore taxes and assume a perfect capital market environment.

B5. A company has 20 million common shares outstanding. It currently pays out $1.50 per share per annum in cash dividends on its common stock. Historically, its payout ratio has ranged from 30% to 35%. Over the next 5 years it expects the following earnings and discretionary cash flow:

	1	2	3	4	5	>5
Earnings	100	125	150	120	140	150+/year
Discretionary cash flow	50	70	60	20	15	50+/year

  a. Over the 5-year period, what is the maximum overall payout ratio the company could achieve without triggering a securities issue.
  b. Recommend a reasonable dividend policy for paying out discretionary cash flow in years 1 through 5.

B6. Aluminum Co. of America recently announced a new dividend policy. The company said it would pay a base cash dividend of 40 cents per common share each quarter. In addition, the company said it would pay 30% of any excess in annual earnings per share above $6.00 as an extra year-end dividend.
  a. If Alcoa earns $7.50 per share in 1991, what percentage of its 1991 earnings would it pay out as cash dividends under the new policy?
  b. For what types of companies would Alcoa's new dividend policy be appropriate. Explain.

B7. Gotham Manufacturing Corporation (GMC) pays quarterly cash dividends on its common stock at an annual rate of $1.00 per share. GMC's cost of common equity capital is 12% APR, compounded quarterly.
  a. Calculate GMC's effective annual cost of common equity.
  b. If GMC's stockholders expect the firm to maintain the same dollar dividend rate forever, what should be the value of a share of GMC?
  c. If GMC changes its dividend policy so as to pay cash dividends at annual intervals and the firm's stockholders expect it to pay $1.00 per share forever, what should be the value of a share of GMC? If your answer is different from what you computed in part b, why is it different and should this difference exist?

d. Suppose GMC projects earnings per share of $3.00 this year and $2.70, $3.30, $3.90, and $3.60 over the next succeeding four years, respectively, and believes it can maintain a long-term payout ratio of ⅓. Which of the following dividend patterns would your recommend:
1. $1.00, $1.00, $1.00, $1.30, $1.20
2. $1.00, $0.90, $1.10, $1.30, $1.20
3. $1.00, $1.00, $1.10, $1.20, $1.20
4. $1.00, $0.90, $1.20, $1.20, $1.20

B8. Briefly describe a typical life cycle of dividend policy for a firm from its creation to its demise. (Penn Central Railroad might be considered to be typical of this pattern.)

B9. In October 1987, Allegis Corporation (now UAL Corp.) announced that it expected to declare a special dividend of not less than $50 per share to be paid out of the after-tax proceeds from the sale of its Hilton International and Westin Hotels & Resorts hotel subsidiaries and Hertz Corp. car rental subsidiary. Its quarterly common dividend rate at the time was $0.25 per share.

a. What does the special dividend announcement tell you about Allegis Corporation's ability to reinvest profitably the after-tax proceeds from the sale of its subsidiaries?

b. Why do you suppose Allegis Corporation planned to pay a special dividend, rather than increase the regular dividend?

c. Allegis Corporation eventually used the after-tax proceeds to repurchase approximately $3 billion worth of its common stock. It acted at the behest of at least one large shareholder. What does the large shareholder's preference for a share repurchase rather than a special dividend seem to indicate about that shareholder's tax position?

B10. Suppose a firm has $10 million available for distribution to its common stockholders. It has 5 million shares outstanding, which are worth $20 each.

a. How large a special dividend could the firm afford to pay? What would happen to its share price?

b. How many shares could the firm afford to purchase if it repurchases shares at the current market price instead of paying a special dividend?

c. If the firm would earn $2.00 per share it it did not distribute the $10 million cash, how would the two methods of cash distribution in parts a and b affect earnings per share? How would an efficient market react to the change in EPS?

d. Show that in a perfect capital market, both methods of cash distribution leave shareholder wealth unchanged. What does this tell you about the dividend versus repurchase decision in a perfect capital market?

B11. Reconsider problem B10. Suppose that all shareholders must pay tax on dividend income at the rate of 50% and on capital gains at the rate of 25% and that all shareholders have a tax basis (cost) of $10 per share.

a. Calculate the impact on shareholder wealth of the special dividend and the share repurchase, assuming that if there were no share repurchase, shareholders would continue to hold their shares forever.

b. Calculate the impact on shareholder wealth of the two cash distribution methods, assuming that if there were no share repurchase, shareholders would hold their shares for exactly 5 years. Assume a required rate of return on the stock of 12% aftertax per year for the 5-year period.

c. How do tax considerations affect the decision to repurchase or pay a special dividend?

B12. Mega Electric Company has been denied its request for an electricity rate increase. Mega has continued to pay $2 per share per annum in cash dividends in anticipation of receiving permission to increase electric rates. As a result of the denial, Mega's payout ratio will go over 100% within 12 months unless something is done quickly.

    a. Mega Electric's chairman asks you, as the utility's chief financial officer, to study the advisability of paying a $1 cash dividend and a $1 common stock dividend in order to "preserve the dividend and not send a negative signal to the market." How would you respond to the chairman?

    b. Mega Electric's president comes to you with a "better idea." She suggests paying a $1 cash dividend and distributing the "rest" of the dividend as $1 face amount of a new 12% debenture. (Assume the 12% interest rate would make the debenture worth its par value.) How would you respond to the president?

PROBLEM SET C

C1. Suppose a firm is facing the possibility of a necessary dividend rate cut because of poor economic conditions. Suppose further that you are a member of the firm's board of directors. How would you respond to the argument of another board member that the firm should publicly deny the possibility of such a cut until the board has decided that the cut is an unavoidable necessity. The other member's argument is that unless the firm denies the possibility of a dividend cut, its stock price will drop. If the cut can be avoided, the drop will have been unnecessary, and the firm's stockholders will have suffered needlessly.

C2. Suppose two firms, which you perceive to be equivalent, announce share repurchase programs, both saying that the reason for the program is that the firm's stock is undervalued. Both stocks are selling in the capital market for $30 per share. Firm A's program is a tender offer of $33 per share. Firm B's program is an equivalent dollar amount of repurchase but will be accomplished over the next 6 months through open market purchases.

    a. Which firm do you believe is sending the more credible signal?

    b. Suppose that you have private information that the two firms have been, and will be in the future, identical in *every* aspect (except for their repurchase programs). Suppose further that you are contemplating the purchase of shares in one or the other firm and would expect to own those shares for at least three years, during which time all investors will come to know that the two firms are indeed identical. Which firm's shares should you buy and why?

C3. Belmar Iron & Steel currently pays an annual dividend rate of $4 per share on its common stock. Because of a shift in business strategy, it would like to eliminate the dividend entirely. The company is concerned about adverse shareholder reaction.

    a. Suggest how the company could cushion the impact of the dividend elimination on an income-oriented class of investors that holds in the aggregate approximately 10% of the company's common stock.

    b. How would you go about implementing your solution?

c. How would you expect the stock market to react to the announcement of the dividend elimination together with your solution?

C4. A firm's earnings are more stable than its net cash inflow. A firm's dividends are more stable than its earnings. In the context of a separation between the firm's ownership and its control, how might this smoothing, coupled with the reluctance to cut dividends, help convey more accurate information about the firm's prospects than if the firm simply paid out some fixed portion of its net cash inflow to the owners?

C5. When a firm repurchases shares of its common stock from a takeover raider, the payment for the shares is referred to as **greenmail**. The common stock of Trans-World-Dilemma (TWD) has a current price of $30 per share. If TWD has 10 million shares outstanding and it buys back 1 million shares from Karl I. Can, paying Karl $35 per share for the block of shares,

a. What should be the company's share price immediately following the buyback?

b. How has the payment of greenmail affected the holders of the other 9 million shares?

C6. You have graduated from business school and gone to work for a large international investment bank. Your firm has been hired by the government of Poland to advise that country on the privatization of companies formerly owned by the Polish government, including the formulation of an appropriate dividend policy. During one of your meetings in Poland, the finance minister of Poland takes you aside and asks your view on the following question: "With capital such a scarce resource in Poland, I don't see how any Polish company can afford to pay out cash to its shareholders. Yet the Polish people have suffered deprivation for so long that Polish shareholders have a right to receive a steady flow of cash dividends in order to improve their standard of living." How would you respond?

C7. Easy Mark, Inc. has a contentious minority shareholder who owns 10% of the firm's 50 million outstanding shares. Easy Mark's share price is $12 per share, but the minority shareholder wants the firm to repurchase her shares for $15 each. Assume all transactions take place in a perfect capital market (including no taxes).

a. How would such a repurchase affect the minority shareholder's wealth?

b. How would such a repurchase affect Easy Mark's share price?

c. How would such a repurchase affect the wealth of Easy Mark's other shareholders?

d. What do you conclude regarding the impact of greenmail on shareholder wealth?

C8. Consider again the problem facing Washington Chemical which is discussed in Chapter 16 and summarized by the four cases in Table 16-8. How would you recommend Washington Chemical reconcile its apparently conflicting capital structure and dividend objectives?

REFERENCES

Aharony, Joseph, and Itzhak Swary. "Quarterly Dividend and Earnings Announcements and Stockholders' Returns: An Empirical Analysis." *Journal of Finance* 35 (March 1980): 1–12.

Bierman, Harold, Jr. *Financial Policy Decisions.* New York: Macmillan, 1970:158–87.

Bierman, Harold, Jr., and Richard West. "The Acquisition of Common Stock by the Corporate Issuer." *Journal of Finance* 21 (December 1966): 687–96.

Brittain, John A. *Corporate Dividend Policy.* Washington, D.C.: Brookings Institution, 1966.

Charest, Guy. "Split Information, Stock Returns and Market Efficiency—I." *Journal of Financial Economics* 6 (June/September 1978): 265–96.

Dielman, Terry, Timothy J. Nantell, and Roger L. Wright. "Price Effects of Stock Repurchasing: A Random Coefficient Regression Approach." *Journal of Financial and Quantitative Analysis* 15 (March 1980): 175–89.

Elton, Edwin J., and Martin J. Gruber. "The Effect of Share Repurchase on the Value of the Firm." *Journal of Finance* 23 (March 1968): 135–49.

Elton, Edwin J., and Martin J. Gruber. "Marginal Stockholder Tax Rates and the Clientele Effect." *Review of Economics and Statistics* 52 (February 1970): 68–74.

Fama, Eugene F., and Harvey Babiak. "Dividend Policy: An Empirical Analysis." *Journal of the American Statistical Association* 63 (December 1968): 1132–61.

Fama, Eugene F., Lawrence Fisher, Michael Jensen, and Richard Roll. "The Adjustment of Stock Prices to New Information." *International Economic Review* 10 (February 1969): 1–21.

Finnerty, John D. "The Behavior of Electric Utility Common Stock Prices Near the Ex-Dividend Date." *Financial Management* 10 (Winter 1981): 59–69.

Finnerty, John D. *Corporate Financial Analysis.* New York: McGraw-Hill, 1986:228–30.

Grinblatt, Mark S., Ronald W. Masulis, and Sheridan Titman. "The Valuation Effects of Stock Splits and Stock Dividends." *Journal of Financial Economics* 13 (December 1984): 461–90.

Harkins, Edwin P., and Francis J. Walsh, Jr. *Dividend Policies and Practices.* New York: Conference Board, 1971.

Hausman, Warren H., Richard R. West, and James A. Largay, III. "Stock Splits, Price Changes, and Trading Profits: A Synthesis." *Journal of Business* 45 (January 1971): 69–77.

Hong, Hai, Robert S. Kaplan, and Gershon Mandelker. "Pooling vs. Purchase: The Effects of Accounting for Mergers on Stock Prices." *Accounting Review* 53 (January 1978): 31–47.

"Hot Stock," *Fortune,* April 1977:67–68.

Lintner, John. "Distribution of Income of Corporations among Dividends, Retained Earnings, and Taxes." *American Economic Review* 46 (May 1956): 97–113.

Marshall, Wayne S., and Allan E. Young. "A Mathematical Model for Re-Acquisition of Small Shareholdings." *Journal of Financial and Quantitative Analysis* 3 (December 1968): 463–69.

Masulis, Ronald W. "Stock Repurchase by Tender Offer: An Analysis of the Causes of Common Stock Price Changes." *Journal of Finance* 35 (May 1980): 305–21.

Michel, Allen. "Industry Influence on Dividend Policy." *Financial Management* 8 (Autumn 1979): 22–26.

Millar, James A., and Bruce D. Fielitz. "Stock-Split and Stock Dividend Decisions." *Financial Management* 2 (Winter 1973): 35–45.

Rosenberg, Marvin, and Allan Young. "The Performance of Common Stocks Subsequent to Repurchase by Recent Tender Offers." *Quarterly Review of Economics and Business* 16 (Spring 1976): 109–13.

Stewart, Samuel S., Jr. "Should a Corporation Repurchase Its Own Stock?" *Journal of Finance* 31 (June 1976): 911–21.

Vermaelen, Theo. "Common Stock Repurchases and Market Signalling: An Empirical Study." *Journal of Financial Economics* 9 (June 1981): 139–83.

Wallingford, Buckner A, II. "Inter-temporal Approach to the Optimization of Dividend Policy with Predetermined Investments." *Journal of Finance* 27 (June 1972): 627–35.

Woolridge, J. Randall, and Donald R. Chambers. "Reverse Splits and Shareholder Wealth." *Financial Management* 12 (Autumn 1983): 5–15.

INVESTMENT AND FINANCING INTERACTIONS

Adjusting Present Value and Required Rates of Return for Capital Structure Effects[1]

In Chapter 10, we described a basic method of estimating a required rate of return. There, and thus far throughout the book, we described the investment and financing decisions of the firm as though they could be treated independently of each other. For the most part, we presumed that if a firm had a good investment, it would in some way obtain the funds necessary to undertake the investment. While this concept is sound, we showed you in Chapter 15 that a firm's capital structure can affect its value. Since the firm can be viewed as a portfolio of investments, these same reasons imply that the firm's capital structure can affect the value of any investment the firm undertakes. Clearly, then, the analysis in Chapter 15 implies that in some cases these two decisions cannot be completely separated—the decisions interact with one another. In this chapter, we show you how to account for the valuation impact of capital structure.

In practice, discount rates, used for evaluating potential investments, are adjusted to reflect the valuation impact of the capital structure decision on firm value. Although the adjustment may only approximately capture the effects of a complex process, the discount rate adjustment method is particularly appealing because all of the other parts of the valuation procedure can be used entirely as they have been described thus far. The only difference in the procedure is that the discount rate reflects the capital structure decision *in addition to* the risk of the project. In every other respect, the valuation procedure is *exactly the same* as previously described. Of course, we want the approximation to be as accurate as possible because using the wrong discount rate can cause the NPV of an investment to be incorrectly measured, which may in turn cause incorrect investment decisions.

DETERMINANTS OF A REQUIRED RATE OF RETURN

What determines the required rate of return for an investment? Hopefully, at this point, you will say that risk is the primary consideration for determining a discount rate, which is correct. The Principle of Risk-Return Trade-Off is the first, and by far the most important, determinant of a required rate of return. When we look at alternative investments in the marketplace to determine the opportunity cost of capital, comparable risk is what defines an opportunity as a relevant alternative investment. Thus, we point out again that the discount rate used to evaluate a particular project

[1]Ryan, this one's for you. Love, Dad.

will be, in most cases, specific to that project in order to reflect the risk of that project.

As already noted, we concluded in Chapter 15 that a firm's capital structure can affect its value. Therefore, a firm's capital structure is a second determinant of a required rate of return. In all fairness, we must point out that, compared with risk, the magnitude of the change in the required rate of return that is caused by consideration of the firm's capital structure is substantially smaller. Therefore, although financing is not irrelevant, it is a secondary consideration in practice.

Before going any further, there are a few things that might be helpful to review from previous chapters. First, recall that the required rate of return is an **opportunity cost of capital**; it is not a historical cost of funds. It is the rate at which investors would provide financing for the project under consideration *today*. Thus, theoretically, each project has its own required rate of return. Second, value is a function of both expected future cash flows and the required rate of return. Thus, value can remain unchanged even though both the expected future cash flows and the required rate of return change, if the changes offset each other. Such a case was illustrated in our Per-Pet example in Chapter 10 where we showed how financial leverage raised the shareholders' expected rate of return *and* required rate of return, but it did not change the value of their investment in a perfect capital market. Finally, the risk-return trade-off is alive and well. Thus, in an efficient capital market, there is a single rate of return for a each level of risk. Otherwise, arbitrage opportunities would exist.

A REQUIRED RATE OF RETURN FORMULA

Recall that a required rate of return for a project can be described in terms of financing rates. Therefore, it can *always* be represented as the weighted average of the components of *any* financing package that will allow the project to be undertaken. These components are the market value proportions of financing provided in the form of debt and equity. Once again, we define θ as the ratio of debt to total firm value. Recall that θ is based on total project value rather than cost. For example, suppose a project has a total present value of $10,000 and $4,000 of debt will be used to finance the project. Then $\theta = .4$. It is important to note that θ does not depend on the initial investment; θ depends only upon the total value of the project and the amount of debt used to finance it. If this project has an NPV of $2,000, then the initial investment must equal $8,000 since the NPV is the difference between the total value of the project and the cost of undertaking the project. Note also that the shareholders of this project will be putting up $4,000 and getting $6,000 in value because they receive the NPV. They get 60% of the value in this case, even though they will be putting up only 50% of the initial investment. The relationship between the amount of financing supplied and the initial cost is not relevant because it disregards the NPV of the investment. The project is referred to as 40% debt-financed and 60% equity-financed because those proportions reflect the distribution of the value of the project among the claimants.

In Chapter 10, we expressed the required rate of return for a project, $r^*(\theta)$, as

$$r^*(\theta) = (1 - \theta)r_e(\theta) + \theta(1 - \tau)r_d(\theta) \tag{19.1}$$

where τ is the corporate tax rate on income from the project, $r_d(\theta)$ denotes the required rate of return to those who provide the debt financing, and $r_e(\theta)$ denotes the required rate of return to those providing the rest of the financing as equity. We showed that $r^*(\theta)$ is constant in a perfect capital market. Recall that $r^*(\theta)$ is often referred to as the weighted average cost of capital, or WACC, especially when it refers to the firm's entire set of assets.

Although Equation (19.1) is always correct, it can be difficult to apply in some situations. We showed in Chapter 10 that the required rate of return to shareholders, $r_e(\theta)$, depends upon θ in a perfect capital market. In Chapter 15, we showed that the value of the firm depends on the firm's capital structure when certain capital market imperfections exist. Therefore, in addition to depending upon θ, both $r_e(\theta)$ and $r_d(\theta)$ also depend upon tax laws, asymmetric information considerations, and transaction costs associated with a given capital structure. As yet, $r_e(\theta)$ and $r_d(\theta)$ have not been perfectly described in the form of mathematical functions. If accurate functions for $r_e(\theta)$ and $r_d(\theta)$ did exist, they could simply be substituted into Equation (19.1), and our job would be done. Unfortunately, we have been able to create such functions only by making simplifying assumptions about the firm and the world in which it operates.

Since we cannot at this time say exactly how $r^*(\theta)$ varies among financing packages, an alternative approach to specifying $r^*(\theta)$ is to gather empirical evidence. Conceptually, a firm could take each possible financing package to the capital market to establish competitively the optimal mix of funds to undertake the project. This, of course, would be extremely cumbersome, and transaction costs would probably far outweigh the benefits from such a strategy. Even obtaining only one market estimate for each project in order to estimate its basic risk is likely to be prohibitively expensive because of the potentially large number of projects that a firm might evaluate.

In practice, a firm looks at existing market-traded securities of comparable risk to estimate a required rate of return rather than incurring the transaction costs of offering many alternative potential financing packages to the market. The required rate of return for a project is then derived from such market rates by adjusting the market rates for any capital structure differences between the firm considering the project and the firms that issued the market-traded securities. Such a procedure is outlined and an example presented later in this chapter.

CAPITAL STRUCTURE   19.2

The adjustment of a required rate of return to reflect the impact of capital structure on the value of a project is based on the entire firm's financing. Therefore, this adjustment is fundamentally different from the adjustment for risk. In some sense, a project that is undertaken by an ongoing firm has no financial risk; only the firm has financial risk. This is because financial risk is created by issuing financial obligations.

The need to reflect the firm's, rather than project's, capital structure complicates the determination of a required rate of return because we do not have a method of assessing exactly how an individual project contributes to the firm's choice of capital structure. By contrast, consider how an individual project contributes to the total risk of the firm. When a firm undertakes a new project, the risk of the project is not measured by the standard deviation of its return because the standard deviation contains both diversifiable and nondiversifiable risk. The required rate of return should reflect only the nondiversifiable risk, beta, of a project because new projects have a diversification interaction with existing projects.[2] When a project is placed in a port-

---

[2] Recall that the diversification interaction of projects creates an agency problem because of the nondiversifiability of human capital. This problem is discussed further in Chapter 22, which deals with mergers and acquisitions.

folio of investments, the beta of the investment measures what the individual project contributes to the risk of the portfolio. This is distinctly different from the considerations of financial risk.

If a firm is *all*-equity-financed (no money owed at any time, no matter what), then the firm has no financial risk. Note that such a firm would not have even one creditor. All of the risk of this hypothetical firm would be its operating risk because the firm never owes anyone anything. Note also that in such a case there is no possibility of default. In effect, the shareholders' limited liability in such cases is a put option with a strike price of zero, which, if you recall from Chapter 8, is a worthless put option. The firm could go bust, and the shareholders could lose everything they have invested in the firm, but if the firm is financed totally with equity, no loss can ever be inflicted on anyone other than the shareholders. Of course, the shareholders in an all-equity-financed firm cannot lose more than they have invested in the firm. However, at the same time, they cannot benefit from limited liability and its accompanying option to default.

Because financial risk is created by issuing financial obligations, adjusting for the impact of financial risk must be done on the basis of whatever unit has responsibility for the obligation (e.g., debt payments). Except in very special cases, some of which are discussed in Chapters 20–23, the shareholders' obligation is not limited by the results of one investment project. Rather, the financial obligation extends to the results of the whole firm. When one project does poorly, the firm must still pay whatever debts come due from the proceeds of all of the firm's other projects. (Only when the firm's revenue from *all* its operations is inadequate to meet its promised obligations can the shareholders be relieved of their obligation—exercise their option to default.) Thus, financing considerations are generally not accounted for on a project-by-project basis. Instead, because financial obligations are the responsibility of the firm, the impact of financing on the required rate of return is determined by the capital structure of the whole firm.

SUBSIDIARIES   Whenever a firm splits itself into financial parts, each of which has limited liability for its financing, the capital structure of each part is the relevant consideration for assessing the impact of financing on the required rate of return for that project. Therefore, if a firm is considering a new investment where the financing will be obtained by creating a subsidiary for which the firm has limited liability, the required rate of return for that investment should reflect the capital structure of the subsidiary.

19.3   THE IMPACT OF CAPITAL STRUCTURE ON A REQUIRED RATE OF RETURN

Although exact mathematical functions do not exist for $r_e(\theta)$ and $r_d(\theta)$, we can build on Equation (19.1) by examining the behavior of $r_e(\theta)$, $r_d(\theta)$, and $r^*(\theta)$ under various assumptions and for particular values of θ. As with previous analyses, we start by considering the problem in a perfect capital market environment.

A PERFECT CAPITAL MARKET ENVIRONMENT

Recall that, if capital structure is irrelevant, $r^*(\theta)$ must be constant over all values of θ. That is, $r^*(\theta)$ does not vary with θ if the value of an investment is unaffected by the firm's capital structure. Of course, as was shown in the Per-Pet example in Chapter 10, a change in leverage does alter how the risk of the investment is borne by the debtholders and shareholders. Therefore, leverage affects $r_e(\theta)$ and $r_d(\theta)$, even in a perfect capital market. $r^*(\theta)$ does not depend on θ because changes in θ do not affect the total value of the investment or its expected cash flows in a perfect capital market.

Based on the fact that $r^*(\theta)$ is constant in a perfect capital market environment regardless of the value of θ, we can determine the values of $r_e(\theta)$ and $r_d(\theta)$ when θ takes on either of its extreme possible values. When the firm is all-equity-financed, $\theta = 0.0$. Therefore, the second term in Equation (19.1) drops out in the case of an all-equity-financed investment and $r^*(0) = r_e(0)$. At the other extreme, when the firm is all-debt-financed, the first term drops out because $\theta = 1.0$ and $r^*(1) = (1 - \tau)r_d(1)$.[3] With no taxes, $\tau = 0$ and we have $r^*(1) = r_d(1)$. Since $r^*(\theta)$ does not depend upon θ in this environment, $r^*(0) = r^*(1)$ and therefore $r_e(0) = r_d(1)$.

The result that $r_e(0) = r_d(1)$ makes intuitive sense. The debtholders of a firm that is financed totally with debt bear all of the firm's business risk. Accordingly, the debtholders' risk would be the same as the risk borne by the shareholders if the firm were all-equity-financed. In some sense, such debtholders would in effect be shareholders. Therefore, in a perfect capital market, these two rates of return must be equal because the risks are equal.

A second implication that can be drawn from a perfect capital market analysis involves the rate of return that debtholders will require for financing only an infinitesimal fraction of the investment; that is, $r_d(\theta)$ when θ is minutely greater than zero. We established above that a firm that is absolutely 100% equity-financed has no chance of default. Such a hypothetical firm can borrow a *very small* amount of money in a perfect capital market at the riskless rate of interest. Of course, the amount of funds that such a firm could borrow at the riskless rate may be only 1 cent for 1 minute. Still, conceptually, the rate on the first fraction of debt in a perfect capital market *must be* the required rate of return for the riskless asset, r_f.

Based on these two implications from a perfect market analysis (and hypothetical functions for $r_e(\theta)$ and $r_d(\theta)$), Figure 19-1 illustrates the relationships established in a perfect capital market environment. In Figure 19-1, the rate r is defined as the rate that would be required if the investment were financed entirely with equity. That is, $r = r_e(0)$; r is often referred to as the **unleveraged required rate of return**. The rate r is based solely on the business risk of the investment, whereas $r^*(\theta)$ reflects both the business risk of the project and the capital structure of the firm. The use of r allows us to separate conveniently the impact of business risk from that of capital structure.

EXAMPLE ■ Recall the Per-Pet, Inc. example from Chapter 10. In that example we examined two different capital structures: all equity ($\theta = 0$) and half equity, half debt ($\theta = .5$). For the all-equity capital structure, the second term in Equation (19.1) drops out, and $r^*(\theta)$, the weighted average, is simply the value of $r_e(0)$, which in the example is 15%. For the leveraged capital structure, $\theta = .5$, $r_d(.5) = .10$, $r_e(.5) = 20\%$. From Equation (19.1), with $\tau = 0$, $r^*(\theta)$ is

$$r^*(\theta) = (1 - \theta)r_e(\theta) + \theta(1 - \tau)r_d(\theta) = (.5)(.20) + (.5)(1)(.10) = 15\%$$

illustrating that the required rate of return is the same in either case; it is not affected by leverage in a perfect capital market environment (including no taxes). ■

---

[3] We know of no firm that is literally all-debt-financed ($\theta = 1.0$). Strictly speaking, θ is always less than 1.0. For convenience, rather than continuing to indicate that θ is as close to 1.0 as possible, we will simply refer to $\theta = 1.0$.

19.4 MARKET IMPERFECTIONS

Figure 19-1 presents required rates of return as a function of leverage in a perfect capital market environment. However, we concluded in Chapter 15 that, taken in total, existing market imperfections bias the capital structure decision in favor of including debt in the firm's capital structure. In this section, we examine an investment's required rate of return when certain capital market imperfections are taken into consideration.

ASYMMETRIC TAX VIEW

In Chapter 10, we explicitly assumed that net corporate/personal taxes are symmetric. In Chapter 15, we showed how asymmetric net corporate/personal taxes can cause capital structure to affect a firm's value. At this point, we will show you how an asymmetric tax view (what we called the **corporate tax view** in Chapter 15) of capital structure affects required rates of return in an otherwise perfect capital market. We assume that there are only corporate taxes in order to decrease the complexity of an an already sufficiently complex topic.

Equation (19.1) provides one way to determine $r^*(\theta)$. A second method is to adjust r, the unleveraged required rate of return, to reflect the impact of capital structure on the value of the investment. In order to do this, however, additional assumptions are necessary. Suppose that the income from an investment is a perpetuity with an expected value of $\bar{I}$ each period; $\bar{I}$ is paid out each period in three parts. One part goes to the government for corporate income taxes. A second part goes to the debtholders, and the third part is paid out to the shareholders. Each of the two groups of investors values the expected future cash flows they will receive at the required rate of return for that flow.

As with any investment, the value of this investment if it is unleveraged, V_U, can be expressed as the present value of its expected future after-tax cash flows. The ex-

FIGURE 19-1

Required rates of return as hypothetical functions of θ in a perfect capital market.

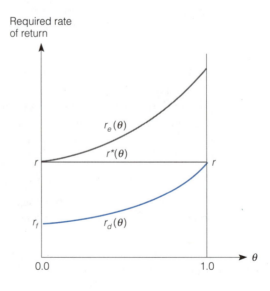

pected future after-tax cash flows are $\bar{I}(1 - \tau)$ each period forever, and r is the unleveraged required rate of return, so

$$V_U = \frac{\bar{I}(1 - \tau)}{r} \qquad (19.2)$$

The value of the same investment if it is leveraged, denoted V_L, can be expressed as the present value of the same expected future after-tax cash flows, but with the present value determined by $r^*(\theta)$, or

$$V_L = \frac{\bar{I}(1 - \tau)}{r^*(\theta)} \qquad (19.3)$$

If capital structure is irrelevant, then $V_U = V_L$ and therefore $r^*(\theta) = r$, just as it does in Figure 19-1. However, if capital structure affects the value of the investment, then we can express $r^*(\theta)$ in terms of r.

Another way to determine the value of a leveraged firm is to compute the present value of the partitioned after-tax cash flows, valuing each according to its required rate of return. In Equations (19.2) and (19.3), the after-tax cash flows used to compute the present value are identical. This is because the adjustment is made to the discount rate *rather* than to the expected future cash flows in Equation (19.3). If we adjust the cash flows instead, we have $\bar{I}$ coming in each period but pay corporate taxes on $\bar{I}$ minus the interest payment. To avoid having to adjust for differences in risk, assume that the debt is created so that it has the same risk as that of unleveraged financing for the investment. So the debtholders earn a risky amount each period with an expected value of rD, where D is equal to the present value of the debt and can be expressed as $D = \theta V_L$. The only difference between this debt and supplying unleveraged equity financing for the investment is that the payments for the debt are not subjected to corporate taxes.[4] Under the conditions just described, the combined expected after-tax cash flow to be paid out to debtholders and shareholders each period is the total income minus the total taxes. The total tax each period has an expected value of $\tau(\bar{I} - rD)$, so the value of the leveraged investment can be expressed as

$$V_L = \frac{\bar{I} - \tau(\bar{I} - rD)}{r} = \frac{\bar{I}(1 - \tau) + \tau rD}{r} = \frac{\bar{I}(1 - \tau)}{r} + \tau D \qquad (19.4)$$

The fraction in the expression on the right-hand side of Equation (19.4) equals the right-hand side of Equation (19.2), so we can rewrite V_L as

$$V_L = V_U + \tau D \qquad (19.5)$$

which is the most common way of mathematically expressing the corporate tax view.

We can build on this result. A value for $r^*(\theta)$ can be derived as a function of r by setting Equations (19.3) and (19.4) equal to each other and solving for $r^*(\theta)$:

$$r^*(\theta) = r - \frac{r\tau D r^*(\theta)}{\bar{I}(1 - \tau)} \qquad (19.6)$$

[4] This is somewhat hypothetical, but it simplifies the analysis so that we can focus on how financial risk affects the required rate of return. A more complex analysis using a more typical debt instrument produces the same result after adjusting for risk differences. (Actually, our debt instrument is not as artificial as it sounds. Income bonds could have been used to create the hypothetical debt instrument in this example up until about 1980 when such securities were essentially eliminated by an IRS ruling.)

FIGURE 19-2

Required rates of return as hypothetical functions of θ with asymmetric net corporate/personal taxes in an otherwise perfect capital market.

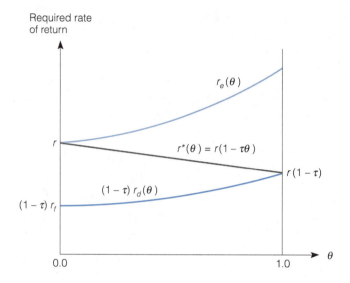

Expressing D as θV_L, substituting Equation (19.3) for V_L, and simplifying leads to the following expression for $r^*(\theta)$:[5]

$$r^*(\theta) = r - \tau\theta r = r(1 - \tau\theta) \qquad (19.7)$$

Note that the function for $r^*(\theta)$ in Equation (19.7), based on the corporate tax view, is linear in θ. That is, the graph of $r^*(\theta)$ versus θ is a straight line. $r^*(\theta)$ decreases as θ increases, and the lowest value of $r^*(\theta)$ ($= r[1 - \tau]$) occurs when the firm is financed entirely with debt (i.e., when $\theta = 1.0$). Thus, because the lowest value for $r^*(\theta)$ maximizes the value of the investment, the optimal capital structure under this view is the one that contains as much debt as possible. Figure 19-2 illustrates how the required rate of return on an investment, $r^*(\theta)$, varies with the degree of leverage, θ, in accordance with Equation (19.7).

EXAMPLE ■   Once again recall the Per-Pet example, this time from Chapter 15. In the extended example in Chapter 15, we showed that with corporate taxes in an otherwise perfect capital market environment, the value of the firm will depend on θ. We examined two different capital structures: (1) all equity ($\theta = 0$) and (ii) borrowing $500 out of a total leveraged firm value of $812.5, or a capital structure of $\theta = .61538$ ($= 500/812.5$) (remember that θ depends upon market values). For the all-equity capital structure, the second term in Equation (19.1) drops out, and $r^*(\theta)$, the weighted average, is simply the value of $r_e(0)$, 15%—the same value for $r^*(\theta)$ that we got with no corporate taxes. However, for the leveraged capital structure,

---

[5] Equation (19.7) is derived by first setting Equation (19.3) equal to Equation (19.4):

$$\frac{\bar{I}(1 - \tau)}{r^*(\theta)} = \frac{\bar{I}(1 - \tau)}{r} + \tau D$$

Cross multiplying and rearranging leads to Equation (19.6), and substituting θV_L for D leads to:

$$r^*(\theta) = r - \frac{r\tau Dr^*(\theta)}{\bar{I}(1 - \tau)} = r - \frac{r\tau\theta V_L r^*(\theta)}{\bar{I}(1 - \tau)}$$

From Equation (19.3) we can see that $r^*(\theta)/\bar{I}(1 - \tau)$ is the inverse of V_L, so it cancels out V_L, and we have

$$r^*(\theta) = r - \tau\theta r = r(1 - \tau\theta)$$

$\theta = .61538$, $r_d(.61538) = .10$, $r_e(.61538) = 20\%$, $\tau = .375$ and, from Equation (19.1), $r^*(\theta)$ is

$$r^*(\theta) = (1 - \theta)r_e(\theta) + \theta(1 - \tau)r_d(\theta) = (.38462)(.20) + (.61538)(1 - .375)(.10)$$
$$= 11.5385\%$$

illustrating that the required rate of return is lowered by leverage with corporate taxes in an otherwise perfect capital market environment.

Extending the example a little further, consider the value of the firm under the two alternative capital structures. The expected after-tax cash flow for the example, the CFAT, with corporate taxes levied at a rate of 37.5%, was found to be $93.75 (an expected before-tax cash flow of $150 times 1 minus the corporate tax rate). With an all-equity capital structure, then, the value of the firm, V_U, is given by Equation (19.2) as

$$V_U = \frac{\bar{I}(1 - \tau)}{r} = \frac{93.75}{.15} = \$625.00$$

which is exactly what we computed the value of the firm to be in Chapter 15. With $\theta = .5$, the value of the leveraged firm, V_L, is given by Equation (19.3) as

$$V_L = \frac{\bar{I}(1 - \tau)}{r^*(\theta)} = \frac{93.75}{.115385} = \$812.50$$

which is the value for the leveraged firm computed in Chapter 15. It is important to note that the CFAT we use is the same for both cases; the change in value is accounted for by the change in the discount rate. Also, once again, *note that the leverage ratio is based on market values.* ■

THE IMPACT OF OTHER MARKET IMPERFECTIONS

Although we now have a function for $r^*(\theta)$, it is a function that is based solely on an asymmetric tax view and on the assumption of a perpetual income stream. Restrictions imposed by assuming that the income stream is a perpetuity will be considered later. For now, consider the view of capital structure presented in Chapter 15 that includes personal taxes, asymmetric information considerations, and transaction costs. When there is little chance of incurring the transaction costs associated with financial distress, the expected value of the costs of financial distress will be low. Therefore, for small amounts of leverage, the value-enhancing considerations of leverage dominate the expected costs of financial distress, and $r^*(\theta)$ decreases with increases in θ. At some point, the expected costs of financial distress become large enough to overcome the other, value-enhancing considerations. The point where $r^*(\theta)$ reaches its minimum determines the optimal capital structure, which minimizes the required rate of return and maximizes the value of the investment. Figure 19-3 illustrates hypothetical functions for the various required rates of return for an investment, based on these considerations.

Figure 19-3 illustrates the collective impact of the valuation considerations associated with capital structure when all of the relevant factors are included. While Figure 19-3 provides a visual aid to understanding, an equation for $r^*(\theta)$ is needed in order to determine precise values. To capture the impact of *all* the relevant dimensions connected with debt financing, define T^* as the **net-benefit-to-leverage factor**. T^* is assumed to be derived from a linear approximation to the actual net-benefit-to-leverage relationship over some relevant range of values for θ.

FIGURE 19-3
Required rates of return as hypothetical functions of θ when relevant capital market imperfections are included.

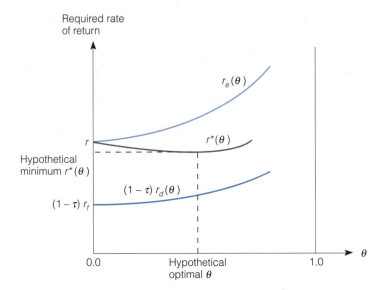

We can now apply the same analysis that was just presented for the corporate tax view to take into account this broader set of capital structure considerations. In this more general case, the value of the leveraged investment can be expressed as

$$V_L = V_U + T^*D \tag{19.8}$$

which is a generalization of Equation (19.5), and the required rate of return on an investment becomes

$$r^*(\theta) = r(1 - T^*\theta) \tag{19.9}$$

which is a generalization of Equation (19.7).

The value of a leveraged investment can be expressed in the form given in Equation (19.8) when the income stream from the investment is a perpetuity with constant expected value. In Equation (19.8), V_L can be viewed as being made up of two components. The first component is the basic value of the investment, V_U. The second component is the net benefit obtained by using the debt financing that the investment is capable of supporting. Each component represents the present value of a stream of expected future cash flows. The first stream is $\bar{I}(1 - \tau)$, the firm's after-tax income each period, its CFAT. The second stream is the net benefit from maintaining an amount D of debt each period. This net benefit can be expressed as T^* times the interest payment each period, or $T^*r_d(\theta)D$. The present value of these cash flow streams can be computed simply by dividing each perpetuity by its required rate of return. Of course, since the risks of the two streams are different, their required rates of return are different. The required rate of return for the firm's (unleveraged) after-tax income stream, its CFAT, is r. Because of lower risk, the required rate of return for the net benefit to leverage is lower than r.

The *net* benefit (or cost) to leverage is composed of net tax advantages, asymmetric information considerations, and transaction costs. For the most part, the net benefit to leverage each period does not depend upon the variance of the firm's income.[6] Because of its dependence upon the likelihood of financial distress, the

[6] This may not hold when the firm is in financial distress. See Chapter 9 for a discussion of financial contracting considerations with respect to financial distress.

riskiness of the cash flows associated with the net benefit to leverage is approximately equal to the riskiness of the firm's debt. Therefore, the stream of benefits from leverage is discounted at $r_d(\theta)$ so that V_L can be expressed as

$$V_L = V_U + T^*D = \frac{\bar{I}(1-\tau)}{r} + \frac{T^*r_d(\theta)D}{r_d(\theta)} \qquad (19.10)$$

It may seem somewhat redundant to represent the second term on the right-hand side of Equation (19.10) in this way since $r_d(\theta)$ could be canceled out. However, identifying the net benefit to leverage as the present value of a cash flow stream provides an important and very useful insight for examining cases where income is not perpetual. In the case of nonperpetual income, the discount rate does not always conveniently cancel out of the equation.

ADJUSTED PRESENT VALUE   19.5

The value of a leveraged investment, given in Equation (19.8), implies the required rate of return given in Equation (19.9). Our interest in a required rate of return is motivated by a desire to be able to value an investment easily and accurately. Although Equation (19.9) is appropriate for investments that are level perpetuities, most investments are not level perpetuities. While Equation (19.9) could be used as an approximation to the required rate of return for an investment whose income stream is not a level perpetuity, better approximations are available. We can derive better approximations to the required rate of return by analyzing the value of an investment under more realistic assumptions.

Frequently, when a firm borrows money, the loan is tied to an asset by an agreement such as a mortgage or lease. In such cases, the debt contract specifies payments of interest and principal over a time period that is less than or equal to the life of the asset. Over that payment period, the value of the asset declines because the project (asset) has a finite life. Finite life projects with contractually specified debt payment schedules are fundamentally different from perpetuity investments because the adjustment of the required rate of return for the effects of capital structure depends upon the life of the project.[7] To take into account this difference, we can apply a procedure called **adjusted present value** (APV).

For finite maturity debt, we can rewrite Equation (19.10) in the form of the present value of a finite stream of net benefits from debt financing, so that the value of an investment, its APV, is

$$APV_0 = \sum_{t=1}^{n} \frac{CFAT_t}{(1+r)^t} + \sum_{t=1}^{n} \frac{T^*INT_t}{[1+r_d(\theta)]^t} \qquad (19.11)$$

where n is the number of periods in the life of the investment and INT_t is the interest payment in period t.

EXAMPLE ■ The Watt Mita-Bean Corporation is evaluating an investment in a new type of soy bean processing plant. The investment would be set up as a wholly owned subsidiary and called Little-Bean and Company. Little-Bean will be financed with $2.5 million of debt and $1.5 million of cash, provided by Watt Mita-Bean as equity financing. The (unleveraged) after-tax cash flows, the CFATs, expected to result from Little-Bean are $1 million per year for 6 years, after which time

---

[7]Myers (1974).

TABLE 19-1 Loan Amortization Schedule for Little-Bean and Company (Dollar Amounts in Millions)

Year:	0	1	2	3	4	5	6
a. Loan balance at start of period	0	2.5000	2.3000	2.1000	1.9000	1.7000	1.5000
b. Interest for the period (13.2% of loan balance)	0	.3300	.3036	.2772	.2508	.2244	.1980
c. Principal repayment	0	.2000	.2000	.2000	.2000	.2000	1.5000
d. Loan balance at end of period (a)–(c)	2.5000	2.3000	2.1000	1.9000	1.7000	1.5000	0

the project is expected to be sold off for a net after-tax $2 million in cash. Little-Bean's debt will be 6-year debt with interest payments of 13.2% per year on the remaining balance. Principal payments will be $200,000 per year with a final principal payment of $1.5 million at the end of year 6. If the net-benefit-to-leverage factor, T^*, for this investment is .25 and the (unleveraged) required rate of return for the Little-Bean project is 20% (i.e., $r_e(0) = r = 20\%$), what is the value of the Little-Bean project to Watt Mita-Bean? In other words, what is the *net adjusted present value* of this project?

Table 19-1 presents an amortization schedule for the Little-Bean loan and identifies the interest payments that Little-Bean will be making over the life of the loan. From Equation (19.11), then, we have

$$APV = \sum_{t=1}^{6} \frac{1.0}{(1.2)^t} + \frac{2.0}{(1.2)^6}$$

$$+ \left[\frac{.3300}{1.132} + \frac{.3036}{(1.132)^2} + \frac{.2772}{(1.132)^3} + \frac{.2508}{(1.132)^4} + \frac{.2244}{(1.132)^5} + \frac{.1980}{(1.132)^6} \right] [.25]$$

$$= 3.325510 + .669796 + .271775 = \$4.267 \text{ million}$$

The net adjusted present value (APV minus the initial cost), then, equals $0.267 million (= 4.267 − 4.0). ∎

19.6   MANAGING CAPITAL STRUCTURE AND ITS IMPACT ON FIRM VALUE

In Chapters 20 and 21, we examine many of the situations where the APV method is very useful. For the most part, these are situations where the financing and investment decisions simply cannot be separated. A lease is an example of such a situation. By contrast, capital budgeting decisions do not typically involve financing that is tied to the project. However, even if the firm's financing decisions are separate from its capital budgeting decisions, if T^* is positive, capital structure affects the value of the firm's investments. To incorporate that effect into the measure of investment value, the *pattern* in interest payments must be known. While it would be difficult to incorporate the exact pattern of every situation into a measure of value, we can make a generalizing assumption about how firms manage their capital structure over time and incorporate that assumed pattern into our measure of investment value.

REBALANCING THE FIRM'S DEBT LEVEL

Typically, a firm establishes a capital structure policy that involves a target level of debt, θ^*. The firm's actual level of debt, θ, might be above or below θ^* at any point in time. While the firm does not maintain $\theta = \theta^*$ at all times, periodically, the firm adjusts its capital structure back to $\theta = \theta^*$. Such adjustments are especially common when a firm has additional reasons for making a major financial transaction, such as issuing bonds. When a firm adjusts its capital structure back to θ^*, it is referred to as **rebalancing the debt level**.

Unintended changes in a firm's capital structure may necessitate rebalancing the firm's debt level. Unintended changes in a firm's capital structure can occur for a number of reasons, but most often such changes occur because new information arrives. For example, an innovation in technology can cause an increase or decrease in the value of a firm. Since θ is the ratio of debt to the total market value of the firm, a change in the firm's value causes a change in θ. (You might recall AT&T's unintended change in capital structure that we noted in the solution to AT&T's capital structure decision in Chapter 15.)

A GENERAL PATTERN FOR DEBT PAYMENTS

The observation that managers have target debt levels for their firms and that they periodically rebalance the capital structures of their firms to that target, lead James Miles and John Ezzell (1980; 1985) to investigate the value of an investment under a general pattern of debt payments. The pattern they explore involves rebalancing the debt level each period on the basis of the project's realized market value. This sounds much more complex than it turns out to be. Miles and Ezzell discovered that under this policy, there is a simple adjustment to the unleveraged required rate of return that produces a single discount rate for correctly computing the NPV of an investment, even when the project's CFAT stream is not a level perpetuity. The Appendix to this chapter examines an alternative general pattern for debt payments.

When the debt level is rebalanced each period on the basis of the realized value of the project, the net benefit to leverage in future periods will vary with the value of the project. So the net benefit to leverage in future periods is more risky under the debt rebalancing pattern than it is with a fixed debt payment schedule. As the debt payment pattern actually unfolds, it can be quite different from what it was expected to be at the start of the project. In fact, the actual debt pattern will vary in the same way that the project value varies.

Under the rebalancing assumption, the stream of net benefits to leverage is not discounted at $r_d(\theta)$ throughout the life of the project. Only the net benefit from the *first* period is discounted at $r_d(\theta)$, since only the amount of debt for the first period is fixed at $t=0$. The net benefit to leverage in subsequent periods must be discounted at the unleveraged required rate of return because this net benefit will vary as the project value and amount of debt vary in future periods. Using this notion, we can derive the adjustment to the unleveraged rate of return that produces the correct project NPV. We will derive this adjustment assuming a perpetual income stream because it is easier to understand, but the derived adjusted rate also applies to projects that have finite lives.

With a perpetual income stream, we have an expected after-tax cash flow of $\bar{I}(1 - \tau)$ each period plus an *expected* (mathematical expectation) net benefit to leverage each period of $T^*\theta r_d(\theta)E(V_L)$, where $E(V_L)$ is the expected value of the project.

Note that the actual value of the project at each point in the future can differ from this expectation. We know from Equation (19.10) that the total value of the leveraged investment is the sum of the present values of the two streams. However, to compute these present values, we need to know the required rate of return for each income stream. The required rate of return for, and present value of, the first stream is straightforward. The required rate of return is the unleveraged rate of return, and the present value is the value of the unleveraged investment given in Equation (19.2).

Determining the required rate of return for, and present value of, the second stream is more complex. As already noted, when the debt level is constant forever, the required rate of return for the stream of net benefits from leverage equals the required rate of return on debt, $r_d(\theta)$, because the net benefit stream belongs to the same risk class as the debt. (This is how we derived the formula for the required rate of return under the corporate tax view of capital structure given in Equation (19.7).) The net benefit to leverage in the first period of the project is $T^*\theta r_d(\theta) V_L$, based on a debt level of θV_L, where V_L is the value of the project at $t=0$. Because V_L is not an expected value, the net benefit to leverage in the first period of the project has the same risk as the debt. However, the net benefits to leverage in subsequent periods are based on the expected value $E(V_L)$ and are therefore riskier. When the amount of debt in future periods depends on what the project's value turns out to be at that time, the risk of those flows is comparable to the risk of the investment itself. That is, the risk is comparable to that of the unleveraged cash flows. Let us denote the net benefit to leverage in the first period of the project as $\Delta = T^*\theta r_d(\theta) V_L$ and the expected net benefit to leverage in all periods after the first as $\bar{\Delta} = T^*\theta r_d(\theta) E(V_L)$. The stream of net benefits due to leverage and the present value calculation for them are illustrated in Figure 19-4.

At time $t=1$, the stream of future net benefits to leverage constitutes a perpetuity with an expected value of $\bar{\Delta}$ each period. So the value, at $t=1$, of future benefits in periods 2, 3, 4, . . . is simply $\bar{\Delta}/r$—the present value of a perpetuity. The total value attributable to leverage, then, at $t=1$, equals this value plus the benefit to leverage in period 1 (Δ), or $\Delta + \bar{\Delta}/r$. To get the total value at $t=0$, we simply compute the present value of this total amount by discounting it back one period at $r_d(\theta)$ because it belongs to the same risk class as the debt itself. The present value of the total stream of benefits resulting from leverage over the life of the project is then

$$\text{present value of the net benefit to leverage} = \frac{\Delta + \bar{\Delta}/r}{1 + r_d(\theta)} \quad \text{(19.12)}$$

and the total value of the leveraged investment, V_L, expressed as the sum of V_U and the present value of the net benefit to leverage, is

$$V_L = \frac{\bar{I}(1 - \tau)}{r} + \frac{\Delta + \bar{\Delta}/r}{1 + r_d(\theta)} \quad \text{(19.13)}$$

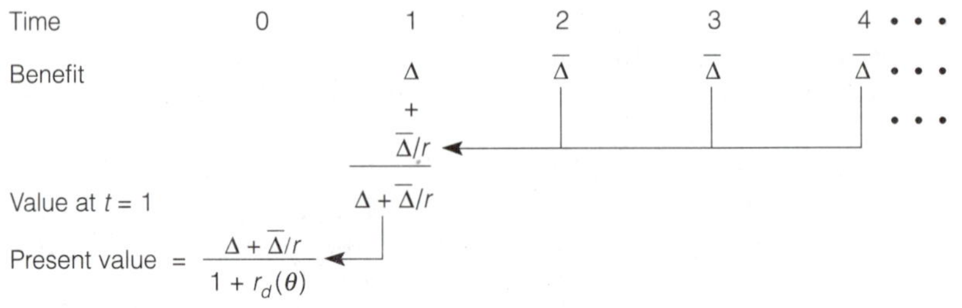

FIGURE 19-4

Present value calculation for the net benefit to leverage.

Time	0	1	2	3	4 • • •
Benefit		Δ	$\bar{\Delta}$	$\bar{\Delta}$	$\bar{\Delta}$ • • •
		$+$			• • •
		$\bar{\Delta}/r$			
Value at $t = 1$		$\Delta + \bar{\Delta}/r$			
Present value $= \dfrac{\Delta + \bar{\Delta}/r}{1 + r_d(\theta)}$					

Since $\bar{I}$ is a level expected perpetual stream, the expected value of the stream at any future point in time is the same as its current expected value, which is the project's current value; that is, $E(V_L) = V_L$. Therefore, $\bar{\Delta} = \Delta$, and both can be expressed as $T^*\theta r_d(\theta)V_L$. Substituting, we have

$$V_L = \frac{\bar{I}(1 - \tau)}{r} + \frac{(1 + 1/r)\,T^*\theta r_d(\theta)\,V_L}{1 + r_d(\theta)} \tag{19.14}$$

Rearranging,

$$V_L\left[1 - \frac{(1 + 1/r)\,T^*\theta r_d(\theta)}{1 + r_d(\theta)}\right] = \frac{\bar{I}(1 - \tau)}{r} \tag{19.15}$$

so that,

$$V_L = \frac{\bar{I}(1 - \tau)}{r - \left[\dfrac{(r + 1)\,T^*\theta r_d(\theta)}{1 + r_d(\theta)}\right]} \tag{19.16}$$

Equation (19.16) is written so that V_L is expressed as the present value of a perpetuity consisting of CFAT $= \bar{I}(1 - \tau)$. Therefore, the denominator must be the required rate of return for this perpetuity, or

$$r^*(\theta) = r - T^*\theta r_d(\theta)\left[\frac{1 + r}{1 + r_d(\theta)}\right] \tag{19.17}$$

Equation (19.17) is the Miles-Ezzell formula for the (weighted average) required rate of return on an investment where the firm follows a policy of rebalancing its capital structure each period based on the project's realized market value.

EXAMPLE ■ Suppose the unleveraged required rate of return, r, for the Watt Mita-Bean Corporation's entire portfolio of assets is 18% and Mita-Bean rebalances its capital structure each year to a target of $\theta = .35$. If $T^* = .25$ and Watt Mita-Bean can borrow currently at a rate of $r_d(.35) = 11.5\%$, what is the weighted average required rate of return, $r^*(\theta)$, for the Watt Mita-Bean Corporation?

From Equation (19.17), we have

$$r^*(\theta) = r - T^*\theta r_d(\theta)\left[\frac{1 + r}{1 + r_d(\theta)}\right] = .18 - .25(.35)(.115)\left[\frac{1.18}{1.115}\right] = 16.935\%$$

■

ESTIMATING THE RISK OF A PROJECT   19.7

Equation (19.17) defines the required rate of return for an investment, based on the unleveraged required rate, r. Since r has the largest impact on the required rate of return, it is important to consider various methods of estimating r. If capital structure were irrelevant, the required rate of return would be constant across all values of θ, and we could simply use the weighted average cost of capital (WACC) formula given in Equation (19.1) for firms investing in projects of the same risk. (Of course, even if capital structure were irrelevant, differences in $r_e(\theta)$ and $r_d(\theta)$, due to the difference in risk bearing, would still have to be taken into account.) But when T^* is positive, the analytical process becomes more complex. Equations (19.1) and (19.17) can be used to derive a formula for r.

We know that the expression for the required rate of return given in Equation (19.1) is always correct. And we have said that the debt management pattern assumed in Equation (19.17) is a fairly accurate characterization of typical corporate policy. Therefore, setting these two equations equal to each other and solving for r will provide a formula for r based on $r_e(\theta)$ and $r_d(\theta)$. Setting the equations equal to each other, we have

$$r - T^*\theta r_d(\theta)\left[\frac{1 + r}{1 + r_d(\theta)}\right] = (1 - \theta)r_e(\theta) + \theta(1 - \tau)r_d(\theta) \qquad \text{(19.18)}$$

and rearranging gives

$$r\left[1 - \frac{T^*\theta r_d(\theta)}{1 + r_d(\theta)}\right] - \frac{T^*\theta r_d(\theta)}{1 + r_d(\theta)} = (1 - \theta)r_e(\theta) + \theta(1 - \tau)r_d(\theta) \qquad \text{(19.19)}$$

To simplify this expression, define $H(\theta)$ as

$$H(\theta) = \frac{T^*\theta r_d(\theta)}{1 + r_d(\theta)} \qquad \text{(19.20)}$$

Then

$$r[1 - H(\theta)] - H(\theta) = (1 - \theta)r_e(\theta) + \theta(1 - \tau)r_d(\theta)$$

The right-hand side of this equation equals the weighted average cost of capital given in Equation (19.1). Denoting this as WACC(θ) and solving for r, we have

$$r = \frac{\text{WACC}(\theta) + H(\theta)}{1 - H(\theta)} \qquad \text{(19.21)}$$

While Equation (19.21) provides a conceptual basis for estimating the basic risk of an investment, accurate estimates of the parameters necessary to use Equation (19.21) are not always easily obtained. For corporations with debt and equity securities that are widely market-traded, θ and $r_d(\theta)$ can be estimated fairly accurately from the value of those securities. The yield to maturity on the firm's outstanding debt, adjusted for tax factors if the current market value of the debt differs from its principal amount, can be used to estimate $r_d(\theta)$. The total market value of the firm's debt and outstanding equity can be used to estimate θ. The estimate of θ is the market value of the debt divided by the sum of the two market values. Estimating $r_e(\theta)$ is more difficult and requires professional judgement. Four methods of estimating $r_e(\theta)$ are outlined below. Finally, the most difficult parameter to estimate is T^*. Until more precise theory is developed, the estimate of T^* involves very subjective judgment.

UNLEVERAGED BETAS

In Chapter 10, we examined the impact of financial leverage on a stock's beta. We noted that each security is valued according to its nondiversifiable risk and that its risk includes both business and financial risk. Therefore, each security—equity *and* debt—has its own beta, and the firm's beta, β_F, is a weighted average of the betas of the securities issued to finance the firm. In a perfect capital market environment, β_F does not depend on how the firm is financed since the firm's beta reflects only the nondiversifiable business risk of the firm's assets. In Chapter 10, we specified a simple function for estimating β_F using $\beta_e(\theta)$, the stock's beta, by assuming that $\beta_d(\theta)$ (the beta of the firm's debt) equals zero. Our purpose in estimating β_F was to provide a measure of the "basic" risk—the business risk—of the firm's portfolio of assets.

In the environment we are examining in this chapter, an environment where capital structure affects the value of the firm, such a measure of the basic risk of the firm's portfolio of assets is provided by the firm's **unleveraged beta**, the firm's beta if the firm was all-equity-financed. The firm's unleveraged beta is simply the stock's beta when $\theta = 0.0$. Therefore, we can estimate $\beta_e(0)$ using r, as given in Equation (19.21). From Equation (10.6) with $\theta = 0.0$, we have

$$r_e(0) = r_f + \beta_e(0)(r_m - r_f) = r \qquad \text{(19.22)}$$

Rearranging Equation (19.22), the unleveraged beta can be expressed as

$$\beta_e(0) = \frac{r - r_f}{r_m - r_f} \qquad \text{(19.23)}$$

ESTIMATING THE REQUIRED RATE OF RETURN ON EQUITY

We describe below four methods for estimating the required rate of return on equity. Market-traded shares are necessary inputs to the first three methods. As such, it is important to identify one or more firms with market-traded shares of common stock that have most of their investments in the same industry as the investment under consideration. If possible, it is desirable to identify several firms in this category. The fourth method is based on the rate at which the firm can borrow. Because all of the methods are subject to random variation, it is advisable to use multiple methods, perhaps all of them, especially if there are problems that make using the market model method particularly difficult.

THE MARKET MODEL   The best method for estimating a required rate of return on equity is to use an asset pricing model such as those described in Chapter 7. Commercial financial data services, such as Value Line, provide estimates of betas for many stocks. Such estimates are obtained using linear regression to regress the historical returns from a stock against the historical returns from a proxy for the market portfolio, such as the Standard & Poor's 500 Index. Such a procedure is based on a one-factor market model similar to the capital asset pricing model (CAPM). More complex multiple-factor models in an arbitrage pricing model (APT) framework can also be used. In the case of the one-factor market model, once a value for beta has been estimated for the project via a surrogate, estimates of the rate of return on the riskless asset, r_f, and the rate of return on the market portfolio, r_m, can be used with that beta to estimate the leveraged required rate of return on equity for that project:

$$r_e(\theta) = r_f + \beta_e(\theta)(r_m - r_f) \qquad \text{(19.24)}$$

THE DIVIDEND GROWTH MODEL   For relatively stable growth industries, the past growth in dividends can be used to estimate the growth factor, g, in the Gordon Dividend Growth Model, which was discussed in Chapter 6. In Chapter 6, we presented a hypothetical calculation of the capitalization rate for General Motors common stock by applying Equation (6.12). The capitalization rate is another name for $r_e(\theta)$. Once we have an estimate for g, Equation (6.12) can be used to estimate $r_e(\theta)$:

$$r_e(\theta) = \frac{D_1}{P_0} + g \qquad \text{(19.25)}$$

THE P/E RATIO METHOD   Recall also from Chapter 6 that when the expected rate of return is equal to the required rate of return on the firm's future investments, the inverse of the P/E ratio equals the capitalization rate for the common stock. This means that in some cases, *with careful judgment,* the inverse of the P/E ratio can be used as an estimate of $r_e(\theta)$. However, as was pointed out in our important warning about P/E ratios, a *great deal* of care is needed to apply this concept. There can be substantial time lags between earnings and price movement; price movement precedes changes in recorded earnings because market participants anticipate changes in earnings and the market price of the stock reflects this anticipation. Furthermore, whenever the firm's earnings are sufficiently small or negative, the capitalization rate implied by the inverse of the P/E ratio will be inaccurate. Finally, when firms are introducing new ideas and have investment opportunities with substantially positive NPVs, it is necessary to estimate the expected net present value of the firm's future investments (NPVFI) and rearrange Equation (6.18) so that the estimate of $r_e(\theta)$ is

$$r_e(\theta) = \frac{\text{EPS}_1}{P_0 - \text{NPVFI}} \qquad (19.26)$$

The P/E ratio method is generally the least reliable of the methods based on market-traded shares, and *it should be used only as a last resort.*

    THE BORROWING RATE METHOD   When all else fails, a crude estimate of $r_e(\theta)$ can be developed from the firm's borrowing rate, $r_d(\theta)$. This is one way that an estimate can be created when the only surrogates that can be identified for an investment opportunity do not have market-traded shares of common stock. We know that, because of risk differences, the required rate of return for equity must exceed the required rate of return for debt for any level of θ. Empirically, we note that for major corporations that have securities traded on the NYSE and outstanding investment-grade bonds (bonds rated BBB, Baa, or higher), estimates of $r_e(\theta)$ are in a range of approximately 1.4 to 2.0 times the yield to maturity on their long-term bonds.[8] One strategy, then, is to multiply an estimate of $r_d(\theta)$ for a project obtained from private sources by a factor F:

$$r_e(\theta) = Fr_d(\theta) \qquad (19.27)$$

Although judgment is necessary to determine the exact value to use for F, a good rule of thumb—Emery's rule—is to use 1.5. In any case, most values would fall in a range between 1.5 and 1.75.

| 19.8 | ## ESTIMATING A REQUIRED RATE OF RETURN FOR AN INVESTMENT |

The process for estimating a required rate of return can be outlined as follows:

1. Choose one or more surrogate firms that have similar risk and industry characteristics as that of the investment.
2. For each surrogate:
   a. estimate θ based on market values for the firm's debt and equity;
   b. estimate $r_d(\theta)$ from the yield to maturity on the firm's outstanding debt;
   c. estimate $r_e(\theta)$ using one or more of the methods cited above;

---

[8] Note that higher beta firms (with higher risk because of either operating risk *or* financial leverage) will tend to have a higher required rate of return on their debt, which corresponds to the higher beta on their stock. Apparently, as a result of this, the regularity noted holds for a fairly broad range of firms.

d. estimate the firm's marginal tax rate, τ, using publicly reported data; and finally

e. estimate the net-benefit-to-leverage factor for the firm, T^*.

The estimate of T^* will involve considerations such as the firm's marginal tax rate, the uniqueness of the product, the amount of nondebt tax shields, among others discussed in Chapter 15. The estimate of T^* is based on professional judgment and is admittedly subjective, but based on empirical research, we would expect most estimates to fall within a range between .05 and .25.[9]

3. For each surrogate, use the parameter estimates in point 2 above to estimate $H(\theta)$ in Equation (19.20) and WACC(θ) in Equation (19.1), which are in turn used as parameter inputs to estimate r using Equation (19.21).

4. Based on the set of one or more estimates of r from surrogate firms, make a single estimate of r. Usually an average can be used, however, judgment is necessary when the variance in the estimates is large and/or some of the estimates are very different from each other. r is based on the project's business risk.

5. The estimate of the required rate of return for the investment, $r^*(\theta)$ (which includes both business risk and the effects of capital structure), can now be computed using the Miles-Ezzell formula given in Equation (19.17), the single estimate of r derived above, and estimates for the firm considering the investment:

a. the target capital structure, θ^*, the firm will be using over the life of the investment;

b. the firm's current $r_d(\theta^*)$; and

c. the net-benefit-to-leverage factor, T^*, for the firm.

A REQUIRED RATE OF RETURN ESTIMATION EXAMPLE

The Chalko Co. is considering an investment opportunity in an area in which it has no previous experience. Chalko has identified several companies whose investments are primarily in the same industry as the one they are considering. One of these companies is Boardon, Inc. Boardon common stock and bonds are traded publicly on the NYSE. Currently, the market value of Boardon common stock is $27 per share, and there are 10 million shares outstanding. Boardon's latest earnings were $3.40 per share, and next year's dividend is expected to be $1.60 per share. Five years ago, Boardon paid a dividend of $.73 per share. Boardon has long-term bonds with a total market value of $120 million, and their bonds, maturing in 2009 with a 9% coupon, are currently selling for $860. In addition to long-term bonds, Boardon has $20 million in notes payable and $40 million in other current liabilities. Summarizing the information:

bond price = $860.00   stock price = $27.00   next year's dividend = $1.60

\# bonds = 139,535   \# shares = 10 million   dividend 5 years ago = $0.73

current liabilities = $60 million; beta = 1.25; r_m = 15%; r_f = 7%; EPS = $3.40

Using this and other information, the required rate of return for the investment that Chalko is considering can be estimated via the procedure outlined above.

Boardon has total liabilities of $180 million made up of long-term bonds (market value = $120 million) and current liabilities (total book value = $60 million). Current liabilities mature soon enough that the book and market values are sufficiently close to ignore the difference and simply use the book value in our calculations. With

[9]Cordes and Sheffrin (1983); Masulis (1983).

a total equity value of $270 million ($27 times 10 million), the total market value of Boardon is $450 million (= 120 + 60 + 270), and $\theta = .40$ (= 180/450). Boardon's 9% coupon bonds of 2009 mature in 18 years and have a market value of $860, which implies a 5.4% effective semiannual rate, a 10.8% yield to maturity, and an 11.09% effective annual rate. Because the bonds are selling at a discount and will incur lower taxes due to capital gains tax deferral, we estimate that new debt for Boardon has a required rate of return that is slightly higher than the 11.09% annual rate; $r_d(\theta)$ is estimated to be 11.25% effective annual.

Lasser Financial Services estimates the beta for Boardon to be 1.25, short-term U.S. government securities are currently earning 7%, and the required rate of return on the market portfolio is estimated to be 15%, so that the market model estimate of Boardon's required rate of return on equity is $r_e(\theta) = .07 + 1.25(.15 - .07) = .17$, or 17%. During the 6-year period from 5 years ago until next year, Boardon's cash dividend grew from $.73 to $1.60, which represents an annual growth rate of $g = 14\%$. With a current market value of $P_0 = \$27$ and expected next dividend of $D_1 = \$1.60$, the dividend growth model estimate of the required rate of return for equity is $r_e(\theta) = (1.6/27) + .14 = .20$, or 20%. Boardon's P/E ratio is 8 (= 27/3.4), so the inverse of the P/E ratio is $r = \frac{1}{8} = .125$, or 12.5%. Finally, 1.5[11.25%] = 16.875%.

Of these estimates, the inverse of the P/E ratio is the least reliable. The difference between 12.5%, and the market model estimate of 17% may be due to the net present value of future investment opportunities. For example, if Boardon expects to earn $3.91 per share next year and $4 of the current market price per share of $27 represents the NPV of future investments (NPVFI), then, from Equation (19.26), the estimate would be $r_e(\theta) = 3.91/(27 - 4) = .17$, or 17%. The estimate obtained from the dividend growth model is based on a growth rate that is almost as large as the return to the market portfolio, and considerably larger than the return on the riskless asset. It is unlikely that growth of this magnitude can be maintained "forever into the future." Thus, the dividend growth model estimate of $r_e(\theta)$ is probably too large, and yet it is plausibly close to the market model estimate. Therefore, the three estimates do not appear to contradict one another. Because the market model estimate is most reliable, it will be used as the estimate of Boardon's required rate of return on equity.

The relevant marginal tax rate and net-benefit-to-leverage factor for Boardon have been estimated to be $\tau = 35\%$ and $T^* = .2$. Thus, based on estimates of the parameters for Boardon, the unleveraged required rate of return for the project Chalko is considering is estimated to be 14.05% in the following manner. From Equation (19.20),

$$H(\theta) = \frac{T^*\theta r_d(\theta)}{1 + r_d(\theta)} = \frac{(.2)(.4)(.1125)}{1.1125} = .00809$$

from Equation (19.1),

$$\text{WACC}(\theta) = (1 - \theta)r_e(\theta) + \theta(1 - \tau)r_d(\theta) = .6(.17) + .4(.65)(.1125) = .13125$$

and thus, from Equation (19.21),

$$r = \frac{\text{WACC}(\theta) + H(\theta)}{1 - H(\theta)} = \frac{(.13125 + .00809)}{(1 - .00809)} = .1405$$

Assume that the above procedure was followed for other surrogates in addition to Boardon, and the single estimate of r based on the set of surrogates is 14%. We can now estimate $r^*(\theta)$ based on this "best" estimate of r and the following estimates of Chalko's financial parameters: $r_d(\theta) = 11\%$, $\theta^* = .3$, and because of its unique tax situation, T^* for Chalko has been estimated to be .15. From Equation (19.17), then, $r^*(\theta)$ is estimated to be

$$r^*(\theta) = r - T^*\theta r_d(\theta) \left[\frac{1 + r}{1 + r_d(\theta)}\right] = .14 - (.15)(.3)(.11)\left[\frac{1.14}{1.11}\right] = .135 = 13.5\%$$

Thus, the required rate of return that Chalko should use to compute the NPV of the investment under consideration is 13.5%.

Because of all the possible rates of return that have been considered, we feel it is important to note specifically some of the rates of return that should *not* be used by Chalko to compute the NPV of the investment and how different those rates are from our estimate of 13.5%. Assuming Chalko has the same tax rate as Boardon, the corporate tax view specifies in Equation (19.7) that $r^*(\theta) = r(1 - \tau\theta) = .14(1 - .35(.3)) = 12.5\%$, which is 1 percent lower than our estimate of $r^*(\theta)$. Use of this rate would overstate the NPV of this project, and Chalko would risk taking on a bad project. Boardon's required rate of return to equity, which was estimated to be 17%, is 3.5% above our estimate of $r^*(\theta)$, and Chalko would risk rejection of a good project if this rate was (incorrectly) used to compute the NPV of the project. Boardon's WACC(θ) is closest to our estimate of $r^*(\theta)$, but 13.125% still understates it by .4% and would overstate the NPV in this case.[10] Finally, we point out once again that the weighted average cost of capital for Chalko plays no direct role in the analysis.

SUMMARY

In this chapter, we described a method for determining a required rate of return for an investment, taking into account the impact of capital structure. The determinants of this required rate of return were discussed in previous chapters. Because of the risk-return trade-off, the critical dimension of a required rate of return on an investment is the nondiversifiable operating risk of the particular investment. Other determinants include certain capital market imperfections, which were discussed in Chapter 15. While operating risk is project-specific, considerations of financial risk require that the impact of capital structure on the value of an investment be accounted for on a firm-wide basis.

This chapter described and illustrated the application of an important method of adjusting for the impact of capital structure, called the adjusted present value method. Additional applications and further discussion of the APV method are presented in the other chapters in Part 3. Building on the basic APV method, Miles and Ezzell developed an especially useful method for determining required rates of return for capital budgeting projects. They showed that there is a simple adjustment that can be made to the unleveraged required rate of return when a firm is assumed to rebalance its debt level each period on the basis of the project's realized market value, which is a capital structure management policy that is similar to those that are widely observed in practice. Their estimation procedure represents a very important improvement upon the corporate-tax-rate-based adjustment developed by Modigliani and Miller. This chapter also presented an example based on the Miles-Ezzell formula, along with methods for estimating the required rate of return on equity, drawn from Chapters 6 and 7.

---

[10] There is not a consistent bias toward over- or understating the required rate of return from simply using a surrogate's WACC(θ). This is unlike the problem that arises from applying the corporate tax view. The rate of return derived from that approach will always understate the rate of return calculated by applying the Miles-Ezzell procedure.

DECISION SUMMARY BOX

The value of an investment can be affected by how it is financed because of capital market imperfections. Adjusting for the effect of financing on the value of the investment can be done in two different ways. The usual method adjusts the required rate of return for the benefits of debt financing and uses that adjusted rate—the weighted average cost of capital—to compute the NPV of the investment. In some cases, there is no simple adjustment that can be made to the required rate of return. When no simple rate adjustment exits, an alternative method, **adjusted present value**, computes the present value, assuming no benefit from debt financing, and then adds to—adjusts—that basic value by adding the total additional value derived from debt financing. It is important to remember that

- The required rate of return is the current opportunity cost of capital. It is not a historical cost of funds.
- Risk is by far the most important determinant of a required rate of return.
- The risk of the investment is determined by its nondiversifiable risk. Thus, the required rate of return for an investment, $r^*(\theta)$, depends primarily on the nondiversifiable risk of the investment. In a perfect capital market, $r^*(\theta)$ does not depend on θ; the business risk is the only determinant of $r^*(\theta)$.
- The business risk of a firm is apportioned between the equityholders and debtholders. The firm's

mix of debt and equity determines its financial risk. Thus, the required rates of return to equity and debt ($r_e(\theta)$ and $r_d(\theta)$, respectively) depend on both the business risk and the financial risk of the firm. Financial risk affects $r_e(\theta)$ and $r_d(\theta)$ even in a perfect capital market.

- Capital structure is an important secondary determinant of a required rate of return that results from capital market imperfections, including asymmetric taxes, asymmetric information, and, to a lesser extent, transaction costs.
- The frequency of rebalancing the firm's capital structure affects the expected value of future net benefits from debt financing.
- Theoretically, each project has its own required rate of return.
- In practice, the use of risk classes (where the required rate of return used for a potential investment is specified by a standardized risk class that investments can be classified into) is an effective method for dealing with differences in the risk and required rate of return for potential investments.
- When in doubt, use Equation (19.1) if possible. Equation (19.1) is always correct, provided that $r_e(\theta)$ and $r_d(\theta)$ accurately reflect the degree of financial risk bearing and the current market-required rate of return for that level of risk.

PROBLEMS

PROBLEM SET A

A1. William Bates is contemplating starting a new firm that will provide background music for elevators, dentist offices, and the like. He estimates a positive NPV of $270,000 for the investment. Mr. Bates plans to call the firm Tarry-Tune, Unlimited, estimates that the initial investment needed to start Tarry-Tune is $325,000, and plans to borrow $200,000 of the initial investment. What is the expected leverage ratio (θ) for Tarry-Tune?

A2. Since the weighted average given in Equation (19.1) is always a correct measure of a required rate of return, why don't firms create securities to finance each project and offer them in the capital market in order to determine accurately the required rate of return for the project?

A3. Explain why there are circumstances in which it is useful to express the value of the leveraged firm as the sum of (1) the value of the firm unleveraged plus (2) the present value of the net benefit to leverage.

A4. Suppose a firm is unleveraged and has a required rate of return on equity, $r_e(0)$, of 15%. If the firm borrows 30% of the value of the firm at $r_d(.3) = 8\%$, and because of the financial leverage, $r_e(.3)$ is 18%, what is the firm's weighted average required rate of return, $r^*(.3)$:

   a. Assuming the firm is operating in a perfect capital market (including no taxes)?

   b. Assuming there are only corporate taxes at a rate of 35% in an otherwise perfect capital market?

A5. Suppose a firm is evaluating a potential new investment. The investment will be financed with $100,000 of debt and $100,000 of equity financing. The (unleveraged) after-tax cash flows, the CFATs, expected to result from the investment are $150,000 per year for 4 years, after which time the project is expected to be sold off for a net after-tax $100,000 in cash. The debt financing will be 4-year debt with interest payments of 14% per year on the remaining balance. Principal payments will be zero in year 1, $20,000 in year 2, $30,000 in year 3, and a final principal payment of $50,000 at the end of year 4. If the net-benefit-to-leverage factor, T^*, is .20 for this investment and the (unleveraged) required rate of return for the project is 20% (i.e., $r_e(0) = r = 20\%$), what is the net adjusted present value for this project?

A6. Jumping Gym's Uni-sexercise Club is a coed health club in northern Southampton that has an unleveraged required rate of return of 43% $= r_e(0) = r$. Gym rebalances its capital structure each year to a target of $\theta = .52$. If $T^* = .20$ and Gym can borrow currently at a rate of $r_d(.52) = 26\%$, what is the weighted average required rate of return, $r^*(\theta)$, for Jumping Gym's Uni-sexercise Club?

A7. Why is it so important to note that the required rate of return is not a historical cost of funds? Cite two factors that can render the use of a firm's historical cost of funds (to evaluate a new investment) to be potentially damaging to the firm.

A8. What are the major factors that will determine the **net-benefit-to-leverage factor**, T^*?

A9. Maxicomputer Corporation is considering building a new manufacturing facility in Taiwan. Maxicomputer's debt ratio is $\theta = 0.5$. Maxicomputer's cost of debt is $r_d(.5) = 10\%$. Maxicomputer estimates that the leveraged cost of equity capital for the project is $r_e(.5) = 16\%$. The net-benefit-to-leverage factor is $T^* = .25$. Maxicomputer's marginal ordinary income tax rate is 40%. Calculate the unleveraged cost of equity capital for the project.

A10. Suppose a firm currently has an unleveraged required rate of return of 10% and perpetual unleveraged after-tax income of $140,301 per year. The firm has come up with an investment opportunity that would alter the firm's asset makeup so that it would increase its perpetual unleveraged after-tax income to $170,650 per year. Since the new asset mix is riskier, the firm's unleveraged required rate of return would also increase to 12.165%. Should the firm undertake this investment opportunity?

A11. The Alaisa Corporation has a perpetual expected annual income of $158,608.70 per year, pays corporate taxes at the rate of 31%, is currently unleveraged, and has a required rate of return of 12%. If Alaisa borrows $400,000 worth of perpetual debt and the corporation's net-benefit-to-leverage factor, T^*, is .22, what will the Alaisa Corporation be worth? What will θ and $r^*(\theta)$ be for Alaisa after the $400,000 is borrowed?

A12. What does it mean to say that a firm follows a capital structure policy of periodically **rebalancing its debt level**?

A13. Reconsider the Chalko example. Chalko has identified a second company that is closely comparable to Boardon. United Industries has a debt ratio of $\theta = .60$, a cost of debt of $r_d(.6) = 12\%$, a leveraged cost of equity capital of $r_e(.6) = 20\%$, a 40% marginal tax rate, and a net-benefit-to-leverage factor of $T^* = .20$.

a. Calculate United's unleveraged cost of equity capital.

b. Calculate the unleveraged cost of equity capital for the investment project Chalko is considering.

c. What is the required rate of return that Chalko should use to compute the NPV of the investment project?

PROBLEM SET B

B1. Jip-Sum Corporation management has pointed out to its shareholders that leverage will raise their expected rate of return. Specifically, Jip-Sum is unleveraged, and shareholders have an expected rate of return equal to their required rate of return of 20%. Jip-Sum can borrow 40% of the value of the firm at an interest rate of 14%. In a perfect capital market with no taxes, what will the shareholders' expected rate of return be if Jip-Sum alters its capital structure by borrowing the 40% of the value of the firm? What will the required rate of return to the shareholders become with this capital structure change? How will the total value of the firm change under these conditions?

B2. Don Ho Ho, Inc., purveyors of Christmas clothing, are $\theta = 55\%$ debt-financed and the required rate of return on that debt $r_d(.55)$ is 16.2%. If Don Ho Ho's corporate tax rate is 37% and the required rate of return on equity, $r_e(.55)$ is 25%, what is Don Ho Ho's required rate of return for the firm, $r^*(.55)$? If Don Ho Ho is operating in a perfect capital market with no asymmetric taxes (i.e., personal taxes eliminate the asymmetry of the corporate tax), what is Don Ho Ho's unleveraged required rate of return to equity, $r_e(0)$?

B3. The Query Company has identified two alternative capital structures. If the firm borrows 15% of the value of the firm it can borrow the money at $r_d(.15) = 10\%$, and the shareholders will have a required rate of return equal to 18%. If the firm borrows 45% of the value of the firm, it can borrow the money at $r_d(.45) = 12\%$, and the shareholders will have a required rate of return equal to 23.21%. If Query pays corporate taxes at the rate of 35%, which capital structure should Query adopt? If Query is operating in an essentially perfect capital market except for taxes, are the taxes approximately symmetric, or are the taxes asymmetric?

B4. Explain in your own words why the P/E ratio method of estimating $r_e(\theta)$ should be used only as a last resort. (*Hint*: You might look back at our warning about stock value and P/E ratios in Chapter 6.)

B5. Rusty-Sell, Inc., a midstate Pennsylvania recycling facility, is $\theta = 27\%$ debt-financed, pays corporate taxes at the rate of 35%, and the firm's (leveraged) beta is 1.45. If $T^* = .21$, $r_d(.27) = 12\%$, $r_f = 8\%$, and $r_m = 15\%$, assuming annual capital structure rebalancing,

a. What is Rusty-Sell's required rate of return to (leveraged) equity, $r_e(.27)$?

b. What is Rusty-Sell's after-tax weighted average cost of capital, $r^*(.27)$?

c. What is Rusty-Sell's unleveraged required rate of return to equity, $r = r_e(0)$?

d. What unleveraged beta is implied by r?

B6. The RTE Corporation expects to pay a dividend next year of $2.22 and expects a growth in its cash dividends of 5% per year forever. RTE has debt financing of $\theta = 35\%$ with $r_d(.35) = 9\%$, and RTE pays corporate taxes at the rate of 30%. If $r_f = 6\%$, $r_m = 12\%$, and RTE's common stock is currently selling for $20 per share:

a. What is the current (leveraged) required rate of return on RTE's common stock?

b. What is RTE's after-tax weighted average cost of capital, $r^*(.35)$?

c. What is RTE's unleveraged required rate of return to equity, $r = r_e(0)$?

d. What unleveraged beta is implied by r?

e. What would you say about the estimates in parts a–d if you learned that the market model estimated a (leveraged) beta of 2.2 for RTE's common stock?

B7. Both the common stock and long-term bonds of Crib-Tick, Inc., makers of baby furniture, are traded publicly on the NYSE. Currently, the market value of Crib-Tick common stock is $14 per share and there are 4 million shares outstanding. Crib-Tick's latest earnings were $2.09 per share, and next year's dividend is expected to be $1.02 per share. Five years ago, Crib-Tick paid a dividend of $.72 per share. Crib-Tick has long-term bonds with a total market value of $30 million, and their bonds, maturing in 2002 with an 8% coupon, are currently selling for $880. (Assume the bonds have 22 more coupon payments until maturity.) In addition to long-term bonds, Crib-Tick has $5 million in notes payable and $10 million in other current liabilities. Current market conditions are $r_f = 6\%$, $r_m = 13.75\%$, Crib-Tick has a beta of 1.1, pays corporate taxes at a rate of 30%, and has an estimated $T^* = .18$. What would you estimate is Crib-Tick's required rate of return to unleveraged equity, $r_e(0)$? What unleveraged beta does this imply?

B8. Lucy's Cross-Stitch, Inc., is a small retail craft shop in Bridgetown. Lucy is contemplating an expansion of the shop and needs help in determining the required rate of return for the expansion. Recently, she was offered $65,000 for all of the equity in the business (she is the sole owner). There is $35,000 in debt on her balance sheet, which is borrowed from the local bank at a variable interest rate, that is currently at an annual effective rate of 13%. The shop averages $21,500 per year before taxes and pays corporate taxes at the rate of 24%. What required rate of return would you recommend she use to evaluate her potential expansion project?

B9. Managers of the Stan Lee Martin Corporation are considering a capital investment project that is unrelated to their current investments. The proposed project will be 40% debt-financed at $r_d(.4) = 11.25\%$. They have identified three firms that they believe are basically comparable to the capital investment project under consideration, and they have collected the following information about those comparable firms:

Firm	Stock beta	Stock price	# shares	Bond price	Coupon	# bonds
A	1.10	$25	1 million	$1100	12%	10,700
B	1.20	$30	2 million	$900	10%	67,000
C	1.15	$22	5 million	$850	8%	32,350

Assume the following hold for all firms: (1) $r_m = 15\%$, (2) $r_f = 7\%$, (3) $\tau = .35$, (4) $T^* = .2$, (4) the total debt is the number of bonds indicated, each with a par value of $1,000 and 10 years to maturity. What required rate of return would you recommend the managers of Stan Lee Martin Corporation use to evaluate the proposed investment project?

B10. Why is the stream of net benefits to leverage riskier when a firm follows a policy of periodically rebalancing its capital structure than it is if the firm never rebalances?

B11. Cans-R-Us, Inc (CRU) is a recycling company located in the suburbs of Missouri City, Kansas. CRU is currently evaluating a potential new investment. The investment will be financed with $700,000 of debt and $1,200,000 of equity financing. The (unleveraged) after-tax cash flows, the CFATs, expected to result from the investment are $1 million per year for 3 years, after which time the project is expected to be sold off for a net after-tax $1 million in cash. The debt financing will be 3-year debt with interest payments of 15% per year on the remaining balance. Principal payments will be $100,000 in year 1, $200,000 in year 2, and a final principal payment of $400,000 at the end of year 3. If the net-benefit-to-leverage factor, T^*, is .25 for this investment and the (unleveraged) required rate of return for the project is 25% (i.e., $r_e(0) = r = 25\%$), and the corporate tax rate is 30%:

a. What is the net adjusted present value for this project?

b. Based on the net APV computed in part a, what is θ for this project?

c. Also based on the net APV computed in part a, what is the weighted average required rate of return, $r^*(\theta)$, for this project? (*Hint*: you will need to use trial and error to solve for $r^*(\theta)$.)

d. Based on $r^*(\theta)$ computed in part c, what is the required rate of return for leveraged equity, $r_e(\theta)$, for this project?

PROBLEM SET C

C1. Based on the information given in problem A4, what would be the firm's weighted average required rate of return, $r^*(.3)$, assuming there are corporate taxes at a rate of 35%, personal taxes at the rate of 32% on income from debt securities, and personal taxes at the rate of 14% on income from equity securities, in an otherwise perfect capital market?

C2. We have emphasized that valuation effects on firm value due to capital structure considerations are much less pronounced than are the valuation effects due to the business risk of the investment. In Chapters 17 and 18, we showed how dividend policy can also affect the value of the firm. The valuation effect of dividend policy could, like the effects of risk and capital structure, be incorporated into the required rate of return. What is the relative size of the effect that dividend policy is likely to have on the required rate of return, as compared with business risk and capital structure?

C3. Stowe-Away Travel, Inc. has decided to float a 30-year $20 million debt issue. The issue will be handled (but not underwritten) by an investment firm. The advisor from the investment firm has recommended a coupon rate of 9.25%. The investment firm believes strongly that the issue would sell at par within 2 to 3 days if the coupon is 9.25%. The financial officer wants to consider a coupon rate of 9.0%. The investment firm has recommended against the 9% and in favor of the 9.25% because its marketing department anticipates difficulty selling the issue with a 9% coupon rate so that some of the issue would have to be sold at discount. Specifically, with a 9% coupon rate, they estimate that only 40% of the issue could be sold at par within the first 2 to 3 days, whereas 20% would be sold at $990 in the second week after issue, 20% would be sold at $975 in the third week, and the last 20% could be sold for only $950 in the fourth week after issue. Based on the following assumptions, what coupon rate is best for Stowe? (*Hint*: There may be extraneous information given below.)

    a. The investment firm's estimates are correct.

    b. The market return for stocks is 13%.

    c. Stowe has a 40% marginal tax rate.

    d. Stowe has a beta of .9.

    e. Stowe uses straight–line depreciation.

    f. The riskless rate is 7%.

    g. Stowe's debt ratio after the issue will be 45%.

    h. Stowe can issue or invest in commercial paper at 8%.

C4. Ida Rather's Knot Corporation, a little rope manufacturing firm in the northeast corner of the Yukon, has been contacted by Wile E. Coyote and offered an investment opportunity that will pay her $2,500 per month for 60 months. Ida must invest $10,000 now and borrow $90,000 from Wile E. at 16% APR, with the entire loan paid back at the end of the 60 months (principal and interest total $199,242.62), for a total initial investment of $100,000. Assume that there are no taxes and also assume that this investment is riskless, as Wile E. Coyote has claimed. Under what conditions would you recommend that Ida undertake this investment?

C5. Alpha Manufacturing is considering building a new distribution center that would cost $1 million. Alpha would finance the investment with $250,000 of equity and $750,000 of debt. The (unleveraged) after-tax cash flows, the CFATs, expected to result from the investment are $400,000 per year for 10 years, after which time the distribution center will be sold off for a net after-tax amount of $200,000 cash. The loan will bear interest at a rate of 12% payable annually. It will be repaid in equal annual installments of $75,000, beginning at the end of year 1. The corporate tax rate is 35%, the net-benefit-to-leverage factor is $T^* = .30$, and the unleveraged cost of equity for the project is 17%.

    a. Calculate the net adjusted present value of the project.

    b. Calculate the weighted average cost of capital and the leveraged cost of equity for the project.

    c. Calculate the NPV of the project.

    d. Reconcile your answers to parts a and c.

C6. **a.** How would you interpret financially the ratio $H(\theta)$ given by Equation (19.20)?

    b. Show that the unleveraged cost of equity capital, r, given by Equation (19.21), is a monotonically increasing function of $H(\theta)$.

    c. Show that $WACC(\theta) < r$ whenever $H(\theta) > 0$.

    d. Explain why $WACC(\theta)$ should be less than r and why the difference between the two should increase as $H(\theta)$ increases.

APPENDIX

APV ASSUMING AN ALTERNATIVE GENERAL DEBT PAYMENT PATTERN

While each project might be valued according to its unique pattern of interest payments, as noted in the chapter, it is useful to assume a *general* pattern that approximates the pattern for many projects. One general pattern was illustrated in the chapter. Another pattern that can be assumed by the APV method is that the amount of debt at the start of each period equals θ times the *then* remaining present value of the project.[11] Therefore, as the value of the project declines each period, the amount of borrowed funds for that project also declines. Under this assumed pattern, it is as though the firm set up a separate project-specific debt payment schedule for interest and principal payments at the start of each project. This hypothetical debt payment schedule is based on the values of the project for each period that are forecast at the start of the project. Economically, this is equivalent to the firm attempting to impose a constant θ over the life of the project before the project starts.

As already noted in the chapter, the net benefit to leverage is a function of the interest payments. Whatever the debt level is at time t, an interest payment based on that level is required at time $t + 1$. Therefore, at time $t + 1$, the net benefit to leverage equals T^* times the interest payment that will be made at time $t + 1$, or $T^* r_d(\theta) D_t$. The amount of debt during period $t + 1$, D_t, is determined by θ and by the value of the investment that is expected at time t, APV_t. It is the product of the two, or

$$D_t = \theta APV_t \qquad (19.28)$$

So the net benefit to leverage in period $t + 1$ can be expressed as

$$T^* r_d(\theta) D_t = T^* \theta r_d(\theta) APV_t \qquad (19.29)$$

and APV_0 can be expressed as

$$APV_0 = \sum_{t=1}^{n} \frac{CFAT_t}{(1 + r)^t} + \sum_{t=1}^{n} \frac{T^* \theta r_d(\theta) APV_{t-1}}{[1 + r_d(\theta)]^t} \qquad (19.30)$$

where n is the number of periods in the life of the project.

The difficulty that arises with this expression for APV_0 is that it depends upon the value of the project at each period of its life. Therefore, to solve for APV_0, we must first solve for APV_1, APV_2, . . . , APV_n. To do this, we start with APV_{n-1}, the project's value at the end of the next to last period. (Recall that the end of period $n - 1$ is the same as the beginning of period n.) APV_{n-1} is a function of the final after-tax cash flow, $CFAT_n$, and the net benefit to leverage in period n. $CFAT_n$ includes in it the salvage value of the project, which can be thought of as APV_n. APV_{n-1} equals the present value of these two expected final cash flows, as of $t = n - 1$, so

$$APV_{n-1} = \frac{CFAT_n}{(1 + r)} + \frac{T^* \theta r_d(\theta) APV_{n-1}}{[1 + r_d(\theta)]} \qquad (19.31)$$

This expression is not easy to evaluate since APV_{n-1} is a function of itself. So we rearrange this equation and solve for APV_{n-1}:

$$\left\{ 1 - \frac{T^* \theta r_d(\theta)}{[1 + r_d(\theta)]} \right\} APV_{n-1} = \frac{CFAT_n}{(1 + r)}$$

$$APV_{n-1} = \frac{CFAT_n}{[1 + r] \left\{ 1 - \dfrac{T^* \theta r_d(\theta)}{[1 + r_d(\theta)]} \right\}} \qquad (19.32)$$

After determining APV_{n-1}, APV_{n-2} can be computed. APV_{n-2} is the present value as of $t = n - 2$, of the CFATs and net benefits to leverage in periods n and $n - 1$, or

$$APV_{n-2} = \frac{CFAT_n}{(1 + r)^2} + \frac{CFAT_{n-1}}{(1 + r)} + \frac{T^* \theta r_d(\theta) APV_{n-1}}{[1 + r_d(\theta)]^2} + \frac{T^* \theta r_d(\theta) APV_{n-2}}{[1 + r_d(\theta)]} \qquad (19.33)$$

[11] Myers (1974).

Values for APV_1 through APV_{n-1}, denoted APV_{n-m} ($m = 1$ through $n - 1$), can be computed in a similar manner:

$$APV_{n-m} = \sum_{i=0}^{m-1} \left[\frac{CFAT_{n-i}}{(1 + r)^{m-i}} + \frac{T^*\theta r_d(\theta)APV_{n-1-i}}{[1 + r_d(\theta)]^{m-i}} \right] \qquad (19.34)$$

EXAMPLE ■ At this point, let us consider the following example to illustrate APV valuation assuming this alternative general debt payment pattern. The initial cost of the asset, C_0, is $10,000. The asset will generate $7,500 in pretax revenue at the end of each of the next 2 years. The tax rate on the revenue, τ, will be 40%, and the asset will be depreciated to a book value of zero on a straight-line basis, so depreciation will be $5,000 per year. Therefore, with a zero expected salvage value, the expected future unleveraged after-tax cash flows (CFATs) for the project will be $6,500 [$= \$7,500(1 - .4) + \$5,000(.4)$] per year for 2 years. The investment has a required rate of return, r, of 15% if it is financed entirely with equity. Part of the actual financing will come from borrowing half of the value of the investment at a rate of $r_d(\theta) = 10\%$, so $\theta = .5$. Finally, the net benefit to leverage, T^*, is estimated to be .2.

In this example, the project life is two periods, so $n = 2$. From Equation (19.32) we have

$$APV_{n-1} = APV_1 = \frac{CFAT_n}{[1 + r]\left\{1 - \dfrac{T^*\theta r_d(\theta)}{[1 + r_d(\theta)]}\right\}} = \frac{6,500}{[1.15]\left\{1 - \dfrac{(.2)(.5)(.1)}{1.1}\right\}}$$

$$= 5,704.03$$

This means that, at time $t=1$, the present value of the remaining expected future cash flow is $5,704.03. Following the debt policy set out above, the firm will arrange to have borrowed at the start of period 2 (which is the same as the end of period 1, i.e., time $t=1$) a net amount of θ times APV_1 or 50% of $5704.03 = $2852.01. Continuing on, from any one of Equations (19.30), (19.33), or (19.34), we have

$$APV_{n-2} = APV_0 = \frac{CFAT_2}{(1 + r)^2} + \frac{CFAT_1}{(1 + r)} + \frac{T^*\theta r_d(\theta)APV_1}{[1 + r_d(\theta)]^2} + \frac{T^*\theta r_d(\theta)APV_0}{[1 + r_d(\theta)]}$$

and, substituting values and rearranging, APV_0 is computed as

$$APV_0 = \frac{10,614.25}{\left[1 - \dfrac{(.2)(.5)(.1)}{1.1}\right]} = \$10,711.63$$

Since the initial amount borrowed for this project is θ times the project's value, D_0 will be $5,355.81 [$= .5(10,711.63)$]. An amortization schedule for the hypothetical debt for this investment under the APV assumption is contained in Table 19-2. Notice that the total debt payments for each period (interest plus principal repayment) are not equal. This is because the assumed debt schedule is based on maintaining the debt level at the level given in Equation (19.28), θ times the project's remaining value each period, rather than having equal payments each period (as would be the case for a typical car loan). Also, notice once again that the debt level each period depends on project value that period, *not* on the initial cost.

While the debt level does not, the net value of the project does depend upon the initial cost. Since the project costs $10,000 and has an APV_0 of $10,711.63, the *net* APV of the project is $711.63. This number, of course, corresponds to the NPV of

TABLE 19-2 Loan Amortization Schedule

	Year 1	Year 2
a. Principal at start of period	$5,355.81	$2,852.01
b. Interest for the period (10% of starting principal)	535.58	285.20
c. Principal repayment	2,503.80	2,852.01
d. Total debt payment b + c	3,039.38	3,137.21
e. Principal at start of next period a − c	2,852.01	0

the project with capital structure effects taken into account. The NPV will equal the net APV if the exact required rate of return is used to compute the NPV. ■

A SIMPLIFIED PROCEDURE FOR APV COMPUTATIONS ASSUMING THE ALTERNATIVE GENERAL DEBT PAYMENT PATTERN

You can see that the computation procedure illustrated in the example given above is very cumbersome for projects with a large number of periods. However, a shortcut formula for computing APV_0 under this assumption has been developed by Ashton and Atkins (1978). The Ashton and Atkins formula for APV_0 is a weighted average of two easily computed present values: The present value of the CFATs for the investment, computed at two different discount rates. One discount rate is r, the unleveraged required rate of return for the project, and the other rate is an adjusted debt rate. The second rate has a familiar look to it. It looks like the adjusted rate of return for a level perpetuity given in Equation (19.9), except that the basic rate is $r_d(\theta)$, rather than r. The second rate in the Ashton and Atkins formula is

$$(1 - T^*\theta)r_d(\theta) \tag{19.35}$$

The Ashton and Atkins formula is

$$APV_0 = \alpha \sum_{t=1}^{n} \frac{CFAT_t}{(1 + r)^t} + (1 - \alpha) \sum_{t=1}^{n} \frac{CFAT_t}{[1 + (1 - T^*\theta)r_d(\theta)]} \tag{19.36}$$

where the weights are α and $(1 - \alpha)$, and α is defined as

$$\alpha = \frac{r - r_d(\theta)}{r - (1 - T^*\theta)r_d(\theta)} \tag{19.37}$$

EXAMPLE ■ In the example considered above, we have

$$\alpha = \frac{r - r_d(\theta)}{r - (1 - T^*\theta)r_d(\theta)} = \frac{.15 - .10}{.15 - [1 - (.2)(.5)].10} = .83333$$

The present value of $6,500 each year for 2 years at $r = 15\%$ is $10,567.11 whereas, at $(1 - T^*\theta)r_d(\theta) = 9\%$, the present value is $11,434.22. From Equation (19.36) then,

$$APV_0 = .83333(10,567.11) + (1 - .83333)(11,434.22) = \$10,711.63$$

which is, of course, the same value computed previously for APV_0. ■

REFERENCES

Ashton, D., and D. Atkins. "Interactions in Corporate Financing and Investment Decisions—Implications for Capital Budgeting: A Further Comment." *Journal of Finance* 33 (December 1978): 1447–53.

Bar-Yosef, Sasson. "Interactions of Corporate Financing and Investment Decisions—Implications for Capital Budgeting: Comment." *Journal of Finance* 32 (March 1977): 211–17.

Chambers, Donald R., Robert S. Harris, and John J. Pringle. "Treatment of Financing Mix in Analyzing Investment Opportunities." *Financial Management* 11 (Summer 1982): 24–41.

Cordes, Joseph J., and Steven M. Sheffrin. "Estimating the Tax Advantage of Corporate Debt." *Journal of Finance* 38 (March 1983): 95–105.

Ezzell, John R., and James A. Miles. "Capital Project Analysis and the Debt Transaction Plan." *Journal of Financial Research* 6 (Spring 1983): 25–31.

Lewellen, Wilbur G., and Douglas R. Emery. "Corporate Debt Management and the Value of the Firm." *Journal of Financial and Quantitative Analysis* 21 (December 1986): 415–26.

Masulis, Ronald W. "The Impact of Capital Structure Change on Firm Value: Some Estimates." *Journal of Finance* 38 (March 1983): 107–26.

Miles, James A., and John R. Ezzell. "The Weighted Average Cost of Capital, Perfect Capital Markets, and Project Life: A Clarification." *Journal of Financial and Quantitative Analysis* 15 (September 1980): 719–30.

Miles, James A., and John R. Ezzell. "Reformulating Tax Shield Valuation: A Note." *Journal of Finance* 40 (December 1985): 1484–92.

Myers, Stewart C. "Interactions in Corporate Financing and Investment Decisions—Implications for Capital Budgeting." *Journal of Finance* 29 (March 1974): 1–25.

Taggart, Robert A., Jr. "Consistent Valuation and Cost of Capital Expressions with Corporate and Personal Taxes." Presented at the New Jersey Center for Financial Studies Conference on Capital Budgeting, Rutgers University Graduate School of Business, May 14, 1990.

20

LIABILITIES MANAGEMENT

When a firm issues debt securities, it agrees contractually to make a set of debt service payments (interest and principal) over the life of the issue. Some issuers make the mistake of treating their debt issues passively, leaving the securities outstanding and meeting each payment obligation as it comes due. Toward the goal of enhancing shareholder wealth, a firm should seek out opportunities to reduce its cost of funds. Such opportunities may include refunding high-coupon bonds with lower-cost debt, repurchasing debt securities that are trading at a discount to satisfy sinking fund obligations, or forcing the conversion of convertible securities.

Volatile interest rates create profitable bond refunding opportunities. Figure 20-1 illustrates that between 1977 and 1981, interest rates on corporate bonds rose sharply, driving the prices of debt issued before 1977 well below par and offering firms the opportunity to repurchase bonds for sinking fund or other purposes at significant discounts. The drop in interest rates between 1984 and 1986 also created a significant opportunity for firms to call or buy back high-coupon debt and refund it with new debt requiring lower total coupon payments.

A firm must evaluate such opportunities carefully to determine whether it is profitable to undertake a refunding and whether postponing refunding to a later date might yield even greater net benefits. Evaluating these opportunities requires a thorough financial analysis of the benefits and costs.

SOUTHERN BELL'S REFUND-OR-WAIT DECISION [1]

Late in 1985, Southern Bell Telephone Company recognized that it had an opportunity to redeem its 12.875% debentures due 2020 and replace them with another issue of long-term bonds bearing a coupon rate of 10.75%. The issue consisted of $300 million principal amount. The refunding would save $6,375,000 of pretax interest expense each year. But the redemption would require Southern Bell to pay (a strike price of) $1,106.10 per $1,000 bond to call them for redemption. The aggregate redemption premium would cost $31,830,000 before taxes.

Southern Bell had to resolve the following issues before it could decide what course of action to take concerning the 12.875% debentures:

1. Would it be profitable to refund the 12.875% debentures immediately? Would the interest savings, net of any tax effects, more than offset the very substantial call premium, as well as the other expenses Southern Bell would incur in connection with the refunding?

[1] The problem in this section is taken from Finnerty, Kalotay, and Farrell (1988), chapter 3.

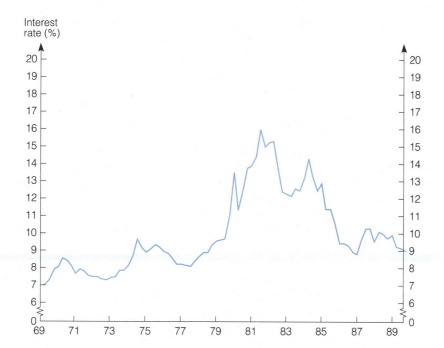

2. Even if refunding the 12.875% debentures immediately would be profitable, could Southern Bell reasonably expect to realize even greater savings by postponing the refunding? In particular, the redemption (strike) price declines over the life of the debt issue. However, an increase in interest rates could more than wipe out the gain from a lower strike price.

3. If Southern Bell decided to refund the 12.875% debentures immediately, it would have to implement that decision. The bond indenture for the 12.875% debentures required Southern Bell to give debtholders at least 30 days' notice prior to a redemption. But if Southern Bell waited 30 days to sell the refunding bonds, a rise in interest rates during that period could reduce, or perhaps even eliminate, the profitability of the refunding.

What should Southern Bell do?

This chapter presents the most widely accepted methods for evaluating bond refunding opportunities. At the end of the chapter we apply these methods to evaluate the profitability of refunding the 12.875% debentures immediately. The timing question is the most complex of the three. For interested readers, we develop an approach to the timing problem and apply it to the Southern Bell debentures in the appendix to this chapter.

DEBT SERVICE PARITY   20.1

When one liability (or other component of a firm's capital structure) is refinanced by another securities issue, often there are simultaneous side effects that occur. The most important (and common) one is a change in the firm's capital structure that may accompany such a refinancing. Side effects, such as an inadvertent change in the firm's capital structure, complicate the process of accurately determining the net benefit to the firm's shareholders of undertaking a refinancing.

One method of neutralizing the side effects of a proposed bond refunding or liability refinancing is called the **debt service parity (DSP) approach**.[2] The basic idea underlying the concept of debt service parity, as applied to a debt refunding, is as follows. When a firm considers refinancing an outstanding debt obligation, a replacement debt obligation is first constructed, *for analytical purposes*, such that the after-tax payments that will be made, if the refinancing is undertaken, will be *identical*, period-by-period, to those which would have been made under the existing debt obligation. If the stream of after-tax debt service payments will support sufficient new debt (with the same period-by-period after-tax debt service requirements) to cover the cost of retiring the outstanding issue *and* cover all transaction costs, then refinancing will provide a net benefit (measured by the surplus that is left over) to the firm's shareholders. The DSP approach neutralizes side effects by holding fixed, *for analytical purposes*, the amount of after-tax cash flow from operations required to service the obligation.

Under the DSP approach, whether or not the new obligation undertaken will *actually* have an identical set of after-tax payments is not important. In order to isolate the refinancing decision and correctly measure the benefits, the net benefit from the refinancing is *measured* on a debt-service-parity basis by holding the period-by-period after-tax debt service payments fixed. Only after the net benefit (or cost) of the refinancing has been accurately measured on this basis should the firm consider other potential simultaneous changes. Such other potential changes might include borrowing a larger or smaller amount with the *actual* replacement liability (than the liability that would allow for debt service parity). The choice of amount to borrow and the specific terms on which to borrow, however, are separate from the decision to undertake the refinancing, and should be evaluated on their own respective merits.

The advantage of using the DSP approach to analyze a refinancing decision is revealed by the Principle of Incremental Benefits: Under DSP, the incremental cash flows that will result directly from choosing to replace the outstanding liability are made explicit and obvious. This chapter is concerned with a special form of refinancing to which the DSP approach is especially well suited, the replacement of outstanding debt with a new issue of debt. DSP can be applied to a variety of decisions in addition to liabilities management, several of which are illustrated in subsequent chapters.

20.2   NET ADVANTAGE OF REFUNDING

Replacing an outstanding bond with a new bond prior to its scheduled maturity is referred to as a **refunding**. The firm can **retire** outstanding debt in any of three ways: (1) It can **call** the bonds, paying bondholders the cash call (strike) price if the bond indenture includes a call provision; (2) it can repurchase the bonds in the open market; or (3) it can exchange new securities for the bonds, provided that bondholders agree to the exchange. When a firm sells new bonds to raise cash to finance a repurchase or redemption, or when it exchanges new bonds for old bonds, the old bonds are said to be **refunded** with new debt. As with other corporate decisions, a refunding should be undertaken only if it will increase shareholder wealth.

When the coupon on the refunded issue is greater (less) than the coupons of cur-

---

[2]Lewellen and Emery (1981).

rently issued bonds of the same risk class and **duration**, the refunding is classified as a **high-coupon** (**low-coupon**) refunding. The former situation is caused by a decline in interest rates, whereby the existing debt sells for more than par value due to its high coupon. A high-coupon refunding is sometimes referred to as refunding premium debt because the debt is selling at a premium above par. A low-coupon refunding occurs when interest rates have risen, causing the existing debt to sell for less than par value due to its low coupon. A low-coupon refunding is sometimes referred to as refunding discounted debt because the debt is selling at a discount below par.

There are three primary reasons why a borrower may find it advantageous to refund one of its issues. It may wish to eliminate restrictive bond covenants (by writing more favorable covenants in the new issue's indenture), lengthen the maturity of the outstanding issue, or, as is more frequently the case, take advantage of a change in interest rates and reduce its cost of borrowing.

While the analysis in this chapter is limited to the third reason, it should be understood that the analytical framework developed here also has direct application to the other two motives. For example, if a refunding is intended to eliminate restrictive bond covenants, and it has been determined that the net advantage (NA) of the refunding is negative, that negative amount is a cost that must be weighed against the benefit of eliminating the old covenants in order to determine whether the refunding is worthwhile.

The decision to refund involves two basic questions. First, will the refunding be profitable; and second, if it is profitable, would it be more advantageous to wait and refund at some time in the future? Financial experts have long disagreed over how to analyze correctly a proposed bond refunding. The early refunding literature reflects disagreement concerning (1) whether the interest savings should be calculated pretax or after-tax; (2) whether the cash flows should be discounted at the pretax cost of the refunding issue, the after-tax cost of the refunding issue, or the firm's cost of capital; and (3) the determination and neutralization of the impact any simultaneous change in capital structure might have on the profitability of refunding.[3] Much of the controversy stemmed from the fact that most early refunding methodologies lacked an analytical framework explicitly derived from or shown to be consistent with the objective of maximizing shareholder wealth. The above controversies are addressed by the DSP approach.[4]

One must be careful not to make the mistake of treating a refunding operation as a capital investment. Making a capital investment involves the purchase of an operating asset whose net cash flows are, in various degrees, uncertain and involve operating risk. Furthermore, a capital investment affects both sides of the firm's balance sheet and is not connected with any specific means of financing. In contrast, a refunding involves the replacement of one debt service stream with another debt service stream that is identical period-by-period on an after-tax basis. The decision affects only the liability side of the firm's balance sheet and is directly connected with a particular means of financing (the refunding issue). Recall that the opportunity cost of capital is the required rate of return under current capital market conditions. Therefore, although we will be more specific below, loosely speaking, the opportunity cost of capital for a refunding is the required rate of return on the refunding issue itself.

[3] This controversy is reviewed in Finnerty, Kalotay, and Farrell (1988).
[4] Lewellen and Emery (1981); Reiner (1980); Finnerty (1986).

ANALYTICAL FRAMEWORK

As with every other corporate decision, the value of a refunding is its net present value to the firm's shareholders. In order to distinguish the net benefit of a bond refunding from the net present value of a capital investment project, we speak of the net advantage (NA) of refunding a bond issue to describe the net present value of the savings from the refunding. If the present value of the cash savings from a refunding exceeds the present value of all of the costs of refunding (i.e., if the NA of a refunding is positive), the operation is profitable.

As previously noted, the principal tenet of the DSP approach is that the decision to refund must be evaluated *as though* the firm's total after-tax debt service obligation will be exactly the same *after* a refunding as before it. By maintaining debt service parity, the evaluation of the refunding decision avoids the complications of other possible simultaneous decisions which would bias the calculation of the net advantage of refunding. For example, if an increase in leverage would increase firm value and the refunding would decrease firm value, the combination could incorrectly make the refunding decision look attractive, although it would be better if the firm increased its leverage using transactions other than refunding the debt. Of course, after the refunding decision (and any others) has been evaluated, the firm may implement multiple decisions simultaneously in order to reduce transaction costs.

The methodology of the DSP approach is straightforward: Determine the amount of new debt that can be issued *today*, if the *after-tax* debt service payments for the new issue (the refunding issue) are exactly the same, period-by-period, as those of the old issue (the refunded issue). One way to view the amount of new debt that could be issued today is to think of the after-tax debt service payments as a set of promised future cash flows that could be "auctioned off" in the capital market. The amount of new debt the firm can issue today is then the amount it would receive in exchange for that set of promised future cash flows. If the proceeds of the new debt issue are more than enough to repurchase the old issue and pay any transaction costs, then the refunding has a positive NA and should be undertaken. Of course, if the new issue proceeds are not sufficient to repurchase the outstanding issue and pay all transaction costs, then the operation would decrease shareholder wealth and should not be undertaken.

EXAMPLE ■   An outstanding debt issue with a $100 million face amount bears interest at the rate of 8% per annum payable annually for 10 years with repayment in full at maturity. The issuer's marginal income tax rate is 40%. What is the after-tax debt service payment stream for the debt issue?

For each year 1 through 9 it will be $4.8 million (= [1−.4][.08]100). For year 10 it will be the same after-tax interest payment plus the principal repayment, for a total of $104.8 million (= 4.8 + 100). Under the DSP approach, the refunding issue would be constructed for analytical purposes so as to have a total after-tax debt service obligation of $4.8 million for each of years 1 through 9 and $104.8 million for year 10. ■

For analytical purposes, it is important to note that the principle of debt service parity extends beyond just cash flows. Parity implies that all rights and obligations of the old issue must also be maintained in the new issue. Therefore, the sinking fund schedule and maturity of the hypothetical new issue used for comparative purposes must be identical to those remaining on the old issue. For example, a debt issue with a remaining life of 6 years will be evaluated against a hypothetical refunding issue with a 6-year life. Note that, were the refunding to be undertaken, the actual new issue may have a life quite different from 6 years. The maturity choice for the actual new issue is a separate decision from the refunding decision. As with other simultaneous decisions, the choice of debt maturity should be made only *after* the firm has accurately determined the benefit or cost of the refunding.

TAX AND ACCOUNTING CONSIDERATIONS

When undertaking a refunding analysis, it is important to reflect the related tax consequences correctly in the analysis. This involves adjusting the cash flows and the discount rate appropriately. As was noted in Chapter 12, the provisions of the tax code are susceptible to change. Therefore, it is important when undertaking a refunding analysis to check the tax consequences carefully and ensure that the *current* tax treatment is reflected accurately in the analysis.

All expenses connected with a refunding are eligible for certain tax deductions to be taken either during the year of the refunding or over the life of the new issue. The basic rule is that expenses connected with retiring the old issue may be deducted in the year of the refunding, and all expenses connected with the new issue (including any discount or premium) must be amortized over its life.

Those expenses that are deductible in the year the refunding occurs include: the call or tender premium—the difference between the call or tender price and par value—in a high-coupon refunding; the unamortized balance of issuance expenses plus original issue discount (or minus original issue premium); legal fees, printing costs, or fees paid to the trustee for canceling the refunded bonds; and when the new bonds are sold before the old bonds are retired, the difference between the interest cost of and the investment return on the surplus funds during the period between the issuance of the refunding bonds and the retirement of the refunded bonds. (If the investment return exceeds the interest cost, of course, the surplus is taxable.)

In a low-coupon refunding, there is no tax-deductible premium because the low-coupon debt is repurchased at a discount. Under the Internal Revenue Code, this discount gives rise to a gain which is considered for tax purposes a "discharge of indebtedness" and is taxed as ordinary income. Usually, this tax liability is so substantial that it makes a potential low-coupon refunding unprofitable. However the code also provides that if the corporation had originally incurred or assumed the refunded debt in connection with property used in its business, the corporation may elect to reduce the taxable basis of its depreciable property, which defers the tax liability.[5] The deferral is beneficial because it reduces the present value of the tax liability.

Refunding high-coupon debt or low-coupon debt thus gives rise to tax consequences that directly affect the profitability of a refunding. In general, the current tax law contains a bias in favor of refunding high-coupon debt because it allows the call (or tender offer) premium to be deducted, but it contains a bias against low-coupon

[5] Section 108 of the code requires a firm that reacquires its own debt at a discount to include the gain—the difference between book value for tax purposes and the reacquisition cost—in its ordinary income in the year it reacquires the debt, unless the firm elects under Section 1017 to reduce the tax basis of any depreciable assets that qualify for such treatment by the amount of the gain. Under the code, the gain should be allocated to assets in the following order of decreasing priority: (a) assets securing the bonds, (b) assets other than those securing the bonds that were purchased with the bond's proceeds, and (c) other depreciable assets.

debt refundings because it taxes the accounting gain generated by refunding discounted debt.[6]

Turning to accounting issues, generally accepted accounting principles require a bond issuer to account for outstanding bonds on the basis of their historical cost. Under this accounting treatment, any changes in a bond's market price subsequent to issuance are ignored. Consequently, changes in market interest rates can give rise to a significant difference between the book value of a bond and its market price. For example, if current market rates are higher than they were at the time of the bond's issuance, the debt obligation will have a market value that is lower than its book value. Accounting Principles Board Statement 26 (APB 26) requires an issuer who reacquires outstanding debt to recognize the difference between the extinguished debt's reacquisition price and its net carrying amount in income as a gain or a loss in the period the debt is reacquired. Consequently, reacquiring high-coupon debt results in a "loss" and reacquiring low-coupon debt results in a "gain"—for financial reporting purposes. It is important to note that the reported accounting gain or loss bears no direct relation to the impact of the refunding on shareholder wealth. It reflects simply the difference between a refunded bond's market value and its historical cost adjusted for any book amortization. In particular, a profitable high-coupon refunding will lead to an accounting loss because of the premium paid whereas an unprofitable low-coupon refunding will lead to an accounting gain because of the discount price paid to reacquire the bonds.

EXAMPLE ■ A firm has two 10-year debt issues outstanding that were issued several years ago. One is selling at a price of $700 per $1,000 face amount due to its below-market interest rate, and the other is selling at a price of $1,200 per $1,000 face amount due to its above-market interest rate. The firm's marginal ordinary income tax rate is 40%. What would be the effect on the firm of reacquiring these debt issues?

If the firm reacquires the low-coupon debt, it will record a *gain* for financial reporting purposes (net of taxes) amounting to $180 per bond (= [1−.4][1,000 − 700]) *regardless of whether the NA of the refunding operation is positive, zero, or negative.* If the firm reacquires the high-coupon debt, it will record a *loss* for financial reporting purposes (net of taxes) amounting to $120 per bond (= [1−.4][1,200 − 1,000]) *regardless of whether the NA of the refunding operation is positive, zero, or negative.*

We show below that in many refunding situations, the accounting gain or loss is the **exact opposite** in algebraic sign to the NA of the refunding operation.   ■

The provisions of APB 26 are somewhat controversial. Critics claim that APB 26 is misleading and can create opportunities for misuse and abuse. This reflects, of course, yet another agency problem wherein financial managers who are eager to report a "gain" may be tempted to engage in a refunding of low-coupon debt that will decrease shareholder wealth, while managers who want to avoid reporting a loss may forgo a profitable opportunity to refund high-coupon debt. One possible remedy would be to amortize the gain or loss over either (1) the life of the new issue or (2) what would have been the remaining life of the refunded issue, thereby reducing the one-time accounting impact. Of course, the Principle of Capital Market Efficiency holds that market participants will assess correctly the valuation implications of refundings by publicly-traded firms in any case. However, as with other corpo-

[6]This difference in tax treatment gives rise to a tax asymmetry, and a valuable tax-timing option for the firm (Emery and Lewellen, 1984). See Chapter 15 for a discussion of the concept of a tax-timing option.

rate decisions, it is important to base the decision to refund on the transaction's impact on shareholder wealth, not on the immediate earnings impact.

AN EXAMPLE OF REFUNDING HIGH-COUPON DEBT

The DSP approach to evaluating the profitability of a proposed high-coupon bond refunding can be illustrated by the following example. Consumer Refinancing Corporation (CRC), which specializes in helping consumers refinance their personal debt, has decided that "charity begins at home." CRC has outstanding a $100 million bond issue that is scheduled to mature in a single lump sum (a so-called **bullet maturity**) 15 years from today. This issue has a 12% coupon rate (6% semiannual) and, at the current time, the bonds are selling in the capital market for $1,035 each and can be called by CRC at a strike price of $1,050 each. The outstanding bonds cost $1 million to issue 5 years ago, and CRC is amortizing this cost on a semiannual straight-line basis ($25,000 [= 1,000,000/40] in expense every 6 months) over the 20-year total life of the bonds.[7] CRC's marginal tax rate is 34%. Figure 20–2 depicts the outstanding debt issue's after-tax debt service stream, and Table 20–1 summarizes the results of applying the DSP approach to evaluate the net advantage to CRC's shareholders of refunding this debt issue.

Current capital market conditions are as follows: (1) CRC can sell 15-year non-callable bullet-maturity debt with an otherwise identical bond indenture as the outstanding bonds at par value if they carry a 10.4% coupon rate (5.2% semiannual); (2) the issuance expenses for the replacement debt that would have to be amortized over the life of the new bonds are $1 million; (3) the issuance expenses for the replacement debt that could be expensed immediately, in addition to the call premium, amount to $350,000; (4) up to $10 million worth of 15-year semiannual installment debt can be borrowed by CRC at an effective semiannual interest rate of 5.15%, with negligible transaction costs.

If CRC does nothing to the outstanding bonds, it is obligated to pay the bondholders a tax-deductible $6 million twice a year for the next 15 years and a non-tax-deductible $100 million principal repayment at the end of 15 years. Also, every 6 months for the next 15 years, CRC can claim, as a tax-deductible expense, part of the original cost of issuing those bonds. Therefore, CRC's scheduled obligation of after-tax payments for the outstanding debt, its CFAT's, is $3,951,500 (= [1−.34]6,000,000 − [.34]25,000) every 6 months plus $100 million 15 years from now. This set of CFAT's is shown in Figure 20–2, and the semiannual after-tax expense is shown on line (c) in Table 20–1.

If CRC issues $100 million worth of new 15-year noncallable bullet-maturity debt, it would claim a tax deduction of $33,333 every 6 months (= 1,000,000/30) based on the issuance expenses, and the total after-tax payments on that debt would be $3,420,667 (= [1−.34]5,200,000 − [.34]33,333) twice a year for 15 years plus a single payment of $100 million 15 years from now. This set of CFAT's is shown in Figure 20–3 as an over-lay on the CFAT's for the outstanding bonds, and the semiannual after-tax expense for this debt issue is shown on line (a) in Table 20–1. The clear area in Figure 20–3 represents the difference between the CFAT's and equals $530,833 per year (= 3,951,500 − 3,420,667), which is the "savings" from issuing

---

[7] Amortization of this issuance cost parallels the treatment of depreciation on new equipment in a capital budgeting project. That is, the cost is incurred at issuance but the tax deduction is spread over the life of the bond issue. Just as in the case of depreciation on a piece of machinery that is sold, when the bonds are repurchased the remaining amount of the cost not yet expensed can be immediately expensed.

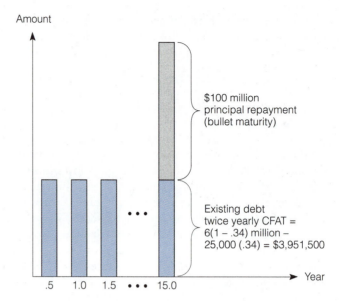

Amount

$100 million principal repayment (bullet maturity)

Existing debt twice yearly CFAT = 6(1 − .34) million − 25,000 (.34) = $3,951,500

Year

.5 1.0 1.5 • • • 15.0

TABLE 20-1 Illustration of the DSP Approach Applied to a High-Coupon Debt Refunding

	After-Tax Debt Service Per Period	Savings/Cost
Refunding Issues:		
(a) Conventional (5.2% semiannual)	$3,420,667	$100,000,000
(b) Installment (5.15% semiannual)	530,833	9,886,584
Total	$3,951,500	$109,886,584
(c) Refunded Issue (6% semiannual)	$3,951,500	100,000,000
Present Value Savings (PVS)		$ 9,886,584
Transaction Costs:		
(d) After-Tax Redemption Premium		$ 3,300,000
(e) Write-Off of Unamortized Discount		(255,000)
(f) New Issue Expenses		1,000,000
(g) Opportunity Cost (the time value of the extinguished option)		1,500,000
Total After-Tax Transaction Costs (TC)		$ 5,545,000
Net Advantage of Refunding (NA)		$ 4,341,584

the new and retiring the old issue. To enforce debt service parity, by maintaining an identical schedule of after-tax payments under the refunding alternative, the set of savings CFAT's will be "auctioned off" in the capital market.

What can the savings CFAT's be sold for in the capital market? Because the savings CFAT's are identical each period, with no final large payment, the debt obtained in exchange for promising the savings CFAT's *must be installment debt* in order to maintain debt service parity. Otherwise, the payment pattern would differ from that

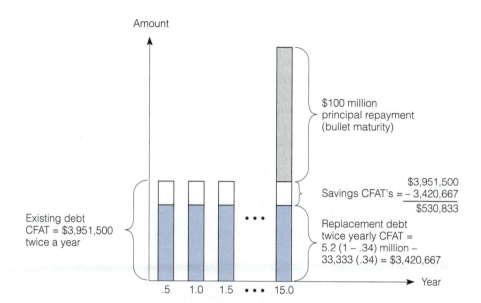

FIGURE 20-3
The schedule of CFAT's for
Consumer Refinancing
Corporation's replacement debt
overlaid on the CFAT's for the
outstanding bonds.

of the outstanding debt obligation. The amount of installment debt for which the savings CFAT's can be exchanged is simply the present value of the savings CFAT's. But what is the required rate of return on these cash flows that correctly determines their present value? Because of simultaneous capital structure effects, the required rate of return for these cash flows is the *after-tax cost of new installment debt*. Recall that current capital market conditions allow CRC to issue new installment debt at a before-tax cost of 5.15%. Therefore, the savings can be sold for $9,886,584, which is the present value of $530,833 twice a year for 15 years at 3.40% (= [1−.34]5.15), and which is shown on line (b) of Table 20–1. Note that the combined after-tax debt service on the two new issues exactly equals the after-tax debt service on the old issue, as the DSP approach requires.

The *net* advantage to refunding then equals the debt proceeds obtained from selling the savings CFAT's *minus* the after-tax cost of the transaction. This can be expressed in equation form as

$$NA = PVS - TC \qquad (20.1)$$

where NA equals the net advantage of refunding; PVS is the present value of the savings; and TC is the total after-tax transaction costs required to undertake the refunding.

TRANSACTION COSTS   There are four transaction costs a firm will incur when it exercises its call option on outstanding debt and replaces the debt with new lower-cost debt.

1. When the call (strike) price is above the par value, that premium above the par value is both a cash cost and a tax-deductible expense at the time the firm exercises its option. In our example, the call price on the outstanding bonds is $50 greater than the par value of each bond. With 100,000 bonds ($100 million = $1,000 times 100,000) outstanding, CRC will incur an after-tax cost of $3,300,000 (= [1−.34][50]100,000), which is shown on line (d) in Table 20–1.

2. CRC can expense immediately any issuance expense that has not yet been claimed on the outstanding bonds. In our example, CRC has already claimed 5 years' worth, or 25%, of the original issuance expense. Therefore, $750,000

(= [.75]1,000,000) can be claimed immediately as a tax-deductible expense, generating a tax credit of $255,000 (= [.34]750,000),[8] which is shown on line (e) in Table 20–1. CRC can also deduct immediately the costs of retiring the outstanding issue, such as the cost of publishing the redemption notice in newspapers and paying the bond trustee's fees for cancelling the old bonds. We are assuming these costs are zero in this example for simplicity's sake.

3. CRC will have a cash outlay of $1 million in issuance expenses for the underwriting commission and various other expenses associated with issuing the new bonds. These expenses will be amortized over the life of the new bonds, so that CRC will have an immediate after-tax expense of $1 million, which is shown on line (f) in Table 20–1. Part of this expense may be what is referred to as overlapping interest. Overlapping interest is caused by the practical necessity of issuing the replacement debt and having the net proceeds available *prior* to calling the outstanding debt. Of course, this cost is a *net* cost since only an incompetent financial manager would leave the $100 million worth of cash from the new issue in a non-interest-bearing investment for the overlapping period. Therefore, the net cost is the difference between the interest cost on the old bonds and the interest earned from temporarily investing the proceeds from the new bonds. The "extra" cost is based on the interest rate on the *old* bonds when the savings are computed from the date the new bonds are issued.[9]

4. Recall from Chapter 8 that it is generally better to sell rather than exercise an American call option. This is true for the firm in this example as well. The outstanding bonds are selling in the capital market for $1,035, but the firm will be paying $1,050 for each bond when it exercises its option. Therefore, by exercising its option (rather than selling the option), CRC will be paying $15 per bond above the bonds' current market value. The difference between the call price of $1,050 and the market price of $1,035 measures the **time value of the (unexpired) call option**.[10] This is a real opportunity cost, but it is not a tax-deductible expense. Therefore, CRC will be incurring a total after-tax cost of $1,500,000 (= [15]100,000), which is shown on line (g) in Table 20–1. This transaction cost accounts for the fact that the outstanding bonds are callable whereas the hypothetical new bonds are noncallable. Of course, the new bonds that CRC decides to issue may well be callable but, once again, that is a separate decision.

The total transaction costs that CRC will incur under our hypothetical refunding then equals $5,545,000 (= 3,300,000 − 255,000 + 1,000,000 + 1,500,000) and the net advantage of refunding is given by Equation (20.1) as $4,341,584 (= 9,886,584 − 5,545,000).

Let's review. Under the hypothetical refunding, (1) CRC issues two types of new debt, $100 million noncallable bullet-maturity bonds issued at par value and $9,886,584 worth of installment debt. (2) $5,545,000 of the installment debt proceeds cover the after-tax transaction costs of the refunding. (3) The future after-tax debt payment schedule to which CRC will be obligated is *identical* to the payment schedule to which it is currently obligated. (4) Therefore, CRC would have a net advantage of $4,341,584 if it undertook the hypothetical refunding. Any actual re-

---

[8] This is similar to the writeoff for tax purposes of a machine that is being discarded at a zero salvage value.

[9] Emery (1978). Equivalently, the "extra" interest is based on the interest on the *new* bonds when the savings are computed from the date the old bonds are retired.

[10] Emery and Lewellen (1990) develop the appropriate decision rule to follow in such a situation, which is to subtract the opportunity cost of $15 per bond in calculating NA.

placement debt resulting from a refunding by CRC, however, may differ from our hypothetical replacement debt if such differences would be in addition to the (positive) net advantage of the refunding. Therefore, in the example just given, it would not be at all unusual for the actual replacement debt to be $120 million worth of callable 25-year maturity bonds—but the additional $20 million, the call provision, and the 25-year (as opposed to 15-year) maturity are *separate* decisions and must be individually justified.

REFUNDING HIGH-COUPON DEBT IN PRACTICE

20.3

Several of the factors noted in the previous section, especially those that have a relatively small impact on the net advantage of refunding, are often ignored in practice. For example, the cost of the overlapping interest is often small enough to ignore in practice as long as the proceeds from the new debt are invested for the overlapping period. Also, the distinction between the installment debt rate and the rate that would make the replacement debt sell for par value is often ignored in practice. Instead, the net advantage of refunding is commonly computed on the basis of issuing additional replacement debt at the new rate. Such an approach, of course, does not strictly maintain debt service parity. However, the primary insight that results from the DSP approach remains: It is the recognition that when capital structure side effects are taken into account, the present value of the savings is determined by discounting at the *after-tax rate on newly issued debt*. As long as a current new issue rate is used, typically, the difference between installment and bullet maturity debt will not be particularly significant.

Note that the after-tax debt service per period for the installment debt in Table 20–1 equals *by design* the difference between (1) the after-tax debt service per period for the refunded issue and (2) the after-tax debt service per period for the conventional refunding issue. The proceeds from the sale of the installment debt issue can be interpreted as the present value of the savings when (1) an issue of high-coupon debt is replaced by an equivalent principal amount of current-coupon conventional debt and (2) the period-by-period after-tax savings are discounted at the after-tax cost of a suitable installment debt issue (or the after-tax cost of the refunding issue when the two costs do not differ significantly).[11] Practitioners usually find this interpretation of the installment debt issue appealing and calculate the NA by discounting the after-tax debt service savings and subtracting the transaction costs.

In practice, then, the net advantage of refunding high-coupon debt can be expressed in equation form as

$$NA = \sum_{n=1}^{N} \frac{(1 - \tau)(r - r')D + \tau([E - U]/N)}{[1 + (1 - \tau)r^*]^n}$$
$$- (1 - \tau)(P - D) - [E + (1 - \tau)F - \tau U] - (P - B) \quad \textbf{(20.2)}$$

where the variables are defined in alphabetical order as

B = the market price of the refunded (i.e., old) debt issue (excluding accrued interest);

---

[11] Lewellen and Emery (1981). They also show that the net advantage of refunding could also be calculated by discounting at the pretax cost *if* the respective numerators were modified to reflect the value to the corporation's shareholders of having the capacity to service an additional amount of debt as a result of the refunding. That is, either the cash flows *or* the discount rate could be adjusted to reflect the capital structure side effects, but one and only one such adjustment is required. Adjusting the discount rate is the simpler procedure.

$D =$ the par value of the old debt;

$E =$ the underwriting commissions and other expenses associated with the refunding (i.e., new) debt issue;

$F =$ the tax-deductible out-of-pocket expenses associated with the refunding operation;

$N =$ the number of periods until the old debt is scheduled to mature;

$P =$ the call (strike) price of the old debt (excluding accrued interest);

$r =$ the coupon rate on the old debt;

$r' =$ the coupon rate on a conventional new debt issue sold at par;

$r* =$ the coupon rate on a new N-period installment debt issue sold at par;

$\tau =$ the issuer's marginal ordinary income tax rate; and

$U =$ the unamortized balance of issuance expenses plus original issue discount (or less original issue premium) on the old debt.

Equation (20.2) states that the net advantage of refunding high-coupon debt equals the present value of the semiannual savings minus (1) the after-tax call premium, $(1 - \tau)(P - D)$, (2) the issuance and other expenses net of the write-off of the unamortized discount, $E + (1 - \tau)F - \tau U$, and (3) the opportunity cost that is incurred if the call option is exercised prior to its expiration (i.e., the time value of the unexpired call option), $P - B$.

Equation (20.2) is equivalent to the DSP approach illustrated in Table 20–1.

EXAMPLE ■   Returning to the Consumer Refinancing Corporation (CRC) example in the previous section, the parameter values are

$D = \$100$ million	$r = .06$	$\tau = .34$
$E = 1$ million	$r' = .052$	$U = \$750,000$
$N = 30$	$r* = .0515$	

The savings per period amount to

$$(1 - \tau)(r - r')D + \tau([E - U]/N) = \frac{(1 - .34)(.06 - .052)100,000,000 + .34(1,000,000 - 750,000)}{30}$$

$$= 528,000 + 2,833 = \$530,833$$

as indicated in Table 20–1. The present value of the stream of savings when discounted at the after-tax cost of the installment debt, 3.4% ($= [1 - .34]5.15$), is

$$\sum_{n=1}^{N} \frac{(1 - \tau)(r - r')D + \tau([E - U]/N)^N}{[1 + (1 - \tau)r*]^n} = \sum_{n=1}^{N} \frac{530,833}{(1.034)^n} = \$9,886,584$$

The values of the other parameters required to evaluate Equation (20.2) are $B = \$103,500,000$; $F = 0$; $P = \$105,000,000$. The net advantage of the CRC refunding is then

$$NA = \$9,886,584 - (1 - .34)(105,000,000 - 100,000,000) - (1,000,000 - [.34]750,000) - (105,000,000 - 103,500,000)$$

$$= \$9,886,584 - 3,300,000 - 745,000 - 1,500,000 = \$4,341,584$$

the same as we determined under the DSP approach.

Suppose the coupon rate on the conventional refunding debt issue is used to discount the after-tax debt service savings. Only the sum in Equation (20.2) changes. The discount rate used in this modified calculation is 3.43% (= [1 − .34]5.2), and the sum becomes $9,849,296 (= present value of 530,833 per period for 30 periods at 3.43% per period), so that NA becomes $4,304,296 (= 9,849,296 − 5,545,000), which is within 1% of the true NA (= [4,341,584 − 4,304,296]/4,341,584 = .0086).

A few additional points should be noted. First, even though the time value of the extinguished option is relevant, if the refunded debt is called at the time the call is theoretically most advantageous, the time value of the option will be zero.[12] Second, as noted in Chapter 6, interest rates are customarily expressed on an annual basis, while interest is paid semiannually on domestic U.S. debt issues. Hence, to be most precise, one should work with semiannual rather than annual cash flows (except in the case of Eurobond issues, which pay interest annually) as we did in the preceding example. In practice, however, little accuracy is lost by assuming annual cash flows.

Finally, notice that Equation (20.2) can be modified to provide a "back-of-the-envelope estimate" of the net advantage of refunding high-coupon debt, simply by ignoring all of the transaction costs ($E = F = U = 0$), using r', and working on an annual basis. In that case the estimate of NA is simply the present value of the change in the after-tax interest payments minus the after-tax redemption premium and the opportunity cost, which is:

$$\text{NA} = \sum_{n=1}^{N} \frac{(1 - \tau)(r - r')D}{[1 + (1 - \tau)r']^n} - (1 - \tau)(P - D) - (P - B) \qquad (20.3)$$

EXAMPLE ■   Continuing our CRC example, Equation (20.3) leads to the following approximation to the true NA:

$$\text{NA} = \sum_{n=1}^{15} \frac{(1 - .34)(.12 - .104)100,000,000}{[1.0686]^n}$$

$$- (1 - .34)(105,000,000 - 100,000,000) - (105,000,000 - 103,500,000)$$

$$= 9,703,586 - 3,300,000 - 1,500,000 = \$4,903,586$$

which overstates the true NA in this case by $562,002.   ■

THE CALL PROVISION

Virtually all corporate bonds are callable for some period prior to their scheduled maturities. Indentures for long-term debt issues typically require the issuer to pay a premium above par value in order to redeem them prior to maturity. The premium is greatest when the bonds first become callable and decreases by equal annual amounts to zero for the last few years just prior to maturity. In a perfect capital market, the inclusion of a call provision would be a zero-sum game. In such an environment, any gain to the party on one side of the transaction would be exactly offset by a loss to the party on the other side of the transaction. However, if you recall our discussions of capital market efficiency, you will remember that we identified three capital market imperfections. Those imperfections have been suggested as reasons for the pervasive inclusion of a call provision in corporate bonds.

Asymmetric information and the possibility of wealth expropriation from debt-

---

[12] Vu (1986). Emery and Lewellen (1990) point out that following this perfect capital market rule will always render the time value of the option zero.

holders by the stockholders provides one reason why firms might be better off including a call provision.[13] When a firm borrows, debtholders may require a higher rate of interest because of the possibility of **asset substitution**. Later on, when a firm has *not* engaged in asset substitution, the debt can increase in value. The firm may be able to recoup this increase in value from the debtholders by exercising its call option.

Also, it can be advantageous for a corporate issuer to include a call option in its debt issues when the corporation is taxed at a higher marginal rate than bondholders.[14] When this is so, the call option is worth more to the issuer than the after-tax cost of the interest rate premium it must pay bondholders to obtain this privilege. This is another case of a non-zero-sum game because of a tax asymmetry.

Finally, the transaction costs associated with calling are less than those connected with capital market repurchases of the bonds. Therefore, if a firm expects to replace a debt issue prior to its maturity for any number of reasons, lower transaction costs provide an incentive for including a call provision in the bond indenture.

TIMING CONSIDERATIONS

Although refunding a debt issue immediately would be profitable, it might be more profitable to postpone the action. If the call price exceeds the market price of the bonds, then calling the bonds immediately involves a transfer of wealth—equal to the difference between the aggregate redemption price for the bonds and their aggregate market value immediately prior to the announcement of the call—from the shareholders to the bondholders. If markets were perfect, this transfer of wealth could be avoided by following a simple decision rule: Call a (nonconvertible) bond issue when, and only when, the market price of the bonds (including accrued interest) reaches the effective call price, that is, the stated call price plus accrued interest. However, since transaction costs are not zero, the timing issue is not so simply resolved.

In practice, companies often call their high-coupon bond issues for redemption before their market value reaches the call price.[15] Issuers thus face a call-or-wait decision. Even if immediate refunding is (apparently) profitable, shareholders might realize an even greater increase in wealth if the firm postpones the refunding. The decision as to whether to refund or to wait thus requires an assessment of the relative likelihood of the levels and changes in levels of future interest rates. The appendix to this chapter describes three approaches to dealing with the timing problem.

SINKING FUND COMPLICATIONS

Long-term corporate bond issues typically provide for a sinking fund that retires a significant portion of the issue at annual intervals prior to the issue's scheduled maturity. The sinking fund provision specifies the amount of debt the issuer must redeem on each sinking fund date. Bond indentures typically specify that the issuer can redeem bonds for sinking fund purposes at their par value (i.e., $1,000 per bond), whereas the issuer must normally pay a premium over the bonds' par value when calling the bonds for optional redemption (except typically in the last few years prior to maturity). A sinking fund provision is valuable to an issuer when interest rates

[13] Bodie and Taggart (1976).
[14] Boyce and Kalotay (1979a) and Brick and Wallingford (1985).
[15] Vu (1986).

decline below the coupon rate because it enables the issuer to call part of the issue at par.

A typical long-term industrial bond issue has the following sinking fund provisions: $100 million principal amount, 30-year maturity, principal to be retired in equal $5 million installments beginning at the end of the eleventh year. Some debt issues specify unequal sinking fund amounts, and others call for semiannual rather than annual payments. In some cases, the final installment, called the **balloon**, is significantly larger than any of the other payments; in fact, sometimes it is larger than all the other payments combined.

For a typical domestic public debt issue, the issuer can meet the sinking fund requirement in either of two principal ways: The issuer can make a cash payment to the trustee equal to the face amount of the debt to be retired, or it can deliver actual securities in the required face amount in lieu of cash. When the issuer delivers cash, the trustee determines, usually randomly, the specific bonds to be retired and notifies the holders of those bonds.

The sinking fund provision often includes an acceleration feature, which permits the issuer to retire at par some specified multiple of the mandatory amount on any sinking fund date. For example, a "double-up" option allows the issuer to call at par up to twice the mandatory amount. The multiplication factor is usually between 1.5 and 3.0. The acceleration feature is structured as a series of European call options that expire sequentially on the sinking fund dates; when one expires unexercised, it cannot be reclaimed in the future.

Certain electric utility bond issues contain a "funnel" sinking fund provision, which requires the issuer to retire annually a specified percentage of the *aggregate* outstanding amount of bonds issued under a particular indenture. For example, the indenture may cover 10 issues totalling $1 billion with the issuer being required to retire 1 percent of the total, i.e., $10 million, each year. When a series of debt issues has a funnel sinking fund provision, it is usually most cost-effective to call the highest-coupon bonds first. In determining which bonds to retire, the issuer must also take into account the optional redemption provision of each issue because of the interdependence of the sinking fund and optional redemption provisions. This interaction makes the analysis of a funnel sinking fund very complicated.

Privately placed debt issues normally do not give the issuer the flexibility to deliver certificates in lieu of cash. This limitation prevents the issuer from designating repurchased bonds toward a specific sinking fund payment obligation. Moreover, bonds must normally be redeemed from all holders on a pro rata basis. Because of these features, private placements allow issuers less sinking fund management flexibility than public issues.

When a bond issue provides for a sinking fund and the call price exceeds the sinking fund price, it may be more profitable for the issuer to call only a portion of an issue for immediate optional redemption and to wait to redeem the balance at the lower sinking fund price, rather than to call the entire issue immediately.

EXAMPLE ■ Suppose that an issuer with a 40% marginal tax rate has $20 million principal amount of debt outstanding that pays interest annually at a 14% rate and that amortizes in two equal installments 1 year and 2 years hence, each of which is paid at par. Further suppose that the optional redemption premium is 2% and that a new 1-year issue and a new 2-year issue would each require a 12% coupon. Refunding the first sinking fund payment would produce 1 year of interest savings. Ignoring issuance expenses in order to focus the example on the central issue and applying

Equation (20.3), the net advantage of refunding an amount representing the first sinking fund payment is:

$$NA = \frac{(1 - .4)(.14 - .12)(10,000,000)}{1 + (1 - .4)(.12)} - (1 - .4)(.02)(10,000,000)$$

$$= -\$8,060$$

Refunding the second sinking fund payment would produce 2 years of interest savings. The net advantage of refunding the second $10 million sinking fund payment is:

$$NA = \left[\frac{(1 - .4)(.14 - .12)}{(1.072)} + \frac{(1 - .4)(.14 - .12)}{(1.072)^2} - (0.60)(0.02) \right][10,000,000]$$

$$= \$96,362$$

The net advantage of refunding the entire issue is just the sum of these two amounts, $88,302. But it is only profitable to refund the second sinking fund amount; the firm's shareholders are better off if the firm calls only the final $10 million of the issue for immediate redemption and waits 1 year to redeem the other $10 million at par through normal operation of the sinking fund. Such a strategy produces a net advantage of $96,362. ■

The above example also illustrates the correct procedure for evaluating the net advantage of refunding a high-coupon debt issue that contains a sinking fund: Separate the issue into a serial debt obligation with each series maturing on one of the sinking fund payment dates. This procedure is appropriate because typically the issuer can call less than the full amount of an outstanding issue. Further, if it is profitable for an issuer to call a bond that it would otherwise have redeemed on any particular sinking fund payment date, it must also be profitable for the issuer to call all the bonds that it would otherwise have redeemed on that date. Thus, as long as it contains this option, a sinking fund issue can be decomposed into a serial issue, and each series can be analyzed separately to determine whether an immediate call is advantageous.

TENDER OFFERS AND OPEN MARKET PURCHASES

Long-term bonds typically contain a "no-call" period, during which the firm cannot call or is restricted in its ability to call the debt. Nevertheless, a corporation can refund such call-protected high-coupon debt by purchasing bonds in the open market or by tendering for them.[16] A portion of the potential net advantage to the issuer arises from a tax arbitrage opportunity. The purchase premium can be deducted for tax purposes in the year of repurchase whereas an investor must amortize it over the life of the issue. Second, the issuer also can deduct the unamortized balance of expenses plus original issue discount in the year of repurchase, which generates a tax shield.

Repurchasing high-coupon debt generally is most profitable when the yield curve is upward-sloping and investors think a call is likely as soon as the period of call protection expires. The prospect of an imminent call serves to hold down a bond's price because investors will value the bond on a **yield-to-call basis**.

[16] Emery and Lewellen (1984).

EXAMPLE ■ Suppose a 12% debt issue has a remaining life of 30 years but becomes callable at a price of $1,100 per bond in 1 year. Further suppose that the firm's new issue rates are 8% for 1-year debt and 10% for 30-year debt because of the upward slope of the yield curve. If investors believe that the firm will never call the issue, its price will be $1,189.29:

$$\$1,189.29 = \sum_{t=1}^{60} \frac{1,000 \, (.12)/2}{(1.05)^t} + \frac{1,000}{(1.05)^{60}}$$

But if they expect the firm to call it in 1 year, its price will be $1,130.18:

$$\$1,130.18 = \sum_{t=1}^{2} \frac{1,000 \, (.12)/2}{(1.04)^t} + \frac{1,100}{(1.04)^2}$$ ■

With three adjustments, the method of analysis illustrated in the CRC example applies also to refundings accomplished through open market purchases or a tender offer. First, the issuer must pay the market price or, in the case of tender offer, some premium over this price, rather than a preset call price. Second, holders are free to accept or reject the issuer's offer. Consequently, both the amount of debt refunded and the effective redemption premium are subject to some degree of uncertainty. These factors can be taken into account by estimating the amount of the issue that can be reacquired at a given price and proceeding with the analysis of refunding this portion of the issue. Third, there are often added transaction costs associated with a repurchase program or a tender offer, such as soliciting dealers' fees when securities firms are engaged to assist with the program.

A critical issue that arises in connection with a tender offer concerns the appropriate premium. It will depend on such factors as investors' interest rate expectations, the composition of the bondholder group, and the yields available on alternative investments. It is often calculated so as to achieve a tender price that provides a yield-to-first-call slightly higher than the yield an investor could realize by investing in United States government agency issues over the same time horizon.[17] Once the tender is announced, the market price of the bonds will increase to the tender price. By tendering at such a price and then reinvesting the proceeds in a government agency issue, a bondholder can realize approximately the same yield that continuing to hold the corporate bonds would provide but with less credit risk. Not surprisingly, this condition normally leads to a very high proportion of bonds being tendered.

It should be noted that the open market purchase method generally is cheaper than a tender offer when the market for the bonds is liquid enough that the repurchase program does not exert much upward pressure on price. Bonds can be repurchased from different holders at a price each is willing to accept. For larger programs, however, companies often prefer the tender offer method because it treats all bondholders equally, that is, each bondholder who tenders receives the same price.

REGULATORY CONSIDERATIONS

Bond refunding does not affect a nonregulated firm's revenue stream. Consequently, it is appropriate to evaluate the profitability of a refunding by a nonregulated firm solely in terms of the present value of incremental debt service. But the amount of revenue a regulated firm is allowed to collect depends upon the firm's permitted cost

---

[17] Finnerty, Kalotay, and Farrell (1988).

of capital. In general, a high-coupon bond refunding reduces a regulated firm's cost of capital. Calling high-coupon debt at a premium and refunding it with current-coupon debt reduces the average interest cost of debt on the utility's books and increases the utility's debt-to-equity ratio due to the after-tax redemption premium. Because the cost of debt is lower than the cost of equity, the higher proportion of debt, which is reduced in cost through the refunding, reduces the utility's cost of capital.

Most public utilities, for example, telephone, electric, and gas companies, are subject to rate base regulation. The revenues these firms are permitted by their regulators to collect from their customers include allowances for operating expenses and for capital costs. But the regulated firm does not recover its capital costs dollar for dollar. Instead, it is allowed to earn a rate of return on its physical assets (called the rate base) based on its average cost of capital. A refunding does not alter a utility's physical assets. Hence the reduction in the allowed cost of capital reduces the utility's revenue stream. At the same time, of course, the utility's interest payments also decline. A commensurate reduction in revenue would be appropriate because the utility's customers pay the utility's capital costs.

Traditional regulatory treatment reduces revenue requirements *by more than* the reduction in interest payments.[18] Some of the benefit of the refunding to the customer comes at the expense of the utility's equity investors. In the absence of corporate income taxes, the penalty imposed on the utility's equity investors equals the product of the premium over book value paid for the debt and the utility's cost of capital following the refunding. In order for the refunding not to occur at the expense of the utility's common stockholders, the premium should be included in the utility's rate base so that the utility can earn its cost of capital on it.[19] When this occurs, the bond refunding is neutral to the utility's common stockholders, and the equations developed at the beginning of the chapter can be used to calculate the net advantage of refunding to the utility's customers.

20.4 REFUNDING DISCOUNTED DEBT

One of the most controversial issues in bond refunding concerns whether a firm can refund an issue of discounted (low-coupon) debt profitably. Such debt bears a below-market coupon rate of interest and consequently sells in the market at a discount from its face amount. As noted earlier in the chapter, reacquiring discounted debt results in a gain for financial reporting purposes, which equals the difference between the book value of the debt and the reacquisition price. But this "gain" bears no direct relation to the net advantage of refunding discounted debt.

WHEN IS IT PROFITABLE TO REFUND DISCOUNTED DEBT?

Refunding discounted debt can be profitable if it increases the proportion of the debt service stream that is tax-deductible.[20] The profitability is due to a tax asymmetry that arises because the bulk of investors in the corporate bond market are either pen-

---

[18] Finnerty, Kalotay, and Farrell (1988).

[19] Alternatively, the cost of capital may be adjusted upwards by subtracting the premium paid for the debt from the book value of the utility's debt. This adjustment decreases the utility's debt-to-equity ratio and hence increases its regulation-specified "cost of capital." See Finnerty, Kalotay, and Farrell (1988), chapter 6.

[20] Finnerty (1986).

sion funds, which are tax-exempt, or life insurance companies, which pay tax at a rate that is lower than the full corporate tax rate. The following example illustrates how the creation of additional tax shields can make the net advantage of refunding discounted debt positive.

EXAMPLE ■ Suppose a bond that was originally issued at par matures in 1 period; interest rates have risen from 8% to 13% since its issuance; and the firm has a 40% marginal tax rate. The outstanding bond's market value is $955.75 (= [1,000 + .08(1,000)]/1.13). Retiring the old bond will free up $1,048 (= 1,000 + [1 − .4] [.08]1,000) of after-tax debt service, which will support the issuance of $972.17 (= $1,048/[1 + (1 − .4).13]) of new debt. The difference between the new issue proceeds and repurchasing the bond at its market value is $16.42 (= 972.17 − 955.75). Suppose that flotation costs for the new issue are $10.00. After subtracting the $6.00 after-tax flotation cost (= [1 − .4]10), there is a positive NA of $10.42 (= 16.42 − 6).

Notice that while only $80 (or 7.4%) of the $1,080 (= 1,000 + [.08]1,000) pretax debt service of the old issue is tax-deductible, $126.38 (= [.13]972.17) (or 11.5%) of the $1,098.55 (= 972.17 + 126.38) pretax debt service of the new issue is tax-deductible. Thus, the new issue has a tax shield benefit of $50.55 (= [.4]126.38) whereas the old issue has a tax shield benefit of only $32.00 (= [.4]80). ■

When the firm sells just enough new debt to retire the outstanding discounted debt, it turns out that the present value of the pretax debt service payments increases as a result of the refunding. That is, the present value of the increase in annual interest expense exceeds the present value of the decrease in principal repayment. The principal source of the increase in shareholder wealth is thus the value contributed by the tax shields created through the refunding. Consequently, refunding discounted debt has a positive NA only if the value of the additional tax shields exceeds the sum of (1) the present value of the increase in pretax debt service requirements, (2) the transaction costs that must be paid, and (3) any tax incurred on the gain. In general, because of transaction costs, it will not be advantageous for a corporation to refund discounted debt if it is not a taxpayer.

The tax treatment accorded the gain (point 3 just noted) is crucial to the economics of refunding discounted debt. In the example just given, we assumed the gain was not taxed. However, because of the usual tax treatment, refunding discounted debt is not normally profitable.[21] In the forgoing example, the gain equals the difference between the issue price ($1,000) and the repurchase price ($955.75) and amounts to $44.25. Taxing the gain at a 40% rate creates a $17.70 (= [.4]44.25) tax liability, which would render the net advantage of refunding negative:

$$NA = 16.42 - 6.00 - 17.70 = -\$7.28$$

The net advantage of refunding discounted (low-coupon) debt can be evaluated in much the same manner as the net advantage of refunding high-coupon (premium) debt. Glance back at Equation (20.2). Note that the sum represents the present value of the annual change in after-tax debt service where the discount rate is the after-tax cost of the refunding issue. The net advantage of refunding equals the present value debt service savings minus transaction costs. Similarly, the net advantage of refunding discounted debt equals the present value of the after-tax change in debt service payments minus transaction costs, where the discount rate is the after-tax cost of the

[21] Finnerty (1986).

refunding issue.[22] Note that in the case of discounted debt, refunding reduces the principal repayment obligation because the debt is repurchased at a discount from its face amount.

The net advantage of refunding discounted debt is given in equation form as

$$NA = \sum_{n=1}^{N} \frac{(1 - \tau)(rD - r'B) + \tau([E - U]/N)}{[1 + (1 - \tau)r']^n} + \frac{D - B}{[1 + (1 - \tau)r']^N}$$
$$- \tau'(D - B) - [E + (1 - \tau)F - \tau U] \quad (20.4)$$

where the parameters B, D, E, F, N, r, r', τ, U are as defined in Equation (20.2) and τ' denotes the present value tax rate on the gain $(D - B)$. Equation (20.4) can be used to evaluate a prospective discounted debt refunding to determine its net advantage. As previously noted, the crucial factor is the tax treatment of the gain, reflected in the term $\tau'(D - B)$.

AN EXAMPLE OF REFUNDING DISCOUNTED DEBT

The application of Equation (20.4) to evaluating the profitability of a proposed low-coupon (discounted) debt refunding can be illustrated by the following example. Consumer Refinancing Corporation (CRC) has outstanding a $50 million bond issue that is scheduled to mature in a single lump sum 10 years from today. The issue has a 6% coupon rate (3% semiannual). The outstanding bonds cost $500,000 to issue 10 years ago, and CRC is amortizing this cost on a semiannual straight-line basis ($12,500 [= 500,000/40] in expense every 6 months) over the 20-year total life of the bonds. CRC's marginal tax rate is 34%.

CRC can sell a new 10-year debt issue at par if the issue bears a 12% coupon rate (6% semiannual). Issuance expenses would amount to $300,000. The outstanding issue is currently trading at a 12% yield to maturity and at a price of $655.90:

$$\$655.90 = \sum_{t=1}^{20} \frac{(.03)(1,000)}{(1.06)^t} + \frac{1,000}{(1.06)^{20}}$$

per bond. Reacquiring the entire issue at this price would cost $32,795,000 (= [655.90]50,000). Table 20–2 summarizes the net advantage calculation assuming no tax on the gain.

The $12,500 before-tax semiannual expense amortization on the old bonds gives rise to a $4,250 (= [.34]12,500) after-tax cash flow per semiannual period. The new bonds have semiannual expense amortization of $15,000 (= 300,000/20) before taxes, and this gives rise to a $5,100 (= [.34]15,000) after-tax cash flow per semiannual period. Refunding thus increases the after-tax cash flow associated with expense amortization by $850 (= 5,100 − 4,250) per semiannual period. The after-tax cost of the new debt is 3.96% (= [1 − .34][12]/2) per period so that the present value of the increase in expense amortization is $11,593 (present value of 850 per period for 20 periods at 3.96% per period).

Issuing sufficient new debt to repurchase the outstanding bonds requires $32,795,000 of new 12% bonds. The reduction in principal amount is $17,205,000 (= 50,000,000 − 32,795,000), the present value of which is $7,912,783 (= 17,205,000/[1.0396]^{20}). The total benefits are then $7,924,376 (= 7,912,783 + 11,593).

Turning to the costs of the refunding, the refunded issue had after-tax interest

---

[22] Finnerty (1986) shows that discounting at the after-tax cost of money for the refunding issue is consistent with the DSP approach.

TABLE 20-2 Illustration of the Calculation of the Net Advantage
of Refunding Low-Coupon Debt

	Refunded Issue	Refunding Issue
Assumptions:		
Principal Amount	$50,000,000	$32,795,000
Coupon Rate	6%	12%
Remaining Life	10 years	10 years
Unamortized Discount	$250,000	$300,000
	Pretax	**After-Tax**
Benefits of Refunding:		
Semiannual Expense Amortization:		
Refunding Issue	$15,000	$5,100
Refunded Issue	12,500	4,250
Savings (Cost)	$2,500	$850
Present Value of Semiannual Savings (Cost)[a]		$11,593
Present Value of Decrease in Principal Repayment Obligation[a]		7,912,783
Total Benefits		$7,924,376
Costs of Refunding:		
Semiannual Interest Expense:		
Refunding Issue	$1,967,700	$1,298,682
Refunded Issue	1,500,000	990,000
Semiannual Increase	$467,700	$308,682
Present Value Increase in Semiannual Interest Expense[a]		$4,209,987
New Issue Expense		300,000
Less Write-Off of Unamortized Balance of Issuance Expenses on Refunded Issue		(85,000)
Total Costs		$4,424,987
Net Advantage:		
Total Benefits		$7,924,376
Total Costs		4,424,987
Net Advantage of Refunding		$3,499,389

[a]Discounted at the after-tax cost of money for the refunding issue (3.96% (= [(1 − .34) 12/2]) per
semiannual period).

expense of $990,000 (= [1 − .34][.03]50,000,000) per period. Issuing $32,795,000 of
new 12% bonds gives rise to after-tax interest expense of $1,298,682 (= [1 −
.34][.06]32,795,000) per period, an increase of $308,682 (= 1,298,682 − 990,000).
The present value of the increased interest expense at a 3.96% discount rate is
$4,209,987 (308,682 per period for 20 periods).

The new debt entails $300,000 of new issue expenses. Writing off the unamortized balance of issue expenses on the old debt produces a tax shield of $85,000 (= [.34]250,000). Total costs of the refunding are $4,424,987 (= 4,209,987 + 300,000 − 85,000). The net advantage of refunding is $3,499,389 (= 7,924,376 − 4,424,987).

Note once again that in this example, the firm is a tax-paying corporation that avoids tax on the refunding's "gain." Although this is not routinely possible, it illustrates the value of active liabilities management since this situation has occurred at times.

SINKING FUND MANAGEMENT

Sinking fund bonds are among the most complicated debt securities to analyze. Effective sinking fund management involves elements of option strategy and game theory. Recall the Principle of Two-Sided Transactions. While the issuer of a sinking fund obligation tries to manage the debt obligation so as to maximize shareholder wealth, so the bondholders try to follow strategies that will maximize their own wealth.

The analysis of a sinking fund issue is considerably more complicated than the analysis of a non-sinking fund issue because of this inherent issuer-bondholder conflict and also because of the interaction between the sinking fund (mandatory redemption) and call (optional redemption) provisions, as illustrated earlier in the chapter. But there are two fundamental aspects of sinking fund management. Consider again the 30-year sinking fund issue with level $5 million sinking fund beginning at the end of year 11. Suppose that 7 years after issuance the firm has decided to retire $5 million principal amount of the bonds. Which future sinking fund obligation should be eliminated by this reacquisition?[23]

First, suppose that interest rates on newly issued debt of the same risk class are significantly higher than the coupon rate and that interest rates are expected to remain unchanged. From the issuer's perspective, it is clearly advantageous to keep the low-coupon debt outstanding as long as possible. In contrast, the bondholders would like to have the bonds redeemed as soon as possible. The issuer can maximize the average life of the portion of the issue that remains outstanding by designating the $5 million block to the first sinking fund payment—the one due in year 11. As a practical matter, the issuer, just like any other market participant, has the right to purchase bonds in the open market, that is, to "buy ahead" of sinking fund requirements. Doing so may be profitable when the bonds are trading at a discount from their face amount.

On the other hand, suppose that current interest rates on comparable debt are much lower than the coupon rate. In this case, it is most advantageous for the issuer to redeem the high-coupon debt as quickly as possible, and again bondholders have the opposite preference. To minimize the average life of the remaining portion of the issue, the issuer can designate the $5 million bonds to the balloon payment at the end of the thirtieth year. In this case, the most distant sinking fund payments are the most profitable to extinguish.

The issuer of publicly-traded debt has a great deal of flexibility in designating bonds to meet specific sinking fund obligations. As a general rule, reacquired low-coupon bonds are designated to the earliest remaining while reacquired high-coupon bonds are designated to the latest remaining sinking fund payment obligation.

---

[23] While the analytical framework assumes that the reacquired debt is refunded with debt of like maturity, in practice, the advance purchase of small blocks of bonds is often funded out of cash on hand. Due to the existence of transaction costs, this method of immediate funding is typically the most cost-effective.

DEFEASANCE

In mid-1982, Exxon Corporation announced that it had defeased, or eliminated from its balance sheet, six Exxon debt issues representing approximately $515 million principal amount of indebtedness. Exxon accomplished this by depositing irrevocably with a trustee a portfolio containing approximately $312 million worth of U.S. Government and federal agency securities the interest and principal payments from which would be sufficient to discharge fully the debt service requirements of the six debt issues. Exxon also reported additional earnings of roughly $130 million after provision for taxes that would have to be paid on income generated by the defeasance portfolio. Firms defease outstanding debt in order to restructure their balance sheets and improve their credit standing (as Exxon indicated it did), to free themselves of restrictive covenants, or to refund discounted debt.

Defeasing an outstanding debt obligation involves the substitution of the issuer's promise to pay for a package of U.S. Government obligations (consisting of U.S. Treasury securities and/or U.S. Government-guaranteed securities) and perhaps also some cash sufficient to discharge the debt obligation in full. There are two types of defeasance. In a **legal defeasance**, the debt issuer's obligations under the indenture are discharged, and the debt is eliminated from the issuer's books for tax as well as financial reporting purposes. Municipalities have used legal defeasance for many years to refund high-coupon debt prior to the date it could first be called for redemption.[24] In an **in-substance**, or **economic**, **defeasance**, the debt is only eliminated for financial reporting purposes; the debt obligation is neither legally discharged nor removed from the issuer's books for tax purposes.[25] Only a legal defeasance can free a firm from restrictive debt covenants. However, because an in-substance defeasance is not a taxable event, that form of defeasance involves no discharge of indebtedness income. This nontaxable "gain" is undoubtedly tempting to firms, but as with any other transaction involving discounted debt, the "gain" for financial reporting purposes bears no direct relation to the net advantage (or lack thereof) of the transaction. Legal defeasance can be accomplished only if the bond indenture permits it; in-substance defeasance is governed purely by accounting rules.

When a firm issues debt to fund the purchase of the defeasance portfolio, the defeasance operation is tantamount to a bond refunding. Most firms that have used in-substance defeasance have defeased discounted debt. Such transactions, when they are financed with new debt, can be analyzed using the techniques described in this chapter with one modification. The firm must pay tax on income generated by the portfolio of securities deposited with the trustee. However, at least partially offsetting this tax obligation, the corporation can continue to deduct the interest payments on the defeased debt provided the deductions do not exceed the amount of interest income from the defeasance portfolio period-by-period. Any period's excess can only be deducted when the defeased issue matures.

When a firm defeases outstanding debt, it purchases a stream of U.S. Government debt service payment obligations, which it uses to service the defeased debt. The purchase price corresponds to the yield at which the U.S. government obligations are trading on the purchase date. U.S. government debt obligations generally trade at a lower yield than corporate debt of the same maturity. Thus, through a

---

[24] Finnerty, Kalotay, and Farrell (1988), chapter 7.

[25] Although in-substance defeasance eliminates debt from the issuer's financial statements, the issuer is required to provide details of the defeasance in a footnote to its financial statements. Consequently, investors are able to determine the amount of debt for which the issuer remains contingently liable following an in-substance defeasance.

defeasance, a firm effectively reacquires its debt at a premium price which corresponds to the lower yield at which U.S. government obligations trade relative to the firm's debt. In addition, the firm is liable for the tax obligations generated by the defeasance portfolio, which creates an added tax drain when the present value of these tax obligations exceeds the present value of the tax shields on the defeased debt. For these reasons, in-substance defeasance is seldom a profitable means of refunding discounted debt.[26]

The most cost-effective strategy for forming the defeasance portfolio involves acquiring those eligible securities that are the highest yielding and that have a cash flow stream which matches as closely as possible the debt service stream of the debt to be defeased. Adapting Equation (20.1), the net advantage of in-substance defeasing a debt issue is

$$NA = NI - D - TC \qquad (20.5)$$

where NI equals the new issue proceeds, i.e., the pretax debt service stream for the defeased debt net of the tax liability associated with the income from the defeasance portfolio discounted at the after-tax cost of the new issue, D equals the cost of the Treasury securities that comprise the defeasance portfolio, and TC is the after-tax transaction costs, including any additional tax liabilities. The pretax debt service stream, rather than the after-tax stream, is discounted because the interest payments of the defeased debt continue to be tax-deductible; the entire pretax debt service stream is thus available to support new debt.

EXAMPLE ■ Table 20–3 illustrates the application of Equation (20.5). For simplification, issuance expenses have been ignored. Defeasing a $10 million 7% coupon non-sinking fund issue with a 2-year remaining life frees up a cash flow stream consisting of $350,000 (= [.07]10,000,000/2) for each of 3 periods and $10,350,000 (= 10,000,000 + 350,000) for the fourth and final period. With new debt at 10%, the present value of this stream, discounted at the after-tax cost of money for the new debt, 3% (= [1 − .4]10/2) per period, is

$$\frac{350,000}{1.03} + \frac{350,000}{(1.03)^2} + \frac{350,000}{(1.03)^3} + \frac{10,350,000}{(1.03)^4} = \$10,185,855$$

With a current Treasury bond yield of 9.75%, the cost of the defeasance portfolio is $9,511,013:

$$\sum_{t=1}^{4} \frac{10,000,000(.07)/2}{(1 + .0975/2)^t} + \frac{10,000,000}{(1 + .0975/2)^4} = \$9,511,013$$

There is $488,987 (= 10,000,000 − 9,511,013) of market discount on the Treasury bonds. Tax on the discount can be deferred until the 2-year maturity of that debt issue. The coupon on the Treasury bonds gives rise to a tax liability of $140,000 (= .4[.07]10,000,000/2) per semiannual period, and the market discount gives rise to a tax liability of $195,595 (= [.4]488,987). The present value of the defeasance portfolio tax liability is then

$$\frac{140,000}{1.03} + \frac{140,000}{(1.03)^2} + \frac{140,000}{(1.03)^3} + \frac{140,000 + 195,595}{(1.03)^4} = \$694,177$$

The net advantage of the defeasance is then −$19,335 (= 10,185,855 − 694,177 − 9,511,013). Because the net advantage is negative, the in-substance defeasance would

[26]Peterson, Peterson, and Ang (1985).

TABLE 20-3 Discounted Cash Flow Analysis of In-Substance Defeasance

	Defeased Issue	Refunding Issue	Treasury Issue
Assumptions:			
Principal Amount	$10,000,000		$10,000,000
Coupon	7%	10%	7%
Yield to Maturity	10	10	9.75
Remaining Life	2 years	2 years	2 years
Issuer's Tax Rate	40%	40%	40%
Purchase Price			$ 9,511,013[a]
Net Advantage of Refunding:			
New Issue Proceeds:			
Present Value of Pretax Debt Service Stream[b]			$10,185,855
Present Value of Defeasance Portfolio Tax Liability			(694,177)
Cost of the Defeasance Portfolio			(9,511,013)
Net Advantage (Disadvantage)			$ (19,335)

[a] The market discount on the Treasury bonds ($488,987) is taxable as ordinary income at maturity.
[b] Represents the pretax debt service stream (7% coupon rate) discounted at the after-tax cost of the refunding issue (3% per semiannual period).

decrease shareholder wealth. Note that the negative net advantage is very sensitive to the spread between the yield on the new issue (10%) and the Treasury bond yield (9.75%). Only if the spread were roughly 5 basis points or less (e.g., Treasury yield of 9.95% or greater) would the net advantage be positive. That is, if the Treasury yield were 9.95%, the cost of the defeasance portfolio would be $9,476,668, and the net advantage of defeasance, after adjusting for the higher tax liability at maturity due to the greater market discount, would be $2,804 (= 10,185,855 − 706,383 − 9,476,668). Despite the tax-free nature of the "gain," in-substance defeasance is seldom profitable, with its profitability generally limited to those situations in which the cost of the defeasance portfolio closely approximates the market value of the debt to be defeased. ∎

REFUNDING PREFERRED STOCK   20.5

The profitability of refunding preferred stock (or preference stock) can be analyzed in much the same manner as the refunding of debt because the two instruments are similar in structure. Preferred stock calls for specified payments at regular intervals, and often has a fixed maturity and amortization schedule just like debt. However, there are some important differences between preferred stock and debt that must be reflected correctly in any preferred stock refunding analysis. Preferred stock dividends and the redemption premium, if any, generally are not tax-deductible. Expenses associated with retiring the old issue and marketing the new issue cannot be deducted for tax purposes. Preferred stock dividends are payable quarterly. Consequently, to be precise, the cash flows associated with a preferred stock refunding should be calculated and then discounted on a quarterly basis. As with semiannual payments, in practice, little accuracy is lost by assuming annual payments.

In any bond refunding analysis it is important to neutralize financial structure side effects and maintain debt service parity. It is equally important to neutralize financial structure side effects in analyzing a proposed preferred stock refunding. Preferred stock involves no default risk, because preferred stockholders cannot have a firm declared in default if the firm misses a dividend payment. But preferred stock provisions typically permit preferred stockholders, voting as a separate class, to elect one or more directors after the issuer fails to make a half dozen or so consecutive dividend payments. A viable business enterprise will almost always treat its preferred stock dividend requirements in the same way it treats debt obligations and pay preferred stock dividends regularly. When a corporation treats its preferred stock obligations like debt obligations, Equations (20.2), (20.3), and (20.4) can be used to evaluate the net advantage of refunding preferred stock so long as the adjustments described in the preceding paragraph are made.

20.6 FORCED CONVERSIONS

The call provision associated with a convertible debt issue (or with a convertible preferred stock issue) gives the issuer a means to force holders to convert the debt (or preferred stock) into common stock whenever the conversion value exceeds the call price. Most convertible bond indentures require the issuer to notify bondholders of the call prior to the redemption date, typically 30 days in advance. Securityholders can convert at any time during this notice period. As we noted in Chapter 14, the market value of a convertible bond will always exceed its conversion value, unless the conversion option is about to expire. The difference between the market value and the conversion value reflects the time value of the conversion option. If the underlying common stock is non-dividend-paying, convertible bondholders will never voluntarily convert, no matter how high the conversion value becomes, because they can always realize a greater value for the bond by selling it in the market. Even when the underlying common stock is paying cash dividends, convertible bondholders will not voluntarily convert if the dividends they would receive after conversion are less than the interest (or preferred stock dividends) they now receive. Consequently, convertible bonds are normally callable subject to a schedule of fixed redemption prices that provide for declining call premiums over the life of the securities.

When the market value of the common stock they would receive exceeds the call price, announcing a call of the convertible issue will motivate holders to convert because that is more profitable to them than tendering the bonds for cash redemption. A firm should follow the forced conversion strategy that maximizes shareholder wealth. In a perfect market environment, a firm should call convertible bonds when their conversion value reaches the **effective call price** (optional redemption price plus accrued interest). If the firm calls convertible bonds when their conversion value is less than the effective call price, the bonds will not be converted, and wealth will be transferred from shareholders to bondholders. If the firm calls convertible bonds when the conversion value exceeds the call price, bondholders will simply convert. The forced conversion strategy that maximizes shareholder wealth is the one that minimizes bondholder value: In a perfect capital market, call the convertible bonds when their conversion value reaches the effective call price.[27]

Empirical evidence indicates that most companies appear to wait "too long"

[27] Brennan and Schwartz (1977); Ingersoll (1977a). This decision rule assumes that the bond's conversion value exceeds its bond value at the time of the call. If interest rates decline following the bond's issuance

(based on the perfect capital market rule just cited) to call their convertible bonds.[28] Of course actual markets are not perfect. In addition, if the market price of the issuer's common stock decreases—and remains—below the conversion price during the 30-day notice period, the redemption value will exceed the conversion value, and bondholders will surrender their bonds for cash rather than convert. In that case, the firm may have to raise enough cash to cover the cash redemption value on short notice, which could involve significant transaction costs. We suspect that this is the reason why companies normally wait to call their convertible bonds until the conversion value exceeds the effective call price by a comfortable margin.

We noted in Chapter 14 that a convertible bond can be modeled alternatively as (1) a straight bond together with a nondetachable call option or (2) the underlying common stock together with a nondetachable put option. According to the second interpretation, if the common stock price does not rise above the conversion price, the convertible bondholders can *put* the stock back to the issuer for the bond's redemption value at maturity. When the bond's conversion value exceeds the bond's redemption value, the put option is out-of-the-money. When a firm forces conversion, it expropriates the remaining time value of a deep-out-of-the-money put option. Therefore, the aforementioned empirical findings may simply reflect management's weighing the value it can expropriate if the forced conversion succeeds against the cost it will incur if the forced conversion attempt fails because of a subsequent fall in the firm's share price.

EXAMPLE ■ Time Incorporated called its Series C $4.50 Cumulative Convertible Preferred Stock for redemption on November 3, 1982, at a redemption price, including accrued dividends, of $54.9375. The issue was convertible into 1.5152 shares of Time Incorporated common stock at a conversion price of $33 per share. The market price of the common stock was $46\frac{3}{8}$, representing a 40.5% premium over the conversion price. But because the firm was paying dividends on its common stock at the rate of $1.00 per share per annum, a holder who converted at that time would suffer a decrease in annual dividend income amounting to $2.98 ($= 4.50 - [1.5152]1.00$) per preferred share. Consequently, few holders had converted voluntarily.

The market value of the common stock provided a **redemption cushion** over the redemption price amounting to:

$$\text{Redemption Cushion} = \frac{\left(\genfrac{}{}{0pt}{}{\text{Conversion}}{\text{ratio}}\right)\left(\genfrac{}{}{0pt}{}{\text{Market price of}}{\text{common stock}}\right) - \text{Redemption price}}{\text{Redemption price}} \tag{20.6}$$

$$= \frac{1.5152(46.375) - 54.9375}{54.9375}$$

$$= 27.9\%$$

This cushion gave holders a strong incentive to convert when Time called the issue. With the assistance of investment bankers, the entire issue was converted. ■

TIMING THE FORCED CONVERSION Investment bankers generally recommend that a firm not call a convertible issue unless the redemption cushion is 20% or

---

and the underlying share price also falls, causing the conversion option to have little value, the convertible bond will behave like a nonconvertible bond, and the decision to redeem the convertible bond will be based on the same criteria as the decision to call a nonconvertible bond.

[28] Ingersoll (1977) studied the call policies of 124 companies that called their bonds between 1968 and 1975 and found that the median premium of the conversion value over the call price was 44%.

greater. The higher the redemption cushion, the lower the risk of cash redemption. To eliminate this possibility altogether, the firm can engage the services of an investment banker (as Time Incorporated did) to underwrite the redemption. In return for a standby fee (generally between 0.5% and 1.5% of the underwriting commitment), the banker agrees to purchase from the firm the number of shares of common stock that would have been issued if bonds (or preferred stock) that were tendered for redemption had instead been converted. Typically, the banker pays a purchase price equal to the effective conversion price and agrees to remit to the firm 80% of the profit the banker realizes by reselling the shares at the higher market price. The banker also normally receives a take-up fee (generally between 2.5% and 5.0% of the effective conversion price) if the standby arrangement results in the banker having to purchase from the firm more than 5% of the issue. Most redemptions of convertible securities are underwritten.

SOLUTION TO SOUTHERN BELL'S REFUND-OR-WAIT DECISION

We can apply Equation (20.2) to the Southern Bell Telephone Company refunding discussed at the beginning of the chapter. On January 6, 1986, Southern Bell Telephone Company redeemed all $300 million principal amount of its 12.875% Debentures due 2020 at a price of 110.61%, or $1,106.10 per bond. In anticipation of the refunding, Southern Bell had issued $300 million principal amount of its 10.75% Debentures due 2025 on December 5, 1985. The new bonds sold at a small discount. With a coupon of approximately 10.86% they would have sold at par value. Underwriting expenses amounted to $8.75 per bond. Table 20–4 provides a net advantage of refunding analysis for this refunding. For illustrative purposes, the net advantage is calculated assuming a 40% marginal tax rate and that the bonds were selling at approximately the call price at the time of the call.

At the time of the refunding, a 35-year Southern Bell issue required roughly the same coupon as a forty-year issue. The refunding issue, however, was callable after 5 years, as is customary for telephone utility debt issues. Thus, the 10.86% coupon rate that would have caused the bonds to sell at par value overstates the interest rate that a noncallable issue would have required. Boyce and Kalotay (1979b) estimate that the call option costs large telephone utility debt issuers an extra 30 basis points. Subtracting this amount from 10.86% implies a 10.56% coupon rate for a noncallable issue.

Refunding the 12.875% issue would produce semiannual interest savings of $3,472,500 (= 300,000,000[.12875 − .1056]/2) before taxes and $2,083,500 (= [1 − .4]3,472,500) after taxes. It would lead to lower amortization expense. Each refunded bond had a current tax basis of $987.97, which would lead to amortization deductions of $0.171857 (= [1,000.00 − 987.97]/70) per bond per semiannual period and a total of $51,557 (= [0.171857]300,000) for the entire issue (300,000 bonds). The refunding issue would have semiannual amortization expense amounting to $37,500 (= 300,000[1,000.00 − 991.25]/70). Total amortization expense would decrease by $14,057 (= 51,557 − 37,500), which would reduce the amortization tax shield by $5,623 (= [.4]14,057).

Subtracting the reduction in amortization tax shields, the semiannual savings amount to $2,077,877 (= 2,083,500 − 5,623). The appropriate discount rate is the after-tax cost of money for the refunding issue. A 35-year issue bearing a 10.56% coupon, with interest payable semiannually, and providing net proceeds of $991.25

TABLE 20-4 Net Advantage of Refunding the Southern Bell 12.875%
Debentures

	Refunded Issue	Refunding Issue
Assumptions:		
Principal Amount	$300,000,000	$300,000,000
Coupon	12.875%	10.56%
Remaining Life	35 years	35 years
Original Net Proceeds per Bond	$986.25	$991.25
Current Tax Basis per Bond	$987.97	$991.25
	Pretax	**After-Tax**
Benefits of Refunding:		
Semiannual Interest:		
Refunded Issue	$19,312,500	$11,587,500
Refunding Issue	15,840,000	9,504,000
Interest Savings	$ 3,472,500	$ 2,083,500
Semiannual Expense Amortization:		
Refunding Issue	$37,500	$15,000
Refunded Issue	51,557	20,623
Amortization Savings (Cost)	$ (14,057)	$ (5,623)
Semiannual Savings		$ 2,077,877
Present Value of Semiannual Savings[a]		$57,848,005
	Pretax	**After-Tax**
Costs of Refunding:		
Redemption Premium	$31,830,000	$19,098,000
Write-Off of Unamortized Discount	(3,609,000)	(1,443,600)
New Issue Expenses	2,625,000	2,625,000
Out-of-Pocket Expenses[b]	900,000	540,000
After-Tax Costs of Refunding		$20,819,400
Net Advantage:		
Present Value of Semiannual Savings		$57,848,005
After-Tax Costs of Refunding		20,819,400
Net Advantage of Refunding		$37,028,605
Break-Even Refunding Rate[c]		11.96%

[a] Discounted at the after-tax cost of money for the refunding issue (3.1944% per semiannual period).
[b] Calculated as $3.00 per bond.
[c] For a noncallable debt issue, which corresponds to a new issue rate of 12.26% for a conventional
callable debt issue.

per bond ($1,000 face amount minus $8.75 underwriting spread) has an after-tax cost of 3.1944% per semiannual period:

$$991.25 = \sum_{n=1}^{70} \frac{(1 - .4)\,1,000\,(.1056)/2 - .4\,(1,000 - 991.25)/70}{(1 + c)^n} + \frac{1,000}{(1 + c)^{70}}$$

$$c = 3.1944\%$$

Discounting the $2,077,877 of semiannual savings to be realized over 70 periods at a rate of 3.1944% per semiannual period indicates present value savings amounting to $57,848,005.

Refunding the 12.875% issue costs approximately $20,819,400 net of taxes. The $1106.10 call price implies a call premium of $106.10 above par per bond. The aggregate call premium is $31,830,000 (= [106.10]300,000) before taxes and $19,098,000 (= [1 − .4]31,830,000) after taxes. Writing off the unamortized discount on the old issue produced an immediate tax credit amounting to $1,443,600 (= .4[1,000 − 987.97]300,000). Assuming the bonds were selling for exactly the call price at the time of the call implies a time value of the firm's option of zero. With after-tax miscellaneous out-of-pocket expenses of $540,000 to cancel the old issue, the total costs of the refunding were: 19,098,000 − 1,443,600 + 2,625,000 + 540,000 = $20,819,400.

Subtracting the total costs from the $57,848,005 present value savings indicates a net advantage of refunding amounting to $37,028,605. Since the net advantage is positive, refunding the 12.875% issue would be profitable. The firm would have realized a positive net advantage so long as the cost of the noncallable refunding issue were below the break-even rate of 11.96%, or 12.26% (= 11.96% + 30%) for an otherwise identical callable issue. The "break-even" calculation is illustrated in the appendix to this chapter.

The second question is more difficult to answer because it concerns timing. We develop procedures for dealing with the timing problem in the appendix to this chapter. The call price is 110.61%, or $1,106.10 per bond. To the extent the 12.875% debentures were trading just prior to the call announcement at a price below the call price, the call may have been somewhat premature, despite the large immediate savings. (The analysis in the appendix provides additional evidence of this possibility.) Nevertheless, one must also take into account the issuer's degree of risk aversion. Southern Bell officials apparently felt that locking in $37 million of refunding savings immediately was preferable to waiting and incurring the risk that interest rates might rise and wipe out some, or perhaps even all, of this gain.

In response to the third question, Southern Bell followed a very prudent course of action by selling the refunding issue prior to announcing the call. Firms frequently act in this manner so as to know beforehand the true cost of the refunding issue.

SUMMARY

A corporation can increase shareholder wealth by managing its outstanding debt obligations effectively. This process involves exploiting profitable opportunities to

1. call and refund high-coupon debt and preferred stock;
2. reacquire and refund discounted debt;
3. exercise the option to increase the amount of sinking fund payments; and
4. prepurchase future sinking fund requirements at a discount.

DECISION SUMMARY BOX

The following guidelines should be followed when evaluating bond refunding opportunities:

- As in the case of other corporate decisions, a bond refunding should be undertaken only if it will increase shareholder wealth, i.e., has a positive NA.
- Refunding decisions should first be analyzed on a debt-service-parity basis to determine whether the decision is advantageous. Other decisions can then be analyzed in combination with the refunding decision in order to establish the most profitable combination of decisions.
- Discount the change in after-tax debt service payments at the after-tax cost of money for the refunding issue and subtract the after-tax costs and expenses associated with the refunding.
- When the indenture for a sinking fund bond issue permits partial calls or permits the issuer to deliver certificates in lieu of cash on sinking fund payment dates (as usually is the case for publicly-traded debt issues), treat a sinking fund issue as if it were a serial debt obligation and evaluate separately the profitability of refunding each sinking fund amount.
- When reacquiring sinking fund debt, designate each reacquired low-coupon bond toward the earliest sinking fund payment obligation of its issue and designate each reacquired high-coupon bond toward the latest sinking fund payment obligation of its issue.
- In the case of a refunding by a regulated firm, ensure that the shareholders are not subsidizing the refunding.
- Under the assumption that the issuer will always treat its preferred stock obligations just like debt, a preferred stock refunding can be analyzed in the same manner as a bond refunding, except that preferred stock dividends and preferred stock issuance and refunding expenses are not tax-deductible.
- A high-coupon debt issue should be called for optional redemption when its market value reaches its redemption value (or call price).
- In a perfect capital market, a convertible debt issue should be called for redemption, in order to force its conversion into common stock, when its conversion value reaches its effective redemption value (the call price, including accrued interest). With costly transactions, including the chance of a "failed conversion," firms typically call only when the conversion value exceeds the effective redemption value by at least 20%.

Preferred stock and debt have similar financial structures, which allows us to apply the frameworks for evaluating bond refunding opportunities to preferred stock refundings.

The profitability of refunding high-coupon debt stems chiefly from the option to call the bonds away from holders at a fixed price and from the tax-deductibility of the call premium. The profitability of refunding discounted debt, on the other hand, results from the opportunity to increase the proportion of debt service payments that are tax-deductible. The sources of profitability are different but the basic analytical approach to evaluating either type of refunding opportunity is the same: discount the change in after-tax debt service payments at the after-tax cost of money for the refunding issue, and subtract the after-tax costs and expenses associated with the refunding.

The presence of a sinking fund adds a degree of complexity to the refunding analysis. More important, it creates profitable opportunities for the issuer. Debt issues generally permit partial calls, and publicly-held debt issues typically give the issuer a delivery option. In a low-interest-rate environment, it may be more profitable for a corporation to call less than an entire issue and redeem the balance through the sinking fund. In a high-interest-rate environment, it may be profitable for the issuer to buy bonds at a discount in anticipation of future sinking fund requirements. Reacquired bonds of a sinking fund issue should be designated toward the earliest sinking fund payment obligation in the case of a low-coupon debt issue and toward the latest sinking fund payment obligation in the case of a high-coupon issue. Active sinking fund management involves elements of both option strategy and game theory, making it one of the more challenging aspects of corporate financial management.

Regulation of the issuer also adds complexity to the refunding decision. Under traditional rate base regulation, shareholders subsidize the refunding. Proper inclusion of the unamortized premium in the firm's rate base or adjusting both the debt ratio and the cost of debt to reflect the unamortized premium will prevent such subsidization from occurring.

As in the case of other corporate decisions, a bond refunding should be undertaken only if it will increase shareholder wealth. It is very important to analyze a proposed debt refunding on an after-tax basis and to neutralize all financial structure side effects. Certain refunding transactions may be advantageous to a firm's shareholders principally because of tax asymmetries. One must understand the tax consequences and true economic benefits, as distinct from the purely accounting benefits, of a proposed refunding in order to determine whether it will increase shareholder wealth.

PROBLEMS

PROBLEM SET A

A1. What is a **high-coupon bond refunding**? What is a **low-coupon bond refunding**?

A2. Explain briefly the **debt service parity** approach to evaluating the net advantage of a proposed bond refunding.

A3. Explain why the manner in which a company must account for the early retirement of a debt issue is not necessarily indicative of the profitability of bond refunding. How can the accounting treatment give rise to an agency cost?

A4. Explain why a company should not necessarily refund an outstanding debt issue the instant the net advantage of refunding first becomes positive.

A5. Calculate CRC's net advantage of refunding the 12% debt issue under the assumption that the installment debt requires a 5.2% semiannual coupon rate.

A6. What is the opportunity cost of calling bonds for refunding when the market price of the bonds (immediately prior to the call announcement) equals the call price.

A7. Explain the reasons for including a call option in a corporate bond issue.

A8. Explain why an instantaneously callable high-coupon bond would never trade in a perfect capital market environment at a price (including accrued interest) in excess of the effective call price.

A9. Which future sinking fund obligations are most profitable to retire first in the
   a. high-coupon case?
   b. low-coupon case?

A10. Explain why it may not be most advantageous for a company to call and refund an entire sinking fund debt issue immediately.

A11. Explain the difference between the factors that make it profitable to refund high-coupon debt and the factors that might, under the right circumstances, make it profitable to refund low-coupon debt.

A12. A company has outstanding a 3-year sinking fund issue that amortizes in three equal annual installments of $20 million each, payable at par. The bonds pay interest annually at the rate of 10%. They are callable at 103% of par. The company's new issue rate is 8% for debt maturing in up to 3 years, and its tax rate is 34%. Ignore issuance expenses.

    a. Calculate the net advantage of refunding each sinking fund amount immediately.

    b. How much of the 10% issue should the company call for immediate redemption?

A13. How should the optional redemption premium be treated by regulators in order to make refunding high-coupon debt neutral to a utility company's common stockholders?

A14. Explain the difference between **in-substance defeasance** and **legal defeasance**. Which type of defeasance can free a firm of restrictive debt covenants?

PROBLEM SET B

B1. A company has outstanding a $50 million debt issue that bears a 15% coupon (7.5% semiannual) and that matures in a lump sum at the end of 10 years. The unamortized balance of issuance expenses is $800,000, which the company is amortizing on a straight-line basis. The call price is $1,100 per bond, and the bonds are selling in the capital market for $1,080 each. A noncallable 10-year bullet-maturity debt issue would require a 12.5% coupon (6.25% semiannual) and $1,000,000 of underwriting and other expenses, and 10-year installment debt would require a 12% coupon (6% semiannual). The company's marginal income tax rate is 40%.

    a. Calculate the period-by-period after-tax debt service on the 15% debt issue.

    b. Calculate the semiannual after-tax savings that would result if the company issued $50 million of 12.5% debt.

    c. How much installment debt can the company issue?

    d. Calculate the net advantage of refunding the 15% debt issue.

B2. Calculate the $83,037,494 present value savings Southern Bell would have realized if it had waited 1 year to refund the 12.875% debentures *and* the refunding rate had fallen to 9%.

    a. Calculate the semiannual savings.

    b. Calculate the after-tax cost of money for the refunding issue.

    c. Calculate the present value of semiannual savings.

    d. Calculate the after-tax costs of refunding.

    e. Calculate the net advantage of refunding as of the delayed refunding date.

    f. Calculate the present value of the net advantage of refunding.

B3. Northern Gas Company has outstanding $100 million principal amount of 12% debentures (6% payable semiannually) that mature in a lump sum at the end of 20 years. The unamortized balance of issuance expenses is $500,000. A par-value $100 million noncallable refunding issue would require a 10% coupon (5% semiannual) and $750,000 of issuance expenses. The 12% issue is callable at a price of $1,020 per bond (pretax), and miscellaneous debt retirement costs amount to $3.00 per bond. Northern Gas's marginal income tax rate is 40%.

a. Calculate the net advantage of refunding assuming the bonds had a market value of $1,020 each.

b. How would your answer to part a change if the 12% debentures were selling at a market price of $1,017 per bond.

B4. Tara Corporation has $70 million of 12% bonds outstanding that are selling for $1,060. The bonds can be called at a price of $1,100 per bond and the bonds have a remaining life of 10 years. Tara is considering refunding the issue with a new $70 million issue of 25-year, 11% coupon bonds. Flotation costs for the new issue would be $500,000 and those of the old issue were $350,000. Tara's tax rate is 40% and no overlapping interest payments are expected. What is the net advantage to refunding the outstanding bonds for Tara? Assume that the term structure of interest rates is currently flat.

B5. The Kaplan Corporation sold $50 million of 25-year, 15% coupon bonds during a period of very high interest rates 10 years ago. Because of changing financial market conditions, the bonds are now selling for $1,055. Kaplan can now refund that bond issue with 15-year, 11% coupon bonds, which would sell at par value. The flotation costs for a new bond issue will be $400,000 compared to the $300,000 of unamortized costs for the old bonds. The firm expects a one-month overlap between the sale of the new bonds and the redemption of the existing bonds. There is a 5% call premium, the firm's tax rate is 40%, and Kaplan can earn 8% APR on short-term marketable securities. What is the NA to Kaplan from refunding the outstanding bonds?

B6. Show the equivalence of Equations (20.2) and (20.4) when $P = B$, $\tau' = \tau$, and $r^* = r'$.

B7. The Solamax Corporation issued $20 million worth of 40-year, 10% coupon bonds 14 years ago. Solamax can call the bonds today for $1,020 per bond, even though the bonds are selling for $1,030 a piece. The management of Solamax is considering issuing $50 million of new 26-year 9.2% coupon bonds, with the proceeds being used for an expansion of facilities and to refund their outstanding bonds. Flotation costs for the new bond issue are expected to be $480,000. The old bonds have $185,000 in flotation costs yet to be amortized. An overlap period of 1.5 months is anticipated if the new bonds are issued, Solamax has a tax rate of 35%, and short-term marketable securities are currently yielding 10%. What is the net advantage of refunding to Solamax? (*Hint:* If Solamax can call bonds for redemption at a price less than their current market value, shareholder wealth is enhanced at the expense of bondholder wealth.)

B8. Southern Manufacturing Corporation has $10 million of 14% sinking fund debentures outstanding. The issue amortizes in equal annual amounts at the end of each of the next 5 years. Southern can call the bonds for immediate redemption at a price of 102%. Southern's new issue rate is 12% for 1- and 2-year debt and 13% for 3-, 4-, and 5-year debt. Southern's marginal income tax rate is 34%. Ignoring transaction costs, how much of the issue could Southern economically call for immediate redemption? Which sinking fund payments?

B9. Astro Trucking Corporation has $25 million principal amount of 8% debt (4% semiannual), which matures in a lump sum at the end of 5 years and which Astro would like to defease. The debt is trading at a 10% yield to maturity (5% semiannual). Astro can purchase $25 million principal amount of 8% 5-year Treasury debt (4% semiannual) yielding 9.70% (4.85% semiannual). Astro's marginal income tax rate is 40%.

a. Calculate the net advantage of in-substance defeasance.

b. Should Astro defease the 8% issue? Explain.

B10. Martin Aerospace Inc. has $50 million of 20-year non-sinking fund preferred stock outstanding that pays dividends quarterly at the rate of 16% per annum. A new issue of 20-year non-sinking fund preferred stock would require a quarterly dividend rate of 12% per annum and $1 million of issuance expenses. The 16% issue is callable at an aggregate cost of $455 million.

a. Calculate the net advantage of refunding.

b. How would your answer to part a change if both preferred stock issues were perpetual?

PROBLEM SET C

C1. On March 21, 1986, Mountain States Telephone & Telegraph Company tendered at a price of 114.5% for its $250 million principal amount of 11⅝% debentures due June 8, 2023. At the time of the tender, Mountain States could have issued new 37-year noncallable debt bearing a 9% coupon and requiring $15.00 per bond of issuance expenses. Bondholders tendered $190 million principal amount of the issue. Tax-deductible refunding transaction costs amount to $3.00 per bond. Assume a 34% marginal income tax rate. Interest is payable semiannually and just prior to the tender the bonds were selling for $1120 each.

a. As of June 8, 1986, Mountain States would have had a tax basis in the 11⅝% debentures of $965.31 per bond. (The difference between this amount and $1,000 represents the unamortized balance of discount and expenses.) Calculate the net advantage of refunding via tender.

b. The 11⅝% debentures were initially callable on June 8, 1988, at a price of 107.50% per debenture. By that date, Mountain States' tax basis in the 11⅝% debentures would have decreased to $967.19 per bond. Calculate the net advantage of waiting until June 8, 1988 to call the bonds assuming (1) the same new issue rate and issuance expenses as on June 8, 1986, and (2) a flat yield curve on June 8, 1986.

c. What procedure could Mountain States have followed in order to determine whether it could expect waiting and calling to be more advantageous than tendering immediately?

C2. A corporation is considering refunding $50 million principal amount of its 10% debentures (5% semiannual) that mature in a lump sum in 10 years. The 10% issue has a market price of $777.05 per bond. The unamortized balance of issuance and other expenses is $400,000. The corporation's marginal income tax rate is 34%. Debt retirement expenses amount to $150,000. A new issue of 10-year bullet-maturity debt would require a 15% coupon rate (7.5% semiannual) and $380,000 of issuance expenses. Calculate the net advantage of refunding the 10% issue assuming:

a. the gain is nontaxable.

b. the gain is taxable immediately at a 34% rate.

c. the gain is taxable at a 34% rate at the time the 10% issue would have matured.

d. Under what conditions is the refunding profitable?

C3. Suppose the 1-year after-tax discount rate is 7% (3.5% semiannual) and that the gain on the refunding in problem C2 is nontaxable. Calculate the break-even refunding rate 1 year hence.

C4. Gotham Airlines is considering whether to refund its outstanding $100 million principal amount of 6% subordinated debentures, which are scheduled to mature in one lump sum at the end of 6 years. Interest is payable semi-annually. The unamortized balance of new issue expenses is $600,000. Debt retirement expenses amount to $100,000 after taxes. A 6-year refunding issue would require a 12% coupon and $1,200,000 of issuance expenses. Gotham's tax rate is 34%.

    a. If the outstanding bonds also yield 12%, what is their market price? Assume the bonds can be repurchased at this price.

    b. Suppose the gain is nontaxable. Calculate the net present value of refunding.

    c. Suppose the gain is taxable at the end of 6 years at a 34% rate. Calculate the net advantage of refunding.

    d. What is the net advantage of refunding if the gain is currently taxable at a 34% rate?

C5. Hoosier Industries has outstanding $40,000,000 principal amount of an 8% debt issue that has a 4-year remaining life and provides for level sinking fund payments of $10,000,000 each at annual intervals. Hoosier's new issue rate is 10% for all maturities up to 4 years, and Hoosier has outstanding debt issues within this maturity range that are all trading at a 10% yield. Hoosier's marginal income tax rate is 34%. Ignoring issuance expenses, how far ahead should Hoosier prepurchase its future sinking fund payment obligations?

C6. **a.** Develop a general expression for the net advantage of refunding perpetual preferred stock.

    b. Develop from the net advantage expression in part a a general expression for the break-even dividend rate for refunding perpetual preferred stock.

C7. Calculate the break-even refunding rate for the Northern Gas Company refunding in problem B3.

C8. Calculate Southern Bell's 5-year break-even refunding rate.

C9. Give an example to illustrate when an issuer would find it advantageous to call a convertible bond in order to force conversion.

APPENDIX

This appendix deals with two complications that arise in practical bond refunding situations. First, we show how to calculate the break-even refunding rate and explain how to determine the optimal time to refund a bond issue. Second, we describe how to take into account properly in a sinking fund prepurchase analysis the possibility that the issuer may be able to prepurchase bonds in the future at a discount from their face amount.

BREAK-EVEN CALCULATION

The break-even refunding rate—the rate at which NA = 0—is calculated in the following manner. We use the Southern Bell 12.875% issue in the illustration. In Table 20–4 we show a break-even refunding rate of 11.96%. Let b denote the break-even refunding rate; NA = 0 when $r' = r^* = b$ in Equation (20.2). The only parameter that changes in Table 20–4 is b, which equals the coupon rate on the refunding issue. Semiannual after-tax interest expense on the refunding issue is $(1 - .4)(300,000,000)$ $b/2 = 90,000,000b$. The after-tax interest savings are $11,587,500 - 90,000,000b$. Subtracting the reduction in amortization tax shields, the semiannual savings are

$$11,587,500 - 90,000,000b - 5,623 = 11,581,877 - 90,000,000b$$

The after-tax cost of the refunding issue is $(1 - .4)b/2 = .3b$ per semiannual period if we ignore the effect of transaction costs. Thus the present value savings equal

$$\sum_{n=1}^{70} \frac{11,581,877 - 90,000,000b}{(1 + .3b)^n}$$

$$= \left[\frac{11,581,877 - 90,000,000b}{.3b} \right] \left[1 - \left(\frac{1}{1 + .3b} \right)^{70} \right]$$

where we have used Equation (3.6) to evaluate the present value of the annuity $(11,581,877 - 90,000,000b$ per period for $n = 70$ periods when the discount rate is $r = .3b$).

The after-tax costs of the refunding, \$20,819,400, do not change. Thus, the break-even refunding rate solves the equation

$$0 = NA = \left[\frac{11,581,877 - 90,000,000b}{.3b} \right] \left[1 - \left(\frac{1}{1 + .3b} \right)^{70} \right] - 20,819,400$$

$$(20.7)$$

Equation (20.7) must be solved by trial and error. When $b = .1056$, we know from Table 20–4 that NA = \$37,028,605. Thus, the break-even refunding rate exceeds 10.56%. We arbitrarily select $b = .11$ and $b = .12$ to test for a solution to Equation (20.7). When $b = .11$, NA = \$24,895,379, and when $b = .12$, NA = −\$927,235. The break-even refunding rate must be between .11 and .12 and lie "close to" .12. By further trial and error, using successively closer approximation, we find that $b = .11965$ produces NA = −\$78,863, which we deem "close enough" to say that the break-even refunding rate is 11.965%.

ANALYZING THE TIMING PROBLEM

We use the Southern Bell 12.875% issue to illustrate three approaches to determining when to call a bond issue for refunding. Suppose Southern Bell postponed the refunding 1 year and that the new issue rate required at that time on a noncallable 34-year issue was only 9%. The redemption premium, specified in the bond indenture, would decrease to 10.26%. Assume the same debt retirement and new issue expenses as in Table 20–4. Substitute the 9% new issue rate for 10.56%, the 10.26% redemption premium 1 year later for 10.61%, and 34 years for 35, and reduce the unamortized balance of issuance expenses on the outstanding issue to reflect an additional year's amortization. The net advantage calculation is similar to the one in Table 20–4. Table 20–5 compares the two calculations. The net advantage of refunding as of 1 year hence would have been \$87,071,123. Assuming the new issue rate for a 1-year Southern Bell issue on January 6, 1986, was approximately 8%, the present value of the net advantage of refunding 1 year hence at a 9% new issue rate would have been \$83,037,494 (= 87,071,123/[1.024]^2), which is more than double the \$37,028,605 net advantage of refunding immediately calculated in Table 20–4. However, if the firm had postponed the refunding 1 year and if interest rates had instead increased, say, 250 basis points (to 13.06%), refunding would no longer be profitable.

One approach to the timing problem involves making the market value adjustment noted in Equation (20.2): subtract the difference between the bonds' aggregate call price and their aggregate market value just prior to the announcement of the call.

For example, Southern Bell called the 12.875% debentures for redemption on

TABLE 20-5 Comparison of Refunding Immediately and One Year Hence

	Immediate Refunding	One-Year Delay
Assumptions:		
Coupon on Refunding Issue	10.56%	9.00%
Remaining Life	35 years	34 years
Current Tax Basis Per Refunded Bond	$987.97	$988.31
Net Proceeds Per Refunding Bond	991.25	991.25
After-Tax Cost of Money for Refunding Issue (Per Semiannual Period)	3.1944%	2.7232%
After-Tax Benefits of Refunding:		
Semiannual Interest:		
Refunded Issue	$11,587,500	$11,587,500
Refunding Issue	9,504,000	8,100,000
Interest Savings	$2,083,500	$3,487,500
Semiannual Expense Amortization:		
Refunding Issue	$15,000	$15,441
Refunded Issue	20,623	20,629
Amortization Savings (Cost)	(5,623)	(5,188)
Semiannual Savings	$2,077,877	$3,482,312
Present Value of Semiannual Savings	$57,848,005	$107,301,323
After-Tax Costs of Refunding:		
Redemption Premium	$19,098,000	$18,468,000
Write-Off of Unamortized Discount	(1,443,600)	(1,402,800)
New Issue Expenses	2,625,000	2,625,000
Out-of-Pocket Expenses	540,000	540,000
After-Tax Costs of Refunding	$20,819,400	$20,230,200
Net Advantage:		
Present Value of Semiannual Savings	$57,848,005	$107,301,323
After-Tax Costs of Refunding	20,819,400	20,230,200
Net Advantage of Refunding as of the Refunding Date	$37,028,605	$87,071,123
One-Year Discount Rate (Per Semiannual Period)	—	4.80%
		(2.40)
Present Value Net Advantage	$37,028,605	$83,037,494

December 5, 1985. The bonds had most recently traded at a price of around 110%, or $1,100 per bond. The market value adjustment is $1,830,000 (= [6.10]300,000), which reduces the net advantage of the refunding to $35,198,605 (= $37,028,605 − 1,830,000).

A second approach to dealing with the timing problem is break-even analysis: If the issuer can realize a net advantage amounting to X by refunding immediately, what future new issue rates will produce the same net advantage? The use of break-even analysis can be illustrated by continuing the Southern Bell example.

Suppose, for example, Southern Bell believed that interest rates were likely to decrease over the next 5 years. How much would interest rates have to decrease in order for refunding in 5 years to be more profitable than refunding immediately? If Southern Bell's 5-year new issue rate for noncallable debt on January 6, 1986, was 10%, and the 5-year after-tax discount rate is 3% (= 10[1−.4]/2) per semiannual period, the question becomes: What new issue rate is required in 5 years to provide a net advantage at that time of $49,763,349 (= $37,028,605[1.03]^{10})? The call price 5 years hence is 108.84%.

As in the first section of the appendix, let b denote the break-even refunding rate, in this case 5 years hence. Table 20–5 furnishes a format for the break-even analysis. The coupon on the refunding issue is b; the remaining life is 30 years; the current tax basis of the refunded bonds is $989.69 (= 987.97 +[5/35][1,000 − 987.97]); the net proceeds per refunding bond is $991.25; and the after-tax cost of money for the refunding issue is $.3b$ (= [1−.4]b/2) per semiannual period.

The semiannual after-tax interest savings are 11,587,500 − 90,000,000b; the reduction in semiannual expense amortization is the difference between amortization of $20,620 (= [1,000 − 989.69][300,000][.4]/60) on the old debt and amortization of $17,500 (= [1,000 − 991.25][300,000][.4]/60) on the new issue. Thus, the semiannual savings are

$$11,587,500 - 90,000,000b - (20,620 - 17,500) = 11,584,380 - 90,000,000b$$

and the present value of the semiannual savings is

$$\sum_{n=1}^{60} \frac{11,584,380 - 90,000,000b}{(1 + .3b)^n}$$

$$= \left[\frac{11,584,380 - 90,000,000b}{.3b} \right] \left[1 - \left(\frac{1}{1 + .3b} \right)^{60} \right]$$

The after-tax redemption premium is $15,912,000 (= [1 − .4][88.40]300,000); the after-tax write-off of the unamortized discount is $1,237,200 (= [1,000 − 989.69][.4]300,000); new issue expenses are again $2,625,000; and miscellaneous out-of-pocket expenses are again $540,000. The after-tax costs of the refunding are $17,839,800 (= 15,912,000 − 1,237,200 + 2,625,000 + 540,000).

The break-even refunding rate solves the equation

$$NA = \$49,763,349 = \left[\frac{11,584,380 - 90,000,000b}{.3b} \right] \left[1 - \left(\frac{1}{1 + .3b} \right)^{60} \right] - 17,839,800$$

which is analogous to Equation (20.7) and is solved by the same trial-and-error procedure. Solving for the break-even new issue rate that results in a net advantage of $49,763,349 gives 10.13% (for a 30-year noncallable issue). Thus, interest rates would have had to fall 43 basis points (10.56% minus 10.13%) over the next 5 years in order for Southern Bell to be able to realize greater savings from waiting to refund.

A third approach to the timing problem uses dynamic programming.[29] Dynamic programming enables the decision-maker to compare the profitability of each refunding opportunity with all possible future refunding opportunities for the same issue. The primary output of this analysis is a **stopping curve**, which takes into account taxes and transaction costs and which indicates for each particular time the refunding rate on the new issue at which the issuer should be indifferent between refunding immediately and waiting. If markets were perfect, the stopping curve would simply coincide with the yields to maturity that correspond to the schedule of call prices for the debt issue.

Figure 20–4 provides the stopping curve for the 40-year Southern Bell debt issue. The issue is noncallable for 5 years. The stopping curve extends over the 35-year call period. At new issue rates that lie below the stopping curve, Southern Bell should call and refund the issue immediately, because the resulting savings exceed the savings the firm could expect to realize by waiting.

Constructing a stopping curve involves working backward in time from the maturity date of the issue. The reason for proceeding in this manner is quite simple. At each moment in time we wish to calculate the value of the "call and refund" strategy and of the "postpone" strategy and then compare the two values to determine which strategy is preferable. But the value of the "postpone" strategy in turn depends on what happens in the future. By proceeding backward in time, we can use the values of "calling" and "postponing" from the previous step (i.e., one period later in time) to calculate the values for "calling" and "postponing" for the current step. Each calculation thus reflects what might happen in all future periods up to maturity. In this manner, dynamic programming simplifies the overall problem to a sequence of one-period decision problems.

Table 20–6 illustrates the procedure for constructing the stopping curve for the Southern Bell debt issue. To simplify the example, suppose that the firm could call the issue at either of only two moments in time: in 2010 or in 2015. To further simplify, we assume that the new issue expenses for the refunding issue and retirement expenses for the refunded issue collectively amount to $10.00 per bond net of tax savings from the refunding. Working backward in time, first consider what might happen in 2015, the final opportunity to refund. The firm could refund each 12⅞% bond profitably in 2015 if the new issue rate on a conventional issue is lower than the 12.47% break-even rate at that time. The variable NA measures the present value savings that correspond to the optimal strategy for different possible interest rates. The value of NA is the greater of (1) the net advantage from refunding, which is positive if refunding is profitable, and (2) zero, which corresponds to the net advantage of waiting because, if the issue is not refunded in 2015, it will never be refunded. If R < 12.47%, the present value savings are positive.

Next consider what might happen in 2010. First, calculate the break-even refunding rate. According to the indenture for the 12⅞% bonds, the call price in 2010 is $1017.69 per bond. The call premium is $17.69 per bond before taxes, or $10.61 per bond after taxes. Again assuming the other costs net of taxes amount to $10.00 per bond, total refunding costs are $20.61 per bond. The break-even refunding rate is 12.38%.

The refund-or-postpone analysis for 2010 is more complex than for 2015 because the firm might wish to pass up a profitable opportunity in 2010 if it expects a more profitable opportunity in 2015. But the desirability of postponing a profitable refunding might change between 2010 and 2015. Suppose that the firm's financial staff

---

[29]Bierman (1966); Boyce and Kalotay (1979b); Elton and Gruber (1971); Kalymon (1971); Kraus (1973); Weingartner (1967).

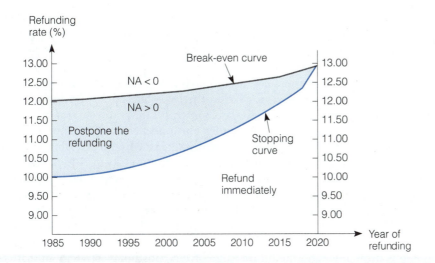

TABLE 20-6 Sample Calculation of Points on the Stopping Curve

Refunding decision in 2015

The call price is par. The issuer will refund if and only if the refunding rate (R) is below the break-even refunding rate (BERR), which is the refunding rate for which the net advantage of refunding is zero. BERR solves the equation:

$$0 = \sum_{t=1}^{10} \frac{.6[128.75 - \text{BERR}(1000)]/2}{[1 + .6\text{BERR}/2]^t} - 10.00$$

$$\text{BERR} = 12.47\%.$$

Therefore, the net advantage of refunding (NA) is:

$$\text{NA} = 0; \text{ if } R \geq 12.47\%$$

$$\text{NA} = \sum_{t=1}^{10} \frac{38.625 - 300R}{[1 + .3R]^t} - 10.00; \quad \text{if } R < 12.47\%.$$

Refunding decision in 2010

If the bond is refunded in 2010 at refunding rate R, then

$$\text{NA} = \sum_{t=1}^{20} \frac{38.625 - 300R}{[1 + .3R]^t} - 20.61.$$

The break-even refunding rate BERR is the value of R for which NA = 0:

$$\text{BERR} = 12.38\%.$$

However, if the issuer waits and refunds in 2015 (if it is profitable at that time), the expected present value savings (discounted back to 2010) are

$$\text{EPVS} = (1 + .3R)^{-10} \left\{ 0.5(0) + 0.5 \left[\sum_{t=1}^{10} \frac{38.625 - 219.6R}{[1 + .22R]^t} - 10.00 \right] \right\}$$

The issuer should refund in 2010 only if NA in 2010 exceeds EPVS in 2010, which happens only if

$$SCRR < 11.51\%,$$

where 11.51% is the *stopping curve refunding rate,* the point on the stopping curve that corresponds to 2010.

has analyzed historical interest rate movements and found that the new issue rate for long-term telephone bonds at the end of a 5-year period varies relative to the new issue rate at the beginning of the period within a range that has a standard deviation equal to 0.268 of the interest rate at the beginning of the 5-year period.[30] Such interest rate changes can be incorporated into the analysis by using the same type of decision tree approach that we used to develop the two-state option pricing model in Chapter 8. We assume that for each possible interest rate in the current period, the interest rate in the following period is either plus one standard deviation or minus one standard deviation from this period's interest rate, each with probability 1/2.[31] In our example, if the interest rate in 2010 is $R\%$, the interest rate in 2015 is either $R + 0.268R$ or $R - 0.268R$, each with probability 0.5. In moving along the stopping curve, it is reasonable to assume that if the future interest rate is $R + 0.268R$, refunding is unprofitable but if it is $R - 0.268R$, refunding is profitable. If the interest rate in 2015 is $R + 0.268R$, refunding is unprofitable so that the future value of the "postpone" strategy in that case is zero. If the interest rate is 2015 is $R - 0.268R$, refunding is profitable, and the future value of the "postpone" strategy in that case equals the net advantage of refunding in 2015:

$$\sum_{t=1}^{10} \frac{.6[128.75 - (R - .268R)\, 1{,}000]/2}{[1 + .3(R - .268R)]^t} - 10.00$$

The expected future value of the "postpone" strategy in 2010 would be

$$0.5(0) + (0.5)\left[\sum_{t=0}^{10} \frac{38.625 - 300(R - .268R)}{[1 + .3(R - .268R)]^t} - 10.00 \right]$$

These savings are discounted back to 2010 at the after-tax refunding rate $.3R$ per semiannual period to obtain the expected present value savings EPVS of waiting until 2015 to refund.

The firm should refund the 12⅞% issue in 2010 only if NA > EPVS, that is, only if the present value savings the firm can "lock in" in 2010 exceed the present value savings it could expect to realize by postponing the refunding. NA > EPVS provided the **stopping curve refunding rate** (SCRR) is less than 11.51%. At interest rates lower than 11.51%, the optimum strategy is to call immediately and refund. At interest rates higher than 11.51%, the optimum strategy is to postpone the refunding. In particular, at interest rates between 11.51% and 12.38% (the break-even rate) in 2010, it is profitable for the firm to refund the 12⅞% issue immediately but the optimum strategy is to wait. Performing the analysis just illustrated based on monthly intervals between 1985 and 2020 would produce the stopping curve in Figure 20–4.

ANALYZING SINKING FUND PREPURCHASES

Equation (20.4) can be used to evaluate the net advantage of making an advance sinking fund purchase of low-coupon debt. Note that designating a low-coupon bond to

---

[30] Such a relationship holds when interest rates follow a geometric random walk. Past studies have found that interest rate movements approximate a geometric random walk. When interest rates are equally likely to rise or fall each period by a constant percentage amount (i.e., the absolute value of $[r_{t+1}/r_t] = 1 + k$, where k is a constant), the distribution of the logarithms of interest rates at any moment in time will be normal (at least for large t) and can be approximated by a binomial distribution in which the interest rate at the end of period t differs from the interest rate at time 0 by plus or minus an amount equal to the interest rate at time $t=0$ multiplied by $kt^{1/2}$. In the example in the text, $kt^{1/2} = .268$, which implies $k = .12$ when $t = 5$, which characterizes the interest rate movements for long-term telephone utility bonds in recent years.

[31] This approach is illustrated in Finnerty, Kalotay, and Farrell (1988).

fill the first open sinking fund slot determines the appropriate refunding rate for the analysis. When the issuer has achieved its optimal capital structure, the debt service parity approach should be used to evaluate the proposed repurchase regardless of the immediate source of cash used to fund the repurchase.

Table 20–7 illustrates the application of Equation (20.4) to the prepurchase of a $10 million sinking fund amount 1 year ahead of the first sinking fund payment date for a $100 million debt issue that amortizes in ten equal annual installments. Suppose the outstanding debt bears a 10% coupon rate but that the debt issue's current yield to maturity is 15%. Suppose that because of the upward slope of the yield curve, the firm can borrow on a 1-year basis at an interest cost of 12.5% by drawing down on an existing credit line, which involves no issuance expenses. We evaluate the net advantage of the prepurchase transaction using this interest cost of the refunding debt to calculate the discount rate.

Suppose that the only alternative to current prepurchase is to buy bonds just prior to the sinking fund date at the price P that will prevail at that time. Note that the higher the future price P, the greater the savings from advance purchase. But note also that from the issuer's perspective, the future price P cannot exceed $1,000 per bond because the issuer has the option to call the bonds at par. Assuming that the future price will be exactly $1,000 favors prepurchase. One method of dealing with this problem is to assume that the issue's yield to maturity remains constant and then calculate the implied price. Based on the 15% semiannually compounded yield to maturity, the current price is 83.043%, or $830.43 per bond, and the price after 1 year (but *immediately prior* to prepurchase) will be 85.592%, or $855.92 per bond.

In Table 20–7, it is assumed that the issuer can repurchase the bonds today or 1 year from today at the same 15% yield to maturity. The net advantage calculated in Table 20–7 is therefore the net advantage of prepurchasing the sinking fund amount immediately rather than waiting 1 year. Consequently, savings and costs are calculated with respect to the 1-year waiting period, and the decrease in principal repayment obligation is calculated relative to the price expected to be paid 1 year hence.

Prepurchase reduces semiannual expense amortization tax shields by $20,000 per period for two periods. The decrease in expense amortization tax shields is discounted at the after-tax cost of money for the refunding issue, 3.75% (= [1 − .4][12.5]/2). The present value is −$37,857 (= [−20,000/1.0375] + [−20,000/(1.0375)^2]). Prepurchase reduces the principal repayment obligation by $254,900 (= 8,559,200 − 8,304,300), the difference between what it costs to retire the debt today and what it would cost to retire it 1 year from today. The present value of this amount is $236,807 (= 254,900/[1.0375]^2). The total benefits of prepurchase are $198,950 (= 236,807 − 37,857).

Turning to the costs of prepurchase, prepurchasing the $10 million sinking fund amount at an aggregate cost of $8,304,300 results in higher interest expense. The refunded debt had interest expense of $500,000 (= [.10]10,000,000/2) before taxes and $300,000 (= [.6]500,000) after taxes per semiannual period. The $8,304,300 of 12.5% debt has interest expense of $519,019 (= [.125]8,304,300/2) before taxes and $311,411 (= [.6]519,019) after taxes per semiannual period. The increase in interest expense is $11,411 (= 311,411 − 300,000). The increase in semiannual interest expense has a present value of $21,600 (= 11,411/1.0375 + 11,411/[1.0375]^2). Buying back the debt today leads to a taxable gain amounting to $1,695,700 (= 10,000,000 − 8,304,300), the tax on which is $678,280 (= [.4]1,695,700). Buying back the debt 1 year from today leads to a taxable gain amounting to $1,440,800 (= 10,000,000 − 8,559,200), the tax on which, payable in 1 year, is $576,320 (= [.4]1,440,800). The present value of this tax liability is $535,411 (= 576,320/[1.0375]^2). The incremental present value tax on the gain is therefore $142,869 (= 678,280 − 535,411). Subtract-

TABLE 20-7 Discounted Cash Flow Analysis of the Economics of a Sinking Fund Prepurchase

	Prepurchased Amount	Refunding Issue
Assumptions:		
Principal Amount	$10,000,000	$8,304,300
Coupon Rate	10%	12.5%
Issue Yield	15%	12.5%
Price	$830.43	$1,000.00
Remaining Life	1 year	1 year
Price after 1 year	$855.92	$1,000.00
Issuance Expenses Plus Original Issue Discount (Less Original Issue Premium)	$100,000[a]	—
Issuer's Tax Rate	40%	

	Pretax	After-Tax
Benefits of Prepurchase:		
Semiannual Expense Amortization:		
Refunding Issue	—	—
Refunded Issue	$50,000	$20,000
Savings (Cost)	$(50,000)	$(20,000)
Present Value of Semiannual Savings (Cost)[b]		$(37,857)
Cost of Repaying Principal after 1 Year:		
Refunded Issue		$8,559,200
Refunding Issue		8,304,300
Savings (Cost)		$254,900
Present Value of Decrease in Principal Repayment Obligation[b]		$236,807
Total Benefits		$198,950
Costs of Prepurchase:		
Semiannual Interest Expense:		
Refunding Issue	$519,019	$311,411
Refunded Issue	500,000	300,000
Semiannual Increase	$19,019	$11,411
Present Value of Increase in Semiannual Interest Expense[b]		$21,600
Tax on the Gain:		
Immediate Prepurchase		$678,280
Repurchase after 1 Year[b]		$535,411
Present Value Increase in Tax on Gain		$142,869
New Issue Expense		—
Debt Retirement Expenses		—
Less Write-Off of Unamortized Balance of Issuance Expenses on Refunded Issue	$(100,000)	$(40,000)
Total Costs of Prepurchase		$124,469
Net Advantage of Refunding		$74,481

[a] Unamortized balance attributable to the sinking fund payment.
[b] Discounted at the semiannual after-tax cost of a new full-coupon issue (3.75% semiannually).

ing the write-off of the unamortized balance of issuance expenses on the refunded issue, the total costs of repurchase are $124,469 (= 21,600 + 142,869 − 40,000).

The net advantage of prepurchasing the initial sinking fund amount immediately, rather than waiting 1 year, is $74,481 (= 198,950 − 124,469). The positive net advantage implies that the issuer should make the prepurchase.

This method of analysis can be extended to consider other possible prepurchase dates, for example, 6 months hence. While the basic approach illustrated in Table 20−7 can be used, the analysis of multiple possible prepurchase dates does complicate the analysis.[32]

REFERENCES

Agudelo, Jamie, and Jeff M. Harmon. "Debt Defeasance: Its Impact on Corporate Financial Reporting." *The Ohio CPA Journal* 43 (Spring 1984): 61–65.

Alexander, Gordon J., and Roger D. Stover. "The Effect of Forced Conversions on Common Stock Prices." *Financial Management* 9 (Spring 1980): 39–45.

Ang, James S. "The Two Faces of Bond Refunding." *Journal of Finance* 30 (June 1975): 869–74.

Bierman, Harold, Jr. "The Bond Refunding Decision as a Markov Process." *Management Science* 12 (August 1966): 545–51.

Bierman, Harold, Jr. "Defeasance is Not a Free Lunch." *Journal of Corporate Finance* (Spring 1985): 13–16.

Bodie, Zvi, and Benjamin M. Friedman. "Interest Rate Uncertainty and the Value of Bond Call Protection." *Journal of Political Economy* 86 (February 1978): 19–43.

Bodie, Zvi, and Robert A. Taggart, Jr. "Future Investment Opportunities and the Value of the Call Provision on a Bond." *Journal of Finance* 31 (March 1976): 1187–1200.

Bowlin, Oswald D. "The Refunding Decision: Another Special Case in Capital Budgeting." *Journal of Finance* 21 (March 1966): 55–68.

Boyce, William M., and Andrew J. Kalotay. "Tax Differentials and Callable Bonds." *Journal of Finance* 34 (September 1979a): 825–38.

Boyce, William M., and Andrew J. Kalotay. "Optimum Bond Calling and Refunding." *Interfaces* 9 (November 1979b): 36–49.

Brennan, Michael J., and Eduardo S. Schwartz. "Convertible Bonds: Valuation and Optimal Strategies for Call and Conversion." *Journal of Finance* 32 (December 1977): 1699–1715.

Brick, Ivan E., and Buckner A. Wallingford. "The Relative Tax Benefits of Alternative Call Features in Corporate Debt." *Journal of Financial and Quantitative Analysis* 20 (March 1985): 95–105.

Caks, John. "Corporate Debt Decisions: A New Analytical Framework." *Journal of Finance* 33 (December 1978): 1297–1315.

Dietrich, J. Kimball. "Effects of Early Bond Refundings: An Empirical Investigation of Security Returns." *Journal of Accounting and Economics* (April 1984): 67–96.

Elton, Edwin J., and Martin J. Gruber. "Dynamic Programming Applications in Finance." *Journal of Finance* 26 (May 1971): 473–505.

Elton, Edwin J., and Martin J. Gruber. "The Economic Value of the Call Option." *Journal of Finance* 27 (September 1972): 891–902.

Emery, Douglas R. "Overlapping Interest in Bond Refunding: A Reconsideration." *Financial Management* 7 (Summer 1978): 19–20.

Emery, Douglas R., and Wilbur G. Lewellen. "Refunding Noncallable Debt." *Journal of Financial and Quantitative Analysis* 19 (March 1984): 73–82.

Emery, Douglas R., and Wilbur G. Lewellen. "Shareholder Gains from Callable-Bond Refundings." *Managerial and Decision Economics* 11 (1990): 57–63.

[32]Kalotay (1981) describes an analytical procedure for handling multiple possible prepurchase dates.

Finnerty, John D. "Evaluating the Economics of Refunding High-Coupon Sinking-Fund Debt." *Financial Management* 12 (Spring 1983): 5–10.

Finnerty, John D. *An Illustrated Guide to Bond Refunding Analysis.* Charlottesville, VA: The Financial Analysts Research Foundation, 1984a.

Finnerty, John D. "Preferred Stock Refunding Analysis: Synthesis and Extension." *Financial Management* 13 (Autumn 1984b): 22–28.

Finnerty, John D. "Stock-for-Debt Swaps and Shareholder Returns." *Financial Management* 14 (Autumn 1985): 5–17.

Finnerty, John D. "Refunding Discounted Debt: A Clarifying Analysis." *Journal of Financial and Quantitative Analysis* 21 (March 1986): 95–106.

Finnerty, John D., Andrew J. Kalotay, and Francis X. Farrell. *The Financial Manager's Guide to Evaluating Bond Refunding Opportunities*, Ballinger Publishing Company, Boston, 1988.

Franks, Julian R., and Stewart D. Hodges. "Valuation of Financial Leases—A Note." *Journal of Finance* 33 (May 1978): 657–69.

Ingersoll, Jonathan E., Jr. "A Contingent-Claims Valuation of Convertible Securities." *Journal of Financial Economics* 4 (May 1977a): 289–321.

Ingersoll, Jonathan E., Jr. "An Examination of Corporate Call Policies on Convertible Securities." *Journal of Finance* 32 (May 1977b): 463–78.

Kalotay, Andrew J. "On the Advanced Refunding of Discounted Debt." *Financial Management* 7 (Summer 1978): 14–18.

Kalotay, Andrew J. "On the Management of Sinking Funds." *Financial Management* 10 (Summer 1981): 34–40.

Kalotay, Andrew J. "Refunding Considerations Under Rate Base Regulation." *Financial Management* 13 (Autumn 1984): 11–14.

Kalymon, Basil A. "Bond Refunding with Stochastic Interest Rates." *Management Science* 18 (November 1971): 171–83.

Kraus, Alan. "The Bond Refunding Decision in an Efficient Market." *Journal of Financial and Quantitative Analysis* 8 (December 1973): 793–806.

Levy, Haim, and Marshall Sarnat. "Leasing, Borrowing, and Financial Risk." *Financial Management* 8 (Winter 1979): 47–54.

Lewellen, Wilbur G., and Douglas R. Emery. "On the Matter of Parity Among Financial Obligations." *Journal of Finance* 36 (March 1981): 97–111.

Livingston, Miles. "Measuring the Benefit of a Bond Refunding: The Problem of Non-marketable Call Options." *Financial Management* 16 (Spring 1987): 38–40.

Lovata, Linda M., William D. Nichols, and Kirk L. Philipich. "Defeasing Discounted Debt: An Economic Analysis." *Financial Management* 16 (Spring 1987): 41–45.

Masulis, Ronald W. "The Effects of Capital Structure Change on Security Prices." *Journal of Financial Economics* 8 (June 1980): 139–78.

Masulis, Ronald W. "The Impact of Capital Structure Change on Firm Value: Some Estimates." *Journal of Finance* 38 (March 1983): 107–26.

Mayor, Thomas H., and Kenneth G. McCoin. "Bond Refunding: One or Two Faces?" *Journal of Finance* 33 (March 1978): 349–53.

Mikkelson, W.H. "Convertible Calls and Security Returns." *Journal of Financial Economics* 9 (September 1981): 237–64.

Miller, Alexander B. "How to Call Your Convertible." *Harvard Business Review* 49 (May-June 1971): 66–70.

Ofer, Aharon R., and Robert Taggart, Jr. "Bond Refunding: A Clarifying Analysis." *Journal of Finance* 32 (March 1977): 21–30.

Peterson, Pamela, David Peterson, and James Ang. "The Extinguishment of Debt Through In-Substance Defeasance." *Financial Management* 14 (Spring 1985): 59–67.

Pye, Gordon. "The Value of Call Deferment on a Bond: Some Empirical Results." *Journal of Finance* 22 (December 1967): 623–36.

Reiner, Kenneth D. "Financial Structure Effects of Bond Refunding." *Financial Management* 9 (Summer 1980): 18–23.

Shannon, Donald S., and William P. Stevens. "How Debt Refunding Can Cause Decision Conflicts." *Management Accounting* 65 (December 1983): 40–44.

Stevenson, Richard A. "Retirement of Non-Callable Preferred Stock." *Journal of Finance* 25 (December 1970): 1143–52.

Vu, Joseph D. "An Empirical Investigation of Calls of Non-Convertible Bonds." *Journal of Financial Economics* 16 (June 1986): 235–65.

Weingartner, H. Martin. "Optimal Timing of Bond Refunding." *Management Science* 13 (March 1967): 511–24.

Yawitz, Jess B., and James A. Anderson. "The Effect of Bond Refunding on Shareholder Wealth." *Journal of Finance* 32 (December 1977): 1738–46.

21

Asset-Based Financing Techniques

Most companies raise funds by retaining earnings or by selling new issues of bonds or common or preferred stock. They raise such funds on their general credit. Investors or lenders, as the case may be, look principally to the cash flow from the firm's total asset portfolio, rather than any single asset or collection of assets, to provide the return of and a return on their investment or loan. In contrast, the investors and lenders involved in **asset-based financing** look principally to the cash flow from a specific asset or collection of assets to provide for the return of and a return on their investments and loans. In many cases, the lenders in asset-based financings extend loans **without recourse** to the owner(s) of the asset(s); such lenders look exclusively to a specific asset pool for the cash flow to service their loans.

There are a number of types of asset-based financing, including leasing, project financing, production payment financing, and corporate real estate financing. This chapter discusses methods of long-term asset-based financing, describes conditions under which asset-based financing is particularly appropriate, and reviews the advantages of each asset-based financing technique.

There are a variety of contradictory models for leasing analysis. Similar to models of bond refunding, the assumptions underlying leasing models have not always been clear. Some recent studies have helped clarify these differing assumptions and developed frameworks for leasing analysis that place the comparison between alternatives on a comparable basis—a "level playing field" so to speak. The key to a proper leasing analysis is the same as the key to a proper liabilities management analysis: ensuring the comparability of alternatives. In other words, the alternatives must be compared on an equivalent basis. As we did in the previous chapter, we will ensure comparability using the concept of *debt service parity (DSP)*. Debt service parity refers to making comparisons among alternatives where the after-tax payment schedule is identical under all the alternative actions.[1]

WESTERN'S LEASE OR BUY DECISION

Western Metals and Mining Corporation has a coal mine project under consideration. The project would cost $100 million. Among the required equipment, Western needs three electric shovels, which cost $10 million each. If Western purchases an electric shovel, it plans to use it for 10 years before selling it. Western expects the market value of an electric shovel at the end of 10 years to be $500,000. An electric shovel can be depreciated for tax purposes on a straight-line basis over 10 years. A finance company has offered to lease each electric shovel to Western for 10 years in

---

[1] Debt service parity is explained and discussed in Chapter 20. It would be helpful to reread the section entitled Debt Service Parity in Chapter 20, or read it now if you have not covered Chapter 20.

return for annual payments amounting to $1.745 million (payable at the end of each year) for each shovel leased.

Should Western buy the electric shovels or lease them? Western's future tax situation is uncertain. How would Western's ability to utilize the tax deductions that result from asset ownership affect the buy-or-lease decision? Under the lease arrangement the finance company will reap the residual value of the electric shovels. How will the residual value Western must forgo affect the desirability of leasing the electric shovels?

LEASE FINANCING   21.1

You may have rented an automobile, a tool, or other item. Such rentals are typically for short periods, perhaps for only a day. But corporations often rent equipment and real estate, and sometimes entire plants, for much longer periods.

Leasing originated some 3,000 years ago when the Phoenicians began chartering ships. Since that time, chartering, a form of ship leasing, has played a major role in the financing of maritime activities. Lease financing has also expanded to cover virtually any type of capital equipment, and its use has grown very rapidly since World War II. Several factors are responsible for this growth. Capital equipment has become increasingly complex and costly, which has increased the risk of technical obsolescence. This accounts for much of the growth in computer leasing. But more important, firms in capital intensive industries, such as railroads, airlines, and utilities, have been unable to utilize fully the tax deductions that result from asset ownership. Lease financing provides a mechanism for effectively transferring tax deductions from those who cannot use them to those who can. The liberalization of the tax deductions associated with asset ownership in the early 1980s provided a strong impetus to lease financing. The lessening of these tax deductions under the Tax Reform Act of 1986, which eliminated the investment tax credit and "slowed down" accelerated depreciation, has made leasing less attractive than it previously had been.

WHAT IS A LEASE?

A **lease** is a rental agreement that extends for 1 year or longer under which the owner of an asset (the **lessor**) grants another party (the **lessee**) the exclusive right to use the asset during the specified **term of the lease** in return for a series of fixed payments.

Payments are typically made monthly, quarterly, or semiannually. The first lease payment is typically due the date the lease agreement is signed, although this is not always the case. Payments are normally level, like a residential mortgage loan, but this time pattern can be altered, for example, to provide for lower payments during the early years before the asset reaches its full cash flow generating potential.

Lease agreements also often give the lessee the option to renew the lease or to purchase the asset, sometimes at a prespecified fixed price but usually at the asset's fair market value as of the date the lessee exercises the option to purchase the asset. Otherwise, the leased asset belongs to the lessor.

Leases differ in terms of the burdens of ownership the lessee must bear. Under a **full-service lease**, the lessor (owner) is responsible for maintaining and insuring the assets and paying any property taxes due on the assets. Under a **net lease**, the lessee is responsible for these items.

Leases also differ with respect to their term and the right of the lessee to cancel the lease during the contract period. **Operating leases** are short-term and are generally cancelable at the lessee's option prior to the end of the lease term. **Financial**, or **capital**, **leases** are long-term, generally extending over most of the estimated useful economic life of the asset, and are generally not cancelable by the lessee before the end of the basic lease period. Those financial leases that are so cancelable require the lessee to reimburse the lessor for any losses occasioned by the cancellation. The focus of this chapter is on financial leases.

Financial leases represent an important source of long-term financing. Entering into a financial lease is like entering into a loan agreement. There is an immediate cash inflow equal to the value of the asset. The firm realizes this value because it gets the exclusive use of the asset without having to purchase the asset; it will thus realize the same stream of economic benefits (other than tax deductions) that it would have if it had purchased the asset. On the other hand, the lease agreement calls for fixed periodic payments, just like a loan agreement. Moreover, if the lessee fails to make timely lease payments, it runs the risk of bankruptcy, just as it would if it missed an interest payment or principal repayment on a loan. Thus, the cash flow stream associated with a financial lease is similar in financial effect to the cash flow stream of a loan. Accordingly, the appropriate starting point for analyzing a financial lease is the alternative of borrowing to finance the purchase price of the asset and repaying the loan over the lease term.

Leased equipment includes aircraft, ships, railroad cars, mining equipment, computers, and many more items—even entire electric generating plants. Virtually any asset can be leased. The principal lessors are equipment manufacturers, such as General Motors Acceptance Corporation (automobiles) and IBM (computers); commercial banks; finance companies, most notably General Electric Capital Corporation; and independent leasing companies. Equipment manufacturers are motivated principally by a desire to ease the financing burden equipment purchases might impose on their customers (i.e., to encourage sales).

TYPES OF LEASE FINANCING

Virtually all financial leases fall into one of three categories: direct leases, sale-and-leaseback arrangements, and leveraged leases (see Figure 21-1).

DIRECT LEASES   Assets covered by financial leases are generally new. Under a **direct lease**, the lessee identifies the asset it requires and either leases it directly from the manufacturer or else arranges for some other lessor to buy it from the manufacturer and lease it to the lessee.

SALE-AND-LEASE-BACK   A firm may instead sell an asset it already owns and lease it back from the purchaser. Such arrangements are common in real estate. For example, during the 1974–1975 recession, many companies discovered sale-and-lease-back arrangements as an attractive means of long-term financing. Under a **sale-and-lease-back** arrangement, the owner of an asset sells it, usually at market value, for cash. The purchaser assumes legal ownership, and thus the right to the tax deductions associated with ownership and to the residual value. The seller gets the exclusive right to use the asset during the basic lease period in return for periodic lease payments.

LEVERAGED LEASING   A lessor who provides lease financing for an expensive piece of equipment, such as an aircraft, may wish to leverage that investment. Under

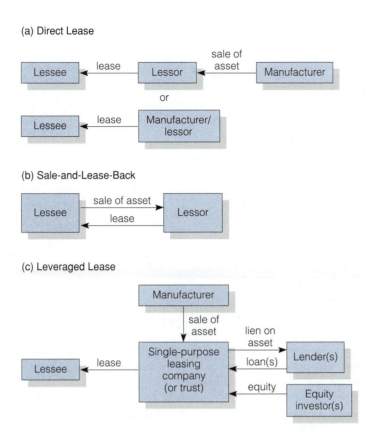

FIGURE 21.1
Illustration of the types of lease financing.

a **leveraged lease** arrangement, the lessor borrows a substantial portion of the purchase price of the asset, generally up to 80%. The lessor provides the balance of the purchase price in the form of equity. To secure the loan, the lessor grants the long-term lender(s) a mortgage on the asset and assigns the lease contract to the lender(s). Lenders thus have a prior claim on the lease payments as well as what is called a **perfected first lien** on the asset. Under such a lien, if the lessee fails to make timely lease payments, the lenders are entitled to seize the asset (and presumably sell it to recover some portion of their capital).

EXAMPLE OF A FINANCIAL LEASE   The problem posed at the beginning of the chapter illustrates a financial lease. Western Metals and Mining Corporation can either purchase an electric shovel for $10 million or lease it under an agreement requiring Western to pay $1.745 million at the end of each year for 10 years and also requiring Western to forgo the tax deductions associated with asset ownership.

Table 21-1 illustrates the direct cash flow consequences to Western of lease financing an electric shovel. Western does not have to spend $10 million to purchase the electric shovel. The effect is equivalent to a cash inflow of $10 million. However, Western must make periodic lease payments and must forgo the depreciation tax deductions and residual value it could realize by owning the electric shovel. Partially offsetting the impact of these cash outflows, the lease payments are tax–deductible. The combined effect of these factors is an effective initial net cash inflow of $10.0 million followed by effective net cash outflows of $1.427 million in each of years 1 through 9 and $1.927 million in year 10.

In Table 21-1, it is assumed that Western expects to pay taxes at a 40% marginal

TABLE 21-1   Direct Cash Flow Consequences to Western of Lease Financing an Electric Shovel (Dollar Amounts in Thousands)

Year	0	1	2	3	4	5	6	7	8	9	10
Benefits of Leasing:											
Initial outlay (avoided)	+10,000										
Costs of Leasing:											
Lease payments[a]		−1,745	−1,745	−1,745	−1,745	−1,745	−1,745	−1,745	−1,745	−1,745	−1,745
Lease payment tax credit[b]		+698	+698	+698	+698	+698	+698	+698	+698	+698	+698
Depreciation tax credits forgone[c]		−380	−380	−380	−380	−380	−380	−380	−380	−380	−380
Salvage value forgone											−500
Net cash flow to lessee	+10,000	−1,427	−1,427	−1,427	−1,427	−1,427	−1,427	−1,427	−1,427	−1,427	−1,927

[a] Lease payments made annually in arrears.
[b] Assumes the lessee's marginal income tax rate is 40%.
[c] Assumes straight-line depreciation to a $500,000 terminal book value for tax purposes.

rate over the next 10 years. If Western does not expect to pay taxes during that period, the value of the depreciation tax deductions forgone would be zero, and the net cash flow column would change accordingly.[2]

Table 21-1 provides only the direct cash flow consequences of the financial lease. As already noted, a financial lease has many of the attributes of a secured loan.[3] In particular, a financial lease displaces a portion of the lessee's debt capacity. We show below how to take into account these debt capacity side effects when valuing a financial lease.

LEASING VERSUS BORROWING AND BUYING

Lease analysis is similar to bond refunding analysis because, just as one bond issue displaces another, lease financing displaces debt. A firm that leases a piece of equipment reduces its borrowing capacity because it must meet its lease payment obligations on time in order to have uninterrupted use of the leased asset. If the lessee misses a lease payment, the lessor can reclaim the asset (which it legally owns) and sue the lessee for the missed lease payment. The consequences of failing to make a lease payment are the same as the consequences of failing to pay interest or repay principal on outstanding debt. The lessor becomes a creditor who can force the lessee into bankruptcy. Consequently, for purposes of financial analysis, a firm's lease payment obligations belong in the same risk category as the firm's interest and principal repayment obligations.

Table 21-2 illustrates the interrelatedness of leasing and borrowing. Suppose that

[2] If the tax deductions could not be taken currently, but could be carried forward and taken in the future, of course their value would not be zero. In that case, the present values of the respective depreciation tax credits (i.e., tax savings) would be reported in Table 21-1.
[3] Under bankruptcy law, a true financing lease—one whose payments the bankruptcy court determines to be the essential equivalent of the payment of interest and principal on a loan—is treated in virtually the same manner as a secured loan. However, there are important differences in the case of operating leases. An operating lease is an executory contract, which the debtor in a bankruptcy can reject (although the lessor can seek damages). In the case of an operating lease involving land or buildings, bankruptcy law limits the amount of damages a lessor can claim. Special provisions of bankruptcy law apply to aircraft and ships, which give the lessor greater flexibility to seize them in the event the lessee defaults.

TABLE 21-2   A Financial Lease Displaces Conventional Debt
(Dollar Amounts in Millions)

	Initial Capitalization	Conventional Financing	Lease Financing	Target Debt Ratio Restored
Long-term debt:				
Conventional debt	$100	$105	$100	$ 95
Financial lease obligations	—	—	10	10
Total long-term debt	100	105	110	105
Shareholders' equity	100	105	100	105
Net assets	$200	$210	$210	$210
Debt ratio	50%	50%	52.4%	50%

Western Metals and Mining Corporation currently has net assets worth $200 million and a debt ratio (θ) of 50%. If Western financed the $10 million electric shovel on a conventional basis without altering its capital structure, it would borrow $5 million and raise $5 million of equity funds. That would leave Western with $105 million of debt and $105 million of equity in keeping with its 50% target debt ratio. If instead Western leases the electric shovel and the associated lease obligations have a present value of $10 million, Western's debt—including this lease obligation—increases to $110 million. No equity funds are required; the lease provides what practitioners like to refer to as "100% financing." However, you can see that in this leasing case, Western will have changed its capital structure by increasing its debt ratio from 50% to 52.4% (= 110/210). Thus, the alternatives just described are not comparable because they do not leave the firm with identical capital structures. Western can restore its capital structure to 50% debt only if it issues $5 million of equity and reduces its other borrowing by $5 million.[4] In that case, its debt will consist of $95 million of preexisting debt plus the $10 million new lease obligation. Under both alternatives, Western has total debt of $105 million, but under the leasing alternative, $10 million of that total consists of the new lease obligation. It is in this sense that a financial lease displaces conventional debt *dollar-for-dollar*.

Only when the lease and borrow-buy alternatives are placed on a comparable basis can there be an accurate comparison between the alternatives. Such comparability includes the firm's capital structure. Whether the firm will, in fact, have identical capital structures after implementation of either alternative is a separate decision, and should be evaluated on its own merits. The important point is to isolate the decision under consideration and not to confuse a lease versus borrow-buy decision with a capital structure decision.

ADVANTAGES AND DISADVANTAGES OF LEASE FINANCING

Leasing offers a number of purported advantages. Some are real but others, such as the purported accounting benefits, are illusory.

[4]The two alternatives could also be made comparable by specifying under the borrow-buy alternative that the firm borrow the entire $10 million, say $5 million on a secured basis and the other $5 million unsecured. The firm's capital structure would be the same under both alternatives, although it would deviate from the firm's target capital structure.

■ *More efficient utilization of tax deductions and tax credits of ownership.* The principal motivation for lease financing is the lessor's ability to utilize the tax deductions and tax credits associated with asset ownership more efficiently than the lessee can. The tax advantages that can result from leasing are illustrated in the next section of this chapter.

■ *Reduced risk.* Most leases are short-term operating leases. Such leases provide a convenient means of obtaining the use of an asset for a relatively short period of time. Cancelable operating leases, for example, computer leases, relieve the lessee of the risk of product obsolescence, which the lessor, such as the equipment manufacturer, might be in a better position to assume. This motivation for leasing reflects the Options Principle: the cancellation option is valuable.

■ *Reduced cost of borrowing.* Lessors of readily saleable assets, such as vehicles, generally do not have to perform credit analyses quite as detailed as those conducted by general lenders. They are also more likely to be able to use "standardized" documentation. Both factors reduce transaction costs and can thus result in a lower cost of borrowing for the lessee, particularly a smaller firm that may face restricted access to conventional sources of funds.

Bankruptcy considerations may also be important. In the case of aircraft and vessels, special provisions of the bankruptcy law give a lessor greater flexibility than a secured lender has to seize the asset in the event of bankruptcy because the lessor owns the asset. Suppliers of capital to smaller companies or to less creditworthy companies, for which the risk of financial distress is greater, often prefer to advance funds through a lease rather than a loan because under a lease the lessor retains ownership of the asset and can seize the asset if the lessee defaults on the lease payments.

Lease financing may permit a lessee to tap a new source of funds, for example, finance companies that do not customarily purchase the lessee's securities. Such a new source of funds is only beneficial, of course, if it results in a truly lower cost of borrowing. The extent of this advantage is virtually impossible to quantify, however.

■ *Circumvent restrictive debt covenants or other restrictions.* Unless the firm's bond indenture(s) or loan agreement(s) contain limitations on leasing, a firm can effectively borrow funds through a lease financing even when conventional debt financing is prohibited by debt covenants.[5] In such situations, leasing represents a disguised form of debt financing. Leasing thus may affect the lessee's agency costs. However, recently drafted indentures and loan agreements generally contain limitations on leasing that foreclose this loophole.

■ *Off-balance-sheet financing.* Companies often go to great lengths to design lease structures that achieve off-balance-sheet treatment so as to minimize the impact of the financing on the firm's apparent degree of leverage (as reflected on the face of the firm's balance sheet). Many companies also try to keep lease payments as low as possible during the early years of the lease term so as to minimize the impact on reported earnings per share. Based on the Principle of Capital Market Efficiency, however, you would expect the leasing information disclosed in the footnotes to the firm's financial statements to enable market participants to gauge the true financial impact of the leasing arrangements. In fact, empirical evidence shows that investors correctly evaluate the financial impact of com-

---

[5]In a highly publicized leasing arrangement, the U.S. Navy once leased a fleet of oil tankers instead of seeking congressional appropriations to finance the purchase of the vessels.

panies' financial lease obligations.[6] The apparent income statement and balance sheet benefits are thus of highly dubious value.

Of course, as you might also expect, a market imperfection can cause the accounting treatment to affect value, so that off-balance-sheet treatment can prove beneficial to a regulated firm, such as a bank, in certain situations. Banks are required to maintain a minimum ratio of capital to total assets based on balance sheet figures. Given any particular amount of capital, the minimum required capital-to-assets ratio determines the maximum amount of assets, as reported in the bank's balance sheet. But by leasing assets off-balance-sheet a bank can increase its assets above the constrained amount. When a bank's assets are already at the permitted maximum, the incremental after-tax cash flow the bank will realize by employing the leased assets in its business should be included in calculating the benefits of leasing.

- *Preservation of capital.* By entering into a lease arrangement, a company avoids having to borrow from its banks or having to invest internally generated funds. However, we showed in Table 21-2 that entering into a lease arrangement displaces conventional debt dollar-for-dollar. Because of the consequent reduction in the lessee's borrowing capacity, capital is not really preserved. There may be a benefit to leasing if market imperfections preclude other forms of borrowing, but that is different from truly preserving capital. In general, the preservation-of-capital argument is of dubious validity.

POTENTIAL DISADVANTAGES OF LEASING   The principal disadvantages of leasing are the lessee's forfeiture of the tax deductions associated with asset ownership and, in most cases, loss of residual value. It is therefore essential that a prospective lessee evaluate carefully the cost of forgoing these benefits and determine whether, in light of this cost and the impact of the leasing arrangement on its debt capacity, leasing is really cheaper than the alternative of borrowing and buying.

It is also important to bear in mind that the tax benefits of leasing to the lessor are offset to some extent by certain tax detriments. The lessor must recognize the full amount of each lease payment as taxable income. A lease is like a loan, but a loan in which the entire debt service payment—principal as well as interest—is tax-deductible to the borrower/lessee and is taxable to the lender/lessor. Leasing is only beneficial when the present value of the benefits of leasing, including the present value of transferring depreciation and other tax deductions and tax credits associated with asset ownership from the lessee to the lessor, exceeds the present value of the costs of leasing, including the present value of the aforementioned tax cost.

TAX AND ACCOUNTING TREATMENT OF FINANCIAL LEASES

21.2

This section reviews the tax and accounting provisions that relate to financial leases.

TAX TREATMENT OF FINANCIAL LEASES

The Internal Revenue Service has established guidelines that it applies to distinguish **true leases** from installment sales agreements and secured loans. If the terms of the leasing arrangement satisfy the guidelines, the lessee is entitled to deduct for tax pur-

---

[6] Martin, Anderson, and Keown (1979) show that there was no significant stock market reaction to the announcement of lease capitalizations by a sample of companies each of which announced significant capitalized lease obligations just after a change in accounting rules—FASB 13—became effective. In addition,

poses the full amount of each lease payment and the lessor is entitled to the tax deductions and tax credits of asset ownership. In particular, the lessor can claim the accelerated depreciation deductions and any tax credits, such as investment tax credit (eliminated by the Tax Reform Act of 1986), that may be available.

These guidelines establish the following principal requirements for a lease to qualify for an advance IRS ruling as a "true lease":

- The term of the lease, including all renewal or extension periods other than renewals or extensions that are (1) at the option of the lessee *and* (2) at the fair market rental prevailing at the time of renewal or extension, cannot exceed 80% of the useful life of the asset;

- The lessor must maintain a minimum equity investment in the asset throughout the term of the lease of no less than 10% of the asset's original cost;

- The lessor can grant the lessee a purchase option, but only if the option price is equal to the asset's fair market value at the time the purchase option is exercised. Certain lease transactions do take place with a purchase option that provides for a fixed price equal to the estimated future fair market value—but the lease in that case does *not* conform to the guidelines and therefore does not qualify for an advance ruling.

- The lessee does not pay any portion of the purchase price of the asset and, if the lease is a leveraged lease, does not lend the lessor funds with which to purchase the leased asset or guarantee loans from others to the lessor for this purpose; and

- The lessor must hold title to the property and must represent and demonstrate that it expects to earn a pretax profit—that is, profit apart from any tax deductions and tax credits it will realize—from the lease transaction.

These and the other requirements the IRS establishes are subject to change from time to time. As we noted in Chapter 12 with respect to other capital investment decisions, it is important to review the applicable tax rules prior to undertaking a financial lease analysis to verify that a proposed lease arrangement would qualify as a true lease under then current law and also to determine whether there is a more advantageous lease structure that would qualify.

ACCOUNTING TREATMENT OF FINANCIAL LEASES

The accounting treatment accorded leases has undergone significant changes in recent years. Prior to 1976, leases represented **off-balance-sheet financing**. That is, neither the leased asset nor the associated lease obligations were recorded on the face of the lessee's balance sheet. However, generally accepted accounting principles did require a lessee to disclose certain details regarding lease transactions in the footnotes to the lessee's financial statements.

Since January 1, 1977, Financial Accounting Standards Board Statement No. 13 (FASB 13) has required lessees to **capitalize** on their balance sheets all leases entered into on or after that date that meet any one of the following requirements:

- The lease transfers ownership of the asset to the lessee before the lease expires;

- The lease agreement grants the lessee the option to purchase the asset at a "bargain" price;

Bowman (1980) furnishes evidence that stock market investors view capitalized lease obligations (correctly) as debt equivalents.

■ The term of the lease equals or exceeds 75% of the estimated useful economic life of the asset; or

■ The present value of the minimum lease payments, discounted to the beginning of the lease period at the lesser of (1) the lessee's incremental borrowing rate and (2) the interest rate implicit in the lease payment stream (the **lease rate**), equals or exceeds 90% of the asset's value (net of any investment tax credit claimed by the lessor).

Leases that "fail" all four tests are **operating leases** from an accounting standpoint and do not have to be capitalized on the face of the balance sheet.

FASB 13 presumes that if one of the four aforementioned conditions is met, the lease arrangement is tantamount to the purchase of the asset with borrowed funds. Accordingly, FASB 13 requires the lessee to report the present value of the lease payments under capital leases next to long-term debt on the right-hand side of the balance sheet with a corresponding amount reported as an asset on the left-hand side of the balance sheet. The lessee amortizes the leased asset over the term of the lease. Correspondingly, under the "interest" method, the lessee separates each lease payment into an interest component and a principal repayment component. The amortization amount and the interest component of the lease payment are deducted from income for financial reporting purposes, and the principal repayment component reduces the amount of the capitalized lease obligation reported on the lessee's balance sheet.

VALUING A FINANCIAL LEASE   21.3

This section deals with how a firm can value a financial lease and incorporate lease financing into its capital budgeting analysis. As already noted, leasing analysis is complex, especially because of a lease financing's potential impact on a firm's capital structure. Because of its complexity, leasing analysis has been one of the more controversial issues in financial management.[7] In particular, there has been considerable debate over the correct discount rate, just as there has been in connection with bond refunding analysis, as we noted in Chapter 20. However, also as in the case of bond refunding analysis, the past controversy has been essentially resolved. Therefore, we focus the discussion in this chapter on the current, generally accepted methods of leasing analysis. One aspect of this analysis that is particularly important reflects the investment-financing interaction present in the lease-versus-borrow-and-buy decision. Under certain circumstances, the net present value of a capital investment project may be negative if the project is financed on a conventional basis but positive if the asset is leased. Because of this interaction, a firm should not necessarily limit its lease-versus-borrow-and-buy analysis just to those projects that it can justify on a purchase basis.

BASIC ANALYTIC FRAMEWORK

The application of the debt service parity (DSP) approach to leasing analysis differs only slightly from its application to the bond refunding decision. The principal tenet of the DSP approach is that the two alternatives must be evaluated as though the firm's total after-tax obligation (either lease payments or debt service payments) will

[7]Bower (1973); Lewellen and Emery (1981); Lewellen, Long, and McConnell (1976); Long (1977); Miller and Upton (1976); Myers, Dill, and Bautista (1976); and McConnell and Schallheim (1983).

be exactly the same under *either* alternative. By maintaining such parity, the evaluation of the lease-versus-borrow-and-buy decision avoids the complications of other possible simultaneous decisions that would bias the calculation of the net advantage of leasing. For example, if an increase in leverage would increase firm value and the project with lease financing would otherwise decrease firm value, the combination could make the leasing choice look attractive, even though the firm would be better off if it simply increased its leverage without undertaking the project with lease financing.

In the case of leasing, the basic question concerns the accurate determination of the market value of the promised lease payments. That is, the DSP approach determines the amount of debt that can be issued *today*, if the obligation connected with the *after-tax* period-by-period debt service payments for the borrow-buy alternative is exactly the same as those of the lease alternative. One way to view the amount of debt that could be issued today is to think of the after-tax lease payments as a set of promised future cash flows that could be "auctioned off" in the capital market. The amount of debt the firm can issue today is then the amount it would receive in exchange for that set of promised future cash flows. If the proceeds of the debt are not enough to purchase the equipment, then the leasing alternative has a positive NPV and should be undertaken. Of course, if the debt proceeds are greater than the cost of purchasing the equipment, then leasing would decrease shareholder wealth and should not be undertaken.

The relevant incremental cash flows associated with a lease-versus-borrow-and-buy decision include:

1. the cost of the asset (savings);
2. the lease payments (cost);
3. the depreciation tax deductions (forgone benefit);
4. the expected net residual value (forgone benefit);[8]
5. any incremental differences in operating or other expenses between the leasing and buying alternatives (cost or savings);
6. any investment tax credit or other tax credits (forgone benefit).

The **net advantage to leasing** equals the purchase price *minus* the present value of the incremental after-tax cash flows, the CFAT's, associated with the lease. The net advantage to leasing (NAL) can be expressed in equation form as:

$$\text{NAL} = P - \text{PV(CFATs)} \tag{21.1}$$

where P denotes the purchase price and PV(CFATs) is the present value of the CFATs.

The appropriate discount rate for determining the present value of the lease payments, any after-tax change in operating or other expenses (due to the lessor becoming responsible for paying them under the terms of the lease), and depreciation tax deductions is the lessee's after-tax cost of similarly secured debt,[9] assuming 100% debt financing for the asset. Recall from Chapter 14 that secured debt is debt that

---

[8] The asset's residual value at the end of the lease term is also important for tax reasons. If the asset's residual value is expected to be insignificant, the Internal Revenue Service may take the position that the lease is not a true lease and deny the tax-deductibility of the portion of the lessee's lease payments that effectively represents principal repayments.

[9] As shown by Franks and Hodges (1978) and Levy and Sarnat (1979), using the after-tax cost of debt to discount the after-tax cash flows captures the impact of capital structure valuation effects.

provides lenders with a lien on certain assets (i.e., the leased asset(s)). This is also the required rate of return for the lease payments because a firm's lease payments belong to the same risk class as the firm's debt payments. In addition, the lease obligation is secured because the lessor retains ownership of the asset. However, the lessee is effectively borrowing 100% of the purchase price, that is, the financial lease obligation is not *over*collateralized, as is typically the case with conventional secured debt financing. (That is, typically, the amount of the loan is less than the initial market value of the asset. Thus, the collateral value exceeds the amount of the loan.) Accordingly, the secured debt rate used in the financial lease valuation should reflect the absence of overcollateralization. Typically, it will be a weighted average of the cost of fully secured debt and the cost of unsecured debt.

The present value of the expected residual value of the asset—the salvage value—is determined by discounting at a higher required rate of return to reflect its greater riskiness. Residual value is more closely related to overall project economic risk than to financing risk. Therefore, the required rate of return for the project is used to determine the present value of the expected residual value.

The net advantage to leasing can be rewritten as

$$\text{NAL} = P - \sum_{t=1}^{N} \frac{(1 - \tau)(L_t - \Delta E_t) + \tau D_t}{[1 + (1 - \tau)r']^t} - \frac{\text{SAL}}{[1 + r]^N} - \text{ITC} \qquad \text{(21.2)}$$

where the variables are defined in alphabetical order as:

D_t = the depreciation deduction (for tax purposes, *not* financial reporting purposes) in year t;

ΔE_t = the total incremental difference in operating or other expenses in year t between the leasing and buying alternatives;

ITC = investment tax credit, if available;

L_t = lease payment in year t;

N = the number of periods in the life of the lease;

NAL = the net advantage to leasing;

P = the purchase price of the asset;

r = the required rate of return for the asset (its after-tax weighted average cost of capital);

r' = the after-tax cost of debt, assuming 100% debt financing for the asset (typically, this will be a weighted average of fully secured and unsecured debt rates);

SAL = expected residual value of the asset at the end of the lease;

τ = the lessee's (asset user's) marginal ordinary income tax rate.

Note that Equation (21.2) assumes that the lease payments are made in arrears (i.e., at the end of each period), not in advance (at the beginning of each period) and that the lessor claims any investment tax credit (ITC). Lease agreements often provide for lease payments to be made in advance, which requires adjusting Equation (21.2), as well as the other equations presented in this section, appropriately to reflect properly the exact timing of the lease payments. Also, when ITC is available, lease agreements sometimes permit the lessee to claim it. Before performing a leasing analysis, you should check the proposed lease terms to determine the timing of the lease payments and who is entitled to claim any available ITC.

ANALYZING WESTERN'S LEASE OR BUY DECISION

The DSP approach to evaluating the desirability of lease financing can be illustrated using the Western Metals and Mining Corporation example given earlier in the chapter. But before proceeding, we need to specify current capital market conditions, which are as follows: (1) Western can borrow 10-year secured installment debt in the amount of 80% of the value of each electric shovel at a pretax interest rate of 11.5% per year; (2) Western can borrow unsecured installment debt in the amount of the remaining 20% of the value of each electric shovel at a pretax interest rate of 14.0% per year. Finally, the after-tax required rate of return (weighted average cost of capital) for this project is 15% per year. Western's marginal tax rate is 40%.

If Western leases an electric shovel, it will not have to pay the purchase price but it will have to make the lease payments. Also, Western will not be able to claim the depreciation expense and it will not own the asset at the end of the lease term thereby forgoing the asset's residual value. In this case, there are no incremental differences in operating expenses between the alternatives and there is no investment tax credit.

EXAMPLE ■ Western's cost of debt at this time, assuming 100% debt financing with 80% secured and 20% unsecured, will be 12.0% (= [.8]11.5% + [.2]14.0%) before-tax and 7.2% after-tax (= [1 − .4]12.0%). The amount of the depreciation tax deductions forgone is $950,000 per year (= [10,000,000 − 500,000]/10), and the related tax savings forgone is $380,000 per year (= [.4]950,000). Therefore, applying Equation (21.2), the net advantage to leasing for Western is:

$$\text{NAL} = \$10,000,000 - \sum_{t=1}^{10} \frac{(1 - .4)1,745,000 + 380,000}{[1 + (1 - .4).12]^t} - \frac{500,000}{[1 + .15]^{10}}$$

$$\text{NAL} = \$10,000,000 - \$9,930,644 - \$123,592 = -\$54,236$$

The net advantage to leasing is negative. Western's ability to utilize the tax deductions associated with asset ownership fully itself is largely responsible for this negative value. Western should borrow and buy rather than lease the electric shovel. ■

OTHER ANALYTIC APPROACHES

As in the case of capital budgeting analysis, there exist alternative approaches to net-present-value analysis. These alternative approaches have certain perceived advantages in some situations but the DSP net-present-value approach is the universally most valid analytic method and the one we recommend you use. Nevertheless, because the internal-rate-of-return approach is widely used by practitioners, we will discuss it briefly. A third approach, called the equivalent-loan approach, is really equivalent to the net-present-value approach but yields some interesting insights.

INTERNAL-RATE-OF-RETURN APPROACH The internal-rate-of-return approach to leasing bears the same relation to the net-present-value approach to leasing as do the two approaches to capital budgeting analysis. The internal rate of return, denoted IRR, is the discount rate that makes the net advantage to leasing in Equation (21.2) equal to zero:

$$\text{NAL} = P - \sum_{t=1}^{N} \frac{(1 - \tau)(L_t - \Delta E_t) + \tau D_t}{[1 + \text{IRR}]^t} - \frac{\text{SAL}}{[1 + \text{IRR}]^N} - \text{ITC} = 0 \qquad \textbf{(21.3)}$$

where the variables are defined as in Equation (21.2).

The internal rate of return represents the **cost of lease financing**. It is an after-tax cost. If the lessee is taxable, the cost of lease financing includes the interest tax deductions lost on displaced debt as well as the tax deductions and tax credits and the residual value forgone as a result of lease financing rather than borrowing and buying the asset. If the cost of lease financing is less than the prospective lessee's after-tax cost of secured debt, the company should lease finance the asset. Otherwise it should borrow funds and buy the asset.

EXAMPLE ■ In the case of Western's proposed lease financing, IRR solves the equation

$$0 = \$10,000,000 - \sum_{t=1}^{10} \frac{1,427,000}{(1 + \text{IRR})^t} - \frac{500,000}{(1 + \text{IRR})^{10}}$$

Solving this equation for IRR gives an IRR = .0758 or 7.58%. Since the cost of lease financing is greater than Western's 7.20% after-tax cost of secured debt, Western should borrow funds and buy the asset according to the internal-rate-of-return criterion. ■

EQUIVALENT-LOAN APPROACH   The equivalent-loan approach has no analogue in capital budgeting analysis. It involves simply comparing the amount of financing provided by the lease to the amount of financing provided by the **equivalent loan**. The equivalent loan is the maximum amount the lessee could borrow if it dedicates the future incremental cash flow stream (i.e., beginning at the end of the first period) to service conventional secured debt. The equivalent loan, by design, involves the same period-by-period after-tax debt service requirements as the lease—which conforms to the DSP principle. In effect, the equivalent loan is the amount for which the after-tax payments could be "auctioned off."

The equivalent loan, denoted EL, can be written

$$\text{EL} = \sum_{t=1}^{N} \frac{(1 - \tau)(L_t - \Delta E_t) + \tau D_t}{[1 + (1 - \tau)r']^t} + \frac{\text{SAL}}{[1 + r]^N} \tag{21.4}$$

where the variables are defined as in Equation (21.2). Note that under the equivalent-loan approach, the expected residual value of the asset is discounted at the after-tax required rate of return for the project to reflect its greater riskiness and consequently lower capacity to support project debt. If the purchase price of the asset less ITC, $P - \text{ITC}$, exceeds the amount of the equivalent loan, the lease effectively provides the greater amount of financing (for the same after-tax debt service stream), so the asset should be leased. Otherwise, the asset should be financed on a conventional basis.

EXAMPLE ■ In the case of Western's proposed lease financing, the amount of the equivalent loan is

$$\text{EL} = \sum_{t=1}^{10} \frac{1,427,000}{(1.072)^t} + \frac{500,000}{(1.15)^{10}} = \$10,054,236$$

which exceeds the $10 million cost of the asset. Thus, conventional financing is more advantageous than lease financing. ■

Note that the cost of the asset minus the amount of the equivalent loan equals $-\$54,236$, the net advantage to leasing. Thus, the equivalent-loan approach is perfectly equivalent to the net-present-value approach. We think the equivalent-loan approach is useful because it makes it easier to interpret the net advantage to leasing: NAL represents the amount by which the magnitude of the funds provided by the lease exceeds (when NAL > 0) or falls short of (NAL < 0) the magnitude of the funds provided by conventional debt financing when debt service parity is preserved.

The equivalent-loan approach has a further advantage. It explicitly calculates the amount of conventional debt that the lease financing displaces. The adjusted-present-value approach, discussed in Chapter 19, could also be used to take into account the value of displaced debt but the equivalent-loan approach is much simpler computationally. Moreover, the equivalence of the equivalent-loan approach and the net-present-value approach under DSP reaffirms that the net-present-value approach under DSP is perfectly equivalent to the adjusted-present-value approach. The adjusted-present-value method measures the net present value of the lease under debt service parity.

WHEN IS LEASE FINANCING ADVANTAGEOUS?

As you would expect, leasing would be a zero-sum game between lessor and lessee in a perfect capital market environment. Even with taxes, in an otherwise perfect capital market environment, it will be a zero-sum game if both parties have the same marginal tax rate. In such an environment, the negative of the benefit to the lessee (−NAL) will be the cost to the lessor. Thus, in the example just given, if the lessor has the same marginal tax rate as Western, the lessor would have a positive NPV of $54,236 if Western undertakes this lease:

$$\text{NPVL} = -P + \sum_{t=1}^{N} \frac{(1 - \tau')(L_t - \Delta E_t) + \tau' D_t}{[1 + (1 - \tau')r']^t} + \frac{\text{SAL}}{[1 + r]^N} + \text{ITC} \qquad (21.5)$$

$$\text{NPVL} = -\$10{,}000{,}000 + \sum_{t=1}^{10} \frac{1{,}427{,}000}{(1.072)^t} + \frac{500{,}000}{(1.15)^{10}} = \$54{,}236$$

where NPVL denotes the net present value of the lease to the lessor, τ' denotes the lessor's marginal ordinary income tax rate, and the other variables are defined as in Equation (21.2). Note the symmetry between Equations (21.2) and (21.5). Note also that the discount rates r' and r are the same in both equations because r' measures the riskiness of the lease payments, as determined in the capital market, and r measures the riskiness of the overall project, also as determined in the capital market.

In an imperfect capital market environment, there is a possibility that a tax asymmetry, information asymmetries, or transaction costs may cause leasing to be favorable for both lessor and lessee. For example, if the lessor and the lessee have different marginal income tax rates, the CFAT's can have different present values to the two parties.

EXAMPLE ■   Suppose Western will never be able to utilize the tax deductions that are potentially available from owning the electric shovel. If Western were a non-tax-paying corporation and if it would never pay any income taxes, then its cost of entering into the lease would be calculated by discounting the pretax lease payments and the forgone residual asset value. The discount rates for determining the present values of these two costs would be the cost of debt, 12%, and the before-tax required rate of return for the project, which we will specify as 17.5%, so that

$$\text{NAL} = \$10{,}000{,}000 - \sum_{t=1}^{10} \frac{1{,}745{,}000}{(1.12)^t} - \frac{500{,}000}{(1.175)^{10}} = \$40{,}685$$

■

BREAK-EVEN LEASE RATE   Equations (21.2) and (21.5) can be used to determine a **break-even lease rate** for each of the lessee and the lessor. The lessee's break-even lease rate, L_E, is the lease rate that makes the lessee indifferent between leasing the asset and borrowing the necessary funds on a conventional basis and buying it; NAL = 0 when $L_t = L_E$ for all periods t. The lessor's break-even lease rate, L_R, is calculated and interpreted similarly.

EXAMPLE ■   To continue our example, if Western never expects to pay income taxes, $L_E = \$1,752,200.54$ because

$$\text{NAL} = \$10,000,000 - \sum_{t=1}^{10} \frac{1,752,200.54}{(1.12)^t} - \frac{500,000}{(1.175)^{10}} = 0$$

The lessor's break-even lease rate, assuming $\tau' = .4$, is $L_R = \$1,732,010.75$ because

$$\text{NPVL} = -\$10,000,000 + \sum_{t=1}^{10} \frac{.6(1,732,010.75) + 380,000}{(1.072)^t} + \frac{500,000}{(1.15)^{10}} = 0$$

So long as $L_R < L_E$, it is possible to find a lease rate (or set of lease rates, one for each period t) L_t such that $L_R < L_t < L_E$ and leasing is mutually advantageous to lessor and lessee. Where L_t lies in relation to L_R and L_E will determine how the net (tax) advantage to leasing is allocated between lessee and lessor, respectively.   ■

   Therefore, you can see that tax considerations can alter the otherwise zero–sum game and, in some cases, make lease financing more advantageous than conventional debt financing for both lessee and lessor. In this example, leasing is advantageous to Western if Western cannot realize the tax deductions associated with asset ownership; the leasing arrangement effectively allows Western to sell these tax deductions, which would otherwise expire worthless due to Western's inability to claim them itself. The value of these tax deductions to the lessor, which is reflected in the lease rate, is sufficient to make lease financing advantageous for both parties. On the other hand, if Western can claim the tax deductions, leasing is not advantageous because the value of the tax deductions reflected in the lease rate is lower than the value Western realizes by claiming the tax deductions itself.

   ASYMMETRIC TAXES   It is not possible to conclude in every case that a low-, or non-, taxpayer should lease from a relatively high taxpaying entity. Whether it is advantageous depends on the lease rate, which reflects the value the lessor is effectively willing to pay for the tax deductions transferred under the lease. In the example just given, leasing would be favorable for Western if it were an entirely tax-free entity. But consider the following example.

EXAMPLE 1 ■   Suppose Western expects to pay income taxes at a 40% rate and that it has been offered a lease with payments of $1,792,000 required at the end of each of the next 10 years. Assume that all the other information given previously, including the depreciation schedule and capital market conditions, is identical. Under such conditions, the net advantage to leasing for Western would be

$$\text{NAL} = \$10,000,000 - \sum_{t=1}^{10} \frac{(1 - .4)1,792,000 + 380,000}{[1 + (1 - .4).12]^t} - \frac{500,000}{[1 + .15]^{10}}$$

$$\text{NAL} = \$10,000,000 - \$10,126,891 - \$123,592 = -\$250,483$$

Thus, Western's net advantage to leasing is negative under this lease arrangement if Western pays taxes at a 40% tax rate. Next consider what happens if Western expects never to pay income taxes.

If Western expects never to pay income taxes, its net advantage to leasing under the given conditions with lease payments of $1,792,000 at the end of each year would be

$$NAL = \$10,000,000 - \sum_{t=1}^{10} \frac{1,792,000}{(1.12)^t} - \frac{500,000}{(1.175)^{10}} = -\$224,876$$

In this case, Western should not lease even if it expects never to pay income taxes. The reason is quite simple: The payments of $1,792,000 are "too large," and therefore the lease rate exceeds Western's break-even lease rate. ■

The potential tax asymmetry between lessee and lessor is situation-specific.[10] As a result, there may exist lease rates in certain situations at which the lessee would prefer leasing to borrowing and buying when the lessee is fully taxable *but* would prefer borrowing and buying to leasing when the lessee is not a taxpayer. Consider the following example.[11]

EXAMPLE 2 ■ Suppose Western expects to pay income taxes at a 40% rate and that it has been offered a lease calling for payments of $1,570,000 *at the beginning* of each of the next 10 years. If none of the other conditions has changed, except that tax deductions are realized at the beginning rather than at the end of each period, the net advantage to leasing for Western would be

$$NAL = \$10,000,000 - \sum_{t=0}^{9} \frac{(1-.4)1,570,000 + 380,000}{[1 + (1-.4).12]^t} - \frac{500,000}{[1 + .15]^{10}}$$

$$NAL = \$10,000,000 - \$9,862,333 - \$123,592 = \$14,075$$

Thus, Western's net advantage to leasing is positive; Western should lease rather than borrow and buy even though Western pays income tax at a 40% rate.

If Western expects never to pay income taxes, its net advantage to leasing would be

$$NAL = \$10,000,000 - \sum_{t=0}^{9} \frac{1,570,000}{(1.12)^t} - \frac{500,000}{(1.175)^{10}} = -\$35,028$$

In this case, with lease payments required in advance, Western should not lease if it expects never to pay income taxes, but it should lease if it expects to pay income taxes at a 40% rate! ■

The critical difference between example 1 and example 2 lies in the timing of (1) the lease payments, (2) the tax deductions, and (3) the tax liabilities. The timing of these items has an effect on the value of the lease to each party. In general, the timing of each of these factors, the nature of the depreciation schedule for the asset, and the existence (or lack) of an investment tax credit, will affect the ability of the parties to create a lease contract that is mutually beneficial. Note that in all cases, however, the proper neutralization of the capital structure side effects is absolutely necessary to isolate, and accurately measure, the value of the financial lease.

In any case, there may be potential for taxpaying entities and non-taxpaying en-

---

[10] Brick, Fung, and Subrahmanyam (1990).
[11] The idea for this example came from Daniel Weaver.

tities to engage in leasing contracts that are favorable for both parties. The key is to evaluate each specific situation to identify the existence and favorable direction of any potential tax asymmetry.

LEASING AND CAPITAL BUDGETING

As we saw in the case of capital structure, lease financing can affect the value of an investment project by enabling a lessee to take advantage of any potential tax asymmetry. It is possible for a project that would have a negative NPV if the firm financed it on a conventional basis to have a positive NPV if it is lease financed. If one party can benefit from tax deductions and credits and their timing but the other cannot, leasing can enhance the value of the project. The reason is very simple. As illustrated above, tax deductions and credits, tax liabilities, and the timing of each constitute a significant source of potential value.

EXAMPLE ■ Table 21-3 illustrates the cash flow streams for a project that would be desirable if lease financed but undesirable if financed on a conventional basis. The firm will never be able to claim the tax deductions associated with asset ownership. The firm has determined that debt financing is of no benefit because the firm is unable to claim the interest tax deductions. The firm's investments require a 15% rate of return (zero leverage). The NPV of the project is −$1,907,113. The project would thus be unprofitable if it were financed on a conventional basis.

Suppose instead that the project is financed under a lease arrangement that calls for lease payments of $10,300,000 at the end of each year. The calculation of the NPV of the project must take into account project-related side effects in the form of any savings resulting from the lease financing:

$$\text{NPV (leased)} = \text{NPV (conventional)} + \text{NAL} \qquad (21.6)$$
$$= -\$1,907,113 + 2,241,434 = \$334,321$$

In this case, the lease rate ($10,300,000 per annum) is low enough that the net advantage to leasing outweighs the negative net present value of the project when it is

TABLE 21-3 Illustration of How Lease Financing Can Turn a Project Profitable

Time	Item	CFBT	CFAT	PV @ 15%
0	Initial outlay	−50,000,000	−50,000,000	−50,000,000
1–7	ΔRev.–ΔExp.	11,378,903	11,378,903	47,341,013
7	Residual value	2,000,000	2,000,000	751,874
				NPV = −$1,907,113

Time	Item	CFBT	CFAT	PV @ 12%[a] (15% for residual value)
0	Initial outlay	50,000,000	50,000,000	50,000,000
1–7	Lease payments	−10,300,000	−10,300,000	−47,006,692
7	Residual value	−2,000,000	−2,000,000	−751,874
				NAL = $2,241,434

Total net present value = −$1,907,113 + 2,241,434 = $334,321

[a] Assumes a new issue rate of 12.00% for the firm's debt.

financed on a conventional basis. In effect, the lessor is willing to pay enough for the tax deductions to make the project desirable.   ■

Note that the project's residual value could also play an important role in the economics of leasing. If the residual value in the example just given were, say, $10 million, the net present value of the project when financed on a conventional basis would be $1.10 million and the net advantage to leasing would be −$0.77 million. The sponsor should finance the project in that case on a conventional basis even though it does not expect to be able to utilize any of the tax deductions associated with asset ownership.

21.4   PROJECT FINANCING

Companies often find it advantageous to finance large capital investment projects that involve discrete assets on a project, or stand-alone, basis. **Project financing** is generally possible when a project possesses the following two characteristics:

1. The project consists of a discrete asset or a discrete set of assets that are capable of standing alone as an independent economic unit; and

2. The economic prospects of the project, combined with commitments from the sponsors and/or from third parties, assure that the project will generate sufficient revenue net of operating costs to service project debt.

Mines, mineral processing facilities, electric generating facilities, pipelines, dock facilities, paper mills, oil refineries, and chemical plants are examples of assets that companies have financed on a project basis. In each case, the project's assets and the related debt obligations are separated from the sponsoring companies' other assets and liabilities, respectively, and the project is analyzed as a separate (though not necessarily independent) unit.

PROJECT STRUCTURE

Each project is unique in certain respects, and the financing arrangements are designed to suit the project's special characteristics and to resolve potential agency problems. The following example will help draw the distinction between project financing and financing on the sponsoring firm's general credit.

EXAMPLE ■   Suppose that Western Metals and Mining Corporation wishes to develop the coal mine property discussed previously in order to obtain coal to sell to Electric Generating Company. On the one hand, Western might finance the mine on its general credit by selling shares of its common or preferred stock or general obligation debentures and investing the proceeds in the project. Suppose, however, that in return for an assured source of coal supply, Electric is willing to enter into a long-term coal purchase contract with Western. The mine will cost $100 million, which Western would like to borrow. The terms of the coal purchase contract can be drawn in such a way that the contract will provide support for the loans Western will arrange to finance development of the mine and minimize potential agency costs. In the extreme case, the loans may be **non-recourse** to Western so that lenders will look solely to payments under the coal purchase contract for the payment of interest and the repayment of principal on their loans. In that case, these loans would be designed to be self-liquidating from the revenues to be derived from coal sales to Electric, and the project financing would have little impact on Western's borrowing capacity.

The coal mine is capable of standing alone as an independent economic unit because of the long-term coal purchase contract, which will guarantee a market for its output. Normally, the project sponsor would have to make additional commitments to lenders as a condition for their agreeing to lend to the project.   ■

Projects like the mine project are typically financed with between 65% and 75% debt. The level of borrowing and the repayment terms are linked directly to the inherent economic value of the project's assets and to the extent of credit support provided by sponsors, suppliers, customers, governments, and other entities related to the project. This credit support takes the form of contractual arrangements to supply raw materials or take output, such as the coal purchase contract mentioned earlier; debt guarantees; insurance; and undertakings such as an obligation by Western to *complete* the mine (i.e., to bring it into production). For example, the coal in the forgoing example has collateral value. Lenders would normally be given a first lien on the project's assets so that if the borrower defaults, they could seize the asset, in this case the mine and related coal reserves, and sell them and apply the proceeds toward repayment of the loan. The coal purchase contract provides credit support, which can be very valuable if, for example, it obligates Electric to purchase all contract quantities that are made available for delivery. Such a contract reduces the risk that the mine will be rendered unprofitable; it transfers a portion of the economic risk of the project from Western to Electric.

PROJECT RISKS   One of the more crucial aspects of project financing involves identifying project risks and then designing contractual arrangements to allocate those risks among the various parties involved with the project so as to minimize total agency costs. Projects typically involve the following classes of risk:

■ *Completion risk*, the risk that the project will not be brought into operation successfully either because there is a technical failure (e.g., it fails to operate at its design capacity) or because cost overruns make it unprofitable to complete construction or impossible for sponsors to raise the additional funds. Lenders are seldom willing to assume completion risk, but banks may be willing to assume it when the sponsor has sufficient equity invested and the economics are so compelling that noncompletion is very unlikely. Alternatively, the engineering firm responsible for designing and constructing the project may be willing to assume the completion risk by entering into a **turnkey construction contract**—but normally only if the facilities are sufficiently similar to others it has constructed. Under a turnkey contract, the construction firm undertakes to build the project facilities and demonstrate that they perform according to previously agreed specifications for a price that is fixed as of the date the contract is signed.

■ *Technological risk*, the risk that technology of the type, or on the scale proposed, will not perform as planned or that the technology embodied in the project will become prematurely obsolete.

■ *Economic risk*, the risk that the project's output will not be saleable at a price that will cover the project's operating and maintenance costs and its debt service requirements.

■ *Raw material supply risk*, the risk that the raw materials or other factors of production required to operate the project at its design capacity will become depleted or become unavailable during the life of the project.

- *Force majeure risk*, the risk that there will be an interruption of operations for a prolonged period after the project has been completed due to fire, flood, storm, or some other factor beyond the control of the project's sponsors.

- *Political risk*, the risk that the host political jurisdiction will change its tax laws or other regulations in a way that materially harms the profitability of the project and, in the extreme case, the risk of expropriation without adequate compensation. In the case of a project in a foreign country, a sponsor can reduce its exposure to political risk either by arranging insurance to cover expropriation risk or by including among its lenders, banks that are major creditors of the host country (assuming the host country would be unwilling to take actions that would jeopardize its relationship with its principal lenders).

Often the risks of a project are so large that it would be imprudent for one party to bear them alone. Project financing provides a means of risk-sharing that is beneficial when there are significant costs of financial distress.

PROJECT FINANCING ARRANGEMENTS

Another crucial aspect of project financing is the design of contractual arrangements to allocate risks among entities involved with the project, to convey the credit strength of creditworthy companies to support project debt, and to minimize agency costs. These credit support arrangements typically include the following:

- *Completion undertaking*. Such an undertaking obligates the sponsors or other creditworthy entities either (1) to assure that the project will pass certain performance tests by some specified date, or (2) to repay the debt. As an example of the former, the coal mine mentioned earlier might be required to produce a certain number of tons of coal per month for a certain specified number of months prior to some specified date. Completion undertakings are designed to control the equityholders' tendency to pursue high-risk projects at the expense of lenders and to prevent them from abandoning a project without fully compensating lenders if a project becomes unprofitable.

- *Purchase, throughput, or tolling agreements*. These obligate one or more creditworthy entities to purchase the project's output or use its facilities. They operate in a manner similar to completion undertakings by preventing equity investors from abandoning a completed project when it is advantageous to them, and detrimental to project lenders, to do so. Purchase agreements that are capable of supporting project financing take the form of **take-or-pay contracts**, which obligate the purchaser to take the project's output or else pay for it if the product is offered for delivery (but normally only if the product is available for delivery), or **hell-or-high-water contracts**, which obligate the purchaser to pay in all events, that is, whether or not any output is available for delivery. The latter is, of course, stronger and therefore provides greater credit support. **Throughput agreements** are often used in pipeline financing. They require shippers to put some specified minimum amount of product (e.g., oil) through the pipeline each month (or interest period) in order to enable the pipeline to generate sufficient cash to cover its operating expenses and its debt service requirements. They can take the form of either ship-or-pay or hell-or-high-water undertakings. **Tolling agreements** are often used in financing processing facilities when the user retains ownership of the item throughout the production process. Such arrangements require users to process a certain specified minimum amount of raw material each month (or interest period).

■ *Raw material supply agreements*. These require the sponsors or other creditworthy entities to supply the facility's raw material needs or else make compensatory payments.

■ *Cash deficiency agreements*. Unless the purchase, throughput, or tolling agreement is of the hell-or-high-water variety, interruptions in availability or deliverability can result in the project realizing insufficient cash to meet its debt service obligations. Sponsors may therefore have to provide supplemental credit support in the form of an **equity contribution agreement**, which obligates them to invest additional cash as equity as required by the project to meet its debt service obligations; a **dividend clawback** or **tax clawback agreement**, which obligates the sponsors to repay cash dividends previously received from the project or to contribute the cash value of project-related tax credits they realize from their participation in the project; or some other form of **cash deficiency agreement** that will provide cash flow to meet the project's obligations to lenders. The stronger the cash deficiency agreement, the greater the proportion of economic risk borne by the project's sponsors and the lower are the agency costs faced by lenders.

The contractual arrangements will determine how much of the project risks are transferred to other parties. It is important for a project sponsor and its advisors to analyze carefully a proposed set of contractual arrangements to ensure that the risks the sponsor will have to bear are tolerable and that the allocation of the economic rewards of the project are commensurate with the allocation of project risks.

ADVANTAGES AND DISADVANTAGES OF PROJECT FINANCING

When applied appropriately, project financing affords a number of significant advantages relative to financing on the sponsors' general credit:

■ *Risk-sharing*. A sponsor can enlist one or more joint venture partners to share the equity risk. Such risk sharing is beneficial in the presence of significant costs of financial distress. Under certain circumstances, a project sponsor can transfer risks to suppliers, purchasers and, to a limited degree, to lenders through contractual arrangements like those just discussed. Risks can be allocated to parties who are willing to bear them at the lowest cost.

■ *Expanded debt capacity*. By financing on a project basis rather than on its general credit, a firm may be able to achieve a higher degree of leverage than would be consistent with its senior debt rating objective if it financed the project entirely on its own. Project-related contractual arrangements transfer portions of the business and financial risk to others, which permits greater leverage. In addition, if a firm's joint venture partners own at least 50% of project equity, under current accounting practice, project debt would not normally appear on the firm's balance sheet, which some companies find attractive in spite of the questionable benefit that supposedly results.[12] Any expansion in debt capacity is generally

---

[12]Footnote disclosure of any contingent liabilities or of any take-or-pay or similar undertakings would normally be required. Lenders and the rating agencies can therefore gauge the impact of project financing arrangements on a firm's credit capacity. Martin, Anderson, and Keown (1979) found that capitalizing lease obligations that had previously been described in footnotes did not have a significant market impact. This would suggest that there are no significant informational asymmetries between thorough footnote disclosure of project financing obligations and capitalization of these obligations on the face of the balance sheet. Nevertheless, there may be some informational asymmetries in practice. The rating agencies generally ignore off-balance-sheet financing obligations that represent less than 5% of a firm's capitalization.

greater when project loans are non-recourse to project sponsors. In addition, project financings can usually be structured so that they fall outside the debt restrictions contained in the sponsoring firm's bond indentures and loan agreements, which can reduce the agency costs the sponsors would otherwise face as a result of these agreements.

■ *Lower cost of debt.* In some cases, the purchasers of the project's output will have a higher credit standing than project sponsors. In that case, financing on the purchasers' credit rather than on the sponsors' credit can lead to a lower cost of debt. Such a benefit is more likely to occur when the output of the project will create a positive NPV for the purchaser that can only be realized if the sponsor undertakes the project. The project sponsor is effectively realizing a portion of the purchaser's positive NPV through the lower cost of borrowing it achieves.

DISADVANTAGES   Project financing also involves costs in addition to those incurred in connection with financing on a firm's general credit. The contractual arrangements mentioned above are often complex. Consequently, arranging a project financing generally involves significant transaction costs in the form of lawyers' and investment bankers' fees. In addition, lenders generally require a yield premium in return for accepting credit support in the form of contractual undertakings rather than a firm's direct promise to pay because of the higher agency costs. Moreover, they require additional yield premiums to compensate for any business risk they assume. Empirical evidence shows that project borrowings generally involve a yield premium of between one and two percentage points.[13]

WHEN TO FINANCE ON A PROJECT BASIS   Two critical steps in deciding whether to finance on a project basis are

■ Would the firm be willing to finance the project on its general credit? If the project's expected profitability is satisfactory but the project is "too big" (in the sense that it is large enough relative to the firm that it significantly increases the expected present value cost of financial distress if the firm finances the project entirely on its own) for the sponsor to pursue on its general credit, project financing should be considered.

■ Project financing should also be considered if (1) the firm would be willing to finance the project on its general credit, (2) the project involves a discrete set of assets, (3) there is a readily identifiable set of purchasers for the project's output who would be willing to enter into contractual commitments strong enough to support project financing, and (4) lenders are willing to advance funds against these contractual commitments without recourse to the project sponsor.

A project that could be financed on either a project basis or on the sponsor's general credit should be financed on a project basis only if that method of financing maximizes shareholder wealth. This will generally be the case when project financing facilitates a higher degree of leverage than conventional financing *and* the tax effects owing to the higher degree of leverage exceed the sum of the costs associated with the yield premium lenders require plus the higher after-tax transaction costs associated with the financing.

Also lenders may not fully take these obligations into account in reaching their credit decisions, according to the results of a survey reported by Wynant (1980).

[13] Wynant (1980).

PRODUCTION PAYMENT FINANCING

Projects that involve the development of natural resources, particularly oil and gas projects, are often financed through a special form of non-recourse asset-based financing known as **production payment financing**. A production payment involves a right to a specified share of the revenue from the production of a particular mineral property. A firm normally borrows against a production payment contract by selling the contract to a special purpose trust or corporation, which borrows the purchase price from one or more banks. (Banks are generally not permitted to own mineral interests directly.) This loan is secured by the production payment contract and is repaid exclusively from revenues generated from the production and sale of the minerals.

For the production payment contract to be valuable as collateral, the mineral deposit covered by the production payment must contain adequate proven reserves, the reserves must be recoverable at reasonable cost, and there must be an assured market for the production. When the collateral value is deemed adequate and the operator provides a completion undertaking satisfactory to lenders, a firm can typically borrow between 50% and 80% of the present value of the future cash flow expected from the sale of production from the reserves. The liquid nature of the assets accounts for the high degree of leverage. As we noted in Chapter 16, the greater an asset's liquidity the higher the degree of leverage it generally tends to support.

Production payment financing can afford two advantages relative to direct financing on a firm's general credit:

- Production payment loans are typically non-recourse to the sponsor. In such instances, because of market imperfections, it may be possible to achieve a higher overall degree of leverage for the firm by arranging production payment financing for some portion of the firm's assets.

- Debt service is generally tied to production, which enables the firm to defer its debt service obligations until production has begun. Because of market imperfections, it may be cheaper to achieve the tailored debt service stream through a production payment loan than through a conventional loan.

There are at least two potential disadvantages of production payment financing. Lenders typically require a yield premium to compensate for the risk that production will be inadequate to cover debt service fully as well as the added agency costs they face, and borrowers suffer some reduction in operating flexibility because the production payment contract may require production during periods when production is unprofitable, for example, due to low mineral prices. Lenders impose these restrictions in order to reduce the agency costs they face.

As in the case of project financing, production payment financing will be preferable to direct financing when production payment financing leads to a higher adjusted present value of developing the mineral deposit. Also as in the case of project financing, this will generally be the case when the value of the tax effects owing to the higher degree of leverage exceeds the cost of the yield premium plus the incremental expenses associated with arranging the loan and maintaining the special purpose trust.

LIMITED PARTNERSHIP FINANCING   **21.5**

It was noted earlier in this chapter that leveraged lease financing represents a cost-effective alternative to debt financing when the lessee is unable to utilize fully the tax deductions and tax credits of asset ownership. Limited partnership financing represents another form of tax-oriented financing. But unlike leasing, the sale of limited partnership units represents a form of equity financing.

Limited partnerships have been formed to finance real estate projects, oil and gas exploration, film-making, research and development projects, the construction of cable television systems, and various other ventures.

CHARACTERISTICS OF LIMITED PARTNERSHIPS

A **limited partnership** is a special form of partnership in which certain partners, called **limited partners**, enjoy limited liability; their liability is limited to the funds they have invested or otherwise have put at risk in the limited partnership.[14] The limited partners are passive investors like the stockholders of a corporation. But a limited partnership, like partnerships generally, does not pay income taxes; income or losses for tax purposes flow through to the partners. Thus, a firm that plans a tax-intensive investment, such as oil and gas drilling, but believes it will not have sufficient taxable income to utilize fully the tax deductions and tax credits of the venture, could form a limited partnership to flow the tax benefits through to the investors. Particularly in risky projects like oil exploration, these tax benefits can offer a substantial inducement to individual investors to share the investment risks inherent in such projects. In recent years, many companies formed publicly traded **master limited partnerships**, rather than incorporating new subsidiaries, in order to avoid corporate taxation or, in the case of ventures that were incurring losses for tax purposes, in order to let the investors benefit from these tax losses directly.[15]

The limited partnership is operated by a **general partner**, who is responsible for the liabilities of the limited partnership (except for those liabilities specifically assumed or guaranteed by the limited partners). The general partner often invests only a small percentage of the total equity of the limited partnership, typically between 1% and 10% for limited partnerships that are sold to individual investors. Income, losses, tax credits, and distributions are allocated among the partners in accordance with a sharing formula specified at the time the limited partnership is formed. Typically, cash is distributed between the general partner and the limited partners in proportion to their respective equity investments until the limited partners have recovered their capital. Thereafter, the percentage of cash allocated to the general partner increases, often substantially. For example, Cinema Group Partners was formed in 1981. The general partner contributed 10% of the partnership capital. The limited partners were promised 98% of profits, losses, tax credits, and cash distributions until they had recovered their investment; thereafter, 80% until they had received cash representing in the aggregate 200% of their investment; thereafter, 70% until they had received cash representing in the aggregate of 300% of their investment; and 60% of any subsequent cash distributions.[16] In addition, the general partner typically receives a management fee, which was calculated as 4% of the

[14] For example, the limited partners might guarantee a portion of the limited partnership's debt to increase the amount of funds they have "at risk" and thereby increase the amount of partnership losses they can deduct for tax purposes.

[15] Collins and Bey (1986) note that the tax advantages of the limited partnership form relative to the corporate form of organization are greatest for companies with high tax rates and low retention rates (i.e., those in "mature" industries) and may be negative for very rapidly growing companies that need to reinvest all their earnings and have low corporate tax rates. The Revenue Act of 1987 essentially eliminated the tax advantage of the master limited partnership except in the natural resource extraction and oil and gas pipeline industries.

[16] Cinema Group Partners, prospectus, April 17, 1981, 4.

limited partnership's net worth in the case of the Cinema Group Partners limited partnership.

The provisions of the Internal Revenue Code relating to partnership taxation are very complex and a discussion of the tax consequences to the limited partners is beyond the scope of this book. Nevertheless, it is important to appreciate that the terms of the limited partnership, in particular the formula for sharing income, losses, tax benefits, and cash distributions, must be designed so as to provide prospective limited partners an acceptable *after-tax rate of return* on their investment.

TYPES OF LIMITED PARTNERSHIP STRUCTURES   Aside from master limited partnerships (which are really corporations in disguise), there are two basic types of limited partnership structures, depending on whether tax-loss-seeking individual investors or institutional investors are being solicited, that is, the market for limited partnership interests is segmented to a certain degree. These two classes of investors have different investment objectives, appear to exhibit different attitudes toward risk, and appear to differ in their sensitivity to agency costs. Table 21-4 compares their preferences. The economic characteristics of the investment will determine to a large extent whether it is more appropriate for individual or institutional limited partnership financing. Once that decision has been made, the limited partnership must be structured accordingly.

In general, individual investors are more tax-motivated than institutional investors. They look for tax deductions in the early years for the return of their invest-

TABLE 21-4 Comparison of Investor Preferences in Retail and Institutional Limited Partnerships

	Retail/Individual	**Institutional**
Tax Benefits of Ownership	Tax deductions and tax credits of ownership represent a very important factor. Retail limited partnerships are typically tax-driven, as for example, in oil and gas limited partnerships.	Attribute relatively little value to tax deductions and tax credits of ownership in most cases. Institutional investors typically have lower income tax rates than individual investors so that tax benefits are less valuable to institutions.
Rate of Return Objective	Typically look for an after-tax rate of return in the range from 15% to 25% per annum, depending on the nature of the partnership's investment.	Typically look for a target rate of return exceeding 20% per annum on a cash basis and often require a minimum rate of return equal to their own "prime" lending rates.
Sharing of Investment Returns	Willing to contribute as much as 99% of limited partnership capital and to accept heavy promotion by sponsors provided the limited partners' rate of return objective is met.	Want the sponsor to have a substantial economic interest (e.g., at least 25% to 50%) and also want proportionate distribution of economic benefits between sponsor and outside investors.
Investment Income Stream Profile	Want tax deductions in early years to cover the cost of the investment and are willing to wait several years for cash payout, as for example, in real estate limited partnerships.	Willing to invest cash up front but want cash income stream over the life of the investment.
Tolerance for Risk-Bearing	Because investors look to tax deductions in the early years for the full recovery of their investment, retail limited partnerships can invest in riskier projects than institutional limited partnerships, as for example, research and development partnerships.	Lower tolerance for bearing economic risks than retail investors because institutional investors' returns are more dependent on the profitability of the partnership's investment—and less dependent on tax deductions—than in the case of a retail limited partnership.

ment. They are more willing than institutional investors to wait until the later years for actual cash distributions provided the flow of tax benefits is adequate. Institutional investors exhibit a lower tolerance for bearing project economic risks than individual investors, appear to be more sensitive to agency costs, and prefer limited partnership investments that will afford more or less regular cash distributions throughout the productive life of the project.

Thus, tax-intensive limited partnership investments, such as those in oil and gas exploration, film-making, or research and development, are marketed almost exclusively to individual investors. They are designed so as to channel the bulk of the available tax deductions and tax credits to investors. They are also designed in such a way that the limited partners bear a substantial share of the economic risks of the project the limited partnership finances.

Limited partnerships that do not involve special tax incentives (e.g., oil depletion deductions or energy tax credits) are typically marketed to institutional investors. In order to reduce agency costs to a tolerable level, institutions normally require (1) a significant equity investment by the general partner(s), (2) the promise of regular cash distributions over the life of the project comparable to what they would earn on a bond investment of the same magnitude as its investment in the limited partnership and (3) a "fair sharing" of the economic risks and rewards associated with the investment. This fair sharing is governed by the provisions of the partnership agreement which places certain restrictions on project sponsors.

MEASURING THE COST OF LIMITED PARTNER CAPITAL

A corporation that sets up a limited partnership and serves as general partner effectively experiences the following cash flow benefits and costs:

- Initial cash inflow equal to the net proceeds from the sale of units of limited partnership interest.

- Annual cash inflows equal to the taxes payable on the portion of partnership taxable income allocated to the limited partners.

- Initial cash outflow equal to the amount of the investment tax credit, if any, allocated to the limited partners.

- Annual cash outflows equal to (1) the cash distributions to the limited partners plus (2) the tax shield resulting from the portion of partnership losses for tax purposes allocated to the limited partners.

- Terminal cash outflow equal to the residual value of the limited partnership's assets allocated to the limited partners.

In addition, if the limited partnership borrows funds with lenders having recourse to the general partner (but not the limited partners) for payment of interest and repayment of principal, such financing impinges upon the general partner's debt capacity. This imposes a cost, like that experienced in connection with leasing, equal to the value of the tax credits forgone as a result of this loss of debt capacity.

EXAMPLE ■ We consider here the impact of limited partnership financing on an all-equity basis. The calculations in the leveraged case are performed similarly. Table 21-5 illustrates the incremental cash flows associated with financing a new cable television system through a limited partnership that the general partner intends to terminate after 10 years. The financing involves the sale of $50 million of units of limited partnership interest that raises $45 million net of issuance expenses. The general

TABLE 21-5   Calculation of Cost of Limited Partner Capital (Dollar Amounts in Millions)

End of Year	(1) Net Proceeds of Financing[a]	(2) Partnership Operating Cash Flow	(3) Partnership Taxable Income[b]	(4) Distribution to Limited Partners[c]	(5) Tax on Income (Loss) Forgone[d]	(6) Residual Value Forgone[e]	(7) Net Cash Flow to Sponsor[f]
0	$45.0	—	—	—	—	—	$45.00
1	—	$1.5	−$3.5	$1.35	−$1.26	—	−2.61
2	—	3.0	−2.0	2.70	−0.72	—	−3.42
3	—	3.5	−1.5	3.15	−0.54	—	−3.69
4	—	7.0	2.0	6.30	0.72	—	−5.58
5	—	10.0	5.0	9.00	1.80	—	−7.20
6	—	12.0	7.0	10.80	2.52	—	−8.28
7	—	14.0	9.0	12.60	3.24	—	−9.36
8	—	16.0	11.0	9.82	2.70	—	−7.12
9	—	17.5	12.5	8.75	2.50	—	−6.25
10	—	19.0	14.0	9.50	2.80	$51.30	−58.00

Cost of limited partner capital[g] = 12.88%

[a] Calculated as gross proceeds of $50 million less 10% issuance expenses.
[b] Calculated as operating cash flow less straight-line depreciation amounting to $5 million per year.
[c] Calculated as 90% of operating cash flow until limited partners recover their $50 million investment (during year 8) and 50% of operating cash flow thereafter.
[d] Taxes payable (credit) by the general partner if the income allocated to the limited partners had instead been included in its income. Limited partners are allocated the same percentage of partnership taxable income as their percentage of partnership operating cash flow. Amount is calculated by multiplying column 3 by allocation percentage and by the tax rate: for year 3, $-1.5 \times .9 \times .4 = -.54$.
[e] Assumes the cable television system is sold for 9 times year 10 operating cash flow, or $171.0 million. Residual value is net of taxes (at a 40% marginal rate) on the half of terminal value that is forgone.
[f] Calculated as the net proceeds of financing plus tax on income (loss) forgone less distribution to limited partners less also residual value forgone.
[g] Calculated as the internal rate of return of the net cash flow stream.

partner will invest $5 million for a 10% ownership interest. The limited partnership agreement calls for the limited partners to pay all the issuance expenses and contribute 90% of partnership capital; to receive 90% of partnership income, losses, tax credits (if any), and cash distributions until they have received aggregate cash distributions equal to their original $50 million investment; and to receive 50% of partnership income, losses, tax credits (if any), and cash distributions thereafter. Allocating taxable income to limited partners eliminates corporate taxation of the allocated income. The sponsor's marginal ordinary income tax rate is 40%.

The initial cash flow is the $45 million inflow representing the net proceeds from the sale of the units of limited partnership interest (column 1). Each annual cash flow thereafter (column 7) except the last year's is equal to the amount of income taxes saved (tax credits lost) on the portion of partnership income (loss) allocated to the limited partners (column 5) less the cash distributions to limited partners (column 4). Note that in year 8 the limited partners reach $50 million in aggregate cash distributions after the payment of $4.1 million that year. The $4.1 million payment represents 90% of $4.56 million. The remaining $11.44 million of year 8 operating cash flow is divided equally between the general partner and the limited partners, giving the limited partners total cash distributions of $9.82 (= 4.1 + 5.72) million for the year. It is assumed in Table 21-5 that the limited partnership sells the cable television system for nine times the last year's operating cash flow, or $171 million, half of which it must distribute to the limited partners. The general partner thus forgoes $85.5 million. Since the cable television system has been fully depreciated, there is a $171 million gain on the transaction, half of which is borne by the limited partners. After-tax residual value forgone (column 6) is therefore $51.3 million (= [0.6]85.5).

The cost of limited partner capital (i.e., raised from the limited partners) (CLPC) is just the discount rate that equates the present value of the cash outflows in Table 21-5 to the initial $45 million cash inflow:

$$NP = \sum_{t=1}^{T} \frac{CF_t}{(1 + CLPC)^t} = \$45.0 \text{ million} \qquad CLPC = 12.88\% \qquad \textbf{(21.7)}$$

In Equation (21.7), NP denotes the net proceeds from the limited partnership financing, CF_t denotes the net cash flow in year t, CLPC is the cost of limited partner capital, and T is the term of the limited partnership. Equation (21.7) is just the standard approach to measuring the cost of funds from a particular financing source. As before, the formula is adjusted according to the frequency with which the net cash flows occur.

The cost of limited partner capital in Equation (21.7) should be compared with the unleveraged required rate of return for the project because limited partnership financing in this case represents an alternative to all-equity financing. For example, if the capital investment project has a 15% unleveraged required rate of return, limited partnership financing is cheaper than all-equity financing. Alternatively, limited partnership financing will be cheaper than all-equity financing if the net present value of the net cash flow stream is positive when the unleveraged required rate of return is used as the discount rate. That is, the cost of raising common equity capital (the unleveraged required rate of return) represents the opportunity cost, or cost associated with the 'next best' alternative, in this case. Discounting the net cash flows in Table 21-5 at a 15% rate gives a net present value of NPV = $5,408,796. The positive net present value indicates that limited partnership financing is cheaper than financing with the general partner's common equity. It reflects the benefits realized by eliminating a layer of taxation. ∎

The cost of limited partner capital depends importantly on the limited partners' tax position and on the asset's residual value. In particular, the higher the tax rate on the limited partner's income, the greater the value of the tax credits transferred to them. Hence, the lower is likely to be the corporation's cost of raising funds through limited partnership financing. In addition, the lower the portion of residual value that needs to be allocated to limited partners, the lower becomes the cost of funds, as was the case with lease financing. Similarly, if the residual value proves to be unexpectedly high, so will the cost of limited partnership financing.

ADVANTAGES AND DISADVANTAGES OF LIMITED PARTNERSHIP FINANCING

Limited partnership financing provides an alternative means of "selling" the tax deductions and tax credits associated with asset ownership. Because the value of these tax benefits depends on the timing of their realization, selling them through a limited partnership can lower the financing costs for a firm that cannot claim them currently. As in the case of lease financing, limited partnership financing can be mutually beneficial to the firm and to the investor when the investor pays income tax at a higher marginal rate than the firm. In that case, the tax benefits of asset ownership are more valuable to the investor even when both can claim them on a timely basis.

Also as in the case of lease financing, the firm must sacrifice a portion of the asset's residual value. When the forgone residual value is taken into account, limited partnership financing may prove to be more expensive than conventional equity financing.

In contrast to lease financing, limited partnership financing can also be advantageous to profitable companies. A partnership is nontaxable. Organizing a project (or a business) as a limited partnership, rather than having a corporation own it, eliminates a layer of taxation. Achieving such tax reduction was one of the principal motives that led to the formation of publicly-traded master limited partnerships.[17] While recent tax legislation has essentially eliminated the tax advantages that master limited partnerships used to afford, the elimination of a layer of taxation may still be accomplished through a private limited partnership (i.e., one with fewer than 35 limited partners and whose limited partnership units are not registered with the Securities and Exchange Commission).

FINANCING CORPORATE REAL ESTATE   21.6

Corporate real estate represents a significant component of companies' asset portfolios yet one that most companies do not manage actively.[18] As many companies discovered during the 1974–1975 liquidity crisis, corporate real estate represents a store of value that can provide substantial borrowing power during difficult periods. In 1974–1975, companies found sale-and-lease-back financing of their corporate headquarters buildings and certain other facilities to be a cheaper source of financing than borrowing on their general credit.

CRITICAL FACTORS IN CORPORATE REAL ESTATE FINANCING There are two important aspects to the financing of corporate real estate. First, at the time it builds a facility a firm must decide whether to finance the facility on its general credit and own it or instead to lease the facility. The lease-versus-borrow-and-construct decision involves the same principal considerations as the lease-versus-borrow-and-buy decision just discussed in connection with machinery and equipment investments. The tax considerations are different because there are special provisions of the tax code that apply to real estate. Nevertheless, a firm must still decide whether it should, in effect, sell project-related tax deductions, tax credits, and the asset's residual value.

Second, if the firm decides to borrow and construct, it must decide whether to borrow on its general credit or to arrange mortgage financing. This is basically the decision as to whether to use secured financing or unsecured financing. But more important, mortgage financing can typically be arranged on a non-recourse basis to cover up to 70% to 80% of the cost of the facility. Thus, mortgage financing may reduce the firm's operating flexibility with respect to the facility but have a smaller impact on the firm's debt capacity than borrowing on the firm's general credit. In addition, if the cost of the facility is financed on the firm's general credit, the firm's

---

[17] Collins and Bey (1986).

[18] Zeckhauser and Silverman (1983) estimate that real estate represents 25% of the assets of American companies, worth in the aggregate between $700 billion and $1,400 billion, but that only 20% of American corporations manage their real estate for profit.

ability to arrange sale-and-lease-back financing in the future provides an option, thus giving the firm additional future financing flexibility.

SIGNIFICANCE OF MORTGAGE FINANCING   Mortgage financing may facilitate a lower cost of debt and a higher degree of leverage than a firm's financing on its general credit. In evaluating a proposed capital investment project that contains a significant amount of real estate for which mortgage financing can be arranged on attractive terms, the adjusted-present-value approach can be used in order to factor into the evaluation any special benefits attributable to mortgage financing. In particular, the present value of any interest cost savings plus the present value of the tax credits that result from financing with higher-than-the-firm's-overall degree of leverage will increase the project's adjusted present value.[19]

SOLUTION TO WESTERN'S LEASE-OR-BUY DECISION

Western should lease the electric shovels only if leasing will increase its shareholders' wealth. The net advantage to leasing depends on two critical factors: Western's ability to claim the tax benefits of asset ownership on a timely basis and the amount of the residual value Western forgoes as a result of leasing.

We found in the text that the net advantage to Western of leasing an electric shovel is negative ($-\$54,236$) if Western can utilize the tax benefits of asset ownership fully. But if Western can never utilize these tax benefits, the net advantage to leasing is $\$40,685$. Therefore, Western must evaluate its likely future ability to realize the tax benefits of asset ownership before it can reach the buy-or-lease decision.

SUMMARY

A firm can finance a project either on its general credit, by promising investors and/ or lenders a share of the future cash flow from its entire portfolio of assets, or on an asset-based basis, by promising providers of capital a share of the future cash flow from a discrete (set of) asset(s). Asset-based financing techniques include leasing, various forms of project financing, limited partnership financing, and real estate mortgage financing.

Lease financing involves an extended rental agreement under which the lessor grants the lessee the exclusive right to use the asset for a specified period in return for a series of fixed lease payments, the right to claim certain tax deductions and tax credits of ownership, and the right to realize at least a specified portion of the asset's residual value at the end of the lease term. Lease financing can be mutually advantageous to both lessor and lessee when the parties are taxed at different rates, or when the lessor is better able to bear the risks of obsolescence of the leased items than the lessee. In the case of short-term cancelable operating leases, the lessee benefits from the cancellation option. In addition, lease financing often affords certain

---

[19] It is important, of course, to distinguish between the project's leverage and the contribution of the project to the firm's debt capacity. As discussed in Chapter 19, a firm may decide to finance a particular asset with, say, 90% debt when it customarily employs, say, 50% debt. The present value of the tax credits attributable to the incremental 40% debt should be added to the project's adjusted present value only if 90% debt financing does not require less than 50% debt financing of other projects. To the extent it does adversely affect the leverage achievable for other projects, the cost of the loss of debt capacity for other projects should be subtracted from the adjusted present value of the project that is 90% debt-financed.

DECISION SUMMARY BOX

- Asset-based financing should be utilized only if it increases shareholder wealth.
- Lease financing is equivalent to borrowing to buy the asset. The decision whether to lease must therefore be evaluated relative to the borrow-and-buy alternative, while neutralizing the capital structure side effects.
- Lease financing can be cheaper than conventional secured debt financing for a firm due to a potential tax asymmetry. Lease financing will have a positive net advantage only if the net present value of the net cash flows to the lessee is positive, or equivalently, only if the lease financing provides a greater amount of funds to the lessee than an equivalent loan.
- Lease financing may be beneficial when the lessor is better able to bear the risks of asset obsolescence than the lessee, as may be the case with lessor/manufacturers of high technology assets such as computers.
- Project financing should be considered whenever a capital investment project (1) consists of a discrete asset (or set of assets) *and* (2) has a positive

expected net present value *and* (3) is so large relative to the sponsor's existing asset portfolio that pursuing it alone would increase the sponsor's risk of bankruptcy to an unacceptable level.
- Project financing should also be considered whenever there is a readily identifiable set of purchasers for the project's output who would be willing to enter into contractual commitments against which the sponsor could borrow funds for the project on a non-recourse basis.
- Limited partnership financing can be cheaper than conventional equity financing for a firm that cannot utilize fully the tax benefits of asset ownership or for a profitable firm that can operate a portion of its business in a separate partnership entity and thereby eliminate corporate taxation of the separate entity's income. Limited partnership financing will have a positive net advantage to a firm only if the net present value of the net cash flows to the firm is positive when discounted at the firm's cost of capital for equivalent conventional financing, in particular, the unleveraged cost of equity capital in the case of a limited partnership with no debt.

advantages over secured lending to providers of capital in the event of bankruptcy. The sale of the tax deductions and tax credits of asset ownership is principally responsible for the widespread use of lease financing.

Lease financing displaces conventional debt. Lease financing should therefore be analyzed as an alternative to borrowing to buy the asset, while neutralizing any capital structure side-effects.

Project financing is generally possible when a project involves a discrete (set of) asset(s) that is capable of standing alone as an independent economic unit. Project loans are designed to be self-liquidating from the project's cash flow. Designing a project financing requires careful financial engineering to allocate the project-related risks among the parties who will bear them at the lowest cost, allocating the project's economic rewards in a manner commensurate with the allocation of project risks, and minimize total agency costs. Under certain circumstances, project financing can lead to more efficient risk-sharing, expanded debt capacity for the project's sponsor(s), and a lower overall cost of funds than direct financing by the project's sponsor(s).

Limited partnership financing provides an alternative means of "selling" the tax benefits of asset ownership. A limited partnership is a special form of partnership in which certain partners, called limited partners, receive a share of partnership profits, losses, tax credits (if any), and cash distributions but enjoy limited liability (just like the shareholders of a corporation). Whereas leasing represents a form of debt financing, limited partnership financing represents a form of equity financing.

Corporate real estate represents a store of value that can serve as collateral to support corporate borrowing. During the 1974–1975 liquidity crisis, many companies found that real estate mortgage financing could be accomplished on terms more favorable than conventional debenture financing.

PROBLEMS

PROBLEM SET A

A1. Define the terms **lease**, **lessor**, and **lessee**. What is the relationship between a lessor and a lessee?

A2. Explain the principal differences between a **direct lease**, a **sale-and-lease-back**, and a **leveraged lease**.

A3. What are the principal advantages and principal disadvantages of lease financing? Which of the purported advantages are really of dubious value?

A4. Explain why a dollar of lease financing displaces a dollar of conventional debt financing.

A5. What are the principal tax benefits associated with asset ownership?

A6. What requirements must a lease satisfy to qualify as a **true lease** for tax purposes?

A7. Describe how the **net advantage to leasing** is measured.

A8. What is the appropriate discount rate to use in calculating the present value of the incremental after-tax cash flows associated with a lease financing? Why is the expected residual value of the asset discounted at a higher rate?

A9. In the Western Metals and Mining Corporation example, suppose the lease rate is $1.7 million payable annually in arrears, the cost of secured debt is 11%, and the required rate of return for the project is 14% assuming Western's tax rate is 40% and 17% assuming Western's tax rate is zero. The depreciation schedule and residual value are unchanged.
    a. Calculate the net advantage to leasing assuming Western's tax rate is 40%. Should Western lease, or borrow and buy?
    b. Calculate the net advantage to leasing assuming Western will never be able to utilize the tax deductions associated with asset ownership. Should Western lease, or borrow and buy?

A10. a. Explain the equivalent-loan approach to the lease-versus-borrow-and-buy decision.
    b. An asset costs $25 million. If it is leased for a 5-year period, the net cash flow to lessee is $20 million at the end of year 0, −$10 million at the end of year 1, and −$7 million at the end of each of years 2 through 5. The company's pretax cost of secured debt is 10% and its tax rate is 34%. Calculate the amount of the equivalent loan.

A11. Allied Metals Inc. is considering leasing $1 million worth of manufacturing equipment under a lease that would require annual lease payments in arrears for 5 years. The net cash flow to lessee over the term of the lease (with zero residual value) is:

Year	0	1	2	3	4	5
Net cash flow ($000)	1,000	−300	−275	−250	−225	−200

Allied's cost of secured debt is 12%, and its cost of capital is 16%. Allied pays taxes at a 34% marginal rate.
    a. Calculate the net advantage to leasing.
    b. Calculate the internal rate of return for the lease.

c. Calculate the amount of the equivalent loan for the proposed Allied lease.

d. Should Allied lease, or borrow and buy?

A12. Define the term **project financing**. Under what circumstances is project financing an appropriate method of financing a capital investment project?

A13. Explain how the contract provisions in a project financing debt instrument can be designed so as to cover the following contingencies:

a. completion risk

b. technological risk

c. economic risk

d. raw material supply risk

e. force majeure risk

A14. What are the principal advantages and disadvantages of project financing?

A15. What do lease financing and limited partnership financing have in common?

A16. What are the two basic types of limited partnership structures? Describe the distinguishing features of each and explain how each type of partnership is designed to suit the preferences of a particular class of investors.

A17. Suppose the cable television limited partnership discussed in the text instead enabled the limited partners to receive 90% of partnership income, losses, tax credits, and cash distributions for the life of the limited partnership. Calculate the cost of limited partner capital.

PROBLEM SET B

B1. Leasing enables a company to acquire the use of an asset just as a cash purchase would. So the asset acquisition/lease decision should be evaluated by using the lessee's required rate of return for the asset as the discount rate. But lease financing displaces conventional debt financing. So the asset acquisition/lease decision should be evaluated by using the lessee's cost of secured debt as the discount rate. How would you resolve these apparently contradictory arguments?

B2. A lessor purchases an asset and immediately enters into an agreement to lease the asset to another company. Because the lease obligation is a form of secured debt obligation, should the lessee's cost of secured debt (as determined in the capital market) be used in the analysis of the net advantage to the lessor of entering into the lease? Alternatively, because the lessor must finance its purchase of the asset somehow, should the lessor instead use its own cost of capital in evaluating the net advantage to the lessor of entering into the lease?

B3. Lake Trolley Company is considering whether to lease or buy a new trolley that costs $25,000. The trolley can be depreciated straight-line over an 8-year period to an estimated residual value of $5,000. Lake Trolley's cost of 8-year secured debt is 12% and its required rate of return for the project is 16% after-tax and 20% pretax. National Trolley Leasing Corporation has offered to lease the trolley to Lake Trolley in return for annual payments of $5,000 payable at the end of each year.

a. Specify the incremental cash flow stream associated with the lease assuming Lake Trolley's marginal income tax rate is 40%.

b. Calculate the net advantage to leasing assuming Lake Trolley's tax rate is 40%. Should Lake Trolley lease, or borrow and buy?

c. Calculate the net advantage to leasing assuming Lake Trolley's tax rate is zero. Should Lake Trolley lease, or borrow and buy?

d. How would your answers to parts b and c change if the residual value at the end of 8 years is $500?

B4. Show how to modify Equations (21.2), (21.3), and (21.4) to reflect the timing of lease payments when the lease calls for payments *at the beginning* of each year.

B5. New Horizon Natural Food Company is considering whether to lease a delivery truck. A leasing company has offered to lease the truck, which costs $35,000, under a 5-year lease that calls for annual payments of $7,850 *at the beginning* of each year. New Horizon could depreciate the truck to $5,000 at the end of 5 years on a straight-line basis and claim depreciation tax deductions at the beginning of each year. Its marginal tax rate is 34%; its cost of 5-year secured debt is 10%; and its required rate of return for the project is 12% after-tax and 16% pretax.
  a. Should New Horizon lease the truck, or borrow and buy?
  b. Suppose instead that New Horizon does not expect to pay income taxes in the foreseeable future. Should New Horizon lease the truck, or borrow and buy?
  c. How do you reconcile your answers to parts a and b?

B6. Neighborhood Savings Bank is considering leasing $100,000 worth of computer equipment under a 4–year lease that calls for payments in advance of $22,000 per year. The bank does not currently pay income taxes and does not expect to have to pay income taxes in the foreseeable future. If the bank purchased the computer equipment, it would depreciate the equipment on a straight-line basis down to an estimated salvage value of $20,000 at the end of the fourth year. The bank's cost of secured debt is 14%, and its cost of capital is 20%.
  a. Calculate the net advantage to leasing.
  b. Calculate the amount of the equivalent loan.
  c. Calculate the internal rate of return for the lease.

B7. William Burn, the president of Surf-side Beer Distributors of Salina, Kansas, has decided that his firm must acquire a new machine which costs $800,000. The firm's corporate borrowing rate is 12%. The machine can be leased for $110,000 per year for its 10-year life. If the company leases it gets no salvage value. If it owns, the expected salvage value is $50,000. Maintenance costs will be the same whether Surf-side leases or buys. The company uses straight-line depreciation (to the salvage value), and its tax rate is 40%. Can you help Will out by showing him which is better, leasing or buying?

B8. Empire Excavation Company plans to acquire a fleet of 10 dump trucks. Each truck costs $75,000. Empire can borrow $750,000 on a secured basis at a pretax cost of 14%. The dump trucks can be depreciated for tax purposes on a straight-line basis to zero over a 5-year useful life. Truck Leasing Corp. has offered to lease the fleet of trucks to Empire under a 5-year lease that calls for lease payments of $190,000 at the end of each year. Empire estimates that forgone residual value would be $10,000 per truck (net of taxes). Empire's tax rate is 34%. Its cost of capital is 16%.
  a. Calculate the stream of net cash flow to Empire under the lease financing.
  b. Calculate the net advantage to leasing.
  c. Calculate the amount of the equivalent loan.
  d. Should Empire lease, or borrow and buy? Justify your answer.

B9. A 3-year lease entails the following stream of net cash flow (in millions of dollars) to the lessee: $10.5, −$3.0, −$5.0, −$5.0. The lessee's pretax cost of secured debt is 13%, and the lessee does not pay taxes and does not expect to become a taxpayer in the near future. The item will have zero residual value at the end of the lease term.

   a. Calculate the net advantage to leasing. Is leasing advantageous?

   b. Calculate the amount of the equivalent loan.

   c. Calculate the IRR of the lease.

   d. Do the three approaches yield consistent results? Explain why you would normally expect them to yield consistent results.

B10. A lease calls for payments of $1 million at the end of each of the next 5 years and payments of $2 million at the end of each of the following 5 years. The asset to be leased costs $10 million and can be depreciated in the following manner to a residual value of $500,000 at the end of the lease term:

Year	1	2	3	4	5	6	7	8	9	10
Depreciation (000)	2,000	1,750	1,500	1,250	1,000	400	400	400	400	400

The lessee's marginal income tax rate is currently 40%. Its cost of 10-year secured debt is 12.5%. Its required rate of return for the project is 15% after-tax and 17.5% pretax.

   a. Calculate the net advantage to leasing.

   b. How would your answer to part a change if the lessee did not expect to pay any income taxes for the next 3 years but to pay income taxes each year thereafter at a 40% rate? (*Hint*: Any tax losses in years 1–3 can be carried forward and realized in year 4.)

B11. Amalgamated Leasing Corp. would like to submit a leasing proposal to the Johnson Hardware Manufacturing Company. Johnson has asked to lease $5 million worth of equipment under a 6-year lease. Amalgamated can depreciate the equipment for tax purposes on a straight-line basis over the 6-year term to an estimated residual value of $250,000. The leasing company's income tax rate is 40%. Amalgamated has estimated Johnson's 6-year cost of funds to be 10% for fully secured debt (120% collateralized) and 12% for unsecured debt and has estimated the required after-tax rate of return for an investment in the assets to be 15%.

   a. Calculate Amalgamated's break-even lease rate.

   b. If Johnson pays income taxes at a 30% rate, calculate Johnson's net advantage to leasing at Amalgamated's break-even lease rate.

   c. Calculate Johnson's break-even lease rate.

   d. Is it possible for Amalgamated and Johnson to find a mutually beneficial lease rate?

B12. The Light Rock Cafe plans to raise capital to finance a new restaurant through the sale of limited partnership interests. The company, as general partner, plans to raise $5.25 million of which $5 million will be invested in the restaurant and the balance will be used to pay issuance expenses. The assets can be depreciated to zero over 8 years on a straight-line basis. The partnership will be terminated at the end of 8 years, at which time the general partner will buy out the limited partners at a price equal to 7 times the last year's operating cash flow. The projected operating cash flow for the partnership is:

Year	1	2	3	4	5	6	7	8
Cash flow ($ thousands)	250	1,000	1,500	2,000	2,250	2,500	2,750	3,000

The limited partners will be entitled to receive 75% of each year's partnership income, losses, tax credits (if any), and cash distributions, and they will also be entitled to receive 75% of the residual value. The Light Rock Cafe will not invest cash but will contribute its name and "know-how" (i.e., its experience) to the project in return for a 25% ownership interest. Assume the general partner's marginal ordinary income tax rate is 40%. Calculate the cost of limited partner capital.

PROBLEM SET C

C1. The **break–even tax rate** is the income tax rate for the lessee that would make the lessee indifferent between leasing an asset on the one hand and borrowing and buying it on the other.

   a. Calculate the break–even tax rate for the Lake Trolley Company in problem B3 under the assumption that the residual value is $500.

   b. If the statutory income tax rate is 40% and is expected to remain 40% for the foreseeable future, how would you give the break–even tax rate a practical interpretation?

C2. The lessor can claim the tax deductions associated with asset ownership and realize the leased asset's residual value. In return, the lessor must pay tax on the rental income.

   a. Explain why a financial lease represents a secured loan in which the lender's entire debt service stream is taxable as ordinary income to the lessor/lender.

   b. In view of this tax cost, what tax condition must hold in order for a financial lease transaction to generate positive net present value tax benefits for lessor and lessee combined?

   c. Suppose the lease payments in Table 21–1 must be made in advance, not arrears. (Assume that the timing of the lease payment tax deductions/obligations changes accordingly but the timing of the depreciation tax deductions does not change). Show that the net advantage to leasing for Western must decrease as a result. Explain why this reduction occurs.

   d. Show that if Western is nontaxable, the net advantage to leasing for Western is negative and greater in absolute value than the net advantage of the lease to the lessor.

   e. Either find a lease rate that will give the financial lease a positive net advantage for both lessor and lessee, or else show that no such lease rate exists.

   f. Explain what your answer to part e implies about the tax costs and tax benefits of the financial lease when lease payments are made in advance.

C3. Derive Equation (21.4) from the debt service parity principle.

C4. Let C denote the cost of equipment, L the amount of each annual lease payment, T_R the lessor's marginal income tax rate, T_E the lessee's marginal income tax rate, and D the lessee's marginal cost of secured debt. Consider a 2-year lease with lease payments in advance, tax depreciation calculated on a straight-line basis (tax deductions realized at year end), and zero residual value.

   a. Show that the net present value of the lease to the lessor, NPV_R, can be expressed as

$$NPV_R = -C + \frac{(1 - T_R)L[1 + (1 - T_R)D] + T_R C/2}{(1 - T_R)D} \left\{ 1 - \left[\frac{1}{1 + (1 - T_R)D} \right]^2 \right\}$$

   b. Show that the net present value of the lease to the lessee, NPV_E, can be expressed as

$$NPV_E = +C - \frac{(1 - T_E)L[1 + (1 - T_E)D] + T_E C/2}{(1 - T_E)D} \left\{ 1 - \left[\frac{1}{1 + (1 - T_E)D} \right]^2 \right\}$$

c. If $T_E = T_R$, is leasing a zero-sum game? Might there be other reasons to lease?

d. If $T_E = 0 < T_R$, is it possible to find a lease payment L for which $NPV_R > 0$ and $NPV_E > 0$ hold simultaneously?

e. Suppose instead that lease payments are made in arrears each year. Recalculate NPV_R and NPV_E. Can you find an annual lease payment amount L for which $NPV_R > 0$ and $NPV_E > 0$ hold simultaneously when $T_R = .4$ and $T_E = 0$?

C5. A bank wishes to enter into an operating lease for certain equipment it needs because the lease obligation would not appear on the face of the bank's balance sheet in that case. The bank must maintain a ratio of capital-to-assets of 8%, and this ratio calculation ignores leases that qualify as opearating leases under generally accepted accounting principles.

a. If the bank's ratio of capital-to-assets is currently exactly 8%, explain why one dollar of capitalized lease obligations would displace one dollar of earning assets (i.e., loans or securities).

b. Explain how the net advantage to leasing through an operating lease should be calculated in order to reflect the avoidance of the capital constraint. How would you modify Equation (21.2)?

c. The Binghamton Thrift can lease $736,000 of office equipment under an operating lease that calls for monthly rental payments in arrears of $13,600 for each of 30 months followed by monthly rental payments in arrears of $16,600 each for an additional 30 months. The residual value of the equipment at the end of the lease term is expected to be 10% of its original cost. Binghamton Thrift's estimated cost of secured debt is 13% per annum, semiannually compounded, and the bank is not, and does not expect to become in the foreseeable future, a taxpayer. The bank earns a "spread" of 2% (marginal interest income minus interest payments) on each dollar of deposits that are loaned out to customers. Calculate the net advantage to leasing assuming the bank's capital-to-assets ratio currently equals the required minimum.

d. How would your answer to part c change if the bank's capital-to-assets ratio exceeds the required minimum by a wide margin?

REFERENCES

Anderson, Paul F., and John D. Martin. "Lease vs. Purchase Decisions: A Survey of Current Practice." *Financial Management* 6 (Spring 1977): 41–47.

Ang, James S., and Pamela P. Peterson. "The Leasing Puzzle." *Journal of Finance* 39 (September 1984): 1055–65.

Bower, Richard S. "Issues in Lease Financing." *Financial Management* 2 (Winter 1973): 25–34.

Bowman, Robert G. "The Debt Equivalence of Leases: An Empirical Investigation." *Accounting Review* 55 (April 1980): 237–53.

Brick, Ivan E., William K. H. Fung, and Marti Subrahmanyam. "Leasing Preferences." Unpublished manuscript, Graduate School of Management, Rutgers University, January 1990.

Collins, J. Markham, and Roger P. Bey. "The Master Limited Partnership: An Alternative to the Corporation." *Financial Management* 15 (Winter 1986): 5–14.

Crawford, Peggy J., Charles P. Harper, and John J. McConnell. "Further Evidence on the Terms of Financial Leases." *Financial Management* 10 (Autumn 1981): 7–14.

Doenges, R. Conrad. "The Cost of Leasing." *Engineering Economist* 17 (Fall 1971): 31–44.

Dyl, Edward A., and Stanley A. Martin, Jr. "Setting Terms for Leveraged Leasing." *Financial Management* 6 (Winter 1977): 20–27.

Elgers, Pieter T., and John J. Clark. *The Lease/Buy Decision.* New York: The Free Press, 1980.

Fabozzi, Frank J., and Uzi Yaari. "Valuation of Safe Harbor Tax Benefit Transfer Leases." *Journal of Finance* 38 (May 1983): 595–606.

Franks, Julian R., and Stewart D. Hodges. "Valuation of Financial Lease Contracts: A Note." *Journal of Finance* 33 (May 1978): 647–69.

Gritta, Richard D. "The Impact of the Capitalization of Leases on Financial Analysis." *Financial Analysts Journal* 30 (March–April 1974): 1–6.

Idol, Charles R. "A Note on Specifying Debt Displacement and Tax Shield Borrowing Opportunities in Financial Lease Valuation Models." *Financial Management* 9 (Summer 1980): 24–29.

Keller, Thomas F., and Russell J. Peterson. "Optimal Financial Structure, Cost of Capital, and the Lease-or-Buy Decision." *Journal of Business Finance and Accounting* 1 (Autumn 1974): 405–14.

Kensinger, John W., and John D. Martin. "Royalty Trusts, Master Partnerships, and Other Organizational Means of 'Unfirming' the Firm." *Midland Corporate Finance Journal* 4 (Summer 1986): 72–80.

Kim, E. Han, Wilbur G. Lewellen, and John J. McConnell. "Sale-and-Leaseback Agreements and Enterprise Valuation." *Journal of Financial and Quantitative Analysis* 13 (December 1978): 871–83.

Lee, Wayne Y., John D. Martin, and Andrew J. Senchack. "The Case for Using Options to Evaluate Salvage Values in Financial Leases." *Financial Management* 11 (Autumn 1982): 33–41.

Levy, Haim, and Marshall Sarnat. "Leasing, Borrowing, and Financial Risk." *Financial Management* 8 (Winter 1979): 47–54.

Lewellen, Wilbur G., and Douglas R. Emery. "On the Matter of Parity among Financial Obligations." *Journal of Finance* 36 (March 1981): 97–111.

Lewellen, Wilbur G., Michael S. Long, and John J. McConnell. "Asset Leasing in Competitive Capital Markets." *Journal of Finance* 31 (June 1976): 787–98.

Long, Michael S. "Leasing and the Cost of Capital." *Journal of Financial and Quantitative Analysis* 12 (November 1977): 579–86.

McConnell, John J., and James S. Schallheim. "Valuation of Asset Leasing Contracts." *Journal of Financial Economics* 12 (August 1983): 237–61.

Martin, John D., Paul F. Anderson, and Arthur J. Keown. "Lease Capitalization and Stock Price Stability: Implications for Accounting." *Journal of Accounting, Auditing and Finance* (Winter 1979): 151–63.

Miller, Merton H., and Charles W. Upton. "Leasing, Buying, and the Cost of Capital Services." *Journal of Finance* 31 (June 1976): 761–86.

Myers, Stewart C., David A. Dill, and Alberto J. Bautista. "Valuation of Financial Lease Contracts." *Journal of Finance* 31 (June 1976): 799–819.

Nevitt, Peter K. *Project Financing,* 2nd ed. San Francisco: Advanced Management Research, 1979.

Nevitt, Peter K., and Frank J. Fabozzi. *Equipment Leasing,* 3rd ed. Homewood, Ill.: Dow Jones-Irwin, 1988.

Phillips, Paul D., John C. Groth, and R. Malcolm Richards. "Financing the Alaskan Project: The Experience of Sohio." *Financial Management* 8 (Autumn 1979): 7–16.

Rice, Michael Downey. *Equipment Financing.* New York: Salomon Brothers, 1981.

Schall, Lawrence D. "The Lease-or-Buy and Asset Acquisition Decisions." *Journal of Finance* 29 (September 1974): 1203–14.

Schallheim, James S., Ramon E. Johnson, Ronald C. Lease, and John J. McConnell. "The Determinants of Yields on Financial Leasing Contracts." *Journal of Financial Economics* 19 (September 1987): 45–67.

Smith, Clifford W., Jr., and Lee M. Wakeman. "Determinants of Corporate Leasing Policy." *Journal of Finance* 40 (July 1985): 896–908.

Sorenson, Ivar W., and Ramon E. Johnson. "Equipment Financial Leasing Practices and Costs: An Empirical Study." *Financial Management* 6 (Spring 1977): 33–40.

Wynant, Larry. "Essential Elements of Project Financing." *Harvard Business Review* (May-June 1980): 165–73.

Zeckhauser, Sally, and Robert Silverman. "Rediscover Your Company's Real Estate." *Harvard Business Review* (January-February 1983): 111–17.

22

MERGERS AND ACQUISITIONS

Few financial events attract headlines quite the way a protracted "battle for control" of a very large firm does. On October 25, 1988, the front page of the *Wall Street Journal* carried an article headlined "Bidding War: Offers for RJR Pit KKR and Shearson in a Battle for Turf," which announced Kohlberg Kravis Roberts & Co.'s (KKR) bid for control of RJR Nabisco, Inc.[1] Five days earlier a management-led group had announced its intention to develop a proposal, in conjunction with Shearson Lehman Hutton Inc., to acquire RJR Nabisco in a leveraged buyout valued at $75 per common share. The KKR bid amounted to $90 per share. The battle for control unfolded over the ensuing 6-week period. It involved three bidding groups, no fewer than 10 of the leading investment banks, and a veritable army of lawyers, information agents, accountants, and commercial banks. KKR finally prevailed on November 30, 1988, when it offered to pay $109 per common share, 45% more than the management-led group's original proposal and a staggering aggregate bid of $25 billion, nearly twice the size of the previously largest takeover.[2]

When one firm (the **acquiror**) acquires another firm (the **acquiree**), it makes a capital investment. As with any capital investment, a firm should proceed only if the capital investment will increase shareholder wealth. The **acquisition** investment is often substantial in relation to the acquiror's size prior to the acquisition. Table 22-1 lists the 10 largest merger and acquisition transactions that have taken place in the United States. Because of its size, an acquisition can have a greater impact on shareholder wealth than other forms of capital investment. The analytical tools and basic decision rules of capital budgeting still apply, but particular care must be taken in applying these tools because of the enormous size and complexity of many corporate acquisitions. Buying a firm is more complicated than buying a piece of equipment. Benefits and costs are more difficult to quantify, and there are special legal, tax, and accounting considerations. Consequently, there are a number of other valuation techniques that are applied in practice to supplement discounted cash flow analysis and provide a check on the reasonableness of discounted cash valuations against the prices other companies have paid for acquisitions under comparable circumstances.

This chapter describes how to tailor the techniques of capital budgeting to corporate acquisitions. It also describes other valuation techniques, in particular comparative analysis, that are widely used in practice. The chapter illustrates how to apply these techniques by solving the following problem.

---

[1] "Bidding War: Offers for RJR Pit KKR and Shearson in a Battle for Turf," *Wall Street Journal*, October 25, 1988, 1ff. The article reported that Henry Kravis (the second K in KKR) had told representatives of Shearson that KKR, as the leading leveraged buyout firm, had to participate in the deal in order to protect its leveraged buyout "franchise."

[2] RJR Acquisition Corporation, Supplement to the Offer to Purchase, December 6, 1988. The skirmish for control of RJR Nabisco overshadowed the battle for control of Kraft Inc., which was concluded just after the bidding war for RJR Nabisco had commenced. Philip Morris Cos., RJR Nabisco's principal competitor in the tobacco business, prevailed and purchased Kraft at an aggregate cost of $13.1 billion.

TABLE 22-1 Ten Largest Merger and Acquisition Transactions in the United States[a] (Dollar Amounts in Billions)

Acquiring Company	Acquired Company	Approximate Price Paid[b]	Year Announced
Kohlberg Kravis Roberts & Co.	RJR Nabisco, Inc.	$24.6	1988
Chevron Corp.	Gulf Corp.	13.2	1984
Philip Morris Companies Inc.	Kraft Inc.	13.1	1988
Texaco Inc.	Getty Oil Co.	10.1	1984
DuPont Co.	Conoco Inc.	8.0	1981
British Petroleum Co.	Remaining 45% interest in Standard Oil of Ohio	7.8	1987
U.S. Steel Corp.	Marathon Oil Corp.	6.6	1981
Campeau Corp.	Federated Department Stores Inc.	6.5	1988
General Electric Corp.	RCA Corp.	6.0	1985
Mobil Corp.	Superior Oil Co.	5.7	1984

[a] As of year-end 1988.
[b] Based on the number of shares of common stock acquired.

Source: W. T. Grimm & Co., *Mergerstat Review 1988,* 41.

MONMOUTH'S ACQUISITION ALTERNATIVE

Monmouth Pharmaceuticals Company, a proprietary drug manufacturer with annual sales of $1.2 billion, is considering acquiring another publicly-traded proprietary drug manufacturer, Chicago Drugs Inc., which has annual sales of $600 million. The acquisition would not only increase Monmouth's sales by 50% but would lead to significant economies in marketing and could expand Monmouth's product line more quickly than Monmouth could by developing similar drugs on its own. The net benefit of the potential acquisition depends, of course, on how much Monmouth would have to pay to acquire Chicago Drugs. Monmouth's board of directors has asked the firm's chief financial officer to (1) determine a reasonable price to offer Chicago Drugs' shareholders, (2) estimate the impact on Monmouth's shareholders of making the acquisition at the recommended price, (3) determine the maximum price Monmouth could afford to pay, and (4) recommend the financial package that Monmouth should offer Chicago Drugs' shareholders.

In the chapter we will help Monmouth's chief financial officer respond to the board's request. But before doing that, we will need to explore the possible benefits and costs of a corporate acquisition. We will also review the special legal, tax, and accounting issues involved in corporate acquisitions.

There is one further consideration we have yet to mention that is important in corporate acquisitions: agency problems. How will the target respond? Under the Principle of Self-Interested Behavior, we would expect that management of the prospective acquiree will not normally sit by passively when an acquisition of "their" firm is proposed. In fact, corporate managers go to great lengths to erect barriers so as to forestall unwanted suitors from acquiring their companies (and perhaps eliminating their jobs in the process). We describe these measures and their potential impact on shareholder wealth.

Having said what we intend to do, we should also make clear something we would like to accomplish in the chapter but are unable to do. To date no one has succeeded in establishing a general theory of corporate acquisitions that is capable of explaining, among other things, the wide swings in aggregate merger activity. Figure 22-1 illustrates the cyclical pattern since 1968 but a similar cyclical pattern goes back to the turn of the century. However, there is a wealth of empirical evidence regarding the profitability of corporate acquisitions. We will review this evidence in the course of the chapter.

22.1   WHAT IS SPECIAL ABOUT A MERGER?

A **merger** involves a combination of two companies, the acquiror and the acquiree. The acquiror absorbs all the assets and liabilities of the acquiree and assumes the acquiree's business. The acquiree loses its independent existence, often becoming a subsidiary of the acquiror. A consolidation should be distinguished from a merger. In a **consolidation**, two (or more) companies combine to form an entirely new entity. The distinction between acquiror and acquiree becomes blurred because shares of each of the consolidated companies are exchanged for shares of the new firm. Each of the consolidating companies loses its independent existence, often becoming subsidiaries of the new firm or, in combination, becoming the new firm.

When two companies of roughly equal size combine, they often choose to consolidate. When they are of unequal size, one (usually, but not always, the larger of the two) **acquires** the other through merger. While the distinction between a merger and a consolidation is important in a legal sense, the same analytical techniques apply to both. Accordingly, we assume that one party to a corporate combination can be identified, or at least treated for analytical purposes, as the acquiror, and we shall use the terms **corporate acquisition** and **merger** interchangeably to refer to corporate combinations generally.

A merger involves the acquisition of an entire firm. Buying a firm, with its own portfolio of assets and its own liabilities, is certainly more complicated than buying a new machine or building a new plant. In addition, there are often complex tax issues that must be resolved. For these reasons, estimating the incremental cash flows that an acquiror can expect to result from a merger is inherently more difficult than the measurement problems encountered in capital investment projects of the types discussed in Chapters 10 through 13. Also, when a firm makes a large acquisition, how it finances the acquisition takes on added importance. The economics of the acquisition and how the firm finances the acquisition tend to interact because the acquisition will alter the acquiror's corporate structure. Thus, estimating the required rate of return is also inherently more difficult in the case of corporate acquisitions than in other forms of capital investment. Yet accuracy is often crucial because of the amount of corporate funds that the firm must commit to the acquisition.

There is a fourth reason mergers represent a special form of capital investment. Companies must typically make very quick decisions on the basis of incomplete information. In unfriendly situations, the acquiror may have only publicly available information on which to base a decision. In such cases, discounted cash flow analysis is difficult to apply. Consequently, the other valuation techniques that are used in practice to gauge the reasonableness of an acquisition price take on increased importance in such situations.

There are a number of possible motives a firm may have for seeking to merge with a particular firm. The various motives should be judged against the objective of maximizing shareholder wealth.

WHEN DO MERGERS CREATE VALUE?

Under the Principle of Incremental Benefits, financial decisions are based on incremental benefits. The shareholders of the acquiring firm can benefit from a merger only if the two firms are worth more in combination than they are separately; that is, only if there is an incremental benefit to merging. To provide a framework for discussion, suppose that the acquiror and acquiree are worth V_A and V_B in total market value (i.e., the total market value of their assets), respectively, prior to merging but would be worth V_{AB} in total market value in combination. As discussed further below, the acquiror will normally not be able to purchase the acquiree for V_B but will have to offer the acquiree's shareholders some premium, P_B, above V_B for their shares. The acquiror will also incur various costs and expenses, E, including any financing side effects related to the acquisition (which can be quite large—e.g., in the RJR Nabisco leveraged buyout just the professional fees and expenses amounted to more than $1.1 billion). The net advantage to merging, NAM, to the acquiror's shareholders equals the difference between (1) the total market value of the firm post-merger net of the cost of completing the acquisition and (2) the total market value of the firm pre-merger:

$$NAM = V_{AB} - (V_B + P_B) - E - V_A$$
$$= [V_{AB} - (V_A + V_B)] - P_B - E \qquad (22.1)$$

where P_B is the premium paid to firm B shareholders and E is the total of other transaction costs.

If the net advantage to merging is positive, the merger would increase the wealth of the acquiror's shareholders. The term in brackets in Equation (22.1) represents what is commonly referred to as the **synergistic effect** of a merger; the whole is worth more than the sum of the parts when this expression is positive. Under the Principle of Two-Sided Transactions, the premium P_B that represents a gain to the acquiree's shareholders also represents a cost to the acquiror's shareholders. Even if the synergistic effect is positive, the acquiror's shareholders will benefit only if the premium P_B the acquiror must pay the acquiree's shareholders and the costs and expenses E the acquiror must pay lawyers, bankers, bondholders, and others to complete the transaction do not consume the benefits arising out of the synergy.

In Equation (22.1), the amount $V_{AB} - (V_A + V_B) - E$ must be positive for the merger to have economic justification. When it is positive, it is divided between the shareholders of the acquiree, who realize P_B, and the shareholders of the acquiror, who realize the remaining $V_{AB} - (V_A + V_B) - P_B - E$. One of the more interesting issues in the area of mergers and acquisitions is the size of P_B in relation to $V_{AB} - (V_A + V_B) - E$. If P_B is sufficiently large, NAM might even be negative, in which case the acquiror will have "overpaid" for the acquisition.

EXAMPLE ■ Suppose that Company A, whose total market value is $50 million, is planning to acquire Company B, whose total market value is $15 million. Suppose further that Company A estimates that due to operating and other efficiencies, the merged firm will be worth $75 million. Finally suppose that Company A's investment bankers have advised that Company A will have to pay a $6 million premium in price to acquire Company B and that merger-related costs and expenses will amount to $1 million.

Applying Equation (22.1) indicates that

$$\text{NAM} = [\$75 - (50 + 15)] - 6 - 1 = \$3 \text{ million}$$

Synergy creates $10 million of value (= $75 − [15 + 50]), $6 million of which is paid to Company B's shareholders and $1 million of which goes to cover transaction-related costs and expenses. Company A's shareholders wind up with a net increase in their wealth of $3 million, and the merger is mutually beneficial to the two companies' shareholders.

■

VALID MOTIVES FOR MERGING

A merger can be economically beneficial only if the sum of the parts exceeds the whole.

ACHIEVE OPERATING EFFICIENCIES AND ECONOMIES OF SCALE   Two companies may decide to merge in order to achieve operating efficiencies or to take advantage of economies of scale. The merged companies can eliminate duplicate facilities, operations, or departments.[3] For example, consider two airlines that have overlapping routes. By merging they can combine their operations in those cities they previously served, and they can better coordinate scheduling and eliminate excess capacity on those routes both previously served.

Achieving operating efficiencies is more likely to result from either a horizontal merger or a vertical merger than from a conglomerate merger. A **horizontal merger** involves two companies in the same line of business. A **vertical merger** involves integrating forward toward the consumer or backward toward the source of supply in a particular line of business. A **conglomerate merger** involves companies in unrelated businesses. The airline merger just discussed is an example of a horizontal merger. A firm that purchases one of its parts suppliers is an example of a vertical merger. Most of the mergers that took place during the merger wave at the turn of the century were of the horizontal type. Most of the mergers that occurred during the 1920s merger wave were of either the horizontal or vertical type. Most mergers in the Unites States during the postwar period have been of the conglomerate type.[4]

Two companies in the same line of business might also merge in order to achieve **economies of scale** in production, distribution, or some other phase of their operation. These occur when the average unit cost of goods sold decreases as output expands, as for example when achieving a higher volume of production would permit a firm to build larger more efficient plants than the smaller ones it must build now. Achieving economies of scale in production is a principal motive underlying most

[3]Something to consider if you are thinking of pursuing a career in corporate finance: The financial staff of the acquiree is typically one of the first redundancies to be eliminated!
[4]The Federal Trade Commission reported that approximately 80 percent of the mergers effected between 1965 and 1975 were conglomerate mergers. *Statistical Report on Mergers and Acquisitions* (Washington, D.C.: Federal Trade Commission, 1977), 106.

horizontal mergers. Achieving other forms of economies of scale is often a stated goal in the other two types of mergers.

Achieving operating efficiencies might also result through vertical integration. A manufacturing firm can gain greater control over its production process by acquiring key suppliers. Similarly, it can increase its control over the distribution of its products by acquiring distributors.

Another means of achieving operating efficiencies involves combining two companies that have complementary resources. For example, a small computer firm might have a skilled product engineering staff and one or more unique products but lack management expertise and a strong sales staff. A second computer firm, perhaps older and larger, might have strong management and an established sales network but lack state-of-the-art products. A merger could be mutually beneficial because each firm has something the other needs. But a merger will be beneficial to each only if it enables each firm to obtain what it needs more cheaply than it could if it remained on its own.

A merger may also eliminate inefficiencies when an efficient producer acquires an inefficient one. This is one of the classic justifications for mergers: they weed out inefficient producers.[5] However, a conglomerate merger will result in improved efficiency only if the managers of the acquiror are able to transfer their knowledge and skills to the (unrelated) business of the acquiree, and this often proves extremely difficult. Indeed, as a conglomerate firm becomes more complex, it may require more, rather than less, staff.

Operating efficiencies and economies of scale are the principal sources of any synergy that can result from a merger. But a conglomerate merger, by its very nature, has less potential than horizontal or vertical mergers for generating them. In any case, one must be careful in assessing potential operating efficiencies and potential economies of scale. They may never be realized. For example, merging an insurance broker and a securities broker to achieve economies of distribution may fail to yield the anticipated benefits if the insurance brokers and securities brokers cannot (or simply will not) sell each other's products. Merging two airlines may not yield the intended economies of scale if the two airlines' equipment is so different that the separate maintenance staffs must be maintained and one airline's pilots cannot fly the other airline's planes without going through an expensive retraining program.

EXAMPLE ■ After Sears, Roebuck & Co. acquired Dean Witter Reynolds Inc. in 1981, it placed Dean Witter stockbrokers in more than 300 of its approximately 850 retail stores nationwide. Dean Witter brokers complained about the "socks and stocks" marketing strategy, saying it was difficult to drum up business from people shopping for clothing, vacuum cleaners, and lawn mowers, and Sears reduced the number of Dean Witter outlets by more than two-thirds beginning in mid-1989.[6] ■

REALIZE TAX BENEFITS When a firm has tax loss carryforwards that it cannot fully utilize, merging with a profitable firm that pays income taxes may prove mutually beneficial. Under certain circumstances, the loss company can use its tax loss carryforwards to shelter from income taxation some or perhaps all of the operating

---

[5] Manne (1965) expounds this view and Ellert (1976), Shrieves and Stevens (1979), and Palepu (1986) lend empirical support. Ellert and Palepu found that stockholders of acquired firms earned relatively low rates of return over a period of several years prior to the merger. Shrieves and Stevens found that 15.2% of the firms in their randomly chosen sample of firms acquired during the period 1948–1971 were "near bankruptcy" at the time they were acquired.

[6] "At Dean Witter, Complaints Grow Over Sears Work," *Wall Street Journal* (April 17, 1990), C1.

income of the profitable firm with which it combines. For example, when the Penn Central Corporation emerged from bankruptcy, in effect it was able to utilize its substantial tax loss carryforwards by acquiring taxpaying companies.[7]

Under certain circumstances, a net tax benefit may also result from stepping up to market value the tax basis of the acquiree's assets in a taxable acquisition. The IRS in that case "recaptures" certain tax deductions and tax credits previously claimed, but the acquiror can use the stepped up basis (rather than the historical basis, which will be zero for fully depreciated assets) as the tax basis for future depreciation deductions. If the present value of the added future depreciation deductions exceeds the tax liabilities incurred upon **step up** (increasing the basis for accounting, or in this case, tax purposes), a net tax benefit results.[8]

There are at least two other means of realizing tax benefits through a merger. Consider a firm that is in a mature industry and that is generating a large amount of free cash flow. The firm can distribute the surplus cash to its shareholders in the form of cash dividends or share repurchases or it can invest the cash itself in liquid securities or the shares of other companies. If the cash is distributed to shareholders, they will have to pay tax (unless shares are repurchased at a price that is less than the shareholders' tax basis in the shares). They will be able to invest only the net-of-tax amount. This tax is avoided if the firm invests the cash in the shares of other companies rather than distributing it to shareholders. Whether the acquiror's shareholders truly gain depends on whether the acquisition has a positive net benefit when compared to the other possible alternative uses of the cash.

Instead of surplus cash, a firm may have unused debt capacity in the sense that a significant increase in outstanding debt would generate interest tax shields that the firm could fully utilize but would not lead to a material increase in the risk of bankruptcy. Because claiming the additional tax shields would increase the market value of the firm (assuming the conditions required for a Miller tax equilibrium do not apply), the firm is a potential acquisition candidate. It has not been unusual in recent years to see a firm threatened with takeover significantly increase its leverage and use the borrowed funds together with any excess internally generated cash to repurchase common stock and/or pay a large cash dividend.

EXAMPLE ■ In March 1988, Santa Fe Southern Pacific, a very large railroad, energy, and real estate firm, paid its common stockholders a $4.7 billion special divi-

---

[7]The merger must have a legitimate business purpose, however, in order for the Internal Revenue Service to permit the profitable firm to utilize the other firm's tax net operating loss carryforwards (NOLs). In general, it is easier to survive the scrutiny of the IRS when the acquiror is the one with the NOLs. The Tax Reform Act of 1986 tightened restrictions on one company's ability to utilize another company's NOLs to shelter part of its operating income from taxation following an acquisition. If the ultimate ownership of a company with NOLs changes by more than 50% over a 3-year period, then the amount of the acquiree's NOLs and unused tax credits that the acquiror can utilize in any one year is limited to an amount calculated by multiplying the net worth of the acquiree immediately prior to the acquisition times the long-term tax-exempt bond yield (approximately 7% at year-end 1989). As a result of more recent changes in tax law, it is no longer possible for an acquiring company with NOLs to use its NOLs to shelter gain on the sale of the acquiree's assets (e.g., assets in a subsidiary with a very low tax basis) following the corporate acquisition, which was one of the strategies Penn Central adopted.

[8]The Tax Reform Act of 1986 (TRA 86) greatly diminished the tax benefits realizable from stepping up an asset's tax basis (as well as many other tax-oriented acquisition strategies). Prior to TRA 86, the amount of recapture was limited to the amount of prior depreciation deductions and investment tax credits. As a result of TRA 86, the tax liability incurred on step up is not limited in this manner but is based on the difference between the market value of the asset and its tax basis prior to step up. We show below that because of the Time-Value-of-Money Principle, TRA 86 has essentially eliminated stepping up the tax basis of an asset as a tax-effective strategy.

dend which it financed largely through bank borrowings, to fend off an unwanted takeover bid from the Henley Group. ■

ACCESS SURPLUS CASH   Mergers may be motivated by the acquiror's desire to use the acquiree's cash.[9] Firms with substantial cash and a shortage of capital investment opportunities thus may face the prospect of being acquired unless they can invest the cash or unless they distribute it to their shareholders. Unlocking surplus cash can be beneficial to shareholders by giving them the opportunity to invest the cash in accordance with their own personal investment objectives. Investing under the threat of takeover may lead to unsound investment decisions.

GROW MORE QUICKLY OR MORE CHEAPLY   A firm may find that it can grow more quickly and more cheaply by acquiring other companies than through internal development. For example, it is generally quicker and, depending on the acquisition price, it may prove cheaper to acquire new products, new facilities, or a national distribution network by acquiring a firm that already has developed them. Acquiring a local company may be the most cost-effective means of establishing a secure market position in a foreign market, particularly if the foreign country is planning to implement import quotas. A desire to secure a position in the U.S. market probably is largely responsible for the sharp increase in the number of foreign acquisitions of U.S. companies in the 1980s. External growth is more likely to prove cheaper for the acquiror than internal growth when the acquiror and acquiree each have specific requirements that the other is particularly well-suited to fulfill. In that case, each contributes to the synergy.

It is also possible to find situations where a firm can acquire assets, such as oil and gas reserves, more cheaply by purchasing another firm than by developing its own, in this case by exploring for new reserves. This situation can arise when a firm does not utilize its assets efficiently.

QUESTIONABLE MOTIVES FOR MERGING

There are a variety of other motives that companies have cited upon entering into a merger transaction. Three of the more questionable motives concern diversification, enhancing earnings per share, and reducing the cost of debt.

DIVERSIFICATION   Diversification is typically one of the principal motives behind a conglomerate merger. At first glance, this motive seems reasonable because of the Principle of Diversification. A firm can reduce the cyclicality of its earnings and cash flow by acquiring another firm whose earnings and cash flow exhibit a less than perfectly correlated cyclical pattern. But this diversification will benefit the acquiror's shareholders only if they could not achieve such diversification on their own, that is, by purchasing shares of the acquired firm directly and in whatever amounts each shareholder desires. Because of capital market efficiency, shareholders can engage in "homemade diversification" and, therefore, the supposed benefits of corporate diversification are largely illusory.[10]

The homemade diversification argument, like the "homemade leverage" argument discussed in Chapter 15 and the "homemade dividends" argument discussed in Chapter 17, rests on certain idealized assumptions: no taxes, no transaction costs, no

---

[9]Jensen (1986a) argues that mergers, or the threat of merger, have unlocked stockpiles of surplus cash in the broadcasting, food, forest products, motion picture, oil, and tobacco industries.
[10]Levy and Sarnat (1970).

bankruptcy penalties, and no other market imperfections. Similar to what we found in Chapters 16 and 18, relaxing these assumptions will show why corporate diversification may, in some cases, create value. For example, as already noted, diversifying at the firm level may be more tax efficient than paying out the excess cash to shareholders. Owners of closely held firms are often in just this situation; it may be cheaper for them to achieve diversification through the corporation.[11]

ENHANCED EARNINGS PER SHARE   During the 1960s there were publicly-traded conglomerates that grew at high rates through acquisition and achieved impressive increases in reported earnings per share. They did so by acquiring companies whose shares had lower price-earnings ratios than their own shares. Share-for-share exchanges in such situations increase earnings per share even if no real gain has resulted from the merger. Unfortunately, in many cases, this earnings per share growth was due solely to the conglomerates' careful selection of targets so as to achieve desirable accounting effects, rather than being due to enhanced operating efficiencies or other forms of true economic gain.

FINANCIAL SYNERGY   Even if there were no costs involved in bankruptcy, a merger can produce a sort of financial synergy. A larger (merged) firm can take advantage of economies of scale in issuing securities, which we documented in Chapter 14. If the merged firm makes larger issues than the two firms would separately, the merger may result in lower transaction costs—issuance expenses—and hence lower financing costs. Lower issuance expenses are certainly possible but their contribution to the value of a merger is likely to be quite small.

Another problem that can arise is the reverse of what we called (in Chapter 9) the problem of **claim dilution with respect to capital structure**. Recall that stockholders can expropriate wealth from bondholders by diluting the bondholders' claim on the assets. That is, the bonds will be worth less if other debtholders have equal claim on the firm's assets. This same phenomenon can work in reverse, **against** the stockholders. Diversification via merger can reduce the probability of bankruptcy, thereby raising the expected future cash flow to the bondholders. In such cases, the expected return to each class of debtholders increases while their risk, as measured by the standard deviation of their return, decreases. It follows from the Principle of Risk-Return Trade-Off that the debtholders of each firm are unambiguously better off as a result of such a merger. Since the merger has not altered the two firms' combined returns, the stockholders must be worse off. The bondholders have gained at the expense of stockholders because the merger effectively resulted in each firm guaranteeing the debt of the other firm. In effect, the bondholders will have benefited from the Principle of Diversification.

DO MERGERS CREATE VALUE?

The two most crucial issues raised in connection with mergers are: (1) whether mergers increase value and, if so, (2) how this increase in value is allocated between the shareholders of the acquiring firm and the shareholders of the acquired firm (and, possibly, others, such as bondholders). The preponderance of the empirical

---

[11] The Internal Revenue Code contains an *accumulated earnings tax* provision that taxes "excess retentions" as though they had been distributed as dividends. This provision, together with a *personal holding company tax* provision, is designed to penalize companies that retain earnings specifically to reduce their owners' income tax liabilities.

evidence suggests that the stockholders of acquired firms tend to benefit handsomely, receiving takeover premiums averaging between 30% and 50% for their shares, whereas the shareholders of acquiring firms tend to realize only very modest gains.[12] It has been estimated that takeovers of public companies completed between 1981 and 1986 increased the wealth of the acquirees' shareholders by more than $134 billion and that the average premium paid for the acquirees' shares was 47.8%.[13] Another recent study found that, among 640 acquisitions announced between 1970 and 1985, shareholders of the acquiree realized average cumulative abnormal returns of 29.2% while shareholders of the acquiror realized average cumulative abnormal returns of 3.6%.[14] In addition, several studies have found that mergers produced significant benefits for the target's preferred stockholders and convertible bondholders but did not result in a significant benefit to debentureholders of either the acquiree or the acquiror (although there were some notably large losses in certain transactions).[15]

The empirical evidence collected to date suggests that mergers do tend to produce synergy. However, it also suggests that this net gain tends to be allocated between the shareholders of the two firms in such a way that the shareholders of the acquiror realize nothing, or only modest gains, on average. This is probably due to capital market efficiency, reflecting the impact (actual or potential) of competing acquirors. In several widely publicized situations, such as the competition for RJR Nabisco, Inc., the first bid was followed by a series of higher bids.

The available evidence on the impact of mergers may seem somewhat discouraging. Are acquirors consistently overestimating the benefits to be gained? Are the statistical tests missing something? Is there some other explanation? All we can say at this point is that a merger can benefit the shareholders of the acquiror as well as those of the acquiree under the right circumstances; careful financial analysis can help identify those circumstances.

IMPACT OF STOCK MARKET CONDITIONS

Mergers have come in "waves." Economic historians have identified four periods of relatively intense merger activity: 1893–1904, 1915–1929, the late 1960s, and the 1980s. As noted previously, most of the large mergers in the first period were of the horizontal type; most of those in the second period were of either the horizontal or vertical type; and most of those in the most recent two periods were of the conglomerate type. But all four waves coincided with periods of generally buoyant stock prices. Figure 22-1 illustrates the pattern of merger activity since 1968. There were more than 6,000 transactions announced in the peak year of the late 1960s merger boom. The number of announcements was substantially lower, but the aggregate value was significantly greater, in the 1980s boom. More than $763 billion of acquisitions were consummated during the four-year period 1985–1988, which exceeds the combined value of all merger transactions that took place during the prior

---

[12]Jensen and Ruback (1983), after a detailed review of the evidence, conclude that "corporate takeovers generate positive gains." Weston and Chung (1983) provide a less technical summary of the advantages of mergers and review the available evidence regarding the impact of mergers on securityholders. See also Jarrell and Poulsen (1989).

[13]Black and Grundfest (1988).

[14]Hayn (1989). Hayn found that tender offers resulted in greater abnormal returns for shareholders of both the acquiror and the acquiree than other forms of acquisitions.

[15]Kim and McConnell (1977); Asquith and Kim (1982); Dennis and McConnell (1986); and Marais, Schipper, and Smith (1989).

FIGURE 22-1

Merger and acquisition activity, 1968–1988.

Source: W. T. Grimm & Co., *Mergerstat Review 1988*, 116–117.

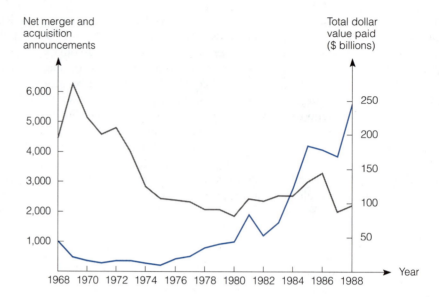

20 years. Perhaps it is the general optimism that accompanies bull markets that spurs acquirors to undertake diversification plans.

22.3 TECHNICAL ISSUES

When one firm acquires another, three sets of technical issues arise: the legal form of the transaction, its tax status, and its accounting treatment. These three sets of issues are interrelated. The basic alternatives are summarized below:

Legal Form	Tax Status	Accounting Treatment
Merger or consolidation	Tax-free	Pooling of interests
Purchase of stock	Taxable	Purchase accounting
Purchase of assets		

LEGAL CONSIDERATIONS

A merger transaction must comply with federal antitrust law, state anti-takeover statutes, the corporate charter of each firm, and federal and state securities laws.

ANTITRUST CONSIDERATIONS There are three principal federal antitrust statutes but the Clayton Act of 1914 has become the principal weapon the government uses to contest mergers that it feels may lessen competition. Section 7 of the Clayton Act forbids a firm to purchase the assets or the stock of another firm if the purchase (1) *might substantially lessen competition* or *tends to create a monopoly* (2) in *any line of commerce* or *in any section of the country*. This test is potentially very broad because it includes transactions that could *potentially* reduce competition in virtually any market. For example, the 1984 merger of Texaco Inc. and Getty Oil Company, at the time the third and twelfth largest oil companies in the United States, was challenged because of the two companies' overlapping gasoline marketing operations in the northeastern Unites States. The actual percentage of potential mergers contested on antitrust grounds is small. Those involving very large companies and horizontal acquisitions appear to be the most likely to be challenged. Many of those that are questioned can survive the challenge by having the acquiror agree to sell assets in the affected market(s) in order to restore competition, as Texaco agreed to do.

The Antitrust Division of the Department of Justice and the Federal Trade Commission (FTC) are the federal agencies responsible for enforcing the antitrust law.[16] The Hart-Scott-Rodino Antitrust Improvements Act requires both parties to a merger to file detailed pre-merger notification reports with the Justice Department and the FTC when both of the following tests are met: (1) one party has $100 million or more of total assets or annual net sales and the other has $10 million or more of total assets or annual net sales and (2) the transaction will involve the purchase of stock and/or assets having an aggregate value of $15 million or more or will involve the acquisition of voting securities giving voting control of a firm with net sales or total assets of $25 million or more.

FORM OF TRANSACTION   There are three basic ways of effecting a corporate acquisition. In a merger, the acquiror absorbs the acquiree. The acquiror automatically obtains all the assets and assumes all the liabilities of the acquiree, which loses its corporate existence. This assumption of liabilities makes it prudent for the acquiror to undertake a **comprehensive due diligence investigation** of the acquiree before the merger to ferret out all significant hidden liabilities. If the acquiror wishes the acquiree to survive as a separate entity, the acquiror can merge the acquiree with a special purpose subsidiary, making the acquiree a wholly owned subsidiary of the acquiror.[17]

A merger or consolidation must comply with each corporation's charter. Many corporate charters, such as those of companies incorporated in Delaware, require only a simple majority whereas others require at least a two-thirds majority of the firm's shareholders to approve any merger or consolidation. A merger or consolidation offers the most flexible means of structuring a tax-free acquisition. It is also generally easier and less costly to complete than either of the other two forms of acquisition.

If instead the acquiror purchases the acquiree's stock, it still obtains the acquiree's assets *and* liabilities but no shareholders' meetings are involved. A prospective acquiror can bypass management, if it so desires, and take its offer directly to the firm's shareholders in the form of a tender offer. Any shareholder who does not like the price offered can refuse to sell his or her shares. This can create problems for the acquiror, however. If the acquiror purchases fewer than 80% of the acquiree's voting securities, it will not be able to consolidate the acquiree for tax purposes, and 20% of the dividends it receives from the acquiree will be taxable.[18] In any case, if any of the

---

[16] The Justice Department issued merger guidelines in June 1982 which set out the criteria it would apply in order to decide which mergers to challenge. The FTC has issued a policy statement expressing views that are very similar to the Justice Department's guidelines with but minor exceptions. Finally, the Justice Department issued amended guidelines in 1984, which acknowledged the globalization of product markets and the appropriateness of taking foreign competition into account when defining a market and assessing a merger's impact on market competition.

[17] The continued corporate existence of the acquiree limits the exposure of the acquiror for liabilities of the acquiree to the acquiree's assets plus any obligations of the acquiree that the acquiror assumes directly.

[18] The dividends received deduction is 70% if the intercorporate dividend recipient owns less than 20% of the paying corporation's voting securities; it is 80% if the recipient owns 20% or more but less than 80% of the voting securities; and it is 100% if the recipient owns 80% or more of the voting securities.

acquiree's shares remain outstanding, there is a minority interest in the subsidiary that could hamper the acquiror's financial or operating flexibility in the future. Consequently, an acquiror that purchases shares from less than all of the acquiree's shareholders, for example through a tender offer, typically follows this purchase with a formal merger in order to eliminate the minority interest.[19]

Under the third structure, the acquiror purchases only the selling firm's assets; the liabilities of the seller, other than those specifically assumed by the buyer, remain the responsibility of the seller. There is thus substantially less likelihood that hidden liabilities will be discovered after the transaction to the detriment of the buyer, and there is no problem with minority shareholders. In addition, the buyer's shareholders do not normally have to approve the transaction, and most corporate charters require only 50% approval by the seller's shareholders. The purchaser pays the seller rather than the seller's shareholders. If the seller disposes of all its productive assets, it can be either liquidated or reconstituted as an investment firm. There are three principal drawbacks to this structure: (1) the conditions necessary to achieve a tax-free transaction are stricter than those for a merger, (2) transferring the title of ownership to individual assets is costly and time-consuming, and (3) the firm rather than its shareholders receives the sale proceeds, and if the purchase price was paid in cash, distributing the cash proceeds to shareholders will normally trigger an income tax liability to the shareholders as well as the selling corporation.

OTHER LEGAL CONSIDERATIONS   There are several other legal issues to address in merger situations. Any purchases of the acquiree's securities by the acquiror must comply with the federal securities laws and federal disclosure requirements.[20] Securities offered to the acquiree's shareholders will normally have to be registered with the Securities and Exchange Commission. As discussed later in the chapter, there are also special rules relating to tender offers. In regulated industries, the acquiror must obtain the approval of the cognizant regulatory authority. For example, if the acquiree is an insurance firm, the insurance commissioner in each state in which the insurance firm is licensed to do business must approve the transfer of the license to do business in that state. Also, state laws and regulations can hamper or prevent mergers.[21] Finally, indenture covenants for the acquiree's outstanding debt may require that the debt be repaid at par upon a change in control. These "poison put" provisions, which have become more commonplace in the wake of the RJR Nabisco leveraged buyout, can impose a substantial financial obligation on the acquiror.

TAX CONSIDERATIONS

The Internal Revenue Service presumes that an acquisition is taxable unless certain stringent conditions are met. In a **tax-free acquisition**, the selling shareholders are treated as having *exchanged* their old shares for substantially similar new shares. The acquiring corporation's tax basis in each asset whose ownership is transferred in the

---

[19] Under Delaware state law, for example, the acquiror can execute a statutory merger, effectively forcing out minority stockholders, without a shareholders' meeting if it owns at least 90% of the voting securities of the acquiree.

[20] For example, a purchaser of 5% or more of a firm's shares must disclose to the SEC and the issuer its holdings within 10 days. The SEC has considered proposals for tightening this and other restrictions on acquirors.

[21] Imperial Group Limited's acquisition of Howard Johnson Company had to contend with state liquor laws that forbade producers or wholesalers of alcoholic beverages, such as Imperial, from selling liquor on the retail level, which many of Howard Johnson's restaurants did.

transaction is the same as the acquiree's, and each selling shareholder who receives only stock does not have to pay any tax on the gain she realizes as a result of the acquisition until the shares are sold. In a **taxable transaction**, the selling shareholders are treated as having *sold* their shares. The acquiror can, if it wants to, increase the tax basis in the assets it acquires to the fair market value of the consideration it pays to acquire them (including the fair market value of the acquiree's liabilities assumed by the acquiror), and unless the sale is an installment sale (i.e., for debt of the acquiror), each shareholder who sells his shares must recognize gain or loss for tax purposes immediately. As a result of the Tax Reform Act of 1986 (TRA 86), an acquisition can qualify as an **installment sale** *only if* the acquiree's common stock was not publicly-traded *and* the installment debt issued to pay the purchase price is not publicly-traded.

From the seller's perspective, the principal benefit of a tax-free transaction is deferral of tax on any gain realized on the sale of the business. The seller who receives stock in the acquiror also has a continuing equity interest in the enterprise and can share in any post-merger benefits. From the buyer's perspective, the principal benefit concerns the acquiror's ability to utilize the existing tax attributes of the acquiree, such as net operating loss carryforwards. However, TRA 86 imposed changes in tax law that restrict the buyer's ability to realize these tax attributes.

With regard to a taxable transaction, a seller generally has three key tax objectives: (1) minimize the taxable income that must be recognized, (2) have as much as possible of the taxable income characterized as capital gain (assuming capital gains are accorded preferential tax treatment), and (3) provide sufficient cash to pay the tax liabilities as they come due. The buyer's principal objective in a taxable transaction is to write up depreciable assets for tax purposes. The write-up increases future depreciation tax deductions, which reduces the buyer's future tax obligations.

REQUIREMENTS FOR TAX-FREE TREATMENT   To qualify as tax-free, the Internal Revenue Code requires that the transaction have a sound business purpose; it can not be solely for tax reasons. The Code also requires the acquiror to continue to operate the acquiree's business and imposes certain requirements on the mode of acquisition and medium of payment.

In the case of a merger or consolidation, the transaction must qualify as a merger or consolidation under applicable state law, and the shareholders of the acquiree must receive at least 50% of the aggregate purchase price in stock of the acquiror, either common or preferred, either voting or nonvoting.[22] This permits a two-step merger: The acquiror can purchase just under 50% of the acquiree through a cash tender offer and then effect a statutory merger in the second step. Any shareholder who receives cash is taxed on the gain immediately; shareholders who receive only stock defer the tax obligation.

In the case of a stock-for-stock acquisition, the acquiror can exchange only its voting stock or the voting stock of its parent and must gain control of at least 80% of the aggregate voting interest in the acquiree and 80% of the total number of out-

---

[22] If the acquiree is merged into a subsidiary of the acquiror (a so-called **subsidiary merger**), the Code requires that (1) the method-of-payment test be met using only stock of the parent company and (2) the subsidiary acquire "substantially all" the assets of the acquiree. Under present IRS guidelines, "substantially all" means at least 90% of the fair market value of net assets and at least 70% of the fair market value of gross assets. If a subsidiary of the acquiror is merged into the acquiree (a **reverse subsidiary merger**), the Code requires that (1) at least 80% of the purchase price must be paid in voting stock and (2) after the transaction the acquiror must hold substantially all of its (pre-merger) assets and substantially all of the acquiree's (pre-merger) assets.

standing shares of each class of nonvoting stock. A stock-for-stock acquisition is the simplest, yet most restrictive, of the three forms of acquisition. Only voting stock of the acquiror or its parent may be used as the medium of payment.

In the case of a stock-for-assets acquisition, the acquiror must obtain "substantially all" of the acquiree's assets in exchange for voting stock of the acquiror or voting stock of its parent. Immediately after the stock-for-assets exchange, this voting stock and any assets not transferred to the acquiror must be distributed to the acquiree's shareholders in liquidation of the acquiree.

TAXABLE TRANSACTIONS   A taxable acquisition can be structured in either of two ways: (1) a purchase of assets or (2) a purchase of stock. In general, in a taxable acquisition, each selling shareholder must recognize gain or loss on the transaction, and the buyer can write up the assets, in a purchase of assets, or stock, in a purchase of stock, acquired in the transaction to the cost paid for them. From a tax standpoint, sellers generally prefer to sell stock, while buyers generally prefer to purchase assets. A sale of stock triggers one level of taxation whereas a sale of assets for cash followed by distribution of the cash proceeds to shareholders triggers two levels of taxation. Buyers prefer to acquire assets, particularly those that can be depreciated, depleted, or amortized for tax purposes, because their tax basis can be stepped up, which leads to increased future tax deductions. The buyer's tax basis in stock is not depreciable.

In a taxable acquisition of assets, the acquiror allocates the purchase price among the acquired assets. To the extent the acquiror has flexibility in allocating the purchase price, tax benefits are maximized by allocating as much of the purchase price as possible to inventory and to assets that are depreciable, depletable, or amortizable over relatively short periods. However, any such allocation must be reasonable. Appraisals assist in the allocation and help substantiate it in the event the Internal Revenue Service challenges the allocation. Since allocation regulations were issued in 1986, both buyers and sellers are required to use the **residual method** for allocating the purchase price. Under this method, the purchase price is allocated first to specific acquired assets based on their respective fair market values. Any balance is allocated to **goodwill** and going-concern value.

EXAMPLE ■   Company A pays $10,000,000 to acquire the stock of Company B and elects purchase-of-assets treatment. Company B has $2 million fair market value of inventory and $7 million fair market value of plant and equipment. Inventory and plant and equipment are assigned their respective fair market values, and $1 million of the purchase price is allocated to goodwill or going-concern value.   ■

TO BE OR NOT TO BE TAX-FREE   A tax-free transaction benefits a shareholder who has a gain because it permits deferral of tax on the gain. A taxable transaction benefits a shareholder who has a loss and also has sufficient taxable income to offset it because it creates a tax shield. A taxable transaction gives the acquiror greater flexibility in financing the acquisition and also benefits the acquiror when the acquiree has substantial depreciable or depletable properties, such as oil and gas reserves, that when written up to market value will generate depreciation and depletion deductions the present value of which exceeds the immediate tax recapture liability triggered by the write up. The interests of the acquiror and the selling shareholders often conflict; the "high" market value of the assets that makes writing up their tax basis advantageous is likely to be reflected in a "high" share price for the acquiree, which creates the capital gain.

Deciding whether to structure a corporate acquisition as a taxable transaction requires comparing (1) the net present value expected from writing up the acquiree's assets and (2) the increase, if any, in the aggregate acquisition cost necessary to compensate shareholders for the increased tax liability:

$$\text{NAT} = \text{NPV} - C \qquad (22.2)$$

where NAT denotes the net advantage of a taxable transaction, NPV denotes the net present value of the tax shields resulting from writing up the assets for tax purposes, and C denotes the incremental cost of the acquisition. When NAT is positive, the acquiror should structure the acquisition as a taxable transaction.

CALCULATION OF NPV The NPV of the tax shields can be calculated in the following manner:

$$\text{NPV} = \sum_{t=1}^{L} \frac{T_c[D^*(t) - D(t)]}{(1 + r)^t} - T_G G \qquad (22.3)$$

where L denotes the period over which the written-up assets will be depreciated (or amortized or depleted) for tax purposes. The tax provision rather than the book provision determines the incremental cash flow benefit to the firm. T_c denotes the corporation's ordinary income tax rate. $D^*(t) - D(t)$ measures the increase during each period t in depreciation, depletion, and amortization deductions, again for tax purposes. The discount rate r in Equation (22.3) is the pretax yield on new debt the firm could issue that matures when the depreciable life of the written-up assets ends. Use of this discount rate assumes that the added depreciation deductions belong to the same risk class as the firm's interest deductions, which seems reasonable. Finally, G denotes the amount of the taxable gain the selling company must recognize for tax purposes, and T_G denotes the seller's tax rate on this gain.

IMPACT OF THE TAX REFORM ACT OF 1986 TRA 86 changed the method of calculating the taxable gain G. Prior to the act, an acquiror could purchase the stock of a company and elect to step up the tax basis of the acquiree's assets to their respective fair market values. The taxable gain, to the purchaser, was limited to the recapture of prior depreciation deductions and investment tax credits—regardless of the market value of the assets. As a result of TRA 86, in any asset acquisition (or stock acquisition treated as an asset acquisition) the taxable gain G equals the difference between the purchase price paid and the acquiree's tax basis in the assets.

Let P denote the purchase price paid and B_S the selling company's tax basis in the assets that are sold. Assuming these assets are fully depreciable for tax purposes,

$$B_S = \sum_{t=1}^{L} D(t) \text{ and } P = \sum_{t=1}^{L} D^*(t)$$

and

$$G = P - B_S = \sum_{t=1}^{L} [D^*(t) - D(t)]$$

Substituting for G in Equation (22.3),

$$\text{NPV} = T_c \sum_{t=1}^{L} \frac{[D^*(t) - D(t)]}{(1 + r)^t} - T_G \sum_{t=1}^{L} [D^*(t) - D(t)]$$

The Time-Value-of-Money Principle ensures that $r > 0$ and hence that NPV < 0 if $T_G = T_c$. Indeed, even if $T_G < T_c$, NPV will be negative except for "small" values of r. Any **goodwill** would render NPV even more negative because goodwill increases the taxable gain but cannot be deducted or depreciated for tax purposes.

As a general rule, structuring an acquisition as a taxable transaction to be able to write up the tax basis of the acquiree's assets is no longer a tax-effective strategy. However, there is one exception to this rule: If the seller has tax net operating loss carryforwards (NOLs) that are sufficient to cover the tax liability, $T_G G$, *and* if the seller or the acquiror could not otherwise use these NOLs (or if their realization would be delayed for some years), it is possible for NPV in Equation (22.3) to be positive. In any case, as we have said many times, the tax code is subject to change. While TRA 86 has virtually eliminated opportunities to derive a net tax benefit from writing up assets in a taxable transaction, future changes in tax law might again create such opportunities. What's important is that you look for such opportunities, and when you think you have found one, calculate the incremental benefits and costs correctly.

CALCULATION OF INCREMENTAL COST   The incremental cost of the acquisition can be calculated in the following manner:

$$C = \left[\frac{T_P[A - B]}{1 - T_P}\right] N \left[1 - \frac{1}{(1 + d)^n}\right] \qquad (22.4)$$

where T_P denotes the selling shareholders' (composite) marginal capital gains tax rate; $A - B$ denotes the difference between the acquisition cost per share in a tax-free transaction (A) and the selling shareholders' average tax basis per share (B); N represents the number of shares of the acquiree's common stock that would be exchanged tax-free if the acquisition were tax-free; d denotes the selling shareholders' (composite) discount rate; and n denotes the average holding period for the shares they would receive in a tax-free acquisition.

Generally, C provides but a rough estimate; except in the case of purchases of closely-held corporations, the detailed information required to calculate a precise value is rarely, if ever, available. Nevertheless, a review of the acquiree's shareholder list will indicate the mix of individuals, corporations, pension funds and other tax-exempt institutions, etc. The acquiror's investment banker can estimate A, as discussed below. A review of the acquiree's share price and trading volume history will provide a rough indication of first, what proportion of the acquiree's shares are unlikely to qualify for long-term capital gains treatment and second, the average tax basis of the acquiree's shareholders. For example, the average price at which the acquiree's shares have traded during the past five years can be used to estimate B. The divisor in Equation (22.4) is needed because the incremental cost C, which is added to the price paid each shareholder, is itself taxable. The second term in brackets is a present value factor, which reflects the fact that the acquiree's shareholders would have to pay tax on their gains at the time they sell their shares. The acquisition accelerates this liability by n years; n might be estimated as the number of years it takes for the cumulative trading volume in the firm's shares to equal the number currently outstanding.

EXAMPLE ■   Suppose for the sake of simplicity that a corporation has a single asset that it purchased for $1 million 10 years ago. The asset is fully depreciated for tax purposes. The asset's current fair market value is $3 million. An acquiror in a taxable transaction could write up the asset to the $3 million purchase price, which it could depreciate in equal amounts over 5 years to a salvage value of zero, but the seller has to pay tax (at the 34% ordinary income tax rate) on the $3 million gain. The acquiror's 5-year new issue debt rate is 10%. Applying Equation (22.3) gives

$$NPV = \sum_{t=1}^{5} \frac{.34(.20)(3,000,000 - 0)}{(1.10)^t} - .34(3,000,000) = -\$246,680$$

The negative NPV illustrates the disadvantage in writing up the asset when the gain is fully taxable as a result of TRA 86. But suppose the selling company has $1,020,000 of NOLs that are about to expire. Since $T_G G = \$1,020,000$ (= [.34]3,000,000), the NOLs will completely shelter the selling corporation's tax liability. Hence, in that case

$$NPV = \sum_{t=1}^{5} \frac{.34(.20)(3,000,000 - 0)}{(1.10)^t} = \$773,321$$

Also suppose for the sake of simplicity that the corporation has a single shareholder who had planned to work for an additional 10 years, then sell her firm and retire. Her marginal capital gains tax rate is 28%. Because of her high income, she invests in high-grade tax-free municipal bonds, which currently yield 10% for a 10-year maturity. Her tax basis in her company stock is her original $1 million investment. To compensate the shareholder for the incremental present value tax liability she will incur in a taxable transaction, the acquiror must pay

$$C = \left[\frac{.28(3,000,000 - 1,000,000)}{(1 - .28)} \right] \left[1 - \frac{1}{(1.10)^{10}} \right] = \$477,911$$

Thus, NAT is −$724,591 (= −246,680 − 477,911) if the gain is fully taxable, and NAT is $295,410 (= 773,321 − 477,911) if the tax on the gain is fully offset by NOLs. In the former case, the acquiror and the acquiree would benefit mutually from a tax-free transaction; in the latter case, they would benefit mutually from a taxable transaction. ■

We have noted that because of recent changes in tax law, there is a net tax advantage to structuring an acquisition as a taxable transaction only in special circumstances. So except in those exceptional cases, shouldn't companies always prefer a tax-free transaction to a comparable taxable one? The answer is "no." The requirements that must be met to qualify for tax-free treatment are restrictive and may conflict with other objectives of the acquiror or the acquiree. For example, a leveraged buyout, because of the high proportion of debt in the capital structure, could not qualify as a tax-free transaction. Second, a foreign acquiror will normally rather pay cash than register with the Securities and Exchange Commission the shares it would need to issue to effect a tax-free acquisition. Third, the shareholders of a financially distressed or otherwise poorly performing company might have a relatively high tax basis in their shares and so prefer a taxable transaction (which will produce capital losses that can shelter from taxation capital gains they have realized on other stocks).

Empirical evidence indicates that the tax attributes of the target firm have been significant in explaining the abnormal returns to shareholders of the acquiror and the acquiree. The amount of the acquiree's net operating loss carryforwards and tax credits that can be transferred to the acquiror only in a tax-free transaction were found to be the most significant tax benefit in tax-free acquisitions. The value of the step up in the acquiree's tangible depreciable assets, net of the cost of depreciation recapture, was found to be the most significant tax benefit in taxable acquisitions.[23]

ACCOUNTING CONSIDERATIONS

Acquisitions often involve difficult accounting issues. One of the more important issues, in practice, is whether to structure the acquisition as a **pooling of interests** or as a **purchase**. In an efficient capital market, the choice of accounting technique should not affect market value because it does not affect cash flows. Nevertheless, professional managers often take great pains to structure transactions so as to achieve a particular accounting treatment.

POOLING VERSUS PURCHASE

In a **pooling of interests**, the respective assets, liabilities, and operating results of the companies involved in the merger are added together without adjustments. The financial statements of the companies are combined as though the companies had always been commonly owned; that is, there are no adjustments made to the recorded values of the companies' assets or liabilities to reflect the merger. The acquiror's financial statements for all disclosed prior fiscal years (typically 5) preceding the merger must be restated to reflect the pooling (if the impact would be material).

Under the **purchase** accounting method, one of the companies is identified as the acquiror, and the acquiror is treated as having purchased the assets of the other firm. The purchase price, after adding the fair market value of the liabilities the acquiror assumes, is allocated to the assets acquired. Any excess of the purchase price over the fair market value of the net assets acquired is recorded as goodwill, which the acquiror must amortize over a period not exceeding 40 years. This represents a noncash charge against the acquiror's net income. If instead of an excess there is a deficiency, the deficiency is assigned as a reduction in the carrying value of long-term assets. The reported net income of the acquiror includes the net income of the acquiree only from the date of the acquisition.

In general, acquisitions that qualify for pooling-of-interests accounting also qualify as tax-free, and taxable acquisitions are accounted for as purchases. However, neither statement is necessarily always true.

ILLUSTRATION OF THE DIFFERENT ACCOUNTING IMPACT

Table 22-2 illustrates the different financial reporting impact of pooling accounting and purchase accounting. ABC Company acquires XYZ Company for $160 million, paying a multiple of 16 times XYZ Company's earnings. In the first case, to qualify for pooling accounting, XYZ shareholders exchange their shares for shares of ABC. ABC Company's shares are trading at $20, a price-earnings multiple of 10. Thus, ABC Company will have to issue 8 million shares in exchange for XYZ Company's 10 million shares. The respective balance sheets and income statements of ABC Company and XYZ Company are simply added item-by-item. As a result of the merger, ABC Company will have pro forma earnings of $50 million and 28 million shares

---

[23]Hayn (1989). Hayn's study covers the period 1970 through 1985. Due to changes in tax law resulting from TRA 86, abnormal returns due to the tax attributes of the target firm will be much less significant in the future (unless future tax law revisions reverse the impact of TRA 86). TRA 86 altered the step-up benefits and the availability of NOLs, as already noted, as well as neutralizing other tax features that had benefited the parties to a merger transaction. TRA 86 substantially reduced the opportunity to exploit tax asymmetries and create value for the shareholders of the acquiror and the acquiree at the expense of the U.S. Treasury.

TABLE 22-2 Illustration of the Different Impact of Pooling Accounting and Purchase Accounting (Dollar Amounts in Millions)

	Before Merger ABC	Before Merger XYZ	Pooling Accounting	Purchase Accounting Adjustments	Purchase Accounting Results
Balance Sheet Impact					
Assets					
Cash & securities	$ 10	$ 10	$ 20	—	$ 20
Inventories	70	30	100	+10[a]	110
Other current assets	20	10	30	—	30
Property, plant, & equipment	200	100	300	+10[b]	310
Goodwill	—	—	—	+30[c]	30
Total assets	$300	$150	$450		$500
Liabilities and Shareholders' Equity					
Current liabilities	$ 50	$ 20	$ 70	—	$ 70
Deferred taxes	50	30	80	−30[d]	50
Long-term debt	50	30	80	−10[e]	70
Equity	150	70	220	−70 + 160[f]	310
Total liabilities and shareholders' equity	$300	$150	$450		$500
Income Statement Impact					
Net revenue	$325	$150	$475	—	$475
Cost of sales	200	113	313	+1[g,j] +10[h,j]	324
Selling, general, and administrative	40	15	55	—	55
Interest expense	5	2	7	—	7
Goodwill	—	—	—	+1[i,j]	1
Pretax income	80	20	100		88
Income tax expense	40	10	50		44
Net income	$ 40	$ 10	$ 50		$ 44
Average shares outstanding (000)	20,000	10,000	28,000		28,000
Earnings per share	$2.00	$1.00	$1.79		$1.57

Pro Forma Adjustments:

[a] Revaluation of inventories to fair market value.
[b] Revaluation of property, plant, and equipment to fair market value.
[c] Goodwill calculated as:

Purchase price	$160
Less XYZ Company equity	(70)
Less XYZ Company deferred taxes	(30)
Plus increase (less decrease) in XYZ Company liabilities to fair market value	(10)
Excess (deficiency) of fair market value of XYZ Company assets over (under) book value of assets	50
Allocated to inventories	10
Allocated to property, plant, and equipment	10
Allocated to goodwill	$ 30

[d] Elimination of XYZ Company deferred income taxes.
[e] Revaluation of XYZ Company long-term debt to fair market value.
[f] Elimination of XYZ Company equity and addition of new ABC Company equity.
[g] To record the impact of additional book depreciation on property, plant, and equipment, which is assumed to be recorded straight-line over 10 years.
[h] Upward inventory adjustment increases the cost of goods sold. Full impact assumed to occur the first year.
[i] To record the amortization of goodwill over 40 years. (The actual value is 0.75, which has been rounded to 1.)
[j] Noncash charges that are not deductible for tax purposes.

(20 million originally issued plus 8 million issued in the merger). Earnings per share are $1.79, representing dilution of 11% from pre-merger earnings per share. Such dilution always occurs under the pooling-of-interests method when the acquiror's shares are valued at a lower price-earnings multiple in the exchange of shares than the acquiree's shares.

In the second case, ABC Company is assumed to effect a two-step merger. It issues $72 million of common stock at a price of $20 per share and uses the proceeds to tender for 4.5 million of XYZ Company's shares. In the second step, ABC Company issues another 4.4 million shares in a merger. As a result, it issues 8 million shares to acquire XYZ Company for $160 million, as before.[24] But the accounting treatment is different. ABC Company must revalue XYZ Company's assets and liabilities and record goodwill. ABC Company has paid $160 million for a company whose book value of equity is only $70 million. Also, the acquiree's deferred taxes must be eliminated under purchase accounting.[25] Finally, it is assumed that the acquiree's debt has a fair market value of only $20 million because interest rates have risen since XYZ Company issued the debt and that the fair market value of XYZ Company's inventories and property, plant, and equipment exceeds the book value in each case by $10 million.[26] Thus, goodwill equals $30 million:

Purchase price		$160 million
Fair market value of assets	$170	
Fair market value of liabilities	40	
Fair market value of net assets		130
Goodwill		$ 30 million

Turning to the income statement, three principal adjustments are made. The higher book value of the fixed assets increases depreciation expense. The increase in depreciation and the upward inventory adjustment increase the cost of sales by $1 million and $10 million, respectively. In addition, the goodwill must be amortized. As a result of these charges, net income and earnings per share are lower under purchase accounting. But because depreciation and amortization are noncash charges, net cash provided (used) by operating activities does not change.[27]

The principal differences between the two methods are (1) the revaluation of assets and liabilities and (2) the creation of goodwill under purchase accounting when the purchase price exceeds the fair market value of the net assets acquired. Because of the negative earnings impact of the goodwill amortization and other expenses, many managers prefer to use the pooling-of-interests method whenever they can.

---

[24] You might recognize from the discussion of tax considerations that such a transaction is tax-free.

[25] Under FASB Statement No. 96 on accounting for income taxes, purchase accounting will not result in elimination of deferred taxes. The statement will require that deferred taxes be separately identified in the purchase accounting balance sheet. Statement No. 96 is scheduled to become effective in 1992.

[26] The degree to which depreciable assets are revalued upward for financial reporting purposes depends on whether the acquisition is taxable or tax-free. In a taxable acquisition, a depreciable asset's tax basis can be written up whereas it cannot be written up in a tax-free acquisition. Writing up the asset's tax basis provides additional depreciation tax deductions, which increase the asset's value.

[27] If instead the acquisition were taxable, net cash provided (used) by operating activities might actually increase as a result of an increase in depreciation expense for tax purposes.

REQUIREMENTS FOR POOLING   Accounting Principles Board Opinion No. 16 specifies the requirements to qualify a transaction for pooling-of-interests accounting treatment, and Accounting Principles Board Opinion No. 17 specifies the accounting treatment for goodwill and other intangibles under purchase accounting.[28] A transaction that meets all of the numerous tests for a pooling must be accounted for as a pooling; otherwise purchase accounting must be used. The conditions that must be satisfied in order to qualify an acquisition for pooling-of-interests accounting include: (1) The acquiror must issue only stock with rights identical to those of the majority of its outstanding voting common stock in exchange for at least 90% of the acquiree's voting common stock; (2) the combination must be completed in one transaction or in accordance with a specific plan within one year after the plan is initiated; (3) no contingent payments are permitted; (4) each firm must have been autonomous (i.e., not a subsidiary or a division of another firm) for at least the preceding two years; (5) none of the companies involved can have sold or spun off a significant portion of its assets within the preceding two years; (6) prior to the combination, none of them can own more than 10% of any of the others involved; and (7) there must not be any plan to reacquire any of the common stock issued to effect the merger or to dispose of a significant portion of the combined companies' assets within the two years following the merger (other than to eliminate duplicate facilities or excess capacity). Thus pooling can be difficult to achieve in many cases, and if pooling is not desired, it is easily avoided by making minor changes to the structure of the transaction.

DOES THE CHOICE OF ACCOUNTING METHOD MATTER?   In practice, firms seem to care because the two methods affect reported earnings differently. In reality, however, the choice of accounting method probably has considerably less significance than most managers realize because of the Principle of Capital Market Efficiency. The choice of accounting method per se does not affect real cash flow. A study of 159 mergers in the 1954–1964 period found that the use of pooling-of-interests accounting generally did not lead to superior share price performance even though reported earnings were higher than under purchase accounting.[29]

ACCOUNTING FOR LEVERAGED BUYOUTS   A leveraged buyout (LBO) presents a difficult accounting issue. LBOs, which are discussed later in the chapter, are acquisitions that are financed principally with debt secured by the target's assets. An LBO will not qualify for pooling-of-interests accounting because of the large amount of non-stock consideration paid in the transaction. But purchase accounting may not be appropriate either. In many LBOs, the target's managers and some of its former shareholders participate in the group that effects the LBO. Often in such situations, accountants have felt that there had not been a sufficient change in ownership and control to justify purchase accounting. Instead they determined that the LBO should be accounted for as a recapitalization of the target (e.g., a repurchase of the target's common shares financed through borrowing).

From the standpoint of lenders and equity investors, recapitalization accounting can have an undesirable effect in highly leveraged transactions: It can result in negative book value of shareholders' equity following the LBO. The cost of repurchasing

---

[28] "Business Combinations," Accounting Principles Board Opinion No. 16, American Institute of Certified Public Accountants, August 1970; "Intangible Assets," Accounting Principles Board Opinion No. 17, American Institute of Certified Public Accountants, August 1970.

[29] Hong, Kaplan, and Mandelker (1978).

shares must be subtracted from shareholders' equity, and the target's assets cannot be written up. Negative shareholders' equity will normally result when (1) the cost of retiring the target's common stock that was financed through borrowing exceeds (2) the target's book value of shareholders' equity prior to the LBO. Lenders to and equity investors in LBOs sought purchase accounting treatment in order to have the target's assets written up to their respective current market values and achieve positive shareholders' equity (or at least smaller negative shareholders' equity than under recapitalization accounting).

The Financial Accounting Standards Board has determined that purchase accounting treatment is appropriate for an LBO *only* in those cases where a new ownership group achieves a controlling interest and such change in control is genuine. To the extent that former shareholders of the target participate in the new control group, the shareholders' equity of the target continues to be recorded at its pre-LBO book value net of any distributions made to remaining shareholders in connection with the LBO. Such accounting treatment results in only partial step up in the value of the target's assets. The method of accounting is effectively a blend of purchase accounting (applied to the equity contributed by the new shareholders) and recapitalization accounting (applied to the continuing equity interest of the pre-LBO shareholders who remain after the LBO).

22.4   FINANCIAL ANALYSIS OF MERGERS

There are two basic approaches to valuing corporate acquisitions: (1) by inference from the prices paid for companies and for individual assets in comparable transactions (comparative analysis) and (2) discounted cash flow analysis. Comparative analysis is the more widely used technique in practice.

The two approaches differ in one fundamental respect. Comparative analysis is used to determine a "reasonable" price to pay. The discounted-cash-flow approach is used to calculate the impact of an acquisition on shareholder wealth given a particular acquisition cost. It can be used to estimate the maximum price an acquiror could pay without harming the wealth of its shareholders. These two approaches are therefore complementary. When used properly together, they will yield more useful information than either approach could separately.

THE MERGER PREMIUM

Two issues make the analysis of acquisitions difficult. The acquiror must normally pay a premium over the price at which the acquiree's shares are trading in the market (or would trade if the target firm were publicly-held). Comparative analysis can be used to determine a "reasonable" premium. Second, in many cases the acquiree is large enough relative to the acquiror that there are significant debt capacity side effects associated with the merger. The adjusted-present-value approach discussed in the next section is ideally suited to handle such situations.

Figure 22-2 illustrates why a merger premium is usually required. The firm's shares are trading at price P determined by the intersection of the demand curve (DD) and the supply curve (SS) for its shares.[30] At that price the market for the

---

[30] The downward-sloping demand curve for common shares is consistent with empirical evidence furnished in Shleifer (1986). The upward-sloping supply curve is consistent with the upward-sloping transactions supply curve in an exchange economy described in Hirshleifer (1984). See also Nathan and O'Keefe (1989).

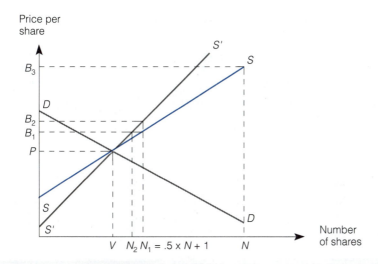

FIGURE 22-2
Illustration of the merger premium.

firm's shares is in equilibrium. Certain investors are willing to sell in the aggregate V shares and other investors are willing to purchase in the aggregate the same number of shares. The firm has a total of N shares outstanding. Typically V is small relative to N (and is even smaller than Figure 22-2 indicates). An acquiror who bids price P would have to compete with all the investors who are also seeking to buy shares at that price but investors would only offer V shares for sale. In order to draw forth more shares from sellers, the acquiror will have to raise its price. How much? If it wants to purchase enough shares for outright control, $.5[N] + 1$, it will have to bid B_1 per share. If it wants to purchase all the shares, it will have to bid B_3. Acquiring a greater number of shares requires a higher bid, thus a higher premium:

$$\text{BP} = \frac{(B - P)}{P} \qquad (22.5)$$

where BP denotes the bid premium, B denotes the bid price, and P denotes the market price before the bid is announced. In terms of Figure 22-2:

$$\text{BP}_c = \frac{B_1 - P}{P}$$

and

$$\text{BP}_{100} = \frac{B_3 - P}{P}$$

where BP_c denotes the bid premium for control and BP_{100} denotes the bid premium for 100% ownership.

Unfortunately, life is not so simple. Potential acquirors cannot be sure just where the supply curve SS lies. For example, if the supply curve were really $S'S'$ instead of SS, a bid of B_1 would draw forth only N_2 shares, not enough for outright control (but perhaps enough for effective control). Potential acquirors would have to bid $B_2 > B_1$ to achieve outright control. To complicate matters, the required premium will tend to vary from one industry to another depending on the industry's prospects and from one firm to another within any industry depending on that firm's relative financial and business characteristics and relative prospects. The required premium may also depend on the state of the stock market.

Table 22-3 shows the distribution of premiums paid in acquisitions for the period

TABLE 22-3 Premiums Paid in Acquisitions of Publicly-Traded Companies, 1974–1988

Year	Number of Acquisitions[a]	Percent Premium Paid Over Market Price[b]								Dow Jones Industrial Avg During Year	
		0.1–40.0		40.1–80.0		Over 80.0		Average	Median	High	Low
		Amount	%	Amount	%	Amount	%				
1974	147	68	46%	47	32%	32	22%	50%	43%	891.66	577.60
1975	129	74	57	38	30	17	13	41	30	881.81	632.04
1976	168	101	60	45	27	22	13	40	31	1014.79	858.71
1977	218	120	55	70	32	28	13	41	36	999.75	800.85
1978	240	116	48	90	38	34	14	46	42	907.74	742.12
1979	229	95	41	91	40	43	19	50	48	897.61	796.67
1980	169	75	44	61	36	33	20	50	45	1000.17	795.13
1981	166	80	48	54	33	32	19	48	42	1024.05	824.01
1982	176	80	45	66	37	30	18	47	44	1070.55	776.92
1983	168	101	60	53	32	14	8	38	34	1287.20	1027.04
1984	199	118	59	68	34	13	7	38	34	1286.64	1086.57
1985	331	231	70	71	21	29	9	37	28	1553.10	1184.96
1986	333	222	67	82	24	29	9	38	30	1955.60	1502.30
1987	237	155	65	66	28	16	7	38	31	2722.42	1738.74
1988	410	255	62	113	28	42	10	42	31	2183.50	1879.14
Total	3320	1891	57	1015	31	414	12				

[a] Number of acquisitions of publicly-traded sellers in which a premium was paid.
[b] Premium paid over the seller's closing share price five business days prior to the initial announcement. Prior to 1979, premium was calculated over the seller's closing share price two business days prior.

Source: W. T. Grimm & Co., *Mergerstat Review 1988*, 94–95.

1974–1988. The annual median premium paid varied between a low of 28% in 1985 and a high of 48% in 1979. The annual median premium paid and also the percentage of premiums that exceed 80% have trended downward, perhaps reflecting the general rise in share prices, since 1982. A recent study found that acquisition premiums during the 1974–1985 period were approximately double those during the 1963–1973 period, which was also a period of generally rising share prices. That study also found that the acquisition premium behaves countercyclically, varying inversely with the Standard & Poor's 500 Index.[31]

COMPARATIVE ANALYSIS

Investment bankers use a table like Table 22-4 to determine a reasonable price for the acquiror to offer for the target firm's shares. The use of such a table reflects the Behavioral Principle: Look to comparable acquisitions for guidance regarding a reasonable price to pay for an acquisition. The table provides the following pricing benchmarks for a carefully selected group of acquisitions of publicly-traded companies:

[31] Nathan and O'Keefe (1989). The reasons for this behavior are not entirely clear. The authors suggest that takeovers reflect undervaluation, which may be more severe during recessions (when share prices are depressed).

$$\begin{array}{ll} \text{Multiple of} \\ \text{Earnings Paid} \end{array} = \frac{\text{Purchase Price Per Share}}{\begin{array}{c}\text{Target's Fully Diluted Earnings Per Share}\\ \text{Before Extraordinary Items}\end{array}} \qquad (22.6)$$

$$\begin{array}{ll} \text{Multiple of} \\ \text{Cash Flow Paid} \end{array} = \frac{\text{Purchase Price Per Share}}{\begin{array}{c}\text{Target's Fully Diluted Cash Flow Per Share}\\ \text{Before Extraordinary Items}\end{array}} \qquad (22.7)$$

$$\begin{array}{ll} \text{Multiple of} \\ \text{Book Value Paid} \end{array} = \frac{\text{Purchase Price Per Share}}{\text{Target's Book Value Per Share}} \qquad (22.8)$$

$$\text{Premium Paid} = \frac{\begin{array}{c}\text{Purchase Price}\\ \text{Per Share}\end{array} - \begin{array}{c}\text{Target's Share}\\ \text{Price Pre-Merger}\end{array}}{\text{Target's Share Price Pre-Merger}} \qquad (22.9)$$

The following ratio is often useful for companies that have substantial manufacturing facilities:

$$\begin{array}{ll} \text{Multiple of} \\ \text{Replacement} \\ \text{Cost Paid} \end{array} = \frac{\begin{array}{c}\text{Aggregate Purchase}\\ \text{Price of Equity}\end{array} + \begin{array}{c}\text{Market Value of}\\ \text{Debt Assumed}\end{array}}{\text{Replacement Cost of Target's Assets}} \qquad (22.10)$$

The following ratio is useful for natural resource companies whose assets often enjoy relatively liquid secondary markets (e.g., oil and gas reserves, timber and timberland, etc.):

$$\begin{array}{ll} \text{Price Paid} \\ \text{Per Unit of} \\ \text{Resource} \end{array} = \frac{\begin{array}{c}\text{Aggregate Purchase}\\ \text{Price of Equity}\end{array} + \begin{array}{c}\text{Market Value of}\\ \text{Debt Assumed}\end{array}}{\text{Number of Units of Resource Target Holds}} \qquad (22.11)$$

In Equations (22.6) and (22.7), if the firm is in a highly cyclical industry, earnings per share and cash flow per share for each firm should be averaged over a period that corresponds to the length of one cycle. Also, if projected earnings are available for each firm as of its acquisition date, it is useful to calculate the multiple of earnings paid on both a historical basis and a projected basis. In Equation (22.9) the target's share price pre-merger is typically measured 30 days before the initial announcement date of the acquisition in order to prevent preannouncement effects from biasing the analysis.

In Equation (22.10), the replacement cost of the acquiree's assets can often be estimated from industry benchmarks, e.g., proved developed crude oil reserves located in Texas have an average "finding cost" of so many dollars per barrel. In Equation (22.11), the number of units of resource the target holds is measured in physical units. Different resources can be combined by adopting some standard of equivalence. For example, an oil and gas company's hydrocarbon reserves can be expressed on a "net equivalent barrel" basis by calculating the number of barrels of oil that would have the same market value as the firm's gas reserves. Then the price paid per unit of resource would be expressed in terms of dollars per net equivalent barrel.

ILLUSTRATION OF COMPARATIVE ANALYSIS   Table 22–4 illustrates the application of comparative analysis to Monmouth Pharmaceuticals Company's possible acquisition of Chicago Drugs Inc. Chicago Drugs currently has 10,000,000 shares outstanding, which are trading at a price of $27. This gives Chicago Drugs a current market value of $270 million. Monmouth's financial staff believes that there has been no merger speculation or other factors that might have inflated Chicago Drugs's

TABLE 22-4 Illustration of Comparative Analysis (Dollar Amounts in Millions Except Per Share Amounts)

| Date Announced | Acquiror/ Acquiree[a] | Information on Acquiree for Latest 12 Months Prior to Acquisition | | | |
		Net Revenue (5 Yr. Growth)	Net Income (5 Yr. Growth)	Cash Flow (5 Yr. Growth)	Book Value
	Monmouth/ Chicago(P)	$600 (12.3%)	$30 (11.2%)	$42 (12.0%)	$196
12/10/x9	Atlantic/ Crescent(P)	630 (10.9)	27 (11.0)	40 (10.3)	177
11/5/x9	Essex/ Trenton	435 (9.8)	20 (10.0)	30 (10.1)	142
9/7/x9	Sussex/ Brooklyn	465 (7.5)	23 (8.0)	35 (8.7)	130
8/3/x9	Madison/ Washington(P)	833 (12.9)	42 (12.6)	60 (13.2)	281
4/30/x9	Jersey/ Philadelphia(P)	610 (11.7)	29 (12.4)	45 (12.7)	197
2/1/x9	Morris/ Neptune(P)	720 (10.1)	32 (9.9)	42 (10.2)	210
11/30/x8	Salem/ Seaside(P)	415 (13.6)	17 (12.6)	22 (11.1)	121
10/19/x8	Worthington/ Homestead(P)	440 (11.4)	22 (11.7)	35 (11.0)	161
8/4/x8	Ludlow/ Quackenbush	515 (11.1)	24 (8.3)	37 (8.3)	160
7/16/x8	Warren/ Bergen	550 (10.8)	25 (8.7)	37 (9.0)	130

For all the Comparables:

High		13.6%	12.6%	13.2%	
Low		7.5	8.0	8.3	
Average	11.0	10.5	10.5		

For the Proprietary Pharmaceutical Manufacturers:

High		13.6%	12.6%	13.2%	
Low		10.1	9.9	10.2	
Average		11.8	11.7	11.4	

[a](P) denotes proprietary pharmaceutical manufacturers.

share price. (If there had been, Monmouth's financial staff would have to reduce the premium to be offered Chicago Drugs's shareholders.)

The comparative analysis table contains data for ten carefully selected recent acquisitions of pharmaceutical companies that are similar to Chicago Drugs in terms of size and business and financial characteristics. Six are also proprietary drug manufacturers like Chicago Drugs.

Purchase Price		Purchase Price as Multiple of			Premium Paid Over Market Price One Month Before Announcement
Aggregate	Per Share	Earnings	Cash Flow	Book Value	
—	—	—	—	—	—
$410	$33.75	15.2x	10.3x	2.3x	60%
270	39.50	13.5	9.0	1.9	45
220	24.50	9.6	6.3	1.7	37
730	55.25	17.4	12.2	2.6	66
450	27.63	15.5	10.0	2.3	55
441	38.25	13.8	10.5	2.1	53
302	43.50	17.8	13.7	2.5	62
320	31.25	14.5	9.1	2.0	50
300	29.88	12.5	8.1	1.9	47
285	44.00	11.4	7.7	2.2	43
		17.8x	13.7x	2.6x	66%
		9.6	6.3	1.7	37
		14.1	9.7	2.2	51
		17.8x	13.7x	2.6x	66%
		13.8	9.1	2.0	50
		15.7	11.0	2.3	58

Comparing the multiples and premiums paid for all ten companies to the respective multiples and premiums paid for proprietary drug manufacturers reveals that the proprietary drug manufacturers have commanded higher multiples and premiums. Monmouth's financial staff therefore decides to base its calculations on the data concerning the proprietary drug firm acquisitions.

In terms of its growth (and other characteristics), Chicago Drugs compares very favorably with the six proprietary drug manufacturers, and "reasonable" acquisition multiples and a "reasonable" acquisition price would fall within the following ranges:

Multiple of earnings paid: 13.8x–17.8x	Aggregate purchase price: $414–$534 million
Multiple of cash flow paid: 9.1x–13.7x	Aggregate purchase price: $382–$575 million
Multiple of book value paid: 2.0x–2.6x	Aggregate purchase price: $392–$510 million
Premium paid: 50%–66 %	Aggregate purchase price: $405–$448 million

The intersection of the four value ranges is $414 million to $448 million. This analysis suggests a price per share in the range of $41.40 to $44.80 per Chicago Drugs share. Any price per share within this range would represent a reasonable price in the sense that it would not be out of line with the prices acquirors have paid in comparable situations, which is in keeping with the Behavioral Principle.

Before closing this discussion, it is only fair to point out that comparative analysis does not always work as smoothly as in the forgoing illustration. In many cases, it is difficult to identify a well-defined group of comparables. For example, the candidates may all be in multiple businesses. In such cases, careful judgment must be applied to determine an appropriate value range, for example, by eliminating less closely comparable companies from the table (as we did in the illustration).

LIQUIDATION APPROACH

The potential liquidation value (or break-up value) of a firm should also be considered in a merger evaluation. A holding company that operates a number of essentially autonomous companies or a firm that owns a number of dissimilar assets, investments, and companies can be valued by estimating the market value of each class of assets and subtracting the cost of repaying all liabilities:

$$LV = A - L - T - E \tag{22.12}$$

where LV denotes the liquidation value of the target, A the liquidation value of all its assets, L the cost of repaying all its debt and preferred stock obligations, T the tax obligation incurred in connection with the liquidation, and E the costs and expenses associated with the acquisition and liquidation.

The liquidation values estimated when applying Equation (22.12) should be based on the values that can be realized within a "reasonable" time frame, say one year, rather than in a "fire sale." Equations (22.6), (22.7), (22.8) and, in the case of subsidiaries that hold substantial natural resources, (22.11) can be used to value subsidiaries that are saleable within this reasonable time frame. Equation (22.9) can be used to value any subsidiaries that are publicly-traded. The cost of repaying debt and redeeming preferred (and preference) stock will be specified in the documents governing those fixed income obligations. Finally, the sale of assets normally will trigger a corporate tax liability, and disposing of assets normally will involve significant expenses.

WEIGHTED-AVERAGE-COST-OF-CAPITAL APPROACH

Table 22-5 illustrates the application of the weighted-average-cost-of-capital approach to the evaluation of the possible acquisition of Chicago Drugs. It is assumed

TABLE 22-5 Discounted Cash Flow Analysis of Acquisition of Chicago Drugs Inc.: Weighted–Average–Cost–of–Capital Approach (Dollar Amounts in Millions)

						Year					
	0	1	2	3	4	5	6	7	8	9	10
Purchase of equity[a]	$480.0	—	—	—	—	—	—	—	—	—	—
Cost of debt assumed	92.6	—	—	—	—	—	—	—	—	—	—
Transaction costs	5.0	—	—	—	—	—	—	—	—	—	—
Acquiree's excess cash	(35.0)	—	—	—	—	—	—	—	—	—	—
Net acquisition cost	$542.6										
Incremental Free Cash Flow:											
Revenue	—	$672	$753	$843	$944	$1,057	$1,184	$1,326	$1,486	$1,664	$1,864
Cost of goods sold[b]	—	336	376	421	472	529	592	663	743	832	932
SG&A	—	251	276	304	334	367	404	444	489	538	591
Depreciation (tax)	—	13	15	15	18	19	22	25	28	30	35
Pretax operating profit	—	72	86	103	120	142	166	194	226	264	306
Income taxes[c]	—	36	43	52	60	71	83	97	113	132	153
Net operating profit	—	36	43	51	60	71	83	97	113	132	153
Depreciation (tax)	—	13	15	15	18	19	22	25	28	30	35
Net operating cash flow	—	49	58	66	78	90	105	122	141	162	188
Net investment in working capital[d]	—	$(15)	$(18)	$(20)	$(25)	$(28)	$(32)	$(36)	$(40)	$(43)	$(50)
Investment in fixed assets	—	(22)	(25)	(30)	(35)	(40)	(45)	(50)	(50)	(50)	(50)
Operating economies net of taxes[e]	—	10	11	12	13	15	15	15	15	15	15
Incremental free cash flow	—	22	26	28	31	37	43	51	66	84	103
Terminal Value of Net Assets:											
Going-concern basis[f]	—	—	—	—	—	—	—	—	—	—	1,473
Disposition basis[g]	—	—	—	—	—	—	—	—	—	—	1,854
Incremental Net Cash Flow:											
Going-concern basis	$(542.6)	$ 22	$ 26	$ 28	$ 31	$ 37	$ 43	$ 51	$ 66	$ 84	$1,576
Disposition basis	$(542.6)	$ 22	$ 26	$ 28	$ 31	$ 37	$ 43	$ 51	$ 66	$ 84	$1,957

Required rate of return $= r^*(\theta) = r - T^*\theta r_d(\theta)\left[\dfrac{1+r}{1+r_d(\theta)}\right] = .1659 - .25\,(\tfrac{1}{3})(.12)\left[\dfrac{1.1659}{1.12}\right] = 15.55\%$

IRR (Going-concern basis) = 15.58%
IRR (Disposition basis) = 17.65%

NPV (Going-concern basis) = $ 1.1 million
NPV (Disposition basis) = $90.9 million

[a] Estimated as 16 times prior year's earnings (a purchase price of $48.00 per share).
[b] Excluding depreciation.
[c] Assumes a 50% marginal income tax rate.
[d] Increase in inventories and receivables net of increase in payables.
[e] Estimated after-tax savings resulting from eliminating redundant overhead and redundant production facilities and from marketing certain of Monmouth's products through Chicago Drugs's distribution network.
[f] Calculated as 9.0 times terminal year's earnings ($142.7 million), which represents the price-earnings multiple at which Chicago Drugs's shares are currently trading, plus the amount of debt outstanding at the investment horizon ($188.3 million).
[g] Calculated as 16 times terminal year's earnings ($142.7 million) plus the amount of debt outstanding at the investment horizon ($188.3 million) and net of capital gains tax at 34% rate (with tax basis of $485 million) and net also of transaction costs ($10 million).

that Monmouth has already decided that it would not be advantageous to elect to step up the tax basis of Chicago Drugs's assets. Monmouth elected to use a 10-year time horizon for its analysis. Projected amounts are rounded to the nearest million.

ACQUISITION COST It is assumed in Table 22-5 that Monmouth purchases all of Chicago Drugs' outstanding stock for cash through a tender offer at a price of $48 per share (16 times earnings, which approximates the midpoint of the range determined in the preceding section). Chicago Drugs currently has $100 million of debt outstanding, which bears interest at a 10% rate, payable annually in arrears. The debt matures in one lump sum at the end of 10 years and is callable at par. Monmouth will be able to assume this debt.

The cost of servicing this debt represents an opportunity cost to Monmouth, which equals the amount of 12% debt displaced by the Chicago Drugs debt that Monmouth assumes and which can be measured by applying the debt service parity (DSP) approach introduced in Chapter 20. Under the DSP approach, the opportunity cost of assuming Chicago Drugs's outstanding debt equals the maximum amount of new 12% debt Monmouth could issue, subject to the constraint that the after-tax period-by-period debt service payments of the hypothetical new issue are the same as those of Chicago Drugs's debt that Monmouth would assume. If Monmouth is permitted to assume the debt and the opportunity cost of assuming the debt is less than the cost of retiring it immediately, Monmouth should assume the debt rather than retire it. The opportunity cost of assuming the debt is included in the cost of the acquisition and is subtracted from the amount of new debt Monmouth could otherwise issue to finance the acquisition. However, if the opportunity cost of assuming Chicago Drugs's debt is greater than the cost of retiring it immediately, the debt should be retired. The cost of retiring it must then be included in the cost of the acquisition.

Monmouth's pretax cost of a new debt issue (before issuance expenses) is 12%. Its marginal ordinary income tax rate is 50% so that, assuming the debt requires after-tax interest payments of $5 million per year, newly issued debt would have an after-tax interest cost of 6% per annum. Under the DSP approach, assuming Chicago Drugs's outstanding debt would have a present value cost to Monmouth of

$$\text{PV (debt displaced)} = \sum_{t=1}^{10} \frac{5}{(1.06)^t} + \frac{100}{(1.06)^{10}} = \$92.6 \text{ million}$$

Since the cost of assuming the debt is less than the $100 million cost of retiring it, Monmouth is better off assuming the debt than retiring it; the net advantage is $7.4 million (= 100.0 − 92.6). The DSP approach would also be used to value any debt instruments (or preferred stock instruments) that an acquiror issues to the acquiree's shareholders in payment for some portion of the acquisition price.

The gross cost of the acquisition is thus $572.6 million (= 480.0 + 92.6). However, based on the analysis of Chicago Drugs's financial statements, Monmouth believes that Chicago Drugs has approximately $35 million of excess cash and marketable securities that it will be able to apply toward the purchase price. (This represents a potential pitfall, however. Companies like to pay as much of the acquisition cost as they can with the acquiree's cash. But what appears as excess cash may in fact be tied up as compensating balances or it may be overseas and repatriating it could trigger a significant tax liability.) Monmouth has estimated that investment bankers' fees and other expenses net of taxes will total $5 million.

The cost to Monmouth of acquiring Chicago Drugs's net assets is:

Cost of purchasing target's common shares	$480.0	
+ Present value of debt acquiror assumes	92.6	
+ Transaction costs and expenses	5.0	**(22.13)**
− Liquidation value of target's excess assets	(35.0)	
Net acquisition cost (NAC)	$542.6	

Note that if the target's debt accelerated as a result of the acquisition, the present value of the debt the acquiror assumes would be the face amount, $100 million, and the net acquisition cost would then be $550 million. Whenever you evaluate the possible acquisition of a firm that has debt outstanding, check whether the acquisition will trigger acceleration (and if it will but assuming the debt would be cheaper than retiring it, you will probably want to find an alternative legal structure that will avoid acceleration).

FINANCING Monmouth's financial staff has studied the capital structure policies of large pharmaceutical companies in the manner described in Chapters 15 and 16. On the basis of that analysis, Monmouth believes that it could finance the acquisition on a long-term basis with a debt-to-total-value ratio of ⅓ without any adverse impact on its senior debt rating or on how it might choose to finance other projects. The amount of new long-term debt Monmouth can issue is the amount it can have outstanding after the acquisition less the amount of debt displaced by the debt it assumes in the acquisition:

$$\text{Added Debt} = \text{NAC}(\theta) - \text{PV (debt displaced)} \qquad \textbf{(22.14)}$$
$$= 542.6(\tfrac{1}{3}) - 92.6 = \$88.3 \text{ million}$$

where θ denotes the acquiror's target debt-to-total-value ratio.

OPERATING ASSUMPTIONS Monmouth believes that Chicago Drugs's revenue will grow at the rate of 12% per annum (the historical growth rate) and that cost of goods sold will grow at the same rate while selling, general and administrative expense (SG&A) will grow at 10% per annum. Annual depreciation expense for tax purposes is estimated from Chicago Drugs's published financial reports and from Monmouth's estimate of Chicago Drugs's required capital expenditure program. The forecast operating economies represent Monmouth's estimate of the benefits it will realize by eliminating redundant overhead and redundant production facilities and from marketing certain of Monmouth's products through Chicago Drugs's distribution network.

Note three important potential pitfalls. It is easy to be too optimistic about (1) the acquiree's growth prospects and about (2) the synergistic benefits from the merger; the more dissimilar the acquiree's and the acquiror's businesses, the more difficult it will be to find true synergies. It is also easy to underestimate (3) the amount of investment that will be required; the older the acquiree's plant and equipment, the higher the required postmerger capital expenditures.

TERMINAL VALUE Terminal value is estimated on two different bases: (1) Monmouth continues to own Chicago Drugs beyond the investment horizon and (2) Monmouth sells all the common stock of Chicago Drugs at the investment horizon. In the first case, Chicago Drugs's terminal value is estimated by applying its current price-earnings multiple, 9.0 (= 27.00/3.00), to Chicago Drugs's pro forma earnings in year 10 estimated as though Chicago Drugs were on a stand-alone basis. In year

10, Chicago Drugs would have $100 million principal amount of 10% debt plus $88.3 million of 12% debt, giving rise to $10.3 million of after-tax interest expense. Subtracting this from Chicago Drugs's estimated year 10 net operating profit of $153 million leaves $142.7 million of earnings. Multiplying by 9.0 gives a terminal value of $1,284.3 million for Chicago Drugs's equity. Adding the terminal value of Chicago Drugs's debt, $188.3 million, gives the terminal value of Chicago Drugs's net assets:

$$\text{TV}(NA) = \text{TV}(E) + \text{TV}(D) - T - E \qquad (22.15)$$
$$= 1,284.3 + 188.3 - 0 - 0 = \$1,472.6 \text{ million}$$

where $\text{TV}(NA)$ denotes the terminal value of net assets, $\text{TV}(E)$ the terminal value of shareholders' equity, $\text{TV}(D)$ the terminal value of long-term debt (and capitalized lease and preferred stock) obligations, T any taxes incurred in realizing the terminal value, and E any other expenses incurred in realizing the terminal value.

In the second case, the estimated $142.7 million of earnings are multiplied by the acquisition multiple Monmouth assumes it will pay for Chicago Drugs, 16, to get gross proceeds of $2,283.2 million. But if Monmouth sells its Chicago Drugs stock, it estimates that it would incur $10 million of transaction costs. It would also realize a long-term capital gain in the amount of $1,788.2 (= 2,273.2 − 485) million.[32] Monmouth's financial staff estimates a future capital gains tax rate of 34%. At a 34% tax rate, Monmouth would incur capital gains tax of $608.0 million (= .34[1788.2]). This leaves

$$\text{TV}(NA) = 2,283.2 + 188.3 - 608.0 - 10 = \$1,853.5 \text{ million}$$

The calculation of terminal value is often critical. By assuming a high enough future multiple, an acquiror can justify any purchase price. It seems prudent to assume that the future acquisition multiple will be no greater than the current acquisition multiple, as we did in the illustration.

ACQUISITION ANALYSIS   Having calculated the incremental net cash flow stream, we can now apply discounted cash flow analysis. The required rate of return for the acquisition $r^*(\theta)$ is estimated by applying the procedure described in Chapter 19 to estimate the unleveraged required rate of return r and using Equation (19.17) to calculate $r^*(\theta)$, which is the weighted average cost of capital for the acquisition

$$r^*(\theta) = r - T^* \theta r_d(\theta) \left\{ \frac{1 + r}{1 + r_d(\theta)} \right\} \qquad (19.17)$$

Based on an analysis of comparable pharmaceutical companies, Monmouth's financial staff estimates the unleveraged required rate of return $r = .1659$. They also estimate the net-benefit-to-leverage factor $T^* = .25$. They previously determined the debt ratio $\theta = \frac{1}{3}$ and the cost of debt $r_d(\frac{1}{3}) = .12$. Substituting these values into Equation (19.17) gives

$$r^*(\theta) = .1659 - .25(\tfrac{1}{3})(.12) \left\{ \frac{1 + .1659}{1 + .12} \right\} = .1555, \text{ or } 15.55\%$$

Note that, as in capital budgeting, the proportions of debt and equity financing are the acquiror's long-run target proportions.

---

[32] Its original tax basis in the shares of Chicago Drugs equals the purchase price for the shares ($480 million) plus transaction costs ($5 million). The net sales proceeds realized upon the sale of the shares equals the sale price ($2,283 million) net of transaction costs ($10 million).

The incremental net cash flow stream is discounted at the required rate of return $r^*(\theta) = .1555$ to obtain the net present value of the acquisition, NPV (acquisition):

$$\text{NPV (acquisition)} = -\text{NAC} + \sum_{t=1}^{T} \frac{\text{CFAT}_t}{(1 + r^*(\theta))^t} \qquad \text{(22.16)}$$

where CFAT_t denotes the (unleveraged) incremental net cash flow during period t and T denotes the investment horizon. CFAT_t includes the terminal value of the acquisition (at the investment horizon).

Applying Equation (22.16) to Monmouth's proposed acquisition of Chicago Drugs indicates NPV (acquisition) = $1.1 million on a going-concern basis and NPV (acquisition) = $90.9 million on a disposition basis. The weighted-average-cost-of-capital approach indicates that the acquisition of Chicago Drugs at a price representing 16 times earnings would be profitable both on a going-concern basis and on a disposition basis, although only marginally so on a going-concern basis. The real worth of the business at the end of 10 years is the higher of the two terminal values, which will normally be the value calculated on a disposition basis.

Calculating terminal value on both bases reveals the sensitivity of the acquisition decision to the terminal value, and in this case, to the multiple applied to terminal year's earnings. Note that the present value of the incremental net cash flow stream, exclusive of terminal value, is $-$346.1 million. The terminal value must be at least $1,468.6 million for the NPV to be positive. Because the NPV of a proposed acquisition is normally very sensitive to the estimated terminal value, it is important to consider carefully the assumptions made in arriving at the estimate. It is also wise to calculate the break-even terminal value, which makes NPV (acquisition) equal to zero.

There is one additional use for discounted cash flow analysis. For any particular incremental net cash flow stream and discount rate, we can calculate the maximum price the acquiror could afford to pay for the target. The maximum price is the one that makes NPV (acquisition) equal to zero. Valuing Chicago Drugs on a disposition basis, Monmouth could afford to pay approximately $570.9 million (the original $480 million price plus the $90.9 million net present value), or $57.09 per share. At that price, Chicago Drugs's shareholders would experience a 111% gain ($57.09 versus $27) while Monmouth's would only expect, at best, to break even.[33] But this calculation assumes that Chicago Drugs can be sold for 16 times earnings at the end of 10 years, and a prospective acquiror might not want to make that sort of bet by offering to pay $57.09 per share.

ADJUSTED-PRESENT-VALUE APPROACH

Monmouth's financial staff has determined that a ⅓ debt-to-total-value ratio is appropriate. This suggests that $88.3 million of the $450 million of cash Monmouth needs to finance the acquisition can be raised through the issuance of new debt without altering Monmouth's debt capacity. The adjusted-present-value approach, which was described in Chapter 19, represents an alternative to the weighted-average-cost-of-capital approach to calculating the NPV of an acquisition.

[33] Strictly speaking, Monmouth could afford to pay an even higher price before NPV becomes zero. A higher price increases Monmouth's tax basis in Chicago Drugs's shares and reduces the future capital gains tax liability. For a purchase price of $570.9 million, the tax liability would be $577.0 million (= .34 [2,273 − 575.9]) versus $608.0 million when the purchase price paid for the stock is $480 million.

Modifying Equation (19.11) to incorporate the net acquisition cost NAC leads to the following expression for the adjusted present value (APV) of an acquisition

$$\text{APV (acquisition)} = -\text{NAC} + \sum_{t=1}^{T} \frac{\text{CFAT}_t}{(1 + r)^t} + \sum_{t=1}^{T} \frac{T^*I_t}{[1 + r_d(\theta)]^t} \quad \textbf{(22.17)}$$

−NAC plus the first sum represents the NPV of the acquisition on an all-equity basis (i.e., as though it was financed entirely with equity). The second sum represents the NPV of the interest tax shields on acquisition-related debt valued by applying the net-benefit-to-leverage factor T^*. We will illustrate the adjusted-present-value approach utilizing the disposition case in Table 22-5.

Monmouth's financial staff calculated the unleveraged required rate of return $r = .1659$. The NPV of the acquisition on an all-equity basis is

$$\text{NPV(all-equity)} = -542.6 + \sum_{t=1}^{10} \frac{\text{CFAT}_t}{(1.1659)^t} = \$43.7 \text{ million}$$

Next, we must calculate the present value of the interest tax shields. The debt pays interest annually. Monmouth's financial staff has been informed by the company's investment bankers that Monmouth can issue 10-year debt for the acquisition without a sinking fund. Issuing \$88.3 million principal amount of 10-year debt bearing a 12% coupon would require interest payments of \$10.60 million (= 88.3[.12]) per annum. The Chicago Drugs debt Monmouth assumes requires interest payments of \$10 million per annum. Total interest expense is \$20.60 million (= 10.60 + 10) per year for 10 years. The net-benefit-to-leverage factor is $T^* = .25$. The second sum in Equation (22.17) is

$$\text{PV(tax shields)} = \sum_{t=1}^{10} \frac{.25(20.60)}{(1.12)^t} = \$29.1 \text{ million}$$

Adding NPV(all-equity) and PV(tax shields) we get

$$\text{APV(acquisition)} = 43.7 \text{ million} + 29.1 \text{ million} = \$72.8 \text{ million}$$

which is less than the \$90.9 million NPV calculated on a disposition basis in Table 22-5. What accounts for the difference between the two figures? The required rate of return $r^*(\theta)$ used in the NPV calculation assumes that Monmouth rebalances its capital structure periodically to maintain $\theta = \frac{1}{3}$ whereas the APV calculation we performed was for a specific debt structure, \$100 million of 10-year debt bearing a 10% coupon and \$88.3 million of 10-year debt bearing a 12% coupon both maturing in a lump sum. But if Chicago Drugs's operating income increases in the manner shown in Table 22-5, Monmouth's debt ratio will gradually decrease. For example, consider year 10. The value of the \$1,957 incremental net cash flow for year 10 as of the beginning of year 10, denoted PV_E, is

$$\text{PV}_E = \frac{1,957}{1.1659} = \$1,678.53 \text{ million}$$

The 10% debt will generate interest tax shields during year 10 the value of which, denoted PV_S, is

$$\text{PV}_S = \frac{.25(10)}{1.12} = \$2.23 \text{ million}$$

at the beginning of year 10. Let D denote the amount of 12% debt outstanding at the beginning of year 10 consistent with a debt ratio of $\theta = \frac{1}{3}$. The amount D of 12% debt will generate interest tax shields during year 10 the value of which, denoted PV_T, is

$$PV_T = \frac{.25(.12)D}{1.12}$$

at the beginning of year 10. The total value of the Chicago Drugs assets at the beginning of year 10 can then be calculated from Equation (19.34)

$$\text{Asset value} = PV_E + PV_S + PV_T$$

$$= 1{,}678.53 + 2.23 + \frac{.25(.12)D}{1.12} \qquad \text{(22.18)}$$

But since $\theta = \frac{1}{3}$ and the value of the 10% debt at the beginning of year 10 is

$$\frac{110}{1.12} = \$98.21 \text{ million}$$

it follows that

$$\text{Asset value} = 3\,(D + 98.21) \qquad \text{(22.19)}$$

Equating Equations (22.18) and (22.19) and solving for D gives

$$D = \$466.21 \text{ million}$$

which is more than double the $198.17 million ($98.17 million of 10% debt plus $100 million of 12% debt) assumed in the APV calculation. The NPV calculation explicitly takes into account the additional future debt capacity created by the acquisition. The true APV(acquisition) when this debt capacity side effect is taken into account must equal the NPV so that[34]

$$\text{APV(acquisition)} = \text{NPV(all-equity)} + \text{PV(tax shields)} + \text{NPV(side effects)} \qquad \textbf{(22.20)}$$
$$= 43.7 + 29.1 + 18.1 = \$90.9 \text{ million}$$

Note that if Monmouth had decided, say for tax reasons, to finance the acquisition of Chicago Drugs on an all-common-stock basis, there would still have been a positive impact on Monmouth's debt capacity that should not be ignored. Equation (22.20) would give in that case

$$\text{APV(acquisition)} = 43.7 + 14.1 + 33.1 = \$90.9 \text{ million}$$

since the present value of the interest tax shields on the 10% debt is $14.3 million.

WHICH APPROACH TO USE

Either the weighted-average-cost-of-capital approach or the adjusted-present-value approach can be used to calculate the NPV of an acquisition. Applied correctly, the two approaches will provide the same NPV. In particular, it is important to hold the acquiror's debt ratio θ constant, which requires taking an acquisition's debt capacity side effects into account. Such a procedure is consistent with **debt service parity**.

We have found the Miles-Ezzell formula for the (weighted average) required rate of return to an investment easier to apply than the APV approach because the Miles-Ezzell formula involves adjusting the discount rate to reflect debt capacity side effects rather than estimating these effects period by period, which the APV method would require. As we noted in Chapter 19, the Miles-Ezzell formula assumes periodic capital structure rebalancing, which is generally consistent with corporate prac-

---

[34] The procedure outlined in the appendix to Chapter 19 could be adapted to calculate NPV(side effects) directly.

tice. It thus provides a reasonably accurate adjustment for debt capacity side effects that can result from an acquisition.

SIGNIFICANCE OF THE METHOD OF PAYMENT

Acquirors typically pay for acquisitions either in cash or in stock, or in some combination of the two. It was noted earlier that achieving tax-free treatment requires that the acquiror pay at least 50% of the purchase price in its stock although in many cases the acquiror has the flexibility to issue preferred stock instead of common stock.

CHOICE OF MEDIUM OF PAYMENT

Figure 22-3 breaks down merger transactions during the period 1964–1988 according to the method of payment. Overall during this period, 42% of the acquisitions were cash only, 42% were stock only, 1% were debt only, and the other 15% were paid for in a combination of stock, cash, and debt.[35] The proportion of transactions involving a combination of stock, cash, and debt generally increased throughout the period. Combinations of stock and debt arise in two-tiered tender offers, where shareholders of the target typically get debentures in the second tier of the transaction. Combinations of cash and debt are common in acquisitions of privately held companies where the sellers often take a note from the buyers as part of the purchase price.

Common stock tends to become a more popular medium of payment among acquirors during periods of rising stock prices, but the shareholders of publicly-traded acquirees, particularly the arbitrageurs who typically replace a significant portion of the public shareholders as soon as an acquisition is announced, prefer cash as the medium of payment. The large leveraged buyouts of the 1980s, of which the RJR Nabisco LBO is the most striking example, often took the form of cash tender offers financed with a combination of bank borrowings and high-yield bonds. During 1988, as the LBO boom crested, 76% of the acquisitions of publicly-traded companies were cash-only transactions.

COMMON STOCK AND NET ACQUISITION COST

The medium of payment is certainly not a matter of indifference to acquirors. They often decide to pay in common stock when they think their share price is attractive; they think it is "cheaper" to pay in common stock than to pay in cash. But whether it is really cheaper depends on how the transaction is structured and on what happens to their share price after the transaction is announced.

Suppose Monmouth wished to buy Chicago Drugs in an exchange of common stock. If Monmouth's management and Chicago Drugs's management agreed on a firm price of $480 million payable in Monmouth common stock, the net acquisition cost would remain $542.6 million regardless of what happened thereafter to Monmouth's share price. But in stock-for-stock acquisitions it is customary to negotiate an exchange ratio, that is, so many shares of Monmouth for each share of Chicago Drugs. If the acquiror's share price then increases, so does the net acquisition cost. Of course, if the acquiror's share price falls, so does the net acquisition cost.

---

[35] *Mergerstat Review 1988* (Chicago: W. T. Grimm & Co., 1989): 50. The Internal Revenue Code imposes certain restrictions on the use of debt to finance acquisitions. For example, in certain situations interest deductions are limited to $5 million per year when the acquiror issues convertible subordinated debt to finance the acquisition and fails to meet certain debt-to-equity ratio and interest coverage standards. Also, there are restrictions on the issuer's ability to claim interest tax deductions in highly leveraged acquisitions when non-investment-grade zero-coupon bonds or so-called payment-in-kind bonds, which pay interest in the form of additional bonds rather than cash, are issued to finance the takeover.

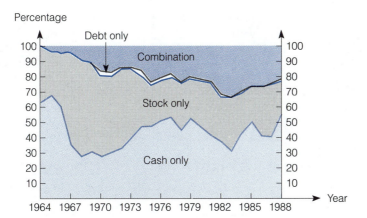

FIGURE 22-3
Trend in method of payment,
1964–1988.
Source: W. T. Grimm & Co.,
Mergerstat Review 1988, 50.

To continue the Monmouth/Chicago Drugs example, suppose that Monmouth has 50 million shares outstanding that are trading at a price of $32 each. Chicago Drugs has 10 million shares outstanding. If Monmouth offers to pay $48 for each Chicago Drugs share, it will have to exchange 1.5 (= 48/32) of its shares for each Chicago Drugs share. Monmouth will have to issue 15 million (= [1.5]10 million) new shares. As a result, Chicago Drugs's former shareholders will own 23% (= 15 million/[15 million + 50 million]) of Monmouth after the acquisition. If the exchange ratio is fixed and if stock market investors believe that the market value of Monmouth's equity should be $2,170.9 million after the acquisition, which equals Monmouth's current market value ($1,600 million) plus what it will pay to acquire Chicago Drugs's equity ($480 million) plus the NPV in the disposition case ($90.9 million), then Monmouth's share price will rise to $33.40 per share (= $2,170.9/65), and its cost of purchasing Chicago Drugs's shares will increase to $501.0 million (= $33.40[1.5]10). The fixed exchange ratio effectively appropriates 23% of the NPV for Chicago Drugs's former shareholders.

On the other hand, if investors believe that the market value of Monmouth's equity after the merger should be $1,950 million, then Monmouth's share price will fall to $30 (= 1,950/65), and its cost of purchasing Chicago Drugs's shares will fall to $450 million (= $30[1.5] 10). In this case, Chicago Drugs's former shareholders share the burden of the fall in value of Monmouth's shares.[36] Thus, an acquiror's shareholders are better off in a stock-for-stock transaction than in a cash-for-stock transaction if the acquiror overpays.

DILUTION IN EARNINGS PER SHARE A publicly-traded acquiror is usually concerned about the impact an acquisition will have on its future reported earnings per share. As noted earlier, an acquisition can increase earnings per share under pooling-of-interests accounting when the acquiror's price-earnings multiple exceeds the target's. However, when the acquiree's price-earnings multiple exceeds the acquiror's, the accounting impact is just the opposite. Table 22-6 illustrates the dilutive case. Absent any operating economies or other synergistic benefits, the market value of the combined entity is just the sum of the market values of the acquiror and the acquiree. Because the acquiror has the lower price-earnings multiple, its earnings per

---

[36]Realizing this possibility, acquirees often try to negotiate a flexible exchange ratio designed to assure them a fixed dollar price for their shares. For example, if Monmouth's share price falls to $30 upon the announcement of the acquisition but the exchange ratio adjusts to 1.60 Monmouth shares per Chicago Drugs share, Chicago Drugs's shareholders would still realize $48 (= 1.60 x $30) per share.

TABLE 22-6   Illustration of Dilutive Impact of an Acquisition on Reported Earnings Per Share

	Acquiror	Acquiree	Combined
Total Earnings	$50,000,000	$10,000,000	$60,000,000
Number of shares	10,000,000	5,000,000	14,000,000[a]
Earnings per share	$ 5.00	$ 2.00	$ 4.29
Share price	$50.00	$40.00	$50.00
Price/Earnings ratio	10.0x	20.0x	11.7x

[a] Acquiror exchanges 0.8 common share for each of the acquiree's common shares, issuing a total of 4 million new shares.

share are diluted from $5.00 per share to $4.29 per share but its price-earnings multiple increases from 10.0x to 11.7x.

You should appreciate that as long as transactions take place in an efficient capital market, dilution in earnings per share will have only an accounting impact; it is not an indicator of a proposed acquisition's impact on shareholder wealth.

22.5   MERGER AND ACQUISITION TACTICS

A large percentage of merger and acquisition transactions are done on a "friendly" basis. The two parties agree to merge and then negotiate the legal form of the transaction, price, method of payment, and other terms. But not all transactions are friendly. Management of the target may resist the potential acquiror's overtures. As discussed below, managers and boards of directors of publicly-traded companies have gone to great lengths in recent years to erect defensive barriers to help fend off unwanted suitors. Such resistance no doubt reflects, at least in part, the Principle of Self-Interested Behavior. But if management refuses to negotiate, the potential acquiror can take its offer directly to the target's shareholders along either of two avenues: a tender offer or a proxy contest. Managers and boards of directors have exhibited remarkable creativity in designing takeover defenses to thwart such threats to their security. Such tactics have been termed **shark repellents** in the media.

TENDER OFFERS

Few events in business pack as much drama—or engender as much bitterness—as a hostile tender offer by one firm for the shares of another. A **tender offer** is an offer to purchase shares of stock at a stated price from shareholders who are willing to "tender" shares at that price. In a hostile tender offer, the management of the target firm takes steps, often including litigation, to contest the offer. Hostile "raids" became an established acquisition strategy in 1974 when one of the leading securities firms assisted International Nickel Co. of Canada in a successful hostile tender offer for ESB, Inc.

Tender offers are often employed when incumbent management refuses to negotiate with the prospective acquiror. In other cases, management may be ambivalent to a proposed acquisition, and a tender offer lets the shareholders decide for themselves whether they like the acquiror's offer. Typically, the tender price represents a substantial premium over the target's prevailing share price, and tender offers are almost always made exclusively in cash.

EXAMPLE ■   The 3-month battle in mid-1981 for control of Conoco Inc., at the time the ninth largest oil company in the United States, is one of the classic battles for corporate control in the history of American business. In addition to Conoco, it involved DuPont Co., Mobil Corp., Seagram Co. Ltd., Texaco Inc., and several leading Wall Street investment banks and law firms. It culminated in DuPont's acquiring Conoco for $8.0 billion in spite of a higher cash bid by Mobil. At the time, it was the largest acquisition in U.S. history.

The drama began to unfold in May 1981.[37] Conoco had decided to sell its 53% controlling interest in Hudson's Bay Oil & Gas Co. On May 5, Dome tendered for 20% of Conoco's common stock at a price of $65 per share. Dome hoped to persuade Conoco to exchange the Hudson's Bay stock for its own shares, which Dome believed would be a tax-free transaction. Conoco shareholders tendered 51% of the outstanding Conoco stock, even though the $65 tender price represented only a 30% premium over the approximately $50 price at which Conoco's shares had been trading and was substantially below the $150 estimated liquidation value per share. The Dome tender put Conoco "in play."

After attempts to negotiate a friendly deal failed, Seagram launched a cash tender offer on June 25 for 41% of Conoco's stock at $73 per share. Conoco approached DuPont to serve as a **white knight**. DuPont insisted on receiving the option to purchase 16 million shares (18.5% of the firm) directly from Conoco for $87.50 per share. DuPont then tendered for 40% of Conoco's stock also at $87.50 per share on July 6 and promised to exchange DuPont shares for the other 60% of Conoco's stock. Seagram countered with a cash bid of $85 per share for 51% of Conoco's stock on July 13. The next day DuPont raised its bid to $95 per share in cash for 40% of Conoco's stock. Mobil jumped into the battle July 17, bidding $90 per share for 50% of Conoco's stock. Ten days later DuPont raised its bid to $95 in cash for 45% of Conoco's stock and Mobil raised its to $105. (Seagram's final bid occurred a few days earlier, $92 per share.) Mobil raised its offer to $115 and then to $120 per share, but most investors were unwilling to tender to Mobil for fear that the U.S. Justice Department would delay or perhaps block the deal for antitrust reasons. When DuPont raised its bid on August 4 to $98 per share for 45% of the stock, and securities for the balance, the prize was totally theirs.

Some observers said that Mobil failed to win Conoco because the "antitrust premium" it offered Conoco shareholders was not large enough. Others said that DuPont prevailed because the chemistry was better in a DuPont-Conoco merger. ■

ADVANTAGES OF TENDER OFFERS   There are a number of potential advantages to cash tender offers as compared to alternative acquisition methods. First, a cash tender offer represents the quickest means of obtaining control of another firm. There are no terms to be negotiated and no securities to be registered. The buyer decides on a tender price and other terms of the offer and files the tender offer documents with the Securities and Exchange Commission. Tender offers also have a shorter minimum waiting period for government antitrust review.[38] However, tender offers are regulated under the Williams Act amendments to the Securities Ex-

---

[37]The following account is based on "The Making of the Megamerger," *Fortune*, September 7, 1981, 58–64.

[38]The minimum waiting period under the Hart-Scott-Rodino Act is 15 calendar days for cash tender offers and 30 calendar days otherwise.

change Act of 1934, and Securities and Exchange Commission rules do not permit an all–out blitzkrieg. The Williams Act requires disclosure (within 10 days of reaching the threshold) of all acquisitions of 5% or more of any class of a firm's equity securities as well as disclosure of tender offers or exchange offers to acquire a class of equity securities of a publicly-traded company.

Second, a tender offer provides greater flexibility than other acquisition strategies. A firm can tender for just enough shares to give it effective control. In the case of a publicly-traded company whose shares are widely held, this may require tendering for only 20% to 40% of the outstanding shares. The acquiror can set conditions of the offer so that, for example, it does not have to buy any shares unless the required minimum number are tendered. Once the acquiror has purchased these, resistance on the part of the acquiree's management will normally lessen. The acquiror can then effect a merger structured as a tax-free reorganization to achieve 100% ownership.

Third, a cash tender offer represents the simplest way for a foreign company to buy an American company. American investors would generally be reluctant to swap shares of a U.S. company for securities of a foreign company for legal and other reasons. A cash tender offer gets around this problem.

Fourth, open market purchases of the target firm's stock followed by a cash tender offer give the potential acquiror an opportunity for profit. The cash tender price effectively puts a floor under the target's share price and alerts the financial community that the target firm is "in play." If a higher bidder emerges, the original bidder can take some consolation from the profits it realizes on the shares of the target it holds.

CONTESTED TENDER OFFERS   Tender offers are often contested by the target's management. Such resistance typically takes the form of mounting an aggressive public relations campaign, filing lawsuits, bidding for the other firm's shares (the so-called Pac-Man defense), as well as other steps. Table 22-7 provides a perspective on the relative success of these efforts. Just over one-quarter of the tender offers launched within the past 10 years have been contested. The target's management succeeded in keeping the target independent in approximately one-fourth of the contested situations. The bidder prevailed in approximately one-half of the contested tender offers. Overall, the original bidder succeeds in roughly 75% to 80% of all tender offers. But it is the other 20% to 25% of the tender offers that capture much of the headlines.

Unexpected tender offers are a source of concern to management. Not only does the 20-day minimum period the tender offer must remain open seem awfully short to a firm that gets caught by surprise but current tender offer regulations require the target firm to disclose its response—including the reasons for the particular response—within 10 business days of the commencement of the offer. To prepare themselves for the unexpected, many companies have directed their investment bankers to gather the necessary valuation data and to stand ready to render a valuation judgement on the firm quickly should another firm announce a tender offer.

PROXY CONTESTS

Tender offers are expensive because the bidder must purchase a sufficient number of shares to secure control. Alternatively, one or more individuals who oppose incumbent management can initiate a **proxy contest**. They solicit shareholders' proxies— a proxy conveys the right to vote the shares of the person who grants the proxy—to

TABLE 22-7 Tender Offers for Publicly-Traded Companies, 1979–1988

	1979	1980	1981	1982	1983	1984	1985	1986	1987	1988	10-Year Total
Number attempted	106	53	75	68	37	79	84	150	116	217	985
Contested by Target:											
Number	26	12	28	29	11	18	32	40	31	46	273
Percentage of total	25%	23%	37%	43%	30%	23%	38%	27%	27%	21%	28%
Number Contested and Bidder Prevailed:											
At original bid	3	1	7	10	3	2	5	5	4	5	45
At higher bid	5	2	6	7	4	8	9	10	14	22	87
Number Contested and Bidder Failed:											
Target remained independent	9	3	6	10	1	6	9	10	6	6	66
Target acquired by 'white knight'	9	6	9	2	3	2	9	15	7	13	75
Survival percentage[a]	35%	25%	21%	34%	9%	33%	28%	25%	19%	13%	24%
Canceled for other reasons	10	5	1	5	1	8	3	8	10	31	82
Completed or Pending at Year-End:											
Number	78	39	59	51	32	63	63	117	93	167	762
Percentage of total	74%	74%	79%	75%	86%	80%	75%	78%	80%	77%	77%

[a] Number of contested tender offers in which the target remained independent expressed as a percentage of the number of contested tender offers.
Source: W. T. Grimm & Co., *Mergerstat Review 1988*, 85–86.

vote their shares at the next annual meeting of stockholders in favor of a dissident slate of directors. However, a proxy fight is expensive and time-consuming, and few proxy contests succeed.

Shareholders seem to prefer cash in hand—especially when it represents a large premium over the prevailing share price—to the mere promise that the firm's financial prospects will improve in the future under new management. This observation is consistent with the Principle of Risk-Return Trade-Off. It is not surprising then that the vast majority of contests for control take the form of cash tender offers rather than proxy fights.

DEFENSIVE TACTICS

Corporate managers often react negatively to unsolicited takeover bids. One would hope that their motive in doing so is to achieve the highest possible value for the firm's shares rather than merely exhibiting the Principle of Self-Interested Behavior. Contested takeovers tend to produce a higher price than uncontested transactions. But in some situations, managers appear more intent on protecting their jobs than on maximizing shareholder value. We hope that such situations are the exception rather than the norm.

The courts have generally held that the directors of a firm have a responsibility to obtain maximum value for shareholders. For example, the Delaware courts ruled in a landmark case involving Revlon Inc. that once a board of directors decides to sell or dramatically restructure the firm, it must act neutrally and strive to achieve the highest possible price. But the Delaware Chancery Court's decision, upheld by the

Delaware Supreme Court in connection with the battle for Time Inc., permits a board of directors to reject an unsolicited bid if it believes that the firm's long-term strategy will produce greater value for shareholders.[39] Time shareholders had sued Time because the firm intended to proceed with its purchase of Warner Communications Inc. without a shareholder vote. The acquisition of Warner would preempt a $200 per share bid for Time that Paramount Communications Inc. had announced. Time's shares were trading at around $144 at the time of the court decision. The Time ruling seems to lend additional support to the use of defensive tactics to ward off unwanted suitors.

Corporate managers have devised a host of defensive tactics, all in the name of promoting shareholder value, of course. Table 22-8 lists some of the more popular ones. These tactics include anticipatory steps that management and the board take in order to reduce the risk of getting blind-sided. But they can also entrench management. The **poison pill** has become controversial, and in at least two cases the Delaware Chancery Court ordered the board of directors to redeem poison pills in order to let shareholders choose between a restructuring plan supported by the board and an outside bidder's cash tender offer. The responsive tactics are more extreme, and many involve the sale of assets or securities.

IMPLICATIONS FOR SHAREHOLDER WEALTH   The use of defensive tactics raises serious questions about how they affect shareholder wealth. If they entrench inefficient management, shareholder wealth must suffer. Two studies conclude that corporate charter amendments that authorize a staggered election of directors or supermajority voting do not adversely affect stock prices.[40] Other studies of targeted share repurchases (i.e., **greenmail**) find that the other shareholders, who do not receive favored treatment, suffer a loss of wealth.[41]

THE AGENCY PROBLEM IN THE BID RESPONSE   The managers' role in determining the corporation's response to an unsolicited takeover bid reflects a potentially serious agency problem. A bid at a large premium to the current share price might benefit shareholders but, at the same time, could cost the managers their jobs. Unless the managers will benefit from the merger, they would have a strong incentive (their jobs) to reject the bid. (Recall the Principle of Self-Interested Behavior.) Many companies have established "golden parachutes" in order to reduce potential conflicts of this sort. The golden parachutes provide generous payments to managers who lose their jobs as a result of a takeover of the company. In some cases these payments have been substantial. For example, the RJR Nabisco, Inc. leveraged buyout resulted in payments to employees totaling $166 million. Golden parachutes are designed to align the objectives of shareholders and managers. However, if they are too generous, under the Principle of Self-Interested Behavior, they could give management an incentive to sell the firm on terms that may not be the most advantageous ones for shareholders.

---

[39] The Chancery Court ruled that "the financial vitality of the corporation and the value of the firm's shares is in the hands of the directors and managers of the firm. The corporation law does not operate on the theory that directors, in exercising their powers to manage the firm, are obligated to follow the wishes of a majority of shares." "Pity the Poor Shareholder in Wake of Time Decision, Advocates Say," *Wall Street Journal*, August 1, 1989, Cl ff. The Chancery Court did not apply the Revlon precedent because Time had not put itself up for sale.

[40] DeAngelo and Rice (1983); Linn and McConnell (1983).

[41] Dann and DeAngelo (1983); Bradley and Wakeman (1983); and Mikkelson and Ruback (1985).

TABLE 22-8 Frequently Employed Takeover Defensive Tactics

Defensive Tactic	Description
Anticipatory tactics:	
Dual class recapitalization	Company distributes a second class of common stock that possesses superior voting rights (e.g., 10 votes per share). New shares cannot be sold. Shareholders who wish to sell must exchange new shares for regular shares. Over time, management's voting power increases as other shareholders sell their shares.
Employee stock ownership plan (ESOP)	Company sells a large block of common stock (or voting preferred stock) to a company-sponsored ESOP and repurchases an equivalent number of common shares in the open market. Company votes the ESOP's shares until they are distributed to employees, which typically takes place over several years.
Poison pill	Company issues rights to its shareholders (typically, one nondetachable right per common share) which entitle the shareholders to purchase at one-half the market price (1) shares of the company's common stock if a potential acquiror buys more than a specified percentage of the company's shares (flip-in poison pill) or (2) shares of the acquiror's common stock following an acquisition of the company (flip-over poison pill). The acquiree's board of directors can redeem the rights for a nominal sum (typically, $0.05 per right) if it approves of the acquisition.
Staggered election of directors	Company's board of directors is divided into three equal classes. Only one class stands for reelection each year. A hostile raider cannot obtain control through a single proxy context.
Supermajority voting/fair price provision	Company's charter is amended to require a supermajority (e.g., 80%) of the company's common shares to be voted in favor of a merger that has not been approved by the company's board of directors. (If it is board-approved, a simple majority usually applies.) A fair price provision waives the supermajority voting provision provided the acquiror agrees to pay all shareholders the same price. The fair price provision is designed to prevent two-tier bids.
Responsive tactics:	
Asset purchases or sales	Company purchases assets that the bidder does not want or that would block the bidder by creating an antitrust problem. Company sells the "crown jewel" assets that the bidder wants.
Leveraged recapitalization	Company borrows a large sum of money and distributes the loan proceeds along with any other excess cash to its shareholders as a dividend. A recapitalization is designed to make it more difficult for a takeover raider to make the acquisition with borrowed funds.
Litigation	Company files suit against the bidder alleging violation of state takeover statute(s), antitrust laws, securities laws, or other laws or regulations.
Pac-Man defense (or Counter tender offer)	Company makes a counterbid for the common stock of the potential acquiror.
Share repurchases or sales	Company uses excess cash or borrows cash with which to finance a large share repurchase program. Alternatively, the company might instead only repurchase shares from the takeover raider, any premium over fair market value representing "greenmail." As a third alternative, the company can sell shares to a "friendly" third party.
Standstill agreement	Prospective acquiror agrees during the term of the agreement (1) not to increase its shareholdings above a specified percentage and, in many cases, (2) to vote its shares with management.

CORPORATE RESTRUCTURING

When threatened by a takeover bid by the Henley Group in March 1988, Santa Fe Southern Pacific announced a leveraged recapitalization, which included a dividend of $25 per share in cash and $5 face amount per share of a 16% senior subordinated debenture to the holders of its common stock. Santa Fe Southern Pacific's $7.3 billion leveraged recapitalization was financed largely through bank borrowings. It eliminated the firm's excess cash and virtually ensured that for many years to come the firm would have relatively little cash for discretionary investment, such as diversification into new businesses. Michael Jensen has argued that getting corporate cash into shareholders' hands where it can be invested as the shareholders see fit is one of the principal benefits of mergers and merger threats.[42] He also argues, quite persuasively, that the increase in leverage that results from corporate restructurings (and leveraged buyouts) tends to boost managerial efficiency because of the need to generate on a regular basis sufficient operating cash flow to service the firm's debt.[43]

One empirical estimate is that shareholders realized an aggregate gain of $5.3 billion from just eight leveraged recapitalizations that took place in 1985 and 1986.[44] Another indicates that the shareholders in eight recapitalizations that took place in the 1985–1987 period experienced an average return of 33.3% during the 60-day period prior to the announcement.[45] A majority of the companies in these studies had already received a takeover bid or were aware of an impending bid. This empirical evidence suggests that the leveraged recapitalization is one takeover response that appears to work to the shareholders' benefit.

22.6   LEVERAGED BUYOUTS

Kohlberg Kravis Roberts & Co. (KKR) acquired RJR Nabisco, Inc. in 1988 in a leveraged buyout costing $26 billion (including over $1 billion of transaction costs). Its common equity investment was a mere $1.5 billion, just 5.8% of the cost of the acquisition. A **leveraged buyout** is an acquisition that is financed principally, sometimes more than 90%, by borrowing on a secured basis; lenders look to the collateral value of the firm's assets as security for their loans and to the operating cash flow these assets are expected to generate as the source of cash to service these loans.

THE RJR NABISCO, INC. LEVERAGED BUYOUT

On October 20, 1988, RJR Nabisco announced that a management group, which included its president and chief executive and the chief executive of its tobacco subsidiary, had advised the board of directors that they "intend to seek to develop with a financial partner a proposal to acquire the firm in a leveraged buyout."[46] The financial advisor was Shearson Lehman Hutton Inc. The press release noted that the management group contemplated paying about $75 per share in cash, for an aggregate value of $17.6 billion. An outside committee of the board had been formed to evaluate any proposal that might be forthcoming, and the committee had hired two investment banking firms to advise it. With the announcement, RJR Nabisco was in play.

THE BIDDING FRENZY   Four days later KKR announced that it was offering to acquire the firm for $90 per share in cash and securities (plus $108 for each outstanding share of preferred stock) and that it had hired four investment banking firms to assist it in this effort. The press reported that Henry Kravis (the second K in KKR) had told Shearson executives that KKR had to participate in the RJR Nabisco buyout

---

[42] Jensen (1984).
[43] Jensen (1986a, 1986b).
[44] Black and Grundfest (1988).
[45] Kleiman (1988).
[46] RJR Acquisition Corporation, Offer to Purchase, October 27, 1988, 18.

in order "to protect its franchise" as the leading LBO firm.[47] On October 27, KKR tendered for up to 87% of RJR Nabisco's stock at $90 per share and stated that it would issue securities worth $90 per share in a second-stage transaction. On November 2, the outside committee of the board requested proposals to acquire the firm from "all credible parties." The next day the management group announced that it had held discussions with KKR regarding a joint bid, that it had terminated discussions, and that it had decided to bid $92 per share. By this time, at least eight leading investment banks and several leading law firms were involved in the battle. The outside committee issued a set of bidding rules and procedures on November 7 in order to "elicit the highest and best offers for the company from all credible interested parties."[48] The announcement specified a November 18 due date.

On November 20, the outside committee announced that it had received three bids: (1) KKR's bid for 80% of the common stock for $94 cash and securities for the balance, (2) the management group's bid for 79% of the common stock for $100 cash, and cash and securities for the balance, and (3) a bid from a group led by The First Boston Corporation (at least the ninth investment bank to enter the fray) that proposed selling the firm's food business by year-end 1988 for the account of RJR Nabisco's common stockholders and having the First Boston-led group buy the firm's tobacco business in 1989. Due to the complexity of the third bid, the outside committee extended the deadline to November 29. On November 29, KKR raised its bid to $106 cash for 75% of the common stock and $106 of securities for the remaining shares; the management group raised its bid to $101 per share; and the First Boston-led group submitted a revised proposal that it valued at between $103 and $115 per share. The outside committee entered into all-night negotiations with KKR that night to "clarify" certain aspects of KKR's revised offer. Meanwhile, the management group prepared yet another bid, this one for $108 per share, which it submitted November 30. When the outside committee notified KKR that it intended to consider management's $108 per share bid, KKR promptly raised its bid to $108 per share. Incredibly, the outside committee then asked KKR and the management group to make their "highest and best offers." KKR raised its bid to $109 per share ($81 of it in cash), and the management group submitted a bid which it valued at $112 per share ($84 of it in cash) but which the outside committee's investment bankers valued at $109 per share. Bear in mind the Principle of Self-Interested Behavior and that management had indicated initially its intention to bid $75 per share. RJR Nabisco's board voted unanimously to accept the KKR offer.

FINANCING FOR THE LEVERAGED BUYOUT   On December 6, KKR tendered for up to 165.5 million shares of RJR Nabisco's common stock (74% of the outstanding shares) at a price of $109 per share and for the 1.25 million outstanding preferred shares at $108 per share. Common stockholders tendered 98.7% of the outstanding common shares, and KKR purchased 75.2% of these shares at a cost of $18 billion.[49] The transaction was so large that it caused a small blip in the U.S. money supply. The balance of the common stock was eliminated in exchange for a

---

[47]"Offers for RJR Pit KKR and Shearson in a Battle for Turf," *Wall Street Journal*, October 25, 1988, A1.
[48]RJR Nabisco, Inc., Amendment No. 6 to Schedule 14D-9, December 7, 1988.
[49]"RJR Holders Get Payment in $25 Billion Takeover," *Wall Street Journal*, February 22, 1989, A4. When the first step in the acquisition closed February 9, KKR's escrow agent received $18.9 billion during the morning. Because the Fed wire system cannot handle amounts larger than $999 million, the banks and securities firms had to make multiple wire transfers. In addition, Citibank wired in money to the escrow bank in $800 million chunks, Chase Manhattan Bank wired in funds in $900 million amounts, and Bankers Trust Company wired in money in $950 million pieces, in order to help minimize confusion. Drexel Burnham, which raised a mere $5 billion, hand delivered a check (in good-the-same-day Fed funds).

combination of preferred stock and convertible debt through a merger effected April 28, 1989. Table 22-9 shows how KKR financed the $25.96 billion net cost of the leveraged buyout. Senior bank borrowings provided 49% of the funds. Subordinated lenders provided 19% by privately purchasing two series of increasing rate notes, whose respective interest rates increase by specified amounts at quarterly intervals. The new common stockholders provided 8% of the funds consisting of $500 million invested in pay-in-kind extendible debt securities and $1.5 billion invested in common stock. The pay-in-kind extendible debt securities are subordinated to the increasing rate notes, can not be repaid until a variety of conditions have been met, and earn interest in the form of additional notes rather than cash. The securities issued in the merger step account for the 24% balance of the funds.

Figure 22-4 shows the legal ownership structure KKR created for the buyout. The layering of ownership entities is designed to rank the claims of the various classes of securities holders on RJR Nabisco's cash flow and assets. The lower the tier the relatively more senior the claim. For example, holders of the exchangeable preferred stock can get cash only if RJR Holdings Capital Corp. pays cash dividends, which are severely restricted under the terms of the debt issues RJR Holdings Capital Corp. has outstanding.

PROFITABILITY OF THE LEVERAGED BUYOUT It goes without saying: $26 billion is an enormous capital investment. On October 19, 1988, the last day prior to the announcement that certain members of management were contemplating a leveraged buyout, RJR Nabisco common stock closed at $55⅞. Common stockholders who held on to their shares and tendered them to KKR for $109 realized a 95% premium. Clearly they profited handsomely. But how profitable was KKR's investment?

Table 22-10 reports the estimated break-up value of RJR Nabisco at the time of the leveraged buyout, as estimated by KKR's investment bankers. We said earlier in this chapter that a firm with multiple businesses can be valued by considering each line of business separately and by examining the prices paid in comparable trans-

TABLE 22-9 Sources of Permanent Financing for the Acquisition of RJR Nabisco, Inc.
(Dollar Amounts in Millions)

Investment:		Sources of Financing:	
Purchase of common stock	$24,589	Senior bank debt	$12,634
Purchase of preferred stock	135	Subordinated debt	5,000
Fees and expenses	1,100	Junior subordinated notes [a]	500
Interest to date of merger	570	Convertible debentures [b]	2,259
Payments to employees	166	Exchangeable preferred stock [b]	4,067
Other	70	Common stock	1,500
Excess cash	(670)		
Total investment	$25,960	Total funds invested	$25,960

[a] Pay-in-kind extendible debt securities purchased by certain equity investors.
[b] Issued in exchange for common stock in the second step of the transaction.
Source: RJR Holdings Capital Corp., Prospectus, May 12, 1989.

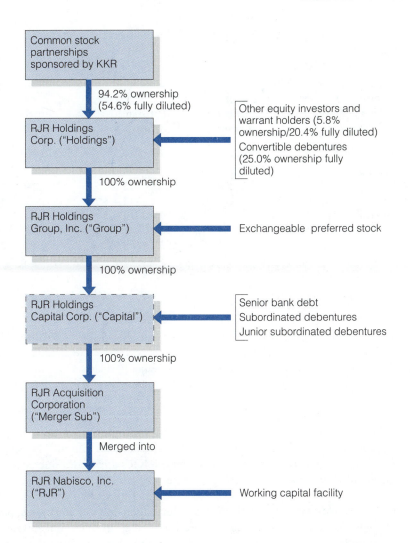

FIGURE 22-4
Ownership and financing
structure for the acquisition
of RJR Nabisco, Inc.

actions for each line of business. That approach was taken in preparing the estimates in Table 22-10.

The estimated pretax value of the assets, on a disposition basis, is between $32.54 billion and $37.91 billion before transaction costs. At December 31, 1988, RJR Nabisco had $4.98 billion of non–LBO-related long-term debt and $1.62 billion of other noncurrent liabilities outstanding. Current assets would be adequate to cover current liabilities even after stripping away excess cash, assuming the carrying value of the current assets accurately reflects their current market value. The net acquisition cost equals the amount of funds invested shown in Table 22-9 plus the cost of assuming outstanding liabilities, approximately $32.56 billion in all. Comparing this cost to the estimated pre-tax values in Table 22-10, the RJR Nabisco leveraged buyout appears at worst to be a zero–net-present-value investment. At best, it would have a net advantage of several billion dollars.

We would need more information than we have to calculate the present value of the future interest tax shields, which would increase the net present value. In addition, press reports indicated that RJR Nabisco's debt fell in price by approximately

TABLE 22-10   Estimated Break-up Value of RJR Nabisco, Inc. at the Time of the Leveraged Buyout
(Dollar Amounts in Millions)

Segment	Est. 1989 Operating Income	Estimated Multiple	Estimated Pretax Value[a]
Tobacco products	$2,351	7.4x– 8.5x	$17,400–19,980
Food products:			
Nabisco Biscuit Co.	400	10.6 –12.5	4,240– 5,000
Nabisco Foods Co.	275	11.1 –12.4	3,050– 3,410
Nabisco Brands Int'l.	195	11.8 –14.4	2,300– 2,810
Nabisco Brands Canada	54	10.2 –11.1	550– 600
Del Monte Foods	284	8.1 – 9.9	2,300– 2,810
Planters Life Savers Co.	191	11.0 –13.1	2,100– 2,500
Total food products	1,399		
Ownership interest in ESPN			300– 400
Other assets			300– 400
Total estimated break-up value			$32,540–37,910

[a] Estimated on a disposition basis. Values are rounded to the nearest 10 million.

Source: RJR Holdings Capital Corp., Offering Brochure, December 1988.

20% to 30% in response to the leveraged buyout announcement, so that the outstanding long-term liabilities cost significantly less than $6.6 billion.[50] Nevertheless, these very rough calculations help us understand KKR's apparent reluctance in raising its $108 bid to its final bid of $109 per share.

AGENCY PROBLEMS   The RJR Nabisco leveraged buyout illustrates two significant agency problems. First, the management-led group announced that it was contemplating bidding $75 per share, far below the $109 acquisition price. The relatively low initial bid undoubtedly reflects the Principle of Two-Sided Transactions: The better the deal for the managers, the worse the deal would be for the shareholders. If shareholders had sold their shares to the management-led group, that group would have reaped a windfall of $34 per share, or more than $7.5 billion in the aggregate. Fortunately, the board of directors immediately formed a special outside committee and took steps to enable the firm's shareholders to realize "full value" for their shares.

Second, as already noted, the leveraged buyout caused RJR Nabisco's bonds to plummet in value. The fall in bond value reflected a transfer of wealth to the shareholders from the bondholders. This is an example of the problem of **claim dilution with respect to capital structure**, a concept we discussed in Chapter 9. Soon thereafter, Moody's Investors Service Inc. downgraded the bonds to Ba-2, from A-1.[51] Worse, the transaction sent shock waves through the corporate bond market as bond investors became concerned that other corporate bonds might be subject to

---

[50] "Two Underwriters Demand RJR Call Swiss Franc Bonds," *Wall Street Journal*, February 7, 1989, C1, and "Metropolitan Life is Set Back in Suit Over RJR Bonds," *Wall Street Journal*, June 1, 1989, A14.

[51] The bonds were downgraded from the third highest category (A) and investment-grade status to the fifth highest category (Ba) and junk-bond-grade status.

similar "event risk." Investors began to demand new protective bond covenants, called "super poison puts," that would force issuers to redeem bonds at par in the event a change in control occurs.[52] Event risk is, of course, another form of agency cost, and the demand for super poison puts represents the bondholders' attempt to reduce this cost.

CHARACTERISTICS OF LEVERAGED BUYOUTS

The RJR Nabisco acquisition illustrates the distinctive features of a leveraged buyout:

■ A well-established firm (RJR Nabisco is the second largest U.S. producer of cigarettes and is also a leading producer of food products) that, in many cases, is a division or subsidiary of a large publicly-traded company that would like to dispose of it;

■ Very high leverage;

■ Multiple layers of secured debt with the most junior class(es) and/or the class providing the largest portion of the debt financing being given a significant equity interest to induce lenders to take this risk;

■ Operating cash flow is dedicated to repaying debt, the senior-most debt first, as quickly as possible;

■ Company management is given a substantial equity stake, typically 10% to 20%, in the form of common stock and stock options, to give them a strong economic incentive to operate the business profitably (RJR Nabisco's management owns approximately 6% of the firm on a fully diluted basis but that stake is worth $155 million when valued at the $5 price per share at which the LBO investors purchased their shares); and

■ Outside equity investors and lenders who receive an equity interest look to the public offering of their shares within 5 to 7 years for the return on their investment. There are very tight restrictions limiting cash dividend payments.

"IDEAL" LEVERAGED BUYOUT CANDIDATES   Ideal leveraged buyout candidates have:

■ Multiple product lines with secure leading market position, strong brand identity, and broad customer base in each (RJR Nabisco's established brand names include Winston and Salem cigarettes, Life Savers candy, Planters peanuts, Blue Bonnet margarine, Ritz crackers, and Nabisco Shredded Wheat);

■ Industry characterized by low rate of technological change and not affected by fashion trends;

■ Assets with good collateral value (e.g., good quality receivables and readily marketable non-perishable inventory);

■ Historical record and projections indicate stable profitability and stable cash flow (i.e., relatively noncyclical business);

■ Purchase price represents a relatively low multiple of earnings, preferably no more than eight times (the higher the multiple, the more difficult it will be for the available operating cash flow to service debt incurred to finance a high percentage of the purchase price);

[52] "Shock Still Clouds Blue-Chip Corporate Bond Market," *Wall Street Journal*, March 22, 1989, C1.

- Minimal capital expenditure requirements (operating cash flow must be used to repay debt);
- Very capable management; and
- Low leverage currently (so as to facilitate the maximum use of debt capacity to buy out existing shareholders).

FINANCING A LEVERAGED BUYOUT

The aforementioned qualities characterize a firm that has relatively low operating risk. It is this low operating risk that permits the firm to take on an unusually high degree of financial risk. In addition, layers of subordinated debt provide comfort to senior lenders much like true equity. Since subordinated lenders often have an equity interest as well, the subordinated debt really represents a mechanism for getting them an interim flow of cash while creating interest tax shields for the firm.

The actual financing structure for a leveraged buyout will depend crucially on the perceived riskiness of the firm's business, its cash flow characteristics, and the quality of its assets, all of which determine how much debt the firm can support. The following rough parameters characterize the financial structure of many leveraged buyouts:

- Senior debt, typically provided by banks and finance companies, which has a maturity of between 6 and 10 years and carries a floating interest rate that represents a premium of 100 to 400 basis points over prime rate, depending on the nature of the firm and the degree of leverage. Senior debt often includes special short-term credit facilities with designated purposes. For example, the RJR Nabisco bank debt included an 18-month $6 billion asset sale bridge facility to be repaid out of the net proceeds from the sales of certain assets and a 2-year $1.5 billion refinancing bridge facility to be repaid out of the proceeds of long-term financing. Senior debt typically represents between 50% and 75% of the total financing.

- Subordinated debt, typically provided by life insurance companies, special leveraged buyout funds (many of which pool moneys invested by pension funds), and other junk bond investors. The subordinated debt typically has a maturity of between 10 and 20 years and carries a fixed interest rate that represents a premium of 200 to 500 basis points over the rate at which the lender would normally be willing to lend to a triple-B-rated firm. Subordinated debt often consists of two or more classes with different levels of subordination. For example, the RJR Nabisco subordinated debt consisted of three classes, the most junior of which was purchased by certain equity investors. This most junior layer consisted of pay-in-kind notes, which pay interest in the form of additional notes rather than cash. Such securities are frequently used in very highly leveraged acquisitions. Subordinated debt typically represents between 10% and 25% of the total financing.

- Preferred equity, typically provided by life insurance companies or leveraged buyout funds, which is used when the debt layers exhaust the firm's ability to use interest tax shields. As in the RJR Nabisco LBO financing, the preferred equity is often exchangeable at the issuer's option for debt, so that the issuer can claim interest tax deductions after it becomes taxable.

- Common equity, which is typically provided by the acquiror, leveraged buyout funds, management, and to a lesser extent, subordinated lenders and other investors. In the RJR Nabisco LBO, partnerships sponsored by KKR invested $1.424

billion (95% of the common equity), and two securities firms invested $76 million.

Within these parameters, investment bankers try to determine the maximum level of debt the firm's operations can support. The analysis-of-comparables approach together with the discounted-cash-flow approaches will suggest a reasonable purchase price. This price together with the firm's borrowing capacity will indicate the maximum degree of leverage for the buyout.

SOLUTION TO MONMOUTH'S ACQUISITION ALTERNATIVE

At the beginning of the chapter we posed four questions with respect to Monmouth Pharmaceuticals Company's proposed acquisition of Chicago Drugs Inc.: (1) reasonable price to pay, (2) impact of the acquisition on Monmouth's shareholders, (3) maximum price Monmouth can afford to pay, and (4) recommended financial package to offer Chicago Drugs's shareholders.

During our discussion of comparative analysis, we estimated a reasonable acquisition price range of between $414 million and $448 million based on a review of recent comparable acquisitions of proprietary pharmaceutical manufacturers.

During our discussion of discounted cash flow analysis, we estimated that even if Monmouth offered to pay $48 per share—a price slightly above the estimated reasonable range—the acquisition would have a net present value of $1.1 million on a going-concern basis and a net present value of $90.9 million on a disposition basis.

Based on this NPV, it appears that Monmouth could afford to pay up to $9.09 per share (= $90.9 million/10 million shares) more than the $48 price contemplated, for a total of up to $57.09 per share. Actually, Monmouth would still have a positive NPV at that price because the preceding calculation did not take into account the effect of the higher tax basis Monmouth would have in Chicago Drugs's stock.

Monmouth has decided there is no benefit to stepping up the tax basis of Chicago Drugs's operating assets so it may decide to pursue a tax-free transaction. In that case, at least 50% of the consideration it offers Chicago Drugs's shareholders would have to consist of equity securities. Depending on the form of tax-free transaction, Monmouth might be limited to using common stock to pay 100% of the purchase price. If Monmouth does decide to initiate a tender offer, it should offer Chicago Drugs's shareholders cash, in order to maximize the likelihood of a successful tender offer, and it should issue securities to raise the needed cash. The mix of securities should be consistent with its long-term capital structure objective.

SUMMARY

A merger represents a special form of capital investment. One firm acquires the entire portfolio of assets and, typically, the liabilities of another firm. Such a transaction has special legal, tax, and accounting consequences. A merger is larger, more complex, and thus more difficult to analyze than the purchase of a building or a single machine. Nevertheless, discounted cash flow analysis, when supplemented by an analysis of comparable merger transactions, will indicate what net acquisition price is reasonable to pay and can indicate whether a proposed transaction at that price is likely to benefit the acquiror's shareholders.

Companies have a variety of motives for merging but a merger will benefit both the acquiror's shareholders and the acquiree's shareholders only if (1) the two com-

DECISION SUMMARY BOX

- When one firm acquires another firm it makes a capital investment. The tools of capital budgeting can be used to evaluate proposed acquisitions. But the size and complexity of acquisition transactions make it more difficult to apply these analytical tools to acquisitions than to an investment in a plant or a piece of equipment.

- The acquiror must select its target. A firm must have a valid motive for acquiring another firm. The benefits of the acquisition for the acquiror's shareholders should be assessed realistically. Pure conglomerate mergers whose only benefit is diversification are only beneficial if the acquiror's shareholders cannot achieve such diversification as cheaply on their own, which will seldom be the case. The acquiror must assess the antitrust and other regulatory consequences of the proposed acquisition in order to determine its feasibility and advisability.

- The acquiror must choose the legal form the acquisition should take: merger or consolidation, purchase of stock, or purchase of assets.

- The acquiror must evaluate its tax position, the target's tax position, and the tax position of the target's shareholders and decide whether it prefers a tax-free transaction or a taxable transaction.

- The acquiror is also normally concerned about the accounting impact of an acquisition, even though the available evidence indicates that the choice of accounting method does not affect valuation. It can choose between pooling of interests and purchase accounting treatments. Acquirors also often place a constraint on how much dilution in earnings per share they are willing to accept.

- The acquiror must decide how it wishes to pay for the acquisition: cash, common stock, other securities, or some combination. Its choice will be restricted by the legal form of transaction, tax status, and accounting treatment it chooses. Common stock has a potential advantage in that the target's shareholders bear part of the risk that the acquiror has overpaid.

- The acquiror can use comparative analysis to determine a range of reasonable acquisition prices.

- If sufficient information is available the acquiror can use discounted cash flow analysis to evaluate the net present value of the acquisition. Discounted cash flow analysis or comparative analysis should also be used to determine the maximum price the acquiror can afford to pay (which is likely to depend on the legal form and tax status of the acquisition).

- Considering all its prior decisions and the likely response(s) of the target, the acquiror must decide how to proceed with the transaction: cash tender offer, friendly proposal to merge, one-step or two-step transaction, etc. The defensive barriers the target has already erected will affect this decision. Prior to proceeding with the transaction, the acquiror must comply with all applicable legal and regulatory requirements.

- As the transaction proceeds—or as the battle for control unfolds—the acquiror may have to alter some of its earlier decisions if it finds that its objectives conflict with those of the target. But throughout this process the acquiror must not lose sight of the fact that its ultimate objective is to maximize the wealth of its stockholders.

panies are worth more together than they are apart and (2) the increase in value is large enough to offset the transaction costs involved. Merging will benefit the acquiror's shareholders only if they can realize some of this net gain. Factors that might give rise to a net gain and thus represent valid motives for merging include opportunities to (1) realize operating efficiencies and economies of scale, (2) utilize tax deductions and tax credits more efficiently, and (3) grow more rapidly or more cheaply. Corporate managers often cite a fourth motive: diversification. Diversification at the corporate level can benefit shareholders by reducing bankruptcy risk or by avoiding the taxation of dividend distributions. But diversification to reduce earnings cyclicality or to create financial synergy is a highly questionable motive. Pure conglomerate mergers, without any synergistic benefits, are unlikely to do anything for shareholders that they can not already do by diversifying their own portfolios. And the financial synergy that is often sought is really illusory; corporate debt capacity increases because shareholders of the merged firms have effectively guaranteed each other's debt.

A proposed merger must satisfy certain legal requirements, in particular, compliance with the federal antitrust and securities laws and with each firm's charter. An acquiror can merge or consolidate with the acquiree or instead purchase the acquiree's stock or instead purchase only (some portion of) the acquiree's assets. An acquiror can structure an acquisition so that it is either taxable or tax-free. In a taxable transaction, the acquiree's shareholders are taxed on their gains but the acquiror can step up the tax basis of the acquiree's assets. In a tax-free transaction, the acquiree's shareholders who receive stock of the acquiror can defer tax on their gains but the acquiror gets no step up in tax basis. The tax treatment of the acquisition can have significant cash flow consequences for the acquiror.

An acquiror can also structure an acquisition so that it qualifies for purchase accounting treatment or pooling-of-interests accounting treatment. The former treats the acquisition like a purchase of assets, and the latter combines the two companies as though they had been together since inception. While the choice of accounting method can have a significant impact on the acquiror's reported earnings per share, empirical evidence indicates that the choice of accounting technique will not affect the acquiror's market value significantly.

There are two basic approaches to valuing corporate acquisitions: comparative analysis and discounted-cash-flow analysis. The former is more widely used in practice but the two can be used effectively in concert. Comparative analysis is used to gauge a reasonable acquisition price. This is done by analyzing the price-earnings multiples, cash flow multiples, book value multiples, and premiums paid in comparable acquisitions and inferring from these reasonable multiples at which to value the target.

The discounted-cash-flow approaches are designed to measure the net present value of an acquisition to the acquiror's shareholders. The two discounted-cash-flow approaches introduced in previous chapters, the weighted-average-cost-of-capital approach and the adjusted-present-value approach, were modified in this chapter to handle corporate acquisitions.

When a firm wishes to make its offer to purchase directly to the target firm's shareholders, it makes a tender offer. That represents the quickest means of obtaining control. Two-step mergers have become an effective acquisition technique: a cash tender offer for just under 50% of the target followed by a tax-free merger.

Under the right circumstances, an acquisition can be financed on a highly leveraged basis. In these so-called leveraged buyouts, lenders look to the collateral value of the assets as the security for their loans and to the operating cash flow those assets are expected to generate as the source of cash to service those loans. Only companies with secure market positions, stable profitability and cash flow, low operating risk, minimal capital expenditure requirements, and very capable management need apply.

PROBLEMS

PROBLEM SET A

A1. Define the following terms:
   a. Merger
   b. Consolidation

c. Horizontal merger
d. Vertical merger
e. Conglomerate merger

A2. Explain the valid motives two companies may have for merging.

A3. The Diversification Principle states that diversification is Beneficial. Diversification is one of the principal justifications managers give when undertaking conglomerate mergers. Explain why the justification is usually invalid notwithstanding the Diversification Principle.

A4. How can a merger create financial synergy? How can it create business synergy? What is the difference between these two types of synergy?

A5. Ace Homebuilding and Brace Homebuilding will merge. Ace has a total market value of $50 million; Brace has a total market value of $75 million; and their merger will lead to operating efficiencies and produce a present value savings of $10 million.
a. What is the total market value of the merged companies?
b. If the merger would entail expenses amounting to $5 million, is there a net advantage to merging?
c. If Ace buys Brace's outstanding shares, paying Brace's common stockholders a $3 million premium, would the acquisition be advantageous to Ace's shareholders. How is the net advantage to merging divided between the two companies' shareholders?

A6. Two companies plan to merge. Prior to the merger, the acquiror has earnings per share of $5 and a price-earnings ratio of 20. The acquiree has earnings per share of $2 and a price-earnings ratio of 10. The acquiror has 10 million shares of stock, and the acquiree has 5 million shares.
a. How many shares must the acquiror exchange for each of the acquiree's shares if the shares are exchanged at their respective market values (i.e., no premium).
b. Calculate the acquiror's earnings per share after the merger.
c. Calculate the acquiror's price-earnings ratio after the merger.
d. What conclusion can be drawn from parts b and c?

A7. How is the net advantage to merging typically divided between shareholders of acquirors and shareholders of acquirees?

A8. Describe the three basic ways of effecting a corporate acquisition and explain the distinguishing features of each.

A9. Describe the principal differences between a **tax-free acquisition** and a **taxable acquisition**. Which of these does a seller generally prefer and which does a buyer generally prefer?

A10. What are the basic requirements to achieve tax-free treatment of a corporate acquisition?

A11. Describe the principal differences between the **pooling of interests** and the **purchase** methods of accounting for acquisitions. Should the choice of accounting technique affect market value in an efficient market?

A12. The purchase price in an acquisition is $275 million. Consultants estimate that the fair market value of the assets acquired is $180 million. Investment bankers estimate that the fair market value of the liabilities assumed in the acquisition is $30 million. Calculate the amount of goodwill.

A13. Define the term **tender offer** and explain how a company can acquire another company through a tender offer. What are the principal advantages of a tender offer relative to other acquisition methods?

A14. Define the term **proxy contest** and explain how an investor group can gain control of a company through a proxy contest. What are the principal disadvantages of a proxy contest relative to a cash tender offer?

A15. Describe the principal defensive tactics that companies have used in an effort to fight off unwanted suitors. How would you expect the use of such tactics to affect shareholder wealth? Describe the agency problem that arises in connection with defensive tactics to thwart unwanted bids.

A16. What distinguishes a **leveraged buyout** from other types of acquisitions?

PROBLEM SET B

B1. Company A intends to acquire Company B. The acquisition will cost Company A $100 million. Company A plans to install new management, "fix" the company, and sell it at the end of 5 years. The projected incremental free cash flow stream Company A expects to realize from the acquisition, which reflects the anticipated operating improvements, is:

Year	1	2	3	4	5
Cash flow ($ millions)	10	20	30	40	50

In addition, the projected after-tax sales proceeds amount to $200 million.
   a. Calculate the NPV of the acquisition assuming a 20% cost of capital.
   b. Calculate the internal rate of return for the acquisition.
   c. Calculate the payback period for the acquisition.
   d. Should Company A proceed with the acquisition?

B2. Two companies merge in a stock-for-stock transaction. What happens to stockholder wealth and bondholder wealth as a result of the merger? Must this *always* be the case in a stock-for-stock transaction?

B3. A corporation owns two plants that it purchased 10 years ago for $5,000,000. The two plants have been depreciated to zero but have a current fair market value of $6,000,000. An acquiror has offered $8,000,000 to buy the corporation. Following the acquisition, it could depreciate the plants straight-line over 5 years. The acquiror's income tax rate is 40%, and its 5-year new issue debt rate is 12%. The selling corporation has two shareholders whose tax basis in their shares is their original $5,000,000 investment to purchase the two plants. Their capital gains tax rate is 28%, and they invest most of their funds in municipal bonds yielding 7%. They had originally planned to sell their business and retire in 2 years, but the $8 million offers seems "too good" to refuse.
   a. Calculate the net present value of the tax shields that would result from writing up the tax basis of the plants. Would the acquiror prefer a taxable transaction?
   b. Calculate the incremental cost of a taxable transaction. Would the sellers prefer a tax-free transaction?
   c. Calculate the net advantage of a taxable transaction. Would the acquiror and the sellers benefit mutually from a tax-free transaction?

B4. Explain why certain shareholders of the acquiree might incur an income tax obligation even though the acquisition qualifies under the Internal Revenue Code as a tax-free acquisition. Must every shareholder of the acquiree necessarily incur an income tax obligation in connection with a taxable acquisition?

B5. National Permanent Credit Corporation just acquired Specific Capital Corporation. National paid $50 per Specific share. Specific's latest 12 months' fully diluted earnings per share before extraordinary items was $5 and fully diluted cash flow per share before extraordinary items was $6.25, the most recent book value per share was $20, and the closing share price 30 days prior to the merger announcement was $35. Calculate the following ratios:

   a. Multiple of earnings paid
   b. Multiple of cash flow paid
   c. Multiple of book value paid
   d. Premium paid

B6. Is it necessarily true that

   a. An acquisition that satisfies the requirements for pooling of interests accounting treatment will qualify as a tax-free reorganization? Explain.
   b. An acquisition that satisfies the requirements for a tax-free reorganization will qualify for pooling of interests accounting treatment? Explain.

B7. International Oil Company has oil and gas reserves consisting of 25 million barrels of oil and 60 billion cubic feet of natural gas. Based on the prices at which oil and gas reserves have recently sold, 1 barrel of oil is equivalent to 6,000 cubic feet of natural gas.

   a. Calculate the number of barrels of oil equivalent in International's reserves.
   b. Regal Oil Corporation is contemplating a bid for International based on the value of International's assets. Petroleum reserves have recently sold for $8.50 per barrel of oil equivalent and Regal estimates that International's other assets are worth $52.5 million. Calculate the estimated value of International's assets.

B8. Big Blue Computer Corporation is preparing to make a bid for the common shares of Macrohard Software Company. Big Blue would acquire the shares for cash but not write up Macrohard's assets. Macrohard has 5 million shares outstanding, which are trading at a price of $30 per share and a price-earnings multiple of 10. Macrohard has $50 million principal amount of 8% debt, which pays interest annually in arrears and matures in a lump sum at the end of 6 years. Big Blue's marginal income tax rate is 40%. Big Blue estimates that it will have to pay a 50% premium to acquire Macrohard and also pay $3 million of after-tax transaction costs. Macrohard has no excess cash. Big Blue's target debt-to-equity ratio is ⅓, its pretax cost of new debt is 10%, its cost of capital for the acquisition is 16.5%, and the incremental free cash flow stream for the next 6 years is

Year	1	2	3	4	5	6
Cash flow ($ millions)	25	30	35	40	45	50

   a. Calculate the NPV and IRR of the acquisition on a going-concern basis, assuming the estimated year 6 net operating profit is $75 million.
   b. Calculate the NPV and IRR of the acquisition on a disposition basis assuming a 6-year investment horizon.
   c. Should Big Blue make the acquisition if it has to pay $45 per share?
   d. What is the maximum price Big Blue can afford to pay on a disposition basis with a 6-year investment horizon?

B9. Big Blue Computer Corporation in problem B8 has a leveraged beta of 1.25. The risk-free rate is 10% and the risk premium on the market portfolio is 8%.

   a. Calculate the unleveraged cost of equity capital for Big Blue.
   b. Calculate the APV of the acquisition on a going-concern basis assuming the debt issued to finance the acquisition matures in a lump sum at the end of 6 years.

c. Calculate the APV of the acquisition on a disposition basis assuming the debt issued to finance the acquisition matures in a lump sum at the end of 6 years.

B10. With regard to Monmouth's acquisition of Chicago Drugs, suppose Monmouth's new issue rate is 13%.
   a. What is the market value of the $100 million of outstanding bonds?
   b. Would the acquisition help or hurt Chicago Drugs's bondholders?
   c. What is the cause of this transfer of wealth?

B11. Big Sky Airlines would like to acquire Far West Commuter Air and integrate Far West's route structure into its system. Big Sky would acquire Far West's shares for cash but not write up Far West's assets. Far West has 2 million shares outstanding; its share price is $24; its earnings per share are $4; and it has no debt and no excess cash. Big Sky's debt-to-equity ratio is 2-to-1; its pretax cost of debt is 14% (annual interest); its cost of equity is 20%; and its marginal income tax rate is 40%. If Big Sky acquires Far West, it projects a year 8 net operating profit of $45 million and incremental free cash flows of:

Year	1	2	3	4	5	6	7	8
Cash flow ($ millions)	6	10	12	14	18	22	25	30

   a. Calculate the NPV and IRR of the acquisition on a going-concern basis assuming Big Sky pays a ⅓ premium for Far West's shares and $500,000 of after-tax acquisition expenses.
   b. Calculate the NPV and IRR of the acquisition on a disposition basis under the same assumptions as in part a and assuming an 8-year investment horizon with an estimated year 8 net operating profit of $45 million.
   c. Should Big Sky make the acquisition if it has to pay a ⅓ premium for Far West's shares?

B12. Big Sky's unleveraged cost of equity capital is 16%. Calculate the adjusted present value of Big Sky's acquisition of Far West Commuter Air under the assumptions stated in problem B11 and assuming the debt issued to finance the acquisition matures in a lump sum at the end of 8 years.

B13. Ajax Air Products and Central Combustion have agreed to an exchange of common stock under which Ajax would acquire Central. Ajax's common stock is trading at $40 per share, and Central's common stock is trading at $20 per share. Each company has 10 million shares outstanding.
   a. Calculate the exchange ratio assuming Ajax does not pay a premium.
   b. Calculate the exchange ratio assuming Ajax pays a 25% premium to acquire Central.
   c. If the exchange ratio determined in part b is fixed and the announcement of the merger causes Ajax's share price to fall 10%, by how much would you expect Central's share price to change?

PROBLEM SET C

C1. Arnold Electronics and Beard Oil and Gas plan to combine through merger. Neither company has any debt. The merger will involve a share-for-share exchange, and there will be no transaction costs. Arnold has total market value $V_A = \$100$ million, and Beard has total market value $V_B = \$200$ million. There are no synergistic effects that will result from the merger.
   a. What is the maximum value the combined companies could have following the merger?
   b. Suppose that if there were no merger, Arnold's shares and Beard's shares

would be expected to provide annual rates of return of 20% and 25%, respectively. Further suppose that there exist two other companies, one of whose shares are a perfect substitute for Arnold's and the other of whose shares are a perfect substitute for Beard's. What must be the expected rate of return on the shares of the merged firm in a perfect market environment?

c. Show that if the shares of the merged firm were trading at a price that would provide an expected annual rate of return of 23%, market agents could earn a pure arbitrage profit. Explain how this could be accomplished, and quantify the profit.

d. Suppose instead that neither the Arnold shares nor the Beard shares has a close substitute. Show that the value of the combined companies following the merger must be less than $300 million.

C2. Two companies are identical, including their capital structures. Each faces two possible states of nature, which are equally likely and which are denoted F (favorable) and U (unfavorable). The returns to the stockholders of each firm and the returns to debtholders are identical in each state but the likelihood that state F will occur for company A and the likelihood that it will occur for company B are uncorrelated. For each company, debtholders have a prior claim to the first 140 of income. The returns in each state are:

	Return in State		Expected	Standard
Return to	F	U	Return	Deviation
Firm	200	100	150	50
Debtholders	140	100	120	20
Stockholders	60	0	30	30

a. Specify the set of possible outcomes for the merged firm, for the former debtholders of each company, and for the former stockholders of each company following a merger through an exchange of shares.

b. Show that each class of debtholders is better off as a result of the merger.

c. Show that each class of stockholders is worse off as a result of the merger.

d. What conclusions can be drawn from parts b and c?

C3. American Car Rental has agreed to acquire Big Apple Car Rental. American's financial staff has gathered the following data regarding acquisitions involving companies in the automobile industry:

Acquiree	Business	Price/ Earnings	Price/ Cash Flow	Price/ Book Value
Central	rental	10x	5.8x	1.5x
Eastern	manufacturing	7	4.3	1.2
Western	manufacturing	6	4.0	1.1
South Central	rental	11	6.7	1.6
Southwestern	rental	12	7.8	1.4
Panhandle	manufacturing	8	4.9	1.3

Price denotes the price paid in the acquisition. Big Apple's latest 12 months' earnings are $25 million, latest 12 months' cash flow is $40 million, and current aggregate book value is $175 million. Calculate a reasonable range of acquisition values for Big Apple.

C4. Radnor Publishing would like to acquire Excelsior Publishing from The Miami Media Group. Radnor estimates that the net acquisition cost, before any depreciation recapture, would be $125 million. Radnor estimates that Excelsior's incremental free cash flow is currently $15 million and is growing at 15% per annum into the foreseeable future before allowing for any asset write-up. Radnor believes it could sell Excelsior at the end of 10 years at a multiple of $^{125}/_{15} = 8\frac{1}{3}$ times incremental free cash flow. The Miami Media Group acquired Excelsior 1 year ago for $100 million, which represents its current tax basis in Excelsior's stock. Excelsior's tax basis in its assets is $25 million because Excelsior's assets consist primarily of goodwill. Radnor's marginal income tax rate is 40%, and its cost of capital for the acquisition is 16%.

    a. Calculate Radnor's NPV of acquiring Excelsior's common stock for $125 million cash assuming that Radnor can write up Excelsior's assets to $50 million and pay only $10 million in depreciation recapture taxes.

    b. Calculate Radnor's NPV of acquiring Excelsior's common stock for $125 million common stock. [Hint: the transaction is tax-free].

    c. Would Miami Media prefer a taxable transaction or a tax-free transaction? Calculate the difference in taxes payable.

    d. How would you recommend that Miami Media and Radnor structure the acquisition: taxable or tax-free?

C5. An investment group acquires the Spring Lake Greeting Card Company in a leveraged buyout. The investment group pays $100 million for Spring Lake, 90% of which it borrows at a 14% annual interest rate. The $100 million purchase price represents a multiple of 8 times incremental free cash flow. Spring Lake's marginal income tax rate is 40%. Spring Lake's incremental free cash flow is expected to grow at the rate of 10% per annum into the foreseeable future. All available free cash flow will be used first, to pay interest, next, to repay principal (until the acquisition loan is fully repaid), and then to pay dividends. The unleveraged cost of equity capital for similar acquisitions is 14%. Calculate the NPV of the leveraged buyout assuming a 6-year investment horizon.

C6. At the time the Delaware Chancery Court ruled in favor of Time Inc. and let it proceed with its purchase of Warner Communications, Time's shares were trading at around $144 per share. Paramount Communications had bid $200 per share for Time's common stock. Time's board of directors refused to let the shareholders vote on the proposed Warner Communications transaction and argued that their long-term strategy had greater value for the Time shareholders. After the court decision, Paramount withdrew its bid.

    a. What do Time's actions reveal about the existence of agency costs?

    b. How could you reconcile the board's argument that its long-term strategy has a present value in excess of $200 per share with the fact that the stock was trading at just $144 per share?

REFERENCES

Alberts, William W., and Joel E. Segall, eds. *The Corporate Merger.* Chicago: University of Chicago Press, 1966.

Aranow, Edward R. *Tender Offers for Corporate Control.* New York: Columbia University Press, 1973.

Arthur Andersen & Co. *Guide to Mergers and Acquisitions.* Chicago: Arthur Andersen & Co., 1988.

Asquith, Paul, Robert F. Bruner, and David W. Mullins, Jr. "The Gains to Bidding Firms from Merger." *Journal of Financial Economics* 11 (1983): 121–40.

Asquith, Paul, and E. Han Kim. "The Impact of Merger Bids on the Participating Firms' Security Holders." *Journal of Finance* 37 (December 1982): 1209–28.

Benjamin, Harvey E., and Michael B. Goldberg. *Leveraged Acquisitions: Private and Public.* New York: Practising Law Institute, 1984.

Bhagat, Sanjai, James A. Brickley, and Uri Loewenstein. "The Pricing Effects of Interfirm Cash Tender Offers." *Journal of Finance* 42 (September 1987): 965–86.

Black, Bernard S., and Joseph A. Grundfest. "Shareholder Gains from Takeovers and Restructurings Between 1981 and 1986: $162 Billion is a Lot of Money." *Continental Bank Journal of Applied Corporate Finance* 1 (Spring 1988): 5–15.

Bradley, Michael, Anand Desai, and E. Han Kim. "Synergistic Gains from Corporate Acquisitions and their Division Between the Stockholders of Target and Acquiring Firms." *Journal of Financial Economics* 21 (1988): 3–40.

Bradley, Michael, and L. MacDonald Wakeman. "The Wealth Effects of Targeted Share Repurchases." *Journal of Financial Economics* 11 (April 1983): 301–28.

Bruner, Robert F. "Leveraged ESOPs and Corporate Restructuring." *Continental Bank Journal of Applied Corporate Finance* 1 (Spring 1988): 54–66.

Dann, Larry Y., and Harry DeAngelo. "Standstill Agreements, Privately Negotiated Stock Repurchases, and the Market for Corporate Control." *Journal of Financial Economics* 11 (April 1983): 275–300.

Dann, Larry Y., and Harry DeAngelo. "Corporate Financial Policy and Corporate Control: A Study of Defensive Adjustments in Asset and Ownership Structure." *Journal of Financial Economics* 20 (1988): 87–128.

Davidson, Sidney, and Roman L. Weil, eds. *Handbook of Modern Accounting,* 3rd ed. New York: McGraw-Hill Book Company, 1983, chapter 33.

DeAngelo, Harry, and Linda DeAngelo. "Proxy Contests and the Governance of Publicly Held Corporations." *Journal of Financial Economics* 23 (June 1989): 29–59.

DeAngelo, Harry, Linda DeAngelo, and Edward M. Rice. "Going Private: Minority Freezeouts and Shareholder Wealth." *Journal of Law and Economics* 27 (1984): 367–401.

DeAngelo, Harry, and Edward M. Rice. "Antitakeover Charter Amendments and Stockholder Wealth." *Journal of Financial Economics* 11 (April 1983): 329–60.

Dennis, Debra K., and John J. McConnell. "Corporate Mergers and Security Returns." *Journal of Financial Economics* 16 (1986): 143–87.

Dodd, Peter, and Jerold B. Warner. "On Corporate Governance: A Study of Proxy Contests." *Journal of Financial Economics* 11 (April 1983): 401–38.

Eger, Carol Ellen. "An Empirical Test of the Redistribution Effect in Pure Exchange Mergers." *Journal of Financial and Quantitative Analysis* 18 (December 1983): 547–72.

Elgers, Pieter T., and John J. Clark. "Merger Types and Shareholder Returns: Additional Evidence." *Financial Management* 9 (Summer 1980): 66–72.

Ellert, James C. "Mergers, Antitrust Law Enforcement and Stockholder Returns." *Journal of Finance* 31 (May 1976): 715–32.

Haugen, Robert A., and Terence C. Langetieg. "An Empirical Test for Synergism in Merger." *Journal of Finance* 30 (September 1975): 1003–14.

Hayn, Carla. "Tax Attributes as Determinants of Shareholder Gains in Corporate Acquisitions." *Journal of Financial Economics* 23 (June 1989): 121–53.

Higgins, Robert C., and Lawrence D. Schall. "Corporate Bankruptcy and Conglomerate Merger." *Journal of Finance* 30 (March 1975): 93–113.

Hirshleifer, Joseph. *Price Theory and Applications.* Englewood Cliffs, NJ: Prentice-Hall, 1984.

Hong, Hai, Robert S. Kaplan, and Gershon Mandelker. "Pooling vs. Purchase: The Effects of Accounting for Mergers on Stock Prices." *Accounting Review* 53 (January 1978): 31–47.

Jarrell, Gregg A., and Annette B. Poulsen. "The Returns to Acquiring Firms in Tender Offers: Evidence from Three Decades." *Financial Management* 18 (Autumn 1989): 12–19.

Jensen, Michael C. "Takeovers: Folklore and Science." *Harvard Business Review* 62 (November-December 1984): 109–21.

Jensen, Michael C. "Agency Costs of Free Cash Flow, Corporate Finance, and Takeovers." *American Economic Review* 76 (May 1986a): 323–29.

Jensen, Michael C. "The Takeover Controversy: Analysis and Evidence." *Midland Corporate Finance Journal* 4 (Summer 1986b): 6–32.

Jensen, Michael C. "Eclipse of the Public Corporation." *Harvard Business Review* (September-October 1989): 61–74.

Jensen, Michael C., and Richard S. Ruback. "The Market for Corporate Control: The Scientific Evidence." *Journal of Financial Economics* 11 (April 1983): 5–50.

Kim, E. Han, and John J. McConnell. "Corporate Mergers and the Co-Insurance of Corporate Debt." *Journal of Finance* 32 (May 1977): 349–63.

Kleiman, Robert T. "The Shareholder Gains from Leveraged Cash-Outs: Some Preliminary Evidence." *Continental Bank Journal of Applied Corporate Finance* 1 (Spring 1988): 46–53.

Levy, Haim, and Marshall Sarnat. "Diversification, Portfolio Analysis and the Uneasy Case for Conglomerate Mergers." *Journal of Finance* 25 (September 1970): 795–802.

Lewellen, Wilbur G. "A Pure Financial Rationale for the Conglomerate Merger." *Journal of Finance* 26 (May 1971): 521–37.

Linn, Scott C., and John J. McConnell. "An Empirical Investigation of the Impact of 'Anti-takeover' Amendments on Common Stock Prices." *Journal of Financial Economics* 11 (April 1983): 361–99.

Mandelker, Gershon. "Risk and Return: The Case of Merging Firms." *Journal of Financial Economics* 1 (December 1974): 303–35.

Manne, Henry G. "Mergers and the Market for Corporate Control." *Journal of Political Economy* 73 (April 1965): 110–20.

Marais, Laurentius, Katherine Schipper, and Abbie Smith. "Wealth Effects of Going Private for Senior Securities." *Journal of Financial Economics* 23 (June 1989): 155–91.

Mergerstat Review 1988. Chicago: W. T. Grimm & Co., 1989.

Mikkelson, Wayne H., and Richard S. Ruback. "An Empirical Analysis of the Interfirm Investment Process." *Journal of Financial Economics* 14 (December 1985): 523–53.

Mueller, Dennis C. "The Effects of Conglomerate Mergers: A Survey of the Empirical Evidence." *Journal of Banking and Finance* 1 (December 1977): 315–47.

Nathan, Kevin S., and Terrence B. O'Keefe. "The Rise in Takeover Premiums: An Exploratory Study." *Journal of Financial Economics* 23 (June 1989): 101–19.

Palepu, Krishna G. "Predicting Takeover Targets: A Methodological and Empirical Analysis." *Journal of Accounting and Economics* 8 (March 1986): 3–36.

Shleifer, Andrei. "Do Demand Curves for Stocks Slope Down?" *Journal of Finance* 41 (July 1986): 579–90.

Shrieves, Ronald E., and Donald L. Stevens. "Bankruptcy Avoidance as a Motive for Merger." *Journal of Financial and Quantitative Analysis* 14 (September 1979): 501–15.

Steiner, Peter O. *Mergers: Motives, Effects, Policies*. Ann Arbor: University of Michigan Press, 1975.

Stewart, G. Bennett, III, and David M. Glassman. "The Motives and Methods of Corporate Restructuring." *Continental Bank Journal of Applied Corporate Finance* 1 (Spring 1988): 85–99.

Travlos, Nickolaos G. "Corporate Takeover Bids, Methods of Payment, and Bidding Firms' Stock Returns." *Journal of Finance* 42 (September 1987): 943–63.

Weston, J. Fred, and Kwang S. Chung. "Do Mergers Make Money?" *Mergers & Acquisitions* 18 (Fall 1983): 40–48.

23

INTERNATIONAL CORPORATE FINANCE

We have employed a theoretical foundation firmly grounded on the Principles of Finance to construct a set of analytical tools for solving financial problems you are likely to encounter. Thus far we have confined our attention to the domestic market because it was convenient to do so. In this chapter we broaden our perspective to include the international dimension. Our discussion will revolve around **multinational corporations**, firms that operate in more than one country.

Let us begin by pointing out that the Principles of Finance are equally valid in international and domestic finance. For the most part, the international dimension merely complicates the application of the Principles. The fundamental goal of the firm also remains unchanged: Maximize shareholder wealth. Firms seek out positive-NPV projects in foreign as well as domestic markets, and the analytical tools developed in earlier chapters can also be applied in an international context when we take into account certain complications.

The primary complication concerns foreign currencies. A firm headquartered in the United States keeps its accounts in U.S. dollars. When it pursues a project in a foreign market, it will invest in assets in the foreign country and incur costs and realize revenues in the local currency. Certain currencies, such as the British pound, German mark, and Swiss franc, are freely convertible into U.S. dollars. But the nonsynchronous timing of revenues and expenses and the fluctuation in exchange rates lead to foreign exchange risks that the firm will want to manage. Other currencies are not freely convertible into U.S. dollars, which exposes the U.S. firm to even greater foreign exchange risk. We will help you understand how the foreign exchange markets operate and the methods they afford for handling foreign exchange risk. We will also show you how to take foreign exchange risk into account when evaluating proposed capital investment projects and analyzing foreign-currency-denominated financing alternatives.

The international market offers a variety of financing alternatives in addition to those available to a firm in the United States. In addition to the various national capital markets in Great Britain, France, Switzerland, and elsewhere, there are vibrant transnational Eurocurrency markets for U.S. dollars, Canadian dollars, British pounds, and several other currencies. The treasurer of a multinational corporation based in the United States not only has available the panoply of domestic financing alternatives we have already discussed but can also borrow by issuing U.S. dollar-denominated bonds to foreign investors in the Eurobond market or by issuing foreign-currency-denominated bonds in any of several domestic markets or in one of the Eurocurrency bond markets. Once again, foreign exchange considerations play an important role in choosing among these alternatives. We will explain the relationship among foreign exchange rates, interest rates in different countries (and different currencies), and national inflation rates. We will then describe how market imperfections that impede the free flow of capital across national boundaries can give rise to positive-NPV financing opportunities in foreign capital markets.

Our basic objective throughout this chapter is to broaden your perspective, to give you a global financial orientation. Of course, we cannot hope to cover the entire subject of international corporate finance in just a single chapter. But we hope to convince you that maintaining an international perspective can yield important benefits in the form of finding positive-NPV projects or identifying positive-NPV financing alternatives not available in the domestic market. Also we will suggest additional readings that will enable you to explore the topics covered in this chapter in greater depth.[1]

NONSTANDARD OIL'S FINANCING ALTERNATIVES

Nonstandard Oil Company, a multinational oil refining and marketing firm, wishes to borrow $100 million or the foreign-currency equivalent to help pay the cost of a new refinery the firm is constructing. The firm's investment bankers have advised the firm's treasurer that Nonstandard can raise funds in the domestic market by issuing at par 5-year bonds bearing a 9% interest rate (interest payable annually in arrears) and that the firm could instead sell Swiss-franc-denominated bonds in Switzerland where the firm maintains its international headquarters. The Swiss franc issue would require a 4% interest rate (interest payable annually in arrears) to be worth par.

The 4% interest rate looks very attractive to Nonstandard's treasurer, but she wonders why the Swiss franc borrowing rate should be so much lower than the U.S. dollar borrowing rate. The answer lies in the relationship among exchange rates, interest rates, and inflation rates. After we have explained these relationships and developed a procedure for taking foreign exchange rates into account in the cost of debt calculation, we will help Nonstandard's treasurer decide which alternative to choose.

THE FOREIGN EXCHANGE MARKET   23.1

A large American department store chain has signed an agreement to import fine English china. The contract calls for the American firm to pay the British exporting firm in British pounds. To do so, the American firm must purchase British pounds in the foreign exchange market. The **foreign exchange market** is the market within which one country's currency is traded for another country's currency. In our example, the American firm would exchange U.S. dollars for British pounds in the foreign exchange market and pay the exporter's invoice. Alternatively, if the contract had specified payment in U.S. dollars, the exporter would have received dollars and then sold the dollars for British pounds in the foreign exchange market.

The foreign exchange market is the world's largest financial market. It is a world-

---

[1] Good textbooks in international finance include David K. Eiteman and Arthur I. Stonehill, *Multinational Business Finance*, 3rd. ed. (Reading, Mass: Addison-Wesley, 1982); Maurice Levi, *International Finance: Financial Management and the International Economy* (New York: McGraw-Hill, 1983); Rita Rodriguez and Eugene Carter, *International Financial Management*, 3rd ed. (Englewood Cliffs, N.J.: Prentice-Hall, 1984); and Alan C. Shapiro, *Multinational Financial Management*, 2nd ed. (Boston: Allyn and Bacon, 1986). An excellent more practitioner-oriented approach to international finance is Alan C. Shapiro, *International Corporate Finance*, 2nd ed. (Cambridge, Mass: Ballinger, 1988).

wide market but London, New York, and Tokyo are the major centers of activity. The larger commercial banks and the central banks are the principal market participants, and corporations generally buy and sell currencies through a commercial bank. Most of the trading takes place in six currencies: U.S. dollar ($), West German deutschemark (or simply, mark) (DM), French franc (FF), Swiss franc (SF), Japanese yen (¥), and British pound sterling (£).

EXCHANGE RATES

An **exchange rate** is the price of one country's currency expressed in terms of another country's currency. For example, a rate of $1.70/£ means that 1 pound costs $1.70 (£1 = $1.70). Put somewhat differently, 1 U.S. dollar costs 0.5882 pounds since 1/1.70 = 0.5882 ($1 = £0.5882). The exchange rate can be expressed equivalently in terms of either dollars per pound or pounds per dollar. The exchange rates could also be expressed indirectly in terms of a third currency, say, the Swiss franc: SF1.50/$ and SF2.55/£.

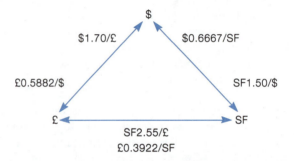

The direct and indirect methods of expressing an exchange rate are equivalent. In our example, the dollar-pound exchange rate implicit in the exchange rates SF1.50/$ and SF2.55/£ is $1.70/£ (or equivalently £0.5882/$) because
In particular,

$$\left[\frac{\$1.70}{£}\right]\left[\frac{£0.3922}{SF}\right] = \$0.6667/SF$$

If the equivalence did not hold, there would be a riskless arbitrage opportunity. For example, suppose pounds were trading at a price of SF2.60/£ in Switzerland and $1.70/£ in New York while Swiss francs were trading for SF1.50/$ in New York. In that case, the pound would be overvalued in Switzerland relative to the other two currencies. A foreign exchange trader who purchased $100 worth of pounds in New York would obtain £58.82 (= [100]0.5882). Selling the pounds in Switzerland would yield SF152.93 (= [58.82]2.60), which could be sold in New York for $101.96 (= [152.93]0.6667), yielding a riskless arbitrage profit of $1.96 per $100 invested.

In practice in foreign exchange trading, all exchange rates are expressed in terms of the U.S. dollar, as for example, SF1 = $0.66, DM1 = $0.60, £1 = $1.70, and so on. Traders find it convenient to quote exchange rates indirectly in terms of a single currency, the U.S. dollar.

TYPES OF FOREIGN EXCHANGE TRANSACTIONS

There are four types of foreign exchange transactions. **Spot trades** involve the purchase and sale of a currency for "immediate" delivery. We put the word immediate in quotation marks because spot trades actually settle 2 days after the trade takes place. Figure 23-1 reproduces a table of foreign exchange rates that appeared in *The Wall Street Journal* on February 16, 1990. The table furnishes the **spot foreign exchange rates** quoted by Bankers Trust Co. for trading amounts of $1 million or greater as of 3 P.M. the preceding two trading days. For example, the British pound is quoted in the table at £1 = $1.6865 for February 15 and £1 = $1.6950 for February 14, indicating a slight decrease in the value of the pound (relative to the dollar) between February 14 and February 15. The table also reports currency **cross rates** for actively traded currencies, which show the value of any currency in terms of any other currency. For example, considering the Canadian dollar (C$)-US dollar ($) exchange rate, C$1.2035 = $1 (in the upper left-hand corner) is equivalent to $0.83091 = C$1 (in the lower right-hand corner).

Forward trades involve the purchase and sale of a currency for future delivery based on exchange rates that are agreed to today. Figure 23-1 shows **forward exchange rates** in addition to spot exchange rates for British pounds, Canadian dollars, French francs, Japanese yen, Swiss francs, and German marks, in each case for 30-day, 90-day, and 180-day forward contracts. Forward contracts typically have a term between 1 and 52 weeks. For example, as noted above, a corporation could have purchased pounds for immediate delivery at an exchange rate of £1 = $1.6865 on Thursday, February 15, 1990. On that same day, a corporation could also have contracted for 30-day delivery (i.e., 30 days after 2-15-90) at an exchange rate of £1 = $1.6779, called the **forward rate**, and for 180-day delivery at a forward rate of £1 = $1.6341. A corporation entering into a 30-day forward contract on February 15 to purchase British pounds would agree to exchange $1.6779 per pound on March 17 when the contract settles.

Note that the forward rates for pounds are lower than the spot rate. In the next section we will look at why this might occur. If a corporation purchased pounds for 30-day delivery, it would get more pounds for its dollar than it would in a spot purchase (£0.5960/$ versus £0.5929/$). The pound is therefore said to trade at a **forward discount** relative to the dollar because forward pounds are "cheaper" than spot pounds. This forward discount can be expressed on a nominal annualized basis as

$$\text{forward discount} = 12 \left[\frac{0.5960 - 0.5929}{0.5929} \right] 100 = 6.27\% \qquad \textbf{(23.1)}$$

Note that the Japanese yen is trading at a **forward premium** relative to the dollar because forward yen are more expensive than spot yen (i.e., in buying yen forward you would get fewer yen per dollar than in a spot purchase).

Forward contracts can be customized to suit a corporation's particular requirements as to amount, currency, settlement date, etc. Voiding a forward contract is difficult and is subject to negotiation with the other party to the contract. There are also currency futures markets. A **currency future** is really a standardized forward contract that is exchange-traded. Because of this standardization, currency futures generally are less costly and enjoy more liquid markets than (non-exchange-traded) forward contracts. With a futures contract, a corporation can close out its position at any time simply by selling the contract (or repurchasing the contract if it has sold **short**). The choice between a forward contract and a futures contract thus involves a trade-off between the customization the forward contract provides and the low transaction costs and liquidity a futures contract provides.

The third type of foreign exchange transaction is a **currency swap**. In a currency swap one party purchases foreign currency from the other and agrees to resell it in

FIGURE 23-1

Foreign exchange rate tables.

Source: Reprinted by permission of *The Wall Street Journal,* © Dow Jones & Company, Inc., 1990. All Rights Reserved Worldwide.

Key Currency Cross Rates — Late New York Trading Feb. 15, 1990

	Dollar	Pound	SFranc	Guilder	Yen	Lira	D-Mark	FFranc	CdnDlr
Canada	1.2035	2.0283	.79834	.63027	.00831	.00096	.71024	.20896	....
France	5.7595	9.706	3.8206	3.0162	.03976	.00458	3.3989	....	4.7856
Germany	1.6945	2.8557	1.1240	.88741	.01170	.00135	....	.29421	1.4080
Italy	1258.7	2121.3	834.96	659.18	8.689	....	742.81	218.54	1045.9
Japan	144.86	244.13	96.093	75.863	....	.11509	85.488	25.151	120.37
Netherlands	1.9095	3.2181	1.2667	....	.01318	.00152	1.1269	.33154	1.5866
Switzerland	1.5075	2.5406	....	.78947	.01041	.00120	.88964	.26174	1.2526
U.K.	.59337	....	.39361	.31074	.00410	.00047	.35017	.10302	.49303
U.S.	....	1.6853	.66335	.52370	.00690	.00079	.59014	.17363	.83091

Source: Telerate

EXCHANGE RATES
Thursday, February 15, 1990

The New York foreign exchange selling rates below apply to trading among banks in amounts of $1 million and more as quoted at 3 p.m. Eastern time by Bankers Trust Co. Retail transactions provide fewer units of foreign currency per dollar.

Country	U.S. $ equiv. Thurs.	Wed.	Currency per U.S. $ Thurs.	Wed.	Country	U.S. $ equiv. Thurs.	Wed.	Currency per U.S. $ Thurs.	Wed.
Argentina (Austral)	.0003597	.0003597	2780.02	2780.02	Malaysia (Ringgit)	.3704	.3698	2.6995	2.7045
Australia (Dollar)	.7503	.7450	1.3328	1.3423	Malta (Lira)	3.0534	3.0534	.3275	.3275
Austria (Schilling)	.08397	.08478	11.91	11.80	Mexico (Peso) Floating rate	.0003670	.0003670	2725.02	2725.02
Bahrain (Diner)	2.6522	2.6522	.3771	.3771	Netherland (Guilder)	.5244	.5299	1.9070	1.8870
Belgium (Franc) Commercial rate	.02828	.02856	35.36	35.01	New Zealand (Dollar)	.5850	.5825	1.7094	1.7167
Financial rate	.02828	.02856	35.36	35.02	Norway (Krone)	.1544	.1548	6.4775	6.4605
Brazil (Cruzado)	.04129	.04264	24.22	23.45	Pakistan (Rupee)	.0471	.0471	21.25	21.25
Britain (Pound)	1.6865	1.6950	.5929	.5900	Peru (Inti)	.00008676	.00008676	11526.05	11526.05
30-Day Forward	1.6779	1.6865	.5960	.5929	Philippines (Peso)	.04533	.04533	22.06	22.06
90-Day Forward	1.6595	1.6683	.6026	.5994	Portugal (Escudo)	.006769	.006769	147.73	147.73
180-Day Forward	1.6341	1.6427	.6120	.6088	Saudi Arabia (Rival)	.26681	.26681	3.7480	3.7480
Canada (Dollar)	.8299	.8288	1.2050	1.2065	Singapore (Dollar)	.5365	.5366	1.8640	1.8635
30-Day Forward	.8269	.8261	1.2093	1.2105	South Africa (Rand) Commercial rate	.3927	.3931	2.5465	2.5439

the future on terms that are agreed to at the time the currency swap is negotiated. Currency swaps typically require interim cash payments at regular intervals from one party to the other to compensate for the difference in interest rates on loans denominated in the currencies involved in the swap.

EXAMPLE ■ Consider the following example. North Sea Marine, a British firm that has borrowed only in pounds, would like to make an investment in the United States. Eastern Scientific Instruments, an American firm that has borrowed only in U.S. dollars, would like to make an investment in the United Kingdom. They can both borrow in their respective national currencies and swap. But suppose a 10-year pound loan requires a 12% interest rate while a 10-year U.S. dollar loan requires a 9% interest rate. Eastern will have to agree to make payments to North Sea sufficient to enable North Sea to service its loan and vice versa.

90-Day Forward	.8207	.8201	1.2185	1.2193
180-Day Forward	.8125	.8123	1.2307	1.2310
Chile (Official rate)	.003448	.003448	290.03	290.03
China (Yuan)	.211757	.211757	4.7224	4.7224
Colombia (Peso)	.002208	.002208	453.00	453.00
Denmark (Krone)	.1532	.1547	6.5295	6.4625
Ecuador (Sucre) Floating rate	.001445	.001445	692.00	692.00
Finland (Markka)	.25310	.25336	3.9510	3.9470
France (Franc)	.17375	.17558	5.7555	5.6955
30-Day Forward	.17342	.17525	5.7664	5.7060
90-Day Forward	.17252	.17437	5.7965	5.7350
180-Day Forward	.17132	.17313	5.8370	5.7760
Greece (Drachma)	.006266	.006333	159.60	157.90
Hong Kong (Dollar)	.12802	.12806	7.8110	7.8090
India (Rupee)	.05907	.05907	16.93	16.93
Indonesia (Rupiah)	.0005568	.0005568	1796.01	1796.01
Ireland (Punt)	1.5785	1.5830	.6335	.6317
Israel (Shekel)	.5378	.5378	1.8594	1.8594
Italy (Lira)	.0007955	.0008034	1257.01	1244.76
Japan (Yen)	.006911	.006930	144.70	144.30
30-Day Forward	.006919	.006938	144.53	144.13
90-Day Forward	.006929	.006948	144.33	143.93
180-Day Forward	.006943	.006965	144.04	143.57
Jordan (Dinar)	1.5328	1.5328	.6524	.6524
Kuwait (Dinar)	3.4596	3.4596	.2891	.2891
Lebanon (Pound)	.001825	.001825	548.00	548.00
Financial rate	.2713	.2836	3.6860	3.5261
South Korea (Won)	.0014584	.0014584	685.70	685.70
Spain (Peseta)	.009153	.009234	109.25	108.30
Sweden (Krona)	.1637	.1632	6.1100	6.1275
Switzerland (Franc)	.6647	.6693	1.5045	1.4940
30-Day Forward	.6642	.6688	1.5055	1.4952
90-Day Forward	.6624	.6673	1.5097	1.4986
180-Day Forward	.6607	.6649	1.5135	1.5040
Taiwan (Dollar)	.038387	.038461	26.05	26.00
Thailand (Baht)	.03911	.03911	25.57	25.57
Turkey (Lira)	.0004264	.0004264	2345.05	2345.05
United Arab (Dirham)	.2723	.2723	3.6725	3.6725
Uruguay (New Peso) Financial	.001247	.001247	801.75	801.75
Venezuela (Bolivar) Floating rate	.02137	.02137	46.80	46.80
W. Germany (Mark)	.5908	.5970	1.6925	1.6750
30-Day Forward	.5909	.5970	1.6924	1.6750
90-Day Forward	.5904	.5966	1.6937	1.6763
180-Day Forward	.5892	.5953	1.6971	1.6797
SDR	1.32768	1.32790	75319	75307
ECU	1.21633	1.21899	....	....

Special Drawing Rights (SDR) are based on exchange rates for the U.S., West German, British, French and Japanese currencies. Source: International Monetary Fund.

European Currency Unit (ECU) is based on a basket of community currencies. Source: European Community Commission.

Suppose each firm needs $100 million or the dollar equivalent. The earliest and simplest form of currency swap is the back-to-back loan. Two firms agree to swap loan obligations. Eastern's debt-service stream (assuming a **bullet maturity** and annual interest payments) under a back-to-back loan arrangement with North Sea is given in Table 23-1.

In this example, Eastern borrows $100 million and exchanges the $100 million with North Sea for £62.5 million. In each of the subsequent 10 years, Eastern pays North Sea £7.5 million, receives $9 million from North Sea and makes an interest payment of $9 million. At the time of the last interest payment, Eastern pays North Sea £62.5 million, receives $100 million from North Sea, and pays $100 million to extinguish its loan.

The back-to-back loan effectively converts the $100 million 9% dollar loan into a £62.5 million 12% pound sterling loan. North Sea's payments and receipts under the

TABLE 23-1 Eastern's Debt Service Stream

	Year 0		Years 1–10		Year 10	
	$	£	$	£	$	£
Borrow $	+100					
Swap $ for £	−100	+62.5				
Interest on $ Loan			−9			
Swap Payments			+9	−7.5	+100	−62.5
Repay $ Loan					−100	
Net Cash Flow	0	+62.5	0	−7.5	0	−62.5

currency swap are the opposite of Eastern's. The currency sway converts North Sea's sterling loan into a U.S. dollar loan. ∎

The back-to-back loan was developed in response to a variety of foreign exchange controls imposed by the British government. There were a number of different controls, but the net effect of the controls was essentially to prohibit foreign (to Britain) companies from borrowing pounds sterling on a fixed-rate basis within the United Kingdom. The restrictions were removed in 1979, but the demand for long-term foreign exchange risk hedging vehicles endured, probably due to lower transaction costs.

Currency swaps evolved from back-to-back loans. Today a corporation can enter into a currency swap with just about any major money center bank and not have to search for a counterparty. Commercial banks, which used to act as agents in putting together back-to-back loans, now act as principals in currency swaps. They use the forward and futures foreign exchange markets to hedge their foreign currency risk exposure.

The question that remains is Why does a currency swap offer a cost advantage over simply borrowing the needed foreign currency directly in the foreign capital market? We need to say more about how the international capital markets operate before we can answer that question. But, briefly, the answer is that market imperfections, such as tax asymmetries and national regulations that restrict international capital flows, have segmented the world capital markets and impeded the free flow of capital across national boundaries. This segmentation in turn can confer a comparative advantage on two firms, or (as is more often the case recently) on a firm and one of its commercial banks, in the form of differences in relative borrowing costs that make currency swaps advantageous.

The fourth type of foreign exchange transaction is the foreign currency option. A forward contract or a futures contract obligates the parties to make the foreign-currency exchange specified in the contract. As discussed in Chapter 8, options convey a right but not an obligation. A **foreign currency option** conveys the right to buy (in the case of a call option) or sell (put option) a specified amount of specified foreign currency at a specified price within a specified time period. Commercial banks sell customized foreign currency options, and standardized foreign currency options are traded on option exchanges. In addition, a number of foreign currency options on futures contracts are traded on the International Monetary Market (IMM) at the Chicago Mercantile Exchange, which is the principal foreign currency futures exchange in the United States.

INTERNATIONAL FINANCIAL PARITY RELATIONSHIPS

We introduced the concept of a perfect capital market in Chapter 4. If the international capital markets were perfect, each financial asset would provide the same risk-adjusted expected rate of return in every market in which it is traded. A financial asset that is traded in two different markets would therefore have the same price in both markets. Otherwise there would be opportunities for arbitrageurs to earn riskless profits. Economists refer to this principle as the **Law of One Price**. We also mentioned the Law of One Price in explaining the Principle of Capital Market Efficiency in Chapter 2.

You know from our discussion of the domestic capital markets that there are transaction costs and other market imperfections that cause departures from the predictions of the perfect market model. Nevertheless, by assuming a perfect capital market environment and examining the implications of that assumption, and then exploring the effect of market imperfections, we were able to draw useful conclusions regarding capital structure choice, dividend policy, and other aspects of corporate financial management. So too with international corporate finance.

We begin by assuming that the international capital markets and foreign exchange markets are perfect. Arbitrage activity enforces the Law of One Price throughout these markets. We can characterize the resulting equilibrium relationships among exchange rates, interest rates, and inflation rates. For ease of reference we have summarized the four key parity relationships in Figure 23-2:

1. **Interest rate parity**
2. **Purchasing power parity**
3. **Expectations theory of forward exchange rates**
4. **International Fisher effect**

These relationships give rise to the combined market equilibrium conditions, also shown in Figure 23-2.

INTEREST RATE PARITY

EXAMPLE ■ Suppose you have the following two investment alternatives. You can buy a 1-year U.S. dollar-denominated note that pays 10% interest at maturity. Alternatively, you can buy a 1-year British-pound-denominated note that pays 12% interest at maturity. Which would you select? You cannot answer the question until you take into account how many pounds you get for your dollars today and how many dollars you would get for your pounds 1 year from today. The forward exchange market provides the needed information.

Suppose the dollar-pound spot rate is $1.70/£ and the 1-year forward rate is $1.60/£. The pound is trading at a forward discount. This example will demonstrate why. If you invest $1,000 in the U.S. dollar-denominated note you will receive $1,100 at maturity. If you instead convert the $1,000 into British pounds at the spot rate, receiving £588.24 (= 1,000/1.70), and purchase the British-pound-denominated note, then you will receive £658.83 (= [588.24]1.12) at maturity. By selling the pounds forward, you would ensure that the £658.83 would purchase $1,054.13. The dollar-denominated note is the more profitable investment. Moreover, you can earn a riskless arbitrage profit by borrowing British pounds, selling

FIGURE 23-2
Key parity relationships in
international financial
market equilibrium.

FIGURE 23-2
Key parity relationships in
international financial
market equilibrium.

Interest Rate Parity

$$\frac{1 + r_F(t)}{1 + r_D(t)} = \frac{s_{D/F}}{f_{D/F}(t)}$$

Purchasing Power Parity

$$\frac{E[1 + i_F(t)]}{E[1 + i_D(t)]} = \frac{s_{D/F}}{E[s_{D/F}(t)]}$$

Expectations Theory of Forward Exchange Rates

$$E[s_{D/F}(t)] = f_{D/F}(t)$$

International Fisher Effect

$$\frac{1 + r_F(t)}{1 + r_D(t)} = \frac{E[1 + i_F(t)]}{E[1 + i_D(t)]}$$

Combined Market Equilibrium Conditions

$$\frac{1 + r_F(t)}{1 + r_D(t)} = \frac{E[1 + i_F(t)]}{E[1 + i_D(t)]} = \frac{s_{D/F}}{E[s_{D/F}(t)]} = \frac{s_{D/F}}{f_{D/F}(t)}$$

Definitions of Variables

$r_F(t)$ = t-period foreign currency interest rate
$r_D(t)$ = t-period domestic currency interest rate
$s_{D/F}$ = spot exchange rate between the domestic and foreign currencies
$f_{D/F}(t)$ = t-period forward exchange rate between the domestic and foreign currencies
$i_F(t)$ = average annual inflation rate over next t periods in the foreign economy
$i_D(t)$ = average annual inflation rate over next t periods in the domestic economy
$s_{D/F}(t)$ = spot exchange rate between the domestic and foreign currencies t periods in the future

them in the spot market for US dollars, investing the dollars at 10%, and selling the dollars you will receive at maturity forward against the pound. Try it!

Borrow £588.24 and buy $1,000 (= [588.24]1.70). The investment of those dollars yields $1,100, which will produce £687.50 (= 1,100/1.60) under the forward contract. There is a £99.26 arbitrage profit. Arbitrage will continue until the interest rate differential is equivalent to the differential between the spot and forward rates. The interest rate differential between U.S. dollars and British pounds for investments of identical risk maturing at time t can be expressed as

$$\frac{1 + r_{\pounds}(t)}{1 + r_{\$}(t)} \tag{23.2}$$

where, $r_{\pounds}(t)$ and $r_{\$}(t)$ denote the t-period pound and dollar interest rates, respectively. The differential between the spot exchange rate ($s_{\$/\pounds}$) and the forward exchange rate for t periods forward ($f_{\$/\pounds}(t)$) can be expressed as

$$\frac{s_{\$/\pounds}}{f_{\$/\pounds}(t)} \tag{23.3}$$

Equating Equations (23.2) and (23.3), interest rate parity must hold for every period t in equilibrium:

$$\frac{1 + r_£(t)}{1 + r_\$(t)} = \frac{s_{\$/£}}{f_{\$/£}(t)} \qquad (23.4)$$

In this example, **interest rate parity** would hold if arbitrage activity raises the 1-year forward rate to \$1.67/£, for then

$$\frac{1 + r_£(1)}{1 + r_\$(1)} = \frac{1.12}{1.10} = 1.02 = \frac{\$1.70/£}{\$1.67/£} = \frac{s_{\$/£}}{f_{\$/£}(1)} \qquad \blacksquare$$

When Equation (23.4) holds, interest rate parity ensures that the forward discount offsets exactly the higher interest rate on British-pound investments of comparable duration and risk. If U.S.–dollar-denominated investments provided a higher interest rate, then the British pound would trade at a forward premium. In that case, the larger number of British pounds to be received upon future sale would fully compensate for the lower British interest rate.

Interest rate parity requires the forward-spot exchange rate differential to offset the interest rate differential between two countries. Evidence indicates that interest rate parity normally holds, at least to a close approximation, in the Eurocurrency markets.[2] It probably does not hold nearly so closely for domestic money markets. A variety of government-imposed restrictions and national differences in taxation inhibit investing in foreign currencies in many countries, which inhibits the arbitrage activity needed to maintain interest rate parity.

PURCHASING POWER PARITY

According to the Law of One Price, if a loaf of bread costs \$1 in the United States, \$1 should also buy a loaf of bread in Great Britain and in every other market. This will happen only if the foreign exchange rate between two currencies adjusts by the difference in the rates of inflation in the countries that issued the two currencies. If the rate of inflation is 8% in the United States and 10% in Great Britain, then the British pound will have to fall by (1.10/1.08) − 1, or about 2% per annum, for the (equivalent) dollar price of a loaf of bread to remain the same in both countries. This equilibrium condition is referred to as **purchasing power parity**.[3]

Purchasing power parity is formally stated in terms of expected inflation rates. It requires that the expected difference in inflation rates over some period, expressed as

$$\frac{E[1 + i_£(t)]}{E[1 + i_\$(t)]} \qquad (23.5)$$

(where E denotes the expected value of the quantity in brackets and $i_£(t)$ and $i_\$(t)$ denote the British and U.S. inflation rates, respectively) must equal the differential between the spot exchange rate ($s_{\$/£}$) and the spot exchange rate expected t periods in the future ($E[s_{\$/£}(t)]$) expressed as

[2] Frenkel and Levich (1977).
[3] The implications of purchasing power parity are explored in detail in Officer (1976). Purchasing power parity differs from the law of one price referred to earlier in that the law of one price refers to individual goods whereas purchasing power parity refers to the general price level for all goods, for example, as measured by the consumer price index.

$$\frac{s_{\$/\pounds}}{E[s_{\$/\pounds}(t)]} \tag{23.6}$$

Equating Equations (23.5) and (23.6), purchasing power parity must hold for every period t in equilibrium:

$$\frac{E[1 + i_\pounds(t)]}{E[1 + i_\$(t)]} = \frac{s_{\$/\pounds}}{E[s_{\$/\pounds}(t)]} \tag{23.7}$$

EXAMPLE ■ Continuing the previous example, purchasing power parity would hold if the current spot rate was $1.70 = £1 and the expected spot rate 1 year forward was $1.67 = £1, for then

$$\frac{E[1 + i_\pounds(1)]}{E[1 + i_\$(1)]} = \frac{1.10}{1.08} = 1.02 = \frac{1.70\$/\pounds}{1.67\$/\pounds} = \frac{s_{\$/\pounds}}{E[s_{\$/\pounds}(1)]}$$

■

When Equation (23.7) holds, purchasing power parity ensures that the expected change in the spot exchange rate offsets the expected inflation rate differential. Empirical evidence supports the existence of purchasing power parity, as we have defined it in terms of expectations.[4] Based on the exchange rates of 23 countries between 1957 and 1976, on average, the prevailing spot exchange rate provided the best estimate of the future spot exchange rate adjusted for inflation-rate differentials.[5]

EXPECTATIONS THEORY OF FORWARD EXCHANGE RATES

If foreign exchange market participants could perfectly hedge their foreign currency risks (or if they did not care about risk, i.e., they were **risk neutral**), the forward rate would depend solely on what market participants expect the future spot rate to be. For example, suppose the expected spot rate for British pounds is £1 = $1.50. What would be the forward rate? It would have to be £1 = $1.50. If it were higher than this rate, everyone would want to sell pounds but no one would be willing to sell dollars forward; if it were lower than this rate, everyone would want to sell dollars but no one would be willing to sell pounds forward. Therefore the **expectations theory of forward exchange rates** maintains that the expected spot exchange rate t periods in the future equals the t-period forward rate:

$$E[s_{\$/\pounds}(t)] = f_{\$/\pounds}(t) \tag{23.8}$$

It is important to note that the expectations theory does not require the actual future spot rate to equal the historical forward rate; foreign exchange market participants are not assumed to be perfect forecasters. All that is required is that on average the forward rate should equal the future spot rate. Empirical evidence shows that on average the forward rate does indeed equal the future spot rate; however, the evidence also indicates that when the forward rate predicts a sharp change (either up or down) in the spot rate, the forecast change tends to overstate the actual change in the spot rate.[6] This finding is at variance with the expectations theory. Thus, while it

---

[4]Strictly speaking, the Law of One Price, from which purchasing power parity is derived, requires that the *actual* inflation rate differential is *always* equal to the *actual* change in the foreign exchange rate. Equation (23.7) requires only the equality of expected inflation differentials and the expected change in the spot rate.

[5]Roll (1979).

[6]Cornell (1977).

appears that on average firms that hedge their foreign currency risk by buying or selling foreign currencies forward do not have to bear any added cost for this insurance, it also appears that during unsettled periods when concerns about foreign currency risk would be heightened, firms are willing to sacrifice some expected return in order to transfer the foreign exchange risk to someone else. Such behavior reflects the Principle of Risk-Return Trade-Off.

INTERNATIONAL FISHER EFFECT

The fourth parity relationship follows from the other three. But it is also firmly grounded in the relationship between nominal rates of return and real rates of return. We pointed out in Chapter 12 that the required rate of return in nominal terms (r_n) can be obtained by simply compounding the required real rate of return (r_r) and the inflation rate (π) (see Equation 12.3):

$$(1 + r_n) = (1 + r_r)(1 + \pi)$$

so that on a historical basis

$$r_n = r_r + \pi + \pi r_r \approx r_r + \pi$$

Many years ago, Irving Fisher argued that the nominal rate of interest observed in the financial markets will fully reflect investors' collective expectation regarding the rate of inflation in order to compensate them for the effects of inflation on the real value of their investments.[7] This phenomenon is called the Fisher effect.[8] If follows from the Principle of Self-Interested Behavior that investors will seek out investments that offer the greatest expected risk-adjusted real rate of return. Arbitrage will ensure that in a perfect capital market two debt instruments that are denominated in different currencies and that are of equivalent risk will offer the same expected real rate of return. If in addition the Fisher effect holds, then the difference in nominal interest rates must equal the difference in expected inflation rates:

$$\frac{1 + r_£(t)}{1 + r_\$(t)} = \frac{E[1 + i_£(t)]}{E[1 + i_\$(t)]} \tag{23.9}$$

Because it follows from the (domestic) Fisher effect, we will refer to Equation (23.9) as the **international Fisher effect**.

EXAMPLE ■ Continuing the example, $r_£(1) = .12$, $r_\$(1) = .10$, $i_£(1) = .10$, and $i_\$(1) = .08$. Equation (23.9) holds because[9]

$$\frac{1.12}{1.10} \approx 1.02 \approx \frac{1.10}{1.08}$$

■

Note that Equation (23.9) follows from Equations (23.4), (23.7), and (23.8). Interest rate parity coupled with purchasing power parity and the expectations theory

[7] Fisher (1965).
[8] Evidence supporting the Fisher effect can be found in Fama (1975).
[9] We use the approximation symbol because 1.12/1.10 equals 1.10/1.08 only when the two values are rounded to the second decimal place. Actually 1.12/1.10 = 1.01818 and 1.10/1.08 = 1.01852. The approximation is due to rounding error. If we had worked with continuously compounded interest rates and inflation rates, the two fractions in our example would have had identical values. We give you the opportunity to work this result out in problem C2.

of forward exchange rates implies the international Fisher effect. More generally, the four parity relationships are mutually consistent; if any three of them hold, then so must the fourth.

Empirical evidence concerning the international Fisher effect is meager but we can observe that as a general rule, the countries with the highest inflation rates also tend to have the highest interest rates. We are at least able to say that real rates of interest exhibit considerably smaller variation than nominal rates of interest. We suspect that because of various national impediments to the free international flow of capital, the national capital markets are segmented to some degree, and arbitrage activity is prevented from achieving a single real rate of interest that applies in all market segments.

23.3   HEDGING AGAINST FOREIGN CURRENCY RISKS

When some of the cash flows a firm expects to receive or anticipates having to pay are denominated in a foreign currency, the firm faces **foreign currency risk** (or **foreign exchange risk**). Foreign currency risk is the risk that the receipt or payment, when translated into the domestic currency, will change as a result of a change in the exchange rate. For example, suppose that Pratt and Whitney has a contract to sell aircraft engines to British Airways. The contract calls for delivery in 1 year against payment in pounds sterling. The value of the contract is £100 million. Suppose the spot dollar-sterling exchange rate expected 1 year hence is £1 = 1.60. Then the aircraft engine contract has an expected value of $160 million. But suppose the dollar-sterling exchange rate is £1 = $1.50 when British Airways makes payment. In that case, British Airways will still pay £100 million, but Pratt and Whitney will receive only $150 million when it converts the pounds into dollars.

Pratt and Whitney can eliminate its foreign currency risk exposure by hedging. **Hedging** a particular foreign currency risk exposure involves establishing an offsetting position in the same foreign currency. Designed correctly, the hedging transaction will generate a gain or loss that will offset the loss or gain, respectively, on the original foreign currency exposure. In the preceding example, Pratt and Whitney's hedging strategy would involve entering into a foreign currency transaction that would generate an offsetting gain if the pound's value depreciated relative to the expected future spot rate prior to receipt of payment (e.g., a $10 million gain if the pound were to depreciate to $1.50/£). There are three basic foreign currency hedging techniques:

- forward market transactions
- foreign currency money market transactions
- foreign currency option transactions

We presume throughout our discussion in this section that the financial manager's objective is to reduce foreign currency risk, not to speculate on foreign exchange rate movements. Many banks and consulting services produce exchange rate forecasts. The availability of such forecasts might tempt a financial manager to speculate but such activity has spawned a number of financial disasters.[10] The Principle of

---

[10] In the mid-1980s Volkswagen A.G. lost more than $250 million due to unauthorized foreign currency speculation in its treasury department. Laker Airlines went bankrupt in the 1980s, in part because it borrowed heavily in U.S. dollars while a large percentage of its revenue was in pounds sterling. The sharp appreciation in the dollar relative to the pound in the early 1980s helped to put Laker into a cash bind.

Capital Market Efficiency is apparently relevant to international markets as well as U.S. domestic capital markets. Empirical evidence shows that foreign exchange forecasting models have not been able to provide a more accurate forecast than the forward rate on a consistent basis.[11]

Before describing the techniques given above, we should mention one other strategy for Pratt and Whitney that you have no doubt thought of. Pratt and Whitney could negotiate payment in U.S. dollars.[12] But the Principle of Two-Sided Transactions should indicate why invoicing in dollars does not eliminate foreign currency risk. It eliminates *Pratt and Whitney's* foreign currency risk exposure—but transfers it to British Airways, which must now pay in dollars. British Airways has worldwide operations, and it generates significant dollar revenue. So this risk shifting is beneficial if British Airways is able to bear this risk at lower cost than Pratt and Whitney. But the Principle of Risk-Return Trade-Off implies that the risk transfer will require compensation to British Airways in the form of a reduced transaction price. Under the Principle of Risk-Return Trade-Off, shifting foreign currency risk between the parties to a commercial transaction will lead to adjustments in contract price to compensate for the risk shifting. The three hedging techniques also involve risk shifting, but to third parties not involved in the commercial transaction. As always, only market imperfections can make the transaction something other than a zero-sum game.

FORWARD MARKET TRANSACTIONS

EXAMPLE ◼   Pratt and Whitney could hedge its foreign currency risk exposure by selling a £100 million forward contract for delivery in 1 year. That strategy converts the 100 million receivable into a known dollar amount. Suppose the 1-year forward rate is £1 = $1.60. Then the forward sale will net Pratt and Whitney $160 million 1 year hence. Table 23-2 shows the consequences to Pratt and Whitney of hedging in this manner in three different future exchange rate scenarios.

If pound sterling depreciates to £1 = $1.50, Pratt and Whitney receives £100 million from British Airways, which is worth $150 million. But Pratt and Whitney delivers the £100 million under the forward contract for $160 million. There is a $10 million profit ($160 − 150) on the forward contract that restores the value of the contract to the originally expected $160 million value. If pound sterling appreciates to £1 = $1.70, the £100 million Pratt and Whitney receives is worth $170 million. But it must deliver pounds at an exchange rate of £1 = $1.60 to settle the forward contract. The $10 million loss on the forward contract leads to a net (of gain or loss on hedging) realized value of $160 million on the engine contract. Indeed, regardless of what happens to the spot rate 1 year hence, Pratt and Whitney will realize $160 million because of the forward contract—that is, losses are avoided but gains are forgone under a forward contract hedge.   ◼

What is the cost of a forward contract? Managers often calculate the cost of a forward contract by annualizing the forward discount or premium. That procedure is wrong; that calculation is based on the difference between the current spot rate and the forward rate, as shown in Equation (23.1). The true cost of a forward contract is its opportunity cost, which depends on the proceeds the firm would realize if it did

---

[11]Levich (1978).

[12]Equivalently, the engine contract could contain a price adjustment clause that would adjust the sterling price for changes in the dollar-sterling exchange rate.

TABLE 23-2 Possible Outcomes of Forward Market Hedge

Spot Exchange Rate, 1 Year Hence	Value of Original Contract (millions)	Gain (Loss) on Forward Contract (millions)	Net Realized Dollar Value (millions)
£1 = $1.50	£100 = $150	$10	$160
£1 = $1.60	£100 = $160	—	160
£1 = $1.70	£100 = $170	(10)	160

not hedge. That cost depends on the difference between the forward rate and the *expected* future spot rate:

$$c = \left[\frac{365}{n}\right]\left[\frac{E[s_{D/F}(n)] - f_{D/F}(n)}{s_{D/F}}\right] \qquad (23.10)$$

where n denotes the length of the forward contract measured in days, $E[s_{D/F}(n)]$ denotes the expected spot rate n days hence, $f_{D/F}(n)$ denotes the forward rate specified in an n-day forward contract, and $s_{D/F}$ denotes the current spot rate.

EXAMPLE ■ If the current spot rate is £1 = $1.70, the cost to Pratt and Whitney of a 1-year ($n = 365$) forward contract is

$$c = \left[\frac{365}{365}\right]\left[\frac{\$1.60 - 1.60}{1.70}\right] = 0$$ ■

Under the expectations theory of forward exchange rates, the forward rate equals the expected future spot rate, and so in an efficient market the cost of a forward contract is zero. The foreign exchange market seems reasonably efficient, so that while the cost of insuring against foreign exchange risk may not be exactly zero in practice, such insurance is nevertheless quite cheap. A firm can use Equation (23.10) to gauge the true cost in any particular situation in which it believes the forward rate is not a good predictor of the future spot rate. However, the available empirical evidence suggests that by and large the forward rate, at least in the case of the world's major currencies, is generally the most reliable predictor of the future spot rate.

Forward contracts enable a corporation to separate the management of foreign currency risk exposure from the process of negotiating international commercial contracts. This simplifies the contracting process because foreign currency risk is borne by third parties. Moreover, the cost of insurance through the forward market is cheap, even when transaction costs are taken into account. Large commercial banks are prepared to enter into forward contracts in marks, French francs, Swiss francs, yen, pounds, Canadian dollars, and certain other currencies. However, forward contracts may be very expensive to arrange and may not be available at all for a third world currency.

FOREIGN CURRENCY MONEY MARKET TRANSACTIONS

Pratt and Whitney could instead hedge its foreign currency risk exposure by borrowing in pounds sterling for 1 year against its future receivable, exchanging at the current spot exchange rate into dollars, and investing the dollar proceeds in a 1-year financial instrument.

EXAMPLE ■   Suppose the current spot exchange rate is £1 = $1.70 and that 1-year interest rates are 10% in dollars and 16.875% in pounds sterling. Pratt and Whitney could borrow £85,561,497 (= 100/1.16875) for 1 year, convert it into $145,454,545 (= [85,561,497]1.70) in the spot market, and invest the dollar proceeds at 10% interest for 1 year to realize $160 million (= [1.10]145,454,545). Pratt and Whitney then uses the £100 million it receives from British Airways to pay interest and repay principal on its sterling loan. Table 23-3 shows the consequences to Pratt and Whitney of hedging in this manner in three different future exchange rate scenarios.

As in the case of the forward market hedge, the gain or loss on the money market hedge fully offsets the loss or gain, respectively, on the value of the original contract. Pratt and Whitney's net realized dollar value is the same regardless of the future dollar-pound spot exchange rate. For example, if the spot exchange rate falls to £1 = $1.50 1 year hence, the £100 million of principal and interest will cost $150 million to repay. The dollar investment returns $160 million, giving a profit of $10 million.   ■

The fact that the net realized dollar value is the same under the two different hedging methods is not a coincidence. Under interest rate parity, any difference between selling a foreign currency forward (as in the forward market hedge) and selling it spot (as in the foreign currency money market hedge) will be fully offset by the difference between the interest rates in the two currencies. The foreign currency money market hedge might be thought of as a "homemade" forward contract. Which form of hedging is more effective in practice will depend, to a large extent, on whether government restrictions on forward selling or on foreign-currency-denominated borrowing favor one method over the other.

FOREIGN CURRENCY OPTION TRANSACTIONS

The hedging techniques discussed so far are useful for hedging foreign currency risk exposures that are certain as to amount and timing. But life is not always quite so simple. Suppose that Pratt and Whitney and General Electric are competing for the order and that British Airways will not make a decision for several weeks (while it studies the bids). If Pratt and Whitney sells pounds forward but does not win the contract, it will lose money if sterling appreciates. Pratt and Whitney can avoid this outcome and still hedge its foreign currency risk by purchasing a pound sterling put

TABLE 23-3   Possible Outcomes of Foreign Currency Money Market Hedge

Spot Exchange Rate, 1 Year Hence	Value of Original Contract (millions)	Gain (Loss) on Money Market Hedge (millions)	Net Realized Dollar Value (millions)
£1 = $1.50	£100 = $150	$10	$160
£1 = $1.60	£100 = $160	—	160
£1 = $1.70	£100 = $170	(10)	160

option, which will let it sell £100 million at a stated exchange rate in 1 year. The most Pratt and Whitney can lose in that case is the cost of the option.

Foreign currency options, like all options, are of two basic types: call options, which convey the right (but not the obligation) to buy, and put options, which convey the right (but not the obligation) to sell. The basic features of options, which were discussed in Chapter 8, are the same for foreign currency options as for other types of options. Foreign currency options represent a useful hedging tool when the quantity of foreign currency to be received or paid is uncertain. The following rules indicate how to choose between forward contracts (or foreign currency money market hedging) and foreign currency options:[13]

- When the quantity of foreign currency to be received (to be paid) is known, sell (buy) the currency forward and

- When the quantity is unknown, buy a put option (call option) on the foreign currency sufficient to cover the maximum amount of foreign currency that might be received (paid).

Our discussion of hedging foreign currency risk has four useful practical implications. First, an important consequence of the expectations theory of forward exchange rates is that the forward rate is a reliable indicator regarding how to allow for foreign exchange risk when pricing goods for future delivery against payment in a foreign currency; the forward rate equals the future spot rate on average. Second, the expectations theory also implies that the insurance that forward contracts provide can be purchased cheaply (at least in the case of the world's major currencies). Third, as a consequence of interest rate parity, it may be possible to create a "homemade" forward contract if actual forward contracts are not available for the particular currency, amount, and term desired. Fourth, as a consequence of the four key parity relationships and the Principle of Capital Market Efficiency, foreign currency speculation is a zero-expected-net-present-value activity. Since foreign currency speculation is certainly not riskless, the Principle of Risk Aversion together with the Principle of Risk-Return Trade-Off and the availability of cheap insurance suggest the following simple rule for corporate financial managers: Hedge whenever possible, don't speculate.

23.4   INTERNATIONAL CAPITAL INVESTMENT DECISIONS

Specific Electric Company, a U.S.-headquartered diversified multinational manufacturing firm, is considering building a plant in West Germany to manufacture electric motors for the Central European market. The plant is expected to cost DM50 million. As you know by now, Specific Electric should choose the alternative with the largest positive NPV from among mutually exclusive alternatives. The same rule applies to international capital investment projects. But a foreign project involves several complications, among the more important of which are (1) the incremental after-tax cash flows are (for the most part at least) denominated in foreign currencies; (2) the foreign currencies may not be freely convertible into U.S. dollars; (3) foreign investment projects often entail a risk of expropriation by the host country's government; (4) there are foreign taxes to consider; (5) the cost of capital for a foreign project may differ from the cost of capital for an otherwise identical domestic proj-

---

[13]Giddy (1983) describes in greater detail the use of foreign currency options to eliminate foreign currency risk exposure.

ect; and (6) there may be a cost advantage to raising funds for a foreign project in the foreign country or in the international capital markets.

The net-present-value criterion involves discounting the incremental after-tax cash flows at the required rate of return for the project and accepting the project if the NPV is positive. There are two alternative methods of applying the NPV criterion to foreign projects: (1) calculate the incremental cash flows in the local currency; convert nondollar incremental cash flows into dollars at appropriate projected foreign exchange rates; and discount at the dollar-denominated required rate of return, or (2) do the entire NPV calculation in the local currency and then convert the foreign-currency-denominated NPV into dollars at the current exchange rate. The two procedures, applied correctly, will produce the same NPV.

ESTIMATING THE INCREMENTAL CASH FLOWS

So long as Specific Electric can hedge its foreign currency risk exposure, it should refrain from basing its investment decision on its internal foreign exchange forecasts. Specific Electric would be wise to apply the Principle of Capital Market Efficiency and base its decision on the foreign exchange market's consensus forecast, which can be obtained by applying the key parity relationships in Figure 23-2. If it wishes to speculate on foreign currency movements, it should do so by trading in the foreign currency market, not by building an electric motor plant.

Specific Electric's project staff has projected the following incremental after-tax cash flows in marks:

Year	1	2	3	4	5
Cash flow (DM millions)	15	17	20	20	17

The current dollar-mark exchange rate is DM1 = $0.60, implying a $30 million project cost. Specific Electric can project future exchange rates by applying interest rate parity, purchasing power parity, and the expectations theory of forward exchange rates.

Suppose the 1-year riskless rate is 8% in the United States (the equivalent annual 1-year Treasury note rate) and 6% in West Germany and that the expected inflation rate in the United States is 5% per annum for each of the next 5 years. Under interest rate parity, Equation (23.4), and the expectations theory, Equation (23.8), the expected spot rate 1 year hence satisfies

$$\frac{1.06}{1.08} = \frac{\$0.60}{E[s_{\$/DM}(1)]}$$

$$E[s_{\$/DM}(1)] = \$0.6113$$

Under purchasing power parity, Equation (23.7),

$$\frac{E[1 + i_{DM}(1)]}{1.05} = \frac{0.60}{0.6113}$$

$$E[1 + i_{DM}(1)] = 1.0306$$

The expected inflation rate in West Germany for the next year is 3.06%. Suppose the real interest rate is expected to remain constant over the next 5 years in each country.

Then the projected West German inflation rate is 3.06% per annum for each of the next 5 years. Specific Electric should check to make sure that its cash flow forecast is consistent with a 3.06% West German inflation rate.

Under purchasing power parity, Equation (23.7), the expected spot rate t years hence ($1 \le t \le 5$) satisfies

$$E[s_{\$/DM}(t)] = \$0.60 \, (1.05/1.0306)^t \qquad \text{(23.11)}$$

Applying Equation (23.11), the projected Deutsche mark cash flows can be converted into U.S. dollars:

Year	1	2	3	4	5
Cash flow (DM million)	15	17	20	20	17
Exchange rate ($/DM)	.6113	.6228	.6345	.6465	.6586
Cash flow ($ millions)	9.17	10.59	12.69	12.93	11.20

LACK OF CONVERTIBILITY Many foreign countries place restrictions on a firm's ability to convert local currency into dollars or other "hard" currencies. This is often the case in third world countries that have very limited hard currency reserves. If the free cash flow is not freely convertible into U.S. dollars—that is, if the U.S. parent is not free to convert the foreign currency into U.S. dollars and transfer the dollars outside the foreign country—the annual cash flows may overstate the true benefits the project sponsor can expect to realize. Recall from Chapter 11 that the NPV calculation implicitly assumes that interim cash flows can be reinvested at the hurdle rate. When the local currency is not freely convertible into U.S. dollars, the incremental cash flow stream should reflect the actual expected U.S. dollar cash remittances (including interest on reinvested balances that can be remitted in U.S. dollars) at the time the project sponsor expects to realize these U.S. dollar flows.

Firms have a variety of methods available to make cash remittances, including dividend payments, interest payments, principal repayments, management fees, royalty payments, and adjusting prices charged for goods and raw materials supplied to the foreign project. Dividend payments are generally more sensitive politically than interest or principal payments, so it is generally preferable to lend funds rather than invest equity. Management fees and royalty payments are generally less sensitive politically than debt service payments. In any case, if possible, it is always advisable to reach an agreement with the foreign government prior to initiating a capital investment project that covers currency convertibility and cash remittances.

EXPROPRIATION AND OTHER POLITICAL RISKS Investing in a foreign country entails political risk—the risk that a foreign government may not honor a previous government's agreement to permit convertibility, a foreign government's imposing discriminatory taxes or, worst of all, a foreign government's expropriation of a firm's property for its own use (euphemistically often called "nationalization").

Political risks should be incorporated in discounted cash flow analysis by adjusting the incremental cash flows, rather than by adjusting the discount rate. Suppose that the expected cash flows for a project are

Year	1	2	3	4
Cash flow ($ millions)	20	30	30	40

Suppose that the project sponsor fears that there is a 50% probability that the project will be expropriated at the end of 2 years when a new government may come to power. The expected cash flow stream to be discounted is

Year	1	2	3	4
Cash flow ($ millions)	20	30	15	20

Calculating the probability of expropriation is highly subjective. But that does not mean the risk should be ignored. If expropriation risk is significant, it is important to gauge the sensitivity of NPV to the probability of expropriation. Break–even analysis—determining the probability of expropriation during any particular year that would reduce the NPV to zero—is often used.

Multinational firms can take steps to reduce expropriation risk:

■ Make the local project dependent on the multinational parent for technical support, raw materials, etc., so that it cannot be operated on a stand–along basis;

■ Set up a foreign subsidiary that borrows from a local government agency or local banks in order to minimize the amount of parent capital that is at risk; that is, in the event of expropriation the local government agency or local banks would face the prospect of their loans not being repaid by the foreign subsidiary; or

■ Have the foreign subsidiary borrow from the same major international banks that lend to the country in question and either (1) specify in the subsidiary's loan agreement that the parent company will guarantee the loan so long as the subsidiary's assets are not expropriated or (2) have the banks specify in the country's loan agreement that default by the foreign subsidiary will trigger a **cross-default** under the country's loan agreement with the same banks.

FOREIGN TAXES   The method of cash remittance can affect the amount of taxes. In addition to local income taxes, countries generally levy **withholding taxes** on dividend and interest payments, often at different rates. Management fees and royalty payments are not generally subject to withholding taxes and are generally tax-deductible in the foreign country. Dividends, interest, management fees, and royalty payments are subject to U.S. taxation if the payments are remitted to the United States. If may be possible, however, to remit payments from a high-tax jurisdiction to a low-tax jurisdiction and thereby reduce worldwide corporate taxes. Multinational firms spend considerable sums on worldwide tax planning and on structuring payments so as to minimize overall taxes. The incremental after-tax cash flow stream should be calculated taking into accounting the incremental U.S. and foreign taxes the project sponsor will have to pay on account of the project.

ESTIMATING THE COST OF CAPITAL FOR A FOREIGN PROJECT

Should the required rate of return on a foreign project be greater than the required rate of return on an otherwise identical domestic project? Many financial executives believe the answer is yes because of the additional economic and political risk associated with foreign projects. However, this view is not necessarily correct.

According to the capital asset pricing model, which we presented in Chapter 7, the riskiness of an investment must be measured relative to the riskiness of a diversified portfolio of stocks, and the only component of risk for which an investor needs to be compensated is systematic risk, which cannot be diversified away. Suppose there exists a single, integrated worldwide capital market. If every investor in each country holds a well-diversified international portfolio, the riskiness of any security or project should be measured in relation to the world market portfolio. In such a market, most of the economic and political risk specific to a particular foreign project could be eliminated through diversification. In that case, a firm's shareholders would face the same risk on a foreign project as on an otherwise identical domestic project. The cost of capital for the two projects would therefore be the same.

Suppose instead that the national capital markets are perfectly segmented. American investors own only American stocks; West German investors own only West German stocks; and so on. In that case, an American firm should measure project risk against the riskiness of the American market portfolio; a West German firm should measure project risk against the riskiness of the West German market portfolio; and so on. Under the Principle of Diversification, so long as the returns from a West German project are not perfectly correlated with the returns on any subset of the American market portfolio, there can be significant gains from diversification.[14] The American firm's shareholders would accept a lower rate of return on the foreign project than on an otherwise identical domestic project.

Corporate international diversification is beneficial to shareholders only if they cannot accomplish such diversification as easily and as cheaply on their own. This does appear to be the case. American investors, while free to own foreign common stocks, invest only a small portion of their portfolios in foreign stocks. A combination of currency restrictions, tax regulations, comparative lack of readily accessible and reliable financial information, and other factors serve to segment the American stock market and foreign stock markets. In recent years, American institutional investors have increased their overseas stock investments, and a variety of foreign-country-specific international mutual funds have started up to offer individual investors additional foreign stock investment opportunities.[15] But U.S. investment portfolios are generally not well diversified internationally—which means that there probably remain unexploited opportunities for firms to reduce shareholder risk through international investing. It also means that there are probably opportunities to find international capital investment projects whose required rate of return is smaller than a comparable domestic project's required rate of return.[16]

It has been concluded that American investors behave as though investing in foreign common stocks entails an added cost of between 2% and 4% per annum; that is, the higher transaction costs associated with purchasing foreign shares and the added monitoring costs due to the more lax financial disclosure standards in foreign jurisdictions reduce the rate of return on direct investments in foreign common stocks.[17] If so, then American investors should be willing to tolerate an American

---

[14] Note that it is not sufficient in order for international diversification to be beneficial that the returns from the different national equity markets be less than perfectly correlated. (See Shapiro (1988) for evidence concerning imperfect correlation.) The systematic risk of a foreign project, such as a gold mine, could nevertheless be equal to the systematic risk of a comparable domestic project if the output from both is sold in a single worldwide product market.

[15] The Austria Fund is one such mutual fund. The Austria Fund, Inc. prospectus, February 23, 1990. The fund's investment objective is long-term capital appreciation through investment primarily in equity securities of Austrian firms. Similar funds exist for more than a dozen different national equity markets.

[16] In the year following the collapse of the Hungarian Communist government in 1989, more than 100 American firms that had not invested there previously, established joint ventures in Hungary. "Business Stakes East Bloc Claims and a 'Gold Rush' Hits Hungary," *New York Times*, March 17, 1990, 1, 45.

[17] Cooper and Kaplanis (1986). The introduction and expansion of international stock mutual funds would tend to mitigate the effect. See footnote 15.

firm earning a rate of return on an overseas project that is between 2% and 4% lower than the rate of return a local firm could realize on the same project. Unfortunately, this does not tell us how to determine the appropriate cost of capital for any particular foreign investment project, only that you should not simply calculate the cost of capital for a domestic project and "tack on" a premium.

APPROXIMATE BETA CALCULATION   We are unable to give you a precise procedure for calculating the project beta, and hence the cost of capital, for a foreign project because the relevant portfolio for purposes of calculating beta depends on the sponsoring firm's shareholders' degree of international diversification. In view of the limited international diversification of most American firms' shareholders, we recommend using the American market portfolio (with the Standard & Poor's 500 Index serving as a useful proxy) in the project beta calculation:

1. Find a set of comparable publicly-traded firms located in the same country and in the same industry as the project under consideration;

2. Calculate the historical total returns adjusted for exchange rate changes (the sum of (a) end-of-period share value converted to U.S. dollars minus beginning-of-period share value converted to U.S. dollars and (b) dividends paid converted to U.S. dollars all divided by (c) beginning-of-period share value converted to U.S. dollars); and

3. Calculate beta using linear regression in the same manner as for a domestic project.

If no comparable publicly-traded foreign firms can be identified, use the beta calculated for domestic projects of the same type. This will normally lead to a conservative (somewhat higher) estimate of the foreign project's required rate of return because international corporate diversification tends to involve lower systematic risk, hence lower beta and a lower required rate of return, than an otherwise identical domestic project.

EXAMPLE ■   Let us return to the problem facing Specific Electric. Specific Electric's marginal income tax rate for the project is 23.8%; the pretax cost of debt for the project is 10% based on a project debt ratio (θ = Debt/[Debt + Equity]) of 25%, or $r_d(\theta) = .10$, which is consistent with Specific Electric's capital structure objective. Specific Electric calculates a (leveraged) project beta of 1.10. The riskless rate is 8%, and the expected rate of return on the market portfolio is 16.6%, so the (leveraged) required rate of return on equity for the project is

$$r_e(.25) = 8 + 1.10(8.6) = 17.46\%$$

The required rate of return for the dollar-denominated incremental cash flow stream is then the weighted average:

$$r^*(.25) = 0.25(.762)(.1) + 0.75(.1746) = 15.00\%$$

The project NPV is

$$\text{NPV} = -\$30.0 + \frac{9.17}{1.15} + \frac{10.59}{(1.15)^2} + \frac{12.69}{(1.15)^3} + \frac{12.93}{(1.15)^4} + \frac{11.20}{(1.15)^5}$$

$$= \$7.29 \text{ million}$$

To verify that calculating the project NPV in Deutsche marks does not alter the dollar NPV, first calculate the approximate Deutsche mark hurdle rate. We give you the opportunity in problem C8 to verify that the required rate of return in Deutsche marks must satisfy the relationship

$$\frac{1 + r_{DM}(1)}{1 + r_{\$}(1)} = \frac{1 + r^*_{DM}(\theta)}{1 + r^*_{\$}(\theta)} \tag{23.12}$$

where $r_{DM}(1)$ and $r_{\$}(1)$ denote the 1-year riskless rates, and $r^*_{DM}(\theta)$ and $r^*_{\$}(\theta)$ denote the required rates of return in DM and \$, respectively. Applying Equation (23.12) gives

$$\frac{1.06}{1.08} = \frac{1 + r^*_{DM}(.25)}{1.15} \quad \text{or} \quad r^*_{DM}(.25) = 12.87\%$$

The NPV of the project in Deutsche marks is

$$NPV = -DM50.0 + \frac{15.00}{1.1287} + \frac{17.00}{(1.1287)^2} + \frac{20.00}{(1.1287)^3} + \frac{20.00}{(1.1287)^4} + \frac{17.00}{(1.1287)^5}$$

$$= DM12.15 \text{ million}$$

Converting this amount to U.S. dollars gives

$$DM12.15 \text{ million}(\$0.60/DM) = \$7.29 \text{ million} \qquad \blacksquare$$

23.5   ## FINANCING FOREIGN INVESTMENTS

A firm that wishes to borrow funds to finance a foreign capital investment project can pursue any of four strategies: (1) borrow U.S. dollars in the United States and export the funds to the foreign country; (2) borrow U.S. dollars in the Euromarket, which is outside the United States; (3) borrow in the foreign country; or (4) borrow in whichever currency and in whichever market affords the lowest interest cost. The fourth strategy is particularly tempting, but also very risky, as many *former* corporate treasurers will attest.

FINANCING IN THE EUROMARKET

In addition to the separate domestic capital markets, there is a large supranational Euromarket. The prefix "Euro" means "outside of." The **Eurodollar** bond market consists of bonds that are denominated in U.S. dollars that are issued, held, and traded outside the United States, essentially beyond the reach of U.S. regulatory authorities, such as the U.S. Securities and Exchange Commission. Similarly, there are Euromarkets for bonds denominated in pounds sterling, French francs, yen, and several other major currencies.

The Euromarket is largely unregulated. It offers a viable alternative to the domestic capital market for a firm that wishes to raise either short-term funds or long-term funds. Commercial banks extend Eurodollar loans, which carry interest rates that float off one or more specified London Interbank Offered Rates (LIBOR). In recent years, financial institutions in the Euromarket have created Note Issuance Facilities (NIFs) and other financing mechanisms that are similar to U.S. commercial paper. In addition, with increasing frequency in recent years, large U.S. multinational firms that have needed to sell common stock have divided the issue into two or more **tranches**. The bulk of the common stock is sold domestically, and the balance is sold overseas in the Euromarket.[18] Also, from time to time, U.S. firms have found it advantageous to sell entire bond issues in the Eurobond market, rather than domestically. In 1989, the World Bank introduced **global bonds**, which are designed to qualify for immediate trading in any domestic capital market and in the Euromarket and hence to reach the broadest group of investors when they are issued.[19] In all these cases, the issuer enters the Euromarket hoping to exploit an opportunity to raise funds at a lower cost than funds can be raised domestically.[20]

EURODOLLAR BOND MARKET   Eurobonds are typically issued in **bearer** form; firms issuing bonds in the United States are required to issue them in registered form. Eurobonds generally pay interest annually, whereas domestic bonds typically pay interest at least semiannually. Also, underwriting expenses tend to be higher in the Euromarket. Finally, Eurobonds tend to involve lower overall cost than comparable domestic issues during periods when the U.S. dollar is appreciating relative to other currencies. We suspect that this reduced cost results from portfolio rebalancing. The appreciating dollar encourages Euromarket participants to switch funds from non-U.S.-dollar-denominated to U.S.-dollar-denominated bonds, which reduces the relative yields of U.S.-dollar-denominated bonds.

We must remind you that when you compare domestic bond and Eurobond financing alternatives, you must be sure to express the cost of each alternative on a comparable basis: Either convert the Eurobond cost of debt to an equivalent semi-annually compounded basis or convert the domestic cost of debt to an equivalent annually compounded basis. We explained how to accomplish these adjustments in Chapter 14.

CHOICE OF CURRENCY

Specific Electric could borrow $30 million and purchase DM50 million, or it could borrow DM50 million. Borrowing dollars to fund a Deutsche mark investment entails foreign exchange risk. If Specific Electric borrows dollars and the Deutsche mark depreciates relative to the dollar, Specific Electric's West German electric motor plant will be worth fewer dollars, and Specific Electric will have to dedicate a larger proportion of its Deutsche-mark-denominated project cash flow to service its U.S. dollar-denominated debt. The opposite would occur if the Deutsche mark appreciated relative to the dollar. Specific Electric can hedge against this foreign exchange risk either by borrowing in dollars and selling Deutsche marks forward or by borrowing in Deutsche marks. The latter strategy will result in a Deutsche mark liability that at least partially offsets the Deutsche mark asset. We use the qualifier "at least partially" because Specific Electric will still face foreign exchange exposure on any equity (DM assets minus DM liabilities) that it has invested in the plant.

Not all foreign investments involve foreign exchange risk. Suppose a foreign project's revenues are denominated in U.S. dollars, as is the case with international oil and gas projects because petroleum products are typically invoiced in U.S. dol-

---

[18] In 1989, The Walt Disney Company sold 42,940,000 shares (worth the equivalent of $483.5 million) of a new subsidiary company, Euro Disneyland S.C.A., entirely outside the United States. Disney formed the subsidiary (and incorporated it in France) to finance, build, and operate a new theme park outside Paris.

[19] International Bank for Reconstruction and Development, 8⅜% U.S. Dollar Bonds of 1989, due October 1, 1999, prospectus, September 19, 1989.

[20] Merton (1987) shows that expanding a firm's investor base can lower its cost of equity capital. Alexander, Eun, and Janakiramanan (1987) found that foreign firms that listed their common stock on a U.S. stock exchange experienced a reduction in their expected rate of return.

lars. Then, for example, the value of Phillips Petroleum Company's oil field investments in the British North Sea will not be very sensitive to changes in the U.S. dollar-pound sterling exchange rate. So Phillips Petroleum and other U.S. oil firms involved in the British North Sea should borrow in U.S. dollars rather than pounds sterling—as should British Petroleum and other non-U.S. firms that also invest there.

More generally, the Law of One Price implies that the price of a foreign good, denominated in the local currency, will adjust to offset exchange rate changes. In our example, the Deutsche mark price of Specific Electric's motors would adjust under the Law of One Price to preserve the dollar price. The Law of One Price does not hold exactly, although it is probably not too bad an approximation in the case of goods that enjoy an active international trade. To the extent the Law of One Price does hold for a particular project, the project sponsor is best off borrowing in its currency of account. Specific Electric should borrow a mixture of U.S. dollars and Deutsche marks, with the dollar proportion directly related to the extent to which Specific Electric expects to be able to preserve the price of its electric motors in dollars in the face of dollar-Deutsche mark exchange rate changes.

INTEREST RATE PARITY   One of the important implications of interest rate parity, Equation (23.4), is that when credit risk is held constant, any difference in nominal pretax yields between two different currencies is exactly offset by the expected change in the spot exchange rate during the term of the loan. If one currency affords a relatively low interest rate, it is because market participants expect the country to have a relatively low inflation rate and its currency to appreciate in value. Nominal interest cost savings will be offset exactly by expected exchange rate changes; the currency of borrowing does not matter.

FOREIGN CURRENCY BORROWING   In practice, there are international capital market frictions that may make it advantageous to borrow in one currency rather than another. Tax asymmetries, government-mandated capital and credit controls, and other market frictions can create opportunities to reduce a borrower's after-tax cost of debt (expressed in terms of the borrower's currency of account) by choosing one currency rather than another in which to borrow.

EXAMPLE ■ Suppose that Specific Electric can borrow 5-year funds in U.S. dollars for its new plant at an interest rate of 10% or 5-year funds in Deutsche marks at an interest rate of 8%. The Deutsche mark-denominated loan calls for sinking fund payments of DM10 at the end of years 2 and 3 and DM15 at the end of years 4 and 5. First we verify that the pretax dollar cost of debt (before transaction costs) is 10%. Table 23-4 presents Specific Electric's debt service in U.S. dollars. The cost of debt is the rate of return c that solves:

$$0 = -30.0 + \frac{2.4452}{(1 + c)} + \frac{8.7192}{(1 + c)^2} + \frac{8.3754}{(1 + c)^3} + \frac{11.2491}{(1 + c)^4} + \frac{10.6693}{(1 + c)^5}$$

so that $c = 10.0\%$.

Specific Electric's marginal ordinary income tax rate is 50% on both its U.S. income and its West German income. Its after-tax cost of debt on the U.S. dollar loan (before transaction costs) is

$$.10(1 - .5) = 5.00\%$$

TABLE 23-4   Specific Electric's Debt Service in U.S. Dollars

Year	1	2	3	4	5
Principal amount (DM millions)	50	50	40	30	15
Interest @ 8% (DM millions)	4	4	3.2	2.4	1.2
Principal payment (DM millions)	—	10	10	15	15
Total debt service (DM millions)	4	14	13.2	17.4	16.2
Exchange rate ($/DM)	.6113	.6228	.6345	.6465	.6586
Debt Service ($ millions)	2.4452	8.7192	8.3754	11.2491	10.6693

TABLE 23-5   After-Tax Debt Service for Specific Electric's Deutsche Mark Loan

Year	1	2	3	4	5
Debt Service (DM millions):					
Principal payment	—	10	10	15	15
Interest payment	4	4	3.2	2.4	1.2
Tax saving (at 50%)	(2)	(2)	(1.6)	(1.2)	(0.6)
Total	2	12	11.6	16.2	15.6
Exchange rate	.6113	.6228	.6345	.6465	.6586
Debt service ($ millions)	1.2226	7.4736	7.3602	10.4733	10.2742

If instead Specific Electric borrows and repays the Deutsche marks through its West German subsidiary (which recognizes no foreign exchange gains or losses for tax purposes but can only deduct its actual Deutsche Mark interest expense), its after-tax cost of debt, expressed in terms of dollars, is given in Table 23-5. In this case, the cost of debt is the rate of return c that solves:

$$0 = -30.0 + \frac{1.2226}{(1+c)} + \frac{7.4736}{(1+c)^2} + \frac{7.3602}{(1+c)^3} + \frac{10.4733}{(1+c)^4} + \frac{10.2742}{(1+c)^5}$$

so that $c = 5.96\%$

The after-tax cost of the Deutsche mark loan exceeds the after-tax cost of the U.S. dollar loan. Note that the Deutsche mark is appreciating relative to the dollar but that only the actual interest expense, not the cost to Specific Electric of repaying the more expensive Deutsche marks, is tax-deductible. ■

As a general rule, other things being equal, borrowing in the weaker currency will minimize the expected after-tax cost of debt. That is, interest rate parity equilibrates exchange-rate-adjusted pretax yields but not after-tax yields. As a second general rule, other things being equal, it is normally cheaper to borrow in high-tax-rate countries. However, other things may not be equal, so we recommend that when evaluating alternative currency borrowing options you calculate the after-tax cost of each before deciding which to select.

INVESTMENT-FINANCING INTERACTIONS   The net present value of a foreign investment project generally depends to some extent on the manner in which it is financed. This is true principally for two reasons: The manner of financing will affect the project sponsor's ability to repatriate funds, for the reasons noted earlier in the chapter, and the manner of financing can have important tax consequences because of the complex interplay of domestic and foreign taxes. We cannot discuss these tax factors here, but we do wish to emphasize their importance to project NPV. Because of these factors, international projects often have significant financing side effects.

When financing side effects are significant, we recommend using the adjusted-present-value approach:[21]

- Calculate the base case NPV assuming all-equity financing from the U.S. parent and assuming that all incremental free cash flow is repatriated to the U.S. parent in the form of dividends;

- Determine how much debt the project is capable of supporting without compromising the firm's target capital structure and calculate the present value tax shields that would result (1) if funds were borrowed in the United States, (2) if funds were borrowed in the foreign country, or (3) if funds were borrowed in the Euromarket, and select the most advantageous alternative;

- Calculate the present-value benefit of any support provided by the host country in the form of loan guarantees, subsidized loans, loans obtained from the World Bank or other organizations to finance infrastructure improvements, etc.;

- Calculate the present-value benefit (chiefly in the form of reduced taxes) of alternative forms of remitting funds or of remitting funds to low-tax jurisdictions, rather than to the United States;

- Calculate the present-value benefit of any other side effect; and

- Add the present-value amounts to obtain project NPV.

We cannot give you a complete checklist. But we can remind you to *bear in mind the Principle of Incremental Benefits when you evaluate a foreign investment project*. Think through carefully the incremental costs and benefits of the project and try to devise ways to enhance each incremental benefit and reduce each incremental cost.

SOLUTION TO NONSTANDARD OIL'S FINANCING ALTERNATIVES

Nonstandard Oil must avoid the temptation to borrow in Swiss francs simply because the interest rate is so much lower than the dollar interest rate. As a consequence of interest rate parity and purchasing power parity, the interest rate differential reflects the expectation that the rate of inflation in the United States will exceed the rate of inflation in Switzerland by 5% per annum over the next 5 years, and the Swiss franc is expected to appreciate by 5% per annum relative to the U.S. dollar. Since all of Nonstandard Oil's revenues are in U.S. dollars, borrowing in Swiss francs does not provide a hedging benefit. Unless there are special tax advan-

---

[21] See Lessard (1986).

tages or transaction cost savings that might result from borrowing in Switzerland, Nonstandard Oil should borrow in U.S. dollars.

SUMMARY

A multinational corporation's objective is the same as a purely domestic corporation's: To maximize shareholder wealth. But an international financial manager needs additional analytical tools to cope with complications in the form of cash flows denominated in foreign currencies, foreign political risk, foreign government regulations and capital constraints, and foreign tax systems. She needs these tools to take advantage of opportunities that are available in the foreign exchange market and in foreign capital markets to reduce foreign exchange risk. Information can be obtained from those markets that enables a financial manager to ensure that financial decisions are not biased, perhaps unknowingly, by foreign exchange rate factors.

A critical first step toward developing these tools involves understanding the four key parity relationships in international financial market equilibrium: interest rate parity, purchasing power parity, the expectations theory of forward exchange rates, and the international Fisher effect. Interest rate parity requires the forward-spot exchange rate differential to offset the interest rate differential between two countries. Purchasing power parity states that the differential between the expected inflation rates in two countries equals the differential between the current and expected future spot exchange rates. The expectations theory states that the forward exchange rate equals the expected future spot exchange rate. The international Fisher effect holds that real rates of interest must be the same in all the world's capital markets.

The four key parity relationships do not hold exactly because of government regulations, particularly capital controls, asymmetric taxes, and other market imperfections. But the parity relationships are a useful approximation to reality and represent a good starting point for analysis. For example, interest rate parity tells us that the two methods of hedging foreign exchange risk, buying or selling foreign currencies forward, or borrowing or lending in a foreign currency, are equivalent strategies.

The foreign exchange market offers a low-cost means of hedging foreign exchange risk. International financial managers would be wise to utilize this relatively cheap insurance and not speculate on exchange rate movements. We explained how to use forward contracts and foreign currency options to eliminate foreign exchange risk.

International capital investment projects involve foreign exchange considerations. But because of the key parity relationships, it makes no difference which currency is used in the calculations. However, it is important that the parity relationships be observed closely when calculating the incremental free cash flow stream. The incremental free cash flow stream should be adjusted for any political risks and/or tax differences, and it should reflect the actual timing of the repatriation of funds from the foreign country. The discount rate should reflect appropriately the opportunity cost of funds to the sponsoring firm's shareholders. As a result of the limited degree of international portfolio diversification of U.S. investors, the cost of capital for a foreign project may actually be less than the cost of capital for a comparable domestic project.

A foreign project can be financed in the sponsoring firm's domestic capital market, in the Euromarket, in the host country's capital market, or in some other coun-

DECISION SUMMARY BOX

- The four key parity relationships provide a useful framework for gauging future foreign exchange rate movements.
- It is best to use the adjusted-present-value approach when evaluating foreign capital investment projects because of the presence of significant financing side effects.
- The incremental cash flow stream and the discount rate should be calculated with respect to the same currency; which currency does not matter so long as the key parity relationships all hold.
- The key parity relationships should be invoked to project future exchange rates when calculating the incremental cash flow stream; in particular, ensure that the inflation rate implicit in the forecast cash flow stream is consistent with purchasing power parity.
- Base the cash flow calculation on the timing of the repatriation of funds from the foreign country and plan how to accomplish the intended timing.
- In applying the CAPM, beta should be calculated based on (1) a set of comparable publicly-traded firms in the host country that are in the same industry as the project and (2) unless there is reason to believe that the sponsoring firm's shareholders are well diversified internationally, a domestic proxy, such as the Standard & Poor's 500 Index, should be used as the market portfolio. Using the domestic beta is likely to overstate the true beta and understate the project's present value.
- Adjust cash flows, not the discount rate, for any political risk.
- Foreign currency risk should be hedged whenever possible either by entering into forward currency transactions or by borrowing in the host country's capital market.
- A firm should evaluate each feasible borrowing alternative, particularly borrowing in the Euromarket. The cost of funds for each alternative should be calculated after-tax on a consistent basis, i.e., expressed in terms of the same currency, the same frequency of compounding, etc. The firm should select the lowest-cost alternative, taking into consideration any particular benefit from hedging foreign exchange, political, or other risks.

try's capital market. An international financial manager should maintain a global financing perspective and not restrict financing to the firm's domestic market. A firm should *not* simply borrow in whichever currency affords the lowest interest rate. Under the parity relationships, that currency is likely to appreciate and offset the apparent saving. Nevertheless, largely due to tax considerations, there may be a cost advantage to borrowing in one country (and currency) rather than another. Borrowing in the host capital market hedges the sponsor's foreign exchange risk and, if structured properly, can also hedge much of the sponsor's political risk. If that country has a relatively weak currency and a relatively high income tax rate (and interest is tax-deductible), the relative advantage of local financing increases.

International projects involve an investment-financing interaction. Consequently, the adjusted-present-value approach is often very useful in the evaluation of an international investment project.

PROBLEMS

PROBLEM SET A

A1. Explain the important differences between a forward contract for a particular foreign currency and a futures contract for the same currency. What are the relative advantages of each?

A2. Using the foreign currency cross rates in Figure 23-1:
  a. Find the price of a Canadian dollar in Swiss francs.
  b. Find the price of a Swiss franc in Canadian dollars.
  c. Show that the currency cross rates in a and b are equivalent.

A3. Using the foreign exchange rates for Thursday in Figure 23-1:
  a. Is the West German mark trading at a forward discount or at a forward premium to the U.S. dollar? Calculate the 30-day, 90-day, and 180-day forward premium or discount.
  b. Is the Japanese yen trading at a forward discount or at a forward premium to the U.S. dollar? Calculate the 30-day, 90-day, and 180-day forward premium or discount.

A4. Explain each of the following parity relationships:
  a. Interest rate parity
  b. Purchasing power parity
  c. Expectations theory of forward exchange rates
  d. Equality of expected real rates of return

A5. The Swiss franc–Japanese yen exchange rate is SF1 = ¥96.18. The Swiss franc–German mark exchange rate is SF1 = DM1.125. What is the Japanese yen–German mark exchange rate?

A6. The dollar-pound exchange rate is £1 = $2.00. The expected rates of inflation in the United States and Great Britain are 4% and 8%, respectively. Calculate the forward exchange rate required under purchasing power parity.

A7. What would happen if the conditions required for the expectations theory of forward exchange rates to hold are satisfied in the market for US dollars and British pounds but
  a. The forward rate (expressed as $ per £) is greater than the expected future spot rate (expressed as $ per £).
  b. The forward rate (expressed as $ per £) is less than the expected future spot rate (expressed as $ per £).

A8. Explain which of the following represents the stronger requirement:
  a. The forward rate always equals the expected future spot rate; or
  b. The forward rate always equals the future spot rate.

A9. If the interest rates in the United States and Switzerland are 8% and 4%, respectively, and the projected inflation rates are 5% and 1%, respectively, verify that Equation (23.9) holds. What is the real rate of interest?

A10. Explain why the difference between the current spot exchange rate and the forward exchange rate is not an accurate measure of the cost of a forward contract.

A11. In what sense can a foreign currency money market hedge be thought of as a "homemade" forward contract? Discuss the significance of this relationship for practical foreign currency risk management.

A12. Using the Pratt and Whitney example, show that if the future spot rate is £1 = $1.25, both the forward contract hedge and the foreign currency money market hedge will produce a net realized dollar value of $160 million. Show that the same result occurs in each case if the future spot rate is £1 = $2.00.

A13. Calculate the U.S. dollar and Deutsche mark internal rates of return for Specific Electric's electric motor plant and apply the IRR criterion. Which criterion is superior: IRR or NPV?

A14. Explain why a corporate treasurer would be unwise to follow a policy of always borrowing in whichever currency affords the lowest interest rate.

A15. A firm faces two borrowing alternatives. It can issue 6-year debt domestically that bears a 10% coupon and that matures in a lump sum at the end of 6 years. Issuance expenses are 1% of the principal amount. It can also issue a 10¼% Eurobond that matures in a lump sum at the end of 6 years. Issuance expenses are 1.25% of the principal amount. The issuer's tax rate is 50%.
  a. Calculate the after-tax cost of the domestic issue.
  b. Calculate the after-tax cost of the Eurobond issue and express this cost on an equivalent semiannually compounded basis.
  c. Which issue is cheaper? Explain.

A16. Suppose Specific Electric Company's marginal ordinary income tax rate is 34%. Ignore issuance expenses.
  a. Calculate the after-tax cost of the U.S. dollar-denominated issue.
  b. Calculate the after-tax cost of the Deutsche-mark-denominated issue expressed in U.S. dollars.

PROBLEM SET B

B1. The 3-month risk-free interest rate in U.S. dollars is 8%. The 3-month risk-free interest rate in Swiss francs is 3%. The dollar-franc exchange rate is SF1 = $0.66.
  a. Calculate the 3-month forward rate required under interest rate parity.
  b. If the 3-month forward rate is SF1 = $0.68, describe how a riskless arbitrage profit could be earned and quantify the profit in both dollars and Swiss francs.

B2. The spot rate for U.S. dollars and German marks is $1 = DM1.50. The 1-year forward rate is $1 = DM1.40.
  a. Under interest rate parity, what is the 1-year U.S. dollar interest rate if the 1-year German mark interest rate is 5%?
  b. Under interest rate parity, what is the 1-year German mark interest rate if the 1-year U.S. dollar interest rate is 10%?
  c. What mathematical relationship must hold between the U.S. dollar and German mark 1-year interest rates if interest rate parity prevails?

B3. Gold is selling for $450/oz. in New York and £300/oz. in London.
  a. If it were costless to transport gold between New York and London, what would the dollar-pound exchange rate have to be if the Law of One Price is to hold?
  b. Suppose the dollar-pound exchange rate is £1 = $1.70. Describe how arbitrageurs could realize a riskless arbitrage profit and quantify the profit in both dollars and British pounds.

B4. Show that if interest rate parity, purchasing power parity, and the expectations theory of forward exchange rates all hold, then so does the international Fisher effect. What happens when any one of the first three parity relationships fails to hold?

B5. The Swiss franc-German mark spot exchange rate is SF1 = DM1.20. The 1-year forward rate is SF1 = DM1.30.
  a. What is your best estimate of the spot rate expected 1 year from now?
  b. If the expected spot rate were SF1 = DM1.40, would anyone want to sell Swiss francs forward? Sell German marks forward?
  c. If the expected spot rate were SF1 = DM1, would anyone want to sell Swiss francs forward? Sell German marks forward?

B6. If the Japanese yen–German mark spot exchange rate is ¥1 = DM0.012 and the expected spot rate 1 year hence is ¥ = DM0.015, what is the relationship between the expected inflation rates in Japan and West Germany for the coming year?

B7. If the expected average annual inflation rates in Canada and Great Britain over the next five years are 7% and 10%, respectively, and the first three parity relationships in Figure 23-2 hold, what is the relationship between the 5-year interest rates in Canada and Great Britain?

B8. TransAtlantic Airlines expects to receive DM5 million from a German tour operator in 30 days. Because TransAtlantic's expenses are in U.S. dollars, the firm wishes to hedge its foreign currency risk. The current spot exchange rate is DM1 = $0.60, and the 30-day forward exchange rate is DM1 = $0.58.

   a. How many U.S. dollars should TransAtlantic expect to receive if it does not hedge?

   b. Suppose the spot exchange rate at the time the tour operator pays is DM1 = $0.56. How much would hedging have saved TransAtlantic?

   c. If 30-day interest rates are 10% in the United States and West Germany, which method of hedging would you recommend?

   d. If the 30-day interest rates in the United States and West Germany are 10% and 14%, respectively, which method of hedging would you recommend?

B9. In problem B8, if the 30-day interest rate in the United States is 12%, what would the 30-day interest rate have to be in West Germany in order for TransAtlantic to be indifferent between entering into a 30-day forward contract and effecting a 30-day foreign currency money market hedge?

B10. Consider again Specific Electric's proposed electric motor plant. What are the expected real rates of interest in West Germany and in the United States? Why must these rates of interest be equal when interest rate parity, purchasing power parity, and the expectations theory of forward exchange rates hold?

B11. Consider again Specific Electric's proposed electric motor plant. Suppose that the projected risk-free interest rates in the United States and West Germany were

	Maturity (years)				
	1	**2**	**3**	**4**	**5**
	Interest Rate (% per annum):				
United States	8%	9%	9%	10%	10%
West Germany	6%	7%	8%	9%	10%

   a. Calculate the spot exchange rates expected 1, 2, 3, 4, and 5 years hence.

   b. Calculate the projected incremental cash flow stream in dollars based on the projected spot exchange rates in part a.

   c. Calculate the NPV of the project based on the cash flow stream in part b.

B12. Northern Chemical Company is considering building a petrochemical plant in Scotland. The plant would cost $100 million. The projected incremental cash flow stream is

Year:	1	2	3	4	5	6	7
Cash Flow (£millions)	30	40	40	50	50	50	50

The current spot exchange rate is £1 = $1.50. The 1-year risk-free rate is 8% in the United States and 12% in the United Kingdom. The expected inflation rate in the United States is 5% per annum for the next 7 years.

    a. What is the expected inflation rate in the United Kingdom for the next 7 years?

    b. Calculate the expected spot exchange rates for each of the next 7 years.

    c. Calculate the projected incremental cash flow stream in dollars.

    d. If the dollar hurdle rate is 14%, what is the NPV in dollars?

    e. Calculate the pound sterling hurdle rate.

    f. Calculate the NPV in pounds.

    g. Are the project NPVs in parts d and f equal? Explain.

B13. Verify that if Specific Electric can deduct for tax purposes the appreciation in the cost of Deutsche marks that must be repaid, its after-tax cost of the Deutsche-mark-denominated loan, expressed in U.S. dollars, closely approximates the after-tax cost of the U.S. dollar-denominated loan, 5.00%.

PROBLEM SET C

C1. The 2-year interest rate is 10% per annum semiannually compounded. The 1-year interest rate is 8% per annum semiannually compounded. If there is no opportunity for riskless arbitrage, what is the 1-year forward interest rate?

C2. **a.** If the interest rates $r_£(t)$ and $r_\$(t)$ are continuously compounded interest rates, reexpress Equations (23.2) and (23.4).

    b. If the inflation rates $i_£(t)$ and $i_\$(t)$ are continuously compounded inflation rates, reexpress Equations (23.5) and (23.7).

    c. Derive Equation (23.9) from Equation (23.8) and the modified Equations (23.4) and (23.7).

    d. Given $r_£(1) = .12$, $r_\$(1) = .10$, $i_£(1) = .10$, and $i_\$(1) = .08$, show that Equation (23.9) holds as a strict equality.

    e. What is the real rate of interest? Show that the international Fisher effect implies that a single real rate of interest exists in the two markets.

C3. Show that if any one of the four parity relationships in Figure 23–2 fails to hold, at least one other must also fail to hold.

C4. Use the key parity relationships in Figure 23–2 to demonstrate the perfect equivalence of a forward contract and a foreign currency money market hedge.

C5. Generalize the Pratt and Whitney example to demonstrate that

    a. The net realized dollar value will be $160 million regardless of the future spot exchange rate when the pounds sterling are sold forward.

    b. The net realized dollar value will be $160 million regardless of the future spot exchange rate when the pounds sterling are sold spot and the dollar proceeds invested at an interest rate that satisfies interest rate parity.

C6. Let $^F R_t$ denote the total return on a foreign security when the share price and dividend payments are measured in the local currency. Let $^\$ R_t$ denote the total return when the components are measured in U.S. dollars. Let $^F R_{mt}$ and $^\$ R_{mt}$ denote the total return on the U.S. market portfolio when the components are measured in the local currency and in U.S. dollars, respectively. By applying the key parity relationships in Figure 23–2, show that in equilibrium:

$$\frac{1 + {}^\$ R_t}{1 + {}^F R_t} = \frac{E[1 + i_\$(t)]}{E[1 + i_F(t)]} = \frac{1 + {}^\$ R_{mt}}{1 + {}^F R_{mt}}$$

C7. Use the relationship between stock returns and expected inflation rates established in problem C6 to show that the following procedures for calculating the beta for a foreign project are equivalent:

    a. Convert $^F R_t$ to $^\$ R_t$ and regress $^\$ R_t$ on $^\$ R_{mt}$ or

    b. Convert $^\$ R_{mt}$ to $^F R_{mt}$ and regress $^F R_t$ on $^F R_{mt}$.

C8. Use the results obtained in problems C6 and C7 together with the key parity relationships in Figure 23-2 to demonstrate that

$$\frac{1 + r_F(t)}{1 + r_\$(t)} = \frac{1 + r^*_F(\theta)}{1 + r^*_\$(\theta)}$$

where $r^*_F(\theta)$ denotes the hurdle rate for the project when the incremental cash flows are expressed in the foreign country's currency and $r^*_\$(\theta)$ denotes the hurdle rate for the project when the incremental cash flows are converted to dollars.

C9. *The Economist* (May 5, 1990) reported the following prices for a Big Mac hamburger in different countries along with recent exchange rates:

Country	Price of Big Mac	Exchange Rate
Australia	A$2.30	A$1.32/US$
Britain	£1.40	£0.61/US$
Canada	C$2.19	C$1.16/US$
France	FF17.70	FF5.63/US$
Japan	¥370	¥159/US$
United States	$2.20	—
West Germany	DM4.30	DM1.68/US$

  a. Calculate the exchange rates implied by the Law of One Price.
  b. Are the prices consistent with the Law of One Price?
  c. How would you interpret your answers to parts a and b? Are exchange rates out of equilibrium? Is the Law of One Price invalid? Or is there some other explanation?

REFERENCES

Adler, Michael. "The Cost of Capital and Valuation of a Two-Country Firm." *Journal of Finance* 29 (March 1974): 119–32.

Alexander, Gordon, Cheol S. Eun, and S. Janakiramanan. "Asset Pricing and Dual Listing on Foreign Capital Markets: A Note." *Journal of Finance* 42 (March 1987): 151–58.

Baldwin, Carliss Y. "Competing for Capital in a Global Environment." *Midland Corporate Finance Journal* 5 (Spring 1987): 43–64.

Cooper, Ian A., and Evi Kaplanis. "Cost to Crossborder Investment and International Equity Market Equilibrium." In J. Edwards, Julian Franks, C. Mayer, and Stephen Schaefer, eds., *Recent Developments in Corporate Finance*. Cambridge: Cambridge University Press, 1986.

Cornell, Bradford. "Spot Rates, Forward Rates and Exchange Market Efficiency." *Journal of Financial Economics* 5 (August 1977): 55–65.

Cornell, Bradford, and Alan C. Shapiro. "Managing Foreign Exchange Risks." *Midland Corporate Finance Journal* 1 (Fall 1983): 16–31.

Eiteman, David K., and Arthur I. Stonehill. *Multinational Business Finance,* 3rd ed. Reading, Mass.: Addison-Wesley, 1982.

Fama, Eugene F. "Short-Term Interest Rates as Predictors of Inflation." *American Economic Review* (June 1975): 269–82.

Fama, Eugene F. "Forward and Spot Exchange Rates." *Journal of Monetary Economics* 14 (1984): 319–38.

Fatemi, Ali M. "Shareholder Benefits from Corporate International Diversification." *Journal of Finance* 39 (December 1984): 1325–44.

Fisher, Irving. *The Theory of Interest.* New York: Augustus M. Kelley, 1965.

Frenkel, Jacob A., and Richard M. Levich. "Covered Interest Arbitrage: Unexploited Profits?" *Journal of Political Economy* 83 (April 1975): 325–38.

Frenkel, Jacob A., and Richard M. Levich. "Transaction Costs and Interest Arbitrage: Tranquil versus Turbulent Periods." *Journal of Political Economy* 85 (November-December 1977): 1209–25.

Garner, C. Kent, and Alan C. Shapiro. "A Practical Method of Assessing Foreign Exchange Risk." *Midland Corporate Finance Journal* 2 (Fall 1984): 6–17.

Giddy, Ian H. "The Foreign Exchange Options as a Hedging Tool." *Midland Corporate Finance Journal* 1 (Fall 1983): 32–42.

Giddy, Ian H., and Gunter Dufey. "The Random Behavior of Flexible Exchange Rates." *Journal of International Business Studies* (Spring 1975): 1–32.

Joy, O. Maurice, Don B. Panton, Frank K. Reilly, and Stanley A. Martin, Jr. "Co-movements of Major International Equity Markets." *Financial Review* 11 (1976): 1–20.

Lessard, Donald R. "World, Country, and Industry Relationships in Equity Returns: Implications for Risk Reduction Through International Diversification." *Financial Analysts Journal* 32 (January-February 1976): 32–38.

Lessard, Donald R. "Evaluating Foreign Projects—An Adjusted Present Value Approach." In Donald R. Lessard, ed., *International Financial Management: Theory and Application*, 2nd ed. New York: John Wiley and Sons, 1986.

Lessard, Donald R., and Alan C. Shapiro. "Guidelines for Global Financing Choices." *Midland Corporate Finance Journal* 1 (Winter 1983): 68–80.

Levi, Maurice. *International Finance: Financial Management and the International Economy.* New York: McGraw-Hill, 1983.

Levich, Richard M. "Tests of Forecasting Models and Market Efficiency in the International Money Market." In Jacob A. Frenkel and Harry G. Johnson, eds., *The Economics of Exchange Rates: Selected Studies.* Reading, Mass.: Addison-Wesley, 1978.

Merton, Robert C. "A Simple Model of Capital Market Equilibrium with Incomplete Information." *Journal of Finance* 42 (July 1987): 483–510.

Officer, Lawrence H. "The Purchasing-Power-Parity Theory of Exchange Rates: A Review Article." *IMF Staff Papers* (March 1976): 1–60.

Rodriguez, Rita, and Eugene Carter. *International Financial Management*, 3rd ed. Englewood Cliffs, N.J.: Prentice-Hall, 1984.

Roll, Richard. "Violations of the 'Law of One Price' and Their Implications for Differentially-Denominated Assets." In Marshall Sarnat and George Szego, eds., *International Finance and Trade, vol. 1.* Cambridge, Mass.: Ballinger, 1979.

Shapiro, Alan C. "Capital Budgeting for the Multinational Corporation." *Financial Management* 7 (Spring 1978a): 7–16.

Shapiro, Alan C. "Financial Structure and Cost of Capital in the Multinational Corporation." *Journal of Financial and Quantitative Analysis* 13 (June 1978b): 211–26.

Shapiro, Alan C. "Currency Risk and Relative Price Risk." *Journal of Financial and Quantitative Analysis* 19 (December 1984): 365–73.

Shapiro, Alan C. *International Corporate Finance,* 2nd ed. Cambridge, Mass.: Ballinger, 1988.

Shapiro, Alan C. *Multinational Financial Management,* 3rd ed. Boston: Allyn and Bacon, 1989.

Smith, Clifford W., Jr., Charles W. Smithson, and L. Macdonald Wakeman. "The Evolving Market for Swaps." *Midland Corporate Finance Journal* 3 (Winter 1986): 20–32.

Stulz, Rene M. "A Model of International Asset Pricing." *Journal of Financial Economics* 9 (December 1981): 383–406.

SHORT-TERM DECISIONS: MANAGING THE FIRM

FINANCIAL STATEMENTS AND RATIO ANALYSIS

The primary source of financial information concerning a firm is its financial statements. The information contained in these statements summarizes the financial performance and financial position of the firm. This chapter reviews the principal financial statements and illustrates their use in financial analysis.

We know from the Principle of Capital Market Efficiency that publicly available information such as that in the firm's financial statements is not likely to be useful for identifying "undervalued" stocks. However, the firm's financial statements can be examined to provide a better understanding of why a widely traded stock is selling at its current price. In addition, for nontraded or infrequently traded (also referred to as **thinly traded**) stocks, the firm's financial statements provide a good starting point for determining the value of the firm.

Financial managers and investors analyze financial statements using a collection of relatively standardized **financial ratios** as a basis for comparison. By comparing the values of selected financial ratios for a particular firm with values of the same ratios calculated on the same basis for comparable firms, the financial analyst can achieve a better understanding of the financial health of the firm. Also, by studying changes in key financial ratios over time, the analyst is better able to discern improvement or deterioration in the firm's financial condition and performance. The calculation and interpretation of several of the more widely used ratios are described in this chapter. The final section of the chapter deals with **discriminant analysis**, a method that has been used to provide a composite measure of the firm's financial condition based on the values of several specified ratios.

FIRST NATIONAL BANK'S CREDIT DECISION

Lincoln Manufacturing Corporation has applied to the First National Bank for a $30 million annually renewable **line of credit**. The vice president in charge of commercial credit lines has been asked to assess the financial health of Lincoln. Recent financial statements for Lincoln Manufacturing are shown in Tables 24-1, 24-2, and 24-3. Based on these statements, do you think First National should grant Lincoln the requested line of credit? Throughout the chapter, we will develop the tools for assessing Lincoln's current financial health. At the end, we will return to this question and provide our opinion.

TABLE 24-1   Income Statements, Lincoln Manufacturing Corporation and Consolidated Subsidiaries (Millions of Dollars Except Per-Share Amounts)

	1990	1989
Revenue:		
Net sales	$743	$663
Other income	7	7
Total revenue	750	670
Costs and Expenses:		
Cost of goods sold (excluding depreciation and amortization)	530	485
Selling, general, and administrative expense	65	58
Depreciation and amortization	39	35
Interest expense	26	25
Capitalized interest	(2)	(2)
Minority interest in earnings of consolidated subsidiaries	1	1
Total	659	602
Net income before taxes and extraordinary items	91	68
Federal and state income taxes	38	29
Net income before extraordinary items	53	39
Preferred stock dividends	2	2
Earnings available for common stock before extraordinary items	51	37
Extraordinary gains (losses) net of taxes	(10)	—
Earnings Available for Common Stock	$41	$37
Average number of common shares outstanding (thousands)	9,360	8,800
Earnings per common share before extraordinary items	$5.45	$4.20
Extraordinary gains (losses) per common share	(1.07)	—
Earnings Per Common Share	$4.38	$4.20
Dividends Per Common Share	$1.92	$1.80

24.1

THE FIRM'S FINANCIAL STATEMENTS

The firm's published financial statements include, at a minimum, an **income statement**, a **balance sheet**, a **statement of cash flows**, and accompanying notes.[1] These statements and their use in financial analysis are reviewed below.

INCOME STATEMENT

The income statement reports the profit (or loss) performance of a business entity for a specific period of time, usually a year or some portion thereof. Net income, or

---

[1] A firm's annual report includes income statements and statements of cash flows for the latest 3 years and balance sheets for the latest 2 years.

TABLE 24-2 Balance Sheets, Lincoln Manufacturing Corporation and Consolidated Subsidiaries (Millions of Dollars)

	1990	1989		1990	1989
Assets			*Liabilities and Stockholders' Equity*		
Current Assets:			Current Liabilities:		
Cash and cash equivalents	$7	$10	Notes and loans payable	$41	$32
Marketable securities	51	45	Current portion of long-term debt	16	10
Accounts receivable	48	43	Accounts payable and accrued liabilities	115	94
Inventories	151	122	Income taxes payable	39	31
Prepaid taxes and other expenses	11	9	Total current liabilities	211	167
Total current assets	268	229	Long-term debt (less current portion)	203	198
Investments:			Capitalized lease obligations due after one year	36	35
Equity in assets of nonconsolidated			Deferred credits	67	55
subsidiaries	32	26	Total liabilities	517	455
Other investments—at cost	43	49	Minority interest in subsidiaries	10	10
Total investments	75	75	Preferred stock not subject to mandatory		
Plant, Property, and Equipment:			redemption (230,000 and 260,000 shares		
At cost	769	689	issued and outstanding)	23	26
Less accumulated depreciation and			Common Stockholders' Equity:		
amortization	290	261	Common stock (15,000,000 shares authorized;		
Net property, plant, and equipment	479	428	9,400,000 and 9,000,000 shares outstanding)	48	46
Other assets	6	6	Capital surplus	69	63
			Retained earnings	164	141
Total Assets	$828	$738	Less treasury stock—at cost (128,000 shares)	(3)	(3)
			Total common stockholders' equity	278	247
			Total Liabilities and Stockholders' Equity	$828	$738

profit, is the difference between total revenue and total cost for the period. The income statement for Lincoln Manufacturing Corporation is shown in Table 24-1. For a manufacturing company, the income statement provides a breakdown of costs into (1) variable, or direct, cost of producing the goods that are sold (chiefly labor and raw materials); (2) other expenses incurred in operating the company, including taxes; and (3) financing costs, including interest and any dividends paid to the holders of the company's preferred stock. Note that certain noncash items, such as depreciation and amortization, are deducted from revenue in arriving at net income. The residual amount, earnings available for common stock, is available for payment to common shareholders as dividends or for reinvestment in the business.

Earnings per share and, in some cases (as in Table 24-1), dividends per share, are provided at the foot of the income statement. Recall that the owners of the outstanding shares of the company's common stock are the residual claimants on the firm's profit; in the long run, cash dividends come from the firm's earnings, net of interest payments and preferred stock dividends. The per-share figures indicate how large the residual pool of net income is relative to the number of common shares, or claims, against it. The number of common shares used in this calculation should be the weighted average number of common shares outstanding during the period adjusted for any **common stock equivalents** in the company's capital structure.

TABLE 24-3 Statements of Cash Flows, Lincoln Manufacturing Corporation and Consolidated Subsidiaries
(Millions of Dollars)

	1990	1989
Cash Flows from Operating Activities:		
Net income before extraordinary items	$ 53	$ 39
Adjustments for noncash transactions:		
Depreciation and amortization	39	35
Deferred income taxes	9	5
Minority interest in earnings of consolidated subsidiaries	1	1
Equity in undistributed earnings of nonconsolidated subsidiaries	(3)	(1)
Interest capitalized	(2)	(2)
Decrease (increase)		
Accounts receivable	(5)	(20)
Inventories	(29)	(12)
Prepaid taxes and expenses	(2)	(1)
Increase (decrease)		
Accounts payable	21	5
Income taxes payable	8	1
All other items—net	(5)	3
Net cash provided (used) by operating activities	85	53
Cash Flows from Investing Activities		
Additions to property, plant, and equipment	(100)	(62)
Sale of property, plant, and equipment	10	5
Additional investments	(3)	(5)
Sale of investments	6	—
Other marketable securities sales (additions)—net	(6)	(5)
Net cash generated (used) by investing activities	(93)	(67)
Cash Flows from Financing Activities:		
Additions to long-term debt and capitalized leases	75	70
Reductions in long-term debt and capitalized leases	(69)	(60)
Additions (reductions) in short-term debt—net	15	21
Cash dividends to stockholders of parent	(20)	(18)
Cash dividends to minority interests	(1)	(1)
Common stock issued	8	10
Preferred stock retired	(3)	—
Net cash provided (used) in financing activities	5	22
Increase (decrease) in cash and cash equivalents	(3)	8
Cash and cash equivalents at beginning of year	10	2
Cash and Cash Equivalents at End of Year	$ 7	$10

Common stock equivalents are convertible securities, stock options, and warrants that are deemed to be the substantial equivalent of common stock. In addition, where the conversion of convertible securities or the exercise of warrants or options not treated as common stock equivalents would, upon conversion or exercise, result in a significant reduction in reported earnings per share, such **dilution** must be disclosed in the form of a **fully diluted earnings per share** figure.[2] This fully diluted figure, although it represents an extreme case of dilution, nevertheless gives the analyst a better feel than the nondiluted figure alone could, of how large each outstanding share's residual claim on the earnings of the business really is.

For valuation purposes, earnings per common share before extraordinary items should be distinguished from the earnings per common share (net of these items) because the former figure is the more meaningful measure of the firm's sustainable profit. Finally, dividends per common share, when taken together with these various measures of earnings per share, indicate the firm's payout ratio for this period, the portion of the available earnings pool that is actually paid out to common shareholders as dividends.

The income statement in Table 24-1 seems to highlight the company's earnings per share. Indeed, that figure and its rate of growth over time are the most widely used measures of a company's performance and, hence, the investment potential of its common stock. It is worth emphasizing, therefore, that generally accepted accounting principles permit companies some latitude in calculating net income and, hence, earnings per share. For example, the last-in-first-out (LIFO) and the first-in-first-out (FIFO) methods are acceptable methods of inventory valuation, but in periods of high inflation, LIFO accounting will produce significantly lower earnings than FIFO accounting. In addition, there are accounting methods followed by particular industries, such as the practice of recognizing allowance for funds used during construction in the utility industry, that can distort interindustry comparisons based solely on earnings per share. You should be careful to note, then, that the earnings per share figure, in spite of the significance some would attach to it, should not be relied upon exclusively to measure a company's performance or the attractiveness of its common stock for investment purposes. Other measures, which are discussed below, are available for obtaining a more comprehensive picture.

Financial analysts find it useful to examine the data provided in the income statement by calculating **profitability ratios** that express the profit earned by the firm as a percentage of various variables (for example, total assets, sales, and owners' equity) and **coverage ratios** that measure the firm's ability to meet its interest and preferred stock dividend obligations. The calculation and interpretation of these important ratios are discussed later in the chapter.

BALANCE SHEET

The balance sheet reports the financial condition of a business entity at a point in time. It is a critical indicator of the fundamental credit strength of a company and therefore the company's capability of financing itself. The balance sheet shows, on a historical cost basis, the **assets** of the firm, which are the productive resources utilized in its operations, and the **liabilities** and **stockholders' equity** of the firm, which are the total claims—divided between the claims of creditors and those of the owners—against those assets.

---

[2] Accounting Principles Board, "Earnings Per Share," APB Opinion No. 15 (New York: AICPA, 1969) and Davidson and Weil (1983), ch. 29.

A typical balance sheet for a manufacturing company is shown in Table 24-2. Note that the basic balance sheet identity,

$$\text{Assets} = \text{Liabilities} + \text{Stockholders' Equity} \qquad (24.1)$$

is satisfied. Note also that assets and liabilities are each broken down into a current component that in the case of assets, matures or is expected to be realized as cash within 1 year and in the case of liabilities, comes due or is expected to be paid out in cash within 1 year. The size of current assets in relation to current liabilities indicates the company's ability to meet its short-term obligations as they come due, and certain measures of this ability are discussed later in this chapter. As discussed below, financial analysts make an important distinction between **liquidity** and the ability to meet short-term needs on the one hand and **profitability** and the ability to remain viable over the longer-term on the other.

Certain balance sheet items are used in conjunction with certain profit items from the income statement to calculate rates of return, which indicate the profitability of the uses to which the firm's assets and the equity investment of its "owners" are being put. The use and interpretation of these measures are discussed below.

STATEMENT OF CASH FLOWS

The statement of cash flows indicates how the cash position of the firm has changed during the period covered by the income statement. As such, it complements the income statement and the balance sheet. Changes in a firm's cash position are due not only to the portion of net income that is retained in the business, but also due to additional borrowings or repayments of debt (both short-term and long-term), additional issues or retirements of capital stock (both common and preferred), additions to or disposals of fixed assets, and several other factors. The statement of cash flows breaks down the sources and uses of cash into 3 components: cash flows from operating activities, cash flows from investing activities, and cash flows from financing activities. In recognition of the need by external users of accounting statements to have information concerning the investing and financing activities of the firm, FASB Statement No. 95 requires firms to issue a statement of cash flows along with the income statement and the balance sheet. But more important from the standpoint of financial analysis, the flows of funds between a business enterprise and investors, creditors, workers, customers, etc., serves as a fundamental starting point for the analysis of the firm, the analysis of capital investment projects, the analysis of corporate acquisitions, and the analysis underlying many other key long-term policy choices.

A typical statement of cash flows is shown in Table 24-3. The sources of cash (and the amount of cash generated by each) and the applications of cash (and the amount of cash used by each) from operating activities, investing activities, and financing activities are itemized. Note that underlying the statement of cash flows is a basic accounting identity:

$$\text{Cash Inflow} - \text{Cash Outflow} = \text{Change in Cash} \qquad (24.2)$$

The statement of cash flows furnishes the information needed to calculate a firm's cash flow (or cash flow from operations). As evident in Table 24-1, various noncash expenses are deducted when calculating a firm's earnings. Cash flow equals earnings plus the noncash expenses:

$$\text{Cash Flow} = \text{Net Income before Extraordinary Items} \\ + \text{Noncash Expenses} \qquad (24.3)$$

Net income before extraordinary items is used in this calculation in order to exclude the effect of extraordinary (i.e., nonrecurring) events. Because noncash items can significantly affect reported earnings, cash flow has taken on increased importance in recent years as an indicator of a firm's performance and a measure of a firm's ability to meet its financial obligations and fund its growth.

The cash flow for Lincoln Manufacturing for 1990 is calculated:

Net income before extraordinary items	$53 million
Depreciation and amortization	39
Deferred income taxes	9
Minority interest in earnings of consolidated subsidiaries	1
Equity in undistributed earnings of nonconsolidated subsidiaries	(3)
Interest capitalized	(2)
Cash flow	$97 million

Deferred income taxes are added back because their payment in cash is deferred; of Lincoln Manufacturing's $38 million tax provision in Table 24-1, only $29 million is payable currently. Minority interest is added back because the earnings do not have to be distributed in cash to the minority shareholders of consolidated subsidiaries; if some portion is distributed, the distribution would be reported separately in the Statement of Cash Flows. But dividends are *not* subtracted out when calculating cash flow because they are a discretionary item associated with the firm's financing activities. Equity in the undistributed earnings of nonconsolidated subsidiaries is subtracted out because that portion of the subsidiaries' earnings is not available to Lincoln Manufacturing (i.e., since Lincoln owns 50% or less of each nonconsolidated subsidiary—which is why the subsidiaries are not consolidated—Lincoln does not have voting control of them). Finally, capitalized interest was subtracted from interest expense when calculating earnings, which increases earnings by a like amount. Because the interest must be paid currently in cash, it is subtracted out in calculating cash flow.

Note that cash flow defined in Equation (24.3) differs from net cash provided (used) by operating activities in Table 24-3. The latter figure includes the cash effect of increases and decreases in various current assets and current liabilities. The adjustments reflect changes in inventory policy, changes in the firm's policy regarding granting and utilizing trade credit, and changes in the size of the firm (e.g., larger sales generally require larger inventories). Cash flow, as defined in Equation (24.3), has a more limited purpose: to reflect the profit (or loss) performance of the firm for a specific period of time on a *cash basis*.

NOTES TO THE FINANCIAL STATEMENTS

The notes to a firm's financial statements are an integral part of those statements. The notes disclose the significant accounting policies used to prepare the financial statements and provide additional detail concerning several of the items in the financial statements. This normally includes

1. more detailed breakdowns of other income, interest and other financial charges, and provision for income taxes;
2. description of the earnings per share calculation;
3. details concerning extraordinary items, if any, and foreign exchange gains or losses;

4. breakdown of inventories, investments (including nonconsolidated subsidiaries), property, plant, and equipment, and other assets;

5. costs and amounts of short-term borrowings;

6. schedules of long-term debt, preferred stock, and capitalized and operating lease obligations;

7. schedule of capital stock issued or reserved for issuance and statement of changes in shareholders' equity (often included as a separate financial statement);

8. details concerning significant acquisitions or disposals of assets;

9. information concerning employee pension and stock option plans;

10. commitments and contingent liabilities;

11. events subsequent to the balance sheet date but prior to the release of the financial statements to the public, which might affect significantly their interpretation;

12. quarterly operating results;

13. business segment information (by line of business and by geographic region); and

14. a 5-year summary comparison of financial performance and financial position.

The notes section also normally includes a discussion by management of recent operating results. As the forgoing list of items suggests, the notes to a firm's financial statements contain a wealth of information that is useful in financial analysis.

HISTORICAL COST VERSUS REPLACEMENT COST ACCOUNTING

Financial decisions should be based on current and expected future conditions. However, financial statements are prepared on a historical cost basis, which can distort the financial statements in important ways. Many different economic factors can cause such distortion. Inflation is one of those factors. As illustrated in Table 24-4, profits tend to be overstated as a result of (1) gains on the inflating value of inventories and (2) understated allowances for depreciation because both inventories and fixed assets will have to be replaced at inflated prices prevailing in the future. Because the tax laws do not permit depreciation to be computed on a replacement cost basis, taxes are paid on these overstated profits, thus impinging on cash flow. The balance sheet is also affected. Assets are valued at what they cost minus accumulated depreciation, not what they are actually worth. Debt is recorded at its principal amount (net of amortized premiums or discounts); no account is taken of the benefit a company and its shareholders realize as inflation reduces the real purchasing power of the company's debt obligations, which are fixed in nominal dollars.

A set of financial statements fully adjusted for the effects of inflation would look very different from those currently prepared in accordance with generally accepted accounting principles. In 1979 the Financial Accounting Standards Board issued Statement No. 33 (FASB 33), which initiated an experiment in inflation accounting by requiring approximately 1,300 large companies to make supplementary disclosure concerning the effect of changing prices on net sales and other operating revenues, income and income per common share from continuing operations, and certain other items.[3] FASB 33 has been superseded, and generally accepted accounting

---

[3]Financial Accounting Standards Board, *Financial Reporting and Changing Prices*, Statement of Financial Accounting Standards No. 33, (High Ridge Park, Stamford, Conn.: Financial Accounting Standards Board, October 1979) and Davidson and Weil (1983), ch. 31.

TABLE 24-4 Historical Cost Accounting versus Replacement Cost Accounting

	Accounting Method		
	Historical Cost	*Constant Dollar*[a]	*Current Cost*[b]
Revenue	$5,313,000	$5,313,000	$5,313,000
Cost of goods sold	3,944,535	4,127,949	4,207,056
Depreciation and amortization	192,465	299,187	416,682
Other operating expenses	630,000	630,000	630,000
Interest expense	168,000	168,000	168,000
Income tax expense	189,000	189,000	189,000
Income (loss) from Continuing Operations	$ 189,000	$ (101,136)	$ (297,738)
Purchasing Power Gain on Excess of Monetary Assets over Monetary Liabilities		$ 195,342	$ 195,342
Annual Increase in Current Cost Amounts of Plant and Inventories ($723,660) less Inflation Component			$ 223,629

[a]Adjusted for general inflation.
[b]Adjusted for changes in specific prices.

principles no longer require supplementary (or any other) disclosure concerning the effects of changing prices. Nevertheless, the FASB 33 experiment produced some interesting results.

The impact of inflation on the 1979 net income of fifteen companies is shown in Table 24–5. FASB 33 required two different methods of inflation-adjustment: the "constant-dollar method," which adjusted inventory costs and depreciation for changes in the consumer price index since the related assets were purchased, and the "current-cost method," which adjusted these items on the basis of the current cost of replacing the company's assets. Under either method, inflation-adjusted earnings are 40% to 70% lower than profits reported under historical-cost accounting, and effective corporate tax rates are 15 to 25 percentage points higher, often far exceeding the then statutory 46% tax rate. The two methods produce different results company-by-company and industry-by-industry, however, depending on how much the replacement cost of specific assets has increased relative to the consumer price index. Interestingly, office equipment producers, such as Burroughs Corp. and NCR Corp., reported inflation-adjusted earnings higher than earnings figured on a historical-cost basis when using the current-cost method, reflecting the reduction in replacement costs resulting from technological advances in that industry. The more capital-intensive companies, particularly those with a higher proportion of much older plant, reported substantially lower net income under both methods, with utilities suffering the greatest negative impact. Unfortunately, the constant-dollar and current-cost methods both have shortcomings, and a consensus as to which method is better, or as to whether some other method should be used, was never reached. While there seems to be general agreement that some account must be taken of the impact of inflation to make financial statements more meaningful, much additional work needs to be done. Nevertheless, FASB 33 was a useful first step because it helped make investors and other financial statement users more aware of the magnitude of the problem.

Table 24-5   Impact of Inflation on the Income from Continuing Operations of Selected Companies
(Millions of Dollars)

Company	Accounting Method		
	Historical Cost	*Constant Dollar[a]*	*Current Cost[b]*
Armco	$ 221.0	$ 117.5	$ 96.6
Burroughs	305.5	192.8	345.0
Celanese	141.0	49.0	46.0
Con Edison	323.9	123.6	43.0
Control Data	118.5	1.7	114.7
Dow Chemical	784.0	722.0	696.0
General Motors	2,892.7	1,776.1	1,803.4
B.F. Goodrich	82.6	9.5	0.3
Merck	382.0	302.0	340.0
NCR	234.6	119.8	310.7
Singer	(92.3)	(173.3)	(142.5)
Southern Company	219.1	(38.4)	(115.2)
Southern Railway	160.6	84.8	69.7
Union Carbide	556.2	394.8	396.3
Xerox	563.1	344.9	427.5

[a] Adjusted for general inflation.
[b] Adjusted for changes in specific prices.
Source: Corporate 1979 annual reports.

The forgoing suggests that in many circumstances the financial analyst will find it necessary to adjust the figures reported in (or calculated on the same basis as those reported in) published financial statements to take into account factors such as the following:

■ Inflation can distort the returns to be realized from any single project just as they do a company's overall financial results. Inflation-adjusted measures are needed to analyze proposed capital investment projects in order to minimize the likelihood that inflation-induced distortions will bias the capital investment decision.[4] As noted in Chapter 12, the analysis should either be entirely in real or entirely in inflated terms.

■ Due to the distortions inherent in reported earnings per share figures, approaches to acquisition valuation based on estimated earnings multiples or capitalizing earnings streams can give misleading results. A more fundamental approach that takes into account the funds needed for replacement and other nondiscretionary purposes is described in Chapter 22.

■ Historical cost accounting can conceal the fact that a company may be worth more in liquidation than as a going concern, particularly when its asset portfolio

[4] A number of firms are already doing this. For example, General Electric Company explicitly notes in its 1979 Annual Report that it follows such a procedure.

contains a high proportion of natural resources or real estate that has appreciated rapidly in value.

■ Net income and the rate of return on stockholders' equity based on traditional historical cost accounting will tend to be overstated in an inflationary environment and can be virtually meaningless because of changes in market values. In that case, the reported profitability measures, earnings growth, and payout ratios of the firm can provide a misleading impression of the potential for future dividend growth.

RECASTING THE FIRM'S FINANCIAL STATEMENTS 24.2

The firm's financial statements contained in Tables 24–1 and 24–2 can be recast into a form that makes them more amenable to careful analysis. In particular, the components of the income statement and balance sheet can be supplemented with ratios that help to highlight changes over time in the financial performance and financial condition of the firm.

INCOME STATEMENT

Table 24–6 contains the income statements for Lincoln Manufacturing Corporation for the years 1989 and 1990, which were provided in Table 24–1, and, in addition, income statements for the years 1986, 1987, and 1988. Note that operating revenue ("net sales") and operating income have been distinguished from nonoperating income ("other income"), which includes such items as equity in the earnings of nonconsolidated affiliates, interest and dividends earned on the company's portfolio of marketable securities, and income from other sources that are incidental to Lincoln's principal (manufacturing) lines of business. Each of the major line items is then expressed as a percentage of yearly net sales, which produces certain measures of profitability that are discussed below. Also, growth rates for certain variables have been calculated. By comparing the ratios from one year to the next and by comparing the growth rates, the financial analyst can obtain a clearer picture than an examination of the absolute quantities alone could provide, of how the performance of Lincoln has changed over the past 5 years. For example, between 1986 and 1990, operating income, net income before extraordinary items, and earnings available for common stock before extraordinary items increased significantly in absolute amount and, more important, increased significantly as a percentage of net sales.

The calculation of the growth rates in Table 24–6 deserves comment. Two methods are widely used, the **simple compound growth method** and the **log-linear least squares method**. Both methods are described in the appendix to this chapter. For our purposes, it is sufficient to note that the log-linear least squares method is generally preferred because it takes all the observations, not just those at the beginning and the end of the period, into account.

BALANCE SHEET

Table 24–7 contains the recast balance sheets for Lincoln Manufacturing Corporation for the years 1989 and 1990. Many summary formats are possible, and Table 24–7 provides one that we have found convenient. The components of assets and liabilities are presented in summary form, and each is expressed as a percentage of net assets (or equivalently, total capitalization). In Table 24–7, cash and marketable se-

TABLE 24-6   Recast Income Statements for Lincoln Manufacturing Corporation and Consolidated Subsidiaries 1986–1990
(Millions of Dollars Except Per-Share Amounts)

| | Twelve Months Ended December 31 | | | | | | | | | | Four-Year Growth Rate |
| | 1990 | | 1989 | | 1988 | | 1987 | | 1986 | | |
	Amount	%	Amount	%	Amount	%	Amount	%	Amount	%	
Net sales	$743	100.0%	$663	100.0%	$579	100.0%	$509	100.0%	$406	100.0%	14.73%
Cost of goods sold	530	71.3	485	73.2	414	71.5	372	73.0	295	72.7	14.37
Gross profit	213	28.7	178	26.8	165	28.5	137	26.9	111	27.3	15.65
Operating Expenses:											
S, G & A	65	8.8	58	8.7	60	10.4	39	7.7	42	10.3	12.70
Depreciation and amortization	39	5.2	35	5.3	32	5.5	28	5.4	23	5.7	12.79
Total operating expenses	104	14.0	93	14.0	92	15.9	67	13.1	65	16.0	12.68
Operating income	109	14.7	85	12.8	73	12.6	70	13.8	46	11.3	19.20
Other income	7	0.9	7	1.1	11	1.9	7	1.3	4	1.0	
Interest expense—net	(24)	(3.3)	(23)	(3.5)	(23)	(4.0)	(21)	(4.1)	(17)	(4.2)	
Minority interest	(1)	(0.1)	(1)	(0.1)	(1)	(0.1)	(1)	(0.1)	(1)	(0.2)	
Pre-tax income	91	12.2	68	10.3	60	10.4	55	10.9	32	7.9	23.02
Income taxes	38	5.1	29	4.4	25	4.4	23	4.6	8	2.0	33.48
Net income before extraordinary items	53	7.1	39	5.9	35	6.0	32	6.3	24	5.9	17.82
Preferred stock dividends	2	0.3	2	0.3	3	0.5	4	0.8	4	1.0	
Earnings available for common stock before extraordinary items	51	6.8	37	5.6	32	5.5	28	5.5	20	4.9	21.51
Extraordinary gains (losses) net of taxes	(10)	(1.3)	—	—	—	—	4	0.8	—	—	
Earnings Available for Common Stock	$41	5.5%	$37	5.6%	$32	5.5%	$32	6.3%	$20	4.9%	15.81
Earnings Per Common Share:											
Before extraordinary items	$5.45		$4.20		$3.92		$3.82		$2.79		14.34
Extraordinary items	(1.07)		—		—		0.46		—		
Net	$4.38		$4.20		$3.92		$4.28		$2.79		8.83
Dividends Per Common Share	$1.92		$1.80		$1.56		$1.52		$1.32		9.18

curities on the one hand and inventories on the other are distinguished from other current assets, while short-term debt is distinguished from other current liabilities.

Under certain circumstances, it would also be appropriate to show some of the other components of current assets and current liabilities separately, as for example, if receivables had increased dramatically. The difference between current assets and current liabilities represents net working capital, or often simply called **working capital**:

$$\text{Working Capital} = \text{Current Assets} - \text{Current Liabilities} \qquad \textbf{(24.4)}$$

TABLE 24-7 Recast Balance Sheets for Lincoln Manufacturing Corporation
and Consolidated Subsidiaries at December 31, 1989 and 1990
(Millions of Dollars Except Per-Share Amounts)

	12/31/90		12/31/89	
	Amount	*%*	*Amount*	*%*
Current Assets:				
Cash and marketable securities	$58	10.5%	$55	10.7%
Inventories	151	27.5	122	23.6
Other current assets	59	10.7	52	10.1
Total current assets	268	48.7	229	44.4
Current Liabilities:				
Short-term debt	57	10.4	42	8.2
Other current liabilities	154	27.9	125	24.2
Total current liabilities	211	38.3	167	32.4
Working capital	57	10.4	62	12.0
Plant, property, and equipment—net	479	87.1	428	82.9
Other Assets:				
Investments	75	13.6	75	14.5
Other	6	1.1	6	1.2
Total other assets	81	14.7	81	15.7
Noncapitalized Long-term Liabilities:				
Deferred credits	(67)	(12.2)	(55)	(10.6)
Net Assets	$550	100.0%	$516	100.0%
Represented by:				
Long-term debt	$203	36.9%	$198	38.4%
Capitalized lease obligations	36	6.5	35	6.8
Minority interest	10	1.8	10	1.9
Preferred stock (involuntary liquidation value of $105 per share)	24	4.4	27	5.2
Common stockholders' equity	277	50.4	246	47.7
Total Capitalization	$550	100.0%	$516	100.0%
Book Value Per Common Share	$29.47		$27.33	

which provides a measure of the business's liquidity, or its ability to meet its short-term obligations as they come due. Next shown are the business's noncurrent assets and noncapitalized long-term liabilities. Adding plant, property, equipment, and other assets to working capital and subtracting the noncapitalized long-term liabilities gives **net assets**, which also equals the sum of the firm's various sources of long-term financing.

Net Assets = Working Capital + Plant, Property, and Equipment + Other Assets
$\qquad$ − Noncapitalized Long-term Liabilities
$\qquad$ = Total Assets − Current Liabilities − Noncapitalized Long-term Liabilities
$\qquad$ = Total Capitalization
$\qquad$ = Long-term Funds Invested in the Business

Some analysts prefer to think of deferred income taxes and other deferred credits as "cost-free capital" and to define net assets more simply as the difference between total assets and current liabilities. Because these deferred credits do not represent financing in any conventional sense but result from tax-timing differences, Equation (24.5) seems more appropriate.

The total capitalization of the business summarizes the distribution of the claims on its net assets among its long-term creditors (including lessors), the holders of minority interests in its consolidated subsidiaries, its preferred stockholders, and its common stockholders. In some cases, the corporate charter specifies that upon liquidation of the business, the preferred shareholders must be paid a premium before any liquidation proceeds can be paid to common stockholders. In that case, it is more appropriate to list the preferred stock at its liquidation value and to adjust common stockholders' equity accordingly (as has been done in Table 24–7). Lincoln Manufacturing Corporation's preferred stock has an **involuntary liquidation preference** of $105 per share, which represents a 5% premium over its $100 par value. Therefore, $1 million (= [5]229,000) has had to be added to book value of the preferred stock in 1990 and subtracted from the book value of common stockholders' equity in 1990 to reflect this liquidation preference.

The adjusted value of common stockholders' equity is divided by the number of common shares outstanding on the balance sheet date to obtain the book value per common share:

$$\text{Book Value per Common Share} = \frac{\text{Common Stockholders' Equity}}{\text{Common Shares Outstanding}} \quad (24.6)$$

This calculation for Lincoln for 1990 is performed in the following manner:

$$\text{Book Value per Common Share} = \frac{277.0}{9.4} = \$29.47$$

The book value per common share would be the residual value per share if the corporation were liquidated and (1) its assets are sold for the amounts shown on the balance sheet; (2) its debt is repaid at its principal amount (as shown on the balance sheet); and (3) its capitalized lease obligations and minority interest are paid their respective **net book values** and preferred stock is redeemed at its involuntary liquidation value.

24.3 RATIO ANALYSIS

Financial analysts find it helpful to calculate **financial ratios** when interpreting a firm's financial statements. The number of financial ratios that might be calculated is virtually limitless, but there are certain basic ratios that are frequently used. These fall into four classes: **liquidity ratios**, **profitability ratios**, **leverage ratios**, and **common stock ratios**. The calculation and interpretation of ratios belonging to the first three classes are discussed below. Those belonging to the fourth class were discussed in Chapters 17 and 18.

24.4 LIQUIDITY RATIOS

Recall that the term *liquidity* refers to how quickly and efficiently (in the sense of low transaction costs) an asset can be exchanged for cash. **Liquidity ratios** are designed to measure the firm's ability to meet its financial obligations on time. Such measures are of three basic types: measures of overall liquidity, turnover ratios, and coverage ratios.

MEASURES OF OVERALL LIQUIDITY

The most widely used measure of overall liquidity is the **current ratio**, which is computed as follows:

$$\text{Current Ratio} = \frac{\text{Current Assets}}{\text{Current Liabilities}} \qquad (24.7)$$

The current ratio measures the number of times that the firm's current assets cover its current liabilities. The higher the current ratio, the greater the firm's ability to meet its short-term obligations as they come due. A widely held but rough rule of thumb holds that a 2:1 current ratio is an appropriate target for most firms.

Current assets include inventories, which are normally more difficult than marketable securities and receivables to turn into cash on short notice to pay off current liabilities. Thus, analysts often exclude inventories from the numerator in Equation (24.7) and calculate the **acid test ratio**:

$$\text{Acid Test Ratio} = \frac{\text{Current Assets} - \text{Inventories}}{\text{Current Liabilities}} \qquad (24.8)$$

EXAMPLE ■ Using the financial statements provided in Table 24-7, the current ratio and acid test ratio for 1990 for Lincoln Manufacturing Corporation are

$$\text{Current Ratio} = \frac{268}{211} = 1.27$$

$$\text{Acid Test Ratio} = \frac{268 - 151}{211} = 0.55 \qquad\qquad ■$$

TURNOVER RATIOS

Turnover ratios can be calculated to measure the degree of liquidity associated with specific current assets. The **receivable turnover ratio**, calculated as

$$\text{Receivable Turnover Ratio} = \frac{\text{Annual Credit Sales}}{\text{Average Accounts Receivable}} \qquad (24.9)$$

measures the number of times the average accounts receivable balance turns over during the year. Note that annual credit sales, which give rise to receivables, are used in the numerator. If a figure for annual credit sales is not available, the firm's net sales figure is used instead. The average accounts receivable is the average of the beginning-of-year and end-of-year amounts.

A measure of liquidity for inventories that is similar to Equation (24.9) is the **inventory turnover ratio**, which is calculated as follows:

$$\text{Inventory Turnover Ratio} = \frac{\text{Cost of Goods Sold}}{\text{Average Inventory}} \qquad (24.10)$$

Net sales may also be used in the numerator of Equation (24.10), although that introduces the possibility that differences in how firms choose to mark up costs of goods sold, rather than inventory policy alone, would affect a comparison based on inventory turnover ratios.

EXAMPLE ■ The turnover ratios for Lincoln Manufacturing Corporation for 1990 are

$$\text{Receivable Turnover Ratio} = \frac{743}{(48 + 43)/2} = 16.33$$

$$\text{Inventory Turnover Ratio} = \frac{530}{(151 + 122)/2} = 3.88$$

■

Note that because receivables turn over 16.33 times per year, the average collection period is $365/16.33 = 22$ days. Thus, Equation (24.9) can be converted easily into a measure of the average collection period. A more accurate picture of the firm's accounts receivable could be obtained by preparing an **aging schedule for accounts receivable**, which would show the amounts of receivables that have been outstanding for different periods—e.g., 0–15 days, 16–30 days, and more than 30 days. An external analyst typically lacks such detailed information, so the rougher calculation embodied in Equation (24.9) must be used instead.

COVERAGE RATIOS

Coverage ratios are designed to measure the firm's ability to pay (cover) any financing charges that will come due. The **interest coverage ratio** measures the number of times the income available to pay interest charges covers the firm's interest expense. It is Earnings Before Interest and Income Taxes (EBIT) divided by the interest expense, or

$$\text{Interest Coverage Ratio} = \frac{\text{EBIT}}{\text{Interest Expense}} \tag{24.11}$$

Because rental payments contain an interest component, the Securities and Exchange Commission prefers the following modified calculation:

$$\frac{\text{Fixed Charge}}{\text{Coverage Ratio}} = \frac{\text{EBIT} + \frac{1}{3}\text{ Rentals}}{\text{Interest Expense} + \frac{1}{3}\text{ Rentals}} \tag{24.12}$$

Interest Expense in Equations (24.11) and (24.12) includes the amortization of debt discount or premium (if any) and the amortization of debt issuance expense. The $\frac{1}{3}$ Rentals in Equation (24.12) approximates the interest component of total rental expense. If the exact interest component is known, that figure should be used instead.[5] The numerators in Equations (24.11) and (24.12) are pretax figures because interest is a tax-deductible expense.

Calculating the Interest Coverage Ratio and Fixed Charge Coverage Ratio requires the calculation of EBIT. The SEC specifies the following formula:

EBIT = Net Income before (i) Income Taxes, (ii) Extraordinary Items,
   (iii) Income (Loss) from Discontinued Operations, (iv) Minority Interest
   + Interest Expense Net of Capitalized Interest
   − Equity in Undistributed Earnings of Nonconsolidated Subsidiaries

---

[5] The SEC defines fixed charges to include also the preferred stock dividend obligations of consolidated subsidiaries to third parties.

Capitalized interest is excluded from EBIT unless the company is a regulated utility company, which will recover capitalized interest through future customer charges.

Preferred dividends are also a financing charge. The associated coverage ratio is

$$\text{Preferred Stock Dividend Coverage Ratio} = \frac{\text{EBIT} + \frac{1}{3} \text{Rentals}}{\text{Interest Expense} + \frac{1}{3} \text{Rentals} + \text{Preferred Dividends}/(1 - \bar{\tau})} \quad \textbf{(24.13)}$$

where $\bar{\tau}$ is the company's average income tax rate. Equation (24.13) reflects the facts that interest expense must be met before preferred stock dividends can be paid and that preferred stock dividends are an after-tax expense.

The coverage calculations in Equations (24.11), (24.12), and (24.13) are based on pretax amounts. Alternatively, the calculations could be done on an after-tax basis. For example, corporate charter requirements for the issuance of additional preferred stock are often based on after-tax amounts.

EXAMPLE ■ Suppose the footnotes to Lincoln Manufacturing Corporation's financial statements for 1990 reveal annual rental expense of $6 million. Lincoln's EBIT would be calculated in the following manner:

$$\text{EBIT} = 91 + 1 + (26 - 2) - 3 = 113$$

since the statement of cash flows in Table 24-3 shows equity in undistributed earnings of nonconsolidated subsidiaries amounting to $3 million. Lincoln's coverage ratios would be calculated in the following manner:

$$\text{Interest Coverage Ratio} = \frac{113}{26} = 4.35\text{x}$$

$$\text{Fixed Charge Coverage Ratio} = \frac{113 + (6/3)}{26 + (6/3)} = 4.11\text{x}$$

$$\text{Preferred Stock Dividend Coverage Ratio} = \frac{113 + 2}{26 + 2 + [2.0/(1 - 38/91)]} = 3.66\text{x} \quad ■$$

PROFITABILITY RATIOS   24.5

Profitability ratios serve as measures of the firm's financial performance. Performance can be measured in relation to either sales or investment, or it can be measured on a per-share basis.

PROFIT MARGINS

Profit margins measure the firm's profitability in relation to sales. Three measures are commonly used.

The **gross profit margin** measures the firm's ability to control expenses. It is calculated as follows:

$$\text{Gross Profit Margin} = \frac{\text{Gross Profit}}{\text{Net Sales}} = \frac{\text{Net Sales} - \text{Cost of Goods Sold}}{\text{Net Sales}} \quad \textbf{(24.14)}$$

The **operating profit margin** measures the surplus that is available after meeting the firm's operating expenses in addition to the cost of goods sold:

$$\text{Operating Profit Margin} = \frac{\text{Operating Income}}{\text{Net Income Sales}}$$

$$= \frac{\text{Net Sales} - \text{Cost of Goods Sold} - \text{Operating Expenses}}{\text{Net Sales}} \quad \textbf{(24.15)}$$

Finally, the **net profit margin** measures the surplus that is available to equity holders after all expenses, including interest and taxes, have been paid:

$$\text{Net Profit Margin} = \frac{\text{Net Income before Extraordinary Items}}{\text{Net Sales}} \quad \textbf{(24.16)}$$

EXAMPLE ■   Lincoln Manufacturing Corporation's profit margins for 1990 are calculated in the following manner:

$$\text{Gross Profit Margin} = \frac{213}{743} = 28.7\%$$

$$\text{Operating Profit Margin} = \frac{109}{743} = 14.7\%$$

$$\text{Net Profit Margin} = \frac{53}{743} = 7.1\%,$$

all of which appear in the recast income statement in Table 24-6.   ■

RATES OF RETURN

Rate of return ratios express profitability in relation to various measures of financing. As such, they attempt to measure the effectiveness with which the firm's assets are being used. Three ratios are commonly used.

The **return on average assets** corresponds to the operating profit margin, replacing net sales with average total tangible assets (total assets less intangibles, such as goodwill) and adding other income to the numerator:

$$\text{Return on Average Assets} = \frac{\text{Operating Income} + \text{Other Income}}{\text{Average Total Tangible Assets}} \quad \textbf{(24.17)}$$

where Average Total Tangible Assets is calculated as the average of the beginning-of-year and end-of-year amounts. Return on Assets is also often calculated on an after-tax and after-interest-expense basis by using net income in the numerator of Equation (24.17).

The **return on average invested capital** measures the percentage return realized on the long-term funds invested in the business:

Return on Average Invested Capital =

$$\frac{\text{Operating Income} + \text{Other Income} - \text{Income Taxes}}{\text{Average Net Tangible Assets}} \quad \textbf{(24.18)}$$

where

Net Tangible Assets = Total Assets − Intangible Assets − Current Liabilities
          − Noncapitalized Long-term Liabilities

          = Total Capitalization − Intangible Assets

Return on Average Invested Capital is also often calculated on a pretax basis by not subtracting taxes in the numerator of Equation (24.18). However, by subtracting taxes, the firm's capital structure (its chosen mix of debt and equity capital) is explicitly taken into account. Also, some analysts prefer to include deferred income taxes and other noncapitalized long-term liabilities in the denominator in Equation (24.18).

Finally, the **return on average common equity** measures the percentage return to the firm's common stockholders:

$$\text{Return on Average Common Equity} = \frac{\text{Earnings Available for Common Stock before Extraordinary Items}}{\text{Average Common Stockholders' Equity}} \qquad \textbf{(24.19)}$$

where Common Stockholders' Equity includes common stock (at par value), capital surplus, and retained earnings.

EXAMPLE ■ Suppose Lincoln's 1990 annual report indicates that Lincoln had no intangible assets at year-end 1990. The 1990 rates of return for Lincoln are calculated as follows:

$$\text{Return on Average Assets} = \frac{109 + 7}{(828 + 738)/2} = 14.8\%$$

$$\text{Return on Average Invested Capital} = \frac{109 + 7 - 38}{(550 + 516)/2} = 14.6\%$$

$$\text{Return on Average Common Equity} = \frac{51}{(277 + 246)/2} = 19.5\% \qquad ■$$

PER-SHARE MEASURES

The three most widely used per-share measures of profitability are **earnings per common share** (EPS), dividends per common share, and **cash flow per common share**. Recall that we used EPS and dividends per share in connection with stock valuation in Chapter 6. Recently, cash flow per common share has begun to receive increasing attention from professional managers and investors. Cash flow per common share is, in some important respects, a more meaningful figure than EPS. To illustrate the difference between the two, Lincoln's earnings per common share (before extraordinary items) for 1990 was

$$\text{Earnings per Common Share} = \frac{51}{9.36} = \$5.45$$

Lincoln's 1990 cash flow was calculated earlier in the chapter and found to be $97 million. Lincoln's 1990 cash flow per common share was

$$\text{Cash Flow per Common Share} = \frac{97}{9.36} = \$10.36$$

The difference between the two measures reflects noncash expense items that decrease reported earnings per common share in the period.

LEVERAGE RATIOS 24.6

Leverage ratios measure the degree of leverage in the firm's capital structure and reflect the degree of financial risk the firm faces. Leverage ratios are of two principal types: **capitalization ratios**, which measure each type of capital relative to the firm's total capitalization, and **debt ratios**, which relate long-term debt or total debt to certain balance sheet and flow of funds quantities.

Capitalization Ratios

The recast balance sheet in Table 24-7 contains, among other things, a **capitalization table**, which breaks down the total capital invested in the firm (total capitalization) into its constituent parts. The relevant sections of Table 24-7 are reproduced in Table 24-8. The associated ratios are called **capitalization ratios**. The capitalization table provides a breakdown of the sources of long-term financing.

Table 24-8 provides one of many possible formats for the capitalization table. Some analysts would include deferred taxes among the sources of long-term funds. Also, long-term debt would be divided into senior debt and subordinated debt, and convertible debt would be shown separately if Lincoln had such classes of debt outstanding. Finally, Table 24-8 breaks down capitalization on a book value basis. Alternatively, each component could be listed on the basis of its market value, which might provide a very different impression, depending on the firm's share price and the level of interest rates.

Debt Ratios

As discussed in Chapters 15 and 16, the firm's choice of capital structure involves several complex issues. But because debt involves certain contractual commitments, a firm's financial risk depends on the amount of debt in its capital structure. Debt ratios are used to measure the extent of the firm's financial risk.

The **long-term debt ratio** measures the percentage of long-term financing that consists of long-term debt. As discussed in Chapter 21, capitalized lease obligations displace conventional long-term debt. Accordingly, the long-term debt ratio includes capitalized lease obligations. It is defined as follows:

$$\frac{\text{Long-Term}}{\text{Debt Ratio}} = \frac{\text{Long-Term Debt} + \text{Capitalized Lease Obligations}}{\text{Total Capitalization}} \qquad (24.20)$$

Table 24-8 Capitalization Table for Lincoln Manufacturing Corporation and Consolidated Subsidiaries
(Millions of Dollars)

	12/31/90		12/31/89	
	Amount	*%*	*Amount*	*%*
Short-Term Debt	$ 57	10.4%	$ 42	8.1%
Long-term debt	$203	36.9%	$198	38.4%
Capitalized lease obligations	36	6.5	35	6.8
Minority interest	10	1.8	10	1.9
Preferred stock (involuntary liquidation value)	24	4.4	27	5.2
Common stockholders' equity	277	50.4	246	47.7
Total Capitalization	$550	100.0%	$516	100.0%

Firms enjoy some discretion in substituting short-term debt for long-term debt (as many firms did when long-term interest rates rose sharply in 1979 and 1980). A more inclusive measure can be obtained by modifying Equation (24.20) in the following manner:

Total-Debt-to-Adjusted-Capitalization Ratio =

$$\frac{\text{Short-Term Debt} + \text{Long-Term Debt} + \text{Capitalized Lease Obligations}}{\text{Total Capitalization} + \text{Short-Term Debt}} \quad \textbf{(24.21)}$$

Equations (24.20) and (24.21) measure debt relative to capitalization. Alternatively, the debt-to-equity ratio measures debt relative to equity as

$$\frac{\text{Debt}}{\text{Equity}} = \frac{\text{Short-Term Debt} + \text{Long-Term Debt} + \text{Capitalized Lease Obligations}}{\text{Preferred Stock} + \text{Common Stockholders' Equity}}$$

$$\textbf{(24.22)}$$

Minority interest is ignored in Equation (24.22), but it might be included among either debt or equity, depending on whether or not the company intends to eliminate it within a few years (as for example, minority interest in a recently acquired subsidiary). Depending on the circumstances, other adjustments to Equation (24.22) might be appropriate; for example, including unfunded pension liabilities in debt if they are substantial and the analyst is trying to measure the risk to creditors if the firm should go bankrupt.[6] Bond rating agencies typically include in long-term debt some portion of off-balance-sheet liabilities (when these are significant), such as those that may arise out of project financing.

The firm must be able to repay its debt obligations as well as meet its interest obligations if it is to remain solvent. The firm's cash inflow relative to the amount of debt it has outstanding provides a measure of the former (interest coverage and fixed charge coverage measure the latter):

Cash-Flow-to-Long-Term-Debt Ratio =

$$\frac{\text{Cash Flow}}{\text{Long-Term Debt} + \text{Capitalized Lease Obligations}} \quad \textbf{(24.23)}$$

Cash-Flow-to-Total-Debt Ratio =

$$\frac{\text{Cash Flow}}{\text{Short-Term Debt} + \text{Long-Term Debt} + \text{Capitalized Lease Obligations}} \quad \textbf{(24.24)}$$

EXAMPLE ■ The debt ratios for Lincoln Manufacturing for 1990 are

$$\text{Long-Term Debt Ratio} = \frac{203 + 36}{550} = 43.5\%$$

$$\text{Total-Debt-to-Adjusted-Capitalization Ratio} = \frac{57 + 203 + 36}{550 + 57} = 48.8\%$$

$$\text{Debt-to-Equity Ratio} = \frac{57 + 203 + 36}{24 + 277} = 98.3\%$$

$$\text{Cash-Flow-to-Long-Term-Debt Ratio} = \frac{97}{203 + 36} = 40.6\%$$

[6] A study of 40 major corporations by Regan (1976) revealed that including unfunded vested pension liabilities in capitalization as debt raised the average debt-to-equity ratio of these firms by 50%.

$$\text{Cash-Flow-to-Total-Debt Ratio} = \frac{97}{57 + 203 + 36} = 32.8\%$$

24.7

USE AND INTERPRETATION OF FINANCIAL RATIOS

The financial ratios described in previous sections are used as benchmarks by analysts, investors, lenders, and managers to judge the financial performance and financial condition of the business enterprise. Which set of ratios will prove most useful in any particular application will depend to a great extent on the user's perspective. A lender to the firm will be most concerned with fixed charge coverage (and liquidity ratios generally); the firm's managers will be concerned with turnover ratios and profitability measures, which indicate how effectively the firm is using its assets; and common stockholders will emphasize return on common equity (and the profitability ratios generally). Lenders are generally most concerned with the firm's liquidity and leverage; in general, the greater the liquidity and the smaller the degree of leverage, the greater the likelihood that interest and principal payments will be made on time. Managers and equityholders are likely to be more directly concerned with the profitability of the enterprise, with shareholders most concerned with the returns earned on their investment.

The financial ratios calculated in the context of any particular study can be judged against industry averages or averages for a selected set of comparable companies. Table 24-9 provides average values for some of the ratios (or slight variations thereon) defined above based on a study of retail and primary manufacturing companies. Table 24-10 provides an interindustry comparison of relative profitability based on operating results for the period 1980–1989. For example, during this period, the profitability of the beverages, drugs, and food processing industries contrasts sharply with that of the domestic oil and gas, railroad, and steel industries.

TABLE 24-9 Selected Financial Ratio Averages by Industry Classification

	Industry Group	
Financial Ratio	*Retail*	*Primary Mfg.*
Liquidity Ratios:		
Current assets/Current liabilities	2.168	2.329
Receivables/Sales	.066	.145
Cost of goods sold/Inventory	8.530	4.187
Profitability Ratios:		
Earnings/Sales	.018	.050
Earnings/Total assets	.040	.066
Earnings/Net worth	.070	.120
Leverage Ratios:		
Long-term debt/Total capital	.297	.271
Long-term debt/Net worth	.541	.568
Cash flow/Total debt	.194	.266

Source: W. Bruce Johnson, "The Cross-Sectional Stability of Financial Ratio Patterns," *Journal of Financial and Quantitative Analysis* 14 (December 1979), 1037–38.

TABLE 24-10   A Comparison of the Profitability of Firms in Selected Industries, 1980–1989

Industry	Median Return on Common Equity[a]			Median Return on Capital[b,c]	Debt/ Capital	Net Profit Margin[c]
	10-Year Average	5-Year Average	Latest 12 Months			
Airlines	12.6%	10.5%	14.6%	8.6%	43%	1.3%
Apparel	17.7	16.2	19.2	12.2	28	4.5
Automotive vehicle	18.7	14.8	14.6	10.5	42	4.0
Banking	14.5	14.7	15.9	13.5	23	3.9
Beverages	20.5	20.2	24.4	13.9	27	8.8
Chemicals	15.0	16.5	17.4	15.7	27	8.5
Computer hardware	12.6	12.1	9.6	7.9	18	5.2
Domestic oil & gas	6.8	7.7	10.4	8.1	40	5.6
Drugs	20.1	20.7	19.3	16.1	7	12.1
Electric utilities	13.0	13.3	12.4	7.1	41	8.7
Food processing	20.0	20.3	20.3	14.0	28	3.9
Forest products & packaging	13.6	15.2	18.8	12.5	30	7.3
International oil	12.5	11.3	12.4	8.9	24	5.1
Personal products	15.6	18.3	20.3	15.4	22	7.2
Property & casualty insurance	14.9	15.9	13.9	12.0	21	4.8
Publishing	18.2	20.9	18.2	13.3	26	8.1
Railroad	6.2	5.5	12.7	7.5	38	7.6
Steel	4.8	5.5	14.9	12.6	25	4.8
Telecommunications	14.0	13.9	15.3	8.6	35	7.0
Tobacco	19.3	19.2	23.2	13.0	29	7.0
All Industries	14.3%	14.3%	14.4%	11.1%	32%	6.3%

[a]Calculated as primary earnings per share divided by beginning-of-year common stockholders' equity assuming the conversion of all convertible preferred stock and including in earnings the gains or losses from discontinued operations but excluding extraordinary items.
[b]Calculated as the sum of after-tax profits and minority interest divided by total capitalization.
[c]Calculated for the latest 12 months.

Source: Forbes, January 8, 1990.

DISCRIMINANT ANALYSIS   24.8

One tool used by financial analysts to interpret better the financial health of a company is called **discriminant analysis**, a statistical procedure that combines the values of a set of variables (such as a firm's financial ratios) into a single observation that is used to classify a firm into one of various groupings.[7] Among the many applications of financial ratio analysis, the detection of company operating and financial difficulties that make bankruptcy more likely and the prediction of a bond rating change have attracted a good deal of interest. Both problems have been approached using discriminant analysis. In the case of bond ratings, the rating predicted by discriminant analysis is compared with the actual rating. For example, a discriminant

[7]Bankers also use discriminant analysis to assess whether a prospective borrower is an acceptable credit risk.

analysis of bonds rated either A or BBB by Standard & Poor's might reveal that a company whose bonds are currently rated BBB has financial characteristics more similar to those companies whose bonds are rated A. This would suggest that the bonds have lower default risk than the BBB rating would indicate.

Discriminant analysis can be used to assess a firm's bankruptcy potential. One research study used data for the 1946–1965 period from two populations of firms, one bankrupt and the other not, selected a paired sample, and estimated the following discriminant function for 1 year prior to bankruptcy:

$$Z = .012\ X_1 + .014\ X_2 + .033\ X_3 + .006\ X_4 + .999\ X_5 \qquad \textbf{(24.25)}$$

where X_1 = working capital/total assets, X_2 = retained earnings/total assets, X_3 = earnings before interest and taxes/total assets, X_4 = market value of equity/book value of total debt, X_5 = sales/total assets, and Z = overall index (discriminant score, or more simply Z-score, for the observation).[8] The study found that Equation (24.25) correctly predicted the bankruptcy of 94% of the firms that were bankrupt within 1 year and correctly predicted that 97% of those that did not fail within the next year would survive. It found that $Z = 2.675$ discriminated best between the bankrupt and nonbankrupt firms (in the sense that it minimized the number of misclassifications) and that the range of Z values could be divided into three intervals:

$Z > 2.99$ firm would not fail within 1 year

$1.81 \le Z \le 2.99$ gray area within which it is difficult to discriminate effectively

$Z < 1.81$ firm would fail within 1 year

The use of discriminant analysis to assess bankruptcy potential has several useful applications. The Z value is a measure of the risk of bankruptcy, which would be useful to potential creditors and potential investors. Management could also use the Z value to measure the company's financial condition relative to that of its competitors. Obviously, one would be unwise to rely too heavily on any single quantitative measure,[9] but a low value for Z could serve as a warning signal and alert the analyst to the need for careful credit analysis. Discriminant analysis, more generally, financial ratio analysis, is thus very helpful in financial analysis.

SOLUTION TO FIRST NATIONAL BANK'S CREDIT DECISION

First National Bank's vice president in charge of commercial credit lines has made it his practice to conduct a thorough financial ratio analysis prior to making a decision whether to grant credit. Lincoln Manufacturing is a client of long standing but he knows that a company's financial condition is subject to change and that it is important to perform a fresh financial ratio analysis each time a new credit application is submitted.

The vice president decides to perform a **pro forma** analysis under the following conservative assumptions: (1) Lincoln Manufacturing will borrow the entire $30 million immediately and keep the credit line fully drawn (rather than just using it for seasonal or temporary purposes); (2) the interest rate on the loan will average 10% (the interest rate on the credit line is First National's prime rate, which is currently 9%, but interest rates can change quickly and Lincoln must be able to meet unforeseen adverse conditions); (3) Lincoln will invest the $30 million in its business and

---

[8] Altman (1968).

[9] This is particularly true when Equation (24.25) is not re-estimated because the estimated values of the parameters in Equation (24.25) may be sensitive to the time period and sample of firms. See Moyer (1977).

TABLE 24-11 First National Bank's Credit Analysis of Lincoln Manufacturing Corporation (Millions of Dollars)

	Average for Comparable BBB-Rated Companies	Actual (12/31/90)		Pro Forma $30 Million Credit Line (12/31/90)	
		Amount	*%*	*Amount*	*%*
Short-Term Debt		$57	10.4%	$87	15.8%
Long-term debt		$203	36.9%	$203	36.9%
Capitalized lease obligations		36	6.5	36	6.5
Minority interest		10	1.8	10	1.8
Preferred stock		24	4.4	24	4.4
Common stockholders' equity		277	50.4	277	50.4
Total Capitalization		$550	100.0%	$550	100.0%

Coverage Ratios:		**1990 Actual**	**Pro Forma**
EBIT		$113	$117.44[a]
Interest expense		26	29[b]
Interest coverage ratio	3.29x	4.35x	4.05x
Fixed charges		$28	$31[b]
Fixed charge coverage ratio	2.48	4.11x	3.85x
Profitability Ratios:			
Average assets		$783	$813
Return on average assets	13.7%	14.8%	14.8%
Average common equity		$261.5	$261.5
Return on average common equity	16.5	19.5%	19.8%[c]
Leverage Ratios:			
Long-term debt ratio	39.5%	43.5%	43.5%
Total-debt-to-adjusted-capitalization ratio	46.7	48.8	51.2
Cash flow		$97	$97.86[c]
Cash-flow-to-long-term-debt ratio	37.6	40.6%	40.9%
Cash-flow-to-total-debt ratio	29.9	32.8	30.0

[a] Investing the $30 million at a 14.8% rate of return increases EBIT by $4.44 million (= [30].148).
[b] Interest at a 10% rate on $30 million of debt increases interest expense and fixed charges by $3 million (= [30].10).
[c] Borrowing $30 million at 10% and investing that sum at 14.8% increases earnings available for common stock before extraordinary items and cash flow by $0.86 million (= 30[.148−.10][1 − .4]).

earn its current return on average assets (14.8%); (4) Lincoln's marginal income tax rate (including state income taxes) is 40%; and (5) the credit application should be approved if the pro forma financial ratios indicate no worse than a BBB credit quality based on comparable companies that have senior debt ratings (Lincoln does not).

Table 24-11 summarizes the vice president's pro forma credit analysis of Lincoln Manufacturing. The 1990 financial ratios for BBB-rated companies, obtained directly from Standard & Poor's Corporation, are included in Table 24-11. Note that Lincoln's $30 million credit line is treated as short-term debt. This treatment is appropriate because credit lines are typically arranged to cover seasonal or temporary cash requirements and are typically reviewed by the bank annually for renewal or cancellation. The vice president treated the loan as outstanding in the full amount for a full year to be conservative in his analysis.

Based on a comparison of the pro forma financial ratios for Lincoln and the average values of the same financial ratios calculated for comparable BBB-rated companies, the vice president concluded that: (1) Lincoln's interest coverage and fixed charge coverage are stronger than the comparable group's coverages; (2) Lincoln is more profitable than the comparable companies are on average; and (3) Lincoln is somewhat more highly leveraged than the comparable companies are on average.

After satisfying himself that Lincoln Manufacturing's prospects are not likely to worsen significantly in the coming year (worsening prospects would increase the risk that Lincoln would not be able to repay the loan if First National Bank refused to renew the credit line), the vice president concluded that Lincoln's greater liquidity and profitability enable it to maintain a somewhat-higher-than-average degree of leverage, and he approved the credit line application.

SUMMARY

The primary source of financial information about a firm is the firm's financial statements. These include, at a minimum, income statements, balance sheets, and statements of cash flows. The information contained in these statements is often supplemented by financial ratios, which identify more clearly the changes over time in the firm's financial performance and financial condition.

Financial ratios are of four principal types: liquidity ratios, profitability ratios, leverage ratios, and common stock ratios. Several examples of ratios belonging to each of the first three classes were described and their calculation illustrated in this chapter. Financial ratio analysis can be applied to a wide range of financial problems. One such application, the use of discriminant analysis in the prediction of bankruptcy, was illustrated in this chapter.

PROBLEMS

PROBLEM SET A

A1. Describe the purpose of each of the following financial statements:
   a. **Income statement**
   b. **Balance sheet**
   c. **Statement of cash flows**

A2. Explain why the notes to a firm's financial statements form an integral part of the financial statements.

A3. Explain why earnings per share should not be relied upon exclusively to measure a company's performance.

DECISION SUMMARY BOX

- Financial ratios calculated from the information contained in a firm's financial statements make that information more meaningful and easier to interpret. When analyzing a firm's historical financial performance and changes in its financial condition, financial ratio analysis serves to highlight significant changes in profitability, liquidity, and leverage. When comparing two firms, financial ratio analysis highlights differences in profitability, liquidity, and leverage. To yield meaningful comparisons, each financial ratio *must be calculated on a consistent basis* for all periods and all firms included in the analysis.
- The set of financial ratios that will prove most useful in any particular application depends to a great extent on the user's viewpoint. Lenders are generally relatively more concerned with liquidity ratios and leverage ratios. Common stock investors are generally relatively more concerned with profitability ratios and common stock ratios. But all four types of ratios are needed to develop a complete perspective on the financial performance

and financial condition of the firm.
- The financial ratios calculated in the context of any particular study should be judged against industry averages or averages for a selected set of comparable companies. For example, in Chapter 16 (see Tables 16-4 and 16-5), we provided financial ratios for companies in different debt rating classes, and we described how to use those averages to establish a target capital structure.
- Discriminant analysis is a useful tool for financial ratio analysis that combines the values of a set of financial ratios into a single measure of the financial condition of a company (e.g., a measure of the risk of bankruptcy). Discriminant analysis is also used by banks and credit companies in credit scoring to determine whether to extend credit.
- Inflation can distort financial analysis just as it does a firm's overall financial results. Inflation-adjusted measures should be used to evaluate proposed borrowing to minimize the likelihood that inflation-induced distortions will bias the credit decision.

A4. What is the basic balance sheet identity?

A5. What primarily distinguishes:
   a. Current assets from the other classes of assets on the balance sheet?
   b. Current liabilities from the other classes of liabilities on the balance sheet?

A6. Define the term **cash flow**. Explain the difference between cash flow and earnings.

A7. Define the term **working capital**. How is working capital calculated? What does working capital measure? How is working capital related to the **current ratio**?

A8. Define the term **net assets**. How is net assets calculated? What is the relationship betweeen net assets and total capitalization?

A9. How is book value per share calculated? How is book value per share interpreted?

A10. What is the difference between a company's **interest coverage ratio** and its **fixed charge coverage ratio**? In view of what we said in Chapter 21 about lease obligations displacing conventional debt, why is fixed charge coverage the better (i.e., more inclusive) measure of a company's ability to meet its interest obligations?

A11. Explain the differences among a company's **gross profit margin**, **operating profit margin**, and **net profit margin**. Why do we need more than one measure of "profit margin"?

A12. Explain the difference between the **long-term debt ratio** and the **total-debt-to-adjusted-capitalization ratio**.

A13. Describe what is meant by the term **discriminant analysis**. Explain how discriminant analysis has been used to predict financial failure.

A14. Why is the **log-linear least squares method** generally preferred to the **simple compound growth method** for calculating the average annual rate of growth in some quantity over a period of several years? (See the appendix to this chapter.)

A15. Verify the calculation of the log-linear least squares growth rates in Table 24-6.

PROBLEM SET B

B1. Compact Computer Corporation has current assets and current liabilities consisting of (in millions of dollars):

Current Assets		Current Liabilities	
Cash and equivalents	$ 25	Notes payable	$ 70
Marketable securities	50	Current portion of long-term debt	30
Accounts receivable	200	Accounts payable	250
Inventories	400	Taxes payable	50
Prepaid expenses	25	Total	$400
Total	$700		

Annual credit sales amounted to $2,250, cost of goods sold amounted to $1,350, and accounts receivable and inventories have each doubled over the past year.

a. Calculate working capital and the current ratio.

b. Calculate the acid test ratio, receivable turnover ratio, and inventory turnover ratio.

B2. Southern Airlines has the following total capitalization (in millions of dollars):

Long-term debt	$100
Capitalized lease obligations due after 1 year	25
Minority interest	25
Preferred stock (at book)	50
Common stock (10 million shares)	200
Total capitalization	$400

The preferred stock carries a 10% liquidation preference.

a. Calculate Southern Airlines's book value per common share.

b. Calculate the company's long-term debt ratio assuming minority interest should be included in long-term debt.

c. If short-term debt equals $50 million, what are the company's total-debt-to-adjusted-capitalization and debt-to-equity ratios?

B3. Blackberry Motor Car Company reported 1990 net income of $120 million, which included a $15 million extraordinary gain and a $25 million loss from discontinued operations. Blackberry reported interest expense of $20 million, of which $2 million was capitalized. Blackberry had $7 million of income from a nonconsolidated subsidiary, of which it received $5 million as a cash dividend. Calculate Blackberry's EBIT.

B4. The 1989 annual report to the shareholders of E. I. du Pont de Nemours and Company reported the following items (in millions of dollars) for 1989:

Earnings before income taxes	$4,324
Interest and debt expense (net of $108 capitalized)	623
Equity in earnings of affiliates	55
Rental expense	406
Preferred dividends	10
Income tax provision	1,844

a. Calculate du Pont's 1989 EBIT.
b. Calculate du Pont's 1989 interest coverage ratio, fixed charge coverage ratio, and preferred stock dividend coverage ratio.

B5. The 1989 annual report to the shareholders of Exxon Corporation reported the following items (in millions of dollars) for 1989:

Sales and other operating revenue (net of excise taxes)	$86,656
Crude oil and product purchases	39,268
Operating expenses	10,535
Selling, general, and administrative expenses	6,398
Depreciation and depletion	5,002
Exploration expenses	872
Other taxes and duties (treat as part of operating expenses)	16,617
Other income	1,112
Minority interest	263
Interest expense	1,265
Income taxes	2,028
Valdez provision (treat as extraordinary cost)	2,545
Effect of accounting change (treat as extraordinary)	+535
Net income	$ 3,510

a. Calculate Exxon's 1989 gross profit, operating income, and net income before extraordinary items.
b. Calculate Exxon's 1989 gross profit margin, operating profit margin, and net profit margin.

B6. The 1989 annual report to the shareholders of General Motors Corporation reported the following items (in millions of dollars) for 1989:

Total net sales and revenues (includes other income of $3,720)	$126,932
Total costs and expenses (includes interest expense of $8,757)	120,534
Income taxes	2,174
Dividends on preferred and preference stock	34
Earnings on common stocks (no extraordinary items)	$ 4,190

The annual report stated the following balance sheet amounts for 1989 and 1988 (in millions of dollars):

	1989	1988
Total assets	$173,297	$164,063
(includes intangibles)	(7,126)	(5,270)
Current liabilities	73,138	72,504
Noncapitalized long-term liabilities	26,557	23,979
Preferred and preference stocks (book value) (assume 5% average liquidation preference)	236	236
Common stockholders' equity (book value)	34,746	35,436

a. Calculate General Motors's 1989 operating income.

b. Calculate General Motors's 1989 net assets and net tangible assets.

c. Calculate General Motors's 1989 return on average assets, return on average invested capital, and return on average common equity.

B7. Brandon Pharmaceutical had net income before extraordinary items of $15 million, and paid $0.5 million of preferred dividends and $10 million of noncash operating expenses. Brandon had 10 million common shares outstanding at the beginning of the year and 11 million outstanding at the end of the year.

a. Calculate Brandon's earnings per common share.

b. Calculate Brandon's cash flow per common share.

B8. The 1989 annual report to the shareholders of Merck & Co., Inc. reported the following items (in millions of dollars) for 1989:

Loans payable	$ 327.3
Long-term debt	117.8
Minority interests	509.9
Stockholders' equity	3,520.6

a. Calculate Merck's long-term debt ratio, total-debt-to-adjusted-capitalization ratio, and debt-to-equity ratio.

b. Merck's 1989 annual report stated deferred income taxes and noncurrent liabilities for 1989 amounting to $701.1 million. Recalculate the ratios in part a, treating deferred income taxes and noncurrent liabilities as part of total capitalization.

c. Recalculate the ratios in part a, treating minority interests as part of long-term debt.

B9. The 1989 annual report to the shareholders of Minnesota Mining and Manufacturing Company (3M) reported the following items (in millions of dollars) for 1989:

Net income	$1,244
Noncash operating expenses	701
Change in inventories	222
Change in accounts receivable	298
Change in accounts payable	279
Long-term debt	885
Short-term debt	455

a. Calculate 3M's cash-flow-to-long-term-debt ratio and cash-flow-to-total-debt ratio.

b. 3M reported 1989 stockholders' equity of $5,378. Calculate 3M's long-term debt ratio, total-debt-to-adjusted-capitalization ratio, and debt-to-equity ratio.

B10. Given the discriminant function

$$Z = .015X_1 + .119X_2 + .230X_3 + .321X_4 + .831X_5,$$

with the variables defined as in Equation (24.25), use the following information (in millions of dollars) to calculate the Z score:

Working capital	$ 30
Total assets	200
Retained earnings	50
EBIT	20
Market value of equity	100
Book value of debt	50
Sales	300

If Altman's Z ranges were still to apply, what would the Z-score just calculated imply?

B11. Mr. G. Wizz, president of Overnight MBA, Inc., reported the firm's earnings per share as $1.75, $1.60, $1.51, $1.32, and $1.65 for 1986, 1987, 1988, 1989, and 1990, respectively.

a. Calculate the simple compound growth rate of earnings per share for Overnight.

b. Calculate the log–linear least squares growth rate of earnings per share for Overnight.

B12. The following table shows the reported net income and dividends per common share before extraordinary items in each of the years 1985 through 1989 for 3 companies.

Net Income:	1985	1986	1987	1988	1989
Exxon Corporation	$3.23	$3.71	$3.43	$3.95	$2.32
General Electric Co.	2.50	2.73	3.20	3.75	4.36
Merck & Co., Inc.	1.26	1.62	2.23	3.05	3.78
Dividends:					
Exxon Corporation	1.72½	1.80	1.90	2.15	2.30
General Electric Co.	1.11½	1.18½	1.32½	1.46	1.70
Merck & Co., Inc.	.53	.63	.82	1.28	1.64

a. Calculate the log–linear least squares growth rate of each company's net income per common share and dividends per common share.

b. Calculate each company's annual payout ratio for each of the years 1985 through 1989.

c. What would you conclude regarding the 3 companies' dividend policies based on your results in parts a and b?

PROBLEM SET C

C1. Some analysts define **net assets** as the difference between total assets and current liabilities.

    a. When net assets is defined in this manner, does it make sense to equate net assets with total capitalization?

    b. In what sense might we think of deferred income taxes as a long-term source of funds?

    c. Obtain copies of the 1990 annual reports for E. I. du Pont de Nemours, Exxon, and General Electric from the library and calculate net assets according to Equation (24.5) and according to the alternative definition.

    d. Which definition of net assets do you prefer? Explain.

C2. Some analysts prefer to calculate total capitalization by including short-term debt net of the amount of cash and cash equivalents.

    a. What might be the rationale for including short-term debt in total capitalization?

    b. What might be the rationale for subtracting cash and cash equivalents?

    c. How would total capitalization be interpreted if the alternative method of calculating total capitalization is used and cash and cash equivalents exceed short-term debt?

    d. How would your answer to part c change if cash and cash equivalents exceed short-term debt by a large amount?

C3. Minority interest consists of the minority equity ownership interest in a consolidated subsidiary.

    a. Suppose the minority interest consists of redeemable preferred stock that the company is obligated to redeem in annual installments over the next 5 years. How would you treat minority interest for the purpose of calculating the company's debt-to-equity ratio?

    b. Suppose instead the minority interest consists of subsidiary common stock that the parent company has no expectation of ever retiring. How would you treat minority interest for the purpose of calculating the company's debt-to-equity ratio?

C4. What limitations, if any, do you perceive in using a company's Z-score as a predictor of bankruptcy risk? Under what assumptions will a company's Z-score serve as an accurate indicator of bankruptcy risk?

APPENDIX

METHODS FOR CALCULATING GROWTH RATES

There are two widely used methods for calculating growth rates: the **simple compound growth method** and the **log-linear least squares method**.

SIMPLE COMPOUND GROWTH RATE

Suppose a quantity grows at a constant annual percentage rate. Let A_0 denote the initial amount and let g denote the constant annual percentage growth rate (expressed as a decimal). The quantity in question grows to $A_1 = A_0(1 + g)$ after 1 year, to $A_2 = A_1(1 + g)^2$ at the end of 2 years, and so on to

$$A_t = A_0(1 + g)^t \qquad (24.26)$$

at the end of t years.

If A_0, A_t and t are given, Equation (24.26) can be solved for g:

$$g = (A_t/A_0)^{1/t} - 1 \qquad \text{(24.27)}$$

The value of g so obtained is called the **simple compound growth rate**.

EXAMPLE ■ A securities analyst would like to calculate the average annual growth rate of earnings per share between 1986 and 1990 for the Monroe Bottling Company. Monroe had earnings per share of $2.75, $2.50, $2.80, $3.15, and $3.60 in 1986, 1987, 1988, 1989, and 1990, respectively.

First note that the growth rate is a 4–year growth rate. Substituting $t = 4$, $A_0 =$ \$2.75 and $A_4 = \$3.60$ into Equation (24.27) gives

$$g = (3.60/2.75)^{0.25} - 1 = .0697, \text{ or } 6.97\% \text{ per annum}$$

Equation (24.27) ignores the intermediate values of A. When the observed values do not all lie along a smooth growth path (as in the preceding example where earnings per share decreased significantly between 1986 and 1987), these intermediate values should not be ignored.   ■

LOG-LINEAR LEAST SQUARES GROWTH RATE

The log-linear least squares method uses all the observed values of the quantity of interest in calculating the average annual growth rate. Suppose that growth occurs continuously so that the quantity A_t satisfies the equation [10]

$$A_t = A_0 e^{gt} \qquad \text{(24.28)}$$

where e is a number approximately equal to 2.71828. Taking the natural logarithm of the expression on each side of Equation (24.28) leads to the equivalent equation

$$\ln A_t = \ln A_0 + \ln e^{gt} = \ln A_0 + gt \qquad \text{(24.29)}$$

The least squares regression method can be used to estimate the growth rate g in Equation (24.29).

LEAST SQUARES REGRESSION The equation

$$Y = A + BX \qquad \text{(24.30)}$$

where A and B are constants, is called a **linear equation**, because its graph is a straight line. Least squares regression is a technique for estimating the constants A and B in a linear equation. The formulas for A and B are

$$B = \frac{[N\Sigma XY - \Sigma X \Sigma Y]}{[N\Sigma X^2 - (\Sigma X)^2]} \qquad \text{(24.31A)}$$

$$A = \frac{\Sigma Y}{N} - B\frac{\Sigma X}{N} \qquad \text{(24.31B)}$$

where N is the total number of observations (of pairs (X, Y)) and where the symbol Σ denotes the sum of the N observed values of the variable immediately to the right of the symbol. To estimate A and B, first use Equation (24.31A) to calculate B and

---

[10] Note that Equation (24.28) is just the compound amount formula we discussed in Chapter 3. The amount A_0 (analogous to the "initial deposit") grows through the continuous compounding of value (analogous to the compounding of interest) at the rate g for t periods.

then substitute that value and the other required quantities into Equation (24.31B) to calculate A. Many handheld calculators contain a statistical package that will perform these calculations. The following example illustrates this procedure.

ESTIMATING THE LOG-LINEAR LEAST SQUARES GROWTH RATE   Consider again Equations (24.28) and (24.29). Note that the initial value of A, A_0, is fixed for purposes of calculating g. Set $A = \ln A_0$. By assumption, g is also a constant. Set $B = g$. Thus Equation (24.29) is in the form of Equation (24.30) with

$$Y = \ln A_t \qquad A = \ln A_0 \qquad B = g \qquad X = t \qquad \textbf{(24.32)}$$

With these substitutions, Equations (24.31A) and (24.31B) can be used to estimate $A = \ln A_0$ and $B = g$, the latter being the desired (average annual) log-linear least squares growth rate. The term **log-linear** describes the process of taking logarithms to convert the given Equation (24.28) into an equivalent linear form, Equation (24.29), to which Equations (24.31A) and (24.31B) can be applied to estimate the values of A_0 and g in the original equation.

EXAMPLE ■   Consider again the problem posed in the preceding example.

A	$Y = \ln A$	$X = t$	X^2	XY
2.75	1.0116	0	0	0
2.50	0.9163	1	1	0.9163
2.80	1.0296	2	4	2.0592
3.15	1.1474	3	9	3.4422
3.60	1.2809	4	16	5.1236
Σ	5.3858	10	30	11.5413

Substituting into Equation (24.31A) gives

$$g = B = \frac{5(11.5413) - 10(5.3858)}{5(30) - 10^2} = .0770$$

or 7.70% per annum   ■

INTERPRETING THE LOG-LINEAR LEAST SQUARES GROWTH RATE   The earnings per share figures in this example are graphed in Figure 24–1. Substituting the quantities just calculated into Equation (24.31B) gives

$$A = \frac{5.3858}{5} - (.0770)\left(\frac{10}{5}\right) = .9232$$

Since $A = \ln A_0$, it follows that

$$A_0 = e^{.9232} = 2.5173$$

Substituting into Equation (24.28), the growth path of earnings per share is

$$A_t = 2.5173 \, e^{.0770t} \qquad \textbf{(24.33)}$$

which has also been graphed in Figure 24–1.

The log-linear least squares growth rate measures the *trend* rate of growth; that is, the growth path described by Equation (24.33) is "fitted to" the observed values in

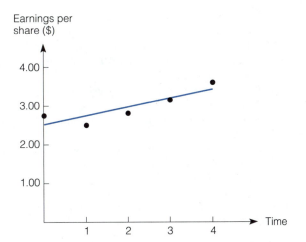

FIGURE 24-1
Trend in earnings per share.

such a way that it mirrors the actual growth in the quantity of interest. In the preceding example, the trend rate of growth of earnings per share is 7.70% per annum. Actual earnings per share growth may have been more or less than this amount (the actual observations do not lie on the growth path in Figure 24-1), but between 1986 and 1990 there was an "average" tendency for earnings per share to increase by 7.70% from one year to the next.

REFERENCES

Accounting Principles Board. *Earnings Per Share*. New York: APB Opinion No. 15, AICPA, 1969.

Altman, Edward I. "Financial Ratios, Discriminant Analysis and the Prediction of Corporate Bankruptcy." *Journal of Finance* 23 (September 1968): 589–609.

Anthony, Robert N. "A Case for Historical Costs." *Harvard Business Review* (November-December 1976): 69–79.

Beaver, William H. "Financial Ratios as Predictors of Failure." In *Empirical Research in Accounting: Selected Studies, Journal of Accounting Research* (supplement to vol. 5, 1967): 71–102.

Davidson, Sidney, and Roman L. Weil, eds. *Handbook of Modern Accounting,* 3rd ed. New York: McGraw-Hill, 1983.

Deakin, E. B. "A Discriminant Analysis of Predictors of Business Failure." *Journal of Accounting Research* 10 (Spring 1972): 167–79.

Deloitte Haskins & Sells. *Financial Reporting and Changing Prices*. New York: Deloitte Haskins & Sells, 1979.

The Dun & Bradstreet Corporation. *1979 Key Business Ratios*. Parsippany, N.J.: Business Economics Division, Dun & Bradstreet, 1980.

Financial Reporting and Changing Prices. Statement of Financial Accounting Standards No. 33, Financial Accounting Standards Board, High Ridge Park, Stamford, Conn., October 1979.

Flynn, Thomas D. "Why We Should Account for Inflation." *Harvard Business Review* (September-October 1977): 145–57.

Foster, George. *Financial Statement Analysis*, 2nd ed. Englewood Cliffs, N.J.: Prentice-Hall, 1986.

Harrington, Diana R., and Brent D. Wilson. *Corporate Financial Analysis*. Plano, Texas: Business Publications, 1986.

Higgins, Robert C. *Analysis for Financial Management*, 2nd ed. Homewood, Ill.: Richard D. Irwin, 1989.

Johnson, W. Bruce. "The Cross-Sectional Stability of Financial Ratio Patterns." *Journal of Financial and Quantitative Analysis* 14 (December 1979): 1035–48.

Johnston, J. *Econometric Methods,* 2nd ed. New York: McGraw-Hill, 1972: 8–55.

Lee, Cheng-Fu. *Financial Analysis and Planning: Theory and Application.* Reading, Mass.: Addison-Wesley Publishing Company, 1985.

Moyer, R. Charles. "Forecasting Financial Failure: A Re-Examination." *Financial Management* 6 (Spring 1977): 11–17.

O'Connor, M. C. "On the Usefulness of Financial Ratios to Investors in Common Stock." *Accounting Review* 48 (April 1973): 339–52.

Pinches, George E., and Kent A. Mingo. "A Multivariate Analysis of Industrial Bond Ratings." *Journal of Finance* 28 (March 1973): 1–18.

Regan, Patrick J. "Potential Corporate Liabilities Under ERISA." *Financial Analysts Journal* 32 (March/April 1976): 26–32.

Statement of Cash Flows. Statement of Financial Accounting Standards No. 95, Financial Accounting Standards Board, High Ridge Park, Stamford, Conn., November 1987.

Vancil, Richard F. "Inflation Accounting—The Great Controversy." *Harvard Business Review* (March–April 1976): 58–67.

WORKING CAPITAL MANAGEMENT

The bulk of the financial manager's time is typically devoted to **working capital management**.[1] In Chapter 24, we defined a firm's **net working capital** as its current assets minus its current liabilities. **Current assets**, principally cash and short-term securities, accounts receivable, and inventories, are assets that can normally be converted into cash within 1 year. **Current liabilities**, principally short-term borrowings, accounts payable, and taxes payable, are obligations that are expected to come due within 1 year. Working capital management involves all aspects of the administration of current assets and current liabilities.

Working capital management can, in theory at least, be treated in the overall context of the analysis of capital investments and the analysis of capital structure discussed earlier in the book. It was noted in Chapter 11 that capital investment projects typically require additional investments in accounts receivable and inventories, and we included the cash flows associated with these investments in the capital budgeting analysis. Also, it was noted in Chapter 15 that short-term borrowings, or at least the permanent component of such borrowings, should be taken into account when evaluating the degree of leverage in the firm's capital structure. In principle, working capital management can be treated within the analytical framework outlined in those chapters. Accordingly, the firm should expand or contract its investments in current assets whenever such a change produces a positive NPV. The most widely followed approaches to working capital management are not nearly this rigorous, however. In practice, firms have a tendency to separate working capital management from the other aspects of financial management. As a result, working capital decisions tend to be made within a partial equilibrium context rather than within the overall context of raising funds and investing in a portfolio of assets to maximize shareholder wealth.

DIVERSIFIED CHEMICAL'S WORKING CAPITAL MANAGEMENT PROBLEM

The following example illustrates the fundamental problem in working capital management. The president of Diversified Chemical Company has asked the company's treasurer to study the appropriateness of that company's policy of maintaining its ratio of current assets to current liabilities (its **current ratio**) at 2.0. Diversified Chemical has already applied the techniques described in Chapter 16 and established a target debt ratio (θ = debt/[debt + equity]) of 25%. In addition, Diversified Chemical's president would like the company's commercial paper to continue to qualify for a P-1/A-1 (Moody's/Standard & Poor's) rating because Diversified Chemical's investment banker has informed her that lower-rated commercial paper is not as readily marketable. After developing a few basic concepts, we will help Diversified's treasurer evaluate the appropriateness of Diversified's choice of current ratio objective.

[1] Gitman and Maxwell (1985).

25.1 ## OVERVIEW OF WORKING CAPITAL MANAGEMENT

Working capital management involves selecting the appropriate levels of cash, marketable securities, receivables, and inventories, and the appropriate level and mix of short-term indebtedness. It is useful to break down the working capital management ment problem into two basic types of decisions: first, the relative levels of current assets and current liabilities; second, the mix of current assets and the mix of current liabilities.

Current assets and current liabilities are related by the firm's need to maintain adequate liquidity. Recall that liquidity refers to the relative ease with which an asset can be converted into cash without loss of value. The firm must ensure that it will have sufficient cash on hand to meet its cash obligations as they come due in order to avoid technical **insolvency**. Liquidity considerations are important because of market imperfections; how quickly an asset must be converted into cash can drastically affect the transaction cost of conversion. For example, a firm that tries to sell inventory or receivables quickly to raise cash may find that it must accept "distress" prices significantly below the true economic value of these assets.

Working capital management involves a risk-return trade-off. Basically, the risk is the risk of illiquidity. This risk is zero for a hypothetical all-equity financed firm (absolutely nothing owed at any time) because the firm has no liabilities. When a firm has only long-term debt financing, this risk is low because only periodically do the firm's debt payment obligations include principal repayment. Even a relatively small amount of current revenue may be sufficient to meet interest-only debt service payments. With short-term debt, however, the likelihood of illiquidity can be much greater because current revenues must be larger to meet the firm's debt payment obligations, including the obligation to repay short-term debt. If current revenues are insufficient, the firm may be able to obtain additional financing to meet the obligations but, because of economy-wide or firm-specific factors, it may be extraordinarily expensive.

HEDGING APPROACH TO WORKING CAPITAL MANAGEMENT

Among the most important current obligations that the firm faces are the required interest payments and principal repayments on its debt. If the firm adopted a hedging approach to financing, it would try to match the maturities of its assets and liabilities. In particular, it would finance seasonal variations in current assets by taking on current liabilities of the same maturity, and it would finance long-term assets by issuing long-term debt and equity securities. In addition, in most cases there is a permanent component of current assets; inventories and receivables will remain above some minimum level. This permanent component would be financed from long-term capital. Under this approach, the borrowing and repayment schedule for short-term borrowing (including temporary increases in payables as well as bank borrowings, commercial paper, etc.) would be set so as to mirror the seasonal swings in current assets. As illustrated in Figure 25–1, short-term borrowings under this sort of policy would fall to zero at the seasonal troughs.

MARGIN OF SAFETY

Under uncertainty, the situation becomes somewhat more complicated than that depicted in Figure 25–1. Cash inflows and outflows cannot be sychronized perfectly.

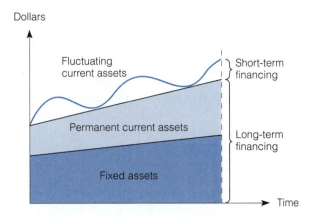

FIGURE 25-1

Mix of short-term debt and long-term sources of capital.

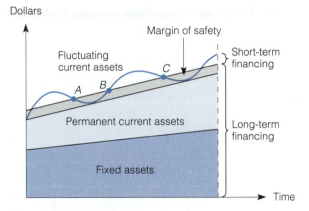

FIGURE 25-2

Margin of safety.

The firm will therefore try to build some **margin of safety** into its debt maturity schedule. In general, the shorter the maturity schedule, the greater the risk that the firm will be unable to meet its debt service obligations. The firm can reduce this risk by lengthening the maturity schedule of its debt. As illustrated by the margin of safety in Figure 25–2, the firm can accomplish this by financing a portion of its seasonal funds needs on a long-term basis. Near the cyclical troughs (e.g., between points A and B), the firm will have excess cash that it can invest on a short-term basis. Near the cyclical peaks (e.g., between points B and C), the firm will have net short-term borrowing requirements. As point B approaches, the firm can liquidate its short-term investments as required to meet its funds requirements. This is likely to be of greater value to the firm when funds needs accelerate rapidly and there is a time lag involved in arranging additional short-term borrowings. In this way, the margin of safety provides a liquidity reserve.

The working capital management policy illustrated in Figure 25–2 is a very conservative one. In particular, the margin of safety results in a higher level of working capital and a higher current ratio than would be the case without it. Many firms, particularly smaller ones, may operate with a negative margin of safety; in that case, the dashed line in Figure 25–2 would lie below rather than above the upper solid line. In that case, the firm utilizes short-term borrowings to finance a portion of permanent current assets and perhaps also fixed assets. As a result, the firm operates with lower working capital and a lower current ratio than firms that follow more conservative policies. The negative margin of safety would increase the firm's exposure to the risk of illiquidity if, among other possibilities, loan agreements are not renewed. Nevertheless, small firms may have to rely heavily on short-term borrowings because market imperfections limit their access to the long-term capital markets.

Management's choice of a margin of safety depends on the trade-off between the cost and the amount of reduction in the risk of illiquidity provided by the margin of safety. Generally, the cost incurred is a higher cost of borrowing. The **yield curve** (the cost relative to the maturity of borrowing) is most often upward-sloping. Therefore, the explicit cost of long-term financing generally exceeds the cost of short-term borrowing. In that case, a positive margin of safety involves a net cost equal to the difference between the actual cost of long-term financing and the (forgone) lower cost of short-term borrowing. Applying the Principle of Risk-Return Trade-Off, you can see that management must weigh these costs against the value of reducing the risk of illiquidity in choosing the appropriate margin of safety.

Because of capital market efficiency, it is unlikely that the firm will be able to achieve a greater reduction in risk than is appropriate for its cost. However, note that mismanagement can result in too large a cost for the amount of risk reduction. That is, it is possible for the firm to "pay too much for" a reduction in risk. This can occur if the risk reduction is unnecessary because the possible negative consequences are "covered" by other mechanisms. Such a situation is just like the overlapping outcome coverage of options illustrated in Figure 8–11.

INDUSTRY DIFFERENCES IN LIQUIDITY

The decision concerning the appropriate current ratio and the appropriate margin of safety will also depend to a great extent on the basic profitability of a company's business and the liquidity of the company's assets. A company's liquid assets provide protection against insolvency, the inability to meet debt obligations as they come due. Greater and more stable profitability and cash flow provide protection against insolvency and reduce the amount of current assets the company needs to maintain. Similarly, the more liquid a company's longer term assets are, the greater the protection those assets will provide against insolvency and the smaller the required level of current assets to achieve the same degree of protection.

There are significant differences in liquidity among industries. This involves the two aspects just mentioned. For example, companies in the textile products, paper, domestic integrated oil, tire and rubber goods, and building materials industries experienced relatively large swings in liquidity between 1970 and 1974, whereas companies in the crude oil production, meat packing, apparel manufacturing, and retail department store industries experienced relatively mild fluctuations in liquidity over the same period.[2]

There are also significant differences across industries in the liquidity of long-term assets. For example, proven oil and gas reserves are more liquid than limited-purpose fixed plant and equipment. There is a fairly active market in proven oil and gas reserves, which accounts for the relatively greater liquidity of these assets.

Because of industry differences in firm liquidity, it is important that any analysis of the alternative values for the current ratio or alternative margins of safety for any particular company start with an analysis of how comparable firms within the same industry have set their current ratios and margins of safety. In other words, as in the case of capital structure choice and dividend policy choice, we can apply the Behav-

[2]Petty and Scott (1980). The fluctuations are evident from a comparison of their Tables 6 and 7.

ioral Principle wherein the policy decisions of comparable firms provide useful benchmarks.

DEBT RATINGS AND LIQUIDITY

The firms in any single industry will not all agree on the appropriate choice of current ratio or the appropriate margin of safety, just as they do not all agree on the appropriate degree of leverage or dividend policy. Not only do their circumstances and prospects differ, but their risk-return choices, including considerations of insolvency, will also differ. Accordingly, some will adopt more conservative working capital management policies than others.

We noted in Chapter 16 that the professional rating services assign ratings to a company's debt securities that reflect their assessment of the financial risks investors bear in holding them. The rating services rate commercial paper as well as long-term debt securities. **Commercial paper** is a short-lived security—the maturity of publicly-issued commercial paper cannot exceed 270 days without registering it with the SEC, but typically the maturity is 90 days or less—and the commercial paper rating reflects principally the agencies' assessment of the fundamental credit quality, relative liquidity, and financial flexibility of the issuer over the next 2 years or so.[3] The financial ratios of companies whose commercial paper bears a particular rating thus indicate the financial structure consistent with the relative degree of liquidity implicit in the particular commercial paper rating.

Table 25–1 illustrates how certain key financial ratios vary from one commercial paper rating category to another, based on Standard & Poor's ratings. Only the four highest rating categories assigned by Standard & Poor's are shown, but the financial ratios also vary systematically for lower-rated commercial paper. More importantly, only commercial paper rated A-1+, A-1, or A-2 can normally be marketed broadly, and at times the market for commercial paper rated A-2 has suddenly contracted. Thus, a rating of A-1+ or A-1 is necessary to ensure uninterrupted market access.

The companies whose commercial paper has the highest rating are generally the most profitable, least leveraged, and most liquid. Interest coverage and fixed charge coverage are highest, and cash flow relative to debt is strongest. Companies whose commercial paper is rated lower on the scale are generally less profitable, more highly leveraged, and less liquid than companies whose commercial paper is more highly rated.[4]

As with the senior debt rating, a company can apply the Behavioral Principle and view the different commercial paper ratings as surrogates for differing levels of financial risk, in this case liquidity risk. The company can establish the degree of liquidity risk it will have to bear by selecting the risk level (i.e., rating category) most consistent with its objectives and aversion to risk. It can then look to the range within which each of the ratios in Table 25–1 and each of the key liquidity ratios (particularly the current ratio) vary across companies within the chosen commercial paper rating category in order to choose a target range for each. Also, as with the

---

[3] *Debt Ratings Criteria: Industrial Overview.* New York: Standard & Poor's Corporation, 1986, 43–45.

[4] As one would expect from comparing Table 25–1 with Table 16–4, there is a strong correlation between a company's senior debt rating and its commercial paper rating (assuming, of course, that it has both types of ratings). In general, it would be unusual for a company whose senior debt is rated AA or higher to have a commercial paper rating lower than A-1+, and it would also be unusual for a company whose senior debt is not rated investment grade (i.e., at least BBB-) to have a commercial paper rating of as high as A-3. Ibid., 43. Generally, a commercial paper rating of A-1 corresponds to a senior debt rating in the A- to AA- range, and a commercial paper rating of A-2 corresponds to a senior debt rating in the BBB to A range (i.e., note that there is some overlap).

TABLE 25-1 Commercial Paper Ratings as Indicators of Relative Liquidity[a]

Commercial Paper Rating[b]	A-1+ *The degree of safety regarding timely payment is "overwhelming."*	A-1 *The degree of safety regarding timely payment is "very strong."*	A-2 *Capacity for timely payment is "strong."*	A-3 *Capacity for timely payment is "satisfactory."*
Interest coverage ratio	8.77x	5.57x	3.14x	2.18x
Fixed charge coverage ratio[c]	4.46	3.15	2.23	1.67
Cash flow/Long-term debt	139.08%	79.46%	50.74%	36.53%
Cash flow/Total debt	92.77	60.06	42.28	31.00
Pretax return on average long-term capital employed	23.15	18.07	11.62	6.64
Operating income/Sales	15.66	11.75	10.05	10.92
Long-term debt/Capitalization	14.91	22.82	29.71	25.58
Total debt/Capitalization including short-term debt	20.40	27.43	33.72	29.55

[a] Median of the 3-year simple arithmetic averages for the period 1983–1985 for companies whose commercial paper had the indicated rating.
[b] As assigned and defined by Standard & Poor's Corporation. The corresponding Moody's Investors Service's ratings are P-1 (for A-1+ and A-1), P-2, and P-3. Standard & Poor's also has three additional commercial paper rating categories, which are designated B, C, and D in descending order of relative liquidity.
[c] Based on full rental charges, rather than the one-third of rental charges used in the SEC fixed charge coverage calculation.

Sources: Bond Guide (New York: Standard & Poor's Corporation, May 1990), 11, and *Debt Ratings Criteria: Industrial Overview* (New York: Standard & Poor's Corporation, 1986), 51.

choice of capital structure, this same basic approach is useful, whether or not the company has rated securities outstanding. The objective is to use the information embodied in the professional rating agencies' assessments together with the company's own objectives and risk tolerances to formulate a specific financial policy in terms of quantifiable targets.

25.2 CHOICE OF CURRENT RATIO OBJECTIVE

Working capital management involves a number of related decisions. First, the corporation must determine appropriate levels of receivables and inventories consistent with the company's sales objectives. Each will contain a fixed component and a variable component. Second, it must establish the appropriate levels of cash and marketable securities consistent with the continual maintenance of adequate liquidity and any compensating balances required under the company's bank loan agreements. Third, the corporation must decide upon the appropriate level of payables consistent with the company's maintaining an acceptable credit record. This too will involve fixed and variable components. Fourth, the company must then determine the mix of short-term and long-term financing for its fluctuating current assets consistent with maintaining an acceptable current ratio (and by implication, an acceptable level of working capital and an appropriate margin of safety).

These four sets of decisions are interrelated. For example, the maximum desired level of bank borrowings will determine the amount of bank lines (that is, pre-arranged contingency loans) the firm must have available and therefore its compensating balance requirements. As a second example, the mix of receivables and comparatively less liquid inventories will affect the overall liquidity of the firm's portfolio of current assets and therefore the amount of cash and marketable securities the firm chooses to maintain.

Figure 25–3 relates the decisions involved in working capital management:

1. The firm determines a current ratio (or working capital) objective based on its debt rating objective and its desired margin of safety. We explain how to choose the current ratio objective later in this section.

2. The firm determines its receivables management and inventory policies. These policies together with its current sales and its sales projections determine the target levels of receivables and inventories. The next section develops proce-

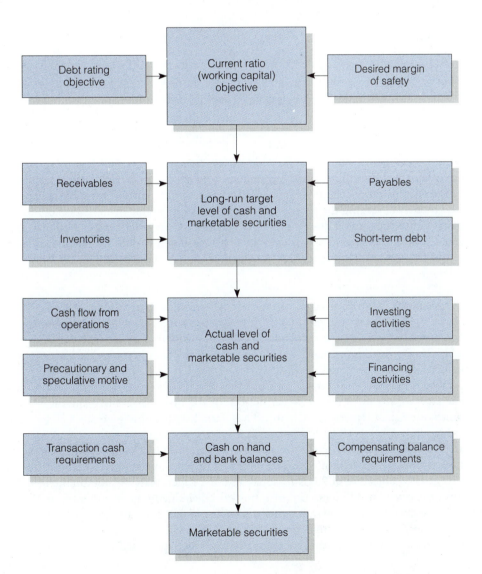

FIGURE 25-3
Overall approach to working capital management.

dures for determining the profit-maximizing receivables amount and the cost-minimizing inventory amount. The current ratio objective, receivables investment, inventory investment, and short-term financing decision (the level of payables and short-term debt) determine the long-run target level of cash and marketable securities. Procedures for evaluating the relative cost of the different sources of short-term funds are developed later in the chapter.

3. The actual level of cash and marketable securities at any time may deviate from the long-run target level depending on the amount of cash generated or used by the firm's operations, the amount of cash generated or used by the firm's financing and investing activities, and the firm's possible desire to maintain added cash balances to satisfy precautionary or speculative motives. Many of the financing and investing activities use or generate large discrete amounts of cash.

4. The actual level of cash and marketable securities is divided between cash on hand and in banks on the one hand and marketable securities on the other. The latter is a residual that is determined once the transaction cash requirements and compensating balance needs have been determined.

THE CURRENT RATIO

In planning and managing its working capital position, the firm will actually use a variety of liquidity measures to guide it. Of the liquidity ratios discussed in the previous chapter, the current ratio is certainly among the more important:

$$\text{Current Ratio} = \frac{\text{Current Assets}}{\text{Current Liabilities}} \qquad (25.1)$$

A higher margin of safety implies that on average, the firm will finance a higher percentage of its working capital requirements on a long-term basis; it thus implies a higher current ratio. The firm can select an appropriate current ratio objective for itself by first observing the current ratios of other comparable firms, especially those firms within the same industry that have whatever commercial paper rating is preferred. The firm's second task is to analyze how different values for its current ratio within or near this "comparable" range might affect its profitability and interest coverage.

EXAMPLE ■ Consider again the task confronting the treasurer of Diversified Chemical. Recall that the president of the company has asked its treasurer to study the appropriateness of the company's policy of maintaining a current ratio of 2.0. Table 25–2 provides a financial analysis relating to this question that Diversified's financial staff has prepared.

Diversified Chemical's treasurer finds that the average year-end value of the current ratio for the most recent 5-year period for the major diversified chemical companies other than Diversified Chemical has varied within a range from 1.50 to 2.50, with a median value of 2.20, for comparable companies whose commercial paper is rated A-1. The median current ratio varies only slightly from one rating category to another but exceeds 2.0 in each case. This evidence alone suggests strongly that a current ratio objective of 2.0 is reasonable, but a fuller analysis should take into account the effect of different current ratios on Diversified Chemical's interest coverage. The average year-end value of the pretax interest coverage for the same companies varied within a range from 4.00 to 7.25, with a median of 5.45, but the coverage ratio was significantly less for commercial paper rated A-2.

TABLE 25-2 Financial Analysis of Alternative Values for the Current Ratio

Commercial Paper Rating[a]	Five-Year Average Current Ratio for Comparable Chemical Companies			Five-Year Average Pretax Interest Coverage for Comparable Chemical Companies		
	High	*Low*	*Median*	*High*	*Low*	*Median*
A1+	2.60x	1.85x	2.30x	8.25x	5.50x	6.75x
A1	2.50	1.50	2.20	7.25	4.00	5.45
A2	2.25	1.45	2.05	5.50	4.25	4.75

	9% Short-Term Int. Rate			13% Short-Term Int. Rate	17% Short-Term Int. Rate		
	2.50x	*2.00x*	*1.50x*		*2.50x*	*2.00x*	*1.50x*
Current assets	$ 90.0	$ 90.0	$ 90.0	$ 90.0	$ 90.0	$ 90.0	$ 90.0
Fixed assets	210.0	210.0	210.0	210.0	210.0	210.0	210.0
Total Assets	$300.0	$300.0	$300.0	$300.0	$300.0	$300.0	$300.0
Short-term debt	$ 36.0	$ 45.0	$ 60.0	$100.0	$ 36.0	$ 45.0	$ 60.0
Long-term debt (at 13%)	64.0	55.0	40.0		64.0	55.0	40.0
Common equity	200.0	200.0	200.0	200.0	200.0	200.0	200.0
Total Liabilities and Equity	$300.0	$300.0	$300.0	$300.0	$300.0	$300.0	$300.0
Earnings before interest and taxes	$ 60.0	$ 60.0	$ 60.0	$ 60.0	$ 60.0	$ 60.0	$ 60.0
Interest	11.6	11.2	10.6	13.0	14.4	14.8	15.4
Pretax income	48.4	48.8	49.4	47.0	45.6	45.2	44.6
Taxes (at 40%)	19.4	19.5	19.8	18.8	18.2	18.1	17.8
Earnings Available for Common	$ 29.0	$ 29.3	$ 29.6	$ 28.2	$ 27.4	$ 27.1	$ 26.8
Return on Beginning Equity	14.5%	14.7%	14.8%	14.1%	13.7%	13.6%	13.4%
Interest Coverage	5.17x	5.36x	5.66x	4.62x	4.17x	4.05x	3.90x
Long-Term Debt/Capitalization	24.2%	21.6%	16.7%		24.2%	21.6%	16.7%
Total Debt/Adjusted Capitalization	33.3%	33.3%	33.3%	33.3%	33.3%	33.3%	33.3%
Safety Margin[b]	$ 14.0	$ 5.0	$(10.0)		$ 14.0	$ 5.0	$(10.0)

[a] Rating assigned by Standard & Poor's Corporation.
[b] Assuming $40 million of current assets are "permanent."

Suppose Diversified Chemical believes that long-term interest rates will average 13% and that short-term interest rates will average 9% over the company's planning horizon. On that basis, increasing the current ratio to 2.50 would reduce interest coverage further below the median value for companies whose commercial paper is rated A-1 and would reduce the return on equity. Diversified Chemical might be tempted to reduce the coverage ratio below 2.0. However, this would expose the company to additional risk from changes in interest rates. At short-term interest rates greater than 13%, reducing the current ratio below 2.0 would lead to decreases rather than increases both in interest coverage and in Diversified Chemical's return on equity. Taking into consideration the median values of the current ratio for the industry as well as this risk, the treasurer recommended that the company try to achieve a minimum current ratio of 2.0 but set its planning target at a slightly higher level.

Finally, note that a current ratio of 2.0 implies a safety margin of $5 million if $40 million of the $90 million of current assets are "permanent" (safety margin = 55 + 200 − [40 + 210] = $5). ∎

The procedure just illustrated is another application of the Behavioral Principle. As in the application of the Behavioral Principle in Chapter 16 to the choice of a capital structure target, the Behavioral Principle is involved only after the firm has selected the risk level it is comfortable with. In the case of capital structure, the chosen risk level is embodied in the long-term debt rating objective. In the case of the current ratio target, the chosen risk level is embodied in the commercial paper (i.e., short-term debt) rating objective.

25.3   MANAGING CURRENT ASSETS

The management of current assets can be broken down into managing (1) cash and marketable securities, (2) receivables, and (3) inventories.

CASH AND MARKETABLE SECURITIES

This section explores the important interaction between cash and marketable securities. In recent years, corporations have placed increasing emphasis on cash management. The liquidity crisis of 1974–1975 made the need for adequate liquidity painfully clear, while the high short-term interest rates in 1979–1981 made the cost just as painfully evident. Corporations now use increasingly sophisticated cash management systems to try to determine the level of cash and marketable securities that achieves the desired degree of liquidity at minimum cost.

It is appropriate to discuss cash and marketable securities together because the firm can convert marketable securities into cash on short notice. Thus, marketable securities satisfy the precautionary motive for holding cash. In addition, they serve as a substitute for cash in satisfying the transactions motive. However, they are not a perfect substitute because this conversion is not entirely costless.

The firm's cash management decision thus involves two closely related decisions. First, what is the appropriate degree of liquidity (cash plus marketable securities)? Second, what is the appropriate distribution of that liquidity between cash and marketable securities in view of the cost of converting marketable securities into cash on short notice? Once we have answered the first question, we can answer the second by determining the desired level of cash transactions balances and required level of compensating balances and then investing the remainder of the corporation's liquid resources in marketable securities.

MOTIVES FOR HOLDING CASH   **Cash** consists of currency and demand deposits. Corporations, like individuals, have three basic motives for holding cash: (1) the transactions motive, (2) the precautionary motive, and (3) the speculative motive. The **transactions motive** involves the need for cash to make payments in the ordinary course of business, such as wages, raw materials, taxes, and interest. Thus, the desired level of transactions balances will depend to a great extent on the size of the firm (because the number of transactions tends to increase with the size of the firm) and the timing of cash inflows and outflows (because the closer the degree of synchronization, the smaller the average level of cash balances required).

The **precautionary motive** reflects the need to hold cash to meet unexpected contingencies. A corporation holds cash balances because its cash inflows and outflows are subject to some degree of uncertainty. Precautionary balances serve as a buffer.

Finally, the **speculative motive** arises in connection with the corporation's desire to have cash on hand to be able to take advantage of profitable opportunities that may arise unexpectedly and require the immediate use of cash. This third motive accounts for a smaller percentage of corporate cash holdings than individual cash holdings; for the most part, corporations hold cash for transactions and precautionary reasons.

SHORT-TERM INVESTMENT ALTERNATIVES There exist a variety of investment alternatives that serve as near-money substitutes. Corporations invest on a short-term basis (maturity of 1 year or less) principally in the following types of securities, which are listed in order of their risk-return level:

- U.S. **Treasury bills**, which have an original maturity of 1 year or less when they are issued, and U.S. Treasury **notes** and **bonds** whose remaining life is 1 year or more. These securities involve the lowest risk of default, the greatest liquidity, but, as the Principle of a Risk-Return Trade-Off holds, they also offer the lowest yield. Corporations often invest in U.S. Treasury securities for very short periods via repurchase agreements, or **repos**, with securities dealers.

- U.S. **federal agency securities**. These securities are backed to varying degrees by the U.S. government, in many cases enjoy markets nearly as liquid as those for U.S. Treasury securities, and provide a slightly higher risk-return level than U.S. Treasury securities of like maturity.

- Negotiable **certificates of deposit** issued by domestic or foreign commercial banks, which evidence time deposits at the respective issuing banks; **bankers' acceptances**, which are drafts that a commercial bank has "accepted" and that consequently are valued in accordance with the accepting bank's credit standing; **commercial paper**, which consists of unsecured promissory notes that corporations have issued; and **medium-term notes**, which are unsecured notes (similar to commercial paper) that are registered with the Securities and Exchange Commission and whose maturities range from 9 months to 30 years. These securities involve some degree of default risk, which varies with the credit standing of the bank or corporation that stands behind the paper, have less liquid markets than U.S. Treasury securities, and consequently offer higher yields than U.S. Treasury securities of like maturity. In addition, **Eurodollar certificates of deposit** generally provide a higher risk-return level than domestic certificates of deposit.

- **Money market preferred stock**, which carries a dividend rate that is reset every 49 days by Dutch auction. Money market preferred stock has special tax advantages for a corporate investor. Preferred stock dividends qualify for a 70% dividends received deduction.

DETERMINING THE DESIRED DEGREE OF LIQUIDITY A corporation will determine the desired degree of liquidity (most importantly, the desired level of cash balances plus investments in marketable securities), with a view to reducing technical **insolvency risk** to an acceptable level. The higher the degree of liquidity, the lower this risk.[5] A financially robust firm will establish a degree of liquidity that makes this risk negligible.[6] A firm that is experiencing some financial difficulty, and thus has limited liquid resources, will try to reduce this risk to as low a level as possible.

ESTIMATING THE DESIRED AMOUNT OF TRANSACTION CASH   One simple yet useful approach to estimating the desired amount of transaction cash balances treats cash management as an inventory management problem. In this model, the corporation manages its inventory of cash based on the cost of holding cash (rather than marketable securities) and the cost of converting marketable securities to cash. The optimal policy minimizes the sum of the present values of these costs.

The simplest version of this model assumes that the corporation can predict its future cash requirements with certainty; that the corporation will need an amount, A, of cash per period (e.g., per month) for transaction purposes spread uniformly over the period; that the interest rate (i.e., the opportunity cost of holding cash) is r per period; and that it will cost the corporation a fixed cost, C, each time it converts securities to cash. Under these assumptions, the cost-minimizing size of each transaction, K, to convert securities to cash is[7]

$$K = \left[\frac{2CA}{r} \right]^{1/2}$$ (25.2)

Equation (25.2) produces a sawtooth pattern of cash balances that runs between K and zero as illustrated in Figure 25–4. The corporation sells marketable securities to raise K. The cash balance decreases steadily to zero as the corporation spends the cash. The corporation then sells additional securities to raise K, and so on. Consequently, the average cash balance is $K/2$.

The model is oversimplified because it ignores uncertainty and assumes that the corporation makes cash disbursements at a uniform rate. More sophisticated models take the random nature of cash flows into account. Nevertheless, Equation (25.2) does yield some useful insights. For example, a higher r or lower fixed cost, C, will lead the firm to reduce its cash balances. Also, the corporation's desired cash balances will decrease if it can take actions, such as speeding up collections from customers or slowing disbursements to suppliers, that will reduce its future cash needs.

EXAMPLE ■   A corporation projects a need for $1 million of cash per month. It believes it can earn 1% per month on funds that are invested on a 30-day basis and that converting marketable securities to cash involves a cost of $312.50 per transaction. Substituting into Equation (25.2) with $C = 312.50$, $A = 1$ million and $r = .01$ gives $K = \$250,000$, so the corporation should sell $250,000 of marketable securities four times per month, or roughly once every week (on average). In that case, its average cash balances would be $125,000 (= 250,000/2). ■

CASH MANAGEMENT WITH UNCERTAIN CASH FLOWS   When there is a high degree of uncertainty regarding future cash flows, the corporation needs more so-

---

[5] Technical insolvency occurs whenever a corporation fails to meet its cash obligations.

[6] Strictly speaking, one can argue that the firm should select the degree of liquidity at which the expected cost of maintaining the optimal degree of liquidity exceeds the expected cost of bankruptcy by a margin large enough to satisfy the corporation's shareholders. As a practical matter, the costs of bankruptcy are probably high enough that the two criteria are essentially equivalent.

[7] Baumol (1952). Essentially, Equation (25.2) provides the optimal trade-off between the fixed cost of converting a financial asset into cash, and the lower return earned on cash (versus marketable securities). More frequent conversions earn a higher return on the funds but cost more in fixed conversion costs.

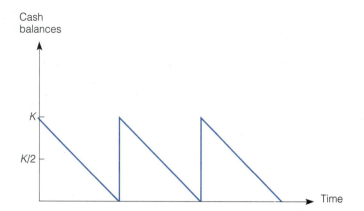

Cash
balances

K

$K/2$

Time

FIGURE 25-4
Time pattern of cash balances
when cash requirements are
uniform and known with
certainty.

phisticated models than Equation (25.2) to handle this uncertainty adequately. The Miller-Orr model offers a useful approach.[8]

The Miller-Orr model determines control limits consisting of an upper control limit, denoted U, and a lower control limit, L. When the firm's cash balance reaches U, it purchases an amount of marketable securities equal to $U - L$. When the cash balance hits zero, the corporation converts an amount of marketable securities equal to L into cash. Both actions restore the firm's cash balances to L.[9]

The values of the upper control limit and the lower control limit depend on the cost per transaction, denoted C, interest rate per period, r, and the variance of the net cash flows, σ^2:

$$L = \left[\frac{3C\sigma^2}{4r} \right]^{1/3} \qquad \text{(25.3A)}$$

$$U = 3L \qquad \text{(25.3B)}$$

Because corporations meet their cash obligations on a daily basis, r and σ^2 are normally expressed in terms of a 1-day time period.

EXAMPLE ■   Returning to the example just discussed, suppose the corporation has estimated the variance of its daily cash flows (outflows minus inflows for the day) to be $\sigma^2 = 2,777,777,778$ per day. Substituting into Equation (25.3), the control limits are

$$L = \left[\frac{3(312.50)(2,777,777,778)}{4(.01/30)} \right]^{1/3} = \$125,000$$

$$U = 3L = \$375,000$$

Figure 25–5 illustrates a time pattern consistent with the control limits just determined. The corporation's cash balance will vary between zero and $375,000, with an average cash balance of approximately $(U + L)/3$, or $166,667. This represents a one-third increase over the average cash balance when future cash requirements are known with certainty. This increase is reasonable: The corporation will generally react to increased uncertainty as to the timing of cash inflows and outflows by increasing the level of cash balances it maintains. ■

[8] Miller and Orr (1966).
[9] A trigger point greater than zero for the sale of securities would be appropriate if there were delays between the sale of securities and the receipt of cash proceeds.

FIGURE 25-5
Time pattern of cash balances
when cash requirements are
uncertain.

FIGURE 25-5
Time pattern of cash balances
when cash requirements are
uncertain.

OPTIMAL AMOUNTS OF CASH AND MARKETABLE SECURITIES Equations (25.2) and (25.3) indicate the desired level of cash transactions balances. However, the corporation may also have to satisfy compensating balance requirements under its bank loan agreements. Particularly during periods of tight money, commercial banks can insist that borrowers keep some percentage of the loan in a demand deposit account with the lender. When a corporation faces such requirements, its optimal average level of cash balances is the greater of its desired average level of transaction cash balances and the aggregate compensating balance requirement. In most cases, the latter will be the greater of the two.

The optimal amount of marketable securities is calculated as a residual after the optimal level of cash balances has been determined, as was illustrated in Figure 25–3. The firm would then invest this amount in some or all of the alternatives listed above by taking into account its possible future cash needs as well as the riskiness, maturities, and yields involved in these various investments.

The amount of marketable securities might exceed the amount just determined. Firms with large profitable foreign operations located in countries that tax certain types of income at low rates, such as Ireland and Puerto Rico, can benefit by investing the cash abroad rather than by repatriating it and paying U.S. income tax on it. Consequently, companies such as pharmaceutical companies maintain what would appear to be unusually large portfolios of marketable securities. These companies can apply the procedures discussed in this section to determine the liquidity and cash balance requirements of their U.S. operations and then reduce the domestic liquidity needs by the amount of cash they would be willing to repatriate in an emergency.

MANAGEMENT OF RECEIVABLES

The two remaining classes of current assets are receivables and inventories. Firms typically have substantial sums tied up in both. Because they are less liquid than cash and marketable securities, overinvestment in either one can be very costly. By the same token, firms must typically extend trade credit in the ordinary course of business, and production is time-consuming. Thus, most companies need to maintain some level of receivables and inventories in order to realize the full profit potential of their businesses. Consequently, underinvestment in either class of current assets is also costly.

IMPORTANT ASPECTS OF RECEIVABLES MANAGEMENT Receivables management involves a number of important decisions, the most critical of which concerns which customers the firm will sell to on credit. The firm must also set its basic terms of sale, decide whether to sell on open account or ask customers to sign IOUs, and establish a procedure for deciding which customers to extend credit to (i.e., which are most likely to pay). The first is generally determined by the terms of sale that are customary in the industry in question. With regard to the second, repeat sales to domestic customers are normally made on open account; corporations generally ask for IOUs only in special cases; e.g., special orders of large value from a new customer, customers requesting an extended repayment period, or export sales. The third area, deciding which customers are likely to repay, is normally handled through credit grading. A corporation can rely on Dun and Bradstreet's ratings of its customers' credit standings or it can form its own credit grading system based on its own collection experience.[10] This section assumes the firm has made these decisions and focuses on the question concerning which customers the company should extend credit to.

RECEIVABLES MANAGEMENT MODEL A company should extend credit to a customer only if its expected profit from doing so is positive. Suppose that the probability of the customer making payment if the corporation grants credit is P_P and that the customer will buy the product only if credit is granted. Further suppose that if credit is granted and repaid, there is probability P_R the customer will make a repeat purchase. Finally, let R represent the revenue, C the cost of one sale, and r the required rate of return per payment period.

If the company does not extend credit, there is no sale and hence no profit. If the company does extend credit, its expected NPV is the expected profit on 1 purchase plus the expected profit on a repeat purchase, or

$$\text{NPV} = P_P\left(\frac{R}{1+r} - C\right) - (1 - P_P)C + P_P P_R\left[P_P\left(\frac{R}{1+r} - C\right) - (1 - P_P)C\right]$$

$$\text{NPV} = \left[P_P\left(\frac{R}{1+r} - C\right) - (1 - P_P)C\right]\left[1 + P_P P_R\right] \tag{25.4}$$

The expected NPV equals (1) the present value of the profit the firm will realize, $[R/(1+r) - C]$ times the probability of payment, P_P, less (2) the present value of the cost, C, times the probability payment will not be made, $(1 - P_P)$, plus (3) the sum of (1) and (2) times the probability that the customer will pay and make a repeat purchase. This approach can be used to develop more sophisticated models that incorporate additional contingencies (such as multiple repeat purchases) and time-value-of-money complexities with respect to revenues and costs.

EXAMPLE ■ Marion Minicomputer Manufacturing sells its new M III personal computer to dealers for $5,000 per machine. The machines cost $4,000 each to manufacture. Marion's prior experience with new direct order customers similar to the one who has just placed an order indicates that they pay 90% of the time in an average of 30 days. Roughly one out of four new credit customers makes repeat purchases. Collection costs average $50 per account, and Marion's required rate of return on receivables is 1.5% per month. In this case, then, we have

$$R = 5,000 \quad C = 4,000 + 50 = 4,050 \quad r = .015 \quad P_P = .9 \quad P_R = .25.$$

Substituting into Equation (25.4), the expected NPV of extending credit is $469.78. Because the expected value is positive, the firm can expect to profit by extending credit and should therefore do so. ■

---

[10] Smith (1964) offers a practical example of how a company can accomplish this.

Management of Inventories

Manufacturing companies generally carry three types of inventory: raw materials, work in process, and finished goods. The sizes of the raw materials inventories depend principally on the anticipated level of production, the seasonality of production, and the reliability of the sources of supply. The sizes of the work in process inventories depend mainly on the overall length of each production run and the number of distinct stages in the production cycle. The sizes of the finished goods inventories depend primarily on the rate of sales (units of product per unit of time), the cost of carrying the inventory, the cost of ordering replacement stocks, and the cost of having run out of an item when an order comes in (in the extreme case, the cost of losing the sale and perhaps also the customer). In general, larger inventories give the firm greater sales and operating flexibility, but they also involve increased storage, handling, insurance, and other costs.

Inventory management model   A simple though still useful inventory management model is the **economic order quantity (EOQ)** model. This model in its simplest form is derived in the following manner. Suppose that units are removed from inventory at the constant rate of S, (the rate at which goods are sold in the case of finished goods inventories); that there is a fixed reordering cost, C_R per order regardless of the number of units reordered; and that it costs C_C to carry a unit in inventory for an entire period. Under these assumptions, the economic order quantity, denoted EOQ, is

$$\text{EOQ} = \left[\frac{2(S)(C_R)}{C_C} \right]^{1/2} \tag{25.5}$$

You will undoubtedly recognize that Equation (25.5) looks very similar to Equation (25.2). That is because the two models were derived under parallel assumptions. As in the case of Equation (25.2), Equation (25.5) results in a sawtooth pattern for the inventory level, similar to the one that was illustrated in Figure 25–4, and the average inventory level over time is EOQ/2.

EXAMPLE ■   Marion Manufacturing's largest dealer is selling Marion's new M III personal computers at the rate of 1,800 units per year. The dealer's cost of placing an order with Marion is $400 per order (including insurance and shipping charges), and its cost of carrying an M III machine in inventory for a year is $100.

Substituting into Equation (25.5), the dealer's economic order quantity from Marion is

$$\text{EOQ} = \left[\frac{2(1800)(400)}{100} \right]^{1/2} = 120$$

This economic order quantity implies a reorder roughly 15 (= 1,800/120) times per year, or every 3.5 weeks, for 120 machines per order. The average inventory level over time is 60 machines.   ■

Like Equation (25.2), Equation (25.5) makes certain simplifying assumptions: future demand is known with certainty, inventory is utilized at a constant rate, and delivery lead times are constant. In fact, each of these factors is subject to uncertainty. A corporation can compensate for this uncertainty by maintaining **safety stocks**, that is, a buffer inventory. In that case, the average inventory level is roughly EOQ/2 + B, where B denotes the amount of safety stocks.

Safety stocks add to the cost of holding inventories but reduce the likelihood that an item will not be available in inventory when it is needed. The appropriate safety stock level is that amount which minimizes the combined cost of stockouts and carrying the additional inventory.

EXAMPLE ■ Marion Manufacturing's largest dealer has found that if it is out of stock when a customer arrives, it will make the eventual sale only 50% of the time. For each lost sale, the dealer loses the net margin of $600 per machine plus the opportunity to earn after-tax profit of $300 from the sale of ancillary items. Lost sales as well as back orders (orders the dealer fills when the next shipment arrives) involve record-keeping costs of $50 per stockout. Thus, each stockout costs $500 (= [.5]950 + [.5]50) on average. It costs the dealer $100 to keep a machine in inventory for a year. The dealer estimates that a safety stock, B, of 10 units will result in 30 stockouts per year, a B of 15 units will result in 25 stockouts per year, and a B of 25 units will result in 24 stockouts per year. These B levels would result in combined stockout and holding costs amounting to

$$10 \text{ units: } \$100(10) + 500(30) = \$16,000$$
$$15 \text{ units: } \$100(15) + 500(25) = \$14,000$$
$$25 \text{ units: } \$100(25) + 500(24) = \$14,500$$

Thus, the dealer should maintain a safety stock of 15 machines. ■

SHORT-TERM LIABILITY MANAGEMENT 25.4

There are three principal sources of short-term funds. A company can (1) arrange **trade credit** from its suppliers, or it can (2) borrow funds from a bank or credit company. Alternatively, if it is sufficiently creditworthy, it can (3) sell short-term IOUs—**commercial paper**—to investors. This section discusses each of these sources of short-term funds, describes how to estimate the cost of funds from each source, and provides a framework for comparing these costs on a consistent basis.

A variety of factors affect the level and mix of short-term indebtedness and, more generally, the overall maturity structure of the firm's debt. The desired level of current assets, the seasonal component of current assets, the extent of hedging employed in the firm's debt structure, and the desired margin of safety are among the more important factors affecting the firm's use of short-term debt. Among the other factors that can affect the actual level of short-term debt are

■ *Flotation costs.* The costs of issuing securities are to some extent fixed and are generally higher than the costs of arranging short-term borrowings. These higher costs lead to less frequent, larger securities offerings. In the interim, firms borrow from banks or issue commercial paper. These short-term borrowings are then "funded out" through the issuance of intermediate-term or long-term securities.

■ *Restricted access to sources of long-term capital.* Legal restrictions limit the types of loans that institutional investors can make. Smaller companies or larger companies whose debt is rated below investment grade may be unable to sell long-term debt securities on acceptable terms, except perhaps under the most favorable market conditions, and therefore have to rely on trade credit and on bank or credit company financing.

■ *Less restrictive terms.* Public and private debt issues normally impose greater cost penalties than bank loan agreements on borrowers who repay the debt before it matures. The greater the likelihood of prepayment, the more attractive becomes bank financing. In addition, banks may be willing to take certain risks that institutional lenders are not willing to take, so firms frequently borrow from commercial banks in connection with **project financings**.

■ *Bankruptcy costs.* Bankruptcy imposes costs on shareholders. The existence of such costs creates a bias in favor of longer maturities and, in particular, discourages overreliance on short-term financing.

■ *The firm's choice of risk level.* The greater the degree of aversion to the risk that interest rates will rise and to the risk that short-term borrowings may not be refunded, the smaller the proportion of (floating-rate) short-term borrowings. This can be an important factor for firms whose shareholders are not well diversified, as is often the case with owner-managed businesses.

SOURCES OF SHORT-TERM FUNDS

The terms **short-term funds** and **intermediate-term funds** are used to refer to the original maturity of the debt obligation. Short-term funds are debt obligations that were originally scheduled for repayment within 1 year.[11] Intermediate-term funds are debt obligations that were originally scheduled to mature between 1 and perhaps as many as 10 years from the date of issue. These definitions are somewhat arbitrary. Moreover, during certain periods, the traditional sources of long-term debt, insurance companies and pension funds, have generally preferred to lend on an intermediate-term rather than on a long-term basis because of the erosion in the value of their long-term fixed-rate bond portfolios caused by persistently higher than expected inflation.

A more useful distinction involves the source of funds from which the loan is to be repaid. Short-term loans are typically arranged to finance seasonal or temporary needs. Intermediate-term loans are to be repaid over a period of years. Thus short-term lenders are principally concerned with the firm's working capital position and its ability to liquidate current assets—collecting on receivables and reducing inventories according to seasonal patterns—to generate cash to meet the firm's current debt service obligations. Intermediate-term (as well as long-term) lenders are more concerned with the longer-term profitability of the firm's operations.

TRADE CREDIT

Trade credit is credit extended to firms by other firms. Trade credit arises in the ordinary course of business; purchasers of raw materials and supplies are typically permitted to wait until after the goods are delivered to pay for them. Trade credit provides a significant amount of financing for firms because it is the largest single source of short-term funds for business collectively, representing approximately 30% of the current liabilities of all manufacturing corporations and approximately 40% of the current liabilities of manufacturing corporations with assets under $25 million. Because suppliers are generally more liberal in extending credit than financial institutions, trade credit is a particularly important source of funds for small companies.

When extending trade credit, the seller specifies the period of time allowed for

---

[11] Note the important distinction between **short-term funds** and the accounting definition of **short-term debt**. Unless refunded earlier, every debt obligation becomes short-term debt within a year of its scheduled maturity. But only short-term funds are also short-term debt at the time the funds are borrowed.

payment and often offers a **cash discount** if payment is made more quickly. For example, the terms "2/10, net 30" are frequently encountered, which means the buyer can take a 2% cash discount if payment is made within 10 days (the **discount period**). Otherwise, the full amount is due within 30 days (the **net period**).

Trade credit illustrates once again the Principle of Two-Sided Transactions. Trade credit gives rise to receivables on the books of the firm that grants credit; it gives rise to accounts payable for the firm purchasing the goods. Because of the Time-Value-of-Money Principle, the purchasing firm should wait until the end of the discount period to pay.

EXAMPLE ■ Suppose that a firm purchases $50,000 worth of supplies each day on terms of 2/10, net 30, and that the firm always pays in exactly 10 days. In that case, the firm will owe its suppliers 10 times $50,000, or $500,000. Thus, suppliers are providing $500,000 of funds (minus $10,000 for the 2% discount) at zero cost that the firm can use in its business.   ■

Cost of Trade Credit

If no discount is offered or if payment is made soon enough that the discount can be taken, there is no cost to the firm for the use of the supplier's credit. When cash discounts are offered but not taken, however, trade credit involves an implicit cost. It should be obvious that when a firm offers a discount for early payment, the discounted price is the "real" price of the goods. That is, if the invoice is for $100 and a 2% discount is offered for early payment, the "real" price is $98. To continue the example, if the firm does not pay its bill within 10 days, it is effectively borrowing $98 and paying $2 interest for the loan by forgoing the 2% discount.

The nominal annualized cost of trade credit can be calculated by applying the following formula:

$$\frac{\text{Annualized Cost}}{\text{of Trade Credit}} = \left[\frac{\%\,\text{Discount}}{100 - \%\,\text{Discount}}\right]\left[\frac{360}{\text{Additional Days}}\right] \quad (25.6)$$

where Additional Days is the time from the end of the discount period until payment is made. For the above example,

$$\frac{\text{Annualized Cost}}{\text{of Trade Credit}} = \left[\frac{2}{100 - 2}\right]\left[\frac{360}{30 - 10}\right] = .3673, \text{ or } 36.73\%$$

As this example illustrates, trade credit can be very expensive when a cash discount is offered but not taken. It may in fact prove considerably more expensive than bank financing. Thus it is important to evaluate the cost implicit in not taking the discount. It can be observed from Equation (25.6) that this implicit cost tends to be greater, the greater the cash discount and the smaller the difference between the net period and the discount period.[12] Notice also that the *effective* annual rate of return is higher than is the nominal annual rate that is given, because of compounding.

EFFECTIVE USE OF TRADE CREDIT   Trade credit offers certain advantages as a source of short-term funds. It is readily available, at least to firms who regularly discharge their obligations to suppliers on schedule. It is informal; if the firm is now paying its bills within the discount period, additional credit can be obtained simply

---

[12] For example, terms of 3/10, net 30, involve an implicit cost of 55.67%, and terms of 2/10, net 20, involve an implicit cost of 73.47%.

by delaying the payment until the end of the net period or perhaps later (but at the cost of forgoing the discount). Trade credit is also more flexible than other means of short-term financing. The firm does not have to negotiate a loan agreement, pledge collateral, or adhere to a rigid repayment schedule. In particular, the consequences of delaying a payment beyond the net period are much less onerous than those resulting from failure to repay a bank loan on schedule. For these and other reasons, trade credit is particularly valuable to smaller firms who typically have difficulty obtaining credit elsewhere.

In this regard, trade credit often serves as an "escape valve" through which the small firm can obtain credit during periods of tight money. To use credit effectively, the firm must weigh these advantages against the associated costs. Delaying payment beyond the discount period involves an explicit cost, as discussed above.

Firms may also "stretch" accounts payable by postponing payment beyond the end of the net period. Such stretching lowers the cost computed in Equation (25.6). For example, paying in 40 rather than 30 days lowers the nominal annual cost from 36.73% to 24.49%. Suppliers may be willing to tolerate such delinquencies during those periods when the buyer has large seasonal funds requirements. To minimize any adverse consequences, however, the buyer should keep the supplier fully informed of its situation to the extent practicable and should keep current on its repayment obligations with the supplier over the balance of the year.[13]

The buyer must be careful to avoid excessive stretching of accounts payable, however. Excessive stretching may cause the firm to incur other implicit costs, such as a deterioration in the credit ratings assigned the firm and/or strained relations with suppliers.[14] These results in turn can lead to less attractive repayment terms in the future and perhaps to higher prices as suppliers attempt to pass through to the buyer the cost of financing the buyer's delinquent payments. These implicit costs of trade credit, while difficult to estimate, should be carefully evaluated. In particular, smaller firms who may at times have to rely exclusively on trade credit for short-term financing should assess the explicit as well as hidden costs of the trade credit offered by alternative suppliers.

SECURED AND UNSECURED BANK LOANS

Commercial bank lending is second in importance to trade credit as a source of short-term financing. Commercial banks also provide intermediate-term financing (maturity between 1 and 10 years). Banks provide loans in a wide variety of forms that are tailored to the specific needs of the borrower. Banks generally lend to their most creditworthy customers on an unsecured basis. When a borrower represents a significant credit risk, the bank may ask it to provide some form of security, such as a lien on receivables or inventory. Finance companies also lend on a secured basis.

SHORT-TERM UNSECURED LOANS   Short-term unsecured bank loans take three basic forms: a **line of credit**, a **revolving credit**, or a specific **transaction loan**. Such loans are generally regarded as "self-liquidating": The lender expects

---

[13] Datings, if available, provide an alternative to stretching accounts payable. Suppliers in seasonal businesses often use "datings" to permit buyers to place orders during the off-peak period (when the buyer's business is a net user of funds) and to repay during the peak selling period (when the business is a net generator of funds). Under this arrangement, the repayment period is longer than normal by prior agreement.

[14] Various mercantile agencies provide such ratings. The most comprehensive of these services is provided by Dun & Bradstreet Business Credit Services (D&B). D&B appraises the credit of a firm relative to that of other firms of comparable financial strength (i.e., net worth) and assigns composite credit appraisal ratings between 1 ("high") and 4 ("limited").

that the assets the company purchases with the loan proceeds will generate sufficient cash to repay the loan within a year. Short-term unsecured loans are evidenced by a promissory note that specifies the amount of the loan, interest rate, and repayment terms. Short-term unsecured loans typically bear interest at a floating rate.

A **line of credit** is an arrangement between a bank and a customer concerning the maximum loan balance the bank will permit the borrower at any one time. Banks normally extend credit lines for a 1-year period subject to 1-year renewals as long as the bank continues to find the borrower's credit acceptable. Banks generally do not like borrowers to use credit lines to cover their long-term funds requirements and so require borrowers to be out of bank debt for some specified period (typically 30 consecutive days). Most credit lines are informal arrangements; if the prospective borrower's credit deteriorates, the bank is not legally obligated to advance funds.

A **revolving credit** agreement represents a legal commitment to lend up to a specified maximum amount any time during a specified period. In return for this legal commitment, the borrower must pay a **commitment fee**, typically between 0.25% and 0.5%, on the difference between the permitted maximum and the amount actually borrowed. Revolving credits are evidenced by short-term notes, typically maturing in 90 days. The borrower can roll these over automatically as long as the notes mature no later than the date the revolving credit agreement expires. Revolving credits often extend beyond 1 year, and the borrower often has the option to convert the revolving credit to a term loan when the revolving credit expires. Bank term loans are discussed below.

A **transaction loan** is a loan the bank extends for a specific purpose. For example, a bank may lend a home builder funds to pay for construction. The loan agreement will require the builder to repay the bank when she sells the house.

TERM LOAN Bank term loans represent intermediate-term debt, but the similarity between their pricing and the pricing of short-term bank loans makes it appropriate to discuss them in this chapter. A bank **term loan** is a loan for a specified amount that requires the borrower to repay it according to a specified schedule. A term loan generally matures in not less than 1 and not more than 10 years, but banks have permitted longer maturities under special circumstances. Repayment is normally at regular intervals in equal installments, but in some cases the loan may provide for a larger final payment, called a **balloon payment**, or simply repayment at maturity in one lump sum, called a **bullet maturity**. Banks often extend revolving credits that the borrower can convert into a term loan. A 3-year revolving credit convertible into a 5-year term loan at the end of the third year is not uncommon. Term loans may carry a fixed rate of interest but more commonly carry a floating interest rate.

COST OF BANK FINANCING Except for a rather small percentage of loans that bear interest at a fixed rate, commercial banks charge interest at a rate that floats. Normally, the interest rate floats with the bank's **prime rate** but it may float instead with some other interest rate that represents the bank's cost of funding the loan. For example, commercial banks often offer their larger more creditworthy customers the option of selecting interest rates based on (1) one of the London Interbank Offer Rates (LIBOR), the rates at which prime banks offer one another deposits in the London market, or (2) the interest rate the bank pays on large certificates of deposit. Nevertheless, the prime rate serves as the base lending rate in most cases.

A bank will adjust its prime rate to reflect changes in its cost of funds. The prime rate is in principle the interest rate the bank charges its largest, most financially sound customers. In practice, commercial banks often offer loans at "money market rates" that are below prime, to compete with the commercial paper market, which is discussed below. Banks charge less creditworthy customers a higher rate, typically expressed as a percentage over prime, depending on the customer's credit standing. For example, if a bank's prime rate is 12%, it might lend to a local manufacturing company at prime plus 0.5%, or 12.5%, and to a local merchant at prime plus 2%, or 14%. The interest rates on these loans would change with changes in the bank's prime rate. If the bank raises its prime rate to 12.5%, the interest rate on the manufacturing company's loan would automatically become 13%, and the interest rate on the merchant's loan would automatically become 14.5%.

In addition to charging interest, banks often require borrowers to maintain a fraction of the loan, typically between 10% and 20%, on deposit with the bank in the form of **compensating balances**. This requirement may take the form of a required minimum but more commonly takes the form of a required average deposit balance during a particular interest period. The latter obviously affords the borrower greater flexibility because a high balance one day can offset a low balance on some other day. Compensating balance requirements tend to be less prevalent during periods of plentiful liquidity. In any case, compensating balances add to the cost of a loan in those instances where the firm's cash balances are higher than they would normally be in the absence of this requirement.

TRUE INTEREST COST   When interest is paid in arrears (i.e., at the end of an interest period) and the bank requires that the borrower maintain compensating balances, the **true interest cost**, TIC, of the loan bearing interest at a stated rate of r is

$$\text{TIC} = \frac{rP}{P - B} \qquad (25.7)$$

where P denotes the amount of the loan, and B denotes the increase in the firm's average cash balances that results from the compensating balance requirement. In Equation (25.7), the corporation pays interest of $r(P)$ (on an annualized basis) but can only use $P - B$ of the loan proceeds in its business.

Equation (25.7) assumes that the compensating balances do not earn interest, which is generally the case. But if the compensating balances earn some yield, y, the interest so earned, yB, reduces the cost of the loan:

$$\text{TIC} = \frac{rP - yB}{P - B} \qquad (25.8)$$

EXAMPLE ■   A company borrows $100,000. The bank charges interest at prime rate plus 0.50% and requires 10% compensating balances, none of which the borrower would otherwise have kept. If the prime rate averages 11.50% during the initial quarter, the true interest cost for that period expressed on an annualized basis is

$$\text{TIC} = \frac{(.12)(100,000)}{100,000 - 10,000} = .1333, \text{ or } 13.33\%$$

In the absence of any compensating balance requirements, the true interest cost would have been simply 12%.

If the borrower could deposit the compensating balances in a time deposit account earning 5% interest, the true interest cost would be only

$$\text{TIC} = \frac{(.12)(100,000) - (.05)(10,000)}{100,000 - 10,000} = .1278, \text{ or } 12.78\% \qquad ■$$

TRUE INTEREST COST OF DISCOUNT NOTES   In Equations (25.7) and (25.8), the borrower pays interest in arrears. Alternatively, the bank may require the borrower to pay interest in advance. It accomplishes this by **discounting** the borrower's note: The borrower signs a promissory note for some amount P but receives only $P - rPf$, where f denotes the fraction of the year the note is to be outstanding. Often, f is computed on the basis of a 360-day year. In this case, the company pays interest expense of rPf but has the use only of P less the amount of interest, and therefore its nominal annual true interest cost is the ratio of these amounts times the number of "periods" in a year, $1/f$, or

$$\text{TIC} = \left[\frac{rPf}{P - rPf} \right] \left[\frac{1}{f} \right] = \frac{r}{1 - rf} \qquad (25.9)$$

Thus, as you would expect because of the Time-Value-of-Money Principle, the true interest cost is higher when interest is paid in advance than when it is paid in arrears. Should the bank also require compensating balances, adjustments like those in Equations (25.7) and (25.8) can be made to Equation (25.9).

EXAMPLE ■   If the borrower in the preceding illustration had to pay interest on a discount basis at the rate of 12% per annum but had not faced compensating balance requirements, the true interest cost for the 90-day loan would have been

$$\text{TIC} = \frac{r}{1 - rf} = \frac{.12}{1 - .12(.25)} = .1237, \text{ or } 12.37\% \qquad ■$$

TRUE INTEREST COST OF AN INSTALLMENT LOAN   Finally, the bank may require the borrower to pay the loan on an installment basis. The true interest cost of such loans is found by calculating the internal rate of return of the relevant cash flows and converting the resulting number to an annualized basis (or whatever other basis is desired).

EXAMPLE ■   Suppose the borrower in the preceding example had to repay the loan in three installments of $25,000 each at the end of the first 2 months and $50,000 at the end of 3 months. The company borrows $97,000 (= $100,000 − [.12][.25]100,000) at the true interest cost of r, that solves

$$0 = -97,000 + \frac{25,000}{(1 + r)} + \frac{25,000}{(1 + r)^2} + \frac{50,000}{(1 + r)^3}$$

$r = 1.3658\%$ is expressed in terms of a monthly unit of time, so that the nominal annual rate is

$$\text{TIC} = 12(1.3658\%) = 16.39\% \qquad ■$$

The preceding examples indicate why it is very important to check the terms of the loan agreement to determine how interest is calculated and when the loan has to be repaid. Two loans with the same nominal interest rate may involve substantially different true interest costs because of differences in how interest is calculated or differences in the timing of repayment.

SECURITY   Commercial banks often ask lenders to provide security for their loans. When the bank is lending on a short-term basis, it may ask the borrower to pledge liquid assets—that is, receivables, inventories, or securities. The pledge of collateral may take the form of a "floating lien" against one or more classes of short-term assets without specifying them in detail, or, more commonly, banks will ask the borrower to specify in detail the collateral for the loan (e.g., to list the receivables it is pledging). Depending on the quality of the receivables, a company can usually borrow between 70% and 90% of the face value of the receivables it pledges. Depending on the quality of the inventories, with readily marketable finished goods possessing the highest collateral value, a company might be able to borrow between 50% and 75% of their fair market value.

For a loan secured by receivables, a commercial bank will normally charge the prime rate plus a premium of up to five percentage points. The rate will be toward the upper end of this range when the bank's cost of processing the receivables is high. However, there are normally no compensating balances on such a loan. The interest cost of a loan secured by inventory varies within a range comparable to that of the interest cost of a loan secured by receivables. The premium is generally lower the higher the quality of the receivables or inventory pledged. Finance companies also make secured loans, but these are generally at rates higher than those commercial banks charge.

The principal benefit the firm derives from pledging security is the opportunity to borrow a greater sum than it could obtain on an unsecured basis. In return, the firm normally pays a higher interest cost at the margin and sacrifices some degree of control over its receivables and inventories.

COMMERCIAL PAPER

The largest most creditworthy companies are able to borrow on a short-term basis by selling **commercial paper**. Currently more than 4,000 companies issue this form of security. Commercial paper consists of unsecured promissory notes that have a maturity of up to 270 days.[15]

MARKET FOR COMMERCIAL PAPER   Commercial paper is sold either directly or through dealers. Large industrial firms, utilities, and medium-size finance companies generally sell their paper through dealers, who typically charge a commission of ⅛ of 1% on an annualized basis. Such dealer-placed paper typically has a maturity of between 30 and 180 days. Principal buyers include other business firms, insurance companies, pension funds, and banks.

Roughly 40% of all commercial paper is sold directly to investors. The large finance companies, such as General Motors Acceptance Corporation, typically sell their paper directly. They tailor the maturities and the amounts of the notes to fit the needs of investors, who consist principally of corporations investing excess cash on a short-term basis. Maturities range from 1 to 270 days. In contrast to most industrial firms, the large finance companies use the commercial paper market as a permanent source of funds because of the finance companies' assets and the lower cost of commercial paper relative to bank financing.[16]

Table 25–3 illustrates the growth of the commercial paper market between 1970 and 1989. The growth pattern reflects surges that occurred in 1973–1974, in 1978–1981, and again in 1984–1989. The first surge resulted from the inability of the commercial banks to meet loan demand during a period of tight money. The two most

---

[15] It is possible for commercial paper to have a maturity longer than 270 days, but such an issue would have to be placed privately or else registered with the Securities and Exchange Commission.
[16] Because of legal lending limits, commercial banks could not fully satisfy the finance companies' short-term borrowing needs in any case.

TABLE 25–3 Size of Commercial Paper Market and Cost of Borrowing through Commercial Paper

Year	Commercial Paper Outstanding, Year-End		Average Interest Rate on 90-Day Prime Commercial Paper[a]	
	Total ($ millions)	*% Dealer Placed*	*Dealer Placed*	*Directly Placed*
1970	$ 33,071	39.3%	7.87%[b]	7.36%
1971	32,126	37.6	5.18	4.97
1972	34,721	39.9	4.71	4.57
1973	41,073	38.5	8.37	7.54
1974	49,144	38.9	10.31	8.81
1975	48,459	35.3	6.36	6.26
1976	53,025	38.7	5.31	5.29
1977	65,051	37.6	5.62	5.57
1978	83,438	38.1	8.10	7.96
1979	112,803	42.6	11.28	10.75
1980	124,374	45.4	13.07	11.83
1981	165,829	50.8	15.93	14.59
1982	166,670	49.5	12.25	11.55
1983	188,057	48.7	9.08	8.89
1984	237,586	53.5	10.36	9.97
1985	298,779	54.7	8.11	7.92
1986	329,991	54.0	6.60	6.48
1987	357,129	51.3	6.94	6.65
1988	455,017	57.7	7.81	7.52
1989	525,266	60.1	9.20	8.91

[a] Expressed on a bond-equivalent-yield basis.
[b] Rate for commercial paper with a maturity of 4–6 months.
Source: Federal Reserve Bulletin, various issues.

recent surges were due to the cost advantage of commercial paper relative to bank borrowing. Also, as illustrated in Table 25–3, the percentage of commercial paper that is dealer-placed has grown more or less steadily over the past 20 years, reflecting the growing participation in the market by industrial borrowers. Nevertheless, as also evidenced in Table 25–3, the finance companies who borrow directly are still generally able to borrow more cheaply than other commercial paper issuers.

COMPUTING THE TRUE INTEREST COST OF COMMERCIAL PAPER As with discount notes, interest on commercial paper is paid on a **discount basis**.

EXAMPLE ■ If the discount rate for 120-day prime commercial paper is 12%, from Equation (25.9), the issuer of a $1 million promissory note would face a nominal annual true interest cost (based on a 360-day year) of

$$\text{TIC} = \frac{r}{1 - rf} = \frac{.12}{1 - .12(120/360)} = .125, \text{ or } 12.5\%$$ ■

True interest cost calculated in accordance with Equation (25.9) is also known as the **bond equivalent yield**.

Note that not all financial instruments earn interest on the basis of a 360-day year. Corporate bonds earn interest on the basis of a 30-day month and a 360-day year, but U.S. Treasury bonds and notes earn interest on the basis of the actual number of days elapsed and a 365-day year. The true interest cost when interest is paid on the basis of a 365-day year is called the **coupon equivalent yield** (CEY) and is calculated by multiplying Equation (25.9) by 365/360:

$$CEY = TIC(365/360) \tag{25.10}$$

COMPUTING THE COST OF BORROWING   Issuers of commercial paper generally find it prudent to maintain a backup line of credit with one or more commercial banks to provide insurance against temporary difficulties in selling commercial paper. For example, for several weeks following the bankruptcy of the Penn Central Railroad in 1970, some large issuers of commercial paper, most notably Chrysler Financial Corporation, found it impossible to market new issues to refund maturing issues. Banks typically charge a fee of ¼ to ½ of 1% for such backup lines. This cost, together with any commissions paid to dealers, must be recognized in the cost of borrowing calculation. Incorporating these costs, Equation (25.9) becomes

$$TIC = \frac{r}{1 - rf - \text{Commission}} + \text{Commitment Fee} \tag{25.11}$$

The true interest cost given by Equation (25.11) should be compared with the costs calculated for alternative sources of funds to determine which is cheapest.

EXAMPLE ■   The issuer of the $1 million note discussed earlier typically sells commercial paper through a dealer who charges a commission of ⅛ of 1%. The issuer also maintains a back-up line of credit requiring a commitment fee of ½ of 1%. The issuer's cost of borrowing is thus

$$TIC = \frac{.12}{1 - .12(120/360) - .00125} + .005 = .1302, \text{ or } 13.02\%$$

Thus, for example, the firm is better off selling commercial paper if it expects the cost of bank borrowing and the cost of trade credit over the next 120 days to exceed 13.02% on an annualized basis.   ■

RATING CONSIDERATIONS   Investors rely upon the commercial paper ratings assigned by Moody's Investors Service and Standard & Poor's Corporation to assess the creditworthiness of an issuer's commercial paper. The two agencies apply similar rating criteria. Moody's has two basic commercial paper rating categories: "Prime" and "Not Prime." The Prime category is subdivided into P-1 (highest quality), P-2, and P-3. Standard & Poor's has four basic commercial paper rating categories, designated A, B, C, and D. The A category is subdivided into A-1+ (highest), A-1, A-2, and A-3.

Issuers whose commercial paper is rated P-1/A-1+ enjoy the lowest cost of borrowing and the least interrupted access to the market. For example, at times the yield differential between commercial paper rated P-1/A-1+ and commercial paper rated P-3/A-3 has exceeded two full percentage points. In addition, following market crises like the bankruptcy of the Penn Central Railroad in 1970, the market for paper rated lower than P-1/A-1 can dry up. Even in the best of times, there is normally no market for commercial paper rated lower than P-3/A-3, and the market for commercial paper rated P-3/A-3 is generally very limited.

As one might expect, commercial paper ratings are closely correlated with senior debt ratings. For example, Standard & Poor's assigns its A-1+ designation when

- The issuer's (or guarantor's) senior debt is rated AA or higher, *or*
- The issuer's (or guarantor's) senior debt is rated A+ or AA-, and the issuer (or guarantor) demonstrates excellent liquidity and substantial near-term financial flexibility.

CREDIT ENHANCEMENT   A company whose commercial paper is rated P-3/A-3, and in some cases a company whose commercial paper is rated P-2/A-2, can lower its cost of borrowing by arranging for a first-class commercial bank to provide credit support in the form of an irrevocable letter of credit. A bank typically charges a fee of between ½ and ¾ of 1% for providing its letter of credit. In addition, there are legal fees and other costs associated with establishing a letter of credit arrangement acceptable to the rating agencies. As a rough rule of thumb, a letter of credit arrangement can reduce the cost of issuing commercial paper when the issuer's direct cost (without letter of credit support) exceeds the prevailing P-1/A-1 commercial paper rate by roughly 75 to 100 basis points.

COMPARING THE COSTS OF SHORT-TERM FUNDS FROM DIFFERENT SOURCES

There are other sources of short-term funds that are less important than those just discussed. For example, bank trust departments will purchase **demand master notes**, which are redeemable upon demand. These typically bear interest at a rate that varies with some readily available benchmark, as for example, the maximum of the 30-day, 60-day, and 90-day commercial paper rates quoted by General Motors Acceptance Corporation. In addition, finance companies also provide lines of credit, generally to less creditworthy companies that might have difficulty borrowing from commercial banks, and even life insurance companies have at times advanced short-term funds on a selected basis. But in most cases, the interest rates on these loans float with the prime rate charged by the largest banks or with the commercial paper rate for "prime quality" commercial paper.

Table 25–4 compares the average annual interest rate on dealer-placed 90-day prime commercial paper, the average annual prime rate charged by money center banks, and the average annual value of 3-month LIBOR (London Interbank Offer Rate) for the period 1970–1989. Except for brief periods, the average prime rate has exceeded the other two rates. Over the 20-year period 1970–1989, the prime rate exceeded the dealer-placed 90-day prime commercial paper rate by an average of 136 basis points (or 1.36%) but in 1980, 1981, and 1982 the average annual difference exceeded two full percentage points (and at times during this period the difference was considerably greater). In general, the differential tends to widen, with commercial paper becoming even cheaper relative to bank loans, during periods of easy money because market forces tend to bring commercial paper rates down more rapidly than banks reduce their prime lending rates.

Thus, even after allowing for the roughly 50-basis-point cost of a backup line of credit, commercial paper has generally proven to be a significantly cheaper source of funds than short-term bank loans for companies that are able to borrow in the commercial paper market. Moreover, the savings are generally greater for the most

Table 25–4 Comparison of Commercial Paper Rate, Prime Rate, and Eurodollar Rate

Year	Commercial Paper Rate[a]	3-Month LIBOR[b]	Prime Rate[c]	Discount to Prime Rate	
				Commercial Paper Rate[d]	3-Month LIBOR[e]
1970	7.87%	8.52%	7.90%	3 b.p.	− 62 b.p.
1971	5.18	6.68	5.81	63	− 87
1972	4.71	5.46	5.25	54	− 21
1973	8.37	9.24	8.02	−35	−122
1974	10.31	11.01	10.80	49	− 21
1975	6.36	6.97	7.86	150	89
1976	5.31	5.57	6.84	153	127
1977	5.62	6.05	6.82	120	77
1978	8.10	8.78	9.06	96	28
1979	11.28	11.96	12.67	139	71
10-yr. Avg.	7.31%	8.02%	8.10%	79 b.p.	8 b.p.
1980	13.07	14.00	15.27	220	127
1981	15.93	16.79	18.87	294	208
1982	12.25	13.12	14.86	261	174
1983	9.08	9.56	10.79	171	123
1984	10.36	10.73	12.04	168	131
1985	8.11	8.28	9.93	182	165
1986	6.60	6.70	8.35	175	165
1987	6.94	7.07	8.21	127	114
1988	7.81	7.85	9.32	151	147
1989	9.20	9.16	10.87	167	171
10-yr. Avg.	9.94%	10.33%	11.85%	191 b.p.	152 b.p.
20-yr. Avg.	8.62%	9.18%	9.98%	136 b.p.	80 b.p.

[a] Average interest rate on dealer-placed 90-day prime commercial paper.
[b] Average of end-of-month values.
[c] Annual average.
[d] Prime rate less bond-equivalent-yield commercial paper rate (measured in basis points, denoted b.p.).
[e] Prime rate less 3-month LIBOR (measured in basis points, denoted b.p.).

Source: Federal Reserve Bulletin, various issues.

creditworthy companies whose commercial paper carries the highest ratings (i.e., P-1/A-1+).

While commercial paper is generally a cheaper source of funds than bank loans, many commercial paper issuers still find it advantageous to maintain some minimum level of bank borrowing. There is always the danger, except for the strongest credits, that the market for the issuer's commercial paper could dry up unexpectedly. Also, commercial banks are more likely than the commercial paper market to help a company that is experiencing temporary financial difficulties. Maintaining some minimum level of bank borrowing can help a company maintain the quality of its banking relationships and thereby help ensure that additional bank financing will be available if needed.

The comparison involving 3-month LIBOR and the prime rate in Table 25–4 is also interesting. The LIBOR rates serve as the benchmarks for pricing **Eurodollar** loans. Three-month LIBOR exceeded prime on average during the period 1970–1974, but the relationship has since reversed. On average, over the 20-year period, prime exceeded 3-month LIBOR by 80 basis points, and during the most recent 10-year period, prime exceeded 3-month LIBOR by 152 basis points. The prime rate–commercial paper rate spread and the prime rate–LIBOR spread have both widened during the past decade as compared to the previous decade. Thus, if a company that would normally borrow at prime has the opportunity to borrow at LIBOR plus a spread of say 1%, the LIBOR-based loan should prove cheaper based on recent experience. More important, banks have, to an increasing extent, offered their U.S. customers the opportunity to select from among several options, including, for example, prime, 3-month LIBOR plus 0.5%, 6-month LIBOR plus 0.5%, etc., at the beginning of each interest period. The rate comparison provided in Table 25–4 demonstrates the Options Principle: having this flexibility can lead to significant cost savings.

SOLUTION TO DIVERSIFIED CHEMICAL'S WORKING CAPITAL MANAGEMENT PROBLEM

In the chapter, we solved Diversified Chemical's working capital management problem. To recap, the company's president had asked the company's treasurer to study the appropriateness of the company's policy of maintaining a current ratio of 2.0. The company's objective is to maintain a P-1/A-1 rating for its commercial paper. Based on a financial ratio analysis of A-1-rated commercial paper issuers, we concluded that Diversified Chemical should try to achieve a minimum current ratio of 2.0, but should set its planning target at a slightly higher level.

SUMMARY

Working capital management involves all aspects of the administration of current assets and current liabilities. This involves two classes of problems: (1) what are the appropriate levels of cash, marketable securities, receivables, and inventories, and (2) the appropriate level and mix of short-term indebtedness. In managing their working capital, companies normally find it prudent to finance the permanent component of current assets on a long-term basis and to maintain a margin of safety besides.

The degree of liquidity varies from one industry to another. These differences are due to differences in profitability, differing degrees of cyclicality, and differences in the relative liquidity of longer-term assets. In general, the lower its relative profitability, the more cyclical its business, and the less liquid its longer-term assets, the greater the amount of liquid assets and the wider the safety margin a firm needs to maintain in order to achieve a particular overall degree of liquidity.

A firm can select an appropriate current ratio objective by studying comparable companies in the same industry that have the desired commercial paper rating to identify a reasonable range of values for this ratio. It can then evaluate the impact of different values within this range on its reported financial results and on its financial ratios in order to decide which specific current ratio objective is most appropriate.

DECISION SUMMARY BOX

- Working capital management involves selecting the appropriate levels of cash, marketable securities, receivables, and inventories, and the appropriate level and mix of short-term indebtedness. It is useful to break down the working capital management problem into two basic types of decisions: (1) the choice of current ratio objective and (2) the mix of current assets and the mix of current liabilities.

- A firm can select an appropriate current ratio objective by observing the current ratios of comparable firms that have the firm's desired commercial paper rating. The commercial paper rating serves as a proxy for the firm's degree of liquidity risk. A firm that wants to maintain a very liquid financial condition (and if it is a commercial paper issuer, to maintain uninterrupted access to the commercial paper market) should strive to achieve a current ratio consistent with a P-1/A-1 commercial paper rating. The firm may wish to set a higher current ratio objective to maintain a margin of safety.

- A firm should extend credit to a customer only if its expected profit from doing so is positive.

- A firm should establish an inventory policy that minimizes its combined costs of reordering and carrying inventories. The EOQ model, which rests on certain simplifying assumptions, provides a good approximation when the unit sales rate is relatively high and relatively uniform over time and the cost of being out of stock is very low. When the cost of being out of stock is significant relative to its profitability, a firm should maintain safety stocks. The appropriate safety stock level is the amount that minimizes the combined costs of stockouts and carrying the additional inventory.

- A firm should establish a cash management policy that minimizes its total cost of maintaining cash balances. With regard to transaction cash balances, such a policy involves balancing the income forgone when funds are held in the form of cash and cash equivalents on the one hand and the transaction costs involved in converting securities into cash on the other. When cash inflows and cash outflows are highly variable, a model such as the Miller-Orr model should be used to determine the optimal level of cash balances commensurate with the uncertainty of the firm's cash requirements.

- A firm should calculate the cost of funds from each available source on a consistent basis, taking into account differences in how interest is calculated, differences in the timing of interest and principal payments, any compensating balance requirements, transaction costs, and any other factors that might affect the cost of funds.

- Commercial paper is generally the cheapest source of funds for large creditworthy companies that have access to this market. Nevertheless, firms normally continue to borrow some amount from commercial banks and use other commercial bank services to have access to bank funding should it ever be needed.

A firm should select a degree of liquidity that will minimize the risk of technical insolvency. It can then employ an inventory approach to estimate the optimal level of transaction cash balances. The firm would hold the remainder of its desired level of liquid resources in the form of marketable securities. The firm chooses the desired level of receivables by balancing the incremental revenues against the incremental costs. It chooses the desired levels of inventories by minimizing the combined cost of carrying inventory and reordering the materials and goods it needs to operate its business.

There are three principal sources of short-term funds: trade credit, bank loans, and commercial paper. Trade credit is the most prevalent but also generally the most expensive. Commercial paper is the cheapest for those firms that can access this market and is growing very rapidly in importance. Nevertheless, firms that can issue commercial paper normally continue to borrow from commercial banks in order to maintain ready access to this source of funds.

This chapter described techniques for estimating the cost of short-term funds from each of these sources. Equation (25.6) provides the annualized cost of trade credit. Equation (25.8) provides the true interest cost of bank borrowings when compensating balances are required, assuming interest is paid in arrears. If interest is paid in advance rather than in arrears, the true interest cost of borrowing funds is higher. This is the case with discounted notes such as commercial paper. Equation (25.11) provides the annualized cost of borrowing for commercial paper on a bond-equivalent basis. This permits a meaningful comparison with the interest costs calculated using Equations (25.6) and (25.8). A prospective borrower who has access to more than one source of short-term funds can use Equations (25.6), (25.8), and (25.11) to compare the costs and determine which source affords the required funds at the lowest cost.

PROBLEMS

PROBLEM SET A

A1. Explain what is meant by the term **working capital management**. What are the different aspects of working capital management, and how do they interrelate?

A2. Define the term **margin of safety**. Explain why a firm would normally want to maintain a positive margin of safety.

A3. What are the three basic motives for holding cash? Explain each motive.

A4. Briefly describe the principal near-money substitutes in which corporations invest.

A5. Explain how the quantity K in Equation (25.2) varies with respect to a change in each of the following:
  a. Fixed transaction cost C.
  b. Rate of cash utilization A.
  c. Interest rate r.

A6. Should a corporation always strive to achieve a target cash balance K given by Equation (25.2)? A target average cash balance $K/2$? Under what circumstances would such a target be appropriate?

A7. Define the term **economic order quantity**. How does the economic order quantity vary with respect to a change in:
  a. Utilization, or sales, rate S.
  b. Reordering cost C_r per order.
  c. Unit carrying cost C_C.

A8. What is meant by the term **safety stocks**? Why would a company normally find it advantageous to maintain safety stocks in its inventory?

A9. What are the three principal sources of short-term funds? Describe the distinguishing features of each. Which of the three is the most flexible?

A10. What are the principal factors that affect a company's choice of an appropriate short-term debt level?

A11. Explain why **trade credit** involves zero cost to the borrower when the funds are repaid before the end of the **discount period**.

A12. Describe the following four basic forms of bank loans:
  a. Line of credit.
  b. Revolving credit.
  c. Transaction loan.
  d. Term loan.

A13. A bank loan agreement calls for an interest rate equal to prime rate plus 1%. If prime rate averages 9% and non–interest-earning compensating balances equal to 10% of the loan must be maintained, what is the true interest cost of the loan?

A14. Explain what it means to sell a note on a **discount basis**. Why does a 10% discount note involve a higher true interest cost than a note that pays 10% interest in arrears?

A15. What is the difference between **bond equivalent yield** and **coupon equivalent yield**?

A16. The discount rate for a 54-day issue of commercial paper is 8.50%. What is the coupon equivalent yield?

PROBLEM SET B

B1. A company's balance sheet contains the following entries:

Assets ($ millions)		Liabilities & Equity ($ millions)	
Cash and marketable securities	$ 20	Notes payable	$ 15
Receivables	40	Long-term debt:	
Inventories	30	Current portion	10
Other current assets	10	Other	40
Plant, property, and equipment	100	Other current liabilities	25
Other assets	25	Other liabilities	10
Total assets	$225	Preferred equity	15
		Common equity	110
		Total liabilities and equity	$225

a. Calculate the **current ratio.**

b. Calculate the amount of **net working capital.**

c. Explain how you would go about determining whether the company has excess liquidity.

d. If 30% of the current assets are permanent, calculate the safety margin.

B2. Explain the steps a firm should follow in selecting an appropriate current ratio objective? What assumptions underlie this procedure?

B3. A company projects a need for $2 million cash per month. Its projected 30-day investment yield is 9% per annum. The cost of converting securities into cash is $300 per transaction.

a. How often should the company plan to sell securities?

b. How much cash would it raise each time it sells securities?

c. What will be the average cash balance?

d. What critical assumptions underlie your answers to parts a, b, and c?

B4. Suppose that the cash flows of the company in problem B3 are uncertain and have an estimated variance of 3.21 billion per day.

a. Calculate the lower and upper control limits.

b. When and in what amounts should the company buy and sell securities?

c. What will be the average cash balance?

d. Relate your answer to part c to your answer to part c in problem B3.

B5. Atlas Manufacturing sells milling machines to textile manufacturers for $50,000 per machine. The machines cost $35,000 each to manufacture, and selling and related expenses per machine amount to $7,500. Atlas has found that new customers for its milling machines pay 85% of the time and in an average of 60 days. Roughly one out of five customers makes a repeat purchase, an average of 10 years after the initial purchase. Collection costs average $50 per account per month, and Atlas's required rate of return on receivables is 1.5% per month compounded monthly. Should Atlas extend credit to Mister Quilter, Inc., a prospective new customer?

B6. Zodiac Sporting Goods maintains inventories of golf bags, which it purchases from an outside supplier. Zodiac sells golf bags at the rate of 5,000 per month. Its cost of placing an order for golf bags is $500 per order, and its cost of carrying a golf bag in inventory for a week is $2.

   a. Calculate the economic order quantity.

   b. How often should Zodiac reorder golf bags?

   c. If the cost of placing an order rises to $1,000, how will the economic order quantity be affected? Explain.

B7. Brown Pontiac maintains an inventory of tires. The dealer uses tires at a constant rate of 1,000 per month. The dealer's cost of placing a new order is $500 per order. The cost of carrying a tire in inventory for a year is $5.

   a. Calculate the economic order quantity.

   b. Calculate the impact on the economic order quantity of a doubling of the (1) usage rate, (2) reordering cost, and (3) carrying cost.

   c. Brown Pontiac has found that if it is out of stock when a customer arrives, it will make the eventual sale only 20% of the time. For each lost sale, Brown Pontiac loses the net margin of $30 per tire. Lost sales as well as back orders involve record-keeping costs of $10 per stockout. It costs Brown Pontiac $12 to keep a tire in inventory for a year. Brown Pontiac has estimated the following benefit of maintaining safety stocks:

Safety stock	100	125	150	175	200
Stockouts per year	75	50	35	30	30

   What level of safety stock should Brown Pontiac maintain?

B8. East Publishing Company offers its authors a 3% discount off the invoice price if they pay for the books they order within 15 days of the invoice date. Otherwise payment in full is due within 25 days of the invoice date.

   a. What is the real price as a fraction of the invoice price?

   b. What is the authors' annualized cost of trade credit if they pay within 25 days?

   c. What is the authors' annualized cost of trade credit if they pay on the 16th day?

   d. What would you conclude based on your answers to parts b and c?

B9. A $10,000 discount note maturing in 63 days is sold at a discount rate of 10.25%.

   a. Calculate the bond equivalent yield.

   b. Calculate the coupon equivalent yield.

   c. How would you interpret your answers to parts a and b?

B10. A corporate cash manager is evaluating three investment alternatives:

   1. 12% discount note maturing in 90 days.

   2. 12.4% CD maturing in 90 days bearing interest on the basis of a 360–day year.

   3. 12.5% Treasury note maturing in 90 days bearing interest based on a 365–day year.

   a. On what basis should the yields be compared?

   b. Calculate the yields on a comparable basis.

   c. Which alternative offers the highest yield?

B11. Zodiac Sporting Goods is considering extending credit to a large department store chain, which is rumored to be facing a liquidity problem. The chain will purchase from Zodiac only if Zodiac extends credit. Zodiac estimates an order size of $100,000 for goods that cost $60,000 to manufacture. Zodiac estimates a 95% likelihood that the chain will pay for the order and expects payment within 30 days. Zodiac estimates an 80% probability of a repeat purchase. Collection costs will be $100, and Zodiac's required rate of return (compounded monthly) is 18% per annum.

    a. Calculate the expected profit of granting credit.

    b. Suppose the chain would make the $100,000 purchase even if credit were not granted. What is the expected profit of granting credit? In that case, should Zodiac grant credit?

    c. What is the break-even probability of payment (expected profit in part a becomes zero)?

B12. Specific Motors Acceptance Corporation sells medium-term discount notes through a dealer who charges a commission of $\frac{1}{10}$ of 1% for 180-day notes. If the discount notes are sold at a discount rate of 11%, calculate:

    a. The TIC on a bond-equivalent basis.

    b. The TIC on a coupon-equivalent basis.

PROBLEM SET C

C1. Let A denote the amount of cash required per period, C the cost per transaction of converting securities to cash, K the quantity of cash to be raised each time securities are sold, and r the interest rate per period.

    a. If cash is used uniformly throughout the period, what is the average cash balance?

    b. What is the interest cost per period of maintaining the average cash balance in part a?

    c. What is the number of securities transactions per period needed to raise the desired amounts of cash?

    d. What are the total transaction costs per period?

    e. Find an expression for the aggregate cost of idle cash balances and securities transactions.

    f. Find the value of K that minimizes the expression in part e and show that it equals Equation (25.2).

C2. Discuss how the firm's inventory management problem could be modeled as a capital investment problem. Discuss how the firm's accounts receivable management problem could be modeled as a capital investment problem.

C3. The following receivables management model is different from Equation (25.4). The customer who is granted credit and pays will make one or more repeat purchases with probability P_Q, and these repeat purchases have present-value profitability Z.

    a. Modify Equation (25.4) to handle this problem.

    b. Reconsider the problem facing Marion Minicomputer Manufacturing. Suppose roughly one out of four customers makes repeat purchases and the expected profitability of these repeat purchases has net present value $1,800. Calculate the expected present value profit of granting credit.

C4. Derive the EOQ model expressed as Equation (25.5).

    a. Find an expression for the annual reordering cost.

    b. Find an expression for the annual inventory holding cost.

    c. Find an expression for the aggregate annual inventory cost.

    d. Find the reorder quantity EOQ that minimizes the annual inventory cost and show that it equals EOQ in Equation (25.5).

C5. Let d denote the actual number of days elapsed until a specified discount note matures, i the discount rate (expressed per annum on a 360-day basis), P the principal (or face) amount of the discount note, and r the bond equivalent yield.

    a. Show that the price required to purchase the discount note is $P - idP/360$.

    b. Show that if the sum determined in part a is invested at the interest rate r calculated on the basis of the actual number of days elapsed in a 360-day year, then $P = (P - idP/360)(1 + rd/365)$.

    c. Solve the expression in part b for the bond equivalent yield r.

C6. Calculate an expression for the equivalent (coupon-bearing debt) cost of a discount note when interest is calculated on the basis of 12 months of 30 days each in a 360-day year.

REFERENCES

Aigner, Dennis J., and Case M. Sprenkle. "On Optimal Financing of Cyclical Cash Needs." *Journal of Finance* 28 (December 1973): 1249–54.

Baumol, William J. "The Transactions Demand for Cash: An Inventory Theoretic Approach." *Quarterly Journal of Economics* 66 (November 1952): 545–56.

Budin, Morris, and Robert J. Van Handel. "A Rule-of-Thumb Theory of Cash Holdings by Firms." *Journal of Financial and Quantitative Analysis* 10 (March 1975): 85–108.

Crane, Dwight B., and William L. White. "Who Benefits from a Floating Prime Rate?" *Harvard Business Review* 50 (January-February 1972): 121–29.

Daellenbach, Hans G. "Are Cash Management Optimization Models Worthwhile?" *Journal of Financial and Quantitative Analysis* 9 (September 1974): 607–26.

Debt Ratings Criteria: Industrial Overview. New York: Standard & Poor's, 1986.

Emery, Gary W. "A Pure Financial Explanation for Trade Credit." *Journal of Financial and Quantitative Analysis* 19 (September 1984): 271–85.

Finnerty, John D. "Bank Discount, Coupon Equivalent, and Compound Yields: Comment." *Financial Management* 12 (Summer 1983): 40–45.

Gitman, Lawrence J., and Charles E. Maxwell. "Financial Activities of Major U.S. Firms: Survey and Analysis of Fortune's 1000." *Financial Management* 14 (Winter 1985): 57–65.

Hayes, Douglas A. *Bank Lending Policies: Domestic and International.* Ann Arbor, Mich.: University of Michigan, 1971.

Kallberg, Jarl G., and Kenneth K. Parkinson. *Current Asset Management.* New York: John Wiley and Sons, 1984.

Miller, Merton H., and Daniel Orr. "A Model of the Demand for Money by Firms." *Quarterly Journal of Economics* 80 (August 1966): 413–35.

Nadler, Paul S. "Compensating Balances and the Prime at Twilight." *Harvard Business Review* 50 (January-February 1972): 112–20.

Petty, J. William, II, and David F. Scott, Jr. "The Heterogeneity of Corporate Liquidity: Industry and Risk Group Effects." *Journal of Economics and Business* 32 (Spring 1980): 206–18.

Robichek, Alexander A., Daniel Teichroew, and J. M. Jones. "Optimal Short-Term Financing Decisions." *Management Science* 12 (September 1965): 1–36.

Sartoris, William L., and Ned C. Hill. "A Generalized Cash Flow Approach to Short-Term Financial Decisions." *Journal of Finance* 38 (May 1983): 349–60.

Schadrack, Frederick C., Jr. "Demand and Supply in the Commercial Paper Market." *Journal of Finance* 25 (September 1970): 837–52.

Smith, Keith B. *Management of Working Capital.* New York: West Publishing, 1974.

Smith, P. F. "Measuring Risk on Consumer Installment Credit." *Management Science* 11 (November 1964): 327–40.

Stigum, Marcia. *Money Market Calculations.* Homewood, Ill.: Dow Jones–Irwin, 1981.

Stone, Bernell K. "The Cost of Bank Loans." *Journal of Financial and Quantitative Analysis* 7 (December 1972): 2077–86.

Stowe, John D. "An Integer Programming Solution for the Optimal Credit Investigation/ Credit Granting Sequence." *Financial Management* 14 (Summer 1985): 66–76.

Stowe, John D., and Adam K. Gehr, Jr. "Contracting Costs and Trade Credit." Presented at the Western Finance Association Meeting, Scottsdale, Arizona, 1985.

FINANCIAL PLANNING AND SHORT-TERM TREASURY MANAGEMENT

Corporate financial planning is essentially the process of establishing a blueprint for the future of the corporation. Planning is necessary to (1) determine the goals of the organization, (2) specify which operating and financial strategies the corporation will follow to achieve those goals, (3) establish a set of projected operating results that can be used to monitor and measure performance, and (4) develop contingency plans to deal with unforeseen circumstances. A firm should not simply react to events as they unfold; it must be prepared to deal swiftly and effectively with adverse developments.

Competitive forces in the capital markets—and in other markets—make it difficult to find and execute positive-NPV decisions. However, mistakes and poor planning make negative-NPV outcomes an ever-present possibility. Factors within the past decade or so have led to increased corporate attention to the need for sound financial planning and corporate cash management. During the 1970s, the rate of inflation and interest rates increased sharply. Higher interest rates increased the opportunity cost of idle cash balances. Since 1980, interest rates have become increasingly volatile, and there has been a pronounced tendency to increase corporate leverage, the latter due in large part to the leveraged buyout phenomenon.[1] Higher leverage coupled with increasingly volatile interest rates increase the financial risk of a firm, thereby making effective planning and cash management imperative. Also, rapidly improving computer technology in the 1970s and the 1980s has made possible significant advances in the cash management services commercial banks provide to corporations. At the same time, the cash management literature blossomed, giving corporate financial officers useful guidance as to how best to use the new cash management tools at their disposal.[2]

This chapter develops a unified framework for corporate financial planning. The chapter describes the corporate financial planning process, discusses the principal components of a financial plan, develops an integrated planning model that incorporates the policy decisions that were analyzed in previous chapters, discusses how the more detailed short-term plan and cash budgets tie into the long-term plan, and describes the interrelationship between cash budgeting and day-to-day treasury cash management. We discuss both long-term planning and short-term planning in the same chapter because the short-term plan, typically an annual plan, is normally a more detailed plan that corresponds to the first year of the long-term plan. We also discuss cash budgeting and Treasury cash management in this chapter because the cash budgets are generally prepared directly from the short-term plan for periods a

---

[1] According to Federal Reserve data, repurchases and redemptions of common stocks exceeded new share issues by $96 billion during 1988 and by $287 billion during the period 1985–1988. "Stock Market Faced Massive Exodus in '88," *Wall Street Journal*, December 29, 1988, C1.

[2] Gentry (1988) provides a review of this literature.

week, a month, a quarter, and a year ahead. The cash budgets are regularly updated, at least weekly at many companies, to reflect the cash management performance of the firm's treasury department.

FINANCIAL PLANNING AT THE YU N. MI TOY COMPANY

Justin Case, the new treasurer of the Yu N. Mi Toy Company (MTC), a privately-held manufacturing firm, discovers on his first day on the job that the firm does not have a formal cash budgeting system. Yu N. Mi, the chairman and principal stock-holder of the firm, reportedly told the treasurer's predecessor not to worry "because we have plenty of money in the bank," most of which the new treasurer discovers is deposited in non-interest-bearing accounts. Mr. Case would like to develop a more effective cash management program to help with the formulation of contingent plans. He believes that the first step in this process is to develop a model of the firm's

TABLE 26–1   Information about the Yu N. Mi Toy Company, Compiled by Justin Case

1. The payment pattern for revenues is estimated to be as follows: 40% of sales are for cash, 10% are paid for 1 month after the sale, 50% are paid for 2 months after the sale, and bad debt is negligible.
2. Justin Case estimates that the cash account should be set to start each month in the amount of $10,000 plus 60% of next month's salaries and wages plus 70% of this month's accounts payable. He plans to adjust the cash account with the short-term investment (borrowing) account, and believes MTC can earn .6% per month on its short-term investments.
3. MTC appears to purchase raw materials each month in the amount of 30% of the predicted sales for the month after next plus 20% of next month's predicted sales plus 10% of this month's sales. Purchases are paid for in the month following their purchase, and there are no discounts available to MTC from its suppliers. The cost of raw materials averages 60% of sales.
4. MTC pays salaries and wages of $7,000 plus 18% of this month's sales.
5. MTC is depreciating its net fixed assets at the rate of 1% of *net* fixed assets per month.
6. MTC pays a cash dividend of $2,000 every month.
7. The long-term debt on the MTC balance sheet carries a 12% A.P.R., and payments are made quarterly in Dec., Mar., June, and Sept.
8. Taxes for MTC are at the rate of 35% of taxable income (including rebates for negative taxes). Taxes are paid monthly.
9. Sales in October and November of this year were $40,000 and $60,000, respectively. Sales forecast for the next 11 months are (in thousands)

Dec.	Jan.	Feb.	Mar.	Apr.	May	Jun.	Jul.	Aug.	Sep.	Oct.
100.00	170.00	150.00	125.00	100.00	70.00	65.00	90.00	175.00	50.00	70.00

Balance Sheet as of November 30

Cash	$ 76.00	Accounts payable	$ 77.00
Short-term investment (borrowing)	70.00	Accrued interest	6.00
Accounts receivable	56.00	Long-term debt	300.00
Inventory	122.00	Common stock	70.00
Net fixed assets	391.00	Retained earnings	262.00
Total Assets	$715.00	Liabilities + Owners' Equity	$715.00

financial activities. (Yu N. Mi agrees that "we need this model, Justin Case.") The firm is a small manufacturer with a stable customer base and stable supplier relationships. Reliable cash inflow and cash outflow data for several years are readily available. The treasurer needs to resolve the following issues:

- What form should the model take?
- What period(s) should it cover, and how frequently should it be updated?

Table 26–1 provides information that Justin Case has gathered about the Yu N. Mi Toy Co., including a current balance sheet. In this chapter we provide the tools to use this information to construct an appropriate model of the firm's financial activities. The solution to Mr. Case's problem is given in a spreadsheet model presented in section 26.5, automating short-term forecasts.

CORPORATE FINANCIAL PLANNING   26.1

WHAT IS CORPORATE FINANCIAL PLANNING?

Corporate financial planning might be defined in the following manner. It is a process in which a firm:

- formulates a set of consistent business and financial objectives for the firm that identifies where management would like to have the firm in the future;

- projects the financial impact of alternative operating strategies (which are identified in the firm's strategic and operating planning processes) under alternative financial policies (capital structure policy, dividend policy, etc.) and under differing assumptions as to the firm's future operating environment;

- weighs these consequences and decides which financial policies to adopt and what sort of long-term financing and short-term financing program to pursue; and

- prepares contingency plans to alter its basic financial strategies in the event future developments should differ from those now expected.

Certain aspects of this definition deserve emphasis.

Financial planning involves analyzing the interactions among the capital investment, capital structure, dividend, liquidity, financing, and liability management options available to a firm. These subjects were treated separately earlier in the book. They come together in financial planning. The whole is not simply the sum of the parts. It is therefore important for a firm to consider explicitly the interactions among the various policy decisions.

Financial planning involves more than forecasting. Forecasting concentrates on the expected outcome. The real value of financial planning is that it helps the firm prepare for *deviations* from the expected outcome.

The emphasis in financial planning is on analysis rather than strict optimization. Financial planning indicates the expected consequences of alternative courses of action. In the end, top management must judge which plan is best. Financial planning helps a firm evaluate anticipated returns and risks and determine a reasonable set of strategies and contingencies, which is embodied in its **financial plan**.

Financial planning typically consists of two phases. First, the firm prepares a **long-term financial plan**. Most companies have a long-term planning horizon of between 3 and 5 years, although some companies, like utilities, involved in industries requiring longer lead times for capital budgeting projects often adopt longer

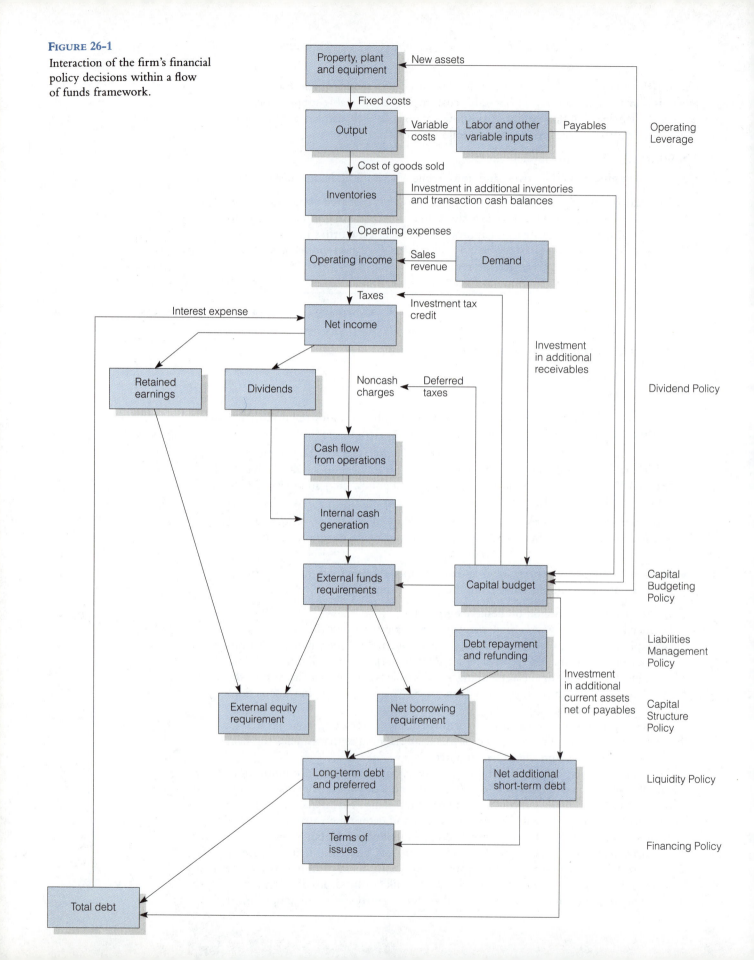

Figure 26-1

Interaction of the firm's financial policy decisions within a flow of funds framework.

planning horizons. Second, the firm also prepares a more detailed **short-term financial plan**, which contains a **cash budget** for the coming year, based on the first year of the long-term plan. The long-term plan reflects the firm's strategic choices and financial policy choices over the planning period, and the short-term plan and cash budget reflect the firm's operating plan for the coming year. Most companies update their financial plan annually.

AN OVERVIEW AND REVIEW OF THE BUSINESS ENTERPRISE OVER TIME

The business enterprise is a dynamic system. Its capital budgeting, capital structure, dividend, liquidity, financing, and liabilities management decisions continually interact. This interaction can be described using the flow of funds framework. Figure 26–1 illustrates this interaction for a typical manufacturing firm.

The principal net source of funds is the firm's operations. The firm utilizes its fixed assets consisting of property, plant, and equipment together with labor, raw materials, and other variable inputs to produce goods for sale. The sales revenue it realizes less the cost of goods sold and operating expenses, such as selling, general, and administrative expenses, equals the firm's operating income. After paying income taxes, the balance is available for distribution to the providers of capital or for reinvestment. An interesting question that arises in connection with financial planning is how operating income responds to increases in output. This depends on the degree of operating leverage in the firm's cost structure. Recall from Chapter 10 that the higher the fixed cost component of total costs, the greater the operating risk.

Net income remains after the payment of interest expense to bondholders and taxes. Net income can be distributed to the firm's shareholders or can be retained for reinvestment in the business. The division of net income between distributions to shareholders and retained earnings depends on the firm's dividend policy. The amount of distribution interacts with both the amount and mix of external financing requirements. A higher distribution proportion increases external financing requirements and, given the firm's capital structure policy, also increases the proportion of funds that must be raised through a new equity issue in order to preserve the desired capital structure.

The volume of external financing is determined chiefly by the size of the firm's capital budget in relation to the amount of funds generated internally. The capital budget is in turn affected by the projected level of sales. Increased sales will eventually require expenditures for planned expansions and additional equipment. In addition, higher production rates cause machines to wear out faster so the need for replacement investment also increases. Higher sales levels will also require additional investment in working capital.

The size of the capital budget, together with the amount of funds generated internally, thus determines the firm's external funds requirements. The addition to retained earnings, together with the firm's capital structure policy, will determine the appropriate debt/equity mix for this new financing. The planned investment in current assets net of the intended increases in payables will determine, in light of the firm's liquidity policy, how large a net increase (decrease) in short-term borrowing is appropriate. The balance of the firm's borrowing requirements should be met on a long-term basis, possibly by issuing some preferred equity in addition to (or in place of) long-term debt, depending on the firm's tax position and capital structure objectives. The firm's tax position will be affected to a large extent by the volume of tax deductions and credits generated by its capital spending program and its level of borrowing.

The total long-term borrowing requirement will include the net additional amount just determined plus amounts to cover debt repayment and early refunding, if any, if the firm wishes to preserve its capital structure. Finally, the terms of the debt (and/or preferred equity) issues will have to be determined in the light of the firm's financing policy. The result of the debt issuance decision is a change in the firm's overall interest expense, which will affect net income and hence cash flow from operations, internal cash generation, external funds requirements, etc.

The process illustrated in Figure 26–1 is a continuing one. Yet the total sources of funds to the firm and the total uses of funds by the firm must be equal for any finite planning period. While it is true that for relatively short periods of time this equality might be achieved by either unintended changes in cash balances or unforeseen short-term borrowing requirements, the firm will attempt through its financial planning efforts to avoid these inefficiencies. It will strive to accomplish all six of the basic financial policies simultaneously, recognizing that it will have to make certain trade-offs. These trade-offs can be analyzed within a corporate financial planning model.

COMPONENTS OF A FINANCIAL PLAN

A firm's financial plan involves a high degree of aggregation. Financial planning is not concerned with specific project-by-project analyses. Rather, it is concerned with the forecasted overall funds position of the enterprise and how the reported financial results of the enterprise would look if everything were to go according to plan.

The principal components of an effective corporate financial plan include

- A clear statement of the corporation's **strategic**, **operating**, and **financial objectives**.

- A clear statement of the business and economic *assumptions* on which the plan is based.

- A description of the **basic business strategies** for each of the firm's principal lines of business and a clear statement of how the managers within each line of business would alter their basic strategies in the event any of the principal contingencies they foresee (e.g., economic adversity, differing responses by competitors, etc.) actually occurs.

- An outline of the **planned capital expenditure program**, including breakdowns by time period (e.g., by year), by division and/or line of business, and by category (e.g., for plant expansion, for replacement of existing equipment, for acquisitions, etc.). The capital expenditure program also often includes a description of the major capital investment projects.

- An outline of the **planned financing program**, including breakdowns by time period, by source of funds (i.e., external versus internal), and by class of security (i.e., senior long-term debt, preferred stock, common stock, etc.).

- A set of **pro forma statements**, including period-by-period income statements, balance sheets, and statements of cash flows. The pro forma income statements will illustrate the projected operating results. The pro forma balance sheets and statements of cash flows will indicate the projected changes in financial condition.

RISK

Chapter 10 introduced the concept of leverage; both **financial leverage** and **operating leverage**. Recall that the amount of leverage is determined by the proportions of fixed costs versus variable costs: A larger proportion of fixed costs versus variable costs creates higher leverage and consequently higher risk; a smaller proportion of fixed costs versus variable costs creates lower leverage and consequently lower risk. We showed that operating leverage affects the total risk of the firm and that financial leverage affects how that total risk is borne by the firm's securityholders.

OPERATING LEVERAGE   As shown in Chapter 10, operating leverage is analogous to financial leverage. However, unlike capital structure decisions, a firm's decisions concerning operating leverage are not generally made in an efficient market environment. Also, the firm often has few alternatives concerning its level of operating leverage. Quite simply, in many cases, production efficiencies require that the firm have a particular degree of operating leverage to be competitive and that degree of operating leverage carries with it a given level of operating risk: The greater the degree of operating leverage, the greater the operating risk. In a sense, then, a firm's operating risk level is often less a choice of risk level and more a result of technological production possibilities and economic conditions.

As noted above, operating leverage increases with the level of fixed costs so that, in general, firms in capital-intensive industries, such as the airline, machinery, mining, and steel industries, have comparatively high degrees of operating leverage and consequently higher operating risk; firms in less capital-intensive industries, such as the service industries, have relatively lower degrees of operating leverage and consequently lower operating risk.

FINANCIAL LEVERAGE   Recall that in a perfect capital market, a firm's choice of capital structure—its financial leverage—does not alter its value but simply reflects the firm's risk-return trade-off; i.e., financial leverage represents a chosen risk level along the capital market's risk-return spectrum. As discussed in Chapters 15 and 16, however, capital market imperfections such as tax asymmetries, information asymmetries, and transaction costs can cause a firm's choice of capital structure to affect the value of the firm. Therefore, a firm may choose its capital structure to maximize its value. Such a capital structure choice carries with it a given level of financial risk: The greater the financial leverage, the greater the financial risk. As in the case of operating risk, then, a firm's financial risk level may result from capital market imperfections rather than simply being a choice of risk level.

COMBINED OPERATING AND FINANCIAL LEVERAGE   From the above discussions of leverage, you can see that a firm's total risk often depends to a large extent on conditions outside the control of the firm. Outside conditions notwithstanding, as we noted in Chapter 10, the firm typically has much more control over its financial risk than it does over its operating risk. As such, financial leverage is typically the tool used to control the total risk of the firm. In the final analysis, however, although the firm may not be entirely free to choose its risk level, it must be managed in accordance with whatever its combined financial and operating risk is. One measure of that risk involves the concept of break-even.

In Chapter 12, we introduced the **break-even** concept with respect to accounting earnings and noted that a firm operating a project at its break-even point for a prolonged period would likely be better off exercising its abandonment option. However, even though the accounting-earnings break-even point is not a desirable target for performance, the break-even concept, applied to cash flow, can provide a pivotal point in connection with the planning process. Over the planning horizon, the **cash-flow break-even point** is the point below which the firm will need to either obtain additional financing or liquidate some of its assets to meet its fixed cost obligations (including such items as fixed salaries and administrative costs, interest and principal payments, and planned cash dividends). The existence of the cash-flow break-even point is pivotal in that it "forces" the firm to address contingency plans for possible but perhaps unlikely bad outcomes. Note that we are not suggesting that forecasting outcomes above this break-even point is all that is necessary to continue in business. Still, a temporary downturn in economic conditions may force a firm below the cash-flow break-even point and possibly even into costly financial distress and perhaps eventually bankruptcy, even if the firm's portfolio of projects has a positive NPV.

The probability of falling below the cash-flow break-even point during the planning horizon can be thought of as a measure of the firm's total risk. This probability depends on both the variability of sales and on how close the firm is to its cash-flow break-even point when adversity begins to set in.

It is important to keep the possible effects of financial leverage and operating leverage in mind when preparing the financial plan for a firm. Both are sources of risk. Thus, to control the risk that it will be unable to meet, for example, its contractual debt payment obligations, a firm can, to whatever extent possible, (1) change the proportion of debt in its capital structure, thereby changing its financial leverage, (2) change the relative proportions of fixed costs versus variable costs in its production function, thereby changing both its operating leverage and its break-even point, or (3) effect some combination of the two. To the extent that, especially, operating leverage cannot be controlled by a firm, the firm should use the planning process to control risk by creating contingency plans for dealing with bad outcomes.

26.2   A FINANCIAL PLANNING MODEL

Most large corporations utilize some form of model to assist them in the financial planning process.[3] These models are generally constructed around the firm's forecast cash flows. They are also typically simulation models, which project the financial impact of alternative strategies and financial policies under specified assumptions regarding the firm's future operating environment. The level of detail and degree of sophistication exhibited by these models vary widely, owing in large part to differences in specific user requirements.

The principal output of the financial modeling process is a set of pro forma financial statements—projected income statements, projected statements of cash flows, and projected balance sheets—for each of the business-environment commercial-strategy financial-policy combinations under consideration. Management reviews these in order to select the most preferred commercial-strategy financial-policy mix. It is important to appreciate that it is the expert judgment of the firm's managers, rather than an optimizing routine contained in the planning model, that ultimately determines which course of action the firm will follow.

This section develops an elementary planning model. The model is less sophisticated than the planning models used by most firms. This is done intentionally. More sophisticated models, while perhaps more useful in practical applications, would contain more detail than we require in order to illustrate the financial planning process.

ROLE OF FINANCIAL FORECASTING

Financial forecasting is a crucial part of the corporate financial planning process. The financial forecast not only furnishes business projections but also quantifies expected

[3] Meyer (1977) provides a more thorough discussion of corporate financial planning models and how to construct and use them than is possible in the limited space available here.

financing requirements and identifies internal and external funds sources to meet those requirements. Typically, each of a firm's various business units will formulate its own plan, and these separate plans will be aggregated to form the firm's business plan. This may involve, for example, each division forecasting its unit sales and the prices it will receive for its products. It is important that these various forecasts be consistent; they should be based on a common forecast of the possible outcomes of inflation, overall level of economic activity, level of interest rates, etc. Achieving consistency requires that top management prepare a forecast of these macroeconomic variables and disseminate this forecast to each of the planning units. It also requires a careful checking of the business unit plans at the corporate level to ensure consistency with the corporate macroeconomic forecast.

Of course, it is also important that the firm's business plan be as accurate as possible, although planning is more art than science. Thus, the best one can realistically hope for is "reasonable" accuracy. Drawing on outside sources, such as the economic consulting firms that generate macroeconomic and industry forecasts, can often improve forecasting accuracy. But ultimately it will be necessary to formulate also contingency plans to guide the corporation when events unfold differently from what was assumed in the preparation of the "base case" plan.

SALES FORECASTING   The sales forecast for each product is normally prepared by the managers of the staff that sells it.[4] Senior management must check the underlying assumptions carefully. In particular, it is important to ensure that the sales forecast is not simply an extrapolation of recent sales results. The sales forecast should include projected market share. When available, market forecasts prepared by a competent economic or marketing forecasting source can be used to test the reasonableness of the sales forecast. The sales forecast should also include projections of unit volume and unit price rather than only a single figure for sales revenue. The forecasters should be required to justify significant changes from current unit volume and price, for example, explaining how competitors will react to a forecast decrease in unit price and how the price change and competitors' reactions have been factored into the unit volume projections.

FORECASTING COSTS   The costs of operating a business can be broken down into fixed costs, which are invariant to the rate of production, and variable costs, which vary directly with unit sales volume. Increasing the production of steel, for example, requires additional electricity, iron ore, labor, etc. The production department prepares the forecast of manufacturing requirements (raw materials, labor, etc.) from the unit sales volume projections. As noted in the preceding section, the firm's operating leverage determines how its total costs respond to a change in unit sales volume.

Fixed costs include indirect overhead costs, such as insurance, rental expense, and wages, salaries, and benefits for the corporate staff (including the planning department!). Each business unit calculates its own fixed costs. Corporate overhead is often charged to the divisions; e.g., for insurance services or funds for working capital that are centrally provided. In addition, a firm's accounting and tax departments prepare the forecasts of depreciation, depletion, and amortization (DD&A) for financial reporting and tax purposes, respectively.

A firm must also project its liability payment obligations. The bond indentures and loan agreements for outstanding debt and existing lease agreements will enable the firm to forecast interest expense and principal repayment obligations under exist-

---

[4]The procedures companies use for preparing sales forecasts are surveyed in Pan, Nichols, and Joy (1977).

ing agreements. One of the more important outputs of the financial planning process is the identification of external financing requirements or excess funds that will be generated. The planning process is iterative. For example, excess cash that is used to pay down debt reduces interest expense, which in turn frees up additional cash which could be used to repay even more debt, and so on. Of course, forecasting interest expense when additional borrowings are planned requires an interest rate forecast. Because of the inherent difficulty in making such forecasts, one of the critical sensitivity analyses a firm must perform is the sensitivity to rising interest rates.

FORECASTING OTHER CASH REQUIREMENTS   The approved capital budgets will indicate the capital expenditure requirements period by period. If the firm has preferred stock outstanding, those agreements specify the preferred dividend requirements. The firm's dividend policy will determine the cash dividend requirements on the firm's common stock. If the firm's strategic plan calls for one or more acquisitions, these are typically included in a supplementary forecast. The most critical aspect of cash planning is the (short-term) daily cash forecast, which is described later in the chapter.

THE MODEL

Table 26–2 lays out a simplified planning model. First we describe the model, and then we will illustrate its use. The model requires various input terms, including the projected change in net sales revenue (entered as ΔREVENUE for each year during the planning period), the projected change in interest rates (entered as ΔINTEREST RATE), the projected change in selling, general, and administrative expense (entered as ΔSG&A), a forecast of annual capital expenditures (entered as CAPEX), specification of critical financial policy variables (WC RATIO—working capital ratio, PAYOUT RATIO, and DEBT RATIO) and various other data.[6] With these data, the income statement equations, statement of cash flows equations, and balance sheet equations generate projected income statements, statements of cash flows, and balance sheets, respectively.

INCOME STATEMENT EQUATIONS   Eight equations generate the projected income statements. Equation (E1) projects future net sales revenue (REVENUE) as the sum of the preceding year's net sales revenue plus the forecast year-to-year change from the preceding year, where REVENUE (-1) denotes the level of net sales revenue in the preceding year. Equations (E3) and (E5) determine the projected level of selling, general, and administrative expense (SG&A) and the projected average interest rate

[5] The model and illustration are taken from Finnerty (1986).
[6] The working capital ratio, WC RATIO, is related to the firm's current ratio in the following manner: Suppose that current assets represent a fixed fraction, A, of net sales revenue,

$$\text{Current Assets} = A(\text{Revenue})$$

and that the current ratio (current assets divided by current liabilities) is fixed, so that

$$\text{Net Working Capital} = \text{Current Assets} - \text{Current Liabilities}$$

$$= (\text{Current Assets})\left(1 - \frac{1}{\text{Current Ratio}}\right)$$

$$= \left[\left(1 - \frac{1}{\text{Current Ratio}}\right)(A)\right](\text{Revenue})$$

The WC RATIO is just the expression in brackets. For example, if Current Ratio = 2 and A = Current Assets/Revenue = 0.4, then WC RATIO = .5(.4) = .2.

TABLE 26–2 A Scaled-Down Financial Planning Model

Input Items:

(I1) Year-to-year changes in net sales revenue (ΔREVENUE).

(I2) Gross profit margin (MARGIN), which is assumed to remain fixed over the planning period.

(I3) Year-to-year changes in selling, general, and administrative expense (ΔSG&A).

(I4) The rate of depreciation of fixed assets for financial reporting purposes (DEPRECIATION RATE), which is assumed to remain fixed over the planning period.

(I5) Embedded cost of long-term debt at the beginning of the planning period (INTEREST RATE[0]).

(I6) Year-to-year changes in the average cost of long-term debt (ΔINTEREST RATE).

(I7) Average tax rate (TAX RATE), which is assumed to remain fixed over the planning period and which is also assumed to be the same for both tax payment and financial reporting purposes.

(I8) A schedule of depreciation rates for tax purposes, which is used together with the amount of planned capital expenditures to determine the amount of depreciation expense for tax purposes for each year during the planning period (DEPRECIATION[TAX]).

(I9) Year-to-year expenditures for new property, plant, and equipment (CAPEX).

(I10) Ratio of the increase in net working capital to the increase in net sales revenue (WC RATIO), which is assumed to remain fixed over the planning period.

(I11) Target payout ratio (PAYOUT RATIO).

(I12) Repayment schedule for the planning period for long-term debt outstanding at the beginning of the period (REPAY).

(I13) Target ratio of long-term debt to total capitalization (DEBT RATIO).

(I14) Values of the following principal income statement and balance sheet items as of the beginning of the planning period: net sales revenue (REVENUE), working capital (WORKING CAPITAL), fixed assets (FIXED ASSETS), other long-term assets (OTHER ASSETS), long-term debt (DEBT), and shareholders' equity (EQUITY).

Income Statement Equations:

(E1) REVENUE = REVENUE[−1] + ΔREVENUE

(E2) COST OF GOODS SOLD = (1 − MARGIN)(REVENUE)

(E3) SG&A = SG&A[−1] + ΔSG&A

(E4) DEPRECIATION[BOOK] = (DEPRECIATION RATE)(FIXED ASSETS[−1])

(E5) INTEREST RATE = INTEREST RATE[−1] + ΔINTEREST RATE

(E6) INTEREST = (INTEREST RATE)(DEBT[−1])

(E7) TAX[BOOK] = (TAX RATE){REVENUE − COST OF GOODS SOLD − SG&A − DEPRECIATION[BOOK] − INTEREST}

(E8) NET INCOME = REVENUE − COST OF GOODS SOLD − SG&A − DEPRECIATION[BOOK] − INTEREST − TAX[BOOK]

Statement of Cash Flows Equations:

(E9) ΔDEFERRED TAXES = (TAX RATE){DEPRECIATION[BOOK] − DEPRECIATION[TAX]}

(E10) CASH FLOW = NET INCOME + DEPRECIATION[BOOK] + ΔDEFERRED TAXES

(E11) ΔWORKING CAPITAL = (WC RATIO)(ΔREVENUE)

(E12) DIVIDENDS = (PAYOUT RATIO)(NET INCOME)

(E13) FUNDS REQUIRED = CAPEX + ΔWORKING CAPITAL + REPAY + DIVIDENDS − CASH FLOW

(E14) NET DEBT ISSUE = (DEBT RATIO){EQUITY[−1] + NET INCOME − DIVIDENDS + DEBT[−1] − REPAY + FUNDS REQUIRED}
           − {DEBT[−1] − REPAY}

(E15) NET STOCK ISSUE = FUNDS REQUIRED − NET DEBT ISSUE

Balance Sheet Equations:

(E16) WORKING CAPITAL = WORKING CAPITAL[−1] + ΔWORKING CAPITAL

(E17) FIXED ASSETS = FIXED ASSETS[−1] + CAPEX − DEPRECIATION(BOOK)

(Continued)

TABLE 26–2   *(Continued)*

Balance Sheet Equations *(continued):*

(E18)   DEFERRED TAXES = DEFERRED TAXES$[-1]$ + ΔDEFERRED TAXES

(E19)   NET ASSETS = WORKING CAPITAL + FIXED ASSETS + OTHER ASSETS − DEFERRED TAXES

(E20)   DEBT = DEBT$[-1]$ − REPAY + NET DEBT ISSUE

(E21)   EQUITY = EQUITY$[-1]$ + NET INCOME − DIVIDENDS + NET STOCK ISSUE

Ratio Definitions:

(E22)   INTEREST COVERAGE = {REVENUE − COST OF GOODS SOLD − SG&A − DEPRECIATION[BOOK]}/(INTEREST)

(E23)   NET MARGIN = (NET INCOME)/(REVENUE)

(E24)   CASH-FLOW-TO-LONG-TERM-DEBT RATIO = (CASH FLOW)/(DEBT)

on the firm's outstanding debt (INTEREST RATE), respectively, in the same manner.[7] Equations (E2), (E4), and (E7) determine various items in the income statement under the assumption that the firm's gross profit margin (MARGIN), book depreciation rate (DEPRECIATION RATE), and book tax rate (TAX RATE) are fixed over the planning horizon. Equation (E6) calculates projected interest expense (INTEREST) under the assumption that any debt repayments or new issues take place at year-end; interest expense thus equals the average interest rate for the year in question multiplied by the amount of debt outstanding at the end of the preceding year (DEBT(-1)). Equation (E8) is just an accounting identity used to calculate net income (NET INCOME).

STATEMENT OF CASH FLOWS EQUATIONS   The next seven equations generate the projected statements of cash flows. Equation (E9) is an accounting identity; deferred taxes represent the timing differences between the recognition of tax expense for financial reporting purposes (DEPRECIATION(BOOK)) and the actual cash payment (DEPRECIATION(TAX)).

Equations (E10), (E13), (E14), and (E15) are accounting identities. Cash flow equals net income plus noncash charges. The amount of funds that must be raised from external sources (FUNDS REQUIRED) equals the amount of funds required for capital expenditure, increased working capital, debt repayment, and dividend purposes less that amount of funds generated internally (CASH FLOW). These required funds can be raised from either of two sources: a new debt issue or a new common stock issue.[8] The mix of new debt and new equity is determined so as to preserve the firm's target debt-to-capitalization ratio (DEBT RATIO). To preserve the capital structure, the year-end debt level should equal the DEBT RATIO times the year-end capitalization (EQUITY(-1) + NET INCOME − DIVIDENDS + DEBT(-1) − REPAY + FUNDS REQUIRED). The difference between this target level and the amount of debt that carries over from the prior year less repayments (DEBT(-1) − REPAY) represents the amount of debt that needs to be issued (or repurchased if NET DEBT ISSUE is negative). The

---

[7] You might interpret INTEREST RATE as the average interest cost of debt for a firm that has only floating-rate long-term debt outstanding. A more sophisticated model would allow for fixed-rate debt and would distinguish between debt outstanding as of the beginning of the planning period and the new debt the firm issues during the planning period.

[8] For the sake of simplicity, the model ignores the other sources of short-term and long-term capital that are available to most firms.

balance of external funds requirements is met from a new stock issue, or if NET STOCK ISSUE is negative, shares are repurchased.

Equations (E11) and (E12) hold by definition. The WC RATIO embodies the firm's current ratio objective, and the PAYOUT RATIO embodies its dividend policy objective.[9]

BALANCE SHEET EQUATIONS   The remaining six equations generate the projected balance sheets. Equations (E16), (E17), (E18), (E20), and (E21) project year-end working capital (WORKING CAPITAL); property, plant, and equipment (FIXED ASSETS); deferred taxes (DEFERRED TAXES); long-term debt (DEBT); and common equity (EQUITY), respectively, as the amount at the end of the prior year plus the change during the year in question. Equation (E19) is just an accounting identity for net assets.

BUILDING MORE SOPHISTICATED MODELS   It is easy to think of ways to improve the model to make it useful in practical situations.[10] We have already suggested a few ways. But there are others; for example, distinguishing between short-term borrowing and long-term borrowing, keeping track of the number of common shares and indicating per-share data, breaking out current assets and current liabilities, among others. Such changes would be useful, but it is important to avoid excessive detail. A financial planning model should provide just enough detail to indicate clearly the financial impact of the alternative strategies and financial policies the firm has under study. Excessive detail is likely to inhibit the planning process by making it more difficult to see these effects clearly.

AN EXAMPLE OF THE APPLICATION OF THE MODEL

To illustrate the use of the model we have just developed, consider the following planning problem. Ata-Boy Corporation is going through its annual planning exercise. Each year Ata-Boy updates its 5-year plan. This year Ata-Boy is forecasting that its net sales revenue will grow at a 10% annual rate. It expects selling, general, and administrative expense to grow at only half this rate. Ata-Boy expects to maintain its 40% gross profit margin, 5% book depreciation rate, and 40% tax rate throughout the planning period. Its embedded pretax cost of debt is 10%, but it is concerned that continuing inflation could raise its pretax cost of debt to 12%. Its target financial policies are WC RATIO = 0.2, PAYOUT RATIO = 0.2, and, in order to maintain its single-A senior debt rating, DEBT RATIO = 0.3.

Table 26-3 shows selected items from Ata-Boy's income statement, statement of cash flows, and balance sheet for the latest year, and the projected financial statements for each of the next 5 years.[11] The latter were prepared by applying Equations (E1) through (E21) from Table 26-2. In addition, we included gross profit, operat-

---

[9] The fixed PAYOUT RATIO would cause dividends to vary as net income varies. A more sophisticated model would incorporate the constraint that dividends per share should not decrease, at least not for planning purposes, for reasons discussed in Chapters 17 and 18.

[10] The more sophisticated financial planning models often take the form of several equations that are solved simultaneously. Francis and Rowell (1978) describe a general simultaneous linear equation model. Davis, Caccappolo, and Chaudry (1973) describe the econometric model the Bell System developed for planning purposes.

[11] In practice, the "latest year" would correspond to the fiscal year in which the 5-year plan is prepared. Companies typically prepare the 5-year plan near the end of the year so that they can estimate the full-year financial results fairly accurately.

TABLE 26-3 Illustration of the Application of the Scaled-Down
Financial Planning Model
(Millions of Dollars)

	Latest Year	Projected Ahead				
		1 Year	2 Years	3 Years	4 Years	5 Years
Income Statement:						
Sales revenue	$ 750.0	$ 825.0	$ 907.5	$ 998.3	$1,098.1	$1,207.9
Cost of goods sold	450.0	495.0	544.5	599.0	658.9	724.7
Gross profit	300.0	330.0	363.0	399.3	439.2	483.2
SG & A	60.0	63.0	66.2	69.5	72.9	76.6
Depreciation	45.0	50.0	56.5	63.7	71.7	80.2
Operating income	195.0	217.0	240.3	266.1	294.6	326.4
Interest expense	32.0	40.3	44.7	49.7	55.2	61.0
Pretax income	163.0	176.7	195.6	216.4	239.4	265.4
Income taxes	65.2	70.7	78.2	86.6	95.8	106.2
Net income	$ 97.8	$ 106.0	$ 117.4	$ 129.8	$ 143.6	$ 159.2
Statement of Cash Flows:						
Net income	$ 97.8	$ 106.0	$ 117.4	$ 129.8	$ 143.6	$ 159.2
Depreciation	45.0	50.0	56.5	63.7	71.7	80.2
Change in deferred income taxes	20.0	22.0	23.0	25.0	27.0	30.0
Cash flow from operations	162.8	178.0	196.9	218.5	242.3	269.4
Capital expenditures	140.0	180.0	200.0	225.0	240.0	250.0
Increase (Decrease) in working capital	14.5	15.0	16.5	18.2	20.0	22.0
Debt repayment	25.0	—	10.0	10.0	20.0	20.0
Dividends	19.6	21.2	23.5	26.0	28.7	31.8
Net funds required	$36.3	$38.2	$53.1	$60.7	$66.4	$54.4
Debt issued (repurchased)	$36.3	$36.9	$51.1	$56.4	$68.3	$68.6
Stock issued (repurchased)	—	1.3	2.0	4.3	(1.9)	(14.2)
Net funds raised (used)	$36.3	$38.2	$53.1	$60.7	$66.4	$54.4
Balance Sheet:						
Working capital	$ 150.0	$ 165.0	$ 181.5	$ 199.7	$ 219.7	$ 241.7
Property, plant, & equipment	1,000.0	1,130.0	1,273.5	1,434.8	1,603.1	1,772.9
Other assets	50.0	50.0	50.0	50.0	50.0	50.0
Deferred taxes	(80.0)	(102.0)	(125.0)	(150.0)	(177.0)	(207.0)
Net assets	$1,120.0	$1,243.0	$1,380.0	$1,534.5	$1,695.8	$1,857.6

TABLE 26-3 *(Continued)*

	Latest Year	Projected Ahead				
		1 Year	2 Years	3 Years	4 Years	5 Years
Balance Sheet *(continued):*						
Long-term debt	$336.0	$372.9	$414.0	$460.4	$508.7	$557.3
Common equity	784.0	870.1	966.0	1,074.1	1,187.1	1,300.3
Capitalization	$1,120.0	$1,243.0	$1,380.0	$1,534.5	$1,695.8	$1,857.6
Ratios:						
Interest coverage	6.09x	5.38x	5.38x	5.35x	5.34x	5.35x
Net margin	13.0%	12.8%	12.9%	13.0%	13.1%	13.2%
Payout ratio	20.0	20.0	20.0	20.0	20.0	20.0
Debt ratio	30.0	30.0	30.0	30.0	30.0	30.0
Cash-flow-to-long-term-debt ratio	0.49x	0.48x	0.48x	0.47x	0.48x	0.48x

ing income, and pretax income in the income statements. These amounts are calculated directly from items generated by the model.

Consider the projections for 1 year ahead. Net sales revenue increases by 10%, from $750 million to $825 million. The gross profit margin is 40%, so that

$$\text{Cost of Goods Sold} = (1 - .4)825.0 \text{ million} = \$495.0 \text{ million}$$

Selling, general, and administrative expense increases by 5%, from $60.0 million to $63.0 million. Depreciation expense is calculated as 5% of beginning-of-year property, plant, and equipment ($1,000 million). The interest rate is 12%, so that interest expense is 12% of beginning-of-year long-term debt ($336.0 million). The tax expense and net income calculations then follow.

The calculation of the change in deferred income taxes is not shown to save space. A separate calculation of depreciation expense for tax purposes would be required. The cash flow calculation involves only addition. The calculation of the increase in working capital uses the assumed WC RATIO:

$$\text{Increase (Decrease) in Working Capital} = 0.2(825.0 - 750.0) = \$15.0 \text{ million}$$

and the dividend calculation uses the assumed PAYOUT RATIO:

$$\text{Dividends} = 0.2(106.0 \text{ million}) = \$21.2 \text{ million}$$

The amount of net funds required is simply the sum of capital expenditures, the increase in working capital, and the amount of common dividends (collectively $216.2 million) less the funds generated internally ($178.0 million), or $38.2 million (= 216.2 − 178.0). Of this amount, $36.9 million must be raised through a new debt issue in order to preserve Ata-Boy's 30% ratio of long-term debt to capitalization.

Turning to the balance sheet, it was found that working capital increased by $15.0 million. Property, plant, and equipment increases by the $180.0 million of gross spending and decreases by the $50.0 million of depreciation, for a net increase of $130.0 million. The calculations of net assets, long-term debt, and common equity require only values previously calculated and simple arithmetic.

Table 26–3 illustrates but one simple iteration in the planning process. Ata-Boy would want to "fine tune" the calculations. For example, it might be impractical to issue $1.3 million of common stock. So Ata-Boy might reduce the payout ratio in years 1, 2, and 3, and possibly increase it in later years.

In this base case, at least, Ata-Boy's financial policies appear sustainable. In particular, the critical financial ratios are consistent with a single-A senior debt rating even under the higher-interest-rate scenario Ata-Boy is assuming in this iteration, and Ata-Boy would have enough free cash flow available to sustain, on average, a 20% payout ratio.[12]

SENSITIVITY ANALYSIS AND ALTERNATIVE COMMERCIAL STRATEGIES

Ata-Boy would also want to repeat this exercise to test the robustness of its financial policies under different assumptions regarding the future operating environment and to evaluate alternative strategies. For example, firms seldom are lucky enough to experience the smooth uninterrupted growth assumed in Table 26–3. Ata-Boy should also consider the financial impact of a temporary downturn in its business. Depending on the likelihood that this might occur, Ata-Boy might wish to reduce its financial leverage. In addition, Ata-Boy might wish to consider the impact of different product pricing strategies and different financial policies.

One of the results of this process might be a set of contingency plans. For example, Ata-Boy might find it prudent to reduce its leverage if interest rates rise sharply in order to protect its senior debt rating. This might necessitate selling additional common stock rather than debt, reducing the payout ratio, or some combination of the two. Rather than wait for interest rates to rise before deciding what to do, Ata-Boy would be wise to plan how to counter this as well as other possible adverse developments in its operating environment.

A FINAL NOTE ON THE PLANNING MODEL

As the forgoing example illustrates, corporate financial planning models are accounting-oriented. They generate a set of accounting statements rather than perform any sort of optimization analysis, discounted cash flow analysis, or risk analysis. These models do not by themselves provide any clear indication as to what constitutes *the* optimal financial policy set; they simply provide a series of snapshots that reveal the accounting impact of certain strategies or financial policy decisions under a specified set of assumptions.[13] But by pointing the "camera" in the right direction

---

[12]Glancing back to Table 16–4 (and also, for short-term debt ratings, Table 25–1) interest coverage is about average (but if Ata-Boy has no lease expense, then its fixed charge coverage would be well above average) and its profitability appears to be well above average, but its debt ratio is above average and its cash-flow-to-long-term-debt ratio is below average for a single-A-rated firm.

[13]Linear programming models have been devised to help find the best financial strategy in terms of a specified set of objectives (embodied in the "objective function" of the model) and subject to specified assumptions and restrictions (embodied in the "set of constraints" of the model). Two such models are described in Maier and Vander Weide (1978) and Myers and Pogue (1974). Nevertheless, the policy prescriptions are only as good as the models that furnish them. Until someone succeeds in identifying the precise relationships among the multiplicity of factors that affect firm valuation, financial planning models, regardless of their degree of mathematical sophistication, will be able to do no better than to suggest "approximate" solutions to the problem of finding the "best" financial policy mix.

and taking a sufficient number of snapshots, managers can see enough of the firm's financial picture to make intelligent financial decisions.

SHORT-TERM FINANCIAL PLANNING   26.3

The projected financial statements in Table 26–3 are useful for long-term planning purposes but not for short-term planning purposes. They lack sufficient detail for closely monitoring the business. To achieve this, a more detailed short-term plan, including a cash budget, is required.

SHORT-TERM FINANCIAL PLAN

The **short-term financial plan** contains a more detailed income statement, statement of cash flows, and balance sheet for each quarter (or, in many cases, for each month) for the coming fiscal year. The short-term plan reflects seasonal factors, which a year-by-year plan cannot. Publicly-owned firms must report their results quarterly, and the short-term plan projects these quarterly results. In addition, the short-term plan is also useful for **financial control** purposes. At the end of each quarter (or month, if the short-term plan is prepared on that basis), management can review the firm's performance relative to the short-term plan. Deviations from the short-term plan may suggest the need for both changes to the projected financial results for the full year and perhaps to the firm's operating strategy and/or financial policies.

The short-term plan must be consistent with the projected first year of the long-term financial plan. The quarterly (or monthly) income statements should add up to the income statement for the full year. The statements of cash flow should add similarly. The balance sheet as of the end of the last quarter should agree with the projected year-end balance sheet for the first year of the financial plan.

CASH BUDGET

The short-term financial plan typically includes a cash budget. The **cash budget** provides a quarterly (or, in many cases, monthly) breakdown of cash receipts and disbursements. It contains a schedule showing the various items that contribute cash and the various items that use cash and the period-by-period cash impact attributable to each. As with the short-term plan as a whole, the cash budget must be consistent with the long-term financial plan.

The cash budget plays a crucial role in financial planning. The firm must have cash available when it is needed for payments to employees, suppliers, creditors, etc. The cash budget enables a firm to monitor closely its sources and uses of cash.

SUPPORTING SCHEDULES

Firms often prepare a variety of supporting schedules to back up the long-term and short-term financial plans. These typically include a detailed capital expenditure budget, which provides a capital expenditure breakdown by project and by year; a detailed operating plan for each principal business unit within the firm; and an advertising budget, among others.

26.4   CASH BUDGETING

Cash budgéting is critically important to the successful operation of a business enterprise. It is an essential part of the financial management function. A business must operate within the limits of the funds that are available to it. The necessary funds must be available at precisely the time they are needed—and must be available at an acceptable cost—to carry out the business activities of the firm. It follows that cash requirements and cash availability must be carefully planned. A firm should not treat cash resources as a residual flow from its operations. In particular, it is important to estimate cash receipts accurately, manage cash collections effectively, control cash disbursements, minimize idle cash balances (for example due to float), and preserve an acceptable degree of flexibility to obtain funds by maintaining an appropriate level of liquid assets and one or more backup lines of credit to meet unexpected needs for cash.

Figure 26–2 illustrates the cash flow time line for a typical manufacturing firm. The need for cash budgeting arises primarily due to the different timing of cash inflows and cash outflows. The operating cash cycle begins with the purchase of raw materials. These are ordered and typically paid for before the manufacturer receives payment for the finished goods. How long management takes to pay for the raw materials depends on its payables management policy, discussed in Chapter 25. Hourly and salaried employees must be paid on a regular basis. Finally, the customer order is received, goods are shipped, the invoice is sent (usually at the time the goods are shipped, although there may be a lag as shown in the figure), the customer sends payment, and the firm gets use of the funds. How long it takes from the time the goods are shipped until the firm has use of the cash depends on the firm's credit policy (also discussed in Chapter 25) and on how effectively the firm monitors and collects its outstanding receivables. Meanwhile, of course, the firm's employees must be paid.

The cash flow time line cuts across the firm's inventory, payables management, credit, and receivables management policies. As these policies change—and as management becomes more effective at implementing them—the relative timing of cash outflows and cash inflows can change. Some decisions may affect just one of these elements, such as a decision to pay production workers biweekly rather than weekly. Other decisions may affect more than one element. For example, a decision to tighten credit terms will speed cash collections but may also reduce total sales and hence the amount of cash needed to purchase raw materials and maintain finished goods inventories. The various policies that affect the length of the cash flow time line must be properly reflected in preparing the cash budget.

FIGURE 26-2
The cash flow time line.

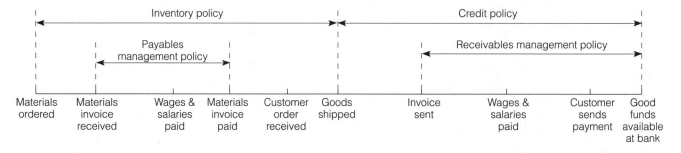

PURPOSE OF CASH BUDGETING

Cash budgeting entails planning for the specific cash needs of the business enterprise and determining how to meet these cash needs in a timely fashion and at an acceptable cost. This activity encompasses

- Projecting the timing and amounts of funds needed to meet operating expenses, cover capital expenditures (including planned increases in working capital), service outstanding debt and preferred stock obligations, pay income and other taxes, and pay dividends (when declared) to the common stockholders. This activity requires taking into account seasonal fluctuations, such as finished goods inventory buildup in anticipation of the Christmas selling season.

- Forecasting the timing and amounts of cash receipts through cash sales and collections on accounts receivable.

- Projecting the amount and timing of excess cash balances and planning how to utilize those funds; for example, by making investments in short-term securities, reducing outstanding indebtedness, or making advance purchases of goods or services to take advantage of special opportunities.

- Forecasting the timing and amounts of short-term borrowing requirements and planning which source(s) of funds to use to satisfy those requirements; in particular, to take advantage of any special opportunities.

- In the case of multinational companies, projecting foreign currency requirements and funds availability to plan foreign exchange hedging transactions.

METHODS OF CASH BUDGETING

There are two principal methods of cash budgeting, which differ in the extent of detail involved. The **direct-estimate method** involves making detailed estimates of cash receipts and cash disbursements category by category. The **statement-of-cash-flows method** uses the recently introduced statement of cash flows[14] to adjust projected net income and identify cash flow generated (used) by operating activities, cash used (generated) by investment (disinvestment) activities, and cash generated (used) by financing (repayment/redemption) activities. The statement-of-cash-flows method is less detailed than the direct-estimate method. It does not show total cash receipts and disbursements; only net receipt of cash from operations is shown.

Both methods are illustrated later in this section. The statement-of-cash-flows method is useful when a summary presentation is desired; for example, for the monthly summaries in the short-term financial plan. The direct-estimate method is more useful for the rolling 30-day (60-day or 90-day) daily cash forecast.[15]

ESTIMATING CASH RECEIPTS

For the purpose of estimating cash receipts, it is useful to distinguish two classes of revenue-generating transactions: (1) relatively large identifiable transactions and (2) relatively small or relatively high-volume transactions. Transactions of the first type include the sale of fixed assets, issuance of securities, or large bulk product

---

[14]"Statement of Cash Flows," Financial Accounting Standards Board Statement No. 95, Financial Accounting Standards Board, High Ridge Park, Stamford, Conn., November 1987.

[15]Some firms use sophisticated simulation and other forms of mathematical models to assist their cash budgeting efforts (Lerner, 1968; Miller and Stone, 1985; and Stone and Miller, 1987).

sales. Transactions of the second type consist primarily of cash sales of individual product items and collections on accounts receivable. Cash receipts from relatively large identifiable transactions are estimated transaction by transaction. Cash receipts from all other transactions are typically estimated from past experience.[16]

PAYMENT PATTERN APPROACH TO RECEIVABLES   Collections on accounts receivable are normally estimated by extrapolating from the historical payment pattern, which may reflect seasonal factors. Table 26–4 illustrates this approach. Suppose that the firm has analyzed monthly collection patterns for the past several years. The analysis revealed the payment patterns for the months of February through June shown in the upper panel of Table 26–4. Suppose that the firm has determined that the payment patterns for February through May of the current year are consistent with the historical pattern and therefore expects June to follow the historical pattern. The estimated June collections are calculated in the lower panel of Table 26–4. Note that June sales are projected to be $350,000, but cash receipts are forecast to be only $288,075, based on the observed historical payment patterns.

If the firm had different divisions or different products, it would be necessary to estimate the payment pattern for each to test for differences. In addition, more sophisticated approaches based on statistical estimation procedures could be used to reflect the variability of the percentages in the upper panel of Table 26–4. One could then identify a range of likely values for, say, June collections rather than just a single point estimate. In any case, it is important that any firm using the payment pattern approach continually monitor the payment patterns to detect changes and update the pattern percentages used in estimating monthly receivable collections.

ESTIMATING CASH DISBURSEMENTS

As in the case of cash receipts, it is useful to distinguish (1) relatively large identifiable transactions from (2) relatively small or relatively high-volume transactions. The first class of transactions includes major capital expenditures, repayment of debt, acquisitions, and common stock dividends and repurchases. The second class includes accounts payable in connection with raw materials and supplies; wage and salary expense; accrued expenses for taxes, interest, professional services, and health and retirement benefits; and prepaid items, such as insurance.

The critical difference between cash disbursements and cash receipts is the firm's control over the timing of cash payment. When raw materials are purchased from a vendor, the firm determines when to make payment based on the payment terms the vendor offers. If the vendor offers a discount for prompt payment, the purchaser can decide whether to pay promptly enough to claim the discount. Well-managed firms maintain payables files, which are typically computerized. These files furnish a daily record of the firm's intended payments on invoices that it has approved for payment.

Similarly, firms establish regular payroll dates and can forecast wage and salary cash requirements with a high degree of accuracy. (The principal source of uncertainty is fluctuation in the level of employment.) The cash required to meet accrued expenses and to cover the cost of prepaid items can be forecast in much the same manner. Any major items would be monitored and provided for separately, as for example, cash to pay for shares the firm was about to repurchase or to make a cash

---

[16] See, for example, Carpenter and Miller (1979); Gentry and De La Garza (1985).

TABLE 26-4 Payment Pattern Approach to Estimating Cash Receipts from Receivables

Month of Sale	Cash Discounts[a]	Collection Pattern					
		Same Month	*Next Month*	*2 Months*	*3 Months*	*4 Months*	*Uncollectable*
February	1%	3.9%	83.2%	7.2%	4.2%	1.0%	0.5%
March	1	3.9	82.8	8.3	3.3	1.2	0.5
April	1	3.7	81.0	10.1	3.7	1.0	0.5
May	1	4.2	85.9	4.9	3.5	1.0	0.5
June	1	4.3	85.6	5.1	3.5	1.0	0.5

[a] Calculated as a percentage of the sales for the month.

Month of Sale	Estimated June Collections		Estimated June Collections
	Collection Percentage	*Monthly Sales*	
February	1.0%	$175,000	$ 1,750
March	3.3	250,000	8,250
April	10.1	300,000	30,300
May	85.9	275,000	236,225
June	4.3	350,000	15,050
Cash discounts[b]	1.0		(3,500)
Total			$288,075

[b] Calculated as a percentage of June sales.

dividend distribution. Generally, interest payment dates and dividend payment dates are known well in advance.[17]

AN EXAMPLE OF AN ANNUAL CASH BUDGET AND ROLLING 30-DAY CASH BUDGET

The short-term financial plan includes an annual cash budget, which typically includes monthly, but at least quarterly, cash budgets. But it is not enough to know that a firm will be a net cash generator during any particular month. A firm needs to be able to monitor its cash position on a daily basis. Consequently, well-managed firms supplement the annual cash budget with a more detailed rolling cash budget. The rolling budget forecasts cash requirements and cash availability on a 30-day basis (or 60 or 90 days) and is updated at least weekly, but often daily.

ANNUAL CASH BUDGET Table 26–5 illustrates an annual cash budget. Each firm will tailor its annual cash budget to suit its particular circumstances. The annual cash budget illustrated in Table 26–5 has the following important features:

■ The factors affecting cash and marketable securities are broken down into operating factors, cash dividends, investment activities, and financing activities.

[17] See, for example, Ferguson and Maier (1982); Gitman, Forrester, and Forrester (1976); Maier, Robinson, and Vander Weide (1981).

Table 26-5 Illustration of Annual Cash Budget
(Dollar Amounts in Thousands)

	January	February	March	Total Quarter I	. . .	December	Total Quarter IV	Annual Total
Cash and Marketable Securities at Beginning of Period	$1,500	$6,365	$5,615	$1,500	. . .	$4,000	$2,675	$1,500
Cash Provided (Used) by Operations:								
Net income	5,100	4,200	3,700	13,000	. . .	5,000	13,500	50,000
Depreciation	250	250	500	1,000	. . .	600	1,800	5,300
Deferred income taxes	25	25	25	75	. . .	25	75	300
Other noncash charges and credits-net	25	—	—	25	. . .	—	50	150
Decrease (Increase) in working capital other than cash and marketable securities	(100)	(500)	(500)	(1,100)	. . .	(300)	(1,000)	(4,500)
Cash Provided (Used) by Operations	5,300	3,975	3,725	13,000	. . .	5,325	14,425	51,250
Cash dividends	—	—	(250)	(250)	. . .	(250)	(250)	(1,000)
Investment Activities:								
Additions to property, plant, and equipment	(250)	(5,500)	(4,000)	(9,750)	. . .	—	(3,000)	(31,575)
Acquisitions of businesses	—	(5,000)	—	(5,000)	. . .	(3,000)	(3,000)	(12,000)
After-tax proceeds from asset sales	—	575	—	575	. . .	—	—	575
Miscellaneous-net	(35)	—	—	(35)	. . .	(25)	(75)	(250)
Cash Used for Investment Activities	(285)	(9,925)	(4,000)	(14,210)	. . .	(3,025)	(6,075)	(43,250)
Financing Activities:								
Increase (Decrease) in short-term debt	—	200	—	200	. . .	—	(500)	(250)
Increase (Decrease) in long-term debt	(100)	5,000	—	4,900	. . .	(2,000)	(6,000)	(3,825)
Common stock issued	—	—	—	—	. . .	75	100	100
Common stock repurchased	(50)	—	—	(50)	. . .	—	—	(150)
Cash Provided by (Used for) Financing Activities	(150)	5,200	—	5,050	. . .	(1,925)	(6,400)	(4,125)
Cash and Marketable Securities at End of Period	6,365	5,615	5,090	5,090	. . .	4,375	4,375	4,375
Increase (Decrease) in Cash and Marketable Securities during Period	$4,865	$(750)	$(525)	$3,590	. . .	$375	$1,700	$2,875

- Cash and marketable securities (i.e., cash equivalents) are shown at the beginning and at the end of each period.
- The impact of each set of factors on cash and marketable securities is reported on a monthly basis, along with quarterly and annual totals.

The format illustrated in Table 26–5 is based on the statement-of-cash-flows method of cash budgeting. This format illustrates the interrelationship between the annual cash budget and the firm's operating budget, which will determine cash provided (used) by operations, its dividend policy, its capital expenditure budget, and its long-term financing plan. For example, if the firm's operating results are weaker than provided for in the operating budget, cash provided by operations will be below forecast, which will reduce the funds available for dividends or investment activities or require an increase in financing or a reduction in cash and marketable securities.

ROLLING 30-DAY CASH BUDGET   Most companies find it useful to maintain a more detailed cash budget for daily or weekly cash planning purposes. The level of detail will depend on the nature of the enterprise. If the firm tends to experience extreme fluctuations in cash receipts or disbursements—for example, as a result of its dependency on a few large customers (e.g., an airplane manufacturer or an automotive parts supplier)—it may wish to identify specific invoices in the rolling cash budget. Also, the time horizon will depend on its credit and short-term investment policies. Table 26–6 illustrates a rolling 30-day cash budget for the firm whose annual cash budget is illustrated in Table 26–5. The firm uses a 30-day time horizon because the bulk of its customers, local distributors, customarily pay their bills within 30 days.

The rolling 30-day cash budget shows the cash and marketable securities at the beginning of each day; the cash receipts other than maturing short-term investments and the cash disbursements anticipated during each day, which together determine the cash surplus or deficit projected for the day; the amount of maturing short-term investments, which provide funds to cover an anticipated shortfall; the net short-term investment (borrowing) required to balance cash needs and cash availability for the day; and the cash and marketable securities at the end of the day, which depend in part on the firm's decision about how to deal with cash surpluses or deficits. Short-term investments and short-term borrowing (i.e., drawing down on credit lines) serve as buffers. As the firm looks 30 days ahead, it can select short-term investments that mature on (or perhaps before) cash will be needed; for example, to meet the payroll on February 2 and to cover a large payment of accounts payable on March 2. The 30-day-forward look also enables the firm to plan for large identifiable cash needs; for example, $5 million to cover the cash cost of an acquisition on February 1 and a $10 million debt rollover on March 2.

CASH BUDGET AND FINANCIAL CONTROLS

Financial control is as important as financial planning and budgeting to the financial management process. Financial control involves monitoring the firm's progress relative to the overall financial plan and cash budget. Significant deviations are identified and analyzed, and then corrective action must be taken. However, the cash budget cannot be used as the sole yardstick of corporate performance versus plan; failure to meet the cash budget is usually the result of failure to meet the operating budget. As soon as significant deviations from the business plan are detected and corrective ac-

TABLE 26-6   Illustration of Rolling 30-Day Cash Budget

	2/1	2/2	. . .	3/2
Cash and Marketable Securities at Beginning of Day	$6,365,000	$6,594,199	. . .	$5,620,317
Cash Receipts:				
Cash sales	45,713	48,750	. . .	42,311
Collections on accounts receivable	2,321,000	2,416,000	. . .	2,216,119
Interest income	75,217	—	. . .	—
Dividend income	—	25,000	. . .	—
Proceeds from sale of fixed assets	—	500,000	. . .	—
Proceeds from sale or liquidation of other assets	—	125,000	. . .	—
Proceeds from incurrence of long-term debt	5,000,000	—	. . .	10,000,000
Proceeds from sale of stock	—	—	. . .	—
All other cash receipts	12,500	17,000	. . .	27,850
Total cash receipts	$7,454,430	$3,131,750	. . .	$12,286,280
Cash Disbursements:				
Cash purchases of materials and supplies	$ 7,517	$ 6,321	. . .	$ 1,790
Payment of accounts payable	1,250,000	755,000	. . .	2,468,950
Payment of wages and salaries	—	4,275,000	. . .	—
Payment of taxes	75,000	—	. . .	—
Payment of prepaid expenses	125,214	—	. . .	78,617
Interest payments	750,000	—	. . .	58,000
Principal repayments	—	—	. . .	10,000,000
Dividend payments	—	—	. . .	250,000
Purchase of treasury stock	—	—	. . .	—
Payments for acquisitions	5,000,000	—	. . .	—
All other cash disbursements	17,500	12,600	. . .	10,000
Total cash disbursements	$7,225,231	$5,048,921	. . .	$12,867,357
Surplus (deficit) cash receipts over cash disbursements	$ 229,199	$(1,917,171)	. . .	$ (581,077)
Maturing short-term investments	275,000	1,850,000	. . .	600,000
Net short-term investment (borrowing)	$ 504,199	$ (67,171)	. . .	$ 18,923
Cash and Marketable Securities at End of Day	$6,594,199	$ 4,744,199	. . .	$5,039,240

tions determined, it is imperative to update the annual and rolling 30-day cash budgets. Underperformance could create a need to borrow from banks or issue additional securities; better-than-expected performance will generate additional cash that also requires a decision as to reinvestment or disbursement.

26.5   AUTOMATING SHORT-TERM FORECASTS

Computer technology has greatly benefited cash budgeting and, as we discuss in the next section, the whole process of cash management. While very large companies with sophisticated cash models use mainframe computers to handle cash budgeting and control, most businesses find that microcomputer technology has advanced to the point where it is adequate to satisfy their entire cash budgeting and control data processing needs.

AVAILABLE SPREADSHEET PACKAGES

A variety of spreadsheet packages are available that lend themselves very nicely to cash budgeting applications. One of the more popular ones has been LOTUS 1-2-3. Perhaps you are already familiar with one of these software systems. In addition, there are a variety of commercially available spreadsheet packages that are specifically designed for cash budgeting applications.

The principal virtue of these packages is their flexibility. They can be updated very easily, which reduces the clerical burden, and they are ideally suited to help you answer "what-if" questions. For example, a change in the February sales projection would ripple through the entire annual cash budget. Such a change can be accommodated in seconds on a microcomputer but would require many tedious time-consuming calculations if done manually.

USING A SPREADSHEET PACKAGE

Table 26–7 presents output from Justin Case's financial planning model of the Yu N. Mi Toy Company, based on the information contained in Table 26–1. As shown in Table 26–7, the short-term investment (borrowing) account is projected to be negative in January and February. Thus, it appears that during January and February, MTC must either (1) obtain additional financing in the amounts indicated (the absolute value of the negative balance) to maintain its target level for the cash account, or (2) allow the cash account to fall below the target.

A short-term investment (borrowing) (S-T) account is a very useful device for simplifying the model-building process. By allowing this account to have a positive *or* negative balance, the problem of automating "conditional" accounts is avoided. Conditional accounts require a more complex set of equations. For example, for our S-T account, if the firm is investing money (the S-T account has a positive balance) the amount invested would be shown as a current asset; if the firm is borrowing (the S-T account has a negative balance) the amount would be shown as a current liability. This simplification results from the Principle of Two-Sided Transactions, the two sides are mirror images: a negative asset is a liability; a negative liability is an asset.

Table 26–8 presents the spreadsheet equations (or data) in the model for the first month of the planning period, December, which is shown in column F. In principle, the general form of such equations is simple:

$$\text{Ending balance} = \text{Starting balance} + \text{Increases} - \text{Decreases} \qquad \textbf{(26.1)}$$

Of course the "trick" to building the model is to identify correctly all of the potential increases and decreases for a given account. For example, the inventory account increases because of the purchase of raw materials and decreases because of selling the inventory. The purchase of raw materials gives rise to an increase in the inventory account, accompanied by a simultaneous increase in accounts payable (or a decrease in the cash account); the sale of inventory gives rise to a decrease in the inventory account, accompanied by a simultaneous increase in cash (or increase in accounts receivable). Recall that whenever a transaction affects two accounts in a double-entry accounting system, when the accounts are on the same side of the bal-

TABLE 26-7 Cash Budget and Pro Forma Income Statements and Balance Sheets for Yu N. Mi Toy Company Based on the Information in Table 26-1
(Amounts in Thousands of Dollars)

	OCT	NOV	DEC	JAN	FEB	MAR	APR	MAY	JUN	JUL	AUG	SEP	OCT
			CASH BUDGET FOR DECEMBER THROUGH AUGUST										
SALES	40.00	60.00	100.00	170.00	150.00	125.00	100.00	70.00	65.00	90.00	175.00	50.00[a]	70.00[a]
A/R COLLECTIONS			66.00	108.00	127.00	150.00	127.50	100.50	83.00	77.50	111.50		
INTEREST INCOME			0.42	0.01	−0.13	−0.06	0.24	0.56	0.76	0.66	0.52		
CASH INFLOW			66.42	108.01	126.87	149.94	127.74	101.06	83.76	78.16	112.02		
PAYABLES PAID			77.00	89.00	84.50	70.00	53.50	43.50	47.00	77.00	59.00		
SALARIES & WAGES PAID			25.00	37.60	34.00	29.50	25.00	19.60	18.70	23.20	38.50	16.00[a]	
TAXES PAID			2.98	8.24	6.66	4.78	2.97	0.79	0.48	2.39	8.90		
INTEREST PAID			9.00	0.00	0.00	9.00	0.00	0.00	9.00	0.00	0.00		
DIVIDENDS PAID			2.00	2.00	2.00	2.00	2.00	2.00	2.00	2.00	2.00		
STARTING CASH			76.00	94.86	89.55	76.70	62.45	52.21	54.12	77.82	74.40		
ENDING CASH			94.86	89.55	76.70	62.45	52.21	54.12	77.82	74.40	53.55		
S-T INVESTMENT CHANGE (cash budget)			−68.42	−23.52	12.56	48.92	54.51	33.27	−17.12	−23.00	24.48		
S-T INVESTMENT CHANGE (balance sheet)			−68.42	−23.52	12.56	48.92	54.51	33.27	−17.12	−23.00	24.48		

	OCT	NOV	DEC	JAN	FEB	MAR	APR	MAY	JUN	JUL	AUG
			MONTHLY PRO FORMA INCOME STATEMENTS								
SALES	40.00	60.00	100.00	170.00	150.00	125.00	100.00	70.00	65.00	90.00	175.00
COST OF RAW MATERIALS			60.00	102.00	90.00	75.00	60.00	42.00	39.00	54.00	105.00
SALARIES & WAGES			25.00	37.60	34.00	29.50	25.00	19.60	18.70	23.20	38.50
DEPRECIATION			3.91	3.87	3.83	3.79	3.76	3.72	3.68	3.64	3.61
INTEREST EXPENSE			3.00	3.00	3.00	3.00	3.00	3.00	3.00	3.00	3.00
INTEREST INCOME			0.42	0.01	−0.13	−0.06	0.24	0.56	0.76	0.66	0.52
TAXABLE INCOME			8.51	23.54	19.04	13.65	8.48	2.25	1.38	6.82	25.42
TAXES			2.98	8.24	6.66	4.78	2.97	0.79	0.48	2.39	8.90
NET INCOME			5.53	15.30	12.37	8.87	5.51	1.46	0.90	4.43	16.52
DIVIDENDS			2.00	2.00	2.00	2.00	2.00	2.00	2.00	2.00	2.00
CHANGE IN RETAINED EARNINGS			3.53	13.30	10.37	6.87	3.51	−0.54	−1.10	2.43	14.52

	OCT	NOV	DEC	JAN	FEB	MAR	APR	MAY	JUN	JUL	AUG
			CURRENT BALANCE SHEET AND MONTHLY PRO FORMA BALANCE SHEETS								
CASH		76.00	94.86	89.55	76.70	62.45	52.21	54.12	77.82	74.40	53.55
S-T INVESTMENT (BORROWING)		70.00	1.58	−21.94	−9.38	39.53	94.04	127.31	110.19	87.19	111.66
ACCOUNTS RECEIVABLE		56.00	90.00	152.00	175.00	150.00	122.50	92.00	74.00	86.50	150.00
INVENTORY		122.00	151.00	133.50	113.50	92.00	75.50	80.50	118.50	123.50	67.00
NET FIXED ASSETS		391.00	387.09	383.22	379.39	375.59	371.84	368.12	364.44	360.79	357.19
TOTAL ASSETS		715.00	724.53	736.33	735.21	719.58	716.09	722.05	744.95	732.38	739.40

TABLE 26-7 *(Continued)*

	OCT	NOV	DEC	JAN	FEB	MAR	APR	MAY	JUN	JUL	AUG
		CURRENT BALANCE SHEET AND MONTHLY PRO FORMA BALANCE SHEETS									
ACCOUNTS PAYABLE		77.00	89.00	84.50	70.00	53.50	43.50	47.00	77.00	59.00	48.50
ACCRUED INTEREST		6.00	0.00	3.00	6.00	0.00	3.00	6.00	0.00	3.00	6.00
LONG–TERM DEBT		300.00	300.00	300.00	300.00	300.00	300.00	300.00	300.00	300.00	300.00
COMMON STOCK		70.00	70.00	70.00	70.00	70.00	70.00	70.00	70.00	70.00	70.00
RETAINED EARNINGS		262.00	265.53	278.83	289.21	296.08	299.59	299.05	297.95	300.38	314.90
LIABS. + OWNERS' EQUITY		715.00	724.53	736.33	735.21	719.58	716.09	722.05	744.95	732.38	739.40

[a] Required for other computations.

TABLE 26-8 Spreadsheet Equations for the Spreadsheet in Table 26-7.
(The months of October through October are shown in columns D through P in the spreadsheet.)

Line	Column A	Column F
3	CASH BUDGET FOR DECEMBER THROUGH AUGUST	
4		DEC
5	SALES	100.00
6	A/R COLLECTIONS	0.4*F5+0.1*E5
7	INTEREST INCOME	0.006*E42
8	CASH INFLOW	+F6+F7
9		
10	PAYABLES PAID	+E48
11	SALARIES & WAGES PAID	7.0+0.18*F5
12	TAXES PAID	+F32
13	INTEREST PAID	+E49+F28 (see footnote a)
14	DIVIDENDS PAID	2.00
15	STARTING CASH	+E41
16	ENDING CASH	+F41
17	S–T INVESTMENT CHANGE (cash budget)	+F15–F16+F8–F10–F11–F12–F13–F14
18	S–T INVESTMENT CHANGE (balance sheet)	+F42–E42
19		
20		
21		
22	MONTHLY PRO FORMA INCOME STATEMENTS	
23		DEC
24	SALES	+F5
25	COST OF RAW MATERIALS	0.6*F24
26	SALARIES & WAGES	+F11
27	DEPRECIATION	0.01*E45

(Continued)

TABLE 26-8   *(Continued)*

Line	Column A	Column F
28	INTEREST EXPENSE	0.01*E50
29	INTEREST INCOME	+F7
30	TAXABLE INCOME	+F24-F25-F26-F27-F28+F29
31		
32	TAXES	0.35*F30
33	NET INCOME	+F30-F32
34		
35	DIVIDENDS	+F14
36	CHANGE IN RETAINED EARNINGS	+F33-F35
37		
38		
39	CURRENT BALANCE SHEET AND MONTHLY PRO FORMA BALANCE SHEETS	
40		DEC
41	CASH	10.0+0.6*G11+0.7*F48
42	S-T INVESTMENT (BORROWING)	+F53-F41-F43-F44-F45
43	ACCOUNTS RECEIVABLE	0.6*F5+0.5*E5
44	INVENTORY	+E44+F48-F25
45	NET FIXED ASSETS	+E45-F27
46	TOTAL ASSETS	+F41+F42+F43+F44+F45
47		
48	ACCOUNTS PAYABLE	0.1*F5+0.2*G5+0.3*H5
49	ACCRUED INTEREST	+E49+F28-F13
50	LONG-TERM DEBT	+E50
51	COMMON STOCK	+E51
52	RETAINED EARNINGS	+E52+F36
53	LIABS. + OWNERS' EQUITY	+F48+F49+F50+F51+F52

[a] This equation repeats every 3 months, with zero for the intervening months.

ance sheet, the transaction causes an increase in one account and a decrease in the other; when the accounts are on opposite sides of the balance sheet, both accounts increase, or both decrease.

Once the equations have been entered into the December column, they can be *block-copied* to subsequent columns for January through August, followed by entering "corrections" for two of the lines in this case: (1) Each sales forecast must be entered separately; and (2) the equation for interest paid on line 13 must have zeros entered into the nonpayment months.[18]

[18] Note that unless otherwise specified, the copy command maintains the relationships among the cells, rather than maintaining specific cell identities. For example, if cell G6 has the equation [E5 + F4] in it and we copy this equation to cell L12, the equation will become [J11 + K10].

In the cash budget, the use of two different equations for the change in the S-T account provides a check on the model. The first equation (cash budget) tracks the actual cash flows. The change is computed as the sum of the increases and decreases in the S-T account. Note that the change in the *cash* account can be an increase or a decrease in the S-T account. The second equation (balance sheet) is the change in the S-T account that results from forcing the balance sheet to balance, this change is computed as simply the ending balance in the S-T account minus its starting balance. If both equations for the change in the S-T account do not produce the same answer, there is an error—the model is not internally consistent.

Three caveats are in order at this point. First, don't be alarmed if the values in the cells are incorrect or show ERR as you are entering the equations for a model. (Only become alarmed when you think you are done, and such things remain.) Second, even a very simple error often causes *many* of the cells to show nonsensical amounts or ERR, or the CIRC indicator to identify circular reasoning (situations where 2 or more cells are functions of one another, simultaneously). This is because the model is a set of interwoven relationships; a single error can have an enormous "ripple" effect. Finally, numbers that look okay are not guaranteed to be correct. We don't mean to be discouraging, but an impressively printed spreadsheet can be deceiving: There can be errors even though the numbers look "fine," so *chek yor model and its output vry carfuly!*

"WHAT-IF" QUESTIONS: THE POWER OF A SPREADSHEET PACKAGE

After building the financial planning model shown in Tables 26–7 and 26–8, it occurred to Mr. Case that actual sales virtually never turn out to be their expected amount. Therefore, he decided to consider the possibilities of higher- or lower-than-expected sales levels. Tables 26–9 and 26–10 present output from his model assuming sales are 80% and 120% of forecast levels, respectively.

Table 26–9 can be produced from Mr. Case's model by following these steps:

1. Insert a blank row between lines 3 and 4 [/, W, I, A4 . . A4].
2. Copy line 6 (old line 5) to new line 4 [/, C, A6 . . P6, A4].
3. Enter .8*F4 in cell F6 (old cell F5).
4. Copy cell F6 to G6 . . P6 [/, C, F6 . . F6, G6 . . P6].

Table 26–10 can be produced from the model for Table 26–9 by following these steps:

1. Enter 1.2*F4 in cell F6.
2. Copy cell F6 to G6 . . P6 [/, C, F6 . . F6, G6 . . P6].

Looking at Table 26–9, it might appear to be a case of "good news" and "bad news." The good news is that with lower-than-expected sales, MTC will not need to obtain additional funds to maintain its target level of cash (in none of the months is the S-T account balance negative). But the bad news is that total projected net income over the planning horizon declines from $70,890 to $41,130. Similarly, looking at Table 26–10, higher-than-expected sales will require an even greater amount of additional financing, but total projected net income increases from $70,890 to $100,660. By now you know that the benefits from a higher sales level far outweigh the costs of obtaining additional financing.

TABLE 26-9 Cash Budget and Pro Forma Income Statements and Balance Sheets for Yu N. Mi Toy Company with 80% of Forecast Sales
(Amounts in Thousands of Dollars)

CASH BUDGET FOR DECEMBER THROUGH AUGUST

SALES 40.00 60.00 100.00 170.00 150.00 125.00 100.00 70.00 65.00 90.00 175.00 50.00 70.00

	OCT	NOV	DEC	JAN	FEB	MAR	APR	MAY	JUN	JUL	AUG	SEP	OCT
SALES	40.00	60.00	80.00	136.00	120.00	100.00	80.00	56.00	52.00	72.00	140.00	40.00[a]	56.00[a]
A/R COLLECTIONS			58.00	92.40	101.60	120.00	102.00	80.40	66.40	62.00	89.20		
INTEREST INCOME			0.42	0.09	0.01	0.06	0.28	0.54	0.69	0.60	0.48		
CASH INFLOW			58.42	92.49	101.61	120.06	102.28	80.94	67.09	62.60	89.68		
PAYABLES PAID			77.00	71.20	67.60	56.00	42.80	34.80	37.60	61.60	47.20		
SALARIES & WAGES PAID			21.40	31.48	28.60	25.00	21.40	17.08	16.36	19.96	32.20	14.20[a]	
TAXES PAID			1.44	5.65	4.40	2.89	1.44	−0.30	−0.54	0.98	6.19		
INTEREST PAID			9.00	0.00	0.00	9.00	0.00	0.00	9.00	0.00	0.00		
DIVIDENDS PAID			2.00	2.00	2.00	2.00	2.00	2.00	2.00	2.00	2.00		
STARTING CASH			76.00	78.73	74.48	64.20	52.80	44.61	46.14	65.10	62.36		
ENDING CASH			78.73	74.48	64.20	52.80	44.61	46.14	65.10	62.36	45.68		
S-T INVESTMENT CHANGE (cash budget)			−55.15	−13.59	9.29	36.57	42.83	25.83	−16.28	−19.20	18.78		
S-T INVESTMENT CHANGE (balance sheet)			−55.15	−13.59	9.29	36.57	42.83	25.83	−16.28	−19.20	18.78		

MONTHLY PRO FORMA INCOME STATEMENTS

	OCT	NOV	DEC	JAN	FEB	MAR	APR	MAY	JUN	JUL	AUG
SALES	40.00	60.00	80.00	136.00	120.00	100.00	80.00	56.00	52.00	72.00	140.00
COST OF RAW MATERIALS			48.00	81.60	72.00	60.00	48.00	33.60	31.20	43.20	84.00
SALARIES & WAGES			21.40	31.48	28.60	25.00	21.40	17.08	16.36	19.96	32.20
DEPRECIATION			3.91	3.87	3.83	3.79	3.76	3.72	3.68	3.64	3.61
INTEREST EXPENSE			3.00	3.00	3.00	3.00	3.00	3.00	3.00	3.00	3.00
INTEREST INCOME			0.42	0.09	0.01	0.06	0.28	0.54	0.69	0.60	0.48
TAXABLE INCOME			4.11	16.14	12.58	8.27	4.13	−0.86	−1.55	2.79	17.67
TAXES			1.44	5.65	4.40	2.89	1.44	−0.30	−0.54	0.98	6.19
NET INCOME			2.67	10.49	8.17	5.38	2.68	−0.56	−1.01	1.82	11.49
DIVIDENDS			2.00	2.00	2.00	2.00	2.00	2.00	2.00	2.00	2.00
CHANGE IN RETAINED EARNINGS			0.67	8.49	6.17	3.38	0.68	−2.56	−3.01	−0.18	9.49

CURRENT BALANCE SHEET AND MONTHLY PRO FORMA BALANCE SHEETS

	OCT	NOV	DEC	JAN	FEB	MAR	APR	MAY	JUN	JUL	AUG
CASH		76.00	78.73	74.48	64.20	52.80	44.61	46.14	65.10	62.36	45.68
S-T INVESTMENT (BORROWING)		70.00	14.85	1.26	10.55	47.12	89.95	115.78	99.50	80.29	99.07
ACCOUNTS RECEIVABLE		56.00	78.00	121.60	140.00	120.00	98.00	73.60	59.20	69.20	120.00
INVENTORY		122.00	145.20	131.20	115.20	98.00	84.80	88.80	119.20	123.20	78.00
NET FIXED ASSETS		391.00	387.09	383.22	379.39	375.59	371.84	368.12	364.44	360.79	357.19
TOTAL ASSETS		715.00	703.87	711.76	709.34	693.51	689.19	692.43	707.43	695.84	699.93

TABLE 26-9 (Continued)

	OCT	NOV	DEC	JAN	FEB	MAR	APR	MAY	JUN	JUL	AUG
CURRENT BALANCE SHEET AND MONTHLY PRO FORMA BALANCE SHEETS											
ACCOUNTS PAYABLE		77.00	71.20	67.60	56.00	42.80	34.80	37.60	61.60	47.20	38.80
ACCRUED INTEREST		6.00	0.00	3.00	6.00	0.00	3.00	6.00	0.00	3.00	6.00
LONG-TERM DEBT		300.00	300.00	300.00	300.00	300.00	300.00	300.00	300.00	300.00	300.00
COMMON STOCK		70.00	70.00	70.00	70.00	70.00	70.00	70.00	70.00	70.00	70.00
RETAINED EARNINGS		262.00	262.67	271.16	277.34	280.71	281.39	278.83	275.83	275.64	285.13
LIABS. + OWNERS' EQUITY		715.00	703.87	711.76	709.34	693.51	689.19	692.43	707.43	695.84	699.93

[a] Required for other computations.

TABLE 26-10 Cash Budget and Pro Forma Income Statements and Balance Sheets for Yu N. Mi Toy Company with 120% of Forecast Sales
(Amounts in Thousands of Dollars)

CASH BUDGET FOR DECEMBER THROUGH AUGUST

SALES	40.00	60.00	100.00	170.00	150.00	125.00	100.00	70.00	65.00	90.00	175.00	50.00	70.00

	OCT	NOV	DEC	JAN	FEB	MAR	APR	MAY	JUN	JUL	AUG	SEP	OCT
SALES	40.00	60.00	120.00	204.00	180.00	150.00	120.00	84.00	78.00	108.00	210.00	60.00[a]	84.00[a]
A/R COLLECTIONS			74.00	123.60	152.40	180.00	153.00	120.60	99.60	93.00	133.80		
INTEREST INCOME			0.42	−0.07	−0.27	−0.18	0.19	0.59	0.83	0.73	0.56		
CASH INFLOW			74.42	123.53	152.13	179.82	153.19	121.19	100.43	93.73	134.36		
PAYABLES PAID			77.00	106.80	101.40	84.00	64.20	52.20	56.40	92.40	70.80		
SALARIES & WAGES PAID			28.60	43.72	39.40	34.00	28.60	22.12	21.04	26.44	44.80	17.80[a]	
TAXES PAID			4.52	10.83	8.92	6.66	4.49	1.87	1.51	3.79	11.60		
INTEREST PAID			9.00	0.00	0.00	9.00	0.00	0.00	9.00	0.00	0.00		
DIVIDENDS PAID			2.00	2.00	2.00	2.00	2.00	2.00	2.00	2.00	2.00		
STARTING CASH			76.00	110.99	104.62	89.20	72.10	59.81	62.10	90.54	86.44		
ENDING CASH			110.99	104.62	89.20	72.10	59.81	62.10	90.54	86.44	61.42		
S-T INVESTMENT CHANGE (cash budget)			−81.69	−33.45	15.83	61.26	66.19	40.70	−17.96	−26.81	30.18		
S-T INVESTMENT CHANGE (balance sheet)			−81.69	−33.45	15.83	61.26	66.19	40.70	−17.96	−26.81	30.18		

MONTHLY PRO FORMA INCOME STATEMENTS

	OCT	NOV	DEC	JAN	FEB	MAR	APR	MAY	JUN	JUL	AUG
SALES	40.00	60.00	120.00	204.00	180.00	150.00	120.00	84.00	78.00	108.00	210.00
COST OF RAW MATERIALS			72.00	122.40	108.00	90.00	72.00	50.40	46.80	64.80	126.00
SALARIES & WAGES			28.60	43.72	39.40	34.00	28.60	22.12	21.04	26.44	44.80
DEPRECIATION			3.91	3.87	3.83	3.79	3.76	3.72	3.68	3.64	3.61
INTEREST EXPENSE			3.00	3.00	3.00	3.00	3.00	3.00	3.00	3.00	3.00
INTEREST INCOME			0.42	−0.07	−0.27	−0.18	0.19	0.59	0.83	0.73	0.56
TAXABLE INCOME			12.91	30.94	25.50	19.03	12.84	5.35	4.31	10.84	33.16

(Continued)

TABLE 26-10 *(Continued)*

	OCT	NOV	DEC	JAN	FEB	MAR	APR	MAY	JUN	JUL	AUG
			MONTHLY PRO FORMA INCOME STATEMENTS								
TAXES			4.52	10.83	8.92	6.66	4.49	1.87	1.51	3.79	11.60
NET INCOME			8.39	20.11	16.57	12.37	8.34	3.48	2.80	7.05	21.55
DIVIDENDS			2.00	2.00	2.00	2.00	2.00	2.00	2.00	2.00	2.00
CHANGE IN RETAINED EARNINGS			6.39	18.11	14.57	10.37	6.34	1.48	0.80	5.05	19.55

	OCT	NOV	DEC	JAN	FEB	MAR	APR	MAY	JUN	JUL	AUG
			CURRENT BALANCE SHEET AND MONTHLY PRO FORMA BALANCE SHEETS								
CASH		76.00	110.99	104.62	89.20	72.10	59.81	62.10	90.54	86.44	61.42
S-T INVESTMENT (BORROWING)		70.00	−11.69	−45.14	−29.31	31.95	98.14	138.84	120.89	94.08	124.26
ACCOUNTS RECEIVABLE		56.00	102.00	182.40	210.00	180.00	147.00	110.40	88.80	103.80	180.00
INVENTORY		122.00	156.80	135.80	111.80	86.00	66.20	72.20	117.80	123.80	56.00
NET FIXED ASSETS		391.00	387.09	383.22	379.39	375.59	371.84	368.12	364.44	360.79	357.19
TOTAL ASSETS		715.00	745.19	760.90	761.07	745.64	742.99	751.67	782.47	768.91	778.87
ACCOUNTS PAYABLE		77.00	106.80	101.40	84.00	64.20	52.20	56.40	92.40	70.80	58.20
ACCRUED INTEREST		6.00	0.00	3.00	6.00	0.00	3.00	6.00	0.00	3.00	6.00
LONG-TERM DEBT		300.00	300.00	300.00	300.00	300.00	300.00	300.00	300.00	300.00	300.00
COMMON STOCK		70.00	70.00	70.00	70.00	70.00	70.00	70.00	70.00	70.00	70.00
RETAINED EARNINGS		262.00	268.39	286.50	301.07	311.44	317.79	319.27	320.07	325.11	344.67
LIABS. + OWNERS' EQUITY		715.00	745.19	760.90	761.07	745.64	742.99	751.67	782.47	768.91	778.87

[a] Required for other computations.

26.6 DYNAMICS OF CASH MANAGEMENT

Cash management involves the management of a firm's existing cash resources and the flow of cash into and out of the firm. Cash management has received increased attention because interest rates were generally higher and more volatile during the 1980s than in prior periods. As a result, cash management has become a separate area of specialization within the Treasurer's departments of many large corporations.

Cash management takes place against the cash budgeting backdrop discussed earlier in the chapter. It encompasses six principal activities: (1) converting accounts receivable into cash, (2) managing accounts payable to make the most cost-effective use of trade credit, (3) managing available cash balances (taking into account compensating cash balance requirements under existing bank loan facilities), (4) investing surplus cash, (5) managing collection float, and (6) controlling cash disbursements. The first four items were discussed in Chapter 25. This section deals with the last two, which are associated with the concept of **float**.

FLOAT

The term **float** refers to a delay in the payee's ability to use funds when a payor makes payment. A firm experiences two principal types of float: **collection float** and **disbursement float**. Float results principally from delays (1) between the time the customer mails a check and the check is received (**mail float**), (2) between the time the check is received and the time it is deposited in a bank (**corporate processing float**), and (3) between the time the check is deposited and the funds are available for the firm's use (**bank collection float**). The latter is due to the time it takes checks to clear, that is, for funds to be collected by the payee's bank from the payor's bank. Effective cash management involves reducing collection float. From the Principle of Two-Sided Transactions you can see that disbursement float and collection float are the same thing viewed from the two sides of the transaction. Effective cash management also includes controlling cash disbursements by taking advantage of reasonable opportunities to exploit disbursement float. We should point out that some of the techniques often used to slow cash disbursement have come under severe criticism from consumer groups and regulatory bodies. Also, the Federal Reserve System has instituted policies to reduce Federal Reserve float, and the Expedited Funds Availability Act of 1988 imposed more stringent standards for funds availability, both of which have significantly reduced bank collection float.

Float is a matter of concern to the cash manager because the cash manager cannot earn interest during the collection float period but does earn interest during the disbursement float period. By speeding cash collections and controlling cash disbursements effectively, a cash manager can increase the amount of funds available for investment (or reduce the amount of funds the firm must borrow) and enhance net income. Cash management activities, while always important, take on increased importance during periods of high interest rates when the opportunity cost of sloppy cash management is greatest.

SPEEDING CASH COLLECTIONS

Commercial banks offer a variety of services that are designed to speed cash collections for corporations. The primary cash collection service is the lockbox collection system.

LOCKBOX COLLECTION SYSTEM   Bankers Trust Company and First National Bank of Chicago developed the first lockbox arrangement in 1947 for Radio Corporation of America (RCA).[19] A lockbox system is designed to reduce collection float by cutting down on mail float and corporate processing float. In the absence of a lockbox system, customers from all over the country would mail their checks to the firm (perhaps to its headquarters), which would process the checks and deposit them into its bank account. Under a lockbox arrangement, a firm selects a set of collection points at strategic locations in different parts of the United States. The firm rents a post office box at each collection point and arranges with a bank located nearby to pick up mail from the post office box several times a day. The firm's customers are instructed to mail payment to the regional collection point, which reduces mail float. The local bank collects the mail, processes the checks, and deposits them in the firm's account immediately, which reduces corporate processing float, and transmits a deposit report to the firm. Using a lockbox collection system can cut a firm's collection float by more than half.

Banks can help firms select the best allocation of collection points. Sophisticated mathematical algorithms have been developed for this purpose.[20] Banks also provide

---

[19] Masonson (1985).

[20] See, for example, Cornuejols, Fisher, and Nemhauser (1977); Fielitz and White (1981); Maier and Van-der Weide (1983).

services beyond depositing the checks and reporting the deposits. For example, sophisticated lockbox systems photocopy customer checks and send these photocopies, along with the contents of the remittance envelopes, to the firm.[21]

Deciding whether a lockbox collection system is economically advantageous involves determining whether the interest that can be earned as a result of increased cash availability plus the value of the reduction in the check processing burden exceed the cost of the services. Most banks charge for their lockbox services on a per-item basis. Consequently, a lockbox collection system tends to be most valuable when the firm receives a relatively small volume of large dollar payments from widely dispersed locations.

OTHER METHODS OF SPEEDING CASH COLLECTIONS Banks offer at least four other methods of speeding cash collections. **Preauthorized checks** (PACs), which are authorized by the payor in advance, are written either by the payee or by the payee's bank and then deposited in the payee's bank account. PACs are generally used for recurring payments, such as mortgage or lease payments.

Preauthorized electronic debits (PADs) work much like PACs. In the case of a PAD, the customer preauthorizes its bank to debit its account and send payment to the payee's bank through the **Automated Clearing House** (ACH) system. The ACH is a collection of 32 regional electronic interbank networks. Each ACH member bank submits to its local ACH each day a computer tape of its ACH debits and credits. These transactions are processed electronically with a guaranteed 1-day collection float (versus 1 or 2 days for PACs). PADs involve less float, and many banks charge less for PADs than PACs because PACs involve paper items. Nevertheless, many firms and individuals prefer PACs because they want paper evidence of payment—a check. In addition, PADs can be used only if all the banks involved in the transaction are ACH members.

PACs and PADs are used for repetitive transactions. Electronic trade payments for separate transactions can be made through the National Automated Clearing House Association. This method of making corporate trade payments is still developing.

The fourth technique for speeding cash collections is the preencoded deposit. Companies that receive a large volume of checks, such as insurance companies and small banks that send checks to their correspondent banks, may find it advantageous to purchase their own encoding equipment to preencode their checks. Depositing preencoded checks speeds check processing at the deposit bank. Significant cost savings can result when the deposit bank charges less for preencoded checks, which is typically the case.

CONTROLLING CASH DISBURSEMENTS

While the goal of cash collection systems is to reduce the lag between the date the check is mailed and the date good funds are available, the goal of cash disbursement systems is to do just the opposite: to extend the lag between the date the check is mailed and the date the firm's checking account is debited. The principal cash disbursement system is remote-controlled disbursement.

Corporate payment terms typically recognize the postmark date on the envelope as the relevant date for the purpose of claiming discounts and determining timely

---

[21] There are two basic types of lockbox systems. A "retail" lockbox system is designed to process a high volume of items of relatively small dollar amount (e.g., monthly utility payments). Such systems generally do not transmit documents back to the firm but a computerized record indicating account information. A "wholesale" lockbox system is designed to process a low volume of items of relatively large dollar amounts. Wholesale systems offer more customized services but are also more expensive.

payment. It is therefore worthwhile for the payor to seek to extend the lag between the mailing date and the ultimate payment of funds from the bank account.

Remote disbursement services exploit the fact that check presentment is more difficult in certain geographic locations (i.e., remote areas) than in major cities. For example, suppose a firm headquartered in New York City can use either a New York City bank or a bank in a remote location to serve as its disbursing bank for payments to suppliers in the New York area. The average presentation time in the case of the New York City bank is 1 day. The average presentation time for the other bank is 3 days. By using the remote disbursement bank, the firm gets an extra 2 days' use of the funds. During the 1970s, some companies went so far as to mail payments to East Coast establishments drawn on West Coast banks in remote locations and vice versa. Part of the disbursement burden fell on the Federal Reserve system, which posts a schedule of guaranteed funds availability. To the extent checks take longer to clear through the Federal Reserve System, the payee bank effectively gets an interest-free loan from the Fed. As a result, the Fed began jawboning against remote disbursement. The jawboning, together with considerable negative publicity, forced most major banks to stop offering the more obvious forms of remote disbursement services.

Controlled disbursement is a service that improves the firm's control over its daily cash disbursements. It does so by providing a single presentation of checks each day. Banks in Federal Reserve cities receive several presentations of checks from the Fed each business day. Items drawn upon a corporate checking account may arrive as late as 4:00 P.M. In such cases, a firm that wished to avoid overdrafts would have to maintain sufficient cash to cover possible debits, which would mean that the firm might not discover that it is in an excess cash position until it is too late in the day to invest the excess cash balances. Controlled disbursement services are now more widely used than remote disbursement services.

Controlled disbursement services are offered through bank branches that are served by regional check processing centers (RCPCs). Banks located in RCPCs receive just one presentation of checks per day from the Fed, usually early in the morning. The firm's bank can use this situation to the firm's advantage by maintaining the firm's account at the RCPC branch. Once the presentment for the day has occurred, the firm knows the exact cash disbursement requirements for the day. The Fed is also trying to discourage this practice to reduce disbursement float. The Fed has announced that it may present checks as late as noon anywhere in the United States where check volume is large enough. Noon presentment, however, will not render controlled disbursement obsolete.

In addition, the Fed has begun capturing on computer tape the magnetic ink character recognition (MICR) line on the bottom of each check that indicates its dollar amount. Early each morning the Fed provides the computer tape to its member banks, which can then inform their customers as to the amount of debits that will be posted to their accounts that day. Each customer then leaves just enough funds in its checking account to cover the checks to be presented that day.

OTHER METHODS OF CONTROLLING CASH DISBURSEMENTS   Three other means are available for controlling cash disbursements. Firms use **payable through drafts** to maintain control over payments made on behalf of the firm by personnel in noncentral locations. Each payable through draft must be approved separately by the account holder, e.g., the division's controller. Mechanically, the payor's bank delivers the payable through draft to the payor, which must approve it and return it to the bank before payment can be made.

Firms use **zero-balance accounts** to give them the flexibility to maintain separate disbursement accounts (for example, one for each of its operating divisions) while retaining central cash management. Each zero-balance account contains just enough cash to cover the day's check presentments. Any excess cash balances are wired to a central concentration account. As a result, the outstanding balance in each zero-balance account is driven to zero by the end of each day.

Electronic trade payments, which were discussed earlier in this section, can also be used to control disbursements. Payments are made electronically at the appropriate time, which can reduce transaction costs. However, firms lose the disbursement float, which has led to some resistance to this method of making corporate trade payments.

CONCENTRATION, INFORMATION, AND INVESTMENT SERVICES

Commercial banks provide three other services that assist corporate cash management: **concentration services**, which facilitate centralized cash management; **information services**, which help a firm monitor its cash position; and **short-term investment services**.

CONCENTRATION SERVICES Most large companies utilize concentration banking. Funds are collected at lockboxes and other locations and then concentrated in a single location (the concentration bank) where they can be used as the corporation requires. Centralization simplifies cash management. It is easier to manage one central account than it is to manage several, some of which may be in far-flung locations. With one concentration account, it is easier to identify excess cash balances. Zero-balance accounts in various locations can be adequately funded and the balance of cash invested. Due to the economies of scale involved in investing, concentration of excess funds in a single account can also lead to enhanced returns on short-term investments.[22]

Figure 26–3 illustrates the flow of funds in a representative concentration banking system. Funds are collected at various locations, some at lockbox locations and the balance at firm offices that deliver the checks to a local bank. Deposit data are collected daily by a third party vendor and transmitted to the firm, which carefully tracks funds availability and determines cash disbursement needs in each location. Excess funds are transferred to the concentration bank through any of three means: **Fed funds wire transfer** (which achieves same-day availability at the concentration bank), **depository transfer check** (DTCs) (which entails writing a check on the corporation's account at the regional location and immediately depositing it into the concentration account whereupon it is processed by the banking system in the usual manner), or **electronic depository transfers** (EDTs) through the ACH system. Automated DTCs and EDTs usually provide 1-day funds availability. As a general rule, DTCs and EDTs are cheaper than wire transfers because the much higher wire transfer charges tend to more than offset the opportunity cost of the 1-day float.

INFORMATION SERVICES Computerized information reporting services, which most money center banks and some nonbank data processing companies offer, are very important to effective cash management. The better information reporting ser-

---

[22]In addition, institutional money market mutual funds typically have minimum investment requirements, certificates of deposit of $1 million or greater generally offer higher yields than smaller CDs, and money market preferred stock usually has a par value of $100,000 per share. When the amount of funds available for investment does not meet the posted minimum, another, perhaps less desirable, investment must be selected. Concentration banking reduces the likelihood of that situation occurring.

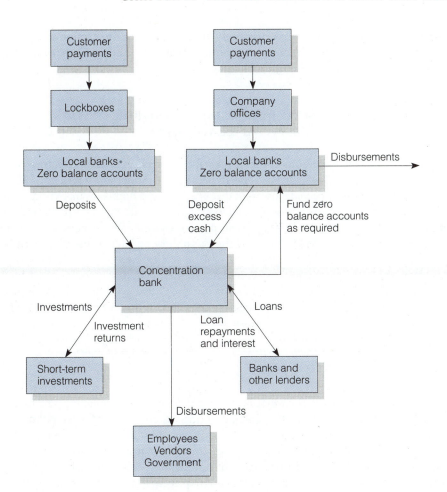

FIGURE 26-3
Flow of funds within a
concentration banking system.

vices normally provide, at a minimum, ledger balance (which includes float), immediately available balance, next day available balance, and balance available thereafter for each of the firm's bank accounts; previous day's debit and credit activity by account; current day's and summary of prior day's lockbox activity; depository transfer and wire transfer reporting; current day's check presentment for each account; and money market data to assist in short-term investment decision-making. Each of these services (as well as others) is offered and priced separately so that a firm can decide which ones it is economically advantageous for the firm to use.

INVESTMENT SERVICES A useful cash management device is the **sweep account**. The account holder specifies an account maintenance level. At the end of each business day, any funds in the account in excess of this maintenance level are automatically "swept" into an interest-bearing account or invested in some other manner that the account holder has previously specified. Typically, several investment alternatives are available. In some cases, it may be possible to split the funds into two or more prespecified investments in accordance with an investment ratio (e.g., 50% in the Dreyfus Cash Management Fund and 50% in the Dreyfus Government Cash Management Fund). Sweep accounts provide convenience, and they reduce idle cash balances. However, they are often expensive.

As with the other cash management services a firm can procure from banks or other outside vendors, the firm must analyze each service to determine whether the benefits from more effective cash management that can be expected to result from using the service exceed the cost of the service.

SOLUTION TO FINANCIAL PLANNING AT THE
YU N. MI TOY COMPANY

Justin Case's financial planning model is presented in section 26.5, automating short-term forecasts. Tables 26–7 through 26–10 present the model and forecasts of MTC's account balances for expected, lower-than-expected, and higher-than-expected sales levels during the upcoming months of December through August. To recap, these tables show that the expected (higher than previous years) sales level may necessitate additional financing for MTC to avoid the possibility of having insufficient cash to meet its obligations, even though the condition is expected to be only temporary. Based on the information presented in these tables, Mr. Case convinced Mr. Mi to allow him to arrange for a line of credit for MTC that would be available just in case additional financing becomes necessary to maintain the smooth operation of the company.

SUMMARY

Financial planning entails formulating financial objectives, projecting the financial impact of alternative operating strategies under alternative financial policies and under alternative operating scenarios, selecting in light of these consequences the "best" financial policies and financial program for the firm, and preparing contingency plans. The completed financial plan outlines the firm's financial strategy and projects the consequences of that strategy. The principal components of an effective corporate financial plan include a clear statement of corporate objectives, a clear statement of assumptions, a description of the basic business strategies, an outline of the planned capital expenditure program, an outline of the planned financing program, and a set of pro forma financial statements that illustrate the projected operating results and the projected impact of the plan on the financial condition of the firm.

Financial planning involves more than forecasting; it entails analyzing the effects of many alternatives under a variety of operating environments rather than just one strategy under the most likely future environment. The output at each step of this process is a set of pro forma financial statements. The ultimate output, the long-term financial plan, embodies the firm's chosen financial policies and financing program. It is important to appreciate that it is the judgment of management—and not some arcane optimization routine contained in a mathematical planning model—that determines the desired financial plan. A financial planning model does not select the best financial strategy; it simply traces the consequences of a particular strategy.

The financial planning process takes place within a flow of funds framework. This chapter developed a financial planning model that can be used to generate pro forma income statements, statements of cash flows, and balance sheets once the values for the various financial policy parameters and the required operating data have been specified. In this simple model, the values assigned to the financial policy parameters embody the firm's financial objectives. The values assigned to the future changes in (1) revenue, (2) selling, general, and administrative expense, and (3) interest rates, together with (4) projected annual capital expenditures and (5) an

DECISION SUMMARY BOX

- A firm should prepare a financial plan on a regular basis, preferably at least annually. Any firm that doesn't plan for its future may not have one.
- A firm's financial plan should consist of (1) a long-term financial plan that covers a period of at least 3 to 5 years, (2) a short-term financial plan that covers the coming year and agrees with the first year of the long-term plan, and (3) a detailed cash budget for the coming year.
- The firm's business units should be intimately involved in the planning process, with each unit preparing its own financial plan. The corporate staff must provide overall guidance by ensuring that all business units base their plans on a consistent set of assumptions (supplied by the corporate staff), checking the business unit plans for reasonableness, and consolidating the business unit plans into the overall financial plan for the firm.

- The firm should regularly monitor its performance against the short-term plan and cash budget, preferably on a monthly basis.
- The cash-flow break-even point over a planning horizon is a pivotal point for addressing contingency plans for possible, even if unlikely, bad outcomes.
- The probability of falling below cash-flow break-even during a planning horizon provides a measure of the firm's total risk.
- A firm should monitor its cash position on a daily basis. It should maintain a rolling cash budget that covers a period of at least 30 days, which it should update at least weekly.
- A firm should seek out ways to improve cash management efficiency by speeding collections and controlling disbursements.

annual long-term debt repayment schedule, embody the firm's assumptions regarding its future operating environment and in the case of the revenue items, the success of its basic commercial strategy in that environment. Repeated iterations of the model based on different values for these variables will indicate how different operating environments, commercial strategies, and financial policies would affect these financial results.

The corporate financial planning process generates a more detailed short-term financial plan in addition to the long-term plan. The short-term plan typically covers the first year of the long-term plan and provides quarterly (in many cases, monthly) financial statements. The short-term plan is useful for control purposes. The short-term financial plan typically includes a cash budget, which provides a breakdown of cash receipts and cash disbursements period by period that correspond to the short-term plan. A firm uses its cash budget to monitor closely its sources and uses of cash.

While the principal output of the corporate financial planning process is the corporate financial plan, the planning process is also useful in other ways. It forces the firm to articulate its financial objectives, to formulate financial policies to meet those objectives, and to test those policies against different operating environments and alternative commercial strategies. The planning process, if done properly, also forces management to contemplate turns of events that might upset its basic strategy and to devise contingent strategies for dealing with such developments. Finally, the financial plan provides a benchmark against which future financial performance may be evaluated.

Cash budgeting is a critically important aspect of corporate financial planning. A firm must have cash available when it is needed to meet the firm's financial obligations. The need for cash budgeting arises because of the uncertain and nonsynchronous timing of cash inflows and cash outflows. Accordingly, a firm needs to be able to monitor its cash position on a daily basis. Firms can use a rolling (30-day, 60-day, or some other interval) cash budget for this purpose. To be useful, the rolling cash budget should be updated at least weekly.

Effective cash management is to cash budgeting what effective operating management is to overall corporate planning. Cash management encompasses converting accounts receivable into cash in a timely fashion, managing accounts payable to optimize the use of trade credit, managing available cash balances to minimize idle unproductive balances while ensuring that the firm pays its bills on time, investing surplus cash to maximize after-tax returns subject to maintaining satisfactory liquidity, taking cost-effective steps to reduce collection float, and controlling disbursement. Firms use lockbox collection systems, preauthorized checks, preauthorized electronic debits, electronic trade payments, and preencoded deposits to speed cash collections. Firms use remote-controlled disbursement, zero-balance accounts, and other techniques to control cash disbursements. Well-managed companies also practice concentration banking in order to centralize their cash management activities. The overriding objective of all these efforts is to utilize the valuable cash resources of a firm in the most efficient manner possible.

Throughout this book, we have stressed the Principle of Capital Market Efficiency. To some, this may seem discouraging—almost as though financial management does not matter. In parting, we want to reassure you that *financial management does matter*. Avoiding disaster in the day-to-day management of the firm is a prerequisite to success. Effective planning and efficient management enhance the firm's chances for success. Remember: While effective planning and optimal day-to-day management cannot ensure the success of the firm, poor planning and mismanagement can easily "snatch defeat from the jaws of victory."

PROBLEMS

PROBLEM SET A

A1. Define the term **corporate financial planning**.

A2. Define the term **financial plan**.

A3. Cite and briefly describe the six principal components of an effective corporate financial plan.

A4. Explain why a firm's **financial leverage** is typically more under its control than is the firm's operating leverage.

A5. Explain why the **cash-flow break-even** point might be of interest to a firm even though, as explained in Chapter 12, the indifference level of sales that will produce a zero NPV is likely to be much higher than the accounting-earnings break-even point, which is in turn generally higher than the cash-flow break-even point.

A6. Which do you think would be more difficult to forecast, costs or revenues? Briefly explain the basis for your conclusion.

A7. Here is a spreadsheet assignment for getting acquainted with LOTUS 1-2-3.

1. Go to a PC with a copy of LOTUS, boot LOTUS, and go into 1-2-3.
2. In cell A1, type: PRACTICE
3. In cell A3, type: Growth
4. In cell A4, type: Acct 1
5. In cell A5, type: Acct 2
6. In cell A6, type: Acct 3
7. In cell A8, type: Total
8. In cell B4, type: 5.0
9. In cell B5, type: 12.3
10. In cell B6, type: 22.1
11. In cell B8, type: +B4+B5+B6
12. In cell C3, type: .20

13. In cell C4, type: (1+C3)*B4
14. In cell C5, type: (1+C3)*B5
15. In cell C6, type: (1+C3)*B6
16. Use the copy command to copy *from* cell B8 *to* C8 (/ key to get menu).
17. Use the copy command to copy *from* cell C3 *to* cells D3, E3, and F3 (use . key to anchor the ranges).
18. Use the copy command to copy *from* cells C3 . . C8 *to* cells D3 . . D8, E3 . . E8, and F3 . . F8.
19. Set the format for the entire worksheet to 2 decimals (worksheet, global, format, fixed, 2).
20. Print your worksheet. It should look like the one given below.

PRACTICE

Growth		0.20	0.20	0.20	0.20
Acct 1	5.00	6.00	7.20	8.64	10.37
Acct 2	12.30	14.76	17.71	21.25	25.51
Acct 3	22.10	26.52	31.82	38.19	45.83
Total	39.40	47.28	56.74	68.08	81.70

A8. What are the principal differences between the **long-term financial plan** and the **short-term financial plan**? Which one contains the **cash budget**?

A9. What is concentration banking? How does it enable a firm to operate its cash management system more efficiently?

A10. What is the purpose of the **cash budget**? Describe the principal elements of the cash budgeting process.

A11. Describe the two principal methods of cash budgeting. What are the major differences between these two methods? Which method is more useful when a summary presentation is desired? When a rolling 30-day daily cash forecast is desired?

A12. Using the information in Table 26–3, project the income statement, balance sheet, and statement of cash flows ahead 6 years, assuming capital expenditures, debt repayment, and the change in deferred income taxes are the same in years 5 and 6.

A13. Describe the six principal aspects of cash management.

A14. Define the term **float**. What are the two basic types of float?

A15. Describe how a **lockbox** collection system works.

A16. What are the primary steps a corporation can take to speed cash collections and control cash disbursements?

PROBLEM SET B

B1. Respond to the following comment: Now that we have such powerful spreadsheet packages and personal computers on which to use them, financial planning should be a snap.

B2. How does **financial planning** help the firm with **financial control**?

B3. Suppose the firm whose recent collection pattern is summarized in Table 26–4 expects its July collections to follow the recent historical pattern and projects the following specific pattern:

Cash discount	Same month	Next month	2 months	3 months	4 months	Uncollectable
1%	4.2%	85.2%	5.0%	3.5%	1.6%	0.5%

Estimate the July collections assuming that July sales are expected to be $275,000.

B4. Suppose the receivables collection pattern for May sales in Table 26–4 was

Cash discount	Same month	Next month	2 months	3 months	4 months	Uncol-lectable
2%	18.7%	71.5%	5.0%	3.3%	1.0%	0.5%

   a. Should you use the May pattern in estimating June collections? Explain.

   b. Given the May receivables collection pattern shown above, describe a procedure for estimating June collections.

B5. Suppose the firm whose recent receivables collection pattern is summarized in Table 26–4 believes that its monthly sales exhibit no seasonal pattern and that the best procedure for projecting its future receivables collection pattern is simply to extrapolate from recent experience.

   a. Suppose the firm decides to base its projected collection pattern on the average pattern for the preceding 3 months. Project the collection pattern for June sales.

   b. Assume the projected collection pattern calculated in part a has been constant over the last 4 months and use it to estimate June collections.

   c. What limitations, if any, are there to the procedure described in part a?

B6. Use the model in Table 26–2 to develop 5 years of projected income statements, statements of cash flows, and balance sheets based on the following information:

ΔREVENUE = 5% per annum

ΔSG&A = 4% per annum

INTEREST RATE[0] = 9%

TAX RATE = 40%

CAPEX = $50 million per year

PAYOUT RATIO = 0.25

REPAY = 0

SG&A[0] = $100 million

FIXED ASSETS[0] = $400 million

WORKING CAPITAL[0] = $150 million

OTHER ASSETS = $50 million

MARGIN = 50%

DEPRECIATION RATE = 8%

ΔINTEREST RATE = 0

DEPRECIATION[TAX] = 12% of book value

WC RATIO = 0.3

DEBT RATIO = 0.4

REVENUE[0] = $500 million

DEBT[0] = $220 million

EQUITY[0] = $330 million

DEFERRED TAXES[0] = $50 million

B7. Use the model in Table 26–2 to develop 5 years of projected income statements, statements of cash flows, and balance sheets based on the following information (dollar amounts in millions).

Forecast:	1 year	2 years	3 years	4 years	5 years
ΔREVENUE =	50	75	75	100	100
INTEREST RATE =	9	10	12	11	9
ΔSG&A =	10	15	20	25	30
CAPEX =	50	60	70	80	90
DEPRECIATION[TAX] =	100	110	120	110	100
TAX RATE =	40	40	50	50	50

PAYOUT RATIO = 0.2   DEPRECIATION RATE = 10%

DEBT RATIO = 0.25   WC RATIO = 0.1

REPAY = 0   REVENUE[0] = $800

SG&A[0] = $140   DEBT[0] = $165

FIXED ASSETS[0] = $550   EQUITY[0] = $495

WORKING CAPITAL[0] = $100   DEFERRED TAXES[0] = $40

OTHER ASSETS = $50   MARGIN = 40%

B8. Midwest Manufacturing can use either wire transfers or depository transfer checks (DTCs) to concentrate funds at its Chicago concentration bank. If Midwest wired out all available funds each day, it would typically wire out $100,000, which consists of $25,000 in immediately available funds it received that day and $75,000 in next-day–available funds received the previous day. A bank wire transfer costs $15 per transaction. If instead Midwest uses DTCs, its cost would consist of (1) forgone interest on the immediately available funds at the rate of 10% per annum (actual number of days elapsed in a 365–day year) and (2) a bank charge of $3.50 per DTC.

   a. Calculate the average daily cost of each concentration method.

   b. Which method should Midwest use?

   c. At what interest rate would Midwest be indifferent between the two concentration methods?

B9. Nonconsolidated Edison Company's bank has furnished the following account analysis for the month of June (through June 30)

	Current month	Year to date
Average daily ledger balance	$100,000	$125,000
Average daily float	10,000	15,000
Reserve requirement (10%)	9,000	11,000
Average daily investable balance	$ 81,000	$ 99,000
Deposit credit (9% APR, simple daily interest based on a 365–day year)	$ 599	$ 4,455

Service	Volume	Unit price	Total cost	Balances required
Maintenance	1	$20.00	$ 20.00	$ 2,703.70
Deposits	21	1.00	21.00	2,838.89
Items deposited	100,000	0.001	100.00	13,518.52
Wire transfers	21	15.00	315.00	42,583.33
Checks written	500	0.10	50.00	6,759.26
			$506.00	$68,403.70

	Price basis	Balance basis
Deposit credit	$599	$81,000
Services rendered	506	68,404
Excess balances available to pay for other bank services	$ 93	$12,596

   a. Nonconsolidated Edison estimates that it could have earned a 10% yield (calculated on the basis of a 365–day year) if it had invested the daily investable balances in a money market fund and paid cash for the bank services. Would Nonconsolidated Edison have been better off under that strategy?

b. If the investment rate of return a company can earn by investing its daily investable balances *always* exceeds the bank's earnings credit rate and there are zero transaction costs, should the company pay cash for bank services or should it pay through deposit credits?

c. How would the existence of transaction costs alter your answer to part b? Formulate a decision rule.

B10. Banks A and B charge for bank services and calculate the deposit credit to pay for those services in the following manner:

	Bank A	Bank B
Monthly service charge	$15.00	$16.00
Monthly balance required to pay monthly service charge	$2,000	$1,920
Earnings credit rate (APR, simple daily interest based on a 365-day year)	9%	10%

a. If a corporate customer pays cash for bank services, which bank has the lower monthly service charge?

b. If a corporate customer pays for bank services through deposit credits, which bank has the lower monthly service charge?

c. If a corporate customer can earn 11% on riskless investments, which bank has the lower monthly service charge?

d. If a corporate customer can earn no more than 8% on riskless investments, which bank has the lower monthly service charge?

B11. Reproduce the spreadsheet output given in Table 26–7, using the model given in Table 26–8.

B12. Modify the model you created for problem B11 to create the spreadsheet outputs shown in Tables 26–9 and 26–10.

B13. Strand PC's, Unlimited makes bulk purchases of PC's, stocks them in conveniently located warehouses, and then ships them to its chain of retail stores. Strand's balance sheet as of 12/31 is shown below (in thousands of dollars).

Cash	$ 20.0	Accounts payable	$ 50.0
Accounts receivable	150.0	Notes payable	100.0
Inventories	330.0	Accruals	50.0
Current Assets	500.0	Current Liabilities	200.0
Net fixed assets	202.0	Mortgage loan	34.0
		Common stock	84.0
		Retained Earnings	384.0
Total Assets	$702.0	Liabilities + Owners' Equity	$702.0

Sales for 1990 were $2 million, while net income after taxes for the year was $56,700. Strand paid dividends of $22,680 to common stockholders. The firm is operating at full capacity.

a. Construct a pro forma balance sheet for next Dec. 31, assuming that sales increase next year by 25%. Assume that all accounts, except notes payable, mortgage loan, common stock, and retained earnings are a function of sales. Assume that all external capital requirements are met by bank loans that are reflected in notes payable.

b. Construct pro forma balance sheets for each of the next 5 years using all of the assumptions in part a except that sales grow by $100,000 per year. Compute the current ratio, debt-to-total assets ratio, and the return on net worth for Strand for each year.

PROBLEM SET C

C1. Mathew T. Box, III, grandson of the founder and currently CEO of the M. T. Box Company, has been concerned about the company's short-term financial management. The treasurer of M. T. Box, Mary Hoover, has gathered the information given below and is asking you to create a cash budget, monthly pro forma income statements, and monthly pro forma balance sheets for the next 6 months for M. T. Box.

1. The payment pattern for revenues is estimated to be as follows: 20% of sales are for cash, 15% are paid for one month after the sale, 55% are paid for two months after the sale, 9% are paid for in 3 months, and 1% are uncollectable.

2. The cash account should be set to start each month in the amount of $15,000 plus 65% of next month's salaries and wages plus 75% of this month's accounts payable. The cash account will be adjusted with the short-term investment (borrowing) account, and Mary Hoover believes M. T. Box can earn 9% A.P.R. on its short-term investments.

3. Purchases of raw materials each month are in the amount of 35% of the predicted sales for the month after next plus 25% of next month's predicted sales plus 8% of this month's sales. Purchases are paid for in the month following their purchase, and there are no discounts available from suppliers. The cost of raw materials averages 68% of sales.

4. The company pays salaries and wages of $15,000 plus 14% of this month's sales.

5. Fixed assets are being depreciated at the rate of 1% of net fixed assets per month.

6. The company pays a cash dividend of $2,000 every month.

7. The long-term debt on the balance sheet carries a 15% A.P.R., and payments are made quaterly in December, March, June, and September.

8. Taxes are at the rate of 35% of taxable income (including rebates for negative taxes). Taxes are paid monthly.

9. Mary Hoover is expecting the company to make a purchase of $150,000 in fixed assets at the end of April.

10. Sales for October, November, and December of this year were $60,000, $90,000, and $150,000, respectively. Sales forecast for the next 8 months are (in thousands)

Jan.	Feb.	Mar.	Apr.	May	Jun.	Jul.	Aug.
250.00	235.00	190.00	160.00	110.00	90.00	135.00	260.00

Balance Sheet as of December 31

Cash	$ 170.00	Accounts payable	$ 160.00
Short-term investment (borrowing)	90.00	Accrued interest	0.00
Accounts receivable	195.00	Long-term debt	600.00
Inventory	157.00	Common stock	120.00
Net fixed assets	615.00	Retained earnings	347.00
Total Assets	$1,227.00	Liabilities + Owners' Equity	$1,227.00

C2. The information given below has been gathered for Dunn Manufacturing, Inc. Ulysses R. Dunn, the founder, manager, and majority shareholder is trying to get a "handle" on financial planning. Use the information given below to create a cash budget, monthly pro forma income statements, and monthly pro forma balance sheets for the next 9 months for Dunn Manufacturing and U. R. Dunn.

1. The payment pattern for revenues is estimated to be as follows: 20% of sales are for cash, 10% are paid for 1 month after the sale, 50% are paid for 2 months after the sale, 18% are paid for 3 months after the sale, and 2% are uncollectable.
2. The cash account is targeted to start each month in the amount of $20,000 plus 70% of next month's salaries and wages plus 75% of this month's accounts payable. The cash account will be adjusted with the notes payable account, which currently costs 1.1% per month on the balance.
3. Dunn purchases raw materials each month in the amount of 40% of the predicted sales for the month after next plus 10% of next month's predicted sales plus 15% of this month's sales. Purchases are paid for in the month following their purchase, and there are no discounts available to Dunn from its suppliers. The cost of raw materials averages 65% of sales.
4. Dunn pays salaries and wages of $27,000 plus 10% of this month's sales.
5. Dunn is depreciating its net fixed assets at the rate of 0.9% of *net* fixed assets per month.
6. Dunn pays a cash dividend of $5,000 every month.
7. The long-term debt on the Dunn balance sheet carries a 12% A.P.R., and payments are made quaterly in December, March, June, and September.
8. Taxes for Dunn Manufacturing are at the rate of 34% of taxable income (including rebates for negative taxes). Taxes are paid quarterly (end of December, March, June, and September) on the basis of what the tax liability is *expected to be over the next quarter*. The model you build must be used in conjunction with trial and error to determine the correct tax payments to avoid encountering the problem of circular reasoning (CIRC). (*Hint*: Initially, just let the taxes "use up" what is currently in the prepaid tax account and go negative.)
9. Dunn expects to purchase $275,000 worth of fixed assets at the end of July.
10. Sales for January, February, and March of this year were $320,000, $345,000, and $365,000, respectively. Sales forecast for the next 11 months are (in thousands)

Apr.	May	Jun.	Jul.	Aug.	Sep.	Oct.	Nov.	Dec.	Jan.	Feb.
410.00	430.00	350.00	325.00	300.00	220.00	265.00	290.00	375.00	350.00	370.00

Balance Sheet as of March 31

Cash	$ 210.00	Accounts payable	$ 177.00
Accounts receivable	256.00	Notes payable (invested)	219.00
Inventory	437.00	Accrued interest	0.00
Prepaid taxes	43.00	Long-term debt	650.00
Other assets	15.00	Common stock	150.00
Net fixed assets	674.00	Retained earnings	439.00
Total Assets	$1,635.00	Liabilities + Owners' Equity	$1,635.00

REFERENCES

Beehler, Paul J. *Contemporary Cash Management: Principles, Practices, Perspectives,* 2nd ed. New York: John Wiley & Sons, 1983.

Brown, Keith C., and Scott L. Lummer. "The Cash Management Implications of a Hedged Dividend Capture Strategy." *Financial Management* 13 (Winter 1984): 7–17.

Brown, Keith C., and Scott L. Lummer. "A Reexamination of the Covered Call Option Strategy for Corporate Cash Management." *Financial Management* 15 (Summer 1986): 13–17.

Carpenter, Michael D., and Jack E. Miller. "A Reliable Framework for Monitoring Accounts Receivable." *Financial Management* 8 (Winter 1979): 37–40.

Cooper, Ian, and Julian R. Franks. "Treasury Performance Measurement." *Midland Corporate Finance Journal* 4 (Winter 1987): 29–43.

Cornuejols, G., M. L. Fisher, and G. L. Nemhauser. "Location of Bank Accounts to Optimize Float: An Analytical Study of Exact and Approximate Algorithms." *Management Science* (1977): 780–810.

Davis, B. E., G. J. Caccappolo, and M. A. Chaudry. "An Econometric Planning Model for American Telephone and Telegraph Company." *Bell Journal of Economics and Management Science* 4 (Spring 1973): 29–56.

Emery, Gary W. "Some Empirical Evidence on the Properties of Daily Cash Flow." *Financial Management* 10 (Spring 1981): 21–28.

Fabozzi, Frank J., and Leslie N. Masonson, eds. *Corporate Cash Management: Techniques and Analysis.* Homewood, Ill.: Dow Jones–Irwin, 1985.

Ferguson, D. M., and Ned C. Hill. "Cash Flow Timeline Management: The Next Frontier of Cash Management." *Journal of Cash Management* (May/June 1985): 12–22.

Ferguson, D. M., and Steven F. Maier. "Disbursement Design for the 1980's." *Journal of Cash Management* (November 1982): 56–69.

Fielitz, Bruce D., and D. L. White. "A Two Stage Solution Procedure for the Lockbox Problem." *Management Science* (August 1981): 881–86.

Finnerty, John D. *Corporate Financial Analysis.* New York: McGraw-Hill, 1986.

Francis, Jack Clark, and Dexter R. Rowell. "A Simultaneous Equation Model of the Firm for Financial Analysis and Planning." *Financial Management* 7 (Spring 1978): 29–44.

Gallinger, George W., and A. James Ifflander. "Monitoring Accounts Receivable Using Variance Analysis." *Financial Management* 15 (Winter 1986): 69–76.

Gentry, James A. "State of the Art of Short-Run Financial Management." *Financial Management* 17 (Summer 1988): 41–57.

Gentry, James A., and Jesus M. De La Garza. "A Generalized Model for Monitoring Accounts Receivable." *Financial Management* 14 (Winter 1985): 28–38.

Gitman, Lawrence J., D. Keith Forrester, and John R. Forrester. "Maximizing Cash Disbursement Float." *Financial Management* 5 (Summer 1976): 15–24.

Gitman, Lawrence J., Edward R. Moses, and J. Thomas White. "An Assessment of Corporate Cash Management Practices." *Financial Management* 8 (Spring 1979): 32–41.

Joehnk, Michael D., Oswald D. Bowlin, and J. William Petty. "Preferred Dividend Rolls: A Viable Strategy for Corporate Money Managers." *Financial Management* 9 (Summer 1980): 78–87.

Kallberg, Jarl G. and Kenneth K. Parkinson. *Current Asset Management.* New York: John Wiley & Sons, 1984.

Kawaller, Ira J. "How and Why to Hedge a Short-term Portfolio." *Journal of Cash Management* (January/February 1985): 26–30.

Kim, Y. H., and V. Srinivasan. "Deterministic Cash Flow Management: State of the Art and Research Directions." *Omega* (1986): 145–66.

Lerner, Eugene M. "Simulating A Cash Budget." *California Management Review* (Winter 1968): 79–86.

Loscalzo, William. *Cash Flow Forecasting*. New York: McGraw-Hill, 1982.

Maier, Steven F., David W. Robinson, and James H. Vander Weide. "A Short-Term Disbursement Forecasting Model." *Financial Management* 10 (Spring 1981): 9–20.

Maier, Steven F., and James H. Vander Weide. "A Practical Approach to Short-Run Financial Planning." *Financial Management* 7 (Winter 1978): 10–16.

Maier, Steven F., and James H. Vander Weide. "What Lockbox and Disbursement Models Really Do." *Journal of Finance* 38 (May 1983): 361–71.

Masonson, Leslie N. "Introduction." In Frank J. Fabozzi and Leslie N. Masonson, eds., *Corporate Cash Management: Techniques and Analysis*. Homewood, Ill.: Dow Jones–Irwin, 1985, ch. 1.

Meyer, Henry I. *Corporate Financial Planning Models*. New York: John Wiley & Sons, 1977.

Miller, Tom W., and Bernell K. Stone. "Daily Cash Forecasting and Seasonal Resolution: Alternative Models and Techniques for Using the Distribution Approach." *Journal of Financial and Quantitative Analysis* 20 (September 1985): 335–51.

Myers, Stewart C., and Gerald A. Pogue. "A Programming Approach to Corporate Financial Management." *Journal of Finance* 29 (May 1974): 579–99.

Pan, Judy, Donald R. Nichols, and O. Maurice Joy. "Sales Forecasting Practices of Large U.S. Industrial Firms." *Financial Management* 6 (Fall 1977): 72–77.

Richards, Verlyn D., and Eugene L. Laughlin. "A Cash Conversion Cycle Approach to Liquidity Analysis." *Financial Management* 9 (Spring 1980): 32–38.

Sartoris, William L., and Ned C. Hill. "A Generalized Cash Flow Approach to Short-Term Financial Decisions." *Journal of Finance* 38 (May 1983): 349–60.

Stone, Bernell K. "The Design of a Company's Banking System." *Journal of Finance* 38 (May 1983): 373–85.

Stone, Bernell K., and Tom W. Miller. "Daily Cash Forecasting: A Structuring Framework." *Journal of Cash Management* (October 1981): 35–50.

Stone, Bernell K., and Tom W. Miller. "Daily Cash Forecasting with Multiplicative Models of Cash Flow Patterns." *Financial Management* 16 (Winter 1987): 45–54.

Zivney, Terry L., and Michael J. Alderson. "Hedged Dividend Capture with Stock Index Options." *Financial Management* 15 (Summer 1986): 5–12.

REFERENCE MATERIALS

GLOSSARY

In the definitions, terms that appear in italics also appear as defined terms in the glossary. The information in brackets refers to places in the text where the term is discussed in context. For example, [10.4] refers to section 4 of Chapter 10.

Abandonment option The ability (option) a firm has to discard or sell an asset or investment project [13.2].

Accelerated depreciation A depreciation method that permits a firm to claim greater depreciation expense than it could under the *straight-line depreciation* method during the early years (and lesser in later years) of an asset's life.

Accounts receivable Money owed to a firm by its customers.

Acid test ratio The difference between current assets and inventories divided by current liabilities [24.4].

Acquiree A firm that is being acquired [Chapter 22, Introduction].

Acquiror A firm or individual who is acquiring something; for example, a firm that is acquiring another firm [Chapter 22, Introduction].

Acquisition *Corporate Acquisition.*

Adjusted present value (APV) A computational method whereby the value of an asset is determined in two parts by adding the present value without regard to capital structure effects plus the value added by capital structure effects [19.5].

Adverse selection A situation where participation appears to convey "negative" information about the participant's product or service [2.6] [5.4].

Affirmative covenant A *bond covenant* that specifies certain actions the firm must take [9.6]. Also called a *positive covenant*.

Agency cost The incremental cost (to the *principal*), above what would be incurred in perfect capital and labor markets, of using an agent [Chapter 9].

Agency problem The possibility that an agent will act in his own self-interest to the detriment of the principal for whom he is acting [Chapter 9].

Agency theory The theoretical analysis of behavior in *principal-agent relationships* [2.1] [Chapter 9].

Agent One who acts on behalf of a *principal* in a *principal-agent relationship* [2.1] [Chapter 9].

Aging schedule (for accounts receivable) Shows the amounts of receivables that have been outstanding for different periods (e.g., 0–15 days, 16–30 days, more than 30 days) [24.4].

American option An option that can be *exercised* at any time during its life [Chapter 8].

AMEX The American Stock Exchange.

Amortize To spread out over a future time period, such as repayment of a loan by installment payments or tax-deductions for depreciation expense [3.4].

Annual percentage rate (APR) A legally specified method for computing a nominal annual rate of return [3.8].

Annuity A series of identical cash flows that are expected to occur each time period for a specified number of time periods [3.4].

Annuity due An *annuity* with n payments but the first payment is made at time $t = 0$ and the last payment is made at time $t = n - 1$.

Antidilutive effect Result of a transaction that increases earnings per common share (e.g., by decreasing the number of common shares outstanding) [17.10].

APB Accounting Principles Board.

APR *Annual Percentage Rate* [3.8].

APT *Arbitrage Pricing Theory* [7.9].

APV *Adjusted Present Value* [19.5].

Arbitrage Buying an asset with the sole purpose of reselling it at a higher price [5.3]. *Riskless arbitrage* is the simultaneous purchase and sale of the asset.

Arbitrage pricing theory (APT) A theory of asset pricing in which the risk premium is based on a specified set of risk factors in addition to (or other than) the correlation with the expected excess return on the market portfolio [7.9].

Arbitrageur A person who engages in some form of *arbitrage* (riskless or risky) [5.3].

Asset Real or personal property that has a value that can be measured in terms of the *present value* of the stream of cash flow the property is expected to generate in the future.

Asset-based financing Methods of financing in which lenders and equity investors look principally to the cash flow from a particular asset or set of assets for a return on, and the return of, their investment [Chapter 21].

Asset-coverage test   A *bond indenture* restriction that permits additional borrowing only if the ratio of assets (typically net tangible assets) to debt (typically long-term debt) does not fall below a specified minimum [14.3].

Asset pricing model   A model for determining the *required rate of return* on an asset [Chapter 7].

Asset substitution   The firm invests in assets that are riskier than those that were expected by the debtholders [9.3].

Asymmetric information   Information that is known to some, but not all, participants [5.4].

Asymmetric taxes   A situation where participants in a transaction have differential net tax rates [Chapter 5].

At-the-money   When the value of the underlying asset equals the *strike price* [Chapter 8].

Auction markets   Markets in which the prevailing price is determined through the free interaction of prospective buyers and sellers, as on the floor of a stock exchange [4.1].

Auction rate preferred stock   Floating-rate *preferred stock*, the dividend rate on which is adjusted every 7 weeks through a *Dutch auction* [14.8].

Authorized shares   (number of) Shares authorized for issuance by a firm's *corporate charter* [14.2].

Automated Clearing House (ACH)   A collection of 32 regional electronic interbank networks used to process transactions electronically with a guaranteed one-day *bank collection float* [26.6].

Average life   The effective maturity of a debt issue, taking into account the effect of sinking fund payments [14.3].

Average rate of return on investment   The ratio of the average annual incremental *free cash flow* to the average investment [11.6].

Back-to-back loan   A form of loan barter arrangement whereby two firms lend each other funds denominated in different currencies for an agreed period [14.5] [23.1].

Balance sheet   A description of the firm's current financial position [1.1] [24.1].

Balloon (payment)   A debt payment that is larger than the loan's other payments. Typically the final payment that repays the outstanding balance of the loan [Chapter 20] [25.4].

Bank collection float   The time that elapses between when a check is deposited into a bank account and when the funds are available to the depositor (during which period the bank is collecting payment from the payer's bank) [26.6].

Bankers' acceptances   *Drafts* that are accepted by a commercial bank [25.3].

Bankruptcy   A formal legal process under which a firm experiencing financial difficulty is protected from its creditors while it works out a plan to settle its debt obligations under the supervision of the bankruptcy court [Chapter 15].

Bankruptcy risk   The risk that a firm will be unable to meet its debt obligations [Chapter 15]. Also called default risk or *insolvency risk*.

Bankruptcy view (of capital structure)   The argument that expected bankruptcy costs preclude firms from being financed entirely with debt [15.1].

Basic business strategies   Key strategies a firm intends to pursue in carrying out its business plan [26.1].

Basis point   1/100 of 1 percent; 1 percent equals 100 basis points.

Bearer bonds   Bonds that are not registered on the books of the issuer; such bonds are held in physical form by the owner, and the owner obtains interest payments by physically detaching coupons from the bond certificate and delivering them to the paying agent [14.7].

Best-efforts   A method of securities distribution in which the securities firm only undertakes to use its best efforts to sell the securities on behalf of the issuer—as contrasted with a *purchase-and-sale* [14.1].

Beta   A linear measure of how much an individual asset contributes to the standard deviation of the market portfolio; calculated as the covariance between the return on the asset and the return on the market portfolio, divided by the variance of the return on the market portfolio [7.6].

Bid-ask spread   The spread, or difference, between the bid price (at which a market agent is willing to buy) and the ask price (at which a market agent is willing to sell) [4.1].

Binomial option pricing model   An option pricing model in which the underlying asset can take on only two possible (discrete) values in the next time period for each value it can take on in the preceding time period [8.8]. Also called the *two-state option pricing model*.

Black-Scholes option pricing model   Formula developed by Fischer Black and Myron Scholes to value a *European option* on a non-dividend-paying stock [8.8].

Block trade   Commonly, a trade involving a large amount of stock. The NYSE defines a block trade as consisting of the lesser of (1) 10,000 or more shares or (2) shares (regardless of the number) with a market value of $200,000 or more, which are sold in a single transaction.

Block-voting   A group of shareholders banding together to vote their shares in a single block [9.2].

Bond   A long-term obligation for money borrowed in the form of a security that the lender purchases from the borrower [14.3].

Bond agreement   A contract for *privately-placed* debt [14.3].

Bond covenant   A contractual provision specified in a *bond indenture*.

Bond equivalent yield   True interest cost expressed on the basis of a 360-day year [25.4].

Bond indenture   A contract for *publicly-traded* bonds [14.3].

Bond value   With respect to a *convertible bond*, the value the security would have if it were not convertible; the value of the security apart from the value of the conversion option [Chapter 14].

Book value   The value as it appears in the accounting records of the firm [14.2].

Book value per common share   The amount of owners' equity on a firm's balance sheet divided by the number of the firm's outstanding shares [14.2].

Break-even concept   The notion of equating costs and revenues; at times this is misleading because computations typically disregard the time value of money [12.5] [26.1].

Break-even lease rate   The lease rate at which a party to a prospective lease is indifferent between entering and not entering into the lease arrangement [21.3].

Break-even point   An accounting term defined as the point at which the total contribution margin equals the total fixed costs of producing a product or service [12.5].

Break-even tax rate   The tax rate at which a party to a prospective transaction is indifferent between entering and not entering into the transaction [Chapter 21].

Broker   One who buys or sells securities on behalf of an investor [4.1].

Bullet maturity   Debt that requires repayment of the entire principal at maturity [14.3] [Chapter 20] [25.4].

Business risk   The inherent or fundamental risk of a business, without regard to *financial risk* [10.4]. The *nondiversifiable risk* of the business. Also called *operating risk*.

Buy   To purchase an asset. Also called *taking a long position*.

Buy orders   Orders for securities purchases [2.4].

Callable   A financial security such as a bond with a call option attached to it (i.e., the issuer has the right to call the security) [14.3].

Call an option   To exercise a call option [Chapter 8].

Call option   The right without the obligation to purchase a specified asset at a specified price within a specified time period [Chapter 8].

Call premium   Premium in price above the par value of a bond (or share of preferred stock) that must be paid holders to redeem the bond (or share of preferred stock) prior to its scheduled maturity date [Chapter 20].

Call price   The price at which the asset specified in an option contract will be purchased if a call option is exercised. Also called *strike price* or *exercise price* [Chapter 8].

Call provision   *Optional redemption provision* [14.3].

Capital   Funds raised for the purpose of investing in a business [21.1].

Capital asset pricing model (CAPM)   A model for determining the *required rate of return* on an asset, taking into account the risk of the asset. A model for specifying the risk-return trade-off in the capital markets [7.6].

Capital budget   A budget for a firm's future capital investment expenditures [11.8].

Capital budgeting   The process of determining the firm's long-term investments [Chapter 11].

Capital expenditure   Investment in additional *assets* [Chapter 11].

Capital gain   Appreciation in the value of an asset [Chapter 17].

Capitalization rate   The *required rate of return* on a stock [6.6].

Capitalization ratio   The ratio of the amount of *capital* raised from a particular source, for example, long-term debt, to the total capitalization of the firm [24.6].

Capitalization table   A table showing the capitalization of a firm, which typically includes the amount of *capital* obtained from each source (e.g., long-term debt, common equity, etc.) and the respective *capitalization ratios* [24.6].

Capitalize   To record on the books of a firm at cost for allocation as an expense over the life of the asset or liability (see *depreciate*) [11.1]. Or, to summarize as the present value of a series of future obligations, as in *capitalize a lease* [21.2].

Capitalized lease obligation   *Capital lease* [21.2].

Capital lease   A lease obligation that has to be capitalized on the face of the balance sheet [21.2].

Capital market   A market in which financial securities are bought and sold [2.7] [Chapter 4] [Chapter 14].

Capital market line   (CML)   The line of investment possibilities extending outward from the *riskless rate*, r_f, and passing through the expected rate of return on the *market portfolio* [7.5].

Capital rationing   The process of imposing a limit (ration) on the amount of new investment undertaken by the firm [13.4].

Capital structure   How a firm is financed. Often meaning simply its proportions of debt and equity financing [2.11] [Chapter 15].

CAPM   *Capital Asset Pricing Model* [7.6].

Cash budget   A budget of expected future cash flows (both inflows and outflows) [26.3].

Cash concentration services   *Concentration services* [26.6].

Cash deficiency agreement   An agreement to invest cash in a project to the extent required to cover any cash deficiency the project may experience [21.4].

Cash discount   An incentive offered to purchasers of a firm's product for payment within a specified time period such as 10 days [25.4].

Cash equivalent   A short-term security that is sufficiently liquid that it may be considered the financial equivalent of cash [Chapter 25].

Cash flow   *Cash flow from operations* [Chapter 18] [Chapter 24].

Cash-flow break-even   The point below which the firm will have insufficient net cash inflow to meet its fixed cost obligations (including such items as fixed salaries and administrative costs, interest and principal payments, and planned cash dividends) [26.1].

Cash flow from operations   A firm's net cash inflow resulting directly from its regular operations (disregarding extraordinary items such as the sale of fixed assets or transaction costs associated with issuing securities), calculated as the sum of net income plus noncash expenses that were deducted in calculating net income [Chapter 18] [Chapter 24].

Cash flow per common share   The difference between *cash flow from operations* and *preferred stock* dividends divided by the number of outstanding common shares [Chapter 18] [24.5].

CBOE   Chicago Board Options Exchange. A securities exchange created in the early 1970s for the public trading of standardized option contracts.

Certainty equivalent   An amount that would be accepted in lieu of a chance at a possibly higher, but uncertain, amount.

Certificate of deposit (CD)   A deposit receipt issued by a bank to evidence the deposit of funds into an account at the bank for a stated period of time paying a stated rate of interest, perhaps subject to certain regulatory restrictions.

CFAT   Cash Flow After Tax [11.1].

Claimant   A party to a an explicit or implicit contract [1.4]. Sometimes also called a *stakeholder* in the *set-of-contracts model*.

Claim dilution   A reduction in the likelihood that one or more of the firm's claimants will be fully repaid, including time-value-of-money considerations [9.3].

Clear a position   Eliminate a *long* or *short position*, leaving no ownership or obligation.

Clientele effect   The grouping of investors who have a preference that the firm follow a particular policy, such as the choice of capital structure [15.7] or dividend policy [17.3].

Closing price   The price at which the last transaction before closing took place.

Collateral   Assets pledged to secure a *bond* or other form of indebtedness [Chapter 14].

Collateral trust bond   A bond that is secured by other securities [14.3].

Collection float   The time between when a customer mails a check and the firm has use of the funds [26.6].

Collective wisdom   The information embodied in a competitive market price [5.5].

Commercial paper   Short-lived (typically less than 270 days) debt security that is created by a firm and can bought and sold by other firms in a public market [25.4].

Commission broker   A broker on the floor of an exchange who acts as an agent for a particular brokerage house and who buys and sells stocks for the brokerage house on a commission basis [4.1].

Commitment fee   A fee paid to a commercial bank in return for its legal commitment to lend funds that have not yet been advanced [25.4].

Common stock   Some form of proportionate ownership in a firm [1.4].

Common stock equivalents   Securities, including certain types of convertible securities, stock options, and warrants, that are considered to be the substantial equivalent of common stock [24.1].

Common stock ratios   Ratios that are designed to measure the relative claims of stockholders to earnings (earnings per share and payout ratio), cash flow (cash flow per share), and equity (book value per share) of a firm [24.3].

Comparative credit analysis   A method of analysis in which a firm is compared to others that have a desired target debt rating in order to infer appropriate financial ratio targets [16.4].

Compensating balance   A cash balance that must be left on deposit at a bank under the terms of a loan agreement entered into with the bank [25.4].

Competitive bidding   A securities offering process in which securities firms submit competing bids to the issuer for the securities the issuer wishes to sell [14.4].

Competitive offering   An offering of securities through *competitive bidding* [14.2].

Complete capital market   A market in which there is a distinct marketable security for each and every possible outcome [4.3].

Completion risk   The risk that a project will not be brought into operation successfully [21.4].

Completion undertaking   An undertaking either (1) to complete a project such that it meets certain specified performance criteria on or before a certain specified date or (2) to repay project debt if the completion test cannot be met [21.4].

Compounding   The process of accumulating the time value of money forward in time. For example, interest earned during one period earns additional interest during each subsequent time period [2.12] [Chapter 3].

Compounding period   The length of the time period (for example, a quarter in the case of quarterly compounding) that elapses before interest compounds [3.5].

Comprehensive due diligence investigation   The investigation of a firm's business in conjunction with a securities offering to determine the adequacy of disclosure of the firm's business and financial situation and its prospects in the *prospectus* for the offering [22.3].

Concentration account   A single centralized account into which funds collected at regional locations (i.e., lockboxes) are transferred [26.6].

Concentration services   Movement of cash from different lock-box locations into a single *concentration account* from which disbursements and investments are made [26.6].

Conditional sales contracts   Similar to *equipment trust certificates* except that the lender is either the equipment manufacturer or a bank or finance company to whom the manufacturer has sold the conditional sales contract [14.3].

Conglomerate   A firm engaged in two or more unrelated businesses.

Conglomerate merger   A merger involving two or more firms that are in unrelated businesses [22.2].

Consol   A type of bond that has an infinite life, but is not issued in the U.S. capital markets [6.3].

Consolidation   Two or more firms combine to form an entirely new entity [22.1].

Contingent claim   A claim that can be made only if specified outcomes occur. For example, a debtholder's right to place a lien on an asset if a debt payment has not been made. Also called an *option* [1.4] [9.1].

Continuous compounding   The process of accumulating the time value of money forward in time on a continuous (or instantaneous) basis. Interest is earned continuously, and at each instant, interest that accrues immediately begins earning interest on itself [2.12] [Chapter 3].

Continuous random variable   A random value that can take on *any* fractional value within specified ranges (as opposed to *discrete* values) [7.1].

Contribution margin   The difference between variable revenue and variable cost.

Control   Fifty percent of the outstanding votes plus one [1.5].

Controlled disbursement   A service that provides for a single presentation of checks each day (typically in the early part of the day) [26.6].

Conversion premium   The percentage by which the *conversion price* in a *convertible security* exceeds the prevailing common stock price at the time the convertible security is issued [Chapter 14].

Conversion price   The contractually specified price per share at which a convertible security can be converted into (exchanged for) shares of common stock [14.6].

Conversion ratio   The number of common shares into which a *convertible security* may be converted; the ratio of the face amount of the convertible security to the *conversion price* [14.6].

Conversion value   The market value of the number of shares into which a *convertible security* can be converted; i.e., the value of the security as common stock.

Convertible bond   A bond that can, at the option of its owner, be converted into (exchanged for) a contractually specified number of shares of common stock. See *convertible security*.

Convertible exchangeable preferred stock   *Convertible preferred stock* that may be exchanged, at the issuer's option, into *convertible bonds* having the same conversion features as the convertible preferred stock [14.6].

Convertible preferred stock   *Preferred stock* that can, at the option of its owner, be converted into (exchanged for) a contractually specified number of shares of common stock. See *convertible security*.

Convertible security (bond or preferred stock)   A security that, at the option of its owner, can be converted into (exchanged for) a contractually specified number of shares of common stock. [4.1].

Corporate acquisition   The acquisition of one firm by another; a merger [22.1].

Corporate bond   A financial security issued by a firm contractually agreeing to make future payments to the bond's owner, typically with a *par value* of $1,000 [6.2].

Corporate charter   A legal document creating a corporation (Chapter 14).

Corporate finance   One of the three areas of the discipline of finance. It deals with the operation of the firm (both the *investment decision* and the *financing decision*) from that firm's point of view [1.1].

Corporate financial planning   Financial planning conducted by a firm that encompasses preparation of both the *long-term financial plan* and the *short-term financial plan* [26.1].

Corporate processing float   The time that elapses between receipt of payment from a customer and the depositing of the customer's check in the firm's bank account; the time required to process customer payments [26.6].

Corporate tax view (of capital structure)   The argument that double taxation of equity returns (corporate and individual) makes debt a cheaper financing method [Chapter 15].

Corporation   Legally treated as a "person" and empowered to own assets, incur liabilities, sell securities, and engage in a range of other specified activities [1.6].

Correlation coefficient   The covariance between two random variables divided by the product of the standard deviations of those random variables [7.1].

Cost-benefit ratio   The NPV of an investment divided by the investment's initial cost [11.5]. Also called the *profitability index*.

Cost of capital   A casual term for the *opportunity cost of capital* [10.1].

Counter trade   The exchange of goods for other goods rather than cash; barter.

Coupon equivalent yield   True interest cost expressed on the basis of a 365-day year [25.4].

Coupon payments (of a bond)   The contractually agreed upon interest payments made by a firm to the bond's owner [6.2].

Coupon rate of interest (for a bond)   The sum of interest payments to be made within one year divided by the *par value* of the bond [6.2] [14.3]. Often called simply coupon or coupon rate.

Covariance   The mathematical expectation of the product of two random variables' deviations from their mean [7.1].

Covenants   Provisions in a *bond indenture* (or *preferred stock agreement*) that require the bond (or preferred stock) issuer to take certain specified actions (*affirmative covenants*) or to refrain from taking certain specified actions (*negative covenants*) [Chapter 14].

Cover   To *clear a position* that was *short* [4.3].

Coverage ratios   Ratios that are designed to measure a firm's ability to cover its financing charges [24.1].

Coverage test   A debt limitation that prohibits the issuance of additional long-term debt if the issuer's interest coverage would, as a result of the issue, fall below some specified minimum [14.3].

Covered call optionwriter   A person who sells (writes) a call option on an asset that she owns [Chapter 8].

Credible signal   A signal that provides accurate information, one that can distinguish among "senders" [9.4].

Cross-default   A provision under which default on one debt obligation triggers default on another debt obligation [23.4].

Cross rates   The *exchange rate* between two currencies expressed as the ratio of two foreign exchange rates that are both expressed in terms of a common third currency [23.1].

Cross-sectional   A statistical methodology applied to a set of firms at a particular point in time [15.8].

Crown jewel   A particularly profitable or otherwise particularly valuable business unit (or asset) of a firm [Chapter 22].

Cumulative dividend feature A requirement that any missed preferred or preference stock dividends be paid in full prior to any common dividend payment being made [14.3].

Cumulative voting A system of voting for directors of a corporation in which a shareholder's total number of votes are equal to her number of shares held times the number of candidates; the shareholder's votes can be cast for candidates in any proportion. In other words, all votes could be cast for a single candidate [1.6] [Chapter 1, footnote 12].

Currency future A *financial future* contract for the delivery of a specified foreign currency [23.1].

Currency swap An agreement to swap a series of specified payment obligations denominated in one currency for a series of specified payment obligations denominated in a different currency [23.1].

Current assets The *short-term* portion of the asset (left-hand) side of the balance sheet [Chapter 25].

Current liabilities The *short-term* portion of the liability (right-hand) side of the balance sheet [Chapter 25].

Current ratio The ratio of current assets to current liabilities [24.4].

Current yield A bond's annual coupon payment divided by its current market price [6.2, footnote 4].

Customary payout ratios A range of *payout ratios* that is typical based on an analysis of comparable firms [18.3].

Date of record Date on which the owners of securities are established for the purpose of determining who is entitled to receive scheduled securities payments, such as dividends on common stock [17.10].

Dealer A person or organization who buys or sells shares for her own account [4.1].

Debenture Long-term bonds not secured by specific assets, typically of longer than 10-year maturity [14.3].

Debt A legal obligation to make contractually agreed upon future payments [1.4] [4.1].

Debt capacity Optimal amount of debt in the firm's capital structure [Chapter 16].

Debt–equity ratio The ratio of total debt (including *short-term debt* and *capitalized lease obligations*) to total *equity* (including *preferred stock*) [24.6].

Debt limitation A *bond covenant* that restricts in some way the firm's ability to incur additional indebtedness [14.3].

Debt ratios Ratios relating a firm's long-term debt or total debt to certain balance sheet or flow of funds quantities [24.6].

Debt service The payment obligations connected with a debt contract [10.6] [Chapter 20].

Debt service coverage ratio The ratio of (1) *EBIT* plus $\frac{1}{3}$ of rental payments to (2) the sum of interest expense plus $\frac{1}{3}$ of rental payments plus principal repayments adjusted for non-tax-deductibility by dividing by 1 minus the tax rate [16.3].

Debt service parity (DSP) approach An analysis where the alternatives under consideration will provide the firm with the exact same schedule of after-tax debt payments (including both interest and principal) [20.1].

Decision tree A diagram that serves to illustrate the interdependence of decisions in situations that require a sequence of decisions, such as the progression of decisions from formulation of an idea for a new product through several stages either to cancellation of the product development project or to market introduction of the product [12.5].

Deductive reasoning The process of inferring something about a specific situation, based on a general fact, as in the case of computing the probability of a particular outcome from probability functions [5.4].

Deep-discount bond A bond that is issued at a price significantly below its par value [14.3].

Defeasance To render null and void [20.4].

Deferred equity A common term for convertible bonds because of their equity component and the expectation that the bond will ultimately be converted into shares of common stock [8.5].

Demand master notes Short-term securities that are repayable immediately upon the holder's demand [25.4].

Dependent (capital budgeting project) Acceptance of the project is contingent upon acceptance of another project. [11.1].

Depository transfer check (DTC) A check on the firm's account at a regional location that is deposited into the *concentration account* to initiate automatically the transfer of funds into that account from another bank account [26.6].

Depreciate To allocate the purchase cost of an asset over its life.

Depreciation A noncash expense claimed for tax or accounting purposes in connection with a capital asset [11.1] [12.4].

Detachable warrant A warrant that can be sold separately from the bond with which it was issued [14.6].

Dilution Reduction in earnings per common share resulting from a financial transaction [24.1].

Dilutive effect Result of a transaction that decreases earnings per common share [14.2].

Direct-estimate method A method of cash budgeting based on detailed estimates of cash receipts and cash disbursements category by category [26.4].

Direct lease A lease arrangement under which the manufacturer of an asset leases it (directly) to some entity [21.1].

Disbursement float The time that elapses between when a firm writes a check to make payment and when its bank account is debited [26.6].

Discount basis (sold on a) To be sold at a price that is less than the face amount of the instrument [5.2] [25.4].

Discount bond A bond with a fair market value that is less than its *principal amount* [Chapter 20].

Discounted cash flow framework A framework for calculating the present value of each payment based on when it will be received and the time value of money [2.12].

Discounting The process of adjusting for the time value of money backwards in time [2.12] [Chapter 3] [25.4].

Discount period   The period during which the discount stated in an invoice can be claimed [25.4].

Discount rate   The generic term for the measure of the time value of money [2.12].

Discrete compounding   *Compounding* the time value of money (e.g., interest) for discrete time intervals (time periods) [2.12] [Chapter 3].

Discrete random variable   A random variable that can take on only a certain specified set of discrete possible values; for example, the positive integers 1, 2, 3, . . . [7.1].

Discretionary cash flow   Cash flow that is available after funding all positive-NPV capital investment projects; it is available for paying cash dividends, repurchasing common stock, retiring debt, etc. [Chapter 18].

Discriminant analysis   A statistical procedure that links the probability of default to a specified set of financial ratios [24.8].

Diversifiable risk   Risk that can be eliminated by diversification [7.7].

Dividend   Periodic payment made to stockholders (of either *preferred stock* or *common stock*) [Chapter 17] [Chapter 18].

Dividend clawback   With respect to a *project financing*, an arrangement under which the sponsors of a project agree to contribute as equity any prior *dividends* received from the project to the extent necessary to cover any cash deficiencies [21.4].

Dividend clientele   A group of shareholders who prefer that the firm follow a particular dividend policy [17.3]. For example, such a preference is often based on comparable tax situations [17.8].

Dividend limitation   A *bond covenant* that restricts in some way the firm's ability to pay cash dividends [14.3].

Dividend policy   A firm policy that governs that portion of the firm's earnings and cash flow that should be paid out to the firm's common stockholders in the form of cash dividends [6.3] [Chapters 17 and 18].

Dividend rate   Dividends paid per common share per annum [14.3].

Dividend reinvestment plan   A firm-sponsored program that enables common stockholders to pool their dividends (plus, in many cases, supplementary cash) for reinvestment in shares of the firm's common stock [14.2].

Dividend rights   A shareholder's right to receive per share dividends identical to other shareholders [1.6].

Dividend yield   Annual dividend rate on a share of common stock divided by the common stock price.

Double-declining-balance   A method of computing depreciation expense [12.4].

Draft   An unconditional written order for payment.

DSAT   *Debt Service* After Tax.

DSP   *Debt Service Parity* [20.1].

Duration   The time until the "average" dollar of present value is received from an asset.

Dutch auction   An auction process in which the market-clearing price is determined by accepting the highest bid, then the next highest bid, and so on, until a price is found

for which all the securities offered for sale will be purchased; all securities transactions then take place at the market-clearing price [Chapter 14] [18.7].

EAA   *Equivalent Annual Annuity* [12.2].

EAB   *Equivalent Annual Benefit* [12.2].

EAC   *Equivalent Annual Cost* [12.2].

Earnings   Earnings available for common stock; net income minus preferred stock dividends.

Earnings per share (EPS)   A firm's annualized *earnings* divided by the share price [6.5] [24.5].

EBIT   Earnings before interest and income taxes [16.3].

Economic defeasance   *In-substance defeasance* [20.4].

Economic dependence   Where the costs and/or revenues of one project depend on those of another [11.1].

Economic order quantity (EOQ)   The reorder quantity that minimizes the annual inventory cost [25.3].

Economic risk (project financing)   The risk that the project's output will not be saleable at a price that will cover the project's operating and maintenance costs and its debt service requirements [21.4].

Economies of scale   The marginal cost of production decreases as a plant's scale of operations increases [22.2].

Effective annual rate (r_a) An annual measure of the time value of money that fully reflects the effects of *compounding* [3.5].

Effective call price   The *strike price* in an *optional redemption provision* plus the accrued interest to the redemption date [20.6].

Effective rate   A measure of the time value of money that fully reflects the effects of *compounding* [3.5].

Effective spread   The *gross underwriting spread* adjusted for the impact of the announcement of the common stock offering on the firm's share price [14.2].

Efficient capital market   A market in which new information is very quickly (within at most a few hours) accurately reflected in share prices [2.7] [Chapter 5] [Chapter 5, footnote 1].

Efficient frontier   The combinations of securities portfolios that maximize expected return for any given level of risk or, equivalently, minimize risk for any given level of expected return [7.4].

Electronic depository transfers   The transfer of funds between bank accounts through the *Automated Clearing House* (ACH) system [26.6].

Employee stock plan   A firm-sponsored program that enables employees to purchase shares of the firm's common stock on a preferential basis [14.2].

Endogenous variable   A value determined within the context of a model [1.3]. Also called simply a variable.

Enhancement   A positive *synergistic effect* of one investment project on another [12.1].

EOQ   *Economic Order Quantity*.

EPS   Earnings Per Share (of common stock).

Equipment trust certificates   Certificates issued by a trust that was formed to purchase an asset and lease it to a lessee;

when the last of the certificates has been repaid, title of ownership of the asset reverts to the lessee [14.3].

Equity   Including some aspect of ownership [1.4] [4.1].

Equity contribution agreement   An agreement to contribute equity to a project under certain specified conditions [21.4].

Equityholders   Those owning some share of a firm. Also called *shareholders* and *stockholders*.

Equivalent annual annuity   The annual annuity whose present value is equal (equivalent) to a present value of some combination of costs and/or revenues [12.2].

Equivalent annual benefit   The *equivalent annual annuity* for the NPV of an investment project [12.2].

Equivalent annual cost   The *equivalent annual annuity* for (1) the total cost of operating an asset over its life or (2) the total cost of undertaking an investment project [12.2].

Equivalent loan   Given the after-tax payment stream associated with a lease, the maximum amount of conventional debt that same period-by-period after-tax debt service stream is capable of supporting [21.3].

Erosion   A negative *synergistic effect* of one investment project on another [12.1].

Eurobond   A bond that is sold outside the country in whose currency the bond is denominated [14.7].

Eurodollar   U.S. dollar denominated deposit account in a bank outside the U.S. [23.5].

European option   An option that can only be exercised at the time of its expiration [Chapter 8].

Event of default   An event that triggers the debtholders' right to demand repayment of the debt [14.3].

EVPI   *Expected Value of Perfect Information.*

Excess return on the market portfolio   The difference between the rate of return on the market portfolio and the riskless rate (i.e., r_m minus r_f) [7.5] [7.6].

Exchange rate   The price of one country's currency expressed in terms of another country's currency [23.1].

Ex-date   *Ex-dividend date* [14.2].

Ex-dividend   To trade without the holder having the right to receive the declared but as yet unpaid dividend [18.2].

Ex-dividend date   The date on which a share of common stock initially trades without the holder having the right to receive the declared but as yet unpaid dividend [18.2].

Exercise   When an optionholder enforces the sale on the terms specified in an option contract. Also called *put* (to exercise a put option) or *call* (to exercise a call option) [Chapter 8].

Exercise price   The price for which the asset will be exchanged in an option contract if the option is exercised. Also called *strike price* [Chapter 8].

Exercise value   The value to an optionholder of exercising the option. In the case of a call, the exercise value is the greater of either 0 or the underlying asset's value minus the option's strike price. In the case of a put, the exercise value is the greater of either 0 or the option's strike price minus the underlying asset's value. Sometimes called intrinsic value [Chapter 8].

Exogenous variable   A variable whose value is determined outside the model in which it is used [Chapter 1, footnote 3]. Also called a *parameter*.

Expectations hypothesis   A theory of the *term structure of interest rates* that holds that each *forward rate* equals the expected future interest rate for the relevant period [4.4].

Expectations theory of forward exchange rates   A theory of foreign exchange rates that holds that the expected future spot foreign exchange rate *t* periods in the future equals the current *t*-period forward exchange rate [23.2].

Expected future cash flows   Projected future cash flows associated with an asset or decision.

Expected future rate of return   The rate of return that is expected to be earned on an asset in the future [7.2]. Also called simply the *expected rate of return*.

Expected rate of return   The rate that is expected to be earned on an investment; that is, the rate that makes the NPV equal zero [6.1]. Also called the *internal rate of return*.

Expected value   The mathematical expectation [7.1].

Expected value of perfect information (EVPI)   The expected value if the future uncertain outcomes can be known minus the expected value with no additional information [12.5].

Expensed   With respect to tax items, deducted for tax purposes in full in the year the expense is incurred [11.1].

Expiration   When an financial contract ceases to exist (be valid). Also called *maturity*.

Expiration date   The date on which a financial security will cease to exist [14.2]. Also called *maturity date*.

Expire   Cease to exist. Also called *mature*.

Ex-rights   In connection with a *rights offering*, shares of stock that are trading without the *rights* attached [14.2].

Ex-rights date   The date on which a share of common stock begins trading *ex-rights* [14.2].

Extendible notes   Notes the maturity of which can be extended by mutual agreement of the issuer and investors [14.3].

Extraordinary positive value   A positive NPV. [2.9].

Factor analysis   A statistical procedure that seeks to explain a certain phenomenon (e.g., the actual rate of return on common stock) in terms of the behavior of a specified set of predictive factors [7.9].

FASB   Financial Accounting Standards Board.

Feasible target payout ratios   *Payout ratios* that are consistent with the availability of excess funds to make cash dividend payments [18.3].

Fed   The Federal Reserve System.

Federal agency securities   Debt securities issued by a federal agency and backed to varying degrees by the federal government [25.3].

Federal funds   Uncommitted reserves that a bank has available to sell to other banks.

Fed funds wire transfer   Electronic transfer of *federal funds* through the Federal Reserve's wire transfer system to achieve same-day availability [26.6].

Financial asset A contract that provides for the exchange of money at various points in time [1.1].

Financial control The day-to-day management of the firm's costs and expenses in order to control them in relation to the budgeted amounts [26.3].

Financial future A contract entered into now that provides for the delivery of a specified asset in exchange for the selling price at some specified time in the future [4.3].

Financial intermediary An institution (such as a bank) or individual that makes transactions that transform funds from one form (such as a savings deposit) into another form (such as a loan) [4.1].

Financial lease *Capital lease* [21.1].

Financial leverage The use of debt financing [10.4].

Financial leverage clientele A group of investors who have a preference for investing in firms that follow a particular financial leverage policy [15.7].

Financial markets and intermediaries One of the three areas of the discipline of finance. It deals with the firm's *financing decision* from a third party's point of view [1.1].

Financial objectives Objectives of a financial nature that the firm will strive to accomplish during the period covered by its *financial plan* [26.1].

Financial plan A financial blueprint for the financial future of the firm [26.1].

Financial planning *Corporate financial planning* [26.1].

Financial press That portion of the media that is devoted to reporting financial news [4.1].

Financial ratios Ratios that can be calculated from a firm's financial statements that enhance our understanding of the firm's financial performance and financial position [24.3].

Financial risk Risk that is created by the use of debt financing [10.4].

Financial security A standardized financial asset such as common stock, preferred stock, bond, convertible bond, or financial future.

Financing decision The firm's choices concerning its liabilities and owners' equity (right-hand side of the balance sheet) [1.1].

Fisher's separation theorem The firm's choice of investments is separate from its owners' attitudes toward investments [4.2]. See also *portfolio separation theorem* [7.5].

Fixed charge coverage ratio The ratio of (1) *EBIT* plus $\frac{1}{3}$ of rental payments to (2) the sum of interest expense plus $\frac{1}{3}$ of rental payments [16.3].

Fixed-price basis An offering of securities at a fixed price [14.2].

Fixed-price tender offer A *tender offer* at a fixed price [17.10].

Flight to quality The tendency for bond investors to sell lower-grade corporate bonds and purchase Treasury bonds during periods of heightened uncertainty [2.2].

Float The difference between the actual balance in a firm's checking account and the account balance shown on the bank's books [26.6].

Floor brokers Independent brokers who are not affiliated with a particular brokerage house and who execute buy and sell orders for commission brokers [4.1].

Floor traders Independent stock exchange members who only buy and sell stocks for their own account [4.1].

Flotation cost The cost of selling a new issue of securities [14.1].

Force majeure risk (project financing) The risk that there will be an interruption of operations for a prolonged period after the project has been completed due to fire, flood, storm, or some other factor beyond the control of the project's sponsors [21.4].

Foreign currency option An option that conveys the right to buy (in the case of a call option) or sell (put option) a specified amount of a specified foreign currency at a specified price within a specified time period [23.1].

Foreign currency risk The risk that the value of one currency expressed in terms of another currency—the foreign exchange rate—may fluctuate over time [23.3].

Foreign exchange market The market within which one country's currency is traded for another country's currency [23.1].

Foreign exchange risk *Foreign currency risk* [23.3].

Formula basis A method of selling a new issue of common stock in which the Securities and Exchange Commission declares the registration statement effective based on a price formula, rather than a specific price [14.2].

Forward contract Contractual obligation to buy or sell a specified amount of a specified commodity, currency, or asset on a specified future date at a specified price, which is agreed to at the time the contract is entered into.

Forward discount The difference between the spot foreign exchange rate and the forward exchange rate when the spot rate exceeds the forward rate [23.1].

Forward exchange rate Foreign exchange rate for a forward trade [23.1].

Forward premium The difference between the forward exchange rate and the spot foreign exchange rate when the forward rate exceeds the spot rate [23.1].

Forward rate An interest rate that will prevail during a future time period, as, for example, the 1-year borrowing rate expected to prevail two periods in the future [4.4] [23.1].

Forward trade The purchase or sale of a foreign currency, commodity, or other item for future delivery based on a price that is agreed to today [23.1].

Fourth market Over-the-counter market in which transactions in financial securities are made directly between institutions [4.1].

Free cash flow *Cash flow from operations* contributed by a particular capital investment project minus net incremental capital expenditures for the project (i.e., net of salvage value and release of working capital) [Chapter 11].

Free-rider Someone who receives the benefit of someone else's expenditure (money, effort, or creativity) simply by imitation [2.11] [9.3].

Friction costs The costs connected with a transaction [5.1].

Full-service lease A lease in which the lessor agrees to pay all costs of maintaining the leased item in good working condition, the cost of insurance, and any property taxes [21.1].

Fully diluted earnings per share   Earnings per share calculated under the assumption that all convertible securities have been converted into common equity and all stock options have been exercised [24.1].

Future   *Financial future* [4.3].

Future value   The amount of cash at a specified date in the future that is equivalent in value to a specified sum today.

Future value annuity factor   The factor multiplied times an annuity to compute the future value of the entire annuity [3.4].

Future value factor   The factor multiplied times a cash flow to compute the future value of the cash flow [3.2].

Future value formula   The formula for computing the future value of a single cash flow [3.2].

General partner   A partner who has unlimited liability for the obligations of the partnership [21.5].

General partnership   A partnership in which all the partners are *general partners* [1.6].

Global bonds   *Bonds* that are designed so as to qualify for immediate trading in any domestic capital market and in the Euromarket [23.5].

Goodwill   Excess of the purchase price over the fair market value of the net assets acquired under *purchase accounting* [22.3].

Greenmail   Repurchasing shares from a single large holder at a premium to the prevailing market price and not extending the repurchase offer to the firm's other shareholders [17.9] [22.5].

Gross profit margin   The ratio of gross profit to net sales [24.5].

Gross spread   The fraction of the (gross) proceeds of an underwritten securities offering that is paid as compensation to the underwriters of the offering [14.1].

Gross underwriting spread   *Gross spread* [14.1].

Hard capital rationing   Severely enforced *capital rationing* [13.6].

Hedge   A transaction that reduces the risk of an investment [4.3] [8.1] [23.3].

Hedging   Reducing the risk of an investment through the use of financial security transactions [4.3] [8.1] [23.3].

Hell-or-high-water contract   A contract that obligates a purchaser of a project's output to make cash payments to the project in all events even if no product is offered for sale (no matter what the circumstances, "come hell or high water") [21.4].

High-coupon bond refunding   *Refunding* a high-coupon bond with a new lower-coupon bond [20.2].

High-yield bond   *Junk bond.*

Homogeneity   The degree to which items are similar [5.3].

Homogeneous   A high degree of *homogeneity* [5.3].

Horizontal merger   A merger involving two or more firms in the same industry that are both at the same stage in the production cycle, that is, two or more competitors [22.2].

Human capital   The unique capabilities and expertise that belong to an individual [9.3].

Hurdle rate   A term for the required rate of return in *capital budgeting* [Chapter 11].

Income bond   A bond contract under which a firm may be allowed to forgo one or more interest payments if the firm has insufficient income [14.3].

Income statement   An accounting statement describing a firm's income over a given time period [1.1] [24.1].

Incremental cash flow   Net increase in the firm's cash flow attributable to a particular capital investment project after allowing for any negative impact the project may have on existing product sales or corporate expenses; the difference between *free cash flow* with the project and *free cash flow* without it [11.1].

Independent projects   A set of capital investment projects that can be evaluated independently; acceptance or rejection of one does not affect acceptance or rejection of any of the others [11.1].

Inductive reasoning   The process of using observations of specific situations to infer a general conclusion, as, for example, using a statistic from a sample observation to estimate a *parameter* [5.4].

Inflation uncertainty   The fact that future inflation rates are not known. A possible contributing factor to the makeup of the *term structure of interest rates* [4.4].

Informational efficiency   The extent to which information is freely available at low cost [2.7].

Information asymmetry   A situation involving *asymmetric information*, that is, information that is known to some, but not all, participants [5.4].

Information services   Organizations that furnish investment and other types of information, such as information that helps a firm monitor its cash position [26.6].

IRR   *Internal Rate of Return.*

Insider   Managers, controlling stockholders, and any other persons who possess privileged nonpublic information regarding a firm [17.9].

Insolvency   When a firm is unable to discharge its debt.

Insolvency risk   The risk that a firm will be unable to discharge its debt. Also called *bankruptcy risk.*

Installment sale   The sale of an asset in exchange for a specified series of payments (the installments) [22.3].

In-substance defeasance   The deposit of cash and risk-free securities into an irrevocable trust sufficient to enable the issuer to remove a debt obligation from its balance sheet [20.4].

Intangible assets   Assets other than *tangible assets*, principally patents, copyrights, trademarks, and goodwill [1.1].

Interest   The cost of borrowed money [1.4].

Interest coverage ratio   The ratio of earnings before interest and income taxes to interest expense [16.1] [24.4].

Interest payments   Contractual debt payments based on the *coupon rate of interest* and the *principal amount* (typically calculated by multiplying these two amounts and dividing by the number of interest periods per year) [6.2].

Interest rate parity A theory of relative exchange rates that states that the difference in interest rates in two currencies for a stated period should just offset the difference between the spot foreign exchange rate and the forward exchange rate corresponding to that period [23.2].

Interest rate swap An agreement to swap interest payment obligations [14.5].

Interest tax shield The reduction in income taxes that results from the tax-deductibility of interest [Chapter 15].

Intermediate-term Typically indicates 1 to 10 years [25.4].

Intermediate-term funds Typically indicates funds that are lent for an initial term of between 1 and 10 years [25.4].

Internal rate of return (IRR) The *discount rate* that makes the NPV of a capital budgeting project zero [11.3].

International Fisher effect A theory that holds that the difference between the interest rates in two currencies should just offset the difference between the expected inflation rates in the two countries that issued the currencies [23.2].

In-the-money An option with a positive *exercise value*. For a call option, this is when the value of the underlying asset exceeds the *strike price*. For a put option, this is when the value of the underlying asset is less than the *strike price* [Chapter 8].

Inventory turnover ratio The ratio of cost of goods sold to average inventory [24.4].

Investment banker A person who assists firms in raising funds by serving as the intermediary between the issuer and the purchasers of securities [14.1].

Investment decision The firm's choices concerning its assets (right-hand side of the balance sheet) [1.1].

Investment grade rating A long-term debt rating in one of the four highest rating categories (Aaa, Aa, A, or Baa from Moody's Investors Service and AAA, AA, A, or BBB from Standard & Poor's) [16.2].

Investment project market line (IMPL) The line of required rates of return for investment projects as a function of beta (nondiversifiable risk) [10.2].

Investments One of the three areas of the discipline of finance. It deals with investing in a firm (the firm's *financing decision*) from the investor's point of view [1.1].

Investment tax credit A provision of the tax code that permits a firm that makes qualifying capital expenditures to credit a specified percentage of those expenditures against its income tax liability for the period in which the qualifying expenditures are made. The Tax Reform Act of 1986 eliminated the investment tax credit, but the credit has been eliminated and restored several times during the postwar period.

Involuntary liquidation preference A premium that must be paid to preferred or preference stockholders if the issuer of the stock is forced into involuntary liquidation [24.2].

IPML *Investment Project Market Line* [10.2].

Issued shares Shares that are currently owned by investors (*outstanding shares*) or have been at one time owned by investors (*treasury shares*) [14.2].

Junk bond A bond with a *speculative grade rating*.

Law of large numbers The fact that the mean of a random sample approaches the mean (expected value) of the population as the sample grows large [7.2].

Law of one price The idea that if two different prices exist for an asset, *arbitrageurs* will execute transactions until the price differential no longer exists [2.7] [23.2].

Lease A long-term rental agreement; a form of secured long-term debt [21.1].

Lease rate The payment per period stated in a lease contract [21.2].

Legal defeasance The deposit of cash and permitted securities, as specified in the bond indenture, into an irrevocable trust sufficient to enable the issuer to discharge fully its obligations under the bond indenture [20.4].

Legal investments Investments that a regulated entity is permitted to make under the rules and regulations that govern its investing activities [16.2].

Lessee An entity that leases an asset from another entity [21.1].

Lessor An entity that leases an asset to another entity [21.1].

Letter of credit A form of guarantee of payment issued by a bank; used to guarantee the payment of interest and repayment of principal on bond issues.

Leverage See *financial leverage* or *operating leverage* [10.4].

Leverage clientele A group of shareholders who, due to their personal leverage, seek to invest in corporations that maintain a compatible degree of corporate leverage [Chapter 15].

Leveraged beta The *beta* of an *leveraged required rate of return* [19.7].

Leveraged buyout The purchase of a firm that is financed with a very high proportion of debt [9.7] [22.6].

Leveraged lease A lease arrangement under which the lessor borrows a large proportion of the funds needed to purchase the asset and grants the lenders a lien on the asset and a pledge of the lease payments to secure the borrowing [21.1].

Leveraged required rate of return The *required rate of return* on an investment if the investment is financed partially by debt [19.3].

Leverage ratio The ratio of the value of the firm's debt to the total value of the firm [Chapter 15].

Leverage ratios A class of financial ratios designed to indicate with how much debt relative to equity a firm has financed itself [24.6].

Liability *Debt*.

LIBOR (London Interbank Offer Rate) The rate of interest major international banks in London charge each other for borrowing [14.5] [23.5].

Lien A security interest in one or more assets that is granted to lenders in connection with a secured debt financing.

Limitation on asset dispositions A *bond covenant* that restricts in some way a firm's ability to sell major assets [14.3].

Limitation on liens A *bond covenant* that restricts in some way a firm's ability to grant liens on its assets [14.3].

Limitation on merger, consolidation, or sale A *bond covenant* that restricts in some way a firm's ability to merge or consolidate with another firm [14.3].

Limitation on sale-and-leaseback A *bond covenant* that restricts in some way a firm's ability to enter into sale-and-leaseback transactions [14.3].

Limitation on subsidiary borrowing A *bond covenant* that restricts in some way a firm's ability to borrow at the subsidiary level [14.3].

Limited liability The fact that shareholder liability for the debts and other obligations of the corporation is limited to the loss of the shareholder's equity in the firm [1.6] [9.3].

Limited partner A partner who has limited legal liability for the obligations of the partnership [1.6] [21.5].

Limited partnership A partnership that includes one or more partners who have *limited liability* [1.6] [21.5].

Linear regression A statistical technique for fitting a straight line to a set of data points [7.6].

Line of credit An arrangement between a bank and a customer concerning the maximum loan balance the bank will permit the borrower at any one time [25.4].

Liquidation rights The rights of a firm's securityholders in the event the firm liquidates [1.6].

Liquidity How easily assets are transferred without loss of value [5.2].

Liquidity preference The argument that greater *liquidity* is valuable, all else equal. A possible contributing factor to the make up of the *term structure of interest rates* [4.4].

Liquidity ratios Ratios that are designed to measure the firm's ability to meet its financial obligations on time [24.4].

Loan amortization schedule A schedule that breaks down each payment on a loan into an interest component and a principal repayment component [3.4].

Lockbox A collection and processing service provided to firms by banks, which collect payments from a dedicated postal box that the firm directs its customers to send payment to. The banks make several collections per day, immediately process the payments, and deposit the funds into the firm's bank account [26.6].

Log-linear least squares method A statistical technique for fitting a curve to a set of data points by transforming one of the variables by taking its logarithm and then fitting a straight line to the transformed set of data points [24.2].

Lognormal probability distribution A standardized probability distribution where the logarithm of the *random variable* follows the *standard normal probability distribution* [7.1, footnote 3].

Long position Ownership of a financial security [4.3].

Long-term With regard to a new securities issue, typically indicates an initial maturity of 10 years or more. With regard to the balance sheet, long-term indicates a remaining maturity of one year or longer. Accounting convention does not distinguish between *intermediate-term* and *long-term* [14.3] [24.1].

Long-term debt Debt that is classified as *long-term*.

Long-term debt ratio The ratio of long-term debt to total capitalization [24.6].

Long-term financial plan Financial plan covering two or more years of future operations [26.1].

Low-coupon bond refunding *Refunding* a low-coupon bond with a new higher-coupon bond [20.2].

Mail float The time elapsed while an invoice or payment of an invoice is in the mail [26.6].

Majority voting A system of voting for directors of a corporation in which each shareholder has one vote for each director and a simple majority can elect each director [1.6].

Management fee The portion of the *gross underwriting spread* that compensates the securities firms who manage a public offering for their management efforts [14.1].

Managers Decision-making employees.

Mandatory redemption schedule Schedule according to which *sinking fund* payments must be made [14.3].

Marginal Incremental [11.1].

Marginal tax rate Rate at which income taxes must be paid on *marginal* income.

Margin of safety With respect to working capital management, the difference between (1) the amount of long-term financing and (2) the sum of fixed assets plus the permanent component of current assets [25.1].

Margin requirements Regulations that specify the minimum portion of the purchase price in a securities transaction that must be paid in cash [8.10].

Market maker A person who facilitates liquidity by transacting in the asset [5.2]. Called a *specialist* in a stock market such as the NYSE.

Market overhang The theory that in certain situations institutions wish to sell their shares but postpone share sales because large sell orders under current market conditions would drive down a firm's share price and that the consequent threat of securities sales will tend to retard the rate of share price appreciation; support for the theory is largely anecdotal [17.9].

Market portfolio A value-weighted portfolio of every asset in a market [7.5].

Market return The return on the market portfolio [7.5].

Market segmentation Theory that the *term structure of interest rates* is determined by the relative demand for and supply of bonds within different maturity ranges. See also *segmented market* [15.7] [17.3].

Market value Value as determined in the capital market.

Master limited partnership (MLP) A publicly-traded limited partnership [1.6] [21.5].

Mature Cease to exist. Also said to *expire*.

Maturity The amount of time a financial security will exist. Also, the point at which a financial security will cease to exist (*expiration*).

Maturity date The date on which a financial security will cease to exist, for example a bond [6.2] [14.2]. Also called the *expiration date*.

Mean The *expected value* of a *random variable* [7.1].

Mean of the sample   The arithmetic average; that is, the sum of the observations divided by the number of observations [7.1].

Medium-term notes   Unsecured notes, similar to *commercial paper*, that are registered with the SEC and whose maturities range from 9 months to 30 years [25.3].

Merger   A combination of two firms in which the *acquiror* absorbs all the assets and liabilities of the *acquiree* and assumes the acquiree's business [22.1].

Mimic   Imitation that sends a false signal [9.4].

Minority interest   An outside ownership interest in a subsidiary that is consolidated (with the parent) for financial reporting purposes [problems].

MLP   *Master Limited Partnership* [1.6] [21.5].

Modeling   The process of creating a depiction of reality, such as a graph, picture, or mathematical representation [1.2].

Money market   Market for short-term financial instruments [25.4].

Money market preferred stock   *Auction rate preferred stock* [14.8].

Monitor   A device providing information about an agent's behavior [9.1].

Monte Carlo simulation   An analytical technique for solving a problem by performing a large number of trial runs (called simulations) and inferring a solution from the collective results of the trial runs [12.5]. Also called simply *simulation*.

Moral hazard   The ability of an agent to take unobserved self-interested actions to the detriment of the *principal* [2.1] [9.1].

Mortgage   A legal document granting a lien on one or more specific assets [14.3].

Mortgage bond   A bond that is secured by a lien on one or more specific assets [14.3].

Multinational corporation   A firm that operates in more than one country [Chapter 23].

Mutual funds   Funds that pool money contributed by individuals or other entities and invest the money in portfolios of securities [7.7].

Mutually exclusive projects   (capital budgeting) Two or more capital investment projects such that acceptance of one precludes acceptance of any of the others [11.1].

NASDAQ   The National Association of Securities Dealers Automated Quotations system [4.1].

Natural logarithm   Logarithm to the base *e* (approximately 2.7183).

Negative covenant   (of a bond) A *bond covenant* that limits or prohibits altogether certain actions unless the bondholders agree [9.6].

Negative pledge clause   A *bond covenant* that requires the borrower to grant lenders a lien equivalent to any liens that may be granted in the future to any other currently unsecured lenders [14.3].

Negotiated markets   Markets in which each transaction is separately negotiated between buyer and seller (i.e., an investor and a *dealer*) [4.1].

Negotiated offering   Offering of securities for which the terms, including underwriters' compensation, have been negotiated between the issuer and the underwriters [14.2] [14.4].

Net adjusted present value   The *adjusted present value* minus the initial cost of an investment [19.5].

Net advantage to leasing   The net present value of entering into a lease financing arrangement rather than borrowing the necessary funds and buying the asset [21.3].

Net assets   The difference between total assets on the one hand and current liabilities and noncapitalized long-term liabilities on the other [24.2].

Net benefit to leverage factor   A simple linear factor used to represent the benefit to the firm per dollar of debt, net of all the positive (e.g., tax asymmetries favoring debt) and negative (e.g., costs of financial distress such as lost product value due to an inability to guarantee future service) factors connected with the use of debt financing [19.4].

Net book value   The current book value of an asset or liability; that is, its original book value net of any accounting adjustments such as depreciation.

Net lease   A lease arrangement under which the lessee is responsible for all property taxes, maintenance expenses, insurance, and other costs associated with keeping the asset in good working condition [21.1].

Net period   The period of time between the end of the *discount period* and the date payment is due [25.4].

Net present value (NPV)   The present value minus the cost; that is, the present value of *all* the cash flows connected with the asset or decision [3.1] [11.2].

Net present value of future investments (NPVFI)   The present value of the total sum of NPVs expected to result from all of the firm's future investments [6.6].

Net profit margin   The ratio of net income before extraordinary items to net sales [24.5].

Net salvage value   The sum of after-tax cash flows, excluding operating revenues and expenses, connected with the termination of a capital budgeting project [11.1].

Net working capital   Literally, current assets minus current liabilities. Often simply referred to as *working capital* [Chapter 25]. See also A Simple Example of Working Capital in [11.1].

Net worth   Common stockholders' equity (consisting of common stock, surplus, and retained earnings).

Nexus (of contracts)   A set or collection of something. [Chapter 9].

Nominal   In name only. Differences in compounding cause the nominal rate to differ from the effective rate [3.5]. Inflation causes the purchasing power of money to differ from one time to another [12.3].

Nominal annual rate   An effective rate per period multiplied by the number of periods in a year [3.5].

Noncash charge   A cost, such as depreciation, depletion, and amortization, that does not involve any cash outflow.

Nondiversifiability of human capital   The difficulty of diversifying one's individual capabilities, expertise, and employment effort [9.3].

Nondiversifiable risk   Risk that cannot be eliminated by diversification [7.7].

Non-recourse   Without recourse, as in a non-recourse lease [21.4].

Nonredeemable   Not permitted, under the terms of the indenture, to be redeemed [14.3].

Nonrefundable   Not permitted, under the terms of the indenture, to be refunded [14.3].

Normal probability distribution   A probability distribution for a *continuous random variable* that is symmetrical around the mean, completely specified once the *mean* and *variance* (or *standard deviation*) are known, and bell-shaped when graphed [7.1].

Normal random variable   A random variable that has a *normal probability distribution* [7.1].

Note   An intermediate-term debt obligation (initial maturity of between 1 and 10 years) [14.3].

NPV   *Net Present Value.*

NPVFI   *Net Present Value of Future Investments.*

NYSE   The New York Stock Exchange.

Odd lot   A number of securities not equal to a *round lot*; in the case of common stock, fewer than 100 shares [4.1].

Odd-lot dealer   A broker who combines *odd lots* of securities from multiple *buy orders* or *sell orders* into *round lots* and executes transactions in those round lots [4.1].

Off-balance-sheet financing   Financing not required to be reported on the firm's balance sheet [21.2].

Offering memorandum   A document prepared to outline the terms of securities to be offered in a *private placement* [14.1].

Open market purchase   The purchase of securities in one or more transactions arranged in the open market [17.9].

Operating lease   A lease obligation that does not have to be capitalized on the face of the balance sheet [21.2].

Operating leverage   The use of a process involving fixed costs in the production of goods and services [10.4].

Operating profit margin   The ratio of operating income to net sales [24.5].

Operating risk   Risk that is created by *operating leverage* [10.4]. Also called *business risk.*

OPM   *Option Pricing Model* [Chapter 8].

Opportunity cost   The difference between the value of an alternative and the value of the best possible alternative [2.1].

Opportunity cost of capital   The price per unit of financial capital that users of funds must pay suppliers of funds in the capital market [4.2] [19.1].

Option   Any right without an obligation attached to it. Often used specifically to mean the right without the obligation to purchase (call option) or sell (put option) an asset [Chapter 8].

Optional redemption provision   Provision of a bond indenture that governs the issuer's ability to call the bonds for redemption prior to their scheduled maturity date [14.3].

Optionholder   The person in the long position side of an option transaction; the owner.

Option pricing model (OPM)   A model for valuing options.

Optionwriter   The person in the short position side of an option transaction; the person with the obligation; the seller of the option.

Organized exchange   A securities marketplace where purchasers and sellers regularly gather to trade securities according to the formal rules adopted by the exchange [4.1].

OTC (over-the-counter)   The over-the-counter market [4.1].

Out-of-the-money   For a call option, this is when the value of the underlying asset is less than the *strike price*. For a put option, this is when the value of the underlying asset exceeds the *strike price* [Chapter 8].

Outstanding shares   Shares that are currently owned by investors [14.2].

Oversubscription privilege   In connection with a rights offering, the opportunity to subscribe for additional shares that other shareholders have not subscribed for [14.2].

Over-the-counter market (OTC)   Any alternative to an *organized exchange*. Often used loosely to refer to NASDAQ, an exchange that is less structured than the NYSE, AMEX, CBOE, and other exchanges [4.1].

Pac-Man strategy   Takeover defense strategy in which the prospective acquiree retaliates to the acquiror's tender offer by launching its own tender offer for the other firm.

Parameter   A representation that characterizes a part of a model (e.g., a growth rate), the value for which is determined outside of the model [1.3]. Sometimes called an *exogenous variable.*

Partnership   Shared ownership among two or more individuals, some of whom may, but do not necessarily, have limited liability. See *general partnership*, *limited partnership*, and *master limited partnership* [1.6].

Par value   A stated or face amount [4.4] [Chapter 14].

Payable through drafts   A method of making payment that is used to maintain control over payments made on behalf of the firm by personnel in noncentral locations. The payer's bank delivers the payable through draft to the payer, which must approve it and return it to the bank before payment can be made [26.6].

Payback   The amount of time it takes for the initial outlay to be recovered, without consideration for the time value of money [11.6].

Payment date   The date on which payment, such as a dividend payment, is actually made [18.2].

Payout ratio   A firm's dividends divided by its earnings [6.3] [Chapters 17 and 18].

P/E ratio   The current stock price divided by the most recent annualized *EPS* [6.6].

Pecking order theory A theory of capital structure choice [15.8].

Perfect capital market A market environment that satisfies a specific set of assumptions given in [4.2] and discussed further in [5.7].

Perfect competition An idealized market environment in which every market participant is too small to affect the market price by acting on its own [4.2].

Perfected first lien A first lien that is duly recorded with the cognizant governmental body so that the lender will be able to act upon it should the borrower default [21.1].

Perfect market view Analysis of a decision assuming a perfect capital market. Capital structure [15.1]. Dividend policy [17.1].

Perpetuity An infinite annuity; i.e., one with a payment every period forever into the future [3.4].

Perquisite A personal explicit or implicit benefit enjoyed by an employee of the firm [9.3].

Personal tax view (of capital structure) The argument that the difference in personal tax rates between income from debt and income from equity eliminates the disadvantage resulting from the double (corporate and personal) taxation of income from equity [15.1].

Planned capital expenditure program Capital expenditure program as outlined in the corporate *financial plan* [26.1].

Planned financing program Program of short-term and long-term financing as outlined in the corporate *financial plan* [26.1].

Poison pill Anti-takeover device that gives a prospective acquiree's shareholders the right to buy shares of the firm or shares of anyone who acquires the firm at a deep discount to their fair market value. Named after the cyanide pill that secret agents are instructed to swallow to avoid imminent capture [22.5].

Pooling of interests A method of accounting for a merger in which the merging entities' financial results are combined as though the two entities had always been a single entity [18.7] [22.3].

Portfolio A group of *financial securities* [2.3] [7.4].

Portfolio separation theorem An investor's choice of a risky investment portfolio is separate from her attitudes toward risk [7.5]. See also *Fisher's separation theorem*.

Position Having a claim on (owning) (long), or obligation concerning (owing) (short), an asset or option; that is, having bought or sold an asset or option.

Positive covenant (of a bond) A *bond covenant* that specifies certain actions the firm must take [9.6]. Also called an *affirmative covenant*.

Post audits Audit of the funds spent on a capital project after the project has been completed to assess the efficiency with which the funds were spent; evaluation of the expected future cash flow estimates; and evaluation of abandonment versus continuing the project [13.6].

Preauthorized checks (PACs) Checks that are authorized by the payer in advance and are written either by the payee or the payee's bank and then deposited in the payee's bank account [26.6].

Preauthorized electronic debits (PADs) Debits to its bank account authorized in advance by the payer. The payer's bank sends payment to the payee's bank through the *Automated Clearing House* (ACH) system [26.6].

Precautionary motive A desire to hold cash in order to be able to deal effectively with unexpected events that require a cash outlay [25.3].

Preemptive right The existing shareholders' right to subscribe for a new share issue before any shares can be offered to other investors [14.2].

Preference stock A security that ranks junior to *preferred stock* but senior to *common stock* in the right to receive payments from the firm; essentially junior preferred stock [4.1].

Preferred stock A hybrid security that combines certain features of debt and common equity and that ranks junior to *debt* but senior to *common stock* in the right to receive payments from the firm [4.1].

Preferred stock agreement A contract for publicly-traded *preferred stock* [14.3].

Preliminary prospectus A preliminary version of the *prospectus* [14.1].

Premium bond A bond with a fair market value that is greater than its *principal amount* [Chapter 20].

Present value The amount of cash today that is equivalent in value to a payment, or to a stream of payments, to be received in the future.

Present value annuity factor The factor multiplied times an annuity to compute the present value of the entire annuity [3.4].

Present value factor The factor multiplied times a cash flow to compute the present value of the cash flow [3.2].

Present value formula The formula for computing the present value of a single cash flow [3.2].

Price-earnings ratio (P/E) The current market price of a share of common stock divided by the firm's most recent annualized earnings [6.6].

Prime rate The interest rate at which banks lend to their most creditworthy customers [25.4].

Principal (1) One of the participants in a *principal-agent relationship*. (2) A *principal amount*.

Principal-agent relationship A situation that can be modeled as one person, an *agent*, who acts on behalf of another person, a *principal* [2.1] [Chapter 9].

Principal amount The face amount of debt; also, the amount borrowed [14.3]. Often called simply *principal*.

Private placement Securities sold directly to investors, often institutions, without a *public offering* [14.1].

Probability The relative likelihood of an outcome among all possible outcomes [7.1].

Probability density function The probability function for a *continuous random variable* [7.1].

Probability function   A function that assigns a *probability* to each and every possible outcome [7.1].

Production payment financing   A method of non-recourse asset-based financing in which a specified percentage of revenue realized from the sale of the project's output is used to pay debt service [21.4].

Profitability index (PI)   The present value of the future cash flows for a project divided by the initial cost of the project [11.5].

Profitability ratios   Ratios that are designed to measure the profitability of a firm [24.5].

Pro forma statement   A financial statement showing the forecast (or projected) operating results or impact of a particular transaction; as in pro forma income statements in the *long-term financial plan* or the pro forma *balance sheet* for a share repurchase [26.1].

Progress review   A periodic review of a capital investment project to evaluate its continued economic viability [11.8].

Project financing   A form of asset-based financing in which a firm finances a discrete set of assets (project) on a stand-alone basis [21.4].

Prospectus   A legal disclosure document that must be distributed to both purchasers and persons whose purchase interest is solicited in connection with a public offering of securities [14.1].

Proxy contest   A battle for the control of a firm in which the dissident group seeks the right from the firm's other shareholders to vote those shareholders' shares in favor of the dissident group's slate of directors [22.5].

Proxy fight   A *proxy contest* [1.6].

Public offering   The sale of registered securities by the issuer (or underwriters acting on behalf of the issuer) in the public market [14.1].

Publicly-traded   Assets that can be traded in a public market, such as the *stock market*.

Purchase   To *buy*, or take a *long position*.

Purchase accounting   Method of accounting for a *merger* in which the *acquiror* is treated as having purchased the assets and assumed the liabilities of the *acquiree*, which are all written up or down to their respective fair market values with the difference between the purchase price and the net assets acquired attributed to *goodwill* [22.3].

Purchase agreement   As used in connection with project financing, an agreement to purchase a specific amount of project output per period [21.4].

Purchase-and-sale   A method of securities distribution in which the securities firm purchases the securities from the issuer for its own account at a stated price and then resells them—as contrasted with a *best-efforts* sale [14.1].

Purchasing power parity   A theory of relative exchange rates that states that the expected difference in inflation rates for two countries over some period must equal the differential between the spot exchange rate currently prevailing and the spot exchange rate expected at the end of the period [23.2].

Pure-discount bond   A bond that will make only one payment of principal and interest [4.4] [5.6]. Also called a *zero-coupon bond* or a *single-payment bond*.

Put an option   To *exercise* a put option [Chapter 8].

Put-call parity   The relationship between the value of a put and the value of a call [Chapter 8].

Put option   The right without the obligation to sell a specified asset at a specified price within a specified time period [Chapter 8].

Put price   The price at which the asset will be sold if a put option is exercised. Also called the *strike price* or *exercise price* [Chapter 8].

Pyramid scheme   A "scam" where a con artist convinces people to invest with the promise of extraordinary return but simply uses newly invested funds to pay off any investors wanting to terminate their investment [5.6].

Randomized strategy   A strategy of introducing a random element into the decision-making process that is designed to reduce the information content of the decision-maker's observed choices [9.4].

Random variable   A function that assigns a real number to each and every possible outcome of a random experiment [7.1].

Range   The difference between the highest and lowest possible values [7.1].

Rate of interest   The rate, as a proportion of the principal, at which *interest* is computed [4.2].

Rate of return ratios   Ratios that are designed to measure the profitability of the firm in relation to various measures of the funds invested in the firm [24.5].

Raw material supply agreement   As used in connection with project financing, an agreement to furnish a specified amount per period of a specified raw material [21.4].

Real assets   Tangible assets and the intangible assets used by a firm to conduct its business [1.1] [4.1].

Real capital   Wealth that can be represented in financial terms such as savings account balances, *financial securities*, and real estate [9.3].

Real rate of interest   The rate of interest excluding the effect of inflation; that is, the rate that is earned in terms of constant purchase-power dollars [12.3].

Rebalancing (a debt level)   The process of making transactions that change the firm's capital structure back to its target [19.6].

Receivable turnover ratio   The ratio of annual credit sales to average accounts receivable [24.4].

Record date   *Date of record* [14.2] [18.2].

Redeemable   Eligible for redemption under the terms of the indenture [14.3].

Redemption cushion   The percentage by which the *conversion value* of a convertible security exceeds the redemption (*strike*) price [20.6].

Red herring   *Preliminary prospectus* [14.1].

Refundable   Eligible for refunding under the terms of the indenture [14.3].

Refunding   Issuing new debt and using the net proceeds to retire previously outstanding debt [20.2].

Registration statement   A legal document that is filed with the Securities and Exchange Commission to register securities for public offering [14.1].

Regression toward the mean   The tendency for subsequent observations of a *random variable* to be closer to its mean.

Remote disbursement   Technique that involves writing checks drawn on banks in remote locations so as to increase disbursement float [26.6].

Reoffering yield   In a *purchase-and-sale*, the yield to maturity at which the *underwriter* offers to sell the bonds to investors [Chapter 14].

Replacement cycle   The frequency with which an asset is replaced by an equivalent asset [12.2].

Repos   An agreement in which one party sells a security to another party and agrees to repurchase it on a specified date for a specified price [25.3].

Repurchase agreements   *Repos* [25.3].

Required rate of return   The rate of return that perfectly reflects the riskiness of the expected future cash flows. The *opportunity cost of capital* for that risk level [6.1].

Residual assets   Assets that remain after dedicating sufficient assets to meet all senior securityholders' claims in full [1.6].

Residual claim   The claim on what is left after all prior claims have been settled. The "last" claim.

Residual method   A method for allocating the purchase price for the acquisition of another firm (a merger) among the acquired assets [22.3].

Residual risk   All the (remaining) risk that is not borne by senior providers of capital; the common stockholders of a firm bear the residual risk of the firm [1.5].

Retained earnings   Accounting earnings that are retained by the firm for investment in its business; earnings that are not paid out as dividends.

Retire   Extinguish a security, as in paying off a debt [20.2]. Also, to *clear a position*.

Return on average assets   The ratio of the sum of operating income and other income to average total tangible assets [24.5].

Return on average common equity   The ratio of earnings available for common stock before extraordinary items to average common stockholders' equity [24.5].

Return on average invested capital   The ratio of the sum of operating income and other income net of income taxes to average net tangible assets [24.5].

Return on investment   *Average rate of return on investment* [11.6].

Reverse stock split   A recombination of outstanding shares of common stock that reduces the number of shares outstanding proportionately. See *stock split* [18.6].

Reverse subsidiary merger   A merger involving a subsidiary of the *acquiror* and an *acquiree* in which the acquiree is the surviving entity (and becomes a subsidiary of the acquiror) [Chapter 22, footnote 22].

Revolving credit   An agreement that represents a legal commitment to lend up to a specified maximum amount any time during a specified period [25.4].

Right   A short-lived (typically less than 90 days) call option for purchasing additional stock in a firm, issued by the firm to all its shareholders on a pro rata basis [14.2].

Rights offerings   The process of issuing *rights* [14.2].

Rights-on   Shares trading with the rights attached [14.2].

Risk   Typically defined as the standard deviation of the rate of return on total investment [7.3].

Risk-adjusted probability   A probability used to determine a "sure" expected value (sometimes called a *certainty equivalent*) that would be equivalent to the actual risky expected value.

Risk-averse   Willing to pay money to transfer risk to others [2.2].

Risk classes   Groups of investments of comparable (sometimes only approximately) risk [10.12].

Riskless arbitrage   The simultaneous purchase and sale of an asset to yield a profit. See *arbitrage*.

Riskless rate   The rate of return earned on a riskless investment. Typically modeled as the rate earned on 90-day U.S. Treasury bills. Denoted r_f.

Risk neutral   Insensitive to risk [23.2].

Risk-prone   Willing to pay money to transfer risk from others [2.2].

Round lot   A standardized number of financial securities, 100 shares in the case of most common stocks (for some high-priced stocks, a round lot consists of 10 shares) [4.1].

Rule 415   Rule enacted in 1982 that permits firms to file *shelf registration* statements [14.1].

Safety stocks   Additional inventory that is maintained in order to reduce the risk of being out of stock [25.3].

Sale-and-leaseback   An agreement to sell an asset and lease it back from the purchaser [21.1].

Salvage value   The expected before-tax difference between the sale price (S) and the cleanup and removal expense (REX) [11.1].

SEC   *Securities and Exchange Commission*.

Secondary market   Market in which previously issued securities are traded.

Secured debt   Debt that identifies specific assets that can be taken over by the debtholder in case of default [14.3].

Securities and Exchange Commission (SEC)   Federal government agency established in 1933 to regulate the public securities markets.

Security   A type of financial asset [4.1].

Security market line (SML)   The linear relationship between required rate of return and beta [7.6].

Segmented market   A market in which participants provide or demand products with only certain attributes, for example, debt of a particular maturity [4.4], firms with a particular capital structure [15.7], or firms with a particular dividend policy [17.7]. See *clientele effect*.

Sell   To sell or *take a short position*.

Selling concession The portion of the *gross underwriting spread* that compensates the securities firms for their efforts to sell the securities [14.1].

Sell order A directive to *sell* one or more financial securities [2.4].

Semistrong-strong form of capital market efficiency A market in which prices fully reflect all publicly available information [Chapter 5, footnote 1].

Senior Having a prior claim; as in senior debt, which has a prior claim to the cash flow and to the assets of the firm in the event of liquidation relative to *subordinated* debt [14.3].

Sensitivity analysis A method of analysis in which key parameters are varied one at a time in order to assess the sensitivity of project NPV (or IRR) to variation in each parameter [12.5].

Separation theorem The choice of investments is separate from investor attitudes. See *Fisher's separation theorem* [4.2] and *portfolio separation theorem* [7.5].

Set-of-contracts model (of the firm) Viewing the firm as a set of implicit and explicit contractual relationships among participants in the firm such as shareholders, debtholders, employees, customers, suppliers, and society [1.4].

Shareholders Those holding some share of the firm's equity. Also called *stockholders* or *equityholders*.

Shark repellents Defensive measures taken by a prospective takeover target to try to ward off potential suitors. See Defensive Tactics in [22.5].

Shelf basis The process of issuing securities that have previously been registered by filing a *shelf registration* statement [14.2].

Shelf registration The process of registering a two-year inventory of securities by filing a single registration statement [14.1].

Shirking When an agent expends less than full effort [9.3].

Short The obligation side of the transaction. With respect to options, the party who must deliver (call option) or take (put option) the asset in the event the option is exercised; responsible for the obligation without the right (to buy or sell) [4.3] [Chapter 8].

Short position The mirror image of owning an asset (a *long position*). A position of obligation, for example, to return borrowed securities [4.3], deliver on a futures contract [4.3], or to sell (call) or buy (put) when the optionholder exercises his option [4.3] [Chapter 8].

Short selling Borrowing an asset, such as a bond or stock, and selling it to a third party [4.2].

Short-term Typically indicates less than or equal to one year.

Short-term debt Debt with one year or less remaining to maturity [Chapter 24].

Short-term financial plan A financial plan covering the coming fiscal year [26.1].

Short-term funds *Short-term debt.*

Short-term investment services Services that assist firms in making short-term investments [26.6].

Signaling The process of conveying information through a firm's actions [5.4].

Signaling view Interpreting the information contained in a firm's actions such as its capital structure choice [15.1] or its dividend policy [17.1].

Simple compound growth method A method of calculating the growth rate by relating the terminal value to the initial value and assuming a constant percentage annual rate of growth between these two values [24.2].

Simple interest Interest is received on the initial principal amount only; interest is not compounded [3.5].

Simulation See *Monte Carlo simulation* [12.5].

Single-payment bond A bond that will make only one payment of principal and interest [4.4] [5.6]. Also called a *pure-discount bond* or a *zero-coupon bond*.

Sinking fund A schedule of debt principal payments that are made prior to maturity, over the life of the debt issue [14.3].

SML *Security Market Line.*

Soft capital rationing Loosely, or not, enforced *capital rationing* [13.6].

Sole proprietorship A business owned by a single individual [1.6].

Span To cover all contingencies within a specified range [4.3].

Specialist A person charged by a stock exchange with the responsibility of maintaining an orderly, continuous market (that is, with smooth changes in prices) in each of the stocks assigned to him by the exchange [4.1].

Speculative grade rating A long-term debt rating other than an *investment grade rating* [16.2].

Speculative motive A desire to hold cash for the purpose of being in a position to exploit any attractive business opportunity requiring a cash expenditure that might arise [25.3].

Speculator One who engages in a speculative activity by taking a position (for example, in a security) in the hope of earning an extraordinary return [5.4].

Spot foreign exchange rate Foreign exchange rate for a spot trade [23.1].

Spot rate The rate that applies in transactions executed for "immediate" delivery [4.4].

Spot trade The purchase or sale of a foreign currency, commodity, or other item for "immediate" delivery [23.1].

Stakeholder A claimant in the *set-of-contracts model* of the firm.

Standard deviation The square root of the *variance* [7.1].

Standard normal probability distribution A *normal probability distribution* in which the *mean* is zero and the *variance* is one [7.1].

Standby agreement Agreement under which a securities firm agrees to stand ready to buy any unsold shares at a predetermined price following a rights offering or to buy any shares resulting from bonds that were not converted during a forced conversion, also at a predetermined price [14.2] [20.6].

Standby fee A fee paid to an underwriter in connection with an underwritten rights offering or an underwritten forced conversion to compensate the underwriter for standing ready (standing by) to take up rights or acquire convertible bonds, exercise the options, and sell the shares obtained upon exercise [14.2].

Stated Specified, as in stated (specified) rate of interest [14.3].

Statement of cash flows A statement required under generally accepted accounting principles that indicates a firm's cash inflows and cash outflows during the accounting period [1.1] [24.1].

Statement-of-cash-flows method A method of cash budgeting that is organized along the lines of the *statement of cash flows* [26.4].

Step up To increase, as in step up (increase) the tax basis of an asset [22.2].

Stock dividends A dividend paid in shares of common stock (rather than cash) [18.6].

Stockholders The firm's proportionate equity owners [1.6]. Also called *shareholders* or *equityholders*.

Stock market Typically refers to the combination of the NYSE, the AMEX, and regularly traded stocks in the OTC.

Stock repurchase A firm repurchasing outstanding shares of its own *common stock* [Chapter 17] [18.7].

Stock split A division of each share into multiple shares, resulting in a proportionate increase in the number of common shares outstanding [18.6].

Stopping curve A curve showing the refunding rates for different points in time at which the expected value of refunding immediately equals the expected value of waiting to refund [Chapter 20, Appendix].

Stopping curve refunding rate A refunding rate that falls on the *stopping curve* [Chapter 20, Appendix].

Straight-line An amount divided into equal per period amounts over some number of periods, for example, *straight-line depreciation* [12.4].

Straight-line depreciation Depreciation calculated under the *straight-line* method, i.e., equal annual amounts.

Strategic Relating to the long-range strategy of the firm [26.1].

Stratified random sampling A sampling procedure in which the population is divided into strata, each with a different set of characteristics, and the sample is drawn randomly from each stratum; the procedure is designed to increase the likelihood of achieving a "representative" sample [7.7].

Strike price The price for which the asset will be exchanged in an option contract if the option is exercised. Also called the *exercise price*, *call price*, or *put price* [Chapter 8].

Strong-form of capital market efficiency A *capital market* in which prices reflect all available information (both public *and* private).

Subjective probabilities Probabilities that are determined subjectively (for example, on the basis of judgment rather than through a statistical sampling procedure) [12.5].

Subordinated Of lesser priority with respect to payment obligations, for example, subordinated debentures [14.3].

Subscribe To purchase financial securities, as in subscribing for additional shares through a *rights offering* [14.2] or subscribing for shares of newly issued securities.

Subscription period The time until the option to *subscribe* expires [14.2].

Subscription price The price at which an investor can *subscribe* [14.2].

Subsidiary merger A merger involving a subsidiary of the *acquiror* and an *acquiree* in which the subsidiary of the acquiror is the surviving entity [Chapter 22, footnote 22].

Sufficient statistic A statistic that contains all of the information pertaining to the value of a parameter that is in a sample [7.6].

Sum-of-the-years'-digits A method of computing depreciation expense [12.4].

Sunk cost A cost that has already been incurred and will not be altered by subsequent decisions [2.5].

Sweep account A non-interest-bearing transaction bank account out of which all funds remaining at the end of each business day are automatically 'swept' and deposited into an interest-bearing account or invested in some other manner that the account holder has previously specified [26.6].

Syndicate A group of securities firms formed to share the underwriting risk in connection with an *underwritten offering* of securities [14.1].

Synergistic effect A violation of value-additivity whereby the value of the combination is greater than the sum of the individual values [22.2].

Systematic risk Risk that cannot be diversified away by combining securities into portfolios [7.7].

Take a position *Buy* or *sell*; that is, to have some amount that is owned or owed on an asset or option.

Take-or-pay contracts A contract that obligates the purchaser to take any product that is offered to it (and pay the cash purchase price) or pay a specified amount if it refuses to take the product [21.4].

Take-up fee A fee paid to an underwriter in connection with an underwritten rights offering or an underwritten forced conversion as compensation for each share of *common stock* the underwriter obtains and must resell upon exercise of rights or conversion of bonds [14.2].

Tangible assets Physical assets, principally cash and equivalents, inventories, receivables, property, plant, equipment, and other long-term investments [1.1].

Taxable acquisition A *merger* or *consolidation* that is not a *tax-free acquisition* [22.3].

Taxable transaction Any transaction that is not tax-free to the parties involved, such as a *taxable acquisition* [22.3].

Tax clawback agreement An agreement to contribute as equity to a project the value of all previously realized project-related tax benefits (not already clawed back) to the extent required to cover any cash deficiency of the project [21.4].

Tax differential view   The argument that shareholders prefer earnings to be retained and reinvested rather than paid out as cash dividends because of the tax differential between capital gains and dividend income [17.1].

Tax-free acquisition   A *merger* or *consolidation* in which (1) the acquiror's tax basis in each asset whose ownership is transferred in the transaction is generally the same as the acquiree's and (2) each seller who receives only stock does not have to pay any tax on the gain he realizes until the shares are sold [22.3].

Tax shield   The reduction in income taxes that results from taking an allowable deduction from taxable income.

Tender offer   A general offer to purchase securities that is made publicly and directly to all holders of the desired securities [17.9] [22.5].

Terminal value   Value of the project remaining at the end of the project's useful life [Chapter 11].

Term loan   A bank loan, typically with a floating interest rate, for a specified amount that matures in between 1 and 10 years and requires a specified repayment schedule [25.4].

Term structure of interest rates   The relationship between the yields on zero-coupon U.S. Treasury bonds and the maturities of those bonds [4.4].

Thinly traded   Infrequently traded [Chapter 24, Introduction].

Third market   Exchange-listed securities trading in the OTC market [4.1].

Throughput agreement   An agreement to put a specified amount of product per period through a particular facility, for example, an agreement to ship a specified amount of crude oil per period through a particular pipeline [21.4].

Time to expiration   The time remaining until a financial security expires. Also called the *time to maturity*.

Time to maturity   The time remaining until a financial security expires. Also called the *time to expiration*.

Time until expiration   The amount of time that will elapse before a contract (e.g., an option) is scheduled to expire [8.2].

Time value of an option   The difference between the market value of an option and its exercise value [Chapter 8].

Time value of money   The idea that a dollar today is worth more than a dollar in the future because the dollar received today can earn interest up until the time the future dollar is received [Chapter 3].

Tolling agreement   An agreement to put a specified amount of raw material per period through a particular processing facility, for example, an agreement to process a specified amount of alumina into aluminum at a particular aluminum plant [21.4].

Trade credit   Credit that firms extend to other firms in the ordinary course of business through the creation of receivables/payables [25.4].

Traders   Those who trade securities [5.3].

Trading posts   The posts on the floor of a stock exchange where the specialists stand and securities are traded [4.1].

Tranches   Two or more quantities of the same loan or security, e.g., the firm issued the new bonds in two tranches 6 months apart [14.6].

Transaction cost   Any explicit or implicit cost connected with making a transaction; for example, a commission (explicit) or the time and effort to read and interpret information (implicit).

Transaction loan   A loan extended for the purpose of financing a particular specified transaction [25.4].

Transactions motive   A desire to hold cash for the purpose of conducting cash-based transactions [25.3].

Transferable put right   A *right*, which is transferable to others, to put *common stock* back to the issuer on specified terms; a form of *put option* issued by firms to repurchase their shares [17.10].

Treasury bill   Discount note maturing in 1 year or less issued by the U.S. Treasury.

Treasury shares   Shares that have been repurchased from investors by the firm [14.2].

True interest cost   For a security such as commercial paper that is sold on a discount basis, the coupon rate required to provide an identical rate of return assuming a coupon-bearing instrument of like maturity that pays interest in arrears [25.4].

True lease   A contract that qualifies as a valid lease agreement under the Internal Revenue Code [21.2].

Turnkey construction contract   A type of construction contract under which the construction firm is obligated to complete a project according to prespecified criteria for a price that is fixed at the time the contract is signed [21.4].

Two-state option pricing model   An option pricing model in which the underlying asset can take on only two possible (discrete) values in the next time period for each value it can take on in the preceding time period [8.8]. Also called the *binomial option pricing model*.

Underlying asset   The asset on which an option contract is based; that is, the asset on which the optionwriter is obligated to transact if the optionholder chooses. The value of an option is contingent upon the value of the underlying asset [Chapter 8].

Underwrite   To guarantee, as, for example, to guarantee the issuer of securities a specified price by entering into a *purchase-and-sale* agreement [14.1].

Underwriter   A securities firm that *underwrites* a *public offering* of securities [14.1] [14.2].

Underwriting   Acting as the *underwriter* in a *purchase-and-sale* [14.1].

Underwriting fee   The portion of the *gross underwriting spread* that compensates the securities firms who underwrite a public offering for their *underwriting* risk [14.1].

Underwritten offering   A *purchase-and-sale* [14.1].

Unleveraged beta   The *beta* of an *unleveraged required rate of return* [19.7].

Unleveraged required rate of return   The *required rate of return* on an investment if the investment is financed entirely by equity [19.3].

Unlimited liability   Full liability for the debt and other obligations of a legal entity; the general partners of a partnership have unlimited liability [1.6].

Unsecured debt   Debt that does not identify specific assets that can be taken over by the debtholder in case of default [14.3].

Unsystematic risk   Risk that cannot be eliminated by diversification [7.7]. Also called *nondiversifiable risk*.

Up-tick   A term used to describe a transaction that took place at a higher price than the preceding transaction (involving the same security) [4.3].

Value additivity   Refers to the *value-additivity principle* [5.6].

Value-additivity principle   The principle that the value of two or more assets that are combined in a single entity is equal to the sum of the respective values of the separate assets [5.6].

Variable   A value determined within the context of a model [1.3]. Also called *endogenous variable*.

Variable cost   A cost that is directly proportional to output.

Variance   The mathematical expectation of the squared deviations from the mean [7.1].

Vertical merger   One firm acquires another that is in the same industry but at another stage in the production cycle, e.g., serves as a supplier to the acquiror or purchases the acquiror's goods or services [22.2].

Voting rights   The right to vote on matters that are put to a vote of securityholders, e.g., the right to vote for directors [1.6].

WACC   *Weighted Average Cost of Capital*.

Warrant   A long-term *call option* issued by the firm whereby its exercise creates new shares of *common stock* [4.1] [8.3].

Weak-form of capital market efficiency   A *capital market* in which prices reflect all of the information contained in past security prices.

Weighted average cost of capital (WACC)   The weighted average after-corporate-tax required rate of return to all financing sources [10.6]. Also used frequently in practice to refer simply to any required rate of return, but especially a *hurdle rate* for a capital budgeting project.

White knight   A firm that steps in at a potential acquiror's behest and acquires the firm in a friendly merger in order to save the firm from a hostile raider [22.5].

Withholding taxes   Taxes that must by law be collected by the paying corporation before payment is made to securityholders [23.4].

Without recourse   Without the lender having any right to seek payment or seize assets in the event of nonpayment from anyone other than the party (e.g., special-purpose entity) specified in the debt contract [21.4].

Working capital   Literally the current assets of the firm. Typically used to mean *net working capital*, which is the difference between current assets and current liabilities.

Working capital management   Management of the firm's current assets and current liabilities in a manner consistent with shareholder wealth maximization [Chapter 25].

Write (an option)   To create and sell an option. Also called *taking a short position* in an option [Chapter 8].

Yield curve   The relationship between the YTMs of coupon-paying bonds selling at *par value* and the maturities of those bonds [4.4].

Yield to maturity (YTM)   The nominal annual rate of return that makes the present value of all expected future payments from a bond equal to its current market value [4.4] [6.2].

YTM   *Yield to Maturity*.

Zero-balance account   A bank account that is managed so as to have just enough cash to cover checks that will be presented for payment during the day, which results in the balance returning to zero at the end of each business day [26.6].

Zero-coupon bond   A bond that will make only one payment of principal and interest [4.4] [5.6]. Also called a *pure-discount bond* or a *single-payment bond*.

Zero-one integer programming   A form of linear programming problem in which each decision variable is constrained to assume a value of either zero or one [13.5].

Zero-sum game   A situation in which one participant can gain *only* at the expense of another participant [2.4] [5.6].

Answers to Selected Problems

Chapter 2

B1. According to the Principle of Self-Interested Behavior, each party to a financial transaction will choose the course of action that is most financially advantageous to that party, given the information that they possess. A particular piece of information may result in a particular action when the decision-maker acts in his own self-interest. In that case, observing the decision-maker's action may allow us to deduce the information that is known to the decision-maker.

B3. Limited liability is a legal concept stating that the financial liability of an asset owner is limited in some manner. For example, a stockholder in a publicly-traded firm such as IBM or General Motors cannot be held responsible for a liability of the corporation. If a borrower's financial liability is limited to a particular amount, that limit gives the borrower the option to default and not fully repay the loan.

B5. According to the Signaling Principle, an action we observe is the optimal action of a self-interested player, given a particular information set. If a second player expects to face the same (or nearly the same) information set but does not know exactly what is in the information set and it is costly (or impossible) to determine the information with accuracy, the second player can infer that the action taken by the first player will also be in the second player's best interest. As a result, we have the Behavioral Principle—when all else fails, look at what others are doing for guidance.

B7. You would want to guard against the free-rider problem in any situation where you expend resources to determine a best course of action and others can receive the same benefits by simply imitating your actions. For example, if you have researched and developed a new cost-saving way to manufacture automobile tires, you would want to apply for a patent so that other firms in the tire industry cannot costlessly imitate your new production process.

B9. $3,259.84

B11. The Principle of Two-Sided Transactions is important to financial decision-making because when we analyze any transaction, we must remember that someone else is analyzing that same transaction from the opposite point of view. This is much like any game of strategy, such as chess.

C1. Assuming that IBM's new "family" was the embodiment of a valuable new idea, the existence of more capable machines would render existing machines less cost effective. With specialized assets to manufacture (old generation, less capable) computers, the common stock prices of other computer manufacturers would decline. This is because the price that can be charged for the less capable computers will be less and therefore the specialized assets owned by the other manufacturing companies would be worth less, leading to a lower value of their common stock.

C3. In our example of selling a used car, it would be virtually impossible to ever know *exactly* what the highest price was that the car *could have been* sold for. Since it would not be possible to know the "best" alternative, the opportunity cost cannot be measured exactly. The majority of situations are like this. Still, measuring alternatives against competitively priced market alternatives provides a very good estimate of the opportunity cost of an alternative.

Chapter 3

B1. $123,365.16
B3. 3.8212%
B5. $10,775.52
B7. 5.5 years
B9. 9.2%
B11. $5,531.66
B13. a. 0.9% **b.** 10.8% **c.** 11.35%
B15. $169.67
B17. $320.65
C1. a. $4,628.21 **b.** $3,441.79
C3. a. $61,857.65 **b.** $32.65
C5. a. $47,912.83 **b.** $49,881.47
C7. $145.13
C9. $1,093.60
C11. $739.33
C13. $566.58

Chapter 4

B1. Limited liability means that the least a corporation's shares can be worth is nothing. The shareholder's liability for the obligations of the corporation is limited to the loss of the shares that they own. In contrast, the owners of a sole proprietorship or general partnership can be held personally liable for the obligations of the firm, so that such a firm could actually have a negative value.

B3. $78,363.64

B5. The asset's increase in value from $50,000 to $75,000 represents a return of 50%. As long as the opportunity cost of capital is less than 50%, you should buy the asset. The fact that you do not have the $50,000 does not affect your decision because you can borrow the money in the capital markets at an interest rate $r < 50\%$.

B7. Fisher's separation theorem is significant to a corporation because it means that the corporation's shareholders will all agree on the single objective of maximizing net present value, regardless of their individual consumption preferences. Thus, the shareholders can delegate decision-making to the managers of the corporation.

B9. 13.01%

B11. Warrants, options, and futures are all contracts that specify financial transactions that may or will occur at some time in the future. An option contract gives its holder the right, without the obligation, to buy (call option) or sell (put option) a specified amount of securities at a specified price within a specified time period. A warrant is simply a long-term call option issued by a corporation on its own stock. A futures contract also specifies a financial transaction in terms of the amount, price, and time period. However, in contrast to the options contract, the futures contract specifies a transaction that *will* take place; neither side has a choice about whether the transaction will occur. The parties to a futures contract can, however, clear their position (eliminate their benefit or obligation connected with the contract) using another transaction prior to expiration of the futures contract. For example, the owner can sell her contract before its transaction is implemented.

C1. Capital markets directly help people who want to buy a house by providing an efficient mechanism by which they can save for a down payment and borrow money against expected future earnings. Indirectly, the capital markets help these savers and borrowers attain the best possible interest rates by providing a setting in which financial intermediaries compete for the business of individuals.

C3. Efficient capital markets bring together the choices for investing in real and financial assets. Self-interested investors would never invest in a real asset if a financial asset of identical risk had a higher return and this is true for corporations as well as for individual investors. Thus, a corporation should never buy an asset with a negative net present value. For a corporation to have a single investment decision rule, the firm's shareholders must agree about that decision rule and this is only possible if individual's investment decisions are *separate* from their consumption preferences and decisions.

C5. A complete capital market is a market in which there are enough distinct securities so that any desired pattern of state-contingent payoffs can be achieved. In a complete market you can profit from having information before anyone else because you can construct any pattern of state-contingent payoffs.

Chapter 5

B1. Six "side" benefits to the existence of capital markets are (1) increased liquidity—capital markets provide an active and readily available forum for the exchange of securities; (2) decreased total transaction costs—arranging securities transactions without the capital markets would require more time and money; (3) providing a measure of value—publicly available transaction prices provide a good estimate of each security's value; (4) creates the ability to smooth an individual's consumption needs over a lifetime of uneven income; (5) improves the access of "small" participants to investments in real assets; and (6) increases the efficiency of total societal investment in real assets.

B3. False. Capital market efficiency and competition among arbitrageurs drives the net present value of being an arbitrageur to zero, which means that they earn a fair return for the effort expended and the risk incurred.

B5. The homogeneity of assets contributes to the efficiency of the capital markets by reducing the evaluation of financial securities to considerations about risk and return. Investors trading to increase the return on their investments (for a given level of risk) will identify the same opportunities that an arbitrageur would, thus increasing the competition for those opportunities and increasing the efficiency of the market.

B7. Inductive reasoning requires inferring the cause from the result. When multiple causes lead to the same result, it is extremely difficult to apply the Signaling Principle and determine the *acutal* cause.

B9. According to the law of value conservation, value is neither created or destroyed when assets (cash flows) are combined or separated or exchanged.

C1. The blessing would be that you would never have to worry about whether you were paying a fair price because all prices would be fair. The curse would be that absolutely no positive NPV investments would ever exist.

C3. APR = 26.25% and r_a = 29.83%

C5. 6.94237%

C7. $57,326.57

C9. The opportunity cost of an alternative is the difference between the value of the alternative and the value of the best possible alternative. Essentially, it is the cost of forgoing the best alternative. For assets of a given risk level, the best alternative is the alternative with the highest rate of return and all investors will choose that alternative. As a result, all assets with the same risk must provide the same rate of return and that required rate of return is the appropriate discount rate for computing the present value of the asset.

C11. The Principle of Capital Market Efficiency results in many ways from the other principles. The actions of self-interested market participants (purchases and sales of securities) provide information. Other self-interested market participants stand ready to interpret that information and free-ride whenever they can by imitating the actions of others. The interaction facilitates the flow of information and helps to enforce the Principle of Capital Market Efficiency.

Chapter 6

B1. a. Fair prices of the 2-, 5-, 10-, and 20-year bonds are $968.61, $930.76, $886.18, and $838.99, respectively. **b.** Fair prices of the 2-, 5-, 10-, and 20-year bonds are $951.24, $893.83, $828.64, and $764.06, respectively. **c.** Fair prices of the 2-, 5-, 10-, and 20-year bonds are $986.39, $969.58, $949.04, and $925.78, respectively. **d.** The change in bond price (as a percentage of the original price) is larger the longer the maturity of the bond. Thus, the longer the maturity of the bond, the more sensitive its price is to changes in the yield to maturity. That is, interest-rate risk increases with increased maturity.

B3. a. YTM = 13.4176% and r_a = 13.8677% **b.** YTM = 13.3996% and r_a = 13.8485% **c.** YTM = 13.398% and r_a = 13.847%

B5. YTM = 8.452% and r_a = 8.631%

B7. $5.13

B9. i = 20% and NPVFI = +$1.78 per share

B11. i = 10%, NPVFI = 0, and expected P_4 = $36.60

C1. −$0.11/share

C3. 10.687%

C5. 9.868%

C7. a. $11/share **b.** 19.09%

Chapter 7

B1. a. $E(X)$ = 4.8% and $E(Y)$ = 3.3% **b.** Var(X) = 57.76 and Var(Y) = 37.41 **c.** Cov(X, Y) = .16 **d.** Corr(X, Y) = $\rho_{X,Y}$ = .00344

B3. This is not a valid criticism because asset pricing models are models of *expected* returns and we would predict that an (after the fact) actual return would not necessarily be equal to its expected value.

B5. 3.92

B7. Both statements are correct. σ measures the total risk of a particular asset, while β measures the risk of that asset

when it is held in a diversified portfolio—the nondiversifiable risk.

B9. 14.14%

B11. 25.92%

B13. β = 1.25 and r_f = 10%

C1. By the portfolio separation theorem, every investor will choose to own a portion of every asset in the portfolio M and will never choose to hold an asset that is not in the portfolio M. Because there is never an owner for an asset that is not in the portfolio M, then M must contain every asset that has an owner—that is, every asset available in the market.

C3. It is not possible that any two of these portfolios have a correlation coefficient between them that is equal to minus 1.0. If this were possible, one possible combination of those portfolios would result in a portfolio of zero risk and the set in Figure 7–8 would touch the vertical axis in at least one place.

C5. Beta measures the risk of the asset when it is held in a diversified portfolio, so the measure of risk for the individual asset depends on how the risk of the portfolio changes when that asset is added to the portfolio. When added to the portfolio, a negative beta asset decreases the risk of the portfolio. In this sense, the asset does have negative risk. An investor would hold an asset like this one because of its ability to decrease the risk of the portfolio. Note, however, that if this asset were held alone, its diversifiable risk would cause it to have positive (and perhaps substantial) risk.

C7. The SML is derived from the CML, in essence, by "inverting" the CML, assuming that the capital markets are perfect and are in equilibrium. The "inversion" simply computes what the rate of return on an individual asset must be if the CML holds. In the process, we consider an asset j and a portfolio M' that is identical to the market portfolio except that M' does not contain the asset j. By considering all the combinations of M' and security j, we find that one possible combination is the market portfolio and, because the market portfolio is on the efficient frontier, the market portfolio dominates all the other combinations. By equating the slope of the risk-return curve for M' and j with the slope of the capital market line, we can derive an expression for the required rate of return on security j that is implied by the CML and this expression is the equation for the SML.

C9. It is important to recall that a zero NPV does not mean a zero rate of return on the investment. It just means that in an efficient market, the rate of return that is earned will be commensurate with the risk of the investment. The reason for investing in financial securities is to earn that (nonzero) rate of return.

Chapter 8

B1. $51.70

B3. $3.34

B5. **a.** $3.50   **b.** $3.12   **c.** $2.74
B7. **a.** $2.48   **b.** $2.66   **c.** $2.84
B9. Call = $6.75, Exercise Value = $4.38, and Time Value = $2.37
B11. **a.** $10.00   **b.** $14.13   **c.** $14.13
C1. $\sigma = 32\%$ yields a value for the call option of $2.028
C3. A synthetic loan could consist of the following portfolio of options that has been sold to a lender for $250,000: 6 put options on the asset, with times to maturity from 1 to 6 years and each with a strike price of $295,001; 5 call options on the asset, with times to maturity from 1 to 5 years and each with a strike price of $250,001; and 1 call option with a 6-year maturity and a strike price of $1. At the end of each of years 1 through 5, the lender would purchase the asset by exercising his maturing call option for $250,001, then immediately sell the asset back by exercising his put option for $295,001, thereby netting interest of $45,000 each year. At the end of year 6, the difference between the strike prices nets the lender $295,000, representing the interest plus the principal.
C5. For an out-of-the-money option, the only value for the option is due to the possibility that it will be in-the-money before it expires and the closer the value of the underlying asset is to the strike price, the greater the probability that the option will become in-the-money before its expiration. Thus, the time value of an out-of-the-money option increases (decreases) as the value of the underlying asset moves toward (away from) the strike price. For an in-the-money option, the time value is due to a combination of (1) the possibility that it will be even deeper in-the-money before it expires, and (2) the forgone opportunity of earning the time value of money on the exercise value (i.e., exercising the option now and reinvesting the proceeds). As the value of the underlying asset moves farther from the strike price, the forgone time value of money on the exercise value grows, but the value of the incremental gain from becoming deeper in-the-money does not grow. Thus, the time value of an in-the-money option decreases (increases) as the value of the underlying asset moves away from (toward) the strike price.
C7. Assume that the values of the assets shown on the balance sheet (a portfolio of real estate loans) are in fact fair market values and that the market value of the liabilities are not in excess of that shown on the balance sheet. Purchase of the thrift institution would be essentially the purchase of a series of call options on the asset portfolio, with strike prices and maturities equal to the debt payment obligations. The value of this investment is thus the value of a call option on a portfolio of loans. If interest rate movement causes the value to increase, the investor gets the net increase in value. If interest rate movement causes the value to decrease (all of the loans are defaulted on in the extreme and the "new" institution collapses), the investor has the option to "walk away." If you make up a few simple hypothetical ex-

amples of the effect of interest rate movement on a $1 billion dollar portfolio of loans, it will quickly convince you of the potential value in this investment. For example, assume the income is a perpetual $140 million per year and the required rate of return on the portfolio is 14% so that the portfolio is currently worth $1 billion (= 140 million/.14). A decline in the required rate of return to 13.8% would cause an increase of about $14.5 million in the present value of the portfolio (= 140 million/.138 = 1,014.493 million).

Chapter 9

B1. Monitoring is not always the best choice because minimizing agency costs involves a trade-off of the three types of agency costs. For example, it may be that monitoring is more costly than costs due to occasional misbehavior on the part of the agent.
B3. The stockholders decision rule for investment projects would be to undertake all positive-NPV projects. Due to the firm's expertise in a particular area, these projects are likely to be highly related to the firm's existing operations. This is not a concern to the stockholders because their investment in the firm is diversified by their other investments. In contrast, because the manager has nondiversifiable human capital invested in the firm, she has the incentive to choose projects that diversify the firm's operations even if these projects are not as profitable for the firm.
B5. The stock of a firm undergoing bankruptcy proceedings is usually positive and never negative because of the limited liability feature of the stock and the view of stock as a call option on the assets of the firm. The worst that the stockholders can do is lose the entire value of their investment in a liquidation. If there is any possibility of the firm recovering in a reorganization, then there is a positive value to the stockholder's option.
B7. If undertaking a low-risk investment reduces the risk of the firm, then it reduces the variability of the rate of return on the firm's assets. A reduction in variability reduces the value of a call option on those assets, thus reducing the value of the firm's shares. In spite of this share value reduction, the firm will increase in value by the NPV of the project (because of the Principle of Risk-Return Trade-Off). If the shareholders' share of the positive NPV is smaller than the share value reduction due to the decrease in firm risk, shareholders will not want the firm to undertake the project. If the project is forgone, the firm's debtholders are the losers.
B9. An optimal contract is one that balances the three types of agency costs so that the total cost is minimized. High contracting costs or high monitoring costs should result in lower costs of misbehavior, and low contracting and monitoring costs may result in higher costs of misbehavior, so there is a trade-off of costs involved. The optimal contract manipulates the trade-off so that the total cost is minimized.

B11. Shareholders can act to align managers' goals more closely with their own goals by providing appropriate financial incentives such as bonus and stock option plans, and by monitoring managerial actions and imposing penalties for failure to act in the shareholders' interest. They also have natural bonding devices such as the right to vote for directors who hire and fire managers and the right to sell their shares, perhaps to bidders in a takeover attempt.

C1. It is not possible to have an agency problem without asymmetric information. If the principal had perfect information about the decisions and actions of the agent, then the agent would never be able to take actions that weren't in the best interest of the principal. If he did, the principal could impose penalties that effectively transfer the total costs of such actions back to the agent. These penalties would cancel out the benefits the agent received from acting in his interest at the expense of the principal, so he would have no incentive to pursue interests other than those of the principal.

C3. Suppose the firm is in financial distress and it is in the best interests of the debtholders to liquidate the firm and payoff the firm's debts. If the managers choose to continue to operate the firm, simply because a large debt payment has not forced the firm into insolvency, there can be a loss to the firm's debtholders. In the case of an otherwise healthy firm, if excessive perquisite consumption were to impair the firm's ability to meet its debt obligations (interest and principal payments), then managers acting in their own interest would be doing so at the expense of *both* the debt- and equityholders. These possibilities create an agency problem between managers and the debtholders.

C5. Convertible debt helps to reduce the agency problem between the shareholders and the debtholders by giving debtholders the option of share ownership. A convertible bond can be modeled as stock plus a put option on the stock of the firm, where the option can be exercised with a strike price equal to the value of the security as debt. This keeps the goals of the shareholders more in line with those of the convertible debtholders because if the shareholders take actions to benefit themselves at the expense of the debtholders, the debtholders can convert their bonds into stock and share in that benefit.

Chapter 10

B1. Invest in stocks B and C because in each case the expected rate of return exceeds the required rate of return.

B3. $r^* = 13.73\%$

B5. In a perfect capital market, this purely financial transaction would be a zero-NPV transaction. The WACC for the firm is irrelevant to the decision because the required rate of return depends only on the risk of the investment—in this case, Treasury notes.

B7. Because the project has the same risk as the market, the project beta is 1.0, and the required rate of return on the project is 15%. With an expected rate of return of 20%, the project has a positive NPV and should be undertaken even though the required rate of return for the firm's current operations is much higher.

B9. 15.2%

B11. APR = 26.4% and r_a = 30.0%

C1. Based only on the two *comparable* oil and gas companies: **a.** 0.668 **b.** 14.008% **c.** r^* = WACC = 14.008%

C3. 1.10

C5. **a.** Because preferred stock dividends, expenses, and discounts are not tax-deductible, the DSAT will simply be the quarterly dividend and NP will be the net proceeds per share from the preferred stock issue. **b.** APR = 10.78% and r_a = 11.23%

C7. 6.17%

Chapter 11

B1. $13,254.32

B3. −$48.75

B5. **a.** $24.90, yes, accept the project. **b.** 20.28%, yes, accept the project. **c.** 2.5 years **d.** 64% **e.** Not very much. Payback provides some indication of the project's risk in that it estimates the time until the initial investment is recovered without regard to the time value of money. ROI can be meaningless. **f.** If the project is one of two mutually exclusive projects and the NPV and IRR criteria led to different choices, the firm should accept the project with the largest NPV.

B7. **a.** $87.75, yes, accept the project. **b.** −31.12%, the *standard* IRR decision rule would say to reject the project. **c.** The IRR is defined to be the discount rate for which the NPV is zero. Because of the nature of the cash flows in this example, that rate happens to have a negative value. **d.** The IRR decision rule is appropriate for evaluating economically independent projects for which all after-tax cash flows but the first are positive. In this case the cash flows are reversed (so to speak): two inflows followed by two outflows. For situations where inflows are followed by outflows (with only one flow reversal) a modified IRR decision rule would be the reverse of the standard rule or, accept the project when the IRR is *less* than the hurdle rate. The rate in this case is negative because the time value of money must cause the inflows in 0 and 1 to *decrease* in value into the future to be exactly worth the required outflows. That is, the total inflow of $150 (= 50 + 100) must decline in value down to $70 (= 20 + 50).

B9. The company should accept project B because its NPV is $52.95, while the NPV of A is $30.11. When considering mutually exclusive projects, the NPV decision rule is the appropriate criterion to apply.

B11. $27.67

B13. −$9,493.80

C1. $4,159,983

C3. $43,579.37

Chapter 12

B1. EAC = \$24,008

B3. Choose machine A because it has an EAC of \$31,691 compared with an EAC of \$31,902 for machine B.

B5. a. 1.5 **b.** \$15,427.58 **c.** \$4,418.44

B7. A decision tree differs from the two-state option pricing model developed in Chapter 8 because, in addition to "forks" representing the set of probabilistic outcomes, a decision tree also has "forks" representing decisions that allow the decision-maker to choose a path.

B9. −\$670,201

B11. a. No. As long as the tax rate is less than 100%, the taxes paid on the revenue will exceed the taxes "saved" on expenses. **b.** \$4,104,087

B13. If the product development has lead to a major advance, the optimal choice is to produce without test marketing. EV in this case is \$2.024 million, while EV doing the test marketing is \$1.74 million (= 1.99 − .25).

C1. a. \$493.85 **b.** \$4,115.43 **c.** Effective 4-year rate = 57.325% so that PV = 1,500 + 1,500/.57325 = \$4,115.43

C3. Yes, NPV = \$18,973

C5. Assuming the equipment for both production methods can be replaced an indefinite number of times into the future, if the project is successful, EV for Method A is \$836,674 and EV for Method B is \$829,213 so J. Hopkins should proceed with the project using Method A.

C7. Yes, doing it himself has an EAC of \$1,970.20 versus an annual after-tax cost of \$2135 (= [1 − .3]3050) for employing the CPA firm.

Chapter 13

B1. 20% and 30%

B3. Billy Bob should buy Machine A because it has the lower equivalent annual cost (\$658.14 vs. \$663.38 for Machine B). Because the machines have the same risk and the same increase in revenues, examining total costs is appropriate. Because they have different economic lives, the EAC should be considered.

B5. Optimal set: 5, 7, 9, 10, 11, 12, 14, 15; cumulative outlay = \$782,000; and total NPV = \$878,500

B7. Optimal set: 1, 2, 5, 7, 8, 9, 10, 11, 12, 13, 14, 15; cumulative outlay = \$1,763,000; and total NPV = \$1,493,500

B9. An after-tax sale price of greater than \$33,333.

B11. \$34,496

C1. As a general rule, it is not likely that a firm can "limit its losses" by selling off a subsidiary that is doing very poorly because of the Principle of Two-Sided Transactions. The potential buyer will only be willing to pay what the subsidiary is worth to them *now*. This is generally not any more than the subsidiary is worth to its current owner. Therefore, in most cases, the loss has already been incurred and will not be "limited" by selling the subsidiary.

C3. Four broad factors that can cause the NPV of a capital budgeting project to be incorrectly measured are (1) difficulty in defining the incremental cash flows—this is especially relevant in cases of economic dependence, (2) difficulty in determining the correct required rate of return—it is crucial that the required return reflect the risk of the proposed investment and not necessarily the average risk of the firm, (3) difficulty in predicting the likelihood of future events such as technological advances that would make the investment obsolete, and (4) difficulty in determing the value of options associated with the investment, such as price setting options, future investment opportunities, abandonment, and postponement options.

C5. Optimal set: 1, 5, 7, 8, 9, 10, 12, 15; cumulative outlay = \$1,195,000; and total NPV = \$1,158,000

C7. Price = $(2,538,000/\text{Demand})^{1/3}$. Let P = Price and D = Demand, then

$$\text{total revenue} = PD = (2,538,000)^{1/3}D^{2/3}$$

Marginal Revenue (MR) = the first derivative of total revenue with respect to demand:

$$\text{MR} = d[\text{Total Revenue}]/dD = [2/3](2,538,000)^{1/3}D^{-1/3}$$

Therefore, MR = MC when

$$\text{MR} = [2/3](2,538,000)^{1/3}D^{-1/3} = .387$$

Solving for D gives $D = \{[\frac{2}{3}](2,538,000)^{1/3}/.387\}^3 = 12,974,330$

Finally, putting demand into our equation for price

$$\text{Price} = (2,538,000/12,974,330)^{1/3} = .5805$$

Chapter 14

B1. 11.78%

B3. a. $r_a = 8.329\%$ **b.** $r_a = 8.399\%$ **c.** $r_a = 8.405\%$

B5. a.

Time	Item	CFBT
0	Proceeds	+1,000
1	Interest	−100
2	Interest	−102.5
3	Interest	−105
4	Interest	−107.5
5	Interest	−110
5	Principal	−1,000

b. 10.45% **c.** 6.91%

B7. a. S = \$21.43 and N = 15 **b.** .098125 **c.** A rights offering is more appropriate than a general public offering when the firm does not have broad market appeal or has concentrated stock ownership. **d.** The principal drawback to a rights offering is that a rights offering generally takes longer to complete.

B9. a. 14.16% **b.** If the firm believes it can refund the 1-year issue at its maturity for a rate less than 14.16%, it should issue the 1-year debt. Otherwise, it should issue the 2-year debt. **c.** 11.45% before-tax or 7.55% after-tax **d.** The two 1-year debt issues would be preferable.

B11. 8.8 years

B13. a. Yes. Because the interest differential on the fixed-rate loan (3%) is greater than the interest differential on the floating-rate loan (1%), it is possible to construct a mutually advantageous interest rate swap. **b.** The manufacturing company should turn down the bank's offer. If they borrow at LIBOR + 1%, receive LIBOR from the bank, and pay the bank 11.5%, the net effect is that they pay 12.5%. Since they can borrow for themselves at a fixed rate of 12%, they should not take the swap offer. **c.** This swap is advantageous for the bank because they can borrow at 9%, receive 10.5%, and pay LIBOR. The net effect is that they can borrow at LIBOR − 1.5% and save 1.5% over the rate they would pay borrowing for themselves at a floating rate (LIBOR). **d.** The bank realizes ¾ of the net cost benefit and the manufacturing company realizes ¼.

C1. a. $r_a = 8.19\%$ **b.** $r_a = 8.61\%$

C3. Shelf registration may lead to a more efficient capital market by increasing the firm's flexibility with respect to the timing of offerings and by reducing the issuance costs associated with individual issues.

Chapter 15

B1. 18.17%

B3. Financial distress adversely affects the value of the firm through its tax credits even when the firm is able to completely use all tax credits via loss carryforwards because of the time value of money. Suppose a firm has $10,000 of depreciation expense, a 40% tax rate, and a required rate of return of 10%. If the firm is able to use the tax credit now, they add $4,000 (= [.4]10,000) to the value of the firm. If the firm is unable to use the tax credits until next year due to financial distress, they add only $3,636 (= 4,000/1.1) to the value of the firm.

B5. a. $40,625 **b.** $7,109

B7. a. $5,000 **b.** $3,500 **c.** $V = \$3,920$ and $\theta = 35.7\%$ **d.** $3,150 **e.** $3,318 **f.** $5,000

B9. a. G_L increases with an increase in τ; G_L increases with an increase in τ_e; G_L decreases with an increase in τ_d. **b.** When $\tau_d = \tau_e$, $G_L = \tau D$ **c.** $G_L = \$0.32$ per dollar of debt

C1. a. No. **b.** While debtholders are promised a fixed payment which provides their entire return, shareholders are proportionate claimants on the residual value of the firm. Therefore, the cash dividends the shareholders receive are only part of their return. The rest of their return is provided by reinvested earnings. Because of the higher risk connected with equity ownership, the required rate of return on common equity (the firm's cost of common equity) is in fact higher than the interest rate paid to the debtholders.

C3. It is true that the required rate of return on equity and the required rate of return on debt are both increasing with increasing leverage. However, the required rate of return on equity is higher than the required rate of return on debt for all degrees of leverage and increasing leverage means that you are using a higher proportion of lower cost debt. Thus, the increase in the rates is offset by the increased usage of the lower cost financing. In a perfect capital market environment, these effects exactly cancel each other out and the net result is that the weighted average of the two remains constant.

C5. You should take the "great" investment alternative. In a perfect capital market, the standard deviation of the market required rate of return for a given risk level is zero. Although the capital markets are not exactly perfect, the Principle of Capital Market Efficiency implies that the standard deviation of the market required rate of return for a given risk level is relatively small. In contrast, the Principle of Valuable Ideas implies that there are positive-NPV opportunities that occur. That is, it implies that the markets for real assets are not nearly as efficient as the capital markets. Therefore, the standard deviation of expected future cash flows is relatively large. Since in either case, your outcome is to be 3 standard deviations in your favor, you want the alternative with the largest standard deviation.

Chapter 16

B1. a. .333 **b.** .385 **c.** .417

B3. a.
Fixed Charge Coverage Target:	3.40–4.00
Cash Flow/Total Debt Target:	55–65%
Long-Term Debt/Capitalization Target:	25–30

b. Additional considerations are the firm's ability to fully utilize non-interest tax credits and debt management considerations such as issuance costs. **c.** The chief financial officer must determine whether Bixton will be able to utilize its larger-than-average research and development and foreign tax credits at debt levels corresponding to the suggested targets.

B5. a.
Long-term Debt/Capitalization Target:	40–45%
Cash Flow/Long-Term Debt Target:	30–40%
Fixed-Charge Coverage Target:	2.50–2.75

b. Firms A, C, and F have senior debt ratings consistent with Sanderson's target so they are good comparables. Of these three, firm C has total capitalization closest to that of Sanderson's. Firm E is a particularly poor comparable due to the significant size difference. **c.** The relatively high ratio of long-term debt to total capitalization and relatively high fixed charge coverage offset each other to some degree. Nevertheless, Sanderson should plan on reducing its long-term debt ratio to the target range within at most a few years.

B7. If the interest coverage ratio > 1, then adding a fixed amount (⅓ of Rentals) to both the numerator and the denominator will cause a larger proportionate increase in the denominator and the resulting fraction (the fixed charge coverage ratio) will be smaller. Comparing the fixed charge coverage ratio with the debt service coverage ratio, the two have the same numerator, but the debt service coverage ratio has a larger denominator, so it must be smaller. All three ratios have the same value when the firm has zero rentals and zero principal repayments during the period.

B9. a. 2.5 **b.** 2.0 **c.** 2.16

B11. a. $300 million **b.** $150 million **c.** The first alternative requires choosing common stock to finance the firm's investment opportunities over time. The result is that the firm may be at debt levels above the desired 50% for a significant time period. The second alternative allows for an immediate readjustment of the debt ratio (with costs such as transaction costs and signaling effects). The exchange offer is probably the better alternative given RWGC's objective of reducing its debt level "as quickly as possible."

C1. Lease financing is a form of secured debt because failure to make the lease payments on time places the firm in default and the owner of the asset can take control of it just as if it were an asset used to secure debt. Consider a firm that has the following capital structure before acquiring an asset:

	Amount ($ millions)
Long-term debt	400
Common equity	600
Total	1,000

The following is a pro forma balance sheet reflecting the replacement of a $10 million dollar debt-financed asset with an identical asset acquired under a lease agreement:

	Amount ($ millions)
Long-term debt	390
Capitalized lease obligation	10
Common equity	600
Total	1,000

C3. a. An investment that is 5% of the common stock of B, financed with 43.75% debt.
b. An investment that is 10% of the common stock of A, financed with 11.11% debt.

C5. Disagree. The existence of a viable junk bond market means that firms do not have to maintain a high credit rating for the sole purpose of ensuring uninterrupted access to the capital markets. Because access to the capital markets is only one of the important factors affecting a firm's choice of capital structure, the existence of a viable junk bond market does not necessarily mean that firms can "comfortably" maintain higher degrees of leverage than they could prior to the development of this market. The higher rate of return on these bonds reflects the other risks inherent in increasing leverage to the point that bond ratings fall below investment grade.

Chapter 17

B1. Dividend policy irrelevance is based on the concept of value conservation and value additivity. In a perfect market environment, a firm that holds its capital investment program and capital structure constant cannot change its value by choosing a particular dividend policy. Three capital market imperfections that might cause dividend policy to affect the value of the firm are (1) taxes, (2) transaction costs, and (3) asymmetric information. An example of how taxes might affect firm value through dividend policy is when investors pay a higher tax rate on dividend income than on capital gains. If all investors had this tax differential, investors would be willing to pay a premium for the stock of low-cash-dividend stocks and the firm could increase its value by retaining and reinvesting earnings. An example of how transaction costs might affect firm value through dividend policy is the high cost of issuing new equity. In this case, firm value is increased by retaining earnings rather than issuing stock to finance a dividend distribution because the transaction cost of issuing the stock is avoided. An example of how asymmetric information might affect firm value through dividend policy is when managers possess more accurate information than investors about the firm's future earnings prospects. In this case, if the firm has better earnings prospects than investors believe and if investors believe that dividend increases signal an increase in expected future earnings, then the firm's value could be increased by increasing dividends.

B3. $2.15

B5. Before the dividend ex-date, the stock is trading with the right to receive the dividend. On the ex-date, the stock begins trading without the right to receive the dividend. Therefore, we would expect the stock price to fall by the amount of the declared dividend. It doesn't matter whether the dividend is paid in cash or additional stock because the dilution of the shareholder's claim in a stock dividend is equal to the value drop due to a cash dividend. That is, a stockholder of record who sells the stock ex-dividend, but before the dividend is paid, still receives the dividend. Since the dividend is valuable, whether it is in cash or additional stock, the stockholder who purchases the stock ex-dividend will not get that value, hence the decline in stock price in either case. The difference between a cash and a stock dividend is that the cash dividend transforms the stockholders' claim from (1) a proportionate claim on a firm into (2) cash plus a proportionate claim on the same firm which now has less cash in its cash account. A stock dividend does not involve such a transformation, it simply breaks the claim into smaller divisions.

B7. To the extent that a dividend reinvestment plan can decrease the transaction costs of a transaction that will take place in any case, it can increase shareholder wealth. The transaction costs might be reduced in at least two ways. First, suppose the firm has a high-dividend-payout policy and the reinvestment plan allows shareholders who would use the cash dividends to purchase more of the firm's common stock. Those shareholders are better off if the dividend reinvestment plan allows them to reinvest the money with little or no brokerage commission. This also might make the stock attractive to a new group of investors who prefer capital gains to dividend income. Second, if the reinvestment plan allows the firm to make fewer new equity issues then all of the shareholders are better off because the firm will have lower issuance costs.

B9. Since the projects are expected to earn their required rate of return, the reinvestment alternative has a zero NPV. Therefore, as we illustrated in section 5 of Chapter 6 in the Indy-Sission example, shareholders will be indifferent to growth versus income when the growth has a zero NPV.

B11. a. Announcement of a share repurchase program should have little effect on the firm's share price. Shareholder value is the same whether the distribution is through a cash dividend or a repurchase of shares and the earnings per share increase is exactly offset by a drop in the P/E ratio. Price effects that do occur are likely to be the result of signaling. For example, if the repurchase signals a lack of positive-NPV projects, then we might expect a price drop. If the repurchase signals undervalued shares, we might expect a price increase. **b.** Tender offer announcements tend to provide a more positive signal since managers are willing to repurchase the shares at a premium over the prevailing market price. As a result, we would expect a price increase upon announcement of a tender offer share repurchase.

B13. a. Ignoring tax effects, stockholder wealth is unchanged in either case. However, stockholders would pay $8 million in taxes on the dividend distribution and only $4 million in taxes on the capital gains realized in the repurchase, so shareholder wealth is $4 million higher with the repurchase alternative than with the cash dividend. **b.** Cardinal's shareholders would be better off having Cardinal retain and reinvest the cash in short-term financial instruments only if the firm anticipates positive-NPV investment opportunities in the near future. In that case, although the short-term financial securities are otherwise zero-NPV investments, the costs that could be avoided by not having to raise external capital in the near future can make them a positive-NPV investment.

C1. a. An increase in the dividend rate might lead to an increase in a company's share price when that dividend increase signals improved expectations for future earnings. **b.** The company would prefer to pay out the cash in the form of a "special" or "extra" dividend when it did not anticipate that the dividend increase could be sustained. In that case, designating the dividend as a "special" distribution might allow the company to avoid the price drop we would expect when the dividend went back down to its normal level the next quarter. **c.** The renewed interest in cash dividends does not imply that dividends are more valuable to investors because they are more certain than expected future earnings. It simply means that companies lacking profitable investment opportunities should distribute excess cash to their investors. Otherwise these cash rich and investment poor companies may become takeover targets for corporate raiders.

C3. a. The stock market normally reacts unfavorably to the announcement of a dividend reduction. **b.** If a dividend reduction signals that future earnings are expected to be insufficient to sustain dividends at the previous level, then the dividend reduction provides a negative signal of the firm's future earnings prospects. **c.** No this is not inconsistent. The price increase upon announcement of the dividend reduction is only inconsistent if the announcement contained no new information. The price increase can be the result of market participants having *expected* a larger decrease in the dividend rate and being surprised that the reduction was only $0.25. **d.** If the reduction is less than expected. Another possibility is that the company released other positive information simultaneous with the dividend announcement. For example, the company might announce a major restructuring or a major new investment program that was to be partially financed with the increased retentions, the positive signal associated with these other announcements might more than compensate for the dividend decrease.

C5. Optimize your firm's capital capital structure. The existence of investor clienteles mitigates many of the potential gains associated with dividend policy, so that the choice of a *particular* policy is often less critical than simply maintaining a stable dividend policy. On the other hand, capital structure optimization requires the analysis of a number of factors (such as agency costs, signaling considerations, and bankruptcy costs) that are likely to be difficult to quantify and may have conflicting impacts on our capital structure decision. As a result, there is a greater potential for gain from capital structure policy and therefore you should ask the good fairy to tell you how to optimize your firm's capital structure policy.

C7. A common method of maintaining a relatively stable capital structure over time is to use retained earnings (equity) and debt issues in the chosen proportion to finance new projects. If the earnings are distributed as dividends, then they are unavailable for financing investment projects and the firm may be forced to forgo a profitable investment opportunity rather than take on additional partners (issue new shares). In that case, the dividend policy would give rise to the opportunity cost of the forgone investment if the capital structure is held constant.

C9. a. $P_E = [NP_R - S]/[N - 1]$ **b.** A shareholder can receive S for her share by purchasing N put rights, exercising the option, and paying taxes of $\tau_g(S - B - NR)$. Thus, ex-rights her share will be worth $P_E = S - NR - \tau_g(S - B - NR)$. Rearranging, we get

$$P_E = (1 - \tau_g)S + \tau_g B - (1 - \tau_g)NR$$

c. Solving the expression in part b, we get

$$R = [(1 - \tau_g)S + \tau_g B - P_E]/[(1 - \tau_g)N]$$

d. Substituting equation (17.3) into the expression in part c and solving for R, we get

$$R = [(1 - \tau_g)S + \tau_g B - P_R]/[(1 - \tau_g)N - 1]$$

Chapter 18

B1. a. 18% **b.** In a perfect capital market environment, shareholder value is not affected by dividend policy, so the share price will remain $25. In a perfect capital market, the value of the firm's stock is the same whether earnings are retained or paid out as dividends financed with new equity offerings.

B3. Consider a firm with 1 million shares outstanding at a current market value of $20 per share. The firm has $2 million to distribute either as a cash dividend ($2/share) or by repurchasing 100,000 shares. In the case of the cash dividend, the share price will drop on the ex-dividend date to $18 per share and shareholders will still have a total value of $20 ($2 in cash plus a share worth $18). In the case of the repurchase, the new share value will be [1,000,000($20) − $2,000,000]/[1,000,000 − 100,000] = $20. In the share repurchase case, shareholders who sell will have $20 cash and those who don't will still have a share worth $20. The net result is the shareholder value is equivalent with the cash dividend and with the share repurchase.

B5. a. 33.86% **b.** Recommended target dividend policy:

Year	Dividend	Payout Ratio
1	$1.70	34.0%
2	1.90	30.4
3	2.10	28.0
4	2.35	39.2
5	2.60	37.1

B7. a. 12.55% **b.** $8.33 **c.** $7.97 The value is different with an annual dividend because of the time value of money. The quarterly dividends of $.25 each can be invested as they are received and are worth more than the single dollar received at the end of the year. **d.** Pattern 3.

B9. a. The special dividend announcement suggests that Allegis did not have profitable investment opportunities in which to invest the proceeds from the sale of its subsidiaries. **b.** By announcing a special dividend, investors will not expect the dividend increase to be sustained so there is no negative information when the dividend returns to its normal level. **c.** This shareholder's preference for a share repurchase rather than a special dividend seems to indicate that she is a high-marginal-tax-rate investor who pays a higher effective tax rate on dividends than on capital gains.

B11. a. The special dividend will cause an aggregate loss of $5 million in shareholder wealth and the share repurchase will cause an aggregate loss of $1.25 million in shareholder wealth. **b.** The special dividend will cause an aggregate loss of $5 million in shareholder wealth and the share repurchase will cause an aggregate loss of $540,716.43 in shareholder wealth. **c.** The firm should select the alternative that minimizes the aggregate shareholder loss to taxes. Therefore, when dividends are taxed at a higher effective rate than capital gains, shareholders may prefer a share repurchase to a special dividend distribution.

C1. In an efficient capital market, the share price will already have dropped as a result of the poor economic conditions and the price will already reflect the possibility that the dividend will be cut. While denial on the part of the board might change the share price movement in the very near-term, it can substantially damage the firm's ability to credibly signal information in the future.

C3. a. The company could offer a swap of either preferred stock for common stock, or debt for common stock, depending on the tax status of the firm and the income-oriented investors. **b.** The plan to eliminate dividends should be announced before any dividend cuts occur, along with the reasons for the cut and a description of the increased profits that are expected from the shift in business strategy. **c.** Although the dividend elimination announcement may still engender a negative stock price reaction, that reaction should be tempered by a positive reaction to the proposed (and profitable) new strategy. In addition, since investors anticipate the elimination over a longer time period, a sudden, sharp drop due to selling by the income-oriented investors should be avoided.

C5. a. $29.44 **b.** The payment of greenmail causes the value of the remaining shareholders' stock to drop by $5 million. It is simply a $5 million wealth transfer from the remaining shareholders to Karl I. Can.

C7. a. The repurchase would increase her wealth by $15 million. **b.** Share price would drop to $11.67 **c.** The aggregate wealth of the other shareholders would drop by $15 million. **d.** Greenmail is an expropriation of the wealth of the remaining stockholders.

Chapter 19

B1. The expected rate of return for the firm will continue to be $r^* = 20\%$ so that the required rate of return to the shareholders, $r_e(.40)$, must be 24%. The total value of the firm is unchanged in a perfect capital market environment.

B3. Query should use the 15% debt-financing alternative because it has an opportunity cost of capital of 16.2750% compared with 16.2755% for the 45% debt alternative. The taxes in this environment seem to be approximately symmetrical since $r^*(\theta)$ for the two alternatives is nearly identical. There appears to be a slight advantage to using the lower-leverage alternative.

B5. **a.** 18.15% **b.** 15.36% **c.** 16.15% **d.** 1.16

B7. $r = 12\%$ and the unlevered beta = 0.77

B9.

	V_D	V_E	θ	r_d
A	11.77M	25M	.32	.1064
B	60.30M	60M	.50	.1207
C	27.50M	110M	.20	.1073

	$r_e(\theta)$	$H(\theta)$	WACC	r
A	.158	.006155	.1296	.1366
B	.166	.010771	.1222	.1344
C	.162	.003876	.1435	.1479

The average r from the 3 firms is 13.96% so that with the projects $r_d(.4) = 11.25\%$, $r^*(.4) = 13.0\%$

B11. **a.** $613,702 **b.** .28 **c.** 23.81% **d.** 29.0%

C1. 16.95%

C3. Stowe should choose the 9% coupon.

C5. **a.** $1,002,919 **b.** $r^*(.5) = 15.68\%$ and $r_e(.5) = 20.31\%$ **c.** $1,003,155 **d.** When financing and investment decisions are interrelated, the net adjusted present value approach adjusts the NPV to reflect the costs and benefits specific to the financing of the project. The NPV calculation assumes permanent debt and no capital structure rebalancing.

Chapter 20

B1. **a.** Years 1–19, CFAT = $2.234 million; Year 20, CFAT = $52.234 million **b.** Semiannual after-tax savings = $379,000 **c.** $5,338,086 **d.** $658,086

B3. **a.** $11,996,650 **b.** $11,696,650

B5. $9,520,497

B7. $1,177,285

B9. **a.** −$118,604 **b.** Astro should not defease the 8% issue because the present value of the tax liability on the defeasance portfolio exceeds the present value of the interest tax shields on the defeased debt and the defeasance would decrease shareholder wealth.

C1. **a.** $24.6 million **b.** Assuming the market value of the bonds is equal to the call price at the time of the call, $43.6 million **c.** Mountain States could have used a break-even analysis or dynamic programming and the

calculation of a stopping curve to determine the optimal timing for the debt refunding.

C3. 14.89%

C5. $NA_1 = -\$25,148$; $NA_2 = -\$49,814$; $NA_3 = -\$74,100$; and $NA_4 = -\$24,590$; so the company should not pre-purchase any of the sinking fund payment obligations.

C7. 5.8532% per semiannual period

Chapter 21

B1. The acquisition of the asset is analyzed by computing the project NPV using the required rate of return on the asset as the discount rate. The choice of financing—leasing versus borrowing—is a separate decision and is analyzed by computing the net advantage to leasing. Because the contractual lease payments are similar in risk to promised debt payment, the appropriate discount rate for the lease/buy decision is the lessee's cost of comparably secured debt. The total NPV of leasing to acquire the asset is the project NPV plus the net advantage to leasing.

B3. **a.**

Year	Net Cash Flow to Lessee
0	+25,000
1–7	−4,000
8	−9,000

b. NAL = −$226.30 (Borrow and buy) **c.** NAL = −$1,001.04 (Borrow and buy) **d.** part b becomes NAL = $597.24 (Lease) and part c becomes NAL = $45.52 (Lease).

B5. **a.** Lease (NAL = $260.31) **b.** Borrow and buy (NAL = −$114.01) **c.** The NAL calculation is situation specific and the timing of lease payments and tax realizations can alter the usual logic that leasing is more advantageous to a lessee who cannot utilize the tax benefits of ownership.

B7. Leasing is better, NAL = $120,592

B9. **a.** NAL = $0.46 million, so leasing is advantageous **b.** $10.04 million **c.** 10.58% **d.** The three approaches yield consistent results. The equivalent loan is simply a mathematical rearrangement of the net advantage of leasing (Cost − EL = NAL) so it must yield the same results. The IRR is the discount rate that causes the NAL to be zero, but ignores the difference in the discount rate for the salvage value. If the salvage value is zero, the IRR method will give results identical to the other two methods.

B11. **a.** $1,140,606 **b.** −$10,840 **c.** $1,137,334 **d.** Because Amalgamated's break-even payment exceeds Johnson's break-even payment, it is not possible for Amalgamated and Johnson to find a mutually beneficial lease payment rate.

C1. **a.** Break-even tax rate = 1.2% **b.** Lake Trolley Company's effective tax rate, rather than the statuatory tax rate is the relevant rate, for this analysis. With a break-even tax rate of 1.2%, leasing at these terms would be advantageous for Lake Trolley Company only if its effective tax rate over the term of the lease is essentially zero.

C3. The debt service parity priciple requires computing the outflows associated with the lease and then "selling" these outflows to determine the amount of debt that could be supported by that stream of debt service payments.

Time	Item	CFBT	CFAT
1–N	Lease payments	L_t/yr.	$(1 - \tau)L_t$/yr.
1–N	Increased expenses	ΔE_t/yr.	$(1 - \tau)\Delta E_t$/yr.
1–N	Depreciation	0	τD_t/yr.
N	Salvage value	SAL	SAL

The expected salvage value could be "sold" at a discount rate equal to the required rate of return on the project, while the other cash flows could be "sold" at the after-tax costs of the loan that is being made. The total present value is then given by Equation (21.4).

Chapter 22

B1. **a.** $59.3 million **b.** 34.45% **c.** 4 years **d.** If the cash flow and net sales estimates are reasonable (not overly optimistic), then the company should proceed with the merger to realize the $59.3 million NPV.

B3. **a.** −$892,943, yes **b.** $147,655, yes **c.** −$1,040,598, yes

B5. **a.** 10 **b.** 8 **c.** 2.5 **d.** 43%

B7. **a.** 85 million barrels of oil equivalent **b.** $775 million

B9. **a.** 16.67% **b.** $169.22 million **c.** $177.66 million

B11. **a.** NPV = $125.59 million and IRR = 32.91% **b.** NPV = $116.13 million and IRR = 32.04% **c.** Yes.

B13. **a.** 0.5 **b.** 0.625 **c.** With the exchange ratio fixed at 0.625, a 10% drop in the price of Ajax (to $36) causes the price paid for Central to be $22.5 (= [.625]36). This is a 12.5% increase from the initial share price of $20.

C1. **a.** $300 million **b.** 23⅓% **c.** For every dollar invested, buy $0.33 of the Arnold substitute and $0.67 of the Beard substitute. Short sell $1 of the merged stock. Your payoff from the substitute stock will be $0.33(1.20) + $0.67(1.25) = $1.2335. Then, pay the $1.23 required return on the merged stock for a net riskless profit of $.0035 per dollar invested. **d.** If neither firm has a close substitute, the merger reduces the set of possible outcomes from investing in the two assets to the single outcome for the merged firm. This reduction in the outcome space spanned by the investment reduces the value of the combined investment from its pre-merger value.

C3. From $250 million to $280 million

Chapter 23

B1. **a.** $0.6921 **b.** Borrow SF1,515.15 and buy $1,000. Invest the dollars to yield $1,080. Exchange this under a 30-

day forward contract for SF1,588.24. Use SF1,560.60 to repay your loan and you are left with a riskless arbitrage profit of SF27.64 or $18.79 for every $1,000 invested.

B3. **a.** $1.50/£ **b.** Buy 1 oz. of gold in New York for $450, transport it to London, and sell it for £300. Exchange the pounds for $510 and you will have a riskless arbitrage profit of $60 or £35.29 for every ounce of gold transported.

B5. **a.** 1SF = DM1.30 **b.** Everyone would want to sell Swiss francs forward but no one would be willing to sell German marks forward. **c.** Everyone would want to sell German marks forward but no one would be willing to sell Swiss francs forward.

B7. $(1 + r_C)/(1 + r_{GB}) = 0.9727$

B9. 15.862%

B11.

Year:	1	2	3	4	5
a. $E[s_{\$/DM}(t)]$	.6113	.6112	.6056	.6055	.6000
b. CF($M)	9.1695	10.3904	12.1120	12.1100	10.2000

B13. The after-tax cost of the Deutsche-mark-denominated debt is 4.992%

C1. The effective annual 1-year forward rate is 12.38%

C3. Suppose the expectations theory of forward exchange rates does not hold. Then $E[s_{D/F}(t)]$ is not equal to $f_{D/F}(t)$. This implies that $s_{D/F}/f_{D/F}(t)$ is not equal to $s_{D/F}/E[s_{D/F}(t)]$. Then if interest rate parity and purchasing power parity do hold, the international Fisher effect cannot hold.

C5. **a.** Total payoff = Forward contract payoff +
Sale Proceeds
= {$160 − [£100 + [£100]$s_{\$/£}(1)$}
= $160 million

b. Total payoff = [£100 million/$(1 + r_£)](s_{\$/£})(1 + r_\$)$;
rearranging,
Total payoff = £100 million $[(s_{\$/£})(1 + r_\$)/(1 + r_£)]$;
if interest rate parity holds,
$[(s_{\$/£})(1 + r_\$)/(1 + r_£)] = f_{\$/£}(1)$ and,
total payoff = [£100 million]$f_{\$/£}(1) = $160 million

C9. **a.**

Country	Implied Exchange Rate
Australia	A$1.05/US$
Britain	£0.64/US$
Canada	C$0.995/US$
France	FF8.05/US$
Japan	¥168.18/US$
W. Germany	DM1.95/US$

b. No **c.** The observed prices do not imply that exchange rates are out of equilibrium or that the Law of One Price is invalid. It simply means that there are transaction costs or other market imperfections that prevent the Law of One Price from holding exactly. For example, in contrast to a financial asset, Big Macs are perishable and it would be impossible to transport them from one market to another without loss.

Chapter 24

B1. **a.** Working capital = $300 and Current ratio = 1.75 **b.** Acid test ratio = 0.75, Receivable turnover ratio = 15, and Inventory turnover ratio = 4.5

B3. $146 million

B5. **a.** Gross profit = $47,388 million, Operating income = $20,236 million, and Net income before extraordinary items = $5,520 million **b.** Gross profit margin = 54.7%, Operating profit margin = 23.4%, and Net profit margin = 6.4%

B7. **a.** $1.38 **b.** $2.38

B9. **a.** Cash-flow-to-long-term-debt ratio = 2.20 and Cash-flow-to-total-debt ratio = 1.45 **b.** Long-term debt ratio = 14.1%, Total-debt-to-adjusted-capitalization ratio = 19.8%, and Debt-to-equity ratio = 24.7%

B11. **a.** −1.5% **b.** −3.1%

C1. **a.** With this definition, net assets includes noncapitalized long-term liabilities so it does not make sense to equate net assets with total capitalization in this case. **b.** Deferred income taxes may be thought of as a long-term source of funds in the sense that they are a liability that has been incurred but payment may be deferred interest-free beyond the current period. **c.** Good luck **d.** The definition of net assets in Equation (24.5) should be preferred because it provides a measure of total capitalization and because the deferred liabilities do not provide financing in a conventional sense they should not be included.

C3. **a.** Because the minority interest in this case represents an obligation of the company, it should be included in the numerator of the debt-to-equity ratio calculation. **b.** Because the parent company has no expectation of ever retiring the minority interest in this case, it would be more appropriately included in the denominator of the debt-to-equity ratio calculation.

Chapter 25

B1. **a.** 2.0 **b.** $50 million **c.** The company should compare its current ratio and other financial ratios with comparable companies in the industry that have commercial paper ratings consistent with the company's risk-return objectives. **d.** $20 million

B3. **a.** 5 times per month **b.** $400,000 **c.** $200,000 **d.** Cash requirements are known with certainty and disbursements occur at a uniform rate each time period.

B5. No, the NPV of extending credit is −$1,385.23

B7. **a.** 1,549 **b.** Doubling either the usage rate or the reordering costs causes the EOQ to increase 41% to 2,191; doubling the carrying cost causes the EOQ to decrease 29% to 1,095 **c.** 150

B9. **a.** 10.44% **b.** 10.58% **c.** If interest is computed on an actual-days-elapsed basis rather than on a 360-days-

per-year basis, the true cost of the discount note is even higher than the 10.44% computed in part a.

B11. **a.** $58,953 **b.** −$13,047, therefore Zodiac should not grant credit if the chain would make the purchase anyway **c.** 61%

C1. **a.** $K/2$ **b.** $r(K/2)$ **c.** A/K **d.** $C(A/K)$ **e.** Aggregate cost (AC) = $r(K/2) + C(A/K)$ **f.** To minimize aggregate cost, take the derivative with respect to K, set it equal to zero, and solve for K:

$$d(AC)/dK = r/2 - CA/K^2 = 0$$
$$r/2 = CA/K^2$$
$$K^2 = 2CA/r$$
$$K = [2CA/r]^{1/2}$$

C3. **a.** NPV = $P_P\{[R/(1 + r)] - C\} - (1 - P_P)C + P_P P_Q Z$ **b.** $788.50

C5. **a.** Price = Principal minus the Interest for a fraction, f, of a 360-day year; i.e. $f = (d/360)$. So Price = $P - iPf = P - iPd/360$ **b.** Future value = Principal = P = Price(1 + rf'), where f' is the fraction of a 365-day year; i.e., $f' = (d/365)$. So $P = (P - iPd/360)(1 + rd/365)$ **c.** multiplying through and rearranging, $r = [i/(1 - if)] \times [365/360]$

Chapter 26

B1. Spreadsheets and personal computers assist but do not in any way replace managerial expertise in the financial planning process. Managers must still formulate their financial objectives, project outcomes under alternative scenarios, choose the "best" financial policies, and formulate contingency plans.

B3. $335,975

B5. **a.**

Cash discount	Same mo.	Next mo.
1%	3.9%	83.2%

2 mo.	3 mo.	4 mo.	Uncollectable
7.8%	3.5%	1.1%	0.5%

b. $273,025 **c.** The procedure in part a ignores the seasonality of the sales and collections and may significantly over- or underestimate collections for months that deviate from the average.

B9. **a.** Yes. **b.** Pay cash **c.** Transaction costs on the firm's investment could deplete the additional earnings. The decision rule would be pay cash if

$$\{[1 + (r_c - r_b)/365]^n - 1\}ADIB - MTC > 0$$

where r_c = company's annual investment rate; r_b = bank's annual earnings credit rate; n = number of days in the month; ADIB = Average daily investable balance; and MTC = monthly transaction costs

Name Index

SUBJECT INDEX

A

Abandonment option, 306, 350–52, G3
Accelerated cost recovery system (ACRS), 325
Accelerated depreciation, 329, G3
Accounting, 3
  for financial leases, 648–49
  for leveraged buyouts, 701–2
  for mergers, 698–701
Accounting model, 10
Accounting Principles Board
  Opinion No. 16, 701
  Statement No. 26, 598
Accounting statements, 240
Accounts receivables, 870, G3
Acid test ratio, 793, G3
Acquiree, 680, G3
Acquiror, 680, G3
Acquisition, 680, G3
Acquisition analysis, in weighted-average cost-of-capital approach to mergers, 712–13
Acquisition cost, in weighted-average-cost-of-capital approach to mergers, 710–11
ACRS (accelerated cost recovery system), 325
Add-on interest, 61
Adjustable rate convertible debt, 412–13
Adjustable rate notes, 412–13
Adjustable-rate preferred stock (ARPS), 86, 411, 412
Adjusted-present value, 582, G3
  and alternative general debt payment pattern, 587–90
  and capital structure, 571–72
  and financial analysis of mergers, 713–15
Adverse selection, 26, 107, G3
Affirmative covenant, G3
After-tax basis, 283
Agency costs, 219, 244, 437–39, 445, G3
Agency problem, 219–20, G3
  in the bid response, 722
Agency theory, 21, 219, 220, G3
Agent(s), 21, 219, G3. *See also* Principle-agent relationships
Aggregate investment opportunities, 79–83

Aging schedule for accounts receivable, 794, G3
Allegheny Corporation, 404
Allied Stores, 439
American Express, 404
American option, 188, 189, 200–2, 214, G3
American Stock Exchange (AMEX), 26, 73, 74, 87, 163, 197
AMEX. *See* American Stock Exchange
Amortization, G3
  in cash flow determination, 285
  of loan, 48
Annual percentage rate (APR), G3
  definition of, 61–62
  legislation on, 61
Annuity, 44, G3
  future value of, 44–46
  with partial time periods, 59
  payments of, 47–48
  as perpetuities, 50–51
  present value of, 46–47
  valuing, not starting today, 48–50
Annuity due, 8, G3
Antidilutive effect, 515, G3
Antitrust considerations, 690–91
APB. *See* Accounting Principles Board (APB)
Apple Computers, 29, 30
APR. *See* Annual Percentage Rate (APR)
APT. *See* Arbitrage Pricing theory (APT)
APV. *See* Adjusted present value (APV)
Arbitrage, 27, 102–3, G3
  definition of, 102
  and irrelevance of capital structure, 432–33
  limits to transaction costs, 104–6
  and the security market line, 173–74
  versus speculation, 106
Arbitrage pricing model (APT), 577, G3
  applying, 180
  versus CAPM, 180–81
  multifactor linear model as, 179–80
Arbitrageur, 103, G3
Asset, G3
  on balance sheet, 783
  differences in ability of, to support debt, 463–64
  financial, 4, 71–73
  illiquidity protected afforded by, 471–72

intangible, 4, 70
investing in part of return distribution of, 191–93
market value of, in an efficient market, 205
option as claim to part of return distribution, 189–91
purchases or sales, 723
real, 4, 70
riskless, 165–70
substitution, 226–29, 606
tangible, 4, 70
uniqueness of, 233
useful life of, 315n
Asset-based financing, 640–72, G3
  arrangements in, 660–61
  of corporate real estate, 669–70
  lease financing, 641–47
    accounting treatment of, 648–49
    advantages and disadvantages of, 645–47, 654–57
    advantages of, 654–57
    versus borrowing and buying, 644–45
    and capital budgeting, 657–58
    tax treatment of, 647–48
    types of, 642–44
    valuation of, 649–58
  limited partnership financing, 663–69, 668
    advantages and disadvantages of, 668–69
    characteristics of, 664–65
    measuring costs of capital in, 666–68
  production payment financing, 663
    advantages and disadvantages of, 668
  project financing, 658–59
    advantages and disadvantages of, 661–63
    arrangements in, 660–61
    project structure in, 658–60
Asset-coverage test, 396, G4
Asset depreciation range (ADR) method, 325
Asset pricing model, G4. *See also* Arbitrage pricing theory; Capital asset pricing model
Asset substitution, 226–29, 268, 606, G4
Asymmetric information, 213, G3
  net effect of, 442–43
  and signaling, 107, 233, 235